The Palgrave Handbook of Russian Thought

Marina F. Bykova • Michael N. Forster
Lina Steiner
Editors

The Palgrave Handbook of Russian Thought

Editors
Marina F. Bykova
North Carolina State University
Raleigh, NC, USA

Michael N. Forster
University of Bonn
Bonn, Germany

Lina Steiner
University of Bonn
Bonn, Germany

ISBN 978-3-030-62981-6 ISBN 978-3-030-62982-3 (eBook)
https://doi.org/10.1007/978-3-030-62982-3

© The Editor(s) (if applicable) and The Author(s) 2021, corrected publication 2021
This work is subject to copyright. All rights are solely and exclusively licensed by the Publisher, whether the whole or part of the material is concerned, specifically the rights of translation, reprinting, reuse of illustrations, recitation, broadcasting, reproduction on microfilms or in any other physical way, and transmission or information storage and retrieval, electronic adaptation, computer software, or by similar or dissimilar methodology now known or hereafter developed.
The use of general descriptive names, registered names, trademarks, service marks, etc. in this publication does not imply, even in the absence of a specific statement, that such names are exempt from the relevant protective laws and regulations and therefore free for general use.
The publisher, the authors and the editors are safe to assume that the advice and information in this book are believed to be true and accurate at the date of publication. Neither the publisher nor the authors or the editors give a warranty, expressed or implied, with respect to the material contained herein or for any errors or omissions that may have been made. The publisher remains neutral with regard to jurisdictional claims in published maps and institutional affiliations.

Cover illustration: Mordolff / Getty Images

This Palgrave Macmillan imprint is published by the registered company Springer Nature Switzerland AG.
The registered company address is: Gewerbestrasse 11, 6330 Cham, Switzerland

PREFACE

This new volume in the series *The Palgrave Handbooks* offers an in-depth survey of the development of Russian thought. It covers Russia's intellectual history from the late eighteenth century to the dissolution of the Soviet Union—from the first inception of a distinctly Russian philosophical and literary tradition through its astonishingly rich development in the nineteenth century to the orthodox Marxism and dissident thought of the Soviet era and beyond. The most lively and influential period in Russia's long intellectual history, this remarkable time produced philosophical, literary, and religious ideas that had a powerful impact on the country's cultural, political, and socioeconomic development, as well as on the intellectual, cultural, and political development of the whole world.

Despite its enormous significance, Russia's intellectual legacy still remains largely unknown to Anglophone readers, who continue to be wary of the Russian tradition and skeptical of its value. This includes not only the Soviet period, which is often perceived as lacking in creativity and original insights, but also the great nineteenth century, which Western historians have often characterized as a period of uncritical absorption and imitation of European ideas. Concerning the Soviet period, the end of the ideological confrontation between East and West and the opening up of the Soviet archives have led to a dramatic increase in the amount of information available concerning Russian thought during this period. However, these discoveries remain largely unknown to the public, which continues to rely on only a handful of texts produced during the Cold War. So there is a whole new world of ideas for the public to discover here. Concerning the nineteenth century, the suggestion that the Russian thought of this period just uncritically absorbed and imitated European ideas is, if anything, even more clearly mistaken.

The present volume was conceived by its editors as a sort of sequel to Isaiah Berlin's 1978 classic, *Russian Thinkers*. One of the best and best-known Anglophone studies of Russian thought, Berlin's collection of essays covered a somewhat limited period from the 1840s to the 1880s, mainly focusing on key figures in Russian literature while disregarding concurrent philosophical developments. Published at the height of the Cold War, his work had a deep, long-lasting impact on the interpretation of Russia's intellectual history in the Anglophone world and on the cultural and diplomatic dialogue between Western countries and the Soviet Union. During the decades that have elapsed since the dissolution of the USSR, it has become clear that the crucial problems that Berlin identified in Russia—for example, the absence of a unified Russian identity, the conflict between the state and the intelligentsia, and the popular allure of the "Russian idea"—have lost none of their relevance. This is reflected in recent intellectual debates in Russia, which have grown ever more intense since the 1980s, when the Soviet ideological regime was relaxed, permitting a resurgence of theories and ideas that had been repressed since the 1920s as well as the development of a variety of new intellectual movements. But the landscape of Russian thought has since changed almost beyond recognition, and understanding it requires a thorough reexamination and new reflection. The lack of relevant publications and information in English has hitherto impeded this, however.

The Handbook of Russian Thought fills this lacuna, offering a reliable presentation and discussion of the broad sweep of Russian thought from the late eighteenth to the late twentieth centuries, including its most recent forms. Recognizing the richness of this subject and the impossibility of grasping it adequately by using any of the traditional reductive interpretations of the history of Russian thought, the book employs a fresh, comprehensive, flexible approach that considers Russian thought in the context of the country's changing historical landscape and takes into account the deep connections between Russian philosophy, literature, religious ideas, politics, and public life. Acknowledging the importance of Western influence on Russian thought, the book also contextualizes Russian thought in relation to the European and, more broadly, Western intellectual tradition that impacted it, updating the relevant data and throwing crucial light on the original ideas, theories, and debates that were generated in Russia.

The aim of this *Handbook* is to help readers to navigate the complex terrain of Russian thought and to learn to appreciate its unique legacy and historical significance. Consisting of thirty-six chapters written by internationally recognized scholars of Russian philosophy, literature, and intellectual history, the volume provides an authoritative account of Russian thought that makes it accessible to a broad readership while also upholding the highest standards of research. The list of contributors includes both distinguished and younger scholars from eight countries (Russia, the United States, Canada, Great Britain, Germany, Switzerland, the Netherlands, and Italy), all of whom are acclaimed for their research, making this volume a valuable source of information based on cutting-edge scholarship. In addition to established accounts of individual figures, schools, and movements within the Russian intellectual tradition, these contributors present many new interpretations of Russian thought and its developmental dynamics. This book also includes detailed critiques of a number of the ideas and arguments that have been developed by Russian thinkers and considers contemporary controversies surrounding their views. The work combines a comprehensive overview of Russia's major thinkers and intellectual currents with specialized contemporary research. It will therefore appeal not only to a broad public seeking to advance its understanding of Russian thought but also to specialists from a variety of human sciences, including philosophy, literary studies, history, political science, and psychology. The editors hope that this *Handbook* will encourage new explorations of the exciting realm of Russian thought and new discussions of the country's rich intellectual and cultural legacy.

Raleigh, NC, USA

Bonn, Germany

Marina Bykova

Michael N. Forster

Lina Steiner

Permissions

An earlier version of Chap. 8 (by Nelly V. Motroshilova) was originally published as "Osnovnye printsipy. Problemnye sfery i izmereniia filosofii V. Solovyova" in *Mysliteli Rossii i filosofiia Zapada. V. Solovyov. N. Berdyaev. S. Frank. L. Shestov* (Moscow: Izdatel'stvo "Respublika"; Izdatel'stvo "Kul'turnaia revoliutsiia," 2007, 83–102). Permission for our English translation has been granted by the publisher as the copyright holder.

An earlier version of Chap. 10 (by Yulia V. Sineokaya and Anton M. Khokhlov) was originally published as "Lev Shestov's Philosophy of Freedom" in *Studies in East European Thought* 68: 213–227 (2016); https://doi.org/10.1007/s11212-016-9257-6. The material is re-used here with permission from the publisher as the copyright holder.

A Note on Transliteration

We have used the Library of Congress Transliteration Table to transliterate Russian terms and names into English. However, a number of proper names are transliterated according to the older convention (e.g., Fyodor Dostoevsky, Vasily Rozanov, and Vladimir Solovyov).

Acknowledgments

The idea for this volume originated in connection with a conference that we organized at the University of Bonn (Germany) in October 2017 with the help of generous financial support from the Alexander von Humboldt Foundation: "Russian Thinkers Between the Revolution and Tradition." Several of the papers presented at that conference have been transformed into chapters for this *Handbook*; additional chapters were commissioned and added subsequently. The Alexander von Humboldt Foundation provided generous funding not only for the original conference but also for required translational work. We would therefore like to thank the Alexander von Humboldt Foundation and the University of Bonn for making both the conference and this volume possible. We would also like to thank the outstanding group of scholars who participated in the conference and/or have contributed to this volume. In addition, warm thanks go to Brad Damaré, Peter Golub, Lucia Pasini, and Valentin Frolov, who translated a number of the articles included in the volume, and to Simon Waskow of the University of Bonn for his editorial assistance. Finally, we would also like to express our gratitude to Phil Getz and the other editors at Palgrave Macmillan, who helped to bring this *Handbook* to life.

CONTENTS

1 Introduction: On Russian Thought and Intellectual Tradition   1
Marina F. Bykova and Lina Steiner

Part I   Russian Philosophical Thought   23

2 Politics and Enlightenment in Russia   25
Gary M. Hamburg

3 Russian Religious Philosophy: The Nature of the Phenomenon, Its Path, and Its Afterlife   51
Sergey S. Horujy

4 Russian Political Philosophy: Between Autocracy and Revolution   73
Evert van der Zweerde

5 Between Aristocratism and Artistry: Two Centuries of the Revolutionary Paradigm in Russia   95
Julia B. Mehlich

6 Kant and Kantianism in Russia: A Historical Overview   115
Alexei N. Krouglov

7 Hegel's Philosophy of Freedom in Nineteenth-Century Russia   139
Jeff Love

xvi CONTENTS

8 Vladimir Solovyov: Philosophy as Systemic Unity 159
Nelly V. Motroshilova

9 Natural Sciences and the Radical *Intelligentsia* in the Late
Nineteenth and Early Twentieth Centuries 179
Daniela Steila

10 Lev Shestov's Philosophy of Freedom 201
Yulia V. Sineokaya and Anton M. Khokhlov

11 Nikolai Berdyaev's Philosophy of Creativity as a Revolt
Against the Modern Worldview 217
Vladimir L. Marchenkov

12 Lenin and His Controversy over Philosophy: On the
Philosophical Significance of *Materialism and
Empiriocriticism* 239
Marina F. Bykova

13 Russian Marxism and Its Philosophy: From Theory
to Ideology 269
Maja Soboleva

14 Between East and West: Russian Identity in the Émigré
Writings of Ilya Fondaminsky and Semyon Portugeis 293
Alexei A. Kara-Murza

15 Ivan A. Ilyin: Russia's "Non-Hegelian" Hegelian 317
Philip T. Grier

16 Gustav Shpet's Path Through Phenomenology to Philosophy
of Language 339
Thomas Nemeth

17 Evald Ilyenkov: Philosophy as the Science of Thought 359
David Bakhurst

18 The "Men of the Sixties": Philosophy as a Social Phenomenon 383
Abdusalam A. Guseynov

CONTENTS xvii

19 The Activity Approach in Late Soviet Philosophy 407
Vladislav A. Lektorsky

**20 A Return to Tradition: The Epistemological Style in Russia's
Post-Soviet Philosophy** 423
Boris I. Pruzhinin and Tatiana G. Shchedrina

Part II   Philosophy in Dialogue with Literature and Art 445

**21 The Russian Novel as a Medium of Moral Reflection in the
Long Nineteenth Century** 447
Lina Steiner

**22 Nikolai Gogol, Symbolic Geography, and the Invention of the
Russian Provinces** 491
Anne Lounsbery

23 Belinsky and the Sociality of Reason 507
Vadim Shkolnikov

**24 The Vocations of Nikolai Grot and the Tasks of Russian
Philosophy** 525
Inessa Medzhibovskaya

25 Chernyshevsky and Dostoevsky: Together in Opposition 549
Vladimir K. Kantor

26 Tolstoy's Philosophy of Life 575
Lina Steiner

27 "Teaching of Life": Tolstoy's Moral-Philosophical Aesthetics 597
Henry W. Pickford

**28 Osip Mandelstam's Poetic Practice and Theory and Pavel
Florensky's Philosophical Contexts** 621
Sofya Khagi

**29 Future-in-the-Past: Mikhail Bakhtin's Thought Between
Heritage and Reception** 643
Vitaly L. Makhlin

xviii CONTENTS

30 Bakhtin, Translation, World Literature 659
Galin Tihanov

31 Alexei F. Losev's Mythology of Music as a Development of the Hermeneutics and Sociology of Music 673
Elena A. Takho-Godi and Konstantin V. Zenkin

32 The Young Marx and the Tribulations of Soviet Marxist-Leninist Aesthetics 693
Edward M. Świderski

33 Mikhail Sholokhov, Andrei Platonov, and Varlam Shalamov: The Road to Hell in Twentieth-Century Russian Literature 715
Sergei A. Nikolsky

34 Yuri Lotman and the Moscow-Tartu School of Semiotics: Contemporary Epistemic and Social Contexts 737
Natalia S. Avtonomova

35 Art as an Instrument of Philosophy 755
Helen Petrovsky

Part III Afterword 775

36 Russian Thought and *Russian Thinkers* 777
Michael N. Forster

Correction to: Art as an Instrument of Philosophy C1
Helen Petrovsky

Name Index 789

Subject Index 797

Notes on Contributors

Natalia S. Avtonomova is Principal Research Associate at the Institute of Philosophy, Russian Academy of Sciences in Moscow (Russia). Her main research interests include philosophy of science, history of contemporary French philosophy, and translation (both as a philosophical problem and from a cross-cultural perspective). She is the author of numerous articles and books, including *Filosofiia iazyka Zhaka Derrida* (Moscow, 2011) and *Poznanie i perevod. Opyt filosofii iazyka* (Moscow, 2008, 2nd expanded ed. 2016).

David Bakhurst is George Whalley Distinguished University Professor and Charlton Professor of Philosophy at Queen's University, Kingston (Canada). His research interests include Russian philosophy and psychology, metaphysics, ethics, and philosophy of education. He is the author of *Consciousness and Revolution in Soviet Philosophy: From Bolsheviks to Evald Ilyenkov* (Cambridge University Press, 1991), *The Formation of Reason* (Wiley-Blackwell, 2011), and numerous articles in books and journals. In 2016, he was elected a Fellow of the Royal Society of Canada.

Marina F. Bykova is Professor of Philosophy at North Carolina State University (USA) and the Editor-in-Chief of the journals *Studies in East European Thought* and *Russian Studies in Philosophy*. Her main research interests lie in the history of nineteenth-century continental philosophy, with a special focus on German Idealism. She has published nine books and numerous research articles, including *The German Idealism Reader: Ideas, Responses, and Legacies* (Bloomsbury, 2019). She is the editor of *Hegel's Philosophy of Spirit: A Critical Guide* (Cambridge University Press, 2019) and *The Bloomsbury Handbook of Fichte* (Bloomsbury, 2020), as well as co-editor (with K.R. Westphal) of *The Palgrave Hegel Handbook* (Palgrave Macmillan, 2020) and (with V.A. Lektorsky) of *Philosophical Thought in Russia in the Second Half of the 20th Century: A Contemporary View from Russia and Abroad* (Bloomsbury, 2019).

Michael N. Forster is Alexander von Humboldt Professor, holder of the Chair in Theoretical Philosophy, and Co-director of the International Centre for Philosophy at the University of Bonn (Germany). His work combines historical and systematic aspects. His historical focus is mainly on ancient philosophy and especially German philosophy. His systematic focus is largely on epistemology (especially skepticism) and philosophy of language (in a broad sense that includes hermeneutics and translation-theory). His publications include *Hegel and Skepticism* (Harvard University Press, 1989), *Hegel's Idea of a Phenomenology of Spirit* (University of Chicago Press, 1998), *Herder: Philosophical Writings* (Cambridge University Press, 2002), *Wittgenstein on the Arbitrariness of Grammar* (Princeton University Press, 2004), *Kant and Skepticism* (Princeton University Press, 2008), *After Herder: Philosophy of Language in the German Tradition* (Oxford University Press, 2010), *German Philosophy of Language: From Schlegel to Hegel and Beyond* (Oxford University Press, 2011), and *Herder's Philosophy* (Oxford University Press, 2018). He is also the co-editor of several volumes, including *The Oxford Handbook of German Philosophy in the Nineteenth Century* (Oxford University Press, 2015), *The Cambridge Companion to Hermeneutics* (Cambridge University Press, 2019), and *Romanticism, Philosophy, and Literature* (Palgrave Macmillan, 2020).

Philip T. Grier is Thomas Bowman Professor of Philosophy and Religion, Emeritus, at Dickinson College (USA) and a past President of the Hegel Society of America. He has written several books (including edited works and translations) as well as numerous essays in such fields as Hegel studies, ethical theory, philosophy of law and politics, the history of philosophy, and Russian philosophy. His published works include *Marxist Ethical Theory in the Soviet Union* (Springer, 1978, 2011), *Dialectic and Contemporary Science: Essays in Honor of Errol E. Harris* (Editor) (University Press of America, 1989), and *Identity and Difference: Studies in Hegel's Logic, Philosophy of Spirit, and Politics* (Editor) (SUNY, 2008), as well as translations of both volumes of Il'in's Hegel commentary (Northwestern University Press, 2010, 2011) and Il'in's *On the Essence of Legal Consciousness* (Wildy, Simmonds & Hill, 2014).

Abdusalam A. Guseynov is Full Member of the Russian Academy of Sciences (RAS). He is Principal Adviser for Academic Affairs at the Institute of Philosophy, RAS in Moscow (Russia). His area of specialization is the history and theory of ethics. He is the author of eleven books and numerous articles and encyclopedia entries. His most recent book publications include *Velikie proroki i mysliteli. Nravstvennye ucheniia ot Moiseia i do nashikh dnei* (Moscow, 2009), *Antichnaia etika* (Moscow, 2011), *Filosofiia—mysl' i postupok: stat'i, doklady, lektsii, interv'iu* (Moscow, 2012), *Problems of Philosophical Ethics* (in Chinese; Beijing, 2018), and *Etika i kul'tura* (St. Petersburg, 2020).

Gary M. Hamburg is Otho M. Behr Professor of European History at Claremont McKenna College (USA). He is the author of *Politics of the Russian Nobility, 1881–1905* (Rutgers University Press, 1984), *Boris Chicherin & Early Russian Liberalism* (Stanford University Press, 1992), and *Russia's Path Toward Enlightenment: Faith, Politics and Reason, 1500–1801* (Yale University

NOTES ON CONTRIBUTORS xxi

Press, 2016). He has also edited numerous volumes, most recently (with Randall Poole), *A History of Russian Philosophy, 1830–1930: Faith, Reason and the Defense of Human Dignity* (Cambridge University Press, 2010).

Sergey S. Horujy (1941–2020) was Professor and Principal Research Associate at the Institute of Philosophy, Russian Academy of Sciences, and Research Director at the Center for Synergetic Anthropology at the National Research University "Higher School of Economics" in Moscow (Russia). His most recent works include *Issledovaniia po isikhaztskoi traditsii*, in 2 vols. (Moscow, 2012), *"Uliss" v russkom zerkale* (St. Petersburg, 2015), *Practices of the Self and Spiritual Practices: Michel Foucault and the Eastern Christian Discourse* (Publ. Co. Grand Rapids, 2015), *Sozium i sinergiia: kolonizatsiia interfeisa* (Kazan', 2016), and *Spiritual Practice as the Base of New Anthropology* (Sidney, 2017).

Vladimir K. Kantor is Professor of Philosophy and Head of the International Laboratory for the Study of Russian and European Intellectual Dialogue at the National Research University "Higher School of Economics" in Moscow (Russia). He is the author of more than twenty books and numerous articles. His most recent books are *Dostoevskij, Nietzsche e la crisi del Cristianismo in Europa* (Venezia-Mestre, 2015), *"Srublennoe derevo zhizni." Sud'ba Nikolaia Chernyshevskogo* (Moscow, St. Petersburg, 2016), *Izobrazhaia, ponimat' ili Sentenial sensa: filosfiia v literaturnom tekste* (Moscow, St. Petersburg, 2017), *Demifologizatsiia russkoi kul'tury* (Moscow, St. Petersburg, 2019), *Russkaia mysl', ili "Samostoian'e cheloveka"* (Moscow, St. Petersburg, 2020).

Alexei A. Kara-Murza is Professor and Principal Research Associate at the Institute of Philosophy, Russian Academy of Sciences, Moscow (Russia). His research mainly focuses on the history of Russian philosophical and political thought. He is the author of *Shveitsarskie stranstviia Nikolaia Karamzina (1789–1790)* (Moscow, 2016) and *Ital'ianskoe puteshestvie Petra Chaadaeva (1824–1825)* (Moscow, 2019), and the editor of *Rossijskii liberalism: Idei i liudi* in 2 vols. (Moscow, 2007, 3rd ed. 2019).

Sofya Khagi is Associate Professor at the Department of Slavic Languages and Literatures, University of Michigan, Ann Arbor (USA). Her research focuses on contemporary Russian literature and culture, nineteenth- and twentieth-century Russian poetry, the intersections of literature and philosophy, and Baltic literatures and cultures. She is the author of *Silence and the Rest: Verbal Skepticism in Russian Poetry* (Northwestern University Press, 2013) and *Pelevin and Unfreedom: Poetics, Politics, Metaphysics* (Northwestern University Press, forthcoming in 2020), as well as the editor of *Companion to Victor Pelevin* (Academic Studies Press, forthcoming in 2021). Her other publications include articles on Russian poetry, post-Soviet fiction and film, science fiction, and Latvian literature.

Anton M. Khokhlov is Russian independent scholar who works on existentialist philosophy, mostly focusing on the philosophical ideas of Jean-Paul

Sartre, Albert Camus, Lev Shestov, and Miguel de Unamuno. He has published journal articles in Russian and international venues.

Alexei N. Krouglov is Professor at the Department of History of Philosophy, Russian State University for the Humanities, Moscow (Russia). His main research interests are in the history of eighteenth- and nineteenth-century philosophy, with a special focus on Kant, German Enlightenment, German Idealism, and Russian philosophy. His works include *Transtsendentalizm v filosofii* (Moscow, 2000), *Tetens, Kant i diskussiia o metafizike v Germanii vtoroi poloviny XVIII veka* (Moscow, 2008), *Filosofiia Kanta v Rossii v kontse XVIII— pervoi polovine XIX vekov* (Moscow, 2009), and *Kant i kantovskaia filosofiia v russkoi khudozhestvennoi literature* (Moscow, 2012). He is also the editor and translator of Tolstoj, L. N. *Gedanken Immanuel Kants* (Stuttgart-Bad Cannstatt, 2016) and co-editor (with H.P. Delfosse) of Tetens, J. N. *Über die allgemeine speculativische Philosophie, neue kritische Ausgabe* (Stuttgart-Bad Cannstatt, 2017).

Vladislav A. Lektorsky is Full Member of the Russian Academy of Sciences. He is Principal Research Associate at the Institute of Philosophy, RAS in Moscow (Russia). His main research interests are in epistemology, philosophy of mind, and philosophy of cognitive science. He has authored more than 500 publications that appeared in a number of languages. He is the author of *Filosofiia, Poznanie, Kul'tura* (Moscow, 2012) and *Chelovek i kul'tura* (Moscow, 2018) and co-editor (with M.F. Bykova) of *Philosophical Thought in Russia in the Second Half of the 20th Century: A Contemporary View from Russia and Abroad* (Bloomsbury, 2019).

Anne Lounsbery is Professor of Russian Literature and Chair of the Department of Russian and Slavic Studies at New York University (USA). Her most recent book is *Life is Elsewhere: Symbolic Geography in the Russian Provinces, 1800–1917* (Cornell University Press, 2019).

Jeff Love is Research Professor of German and Russian at Clemson University (USA). He has written two books on Tolstoy, *The Overcoming of History in "War and Peace"* (Brill, 2004) and *Tolstoy: A Guide for the Perplexed* (Continuum, 2008), along with *The Black Circle: A Life of Alexandre Kojève* (Columbia University Press, 2018). He is the editor of *Nietzsche and Dostoevsky: Philosophy, Morality, Tragedy* (Northwestern University Press, 2016), *Heidegger in Russia and Eastern Europe* (Rowman & Littlefield, 2017), as well as co-translator of F. W. J. Schelling's Philosophical *Investigations into the Essence of Human Freedom* (SUNY Press, 2006) and translator of Alexandre Kojève's *Atheism* (Columbia University Press, 2018).

Vitaly L. Makhlin is Professor of Philosophy at the Moscow State Pedagogical University (Russia). His main research interests include the history of nineteenth- and twentieth-century Western and Russian philosophy, as well as the history and theory of the humanities, both East and West, with a special focus on Mikhail Bakhtin's philosophy, theory of literature and discourse, and methodology of the human studies. He has edited an annual publication *Bakhtinskii sbornik* (1990–2005) and has authored four books and numerous articles. Among his recent books are *Vtoroe soznanie: podstupy k gumanitarnoi epistemologii* (Moscow, 2009) and *Great Time: Approaches to M. M. Bakhtin's Thought* (Siedlice, Poland, 2015).

Vladimir L. Marchenkov is Professor of Philosophy of Art at Ohio University (USA). His research interests include philosophy of art, both Western and Asian, Russian Philosophy, and German Idealism. He is the author of *The Orpheus Myth and the Powers of Music* (Pendragon, 2009), translator of Alexei Losev's *Dialectics of Myth* (Routledge, 2003), and author as well as consulting editor on Russian philosophy for the award-winning *Encyclopedia of Philosophy, Second Edition* (Thomson Gale, 2006). He also edited two volumes of essays, *Between Histories: Art's Dilemmas and Trajectories* (Hampton Press, 2013) and *Arts and Terror* (Cambridge Scholars Publishing, 2014), and co-edited (with S. Bird-Pollan) a collection of essays on *Hegel's Political Aesthetics: Art in Modern Society* (Bloomsbury, 2020).

Inessa Medzhibovskaya is Associate Professor of Liberal Studies and Literature at the New School in New York City (USA). She is the author of *Tolstoy and the Religious Culture of His Time* (Lexington Books, 2008), *Tolstoy's On Life (from the Archival History of Russian Philosophy)* (*Tolstoy Studies Journal* (30), 2019), and editor of the critical edition of Tolstoy's *On Life*, co-translated with Michael Denner (Northwestern University Press, 2018), *Tolstoy and His Problems: Views from the Twenty-First Century* (Northwestern University Press, 2018), and *A Critical Guide to Tolstoy's On Life: Interpretive Essays* (the Tolstoy Society of North America, 2019), and she served as the academic advisor for volumes 267 and 289AC of *Short Story Criticism* (Gale/Cengage, 2019, 2020). Most recently published is her *L.N. Tolstoy* in the Oxford Bibliographies series (Oxford University Press, 2021).

Julia B. Mehlich is Professor of Philosophy at the Faculty of Philosophy, Lomonosov State University in Moscow (Russia). Her main research areas are the history of Russian philosophy in relation to European philosophy of culture. Her recent books include *Personalizm L. P. Karsavina i evropeiskaia filosofiia.* (Moscow, 2003), *Irratsional' noe rasshirenie filosofii I. Kanta v Rossii* (St. Petersburg, 2014), and *Lev Karsavin* (St. Petersburg, 2019). She has also co-edited (with Steffen H. Mehlich) two special issues of the journal *Russian Studies in Philosophy: Neokantianism in Russia* (54(5), 2016) and *Philosophy of Right in Russia* (58(1), 2020).

Nelly V. Motroshilova is Professor and Principal Research Associate at the Institute of Philosophy, Russian Academy of Sciences in Moscow (Russia). Her research interests include German Idealism, especially Kant and Hegel, as well as Husserl, Heidegger, and Russian philosophical thought. Among her recent books are *Russkaia filosofiia v 50-kh–80-kh godakh 20-go stoletiia i zapadnaia* *mysl'* (Moscow, 2012), *Martin Khaidegger i Khanna Arendt: Bytie, vremia, liubov'* (Moscow, 2013), and *Ranniaia filosofiia Edmunda Gusserlia (Halle, 1887–1901)* (Moscow, 2018).

Thomas Nemeth, recently a writer-in-residence at New York University, holds a PhD in philosophy from the University of Louvain. His principal interests are the history of Russian philosophy, Husserl, and Kant. Most recently he has written *The Early Solov'ëv and His Quest for Metaphysics* (Springer, 2013), *Kant in Imperial Russia* (Springer, 2017), *The Later Solov'ëv. Philosophy in Imperial Russia* (Springer, 2019) as well as translated Shpet's *Appearance and Sense* (Springer, 2012), Solov'ëv's *Justification of the Moral Good* (Springer, 2015), and Shpet's *Hermeneutics and Its Problems* (Springer, 2019).

Sergei A. Nikolsky is Principal Research Associate at the Institute of Philosophy, Russian Academy of Sciences (RAS) in Moscow (Russia). His research interests are philosophy of literature and philosophy of Russian history (historiosophy). He has authored a series of books and articles, including *Russkoe mirovozzrenie* in three volumes (vols. 1–2 co-authored with V.P. Filimonov; Moscow, 2008, 2009, 2012), *Gorizonty smyslov. Filosofskie interpretatsii otechestvennoi literatury 19-vo i 20-vo vv.* (Moscow, 2015), *Imperiia i kul'tura. Filosofsko-literaturnoe osmyslenie Oktiabria* (Moscow, 2017), and *Filosofskaia antropologiia Andreia Platonova* (co-authored with S.S. Neretina and V.N. Porus; Moscow, 2019). Since 2006 he has served as the coordinator and editor of the proceedings of an annual national conference "The Problems of Russian Self-consciousness" organized by the Institute of Philosophy, RAS.

Helen Petrovsky is Principal Research Associate at the Institute of Philosophy, Russian Academy of Sciences in Moscow (Russia). Her major fields of interest are contemporary philosophy, visual studies, and North American literature and culture. She is the author of *Neproiavlennoe. Ocherki po filosofii fotografii* (Moscow, 2002), *Antifotografiia* (Moscow, 2003, 2015), *Po tu storonu voobrazheniia. Sovremennaia filosofiia i sovremennoe iskusstvo* (Nizhnii Novgorod, 2009; co-authored with O. Aronson), *Theoriia obraza* (Moscow, 2010), *Bezymiannye soobshchestva* (Moscow, 2012), *Chto ostaetsia ot iskusstva* (Moscow, 2015; co-authored with O. Aronson), and *Vozmushchenie znaka. Kul'tura protiv transtsendentsii* (Moscow, 2019). She is the winner of the 2011 Andrei Bely Prize (category: Theory) and the 2012 Innovation Prize ("Art Theory and Criticism").

Henry W. Pickford is Professor of German and Philosophy at Duke University (USA). He is the author of *The Sense of Semblance: Philosophical Analyses of Holocaust Art* (Fordham UP, 2013), *Thinking with Tolstoy and Wittgenstein: Expression, Emotion, and Art* (Northwestern University Press, 2013), co-author of *In Defense of Intuitions: A New Rationalist Manifesto* (Palgrave Macmillan, 2013), co-editor of *Der aufrechte Gang im windschiefen*

Kapitalismus (Springer, 2018), and editor and translator of Adorno, *Critical Models: Interventions and Catchwords* (Columbia UP, 1998) and Lev Loseff, *Selected Early Poems* (New York: Spuyten Duyvil, 2014).

Boris I. Pruzhinin is Principal Research Associate at the Institute of Philosophy, Russian Academy of Sciences in Moscow (Russia) and Editor-in-Chief of the journal *Voprosy Filosofii*. In his research he focuses on topics central to philosophy and methodology of science, as well as history of Russian philosophy. He is the editor of the book series "Russkaia filsoofiiia pervoi poloviny 20-go veka," which includes 33 volumes, and the author of ten book and more than 200 articles. Among his recent books are *Ratio serviens. Kontury kul'turno-istoricheskoi epistemologii* (Moscow, 2009) and co-authored *Kul'turno-istoricheskaia epistemologiia: problemy i perspektivy* (Moscow, 2014).

Tatiana G. Shchedrina is Professor at the Moscow State Pedagogical University (Russia) and at the Far Eastern Federal University (Russia). She is specialist in the history of Russian philosophy of the nineteenth and twentieth centuries and in the methodology of historical and philosophical research. She has published ten books and more than 200 research articles. Her recent books include *Arkhiv epokhi: tematicheskoe edinstvo russkoi filosofii* (Moscow, 2008) and *Gustav Shpet: filosof v kul'ture. Dokumenty i pis'ma* (Moscow, 2012).

Vadim Shkolnikov is Docent at the Department of Philology, at Higher School of Economics Research University, in St. Petersburg (Russia). He has written numerous articles on Belinsky and the culture of early Russian Hegelianism. He is working on a monograph entitled *Beautiful Souls and Terrorists: A Phenomenology of Conscience in Nineteenth-Century Russia.*

Yulia V. Sineokaya is Corresponding Member of the Russian Academy of Sciences and Deputy Director for Research at the Institute of Philosophy, Russian Academy of Sciences in Moscow (Russia). Her research focuses on interactions between Western philosophy and Russian thought in the late nineteenth and twentieth centuries. She is the author of *Tri obraza Nietzsche v russkoi kul'ture* (Moscow, 2008). She has also edited numerous collections, including *Anatomiia filosofii: kak rabotaet tekst* (Moscow, 2016), *Istoriia filosofii v formate stat'i* (Moscow, 2016), *Filosofskie emanatsii liubvi* (Moscow, 2018), *Nietzsche segodnia* (Moscow, 2019), *Fridrikh Nietzsche: Nasledie i proekt* (co-edited with E. A. Poliakova, Moscow, 2017), and *Filosofiia vo mnozhestvennom chisle* (co-edited with A. V. Smirnov, Moscow, 2020), and *Repliki: filosofskie besedy* (Moscow, 2021).

Maja Soboleva is Associate Professor of Philosophy at the Philipps-University of Marburg (Germany), Senior Research Fellow at the Alpen-Adria University of Klagenfurt am Wörthersee (Austria), and Director of the research project "A Man in His Own Time: Problematization of Temporality in European Intellectual Space in the 1900–1930s" at Ural Federal University (Russia). Her areas of specialization are epistemology, hermeneutics, philosophy of language, and the history of philosophy, in particular the German and Russian philosophical traditions. She is the author of over 100 scholarly publications in English, German, and Russian. Among her books are *A. Bogdanov und der philosophische Diskurs in Russland zu Beginn des 20. Jahrhunderts. Zur Geschichte des russischen Positivismus* (Hildesheim, 2007), *Die Philosophie Michail Bachtins. Von der existenziellen Ontologie zur dialogischen Vernunft* (Hildesheim, 2010), *Filosofskaia germenevtika: poniatiia i pozitsii* (Moscow, 2013), *Leben und Sein. Hermeneutische Bedeutungstheorien von Georg Mish und Josef König* (Wien, 2014), and *Logika zla. Al'ternativnoe vvedenie v filosofiiu* (St. Petersburg, 2019).

Daniela Steila is Professor of Philosophy at the University of Turin (Italy), where she teaches the history of Russian philosophy. She works on such topics as Russian culture in the nineteenth and twentieth centuries, the history of Russian Marxism, Russian epistemology and philosophical historiography, Lev Vygotsky's psychology, and philosophy in the Soviet era. Among her books are *Nauka i revoliutsiia* (Moscow, 2013) and *Gor'kij-Bogdanov e la scuola di Capri* (co-authored with J. Scherrer, Rome, 2017).

Lina Steiner is Leading Research Associate at the International Centre for Philosophy at the University of Bonn (Germany) and Director of the Research Center "Philosophy and Literature." Her research focuses on the intersections of philosophy and literature, particularly in the nineteenth-century novel. Her publications include *For Humanity's Sake: The Bildungsroman in Russian Culture* (University of Toronto Press, 2011), *Romanticism, Philosophy, and Literature* (co-edited with M. N. Forster, Palgrave Macmillan, 2020), and numerous articles that appeared in *Slavic Review, Comparative Literature, Studies in East European Thought*, and other journals and collected volumes.

Edward M. Świderski is Professor of Philosophy of Culture and Aesthetics, Emeritus, at the University of Fribourg (Switzerland) and former Editor-in-Chief of *Studies in East European Thought*. Besides editing for many years *Studies in Soviet Thought* that later became *SEET*, he has widely published on topics in Russian and Soviet philosophy, Polish philosophy, phenomenology, and analytic aesthetics.

Elena A. Takho-Godi is Professor of Russian Literature at the Lomonosov Moscow State University, Leading Research Associate at Gorky Institute of World Literature of the Russian Academy of Sciences, and Department Head at the Library-Museum "A.F. Losev's House" in Moscow (Russia). She is the author of *Aleksei Losev v epokhu russkoi revoliutsii: 1917–1919* (Moscow, 2014) and the editor of *Literatura i religiozno-filosofskaia mysl' kontsa XIX – pervoi treti XX veka. K 165-letiiu Vl. Solov'eva* (Moscow, 2018), *Filosof i ego vremia: K 125-letiiu so dnia rozhdeniia A.F. Loseva* (Moscow, 2019), *Literatura i filosofiia: Ot romantizma k XX veku. K 150-letiiu so dnia smerti V. F. Odoevskogo* (Moscow, 2019), and *Predsimvolizm — liki i otrazheniia* (Moscow, 2020).

Galin Tihanov is the George Steiner Professor of Comparative Literature at Queen Mary University of London (United Kingdom). He has held visiting appointments at universities in Europe, North and South America, and Asia. He is the author of five monographs, including, most recently, *The Birth and Death of Literary Theory: Regimes of Relevance in Russia and Beyond* (Stanford University Press, 2019) which won the 2020 AATSEEL Prize for "Best Book in Literary Scholarship." Tihanov is elected member of Academia Europaea, past president of the ICLA Committee on Literary Theory, and member of the Executive Board of the Institute for World Literature at Harvard University. He is currently writing *Cosmopolitanism: A Very Short Introduction* commissioned for Oxford University Press.

Konstantin V. Zenkin is Professor of Musicology and Vice Rector for Research of the P.I. Tchaikovsky Moscow State Conservatory (Russia). He is the Editor-in-Chief of the musicological journal *Nauchnyi Vestnik Moskovskoi Konservatorii*. His areas of interest include history of European music of the nineteenth and twentieth centuries, philosophy of music, and performing art. He is the author of *Fortepiannaia miniatiura i puti muzykal'nogo romantizma* (Moscow, 1997; 2nd ed. 2019) and *Muzyka — Eidos — Vremia. A.F. Losev i gorizonty sovremennoj nauki o muzyke* (Moscow 2015). His latter book was recently translated into English (Progress-Tradition Moscow, 2018).

Evert van der Zweerde is Professor of Social and Political Philosophy at Radboud University, Nijmegen (Netherlands). He is co-editor of the series *Reframing the Boundaries: Thinking the Political* (Rowman & Littlefield International) and associate editor of *Studies in East European Thought*. His research focuses on political philosophy, especially theory of democracy, and on Russian philosophy. His recent publications include a collection of articles, *Vzgliad so storony na istoriiu russkoi i sovetskoi filosofii* (St. Petersburg, 2017) and "Democratic Repertoires of Political Legitimization: Russian Echoes and European Realities," in *Russia and the EU; Spaces of Interaction*, edited by T. Hoffmann and A. Makarychev (Routledge, 2019).

CHAPTER 1

Introduction: On Russian Thought and Intellectual Tradition

Marina F. Bykova and Lina Steiner

> It is characteristic of the Russian people to philosophize [...].
> The fate of the philosopher in Russia is painful and tragic.
> Nikolai Berdyaev, *The Russian Idea*

This volume is an extensive *Handbook of Russian Thought* that provides an in-depth survey of major figures, currents, and developments in Russian intellectual history, spanning the period from the late eighteenth to the late twentieth centuries. This was the most intense period in Russia's intellectual and political history, witnessing the emergence of original philosophical and social ideas and thinkers, great literature, art, and criticism. All of these together shaped the intellectual, cultural, and political history of Russia as it was making its way into world culture.

Although a century has elapsed since the appearance of the English translation of Thomas G. Masaryk's influential *The Spirit of Russia*, for many Anglophone readers Russian thought is still a conundrum.[1] Meanwhile, scholars specializing on Russian intellectual history have largely come to agree that the distinctive characteristic of Russian thought is its philosophical propensity.

M. F. Bykova (✉)
North Carolina State University, Raleigh, NC, USA
e-mail: mfbykova@ncsu.edu

L. Steiner
University of Bonn, Bonn, Germany
e-mail: lsteiner@uni-bonn.de

© The Author(s), under exclusive license to Springer Nature
Switzerland AG 2021
M. F. Bykova et al. (eds.), *The Palgrave Handbook of Russian Thought*,
https://doi.org/10.1007/978-3-030-62982-3_1

In Russia, the interest in the fundamental problems concerning such matters as existence, cognition, moral values, freedom, and other philosophical questions characterizes not only humanistic disciplines, but also art and culture in the broader sense.

Since the beginning of the 1900s there have been numerous efforts to traverse the vast and unfamiliar terrain of the Russian intellectual tradition by coming to grasp the role of philosophy and philosophical thought in Russian history.[2] Exploring a variety of more or less conventional pathways—from tracing the development of religious philosophy to sketching the clashes between materialism and idealism to scrutinizing Russian thought from the perspective of long-established subjects of philosophical inquiry—these endeavors attempted to throw Russian philosophy into relief by comparing it with, and assimilating it to, the West European philosophical tradition. For those few who expected to find in Russia a further elaboration of classical themes of *pure* philosophy, this comparison might have been disappointing. Russian philosophy may not have achieved such preeminence as its counterpart in ancient Greece, and it may not have created such sophisticated philosophical systems as those developed in German Idealism. And yet, as connoisseurs of Russian cultural and intellectual history have repeatedly pointed out, Russia is a philosophical nation in a more profound sense. In Russia, the term "philosophy" bears a much wider connotation than just an academic discipline. As Mikhail Epstein notes, "in Russia, philosophy is less a noun, a self-sufficient entity (a field, a discipline, a profession), and more an *adjective*, an attribute or a property of various *philosophical* activities: the philosophically oriented humanities, or philosophically inspired cultural creativity, or philosophical aims of sociopolitical undertakings" (Epstein 2019, 5). What "philosophy" signifies in Russia goes far beyond just specialized philosophical studies and surpasses themes and topics usually conceived as purely philosophical—even though, contrary to a still existing bias, as we hope to demonstrate by this volume, philosophy proper has always remained prominent in Russian intellectual discourse. Instead of being limited to one specific discipline, in Russia, "philosophy" is usually associated with an intricate practice of philosophizing.

Many observers explain this attributive usage of the word by the abuse that philosophy in Russia suffered during the Soviet period when it became associated with orthodox Marxism and was turned into ideology. To be sure, the social setting in which philosophy operated under the Soviet regime was hostile and oppressive; any appearance of non-Marxist and free thought was met with malicious attack(s). This led many original thinkers (e.g. Mikhail Bakhtin (1895–1975), Alexei Losev (1893–1988), Lev Vygotsky (1896–1934), etc.) to retreat into other social and humanitarian disciplines—such as aesthetics, theory of classical culture, literary studies, and psychology—which appeared to be relatively immune from ideology and political oppression and thus became means for practicing philosophy in a more sheltered environment.[3]

But in the Russian context, even in the prerevolutionary years, "philosophy" was rarely associated with a specific discipline or highly specialized

1 INTRODUCTION: ON RUSSIAN THOUGHT AND INTELLECTUAL TRADITION

scholarly practice. The influential Russian thinkers of the nineteenth century, including Pyotr Chaadaev (1794–1856), Alexander Herzen (1812–1870), Mikhail Bakunin (1814–1876), Fyodor Dostoevsky (1821–1881), Nikolai Danilevskii (1822–1885), Nikolai Chernyshevsky (1828–1889), Leo Tolstoy (1828–1910), Nikolai Fedorov (1829–1903), Konstantin Leontiev (1831–1891), and Vasily Rozanov (1856–1919), lacked academic affiliations; further, not one of them was an academic scholar. Even the founding father of Russian religious philosophy, Vladimir Solovyov (1853–1900), who lectured at Moscow University in his early years, 1875–1881, was forced to vacate his position after calling upon the tsar for clemency for those responsible for the murder of Alexander II.

Most of those who contributed to the Russian philosophical legacy—in both the nineteenth and twentieth centuries—were writers, critics, journalists, artists, politicians, or civil servants. They pursued philosophy through a variety of intellectual practices where literature, journalism, and literary and social criticism became their own creative means of philosophizing. Hence our focus in this *Handbook* is on *Russian thought*, and not on Russian philosophy or even philosophical thought, which would limit the scope of analysis and present a distorted account of the Russian intellectual tradition. Our goal in this volume is to reconstruct an amazingly vibrant picture of intellectual and cultural life in Russia from the early nineteenth to the late twentieth centuries, presenting it in its enormous complexity and intellectual vigor. This book employs a unifying approach to the subject matter, putting it into the context of Russia's changing historical landscape and considering different forms of its appearance in literature, art, social and political conceptions and theories, dominant moral systems, and religious beliefs, while rejecting any reductive or simplistic narrative that conceals the genuine character of Russian thought.

Russian intellectuals never excelled at producing abstract (pure) ideas that would have no substantiation in the actual world. They always applied themselves to the task of manifesting the most general ideas in Russian social relationships and in the substance of everyday life. Their ultimate goal was to *philosophize reality*, but this was much more than a pure contemplation, and rather required an active, reflective engagement with the existent reality. In this sense, a symbiotic relationship between literature, criticism, art, orthodox Christian faith, and philosophy has typified the Russian intellectual tradition since the early stages of its development. Thus, in order to properly appreciate the scope of Russian thought and unravel its multifaceted content, it is essential to take into account the intimate and intense connections between a variety of Russian intellectual pursuits, such as philosophy, theology, literature, art, cultural studies, politics, and social life. And this is the path this book follows.

Russian thought cannot be properly understood apart from its historical development. Its persistent and fervent immersion in the cultural, social, and political life of the people makes a historical perspective vital for understanding the key issues it debates and the solutions it proposes. Thus, before discussing

Historical Evolution

the structure of this *Handbook*, a brief history of Russian thought considered in the context of Russia's historical development is in order.

The peculiar characteristic of Russian thought, emphasized by many commentators, is that its emergence and early evolution came to be largely motivated by external rather than internal causes and processes. Instead of being a result of an organic national evolution, it grew out of foreign religious and moral precepts that Russian society embraced and assimilated after their acceptance by the country's rulers. Yet, although foreign philosophical and theological ideas profoundly affected Russian thought, the latter was not just a pure imitation or uncritical adaptation of Western ideas and theories of the time. Even those most receptive to foreign ideas adopted them with significant qualifications, which reflected specifically Russian concerns and interests.

The Russian cultural and spiritual tradition is long-standing, and its origin is usually associated with the introduction of Christianity in Kievan Rus' in the ninth century. This differs from Russian philosophy and *philosophically* inclined thought, a complex tradition that emerged only in the nineteenth century. As Russian philosophy matured, it went through several highs and lows, suffering from a number of political and social upheavals and temptations, from violent humiliation and the arbitrariness of the law, during both the tsarist regime and the totalitarianism of the Soviet era. Based on the intensity of philosophical reflection and the level of intellectual achievements, the development of Russian philosophically informed thought can be divided into three main periods: (1) the "philosophical awakening" of the 1830s and 1840s, which overlapped with the beginning of the Golden era of Russian literature; (2) philosophy of the Silver age, which spanned the last two decades of the nineteenth and the first two decades of the twentieth centuries; and (3) the intellectual renaissance of the latter half of the twentieth century. In order to understand the specific significance of these periods and appreciate the accomplishments associated with each of them, we will begin our excursion into the history of Russian thought with a brief characterization of the early stage of its development.

1. The Early Stage

The first philosophical ideas as well as the earliest usage of the term "philosopher" in Russia date back to *The Primary Chronicle*, compiled around 1113 by the semi-legendary Kievan monk Nestor. The *Chronicle* records several stories of Prince Vladimir's (972–1015) conversion of himself and his people to Christianity. According to the most famous among these legends, Vladimir, eager to adopt one of the neighboring countries' religions, was most impressed by a "philosopher" (sometimes described as a "scholar") sent by Byzantium in 986. Skilled in rhetoric and highly knowledgeable in his faith's canons, this missionary not only presented the Kiev Prince with a radiant image of the Old and New Testaments' mysteries, but also persuaded him of the superiority of Orthodox Christianity over all other religious denominations and faiths. Intrigued by this presentation, Vladimir sent his ambassadors to Constantinople, where they were exposed to the most elaborate rituals while attending the liturgy in Saint Sophia cathedral. In 988, upon receiving his ambassadors' glowing reports, Vladimir converted himself and his people to Orthodox Christianity. To reinforce his decision, he married the Byzantine princess Anna Porphyrogenita (see Bushkovitch 2012, 7).

In late Byzantine culture Greek philosophy was losing its prestige as a body of knowledge in its own right and was turning into a handmaiden to Orthodox theology.[4] Nevertheless, Orthodox monks were still the beneficiaries and legatees of Greek *paideia*.[5] After Vladimir's baptism, Kievan Rus' began to absorb the writings of Eastern Church Fathers and through them the legacy of Greek, as well as Jewish, thought. Importantly, notwithstanding their connections to Constantinople, the Rurikovid rulers of Kievan Rus' also developed close political and trade alliances with a number of European kingdoms, including Norway, Britain, France, and Hungary.

The development of the Kievan Rus' was arrested by the Mongolian invasion in 1223. Two and a half centuries of the Mongol yoke left an indelible imprint on Russian civilization by bringing it into closer contact with several Asian civilizations that had been subdued by the Mongols and absorbed into their Empire. Only in 1472 did the Moscow Grand Duke Ivan III, by marrying the niece of the last Byzantine Emperor, Zoe (Sophia) Paleologue (who had been brought up at the Papal court in Rome), reassert Russia's ties with Europe and his readiness to shake off the yoke. Ivan III's vision was to transform Moscow into the "third Rome." During his reign, the country began moving toward establishing a Russian empire, which finally received the title of a *tsardom* during the reign of his grandson Ivan IV (the Terrible). The first Autocrat of All Russia, Ivan IV saw himself as an equal of the Emperor of the Holy Roman Empire. There began to emerge the idea of reconquering Constantinople from the Ottomans and adding it to the Russian *tsardom*, thus transforming it into the greatest Christian Empire of the world. Yet it was Catherine II who officially embraced this goal and made it central to her foreign policy in the 1770s.[6]

By this time, Russia had traveled a long path from being an appendage of the Mongol Empire to a vast and still expanding modern Empire whose German-born Empress had carefully shaped her identity as an enlightened autocrat by combining the traditional claim of being the principal defender of authentic Christianity with the new claim of being a *philosophically* minded monarch whose reason was as strong as her faith. A European brought up during the "philosophical age," Catherine II realized that a more utilitarian Enlightenment championed by her predecessor Peter the Great was insufficient for transforming Russia into a modern empire. She promoted ambitious visionaries and encouraged a number of cultural reforms (Madariaga 1991). Thus, in addition to supporting the Petersburg Academy of Sciences and Moscow University, in

1783 Catherine established the Russian Academy, whose aim was to cultivate the Russian language and literature, and appointed Princess Ekaterina R. Dashkova (1743–1810) as its founding President (Bushkovitch 2012, 129; see also Uspensky 1987).[7] However, the Pugachev uprising, followed by the outbreak of the French Revolution, made the Empress scale back her progressive reforms and become increasingly tyrannical. During this last quarter of the eighteenth century, the government persecuted the champions of the Enlightenment, including two significant philosophical writers of the period: the journalist and publisher Nikolai Novikov (1744–1818) and the writer and philosopher Alexander Radishchev (1749–1802). By imprisoning and exiling these outspoken critics of slavery, the government wished not only to punish them for attacking the status quo, but also to intimidate other potential free thinkers (Lossky 2011, 6–8). Upon his ascension to the throne, Paul I, who had been educated in the spirit of conservative liberalism, proved to be an even more brutal tyrant than his mother Catherine. He introduced an equivalent of the Salic law that banned women from the Russian throne. It went without saying that no woman could aspire to become an administrator or an academic (a situation that lasted until the 1917 Revolution). Paul's reactionary policies were particularly damaging for philosophy, which came to be seen as subversive. Thus since the 1790s the conflict between thinkers who aspired to *libertas philosophandi* and the state has become a recurrent feature of Russian history.

The first department of philosophy opened at Moscow University, Russia's first European-style University, established in 1755 on the initiative of Mikhail Lomonosov (1711–1765) (see [Istoriia MU] 1955, 2). According to Lomonosov's plan, there were originally three Faculties: Law, Medicine, and Philosophy. Viewed as a comprehensive understanding of the fields of science and humanities, philosophy served the purpose of basic (liberal arts) education but also offered several areas for specialization (Zenkovsky 1953, 1: 105–115).[8] Lectures were typically delivered in Latin, and only a few courses were taught in Russian. Lacking adequately trained domestic academics, Russian rulers invited foreign scholars to staff the University and other existing educational institutions (such as the theological educational establishments that had become widespread by the mid-eighteenth century). The majority of the first philosophy professors who served at Moscow University came from Germany. This trend continued into the beginning of the nineteenth century, and when in 1804 the new tsar Alexander I opened two new universities—one in Kazan and another in Kharkov—many professorial positions were filled by Germans. Although many of them were already well-established European scholars, their impact on Russian thought was relatively limited.[9]

Furthermore, after a brief span of liberalization during the first decade of Alexander I's reign, there followed a period of reaction that lasted through the 1860s. It is only logical that from that point on, ethical and socio-political concerns would preoccupy Russian intellectuals and dominate philosophical discourse, arguably to the detriment of what is usually considered pure (or theoretical) philosophy.

1 INTRODUCTION: ON RUSSIAN THOUGHT AND INTELLECTUAL TRADITION

Since the first decades of the nineteenth century, there were a number of "dark ages" when the notion of philosophy in its Western European sense was regarded as a dangerous virus that might undermine the vitality of the Russian nation. In the wake of the Decembrist uprising in 1825, a number of professorial positions in philosophy at the Universities of Moscow, Petersburg, Kazan, and Kharkov were closed or drastically reduced. Throughout the 1830s–1860s the teaching of philosophy was frequently carried out by the faculties of natural science, law, and theology (Koyré 1929, 46–87). Even before 1825, philosophy professors were frequently harassed when their lectures and writings conveyed atheistic or liberal ideas that could be harmful to autocracy. Not only the followers of Kant and Fichte, but even the philosophers who were educated in the systems of Friedrich Schelling and Lorenz Oken, were often purged under Alexander I's reactionary Minister of Education Prince Alexander Golitzin (Koyré 1929, 46–87). Thus, for example, Alexander Galich (1783–1848), a Schellingian philosopher educated in Germany who taught at Petersburg Pedagogical Institute, was charged with atheism and revolutionary sympathies and dismissed from teaching (Sukhov 2012, 80–81).

When, in 1832, Golitzin was succeeded by the more liberal Count Sergei Uvarov, himself a long-term friend of Schelling who was also on friendly terms with Alexander von Humboldt and Johann Wolfgang von Goethe, the situation became somewhat more favorable to students of German Romantic and early idealist philosophy. Uvarov himself exploited this philosophy to substantiate his own formula "Orthodoxy, Autocracy, and the Nation," which served as the core of his doctrine of "official nationalism," used to justify his own policies for public education in Russia (Koyré 1929, 194–207; Whittaker 1984).

By that point, Schelling was already quite well known in Russia, thanks to the work of Daniil Vellanski (1774–1847), Professor of Physiology at the Academy for Medical Surgery in St. Petersburg. As Zenkovsky remarked, "Vellanski's importance to the development of philosophic ideas in Russia is extremely great. His *direct* influence was not significant; nevertheless, when Circles of 'Wisdom-Lovers' were formed in Moscow and St. Petersburg in the 1820's [...], they all acknowledged Vellanski as the leader of Russian Schellingianism" (Zenkovsky 1953, 1: 120). The Circles of "Wisdom-Lovers" (i.e. Philosophers, or in Russian—*Liubomudry*) mentioned above sprang up in the early 1820s, and they were the first philosophical groups in Russia. The facts that the *Liubomudry* had to meet secretly and that their circles existed only for a few years and had to be closed at the end of 1825 in the aftermath of the Decembrist uprising are indicative of the fragile status of philosophy in Russia throughout the 1820s.

The more famous Moscow Circle included Prince Vladimir F. Odoevskii (Russia's first musicologist and a major prose writer), Dmitrii Venevitinov (a talented lyric poet who died at the age of 21), Ivan Kireevsky (the future Slavophile), and other scions of Moscow aristocracy (Zenkovsky 1953, 1: 130–170). The social background of the *Liubomudry* explains why their teacher Vellanski's influence on the development of Russian philosophical thought and its milieu was rather limited. As aristocratic dilettanti, *Liubomudry* did not try to pursue academic careers, and their intellectual activities suffered from their insularity and limited exposure to the complexity of Russian life. Yet, it would be a mistake to underestimate this circle's contribution to the development of Russian philosophy. Despite the largely dilettante character of the movement, it was a crucial part of the Russian Enlightenment whose ideas and theories had an essential impact on the country's intellectual discourse, shaping its theoretical quests and determining its central themes.

2. The "Philosophical Awakening" of the 1830s–1840s

There seems to be a scholarly consensus that Russian philosophy proper began to evolve in the nineteenth century (Hamburg and Poole 2010, 1–5). While scholars are still debating the origins and most essential traits of the Russian philosophical school, many associate its beginning with the debate between Slavophiles and Westernizers prompted by Pyotr Chaadaev's (1991) *First Philosophical Letter* published in the journal *Telescope* in 1836.[10] It should come as no surprise that this debate concerned the question of Russian national identity and its relation to universal humanism. A reflection on the meaning of Russianness has been a recurring theme in Russian discussions since the late eighteenth and early nineteenth centuries, and not only within a narrow philosophically engaged intellectual circle but also among literati, politicians, religious and social thinkers, and other representatives of the new educated elite who came to be known as the *intelligentsia*.

As a quintessentially Russian (and Polish) phenomenon, the intelligentsia arose only in the nineteenth century in response to the inability of the Russian rulers to provide the country with effective intellectual leadership. Russian society had a dire need for a philosophical orientation, and the task of establishing this orientation fell to the intelligentsia, which filled the void while the government and official state institutions failed to offer any adequate guidance. Composed mostly of the *raznochintsy* (the nascent middle class, which included impoverished gentry as well as descendants of merchants and clergymen), this peculiar social group had an acute sense of self-awareness and felt responsibility for the people and the nation at large. Without being professional thinkers, individuals who formed this specific group practiced a variety of intellectual professions, being writers, artists, teachers, priests, lawyers, doctors, scholars, literary critics, and journalists. The influence of the intelligentsia on the life of nineteenth-century Russian society can hardly be overestimated. The intelligentsia's ultimate ambition was to change the entire society and, eventually, all of humanity, by intellectualizing the very substance of social life and the course of history. Philosophical reflection became the most appropriate means toward this end.

Indeed, the 1830s–1840s witnessed an enormous flourishing of philosophical thinking, a kind of "philosophical awakening" which Russia had never experienced before. It was the Russian historian and Orthodox priest Georges

(Georgii) Florovsky (1893–1979) who first used the expression "philosophical awakening" to refer to this period in Russian intellectual history, which largely overlapped with the "Golden Era" of Russian literature. This is how Florovsky describes the atmosphere of this period:

> After a long historical experience and ordeal philosophical life becomes a new mode or a new phase of national existence. [...] One can notice in the generation of that epoch some captivating attraction to philosophy, sense a philosophical passion and thirst, see a kind of magical irresistible tendency toward philosophical themes and issues. (Florovsky 1988, 234–235)

Not only had philosophical thinking enjoyed a revival and reclaimed its public role within Russian society, but philosophy finally evolved into a special academic discipline with its own scope and aims. A characteristic shift in philosophical inquiry toward the questions of human nature, freedom, individual destiny, and social responsibility signaled a beginning of a distinctive Russian tradition of philosophical humanism (Hamburg and Poole 2010). A passionate commitment to the ideals of liberty, self-determination, human dignity, and justice underlay all philosophical discussions of that time, including the seminal debate between the Slavophiles and the Westernizers, the defense of a materialistic worldview by Russian radicals, Russian populists' search for new ethical values, and neoidealists' struggles to envision and describe a new human condition.

The increasing awareness of the contrast between Russia's political power and its social backwardness, and the deeply felt disintegration of Russia's eclectic culture, brought to attention a dire need for modernization which found its expression in extensive intellectual debates about the world's historical progress and Russia's place in universal history. Occupied with the problem of Russia's "whence and whither," Russian intellectuals came to be divided into two conceptually opposed intellectual camps: the Westernizers and the Slavophiles. The Westernizers linked universal progress to universal rationality and the rationalization of society, and the progress of Russia to developing its national identity in accordance with the European (Western) pattern. In contrast to this, the Slavophiles showed a strong opposition to all things Western, insisting on the uniqueness of the Russian legacy and its messianic future. Hence, in the middle of the nineteenth century the means to define Russian national identity (Russianness) became the central point of a passionate search for the meaning of universal history and the place Russia occupied in it.

Both the Westernizers and the Slavophiles recognized that their country was only beginning to emerge from the "dark ages" into which it was plunged by the Mongolian invasion and other historical calamities. But whereas Europe could overcome its "dark ages" by recovering the legacy of Greco-Roman civilization that had never been wholly extinguished thanks to the omnipresence of Latin, Russia, whose connections to Greco-Roman antiquity were tenuous, had to find another path. The Westernizers and the Slavophiles differed substantially in their views regarding the Byzantine legacy, which was interlinked with that of Orthodoxy. For the radical Westernizers, everything that had to do with Byzantium seemed shrouded in darkness and deserved oblivion. Enlightenment for them meant the development of reason and secular culture. The Slavophiles, on the contrary, believed that the Byzantine Orthodox tradition in a broader sense—a set of beliefs, customs, and habits of thought preserved through popular literature and culture—possessed great stores of wisdom which had to be preserved and analyzed.

While the Westernizers believed that an "integral worldview" and a unified vision of history were the essential framework for theorizing about Russia's destiny and place in universal history, the Slavophiles strove to promote *sobornost'*, Russian spirituality in the purity of its origin, as the unique Russian identity and the only way out of Western decline. In Russian, the term "*sobornost'*" means "togetherness" and "spirit of communality" and has theological origins and connotations. It accounts for the spiritual experience of religious faith in what is considered to be its purest form, namely, Russian Orthodoxy. One of the key Slavophiles, Alexei Khomiakov (1804–1860) viewed the Russian *obshchina* (a village commune) as a perfect example of *sobornost'* and commended the Russian peasants for their humility and inherent sense of justice. The Slavophiles insisted on the orthodox spirit of organic "togetherness," uncontaminated by Western rationalism and immorality, as the only model for Russian society and ultimately as the ideal for all of humanity. The Slavophiles thereby laid the foundations for a Russian tradition of cultural and religious messianism which includes Fyodor Dostoevsky (especially his political writings), the Pan-Slavist and Eurasian movements, and the apocalyptic visions of Nikolai Berdyaev (1874–1948).

Armed with a philosophical methodology derived primarily from the study of Schelling, another early Slavophile, Ivan Kireevsky (1806–1856), went on to develop his own metaphysics of "integral knowledge," which he starkly juxtaposed to Hegel's panlogism. In Zenkovsky's opinion, Kireevsky and Khomiakov were the first truly original Russian philosophers, and their approach to philosophy signaled the emergence of a new philosophical trend, for which Nikolai Berdyaev would later use the felicitous phrase "the Russian Idea" (Zenkovsky 1953, 171–237; Berdyaev 1992).[11] Like the early Slavophiles and their immediate followers, the later trend was by no means unified and homogeneous. On the contrary, throughout the rest of the nineteenth century, Russian thinkers continued to struggle for their intellectual identity and recognition vis-à-vis European culture with its well-developed philosophical tradition. They also continued to fight for their academic rights and freedoms within their own state.

The government's repression of philosophy came to a head in 1850 when Nicholas I, frightened by the new revolutionary wave in Europe, ordered the termination of all professorial positions in philosophy. They were re-established only in 1863 under the "Tsar-Liberator" Alexander II (Koyré 1929, 68–153; Walicki 1979, 71–115; Sukhov 2012, 77–149). The fact that throughout most of the nineteenth century philosophical reflection was confined to the semi-public intellectual "circles" and "thick" literary journals left an imprint on both Russian philosophy and literature, which grew accustomed to seeing themselves as interrelated discourses. It is not merely a coincidence that the 1860s and 1870s, which historians describe as the pinnacle of the Russian Enlightenment (the age of *prosvetitel'stvo*), witnessed both the resurgence of philosophical literary criticism (as represented by Nikolai Chernyshevsky, Nikolai Dobrolyubov, Nikolai Strakhov, and a number of others) and the efflorescence of the philosophical novel (represented, first and foremost, by Ivan Turgenev, Leo Tolstoy, Fyodor Dostoevsky, and Ivan Goncharov).

3. The Silver Age

The last decade of the nineteenth and the first two decades of the twentieth century were characterized by the artistic and intellectual boom that came to be known as the "Silver Age of Russian culture." The full range of Silver Age achievements cannot be summarized in a few short paragraphs, and not only because of its great depth and sophistication, but also because of its dichotomous character: optimism coexisted with pessimism and "hopeful anticipation" became interspersed with an increasing "sense of uncertainty and disintegration, of deep skepticism about all received truths and certainties" (Riasanovsky and Steinberg 2011, 450). A list of those associated with the culture of the Silver Age includes the artists Alexandre Benois (1870–1960), Marc Chagall (1887–1985), and Kazimir Malevich (1879–1935), the composers Sergei Rachmaninov (1873–1943) and Alexander Scriabin (1872–1915), the writers Andrei Bely (1880–1934), Dmitrii Merezhkovskii (1865–1941), and Ivan Bunin (1870–1953), the lyric poets Alexander Blok (1880–1921), Anna Akhmatova (1889–1966), Marina Tsvetaeva (1892–1941), and Osip Mandelstam (1891–1938), the *Ballets Russes* choreographers Mikhail (Michel) Fokine (1880–1942) and George Balanchine (1896–1979), and many other artists who have made their way into the canon of Western culture.

Although this period of Russian cultural expansion has traditionally been associated with the arts, the Russian "spiritual Renaissance" (Berdyaev) of the first two decades of the twentieth century also signifies the revival of philosophical thought and the renewal processes occurring in philosophy itself. Indeed, this Renaissance was largely associated with the philosophical collection *Vekhi* (Landmarks) (1909) and the writings of a score of original philosophers and prominent figures of the Silver Age, such as Vasily Rozanov (1858–1919), Nikolai Berdyaev, Sergei Bulgakov (1871–1944), Semyon Frank (1877–1950), Pavel Florensky (1882–1937), Lev Shestov (1866–1938), and others. The ideas and theories of many of them are the focus of specific essays included in this *Handbook*.

This period also saw a rapid development and flourishing of the strong tradition of Russian religious philosophy, including both liberal and radical trends of religious humanism (Sergei Bulgakov, Semyon Frank, Pavel Florensky), as well as the complex teaching of the most systematic Russian philosopher, Vladimir Solovyov (1853–1900). Although different in their assessments of the value of law for guaranteeing personal autonomy and human rights, religious humanists responded to Dostoevsky and Nietzsche, drawing upon Solovyov and further advancing his optimistic doctrine of integration (the philosophy of All-Unity), in which they saw a potential for a renewed wholeness of humanity and a true selfhood.

As art and literature, philosophy of the Silver Age is characterized by a drastic departure from previous (more traditional) currents and topics in philosophical inquiry and a remarkable continuity with previous themes. Describing the "spiritual Renaissance" of the early twentieth century, Berdyaev pointed to symbolism and aestheticism as the distinguishing features of that intellectual period. But there are two other important features that make the philosophy of the Silver Age so unique, especially in comparison to its earlier and later counterparts. This philosophical Renaissance stands out for its persistent futurological intention and for its focus on the personality and concrete individuality, which also includes an interest in exploring human sensual and erotic nature.

Having no chance for practical self-realization in the toxic environment of Russia's social life, intellectuals, including both the artistic elite and philosophers, who at first passively contemplated decadence, suddenly turned their attention to the future, beginning to construct it in an imaginary—symbolic and abstract—way, thus demonstratively breaking with the dull reality and everything that was taken for granted. This is why many Russian intellectuals welcomed the 1905 and 1917 revolutions and perceived them as a practical realization of a grandiose futuristic project. A clearly displayed futurological tendency coincided with what many scholars call an "erotic revolution" in Russian philosophy, which brought to attention the aesthetic and moral significance of Eros and attempted "to unite into one whole the philosophical, religious, psychological, and aesthetics aspects of love" (Shestakov 2017, 30). Some Russian thinkers (such as Vl. Solovyov, Berdyaev, Lev Karsavin (1882–1952), Boris Vysheslavtsev (1877–1954)) conceived love as a way of harmonizing spiritual and bodily principles, overcoming egoistic urges, and leading to a moral revival of man, while others (Florensky, Bulgakov, Ivan Ilyin (1883–1954)) who equated love with the Christian love of humankind [caritas] associated it with compassion and mercy. Yet despite the differences between their approaches, they all maintained a focus on intimacy and emphasized the value of the person and her individual experience (see Tihanov 2009, 115–122). Thus, the Silver Age gave rise to new schools within Russian philosophy that closely intertwined, such as personalism (Rozanov, Lossky) and existentialism (Shestov), creating highly original concepts and theories (e.g. Berdyaev's existential personalism) which are significantly different from their Western counterparts.[12]

Personalism and existentialism were certainly not the only philosophical schools that emerged during the Silver Age. A rich variety of philosophical creeds, circles, and movements (Eurasianism, Marxism, Cosmism,

1 INTRODUCTION: ON RUSSIAN THOUGHT AND INTELLECTUAL TRADITION 13

Neo-Kantianism, etc.) that sprung up within a short period of time flourished side by side with other intellectual inquiries in the environment, which fostered dialogue and interaction among different disciplines and facilitated the birth of a number of new disciplines, such as modern linguistics, comparative literature, and literary theory.[13]

This cultural Renaissance was relatively short-lived and came to a violent end when the Revolutions of 1905/1906, followed by World War I, the Revolutions of 1917, and the civil war claimed millions of lives and drove hundreds of thousands into exile. In the fall of 1922, the Bolsheviks expelled some 220 prominent intellectuals considered "problematic dissidents," sending them on so-called "philosophers' ships" to Germany. Among those forcibly deported from their home country was a wide array of thinkers, including philosophers, economists, scientists, writers, journalists, and other intellectuals. The majority of these individuals were never involved with the counterrevolutionaries or any other active political opposition. They were people who had intellectual differences with Bolsheviks and their general plan for the country. It was a sad irony, because, exiled from Russia, they had lost the homeland that they had tried to improve and civilize throughout their lives.

Those who, like Berdyaev and Shestov, were lucky enough to continue their career in Europe[14] carried on with their philosophical pursuits. For them and other progressively thinking individuals—both in exile and within the country—the future of Russia became an urgent concern. Thus, questions of the fundamental value of individual freedom, protecting individual rights, and affirming the ideal of individual and collective personality continued to play a prominent role in the philosophical discussions of that time, determining further philosophical and intellectual development in Russia.

4. A New Intellectual Awakening: The Mid-1950s and the Early 1990s

The seventy-year-long Soviet epoch left perhaps the most severe imprints on the state of Russian intellectual life and, especially, philosophical thought. Yet it would be a mistake to view this period as entirely dogmatic. While it was largely dominated by orthodox Marxism (and Marxism-Leninism), some original independent thinkers (such as Alexander Bogdanov (1873–1928), Alexei Losev, Mikhail Bakhtin, Lev Vygotsky) endured through the immediate aftermath of the October Revolution of 1917, and their work over the following two decades still resembled free thinking. However, this relatively productive phase in the development of Russian thought came to an end with the rise of Stalin and his autocracy, when "spiritual terror was fully unleashed and gaining its strength, and free thought had been banished and forbidden" (Lektorsky and Bykova 2019, 5). The next quarter-century came to be perhaps the most disastrous in the history of Russian thought. Thus, it is remarkable that at least some components of philosophical and other forms of intellectual culture survived Stalinism and eventually returned. The spiritual and cultural treasures Russia accumulated over its more than thousand-year history proved to be too great to have been lost irretrievably.

Indeed, the second half of the twentieth century brought to light numerous highly original and creative thinkers who not only challenged the state's dogmatism but also openly criticized the status quo, thus contributing to advancing a progressive agenda in the country's political and social life. Having its origins in the Khrushchev "thaw" (the years between 1956 and 1964), when the intellectual, cultural, and social atmospheres were brought back into flux after the death of Stalin, the period from the mid-1950s to the early 1990s saw a new renaissance of philosophy and a rejuvenation of cultural life in the Soviet Union. This renaissance not only involved a return to genuine philosophical thought or its awakening from its forced "dogmatic slumber," but also allowed for the spread of new ideas and the liberalization of all intellectual domains. In philosophy, it was marked by the emergence of new, original philosophical ideas and results that significantly advanced philosophy and remain significant even today. This period of intellectual and cultural flourishing was characterized by the development of new trends of thought independent of, or even opposed to, official orthodox Marxism, leading to Marxism's radical transformation and eventual rejection as a Russian cultural and social project (Lektorsky and Bykova 2019, 8). These new philosophical ideas and theories also provided fertile ground for intellectual inquiries in other human and social sciences, as well as in a variety of other forms of cultural enterprise including art, literature, cinematography, and music. In the 1960s–1980s, forbidden philosophical works—both of the Russian prerevolutionary philosophers and of then contemporary thinkers of both anti-Marxist and creative Marxist trends—made their appearance in the form of manually reproduced or self-published documents, creating a new intellectual discourse shared by academics, literati, artistic elites, and other representatives of the Soviet intelligentsia. Poetry was the first artistic form to experience a Renaissance (represented by Bella Akhmadulina (1937–2010), Evgenii Evtushenko (1932–2017), and a number of other young poets). This epoch also witnessed the emergence of a unique Soviet genre called "author song" (whose key representatives were Bulat Okudzhava (1924–1997) and Vladimir Vysotsky (1938–1980)). Once again, "thick" literary journals became the highpoints of cultural life. But by the early 1970s cultural priorities had changed and from then on philosophical thinkers—both old (such as Mikhail Bakhtin and Alexei Losev) and new (such as Yuri Lotman (1922–1993), Evald Ilyenkov (1924–1979), Merab Mamardashvili (1930–1990), and Alexander Zinoviev (1922–2006))—began to attract the attention of not only a narrow circle of their colleagues and students but also the entire educated society. Thus, philosophical thought significantly grew in its influence, becoming again the intellectual core of Russia's cultural-creative consciousness.

At least three chapters in this volume (Chaps. 17, 18, and 19) focus on this new philosophical renaissance, introducing thinkers and ideas that achieved prominence in the second half of the twentieth century. Until not long ago, the topic of the development of philosophy in Soviet Russia remained unexplored, and Anglophone scholarly literature on the subject was dominated by the conception that official philosophy in Soviet Russia was nothing more than dogma, and that it was rather detrimental to Russian cultural and intellectual life. Only recently has the situation begun to change, giving way to a few timely publications that shed light on that period in Russian intellectual history and clarify the complexity of the philosophical legacy of the Soviet period (see Epstein 2019; Lektorsky and Bykova 2019). We hope that the present volume will further contribute to this important discussion and help to overcome lingering misconceptions about the status quo in philosophy and intellectual life in Russia under the Soviet regime. Not being able to focus here on a detailed analysis of this new renaissance, which, at least to some extent, continues in various fields of culture in contemporary Russia, we would like to emphasize the remarkable character of Russian culture, namely its endurance during times of repression and a unique capacity for self-renewal.

Mikhail Epstein has recently compared the philosophical revival in Russia during the post-Stalinist period to a phoenix (Epstein 2019). A highly expressive and proper metaphor to use in this context, in fact the image of a phoenix could be applied to the Russian intellectual tradition as a whole. This tradition has known many "dark ages" and cataclysms. And yet every time a "tragedy of Russian culture" was lamented, new generations of thinkers would emerge.[15] Sometimes these newcomers tried to obliterate the words of their predecessors or to lock them up in limited access archives. However, without trying to make light of such tragic events as the "philosophers' ships," the Stalinist great purges, and the wars that claimed millions of lives and irrevocably destroyed many intellectual networks, and while recognizing the high price paid—at both the individual and national level—for all these atrocities, we should admit that Russian philosophy and thought have reemerged from all these horrific events. And this was no sheer miracle. Woland in Mikhail Bulgakov's novel *Master and Margarita* was hardly right to claim that "manuscripts don't burn" (Bulgakov 1989, 157), for many remarkable works and even their creators were burnt or otherwise destroyed. But what allowed the tradition to survive was the Russian philosophical discourse that took so many centuries to emerge and is still taking shape. It is worth recalling in this context Mikhail Bakhtin, who said that in human culture "nothing is absolutely dead. Every meaning will have its homecoming festival" (Bakhtin 1986, 170).

The Palgrave Handbook of Russian Thought: Aim, Scope, and Structure

Bakhtin's vision of the human sciences as both a reflection on and an integral part of an ongoing *dialogue* within a single culture and of cultures across millennia describes remarkably well something that constitutes a unique feature of Russian thought.[16] Indeed, in the long run, the obstacles that the Russian intelligentsia had to endure and overcome on its way to intellectual freedom have only broadened its intellectual horizon and made it more receptive to the ideas generated by adjacent disciplines and discourses. Thus, among the most important legacies of the Russian tradition are its unique *multivoicedness* and the breadth of its styles and genres. The recognition of the essential nature of these legacies and the desire to demonstrate Russian thought in all its complexity have guided our decisions about the scope and structure of the present *Handbook*.

From looking at the table of contents, readers will gather that this *Handbook* is neither an introduction to Russian thought nor a comprehensive guide to all its periods, figures, schools, and theories. A score of attempted introductions precedes this *Handbook*,[17] and writing a comprehensive guide to the history, spanning more than a millennium, of the enormously rich Russian intellectual and cultural tradition would be not merely an ambitious task but a futile one. Our volume does not attempt to serve as an encyclopedic history of modern Russian philosophy and culture either. We see our goal in this volume as one of aptly presenting the genuine nature and content of the Russian intellectual and cultural tradition, properly communicating its richness and its profound connection with Russian politics and social life, and simultaneously revealing the specific interconnections between different disciplines, trends, and creeds within Russian culture itself. Anyone who is familiar with the Russian tradition would agree that it is very complex and difficult to navigate, and this volume offers the guidance needed to negotiate the vast and unusually multifaceted philosophical and intellectual terrain of nineteenth- and twentieth-century Russia without neglecting the peculiarities of its ever changing historical context.

While recognizing the central role of philosophy and philosophical inquiry in Russian intellectual discourse, this *Handbook* is not limited to the discussion of Russian philosophy as a scholarly discipline. It adopts an expansive approach which also considers a broader variety of philosophical, intellectual, and cultural movements and trends, including a number of thinkers who not only lacked formal philosophical training but also represented a variety of disciplines, professions, and activities that contributed to the creation and development of Russian cultural discourse. This rationale is exhibited in this book's Table of Contents and its divisions.

The volume is divided into three unequal parts. Part I introduces Russian philosophical thought, beginning with its historical background and discussing its most notable and distinctive legacies: its acute concern with religious problems, which defines the very phenomenon of Russian religious philosophy, and its participation in political discourse, which entails the development of political philosophy closely connected to Russian political history. The rest of this part addresses topics and themes central to Russian philosophical discourse in its multidirectional development and the dynamic interaction of different ideas, concepts, and theories, as well as a variety of external and internal factors that contributed to its evolution. Ordered chronologically, chapters in this section bring to discussion major schools, movements, trends, and figures in Russian philosophy during the period from the early nineteenth to the late twentieth

1 INTRODUCTION: ON RUSSIAN THOUGHT AND INTELLECTUAL TRADITION   17

centuries. Not everything that happened in Russian philosophy in those decades can be covered here. Our focus is rather on the philosophical dynamic of the period, how it was shaped, and what impact it had on the development of Russian thought. In addition to covering the thinkers and movements of the end of the nineteenth and the early twentieth centuries traditionally present in historical surveys on the history of Russian philosophy—such as Vl. Solovyov, Berdyaev, Shestov, Ilyin, Shpet, as well as Russian Kantianism, Hegelianism, and Marxism—our volume also includes chapters relevant to the philosophical renaissance of the latter half of the twentieth century, the period which usually remains outside of scholarly interests. The first part concludes with a chapter with a symbolic title, "A Return to Tradition," which briefly summarizes several important features of Russian post-Soviet philosophy. By including this chapter we want to emphasize that Russian philosophy continues to evolve and search for new topics and innovative approaches to traditional themes.

Part II brings out the organic connections between philosophical inquiry and artistic creativity that are characteristic of Russian culture. It opens with an essay on the classic Russian novel, which has long been considered Russia's most original intellectual achievement. As the essay shows, this reputation was largely due to the depth and originality of the Russian novelists' approach to ethical problems. The rest of Part II is structured chronologically and discusses a number of major writers-thinkers (such as Nikolai Gogol, Fyodor Dostoevsky, Nikolai Chernyshevsky, Leo Tolstoy, Andrei Platonov, Varlaam Shalamov, Mikhail Sholokhov); Nikolai Grot's philosophical theory of human creativity, which applied to both philosophy and art; the philosophical poetry of Osip Mandelstam; philosophically informed literary criticism (here represented by Russia's first professional critic, Vissarion Belinsky); as well as Mikhail Bakhtin's highly original philosophy of literature. Russian thinkers' unique contributions to aesthetic theory are represented by Tolstoy (as a pioneer of the expressive theory of art) and by Soviet-era aesthetic debates, which paved the ground for the emergence of contemporary Russian art. The penultimate chapter is dedicated to Yuri Lotman and the Moscow-Tartu school of semiotics, arguably the most vibrant Soviet intellectual movement in the 1970s and 1980s, whose insights and methodological innovations are still being deployed in a number of fields, including semiotics, literary and cinema studies, philosophy, sociology, and ecology. The concluding chapter of Part II then focuses on contemporary art that conceives of itself as an instrument of philosophy.

The volume closes with an Afterword (Part III), which responds to the volume's presentation of Russian thought by considering it from the vantage-point of Isaiah Berlin's celebrated 1978 collection of essays titled *Russian Thinkers*. The Afterword reevaluates Berlin's book, suggesting that some of his views are questionable, and sketches a new vision of the Russian intellectual tradition from a contemporary Anglophone perspective.

The *Handbook* consists of thirty-six chapters written by a group of internationally recognized scholars working on Russian philosophy and literature who represent a variety of schools and traditions in philosophy and intellectual history. All essays included in the volume are original works that offer scholarly introductions to the subjects under consideration.

Although not intended to be comprehensive, this volume reconstructs the Russian philosophical and intellectual tradition by putting it in its broader historical, social, and political context. The editors' goal is not to celebrate any particular school or trend within the Russian tradition or to argue for any specific interpretation of the Russian philosophical and cultural legacy, but rather to present Russian thought as broadly and objectively as possible. Along with established expositions of Russian intellectual history, new interpretations of its main trends, central philosophical conceptions, and ideas are also included. It is our hope that the mysterious "Spirit of Russia" will finally emerge as a personality that inspires Western scholars to enter into a genuine dialogue with it.

NOTES

1. See Masaryk (1919), which was the English translation of the original German version of the book that appeared a few years earlier. (See Masaryk (1913).) This study provides a sophisticated account of the symbiotic relationship between Russian philosophy and Russian literature.
2. Russian philosophy has been explored more or less systematically in a number of extensive chronologically structured surveys, such as Lossky (2011), Zenkovsky (1953), Levitsky (1981), Copleston (1986), and Kuvakin (1993).
3. See Lektorsky and Bykova (2019), 1–16.
4. For a more detailed discussion, see Sukhov (2012), 28.
5. See Mirsky (1999), 8–19; Picchio (1984), Likhachev (1986). Concerning the relationship between Ancient Greek philosophy and its vision of *paideia* and early Christianity, especially in the Eastern part of the Roman Empire, see Jaeger (1961).
6. Catherine's and Potemkin's "Greek project" is discussed in great detail by Andrei Zorin (see Zorin 2001). The creation of the new capital that resembled Rome by Peter the Great was another major step toward the construction of the modern state ideology of Russia as a nation-Empire that spanned the divide between East and West. Yuri Lotman and Boris Uspensky discuss Peter's manifold imperial ambitions in the context of Russian history since the medieval period in "Otzvuki konzepzii 'Moskva-Tretii Rim' v ideologii Petra Pervogo." See Lotman (1992), 3: 201–212.
7. For a detailed account of her tenure as President of this academy and as Executive Director of the Academy of Sciences, see Dashkova (1995).
8. On philosophical instruction at the Slavic-Greek-Roman Academy and other theological Academies that had existed since the medieval period, see Zenkovsky (1953), 1: 44–50.
9. It is worth mentioning, however, that German scholars, many of whom were well versed in the latest philosophical developments in their own country and Europe in general, sparked interests in contemporary German philosophy among their Russian colleagues and students. This greatly stimulated Russian

1 INTRODUCTION: ON RUSSIAN THOUGHT AND INTELLECTUAL TRADITION 19

attraction to German philosophical and other intellectual achievements and made Russia very receptive to philosophical ideas and theories coming from its philosophically attuned neighbor. On the Russian reception of German philosophy in this and later periods, see Bykova (2019). For a more specific discussion of the reception of Kant in Russia, see Alexei Krouglov's essay in this volume (Chap. 6).

10. See, for example, Copleston (1986), chapter two, "Russia and the West," 26–44.
11. Copleston, writing about Russian philosophy from a Western perspective, is less enthusiastic about the Slavophile's philosophical breakthroughs but nevertheless seems to share Zenkovsky's view of their significance. See Copleston (1986), 45–76.
12. It is also worth mentioning that many Russian philosophers, while in exile, participated in the creation of the Western philosophical movements of the 1930s and 1940s. For example, Berdyaev's ideas became one of the inspirations of the French Personalist movement.
13. The relationship between philosophy and philology, criticism and the new discipline of literary theory, in Russia and other countries of Eastern and Central Europe has recently been illuminated by Galin Tihanov. See Tihanov (2019).
14. At the beginning of the twentieth century, there were two main Russian émigré centers in Europe: one in Berlin, the other in Paris.
15. A sense of tragic fatalism permeates the writings of many Russian émigré thinkers in interwar Europe. See, for example, *The Tragedy of Russian Culture* by P.M. Bitsilli (2000).
16. In "Toward a Methodology for the Human Sciences" Bakhtin writes:

    "The exact sciences constitute a mono-logical form of knowledge: the intellect contemplates a *thing* and expounds upon it. There is only one subject here—organizing (contemplating) and speaking (expounding). In opposition to a subject there is only a voiceless *thing*. Any object of knowledge (including man) can be perceived and cognized as a thing. But a subject as such cannot be perceived and studied as a thing, for as a subject it cannot, while remaining a subject, become voiceless, and consequently, cognition of it can only be *dialogic*. [...] The place of philosophy. It begins where precise science ends and a different science begins. It can be defined as the metalanguage of all sciences (and of all kinds of cognition and consciousness)." Bakhtin (1986), 161.

17. The most complete and chronologically organized studies include Lossky (2011), Zenkovsky (1953), Walicki (1979), Levitsky (1981), Copleston (1986), and Kuvakin (1993). See also Koyré (1929), Berlin (1978), and Shpet (2009).

BIBLIOGRAPHY

Bakhtin, Mikhail M. 1986. *Speech Genres and Other Late Essays.* Translated by Vern W. McGee. Edited by Caryl Emerson and Michael Holquist. Austin: University of Texas Press.

Berdyaev, Nicholas. 1992. *The Russian Idea.* Translated by R.M. French. New York, NY: Lindisfarne Press.

Berlin, Isaiah. 1978. *Russian Thinkers.* Edited by Henry Hardy and Aileen Kelly. London: Penguin.

Bitsilli, Pyotr M. 2000. *Tragedia russkoi kul'tury*. Moscow: Russkii put'.

Bulgakov, Mikhail M. 1989. *Master i Margarita*. Kiev: Molod'.

Bushkovitch, Paul. 2012. *A Concise History of Russia*. Cambridge, UK: Cambridge University Press.

Bykova, Marina F. 2019. On the Reception of German Idealism. In *Philosophical Thought in Russia in the Second Half of the 20th Century. A Contemporary View from Russia and Abroad*, ed. V.A. Lektorsky and M.F. Bykova, 167–186. London: Bloomsbury Academic.

Chaadaev, Pyotr Ya. 1991. *Polnoe sobranie sochinenii i izbrannye pis'ma*. 2 vols. Moscow: Nauka.

Copleston, Frederick C. 1986. *Philosophy in Russia: From Herzen to Lenin and Berdyaev*. Notre Dame, IN: University of Notre Dame Press.

Dashkova, Ekaterina R. 1995. *The Memoirs of Princess Dashkova*. Translated by Kyril Fitzlyon. With an Introduction by Jehanne M. Gheith. Durham and London: Duke University Press.

Epstein, Mikhail. 2019. *The Phoenix of Philosophy: Russian Thought of the Late Soviet Period (1953–1991)*. New York, NY: Bloomsbury Press.

Florovsky, Georges. 1988. *Puti russkogo bogosloviia*. Paris: YMCA-Press.

Hamburg, Gary M., and Randall A. Poole, eds. 2010. *A History of Russian Philosophy 1830–1930. Faith, Reason, and the Defence of Human Dignity*. Cambridge: Cambridge University Press.

[Istoriia MU]. 1955. Istoria Moskovskogo Universiteta, 1755–1955. 2 vols. Moscow: Izdatel'stvo Moskovskogo Gosudarstvennogo Universiteta.

Jaeger, Werner. 1961. *Early Christianity and Greek Paideia*. Cambridge, MA: The Belknap Press of Harvard University Press.

Koyré, Alexandre. 1929. *La philosophie et le problème national en Russie au début du XIX siècle*. Paris: Librairie Ancienne Honoré Champion.

Kuvakin, Valery A., ed. 1993. *A History of Russian Philosophy: From the Tenth through the Twentieth Centuries*. 2 vols. Buffalo: Prometheus Books.

Lektorsky, Vladislav A., and Marina F. Bykova, eds. 2019. *Philosophical Thought in Russia in the Second Half of the 20th Century. A Contemporary View from Russia and Abroad*. London: Bloomsbury Academic.

Levitsky, Sergei A. 1981 [1968]. *Ocherki po istrorii russkoi filosofskoi i obshchestvennoi mysli*. Frankfurt/Main: Posev.

Likhachev, Dmitrii S. 1986. *Issledovania po drevnerusskoi literature*. Leningard: Nauka.

Lossky, Nikolai O. 2011 [1951]. *Istoria russkoi filosofii*. Moscow: Akademicheskii proekt. [In English: Nicholas O. Lossky, *History of Russian Philosophy* (New York: International Universities Press, 1972).]

Lotman, Yuri M. 1992. *Izbrannye stat'ii*. 3 vols. Talinn: Alexandra.

Madariaga, Isabel de. 1991. *Catherine the Great*. New Haven and London: Yale University Press.

Masaryk, Thomas Garrigue. 1913. *Russland und Europa: Studien über die geistigen Strömungen in Russland. Erste Folge. Zur russischen Geschichts- und Religionsphilosophie. Soziologische Skizzen*, 2 vols. Jena: Diederichs.

———. 1919. *The Spirit of Russia: Studies in History, Literature and Philosophy*. Translated by Eden and Cedar Paul. London: George Allen & Unwin; New York, NY: Macmillan. [This is the English translation of the German book listed above.]

Mirsky, Dmitry S. (Sviatopolk-Mirsky) Prince. 1999. *A History of Russian Literature from Its Beginnings to 1900*. Edited by Francis J. Whitfield. Evanston, IL: Northwestern University Press.

Picchio, Riccardo. 1984. The Impact of Ecclesiastical Culture on Old Russian Literary Tradition. In *Medieval Russian Culture*, in 2 vols., ed. Henrik Birnbaum and Michael S. Flier. Vol. 1, 247–279. Los Angeles, CA: University of California Press.

Riasanovsky, Nicholas V., and Mark D. Steinberg. 2011. *A History of Russia*. 8th ed. Oxford and New York: Oxford University Press.

Shestakov, Vyacheslav P. 2017. *Russkii Serebrianyi vek: zapozdavshii renessans*. St. Petersburg: Aleteia.

Shpet, Gustav G. 2009. *Ocherk razvitia russkoi filosofii*. Rekonstruktsia Tat'iany Schedrinoi. Russkie Propilei. 2 vols. Moscow: Rosspen.

Sukhov, Andrei D. 2012. *Russkaia filosofia: kharakternye priznaki i predstaviteli, osobennosti razvitiia*. Moscow: Institut filosofii RAS.

Tihanov, Galin, ed. 2009. *Gustav Shpet's Contribution to Philosophy and Cultural Theory*. West Lafayette, IN: Purdue University Press.

———. 2019. *The Birth and Death of Literary Theory: Regimes of Relevance in Russia and Beyond*. Stanford, CA: Stanford University Press.

Uspensky, Boris A. 1987. *Istoria russkogo literaturnogo iazyka XI–XVII vv*. München: Sagners Slavistische Sammlung.

Walicki, Andrzej. 1979. *A History of Russian Thought: From the Enlightenment to Marxism*. Translated by Hilda Andrews-Rusiecka. Stanford, CA: Stanford University Press.

Whittaker, Cynthia H. 1984. *The Origins of Modern Russian Education: An Intellectual Biography of Count Sergei Uvarov, 1786–1855*. DeKalb, IL: Northern Illinois University Press.

Zenkovsky, Vasily V. 1953. *A History of Russian Philosophy in 2 vols*. Translated by George L. Kline. London: Routledge and Kegan Paul.

Zorin, Andrei L. 2001. *Kormia dvuglavogo orla: literatura i gosudarstvennaia ideologia v Rossii v poslednei treti XVIII—pervoi treti XIX veka*. Moscow: NLO.

PART I

Russian Philosophical Thought

CHAPTER 2

Politics and Enlightenment in Russia

Gary M. Hamburg

GENERAL CONSIDERATIONS: ENLIGHTENMENT IN EUROPE AND RUSSIA

From roughly 1680 to 1789 advocates of Europe's cultural transformation tended to think of themselves as members of an exclusive community bringing light to a benighted intellectual landscape: hence the self-image of French *lumières* and of the Central European *Aufklärer* (Hunt and Jacobs 2005). Although the desire to promote learning through rigorous inquiry was an old one, found in the ancient Greeks, in the Scholastics, and in the boldest thinkers of the Renaissance, countless eighteenth-century continental thinkers followed Bernard de Fontenelle and Jean d'Alembert in picturing themselves as animated by an "almost entirely new philosophical spirit." This new spirit manifested itself in the study of natural phenomena (d'Alembert referred to *les sciences de la nature*), social science [*science de l'homme*], but also theology [*science de Dieu*] (Robertson 2015, 2–4). According to the distinguished historian Jonathan Israel, in the hands of the Enlightenment's most radical adherents, some French and others not, the new philosophy aimed at emancipating human beings "from the collective force of autocracy, intolerance, and prejudiced thinking, [at] establishing a secular morality [based on] ideals of equality (sexual and racial), democracy, individual liberty and a comprehensive toleration" (Israel 2006, 524). To the *philosophes'* later admirers, the eighteenth-century conviction that knowledge is the key to social change constituted nothing less than the banner of progress—a banner deserving defense against

---

G. M. Hamburg (✉)
Department of History, Claremont McKenna College, Claremont, CA, USA
e-mail: gary.hamburg@cmc.edu

© The Author(s), under exclusive license to Springer Nature
Switzerland AG 2021
M. F. Bykova et al. (eds.), *The Palgrave Handbook of Russian Thought*,
https://doi.org/10.1007/978-3-030-62982-3_2

religious reaction, conservatism, fascism, neo-liberalism, and every variety of social conformism (Hunt and Jacobs 2005).

Historians of Russia have disagreed sharply over fundamental questions such as whether the Russian Empire experienced an Enlightenment at all, and if it did, whether the Russian version was a mere "echo" of Western developments. As Michael Schippan has noted, few scholars in the imperial period wrote about the Enlightenment as a stage in Russian development; then, from the 1930s on, Soviet historians tended to equate the Russian Enlightenment "exclusively to the struggle against serfdom, autocracy, Church and religion," an interpretation that "fit" the Western model of radical Enlightenment but that also marginalized the Enlightenment's impact in Russia, since there were so few Russian radicals (Schippan 2012, 26). From the 1960s on, Soviet writers defined the Russian Enlightenment as a peculiar "national" phenomenon, against the background of other national Enlightenments. Meanwhile, in the West until lately, most interpreters have understood Russian developments as belated "translations" of Western ideas or as a moment when Russian culture became more "Europeanized" and when the imperial polity "modernized" itself (Schippan 2012, 33–35; Winter 1953, 1966, 267–347; Städtke et al. 1999; Barran 2002; Hildermeier 2004). A new, but related, Western approach to Enlightenment in Russia has focused on the social and cultural history of language use, especially French language use, in eighteenth-century Russia (Rjéoutski et al. 2014; Grechanaia 2010; Berelowitch 2015). Two questions in this new approach are whether and to what degree French-speaking Russian elites were part of a pan-European audience for the Enlightenment.

The complex problems underlying these historiographical currents have made it difficult for historians to agree on the chronology of the Enlightenment in Russia. Schippan has noted that the periodization of the Enlightenment in Russia extends from 1650 to 1825—that is, from the literary career of Simeon Polotskii to the Decembrist rebellion or from early in the reign of Tsar Alexei Mikhailovich to the death of Alexander I. The more common notions fix the Enlightenment in Russia to the period between Peter I's assumption of autocratic power in 1689 and the death of Catherine II in 1796, with emphasis on Catherine's reign as the Russian Enlightenment's apex (Schippan 2012, 9–41; Walicki 2005, 37–45).

This essay assumes that the enlightenment of Russia was the consequence of two interconnected developments. The first development, largely of domestic origin, stretched over three centuries, from 1500 to 1801. It proceeded from discussion and debate within the Orthodox Church and the community of believers over the roots of knowledge, religious and secular, and over how to construct a just political order on earth. The second development, fed by the first but also linked in part to the importation from Europe of books pertaining to theology, philosophy, history, and science, extended from the mid-seventeenth century to 1801. This second trend accelerated in the early eighteenth century under Peter I and again in the late eighteenth century under Catherine II and Paul I. Some scholars might be tempted to distinguish the gradual Christian Enlightenment from a more precipitous, violent, and predominantly secular one; however, that way of understanding the two developments misses their intimate links (both had religious dimensions; both entailed the consumption of "foreign" books, yet were rooted in native soil; the first development constituted in large measure a pre-condition for the second one).

The interdependence of the two developments can be grasped if we study the Russian term for "enlightenment," *prosveshchenie*. The word descended from Old Russian and Church Slavonic. It connoted the acquisition of spiritual life at baptism, dedication to Christian virtues, and to the goal of *theosis*. By 1750 or so, the word had acquired new connotations, such as possession of specialized knowledge and the practice of secular virtues, so that eighteenth-century Russian speakers invoking *prosveshchenie* might have referred either to the moral or secular sense of the term or to both simultaneously (Hamburg 2016, 16–19). The persistence of the term's moral connotation disencumbered Russian thinkers from regarding themselves as *lumières* after the French fashion, even when the Russians in question were Francophones. Indeed, by most accounts, the appearance of the Russian intelligentsia—that is, of a group of alienated intellectuals committed to the Empire's radical transformation and therefore of a Russian "equivalent" to the *philosophes*—was, at the earliest, a very late eighteenth-century phenomenon, but likelier a nineteenth-century one (Shtrange 1965; Raeff 1970; Ilizarov 1999). For various reasons, and with few exceptions, Russians committed to an enlightenment tended not to advocate for a French-style radical Enlightenment that might destroy the institutional Church, abolish autocracy, and establish a secular morality, democratic government, and individual liberty. Why?

First, the public sphere in Russia was, until the second half of the eighteenth century, virtually monopolized by Church and state. As Gary Marker has demonstrated, before the eighteenth century there existed only one major publishing house in Moscow—the so-called *Pechatnyi dvor*. Before Peter I's death in 1725, the situation had improved only slightly via the addition of the Senate's press in Petersburg and a few monastic publishers (Marker 1985, 19–31). Even under Catherine II, who encouraged university training, study abroad, and learned societies, the public sphere was carefully monitored: some examples of which are the empress's campaign against Freemasonry after 1785 and her arrest of the publicist Nikolai Ivanovich Novikov in 1792, in addition to her decision to arrest Alexander Nikolaevich Radishchev in 1790.

Second, instead of opposing institutional religion, leading intellectuals approved of, and benefitted from, the Church's promotion of education, especially Western learning. Indeed, a case can be made that a handful of key figures in the Russian Church took the lead in advancing Enlightenment in the Empire. Seventeenth-century Churchmen such as the erudite Simeon Polotskii, and his student Sil'vestr Medvedev, championed "Latin learning" through a monastic school they founded in Moscow and through their own references to Western philosophy. Simeon's immense anthology of verses, *The Multi-colored Garden* [*Vertograd mnogosvetnyi*], introduced elements of scholasticism and Western humanism into Muscovite discourse. Simeon even offered an abstract critique of tyranny. Sil'vestr's *Short Meditation on the Years 1682–1684* [*Sozertsanie kratkoe let 7190–7192*], one of the first analytical histories to appear in Russia, explored the psychological and social dimensions of the 1682 popular uprising (Bogdanov 1995, 215–249; Hamburg 2016, 191–230).

The two most influential Orthodox Churchmen of Peter I's reign, Stefan Iavorskii and Feofan Prokopovich, brought knowledge of Western theology and philosophy from the Kievan Academy, where both of them studied and taught. Stefan, who taught rhetoric and philosophy in Kiev, was heavily influenced by scholasticism, but also by Western astrology, cabbalism, and apocalypticism. Between 1702 and 1706, he employed his arcane knowledge in a series of sermons praising the tsar but also defining many paths toward Christian enlightenment (Collis 2012, 211–270). His extraordinary book, *Rock of Faith* [*Kamen' very*] (published in 1727), attempted to explain Church dogma, including the Church's teaching on the role of secular authorities in religious matters, to the imperial Senate (Samarin 1880, 266–267; Stefan Iavorskii 2010).

After 1716, Feofan was the most important Petrine Churchman, having eclipsed Stefan in his influence at court. Feofan wrote the *Primer* [*Pervoe uchenie otrokam*] (1720) used to catechize children for a century. He also wrote the *Spiritual Regulation* [*Dukhovnyi reglament*] (1721) that partially subordinated the Church to the state and aimed to improve clerical education by teaching languages, sciences, philosophy, and dogmatic theology to seminarians. Feofan wanted future priests to spread enlightenment in Russia not only by preaching the gospel, but also by suppressing popular superstitions. Feofan acted as Pyotr's instrument in justifying new policies. His *Justice of the Monarch's Will* [*Pravda voli monarshei*] (1722) served as a preface to Peter's new law of royal succession; it was also the most sweeping defense of royal sovereignty to appear in eighteenth-century Russia. Throughout the early 1720s, Feofan advocated the establishment of a Russian Academy of Sciences (Kopelevich 1977). In carrying out his duties, Feofan drew on wide knowledge of Western philosophy, from Plato and Aristotle through the scholastics and Renaissance humanists, to Dutch theorists like Hugo Grotius and Samuel Pufendorf, and English thinkers such as Thomas Hobbes. He also studied biblical prophecies, the Greek Church fathers, Dionysius the Areopagite, the "wisdom" of Hermes Trismegistus, the cosmology of Tycho Brahe, the occult qualities of gems as described by Daniel Sennert, and alchemy as taught by Innokentii Gissiell. Although Feofan rejected superstition, he believed in miracles as recorded in the bible and those witnessed in the contemporary world, such as the preservation of bodies at the Monastery of the Caves (Collis 2012, 271–354). Because he was a religious traditionalist, alchemist, and man of the Enlightenment rolled into one, Feofan exemplified the capacious limits of the learning he advocated (Florovskii 1937, 92–94).

The erudite strain in Russian Orthodoxy perpetuated itself under Catherine II in the person of Platon (Levshin), who from 1775 to his death in 1812 served as metropolitan of Moscow. Like Feofan, Platon retained his belief in biblical miracles and in those performed by Russian saints, but he also knew modern languages, philosophy, and history. By temperament, Platon was an irenicist who taught that the true Christian spirit is found in forgiveness and charity. In this regard, the historian Elise Wirtschafter has pointed to Platon's 1773 sermon on the feast of Sts. Peter and Paul which asserted that love must be the foundation of good government and of any just authority. According to Platon, "anyone who accepts the call to government must love both the one who entrusts him with power and the people entrusted to his care" (Wirtschafter 2011, 337; Wirtschafter 2013). By conviction, as his *Exhortation* [*Uveshchanie*] to Old Believers showed, Platon confronted religious dissenters not by the sword but with mildness and the language of reason (Platon 1766). In 1785, when Catherine enlisted him to investigate Novikov and the Moscow Freemasons, Platon defended Novikov against the charge of not being a faithful Christian. In 1801, at the coronation of Alexander I, Platon delivered a public address calling on the tsar to "heed the rights of humanity" [*prava che-lovechestva*] (Snegirev 1890, 177–178). He may have been the first Russian prelate to invoke human rights—a crucial principle of the French Enlightenment (Hunt 2008).

Whatever their individual contradictions, the Orthodox erudites from Simeon and Sil'vestr to Platon promoted learning in court circles, raised the level of theological discourse in the Church, and also laid the practical foundations for new schools and academies in Russia.

Third, Russian monarchs from Alexei Mikhailovich (ruled 1645–1676) to Catherine II (1762–1796) aligned themselves, to one degree or another, with the cause of enlightenment. Starting in 1653, Alexei supported the correction of Orthodox ritual books undertaken by Russian patriarchs, a task implying that the efficacy of religious acts depended on philological precision in transcribing ancient Greek texts. Between 1658 and 1667, the tsar confronted Patriarch Nikon over the way the latter had sought to implement the Church reforms. The trial of Nikon at the Church council of 1666–1667 charged the patriarch with various abuses of office (insulting the tsar, insulting Orthodox Christians, unauthorized resignation from the rank of patriarch), but the unarticulated issue was the struggle for ascendancy between tsar and patriarch (Andreev 2003, 315–367). The verdict against Nikon was the first step toward the state's primacy in domestic affairs achieved a half century later under Peter I, but it was also a landmark in the state's effort to control the enlightenment. In 1665, Alexei licensed Simeon Polotskii to establish a monastery school to train translators and government clerks. Judging by its curriculum, the school attempted to familiarize students with Western learning in philosophy, theology, and history, as well as languages. Alexei entrusted to Simeon the instruction of his own children, perhaps including his daughter Sof'ia—the future regent (Hughes 1990, 33–35). It is probably no accident that in her regency (1682–1689), Sof'ia promoted both "Latin" and "Greek" schools. In 1685, she licensed the establishment of the Slavonic-Greek-Latin Academy, the first institution of higher education in Russia (Bogdanov 1986, 177–223; Hughes 1990, 164–165; Chrissidis 2016).

In October 1698 Peter I had already informed Patriarch Adrian of his hope to establish schools combining religious study and training in those "free sciences" useful in state service (Ustrialov 1858, 511–512). Although some historians have characterized this declaration as a plan "for the Academy of Sciences or a university," at this stage Peter may not have been sure how to proceed (Kopelevich 1977, 32). He may have had in mind the British millenarian Francis Lee's proposal for a series of colleges dedicated to experimental learning, one of which was to be modeled on the French *Académie des Sciences* (Collis 2012, 408). In 1712, Peter received a letter from Gottfried Leibniz sketching a plan for a royal *Kunstkammer* and an Academy of Sciences (Ger'e 1871, 132–135). In 1718, the tsar opened his *Kunstkamera*, which was intended to facilitate the study of nature and to advance the religious goal of satisfying interest about God's creatures (Collis 2012, 434–548; Staniukovich 1953). Leibniz probably accelerated this event, but earlier scientific enthusiasts had sparked Peter's fascination with curiosities. Meanwhile, on his second Grand Embassy to Europe in 1717, Peter visited the Sorbonne and French Academy of Sciences. There he met Fontenelle (1727; Kopelevich 1977, 43–44). The tsar's project for a Russian Academy of Sciences only took final shape between January 1723 and January 1724 (Kopelevich 1977, 51–52). The Academy's creation was an example of the way domestic factors (Peter's curiosity about nature, his peculiar religiosity, Feofan's interest in natural philosophy) and external ones (Leibniz's plan for a Russian Academy, Fontenelle's encouragement, Peter's desire to compete with European courts) worked together in the enlightenment of Russia.

The historian James Cracraft has argued in a series of books that Peter I effected a "cultural revolution" in Russia, a kind of top-down "revolution by decree" (Cracraft 1988, 1997, 2003, 2004). This revolution transformed Russian architecture, the Empire's "built world," by altering construction techniques to conform to European models. The Petrine revolution also introduced European visual imagery into Russian books and pictorial arts, partly through state-subsidized publications and partly through state patronage of the arts. Finally, Cracraft has claimed, Peter's "bureaucratic revolution," his military modernization of the country, and Russia's nautical turn introduced new words into Russian written discourse and produced a new set of relationships between printed texts and their readers. These changes accompanied the introduction into Russia of up-to-date mathematics, geometry, astronomy, grammar and rhetoric, philosophy, and secular history. In Cracraft's opinion, the establishment of the Academy of Sciences was the "natural culmination of developments reaching back to the beginning of Peter's reign," but was also the making of the "institutional heart of the onrushing effort to naturalize in Russia […] the very vocabulary of early modern European science" (Cracraft 2004, 193–254). In other words, the Academy's foundation was the centerpiece of the country's enlightenment.

Cracraft's cultural-revolution theory perhaps understated the resiliency of traditional religion and also underestimated what he has called "the persistence of Muscovy," both phenomena he admitted as "countervailing trends" (Cracraft 2004, 309–331). But his emphasis on Petrine coercion and on Peter's successful cooptation of educated elites helps us grasp why radical enlighteners of the Western type were so rare in Petrine Russia: the government had firmly committed itself to the country's enlightenment.

Between 1725 and 1762, Russian monarchs adhered broadly to Petrine policies concerning education. In 1725, Catherine I inaugurated the Academy of Sciences. In the 1730s, Anna Ivanovna applauded research in geology, metallurgy, and astronomy. From the 1740s to the early 1760s, Elizabeth I generously funded the Academy of Sciences. In 1755, she approved the establishment of Moscow University, and, in 1760, the foundation of the Russian Academy of Arts. The historian Andrei Borisovich Kamenskii has rightly noted that, from 1725 to 1741, the government showed little inclination to reevaluate Peter's program in education, state administration, economics, or social policy (Kamenskii 1999, 251). The country's inertial momentum was toward enlightenment. After Elizabeth's accession to the throne in 1741, the government defended Peter's legacy more forcefully, including his program of enlightenment (Kamenskii 1999, 275). As the historian Alexander Vucinich has shown, the Academy of Sciences and Moscow University functioned over the next century in a political environment strongly favorable to science (Vucinich 1963).

In the period between Peter I's death in 1725 and Catherine II's ascension to the throne in 1762, two thinkers personified the achievements of Russia's enlightenment movement: the philosopher-historian Vasilii Nikitich Tatishchev and the polymath Mikhail Vasil'evich Lomonosov.

Tatishchev's "Dialogue of Two Friends on the Utility of Science and Schools" (written 1730–1733, published 1773) was one of eighteenth-century Russia's greatest philosophical texts. It touched on the importance of education, on human nature (Tatishchev was a metaphysical dualist, not a materialist), on the afterlife (Tatishchev was a not altogether orthodox Christian, who accepted the soul's immortality), and on the centrality of reason and of virtue in the well-considered human life. Tatishchev claimed that, to achieve knowledge of the good, human beings must study their entire lives: "Study leads to wisdom, lack of study to darkness" (Tatishchev 1979, 141). He strongly rejected the objections that great learning leads to religious unbelief. While conceding that the student of philosophy must be wary of slick rhetoric and passing intellectual fashion, he maintained: "Necessary philosophy is not sinful" (Tatishchev 1979, 79). Indeed, if the Church and state wanted to avoid the spread of heresy, he thought, the best way of doing so was to advance genuine learning. Tatishchev linked his advocacy of enlightenment with a program of religious toleration based on an awareness of Russia's multi-confessional identity and on the study of languages. Analysis of Russian history convinced him that, "thanks to several hundred years of good and careful government, the differences among the faiths have done no harm" (Tatishchev 1979, 87).

Between 1720 and the end of his life, Tatishchev wrote a multi-volume *Russian History*, of which he finished only parts one and two (covering Old Rus' to the Mongol invasions of the thirteenth century) and fragments of two additional parts. Although he devoted many pages to exploring the spread of Christianity in Kiev and the spread of Christian mores in Rus', he conceived of his grand work as a secular history devoted to Russian politics. In *Russian History*, while conceding there is no universally "best" form of government, Tatishchev maintained that, in Russia, the monarchy had proven itself better than a republic. He also asserted that Russian monarchs tended to succeed when they sought prudent advice from the nobility—evidence for Montesquieu's later notion that intermediate bodies play a positive role in well-functioning monarchies (Tatishchev 1962–1968). In the eighteenth century, Tatishchev's history was not published in its entirety, but Lomonosov, Catherine II, Mikhail Mikhailovich Shcherbatov, and other scholars read it in manuscript. It therefore constituted one of the foundations of political thought in the later stages of the Russian Enlightenment.

Lomonosov played a vital role in the development of the Academy of Sciences at mid-century, in the founding of Moscow University, in the domestication of scientific research in Russia, but also in Russian literature and politics. In the 1740s, he wrote brilliant poetry reconciling science and religious belief (see his "Evening Meditation on God's Majesty on the Occasion of the Great Northern Lights" and "Morning Meditation on Divine Majesty") (Levitt 2009), court odes (e.g., his magnificent "Ode on the Arrival of Empress Elizabeth in St. Petersburg") (Serman 1988, 82), and a glorification of natural philosophy, *Short Guide to Eloquence* (1748) (Lomonosov 1748). Lomonosov's *Ancient Russian History to 1054* (written 1751–1756, published 1766) celebrated the cultural sophistication of the Slavic tribes that founded the Kievan state and also illustrated the importance of autocracy in the development of that polity (Lomonosov 1766). However, Lomonosov alerted his readers that autocracy in Russia had been prone to two problems: degeneration into tyranny, as had occurred under Prince Sviatoslav, and vulnerability to rebellion, such as Novgorod's resistance to Yaroslav the Wise (Lomonosov 1766, 128–133). Thus, Lomonosov's defense of autocracy helped prepare the ground for the notion of "enlightened" monarchy that flourished under Catherine II.

Therefore, from the late seventeenth century till the mid-eighteenth century, the enlightenment movement in Russia was moderate in character. Church and state dominated the public sphere through their control over printing. They maintained control over this sphere not only by exercising a near monopoly, but also by promoting erudition and public instruction. The Russian-educated public, increasingly numerous and influential by mid-century, generally cooperated with progressive Churchmen and monarchs in advancing the country's enlightenment. Although there were points of friction between the authorities and individual intellectuals, before the late eighteenth century Russia did not experience anything like the spirit of opposition that developed in France between the powers that be and leading *lumières*. Consequently, before Catherine II's time, Enlightenment discourse in Russia focused on traditional political issues, such as the range of the sovereign's authority in national life, the importance of piety and the observance of virtue, and, above all, the advancement of knowledge.

Enlightenment Under Catherine II: Early Years

Catherine's interest in the continental Enlightenment manifested itself in many ways. As early as 1758, she became aware through her mother, Princess Johanna von Holstein-Gottorp, of the Paris salon run by Marie-Thérèse Rodet Geoffrin (Ségur 1897, 203–204). That salon featured painters, sculptors, and also well-known writers—in its first years Fénelon and Montesquieu, in its later years d'Alembert, Denis Diderot, and Holbach (Goodman 1994). From 1763 to 1777, Catherine corresponded with Mme. Geoffrin about politics, art, and the activities of Russian diplomatic agents in France (Gamburger 1867; Ségur 1897, 431–462). She used Geoffrin to convey her fascination with Montesquieu's *De l'esprit des lois*, which she described as "the breviary of sovereigns" (Ségur 1897, 444), and to report on her patronage of the sculptor Étiénne de Falconet (Ségur 1897, 460–461). In August 1762, Catherine commissioned Ivan Ivanovich Shuvalov to tell Diderot that she would guarantee his security in finalizing publication of the *Encyclopédie*, either in Riga or elsewhere in the Russian Empire, a plan he rejected; however, in 1766, when Catherine offered to buy his library and papers on favorable terms, he accepted her proposition. From 1763 to 1778, Catherine engaged in a lively correspondence with Voltaire—an exchange of letters that probably burnished her reputation in Russian elite circles but that was also valuable to her political development (Catherine II 1971; Voltaire and Catherine II 2006). In early 1764 the empress subscribed to Friedrich Melchior Baron von Grimm's *Correspondance littéraire, philosophique et critique* (1753–1793), a biweekly literary newsletter he produced for elite subscribers, on a confidential basis (Catherine II and Grimm 2016: civil). In it, Catherine could follow important French cultural events, including commentary on philosophy and painting. In 1772–1773, Catherine sponsored publication of Helvétius' *De l'homme*, a book shepherded to press by her agent, Prince Dmitrii Alekseevich Golitsyn, and dedicated to her (Helvétius 1773). In 1773–1774, Catherine hosted Diderot in Petersburg for a series of conversations on philosophy, politics, religion, and culture (Bil'basov 1884; Bil'basov and Lentin 1972). All these steps testified to the empress's fascination with the *philosophes* and to what Arthur Wilson has labeled "the forthright way in which she sought to recruit influential friends" (Wilson 1972, 443).

From the beginning of her reign, Catherine II focused on the improvement of education at the popular and elite levels. As her biographer Isabel de Madariaga has noted, the empress studied the educational theories of John Locke, François Fénelon, and Jean-Jacques Rousseau. In 1764, Catherine put forth her own pedagogical view through Ivan Ivanovich Betskoi, who sought a system of education for young people of both sexes (Madariaga 1981, 488–492; "General'noe...," 1764). Betskoi wanted to make of his pupils a "new race [...], new fathers and mothers who would be able to inculcate in their children the same correct and sound rules which they themselves had received, so their children would pass them on further [...] from generation to generation to future centuries" (Betskoi 1789–1791, 101; Schönle et al. 2016, 5). Almost simultaneously, the empress received from Diderot a memorandum, *Essai sur les études en Russie,* calling eventually for a national system of education on the model of Protestant German lands, but in the short run for the universal public education of teachers (Diderot 1875). In the 1775 Statute on Local Administration, the empress mandated the establishment of schools at the district and provincial levels. In 1786, she attempted to create a national network of primary and secondary schools (Madariaga 1981, 493–497). One of her goals was to foster a wider pool of potential students for university training and for the Academy of Sciences. It was as if she saw the oddity of Peter I's approach in establishing the Academy first—exactly the opposite of what logically should have happened. The empress also meant for the new schools to inculcate into her subjects respect for the law and crown—that is, to foster in them habits of discipline and obedience (Felbiger 1777).

The most widely disseminated expression of Catherine's enlightened political philosophy, and of its limits, can be found in her *Nakaz* or *Instruction to the Commission for Composition of a New Law Code* (1767), a document published eight times during her reign and read aloud in government agencies at least three times a year (*Nakaz* 1907). In it, Catherine quoted (often verbatim) texts by Western European thinkers—Cesare Beccaria, Jacob von Bielfeld, Johann von Justi, Denis Diderot, François Quenay, and especially Montesquieu, which she artfully arranged and mixed with her own ideas. In the *Nakaz,* the empress insisted on the importance of an autocratic government in Russia, "for no other form of authority can act in a fashion appropriate to such a vast space" (*Nakaz* 1907, 3). But, in article 13 of the *Nakaz,* she also defined autocracy's purpose as ruling in the people's best interests (*Nakaz* 1907, 4). In article 38, she contended that autocratic government is compatible with liberty, where freedom is understood as "the right to do everything that the laws allow" (*Nakaz* 1907, 8). Catherine followed Montesquieu in underlining that law is never the sole determinant of popular behavior; indeed, because custom is often more important than law in affecting conduct, a wise legislator must think carefully about existing *mores* before framing new laws. Sometimes, she observed, a legislator must "prepare people's minds" for innovations by changing customs in advance of the laws (*Nakaz* 1907, 13). This observation followed logically from Catherine's commitment to education as the key to Russia's advancement.

It should be noted that, while Catherine recommended the spread of enlightenment through education, she conceded in the *Nakaz* that, under current Russian conditions, the adoption of a national system of public education was impractical. She therefore temporized by demanding that each head of household provide children with religious instruction, teaching them "God is the source of all wisdom," and inculcating in them knowledge of the ten commandments and of the Orthodox Greek faith (*Nakaz* 1907, 103–104).

Like Beccaria, whose book *Dei delitte e delle pene* (1764) she had read with profit, Catherine recommended a legal code in which punishments are calibrated to fit the severity of the crimes a person has committed, but also in which mild punishments are preferred to severe ones. In articles 96 and 123 of the *Nakaz*, the empress excluded mutilation and torture of accused persons, as a practice "repugnant to reason" (*Nakaz* 1907, 23, 30). Like Diderot and other *philosophes*, Catherine rejected religious persecution, because of the grave harm it inflicts on domestic tranquility and on the security of citizens (*Nakaz* 1907, 134); but, unlike Diderot, she did not recommend the disestablishment of Orthodoxy as the state religion in the Russian Empire. In this respect, her program of religious toleration stopped far short of the radical Enlightenment program.

In the first, unpublished draft of the *Nakaz*, Catherine had argued that the laws should not deprive people of freedom "except in extreme emergencies" and should strive to improve their conditions as much as possible. She suggested that the laws "must bring slaves to the point that they can purchase their own liberty" (Stennik 2006, 140). These passages, which first readers interpreted as attacks on serfdom, were dropped from the published version of the *Nakaz*. However, in articles 250–263 of the *Nakaz*, devoted to the structure of Russian society, Catherine did demand that the laws "ease the lot of subjects insofar as right reason permits," that the laws not reduce people to slavery, and that the laws deter the abuse of slaves (*Nakaz* 1907, 74–77). In article 252, she asserted that the government should follow "natural law, which commands us to contribute [...] to the welfare of all men" (*Nakaz* 1907, 74). However, in article 263, she called for laws that would "prevent the causes that so often have contributed to serfs' revolts against their masters" (*Nakaz* 1907, 76–77). On this crucial aspect of Russian law, Catherine adopted a middle path between abolitionism and all-out defense of the existing system.

Catherine's *Nakaz* was historically significant in three respects. First, it reasserted but also broadened the century-old royal commitment to enlightenment in Russia—that is, it underlined autocracy's progressive role, in alliance with the Orthodox Church, in Russian cultural development; also, it recommended a more humane criminal code; a more extensive plan for religious toleration; and, in principle, better treatment of Russian serfs. Second, as we shall see below, the *Nakaz* triggered an emblematic exchange of opinions with Diderot over the best path for Russia's future—an exchange that amounted, in fact, to an encounter between one variant of moderate enlightenment and a version of radical enlightenment. Third, as we shall note, the *Nakaz* triggered at least three responses that characterized late eighteenth-century enlightenment politics in Russia.

Enlightenment Under Catherine II: The Encounter with Diderot

Diderot spent five months in Russia, from 27 September/8 October 1773 to 22 February/5 March 1774. We do not know precisely when the empress first received him, but over the twenty-one weeks of his Russian visit, Diderot and Catherine met in the Winter Palace forty or more times—usually from three to five o'clock in the afternoon. There was no predetermined script for their conversations. In most meetings, the two interlocutors explored a single subject. Before a day's conversation, Diderot jotted down his ideas and then gave a more-or-less formal "lecture" on the pre-selected topic to Catherine. After this orderly presentation, *philosophe* and empress discussed the day's topic. In the evening, after returning to his apartment, Diderot reviewed his notes and meditated on the day's conversation. The result of the meditation sometimes took the form of a policy memorandum [*mémoire*]; on other occasions, Diderot composed an imaginary dialogue, a sardonic sketch, or a daydream [*rêverie*]. At the end of his stay in Russia, he gave Catherine a large folder, nearly four hundred hand-written pages long, containing these meditations (Diderot 1966).

In his *mémoires* for Catherine, Diderot sketched several criticisms of Russian political and social arrangements. First, at various junctures, he criticized despotism. In the *mémoire* on a permanent Legislative Commission, he wrote: "A despot, be he the best of men, commits infamy in ruling according to his own pleasure. He is a good father who reduces his subject to the condition of beasts; in inducing them to forget their desire for liberty, a desire that is so difficult to recover, he secures for them ten years of happiness at the cost of twenty years of misery. One of the greatest misfortunes that can befall a free people is two or three consecutive reigns of just and enlightened despotism" (Diderot 1966, 117–118). In his fanciful anecdote, "Le postillon de Hamm à Lippstadt," Diderot commented on the absurdity of the Prussian custom forbidding carriage drivers to sound their horns and to pass carriages conveying their social betters. "Under despotism," he quipped, "there is nothing but a long line of slaves, among whom no one dares to sound the horn at his superior" (Diderot 1966, 190–191).

In the *mémoires* for Catherine, Diderot wondered how to change the culture underpinning despotic states. In Russia, he thought, the establishment of a permanent Legislative Commission was essential to put an end to despotism, but to succeed it would have to be accompanied by other initiatives: inculcating in Russian subjects respect for law, promoting officeholders by merit, and encouraging popular education. The last measure was perhaps the most important, according to Diderot, because genuine political change is a consequence of enlightenment—that is, of the "civilized" outlook promoted in schools. Diderot therefore called on Catherine to institute a national system of public schools: "in every large city one school, or, if there is demand, more than one school." The schools should try to form a cohort of "honest and enlightened citizens in every class of society." Because he considered the goal of an educated populace vital to the realm, Diderot demanded that parents be compelled to send their children to school (Diderot 1966, 129–144).

Diderot advocated that schools concentrate on teaching science. He claimed that schools for girls should adopt a science-heavy curriculum, including the study of anatomy. He suggested that the government license teachers of both genders, for subjects like anatomy might be better taught by women than by men (Diderot 1966, 90–91). He opposed the teaching of the fine arts in public schools, because "fine arts give rise in subalterns to [a taste for] opulence." He would have banned dance, music, and gymnastics, "for it is unnecessary for a simple person to be a dancer or musician" (Diderot 1966, 143).

Diderot advertised inculcating respect for law, promoting of officeholders by merit, and encouraging popular education as "conservative" measures, but he also considered them prerequisites of regime change, from above. He tried to persuade Catherine to consider becoming a constitutional monarch of the British sort: "If one were to propose that Her Imperial Majesty immediately oversee transformation of the Russian Empire into the English constitution, I strongly doubt she would refuse. As free as she is to do good and as far from doing evil as she is, what would she lose? And why should she wish to bequeath to her successors a government they will tend to abuse?" (Diderot 1966, 123).

Second, in the *mémoires*, Diderot raised the question of serfdom's abolition. He stopped shy of advocating serfdom's universal abolition, but in order to understand Russian rural life, he sent her a series of questions about life in the countryside. He wondered what proportion of Russian subjects was free peasants [*odnodvortsy*] and what proportion was serfs [*les paysans*] (Tourneux 1899, 535); whether nobles owned all land in the countryside (Tourneux 1899, 539); what privileges were attached to noble status; and how she might describe "conditions between masters and slaves" (Tourneux 1899, 539–540). Catherine responded tersely to these queries in a written document: in it she maintained that "there are entire districts in which peasants never go without meat on the table; in which chicken is too common." She claimed: "I have seen some storage facilities full of six years' harvest, and there grain is not sold, because doing so would drive down prices." She conceded that everywhere the nobility's invocation of the right to property ownership conflicted with the merchantry's pretention to freedom of commerce and with the peasantry's "right to humane treatment" [*droit de l'humanité*]. She also admitted: "There are acts [by serf owners] of despotism and of error against which reason and equity cry out" (Tourneux 1899, 537–538). In his *mémoire*, "*De la ville de Saint-Pétersbourg*," Diderot championed "[a general] emancipation [of serf workers in the capital] or an emancipation under which they would pay a fee each year [to their former masters], or an emancipation through sale of serfs to foreigners." Through these steps he prodded the empress to "form a middle Estate" and thus to advance in the Russian capital "polite mores, a kind of urbanity" (Diderot 1966, 55–56).

During his residence in Petersburg, was Diderot aware of the Pugachev rebellion that raged in the countryside? The evidence that he knew of the uprising is overwhelming, although one cannot be certain exactly when he learned of it. In mid-October 1773, the government debated how best to respond to the rebels but kept secret its initial countermeasures. By late November 1773, rumors that the rebels might seize Orenburg circulated in Petersburg and reached the ears of foreign diplomats. Finally, on 23 December 1773, the government issued a public statement describing the rebellion as a symptom of "a terrible age of ignorance" [*strashnoe nevezhestva vremia*]. The statement characterized Pugachev as a new Grishka Otrep'ev, who had perpetrated "an insane deception" (Dubrovin 1884, 65–66, 168–169, 229, 240). Thus, Diderot may have learned of Pugachev's movement from diplomats as early as late November, but perhaps as late as 23 December, when Catherine's ukase appeared. After Diderot left Petersburg in early 1774, he told European friends that Catherine herself had informed him of the uprising. In a letter to Catherine from Paris on 17 October 1774, he reported sharing her impression of Pugachev with his European acquaintances. Diderot told them: "I never observed her [Catherine's] tranquility shaken […]. She saw in the rebel nothing but a fool awaiting hanging" (Tourneux 1899, 497).

Diderot's awareness of the rebellion forces us to ask whether his very interesting *mémoire*, "*Des révolutions*," alluded to it. In the table of contents, he gave to Catherine with the folder comprising his *mémoires*, Diderot listed this undated document as *mémoire XXIII* (Tourneux 1899, 584). Assuming that the empress and the *philosophe* met three times a week from mid-November (the probable date of their second conversation), their discussion of revolutions would have occurred in early January (seven weeks after mid-November) or mid-January 1774 (nine weeks from mid-November counting a fortnight in which Diderot was ill). In either case, before writing "*Des révolutions*," Diderot would have known of the rebellion from European diplomats and/or from Catherine's public statement of 23 December.

"*Des révolutions*" focused primarily on social-psychological causes of revolution. To the question—"Who stages revolutions?"—Diderot answered: "Those who have nothing to lose in the existing order, and those who have everything to gain." He seemed to assume that revolutionaries are usually dissatisfied members of the possessing classes—"powerful officials and those who have suffered the loss of their fortunes." He therefore advised Catherine to "prevent the ruin of great families, [for] their misery is more dangerous than their opulence" (Diderot 1966, 114–115). Diderot may have been thinking of the seventeenth-century aristocratic conspiracy called the Fronde and perhaps also about eighteenth-century Russia's age of palace coups. He allowed himself to mention the political prominence of the five Orlov brothers, a passing observation that alluded subtly to the events of 1762. This comment indicated Diderot's knowledge of Catherine's coup against her husband Peter III, but it also suggested his awareness that Pugachev was a pretender to the crown under Peter III's name. Diderot's *mémoire* also pointed to an element of "savagery" in Russians: "It seems to me," he wrote, "that a savage traits enters a bit into the national character. The savage is neither father nor spouse nor brother. He is himself, he is a child of nature" [*l'enfant de la nature*] (Diderot 1966, 114). This picture of the rebel as a "child of nature," as "one who has nothing to lose" and "everything to gain," was perhaps predicated on what Diderot had learned of Pugachev. The *philosophe*'s advice to Catherine, to "take all measures to encourage virtue and to discourage vice," applied explicitly to the handling of Russia's great families but implicitly to dealing with *les misérables russes*.

In addition to rendering the empress political counsel, Diderot composed three *mémoires* on religious toleration (Diderot 1966, 97–113). In them he argued that intolerance distorts the life of a polity by falsely emphasizing frivolous things, by creating conditions for denunciations and calumnies, by excluding able individuals from office, and by spreading hatred, prejudice, and lies. He faulted intolerant Christian clergymen but also Deists for their sectarian spirit. Diderot suggested that intolerance, whatever its source, "is never favorable to the truth [...] because truth loves to be tested, while falsehood shrinks from being tested" (Diderot 1966, 97). In other words, he claimed, a religiously intolerant polity can never be a free one.

Catherine received Diderot with good humor and listened for hours without decisively rebuffing him. Her patient demeanor was good politics: after all, pondering Diderot's political and religious program raised her reputation among the *philosophes* by entitling them to hope that their ideas might one day be applied in Russia; in turn, her renown among educated Europeans helped her domestically, by making it more likely that intelligent Russians would heed her political wisdom.

Yet Catherine was not all sweetness and light. She found Diderot's proposal to build an alliance between France and Russia irritating. She neither entirely rejected his outlandish flattery of her person nor accepted it eagerly. In her closing meeting with Diderot, the empress described him as both breathtakingly naïve and occasionally wise: "You sometimes have the sense of a twelve-year-old, and other times of a centenarian" (Necker 1801, 231). In 1787, thirteen years after Diderot had left Petersburg and three years after his death, she told the French ambassador Louis-Philippe Ségur that she had listened to Diderot "with more curiosity than profit." "If I had trusted him," she said, "everything in the Empire would have been turned upside down; legislation, administration, politics, finances—I would have reversed them all for some impracticable theories. However, since I listened more than I spoke, a witness who overheard us might have thought him a strict teacher and me a humble school-girl" (Ségur 1827, 34–35). In fact, Catherine's pose in the conversations with Diderot was that of a discreet, curious but well-informed, prudent head of state. She reminded Diderot that she had read Tacitus, Voltaire, and Montesquieu, but she boasted to Diderot of two supreme teachers, one of them male—misfortune [*le malheur*]—and the other female—enforced isolation [*la retraite*] (Necker 1801, 228).

After returning to The Hague from Petersburg, Diderot drafted a second, more strenuous response to Catherine's version of enlightenment—an extended marginal commentary on her *Nakaz*. Because the *philosophe* rejected various provisions of the empress's signature work, including her premises, and because he exposed her political positions as (insincere) posturing, his *"Observations"* read almost like a revolutionary tract.

Whereas Catherine had begun the *Nakaz* with a prayer for wisdom, a reference to the Church's commitment to the golden rule, and the vague assertion that good citizens seek their country's "prosperity, glory, and tranquility," Diderot's *"Observations"* maintained: "There is no true sovereign besides the nation," "no true legislature besides the people" (Diderot 1963, 343). He insisted that, if the people are to respect the laws, citizens must compose them. To enact the laws the people, and the existing head of state, must swear an oath to obey the laws: according to Diderot, anyone who refuses the oath of obedience "declares himself in advance a despot and tyrant" (Diderot 1963, 344).

Diderot described Catherine as "most assuredly a despot." The only issue was whether she wished to preserve her despotic rule or to abdicate it (Diderot 1963, 345). Diderot had no patience with the empress's prayers or with her flattery of the Orthodox Church. In his opinion, priests "are even more unreliable conservators of the law than magistrates are," because priests pretend that they "answer [not to the state but] to God alone" (Diderot 1963, 346). Besides, he claimed, priestly faith is "a tissue of absurdities," and priests are "purveyors of ignorance" rather than of reason (Diderot 1963, 347). According to Diderot, Catherine confronted a principled choice: either the *philosophe*'s path of reason, or the priest's path of violent "fanaticism," for "every priest is a dagger in the hand of God" (Diderot 1963, 349).

In article 6 of the *Nakaz*, Catherine had proclaimed Russia "a European power." Diderot's response was that "it mattered little" whether Russia was European or Asiatic, but it mattered much whether the country was "great, flourishing, and stable" (Diderot 1963, 349). He conceded that so vast a polity as Russia, where there were "all sorts of barbarians," would not be easy to civilize. But he maintained that, with good laws and intelligent administration, the civilizing mission might well succeed (Diderot 1963, 350–352). On the other hand, bad laws would only multiply the people's wickedness, undercut their prosperity, and lead them toward revolution (Diderot 1963, 352–353).

To Catherine's premise, "It is more advantageous to obey the laws under one master than to submit to many masters," Diderot agreed on the condition that the master had also submitted to the laws. In the *philosophe*'s opinion, one-person rule was usually a recipe for government by "a mad-man, a wicked man, or a fool" (Diderot 1963, 353). Absolute governments "completely subordinate liberty and property to a single person," he wrote. He observed that Russia was more poorly governed than France, precisely "because the natural liberty of the individual has been reduced to naught, while the crown's authority is unlimited." He proposed that any people seeking happiness and good laws must choose "limited government." Diderot ruled out the option of "pure monarchy," for this was just another name for despotism. If Catherine were to impose a new political system, he recommended that she choose something like the English parliamentary system; however, he noted that even limited monarchies tend to slide back into despotism (Diderot 1963, 355–357).

Diderot implied that the best form of government might be a democratic republic, in which power is vested in a popular legislature (Diderot 1963, 357–358). In republics, he noted, genuine liberty exists. In monarchies, unfortunately, there often existed only the "illusion" of liberty. Diderot likened the illusion to "a spider's web, on which the image [of liberty] is painted" but underneath which lurked "the despot's hideous head" (Diderot 1963, 358). Diderot dismissed systems of popular representation in which the elected legislature is subordinated to the crown or in which the legislature is a mere channel for conveying the monarch's will to the people. He also rejected arrangements in which representative bodies convey the people's wishes to the crown, for these written pleas are easily ignored (Diderot 1963, 360–363). He ridiculed institutions like the French *Parlement* and Russian Senate, which supposedly acted as a repository of law. In his opinion, "the Senate is nothing—a voice crying in the wilderness" (Diderot 1963, 363–364).

Diderot advocated equality before the laws. Because he rejected legal privileges attached to birth and occupation (Diderot 1963, 366–367, 378), he demanded that the head of state also submit to the laws. Just as ordinary citizens are not free to do whatever they please, so the crown must act within the law's framework (Diderot 1963, 367–368). Diderot argued that independent courts should hear criminal and civil cases. He worried that if the courts remained under control of the executive branch, then "one will end up submitting to despotism" (Diderot 1963, 377). In all circumstances, he thought, the great threat to citizens comes from the egoistic head of state who, separating himself or herself from the nation, "supposes he or she is at war with it." Diderot warned that departing from the rule of law and imposing ruinous measures on the people can carry a great cost—namely, a revolution (Diderot 1963, 380).

Diderot noted ominously that, in her *Nakaz*, "the Empress said nothing to emancipate the serfs." He asked: "Does she want slavery to endure? Does she ignore the fact that, where liberty does not exist, there can be no order, no laws, no population growth, no agriculture, no commerce, no wealth, no science, neither taste nor art" (Diderot 1963, 386).

In conclusion, Diderot formulaically praised Catherine for her "great soul" and "far-reaching genius," but he told her bluntly that the *Nakaz* had done nothing to ensure the rule of law in Russia: "I see in it the label of 'despot' has been discarded, but the substance is preserved under the label 'monarchy'" (Diderot 1963, 457).

Catherine did not read Diderot's critique of her *Nakaz* until after his death, when she inspected his papers in Petersburg. In a 1785 letter to her friend Friedrich Melchior von Grimm, Catherine declared: "This piece [Diderot's *"Observations"*] is true nonsense [*un vrai babil*], in which one finds neither knowledge of how things are, nor prudence, nor insight; if my *Instruction* had been drafted after Diderot's taste, it would have been applicable to a wholly different state of affairs [than to those in Russia]" (Tourneux 1899, 519–520).

Three Russian Responses to Catherine's Enlightenment Program

Mikhail Mikhailovich Shcherbatov served as a member of the Legislative Commission to which Catherine had directed her *Nakaz*. In its debates, he fretted about what he understood to be the empress's lack of appreciation of the nobility's historical significance in Russia, and he criticized the Petrine Table of Ranks for too easily permitting the promotion of commoners into noble ranks. Shcherbatov grasped that not many members of the commission sympathized with his claim that access to the nobility should be tightened, but he supported the commission itself and bitterly criticized Catherine's decision to dissolve it before the members had managed to draft a new legal code.

In his magnificent *Russian History from Ancient Times* (written 1768 to 1790, first volume published 1770), Shcherbatov traced the political travails of Kievan Rus', when fractious princes divided the country into warring factions, and under the Tatars, who ruled by shrewdly playing off Russian princes against each other. He made the case that Russia prospered in the Muscovite period as a kind of diarchy, in which monarchs ruled in partnership with the nobiliary elites; however, the country foundered when monarchs rejected good advice from the nobility and when noble elites put selfishness above the good of the realm. In the last volume of his history, Shcherbatov alluded to the desirability of some kind of constitutional arrangement when he wrote approvingly of Vasilii Shuiskii's 1606 oath "to impose no punishments without the advice of an assembly" (Shcherbatov 1901–1904, 131).

Throughout his history, Shcherbatov focused on the spread of enlightenment in Russia. Although he praised the Church for cultivating the rudiments of learning in a backward country, Shcherbatov rejected "excessive religiosity" and what he called the "monkish spirit" that had prevailed in Kiev (Hamburg 2016, 681–683). In an unpublished essay, probably written in 1782, he described pre-Petrine Russia as a society in which "lords and the entire people were sunken in superstition, and where other peoples were thought so outlandish that it was regarded as a sin to talk with a person of another faith" (Shcherbatov 1860, 10). His "solution" to Russia's problems may be found in his utopian "novel," *Journey to the Land of Ophir* (written 1783–1784, published 1896), which imagined a national network of schools, organized by social classes, and a constitutional monarchy governed by the motto: "The people do not exist for tsars, but tsars exist for the people, for before there were tsars, there was the people" (Shcherbatov 1897, 979). Thus, Shcherbatov's program combined a traditionalist element, built on recognition of the differences in social origins, and a progressive outlook that embraced enlightenment.

Nikolai Ivanovich Novikov served Catherine on the staff of the Legislative Commission as a scribe responsible for recording subcommittee discussions. Unlike Shcherbatov, he rejected the social exclusivity of the nobility. Over the course of the commission's meetings, he also apparently realized that serfdom would, at some point, have to be abolished—a position that set him at odds with the empress, whose public silence on this issue he likely interpreted as acquiescence to the country's system of forced labor. On leaving the Legislative Commission in December 1768, Novikov threw himself into journalism: between 1769 and 1774, he edited four satirical journals in which he criticized Russian backwardness, including serfdom; a decade later, from 1775 to 1785, he edited several Masonic journals, in which he championed the cultivation of virtue. In the 1770s and 1780s, he became one of Russia's most remarkable publishers. After 1773, he saw into print the *Ancient Russian Library,* a library of Old Russian chronicles and other historical sources; then from 1779 to 1783, he ran the Moscow University Press.

Novikov's extraordinary career as journalist and publisher was an outgrowth of the Catherinian Enlightenment, to the degree that he took seriously her invitation to spread enlightenment among the elites, but his acerbic criticisms of corrupt government officials, of the court, and of serf society threatened to set him at odds with her. In 1777, in the journal *Morning Light [Utrennii svet]*, Novikov used the enlightened principle of human dignity to criticize societies in which a person's standing is determined by class background or birth. Novikov did not reject social hierarchy per se: rather he wanted socially recognized differences among human beings to rest on exceptional virtue in public service and on conscientious discharge of natural roles, such as parenthood (Makogonenko 1951; Jones 1984; Faggionato 2005).

One of Russia's most prominent Freemasons, Novikov had studied the political program outlined in an anonymous text, published privately by the Martinist Ivan Vladimirovich Lopukhin. This book, *A New Outline of True Theology* (1784), advocated religious toleration, the spread of education, the elimination of onerous taxation, and abolition of all forms of slavery. The *New Outline* anticipated that, in the future, somewhere on the globe, a righteous monarch would prepare the foundation of the kingdom of God on earth, which kingdom would take the form of a just republic ([Anon.] 1784; Faggionato 2005). It is by no means clear that Novikov himself yearned for a republican government, but Catherine may have suspected him of doing so. The empress ordered his arrest in 1792. After interrogation, he was charged with offenses against the crown (secretly corresponding with members of a foreign government and trying to draw Crown Prince Paul into Freemasonry) and against the Orthodox Church (publishing books inimical to Orthodoxy and creating religious offices outside of Orthodoxy).

Although Novikov's career ended in imperial disfavor, he and Shcherbatov resembled each other in their commitment to public education, in their belief in knowledge and virtue, and in their caution in political matters. Whatever their disagreements with Catherine, they belonged, in a pan-European context, to the "party" of moderate Enlightenment.

In 1790, when Alexander Nikolaevich Radishchev published his *Journey from St. Petersburg to Moscow*, Catherine confronted radical Enlightenment ideas again, this time on Russian soil. *Journey* had two inspirations: the first was Abbé Raynal's book, *Histoire des deux Indes*, which Radishchev had read in 1780 or 1781; the second was Laurence Sterne's novel, *A Sentimental Journey through France and Italy*, whose hero, Yorick, had rubbed shoulders with people from all walks of life in order to gather material for philosophizing. In *Journey*, Radishchev's traveler meets a cross-section of Russians—coachmen and stationmasters, restaurateurs and merchants, enserfed peasants and prostitutes, and sundry government officials. Each person tells him about some aspect of life in Catherine's Empire, and the traveler faithfully reports what he has learned. Meanwhile, the traveler augments his sketches of social relations by sharing his own hopes, fantasies, and speculations, with all of these packaged together as a moralizing indictment of existing social "reality." Thus, Radishchev's *Journey* was both a work of social criticism and a dream-vision of Russia's shining future.

Radishchev's critique of Russian society focused on inequality in its various manifestations, the most painful of which was serfdom. Near Liubani, the traveler witnesses peasants working on Sunday because they spend the other six days of the week toiling in their master's fields. Shocked by the master's cruelty of heart, the traveler exclaims: "On the brow of each of your serfs, I read your condemnation" (Radishchev 1949, 46). At Mednoe, the traveler watches a serf auction separate members of a nuclear family to different bidders, a spectacle he calls "shameful" (Radishchev 1949, 160). So far as the traveler can see, serf owners profit from greed, theft, and tyranny over the peasants. Furious at members of his own class, the traveler labels them as "greedy beasts, insatiable predators" (Radishchev 1949, 186).

The more he observes, the clearer the traveler sees that peasant women suffer a double burden under serfdom: in addition to economic exploitation, they experience coercion and sexual predation from the masters. The traveler twice mentions rape or attempted rape of serf women, including an egregious case in which a landlord's son tried to force a young woman just before her wedding (Radishchev 1949, 85). The traveler concludes that such acts are not so much exceptional as they are part of a continuum of abuse, which serf women of every age, "grandmothers and young maidens" [*bab i devok docheri*], endure in village fields (Radishchev 1949, 83).

The traveler notes a relationship between the inequality inherent in the serf order and the system of governmental ranks that fosters corruption and abuse in civil service. In his view, officials of higher rank routinely abuse stationmasters, because they assume their rank entitles them to do so. According to the traveler, even petty officials behave callously. He repeats a story about a naval duty-officer outside Sistroretsk who had refused to awaken his unit commander even though a ship had run aground on rocks and passengers faced the possibility of drowning. The traveler accuses the lazy unit commander of being a "would-be murderer" and compares the Sistroretsk incident to one reported by Abbé Raynal in which a Bengal officer arbitrarily mistreated English prisoners in a Calcutta jail (Radishchev 1949, 51–52).

The traveler senses that inequality in the countryside, and in the civil service, is linked to Russia's despotic government. In Spasskaia Polest', he imagines a king wearing radiant clothing and surrounded by *arcana imperii*—a golden scepter, the scales of justice—and by fawning courtiers, who praise the king for his wisdom and just rule. This tableau proves too good to be true, because the king is blind to the reality that his spotless clothing is, in fact, "soaked in blood and wet with tears" of his subjects; that his "loyal" retainers are corrupt bribe takers; that his "wise" policies injure rather than help the poor. In the traveler's reverie, the source who overcomes the king's blindness by removing the scales from his eyes is none other than the mysterious wayfarer Truth (Radishchev 1949, 61–68). According to the traveler, those monarchs who listen to wayfarer Truth will enjoy her counsel, while those who scoff must eternally bear her censure. In this case, Radishchev permits the monarch to express outrage at his deceptive courtiers: "Unworthy criminals! Malefactors! Are you aware that you have taken advantage of your master's trust? You will all be put on trial! You must henceforth put an end to your abuses. What can you say to justify your deeds?" (Radishchev 1949, 68). Thus, the traveler stops short of demanding the violent overthrow of unjust monarchs.

And yet, Radishchev's *Journey* did not entirely reject revolution. In one chapter, he incorporated selected verses from his unpublished "Ode to Liberty," praising Oliver Cromwell for teaching peoples "how they might avenge themselves" (Radishchev 1949, 169). In another chapter, the traveler peruses a project for peasant emancipation, but warns that, if it is not adopted, a terrible fate may be in store for serf owners:

> Do you not grasp, my dear fellow citizens, what destruction awaits us, or the degree of danger we now face? [...] A stream confined to its banks only gains force as it encounters resistance. If it once bursts through the dam, nothing will manage to stand in its way. And so it is with our brothers now confined in chains. (Radishchev 1949, 129)

According to a diary entry for 26 June 1790 by her state secretary, Alexander Vasil'evich Khrapovitskii, the empress regarded the author of *Journey from St. Petersburg to Moscow* as a radical Freemason, a "Martinist," and the book itself as a manifestation of "the French disease" (Borozdin et al. 1907, 298). Catherine later told one of her imperial counselors, Count Alexander Andreevich Bezborodko, that she saw in *Journey* "nothing but schism and destructiveness [*razvrat*]" (Borozdin et al. 1907, 298). On 7 July 1790, she informed Khrapovitskii that, in her view, Radishchev was "a rebel [*buntovsh-chik*] worse than Pugachev" (Borozdin et al. 1907, 300).

Thus, Catherine confronted in Radishchev a Russian instantiation of the radical French Enlightenment, as embodied in Diderot and Abbé Raynal. She rejected the social and political "extremism" preached by these radicals, whom she contrasted to "safe" monarchists like Voltaire. By April 1795, Catherine had decided that "the *philosophes* and boys of that ilk who have taken part in the revolution and who have embraced the *Encyclopédie*, people like Helvétius and d'Alembert, […] have but two goals: the first is to abolish the Christian religion; the second, [to abolish] royalty" (Catherine II 1878, 622). Her commitment to gradual enlightenment did not permit her, or, if she could help it, her Russian elite subjects, to join the radicals. That was a bridge too far.

Conclusion

Except for Radishchev, enlighteners in late eighteenth-century Russia tended to be strikingly moderate when viewed in the broad European context. Catherine's program of seeking "influential friends" amongst *philosophes*, promoting education, and enlightened monarchy built on earlier foundations laid by educated Churchmen and autocrats. Her reformist measures and rhetorical flourishes made it difficult for Russian thinkers to outflank her, even when they defined human dignity, virtue, and righteousness differently. But the empress's encounters with Diderot in the 1770s and with Radishchev in 1790 dramatically illustrated the vulnerabilities of her program, and of the moderate Enlightenment, in a society based on forced labor and riven by inequalities of every sort.

Bibliography

Andreev, Igor' L. 2003. *Alexei Mikhailovich.* Moscow: Molodaia gvardiia.

Anonymous. 1784. *Novoe nachertanie istinnoi teologii.* Moscow: V tipografii I. Lopukhina.

Barran, Thomas Paul. 2002. *Russia Reads Rousseau, 1762–1825.* Evanston, IL: Northwestern University Press.

Berelowitch, Wladimir. 2015. Francophonie in Russia under Catherine II: General Reflections and Individual Cases. *Russian Review* 74 (1): 41–56.

Betskoi, Ivan I. 1789–1791. *Sobranie uchrezhdenii i predpisanii, kasatel'no vospitaniia, v Rossii, oboego pola blagoradnago i meschchanskago iunoshestva, s prochimi v pol'zu obshchestva ustanovleniiami.* St. Petersburg: pechatano v tipografii I. K. Shnora.

Bil'basov, Vasily A. 1884. *Didro v Peterburge.* St. Petersburg: I. N. Skorokhodov.

Bil'basov, Vasily A., and Antony Lentin. 1972. *A Philosopher at the Court of Catherine the Great: Didro v Peterburge.* Cambridge, UK: Oriental Research Partners.

Bogdanov, Andrei P. 1986. K polemike kontsa 60-kh—nachala 80-kh godov XVII v. ob organizatsii vyshego uchebnogo zavedeniia. In *Issledovaniia po istochnikovedeniiu istorii SSSR XIII–XVIII vekov,* ed. Viktor Ivanovich Buganov, 117–223. Moscow: Institut istorii AN SSSR.

―――. 1995. *Ot letopisaniia k issledovaniiu. Russkie istoriki poslednei chetverti XVII veka.* Moscow: RISC.

Borozdin, Alexander K., Ivan I. Lapshin, and Pavel E. Shchegolev. 1907. *Protsess Radishcheva*. Offitsial'nye materialy i svidetel'stva sovremennikov (Iz dela Gosudarstvennago Arkhiva i pechatnykh istochnikov). In *Polnoe sobranie sochinenii A. N. Radishcheva v 2-kh tomakh*, vol. 2, 298–353. Moscow: Izdanie M. I. Akinfieva.

Catherine II. 1878. Pis'ma Imperatritsy Ekateriny II baronu Mel'khioru Grimmu (gody s 1774 po 1796). Edited by Iakov Grot. In *Sbornik Imperatorskago Russkago Istoricheskago Obshchestva. XXIII* (2): 1–695.

———. 1971. *Documents of Catherine the Great. The Correspondence with Voltaire and the Instruction of 1767 in the English Text of 1768*. New York, NY: Russell & Russell.

Catherine II, and Friedrich Melchior Grimm. 2016. *Chastnaia khudozhestvennaia i politicheskaia korrespondentsiia epokhi Prosveshcheniia*. Vol. 1. *1764–1778*. Moscow: Mezhdunarodnyi Tsentr po izucheniiu XVIII veka Fernei-Vol'ter.

Chrissidis, Nikolaos A. 2016. *An Academy at the Court of the Tsars: Greek Scholars and Jesuit Education in Early Modern Russia*. DeKalb, IL: NIU Press.

Collis, Robert. 2012. *The Petrine Instauration. Religion, Esotericism and Science at the Court of Peter the Great, 1689–1725*. Leiden and Boston, MA: Brill.

Cracraft, James. 1988. *The Petrine Revolution in Russian Architecture*. Chicago, IL: University of Chicago Press.

———. 1997. *The Petrine Revolution in Russian Imagery*. Chicago, IL: University of Chicago Press.

———. 2003. *The Revolution of Peter the Great*. Cambridge, MA: Harvard University Press.

———. 2004. *The Petrine Revolution in Russian Culture*. Cambridge, MA: Harvard University Press.

Diderot, Denis. 1875. Essai sur les études en Russie. In *Oeuvres Complètes de Diderot. Tome Troisième*, 415–428. Paris: Garnier Frères.

———. 1963. Observations sur l'Instruction de l'Impératrice de Russie aux deputés pour la confection des lois. In *Oeuvres politiques. Textes établis avec introductions, bibliographies, notes et relevé de variantes*, ed. Paul Vernière, 329–458. Paris: Garnier Frères.

———. 1966. *Mémoires pour Catherine II*. Edited and with an Introduction by Paul Vernière. Paris: Éditions Garnier Frères.

Dubrovin, Nikolai F. 1884. *Pugachev i ego soobshchiki. Epizod iz istorii tsarstvovaniia Imperatritsy Ekateriny II. 1773–1774 gg.* Vol. 2. St. Petersburg: Tipografiia I. N. Skorokhodova.

Faggionato, Raffaella. 2005. *A Rosicrucian Utopia in Eighteenth-Century Russia: The Masonic Circle of N. I. Novikov*. Dordrecht: Springer.

Felbiger, Johann von. 1777. *Anleitung der Rechtsschaffenheit oder das für die in den Trivialschulen lernende slavonisch-servische nicht unirte Jugend bestimmte Lesebuch.* Wien: Wien Kurzböck.

Florovskii, George. 1937. *Puti russkogo bogosloviia*. Paris: YMCA Press.

Fontenelle, Bernard. 1727. *Éloge du Czar Pierre I*. In *Histoire de l'Académie Royale des sciences*. Année MDCCXXV, 105–128. Paris: l'Académie Royale des sciences.

Gamburger, Andrei F. 1867. Pis'ma Imperatritsy Ekaterine II k g-zhe Zheffren. In *Sbornik Imperatorskago Russkago Istoricheskago Obshchestva*. Vol. 1, 253–290. St. Petersburg: Tipografiia Transhelia.

General'noe uchrezhdenie o vospitanii oboego pola iunoshestva. 1764. In *Polnoe sobranie zakonov imperii rossiiskoi*, XVII, 12 (12 marta 1764 goda), 103. [publisher anonymous].

48   G. M. HAMBURG

Ger'e, Vladimir I. 1871. *Otnosheniia Leibnitsa k Rossii i Petru Velikomu po neizdannym bumag Leibnitsa v Ganoverskoi biblioteke.* St. Petersburg: Pechatnia V. I. Golovina.

Goodman, Dena. 1994. *The Republic of Letters: A Cultural History of the French Enlightenment.* Ithaca, NY: Cornell University Press.

Grechanaia, Elena P. 2010. *Kogda Rossiia govorila po-frantsuzski: Russkaia literatura na frantsuzskom iazyke (XVIII—pervaia polovina XIX veka).* Moscow: IMLI RAN.

Hamburg, Gary M. 2016. *Russia's Path toward Enlightenment. Faith, Politics, and Reason, 1500–1801.* New Haven, CT and London: Yale University Press.

Helvétius, Claude-Adrien. 1773. *De l'homme; de ses facultés, et de son éducation, ouvrage posthume (publié par le prince Galitzin).* À Londres (La Haye): Chez la Société Typographique.

Hildermeier, Manfred. 2004. Traditionen der Aufklärung in der russischen Geschichte. In *Interdisziplinarität und Internationalität. Wege und Formen der Rezeption der französischen und der britischen Aufklärung in Deutschland und Russland in 18. Jahrhundert,* ed. Heinz Duchhardt and Claus Scharf, 1–15. Mainz: von Zabern.

Hughes, Lindsey. 1990. *Sophia. Regent of Russia 1657–1704.* New Haven, CT and London: Yale University Press.

Hunt, Lynn. 2008. *Inventing Human Rights: A History.* New York, NY: W. W. Norton & Company.

Hunt, Lynn, and Margaret Jacobs. 2005. Enlightenment Studies. In *Encyclopedia of the Enlightenment, 4 vols.,* ed. Alan Charles Kors et al. New York: Oxford University Press. http://www.oxfordreference.com.ccl.idm.oclc.org.

Ilizarov, Simon S. 1999. *Moskovskaia intelligentsia XVIII veka.* Moscow: Janus-K.

Israel, Jonathan. 2006. Enlightenment: Which Enlightenment? *Journal of the History of Ideas* 67 (3): 523–545.

Jones, W. Gareth. 1984. *Nikolai Novikov: Enlightener of Russia.* Cambridge, UK: Cambridge University Press.

Kamenskii, Andrei B. 1999. *Ot Petra I do Pavla I. Reformy v Rossii XVIII veka. Opyt tselostnogo analiza.* Moscow: RGGU.

Kopelevich, Iudif Kh. 1977. *Osnovaniia Peterburgskoi Akademii nauk.* Leningrad: Nauka.

Levitt, Marcus C. 2009. The Theological Context of Lomonosov's 'Evening' and 'Morning' Meditations on God's Majesty. In *Early Modern Russian Letters: Texts and Contexts Selected Essays,* ed. Marcus C. Levitt, 305–319. Boston, MA: Academic Studies Press.

Lomonosov, Mikhail V. 1748. *Kratkoe rukovodstvo k krasnorechiiu.* St. Petersburg: Akademiia Nauk.

———. 1766. *Drevniaia rossiiskaia istoriia.* St. Petersburg: Akademiia Nauk.

Madariaga, Isabel de. 1981. *Russia in the Age of Catherine the Great.* New Haven, CT and London: Yale University Press.

Makogonenko, Grigorii P. 1951. *Nikolai Novikov i russkoe prosveshchenie XVIII veka.* Moscow: Khudozhestvennaia literatura.

Marker, Gary. 1985. *Publishing, Printing and the Origins of Intellectual Life in Russia, 1700–1800.* Princeton, NJ: Princeton University Press.

Nakaz imperatritsy Ekateriny II, dannyi kommissii o sochinenii proekta novago ulozheniia. 1907. St. Petersburg: Imperatorskaia Akademiia Nauk.

Necker, Susanne Curchod. 1801. *Nouveaux mélanges extraits des manuscrits de Mme.* Necker. Tome I. Paris: C. Pougens [et] Genets.

Platon, Archbishop of Moscow (Levshin). 1766. *Uveshchanie k raskol'nikam s chinop-olozheniem, kak prinimat' obrazuiushchikhsia iz nikh k Pravoslavnoi vere.* St. Petersburg: V Sinodal'noi Tipografii.

Radishchev, Alexander N. 1949. Puteshestvie iz Peterburga v Moskvu. In *Izbrannye filosofskie sochineniia*, ed. I. Ia Shchipanov, 37–199. Moscow: Gosudarstvennoe izdatel'stvo politicheskoi literatury.

Raeff, Marc. 1970. *Origins of the Russian Intelligentsia: The Eighteenth Century.* New York: Harcourt, Brace & World.

Rjéoutski, Vladislav, Gesine Argent, and Derek Offord, eds. 2014. *European Francophonie: The Social, Political and Cultural History of an International Prestige Language.* Oxford: Peter Lang.

Robertson, John. 2015. *The Enlightenment. A Very Short Introduction.* Oxford: Oxford University Press.

Samarin, Yurii F. 1880. *Stefan Iavorskii i Feofan Prokopovich in Sochineniia. 5.* Moscow: Tipografiia A. I. Mamontova.

Schippan, Michael. 2012. *Die Aufklärung in Russland im 18.Jahrhundert.* Wiesbaden: Harrassowitz Verlag.

Schönle, Andreas, Andrei Zorin, and Alexei Evstratov, eds. 2016. *The Europeanized Elite in Russia, 1762–1825.* DeKalb: NIU Press.

Ségur, Louis-Philippe. 1827. *Mémoires ou souvenirs et anecdotes. Tome III.* Paris, London: Chez Henri Colburn.

Ségur, Pierre de. 1897. *Le royaume de La Rue Saint-Honoré.* Paris: Calmann Lévy, Éditeurs.

Serman, Ilya Z. 1988. *Mikhail Lomonosov: Life and Poetry.* Jerusalem: Center of Slavic and Russian Studies, the Hebrew University of Jerusalem.

Shcherbatov, Mikhail M. Prince. 1860. Razmotrenie o porokhakh i samovlastii Petra Velikogo. In *Raznye sochineniia Kniazia M. M. Shcherbatova*, 1–20. Moscow: Universitetskaia tipografiia.

———. 1897. Puteshestvie v zemliu ofirskuiu g-na S.... In *Sochineniia.* 1, 749–1060. St. Petersburg: Tiopografiia M. Akinfieva i I. Leont'eva.

———. 1901–1904. *Istoriia rossiiskaia.* Vol. 7: Chast' 2. St. Petersburg: Izdatel'stvo kniazia B. S. Shcherbatova.

Shtrange, Mikhail M. 1965. *Demokraticheskaia intelligentsiia Rossii v XVIII veka.* Moscow: Izdatel'stvo "Nauka".

Snegirev, Ivan M. 1890. *Zhizn' Moskovskago metropolita Platona. Chast' 2.* Moscow: Tipo-Litografiia I. Efimova.

Städtke, Klaus, Franziska Thun, and Dirk Uffelmann, eds. 1999. *Kultur als Übersetzung. Klaus Städtke zum 65. Geburtstag.* Würzburg: Königshausen & Neumann.

Staniukovich, Tat'iana V. 1953. *Kunstkamera Peterburgskoi Akademii nauk.* Moscow: Idatel'stvo Akademii nauk SSSR.

Stefan Iavorskii. 2010. *Kamen' very Pravoslavnoi-kafolicheskoi Vostochnoi tserkvi.* St. Petersburg: Obshchestvo pamiati igumenii Taisii.

Stennik, Yurii V. 2006. A. P. Sumarokov—kritik 'Nakaza' Ekateriny II. In *XVIII vek. Sbornik 24*, 124–143. St. Petersburg: Nauka.

Tatishchev, Vasily N. 1962–1968. *Istoriia Rossiiskaia v semi tomakh.* Moscow: Izdatel'stvo AN SSSR.

———. 1979. Razgovor dvu[kh] priiatelei o pol'ze nauki i uchilishch. In *Izbrannye proizvedeniia*, 51–132. Moscow: Nauka.

Tourneux, Maurice. 1899. *Diderot et Catherine II.* Paris: Calmann Lévy University Press.

Ustrialov, Nikolai G. 1858. *Istoriia tsarstvovaniia Petra Velikago.* Vol. 3. St. Petersburg: Tipografiia II Otdeleniia Sobstvennoi Imperatorskago Velichestva Kantseliarii.

Voltaire and Catherine II, Empress of Russia. 2006. *Correspondance, 1763–1778.* Edited by Alexandr Stroev. Paris: Non lieu.

Vucinich, Alexander. 1963. *Science in Russian Culture. A History to 1860.* Stanford, CA: Stanford University Press.

Walicki, Andrzej. 2005. *Zarys mysli rosyjskiej od oswiecenia do renesansu religijno-filozoficznego.* Kraków: Wydawnistwo Uniwersitetu Jagiellonskiego.

Wilson, Arthur M. 1972. *Diderot.* New York and Oxford: Oxford University Press.

Winter, Eduard. 1953. *Halle als Ausgangspunkt der deutschen Russlandskunde im 18. Jahrhundert.* Berlin: Akademie-Verlag.

———. 1966. *Frühaufklärung. Der Kampf gegen den Konfessionalismus in Mittel- und Osteuropa und die deutsch-slavische Begegnung.* Berlin: Akademie-Verlag.

Wirtschafter, Elise Kimerling. 2011. Christian Rulership in Enlightenment Russia: Father Platon at the Court of Catherine II. In *The Book of Royal Degrees and the Genesis of Russian Historical Consciousness,* ed. Gail Lenhoff and Ann Kleimola, 334–340. Bloomington, IN: Slavica.

———. 2013. *Religion and Enlightenment in Catherinian Russia: The Teachings of Metropolitan Platon.* DeKalb, IL: Northern Illinois University Press.

CHAPTER 3

Russian Religious Philosophy: The Nature of the Phenomenon, Its Path, and Its Afterlife

Sergey S. Horujy

PREAMBLE: SOME WHY'S AND WHAT'S

The tasks of this text are not historical, at least in the sense of describing historical facts or sources. Today in the factual history of Russian philosophy, there are no great lacunae or enigmas, and in any case, such history is not the focus of my studies. My principal goal is conceptual: it is the comprehension of the phenomenon of Russian religious philosophy both in its diachrony and in its synchrony. A methodological remark: these two aspects will be considered not *nacheinander*, but *nebeneinander*, that is, not in succession, but in parallel to each other. This means that I shall trace the course of (philosophical) events trying not so much to describe factual details as to expose logics and structures of this course, the concepts and ideas involved in it.

Undoubtedly, the subject chosen deserves serious attention. The heritage of Russian philosophy is predominantly religious, and Russian religious philosophy made a valuable contribution to Russian culture as well as Christian thought. Its role was especially important during the Silver Age. In this specific period, which created its own rich and syncretic culture, philosophy was flourishing and quickly advanced to the leading position in cultural life. The philosophical dimension of the cultural process has even been given the special name of the Religious-Philosophical Renaissance. However, we are immediately confronted with difficulties and perplexities when trying to define exactly what Russian religious philosophy is. To start with, what are the chronological borders of this phenomenon? It is indisputable that Russian religious philosophy

S. S. Horujy (✉)
Institute of Philosophy, Russian Academy of Sciences, Moscow, Russia

© The Author(s), under exclusive license to Springer Nature
Switzerland AG 2021
M. F. Bykova et al. (eds.), *The Palgrave Handbook of Russian Thought*,
https://doi.org/10.1007/978-3-030-62982-3_3

was at its peak in the first decades of the twentieth century, in prerevolutionary Russia and then in the emigration between the world wars; it is equally indisputable that now it does not exist anymore and belongs to the past. But when did it start and when exactly did it end? The answers can hardly be found even in special literature, and one of my aims will be to determine them more precisely.

The next question concerns inner, noumenal characteristics of the phenomenon. Evidently, Russian religious philosophy is the part of Russian philosophy which takes up religious positions. But this formula covers a vast manifold of extremely different works and authors. The works of Russian religious thinkers demonstrate drastic differences in their attitude to religion as well as in the character of their philosophizing. Their connection with religion varies from the rigorous following of Orthodox doctrine in all its parts, including ecclesiastic rites and sacraments (as in the late Bulgakov), to the arbitrary selection of discordant religious contents (as in Merezhkovskii or Rozanov), and often these contents belong neither to Orthodoxy nor to Christianity. Their philosophy includes some systematic theories (like those of Nikolai Lossky or Frank) and profound studies (like those of the Dionysian cult by Vyacheslav Ivanov and of the symbol by Losev), but for the most part they demonstrate all kinds of non-academic styles and discourses, essayistic and journalistic, impressionistic and intimate-confessional, and so on. Often philosophy is mixed here with theology and free style essays so that the resulting discourse lacks well-defined methodological rules and has no convincing substantiation of its statements. Thus a recent course of Russian philosophy remarks: "To put the matter bluntly, they [Russian philosophers] may seem to make assertions about what is the case without giving any convincing reasons for believing that reality is what they claim it to be" (Copleston 1986, 354). Due to this discursive vagueness, there are many Russian thinkers who are concerned with religious problems but are, in some way or another, in the neighborhood of religious philosophy, for example, Gershenzon, Bakhtin, Golosovker, Fedorov's followers, and Eurasianists.

As a result, the borders of the phenomenon become even more indeterminate. There are no exact criteria that define these borders, and thus my task of recovering Russian religious philosophy is an enterprise in the spirit of Russian folk tales: *go I do not know where and bring I do not know what*. Let us nonetheless try.

The Birth of Russian Philosophical Discourse as an Epistemological Event

All rules involve exceptions, and this is especially true in the case of philosophy. It is not so difficult to formulate a set of general requirements which should be met by any philosophical discourse as such. These requirements belong to three groups: the presence of method—the preparation of concepts and the work with them—the presence of a cognitive paradigm. But for any such requirements it is surely possible to find some not bad philosophy which does not obey it. Thus, the full triad is not obligatory for each particular philosophy, but all its parts must be taken into account when we trace the emergence of a full-fledged philosophical school or tradition. For a long period, Russian culture created only *proto-philosophical forms* which possessed just some or other isolated elements of a philosophical discourse. Philosophical aspects were present in the literature of the Russian free masons (though this literature was mainly translated), in preaching, as well as in historical, political, and rhetorical texts. There was some philosophical education, chiefly in theological academies, and even some modest scale philosophy was produced, chiefly by professors of these academies. But what matters is that all these elements of philosophical culture and infrastructure were not new creations: they were borrowed from the West together with all the other products of persistent Westernization, the dominant trend of the Russian development since the Petrine reforms. Thus, being imperfect and insufficient epistemologically, these proto-philosophical forms were unsatisfactory also in an even more important respect—they did not serve the cardinal task of philosophical expression of that basic fund of ideas which I shall call the *Eastern Christian discourse*: the spiritual and conceptual fund created by Orthodox Christianity and shaping the Orthodox (first Byzantine and then Russian) mentality and cultural-civilizational organism.

However, the same Petrine reforms gave to Russia powerful historical dynamics, and the cultural process moved on intensely, philosophical dimension included. Soon after the Patriotic War of 1812 philosophical reflection cultivated chiefly in small groups of intellectuals (famous Russian "circles," *kruzhki*) starts to attack key philosophical problems. At first, in such circles as the Lovers of Wisdom in the 1820s and the Stankevich circle in the 1830s, philosophical work is still predominantly of the school character (with the study of Schelling and then Hegel as the main subject). But soon some big problems were moved to the center of discussion, problems connected with Russia's own history and spiritual tradition. Their discussion evolved gradually into creative philosophical work, resulting in the birth of original Russian philosophy. According to the winged words of Mikhail Gershenzon, "the great drifting of the ice of Russian thought has begun" (Gershenzon 1923, 6).

The time of drifting ice was the 1840s, the central place Moscow, and the main protagonists of the process were two disputing groups, which were given the names of the Westernizers and the Slavophiles. As for the problems in the discussion of which the Russian philosophical mind was being formed, they concerned two big themes: Russia, in the specific nature of its history and its relation to the West, and human personality, in its relationship with society. Hot disputes between the Westernizers and the Slavophiles, which took place in 1842–1844, belong to the most colorful and memorable pages of Russian intellectual life. They were very productive philosophically: in the course of them, a number of basic philosophical conceptions were formulated, and two diverging lines in Russian thought were clearly articulated, which have existed ever since, presenting sharply different positions in cultural and social philosophy, on all topical problems of Russian history and contemporary life. In their relation to philosophy these lines were also different. The Western line was predominantly oriented to what we today call human rights, politics, and social action, and much less to purely conceptual issues. Westernizers considered it necessary to present philosophical foundations of their positions, but they thought that it was sufficient to this end to use the available resources of European philosophy. As a result, their philosophical achievements were always modest; the most notable exception is probably Herzen's conception of personhood.

In contrast to this, Slavophiles were inclined to exaggerate the distinctions and contradictions between Russia and the West, but paradoxically such distorted optics turned out to be stimulating and fruitful for creative philosophizing. Indeed, if Russian spirituality, mentality, and development are completely different from all Western models and patterns then obviously *Russia needs its own independent philosophical project!* There must be original Russian philosophy expressing an authentic Russian self-consciousness and mind-set, Russian spiritual and historical experience. And it is easy to see what character this philosophy would have. According to the Slavophiles, Russian consciousness and experience are determined by Orthodox Christianity, and thus in order to express them, philosophy, as Ivan Kireevskii stated clearly, must be rooted in the Orthodox Tradition, in the works of the Orthodox Church Fathers. But, again paradoxically, this connection with the theological thought of the distant past represented, according to Kireevskii, not dogmatic bonds for philosophical reason, but, on the contrary, the necessary condition for the vital force of philosophy, and for its ability to be topical, "responding to questions of the day." Together with Khomiakov's ideas on conciliarity (*sobornost'*), this project, by Kireevskii, is an original contribution lying on the border between philosophy and theology and representing a sound and constructive approach to the comprehension of Russian self-consciousness as well as Russian historical and spiritual experience. Thus Gustav Shpet, although his own position was definitely Westernizing, stated decisively: "Slavophile problems [...] are the only original problems of Russian philosophy" (Shpet 1922, 37).

But notwithstanding the successful discovery of the field of topics for original Russian philosophy, the philosophy itself still did not emerge. Aiming to determine the borders of the phenomenon of Russian religious philosophy, we must look closely at epistemological aspects, and we see that there were no Russian thinkers so far whose work possessed all the necessary epistemological parameters of philosophical discourse listed above. Kireevskii's work approached these epistemological demands, he was sensitive to epistemological and methodological problems, but his philosophical program was only starting to emerge at the time of his sudden death from cholera in 1856. Khomiakov's work was quite disorganized epistemologically, and moreover, his main contribution to Russian thought, the doctrine of *sobornost'*, was much more theological than philosophical. Thus, the task of creating a Russian philosophical tradition or school was still to be fulfilled.

However, it was successfully fulfilled in the next generation by Vladimir Solovyov. It is completely true that Solovyov created the first philosophical system which met the demands of professional philosophical discourse and was based on principles belonging (at least partially) to Eastern Christian discourse. The first of these principles was All-Unity, *hen kai pan*, *vseedinstvo*: an ontological category, which Solovyov made the top principle of his system. It was a happy decision helped by the shrewd philosophical intuition of Solovyov: although his knowledge of the Greek Fathers was poor, he had chosen, unmistakably, the idea which is the best meeting point of classical European metaphysics and Orthodox Tradition. Born in Ancient Greece and having obtained a refined elaboration in Neoplatonism, All-Unity then became one of the central conceptions of Christian Platonism and had a rich history in both Western culture (Eriugena, Nicholas of Cusa, Leibniz, et al., finally Schelling and Hegel) and Eastern Christianity (Gregory of Nyssa, Dionysius Areopagite, et al.), including Russian spirituality and culture (Horujy 1994, 32–66). Moreover, it was noticed repeatedly after Solovyov that the motif of All-Unity has a kind of *Wahlverwandtschaft*, an elective affinity, with the Russian mind-set, deeply inclined as it is to an order of things based on wholeness, union, and unity. Thus, his philosophy of All-Unity found favorable reception. In addition, it had a quite special value for all interested in the development of Russian philosophy.

Having all the elements of classical philosophical discourse, Solovyov's system was at the same time an open system: it represented a large-scale philosophical construction which was far from being finished. It opened up a large spectrum of themes and problems which were all elaborated only in outline; and it offered the philosophical tools needed for their further elaboration. The themes in question embraced almost the whole field of general problems of religious thought; like the idea of All-Unity, they also belonged to the interface of European metaphysics and Eastern Christian discourse. This means that Solovyov's work supplied Russian religious thought with the conceptual and epistemological fund adequate for its themes, and it also identified a number of fields for further development. Evidently, it was an inviting situation. Solovyov was opening up a vast horizon for original Russian philosophy.

The reaction to the appearance of Solovyov's philosophy proved that it was a much needed and long-awaited event. Philosophical works discussing and developing his ideas started to appear almost immediately, and this was not a short-lived reaction, but the birth of a new philosophical tradition: *Russian religious philosophy*. With its creation Russian thought advanced not just to a new stage, but also to a new status on the philosophical scene.

Further development of Solovyov's ideas began in his lifetime, first of all in the works of his closest friend Prince Sergei Trubetskoi (1862–1905). Soon it was understood that Solovyov's philosophy has three principal axes: *All-Unity—Sophia, the Divine Wisdom—the Godmanhood* [*bogochelovechestvo*].

Each of these core ideas was the leading principle of a certain fundamental branch of philosophical and religious thought. All-Unity was the central principle of ontology, and at the same time it served as the universal organizing principle of all Solovyov's system: in each particular section of philosophy Solovyov established the generating principle of its framework, and this principle was a certain representation of All-Unity. Sophia was the heart of religious and mystical life, and the driving force of all Solovyov's work. The Godmanhood was the basic conception of world history as the process of the gradual ascent of mankind to the union with God. Very soon after Solovyov's untimely death in 1900 each of these three axes of his thought became the base of an active philosophical trend. A new philosophical movement was emerging and gaining force quickly.

Characterization of the Newborn Phenomenon

There are few examples in modern philosophy of such a quick appearance and vigorous rise of an important philosophical tradition or school. The early period of Russian religious philosophy can be compared in its intensity and fruitfulness (if not in the scale of its achievements) to the upsurge of German philosophy at the period of Romanticism. In an improbably short time, about one decade at the beginning of the twentieth century, a large group of original thinkers appeared on the philosophical scene: Vasilii Rozanov, Lev Shestov, Vyacheslav Ivanov, Evgenii Trubetskoi, Pavel Novgorodtsev, Sergei Bulgakov, Semyon Frank, Nikolai Lossky, Nikolai Berdyaev, Pavel Florensky, to mention only the principal ones. And in subsequent years new important figures kept on appearing: Vladimir Ern, Ivan Ilyin, Lev Karsavin, Fyodor Stepun, and others. Moscow, St. Petersburg, and Kiev became centers of animated philosophical life. A quickly growing philosophical community established the corresponding infrastructure and institutional aspects: philosophical societies were organized in many cities, philosophical journals were founded, and many philosophical projects aimed at publications, debates, education, and so on emerged and were realized. There were close contacts with European philosophy, and some period of study in Europe was almost a sine qua non in philosophical education. During all the prerevolutionary years Russian philosophy was in an incessant creative ascent, and it was becoming imminent that it would soon replace literature in the role of the leading branch of national culture.

As a whole, this powerful movement was very diversified in its leading ideas; all principal trends of European philosophy had their adepts in Russia. But it included a large and clearly expressed mainstream which was nothing but Russian religious philosophy based on the heritage of Solovyov. This mainstream, usually called the *Russian Religious-Philosophical Renaissance,* is dominant in this period of the history of philosophy and is often considered the main achievement of all Russian philosophy as such. Here the principal themes and problems of philosophical work follow in the tracks of Solovyov's thought with its three axes listed above. Surprisingly, a great number of original philosophical systems is created, and in the majority of them, as in Solovyov's system, the principle of All-Unity keeps the central place, so that all this vast philosophical body obtains the name of *metaphysics of All-Unity*. Let us list the authors of the most important of them approximately following the chronological order of their emergence (although all of them appeared in a very short interval of time after 1905): Evgenii Trubetskoi, Bulgakov, Florensky, Frank, Nikolai Lossky; and, as an epilogue, two more systems, maybe the most mature ones, presented by Karsavin in the diaspora and Losev in Soviet Russia. It is worth adding that this concluding work of the Russian metaphysics of All-Unity was rewarded with the imprisonment and forced labor of both its authors. In their conceptual framework these Russian systems of All-Unity represented typical works of classical metaphysics. They had many connections in European philosophy such as that of Nicholas of Cusa, Leibniz et al., and were especially influenced by German Idealism, so that Lev Karsavin even stated: "Everything done by Russian specialists in philosophy should be included for fairness' sake in the history of European and, most of all, German thought" (Karsavin 1929).

The mythologem of Sophia cherished by Solovyov also had a very rich post-Solovyovian history. Solovyov himself never actualized his endeavor to make Sophia the top principle of an all-embracing philosophical-theological system, but his followers came closer to doing so. A new philosophical-theological discourse or (sub-)discipline called *sophiology* emerged in Russian religious philosophy. It was represented by at least three full-scale systems: those of Evgenii Trubetskoi, Florensky, and Bulgakov, and the influence of sophiology can be found in many other thinkers: Vyacheslav Ivanov, Berdyaev, Lossky, Ern, Durylin, Karsavin et al. In contrast to the metaphysics of All-Unity, sophiology is not, strictly speaking, a philosophical discourse, it has many specific features. I called Sophia a "mythologem," and this vague term implies that it belongs neither to philosophy nor to theology. It is the personified "wisdom" which originally appeared in the Deuterocanonical books of the Old Testament composed in the milieu of Hellenized Jewry, and then sporadically became the subject of mystical ecstasies, theological speculations, and philosophical constructions.[1]

Solovyov's turn to sophiology was the result of his direct mystical "Three Encounters" with Sophia, but later thinkers did not claim such personal encounters and were just producing theories (although they sometimes mentioned certain sophianic inspirations). All these theories were, however, very objectionable since they could not meet the conditions of either philosophical or theological discourse: the vague origins and status of Sophia prevented its turning into a correct philosophical concept, and as for theology, Sophia was not included in the body of the Church dogmas and any attempt to put it at the top position in theological constructions unavoidably led to contradictions with canonical Church teaching. But, on the other hand, Sophia had a place of her own in Russian Christianity (e.g., in icons and the consecration of churches), and the discourse of Sophia was convenient for expressing many aspects and motifs of the relationship between God and world. Combining many heterogeneous elements, mystical, theological, philosophical, sometimes artistic and even lyrical, exploiting freely resources from many heterogeneous schools and traditions, Russian sophiology was a striking and fastidious intellectual phenomenon: if you wish, a quintessence of the whole syncretic culture of the Silver Age. Thus sophiological theories, especially the massive system of Bulgakov, had many adherents; and later on, when Russian thought in the diaspora was gradually coming to the tasks of the critical reassessment of Russian religious philosophy, this reassessment, in the first place, took the shape of the criticism of sophiology. It was the famous "Dispute on Sophia" in Paris in the mid-1930s, which I shall discuss below.

Unlike All-Unity and Sophia, the last of Solovyov's great ideas, the Godmanhood, did not give rise to an independent philosophical trend (although such formulas as "system of Godmanhood" are used sometimes). Nevertheless, it played a very considerable role in Russian religious philosophy, representing the dominant paradigm of philosophy of history. In this paradigm the description of the historical process includes the religious dimension and is complemented with a conception of meta-history describing the direct interference of divine factors. Usually such interference is conceived as concentrated predominantly in the final stages of history, so that meta-history takes the form of eschatology and apocalypticism. Principal examples, in which the idea of the Godmanhood is at work, are provided by the systems of Evgenii Trubetskoi (in his last book *The Meaning of Life* (1918), already finished after the Bolshevik revolution), Bulgakov, and Karsavin. The last big work by Father Sergius Bulgakov, his "great" theological trilogy (1933–1945), has the title *On Godmanhood* and undoubtedly represents the main example of the discourse of the Godmanhood in Russian thought. In this huge theological trilogy Bulgakov presents the idea of the Godmanhood as the "basic truth of Christianity" and describes all its aspects in detail, paying special attention to eschatology. Lev Karsavin pays special attention to the problem of time. He includes historical and meta-historical processes in the framework of his dynamical model of All-Unity combined with Three-Unity as the paradigm of development, and this makes it possible to perform a profound analysis of temporality.

Of course, these three axes did not exhaust the spectrum of the themes and problems of the Religious-Philosophical Renaissance. It was a full-dimensional philosophical movement, and the work of its participants embraced all principal branches of philosophy. Its heritage includes studies and theories in the philosophy of culture (Vyacheslav Ivanov, Berdyaev, Florensky), the philosophy of the state and law (Novgorodtsev, Struve, Bulgakov), the philosophy of economics (Struve, Bulgakov), epistemology (in the first place, Sergei Trubetskoi and the so-called Russian intuitivism of Lossky and Frank), the philosophy of symbol and myth (Vyacheslav Ivanov, Andrei Bely, Florensky, Losev), ethics (Lossky, Ilyin, Vysheslavtsev), aesthetics and philosophy of art (Shestov, Andrei Bely, Florensky, Lapshin, Losev), and so on. There were also studies in the history of philosophy, of which those devoted to the history of Russian thought are of special interest: this history did not exist before, and so a new historical sub-discipline had to be created. It was created successfully; until now the lectures by Vassily Zenkovsky and Nikolai Lossky remain the basic textbooks of the history of Russian philosophy. The movement was not indifferent to burning problems of its time. Some of its members, such as Sergey and Evgenii Trubetskoi, Struve, Bulgakov (in his early period), and Ivan Ilyin, were actively involved in politics, and it tried to achieve philosophical comprehension and find philosophical responses to the developing revolutionary crisis of Russia. The famous collections *Landmarks* (1907) and *Out of the Depths* (1918) remain the most important fruits of the civic concern of Russian religious philosophy.

Proceeding to the assessment of the phenomenon described, one must stress first of all its historical significance. The emergence of Russian religious philosophy was the birth of a full-fledged original philosophical tradition or, to be more precise (regarding all its conceptual and epistemological framework as belonging to classical metaphysics), an autonomous school within the broad Western tradition. In a very short time Russian philosophy grew into a full-dimensional sociocultural institution with all of the necessary components: an organized professional community and influential leaders, a spectrum of trends and groups, professional literature and media, and so on. It included a galaxy of prominent thinkers and was quickly increasing its activity and its influence in Russian society and culture.

However, the rhythms of Russian history in that pre-catastrophic epoch were so accelerated that very soon, even before the catastrophe, the limits of this vigorous growth and some negative features of the newborn tradition started to come to light. For the most part they were generated by the intermediate position of Russian religious philosophy between classical European metaphysics and Eastern Christian discourse: in fact, it could be defined as the combination of the Western framework and the tasks dictated by Eastern Christian discourse and Russian history and mentality. Such a specific position left a strong imprint on this philosophy and produced numerous effects. Both cultural phenomena had deep differences, and it soon turned out that it was impossible to combine them and to reconcile complete belonging to the one with an equally complete belonging to the other. As a result, the relationship of Russian religious philosophy with both classical metaphysics and Eastern Christian discourse had its problems.

Yes, this philosophy was a part of European metaphysics, but a quite special part. It did not join any existing schools or trends in Western thought; it was an autonomous school. Thus, it had to elaborate its own methodological and epistemological framework, but it largely neglected this duty. As a matter of fact, Russian religious philosophy as a certain whole not restricted to the Solovyovian core was hardly a "school" in the proper sense: it was a large and motley group of extremely different theories and conceptions united only by the dependence on classical metaphysics (in conceptual core) and the connection with Eastern Christian discourse in the Russian version (in the motivations and tasks of the philosophizing). Personalities and personal histories of thinkers played a big role, which was not typical at all for professional philosophy in the

West. Thus, philosophical texts could be closer to essayistic, journalistic, confessional, or aphoristic discourse and, as a result, there was no epistemological or methodological discipline (the relatively rigorous discourse of Russian intuitivism of Lossky and Frank was an exception). Very often, Western metaphysical postulates became mixed with Orthodox mystical intuitions, Church dogmas with folklore, and syllogistic proofs with free-style narrative. It was an original, interesting, and picturesque philosophical landscape, but systematic reasoning and reliable proofs were often lacking, and due to this the Religious-Philosophical Renaissance brought forth not so much indisputable achievements and firmly established results (although its disputable statements and daring hypotheses also had their value, and many ideas of Bulgakov, Florensky, or Vyacheslav Ivanov turn out to be topical even today). It should be noted that the conceptual equipment used by Russian religious philosophy was becoming more and more obsolete: for the most part, it did not correspond to the process of the overcoming of metaphysics which was actively developing. Western philosophy was advancing from classical metaphysics to phenomenology and then other new directions, but Russian religious philosophy did not take part in this movement, except for some contributions to the origins of existentialism in the work of Berdyaev and Shestov. It stood completely aside and did not respond to any of the three philosophies—Husserl's, Heidegger's, Wittgenstein's—which created the foundation for contemporary philosophical thinking, and this is the main reason why it is outdated today.

The discursive looseness inherent in Russian religious philosophy was particularly evident in one important problem, that of the relationship between philosophy and theology. Belonging to the field of religious thought, this philosophy could not avoid this problem, but it did not accept or elaborate any general principles for its solution. As a result, the relationship in question became a kind of a "free parameter" chosen by each thinker ad libitum. Each of the big thinkers of the Religious-Philosophical Renaissance had his own spiritual history and religious position and tried to find his own personal solution to the problem adequate to his experience. Thus, the relationship between philosophical and theological discourse varies with a maximal diapason in the systems of Russian religious philosophy. For example, Bulgakov decides that philosophy cannot express Christian truth correctly. He comes to this conclusion in the book *Tragedy of Philosophy* written in Crimea in 1920–1921, and all his subsequent works are purely theological. Frank, on the contrary, conveys Christian truth in philosophical discourse almost devoid of theological elements. In other thinkers, the type of discourse is anywhere between these two poles: it is the mixing of philosophical and theological discourse in varying proportions.

As for the relationship to Eastern Christian discourse, it went without saying for Russian religious philosophy that it should base itself on this spiritual fund, treating universal problems of the philosophical mind in the prism of the experience of Russian history, mentality, and spirituality and trying to achieve the philosophical comprehension of this experience. However, in reality the advance to these goals was unsatisfactory in a number of important aspects. First of all, some essential parts of Eastern Christian discourse remained outside the horizon of Russian religious philosophy. In the first place, they were the parts connected with a rich practical anthropology developed in the Orthodox ascetical tradition, *hesychasm*. The role of hesychasm in Orthodoxy deserves a special remark. It is an Orthodox mystico-ascetical practice developed and translated in Eastern Christian monasticism since the fourth century which created the "spiritual art" centered on a specific school of prayer and realizing the gradual self-transformation of the whole human being toward the union with God. This practice cultivates the quintessential Christian experience of the ascent to and union with Christ conceived as the union of all man's energies with divine energy or God's grace, and for this reason it is recognized as the core of Orthodox spirituality and religious life. In the fourteenth century, Hesychast experience obtained a theological description in the teaching of St. Gregory Palamas which is usually called the theology of divine energies. Hesychast spirituality deeply influenced the Orthodox way of life and thought, but in some periods the hesychast tradition was in decline and its influence hidden and implicit. In sum, there was a large phenomenal and conceptual complex related to hesychasm which included a circle of anthropological and psychological phenomena involved in hesychast practice, many ethical and behavioral patterns, a theology of divine energies, and also a theology of *theosis*, the union with God. For the Westernized cultural community of Russia, including the philosophical community, all of this complex was mostly *terra incognita* because hesychast practice and Palamas' theology were rejected by Western Christianity. But sooner or later it was inevitable that Russian thought would have to address this key part of Eastern Christian discourse.

There were many more lacunae and deficiencies in Russian religious philosophy in its relation to its double basis, Western metaphysics and Eastern Christian discourse. As we see, in retrospect, both its principal axes, the metaphysics of All-Unity and sophiology, were not fully adequate to Eastern Christian discourse. The metaphysics of All-Unity was firmly connected with the line of Christian Platonism and thus it could hardly correspond to Orthodox ontology, which, as today's Orthodox theology stresses, is completely based on un-platonic principles of personality, love, and communion. As for sophiology, it had no basis in the Christian kerygma and entered into contradictions with Christian dogmatism. But I shall not dwell on all of these shortcomings of Russian religious philosophy. What matters for my tracing of its path is that until the time of the Bolshevik revolution they did not yet manifest themselves noticeably. Russian philosophy was in uninterrupted growth, and its most capital works began to appear exactly in the last prerevolutionary years: *The Pillar and Foundation of the Truth* by Florensky (1914), *The Object of Knowledge* by Frank (1915), *The Meaning of Creativity* by Berdyaev (1916), *The Unfading Light* by Bulgakov (1917). However, the Religious-Philosophical Renaissance was broken up violently.

Religious Thought in Diaspora as a Discursive Modulation

Let me start with a brief illustration which clearly shows the general meaning of the whole further path, as I see it. It is well known and has been repeatedly described that the Bolshevik revolution caused the great exodus of Russian philosophy. Almost all leading philosophers, including non-religious ones, emigrated, and the multitude of voluntary departures and unwilling flights was finally complemented by the famous "philosophical ship," the deportation of a large group of prominent thinkers (together with many prominent figures from other fields of culture) by two ships from St. Petersburg to Stettin (then Germany) in the autumn of 1922. As a result, a unique (both in quantity and quality) Russian philosophical community arrived in the West. Furthermore, this community found itself in a period of maximal creative activity. There were high chances that the development of Russian religious philosophy would continue to produce fruitful results, even more significant ones than in the pre-revolutionary period. And these expectations were coming true at first. Leaders of the community wrote new books, often better and more important ones than their previous works, and a well-developed philosophical infrastructure arose, including journals, publishers, professional organizations, educational institutes, and so on. The active presence of Russian philosophy in the West became a noticeable factor of the global philosophical situation. The German *International Journal of Russian Philosophy* [*Der russische Gedanke*] was launched in Germany, and on its pages Boris Iakovenko proposed the following global project: "One must establish twelve or fourteen chairs all over the world and put them at the disposal of Russian philosophers living in exile, with approximately the following distribution: two chairs in Germany, three in the United States, and one in each of the following nine states—France, England, Italy, Japan, Czechoslovakia, Belgium, Switzerland, Sweden, and Austria."[2]

However, the course that things took was quite different. Let us have a look at the global situation of philosophy and religious thought in the present. If we try to see the traces of all that activity of Russian philosophy in the West, we find that there are none. Russian religious philosophy did not continue in the emigration (as well as in Russia) after the generation of the protagonists of the Religious-Philosophical Renaissance. Instead, we find other, different traces of Russian religious thought. There are two important *theological* institutions in the West, established by Russian emigrants, and active and authoritative up to this day: St. Sergius Orthodox Theological Institute in Paris and St. Vladimir's Theological Academy in Crestwood, in the USA. But initially, after the great exodus of Russian culture, the Russian theological presence in the West was almost invisible in comparison to the strong and very visible presence of Russian philosophy. Of course, a number of Russian theologians emigrated, but there was nothing in this emigration comparable to the resounding exodus of Russian philosophy. There was no "theological ship," and no need for Bolsheviks to organize it since Russian theology was basically weak and archaic with no noticeable weight or popularity in national culture. Nevertheless, it is Russian theology and not Russian philosophy that turned out to be present and active in the West, eventually. This is the phenomenon which I call discursive modulation: *in the post-revolutionary period, in diaspora, the dominant discourse of Russian religious thought has been changed from philosophical to theological.*

This phenomenon demonstrates the unusual character of the discursive relations. Traditionally, in the history of Western thought these relations developed in the opposite way: from the subordination of philosophy to theology to the emancipation of philosophy and then gradually to its complete separation from theology; and such an evolution was one of the main aspects of secularization. Thus, the change to the prevalence of theology is a *sui generis* phenomenon of desecularization or, maybe, post-secularism. One must look more closely and comprehend why, and how, such a specific phenomenon occurred.

External circumstances are all visible. One of the principal trends of the Religious-Philosophical Renaissance was, in the words of the popular formula, the "return of the intelligentsia to the Church"; and often such a return of Russian intellectuals led not only to a participation in Church life, but more importantly, to a profound preoccupation with Church teaching, so that philosophical work could evolve from secular to religious philosophy and then to theology. One striking example of such trajectory is the thought of Bulgakov who, as mentioned above, decided firmly to leave philosophy for theology. And it is not surprising that Bulgakov becomes one of the key figures in the discursive modulation. One of main fruits of the ecclesiastization [*vostserkovlenie*] of the émigré intelligentsia was the founding, in 1925, of the St. Sergius Theological Institute, and Bulgakov became its permanent dean and indisputable spiritual authority. Very soon the Institute turned into a theological institution of the new type, in which the cardinal upgrading of Orthodox theology and theological education takes place. Due to this it became the center of theological education, well-known and highly respected in all the Orthodox world. The important detail is that the crucial role in this upgrading of theology and the achievement of the glorious reputation belongs to Russian religious philosophy. All the principal merits of the Institute—the comprehensive curriculum, up-to-date programs, and the unprecedentedly high level of teaching—were ensured by the support of leading Russian philosophers. During the first two or even three decades of its work, the Institute had a genuine star team of teachers, the core of which is represented by such prominent thinkers as Bulgakov, Frank, Nikolai Lossky, Zenkovsky, Vysheslavtsev, Florovsky, Fedotov, and Veidle. After the Second World War, with the decisive help of the Institute another institution of the same type and level, the St. Vladimir's Theological Academy, was organized in the USA. And here again the crucial role belongs to Russian religious philosophers who formed the initial star team of teachers: Nikolai Lossky, Georges (Georgii) Fedotov, Nikolai Arseniev, Evgenii Spectorskii, Georgii Florovsky (who was equally theologian and philosopher). In the same post-war period, the most talented graduates of the St. Sergius Institute—Pavel Evdokimov, Alexander Schmemann, John Meyendorff et al.—began to join the staff of both institutions, representing the new generation of Orthodox theologians and consolidating the new level of Orthodox theology. The proportion of non-Russian students grew, and graduates of both Russian institutions gained high positions in the Church hierarchy and in the establishment of other Orthodox Churches. Thus, Russian theology in the diaspora rose to a new level and achieved a new status in the Orthodox world, and what made this success possible was not the resources of the prerevolutionary Russian theology, but the efforts of Russian religious philosophy. Russian theology was the fruit of the Russian Religious-Philosophical Renaissance.

This upsurge of theology is, however, only one aspect of this discursive modulation. A more important question for us is: What happened to religious philosophy? Why could it not develop successfully, as theology did? For the answer one must come back to its shortcomings as pointed out above and, first of all, to its relation to Eastern Christian discourse. With the upgrading of theological thought these shortcomings attracted more attention, and the profound criticism of Russian religious philosophy followed. It was presented chiefly by two authors of the younger émigré generation, Father Georgii Florovsky (1893–1979) and Vladimir Lossky (1903–1958), son of Nikolai Lossky.

The famous book *Ways of Russian Theology* (1937) by Florovsky was a capital study of Russian religious thought through all of its history in the prism of Eastern Christian discourse: the author very insistently evaluated all of the phenomena of Russian spiritual and intellectual history from the viewpoint of their correspondence to the Orthodox tradition as it is presented in the works of the Greek Church Fathers. He was very strict in his judgments and found deviations from the Tradition almost everywhere, and especially in the prerevolutionary culture of the Silver Age and Religious-Philosophical Renaissance. Thus, the last chapters of the book were a frontal attack on Russian religious philosophy followed by the firm conclusion that Russian thought must (re) turn to the inheritance of the Greek Fathers; however, not out of formal obedience to it, but in order to make the contact with the "mind" of the Fathers, their living experience, which made it possible for them to give a creative response to the problems of their time. Under the name of "Neopatristic synthesis" this conception of the "return to the Fathers" became widely known and served as the leading strategy of Orthodox thought until recent times. But as for the critical part of Florovsky's book, in the pre-war years the main figures of Russian religious philosophy were still dominant on the intellectual scene of the emigration, and a collective decision was made to silence the book. As a consequence, Florovsky's severe verdicts were relatively little discussed, but nevertheless they exercised a not insignificant influence on the situation and destiny of Russian religious philosophy. One notices that his position is close to what I call discursive modulation: according to Florovsky, for Russian religious thought the "return to the Fathers" involves an abandonment of Russian religious philosophy and the (re)turn from philosophical to theological discourse.

The role of Vladimir Lossky also combines both critical and positive contributions. In contrast to Florovsky, his criticism does not embrace all of the phenomena of Russian religious philosophy but concentrates only on the sophiology of Bulgakov, presenting its analysis in a small book (see Lossky 1936). This sophiology is a very specific teaching. In its late version, discussed by Lossky, it belongs to theology and represents the fruit of Bulgakov's deliberate turn from philosophy to theology. But, in Bulgakov's case, this turn did not change the basic properties of his thought; in both philosophical and theological modality this thought is most typical and characteristic of the Russian Religious-Philosophical Renaissance. He openly denied the generative and formative role of hesychast experience in Eastern Christian discourse and saw the tasks of creative thought as lying not in the articulation and comprehension of this discourse (that is, basically, Orthodox Tradition), but in the striving for a new and unprecedented development of Church teaching. His main focus is on unhindered creation in all fields: the classical accent of religious modernism. He considers this creative striving as the "manifestation of the prophetic spirit" and is firmly convinced that it has no laws or rules and should not associate itself with any tradition: "There is no tradition with respect to creative ways of the Christian daring [...] There cannot be any 'Philokalia' for the creation because it is outside of laws and law-governed nature" (Bulgakov 1936, 354–356). Such a position is very much in the spirit of the modernist culture of the Silver Age, with its cult of artistic and spiritual creation and its projects and utopias of the "creation of one's own life" [*zhiznetvorchestvo*]. Following such principles Bulgakov combines in his teaching the in-depth knowledge of Orthodox Tradition and dogmatism with a free treatment of them, the subjective selection of their contents, and arbitrary and self-willed interpretations of their data. Bringing to light such mistreatments and misconceptions Lossky comes to the conclusion that "the confusion between personality and nature is the principal dogmatic error of Fr. S. Bulgakov," and that "the incompatibility of the sophiology of Fr. S. Bulgakov with the dogmas of the Church becomes evident" (Lossky 82, 86). But besides these concrete conclusions, Lossky also exposes and criticizes general properties of Bulgakov's thought which belong to Russian religious philosophy as a whole (e.g., "the denial of the living tradition" that amounts to a formal treatment of tradition as a collection of ancient texts; "all patristic theology is conceived by him [Bulgakov] as a series of philosophical systems produced by individual humans" (ibid., 22)).

Moreover, a few years after his pamphlet on Sophia, V. Lossky published his path-breaking work "The Mystical Theology of the Eastern Church" (1944) outlining a new way of presenting Orthodox theology, which carefully disclosed and systematically traced the role of divine energies and the theology of St. Gregory Palamas. This work initiated a turn of Orthodox thought to the profound study of the theology of divine energies in both its history and its far-reaching implications. Soon after Lossky's works this "palamitic turn" was very successfully continued by works of another Russian émigré theologian, Fr. John Meyendorff, whose capital book *Introduction to the Study of St. Gregory Palamas* (1959) had the most resounding effect. It turned out that such a turn opened up a large working field which included vast patrological and byzantological studies because the abundant theological literature of Palamas' age—the period of so-called Hesychast disputes of the fourteenth century—was very little known and the greater part of it remained unpublished. The study of this huge complex of late Byzantine theological texts, often of high quality and value, became the work of not only the Orthodox, but also the all-confessional theological and byzantological community. It was evident that a new trend of Orthodox theology had emerged, and it was called "neopalamism."

Evidently, this new direction in theological work did not contradict Florovsky's program of the "return to the Fathers" but rather complemented it; in fact, the study of palamitic theology could be considered as one of the realizations of this return. Taken together, Florovsky's and Lossky's contributions look similar and parallel. Both authors criticized Russian religious philosophy and then complemented this criticism with the elaboration of a new direction for Orthodox thought belonging to theological rather than philosophical discourse. Later these directions were widely accepted in Orthodoxy, acquiring (not from their founders) the names of neopatristics and neopalamism. In the meanwhile, the development of Russian religious philosophy ran out. The lifespan of the phenomenon did not spread beyond the heroic generation of its great founders. Of course, they had some followers and disciples (such as N. Lossky's disciple Sergei Levitskii (1908–1983) or Ivan Ilyin's follower Nikolai Poltoratskii (1921–1990)), but their number was small, and there were no significant thinkers among them. By the last decades of the twentieth century, when neopatristics and neopalamism became the leading trends of Orthodox theology, the philosophical movement once launched by the creative thought of Vladimir Solovyov virtually came to its close. In the global context, this is not surprising, since at that time classical metaphysics, to which this movement belonged, represented the distant past of European philosophy. Thus, these theological trends could be considered as a *sui generis* afterlife of Russian religious philosophy. And coming back to Florovsky's and V. Lossky's role, they can be seen now as the Mediators or Guides of Russian religious thought in its transition from philosophical to theological discourse that I call discursive modulation.

Post-Soviet Philosophy: The Palingenesis? The Reverse Modulation?

Evidently, discursive modulation leads beyond the field of Russian philosophy. The trends of neopatristics and neopalamism, which are its outcome, are not philosophical and, moreover, they do not belong to Russian thought anymore: they were initiated by Russian scholars, but later the Russian influence in them became minimal. The same can be said about both high-reputed theological institutions founded by Russian scholars in the West: for a long time the Russian presence in them has been insignificant. The Great Exodus of Russian culture inevitably had to exhaust its resources. In the meantime, however, the communist regime in Russia collapsed, and the freedom of philosophical and theological thought in the country was restored. Now post-Soviet philosophy has been developing for two or three whole decades, and one component of this process is the development of Russian Christian thought in the new Millennium. It is this component that I shall discuss now.

It was inevitable that renewing its work after the forced break, Christian thought in Russia had to start with the restoration of lost connections with Russian religious philosophy. The long period during which this philosophy was a forbidden fruit for Soviet citizens generated mythologized representations about its contents and exaggerated hopes of its possible role in future Russian thought and society. Immediately after the fall of the Soviet regime the big public campaign "The return of forgotten names" was launched, and Russian religious philosophy was advertised and promoted to an incredible extent. However, analyzing these hopes for the religious-philosophical panacea I concluded: "Neither the system of ideas nor the system of values proper to Russian religious philosophy has any chance of being adopted today" (Horujy 2001, 274). Predictably, these hopes failed very soon. The thought of the Religious-Philosophical Renaissance provided neither the ground for a new philosophical development nor a pool of valuable ideas for post-communist society.

What was less predictable, however, was that no new trends or theories unrelated to this old inheritance appeared either. Freedom of thought was regained, but there was no creation. The philosophical work in the field of Christian thought was restricted mainly to historical studies of particular figures and episodes, while general reflections on the phenomena of the Silver Age, Russian religious philosophy, the Religious-Philosophical Renaissance, and the retrospective assessment of their inheritance were all virtually absent. Critical analysis of these phenomena by émigré thinkers such as Florovsky and Vl. Lossky was partly unnoticed and partly misunderstood. As explained above, their assessment of Russian thought was based on their keen vision of Eastern Christian discourse and the quintessential Christocentric experience. But their position was not seen in the proper context of their global tasks so that its meaning was lost completely. As a consequence, their criticism of Russian religious philosophy and their turn away from it caused by the concrete defects in it that they disclosed were repeatedly misinterpreted as a neglect of philosophy and, in particular, philosophy of religion (e.g., "Philosophy of religion is not just absent in the works of V.N. Lossky and the Archpriest G. Florovsky, but it is impossible to imagine it there" (Antonov 2013, 96)). As a result, the comprehension of the religious-philosophical development taken as a whole was absent too, and the basic phenomenon of discursive modulation was not noticed. And in this situation the work in the field of religious-philosophical thought turned unavoidably to retreading old ground.

Religious-philosophical and theological communities began to concentrate on some or other old pieces of Russian religious philosophy, believing unfoundedly that they were still alive and topical. The most popular pieces were sophiology, and the "veneration of the name," the last direction of Russian religious philosophy which included Florenskii, Bulgakov, Ern, Losev, et al. and aimed at providing a theological foundation for the practice of a certain cult of God's Name that emerged among Russian monks and was condemned by the Russian as well as Ecumenical Orthodox Church in 1913, after the sharp conflict provoked by its adepts on the Holy Mount Athos. Both trends have already been discussed in depth and substantially criticized.[3] It was shown that they convey Eastern Christian discourse incorrectly, and in the pan-Orthodox theological context formed by the discursive modulation they were considered as belonging to the past. But all of this development is largely ignored in today's Russian works on Russian religious philosophy. Lots of texts—mostly articles, but also some books—are produced with an apology for sophiology and a veneration of the name. Some other phenomena and figures of Russian religious philosophy such as Ivan Ilyin or Eurasianism also find their adepts and are discussed in the same outdated perspective without considering the critical work produced by Russian thought in the diaspora. In sum, a return to the past takes place in the comprehension of the path of Russian Christian thought. The last stages of this path are largely ignored or misunderstood by post-Soviet thought.

There are, however, two authors whose work can be considered an exception to this rule, Vladimir Bibikhin (1938–2004) and the author of this text, Sergey Horujy. Our relation to Russian religious philosophy is a bit different. My work includes two relatively independent parts. I study the development of Russian religious thought and also present a new anthropological conception, synergic anthropology, with no direct links to preceding Russian philosophy. Bibikhin never wrote on Russian philosophy, except for a few short texts on Rozanov, Solovyov, and Leontiev, but he paid close attention to problems of Russian history, mentality, and spirituality and presented his own original views of them in several lecture courses. Both of us appreciate the turn of Russian thought to theology and consider the results of this theological turn in our philosophical work, especially neopalamitic theology which puts into focus the problem of energy, of key interest to both. Bibikhin even made an important contribution to neopalamism, producing the Russian translation of the most important of Palamas' works, *Triads in the Defense of Saint Hesychasts*. For this reason, in the context of the discursive changes of Russian religious thought the work of both of us can be considered as a sui generis *reverse modulation* of the discourse, from theology to philosophy. Such modulation is, obviously, the straightforward way to resume philosophical work on the ground of Eastern Christian discourse.

In fact, Bibikhin's philosophizing never takes on any tasks related directly to Eastern Christian discourse. His connections with this discourse are mostly implicit, but nevertheless they are strong enough.[4] The main part of his work is a series of about twenty lecture courses delivered at Moscow University in the post-Soviet period and published posthumously (not all of them are yet published). This series is a unique phenomenon in contemporary Russian philosophy. It embraces nearly all philosophical territory: *philosophia prima*; ethics; philosophy of time and history; philosophy of language; philosophy of economics; philosophy of (biological) life; history of philosophy; fundamental studies of Heidegger and Wittgenstein, the main thinkers of the last century and his main dialogical partners. In sum, all this body of work could easily be a comprehensive philosophical system, but Bibikhin is against system and even against method, considering them as fetters restricting the freedom of philosophy. One must add that he avoids the systematic and syllogistic style and very rarely gives strict proofs of his statements, instead using a rich repertoire of rhetorical means. These qualities of his thought make one expect that his philosophizing is close to the loose discourse of Russian religious philosophy which I criticized above. Yet, paradoxically, his discourse is only seemingly loose and arbitrary, in reality it is always checked and reflected upon. Bibikhin is especially careful to avoid the mixing of philosophical and theological discourse and sharply criticizes "theologizing philosophers and philosophizing theologians" which were always typical of Russian philosophy. Thus, he distances himself from the Religious-Philosophical Renaissance, singling out only a few thinkers such as Rozanov (close to him stylistically), Leontiev, Solovyov, and Chaadaev. He pays special attention to the anatomy of philosophical discourse, stressing the role of such principles as the disposition (*die Befindlichkeit* in Heidegger's discourse) and the seizing [*das Greifen*]. Here he continues Heidegger's tradition and gets close to some new philosophical trends, such as a philosophy of atmospheres.

Due to its special character, the analysis of Bibikhin's discourse is a necessary preliminary to the comprehension of his philosophy. There are at least three big subject areas in which this philosophy is of great interest for Russian as well as European thought: philosophy of energy, philosophy of property, and philosophy of life as a biological and social phenomenon. On the first theme, Bibikhin presented a new position which diverges from the Orthodox teaching on divine energies and states the unconditional primacy of the Aristotelian "energy of the rest" over energy as the dynamical principle. The second theme is of acute importance for the chaotic post-Soviet situation in problems of property, the more so in that Bibikhin applies many of his concepts and ideas directly to this situation. Finally, in the lecture course "The Forest [*hyle*]," the thinker develops a very original approach to the phenomenon of life, on the one hand, following Aristotle most closely and, on the other hand, taking into account all data of modern biology and genetics and presenting a daring outline of global ecological philosophy. Today the study of Bibikhin's thought has hardly begun, but there is a permanent interest in it. The first international conference on his work took place in St. Petersburg in 2013, and the second one in 2019 in his native city of Bezhetsk. At the same time, translations of his texts are beginning to appear in the West.

As for my synergic anthropology, it is a large anthropological project in which anthropology combines two roles: the conception of man (the traditional role) and the episteme (the new role). The first stage of the project is the phenomenological description of anthropological experience in its entirety. The description follows the methodology of the "tiny rescued bit" (Husserl's formula): using certain criteria, I choose a starting domain of "pure anthropological experience" and undertake its analytical description. This rescued bit is the experience of hesychast practice which is a holistic practice of the Self oriented to the actual ontological transcendence of the human being. The description results in the reconstruction of the "Organon" of this practice, that is, the complete set of rules which determine the organization, the checking-up, and the interpretation of hesychast experience structured as a ladder (the "Ladder of Paradise") with steps ascending from repentance and struggle with passions to synergy and deification [*theosis*]. The "rescue" of the first bit provides a certain fund of general concepts and principles of which the most important is the *principle of the anthropological unlocking*. The hesychast Organon shows the mechanism of the formation of man's constitution, structures of man's personality and identity: this constitution is shaped in what I call "extreme anthropological manifestations," in which man makes himself open, or unlocked, toward something (or Somebody, in the Christian experience) that is beyond the horizon of his consciousness and existence, and hence is Other with respect to man as such. Hesychast practice realizes such constitutive unlocking toward the other mode of being, that is, the Ontological Other, so that in this case the paradigm of man's constitution is ontological unlocking. This constitution defines the anthropological formation called the Ontological Human.

Extending the analysis to other domains of anthropological experience we discover two more kinds of the constitutive unlocking. One is the ontical unlocking, that is, the unlocking toward the "Ontical Other" which is also beyond the boundary of human experience, but still belongs to the present being. The main example of the Ontical Other is the unconscious, and psychoanalysis gives us abundant and detailed descriptions of human constitutions shaped in the experience of the unlocking toward the unconscious. Ontical unlocking defines the anthropological formation called the "Ontical Human," and the unlocking toward the unconscious, its sub-formation called "Freud's Human." Another sub-formation is "Nietzsche's Human," constituted in the unlocking actualized in practices of the will to power. The distinctive feature of all ontical constitutions is the topological property of singularity studied in detail by Gilles Deleuze, and in the analysis of the Ontical Human synergic anthropology is in dialogue with his thought. Finally, the last kind of constitutive unlocking is the unlocking toward virtual reality actualized in all kinds of virtual and digital practices. This virtual unlocking defines the formation called the "Virtual Human," and one can prove that the ontological, ontical, and virtual unlocking exhaust all the ways of man's constitution shaped in the anthropological unlocking.

The reconstruction of the complete set of paradigms of man's constitution provides a full-fledged framework of "anthropology of the unlocking." The anthropological unlocking is now seen as the universal paradigm of man's constitution which serves as the core of a new conception of man considering the totality and variety of anthropological experience. This conception is radically nonclassical: pluralistic, subjectless, and essenceless. At the next stage I turn this anthropological framework into an episteme or meta-discourse that is the integrating conceptual and epistemological basis for the whole set of human sciences. In this way synergic anthropology must perform the transformation of all principal humanistic discourses in order to become the *science of the human sciences*. Today this big program is still far from completion.

Coming back to our main theme, the way of Russian Christian thought, we see that synergic anthropology is indeed the reverse modulation in this way. Its reconstruction of hesychast anthropology represents the extension of neopalamism to anthropology, joined with the modulation into philosophical discourse. It is not theology or religious philosophy, but it presents the phenomenological description of certain kinds of religious experience in the participative paradigm. Moreover, it outlines a new paradigm of the relationship between philosophical and theological discourse: the dialogue on the common ground of anthropological experience and, more precisely, the hesychast experience. Hesychast practice here obtains an important discursive mission: it appears as the field for a new configuration of philosophical and theological discourse.

Notes

1. A concise reconstruction of these origins and all the further path of Russian sophiology is presented in my work *Pereput'ia russkoi sofiologii*. See Horujy, 2000, 141–168.
2. See B. Jakowenko. "Erklärung des Herausgegebers," quoted by Plotnikov (1999, 337).
3. A concise resumé of this criticism is given in my articles "Pereput'ia russkoi sofiologii" and "Imiaslavie i kultura Serebrianogo veka: fenomen Moskovskoi shkoly khristianskogo neoplatonizma." See Horujy 2018, 274–292.
4. As V.V. Bibikhin has pointed out: "As far as we recognize ourselves as the inheritors of Byzantine Orthodoxy, the claim to the exceptional knowledge of God made by it in its last centuries remains our problem." See Bibikhin 2010, 354. These words about the problem of energy, the key problem of contemporary Orthodox thought, clearly allow us to include Bibikhin's work in the context of the philosophical comprehension of Eastern Christian discourse.

Bibliography

Antonov, Konstantin M. 2013. Filosofiia religii S.N. Bulgakova i problematika konzepzii neopatristicheskogo sinteza V.N. Losskogo. In *Sofiologia i neopatristicheskii sintez. Bogoslovskie itogi filosofskogo razvitia*, ed. K.M. Antonov and N.A. Vaganova, 95–114. Moscow: PSTGUB.
Bibikhin, Vladimir V. 2010. *Energia*. Moscow: Institut filosofii, teologii i istorii Sv. Fomy.
Bulgakov, Sergei. 1936. *Uteshitel'. O bogochelovechestve*. YMCA: Paris.

Copleston, Frederick C. 1986. *Philosophy in Russia. From Herzen to Lenin and Berdyaev.* Notre Dame, IN: Notre Dame University Press.

Gershenzon, Mikhail O. 1923. *Istoriia Molodoi Rossii.* Moscow-Petrograd: Gosudarstvennoe Izdatel'stvo.

Horujy, Sergey S. 1994. Ideia Vseedinstva ot Geraklita do Bakhtina. In *Posle Pereryva. Puti Russkoi Filosofii*, 32–66. St. Petersburg: Aleteia.

———. 2000. *O Starom in Novom.* St. Petersburg: Aleteia.

———. 2001. Breaks and Links. Prospects for Russian Religious Philosophy Today. *Studies in East European Thought* 53 (4): 269–284.

———. 2018. *Opyty iz Russkoi Dukhovnoi Tradizii.* Moscow: Institut filosofii, teologii i istorii Sv. Fomy.

Karsavin, Lev P. 1929. Filosofiia i VKP. *Eurasia* 20 (Paris), April 6.

Lossky, Vladimir N. 1936. *Spor o Sofii. Dokladnaia Zapiska Prot. S. Bulgakova i Smysl Ukaza Moskovskoi Patriarkhii.* Paris.

Plotnikov, Nikolai. 1999. Evropeiskaia tribuna russkoi filosofii. Zhurnal *Der russische Gedanke* (Bonn 1929–1931). *Issledovaniia po Istorii Russkoi Mysli* 3: 331–358.

Shpet, Gustav G. 1922. *Ocherk Razvitia Russkoi Filosofii.* Prague: Kolos.

CHAPTER 4

Russian Political Philosophy: Between Autocracy and Revolution

Evert van der Zweerde

INTRODUCTION

Gary Hamburg and Randall Poole, highlighting the humanist tradition in Russian philosophical thought between 1830 and 1930 as what "is most characteristic and best about Russian philosophy in this period," rightly entitled their book *A History of Russian Philosophy* (Hamburg and Poole 2010, 3). This chapter, too, offers a *specific* history, but, contrary to the example just cited, it arguably is about what was "least characteristic and worst" about Russian philosophy, namely the development of political philosophy.[1] Russia's history is rife with political theories and ideologies, and philosophy is not hard to find, in academic, quasi-academic, and anti-academic forms. However, Russian philosophical culture has been relatively poor in thought that is both "genuinely" philosophical (critical, conceptual, analytical, reflexive, radical), and "seriously" political (acknowledging the reality of the political and of politics). There certainly are exceptions, such as the Silver Age [*Serebriannyi vek*, 1890–1920], when political philosophy did become more prominent. Also, political philosophy picked up steam after the collapse of the essentially anti-political Soviet system. On the whole, however, political philosophy has been underdeveloped in Russia.

Hannah Arendt rightly suggested that "there is a kind of enmity against all politics in most philosophers" (Arendt 1994, 2). This enmity is mutual: the

E. van der Zweerde (✉)
Department of Social and Political Philosophy, Radboud University,
Nijmegen, Netherlands
e-mail: e.vanderzweerde@ftr.ru.nl

© The Author(s), under exclusive license to Springer Nature
Switzerland AG 2021
M. F. Bykova et al. (eds.), *The Palgrave Handbook of Russian Thought*,
https://doi.org/10.1007/978-3-030-62982-3_4

philosophers discussed in this chapter were politically marginal, with the exception of Lenin and, arguably, Ilyin. This suggests that *good* political philosophy remains critically distant from politics. Yet, in order to be relevant, it also must relate to things, politically, as they exist. Metaphorically speaking, political philosophy neither belongs in the political arena itself, where it risks becoming too directly involved, nor on the solitary mountaintop of wisdom and contemplation, but somewhere in between on an often slippery slope. The organizing idea of this chapter is that said "enmity against politics" is itself profoundly political.

Any history of philosophy is written from a particular perspective. Rather than conceal this fact, it is important to make it explicit. This chapter's perspective is Schmittian in assuming that "the political" is the ubiquitous possibility of real conflict in all human domains, without demarcating a particular domain *next to* economy, morality, art, etc. Accordingly, I understand "politics" as an umbrella term for all ways of "dealing with the political" as just defined. The perspective of this chapter is critical both of positions (such as mainstream liberalism) that look at the political as a field next to others and of those positions (like Marxism in most of its variants and most Christian positions) that suggest that a society beyond struggle and strife, and hence beyond politics, is possible.

At the same time, the perspective is *anti*-Schmittian in rejecting the primacy of imposing *order*: it is just as important to counter-pose disorder against existing order. First, any society critically depends on the articulation of the political; secondly, the political is not only the possibility of conflict, but also of concord. Conflict (disagreement, polemics, struggle, hatred, violence, competition, war) and concord (consensus, cooperation, dialogue, friendship, solidarity, peace, love) have a common ontological root in the combination of human plurality, finitude, freedom, and difference.

The interpretative framework employed in this chapter thus assumes that the political is the ubiquitous possibility of real conflict and concord and defines politics as a general term for dealing with it. We can then distinguish four basic forms of politics: denial, suppression, canalization, and unchaining. Between unchaining and canalization we can add mobilization in a variety of forms like street politics and spontaneous organization (strikes, revolts, etc.); between canalization and suppression we can add control, e.g., managed forms of representation and (repressive) toleration; between suppression and denial we can allocate sublimation, e.g., scapegoating and the persecution of ethnic or religious minorities; between denial and unchaining, finally, we can give a place to the orchestrated revolution of the "October" type. Both the full actualization of conflict (like civil war or terror) and the full actualization of concord (like a harmonious construction of socialism or "Kingdom of God") rely on a denial of the political as the possibility of *both* conflict and concord, and hence mark the end of politics.

To this scheme, we can add the contrast between organicist (which includes corporatist) and mechanistic (which includes liberal models of society and polity) views. In the case of Russia, we must add two further contrasts related to

Russia's geographic openness and specific history: the contrast between a "Nordic" model of polyphonic self-rule, a "Byzantine" model of symphonic dualism, and a "Tatar" model of divinely sanctioned monologic absolutism, and the contrast between a "West European" model of bureaucratic statehood and rule of law and an "Asiatic" model of despotic rule. Political reality is always mixed and hybrid, but the specificity of the Russian case is, probably, the fusion of two models of centralized rule: the dualistic Byzantine-Russian tradition (Constantinople, Kiev, Moscow) and the monistic Tatar-Mongol tradition of the Golden Horde, against the backdrop of a "Nordic" model of self-government.[2]

Political philosophy is always connected to a broader philosophical culture with its predominant models and motifs, its positive and negative examples of "good" vs. "bad" philosophy, and is embedded in historical, socio-economic, cultural, and political circumstances that condition it without determining it. Secondly, it is more critically connected to political conditions than other branches of philosophy: established power structures will be quick to monitor what happens in the field of political philosophy—as a result, political philosophers have often been persecuted or banned. Finally, political philosophy often tries to relate actively to politics, by seeking to influence political reality, calling for change, summoning those who rule, or contributing to the legitimization of the existing regime. Political philosophy thus is much more intimately connected to political reality than metaphysics, logic, or ethics.

Russia has been living, for most of its history, under an autocratic and increasingly oppressive, then a revolutionary and increasingly totalitarian, and finally a republican and increasingly authoritarian political system. What then is the space for political philosophy? Where does it find a place? In tsarist times, it largely took place in private circles [*kruzhki*], went abroad, or became revolutionary; in Soviet times, it was domesticated as part of "historical material- ism" while it flourished in emigration and *tamizdat*, in underground *samizdat* and in unexpected niches in the academic world; in post-Soviet time it revived, reaching back to earlier times and picking up on theoretical developments else- where, establishing itself as a discipline with cynical overtones.

The development of political philosophy in Russia is closely connected to its political history. In Russia, philosophy generally, and political thought more specifically, was left to develop according to its own dynamic only during brief periods, which therefore historically appear as episodes. Not accidentally, five of the eight authors chosen for this chapter spent large parts of their life in exile or in voluntary emigration. This chapter traces the development of Russian political philosophy from the nineteenth century to the present day. The chap- ter consists of four sections, each highlighting two philosophers who contrast with one another on relevant points while considering general political trans- formations. The choice of eight authors, Herzen, Bakunin, Vl. Solovyov, Lenin, Ilyin, Frank, E. Soloviev, and Magun involves a degree of arbitrariness, and is motivated by both representation of topics and availability of translations.

Dialectics and Destruction (1825–1881)

The Russian Empire emerged from the Napoleonic Wars not only as a major European and world power, but also as the main agent of restoration, effectively suppressing revolutionary tendencies. After the 1825 Decembrist uprising, the tsarist regime put an end to dreams about a gradual transition to a modern, enlightenment-inspired state. In the mid-nineteenth century, large parts of the European continent were under the spell of revolution, which took place in 1848 as a mostly liberal revolution. The Russian nobility, blocked from political participation, suffered from state censorship and direct repression whenever it tried to bring about change, but was relatively free to travel, study abroad, and receive publications from elsewhere. As a result, philosophical *kruzhki* emerged, in which the latest ideas, especially from Western Europe, were received and discussed. Lively debates took place on the pages of "thick journals" like *Vestnik Evropy* and *Otechestvennye zapiski*. Most importantly, however, political thought was barely transformed into practical politics, which explains its typical combination of abstraction and radicalism.

Particularly important was the influence of Georg Wilhelm Friedrich Hegel and the Left-Hegelians (Planty-Bonjour 1974). Here, Alexander Herzen (1812–1870) and Mikhail Bakunin (1814–1876) stand out as thinkers of lasting significance. In the case of Bakunin, widely published and read outside Russia and one of the founders of the anarchist tradition, this is obvious. Herzen is important because of his rare political sense. What the two friends share, apart from their gentry background, their Hegelian inspiration, and their fresh style of writing, is that they both fell victim to the tsarist regime, spent substantial parts of their lives in exile and prison, and tried to organize opposition and liberation from abroad.

To grasp Herzen's position, there is no better source than *My Past and Thoughts* [*Byloe i dumy*]. Written over a long period (1852–1868), it portrays the life in exile of a Russian philosopher, reflects a considerable part of European history in which he often took active part, and records the development of his ideas. One of the founding fathers of Russian socialism and forerunner of the later populists [*narodniki*] and social revolutionaries (the main competitors of the Bolsheviks), Herzen at the same time sits oddly in that category. Often, his political philosophy is qualified as liberal socialism. This may strike one as an oxymoron signaling the impotence of political opposition against tsarist autocracy and explaining why *all* oppositional forces tended to merge—a situation like the late Soviet period, when dissidents of all feathers jointly rejected the self-proclaimed socialism of the USSR.

Indeed, hopes for liberal reforms had waned after the repression that followed the Decembrist uprising in 1825, while at the same time poverty, illiteracy, and disease were widespread, making it difficult to separate demands for social justice from those for political freedom. Herzen gradually distanced himself from "Westernizers" like Belinsky, from "Slavophiles" like Samarin, and from "liberals" like Granovsky, turning instead to French socialists like Saint

Simon and Proudhon. The journal *Kolokol* [*The Bell*], which he distributed from the West (1857–1867), was a considerable success, but Herzen never became a significant political force himself (von Beyme 2001, 103–112).

Herzen started his philosophical career in the aftermath of Hegelianism, and his early position can be labeled Left-Hegelian, aiming to give a material basis to what was, in Hegel, speculative and idealistic: "Following Hegel he defended the unity of the laws of thought and nature, but in opposition to the great idealist he claimed that the laws of thought [...] did not precede nature but stemmed from its development" (Kuvakin 1994, 223). The thing that singles out Herzen among Russian thinkers is also connected to one of the key issues of nineteenth-century political philosophy: the relationship between theory and praxis, or, more specifically, between positive science and transformative politics. Herzen based himself on nascent evolutionary biology to deny the existence of cosmic determinism (Kelly 2016, 183), or any immutable laws that would determine nature or history. What Aileen Kelly has dubbed Herzen's "discovery of chance" points to the *natural* phenomenon of contingency and hence to the *historical* relevance of the free human will. As he wrote in 1847 in *From the Other Shore* [*S togo berega*]: "The future does not exist: it is made up of the sum total of a thousand conditions, both essential and fortuitous, plus the human will, which supply unexpected denouements and *coups de théâtre*" (Herzen 2003, 360). Contingency is the ontological foundation of free will and of political responsibility.

When the liberal 1848 European revolutions, in which he participated actively, failed to yield socialism (Walicki 1988, 163), Herzen became convinced that the Russian peasant commune could provide the basis for a future socialist society, but his rejection of any teleological understanding of history and his awareness of the "rich and dynamic relation between human beings and the outside world" (Kuvakin 1994, 229) precluded any idea of the inevitability of a socialist revolution. The road to a free and just society is not a matter of a single leap, but of many small and often contradictory steps. This points toward a pluralist and pragmatic understanding of politics: "Herzen would combine the notion of chance in this Darwinian sense with a radical humanism, drawing on a number of sources to shape the concept of limited but real freedom that he would oppose to all teleological narratives of history and human life" (Kelly 2016, 186).

If Herzen's life is exciting, Bakunin's reads like a Russian rollercoaster. Born to a noble family, his life is marked by rebellion against his father, desertion from the army, revolutionary activism in a number of European countries, and detention in equally many prisons. His thought was shaped by Hegelian circles in Moscow and by the Young Hegelians with whom he studied in Berlin. Starting from a Right-Hegelian position, he briefly embraced the idea of a union of all Slavic peoples (liberated from the Ottoman, Prussian, and Habsburg empires). In his fascinating *Confession* [*Ispoved'*], written in 1851 while incarcerated in the Peter and Paul's Fortress in St Petersburg, he exposed his views in a letter to tsar Nicholas I, suggesting that "if you, Sire, had wished at that time to raise the Slav banner, then they unconditionally, without discussion, blindly submitting to your will, they and all others who speak Slavic in the Austrian and Prussian possessions would have thrown themselves with joy and fanaticism under the broad wings of the Russian eagle and would have rushed with fury not only against the hated Germans but against all Western Europe as well," a passage on which the tsar noted in the margin: "I don't doubt it; i.e., I would have stood at the head of the revolution as a Slav Masaniello; thank you!" (Bakunin 1977, 98).

Bakunin's profound disappointment with the revolution of 1848 led him toward radical anarchism and made him a pivotal figure, both theoretically and practically, in the international socialist movement, where he became a major opponent of Marx and Engels. Politics, for Bakunin, is a matter of spontaneous, radically oppositional action. The lasting controversy between him and Karl Marx can be phrased as the opposition between revolutionary will (Bakunin) and socio-economic conditions (Marx), and thus ultimately between freedom and determinism (Bakunin 2005, xxxi). Bakunin opposed the idea of a well-organized revolution in a carefully selected place and at the right moment, leading to a seizure of power and the dictatorship of a revolutionary socialist party. Bakunin: "I […] see no salvation except in revolutionary anarchy, guided on all issues by an invisible collective power—the only dictatorship I accept, because it is the only kind compatible with openness and maximum energy for the revolutionary movement" (Bakunin 1973, 178).

Typical of Bakunin, and connecting him to present-day movements like Occupy, is the conviction that the way in which the revolutionary movement organizes itself should foreshadow the future communist society. Bakunin offered an almost prophetic picture of the "dictatorship of the proletariat" that would follow from the Marxist idea of the "planned" socialist revolution (Bakunin 2005, 181) and contrasted it with his own principle that "Liberty can be created only by liberty, by an insurrection of all the people and the voluntary organization of the workers from below upward" (Bakunin 2005, 179). For Bakunin, the state is not a mere instrument in the hands of the ruling class, but the incorporation of repression; since state and capital are *equally* the enemies of the workers, they must *both* be destroyed, rather than trying to beat the opposing bourgeois class with its own weapons. For Bakunin, "democratic state" is a contradiction in terms: "He who wants […] the establishment of freedom, justice, and peace, he who wants […] the full and complete emancipation of the masses of the people, should also aim toward the destruction of all States and the establishment upon their ruins of a Universal Federation of Free Associations of all the countries in the world" (Bakunin 1953, 222f., 225).

In one of his most famous sentences, Bakunin expresses the key idea of the "negative dialectics" retained from Hegel: "The passion for destruction is also a creative passion" (Bakunin 1973, 58). Although Bakunin did not glorify revolutionary violence, but emphasized the need to clear the ground when preparing for a new society, nor suggested that this was the only creative passion, his emphasis on negation and his frequent reference to passion and instinct in his 1873 *Statism and Anarchy* [*Gosudarstvennost' i anarkhiia*] (Bakunin 2005) do explain why Carl Schmitt ascribed to him a "Scythian rage" (Schmitt 1996, 54). For Bakunin, the human being is characterized by animality, freedom, and thought, and the awareness of freedom is directly connected to an instinct to revolt (Kuvakin 1994, 299). With Scythian rage, Schmitt was referring to Bakunin's second most famous sentence, in which he inverted Voltaire's statement that if God didn't exist, he should be invented: "I reverse the phrase of Voltaire, and say that, *if God really existed, it would be necessary to abolish him*" (Bakunin 1970, 28). His consistent atheist political theology is coupled with a boundless faith in man's capacity to collectively organize their existence.

This joint discussion of two major political thinkers of the mid-nineteenth century not only demonstrates the subversive potential of dialectical thinking or the impotence of political opposition in tsarist Russia, it also illustrates how West European philosophical ideas traveled to Russia, took different shapes under the impact of different circumstances, and then became part of much broader intellectual movements. This is particularly the case with Bakunin, who continues to be, with his later compatriot Pyotr Kropotkin (1842–1921), a source of inspiration of the global anarchist movement. Finally, the discussion highlights one of the paradoxes of political philosophy: the fact that it is occasioned and stimulated by political strife and turmoil is also the reason why many political philosophers did not leave behind a finished and polished body of work.

From Repression to Revolution (1881–1921)

During the late nineteenth century, the Russian Empire was caught in rapid processes of modernization, urbanization, and industrialization—catching up with developments elsewhere. It was a period of great tension: on the one hand, the abolition of serfdom (1861) had created free labor, driven by poverty and famine (1891–1892) to the cities where an industrial proletariat became the natural constituency of trade unions and socialist parties; on the other hand, the rising bourgeoisie joined hands with the landed gentry in demanding political rights, leading to the *zemstvo*, a form of local representative government. The tsarist regime tried to contain these developments by offering limited reforms, leading to *Scheinkonstitutionalismus* (von Beyme 2001, 9). It mostly reacted, however, with control and repression. From 1881 until 1905, opposition increased between the tsarist regime and the revolutionary intelligentsia, while the period from 1905 until 1921 (with three revolutions and a civil war) was not only one of hope and unprecedented intellectual creativity, but also of anxiety and disappointment.

On the face of it, Vladimir Solovyov (1853–1900) and Vladimir Ulyanov [Lenin] (1870–1924) share little more than their first name. Which two thinkers could be further apart than a utopian Christian mystical idealist and a professional atheist revolutionary Marxist? Despite differences, however, they share three features: both pursued philosophy not as an end in its own right, but as a means for the transformation of the world; secondly, both aimed at using tsarist Russia for a grand, world-encompassing project; finally, both built their political philosophy on a denial of the political: they saw the possibility of conflict not as ubiquitous, eternal, and ineradicable, but as temporary, containable, and eradicable. This anti-political stance is paradoxical: Solovyov explicitly advocated a "Christian politics" that would, if successful, engender a harmonious society, and Lenin was a master politician of his era, instrumentalizing everything, including himself, for the cause of the socialist revolution. Solovyov never acquired political influence, nor indeed a following, while Lenin emerged as a victorious Bolshevik leader and founding father of a Soviet Union which existed for seventy years. What unites them is a vision of a global community beyond conflict and partition, based on the genuine concord of humankind, and, moreover, on a true worldview: the universal Christianity of the reunited churches and the scientific ideology of Marxism respectively.

Solovyov was the son of a devout Orthodox-Christian mother and a famous professor of Russian history. Though not of noble descent, he was part of the Moscow cultural and intellectual elite, and his father's position gave him a relatively safe niche: his theological writings did not pass the Holy Synod's censorship and had to be published abroad, but his philosophical writings and interventions in public debate [*publitsistika*] did appear in Russia and were widely read, and he never became the victim of direct oppression. After successful dissertation defenses (1874 and 1880), he did not embark on an academic career: in a public lecture, he had urged tsar Alexander III to prove himself a truly Christian ruler by not executing the death penalties of the murderers of his father, Alexander II. Since then, he led an unorganized life as writer, lecturer, and polemicist, returning to academic work toward the end of his short productive life, with a Plato-translation, two hundred encyclopedia entries, and his philosophical masterpiece, *The Justification of the Good* [*Opravdanie dobra*] (Solovyov 2015).

Solovyov's political philosophy, like his project of integral life and knowledge as a whole, ultimately relies on his repeated interaction with Sophia, understood by him as Divine Wisdom, Eternal Femininity, and World Soul. His mystical experience is expressed in his poetry and in a collection of dialogues, fragments, and schemes that remained unfinished, written in French, and published only posthumously (Solovyov 1978). Solovyov's vison of the "good" state-cum-society is best qualified as a hierarchically organized Christian-Platonic theocracy. Sophia, moreover, revealed to him the organic unity of humankind as a whole (Solovyov 2009, 152f.), a vision that remained central to his thought up to the last chapter of *Justification of the Good*, "The Moral Organization of Humanity as a Whole" (Solovyov 2015, 365–417). From this vision he derives both his utopian conception of a free theocracy, encompassing all of humankind and led by a King (the Russian tsar), a High Priest (the Pope of Rome), and a Prophetic intelligentsia, and a more realistic yet not less normative conception of an ideal Christian state, expounded in *The Justification of the Good* and other later texts. The state, including police, criminal justice, war, etc. is a necessary evil for Solovyov: its purpose is the limitation of evil, not only crime, but also poverty, discrimination, and abuse of power, so that the good can realize itself on the basis of humans' free decision. Conflict, from a Solovyovian perspective, cannot be legitimate, and its manifestation is therefore symptomatic of a not yet fully just society.

The impotency of Solovyov's utopian and realistic ideal theories contrasts with the view of the vast majority of the Russian intelligentsia: that a revolution was the only way forward. Lenin's combination of true theory and professionally organized political practice is the most radical example of this conviction. Nearly all of Lenin's writings are *polemical* in character, not surprisingly given his role in the Marxist movement, and as mastermind of the October Revolution. What may be surprising is that his polemics are not limited to political issues, but extend into the field of theory: one of his best known works, *Materialism and Empiriocriticism* [*Materializm i empiriokrititsizm*] (1909), is a lengthy polemic with Neo-Kantianism, Empiriocriticism (Vladimir Bazarov), and Empiriomonism (Alexander Bogdanov) *within* the party. Lenin vehemently defends a dialectical materialist philosophy of science against any form of idealist empiricism, skepticism, relativism, or non-dialectical materialism.

Lenin is of lasting relevance because of the frightening combination of an alleged scientific worldview and an instrumental perception of political power (i.e., one that separates means from ends). The "sacred" goal of a just, classless society legitimizes all means, while the certainty of an upcoming end of class-struggle, marking the beginning of the real history of a united humanity, is substantiated with a social science that establishes "laws" of the historical development of society with the same degree of certainty as the laws of nature. What is crucial from a Leninist perspective is, from any other perspective, a deathly nexus: political practice receives its justification from a scientistic worldview that leaves no space, other than tactical, for compromise, plurality, or trial-and-error, while academic debates inevitably become political struggle.

The seeds for what later became the *battle on two fronts*, i.e., the political and military front on the one hand, and the ideological and scientific front on the other, are present in Lenin's dogmatic version of dialectical and historical materialism, which he had adopted from his master, the later Menshevik Georgii Plekhanov (1856–1918). If the political has to do with the *possibility* of conflict and concord, then a monolithic conception of positive scientific knowledge leaves no space for either of them. From that angle, Lenin's political philosophy is as radically politicizing as it is radically anti-political. Even if Lenin himself foresaw, toward the end of his life, the development of the USSR into a totalitarian regime headed by Joseph Stalin, who turned his "teaching" into the official Marxist-Leninist ideology, still these developments are explicable from Lenin's conception.

The Lenin case shows, in its excess, key problems of the modern era: the increased truth-monopoly of science combined with the increased governmental and biopolitical capacity of regimes to implement a single best policy: both rely on a denial of the political. In another famous text, *State and Revolution*

[*Gosudarstvo i revoliutsiia*], Lenin argues that the state, including democratic institutions, is a mere instrument in the hands of the ruling class. Its power must be broken, after which the same instrument can be used for the dictatorship of the proletariat and the administration of a nascent socialist society. It is only when the final goal, a classless communist society, is reached that the state becomes obsolete—at that point, it becomes mere administration. Lenin not only applied a radical dualism of means and ends to existing institutions, but he also applied the same dualism to the underground party organization and, ultimately, to himself as a person. As a result, not only was the oppressive state apparatus maintained, and soon expanded, after the Bolshevik victory, but also the organizational forms of the party led by Lenin continued into the Soviet system. The initial council [*soviet*] socialism was replaced by democratic centralism—a denial of the political within the party. With the advantage of hindsight, Bakunin proved, rightly, that the way in which the revolutionary movement organizes itself is a pre-figuration of what comes after a successful revolution, and therefore has to be carefully thought-over: an abstract separation of means and ends strikes back with a vengeance.

It is easy to accuse Lenin of intellectual opportunism, but we have to acknowledge that the basis of this opportunism is a consistent philosophical position. Moreover, as Slavoj Žižek has convincingly argued, Lenin overcame his historical determinism in 1917, between the two Russian revolutions of that year, in the direction of an objective, not subjective voluntarism: "what he insists on is that the exception (the extraordinary set of circumstances, like those in Russia in 1917) offers a way to undermine the norm itself" (Žižek in Lenin 2002, 10). Historical determinism is not the same as automatism: it is about making history on the basis of adequate knowledge of the concrete situation—the latter, however, is objectively what it is.

This discussion of Solovyov and Lenin highlights the key problem of a "religious" vs. "secular" perspective on society. Solovyov and Lenin are each other's opposites when it comes to the nexus of God and man: if to Lenin, Solovyov must appear a religious idealist, of which his key notion of Divine Humanity [*bogochelovechestvo*] is clear proof, conversely for Solovyov the Marxist type of socialism is a case of the Deification of Man [*chelovekobozhestvo*], Man taking the place of God. Solovyov tries hard to incorporate concepts like rule of law, individual rights and liberties (such as freedom of speech), and separation of powers into a framework that, in the final analysis, remains an example of Orthodox-Christian political theology: politics should be organized around the collective human effort to fit into a divinely created order. Lenin, by contrast, represents a radical example of what Carl Schmitt diagnosed as the "secularization" of theological concepts (Schmitt 1996, 43): humanity, incarnate in the revolutionary proletariat headed by the communist party, can realize in historical time what Christian thinkers projected beyond its end. From both a Christian and a Leninist point of view, the difference between *bogochelovechestvo* and *chelovekobozhestvo* is of such paramount importance that it served the rejection and persecution of religion by the Soviet regime on the one hand, and a framing in terms of a struggle with the Antichrist on the other. From the perspective adopted in this chapter, the difference is minor: both perspectives rely on a denial of the political, and ultimately do away with politics (obviously, doing away with politics is itself political) in the name of an "organic" vision of society, and both perspectives also depend on a knowledge of historical good and evil, easily slipping into Manicheism.

Soviet Union and Emigration (1922–1956)

The "short Soviet century" that started with the establishment of the Bolshevik regime at the end of the Civil War in 1922 and ended in 1989 is divided into shorter periods. A period of lively, though increasingly politicized, discussions among Marxists such as Alexandra Kollontai, Anatoly Lunacharsky, Ljubov' Aksel'rod, and Nikolai Bukharin, all explicitly claiming to be Marxists, ended with the establishment toward 1930 of an orthodox, Leninist version of dialectical and historical materialism. The effective suppression of any form of political opposition against the rule of the Bolshevik party went along with the subordination of the entire field of philosophy to the interests of the Party. Around 1956, however, the year of "destalinization" by Khrushchev, Soviet intellectuals awoke from the dream (or nightmare) of an inevitable Soviet reality: even if the clock of "Thaw" was turned back by Brezhnev, the Soviet system, including its official philosophy, henceforth stood out as contingent and, at least in principle, contestable. Until 1956, however, one must look for political philosophy elsewhere, i.e., among émigré philosophers who received their philosophical education before 1917, opposed the Bolshevik regime, and had to leave the country in 1922.

The biography of Semyon Frank (1877–1950) turns him into a truly European twentieth-century philosopher, comparable to Hannah Arendt or Walter Benjamin because of the combination of a Jewish ancestry, a background at the cultural and intellectual forefront, and the experience of totalitarianism. The child of a German Jewish father and an Orthodox Russian mother, he had received a broad education that included the universities of Heidelberg and Munich, and like many of his contemporaries moved from a Marxist socialism to a religiously inspired idealist philosophy. Like Sergei Bulgakov and Nikolai Berdyaev, he was a key author in three edited volumes that marked turning points in Russia's philosophical culture: *Problems of Idealism* [*Problemy idealizma*] (1902, Poole 2003), *Signposts* [*Vekhi*] (1909, Shatz and Zimmermann 1986), and *Out of the Depths* [*Iz glubiny*] (1918, Woehrlin 1986)—together these volumes highlight the trajectory from revolutionary zeal to apocalyptic expectation of those parts of the Russian intelligentsia that involuntarily left Soviet Russia in 1922. He lived in Berlin until 1937, then moved to Paris, which he left for London in 1945.

Not a public figure like Berdyaev, nor embedded in émigré church life like Bulgakov, Frank was one of the less visible émigré philosophers. At the same time, he was also much more systematic, and his major work in social and political philosophy, *The Spiritual Foundations of Society* [*Dukhovnye osnovy obshchestva*, 1930], is a masterpiece of "communalist" thinking with a relevance that exceeds its émigré Russian context. Rooted in so-called Russian religious philosophy, Frank seeks to move, politically, beyond the opposition of Right and Left, conceptually, beyond the contrast between mechanic and organic ways of conceiving society, and, philosophically, beyond the opposition introduced by Ferdinand Tönnies between society [*Gesellschaft, obshchestvo*] and community [*Gemeinschaft, soobshchestvo*], by regarding sociality [*obshchestvennost'*] and communality [*sobornost'*] as two dimensions of all forms of human coexistence (Frank 1987, 54; Boobbyer 1995, 134–147).

Of noble descent, Ivan Ilyin (1883–1954) quickly made a reputation as one of the most brilliant minds of his time, especially with his 1918 dissertation *The Philosophy of Hegel as a Doctrine of the Concreteness of God and Man*. After the 1917 revolutions, he became one of the intellectual leaders of the White opposition to the Bolshevik regime, developing "what might be called a theory of White activism" (Utechin 1963, 272), or, in philosophical terms, a militant right-Hegelian monarchism with emphasis on a strong national state and an equally strong legal order. In 1922, he was, together with Frank, among the intellectuals who had to leave Soviet Russia by "philosophy steamer" (Chamberlain 2006). Enjoying lasting popularity among the right-wing Russian emigrant community, and beyond that in conservative Christian circles, Ilyin (both his ideas and his remains) posthumously returned to his native Russia in the post-Soviet period. Not only have his works been republished in large editions (ranging from cheap paperbacks to posh coffee-table books), but he has also gained semi-official recognition as one of three "Putin's philosophers"—along with his main émigré opponent, Nikolai Berdyaev (equally religious, but leaning toward socialism and anarchism), and the founding father of Russian religious philosophy, Vladimir Soloyvov (Eltchaninoff 2018). What the three thinkers have in common is their general religious-philosophical orientation and their shared embrace of a "Russian idea": while Berdyaev gave the title *The Russian Idea* [*Russkaia Ideia*] to his history of nineteenth-century Russian philosophical thought (Berdyaev 1992), and Ilyin wrote extensively about this "Russian idea" in the series of articles *Our Tasks* [*Nashi zadachi*] (1948–1954), this Russian idea has its roots in Solovyov's 1888 seminal essay "L'idée russe" in which the author famously claimed that "a nation's idea is not what this nation thinks of itself in historical time, but what God thinks about this nation in Eternity" (Solovyov 1978, 83). This not only raises a number of epistemological questions, but from a political-philosophical point of view it also displaces the political from a dimension of self-determination (what Russians think can lead to what they say and then do) to a dimension of eschatology, providence, and prophecy, i.e., to the field of political *theology*. Ilyin's post-Soviet popularity reflects both Russia's current emphasis on a strong state with a "vertical of power" and the anxiety of many Russians who have lost their Soviet "markers of certainty"—a book like Ilyin's *Resistance to Evil by Force* [*O soprotivlenii zlu siloiu*] of 1925 is published today with the support of the

Russian Orthodox Church and has also recently appeared in German translation (Ilyin 2018).

In Frank and Ilyin, we witness two variants of the key element of Russian religious philosophy as political philosophy: the acknowledgment of the possibility of conflict, i.e., the political, ultimately residing in some form of particularization [*obosoblenie*], and the attempt to neutralize or contain this political dimension, either by canalizing it, as Frank does in the form of civil society and parliamentary democracy understood as elected aristocracy (Frank 1987, 142–146, 172–175), or by restraining it, as Ilyin does, in the framework of a strong and authoritarian, nation-based monarchic state (Eltchaninoff 2018, 54–56). What the Russian religious philosophers have in common is their *negative* evaluation of any form of division, partition, or separation in, or from, a society conceived as an organic whole. While Ilyin, not unlike Carl Schmitt, drew the consequences from the perceived necessity of organic unity, Frank went to the greatest possible lengths to accommodate differentiation and diversity, though still emphasizing that, however differentiated it may be, human society ultimately has its foundation in "*living, concrete total-unity*" (Frank 1987, 100). As in Solovyov, this all-unity ultimately contains all of humankind.

Among émigré philosophers, one can draw a distinction. First, there are diaspora thinkers who thought and wrote as if their thought was relevant, mostly if not exclusively, for Russia, as it were preparing themselves for a time when they might return. This applies to the conservative monarchist Ivan Ilyin, who indeed enjoys enormous posthumous popularity in post-Soviet Russia as one of "Putin's philosophers" (Eltchaninoff 2018, esp. Chapter 3), but who found his Western audience mostly among ultraconservative and extremely right-wing, including fascist and anti-Semitic, circles (anti-Semitism defines a watershed between many, including contemporary Russian, thinkers and broad Western audiences). This is quite different in the case of one of the most systematic Russian philosophers, an author of, among others, a mature social and political philosophy: Frank. Frank belongs to another group of thinkers, who, after enforced emigration, adapted to their new condition and wrote, in principle, for a general educated audience, even if some of them, such as Nikolai Berdyaev, still paid considerable attention to Russian and Soviet topics. Berdyaev found a wide audience that was interested in his existential personalism, while another emigrant, Sergei Bulgakov, became influential in Western theology beyond the confines of Orthodoxy, as testified by the writings of Rowan Williams, Paul Valliere, and John Milbank. Berdyaev's works were translated into several European languages, while Frank and Bulgakov have become fully appreciated only recently with a German translation of their collected works.

Late Soviet and Post-Soviet Period (1956–2018)

A period of "thaw" [*ottepel'*], initiated by Nikita Khrushchev, yielded a generation of intellectuals of Soviet upbringing: the Sixtiers [*shestidesyatniki*], who departed from a fuller and more creative reading of Marx and other philosophers. Soviet philosophy became much more alive and interesting than it had been, but political philosophy did not exist as a separate discipline and was eclipsed by the disciplines of scientific communism and historical materialism. As James Scanlan wrote: "Social and political philosophy, the field closest to ideological concerns, is the one fully monolithic and dogmatic field of Soviet philosophy" (Scanlan 1985, 224). The Soviet system had made political philosophy essentially *obsolete* (and thereby illegitimate): the construction of socialism was built on the resolution of the political question, and the gradual development toward a classless communist society meant the eradication of the political altogether. In a communist society, the possibility of conflict would no longer exist, since it would have been "dealt with" once and for all through *full* concord. On the way toward such a society, conflict would only arise as part of international class struggle, or connected to relics from pre-socialist society: stubborn bourgeois, *kulaks*, enemies of the people, etc. The USSR did not hold a place for politics, in paradoxical contrast to its often hyper-politicized discourse. If "the classic Soviet analysis of contemporary society [...] takes its start from Marx's summary of his outlook in the preface to *A Contribution to a Critique of Political Economy*" (Scanlan 1985, 225), then clearly any analysis of "real existing socialism" in terms of a socio-economic foundation with a juridical-political superstructure and a "matching" ideological superstructure to top it off would be devastating—outside the USSR, such Marxist analyses abounded, but inside it a discussion of school, army, or academia as "ideological state apparatuses" (as Louis Althusser would call them) was *anathema*.

Still, this decade was one of lively debate among Marxist and non-Marxist thinkers, stimulated also by Marx's *Economic and Philosophic Manuscripts* of 1844 that had been published in Soviet Russia in 1932, but had remained unaddressed. The *shestidesiatniki* aimed at reform from within by breaking open orthodox Marxism-Leninism, engaging with pre-Marxist philosophical positions, most noticeably Hegel and Kant, and exchanging with their Marxist colleagues in the West. Some of them later became dissidents, but many remained inside Soviet academia, preparing for better times after the regime re-established tight control after 1968, and educating generations of young academics in a spirit of critical thinking combined with political caution.

The period after the downfall of Khrushchev, in 1964, was one of increasing "stagnation" that also affected philosophy. As a result, political philosophy retreated into underground, dissident, and émigré circles, in the form of *samizdat* and *tamizdat*. One famous example is *Iz-pod glyb* [*From Under the Rubble*], (Scammel 1975), a collection of essays by, among others, Alexander Solzhenitsyn, Igor' Shafarevich, and Yevgeni Barabanov, the title of which refers back to the equally gloomy collection of essays *Iz glubiny* [*Out of the*

Depths] already mentioned. Another example is offered by the works of Alexander Zinoviev (1922–2006) who expressed his critical analysis of "real existing socialism" and of the *Homo sovieticus* in the form of sociological novels like *Ziiaiushchie vysoty* [*The Yawning Heights*], *Svetloe budushchee* [*The Radiant Future*], and *Zheltyi dom* [*The Yellow House*]. What singles out most of these contributions is their radical and abstract nature, mirroring the situation in the nineteenth century: radical in the sense of sketching alternative projects for Soviet Russia, and abstract in the sense of not being connected to, or tested by, any concrete political experience or activity (Horvath 2005).

This situation lasted roughly until 1986, when Mikhail Gorbachev's program of *perestroika* and *glasnost'*, launched to save the socialist project and the CPSU's dominance, led to a rapid demise of Marxism-Leninism (Brown 2004) and allowed some *shestidesiatniki* to advocate humanist values, democracy, and civil society; while others, influenced by contemporary positions in Western philosophy (Arendt, Foucault, Deleuze, among others), conceived of political philosophy as a profoundly critical, rather than constructive endeavor. Marx could still play a role, but not Marxism-Leninism (Scanlan 1994, 189–194). However, the Russian Federation that emerged from the breaking up of the USSR not only went through heavy economic crisis, but also saw liberalization and privatization destroy societal structures as well as nascent pluralist democracy, resulting in a wild capitalism the only response to which seemed to be a strong, centralized state, a managed civil society, and a "sovereign" democracy. In the twenty-first century, Russia is not returning to Soviet models; it rather fits a global tendency toward neo-patrimonial illiberal democracy. But it does return to a Russian model of a strong centralized state ruling a grudgingly obedient population with, as Edward Świderski put it, a remarkable "proclivity [...] for anarchic behavior—*Pugachyovshchina*" (Świderski 2010, 295).

The era between 1989 and 2000 was marked not only by an unheard-of degree of academic and intellectual freedom, but also by the anarchy and hardship of a collapsing socio-economic empire as well as humiliation on the international front, weakly compensated by an increasingly presidential system. Finally, the period from 2000 until the present day is determined not only by societal stability, economic prosperity, and a regaining of Russia's position as a world power, but also by a *vertikal' vlasti*, increasing patriotism, autocratic patterns, and the silencing of serious political opposition. In Russia today, the possibility of conflict is fully acknowledged, and the main way of dealing with it is not denial, but a combination of suppression and control. The field of political philosophy, as a result, tends to be populated by, on the one hand, speculative philosophies of history which deny the political in the name of a cohesive society based on traditional values, such as the post-Heideggerian vision of Alexander Dugin, or the revived thought of Ivan Ilyin; and on the other, impotent attempts to unchain the political that recall anarchism, for example by the punk anarchists of Pussy Riot (Alyokhina 2017; Scholder et al. 2013; Tolokonnikova 2016; Tolokonnikova and Žižek 2014).

88 E. VAN DER ZWEERDE

For the late Soviet and post-Soviet period, I focus on the "prototypical" *shestidesiatnik* Erikh Soloviev (b. 1934) and the post-Marxist "left Schmittian" Artem Magun (b. 1974). In both cases, many other authors could have been chosen who at least deserve to be mentioned: Alexander Akhiezer (1911–2000), Yuri Zamoshkin (1927–1993), Nelly Motroshilova (b. 1934), Vadim Mezhuev (1933–2019), Yevgeni Yasin (b. 1934), Vladimir Bibikhin (1938–2004), Yevgeni Rashkovsky (b. 1940), Vladimir Kantor (b. 1945), Valery Podoroga (b. 1946), the analyst of totalitarian aesthetics Boris Groys (b. 1947), the thinker of (post-) terror Mikhail Ryklin (b. 1948), the left-liberal Boris Kapustin (b. 1951), the critical historian of contemporary Western philosophy Vladimir Malakhov (b. 1958), the Right-Heideggerian Eurasianist Alexander Dugin (b. 1962), the republican Oleg Kharkhordin (b. 1964), or identity theorist Veronika Sharova (b. 1981), to name only a few. In this sense, the choice of authors for this section has a considerable degree of arbitrariness.

Erikh Soloviev was among the Soviet philosophers who found refuge in the history of philosophy, a niche that was relatively politically insensitive and offered opportunities to connect to philosophical culture outside the USSR. His 1984 monograph on Martin Luther *Unbeaten Heretic* [*Nepobezhdionnyi eretik*] and his 1991 essay collection *The Past Interprets Us* [*Proshloie tolkuet nas*] make clear, as do his writings on Immanuel Kant and Vladimir Solovyov, that his primary focus is on ethics, philosophy of law, and social and political philosophy (Soloviev 2003). Under post-Soviet conditions, torn between the perverted collectivism of official Marxism-Leninism, and the atomizing tendencies of neoliberal hegemony, to emphasize, as does Soloviev, the notions of conscience and responsibility, the contrast between *individual* [individ] and *person (ality)* [lichnost'], and the need for political power to legitimize itself in moral terms, is to address and articulate the political. It counters the widespread idea that Russia must find a single way forward, guided by a new "idea" to fill the alleged "ideological vacuum" (if anywhere, it is here in its perverted conception of ideology that we witness the devastating effects of the Soviet marriage of politics and philosophy). At the same time, there is a sense of historical irony when it comes to the generation of the sixties: speaking with the authority of their direct experience with the Soviet system and its perverted "Marxism," they became "outdated" as they spoke.

Born in 1974, Magun is one of the political philosophers in contemporary Russia who are "post-Soviet" in the sense that they developed their thought after the breakdown of the Soviet system. For Magun, the period 1985–1999 is a period of revolution, comparable to the "paradigm of the modern revolution," i.e., the French revolution two centuries earlier (1789–1799) (Magun 2013, 15). Key to understanding the modern revolution is its negativity, the *radical* negation of the *ancien régime*, which in the case of Russia was, first, the tsarist, and then the Soviet regime. More broadly, "negativity" in the sense of a denial, if necessary, also destruction, of existing power structures, is what singles out "the Left": the fact that in most languages "left" is connected to notions like inapt, sinister, or wrong, and "right" correspondingly with proper, just, or correct, reflects not only the fact that "the Left" wants to change the existing conditions, but also that hegemonic ideology is also generated, or at least supported, by the powers-that-be. While Gorbachev's policy of *perestroika* and *glasnost'* aimed to preserve the Soviet system through reform, it also presented socialism as a choice, not a historical inevitability (Walicki 1995, 536). This has liberated political philosophy, too. As a pupil of Bibikhin and the Left-Heideggerian Philippe Lacoue-Labarthe, and editor of the bilingual journal *Stasis*, Magun moves smoothly from Russian to Western academic philosophical culture and back; in this respect, he exemplifies a new "Silver Age" which is similar to the previous one, a century earlier, in many respects.

The challenge of post-Soviet Russia is the recognition of the fact that, if humans make their own history, they not only do this on the basis of given conditions rather than freely chosen ones, but they also do it in the plural, divided, among others, along lines of left and right. That Russia took the course of neo-liberal and neo-patrimonial governance in combination with a "guided" democracy and a "managed" civil society is not a matter of destiny or historical inevitability, but, to quote Herzen again, of "a thousand conditions, both essential and fortuitous, plus the human will"—a situation which implies that the current situation is shaped by "the Right" as much as this was the case in Soviet times, when progressive and internationalist rhetoric badly concealed power- and privilege-preserving politics.

In Magun's emphasis on the negative dimension of politics, and of revolutionary politics in particular, we perceive an important leitmotiv in Russian political philosophy: the radical negation of existing power structures. Bakunin on the one hand and Lenin on the other represent the two possible revolutionary options: the negation of power structures as such, and the attempt to posit an alternative power structure, to "conquer the state" in the name of an alternative. From a Western perspective, it is easy to qualify these Russian positions as "extreme" and explain them in the light of the absolutist character of tsarist autocracy. While it is certainly true that the attempts to reform the tsarist system by reformers such as Pyotr Stolypin, by constructive opposition parties such as the Kadets [*konstitutsionnye demokraty*], and even by the tsar-liberator Alexander II failed, thus appearing to lead inevitably to the violent revolutions of 1917, we should realize that there is nothing specifically Russian about this situation.

Conclusion

Ending this discussion of political philosophy in Russia with Magun is arbitrary, but any end would be arbitrary. Starting the chapter with Herzen was just as arbitrary. The aim of this chapter has not been to be complete, or to grasp a core or essence, but rather to offer, from the perspective of a specific understanding of political philosophy, a number of approaches to a rich and interesting field. Other authors might have been chosen, and any suggestion that the chosen pairs somehow demonstrate an organic or dialectical, let alone inevitable development, should be avoided. Like its future, the past of political philosophy is radically open by definition, both because of the inescapable freedom and the indeterminacy of human thought, and because of the unpredictability of political developments. As long a humankind exists, political philosophy will exist, and it will also exist in Russia. The only thing that cannot be predicted is what it will look like.

Political reality in Russia did not so much determine political philosophy as push it to extremes. Conversely, political philosophy never had an impact on political reality, arguably not even in the case of Lenin, whose abstract ideals gave way to the harsh logic of dictatorship. While under different circumstances, radical political philosophy can, for example through the multiple forms of civil society, influence political life without determining it, any attempt to implement political philosophy is detrimental both politically and philosophically. It is not accidental, therefore, that "moderate" thinkers like Herzen and Frank developed their political philosophy abroad and in the wake of a failed revolution, while a third philosopher, Erikh Soloviev, saw his ideals quickly become diluted in the post-*perestroika* period.

Hardly any of the political theories and philosophies that Russia has yielded have ever been seriously tested in political practice. The exception, Leninist-Marxism, inaugurated a minority tyranny of the Bolshevik faction and almost instantly started to eat its own children. Moreover, Marxism-Leninism was constructed *after* the establishment of the Soviet regime and thus already part of its ideological legitimization. Russia's history is often marked by, on the one hand, autocratic, dogmatic, sometimes cynical power play, and, on the other, abstract and often utopian visions of a post-political society.

Political philosophy in Russia is heavily under-researched, for which there are three reasons. The first reason is the relative scarcity of complete critical editions and reliable translations, as well as the spread of the latter over languages such as English, German, and French. Secondly, many scholars, especially in the West, who study Russian philosophy are not professional philosophers, but Slavic study scholars, historians, literary and cultural theorists, often more interested in ideas and influences than in concepts and arguments. Thirdly, those who are philosophers are often more attracted to religious philosophy, metaphysics, and ethics, than to political philosophy. This situation yields many possible topics for further research, including both in-depth analyses of individual thinkers and diachronic and synchronic comparisons. Particularly promising, to my mind, are cross-cultural comparative analyses, e.g., between Lenin and Sayyid Qutb, between Christian thinkers like Vladimir Solovyov or Frank and Muslim or Catholic reformists, between Ilyin and authoritarian, including "fascist," European political thinkers, or, finally, between Herzen and contemporary "skeptical revolutionaries."

To conclude, if one of the tasks of political philosophy is to articulate the political, we can state that the apparent poverty of political philosophy in Russia has everything to do with the fact that, during large stretches of its history, to articulate the political almost immediately meant to enter into conflict with the authorities. When the hindologist and philosopher Alexander M. Piatigorsky (1929–2009), who had involuntarily left the USSR in 1974, briefly returned to Russia and gave a series of lectures in Moscow entitled "What Is Political Philosophy? [*Chto takoe politicheskaia filosofiia*]," he said: "However, the political philosopher is not only a spy, as we already discussed. He, like in general any genuine philosopher, is also a saboteur [*diversant*], in so far as he *objectively* gets to know his object—i.e., *their, your,* and finally, *one's own,* political reflection—as something ineffective, mystified, and mystifying. With this he objectively undermines power, any power, whether his own or someone else's" (Piatigorsky 2007, 59). Political philosophy always has been, is, and always will be a potential threat to the powers that be, because it articulates the contingency of the political order of which those powers are the manifestation. If political philosophy is an accepted part of academia and society, this either means that the hegemonic order has successfully immunized itself against the subversive potential of critical thinking, or that it has become part of the ideology of that order. Just as the political, the ubiquitous and ineradicable possibility of conflict and of concord, can be denied, suppressed, unchained, or canonized, the same four possibilities apply to political philosophy. As a result, it is ineradicably there, but not per se in explicit and manifest forms.

Notes

1. My book-length discussion of political philosophy in Russia will be shortly published by Edinburgh University Press. The title of the forthcoming book is *Russian Political Philosophy: Anarchy, Authority, Autocracy.*
2. At this point Russian political history still has to be rewritten; see, e.g., Anderson (1967) and Kharkhordin (2005).

Bibliography

Alyokhina, Maria. 2017. *Riot Days.* London: Metropolitan Books.
Anderson, Thornton. 1967. *Russian Political Thought. An Introduction.* Ithaca, NY: Cornell University Press.
Arendt, Hannah. 1994. 'What Remains? The Language Remains.' A Conversation with Günter Gaus. In *Essays in Understanding 1930–1954.* Edited by Jerome Kohn, 1–23. New York: Schocken.
Bakunin, Mikhail. 1953. *The Political Philosophy of Bakunin. A Comprehensive Selection from the Writings of Marx's Great Historical Rival.* Compiled and Edited by G.P. Maximoff. New York: Free Press.
———. 1970. *God and the State.* Mineola: Dover Publications.
———. 1973. *Selected Writings.* Edited by Arthur Lehning. New York, NY: Grove Press.
———. 1977. *The Confession of Mikhail Bakunin with the Marginal Comments of Tsar Nicholas I.* Translated by Robert C. Howes, with Introduction by Lawrence D. Orton. Ithaca, NY and London: Cornell University Press.
———. 2005. *Statism and Anarchy.* Edited by Marshall Shatz. Cambridge: Cambridge University Press.

Berdyaev, Nikolai. 1992 [1947]. *The Russian Idea*. Hudson, NY: Lindisfarne.

Beyme, Klaus von. 2001. *Politische Theorien in Russland 1789–1945*. Wiesbaden: Springer Fachmedien.

Boobbyer, Philip. 1995. *S.L. Frank. The Life and Work of a Russian Philosopher 1877–1950*. Athens, OH: Ohio University Press.

Brown, Archie (ed.). 2004. *The Demise of Marxism-Leninism in Russia*. Oxford: Palgrave Macmillan.

Chamberlain, Lesley. 2006. *The Philosophy Steamer; Lenin and the Exile of the Intelligentsia*. London: Atlantic.

Eltchaninoff, Michel. 2018. *Inside the Mind of Vladimir Putin*. London: Hurst & Company. (In original: *Dans la tête de Vladimir Poutine*. Arles: Actes Sud, 2015.).

Frank, Semen. 1987 [1930]. *The Spiritual Foundations of Society*. Athens and London: Ohio University Press.

Hamburg, Gary M., and Randall Poole (eds.). 2010. *A History of Russian Philosophy 1830–1930. Faith, Reason and the Defense of Human Dignity*. Cambridge: Cambridge University Press.

Herzen, Alexander. 2003. *Selected Philosophical Works*. Honolulu: University Press of the Pacific. (1st ed., 1956.)

Horvath, Robert. 2005. *The Legacy of Soviet Dissent*. Abingdon and New York: Routledge.

Ilyin, Ivan. 2018. *Über den gewaltsamen Widerstand gegen das Böse*. Straelen: Edition Hagia Sophia. (Recent Russian edition: 2017, *O soprotivlenii zlu siloiu*. Moscow: Dar.)

Kelly, Aileen M. 2016. *The Discovery of Change. The Life and Thought of Alexander Herzen*. Cambridge, MA and London: Harvard University Press.

Kharkhordin, Oleg. 2005. *Main Concepts of Russian Politics*. Lanham, MD: The University Press of America.

Kuvakin, Valery A. 1994. *A History of Russian Philosophy*. 2 vols. Buffalo, NY: Prometheus.

Lenin, Vladimir. 2002. *Revolution at the Gates. Selected Writings by Lenin from 1917*. Edited by Slavoj Žižek. London and New York: Verso.

Magun, Artemy. 2013. *Negative Revolution. Modern Political Subject and Its Fate After the Cold War*. New York and London: Bloomsbury. (In original: Magun, Artemy. 2008. *Otritsatel'naia revoliutsiia*. St. Petersburg: izd. Evropeiskogo Universiteta.)

Piatigorsky, Alexander. 2007. *Chto takoe politicheskaia filosofiia?* Moskva: izd. Evropa.

Planty-Bonjour, Guy. 1974. *Hegel et la pensée philosophique en Russie 1830–1917*. La Haye: Martinus Nijhoff.

Poole, Randall A. (ed.). 2003. *Problems of Idealism: Essays in Russian Social Philosophy*. Translated by Randall A. Poole. New Haven, CT and London: Yale University Press.

Scammel, Michael (ed.). 1975. *From Under the Rubble*. Translated by Michael Scammel. London: Collins & Harvill Press. (In original: *Iz-pod glyb*. Paris: YMCA Press, 1974.).

Scanlan, James P. 1985. *Marxism in the USSR. A Critical Survey of Current Soviet Thought*. Ithaca and London: Cornell University Press.

——— (ed.). 1994. *Russian Thought after Communism. The Recovery of a Philosophical Heritage*. Armonk, NY: M.E. Sharpe.

Schmitt, Carl. 1996 [1922]. *Politische Theologie*. Berlin: Duncker & Humblot.

Scholder, Amy, et al. (eds.). 2013. *Pussy Riot. A Punk Prayer for Freedom*. New York: The Feminist Press.

Shatz, Marshall S., and Judith E. Zimmermann (eds.). 1986. *Signposts*. Translated by Marshall S. Shatz and Judith E. Zimmermann. Irvine, CA: Charles Schlacks Jr.

Soloviev, Erikh. 2003. The Humanistic-Legal Problematic in Solov'ëv's Philosophical Journalism. *Studies in East European Thought* 55 (2): 115–139.

Solovyov, Vladimir. 1978. *La Sophia et les autres écrits français*. Edited by François Rouleau. Lausanne: L'Age d'Homme.

———. 2009. *Divine Sophia; The Wisdom Writings of Vladimir Solovyov*. Edited by Judith D. Kornblatt. Ithaca, NY and London: Cornell University Press.

———. 2015. *Justification of the Moral Good*. Edited by Thomas Nemeth. Cham: Springer.

Świderski, Edward. 2010. The Cultural Hermeneutic of Russia's Historical Experience: The Case of Alexander Samojlovič Akhiezer. *Studies in East European Thought* 62 (3/4): 279–298.

Tolokonnikova, Nadya. 2016. *How to Start a Revolution*. London: Penguin.

Tolokonnikova, Nadya, and Slavoj Žižek. 2014. *Comradely Greetings. The Prison Letters of Nadya and Slavoj*. London and New York: Verso.

Utechin, Sergej. 1963. *Russian Political Thought. A Concise History*. New York and London: Praeger.

Walicki, Andrzej. 1988. *A History of Russian Thought. From the Enlightenment to Marxism*. Oxford: Clarendon.

———. 1995. *Marxism and the Leap to Freedom*. Stanford, CA: Stanford University Press.

Woehrlin, William F., ed. 1986. *Out of the Depths*. Translated by William F. Woehrlin. Irvine, CA: Charles Schlacks Jr.

Žižek, Slavoj. 2017. *Lenin 2017*. London and New York: Verso.

CHAPTER 5

Between Aristocratism and Artistry: Two Centuries of the Revolutionary Paradigm in Russia

Julia B. Mehlich

INTRODUCTION

Russian historical reckoning as the *conscious* desire to undertake a revolution in the original sense of the word,[1] that is, as a return to the original position or *restoring the true path of the development of the history* of the spirit toward freedom, begins with the formation of secret Decembrist societies in 1816–1817. Recalling the October 1917 revolution in his book *The Decembrists Before the Court of History (1825–1925)* [*Dekabristy pered sudom istorii (1825–1925)*], Sergei Yakovlevich Hessen (1903–1937) had this to say about the centennial of the Decembrist Revolt: "On the one hundredth anniversary of the birth of Russia's first secret society, Russia wove its best wreath for the grave of the Decembrists by striking the final blow against autocracy, completing the struggle that they began" (Gessen 1926, 7). A century later, the year 2017 again saw discussions about revolution as a restoration of Russia's historical path, not from the perspective of "cunning reason," but from eternity, identity, or pragmatism. In the early twentieth century, it was impossible to engage in history without positioning oneself in relation to the Neo-Kantian Baden School's theory of culture and values. Enthusiastically welcoming revolution, Hessen does not apply a deterministic concept of history without a subject, but clearly adheres to a personified theorization of history based on individual

---

J. B. Mehlich (✉)
Department of Philosophy of Natural Sciences, Faculty of Philosophy, Lomonosov State University, Moscow, Russian Federation

© The Author(s), under exclusive license to Springer Nature Switzerland AG 2021
M. F. Bykova et al. (eds.), *The Palgrave Handbook of Russian Thought*,
https://doi.org/10.1007/978-3-030-62982-3_5

95

"*personified*" causality developed by his namesake and distant relative Sergei Yakovlevich Hessen.[2]

Sergei Iakovlevich Hessen formulated the purpose of his book accordingly: "to give a holistic outline of *assessment* of the relationship toward the Decembrists by their contemporaries and descendants" (Gessen 1926, 8; italics mine), thereby positioning it within the Neo-Kantian methodology of transcendental theory of values, whose main methods for comprehending historical and social being were Wilhelm Windelband's idiographic method and Heinrich Rickert's individualizing method. The centennial of the October Revolution saw a renewed understanding of the need to comprehend history not only from the position of social reality's immanence to the laws of economics and historical materialism, but also from the position of *revolution* (return) to the variety of methodologies for interpreting historical beings that existed before the revolution and were tossed aside as invalid after the revolution's success. History's participants perceive, understand, and interpret its progress in different ways, and this interpretation is largely determined by how an individual sees himself in history: as its instrument or its creator, as an aristocrat or an artist.

In this chapter, I consider and apply the personification method to history for the following reasons: first, it theoretically conjures up the image of the revolutionary artist at the beginning of the twentieth century and has enormous significance for the interpretation of the history and culture of that period. Second, applying it allows us to explore the stated topic of this chapter and interpret history, specifically the periods of the Decembrist Revolt and the October Revolution, through a typologizing of individuals as either aristocratic or artistic. These periods will be further analyzed using specific examples to show the presence of individuals corresponding to each period. The *aristos* represents the collective image of the Decembrists who took part in the Revolt, while the exemplary artist of the October Revolution is represented by the real figure of the artist, philosopher, writer, and bohemian Fyodor A. Stepun. I view the revolutionary aristocrat and writer Alexander I. Herzen as a link between the aristocratic and artistic personalities and, accordingly, between the periods of the Decembrist Revolt and the October Revolution.

The Personification Method of Comprehending History

In the late nineteenth and early twentieth centuries there existed various approaches to understanding social reality and history. Among those were Hegel's logicism, the materialism expressed in Marx's economic theories, Herzen's anarchistic individualism and its "shabby improvisation of history," Neo-Kantianism's individual causality and personalistic approach to interpreting cultural worldviews and creative transformation, recreation of reality, developed by Sergei I. Hessen, Dostoevsky's "believed-in meaning of history," and so on. In its own way, each concept addressed the relationship between the meaning of an individual life and the overall meaning of history.

Given the availability of a variety of methodologies, approaches, and theories for comprehending history, including the revolutionary paradigm, I will apply the concept of individual causality, which constitutes the basis of the theory of transcendental values of culture and which most adequately describes modern interpretations from the position of the overall sense of values of various cultures and social realities. It is Neo-Kantianism that develops the idea of human reason constituting and constructing reality, an idea that appears as a sum of technologies, including revolutionary ones. At the same time, the activity of the cognizing subject increases along with his awareness of his own participation in creating what happens around him. Neo-Kantianism offers an individualizing method for interpreting history, a particular type of transition from the singular to the universal. The notion of the "universally valid" [*Allgemeingültiges*] is justified as a complement to the logical notion of the "generic universal." The introduction of the universally valid in contrast to the generic universal makes it possible to introduce the notion of "individual causality," as well, which in turn permits consideration of the validity of the *individual*, the inimitable and irreplaceable in history. The existence of universally binding values and of individual causality explains the influence both of real, individual figures and of artistic images, ideals, and idols on the formation of existing norms of behavior. One of the founders and leading theoreticians of Neo-Kantianism, Heinrich Rickert, believed that history as a science, despite the individualized method, could not describe everyone individually, revealing only what "has *general significance*" and is simultaneously "significant for everyone" through correlation with unconditional values. This value-related approach allows one to use the term "the typical" which, as Rickert uses it, does not mean "the typical as the average" [*das Typische als das Durchschnittliche*] but "the typical as the exemplary" [*das Typische als das Vorbildliche*], "since the average, as the content of a general notion, always contains *less* than any of its individual exemplars, while the exemplary must extend beyond the average and contain *more* than the general notion" (Rickert 1896, 361). What is typical-exemplary includes what ought to be, which is always correlated with ideals and values. Neo-Kantianism thus presents and develops a personifying methodology for comprehending historical reality through individuality and personhood. With that in mind, researchers can use a particular, exemplary person, either real or derived, as the individuality in question. Fyodor Avgustovich Stepun, a colleague of Sergei Hessen whom I will discuss below, likewise argued, "Every literary, philosophical, and social movement is best studied through the particular and, to the extent possible, most typical of its representatives. After all, the issues of history are ultimately resolved by individual, solitary human souls" (Stepun 1910, 173). Thus, disclosing the "ultimate depths [...] of the soul" of this kind of individual also means illuminating the "ultimate essence" of the movement being studied. *O messii* [*On the Messiah*], a 1909 collection of essays on the philosophy of culture published in Leipzig that included contributions from both Hessen and Stepun, examined real historical figures who had become the spokesmen, the messiahs, of their time. For Stepun this was Vladimir Solovyov, and for Sergei Hessen it was Alexander Herzen. "If we are to save humanity," writes Hessen, "we must become revolutionaries. […] A revolutionary in the contemporary sense is a socialist. Socialism alone can save the old world. […] This is no egalitarianism: individualism is the principle behind Herzen's anarchic socialism" (1909a, 49). Herzen himself becomes the exemplary individual with whom Hessen would maintain a dedication and intimacy for the rest of his life, but we also see his methodological approach for comprehending historical being by using emerging typical examples of real people.

The methodological differentiation of science between sciences of nature and sciences of spirit (history) had an enormous influence in Russia that has not yet been adequately reflected in the contemporary literature. This is due to the fact that, following the competing scientific programs and paradigms of pre-revolutionary methodological pluralism, historical materialism dominated for many years. In Russia before the October Revolution, everyone analyzed and applied, or rejected, Neo-Kantian methodology regardless of the philosophical inclinations of the individual thinker. Alexei F. Losev provides evidence of this: "Neo-Kantianism was everything then. Windelband in Heidelberg was considered the primary authority" (Bibikhin 2006, 241). It was with Neo-Kantianism that the division between Neo-Westernizers and Neo-Slavophiles recommenced at the beginning of the twentieth century. The editorial article in the journal *Logos. Mezhdunarodnyi ezhegodnik po filosofii kul'tury* [*Logos. International Yearbook of Philosophy of Culture*], first published in Moscow in 1910 by the publisher Musaget and edited by S.I. Hessen, E.K. Medtner, and F.A. Stepun, caused heated debates among Russia's intellectual-artistic circles. The journal had been conceived in Heidelberg, where Hessen and Stepun defended their dissertations before the Neo-Kantians Rickert and Windelband: *On Individual Causality* [*Über individuelle Kausalität*] (Hessen 1909b) and *Vladimir Solovyov* [*Wladimir Ssolowjew*] (Steppuhn 1910), respectively. To the editorial article, Vladimir Ern (Ern 1911) responded indignantly with the collection of articles *The Struggle for Logos* [*Bor'ba za Logos*], while Hessen (Gessen 1911) published an article in the journal *Rech'* [*The Speech*] with the title "Neo-Slavophilism in Philosophy" ["Neoslavianofil'stvo v filosofii"]. Despite their fundamental difference in viewpoint from Neo-Kantians, a number of authors associated with the publisher "Put'" [The Path], which belonged to the so-called Neo-Slavophile camp of Nikolai Berdyaev, Sergei Bulgakov, Evgenii Trubetskoi, and others, began publishing a series of monographs devoted to Russia's famous figures and clearly applying the personification method. In his book *Alexei Stepanovich Khomyakov*, Berdyaev writes:

> This work is less historical than philosophical, systemic, psychological, and critical. I wanted to provide a holistic image of Khomyakov, what was central and significant to his worldview and world-feeling. […] Since I consider Khomyakov the central figure in Slavophilism, the topic of *Khomyakov* is, at the same time,

about Slavophilism in general, and the topic *Khomyakov and We* is about the fate of Slavophilism. (Berdyaev 2007, 226)

With their philosophical differences but methodological similarities, the representatives of the Neo-Westernizers and Neo-Slavophiles were the creators and participants of one of the most significant and well-known periods of Russian cultural prosperity, what is known as the Silver Age, which stretched from the late nineteenth century to the early 1920s.[3] The main feature of the Silver Age was precisely this polyphony and openness to the world, a receptivity toward other voices and polemics.

From the perspective of the personalistic methodology offered in this chapter, I will analyze the typical-exemplary individuals and images of the Decembrist Revolt of 1825 and the October Revolution of 1917. The former represents more of a collective typical-exemplary image, while the latter will involve a real historical individual central to understanding the October Revolution. Emerging images of Decembrists relate to their bohemian representatives, especially the Decembrist "Northern Secret Society," whose members embodied the literary-philosophical environment of their time. They are known as the "Decembrists" because, on December 14, 1825, they led a revolt in St. Petersburg with the aim of overthrowing the autocracy and establishing a republic, or a constitutional monarchy, as well as abolishing serfdom. The uprising was led by aristocratic officers of the guard who distinguished themselves during the 1812 Patriotic War against the Napoleonic army. On their return from Europe, they had expected socio-political change in Russia, as well, but once they abandoned hope for tsarist reforms, they began creating secret societies and preparing for a coup, including the possibility of regicide to achieve their goals. The conspirators took advantage of a transfer of power when, after the death of Tsar Alexander I, his brother Nicholas was to take the oath. The Decembrists led their guard units to the Senate Square in order to prevent the new tsar, who was unpopular among military circles, from taking his oath, to occupy the Winter Palace, and to arrest the tsar's family. The man chosen as the future Decembrist "dictator," Prince Sergei Petrovich Trubetskoii, was to lead the revolt, but he did not show up in the square, and the intended regicide Petr Grigor'evich Kakhovskii refused to kill the tsar. Nicholas ordered his artillery troops to fire grapeshot at the rebel ranks, and they began to flee. The uprising had been suppressed. Five Decembrists were sentenced to death: Mikhail P. Bestuzhev-Riumin, Petr G. Kakhovskii, Sergeii I. Muraviov-Apostol, Pavel I. Pestel, and Kondratii F. Ryleev (cf. Edel'man 2010). In the verse dedication "In Memory of Ryleev" ["Pamiati Ryleeva"], one of the executed Decembrists whom I will discuss below, the poet Nikolai Platonovich Ogarev, close friend and confidant of Herzen, summarized the entire story in 1859 in the following words:

> The mutiny flared up and froze. Execution awoke.
> Here are the five who were hanged. (Ogarev 1975, 124)

Returning to my description of the literary-philosophical environment of that time, I would note, for example, the Decembrist Mikhail Sergeevich Lunin (1787–1845), lieutenant-colonel of the Imperial Guard and author of a number of social-philosophical treatises, who left for Paris after a temporary resignation in 1916 and met Henri de Saint-Simon. Herzen, who published Lunin's work in his Free Russian Press, called him one of "the finest and most delicate minds." Another Decembrist, Wilhelm Karlovich Küchelbecker, was born into a family of Russian German aristocrats and studied with his friend Pushkin at the Imperial Lyceum in Tsarskoe Selo in 1811. He co-founded the almanac *Mnemosyne* [*Mnemozina*] (1824–1825), the print organ of Russia's first literary-philosophical circle, "The Lovers of Wisdom" (1823–1825). Almost all of them were "talents and poets," the most famous of whom included Kondratii Fedorovich Ryleev and Alexander Alexandrovich Bestuzhev (Marlinskii). The Decembrist memoirs, the volumes of literature about them, and the reminiscences of their friends conjure up the image of a typical-exemplary individual, one who constitutes his era. The central figure of the first half of the nineteenth century is in fact a Decembrist and not a poet. In Russian culture, Pushkin is, of course, the central figure of the Golden Age of Russian literature, but it is the Decembrists who would become the ideal for revolutionaries and predecessors to the events of 1917. Hessen refers to a letter from the Romantic Nikolai Yazykov to his family that reflects the worldview and outlook on the history of Romanticism shared by the Decembrists, especially Ryleev. Yazykov writes about his faith in the "*spirit of the times*" that "*does not obey decrees but always travels its own path and constructs what it needs*" (Gessen 1926, 64). The adoption of "the spirit of the times" relates to Hegel's understanding of the "cunning reason of history," and comprehending it requires, in turn, that one accept playing the role of its *instrument*. The Decembrists were organized into two secret societies: The Northern Society in St. Petersburg (1822–1825) and The Southern Society in Kiev (1821–1825), built on the foundations of the "Union of Welfare" (1818–1821) and the "Union of Salvation" (1816–1817). The latter, more radical and politicized, was led by Pavel Ivanovich Pestel, the Decembrist theoretician and author of "The Russian Truth" ["Russkaia Pravda"], the main programmatic document of the Southern Society, which argued for establishing a republican system. However, the "soul and primary engine of the Northern Society" was the poet Ryleev, and the image of the Decembrist was created in precisely this bohemian environment of Petersburg and Moscow. The Decembrists' own self-evaluation played a role of no small importance in the creation and understanding of that image, as evidenced by Sergei Ya. Hessen in his book chapter entitled "The Decembrists' self-evaluation" ["Samootsenka dekabristov"]. How did the Decembrists see themselves, and how did they self-evaluate? In Ryleev's *The Confession of Nalivaiko* [*Ispoved' Nalivaiki*] (1825), a poem about the legendary Cossack who led a failed uprising against Polish feudal lords in Ukraine in the late sixth century, the poet conveys a vision of his role in events through the mouth of his hero:

I know that death awaits
The one who first rebels
Against the people's oppressors;
Fate has doomed me already.
But tell me, when and where has freedom
Ever been redeemed without sacrifice?
I will die for my native lands—
This I sense, and I know...
And joyfully, Holy Father,
Do I bless my lot in life!
(Ryleev 1919, 5)

In his reminiscences about Ryleev, Nikolai A. Bestuzhev, brother of Aleksander Bestuzhev, writes that Ryleev read the poem to his brother Mikhail after finishing it and replied to the latter's observations with,

> Do you think I doubted my calling even for a minute? Believe me, every day convinces me of the necessity of my actions, and of my future death, by which we must purchase our first attempt at Russia's freedom, and at the same time, of the need to set an example to awaken the Russians who slumber. (Bestuzhev 1919, 5–6)

Bestuzhev continues: "the thought of being an *instrument* or a sacrifice for a dawning freedom filled his entire existence and was his sole purpose in life" (Bestuzhev 1919, 6; italics mine; see also Gessen 1926, 99). Hessen's further commentary on these events is also important:

> When you recreate in your mind a picture of those last days [...] it cannot help but seem that [...] all their discussions about how to act took place only for appearances [...] As if all this had been done for fiction, in the interests of observing form, while everyone was fully conscious of a certain fatalism, and of this great faith in the effectiveness of victimhood [...] It seemed they saw the highest meaning in the most unavoidable failure. (Gessen 1926, 99–100)

This portrait of detachment from the reality of events, this vision of them as more of a performance or an act of formality, is complemented by the memoirs of the Decembrist Prince Evgenii Petrovich Obolenskii. Obolenskii reports how, during his confinement in the Alekseev Ravelin of Peter and Paul Fortress, he found the means of corresponding with Ryleev through a watchman. Olga Edelman, author of the book *The Investigation into the Decembrists* [*Sledstvie po delu dekabristov*], writes that, compared with the notes from "participants of the subsequent generations of revolutionaries, right up to and including the Soviet dissidents, that describe in the greatest detail the nature of their interrogations, how they answered, and what coercive measures were applied to them" (Edelman 2010, 15), "it did not even seem to occur" to Obolenskii and Ryleev "to use this opportunity for practical purposes." Instead, "they exchanged verses and poured out their soulful experiences to each other" (ibid., 17). For example, Obolenskii remembered Ryleev's poems "I am sickened here, as if in a foreign land" ["Mne toshno zdes', kak na chuzhbine"] and "O dear friend, how distinct is your voice" ["O milyi drug, kak vniaten golos tvoi"] and conveyed them in his memoirs. Edelman finds it productive to examine this behavior by addressing the impact of "literary stereotypes on the behavior and actions of people from a particular era" (ibid., 16), referring to Yuri M. Lotman's work on the Decembrists (Lotman 1975). For people of the Decembrist generation, Edelman notes, different types of heroes were established in that era's typical literature of Sentimentalism and Romanticism: "A hero might suffer in prison, might stand valiantly in the face of a triumphant enemy, deliver a monologue in the high style (often inappropriately so from the perspective of everyday common sense), and courageously greet his execution" (Edelman 2010, 16). These are literary ideals and philosophical arguments: a belief in the spirit of the times, a vision of oneself as its instrument, and an acceptance of one's sacrificial role in the name of realizing the true spirit of freedom, that largely create the worldview and define the behavior of the Decembrists while also constituting the era itself.

The Decembrist image comes together rather quickly both in literary and scholarly works. Naturally, this pertains first of all to Pushkin's relationship with the Decembrists and the tenth chapter of his novel *Eugene Onegin*, only fragments of which have reached us: Pushkin destroyed the text. Thirty years later, Lev Tolstoy wrote three chapters of a novel *The Decembrists* before he began working on *War and Peace*. The earlier novel remained incomplete. Hessen notes that Tolstoy halted at the events preceding the revolt, the era of the Napoleonic Wars.[4] At nearly the same time, Nekrasov wrote his poems *The Grandfather*, about a Decembrist who has returned home from Siberia, and *Russian Women*, about the Decembrists' wives. Pyotr Gnedich's play *The Decembrist* enjoyed some success. The novels of Dmitrii Merezhkovskii *Alexander I* (1913) and *December 14th* (1918) drew sharp criticism from Hessen. This is not surprising, given that Hessen, as I have already noted, was a revolutionary, and Merezhkovskii a conservative monarchist. The Decembrist image would remain a dominant one throughout the culture, associated primarily, Edelman notes, with the fact that:

> the Decembrist theme was developed, naturally enough, by researchers opposed to the autocracy; Herzen's publications already surround the Decembrists with the haloes of heroes and martyrs to freedom,[5] and they were enthusiastically revered by representatives from every liberal and revolutionary circle in Russian society. Since then, a sublime, somewhat idealized and romanticized attitude toward the Decembrists has become deeply rooted in Russian culture, and they became perceived as the model of selfless service to the interests of the people, as a *moral yardstick*. (Edelman 2010, 21–22; italics mine)

For these reasons, the Decembrist might be described as an *aristos* [ἄριστος]: the aristocrat, the poet, the best man possible. Hessen fully shares this kind of idealized image of the Decembrists and draws the following conclusion in his research: "And so even now, having traveled so far past the Decembrists, we reverentially honor their memory, the memory of these first revolutionaries, the revolutionary Romantics, the paladins of freedom who were able to die so beautifully for their ideas" (Gessen 1926, 295). He represents the Decembrist as a revolutionary, a poet, and the moral yardstick of his era: as *aristos*. This image would also become a beacon for their successors in the October Revolution in 1917. Located somewhere between the image of the aristos, the participant of the Decembrist Revolt, and the revolutionary artist of October 1917 is the figure of Alexander Ivanovich Herzen, who embodied the image of the aristocrat, the bohemian, and the revolutionary, and who provided the theory for, and vitally contributed to the emergence of, the revolutionary artist, as I will discuss below.

Pointing the Way to Artistry: The Aristocrat, Revolutionary, and Writer Alexander Herzen

The Decembrist Revolt and the Decembrists themselves in Russian cultural self-consciousness are strongly linked to the name of Alexander Ivanovich Herzen (1812–1870), an aristocrat, world-famous writer and revolutionary, bohemian figure, and ideal for many of Russia's revolutionaries. Herzen is universally recognized as the successor to the Decembrists' Romantic ideas and deeds, and he linked their revolt and execution to his own spiritual awakening to the revolutionary struggle for freedom. He himself was a moral yardstick, the *aristos* of revolution, and it is no accident that Sergei Hessen calls him a messiah of the twentieth-century revolutionaries. At the same time, Herzen was under the influence of Hegel's and Marx's philosophy and interpretation of historical objectivity, though the revolutionary events in France in 1848 convinced him that he himself could not become an instrument of revolution, leading him to complete disillusionment both with revolution and with history: "What is all this, ultimately? A joke?" asks the Romantic and Decembrist successor Herzen. "Everything we cherished, that we loved, that we strived for, that we sacrificed to. Life deceived us. History deceived us" (Gertsen 1969a, 726). Herzen faces a difficult choice: elemental life, or reason. He chooses "fara da me" [to bet on oneself] (ibid., 728). He writes the logical confession of a man "of doubt and negation," one who knows the "sickness of truth," weeding out "the root of truth that my whole life cherished" in a number of articles on the history "of this disease through which the insulted idea struggled" in his collection *From the Other Shore*: "By them, I pursued the last idols in myself, and, with irony, I took vengeance on them for the pain and deceit; I did not mock my neighbor, but myself" (Gertsen 1969a, 727). Herzen is disillusioned with history, and with life, but not with reason, and this changes his view of history:

> Neither nature nor history *goes anywhere*, and therefore they are prepared to go *everywhere* [...] Having neither a plan nor a given theme, nor any inevitable outcome, the shabby improvisation of history is ready to go with everyone, everyone can add his verses to it. Human involvement is great and full of poetry, it's a kind of creativity. (Gertsen 1969b, 199–200)

Herzen opens history to creativity, to the participation of its most gifted poets, revolutionaries, and bohemians. Elemental life is shaped and acquires meaning in their work, while history itself has no higher meaning except as the result of their thoughts and ideas. It is this vision of history and life that would become the basis for the worldview of the successors to Herzen's ideas about revolution.

In his Master's thesis *Herzen's Historiosophy* [*Istoricheskaia filosofia Gertsena*], which he defended in Prague in 1923 (the full text has not been located: only the conclusion has survived), Georges (Georgii) Florovsky analyzes Herzen's position. Florovsky was of the generation of the October Revolution, and, to comprehend its significance, he considers it necessary to turn to Herzen. Florovsky analyzes contemporaneous theories for explaining the historical process, taking the problem of history beyond the limits of conceptual formulations in the categories of rational philosophy and examining it in the categories of phenomenology and irrational philosophy. Florovsky traces how, in the history of ideas, historiosophical rationalism, or logicism, historiosophical naturalistic fatalism, and the theory of progress, that is, of the logical predetermination of history, have all been rejected and overcome. He believes this process is related to the Neo-Kantian removal of the laws of causality from the interpretation of history. Florovsky shows that logicism is actually overcome by Herzen himself with the aid of Romantic irrationalism, and he identifies a weakness of Herzen's Romanticism in its opposition to logicism. This weakness consists of the fact that Herzen, "*whose meditations* have reached the impasse of the irrationalistic, and *having thus exposed by his own example the deep flaws of Romantic speculation* [...] posed the issue of a new ascent with lively brilliance, that is, the problem of synthesizing opposites that are irreconcilable either on the basis of pure reason, the abstract and the universal, or on the basis of pure volitional feeling, the solitary and the personal" (Florovsky 1997, 255), which leads him through tormented skepticism to "discord and impassability" (ibid., 251), to "ultimate anarchic individualism" (ibid., 253). Florovsky negatively assesses Herzen's idea of history's openness to creativity as an unresolved issue. Florovsky applies the pluralism of methodologies and worldviews, or Herzen's "discord and impassability," to his description of Russia's pre-revolutionary situation in the early twentieth century. The writer Ivan Bunin interprets these events with a quote from Jeremiah:

Among My people are the wicked; they lie in wait, like bird catchers, press close to the earth, set snares, and catch people. And My people love this. Hear this, earth: I will bring destruction onto My people, *the fruit of their own schemes.* (Bunin 2004, 57; see Jeremiah 5: 26, 31; 6: 19)

Meanwhile, Florovsky replenishes the revolutionary era's pluralism of methodologies and worldviews in his own work by indicating yet another path proposed by Herzen's primary opponent, Fyodor Dostoevsky. According to Florovsky, "the antinomic confrontation between the 'meaning of history' and the 'meaning of life'" was overcome in Dostoevsky's "*consciousness*" only "by *the way* that the very notion of the 'meaning of history' was stratified: alongside a 'cognized' meaning that is logically defined by the coordinates of causality, of immanent purposefulness, there emerges a 'believed-in' meaning, a meaning intuitively grasped when inspired by the timeless experience of real communion with God" (Florovsky 1997, 252). Thus, instead of logical denial, he proclaims man's creative activity, and instead of revolution, a creative reconstruction of reality in "free theurgy." Florovsky seeks to unite the concept of culture with the "believed-in meaning of history," which can include "surprises," "fractures" (one might even say revolutions), and "curves," in short, what Florovsky follows Herzen in calling "creativity" (cf. Florovsky 1995, 35–36). Does this mean that Florovsky considers "mutational eruptions" to be "causeless"? No, because there is an incomprehensible "harmony" in the "cosmic world": "'Improvisations' have their own immanent needs" (ibid., 42), which are mystically comprehended and expressed in Christian historiosophy. But did the idealistic Romantics and materialistic revolutionaries not believe in the higher meaning of freedom and progress? History's openness to individual causality and creativity means that every event in history is the consequence of man implementing his ideals and plans, of which there can be many, including revolution. He who carries out his revolutionary project in the early twentieth century is its creator and performer, its poet and artist on the theatrical stage of history.

The Theatricality of Revolution and the Bohemian

In the early twentieth century, history was examined not only as the inevitable movement of spirit (G.W.F. Hegel) or economic laws (K. Marx), but also as a sum of statistical data (A.A. Chuprov, *Essays on Statistical Theory* [*Ocherki po teorii statistiki*], and "interpretation of the spontaneous (irrational) givenness of the historical fact" (S.I. Hessen), along with "shabby improvisation" (A.I. Herzen) and "believed-in meaning" (F.M. Dostoevsky). This diversity of methodologies suggests various exemplars, types of participants and creators. There is an entire gallery of heroes: the "new," "reforged," "supreme," "super," and "Soviet" man. The abundant presence of new people is primarily related to a feature of the whole twentieth century, a vying to present one's images and ideals: twentieth-century man put himself on the same level as the world and God, treated them as equals, and saw himself as a new creator. Konstantin Chkheidze introduces a whole gallery of "molders," creators of new people in Russian literature in the early twentieth century. He schematizes the literary protagonists of that era, outlining the transformation of "the ideal of man" and society. Here is how he singles out one vector of development:

> the beasts and human wolves of Vs. Ivanov and Pilnyak. The beast heroes of Babel, Ar. Veselii, and in part Libedenskii. […] The heroes with a human face: Tikhonov, Svetlov, Fadeev, Gladkov. […] The hero-creators, creators of a new life, also Gladkov, Panferov, Karavaeva, Sholokhov. […] In their own way, the crowning achievement of this movement, so to speak, are these molders of life, people who dreamed of its, life's, integrated transformation. Among them: Bely, Khlebnikov in part, Esenin ("Inoniia"), Mayakovsky. (Chkheidze 2003, 395)

The world-feeling of early twentieth-century man was aptly conveyed by Andrei Bely:

> In those years I felt an intersection within myself: verse, prose, philosophy, music. I knew that one without the other was a flaw, but I did not know how to combine completeness. I never figured out who I was. A theoretician, a critic and propagandist, a poet, a prose writer, a composer? Some kind of power jostled around in my chest, giving me confidence that everything was available to me and it all depended on me to shape myself; I saw my approaching fate as a piano on which I was hammering out a symphony. (Bely 1990, 24)

Revolution is likewise a theatrical stage where politicians, poets, and artists play the various roles they have chosen, and the revolutionary events performed by bohemians are full of theatricality. Revolution is conceived and carried out as a global event, therefore the way it is perceived and its characteristics are typical not only of Russia, as Victor Klemperer showed in relation to the Munich Revolution of 1919, defining its essential features as "a theatricality of political events," where "politics seems less like a profession than a theatrical stage where dreams (and nightmares) are playing out" (Klemperer 2015, 7).

The typical-exemplary figure in Russia who personified both the bohemian and the revolutionary artist was Fyodor Avgustovich Stepun (1884–1965). Furthermore, he also provided the theoretical basis for the concept of artistic "many-souledness." Stepun "in terms of his genealogical roots […] traced himself back to the Baltic states and to France," writes Nikolai Poltoratskii, "in his everyday life, to the irrevocably vanished Russia of aristocratic landowners, in religion, to Protestantism and Orthodoxy, and in his mental and spiritual life, to German Romanticism, post-Kantian critique, and that aggregate of our pre-revolutionary life after which the name of 'Russian cultural renaissance' of the early twentieth century has already become consolidated" (Poltoratskii 2017, 680). In addition to his aforementioned participation in issuing *Logos*, which provoked heated debates in Russia's intellectual circles, Stepun became more broadly known for a publication entitled *From the Letters of an*

Ensign-Artilleryman [*Iz pisem praporshchika-artillerista*], whose first part appeared in the journal *Severnye zapiski* [*Northern Notes*] 1916 under the pseudonym N. Lugin (Stepun 2000). Stepun would greet the February Revolution of 1917 as an officer in the Russian army, and his published letters from the front made him a popular and active participant in subsequent revolutionary events.

International fame followed Stepun's memoirs, *What Was and What Might Have Been* [*Byvshee i nesbyvsheesia*], written and published in Munich in 1947–1950. After the publication of the second volume in 1948, reviewer Andreas Hügel offered this brief philosophical characterization of Stepun: "We might say of Fyodor Stepun, a sociologist and philosopher of the Vladimir Solovyov school, that he acted wisely and cleverly in allowing time for his memories to mature to the present day, which is the only reason he can reveal his special gift for elevating the past to the timeless."[6] Stepun's recourse to the genre of memoir was related to his inability to find work in academia and politics during the war and early post-war years, which forced him to turn to literature and literary criticism. Our further examination of Stepun's views will also be based largely on his memoirs.

Given his belief in the many-souledness of actors and the ability of poets and philosophers to penetrate the depths of being and to create ideals and values, Stepun could not help participating in the events of the revolution. He is an actor-philosopher, a hero-molder of events. All bohemians see themselves as spiritual leaders, directors as well as performers of the revolution who create certain scenes and place themselves in them. It is primarily himself that Stepun sees, describes, and comprehends in these events. "And I did this," Stepun remembers. "Until now, I cannot without remorse think about my speeches on the front, which I often ended with this dramatic phrase: 'Petersburg has given us freedom, and we will earn victory for Russia!'" (Stepun 1948, 102).

After greeting the revolution, Stepun did not remain fixed but constantly changed his views and roles in the revolution from simple support of the revolutionaries during his stay in Heidelberg in 1909–1910 (here it is worth noting a famous passage involving the organization of a charitable dinner for the revolution's needs) to the ensign-artilleryman's enthusiastic welcoming of news of the February Revolution in Petrograd in 1917: "Oh, if only that turns out to be true!" (Stepun 2000, 190), only to later designate it "a mix of disease and crime" (Stepun 1948, 102). In self-critical summation, he adds, "The months of the February Revolution [...] I remember as a time of evil betrayal of my true self to the 'subject of will,' with which it shared only a distant kinship" (ibid., 102). In his memoirs, Stepun presents himself in various roles: the young Tolstoyan, the *Logos* Westernizer, the ensign-artilleryman, the delegate to the All-Russian Council of Workers, the serviceman under the War Ministry, the head of the "State Demonstrative Theater," the gentleman peasant, the "covert White Guard," the Slavophile publicist, the professor, and the Dresden bohemian. What made this possible?

Stepun's main theoretical position is dividing reality into *life* and *creatorship* from the perspective of the individual. Life is "soulful presence and soulful movement," or experiences; creatorship is the structuring of experiences by products of the spirit, or by values. It is in the creative, aesthetic sphere that Stepun lays out the groundwork that allows him to find an explanation and justification for his behavior. Primarily, it is the fact that creatorship demonstrates the diminutiveness of life, its various forms and paths that must, however, "be traversed in all directions, *but with the sole purpose of decisively rejecting them as a path*" (Stepun 2005, 125). That is, you can follow whichever path you choose, and with whomever you choose, knowing and acknowledging that this may be a mistake, though the mistake is not yours but the mechanism of a *diminished being*. Stepun's personal position and his view of himself in historical reality are more unambiguously formulated in his article "The Nature of the Actor's Soul (On Philistinism, Mysticism, and Artistry)" ["Priroda akterskoi dushi (O meshchanstve, mistitsizme i artistizme)"], in which, proceeding from the idea that the individual's soul is divided into two spheres, life and creatorship, and depending on the ratio between them, he defines three soulful modes or types of worldviews: the philistine, the mystical, or the artistic. The philistine soul is unable to delve deeper into either creatorship or life, therefore it does not consider any contradiction between these spheres a tragedy, and it creates no new forms, merely imitating existing ones. The mystical soul rejects the form in favor of experiencing an ineffable unity that in creatorship is dissociated by the form. The artistic soul manifests itself in an endless variety of shapes or roles "that constitute it as such." For Stepun, many-souledness means "a sin of betrayal" in relation to the desire to "die in facelessness," but he would give preference to "unconditional many-souledness" (see Stepun 2009).

Therefore, it is not that Stepun perceives the reality of the revolution aesthetically "as if it were reality," but that Stepun himself behaves like a literary character for whom participation in the revolution is only a game or a role: "When I was defending my resolutions indefatigably in the trenches and in committees and I was calling on everyone to fight for the Motherland and the Revolution, for the first time in my life I felt myself not who I really was" (Stepun 1948, 102). He writes about "the concealing of my own self" (ibid., 103), that is, accepting only roles and retreating into what was apparently not his self. Following this position, Stepun cannot avoid being a "self-delighted hero," shaping his experiences in various roles. This kind of artistic many-souledness provides Stepun with unlimited opportunities to flirt with reality, even to the point of opportunism, as it appears in a letter to Paul Tillich dated September 29, 1948. At that time, Stepun was terrified of the "Soviets," because he had delivered some three hundred lectures on Russia and Bolshevism as an ardent denouncer and adversary of the latter ever since he was expelled from Soviet Russia and prior to publishing his book *The Image of Russia and the Face of the Russian Revolution* [*Lik Rossii i litso russkoi revoliutsii*] in 1934. As one of those exiled from Russia by the philosophers' ship, he was considered a counterrevolutionary, and his two brothers who remained in Russia were arrested and disappeared into the camps. Stepun's fears were thus not unwarranted. He tried to convince Tillich, who had left for New York in 1933, to help him immigrate to the United States, and also tried to secure a position in Heidelberg, but to no avail. This is an opportune moment to remember the bohemians' flirtations with the proletariat, as Klemperer noted in his assessment of the bohemians' recasting of themselves as "spiritual laborers" (Klemperer 2015, 47). In the aforementioned letter to Tillich, Stepun wrote, "In emigration, I abstained from all active practical politics, because I considered them meaningless; I was subjected to fierce attacks from the right and was labeled an *ultraviolet communist* [italics mine.—J.M.], but none of this serves to legitimize the Soviets" (Stepun 2011, 156). Later, he has already begun to relativize his attitude toward the revolution and the Bolsheviks, no longer seeing them as a mix of "disease and crime," as he had written in his memoirs published that same year: "Nevertheless," Stepun writes in his letter, "Bolshevism was and remains the *creative insanity* [italics are mine] of the era, while national socialism, on the other hand, seemed only hastily assembled nonsense with no future" (Stepun 2011, 158). Is this just a flirtation with the proletarian regime, a mention of himself with reference to the right, and, consequently, an agreement with those who would define him as not even a light pink communist, much less a red, but an *ultraviolet* one? It does not seem so. There is a basis for recognizing the initial diminishment of any role that is explained not by one's own lack of responsibility or principles, but by the sinfulness of being. Fortunately, Fyodor Avgustovich did not have to play this role: instead, he became a brilliant memoirist and literary critic.

In his article "Philosopher-Artist" ["Filosof-artist"], Nikolai Poltoratskii offers an evaluation of Stepun's personality and work, writing that Stepun accurately says in his memoirs of those figures of pre-revolutionary culture he knew: "each man was his own construct" (Poltoratskii 2017, 683). Stepun's definition might be theoretically juxtaposed with the typical-exemplary personality in Rickert. Poltoratskii applies it to Stepun himself: he defines Stepun as a model image and finds in him a duality whose deepest foundation is the insurmountable opposition between life and creatorship. "Fedor Stepun's spiritual orientation is philosophical artistry, not philosophical aestheticism," and Poltoratskii therefore believes that Stepun himself in an artistic self-portrait appears as a "*philosopher-artist*" (Poltoratskii 2017, 684). In other words, Poltoratskii also characterizes Stepun's personality as artistic. Thus, it could be argued that the twentieth-century revolutionary bohemian fashioned an image not of the aristocrat as moral yardstick, but of the artist who preferred the second of the two paths Valery Bryusov once described as leading "to crucifixion or to suffering small whips" (Briusov 1990, 167).

In the hundred years that have passed, global estimates of the October Revolution range contradictorily from enthusiasm to hostility. The centennial compels us to reassess it in Russian society as well. At the same time, the revolutionary paradigm remains not only relevant, but even immediately current. How should we see revolution today, and what examples, personalities, and constructs should represent it? It is evident that today's revolutions, even more so than in Stepun's time, represent the theatricalization of politics, the thoroughly planned staging of scenes that are easily transmitted via the internet and smartphones. The public expects drama, even tragedy, but instead gets farce, a transformation of revolution into buffoonery. Nonetheless, the last remaining bohemian revolutionary on the Russian stage, the author Eduard Limonov, who does not, however, represent the *typical-exemplary* personality of modern revolution passed away in March 2020.

Conclusion

Paradoxically, even those with opposing worldviews agree in their assessments of the revolution, both "people of faith, people of love" and "people of doubt and negation" (cf. Gertsen 1969a, 727). For example, in his book *Cursed Days* [*Okaiannye dni*], Ivan Bunin exclaims, "How identical they are, all these revolutions! [...] It all repeats, mainly because *one of the most distinctive features* of revolutions is this rabid thirst for games, hypocrisy, posturing, and buffoonery. The ape awakens in the man" (Bunin 2004, 80; italics mine). In *My Past and Thoughts*, Herzen writes that history "needs the insane as bread-starter, and does not care what happens to them once they come to their senses; it uses them, then lets them live out the rest of their lives in nursing homes," sick with "offended thought" (Gertsen 1969a, 726–727). Following this interpretation of history in Bunin and Herzen, it might be said that the revolutionary paradigm has an enduring significance, and that revolution will always find a way, since the insane will always be with us, as well as those with a passion for play and buffoonery, for posturing and apishness. To clarify this interpretation of history as shabby improvisation and the individual's ability to create his own ideals and idols and to implement them, I will turn to Nikolai Danilevskii, author of the theory of cultural-historical types, who rejects the idea of universal history. He writes: "progress [...] is not about going entirely in a single direction [...], but in traveling through the entire field that constitutes the space of historical activity of mankind in every direction" (Danilevskii 1991, 109). A century ago, Russia approached the road of economic determinism and traveled down it, showing everyone its falsity, its "sinfulness" as "the wrong path," as Fyodor Stepun would have said, negatively assessing, like Nikolai Berdyaev, any cultural creatorship implemented in reality. This does not, however, mean abandoning revolution as a return to the initial cultural historical situation of a diversity of realities and methodological pluralism.

When we conceptualize both past and ongoing revolutionary events, we maintain a persistent perception of their theatricality, which was initially associated with a bohemianism able to penetrate the essence of things, to live through and to exercise its ideals. The Decembrist embodies the image of *aristos*, the moral yardstick for one's life and deeds. Rejecting the objectivity of the spirit of history and recognizing the spontaneity of experiences, creatively reformulated through the *artist's* many-souledness, only strengthen the staginess and stylization of revolutions.

It is difficult to say which images and faces from today's revolutions will persist over the next century, or which poets' voices will remain heard, but our opportunity to find parallels today with revolutionary events of one or two centuries ago, even while maintaining contradictory assessments of them, allows us to continue thinking about the vitality of the revolutionary paradigm.

Translated by Brad Damaré

NOTES

1. I consider the revolutionary paradigm as beginning with the original scientific meaning of the word "revolution" (turning, rotation, circulation) in Nicolaus Copernicus' work *De revolutionibus orbium coelestium* (1543), which was later used in the sense of a shift in society and worldview and established by the events of the French Revolution. Here I return to the original meaning of the word "revolution" as a rotation, a return to an original position, to the true or original course of history, which corresponds to a return to Russia's centuries-old history.
2. Rickert acted as dissertation advisor for S.I. Hessen (1887–1950) and had a decisive impact on the formation of his concept of theorizing history.
3. The Silver Age ended due to the forced silence of open polemics, a result of the activities of Glavlit, the Main Directorate for Literature and Publishing, established on June 6, 1922 by government decree for the purpose of "unifying all forms of censorship of printed works."
4. Here Hessen cites the editor of Tolstoy's 1913 collected works, P.I. Biriukov (cf. Hessen 1926, 275).
5. One example might be the 1860 London edition of K.F. Ryleev's *Meditations* [*Dumy*], with a dedication by N.P. Ogarev ("In Memory of Ryleev"), published by the Free Russian Press, which Herzen founded in 1853 and managed together with Ogarev to promote the printing of Russian books otherwise banned by the tsar (see Ryleev 1860).
6. A. Hügel, "Rezension." *Neue Zeitung*, Munich. This review is quoted in the dust jacket for the second part of Stepun's memoirs (1948).

BIBLIOGRAPHY

Bely, Andrei. 1990. *Nachalo veka. Vospominaniia. V 3 knigakh*. Book 2. Moscow: Khudozhestvennaia literatura.

Berdyaev, Nikolai A. 2007. Alexei Stepanovich Khomiakov. In *Konstantin Leontiev. Ocherk iz istorii russkoi religioznoi mysli. Aleksei Stepanovich Khomiakov*, 226–445. Moscow: Ast; Ast Moskva; Khranitel'.

Bestuzhev, Nikolai A. 1919. *Kondratii Fedorovich Ryleev. Vospominaniia N.A. Bestuzheva*. Moscow: Al'tsiona.

Bibikhin, Vladimir V. 2006. *Aleksei Fedorovich Losev. Sergei Sergeevich Averintsev*. Moscow: Institut filosofii, teologii i istorii sv. Fomy.

Briusov, Valerii Ya. 1990. "Pis'mo k A. Belomu. Selo Antonovka, 1904." In *Nachalo veka. Vospominaniia. V 3 knigakh*. Book 2, by Andrei Bely, 166-167. Moscow: Khudozhestvennaia literatura.

Bunin, Ivan A. 2004. *Okaiannye dni*. In *Okaiannye dni. Nesvoevremennye mysli*, by Ivan A. Bunin and Maksim Gorky, edited and with an introduction by Oleg N. Mikhailov, 50–172. Moscow: Airis-Press.

Chkheidze, Konstantin A. 2003. Pis'mo k N.A. Setnitskomu. 7 dekabria 1932 g. Praga. In *Iz istorii filosofsko-esteticheskoi mysli 1920–1930-kh godov. Vypusk 1. N.A. Setnitskii*, 394–396. Moscow: IMLI RAN.

Danilevskii, Nikolai Ya. 1991. *Rossiia i Evropa*. Moscow: Kniga.

Edelman, Ol'ga V. 2010. *Sledstvie po delu dekabristov*. "Selecta" Series. Moscow: REGNUM.

Ern, Vladimir F. 1911. *Bor'ba za Logos. Opyty filosofskie i kriticheskie*. Moscow: Put'.

Florovsky, Georgii V. 1995. O narodakh neistoricheskikh (Strana otsov i strana detei). In *Mir Rossii-Evraziia. Antologiia*, ed. Lidiia I. Novikova and Irina N. Sizemskaia, 27–42. Moscow: Vysshaia shkola.

———. 1997. Conclusion to *Istoricheskaia filosofiia Gertsena*. In Appendix to "Utrachennaia dissertatsiia Florovskogo," by Modest A. Kolerov. In *Issledovaniia po istorii russkoi mysli. Ezhegodnik za 1997 g.*, ed. Modest A. Kolerov, 249–257. St. Petersburg: Aleteiia.

Gertsen [Herzen], Alexander I. 1969a. *Byloe i dumy. Chasti 1–5*. Edited by A. Kozlovskii and A. Krakovskaia. Series 2 of "Biblioteka vsemirnoi literatury," Literatura XIX veka. Vol. 73. Moscow: Khudozhestvennaia literatura.

———. 1969b. *Byloe i dumy. Chasti 6–8*. Edited by S. Chulkov. Series 2 of "Biblioteka vsemirnoi literatury," Literatura XIX veka. Vol. 74. Moscow: Khudozhestvennaia literatura.

Gessen, Sergei I. 1911, September 5. Neoslavianofil'stvo v filosofii. *Rech'*, 243.

Gessen, Sergei Y. (Sergei Iosifovich). 1926. *Dekabristy pered sudom istorii (1825–1925)*. With an Introduction by Boris L. Modzalevskii. Leningrad-Moscow: Petrograd.

Hessen, Sergius. 1909a. Herzen. In *Vom Messias. Kulturphilosophische Essays von Richard Kroner, Nikolai von Bubnoff, Georg Mehlis, Sergius Hessen, Friedrich Steppuhn*, 42–59. Leipzig: Verlag von Wilhelm Engelmann.

———. 1909b. *Über individuelle Kausalität. Inaugural-Dissertation zur Erlangung der philosophischen Doktorwürde der philosophischen Fakultät der Albert-Ludwigs-Universität in Freiburg i. B*. Freiburg im Breisgau: Albert-Ludwigs-Universität in Freiburg im Breisgau.

Klemperer, Victor. 2015. *Man möchte immer weinen und lachen in einem. Revolutionstagebuch 1919*. With a foreword by Christopher Clark and a historical essay by Wolfram Wette. Berlin: Aufbau Verlag.

Lotman, Yuri M. 1975. Dekabrist v povsednevnoi zhizni (Bytovoe povedenie kak istoriko-psikhologicheskaia kategoriia). In *Literaturnoe nasledie dekabristov*, 25–74. Leningrad: Nauka.

Ogarev, Nikolai P. 1975. Posviashchenie. Pamiati Ryleeva. In Kondratii F. Ryleev, *Dumy*, edited by Leonid G. Frizman, 124–125. Series "Literaturnye pamiatniki." Moscow: Nauka.

Poltoratskii, Nikolai P. 2017. Filosof-artist. In Fyodor A. Stepun, *Bol'shevizm i khristianskaia ekzistentsiia. Izbrannye sochineniia*, edited by Vladimir K. Kantor, 680–684. Series "Pis'mena vremeni." Moscow-St. Petersburg: Tsentr gumanitarnykh initsiativ.

Rickert, Heinrich. 1896. *Die Grenzen der naturwissenschaftlichen Begriffsbildung. Eine logische Einleitung in die historischen Wissenschaften*. Freiburg i. B.-Leipzig: Akademische Verlagsbuchhandlung von J.C.B. Mohr (Paul Siebeck).

Ryleev, Kondratii F. 1860. *Dumy. Stikhotvoreniia*, with an introduction by Nikolai P. Ogarev. Izdanie Iskandera. London: Trübner & Co.

———. 1919. *Otryvok iz poemy "Nalivaiko"* In *Kondratii Fedorovich Ryleev. Vospominaniia N.A. Bestuzheva*, by Nikolai A. Bestuzhev, 5. Moscow: Al'tsiona.

Steppuhn, Friedrich. 1910. *Wladimir Solowjew. Zeitschrift für Philosophie und philosophische Kritik* 138 (1–2): 1–79; 239–291. Leipzig: Johann Ambrosius Barth.

Stepun, Fyodor A. 1910. Tragediia tvorchestva (Fridrikh Shlegel'). In *Logos. Mezhdunarodnyi ezhegodnik po filosofii kul'tury*, vol. 1, 171–196. Musaget: Moscow.

Stepun, Fedor. 1948. *Vergangenes und Unvergängliches. Aus meinem Leben. Zweiter Teil. 1914–1917*. München-Kempten: Josef Kösel Verlag.

Stepun, Fyodor A. 2005. Zhizn' i tvorchestvo. In *Logos. Mezhdunarodnyi ezhegodnik po filosofii kul'tury* (3–4): 71–126. Reprint. Moscow: Territoriia budushchego.

———. 2009. Priroda akterskoi dushi (O meshchanstve, mistitsizme i artistizme). In *Zhizn' i tvorchestvo. Izbrannye sochineniia*, with an introduction and commentaries by Vladimir K. Kantor, 186–212. Moscow: Astrel.

Stepun, Fedor A. 2011. Brief von Fedor Stepun an Paul Tillich. München, 29. September 1948. *Journal for the History of Modern Theology/Zeitschrift für Neuere Theologiegeschichte* 18 (1): 155–160. (Special issue: *Paul Tillich im Dialog mit dem Kultur- und Religionsphilosophen Fedor Stepun. Eine Korrespondenz im Zeichen von Bolschewismus und Nationalsozialismus*, edited and with an introduction by Alf Christophersen).

Stepun, Fyodor A. (N. Lugin). 2000. *Iz pisem praporshchika-artillerista*. Tomsk: Vodolei.

CHAPTER 6

Kant and Kantianism in Russia: A Historical Overview

Alexei N. Krouglov

INTRODUCTION

The critical reception of Immanuel Kant began in Russia no later than 1789–1790. In 1789, Nikolai M. Karamzin visited Kant in Königsberg and described the experience to a general audience in 1791 (Karamzin 1791, 155–160). A year earlier the famed Königsberg philosopher was mentioned in a Latin speech at Moscow University (Mellmann 1790, 38). In 1795–1797, the first course on Kantian philosophy was taught at Moscow University (Krouglov 2009b, 517–529), and in 1803 the first Russian translation of Kant's work appeared. Kant's philosophical development includes several interesting episodes, such as the Seven Years' War, Kant's Russian citizenship from 1758 to 1762, and his contacts with Russian officers and students in the early period of his work (Krouglov 2016a, 149–164); however, they tell us little about Kantianism in Russia.

In fact, the very term *Kantianism* needs clarification. If we think of Kantianism as a philosophical trend that shares the basic ideas of the critical philosophy, as say in Germany (Johann Schultz, Christian Gottfried Schütz, etc.), then this kind of Kantianism never occurred in Russia. The individual Kantians who worked in Russia were never united by a common philosophical program—Johann Wilhelm Ludwig Mellmann (Krouglov 2015, 365–376) and Valentin F. Asmus (Zhuchkov and Blauberg 2010). This is the essential

A. N. Krouglov (✉)
Russian State University for the Humanities, Moscow, Russia

© The Author(s), under exclusive license to Springer Nature Switzerland AG 2021
M. F. Bykova et al. (eds.), *The Palgrave Handbook of Russian Thought*,
https://doi.org/10.1007/978-3-030-62982-3_6

difference between Russian Kantianism and Russian Schellingianism or Hegelianism, which did exist as relatively cohesive philosophical trends.

Although neo-Kantianism was never as popular in Russia as it was in Western Europe, the scope of its influence and the number of adherents it found are current topics of debate. The achievements of neo-Kantianism in Russia with regard to the development of Kant's ideas and the popularization of his work are still relatively modest. Nevertheless, it is unlikely that any other philosophical doctrine is so comprehensive, ubiquitous, and monumental in Russian philosophy and culture. In this sense, only Plato rivals the Königsberg philosopher. The breadth of Kant's influence includes suicides linked to reading the *Critique of Pure Reason* in the end of the nineteenth century, shootings over disputes about the categorical imperative at the beginning of the twenty-first century, portraits of Kant carried by the opposition during anti-Putin demonstrations of the last decade, popular Kantian souvenirs in Kaliningrad, and wedding photographs taken at Kant's tomb near the Königsberg Cathedral.

Thus, reception of Kant in Russia is not a highly specialized form of Kantianism, but a three-century-long, ongoing philosophical dialogue and debate with Kant in various philosophical traditions and contexts. This includes practically all philosophical disciplines, university departments, and theological seminaries and academies. Outside of the academic community, Kant is discussed in popular magazines, journalism, cinema, and even in politics. The influence of Kant's philosophy in Russia almost always implies polemics, criticism, and the desire to correct or develop certain theses advanced by the German philosopher.

At the end of the eighteenth century, Kant was unable to completely avoid various German epigones who were at times fanatical, dogmatic, and parochial. However, the fact that Kant taught for a very long time in the Albertina[1] and did not produce a single dogmatic Kantian speaks for itself. His pupil Johann Gottfried Herder recalled that Kant "pleasantly insisted on independent thinking" (Herder 1881, 404–405). This paradoxical pedagogic strategy contains something inherent in the very essence of Kant's philosophy. The fact that there were no such dogmatic followers in Russia is an indication that Kantian philosophy was received in the spirit of its creator. In this sense, some Russian critics of Kant are more Kantian in spirit than those who dogmatically and uncritically uphold his tenets.

The above aspects of the reception of Kant's philosophy are what make the figure of Kant in Russia so multifaceted and significant. One area where this is clearly evident is Russian fiction, where Kant has played a major role from the late eighteenth century to the present day.[2] Some Russian authors mentioned Kant's name sporadically, some made him the protagonist of their works,[3] some devoted their poems to him, and still others expressed their assessments in the epistolary heritage or in literary-critical articles. A romantic and a dreamer, a frail intellectual elder, a teacher of humankind, an egoist and philistine individualist, an all-encompassing thinker and aesthete, an exceptional rationalist and mystic—these are just some of the characteristics attributed to Kant in Russian prose and poetry.

A significant contribution to the popularization of Kant in Russia was made by Russian Kant Studies, which emerged at the end of the nineteenth century. The difference between Kant Studies and Kantianism is that Kant Studies implies a scholarly and objective approach to Kant's philosophical ideas without imposing personal philosophical views. Kant Studies scholars do not necessarily subscribe to the key positions of Kant's philosophy. Moreover, some significant Kant Studies scholars have been committed anti-Kantians and, in their works on Kant, tried to show the inconsistency of certain tenets of his philosophy. Although most Kant Studies scholars were at least partially sympathetic to Kant's philosophy, it is necessary to distinguish Kant Studies from Kantianism: the former does not necessarily presuppose the latter, or vice versa.

Today, Russian Kant Studies is the most advanced subfield of the history of philosophy in contemporary Russia: hardly any subfield of the history of philosophy is comparably developed (see Davydova 1996), and this includes Schelling Studies and Hegel Studies. There are three Russian editions of Kant's collected works, including the bilingual German–Russian edition,[4] nine translations of the *Critique of Pure Reason*,[5] and an academic journal, *Kantovskii sbornik*, is published by the Immanuel Kant Baltic Federal University. No other philosopher has such a large presence in the history of philosophy in Russia.

However, there was never a clearly defined Kantian movement in Russia, and Kant's ideas are discussed mainly as part of a larger debate, often within an unambiguously negative existential interpretation. This led to the stereotype and prejudice that Russia rejected Kant entirely, that he never took to Russian soil, and that he existed only in a sinister and devilish guise (Akhutin 1990, 51–69). Contrary to this, an unbiased analysis shows that the Kantian influence in Russia has been more extensive, broad, and consistent than any other foreign philosophical doctrine of the modern era,[6] including Hegelianism and Marxism,[7] the latter of which had a much larger impact on Russian political history than philosophy proper.

The purpose of this chapter is to defend this thesis. However, extensive research would be required for a systematic corroboration of the argument. Thus, I will limit myself to identifying several areas of Kant's philosophical reception in Russia with the intention of demonstrating the depth, scope, and intensity of his influence. After a brief overview of the main stages of the reception of Kant in Russia, I will focus on the meaning of Kant's ideas within ethics and the philosophy of law. I will then consider the problem of Kantian philosophy within the context of Orthodox thought and finish by showing the role Kant has played in a number of political and historical situations in Russia.

The Main Stages of Kant's Reception in Russia

Kant was introduced to Russia during his lifetime. At the end of the eighteenth century, a number of German professors thoroughly familiar with Kantian critical philosophy had already arrived in Moscow. Kant was described warmly and kindly in Karamzin's *Letters of a Russian Traveler*, the publication of which had an enormous influence in Russia. Kant's work in ethics was translated into Russian in 1803 (Kant 1803), and the journal of the Ministry of Internal Affairs published the first detailed article about the Königsberg philosopher referring to him as a "great man" and a "Writer of the State" (Villers 1804, 125). In 1804, the Ministry of National Enlightenment (Education) approved the curriculum for the Pedagogical Institute, which recommended studying a number of subjects using Kantian textbooks. However, a tangible group of young people interested in the new philosophy and capable of deeply penetrating its subtleties had not yet emerged.

The second Kantian wave occurred shortly before the French invasion of Russia in 1812 and is associated with a new generation of German professors who arrived in the universities and theological academies of Moscow, St. Petersburg, Kazan, and Kharkov. Although it too failed to precipitate serious progress in the development of Kant's philosophy, the second wave managed to disseminate and popularize Kant's ideas. During this stage there emerged several Russian dissertations (mostly in Latin) that in one way or another referred to Kantian philosophy. They were of varying quality and appeared primarily in Kharkov due to the influence of Johann Baptist Schad. At this time, several symptomatic Russian criticisms of Kant appeared, beginning with Aleksandr S. Lubkin (Lubkin 1805), who argued in favor of the popular thesis that Kant destroyed everything but built nothing in its place.

The third wave of Russian Kantian philosophy is associated with young Russian professors who were partially educated abroad. However, before they could make any significant headway, their activity was interrupted by administrative repression. Moreover, having mostly overlooked Kant, Russian intellectuals began to gravitate toward Friedrich Schelling, who attracted them much more than Kant, because Schelling seemed loftier, less ambiguous, more poetic, and more modern.[8] For some time, the difference between Kant's and Schelling's transcendental idealism was not well understood in these circles. Kant was clearly overshadowed. Afterwards, philosophical fashions in Russia changed many times: Schelling was replaced by an obsession with Georg W.F. Hegel, positivism, Marxism, phenomenology, and so forth. However, the kaleidoscopic change of philosophical fashions had one important quality: for all the newfangled doctrines that led to the debunking and discarding of previous preoccupations, Kantian philosophy did not disappear and remained as a kind of inconspicuous constant, retaining importance despite the many changes of philosophical fashion in Russia, which is what eventually made its influence so prominent and broad.

In the mid-nineteenth century, as a result of a near prohibition against the teaching of philosophy in Russian universities under the motto "The benefits of philosophy are unproven, but its harm is" (Barsukov 1897, 21), the study of Kantian philosophy for some period moved from the universities to the theological academies of St. Petersburg, Moscow, Kazan, and Kiev. For this reason, Kant's philosophy of religion and ethics played a major role in Russia. Starting from the end of the nineteenth century, this would become true for Russian philosophy of religion outside the academies. In this environment, not only was Kantian philosophy polemicized, but also Kant's image was vilified, which was gradually reflected in Russian fiction and led to a gross image of Kant as a philistine who stank of decrepitude, death, and decay.

In the last third half of the nineteenth century, Russian Kant Studies gradually developed, and by the end of nineteenth century, an interest in Kant's philosophy was fueled by both the influence of neo-Kantianism and an appeal to Kant's philosophy by key figures of Russian philosophy, such as Vladimir S. Solovyov. Kant and German Kantian scholars began to be more actively translated and published, which made the work available to a broader Russian audience. During this period, Plato and Kant were often compared as the two poles of world philosophy—the positive and the negative, representing being and nothingness.

Beginning in the twentieth century, the Russian debate surrounding Kant acquired several new qualities. First, the poetry and literature of the Silver Age began to creatively rethink the transcendental aesthetic—Kant's doctrine of space and time. Second, beginning with Georgii V. Plekhanov, the debate about Kant's thing-in-itself, as well as his idealism and materialism, became a key part of Russian Marxism, and these disputes led to the emergence of orthodox, dogmatic positions in the second half of the twentieth century. Third, already in World War I, discussions about Kantian philosophy acquired an overt political and anti-German tone, leading to the assertion that German militarism was a reflection of Kant's philosophy. These disputes broke out with renewed vigor during World War II in 1943–1944 in connection with the publication of the third volume of *The History of Philosophy* [*Istoriia filosofii*] dedicated to German classical philosophy.

After long and bitter philosophical and political disputes following World War II, Kantian philosophy was finally legitimated within the framework of Marxist–Leninist philosophy as a predecessor and source of Marxism—classical German philosophy—in accordance with the article written by Vladimir I. Lenin (Lenin 1973, 43). Under the name invented by Friedrich Engels, the study of Kant became compulsory in all USSR philosophy departments.[9] The publication of Kant's collected works in the 1960s, as well as Kant's anniversary, were widely celebrated in 1974 in Soviet Kaliningrad (former Königsberg) and gave a new impetus to Kant Studies in the Soviet Union.[10]

After the collapse of the Soviet Union, the situation in Russia changed. Marxist–Leninist philosophy and ideologically inspired Hegelianism disappeared as if they had never existed, while Kant Studies, which had persisted all

Kant's Reception in Russian Ethics and Legal Philosophy

this time, again came to the fore and gained new relevance. However, several difficult challenges arose: how was the extensive prerevolutionary research on Kant (that had been censored or entirely banned in the Soviet period) to be incorporated into the contemporary field? How was Soviet Kant Studies to be incorporated (instead of completely rejected)? How was Russia to re-enter the world of Kant Studies, while retaining its own themes and unique point of view?

Kant's Reception in Russian Ethics and Legal Philosophy

If we exclude physical geography (for which, apart from philosophy, Kant was made a foreign member of the St. Petersburg Academy of Sciences in 1794), natural law was the only philosophically related discipline in which Kant was a major authority among Russian scholars regardless of their university affiliation—St. Petersburg, Kazan, Moscow, or Kharkov. The rise of Kantian-based natural law is related to a decree made by Alexander I on August 6, 1809. The decree required that Russian officials were obligated to take examinations in various disciplines before being promoted, among the most important of which was one on natural law. To prepare for the exams, university lectures and public courses were organized, and various textbooks were published by Russian authors, as well as translations of foreign jurists and philosophers. Government sympathy for Kant was apparently part of an attempt to stymie the "dream of equality and stormy freedom" that had fueled the French Revolution (Kolubovskii 1890, 534).

In Russia, it was actually German professors who made the first headway in Kantian natural law. In his textbook, Philipp C. Reinhard wrote that "having transformed the whole of philosophy, he introduced a new way of thinking about morality and natural law" (Reinhard 1816, 21). A similar sentiment was also expressed by Johann C. Finke: "In my beginnings, I followed the great Königsberg Philosopher although in many places I parted from him" (Finke 1816, 2). Their ideas were picked up directly by their Russian audience and students, as well as other Russian philosophers and jurists (Filimonov 1811, 3, 88; Kunitsyn 1818, 11, etc.). Let us now formulate the basic tenets of the Russian variants of natural law that are dependent on Kant's philosophy: (1) the clear distinction of the law from morality[11] and from politics[12]; (2) the distinction between internal and external freedom; (3) the establishment of law based on external freedom; (4) the derivation of natural law from pure reason without reference to religion[13]; and (5) the use of these laws as the foundation for a positive law postulated by the will of legislators.

However, by the mid-1820s, Kantian-oriented natural law was rebuffed by the conservative-minded statesmen responsible for education in Russia. They initiated administrative persecution of the supporters of natural law, fired a number of teachers from universities in Kazan, St. Petersburg, and other academic institutions, banned a number of books, and tried to achieve a general ban on natural law as such. Their position is well defined by Grigorii N. Gorodchaninov, a professor at Kazan University: "Kant believed that the

6 KANT AND KANTIANISM IN RUSSIA: A HISTORICAL OVERVIEW

source of natural law is practical reason and that the subject of natural law is external human freedom. But what is reason without the foundation of Faith?" (Gorodchaninov 1821, 87). Herein lay Kant's mistake: "man's fallen reason cannot be the *supreme rule* of our actions; the source of dispute and logomachy cannot be the *source* of morality and natural law" (Gorodchaninov 1826, 103).

Mikhail L. Magnitskii, the curator of Kazan University, went further by arguing that Kant's natural law based on reason represented:

> a complete, theoretical system of everything we saw in the French Revolution; in reality, it was the most dangerous substitute for Biblical Revelation [...] having refuted the altar of Christ, [pure reason] strikes a sacrilegious blow against the right of Tsars, the authorities, and the mystery of marriage; it undercuts the three main pillars that support the dome of society. (Magnitskii 1861, 157–158)

If we summarize the criticisms against the Russian adherents of Kantian-oriented natural law, we see that formally they are almost identical to the merits of the supporters of natural law, but only in the opposite direction: the refusal to derive law from Revelation; nonconformity with the Gospel; considering (fallen) reason as the independent source of law; the distinction between morality and (natural) law, interpreted as the immorality of law; and the voluntary or involuntary promotion of revolutionary ideas that undermine autocracy and Orthodoxy. Despite the evident obscurantist overtones of this criticism, there were real reasons why it persisted—for many Kantians in Russia, the connection between Kant's arguments relating to law, ethics, and religion went unnoticed; thus, the religious context of these ideas was misunderstood.

Administrative interference and the persecution of philosophers did serious damage to Kantianism in Russia and for a time hampered its development. However, despite these setbacks, Kantian ideas about the philosophy of law remained important in Russia and have continued to be influential up to the present day. For instance, after considering the legal conflict over the Constitutional Court and its relation to the legality of the 1993 armed conflict between President Boris N. Yeltsin and the Russian parliament, one of the judges of the Constitutional Court expressed his dissenting opinion in connection with the court's decision,[14] ending his statement with a quote from Kant's *The Metaphysics of Morals*: "He who makes himself a worm cannot complain when he is trodden on" (Kant 1914, 437). In fact, there has been recent discussion in Russian Kant Studies about whether Kant can be considered "the father of the Russian Constitution" (Barenboim 2009, 5–9; Belov 2014, 51–59).

Disputes concerning philosophical and legal issues in Russia demonstrate several characteristic features of the interpretation of Kantian philosophy. First, in these discussions, neither side seems much interested in the details of Kant's own philosophy of law (e.g., his views on property, contracts, and family relationships) as expressed in "The Doctrine of Right," the first book of his *The Metaphysics of Morals*. This tendency persists to this day. Thus, Sergey S. Alekseev (one of the authors of the Russian constitution) devoted a special study to the problems of law in Kant and used Kant's quote in his title, but based his study of Kant's writings on the problems of morality or his later articles on socio-political problems. Alekseev even gives preference to Kant's lectures on ethics over "The Doctrine of Right" (Alekseev 1998, 31–32, 71, 151).

Second, in their arguments, the anti-Kantians demonstrated the absence of a clear distinction between the philosophy of law and the philosophy of religion: their arguments against Kantian natural law turned into a polemic with Kant's *Religion within the Limits of Reason Alone.* In turn, the pro-Kantian camp appealed to Kant as, on the one hand, a thinker who clearly distinguished between law and morality and, on the other hand, the author of an ethical doctrine that defended human virtue and human rights. However, it is obvious that appealing to Kant as an ethicist to support one's own legal position is at odds with Kant as a philosopher who clearly distinguished between morality and law. In Russian Kant Studies, the very problem of the interconnection of law and morality in Kant has been the subject of careful discussion only in recent decades. In any case, in the pro-Kantian party, the philosophy of law immediately flows over into ethics. Such a discussion is typical of the Russian interpretation of Kant: in this context, it seems hardly possible to discuss this narrow issue of Kantian philosophy because it almost inevitably turns into a discussion of Kant's philosophy as a whole.

It is not an accident that one of Kant's most illuminating and profound works on ethics, the *Groundwork of the Metaphysics of Morals,* was the first work to be translated into Russian. Thus, it was Kant's theory of morals and not knowledge that from the beginning was at the center of the study of Kant in Russia. Unlike other aspects of Kant's philosophical work, interest in this problem practically never fades or gets interrupted in Russia. During the first century of debate over Kant's ethics, certain positions were formulated and reproduced in one form or another. On the one hand, most Russian philosophers admitted that Kant presented the most systematically rigorous and deep moral philosophy, free of excess and materialistic interpretations; in fact, this position was argued quite passionately. Kant was credited for the consolidation of human virtue, for the development of an elevated theory of duty, and for defending the dignity of the human individual.

However, his excessive strictness was considered an unacceptable form of rigorism that turned into "a philosophical paradox that made sense only in the context of a sect and not the real world" (Lubkin 1814, 32), which "imposes an unbearable burden on people" (Perevoshchikov 1816, 281) and kicks away "the crutch supporting human morality" (Innokentii 1869, 83). The demands of duty out of respect for moral law grew into accusations of egoism in Kant's ethics, disputes over which lasted for more than a decade (Golubinskii 1884, 71), while his autonomy of will was interpreted as "incredible impudence" toward God (Savitskii 1825, 56–57). In the criticism of Kant's ethics, several other important ideas began to appear during these same years: (1) accusations of formalism, (2) appeals to the heart, and (3) a sense of "horror and trembling" upon butting up against Kant's ethics (Savitskii 1825, 57). As will be discussed below, the last two ideas, together with the main criticism that Kant had deduced religion from ethics (instead of the other way around), would play a special role in the theological-academic reception of Kant's philosophy.

This duality in relation to Kant's ethics was also characteristic of one of the best Russian Kant scholars and, perhaps, the most significant Russian philosopher—Vladimir S. Solovyov. The author of one of the best encyclopedic articles on Kant (Solovyov 1990a, 441–479), and the Russian translator of Kant's *Prolegomena*, Solovyov turned to Kant's ethics in his *Critique of Abstract Principles* (1880) and *The Justification of the Good Moral Philosophy* (1897). Highlighting the three main aspects of the good-in-itself—purity, completeness, and strength—Solovyov considered Kantian philosophy to have realized the first aspect, while giving himself the task of realizing the second (Solovyov 1990b, 96–97). In Solovyov's work, Kant is represented as the founder who turned moral philosophy into a science or as the "Lavoisier of moral philosophy" (Solovyov 1990b, 241). Kant is credited with "the great merit of being the first harbinger in the philosophy of unconditional, pure, or autonomous morality. His description and three-part definition of the categorical imperative gave ethics the reliability of the axioms of pure mathematics" (Solovyov 1990a, 473–474). In brief form, Solovyov formulated the positive essence of Kant's philosophy: "the dependence of world phenomena on the mind and unconditional independence of moral principles" (Solovyov 1990a, 471–473).

But as with Kant's comparison of his work to that of Copernicus in the preface to the second edition of the *Critique of Pure Reason*, this comparison with Lavoisier has a flipside for Solovyov. With regard to the Copernican Revolution in Kant's philosophy, Solovyov saw his task as "humbling the proud analogy" (Solovyov 1990c, 822), which requires one to refrain from exaggerating the human subject, deprive humanity of its "central luminary role in knowledge," and overcome false anthropocentrism. In the case of Kant's comparison with Lavoisier, Solovyov emphasized the role of practical reason as an unconditional principle of human behavior. Solovyov reasoned as follows: "it is as if a chemist began to demand or thought it possible that people should use pure hydrogen instead of water" (Solovyov 1990b, 241).

Evgenii N. Trubetskoi tried to develop this line of reasoning in his *Metaphysical Conjectures on Knowledge: Overcoming Kant and Kantianism* (Trubetskoi 1917), in which he took further steps on the path to humbling the human subject. Although his criticism of the exaltation of the subject in the *Critique of Pure Reason* was perhaps unfair, he shrewdly identified the possible ethical consequences of a Copernican Revolution in German idealism and neo-Kantianism—the distortion of the *autonomization* of the subject and the misrepresentation of Kant's idea of *autonomy* (Krouglov 2016b, 408–421).

The most prominent supporter of Kantian ethics in Russia was Lev N. Tolstoy, who considered the *Critique of Practical Reason* to be the German philosopher's greatest work, a temple with respect to which the *Critique of Pure Reason* was only scaffolding (Krouglov 2008, 361–386). Tolstoy was nearly as enthusiastic about Kant's treatise *Religion Within the Limits of Reason*

Alone. Influenced by closely reading Kant in his later years, Tolstoy penned an important and unique description of the German philosopher: "Kant is considered an abstract philosopher, but he is a great religious teacher" (Tolstoy 1958, 51), "a moral, religious teacher," and "a great moralist and deeply religious person" (Makovitskii 1979, 485, 523). Tolstoy sought to convey the profound ideas of Kant's philosophy to the general public in Russia and tried to popularize Kant in his later non-fiction works, as well as in his collection of daily proverbs from famous philosophers. A very special project was Tolstoy's collection of aphorisms *The Selected Thoughts of Kant*, which he published in 1906 (Tolstoy 2016).

For many decades, the problems of Kantian ethics made up the core of Russian Kant Studies. Kant's moral philosophy and the categorical imperative are the subjects of some of the finest works of Russian Kant Studies of the late Soviet and post-Soviet period (Skripnik 1978; Sudakov 1998; Guseynov 2000, 5–36; Soloviev 2005, 2008, 145–152).

Kant's Reception in Russian Religious Philosophy and Orthodoxy

In Western Kant Studies, discussions about the relation of Kantian philosophy and Christianity most often come to the sound conclusion that it exists outside Christian faiths and is trans-confessional. However, for Western philosophers, this implies that Kantian philosophy is neither Protestant nor Catholic (Winter 2000, 11–13), with Orthodoxy completely excluded from these discussions. In Russia, the issue of Kant's attitude toward Orthodox thought in contrast to his attitude toward Catholicism and Protestantism has also not been specifically raised. At the turn of the nineteenth century, under the influence of German thought, the thesis that Kant is a Protestant philosopher was accepted as fact. In Russia, however, a number of Orthodox theologians began to fiercely debate the existence of religion within the limits of reason and to attack Kant's philosophy as a whole.

The exaggeration and extremism of these polemic invectives has contributed to the misconception that all Orthodox thought in Russia categorically rejected Kant—this is clearly untrue. For all their brilliance, the number of sharp anti-Kantian views does not represent all typical Orthodox theory. Moreover, the Orthodoxy of these Russian Orthodox anti-Kantians (including the priests) is itself controversial. The activity of these ardent anti-Kantians spans only four decades after the end of the nineteenth century, while Russian Kant Studies has existed for over 200 years. This view also ignores those Russian Orthodox thinkers who were sympathetic or neutral to Kant. Thus, without a comparative study of Kant's reception in Catholicism, Protestantism, *and* Orthodoxy, the typicality and originality of the sharply negative theories of certain Russian Orthodox anti-Kantians cannot be properly assessed.

The Orthodox world has never had a unified approach to Kant. This is certainly true of the Russian academies: many scholars from the Russian academies are actually closer in their views regarding Kant's philosophy to Russian university professors than to other academy theologians and vice versa. Besides the sharp denunciations of Kantianism, there was also neutrality as well as adulation. The three most significant anti-Kantians are Vasilii N. Karpov, professor at the St. Petersburg Theological Academy; Archbishop Nikanor (Brovkovich), the rector of the Kazan Theological Academy; and Pavel A. Florensky, professor at the Moscow Theological Academy.

Karpov writes, "In his critical philosophy, Kant is essentially a Lutheran theologian disguised as a Lutheran philosopher" (Karpov 1866, 1) and that Kant is one of the most consistent spokesmen of "modern philosophical rationalism," who ignores the independent strength of the heart. Kant's critical philosophy is "cold, freezing the soul," which "a man living a full and harmoniously developed life" could never sympathize with (Karpov 2013, 141). On this interpretation, the "I" is the only sanctuary of truth, the all-absorbing mind which creates the proud idol of rationalism on the fragile pedestal of egoism. The human in critical philosophy is:

> a being (if only a being) woven from concepts, ascending and descending along the gossamer of its categorical web, isolated in the pure forms of space and time, which it can neither escape nor see beyond, and despite the infinite extensibility of these forms, they confine and constrain leaving one feeling as unnatural as a bird in a cage. The human mind demands freedom, to fly beyond all temporal and spatial limitations, to break the frail categorical fabric. But Kant does not allow this, arguing that outside this windowless temple there is a region of ghosts, a country unknown and uninhabited, confounding people; and many who listen to him remain permanently in space, live exclusively in time, and die forever in eternity. (Karpov 2013, 173)

Karpov considered Kant's approach a form of sophisticated sophistry according to which the existence of God is rejected in the theoretical sphere but unquestioningly accepted in the practical sphere.

In a highly polemic work, *A Critique of Kant's Critique of Pure Reason* [*Kritika na kritiku chistogo razuma Kanta*], Archbishop Nikanor claims that Kant "reached the Herculean Straits of philosophical absurdity" (Nikanor 1888, 226). He recognized a "thirst for nothingness" in Kant's philosophy and disparaged him for the "intentional moral misdirection of his thought" (Nikanor 1888, 93–94, 356). Nikanor unequivocally accused Kant of atheism, interpreting Kant's refutation of proofs for the existence of God as the denial of the existence of God (Nikanor 1888, 385–386).

Pavel A. Florensky went so far as to make ad hominem attacks against Kant, referring to the Königsberg philosopher as the "Pillar of God-Resistant Evil" (Florensky 1990, 820). Considering Kant "to be Protestant to the bone," Florensky argued that "his whole system secretly points to one thing—the cult

126 A. N. KROUGLOV

of the impossibility of its existence. How and why this cult is impossible is the primary question of Kantian thought" (Florensky 2004, 105). Hinting at Kant's satanic nature[15]—a theme readily picked up by Russian literature—he argues:

> There is no system more evasively slippery, more "hypocritical," in the sense of the apostle James, more "deceiving," in the words of the Savior, than Kant's philosophy: each of its postulates, every term, every turn of thought is neither a yes nor a no [...] Not a single term has a pure tone, but continues to howl. Kant's system is truly a genius system—the most ingenious, that was, is, and ever will be [...] a system on the side of deception. Kant is a great deceiver. (Florensky 2004, 103)

Florensky's lectures on the history of philosophy at the Moscow Theological Academy are replete with diatribes against Kant that are unworthy of a philosopher, let alone a priest.

These invectives and curses demonstrate another aspect of Kant's reception in Russia: his philosophy was not perceived as an abstract, scientific doctrine, but as a personal, existential threat. Back in 1815, Ilya F. Grinevich penned the following lines in his dissertation:

> I confess that when I first read and carefully contemplated the antinomies of reason proposed by Kant, I shuddered with all my soul, for, all of a sudden, I clearly understood that with the abandonment of the veracity of the first-order principles of thought, there cannot be any reliable knowledge of the truth. Knowledge itself was destroyed, and worse than any ignorance is the knowledge that nothing can really be known! And it seemed to me as if I were falling from heaven into the abyss of hell where only confusion, discord, and horror prevailed. (Grinevich 1982, 137)

In 1897, the *Critique of Pure Reason* was even linked to several suicide attempts (Lapshin 1900, 880–881; Koni 1967, 474). The most revealing case involved the future Komi-Zyrian writer and philosopher Kallistrat F. Zhakov. After reading the *Critique of Pure Reason*, he came to the conclusion that "things in themselves and the essence of nature were unknowable, that science was only a chess game" (Zhakov 1996, 146–147), after which he decided to commit suicide—the attempt was unsuccessful. Although the fate of the German poet Heinrich von Kleist shows that the link between suicide and Kantian philosophy is not just a Russian phenomenon, this existential interpretation of Kantian philosophy did acquire some unique features in Russia.

There were philosophers and theologians in the same theological and academic environment that treated Kant and his philosophy of religion neutrally. At least since Ivan M. Skvortsov's (professor at the Kiev Theological Academy) dissertation *Religions Within the Limits of Reason Alone* [*Religiia v predelakh odnogo tol'ko razuma*], the best representatives of theological-academic philosophy in Russia have eschewed hyperbole, while supporting the idea that constructive criticism should be presented only after an opponent's merits had been noted. Although Skvortsov had many objections to Kantian religious philosophy, he began his research by naming three important truths discovered by Kant: (1) reason is incapable of accessing the supersensory, (2) all morality that begins with the sense of pleasure and happiness is not moral, and (3) humanity by nature is damaged. The significance of these philosophical theses for theology is shown by Skvortsov as follows: "These Truths, known from Revelation were proven by the Philosopher from reason alone, and, therefore, the Christian Theologian and Philosopher when teaching religion to the unbelievers of our times can refer to Kant the same way the Church Fathers referred to classical Plato. But Kant's service to religion does not seem to extend beyond this" (Skvortsov 1838, 44).

The positive influence and use of Kantian ideas are noticeable in the Latin textbook on metaphysics written by St. Petersburg Theological Academy professor Herodion Y. Wetrinskj. The compendium is one of the first textbooks on philosophy and metaphysics written in Russian. In it, a strange interpretation of Kant is eccentrically interwoven with a number of pre-Kantian interpretations of the transcendental. Wetrinskj, who was familiar with Kant's work through Latin translations, does not distinguish between Kant's writings preceding and proceeding the *Critique of Pure Reason*; on the contrary, he connects a nontraditional interpretation of Kant's 1770 dissertation with ideas in the *Critique of Pure Reason*. He uses Kant's views to justify his own theistic position and for developing the "metaphysics of the intelligible world" (Wetrinskj 1821, 73–74; Pozzi 2018, 56–66).

An example of a competent, albeit critical analysis of the Kantian position on religion is the work of Nikolai P. Rozhdestvenskii (professor at the St. Petersburg Theological Academy) on Christian apologetics. Lacking the emotion of accusatory theology, Rozhdestvenskii's work demonstrates a profound understanding of Kantian critical philosophy, on the basis of which he evenly and deliberately analyzes the main flaws and merits of Kant's philosophy.

Rozhdestvenskii concisely describes the theological debates arising from the religious questions in the *Critique of Pure Reason* and the *Critique of Practical Reason*. He arrives at a conclusion that explains much about Kant's reception in Russian: the main results of the first *Critique* "are purely negative, if not for religion in general, then for theology as a science, which arises from man's possibility of knowing God" (Rozhdestvenskii 1884, 88). Kant was not an atheist or opponent of religion, but he did undermine the foundations of theology. This was likely understood not only by Rozhdestvenskii, who addressed it directly, but by all of Kant's numerous critics in Russian theology. However, instead of acknowledging this fact like Rozhdestvenskii, theologians like Nikanor, who lacked serious arguments against Kant's interpretation of theology, simply accused Kant of atheism in the hope of maintaining an acceptable form of theology (which was their livelihood). Rozhdestvenskii believed Kant's general contribution to theology was twofold: Kant weakened Wolffianism's one-sided influence on theology in the form of formalism and dogmatism but contributed another one-sided influence in the form of dry moralism.

However, the theological-academic environment also had thinkers who unambiguously sympathized with Kant. One of the most striking examples is found in the writings of Metropolitan Anthony (Khrapovitskii). The Russian theologian came to a surprising idea within the context of Orthodoxy about how Kantian philosophy was different from Catholicism and Protestantism, and, moreover, how similarity existed between Kantian philosophy and Orthodoxy. After drawing attention to inconsistencies in Kant's writing, Khrapovitskii considers its source: "The answer to such a question must be sought in Kant's striving to firmly establish an autonomous morality as opposed to the moral heteronomy of Catholics and Protestants. In fact, his moral religion has much less similarity with these religions than with the Orthodox ascetic teaching on spiritual perfection" (Anthony 1894, 425). However, even Kantian sympathizers like Metropolitan Anthony were at times critical:

> having committed himself too much to his idea, Kant was afraid of lowering the moral principle by recognizing any external influence on it, even in the case of the Revelations of the Gospel. Having rightly asserted the freedom, the intrinsic value, and the morality of human nature from the very beginnings of the pursuit toward good or evil, Kant did not stop at the truth that the good is freely accepted or rejected by man, and infinitely increases in significance when instead of an indefinite urge to compassionate feeling, it appears to him via a harmonious system of truths, which from the heavenly throne of God encompasses the whole of the cosmos and all ages. (Anthony 1894, 425)

An even more striking position on Kant within the Russian Orthodox Church is represented by its current head, Patriarch Kirill (Gundiaiev) of Moscow. There is hardly a contemporary Christian church leader who so openly and publicly appeals to the ethical teachings of Kant, the categorical imperative, and the moral proof of the existence of God as Patriarch Kirill, who for a long time served as the Metropolitan of Kaliningrad (former Königsberg) (Krouglov 2011, 27–28).

KANT AND THE POLITICAL AND HISTORICAL SITUATION IN RUSSIA

The development of Kantian philosophy in Russia has never been a purely scientific process divorced from the political life of the country; on the contrary, it bears traces of significant involvement in public life. The first Kantian in Russia, Mellmann, was expelled from the country in the eighteenth century with the direct participation of Catherine II. In the first decades of the nineteenth century, during the reign of Alexander I, Kant in Russia unexpectedly turned from a supporter of the state and law into an opponent of its religious foundations, the church, the state, and the family. The Russian ban on the teaching of philosophy in the middle of the nineteenth century also affected Kantianism.

In the twentieth century, the debate was even more urgent and radical. As early as the 1840s, there arose the thesis that German philosophy and Kantianism in particular "was impossible in our country, because it contradicts the religious, civil, and intellectual life of our people" (Davydov 1841, 400). After the outbreak of World War I, along with the desire "to free Russian thought from German dominance" (Vorotynkin 1917), some Slavophiles expressed the conviction that "The internal transcription of the German spirit in Kant's philosophy naturally and fatalistically correlates with the external transcription of the same German spirit into Krupp's guns" (Ern 1991, 309). As a result, a heated debate arose over the question of "Kant's guilt" (Rubinstein 1915).

This controversy was particularly heated within Russian social democracy, where, starting at the end of the nineteenth century (in the context of the debate between materialism and idealism, the interpretation of the thing-in-itself, the immediacy of the categorical imperative, and the interconnectedness of critical philosophy and Marxism), Kantian philosophy became the subject of active disputes, which were articulated in the articles and translations of Georgii V. Plekhanov (Plekhanov 1956, 451–503). First, Plekhanov criticized the Kantian ethic quite sharply, but then at the height of World War I, he appealed to Kant's categorical imperative to argue in favor of stopping hostilities and establishing peaceful relations between different peoples (Plekhanov 1914, 14, 16, 1925, 209).[16] However, at the height of the war, there was also sharp criticism of Plekhanov's view of Kant's ethics, which caused a storm of indignation among the social-democrats, including accusations of perfidy against materialism and Marxism and betrayal of the revolutionary struggle (Martov 1925; 1917). This controversy did not end after World War I, nor after the 1917 October Revolution, nor after Plekhanov's death, but continued in the Soviet Union for a long time (Deborin 1961, 331–332; Axelrod 1927). The lengthy nature of this dispute is explained by the fact that at its core it was a dispute about the existence of ethics within Marxism, where the true historical example of ethical doctrine was precisely Kantian philosophy.

Not only was the categorical imperative a stumbling block for supporters of the class struggle, but until the end of World War II, two sides fought over Kant's philosophy.

According to the first side, Kant's *Prolegomena* (which had been fully represented in the first Soviet edition) showed that his philosophy formed "the basis of opportunism, revisionism, and social fascism" and that it was "[…] one of the main tools in the hands of the bourgeoisie in the struggle against the revolutionary movement of the proletariat, and a subtle instrument of the falsification and the vulgarization of Marxism by the Socialists of the Second International" (Saradzhev 1934, 8). Its study was, however, necessary in order to become personally acquainted with the enemy: "In our day, the exposure of the counter-revolutionary role of Kantianism is one way to accomplish the vital

130 A. N. KROUGLOV

task of the Bolshevik struggle for the purity of revolutionary theory against the bourgeois distortions of Marxism-Leninism" (Saradzhev 1934, 101).

The second side was represented three years later in the second Soviet edition of the *Prolegomena*. In this case, Kant is named the predecessor of "classical German philosophy, which is one of the theoretical sources of Marxism" ("Ot izdatel'stva" 1937, 1). For this reason, the grounds for studying Kantian philosophy were different: "The working people of the country of victorious socialism and the international proletariat are the only legitimate heirs of the whole of world culture and German classical philosophy in particular, while in Germany, in the homeland of classical philosophy, fascist obscurantists burn the immortal, classical works of world culture upon their bonfires" ("Ot izdatel'stva" 1937, 2).

After the outbreak of World War II, the controversy surrounding Kantian philosophy, which had started during World War I, gained new momentum and new features. This time the rhetoric was less concerned with the opposition of the militaristic essence of Germanism and Slavophilia, and more with the ideological struggle of different interpretations of Kantian philosophy. Discussions also revolved around the responsibility of Kantian philosophy and German idealist philosophy, not just for Krupp's guns, but for monstrous crimes against humanity. In 1942, Asmus defended Kant and German philosophy from National Socialist ideologues in his pamphlet *The Fascist Falsification of Classical German Philosophy* (Asmus 1942).[17]

However, it was easier for Asmus to polemicize with Nazi ideologues than with his Soviet counterparts. In 1943, the Institute of Philosophy of the Academy of Sciences of the USSR published the third volume of *History of Philosophy* [*Istoriia filosofii*], most of which was devoted to German classical philosophy. The chapter on Kant was written by Asmus, but, surprisingly, there was no reference to fascist falsification. Asmus's criticism of the "too honest and astute thinker" (Aleksandrov et. al. 1943, 103) is reduced to a minimum. Initially, all three volumes of this edition were awarded the Stalin Prize. However, 1944 saw the publication of "On the Inadequacies and Mistakes in the Description of the History of German Philosophy at the End of the Eighteenth and Early Nineteenth Centuries" ["O nedostatkakh i oshibkakh v osveshchenii istorii nemetskoi filosofii kontsa XVIII i nachala XIX vv."]. This was the decision of the Central Committee of the Communist Party of the Soviet Union and resulted in a prolonged revision of the third volume with the personal involvement of Joseph V. Stalin. The conclusion of the decision reads:

> the chapters of the third volume of *Istoriia filosofii* [*History of Philosophy*] devoted to the philosophy of Kant, Fichte, and Hegel, give an erroneous account of the history of German philosophy, exaggerating its significance. […] The volume does not criticize the reactionary social and political views of the German philosophers of the end of the eighteenth and the beginning of the nineteenth centuries. ("O nedostatkakh i oshibkakh" 1944, 19)

The Stalin Prize Committee stripped the third volume of its award. Only in the mid-1950s, after a series of other debates, was Kant's philosophy finally legitimized within the framework of Marxist–Leninist philosophy, after which its authority and significance were not questioned until the end of the USSR.

However, the echoes of these mid-twentieth-century discussions can be heard in Russia today. In particular, there is periodic debate concerning whether Kaliningrad University should carry the name of the German philosopher Immanuel Kant and whether this is evidence of creeping Germanization in the Kaliningrad region.

Conclusion

Contrary to certain ideas that have spread in post-Soviet Russia, Kant's philosophy has established a firm place in the history of philosophical thought in Russia, which neither administrative and political repression nor tragic historical events have been able to displace. The positive and negative impact of Kant's ideas on various philosophical disciplines in Russia, and Russian culture in general, has been more significant and extensive than previously thought. In Russia, the evolving discussion of certain Kantian problems is an excellent illustration of what Hegel expressed in his concept of *Aufhebung*.

Translated by Peter Golub

Notes

1. This is a reference to the University of Königsberg (in German: *Albertus-Universität Königsberg*), one of the oldest German universities, founded in 1544. It was commonly known as the Albertina—Ed.
2. Similar studies on the influence of Schelling in Russian fiction are virtually non-existent. The available research on the presence of Hegel in Russian poetry (Chyzhevsky 2007) shows that Schelling and Hegel are less influential than Kant in this case.
3. The best examples are Mikhail Bulgakov's novel *The Master and Margarita*, Mark Aldanov's novel *The Ninth Thermidor*, and Sigizmund Dominikovich Krzhizhanovskii's masterful Kantian short-story "The Life Story of a Thought."
4. See Kant (1963–1966, 1994c, 1994–2018). For the latest edition, see also Bykova (2015, 362–380).
5. Vladislavlev 1867, Sokolov [1]1896–1897, [2]1902, Lossky [1]1907, [2]1915; Lossky in the edition edited by Asmus, Gulyga, and Oizerman [1]1964, [2]1994; Lossky, Arzakan'ian and Itkin in the edition edited by Andreeva and Gulyga 1994; Lossky, Arzakan'ian and Itkin in the edition edited by Motroshilova and Tuschling 2006 (Kant 1867, 1896–1897, 1902, 1907, 1915, 1964, 1994a, b, 1998, 2006).
6. The theme of Kant's reception in Russia has been the subject of a rich research tradition during the last half-century. (See Kamenskii 1960, 1971, 1974; Kamenskii and Zhuchkov 1994; Abramov 1995; Pustarnakov 2003; Abramov and Zhuchkov 2005; Kalinnikov 2005; Abramov 1994, 1995, 1998; Nizhnikov

2005; Dmitrieva 2007; Krouglov 2009a, 2012; Mehlich 2014.) For this reason, when Thomas Nemeth (Nemeth 2017) refers to the recent Springer edition as "The first comprehensive study of the Russian reception of Kant's Idealism in any language," he clearly misconstrues the historical reality.

7. Kantianism has been more influential despite the pretentious, little-substantiated statement that "Hegel is the fate of Russia" (Sumin 2005) or Hajo Holborn's observation that the battle of Stalingrad was a battle between right and left Hegelians (Cassirer 1946, 249).

8. Alexander S. Pushkin—who described the character Lensky in his *Eugene Onegin* as "a lover of Kant and a poet" (Pushkin 1937, 33–34)—was clearly in the minority.

9. As far as this can be judged from sketchy data, this subject—perhaps only with a modified name—remains compulsory in all Russian philosophy departments to this day; however, the content has changed significantly. If before Hegel constituted half of the material (see Kuznetsov 1989), now the center of gravity has radically shifted in favor of Kant.

10. Their quantitative analysis is presented by year in the corresponding table (Motroshilova 1994, 53).

11. Christian Thomasius took the first steps on this path.

12. It is likely that the consideration of this triad in Russia, which is alien to Kant, who preferred to juxtapose the law to morality, and morality to politics, comes from the translation of Friedrich Baumeister's textbooks into Russian.

13. To an extent, Hugo Grotius had already started this tradition.

14. Dissenting opinion of Judge Boris Safarovich Ebzeev on the Decision of the Constitutional Court of the Russian Federation of December 1, 1993, No. 88-R, "On the Suspension of Judge V.D. Zor'kin of the Constitutional Court of the Russian Federation."

15. The notion that Kant was accused of Satanism and devilry only in Russian or Orthodox circles is untrue. Such accusations were made in Protestant and Catholic circles in various Western European countries, but several decades earlier than in Russia (Krouglov 2009a, 426–445).

16. Already by 1925, there were no less than 156 Russian language works on the theme of "Kant and Marx" (Rozanov 1925, 209–222).

17. Asmus followed in the footsteps of an earlier article by Grigorii Konstantinovich Bammel', "On the Faschisization of the History of Philosophy in Germany" (see Bammel' 1936).

Bibliography

Abramov, Alexander I. 1994. Kant v russkoi dukhovno-akademicheskoi filosofii. In *Kant i filosofiia v Rossii*, ed. Zakhar Abramovich Kamenskii and Vladimir Aleksandrovich Zhuchkov, 81–113. Moscow: Izdatel'stvo Nauka.

———. 1995. Kant v Rossii. In *Russkaia filosofiia. Malyi entsiklopedicheskii slovar'*, 235–242. Moscow: Izdatel'stvo Nauka.

———. 1998. Kantianstvo v russkoi universitetskoi filosofii. In *Voprosy filosofii*, vol. 1, 58–69. Moscow: Izdatel'stvo Nauka.

6 KANT AND KANTIANISM IN RUSSIA: A HISTORICAL OVERVIEW 133

Abramov, Alexander I., and Vladimir A. Zhuchkov, eds. 2005. *Kant: pro et contra. Retseptsiia idei nemetskogo filosofa i ikh vliianie na razvitie russkoi filosofskoi traditsii. Antologiia*. St. Petersburg: Izdatel'stvo Russkoi Khristianskoi gumanitarnoi akademii.

Akhutin, Anatolii V. 1990. Sofiia i chert (Kant pered litsom russkoi religioznoi metafiziki). *Voprosy filosofii* 1: 51–69.

Aleksandrov, Georgii F., Bernard E. Bykhovskii, Mark B. Mitin, and Pavel F. Yudin, eds. 1943. Filosofiia pervoi poloviny XIX veka. In *Istoriia filosofii*, vol. 3, 1–594. Moscow: OGIZ Gospolitizdat.

Alekseev, Sergei S. 1998. *Samoe sviatoe, chto est' u Boga na zemle. Immanuil Kant i problemy prava v sovremennuiu epokhu*. Moscow: Infra–M.

Anthony, arkhimandrit (Khrapovitskii). 1894. Nravstvennoe obosnovanie vazhneishego khristianskogo dogmata. Prilozhenie k razboru ucheniia Kanta ob opravdanii. *Bogoslovskii vestnik* 3: 423–445.

Asmus, Valentin F. 1942. *Fashistskaia fal'sifikatsiia klassicheskoi nemetskoi filosofii*. Moscow: OGIZ Gospolitizdat.

Axelrod, Liubov' I. 1927. Otvet na 'Nashi raznoglasia' A. Deborina. *Krasnaia nov'* 5: 136–163.

Bammel', Grigorii K. 1936. O fashizatsii istorii filosofii v Germanii. In *Protiv fashistskogo mrakobesiia i demagogii*, ed. Ilya N. Dvorkin, Abram M. Deborin, Mikhail D. Kammari, Mark B. Mitin, and Maksimilian A. Savel'ev, 216–264. Moscow: Gosudarstvennoe sotsial'no–ekonomicheskoe izdatel'stvo.

Barenboim, Petr D. 2009. Kant kak otets Konstitutsii Rossii. *Zakonodatel'stvo i ekonomika* 9: 5–9.

Barsukov, Nikolai P. 1897. *Zhizn' i trudy M.P. Pogodina*, book 11. St. Petersburg: A.D. i P.D. Pogodiny.

Belov, Vladimir N. 2014. Kant i Konstitutsiia RF. *Kantovskii sbornik* 3 (49): 51–59.

Bykova, Marina F. 2015. Novoe slovo v mirovom kantovedenii. O dvuiazychnom izdanii sochinenii Immanuila Kanta na nemetskom i russkom iazykakh. In *Istoriko–filosofskii ezhegodnik*, vol. 2015, 362–380. Moscow: Izdatel'stvo Akvilon.

Cassirer, Ernst. 1946. *The Myth of the State*. New Haven: Yale University Press.

Chyzhevsky, Dmitry I. 2007. *Gegel' v Rossii*. St. Petersburg: Izdatel'stvo Nauka.

Davydov, Ivan I. 1841. Vozmozhna li u nas Germanskaia filosofiia? *Moskovitianin* 2 (3–4): 385–401.

Davydova, Lyudmila S., ed. 1996. *Immanuil Kant. Bibliograficheskii ukazatel' literatury na russkom iazyke 1803–1994 gg*. Moscow: IFRAN.

Deborin, Abram M. 1961. Nashi raznoglasiia. In *Filosofiia i politika*, 303–344. Moscow: Izdatel'stvo Akademii Nauk SSSR.

Dmitrieva, Nina A. 2007. *Russkoe neokantianstvo: "Marburg" v Rossii. Istoriko–filosofskie ocherki*. Moscow: ROSSPEN.

Ern, Vladimir F. 1991. Mech i krest (Ot Kanta k Kruppu). In *Sochineniia*, 308–318. Moscow: Izdatel'stvo Pravda.

Filimonov, Vladimir S. 1811. *Sistema estestvennogo prava*. St. Petersburg: Imperatorskaia tipografiia.

Finke, Iogann Kh. 1816. *Estestvennoe, chastnoe, publichnoe i narodnoe pravo*. Translated from German (anonymous translator). Kazan': Universitetskaia tipografiia.

Florensky, Pavel A. 1990. O Dukhovnoi Istine. Introductory remarks on the defense of a master's degree. Moscow, May 19, 1914. In *Stolp i utverzhdenie istiny*, vol. 1, 817–826. Moscow: Izdatel'stvo Pravda.

—————. 2004. Chteniia o kul'te. In *Sobranie sochinenii. Filosofiia kul'ta (Opyt pravoslavnoi antropoditsei)*, 26–416. Moscow: Izdatel'stvo Mysl'.

Golubinskii, Fyodor A. 1884. *Lektsii po filosofii*. Issue 4. Moscow: Tipografiia L.F. Snegireva.

Gorodchaninov, Grigorii N. 1821. Mnenie khristianina o prave estestvennom. *Kazanskii vestnik pri izd. Imperatorskom Kazanskom Universitete* 2 (6): 65–130, 121–140.

—————. 1826. O zabluzhdeniiakh razuma v izyskanii istiny. *Kazanskii vestnik, izd. pri Imperatorskom Kazanskom Universitete* 17 (6): 91–103.

Grinevich, Ilya F. 1982. Rassuzhdenie vstupitel'noe ob izuchenii filosofii i ob istinnoi prirode onoi. Kharkov, 1815. Published by Zakhar Abramovich Kamenskii. Translated by Aleksandr A. Stoliarov. *Kantovskii sbornik* (7): 122–153.

Guseynov, Abdusalam A. 2000. Etika dobroi voli. Introduction to *Kant, Immanuil. Lektsii po etike*, 5–36. Moscow: Izdatel'stvo Respublika.

Herder, Johann G. 1881. Briefe zu Beförderung der Humanität. *Sämtliche Werke* in 33 Bände. Edited by Bernhard Suphan. Vol. 17, 1–414. Berlin: Weidmannsche Buchhandlung.

Innokentii, arkhimandrit (Borisov). 1869. O religii voobshche. In *Sbornik iz lektsii byvshikh professorov Kievskoi Dukhovnoi Akademii, arkhimandrita Innokentiia, protoiereia I. M. Skvortsova, P. S. Avseneva (arkhimandrita Feofana) i Ia.K. Amfiteatrova, izdannyi akademiei po sluchaiu piatidesiatiletnego iubileia ee (1819–69)*, 1–92. Kiev: Tipografiia gubernskogo upravleniia.

Kalinnikov, Leonard A. 2005. *Kant v russkoi filosofii i kul'ture*. Kaliningrad: Izdatel'stvo RGU im. I. Kanta.

Kamenskii, Zakhar A. 1960. I. Kant v russkoi filosofii nachala XIX veka. *Vestnik istorii mirovoi kul'tury* 1: 19–66.

—————. 1971. *Filosofskie idei russkogo Prosveshcheniia*. Moscow: Izdatel'stvo Mysl'.

—————. 1974. Kant v Rossii. In *Filosofiia Kanta i sovremennost'*. Edited by Teodor I. Oizerman, 289–328. Moscow: Izdatel'stvo Mysl'.

Kamenskii, Zakhar A., and Vladimir A. Zhuchkov, eds. 1994. *Kant i filosofiia v Rossii*. Moscow: Izdatel'stvo Nauka.

Kant, Immanuel. 1803. *Kantovo osnovanie dlia metafiziki nravov*. Translated by Yakov A. Ruban. Nikolaev: Tipografiia Chernomorskogo uchilishcha.

—————. 1867. *Kritika chistogo razuma*. Translated by Mikhail I. Vladislavlev. St. Petersburg: V tipografii N. Tiblena i Komp.

—————. 1896–1897. *Kritika chistogo razuma*. Translated by Nikolai M. Sokolov. St. Petersburg: Izdanie knizhnogo magazina M.V. Popova.

—————. 1902. *Kritika chistogo razuma*. Translated by Nikolai M. Sokolov. St. Petersburg: Izdanie knizhnogo magazina M.V. Popova.

—————. 1907. *Kritika chistogo razuma*. Translated from German by Nikolai O. Lossky. St. Petersburg: Tipografiia M.M. Stasiulevicha.

—————. 1914. *Die Metaphysik der Sitten*. In *Kant's Gesammelte Schriften*. Edited by Royal Prussian Academy of Sciences. Vol. 6. Berlin: Druck und Verlag von Georg Reimer.

—————. 1915. *Kritika chistogo razuma*. Translated from German by Nikolai O. Lossky. St. Petersburg: Tipografiia M.M. Stasiulevicha.

—————. 1964. *Kritika chistogo razuma*. In *Sochineniia v 6 tomakh*. Translated by Nikolai O. Lossky, Tsolak G. Arzakan'ian, and Moisei I. Itkin. Edited by Valentin F. Asmus, Arsenii V. Gulyga, and Teodor I. Oizerman. Vol. 3. Moscow: Izdatel'stvo Mysl'.

6 KANT AND KANTIANISM IN RUSSIA: A HISTORICAL OVERVIEW 135

———. 1963–1966. *Sochineniia v 6 tomakh*. Edited by Valentin F. Asmus, Arsenii V. Gulyga, and Teodor I. Oizerman. Moscow: Izdatel'stvo Mysl'.

———. 1994a. *Kritika chistogo razuma*. Translated from German by Nikolai O. Lossky, Tsolak G. Arzakan'ian, and Moisei I. Itkin. Moscow: Izdatel'stvo Mysl'.

———. 1994b. Kritika chistogo razuma. In *Sochineniia*, trans. Nikolai O. Lossky, Tsolak G. Arzakan'ian, Moisei I. Itkin, and Iskra S. Andreeva, ed. Arsenii V. Gulyga. 3. Moscow: Izdatel'stvo CHORO.

———. 1994c. In *Sochineniia v 8 tomakh*, ed. Arsenii V. Gulyga. Moscow: Izdatel'stvo CHORO.

———. 1998. *Kritika chistogo razuma*. Translated from German by Nikolai O. Lossky, edited by Vladimir A. Zhuchkov. Moscow: Izdatel'stvo Nauka.

———. 2006. *Kritika chistogo razuma*. German-Russian bilingual edition. Translated from German by Nikolai O. Lossky, Tsolak G. Arzakan'ian, Moisei I. Itkin, and Nelly V. Motroshilova, edited by Nelly V. Motroshilova and Burkhard Tushling. Vol. 2. Moscow: Izdatel'stvo Nauka.

———. 1994–2018. *Sochineniia na russkom i nemetskom iazykakh v 5 tomakh*. Edited by Nelly V. Motroshilova and Burkhard Tushling. Moscow: Kami; Izdatel'stvo Nauka; Moskovskii filosofskii fond; Kanon+ ROOI Reabilitatsiia.

Karamzin, Nikolai M. 1791. Pis'ma russkago puteshestvennika. *Moskovskii zhurnal* 1 (2): 155–160.

Karpov, Vasilii N. 1866. *Sistematicheskaia forma filosofskogo ratsionalizma, ili naukouchenie Fikhte*. St. Petersburg: Tipografiia Dukhovnogo zhurnala *Strannik*.

———. 2013. Filosofskii ratsionalizm noveishego vremeni. In *Sochineniia v 3 tomakh*, vol. 1. Melitopol: Izdatel'skii dom Melitopol'skoi gorodskoi tipografii.

Kolubovskii, Yakov N. 1890. Filosofiia u russkikh. In *Iberveg Fridrikh, Geintse Maks. Istoriia novoi filosofii v szhatom ocherke*, translated from the seventh German edition by Yakov N. Kolubovskii, 529–591. St. Petersburg: L.F. Panteleev.

Koni, Anatolii F. 1967. Samoubiistvo v zakone i zhizni. In *Sobranie sochinenii v 8 tomakh*, vol. 4, 454–481. Moscow: Izdatel'stvo Iuridicheskaia literatura.

Krouglov, Alexei N. 2008. Lev Nikolaevich Tolstoj als Leser Kants. Zur Wirkungsgeschichte Kants in Russland. *Kant–Studien* 99: 361–386. Berlin, New York: Walter de Gruyter.

———. 2009a. *Filosofiia Kanta v Rossii v kontse XVIII—nachale XIX vekov*. Moscow: Kanon+ ROOI Reabilitatsiia.

———. 2009b. Pervyi kurs po kantovskoi filosofii v Rossii. In *Sushchnost' i slovo. Sbornik nauchnykh statei k iubileiu professora N.V. Motroshilovoi*, 517–529. Moscow: Fenomenologiia-Germenevtika.

———. 2011. Kant and Orthodox Thought in Russia. *Russian Studies in Philosophy* 49 (4): 10–33.

———. 2012. *Kant i kantovskaia filosofiia v russkoi khudozhestvennoi literature*. Moscow: Kanon+ ROOI Reabilitatsiia.

———. 2015. Die erste Rezeption der Religion innerhalb der Grenzen der bloßen Vernunft in Russland: Der Fall Mellmann. In *Vernunftreligion und Offenbarungsglaube. Zur Erörterung einer seit Kant verschärften Problematik*, ed. Norbert Fischer and Jakub Sirovatka, 365–376. Freiburg: Herder.

———. 2016a. Kant und der Siebenjährige Krieg. *Studies in East European Thought* 68 (2–3): 149–164. Dordrecht: Springer.

———. 2016b. Evgeny N. Trubetskoy and Overcoming the Neo-Kantian Kant. *Russian Studies in Philosophy* 54 (5): 408–421.

Kunitsyn, Aleksandr P. 1818. *Pravo estestvennoe*, books 1–3. St. Petersburg: Tipografiia Ios. Ioannesova.

Kuznetsov, Vitalii N. 1989. *Nemetskaia klassicheskaia filosofiia*. Moscow: Vysshaia shkola.

Lapshin, Ivan I. 1900. O trusosti v myshlenii. Etiud po psikhologii metafizicheskogo myshleniia. *Voprosy filosofii i psikhologii* 5 (55): 817–881. Moscow: Tipo-litografiia of I.N. Kushnerev and K°.

Lenin, Vladimir I. 1973. Tri istochnika i tri sostavnykh chasti marksizma. In *Polnoe sobranie sochinenii v 55 tomakh*, vol. 23, 40–48. Moscow: Izdatel'stvo politicheskoi literatury.

Lubkin, Aleksandr S. 1805. Pis'ma o kriticheskoi filosofii. *Severnyi Vestnik* 7 (8–9): 184–197, 304–306. St. Petersburg: Imperatorskaia tipografiia.

———. 1814. Primechaniia k nravstvennomu veroucheniiu. In *Snell', Fridrikh Vil'gel'm Daniel'. Nachal'nyi kurs filosofii. Nravstvennoe verouchenie i obozrenie istorii filosofii*, vol. 5, 30–33. Kazan': Universitetskaia tipografiia.

Magnitskii, Mikhail Leont'evich. 1861. Mnenie deistvitel'nogo statskogo sovetnika Magnitskogo, o Nauke Estestvennogo prava. In *Chteniia v imperatorskom obshchestve istorii i drevnostei rossiiskikh pri Moskovskom universitete*, vol. 4, 157–159. Moscow: Universitetskaia tipografiia.

Makovitskii, Dushan P. 1979. U Tolstogo 1904–1910. 'Iasnopolianskie zapiski' D.P. Makovitskogo. In *Literaturnoe nasledstvo* 90 (2): 5–687. Moscow: Izdatel'stvo Nauka.

Martov, Yulii O. 1917. *Kant s Gindenburgom, Marks s Kantom (Iz letopisi ideinoi reaktsii)*. Petrograd: Izdatel'stvo Sotsialist.

———. 1925. Prostota khuzhe vorovstva. In *Marksizm i etika. Sbornik statei*, ed. Iakov Samoilovich Rozanov, 232–258. Kiev: Gosudarstvennoe izdatel'stvo Ukrainy.

Mehlich, Julia B. 2014. *Irratsional'noe rasshirenie filosofii Kanta v Rossii*. St. Petersburg: Aleteia.

Mellmann, Johann Wilhelm Ludwig. 1790. *Oratio de communi omnis educationis et institutionis consilio in solennibus anniversariis imperii ab augustissima et potentissima totius Rossiae autocratore Catharina II, optima patriae matre ante annum XXVIII suscepti ab universitate Mosquensi rite ac pie celebrandis A. D. XXVIII. Junii anni MDCLXXXX*. Moscow: Okorocow.

Motroshilova, Nelly V. 1994. Predislovie. In *Immanuil Kant. Sochineniia na russkom i nemetskom iazykakh v 6 tomakh*, ed. Nelly V. Motroshilova and Burkkhard Tushling, vol. 1, 42–73. Moscow: Kami.

Nemeth, Thomas. 2017. *Kant in Imperial Russia*. Cham: Springer.

Nikanor, arkhiepiskop Khersonskii (Brovkovich). 1888. Pozitivnaia filosofiia i sverkhchuvstvennoe bytie. In *Kritika na kritiku chistogo razuma Kanta v skolki tomakh?* 3. St. Petersburg: Tipografiia F. Eleonsky and K°.

Nizhnikov, Sergei A. 2005. *Filosofiia I. Kanta v otechestvennoi mysli*. Moscow: Izdatel'stvo Rossiiskogo universiteta druzhby narodov.

Anonymous. "O nedostatkakh i oshibkakh v osveshchenii istorii nemetskoi filosofii kontsa XVIII i nachala XIX vv." 1944. *Bol'shevik* 7–8: 14–19. Moscow: Izdatel'stvo Pravda.

Anonymous. "Ot izdatel'stva." 1937. *Kant, Immanuil. Prolegomeny ko vsiakoi budushchei metafizike, mogushchei vozniknut' v kachestve nauki*, 1–2. Moscow: Gosudarstvennoe sotsial'no–ekonomicheskoe izdatel'stvo.

Perevoshchikov, Vasilii M. 1816. Opyt o vozbuzhdenii i utolenii strasti. *Vestnik Evropy* 12: 281–294. Moscow: Universitetskaia tipografiia.

6 KANT AND KANTIANISM IN RUSSIA: A HISTORICAL OVERVIEW 137

Plekhanov, Georgii V. 1914. *O voine. Otvet tovarishchu Zakhariiu Petrovu.* Paris: Imprimerie Union.

———. 1925. Eshche o voine (Eshche o prostykh zakonakh nravstvennosti i prava). In *Marksizm i etika. Sbornik statei,* ed. Iakov Samoilovich Rozanov. Kiev: Gosudarstvennoe izdatel'stvo Ukrainy.

Plekhanov, Georgii V. 1956. Predislovie k pervomu izdaniiu ('Ot perevodchika') i primechaniia k knige F. Engel'sa Liudvig Feierbakh i konets nemetskoi klassicheskoi filosofii. In *Izbrannye filosofskie proizvedeniia,* vol. 1, 451–503. Moscow: Gosudarstvennoe izdatel'stvo politicheskoi literatury.

Pozzi, Vera. 2018. 'Institutiones Metaphysicae' I.Ya. Vetrinskogo i Sankt-Peterburgskaia Dukhovnaia Academiia. In *Istoriia filosofii* 23 (1): 56–66. Moscow: IFRAN.

Pushkin, Alexander S. 1937. *Evgenii Onegin. Polnoe sobranie* sochinenii v 16 tomakh. Vol. 6. Moscow, Leningrad: Izdatel'stvo AN SSSR.

Pustarnakov, Valentin F. 2003. *Universitetskaia filosofiia v Rossii. Idei. Personalii. Osnovnye tsentry.* St. Petersburg: Izdatel'stvo Russkogo Khristianskogo gumanitarnogo instituta.

Reinhard, Filipp Kh. 1816. *Estestvennoe pravo.* Translated from Latin by Ivan Sychugov. Kazan': Universitetskaia tipografiia.

Rozanov, Yakov S. 1925. Marksizm i kantianstvo (Opyt bibliograficheskogo ukazatelia) 7: 209–222. Moscow: Knigoizdatel'stvo Materialist.

Rozhdestvenskii, Nikolai P. 1884. *Khristianskaia apologetika. Kurs osnovnogo bogosloviia, chitannyi studentam Sankt–Peterburgskoi dukhovnoi akademii v 1881/2 uchebnom godu.* Posmertnoe izdanie Sankt–Peterburgskoi dukhovnoi akademii, ed. Andrei Ivanovich Predtechenskii, vol. 1. St. Petersburg: Tipografiia doma prizreniia maloletnikh bednykh.

Rubinstein, Moisei M. 1915. Vinovat li Kant? In *Russkie vedomosti* February 11 (33): 5. Moscow: Tipografiia Russkikh vedomostei.

Saradzhev, Artashes Kh. 1934. O 'kriticheskom' metode Kanta. In *Immanuil Kant. Prolegomeny,* ed. Artashes Khorenovich Saradzhev, 7–101. Moscow: Gosudarstvennoe sotsial'no-ekonomicheskoe izdatel'stvo.

Savitskii, Zakharii I. 1825. *Izlozhenie glavneishikh sistem nravstvennosti drevnikh i noveishikh filosofov.* Khar'kov: Universitetskaia tipografiia.

Skripnik, Anatolii P. 1978. In *Kategoricheskii imperativ Immanuila Kanta,* ed. Abdusalam A. Guseynov. Moscow: Izdatel'stvo Moskovskogo universiteta.

Skvortsov, Ivan M. 1838. Kriticheskoe obozrenie Kantovoi Religii v predelakh odnogo razuma. *Zhurnal ministerstva narodnogo prosveshcheniia* 17 (1): 44–99. St. Petersburg: Tipografiia Imperatorskoi Akademii Nauk.

Soloviev, Erikh Yu. 2005. *Kategoricheskii imperativ nravstvennosti i prava.* Moscow: Izdatel'stvo Progress-Traditsiia.

———. 2008. Die zweite Formel des kategorischen Imperativs in der moralisch–rechtlichen Lehre Wladimir Solowjows. In *Kant im Spiegel der russischen Kantforschung heute,* ed. Norbert Hinske and Nelly W. Motroschilowa, 145–152. Stuttgart-Bad Cannstatt: Frommann-Holzboog.

Solovyov, Vladimir S. 1990a. Kant. In *Sochineniia.* Vol. 2, 441–479. Moscow: Izdatel'stvo Mysl'.

———. 1990b. Opravdanie dobra. Nravstvennaa filosofiia. In *Sochineniia v 2-kh tomakh,* ed. Alexei Losev and Arsenii Gulyga, vol. 1, 47–580. Moscow: Izdatel'stvo Mysl'.

———. 1990c. Teoreticheskaia filosofiia. In *Sochineniia v 2-kh tomakh*, ed. Alexei Losev and Arsenii Gulyga, vol. 1, 757–831. Moscow: Izdatel'stvo Mysl'.

Sudakov, Andrei K. 1998. *Absoliutnaia nravstvennost': Etika avtonomii i bezuslovnyi zakon*. Moscow: Editorial URSS.

Sumin, Oleg Yu. 2005. *Gegel' kak sud'ba Rossii*. 2nd ed. Krasnodar: PKGOO Glagol.

Tolstoy, Lev N. 1929–1958. Dnevnik, 1907. In *Polnoe sobranie sochinenii v 90 tomakh*. Jubilee Edition. Vol. 56, 3–87. Moscow: Gosudarstvennoe izdatel'stvo Khudozhestvennaia literatura.

———. 2016. *Gedanken Immanuel Kants. Anhand der Originalvorlagen aus dem Russischen zurückübertragen*. Edited by Alexei N. Krouglov. Stuttgart–Bad Cannstatt: Frommann–Holzboog.

Trubetskoi, Evgenii N. 1917. *Metafizicheskie predpolozheniia poznaniia. Opyt preodoleniia Kanta i kantianstva*. Moscow: Tipografiia Russkaia pechatnia.

Villers, Karl. 1804. Immanuil Kant. *Sankt–Peterburgskii zhurnal* 10: 125–135. St. Petersburg: Meditsinskaia tipografiia.

Vorotynkin, Fyodor. 1917. *Elementy chistogo razuma (Kritika Kant'ovskoi logiki). K voprosu ob osvobozhdenii russkoi mysli ot nemetsko-mozgovogo zasil'ia. Opyt kontsentrirovaniia chelovecheskoi mysli v obstanovke, blizkoi k zhizni pervobytnogo cheloveka. Pis'ma iz okopov*. Lutsk: tri tipografii g. Lutska.

Wetrinskj, Herodion. 1821. *Institutiones metaphysicae*. St. Petersburg: Typis M.C. Iversen.

Winter, Alois. 2000. *Der andere Kant. Zur philosophischen Theologie Immanuel Kants*. Foreword by Norbert Hinske. Hildesheim: Georg Olms.

Zhakov, Kallistrat F. 1996. *Skvoz' stroi zhizni*. Syktyvkar: Komi knizhnoe izdatel'stvo.

Zhuchkov, Vladimir A., and Irina I. Blauberg, eds. 2010. *Valentin Ferdinandovich Asmus*. Moscow: ROSSPEN.

CHAPTER 7

Hegel's Philosophy of Freedom in Nineteenth-Century Russia

Jeff Love

Aside from Karl Marx, no modern philosopher had a broader impact in Russia than G. W. F. Hegel,[1] whose thought was one of the primary contexts in which the pressing questions of nineteenth-century Russian life were posed, debated, and transformed from the 1840s onward. Perhaps foremost among these was the question concerning freedom that exercised the most fertile minds of the nineteenth century, not only in Russia, but throughout Europe. In Russia this question had particular urgency given the oppressive regime of Nicholas I (1796–1855), the institution of serfdom, and the perceived general "backwardness" of the country in relation to its European counterparts. This sense of urgency accompanied the many heated debates over Russian identity and the proper way forward for Russia, leaving a fraught legacy for the twentieth century. Suffice it to say that, at one and the same time, the most diverse personalities, from the tumultuous anarchist Mikhail Bakunin to the conservative Ivan Kireevski, studied Hegel avidly; and they all turned to him for very different purposes in pursuit of their own plans for the creation of a just community in Russia, freed from the sins of the past, whether pre- or post-Petrine.

In this chapter I want to examine Hegel's impact on nineteenth-century Russian thought in terms of three debates that express different but nonetheless interlocking perspectives about freedom.[2] The first of these is the debate

J. Love (✉)
Clemson University, Clemson, SC, USA
e-mail: gjlove@clemson.edu

© The Author(s), under exclusive license to Springer Nature Switzerland AG 2021
M. F. Bykova et al. (eds.), *The Palgrave Handbook of Russian Thought*,
https://doi.org/10.1007/978-3-030-62982-3_7

139

140   J. LOVE

about political freedom, whether genuine freedom lies in individual self-assertion or within the community into which the individual integrates herself. The second is the debate over freedom and nature, in the sense of whether we are free to change or master nature, or unable to do so. The third, and final, is perhaps the most sweeping and influential, the debate whether man should become God or retain a notion of God that orients man in the world and subordinates man to the divine will. The characteristic claim in this latter respect is that there can be no reconciliation between human freedom and divine will: one or the other must prevail.

The "Nature" of Freedom

Hegel emerged in Russia in the 1830s just a few years after the philosopher's death in 1831. Several important figures, like Ivan Kireevskii, had attended Hegel's lectures in Berlin in the late 1820s, but the Russian students who initially disseminated Hegel's thought had studied his work primarily with Hegel's first generation of disciples. Among these Russian students were many of the decisive figures of the 1840s, the era of Russian idealism.

While Hegel's entry into Russian intellectual life at this time has been called superficial or a sort of "fad," the traces it left suggest otherwise: indeed, they suggest that Hegel's thought shook Russian intellectual life to its very foundations, a notion that the subsequent history of the Russian intelligentsia does nothing to refute. It is thus perhaps something of a surprise that this formidable intellectual force came to the fore in the circle that formed around a modest man, Nikolai Vladimirovich Stankevich (1813–1840), who was widely admired for his mildness and generosity of spirit. This circle included several of the leading figures in Russian intellectual history, such as Mikhail Bakunin, Vissarion Belinsky, and Alexander Herzen.

Some have viewed the popularity of Hegel's thought as a response to Romantic mysticism, as well as to the failure of the Decembrist revolt in 1825. These differing accounts amply demonstrate the range of response to Hegel in Russia, not only in the beginning, but throughout the nineteenth century; yet, they also reflect the range of response to Hegel in Germany itself as traditionally divided into two broad tendencies, those of the "left" or "young" Hegelians and the "right" or "old" Hegelians. Given the significance of these two tendencies in the dissemination of Hegel's thought, I want to set out briefly the crucial difference between them as an orientation to the subsequent discussion.[3]

This difference may perhaps be best explained in reference to the question of authority. What is the highest authority in human affairs, the human being herself or God? If the human being is the highest authority, the essential course of Hegelian philosophy is to reveal to human beings that they are responsible for their own destiny and that the notion of God maintained in the Western tradition is an alienated figuration of humanity. Thus, the historical trajectory one might associate with this, the left Hegelian, tendency is one of de-alienation whereby the authority formerly vouchsafed to God alone is assumed by a free and self-governing humanity. If, to the contrary, God is the highest authority, Hegelian thought reveals the course of providential design in history and seeks to convince human beings of its rationality or accessibility to human reason and the consequent necessity to conform human thought and action to that design; once this act of willing submission to providence (and reason) is completed, history will be fulfilled and the error stemming from the human inability to grasp the divine (and reason itself) abolished.

To return to Stankevich and his circle, it is evident that the divide in German Hegelianism was reflected in the differing attitudes toward Hegel's thought taken up by members of that circle.[4] And it is equally evident that the central concept at issue—and readily implied by the reference to authority above—was freedom. Exactly what constitutes freedom? The variation in response to this question was expressed largely along the same lines as the question about authority: Does freedom reside in human self-assertion, the assumption of the divine identity by its putative creator, or in accommodation with an essentially divine identity that is in some basic manner different from the human?

Stankevich appears to have walked on the edge of this difference accepting that the world is governed by reason and that individual action should be directed toward affirmation of an overarching rationality. This attitude becomes problematic, however, the moment one transfers it to political reality: it can be an exhortation to revolution or to accommodation with a given political regime depending on whether one considers that regime as reflecting overarching rationality or contravening it. Within this context both Bakunin and Herzen are emblematic, their thinking reflecting in differing ways the broad tensions in nineteenth-century Russian Hegelianism.

Let me now take a look at these two important figures in order to pursue, respectively, the question above about political freedom and then the question of freedom from nature. I will conclude with a discussion of Solovyov's notion of divine humanity in response to the final question above concerning the relation of human beings to God.

Mikhail Bakunin

Bakunin has the reputation of being a protean figure, ever changing, ever restless.[5] This protean quality is quite evident in his attitude toward Hegel. While Bakunin was initially enthusiastic, impressed by Hegel's ostensibly terminal vision of Western civilization, he seems to have subsequently turned against that vision. While it may be an exaggeration to suggest that Bakunin's anarchism resulted from his opposition to Hegel, this claim is nonetheless appropriate because it suggests that anarchism is more deeply indebted to Hegel than its advocates may admit.[6] Indeed, to claim that Bakunin's encounter with Hegel is at the origin of modern anarchism is both polemical and productive. At issue is an underlying view of freedom, and we may fruitfully grasp Bakunin's engagement with Hegel as one that changed (if it did) due to a change of, or

142   J. LOVE

refinement in, Bakunin's understanding of freedom. Far from opposition in fact, I will argue that Bakunin ends up with a striking affirmation (through negation) of certain aspects of Hegel's thought.

There is thus some dispute as to whether Bakunin changed his mind about Hegel, or pursued, with increasing vehemence, insights that had struck him earlier on in his reading of Hegel.[7] For the purposes of my survey I prefer the latter line of thought—though I believe that Bakunin's encounter with Hegel developed significantly in the late 1830s such that "[t]he idea of man's fusion with God gave way almost imperceptibly to the idea of setting free the divine element in *man*" (Walicki 1979, 119). I prefer this characterization of Bakunin's "development" precisely because it allows emphasis on an important pattern in Russian Hegelianism that would appear somewhat later on in the nineteenth century in the work of Solovyov and in the twentieth century in the work of Alexandre Kojève. This pattern emerges from a crucial ambiguity in the notion of fusion with God to which I have already referred; namely, that fusing with God can be at one and the same time an act of the most radical humility *and* self-assertion. Hence, it is not surprising that Bakunin's understanding of Hegel may be regarded ambiguously as well, with some insisting on a change and others on continuity.

Whatever the case, Bakunin's overt Hegelianism was most evident from 1838 to 1842, as recorded in his correspondence and several famous articles, including "The Reaction in Germany" of 1842. Bakunin's two-part article, "On Philosophy," from 1838, reads almost like a very simplified gloss on the *Phenomenology of Spirit*. Bakunin follows a similar structure, dividing the argument of the *Phenomenology* into three primary segments, the stage of consciousness, self-consciousness, and the trickier final stage of completed self-consciousness, or absolute knowledge. Bakunin defines the basic structure in a simple formulation:

> And for this reason, any man *in his singularity is universal*, and, as having *in himself* the universal, can elevate himself to it, without coming out of his singularity, he can know the universal, truth, and realize it by the strength of his free will.

Bakunin continues:

> We saw that the universal is the single basis, the truth, and the necessity of all being, a necessity to which everything is subject, and which nothing can escape. All being of the physical as well as of the spiritual world takes place, develops, lives, and passes, according to necessary and determinate laws, and these laws, as determinate and particular thoughts, are essentially necessary members of the single, infinite, and indissoluble organism of the *universal*, of *reason*. (Del Giudice 1981, 500—translation modified; Bakunin 1987, 177)

Here Bakunin sounds more oriented to a conservative view, or at least a view that comes close to subsuming the individual human being into the ostensibly universal, and not the virulent left Hegelianism with which he is typically associated. But he also retains a basic ambiguity in the sense that the universal can appear to be what overtakes the individual or the individual the universal—which is which? In other words, what is Bakunin's fundamental orientation: Does the universal become individual or the individual become universal? While controversial, one may conclude that, for Bakunin, both amount to the same thing, a fusion of universal and individual in a collective individual or subject, *Geist*, beyond politics, beyond the state.

The possibility of fusion raises another question that is important and will loom over my subsequent discussion: Is Bakunin in fact more Fichtean than Hegelian?[8] Judging from the language Bakunin uses in his article, he seems at pains to ensure that the universal is rooted in "necessary and determinate laws" that are not merely the work of a productive subjectivity, not even a collective one. By this I mean to suggest that Bakunin's emphasis on the universal suggests that the process of converting singularity into universality is not one of the simple negation of the other, the not-I [*Nicht-ich*], thus leading to the creation of a new subjectivity *ex nihilo*, but the discovery of the basic conditions that must be assumed as the determining elements in the discovery of oneself in other, of the process of de-alienation which is also a kind of suffering. If this is so, Bakunin is hardly a pure voluntarist, as he is often accused of being.[9]

Bakunin goes so far as to claim that this "suffering is the necessary condition of human development." To claim such a role for suffering does not seem all that emancipatory unless one considers suffering in the radical form of liberating oneself from the stake in individual existence that seems to be the very wellspring of suffering—only individuals die after all. There is, however, an intriguing Hegelian point that Bakunin may be making here; namely, that suffering is the essence of the "path of despair" [*der Weg der Verzweiflung*] Hegel himself mentions in his short Introduction to the *Phenomenology* (Hegel 1977, 49). While this despair is typically associated with doubt, and Bakunin's notion of suffering is consistent with this association, there is another reading that can be set alongside this one: despair as the loss of individuality or being taken over by the universal to the extent that different understandings of phenomenal appearances, always relative to a given and incorrect view, prove themselves to be connected with the survival or self-preservation of the individual.

This parable is one of de-individuation: as the individual moves progressively deeper into the realm of the concept, and as the concept becomes more concrete, the phenomenal reality that nourishes individuality recedes as a reality serving survival or self-preservation. This is in fact merely another way of describing the "ascent" to universality that, while maintaining its concrete moments in sublated form, cannot be other than a liberation from the illusions to which the particular and the particular individual are prone in favor of coming to a final view that eliminates the individual in universalizing it. The structure Bakunin describes is thus one that causes the suffering of the individual who must give up its attachments to views that maintain the particular individual as necessarily wrong in some way prior to ascending to the truth whereby the individual becomes universal and the universal individual.

One need not diverge from this view in any significant way to come to Bakunin's later praise of the negative or *Negieren*, a praise that is well anchored in the Hegelian texts themselves (Hegel 1970–1971, 1/21). In his famous article, published in 1842 under a pseudonym, "The Reaction in Germany," Bakunin's emphasis is quite clearly on the negative as the fount of revolutionary activity. Although there is an obvious connection between negation and destruction, and a long theological history of connection between negation and evil, Bakunin is far more equivocal; or we may say that he brings together two facets of negation whose underlying sense becomes clearer if its object is clear. What then is the objective of negation? To be sure, that objective can easily be considered the physical destruction of the oppressive order in Europe, the princes and prelates, bankers and financiers, generals, and courtiers whose lives require the virtual enslavement of the vast majority of people. But Bakunin, I venture, goes further than that and, by doing so, shows his deeper affinity with Hegel. Bakunin's more radical concept of negation and "nothingness," what he refers to as *Nichtigkeit*, involves the universalization of the individual—the universalization of the individual is also the most radical an-archism because no *archē* is needed anymore.

Bakunin's negation carries with it of course the fury of the destroyer but if that destruction can be viewed as the destruction of particular individuality, the source of error and violence (as individuals compete to prove their views correct), then Bakunin is in this sense a proponent of the most fundamental negation, that of placing one's individual or material self before others, of selfishness or original sin, dressed up in Hegelian guise as the pursuit of the universal. My life in the universal, the life not devoted to self-assertion, is the life that dispenses with laws, with the *archē* (at least the human one), with the need for a justification, which is merely a way of justifying coercion, an order, an authority. The most pervasive and thoroughgoing anarchy is the one that dispenses with authority, with the need for a criterion granting privileges to some, and denying them to others.

> The whole significance and the irrepressible power of the Negative is the annihilation of the Positive; but along with the Positive it leads itself to destruction as this evil, particular existence which is inadequate to its essence. Democracy does not yet exist independently in its affirmative abundance, but only as the denial of the Positive, and therefore, in this evil state, it too must be destroyed along with the Positive, so that from its free ground it may spring forth again in a newborn state, as its own living fullness. And this self-change of the Democratic party will not be merely a quantitative change, i.e., a broadening of its present particular and hence evil existence: God save us, such a broadening would be the leveling of the whole world and the end result of all of history would be absolute nothingness—but a qualitative transformation, a new, vital, and life-creating revelation, a new heaven and a new earth, a young and magnificent world in which all present discords will resolve themselves into harmonious unity. (Bakunin 1973, 40)

This "young and magnificent world" is precisely one that no longer needs authority because all particular positions have been negated in the consequent creation of a completely harmonious whole. Very far from being the creation of an internally inconsistent anarchism or one that ends in fiery destruction, Bakunin offers a model in which particularity has been abolished, the particular individual being subsumed in a collective or "universal" individual.[10]

For some this must appear to be a disturbing authoritarian or totalitarian state. The assumptions behind such a claim, however, need to be interrogated: Is the best state one that leaves room for the particular, for self-interest, for the singular broadly defined? Or is the risk of such a state not always that the particular, prizing his or her own above all others, must lead ultimately to domination of one group over another, a domination that requires a viable notion of authority to rule without constant recourse to arms? The other course is one of regulating self-interest or denying that it may be satisfied and deploying this denial as a sort of "negative norm."

ALEXANDER HERZEN

Despite his reputation, Herzen appears in this account as a conservative counterweight to Bakunin, one who embraced and then rejected Hegel in a perhaps more complete way than Bakunin (if, indeed, Bakunin ever really rejected Hegel). I should be careful to explain my use of the term "conservative" here. What I mean is that Herzen did not seek the radical negation of particular individuality or self-interest that I claim Bakunin advocated. To the contrary, Herzen stepped back from what we would now call the totalitarian tendencies in Hegel's thought in favor of thinking that has more than a little resemblance to pragmatism, with its emphasis on moderation and a certain cognitive humility. Thus, it is no surprise that Sir Isaiah Berlin should find in Herzen an important political thinker defending a manner of conceiving politics congenial to the liberal democratic consensus (Berlin 1978, 83). But there is also the other Herzen who goes further than the liberal democratic consensus to stress the fact that we simply do not have access to the truth, even that of the liberal democratic state itself. This Herzen offers us the prospect of an equality and universality based on the denial of any final authoritative view.

As with Bakunin, Herzen's reception of Hegel is often divided into two parts, an initial fascination with Hegel followed by increasing distance.[11] While Herzen participated in the same circles as Bakunin, particularly that of Stankevich, it seems that he began his most serious engagement with Hegel upon reading the *Phenomenology of Spirit* in 1841. Herzen ascribed considerable importance to this reading, and Hegel appears prominently in Herzen's important *Dilettantism in Science* from 1842. While commentators distinguish Herzen's early interest in Hegel as being of the more conservative sort (inclined more to what is approximate to right Hegelianism), his most actively Hegelian period shows an alignment more condign to left Hegelianism (Kelly 2016, 149, 152). What this principally means in Herzen's case is that he moves from

146   J. LOVE

a belief in the need to accept reality as it is to a radical embrace of action as the means of resolving the gaping difference between the reality of his time in Russia and the Hegelian ideal. Remarkably Herzen spots in Hegel a reticence to speak openly about his views:

> But if genuine science is really so simple then why did its greatest representatives, for instance Hegel, use so difficult a language? In spite of the power and grandeur of his genius Hegel was but a human being. He dreaded to express himself straightforwardly in an epoch of twisted language, for he dreaded to follow up the extreme consequences of his fundamental principles. He lacked the heroism of consistency, the self-sacrifice of accepting the full truth regardless of the cost. The greatest men, in fact, shrank from the inferences drawn from their fundamental principles. Some of them were frightened and retracing their steps, sought to obscure their meaning instead of seeking clarity. Hegel realized that much of the conventional should have been sacrificed: he was too merciful to deal mortal blows. On the other hand, he could not but give expression to that which he was destined to express. Drawing an inference, Hegel often dreaded to admit its full consequences and sought not the simple, natural conclusion following of itself, but strove to adjust it to the circumstances. And thus the logical development of his idea became more involved and the meaning more obscure. To this let us add his bad habit of using the language of the school, a habit he involuntarily acquired in his life-long conversation with the German scientists. But here, too, his genius broke to the surface in all its might. In the midst of his tortuous sentences there is suddenly a dazzling word which sheds its radiance far around, a word whose thunder reverberates in the soul and inspires awe. No, we cannot reproach this great thinker. A great man may rise above his age, but not depart from it entirely. And if the younger generations have learned to speak more simply, have dared to lift the last of the veils from Isis, it is precisely owing to the fact that Hegel's outlook already existed and has been assimilated. (Herzen 1956, 70)

If Hegel is in this rather complicated sense an esoteric thinker, what is the esoteric doctrine? For Herzen the esoteric (or secret) doctrine is connected with the death of God and rise of science, this being merely another way of describing the sway that reason may have not only over human beings but over nature and the cosmos as well. Herzen is an advocate here, as elsewhere, of the power of reason to identify the larger structures in our lives that determine them, and our way of looking at them. Herzen is no Fichtean subjectivist; to the contrary, he has marked respect for Hegel's attempt to make the world intelligible. Herzen is thus also not a transcendental thinker: there are no transcendent conditions without which the world as we know it might cease to exist. The world is in this sense ruled by immanent "laws" that are accessible to human intelligence or reason but not made by either.

What is fundamentally at stake here? If the world is an expression of immanent laws completely accessible to reason, we can come to transform ourselves from creatures of potential error into totally rational beings who know what the final order of things is. If, on the other hand, the world is an expression of an origin that is necessarily unintelligible, we can never come to know it finally

7 HEGEL'S PHILOSOPHY OF FREEDOM IN NINETEENTH-CENTURY RUSSIA **147**

and are thus never capable of becoming truly rational beings. The change, or evolution, in Herzen's attitude to Hegel comes down to Herzen's increasing skepticism about the final intelligibility of the world.

This change of course has important political implications. Herzen's most avid Hegelianism is tied to a practical political program that, like Bakunin's, seeks to overcome the reign of particular interest in favor of a community that has overcome such self-interest and egoism. If anything, Herzen is more direct and sweeping than Bakunin:

> The sphere of science is the general, thought, reason as self-cognizing spirit. In this sphere it has achieved the main part of its destiny, while the rest will take care of itself. It has understood, cognized, and evolved the truth of reason as underlying reality: it has liberated the thought of the world from the phenomenon of the world, all things that exist, from the fortuitous. It has dissolved everything solid and immobile, made transparent everything that is obscure, brought light into darkness; it has revealed the eternal in the transient, the infinite in the finite and recognized their necessary existence. Finally, it has destroyed the Chinese wall separating the absolute, the true, from man and has hoisted the banner of the autonomy of reason over the ruins. Proceeding from the simple phenomenon of sensuous authenticity and personal reflections, it develops in him the generic idea, the universal reason disengaged from personality. At the outset it demands the sacrifice of personality, Isaac's offering of the heart; this is its *conditio sine qua non* and however terrible it may seem it is right. (Herzen 1956, 72)

Here indeed is Bakunin's negation viewed in the appropriate light of sacrifice of particular interests for the universal.

Now this is certainly not the Herzen proclaimed by Berlin as a defender of human liberty, as an ardent opponent of the kind of tyranny represented by Stalinism and the Soviet Union that so determined the debates about Russian thinkers during the cold war. No, this is a Herzen who is uncompromisingly radical, who resembles Bakunin, and the most radical forms of Christian thought that seek to suppress self-interest in favor of the community, the individual being subsumed in a collective individuality or subjectivity or personality that is a sort of re-birth as Herzen admits. From this perspective, Hegel is a great liberator from the servitude to self-interest, a point made with equal emphasis by one of the twentieth century's most celebrated interpreters of Hegel, heir to Bakunin and Herzen, Alexandre Kojève:

> The entire sphere of finitude, by the fact that it is itself something, belonging to the senses—collapses into the true-or-truthful faith before the thought and intuition [*Anschauung*] of the eternal, [the thought and intuition] becoming here one and the same thing. All the gnats of subjectivity are burned up in this devouring fire; and *even the conscience* of this giving of oneself [*Hingebens*] and of this annihilation [*Vernichtens*] is annihilated [*vernichtet*].
>
> Hegel knows it and says it. But he also says in one of his letters that this knowledge has cost him dearly. He speaks of a period of total depression that he lived

148   J. LOVE

through between the 25th and 30th years of his life, of a "Hyperchondria" that went "*bis zur Erlähmung aller Kräfte*," "to the point of a paralysis of all his forces" and which arose precisely from the fact that he could not accept the necessary abandonment of Individuality, that is in fact of humanity, that the idea of Absolute Knowledge demands. But, finally, he overcame this "Hyperchondria." And, becoming wise through this last acceptance of death, he published, few years later, the First Part of the "System of Knowledge," entitled, "Science of the Phenomenology of the Spirit," where he reconciles himself with all that is and has been, by declaring that there will never again be anything new on earth. (Kojève 1980, 167–168)

If anything, Kojève is more radical (and more Stalinist, at least within his terms) in regard to the necessity of sacrificing individuality or personality to bring about genuine emancipation and the final utopian state where "there will never again be anything new on earth."

Yet Herzen appears to have recoiled from this sacrifice and comes to a more conservative solution, the one so prized by Berlin as inspirational and original. This solution is expressed in part as an attack on Hegel, seen, as he would so often be seen in the twentieth century, as a totalitarian philosopher or, in rougher terms, as subservient to the prerogatives of the (Prussian) state:

It is abstract because it is absolute; it is the knowledge of being but not being itself; it is above it and therein lies its one sidedness. If it were enough for nature to know, as Hegel inadvertently admits at times, then on attaining self-cognition it would cancel its existence and ignore it; but, in fact, existence is as dear to it as knowledge. It loves life but life is possible only in a Bacchic whirl of the transient; while in the sphere of the general, the tumult and the eddies of life calm down. The human genius wavers between these opposites; like Charon it keeps ferrying back and forth from the temporal abode to the eternal one. This crossing, this alternation is history and this is what matters, after all, and not just crossing to the other side and living in the abstract and universal spheres of pure thought. Nor did Hegel alone understand this. Leibniz, a century and a half earlier, said that unless the monad had a transient, ultimate existence it would dissolve into the infinite and completely lose the possibility of asserting itself. All of Hegel's logic discloses that the absolute is the confirmation of the unity of being and thought. But no sooner do Hegel and Leibniz get down to the crux of the matter than they both lay all that is temporal and existing on the altar of thought and spirit. (Herzen 1956, 125–126)

The richness of this passage lies in part in the contrasts it builds between the transient, temporal existence and the eternal sphere of pure thought. That is, Herzen focusses his concern with Hegel (and Leibniz) on the inadequacy of the abstract and the universal when it comes to dealing with temporal existence. The universal flees from time, and there is, in effect, no easily explicable relation between the temporal and non-temporal or eternal. Thus, rather than bringing us closer to concrete, lived existence, Hegel bids us to flee from it; there is no reconciliation of time and the eternal, the finite and the infinite, but rather the dissolution of one into the other, a dissolution that must be similar to death or a wish for death since it is opposed to time, and life takes place in time not outside of it. The concept cannot understand what it does not itself create, and by linking temporal existence and nature, Herzen formulates a criticism of Hegel that, despite Herzen's general suspicion about Schelling, seems indebted to Schelling's attack on Hegel in his *Lectures on the History of Modern Philosophy* and his later lectures, given in Berlin in 1842–1843, on the philosophy of revelation.

Herzen turns from Hegel as one who turns away from concrete existence and cannot tell us anything about it, preferring to flee from it into abstractions. Herzen thus contributes to a line of criticism of Hegel that continues until this day, extending from Schelling and Kierkegaard to Heidegger and Derrida and Foucault. This line of criticism is not so much concerned with the crucial Hegelian issue of mediating immediacy, of figuring out how human cognition achieves a balance between understanding and "raw" experience or intuition, as with taking account of the latter. Hegel indicates in the *Phenomenology* that there is no raw experience other than as mediated by the concept. While for Hegel the mediation of experience first makes it coherent to us, for his opponents, and for Herzen of course, the concept appears to remove us from experience by denying what is arguably its most crucial single feature: time.

Herzen is one of a long line of opponents to Hegel who seek to save our existence in time from the ostensibly deadening or distorting effect of abstraction. By doing so, Herzen becomes an advocate of resistance to the hegemony of the concept or, indeed, any other form of hegemony that purports to explain existence in terms of a framework of absolute or final truths. Herzen creates a politics of compromise, deeming the sacrifice of self-interest, our "natural" interest in our own particular tangible life in time, too great a price to pay or, indeed, a price in itself too great because what is sought—the eternal and infinite—begs us to turn away from life rather than to embrace it, thus constituting an exhortation to political self-abasement or, more radically, to suicide.

VLADIMIR SOLOVYOV

It is perhaps not clear that Solovyov should be considered Hegelian. One shrewd commentator suggests that Solovyov's thought has much more in common with Schelling than Hegel (Kojève 1934, 540). Another sees in Solovyov a neo-Hegelian (Kline 2015, 2645). I tend to agree with the latter characterization and find Solovyov's thinking, at least around the time of his famed *Lectures on Divine Humanity* (1878–1881), quite Hegelian in spirit. Solovyov undertakes what could be regarded as a reconciliation of the right and left Hegelian positions. More than that, however, he also grants great importance to concrete human life and the creation of a philosophy of practice that is at once less radical than Bakunin's and more inclined to accept ultimate truth than Herzen.

150   J. LOVE

In the *Lectures*, Solovyov begins with the negative and negation. He ends up with a positive philosophy that does not succumb to the negative but is intended in fact to overcome it. While these two orientations recall a distinction made by the later Schelling between positive and negative philosophy (Houlgate 1999, 101–111), they have little to do with Schelling's work but constitute an original philosophical orientation that, typically for Solovyov, is an attempt to create an overarching synthesis of philosophical positions.

At the beginning of the second lecture, Solovyov clarifies this distinction:

> Absoluteness, like the similar concept of infinity, has two meanings, one negative and one positive. Negative absoluteness, which undoubtedly belongs to the human person, consists in the ability to transcend every finite, limited content, not to be limited by it, not to be satisfied with it, but to demand something greater. In the words of a poet, it consists in the ability "to seek raptures for which there is no name or measure." Not satisfied with any finite conditional content, humanity does, indeed, declare itself to be free from any internal limitation. It declares its negative absoluteness, which constitutes the surety of an infinite development. But the dissatisfaction with any finite content, with any partial, limited reality, is itself a demand for all of reality, for full content. And in the possession of all of reality, of the fullness of life, lies positive absoluteness. Without it, or without at least the possibility of it, negative absoluteness has no significance, or rather, it signifies only an unresolvable internal contradiction. The contemporary consciousness finds itself in just such a contradiction. Western civilization has liberated human consciousness from all external limitations, acknowledging the negative absoluteness of the human person and proclaiming absolute human rights. But at the same time, by rejecting every principle that is absolute in the positive sense, that in reality and by its very nature possesses the entire fullness of being, and by circumscribing human life and consciousness with a circle of the conditional and transitory, this civilization has also asserted infinite striving and the impossibility of its satisfaction. (Solovyov 1995, 17–18)

The central object of Solovyov's thinking is to investigate the absolute and to articulate what he refers to as the positive absolute. The negative absolute, to the contrary, is for Solovyov very problematic because it can only lead to dissatisfaction, a sense of impossibility that is indeed akin to Hegel's own notion of bad infinity. Hence, Solovyov, again like Hegel in this respect, does not seek to remain with philosophy as the eternally frustrated pursuit of wisdom, of a final point that lies infinitely distant, now and forever, but rather he seeks to make the transition from the love of wisdom to wisdom itself,[12] from philosophy to sophiology.

This transition is the most distinctive aspect of Solovyov's thinking and Solovyov purports to describe it in the *Lectures* which, in this respect, constructs a path from the negative to the positive that, in barest outline, is not dissimilar from the developmental story Hegel pioneers in the *Phenomenology*. There are indeed several common elements in terms of the path from the negative, a beginning full of apparently unrealized and unrealizable possibility, to

7 HEGEL'S PHILOSOPHY OF FREEDOM IN NINETEENTH-CENTURY RUSSIA   151

the final establishment of the absolute principle. On the way toward the affirmation of this final principle Solovyov weaves together art, philosophy, and theology in a series of grand triads that imitate, perhaps in the most basic manner, the Hegelian dialectics.

The main figure in this transition is of course the human being. The crucial contradiction Solovyov seeks to address is essentially that between absolute or infinite aspiration and finite capacity:

> For human beings today admit, both in life and in knowledge, only a limited, conditional reality, a reality of particular facts and phenomena, and from this point of view a human being is but one of those particular facts. Thus, on the one hand, a human being is a being with absolute significance, with absolute rights and demands. On the other hand, this same human being is only a limited and transitory phenomenon, a fact among the multitude of other facts, limited by them and dependent upon them on all sides. This is true not only of the individual, but also of humanity in its entirety. (Solovyov 1995, 18)

From this contradiction is born the notion of "two absolutes" that is Solovyov's intriguing (and controversial) way of resolving the contradiction. The primary absolute is the divine being who, in Solovyov's Hegelian terms, combines subject and substance into one absolute and absolutely independent being that contains all, but is contained by none. The question, then, is how the absolute being may relate to the contingent flesh and blood human being in a way that is not negative, that is, that does not emphasize its own impossibility, or an infinite distance, but rather harmony and unity.

Solovyov's attempt to resolve this problem is of course well-known: the notion of divine humanity [*bogochelovechestvo*].[13] In this respect, Solovyov appears to lean toward a left Hegelian orientation, and his attempt to resolve the problem of the relation of a contingent being to one that is entirely freed of contingency offers an interesting perspective not only in itself but also in terms of the relation between the left and right Hegelian tendencies. How is it possible in the end for human beings to become God while allowing God to remain God? This most ancient question, posed by the three hypostases, plays a crucial role in the remainder of the *Lectures*, the end of practical (and thus historical) action being the unification of the human being and God. Solovyov gives a hint at his solution in lecture five:

> The will of God must be the law and norm for the human will, not as acknowledged despotism but as the consciously chosen good. Upon this inner relationship is to be established a new covenant between God and humankind, a new divine-human order which is to replace the preliminary and transitional religion that was grounded in the external law. (Solovyov 1995, 72)
>
> In the divine organism of Christ, the acting, unifying principle, the principle that expresses the unity of that which absolutely is, is obviously the Word, or Logos. The second kind of unity, the produced unity, is called Sophia in Christian theosophy. If we distinguish in the absolute in general between the absolute as

such (that which absolutely is) and its content, essence, or idea, we will find the former directly expressed in the Logos and the latter directly expressed in Sophia, which is thus the expressed or actualized idea. (Solovyov 1995, 109–111)

Solovyov then proceeds to identify human beings as a whole as this link:

> A human being contains all possible oppositions, which can all be reduced to the one great opposition between the unconditional and the conditional, between absolute and eternal essence and transitory phenomenon, or appearance. A human being is at the same time divinity and nothingness. (Solovyov 1995, 116)

The pursuit of wisdom is productive, actualizing unity, and in this sense Solovyov carries on an essentially Hegelian project. But, as at least one celebrated commentator has noted, Solovyov retains a structure that makes it impossible for the human being itself to become absolute or to unite completely with the principle of unity: the human being is always in a sense secondary, imitating or unifying itself with something that exceeds it. Hence, the question arises as to whether Solovyov is genuinely Hegelian (and of the "right wing") or more Kantian in the sense that the achievement of the project of unity seems thwarted if the unifying principle is unattainable in itself but remains as a sort of "regulatory" idea to emulate. In other words, the proper point may well be that Solovyov tacitly admits the impossibility of becoming absolute or wise, or even attaining to sophia, and thus only alleviates the skepticism inherent in his solution. For to attain a completion that is necessarily secondary, if the absolute remains independent in some way, is to retain the same essentially negative orientation from which Solovyov begins. The finite being cannot truly encompass the infinite; indeed, the finite being can do little more than what Solovyov originally decries by attempting to eliminate as many limitations as possible.

The question here is whether a positive absolute is possible at all. The sense that Solovyov gives to the notion of the positive absolute brings us to this question and leaves considerable doubt about the possibility of achieving the absolute. Put in simple terms, the key underlying issue, of which Solovyov is fully conscious, is whether a finite being can legitimately claim to absolve itself of all limitation, to be in this perhaps controversial sense, infinite. And, as I suggested, Solovyov in this respect brings up the fundamental debates over the nature of Christ, debates that led to numerous heresies and retain their power today. Moreover, Solovyov's solution goes back deeply into the Platonic question of *methexis*, or the relation of the ideas to their copies in time and space, an issue that animates one of Plato's most influential dialogues, the *Parmenides*, of which Hegel said that it was a supreme display of (negative) dialectical thought.

The basic question is still very much with us also in the sphere of artificial intelligence and modern conceptions of "superintelligence," another projection of infinity as infinite thought in a sense that goes back to Medieval debates

7 HEGEL'S PHILOSOPHY OF FREEDOM IN NINETEENTH-CENTURY RUSSIA

about God and the accessibility of God to the human mind. While various views emerge, analogy, equivocity, and univocity, the essential underlying issue is the same: Is God somehow like us but in an infinitely intensified way or is God transcendent, always beyond us?

PHILOSOPHIES OF ACTION

To conclude—that is the question at issue in the preceding accounts. How to attain to an end, be it absolute freedom, freedom from the absolute, or union with the absolute. In each case the central oppositions, between particular and whole, nature and reason, or finite and infinite have their proximate provenance not only in Hegel but also in the vast tradition he communicated and culminated. Unlike Kant, Fichte, or Schelling, Hegel's thought offered up the central questions that occupied his predecessors within a vast historical panorama, a holistic account of Western thought that must have been irresistible to a generation eager to learn about the West as an alternative to an ugly reality. Moreover, as we have seen, the notion of history as a history of liberation exercised the Russian imagination with as much force as their European counterparts. I have merely examined a few examples of that response in the nineteenth century, avoiding the importance of Hegel for other streams in Russian thought, including the ostensibly more conservative Slavophiles. I have done so because I have sought to focus on a remarkably fecund line of Russian Hegelianism that represents a potent response and counterpoint to the reception of Hegel in the West and arguably culminates with Kojève's very influential lectures on Hegel from the 1930s, given in the heart of the West, the capital of the nineteenth century, Paris.

The primary concern of the Russian reception, even in the case of Solovyov, was action. The most common narrative of the Russian reception of Hegel constructs a story that begins with deploying Hegel to justify a certain quiescence, a reconciliation with an evidently despairing reality, and ends with either a rejection of Hegel or an intensification of the most radical notions of political practice, in pursuit of reconciliation brought about by action. To conclude, let me review the alternatives I have sketched out so briefly above.

Bakunin's notion of practice is understood as negation. In the sense of Solovyov, Bakunin is the negative thinker par excellence. But, as such, he is hardly superficial or precariously glib as some claim (McLaughlin 2002, 9–10); rather, he gets to the heart of one crucial path toward the absolute as a path of shedding one's interest in oneself, in overcoming the self-orientation that cannot but promote one's interests over others. Bakunin's "nihilism" consists in the harshest critique of self-interest, not in the promotion of individual liberty at the expense of all others. If Bakunin referred to himself as a staunch advocate of liberty (Bakunin 1973, 128), I have argued that he viewed liberty as freedom from the narrow confines of self-interest rather than as the essentially bourgeois deification of self-interest. In the end, then, Bakunin's liberty is radical anarchism in the sense that he seeks to free all from the chains of self-interest, creating a community freed from authority. Of course, the problem attending such a utopian plan is that self-negation is extremely difficult to put into practice—as long as we live, we cannot be assured that we have truly freed ourselves of self-interest because every day we continue to live we do so based on appropriating resources to ourselves.

Herzen rejects this radical agenda in favor of a compromise with self-interest placed in the context of nature: we are unable, ultimately, to overcome nature, either cognitively or in practice. Herzen thus repeats the rejection of the most radical utopian positions that one sees at the outset of the modern period in Machiavelli and Hobbes. The ostensibly classical liberal position identifies freedom with self-interest (in Hobbes' case the most pervasive form of self-interest, self-preservation, or the promise of freedom from violent death). Yet, Herzen adds another component that turns infinite dissatisfaction into the engine of a practical political order. By this I mean that Herzen advocates cognitive and practical humility as a means of creating a society where dissatisfaction with the achievement of final freedom becomes satisfaction with attenuated freedom; namely, the effort to persuade all to let go of the most aggressive illusions of self-interest in favor of a mutually supportive society where the inability of any one to claim authority imposes upon all a duty to negotiate disputes without forcing them to end with the conquest or destruction of others—here many years in advance is the sort of polity encouraged in the twentieth century by Hannah Arendt and Jürgen Habermas, among others.

If the notion of divine humanity developed by Solovyov seems to be closer to Bakunin in some respects than Herzen, I suggest that this is not in fact the case. To be sure, Solovyov sees no value in self-interest, but the crucial ambiguity of his "two absolutes" has a practical impact that bears more resemblance to Herzen than to Bakunin, at least as I interpret them. The primary difference on the surface is that both Bakunin and Herzen propose a sort of "negative norm," whereas Solovyov seeks to create a positive one that does not end in radical self-abnegation or an attempt to moderate self-interest through the admission of dissatisfaction. Evidently, Solovyov did not view a societal compact based on the impossibility of satisfaction as a convincing or indeed inspiring political creed. At the same time, however, it is not clear whether Solovyov's positive solution to the essentially negative view is in fact an overcoming of it or merely another myth by which a deeper admission of the inevitability of dissatisfaction is masked.

The enduring aspect of this reception of Hegel, I suggest, lies in its persistent questioning about the possibility of a final, and free, political order and the notion of freedom expressed by that order. And here we come to the heart of the matter: Is freedom to be sought in the liberation of self-interest or in its negation? If Bakunin responds to this question with exceeding radicality, then both Herzen and Solovyov are more circumspect, more skeptical, perhaps, more Kantian in so far as they recognize that the overcoming of self-interest (or inclination in Kantian terms) is a radical form of autonomy that is the negation of the actor in the moment of the final achievement of freedom. To put the point more clearly, both Herzen and Solovyov recognize the basic incoherence that attends the achievement of the most radical self-abnegation, which, as Dostoevsky's Kirillov recognizes, cannot but be literal suicide. Shrinking back from this apparently absurd solution, Herzen and Solovyov offer attempts to minimize the potential for violence that accompanies any assertion of self-interest where what is "mine" necessarily has to claim priority over what is not mine.[14] In doing so, they create alternatives that are still very much with us in the various claims promoting human humility as the solution to political violence and environmental depredation, either as the acknowledgment of the impossibility of satisfaction through technology or as the claim for a new positive mythology of acceptance, the mythology of finitude.

NOTES

1. Nikolai Berdyaev claimed that Hegel's importance for Russia resembled the importance of Plato for the patristics and Aristotle for the scholastics (Berdyaev 1948, 72). The standard accounts are Chizhevsky 1992, Jakowenko 1934, Koyré 1950, and Planty-Bonjour 1974. There are also several recent articles, for example, Frede 2013 and Shkolnikov 2013.

2. In doing so, I am offering a somewhat different picture than most traditional intellectual histories of Russia which, as Alexandre Koyré notes, are organized chronologically (Koyré 1950, 104). Moreover, there is a slightly polemical intent, primarily in regard to Bakunin and Herzen. I wish to highlight the importance of both but in a somewhat different manner than as characterized in Sir Isaiah Berlin's important and pioneering essay. See Berlin 1978, 82–113.

3. See in this connection Toews 1985.

4. Victoria Frede notes that Stankevich himself, and thus the circle as well, was influenced primarily by the older generation of Hegelians, the right Hegelians. This suggestion supports the notion (see below) that Bakunin's view about Hegel underwent a change from an appreciation of Hegel as the architect of the modern rational state to an aversion to his thought based in an aversion to the rational state. See Frede 2013, 159–174.

5. See, for example, Berlin 1978; Carr 1975; Kelly 1982; Leir 2006; Morris 1970.

6. It is intriguing to note that a similar attitude to Hegel was expressed in France by the generation of the 1960s. Some trace this rejection to the interpretation of Hegel presented by a Russian, Alexandre Kojève, whom we may place with the left Hegelians, at least as regards the form of his interpretation.

7. The general view is that Bakunin changed the views he expressed in 1838, though at least one scholar provides a much more nuanced account of Bakunin's development: see Del Giudice 1981, 302–303.

8. This is an issue of some moment since the association with Fichte allows an interpretation of Bakunin's thought as radical nihilism in the sense often applied to Bakunin as a prophet of destruction, or creation through destruction. As I note below, the problem essentially comes down to an understanding of what Bakunin means by destruction: Is destruction the suppression of other in favor of some self that antecedes the other, or, as I will argue, the destruction of oneself as individual in favor of a collective self dispensing with the need for author-

ity. Regarding Bakunin as a Fichtean, see McLaughlin 2002, 23–24. Again, Del Giudice provides a carefully nuanced account—Del Giudice 1981, 151–279. Del Giudice makes an excellent case for the far greater depth and breadth of Bakunin's engagement with Hegel than with Fichte.

9. By "voluntarist" I mean one whose will is creative, not merely *responding* to different choices but *creating* those choices by initiating a series of states. A will that chooses to obey natural laws (as Bakunin seems to bid us to do) is hardly will within this meaning of the term and suggests in fact that Bakunin is more of a right than a left Hegelian in so far as his notion of emancipation is at the same time an exhortation to obey (natural laws): Bakunin does not tell us to impose human rule on nature but, to the contrary, to impose the rule of nature on human beings (an apparently contradictory plan of action if we are already natural beings). Here Bakunin seems to end up in difficulties which his twentieth-century successor in negation, Alexandre Kojève, resolved by making the point of negation nature itself. From this perspective Bakunin creates a secularized Augustinian view whereby will [*voluntas*] is expressed as the power to disobey as well as obey, with God being replaced by natural law.

10. This interpretation of anarchism may not immediately seem to fit well with Bakunin's properly anarchist writings of the later 1860s and early 1870s where the element of self-sacrifice is less clearly evident though the assertion of natural law remains (indeed, it becomes more dominant). Bakunin writes in *God and the State*: "In his relation to natural laws but one liberty is possible to man—that of recognizing and applying them on an ever-extending scale in conformity with the object of collective and individual emancipation or humanization which he pursues" (Bakunin 1973, 129). Is such emancipation a dedication to the subordination of insubordinate particular impulses to these sweeping laws that govern us? In any event, any dedication to universal laws has to bring about the same negation of particular interests as Bakunin seems to promote in "The Reaction in Germany" and thus may be regarded as continuing the program announced in the article.

11. See Harris 2013 and more generally Shpet 1921 and Kelly 2016.

12. "The true shape in which truth exists can only be the scientific system of such truth. To help bring philosophy closer to the form of Science, to the goal where it can lay aside the title '*love* of knowing' and be *actual* knowing" (Hegel 1977, 3).

13. This translation has occasioned some controversy. It is no doubt more literal than God-manhood since the Russian *chelovek*, like the Greek *anthrōpos*, does not indicate gender. The other aspects of the debate have to do with emphasis: Is it God who is humanized or humanity that is divinized? I will not be going into the intricacies of the arguments—suffice it to say that I put more stress on the divinization of the human because this retains, it seems to me, the separation that Solovyov retains between the divine and human absolute.

14. Jean-Jacques Rousseau, whose influence on German Idealism as a whole is hard to overestimate, makes this point eloquently at the beginning of the second part of his *Discourse on Inequality*. See Rousseau 2002, 113.

BIBLIOGRAPHY

Bakunin, Mikhail. 1987. *Izbrannye filosofskie sochinenia i pis'ma*. Moscow: Mysl'.

———. 1973. In *Selected Writings*, ed. Arthur Lehning. London: Jonathan Cape.

Berdyaev, Nikolai. 1948. *The Russian Idea*. Trans. R. M. French. New York, NY: Macmillan.

Berlin, Isaiah. 1978. *Russian Thinkers*, ed. Henry Hardy and Aileen Kelly. Harmondsworth, UK: Penguin.

Carr, Edward H. 1975. *Michael Bakunin*. New York, NY: Octagon.

Chizhevsky, Dmitry. 1992. *Gegel' v Rossii*. Moscow: Nauka.

Del Giudice, Martine. 1981. *The Young Bakunin and Left Hegelianism: Origins of Russian Radicalism and Theory of Praxis, 1814-1842*. PhD diss., McGill University.

Frede, Victoria. 2013. Stankevič and Hegel's Arrival in Russia. *Studies in East European Thought* 65 (3/4): 159–174.

Harris, Robert. 2013. Granovsky, Herzen and Chicherin: Hegel and the Battle for Russia's Soul. In *Hegel's Thought in Europe*, ed. Lisa Herzog, 35–48. London: Palgrave Macmillan.

Hegel, Georg Wilhelm Friedrich. 1977. *Phenomenology of the Spirit*. Trans. A. V. Miller. Oxford: Oxford University Press.

———. 1970–1971. *Werke*, ed. E. Moldenhauer and K. Michel, vol. 20: 1. Frankfurt: Suhrkamp Verlag.

Herzen, Alexander. 1956. *Selected Philosophical Works*. Trans. L. Navrozov. Moscow: Progress.

Houlgate, Stephen. 1999. Schelling's Critique of Hegel's 'Science of Logic'. *The Review of Metaphysics* 53 (1): 99–128.

Jakowenko, Boris. 1934. *Ein Beitrag zur Geschichte des Hegelianismus in Russland*. Prague: Josef Bartl.

Kelly, Aileen. 1982. *Mikhail Bakunin: A Study in the Psychology and Politics of Utopianism*. Oxford: Clarendon Press.

———. 2016. *The Discovery of Chance: The Life and Thought of Alexander Herzen*. Cambridge, MA: Harvard University Press.

Kline, George L. 2015. *George L. Kline on Hegel*. North Syracuse, NY: Gegensatz.

Kojève, Alexandre. 1980. *Introduction to the Reading of Hegel*. Trans. James Nichols, Jr. Ithaca, NY: Cornell University Press.

———. 1934. La métaphysique religieuse de Vladimir Solovyov. *Revue d'histoire et de philosophie religieuses* 14: 534–554.

Koyré, Alexandre. 1950. *Études sur l'histoire da la pensée philosophique en Russie*. Paris: J. Vrin.

Leir, Mark. 2006. *Bakunin: The Creative Passion—A Biography*. New York: Seven Stories Press.

Mclaughlin, Paul. 2002. *Mikhail Bakunin: The Philosophical Basis of His Anarchism*. New York: Algora Publishing.

Morris, Brian. 1970. *Bakunin: The Philosophy of Freedom*. Montreal: Black Rose Books.

Planty-Bonjour, Guy. 1974. *Hegel et la pensée philosophique en Russie 1830-1917*. La Haye: Martinus Nijhoff.

Rousseau, Jean-Jacques. 2002. *The Social Contract and the First and Second Discourses*, ed. Susan Dunn. New Haven, CT: Yale University Press.

Shkolnikov, Vadim. 2013. The Crisis of the Beautiful Soul and the Hidden History of Russian Hegelianism. In *Hegel's Thought in Europe*, ed. Lisa Herzog, 17–34. London: Palgrave Macmillan.

Shpet, Gustav. 1921. *Filosofskoe mirovozrenie Gertzena*. Petrograd: Kolos.

Solovyov, Vladimir S. 1995. *Lectures on Divine Humanity*. Trans. Peter Zouboff, revised by Boris Jakim. Hudson, NY: Lindisfarne Press.

Toews, J.E. 1985. *Hegelianism: The Path Toward Dialectical Humanism 1805-1841*. Cambridge, UK: Cambridge University Press.

Walicki, Andrzej. 1979. *A History of Russian Thought from The Enlightenment to Marxism*. Trans. Hilda Andrews-Rusiecka. Stanford, CA: Stanford University.

CHAPTER 8

Vladimir Solovyov: Philosophy as Systemic Unity

Nelly V. Motroshilova

Vladimir Sergeevich Solovyov (1853–1900) is rightly considered to be one of the most original thinkers and the central figure in Russian philosophy of the nineteenth century. The founder of a tradition of Russian spirituality that brought together ideas of philosophy, mysticism, and theology, combining them with a powerful social message, he was instrumental in the development of Russian philosophy, as well as in the Russian spiritual renaissance of the late nineteenth and the early twentieth century. He was the first Russian thinker who attempted to develop a philosophical system which would offer solutions to core issues in such varying fields as the history of philosophy, ontology, epistemology, scientific cognition, theology, ethics, and politics, thus changing the direction and central discourse of Russian philosophy.

Quite a lot has been written about Vladimir Solovyov's philosophy in Russia and abroad (see Gaidenko 2001; Losev 2009; Kornblatt 2004; Kostalevsky 1997; Kozyrev 2007; Mrówczyński-Van Allen 2013; Nemeth 2014; Valliere 2007).[1] Yet the task of providing a general analysis of his philosophy as a (relatively) integral systemic unity remains current. I see my goal in this chapter as

---

An earlier version of this text was published in Motroshilova 2007, 83–102. Used here with permission of the publisher.

N. V. Motroshilova (✉)
Institute of Philosophy, Russian Academy of Sciences, Russian Federation, Moscow, Russia

© The Author(s), under exclusive license to Springer Nature Switzerland AG 2021
M. F. Bykova et al. (eds.), *The Palgrave Handbook of Russian Thought*, https://doi.org/10.1007/978-3-030-62982-3_8

160 N. V. MOTROSHILOVA

one of examining Solovyov's original systematic approach to philosophical knowledge and identifying the main systemic dimensions of his philosophy.

CAN SOLOVYOV'S PHILOSOPHY BE VIEWED AS A SYSTEMATIC WHOLE?

Some authors believe that Vladimir Solovyov's philosophy does not possess a systemized wholeness, and that, in the course of its development, it gravitated more and more toward an asystemic and even antisystemic form, transforming into a scattered body of works and fragments more essay-like and polemical in construction. For evidence of this, we can turn to Solovyov's own statements aimed against the various system-creating constructions of traditional philosophy, including those against "static pantheism," Spinoza's *ordo geometrico*, or Hegel's many-branched system of philosophical science. In *Theoretical Philosophy* [*Teoreticheskaia filosofiia*], for example, Solovyov writes that "finalized, 'absolute' systems have outlived their age, while much-needed 'collective' philosophy, or more precisely, a philosophy assembled from parts, excludes the very concept of a sole architect, as well as of a sole undertaker" (Solovyov 1988, 824–825). He also criticized positivist classifications of science and philosophy that "cannot represent a true comprehensive system of knowledge" (ibid., 756). In *Critique of Abstract Principles* [*Kritika otvlechennykh nachal*] he demonstrates in detail the untenability of any "external system of science" of the kind that positivism proposes. It is, however, highly important and characteristic that the philosopher does not in the least dismiss in itself the desire to discover and construct a system of science, a system of knowledge. On the contrary, he clearly states,

> The laws of phenomena that constitute the content of particular fields of science present us only with individual aspects of the phenomenal world, not with its overall truth. Approaching the latter requires unifying all these particular laws and, accordingly, particular fields of science *into a single whole, connected system of knowledge. This is the perfectly legitimate demand of positivism.* (Solovyov 1988, 668; italics mine)

In that respect, Solovyov quite definitely outlines a "positive system of science," a project that "is clearly possible only on the basis of the kind of general principle that would embrace all substantial sides of human knowledge, including their internal connection or general meaning (ratio)" (ibid., 756). But is this "legitimate" systematic construction applicable only to the particular fields of science (to "the laws of phenomena") that Solovyov is discussing in this context? Does it in fact relate to philosophy as well?

I believe Solovyov considers systematic construction to be applicable not only to the "positive sciences" but also to philosophical knowledge, applicable moreover due to the very necessity that arises from the inner essence of philosophy. Another issue is that the philosopher is discussing *systemic nature in a renewed understanding* that has broken away, first of all, from any pretense of "absoluteness" among the individual principles at the foundation of this system, principles which are in fact one-sided, and second, from the idea of "sole responsibility," of a single system "architect" (as were, for example, Hegel or Kant). In the former case, Solovyov links systematicity not with any kind of abstracted (discrete, removed) principle, but with the all-unifying principle of All-Unity [*Vseedinstvo*]. In the latter case, he advances the idea not of sole responsibility, that system-creating activity takes place and is completed at some particular time and entirely by some particular person, but of prolonged, sustained *collective aggregative work* produced, of course, by separate individuals, but with an "internally binding plan" (Solovyov 1988, 825) that cannot otherwise be realized than through long-term history.

Solovyov's oeuvre contains no shortage of more concrete attempts at working out the various aspects of a systematic, integral-synthetic construction of philosophy. For example, his polemic with Kant (in *Kritika otvlechennykh nachal*) indicates the "direct dependence of the ethical question on the metaphysical" (Solovyov 1988, 595),[2] and from this perspective, Solovyov's work, from his first steps in philosophy to his last texts, on the problem of the "absolute-existent" as the fundamental basis, as the first principle of philosophy, is especially important. "Our understanding of the absolute-existent, which constitutes the starting point of the first theosophical science and, accordingly, lies at the foundation of *all systems of integral knowledge*, differs *toto coelo* from 'the absolute' of rationalist philosophy" (Solovyov 1989, 232; italics mine). Thus, while dissociating himself from the principles and approaches of system-creating "absolute" rationalist philosophy, Solovyov does not reject the ideal of a systematic construction itself, which he considers *"the entire system of total knowledge,"* where a newly interpreted principle of the absolute also plays a central role. But can we say of Solovyov's systematic philosophical construction that it truly, fundamentally differs from the system of traditional philosophy and above all of rationalist philosophy?

Some differences are in fact apparent, and they may even be considered substantial in a certain sense. They already appear in the Solovyov quotations above. No less substantial, however, are those elements, those aspects that bring Solovyov's philosophy closer to classical thought in terms of systematicity, of the internal unity of philosophy. In what follows, I will first summarize the elements of difference, and then the similarities.

All the evidence suggests that Solovyov was not guided by the ideal of an "encyclopedic" system of philosophy like those historically well-known examples of systematic philosophical constructions from the seventeenth and early eighteenth to nineteenth centuries (Christian Wolff's or Hegel's, for example). Solovyov had no desire to support or continue, much less realize, the project of necessarily constructing philosophy as a unity of special disciplines (rational cosmology, ontology, psychology, epistemology) or as a unity of logic, philosophy of nature, and philosophy of spirit (subdivided in turn into individual sub-categories) or as a unity of theoretical and practical philosophy, overarching metaphysical projects subjected to critique and already substantially overcome in the process of the development of classical philosophy. It was not just an issue of whether, during the last quarter of the nineteenth century, fulfilling this kind of project aimed at elaborating a substantially renewed and monstrously proliferating mass of knowledge was beyond the powers of any individual or even of a generation of philosophers. Repeating a Hegelian "system-creating" intellectual feat was impossible under these new conditions. More importantly, history had confirmed that any kind of individual principle (matter, spirit, the absolute, the self, and so forth) laid at the foundation of a system devalues the truly titanic work aimed at a more or less full explication of a system in its most substantial areas. This perhaps testified to the end of an era that had begun already in ancient Greek thought, when the philosopher sought some initial beginning of the world, its arche. Solovyov, meanwhile, sensitively perceived "the beginning of the end."

Solovyov's critical attitude toward classical metaphysical systems in the second half of the nineteenth century reflected the philosopher's already substantially broad mindset. In the twentieth century, these kinds of mindsets were fated to become truly dominant. By the end of the twentieth century, both asystematicity and antisystematicity were to become almost the main principles of many non-classical philosophical doctrines. For these, the struggle against systematicity was tightly interwoven with the struggle against scientism, or philosophy's orientation toward science and scienticity. The leading slogan was fundamental fragmentariness, the "patchwork quality" of philosophizing. Indeed, the pretense of systemic wholeness was now declared an echo of the totalitarian desire to suppress the freedom of human thought, which they claimed was "naturally" non-systematic in nature. Though Solovyov was both here and in a number of other cases in agreement with some of his contemporaries (like Nietzsche) in partially summarizing but partially anticipating the future line of critique of metaphysical systems of classical thought, he certainly would not have supported antisystemic or antimetaphysical nihilism in philosophy, whatever its source: the forms of positivism he was already familiar with (or saw as possible in the future), or the "essayism," "fragmentarism," or whatever. These sentiments and consequences of the struggle with classical philosophical systematicity are alien to Solovyov. Though speaking out against traditional forms of system-creation in philosophy, Solovyov does not at all dismiss the "positive" significance of a philosophical system; he does not reject those achievements of systematic thinking that he considers integral to philosophical culture. Criticizing the universal rationalism of past philosophy, its headlong focus on science, its insufficient attention to non-scientific, non-rationalist forms of comprehending the world, Solovyov does not, however, break with scientism nor with rationalism as principles of philosophical inquiry.

Thus, while not intending to follow Wolff or Hegel through the debris of their concrete and multidisciplinary systematic classifications, Solovyov does not at all neglect the whole range of principles and findings of systematic thought. What are these? I will identify only a few.

1. Solovyov maintains the traditional distinction between theoretical and practical philosophy. Of course, Solovyov's own development saw him turning toward a "justification of truth" (the outline of *Theoretical Philosophy*) after he had written his essay "Justification of the Good" ["Opravdanie dobra"]; moreover, he was unable to bring his work to a conclusion due to his early death. However, the very intention of bringing theoretical and practical philosophy into a systematic unity undoubtedly testifies to Solovyov's fidelity to this classical principle and to his desire to carry out a renewed effort in both spheres of philosophical knowledge.

2. Nor is there any doubt that Solovyov more or less maintained, in some sense or another, the main, traditionally designated trends of philosophical systematization, though, as literarily gifted and inclined to essays and polemics as this author was, his work essentially embraced the classical subject matter of traditional metaphysics (cosmology, ontology, epistemology, psychology), problems of philosophical anthropology and social philosophy, issues of "practical" philosophy in the classical understanding (ethics, philosophy of law, aesthetics), the set of issues related to philosophy of religion and philosophy of history, and relatively new personal-existential questions.

3. Though some authors have rightly draw attention to his "mobility," to that well-known amorphousness of Solovyov's philosophical output, his substantial difference from, say, Hegelian systemization, these authors would hardly deny that Solovyov strove to permeate all his philosophical inquiry with a *single* principle, of the kind asserted as All-Unity. This is why concepts like collectivity, synthesis, and systematization (on the basis of All-Unity) are so evident in all of Solovyov's main works.

4. Solovyov's systematic construction of philosophy is, I believe, twofold in nature. a) On the one hand, his body of work contains pieces that fulfill his goal of detailed development ("Justification of the Good") or design (*Theoretical Philosophy*), predominantly of some single (ethical, epistemological, ontological, etc.) systemic aspect. b) On the other hand, the kind of construction in which a particular work encompasses various systematic aspects in a defined order or intersection is even more characteristic of Solovyov's body of work. These works (*Philosophical Principles of Integral Knowledge* [*Filosofskie nachala tsel'nogo znaniia*], *Critique of Abstract Principles* [*Kritika otvlechennykh nachal*]) are, in a certain sense, a critical introduction to Solovyov's philosophy, to his innovative reworking of classical thought, taken in the broadest range of systemic aspects. This was the unique "critique of classical reason" that Solovyov performed in the name of clearing the ground and preparing his "project," "materials," and so forth for constructing a new edifice for philosophy. For a number of reasons related not only to Solovyov's own fate and to the state of global philosophy, the thinker was never able to complete or even to sketch the main features of his project, but for the purposes of

our topic, this question is central: were his intentions systematic or asystematic? Is it appropriate to use existing systemic divisions and criteria for analyzing Solovyov's philosophy? As the arguments above have shown, my own answer to these questions would be yes. (Of course, with the important qualification that in a number of works, especially those more purely essayistic, polemical, political, purely religious, and so forth in nature, Solovyov does not pose any systematic nor overall philosophical goals whatsoever.) Let us now move to a more detailed analysis of Solovyov's philosophy as a (relatively) systemic whole based on the principle of All-Unity.

The Main Systemic Dimensions of Solovyov's Philosophy

I consider it both possible and necessary to delineate the following main dimensions in Solovyov's philosophy, grouped into sets of related issues.

I. The "metaphysical" group (general theoretical philosophy)

1) cosmological

a) evolutionary-theoretical and dialectical

2) ontological
3) epistemological and logical
4) psychological

dimensions

II. The "practical philosophy" group

1) moral (ethical)
2) socio-philosophical and sociopolitical

a) philosophical-legal
b) religious-political

3) aesthetic
4) philosophical-historical

dimensions

III. The philosophical anthropology group

1) philosophical-anthropological

a) personal-existential

dimensions

IV. The theological group

It is worth noting that this synthesizing schema does not appear in its full form in any of Solovyov's descriptions of his own system (though I will suggest that certain parts of it appear in a number of his works). Nevertheless, summarizing the material of all the philosopher's major works makes it possible to construct the outline above and apply it in the course of our study. I call the dimensions indicated above the *vertical* system dimensions of philosophy (Solovyov's philosophy, in this case). As the list itself shows, it correlates both to traditional disciplinary system divisions of metaphysical philosophy into rational cosmology, ontology, epistemology, and psychology, as well as to the Hegelian distinctions between logic (a special epistemology), philosophy of nature, and philosophy of spirit, with divisions of philosophy of law into philosophy of the state and society or practical philosophy into ethics, aesthetics, philosophy of history, and history of philosophy. However, the substantial difference in Solovyov's project consists in the fact that it is not like Hegel's "encyclopedic." In other words, Solovyov does not consider it necessary to develop every single area invariably as a specialized discipline, as an individual philosophical science. That said, however, approaches that had previously been focused on disciplines were not lost but preserved in an integral philosophy, and preserved *as dimensions* that *could* be fully present in philosophy, providing it with the *multiplicity, the multidimensionality* of a systematic approach. The "vertical" (quasi-disciplinary) dimensions intersect in the thinker's texts on the basis of *issue* areas of research, which are embraced and synthesized by the concepts of "God," "nature," "man," and "society." These could be called *"horizontal" issue areas of philosophical analysis.*

The most interesting and relatively new features of Solovyov's philosophical systematization are related to *how* the *vertical* system dimensions intersect with the "horizonal" and *how* they themselves are mediated by the main principle of Solovyovian philosophy, namely, the principle of All-Unity. Before moving to the question of this intersection and mediation, I should note that attempting to comprehend the whole system construction requires taking into consideration its multilayeredness, the dialectical intensity of the principle of All-Unity. The latter seems to have two main "vectors" that, at first glance, are aimed in opposite directions, but that also "give shape" to All-Unity through dialectical conjunction. The *first vector* is synthesis, unification: 1) unification of the Good, Truth, and Beauty; 2) synthesis of various philosophical approaches; 3) continuity, unity in philosophy's movement from God to nature, man, and society. The *second vector* is the vector of freedom, individualization, differentiation, isolation, and even schism: 1) isolation of the individual and his (often dramatic) detachment from the whole, from All-Unity; 2) the confrontation of good and evil; 3) the opposition of creative and destructive forces (in the cosmos, in the nature of man, in culture, in philosophy).

In light of this, Solovyov's All-Unity is a kind of unifying, synthesizing principle that makes no guarantee of a serene Unity and that forces its way through intense confrontation and struggle between opposing forces. This in turn leaves its stamp on the fate of system and systematization issues. Whereas Hegel's system seems to march forward in its victorious "procession," Solovyov's system, constructed on the principle of All-Unity, forces its way forward strenuously and without any guarantee of success: synthesis poses great difficulty for philosophy and for philosophers, and only through collective, aggregative work are truly synthesizing, unifying efforts possible, even in the very long term. Here I would also bring in the drama of the philosopher's personal life, an aspect of the analysis that I have discussed in more details elsewhere (see Motroshilova 2007, 8–16). I do believe that Solovyov's tendency toward systematicity, which is central to his philosophical construction, could be—at least to some degree—explained by his truly dramatic personal experience. With all his being, Solovyov was attuned to the sound wave, to the melody of All-Unity that he grasped from the depths of Being with his spiritually sensitive sense of hearing. On the other hand, the tragic melody of freedom as an existential fault line, as discord, as decoupling differentiations, was always audible to him and troubled his soul. This foundational existential opposition, the All-United and the All-Differing, was never an abstract problem for Solovyov as it sometimes has been for emotionally "cold" philosopher-theoreticians, but he experienced it as an inescapable tragedy, touching deeply on his sense of self. To use a verse from Solovyov's own poetry, in his "soul, two eternal forces secretly converged in invisible hostility." Nevertheless, his faith in All-Unity, that is, in wholeness, in the connectedness of everyone and everything in the world, ruled supreme; an All-Unity preserved by none other than the providence of God Himself and overcoming the most formidable and tragic differences.

At this point I will provide a more concrete characterization of the principle of All-Unity on which, like a foundation, the whole systematic construction of Soloyov's philosophy is erected.

All-Unity: The Central Category and Main Principle of Solovyov's Philosophical Doctrine

All-Unity in Solovyov's philosophy is not only a principle of universal connection of the world itself, but also a principle that unifies philosophy, particularly its main divisions. Solovyov presents All-Unity in its two interconnected aspects and meanings related both to the world and to his philosophical inquiry in the following formulation, taken from his conclusion to *Critique of Abstract Principles*:

> In the ethical portion of the present study, we arrived at the affirmation of *a certain order of earthly life*, of all-unity as something undoubtedly desirable; we found that it is only this kind of order (a defining relationship of all creatures as a free theocracy) that can embody the supreme norm for our will and activity. In the second, gnoseological [= epistemological] portion of our study, logical necessity led us to the affirmation of the same absolute order of earthly being not only as something desired but also as something unconditionally true or existent [*sushchee*]. Where our study of abstract principles in the area of ethics led us to all-unity

8 VLADIMIR SOLOVYOV: PHILOSOPHY AS SYSTEMIC UNITY   167

as the supreme demand of the moral will, or as the highest good, our study of abstract principles in the area of theory of knowledge and metaphysics led us to the same all-unity both as the supreme idea of the mind and as existent truth. [...] If all-unity is the absolute good in the moral sphere (for the will), if it is the absolute truth in the cognitive sphere (for the mind), then the effectuation of all-unity in our external reality, the realization or embodiment of it in the sphere of perceptible, material being, is absolute beauty. (Solovyov 1988, 744–745; italics mine)

This quotation from Solovyov is typically evoked by anyone who speaks or writes about the principle of All-Unity.[3] But if we limit ourselves to this quotation alone (which is often the case among those who spend an insufficient amount of time studying the text), I am afraid that we will lose the rich, multidimensional philosophical construction that Solovyov is embedding in this principle, in this concept, in this category.

I see the purpose of the short excerpt provided above as the supreme *textual clarification of the principle of All-Unity* as Solovyov employs and interprets it.

1. Above all, Solovyov considers All-Unity an *idea in opposition to materiality* [*veshchnost'*]. If "materiality is the inertness and impermeability of being," then its direct opposite, All-Unity, is the idea as "positive all-permeability" (Solovyov 1989, 363). This initial characterization, negative in form but positive in substance ("positive all-permeability"), requires further clarification.

2. *All-Unity is the idea-symbol of "the overall connectedness of all creation."* Soloyov describes this connection beautifully and dramatically: "rebellious life," "the gigantic burst of elemental forces" cannot destroy or eliminate "*absolute all-unity,*" but only imbue it with "movement, brilliance, and thunder" (the image of a nighttime sea in the Tyutchev poem that Soloyov cites illustrates not only unity, the wholeness of the world, but also the "stormy excitement" of life and "unquenchable longing of individual being separated from absolute all-unity") (see Solovyov 1989, 367).

2a. No less beautiful, and at the same time no less dramatic, is the *symbolism related to the emergence of All-Unity in nature*. "Earthly all-unity on the part of the material nature that perceives it, reflected light, is the passive feminine beauty of a moonlit night. [...] *Earthly all-unity and its exponent, light,* in its original segmentation into a multiplicity of self-contained loci, embraced, however, by the overall harmony, is the beauty of a starry sky" (Solovyov 1989, 365; italics mine). On the one hand, Solovyov follows this elegant, reflectively artistic course in order, from the outset, to link beauty as the fundamental hypostasis of All-Unity with its other aspects, and on the other hand, he does so in order to include in his metaphysical considerations the aesthetic component of the theme of unity and multiplicity, of Being as such and of particular being. Meanwhile Solovyov endows this aesthetic interaction among the whole, the united, and the individual with existential features, further dramatizing and even personifying the play of nature's vital forces. Despite being constrained by "impermeable" materiality, elemental chaos [*stikhiinost'*], and the occasional lack of beauty, nature is not separated from All-Unity. "The impulses of elemental forces or elemental impotence are in themselves alien to beauty, but give birth to it already in the inorganic world, becoming, willfully or not, in different aspects of nature, the material for a more or less clear and full expression of the *universal idea or positive all-unity*" (Solovyov 1989, 371; italics mine).

Two details are important here. The first is that *positive all-unity* is a different name for the *universal idea*. In other words, we once again find affirmation and continuation of the interpretation of all-unity presented above, that it is an idea, and a "universal" idea besides, that is, an idea that universally unites. This thus argues for *an idealism whose specific type and character require further clarification*. The second detail is what provides that clarification: at this stage of analysis, Solovyov's idealism demonstrates its *metaphysical-cosmological, evolutionary-dialectical* features. Here we see flashes of its original *symbolic-artistic sides*, since all the elements and all the ugliness in nature "reaches upward" toward its beauty, toward "the creative principle of the universe (Logos)" (Solovyov 1989, 371). In any case, these manifestations of elements do not break away from the "real embodiment of the all-whole and indivisible idea," but become a "material and medium" for it. And so, it is neither Good nor Truth but *Beauty that is laid at the very foundation of All-Unity*, since it is attributable even to the elements of inanimate nature. For Solovyov, Beauty is the main thread that God extends through nature; as one of Solovyov's poems puts it, "the divine fire burns everywhere under the impassive guise of matter."

Solovyov's conceptual construction is idealistic because it continues a tradition that might be called *cosmological-aesthetic religious idealism*: inanimate nature is the "material and medium," the "chaotic matter" for the truly divine "universal idea" that organizes and spiritualizes nature (the cosmos), that serves as the "creative principle" (Logos) for the cosmos, and that unites everything through Beauty. This is the tradition established by Plato and developed by the Neoplatonists, continued by the German mystics, appearing in Giordano Bruno, and influencing the Romantics, Schelling, and Hegel. Did Solovyov bring anything new to this tradition?[4] I believe he brought quite a bit. Even the "metaphysical storytelling" style corresponds to Platonic or Plotinian models.

2b. The transition from thinking about inanimate nature to the animal world and to man is simple and smooth, which is unsurprising: it is the Creator himself and the principle of All-Unity he "guarantees" that "vouch" for this pairing. "The very same image of all-unity that the universal creator sketched in the starry sky or in the multicolored rainbow with such massive and simple features is the same as the one he has painted all over vegetative and animal bodies with such subtle detail" (Solovyov 1989, 371). Here Solovyov finds himself in solidarity with those Romantic and poetically inclined metaphysical philosophers, those artists who saw God, in his creation of nature, as a skillful, tireless, and inimitable Artist. Thus, at this stage of the embodiment of All-Unity, it is Beauty as its hypostasis and the "aesthetics of nature" as a part of philosophy united with cosmologism that run the show. Consequently, theoretical and practical philosophy are originally unified with one another. I would also like to highlight once again the personal aspect here. Solovyov as a person had a romantic, poetic soul, and it is no wonder that he wrote not only (very vivid, inspired) philosophical prose, but also verse. Unlike his philosophy, I would not call his poetry major and significant. However, as a concentration of the philosopher's Romantic experience, as an expression of his soul's lyrical chords, it is worthwhile and interesting. One of Solovyov's poems is a tense, dramatic coupling of man's "free spirit" with nature's beauty endowed with light and with spiritual bursts, and of these with *divine spirit, a synonym of pure All-Unity*:

As all of heaven's glory is reflected
In the pure azure of a quieted sea,
So does eternal good appear to us
In the light of free spirit's passion.
But as immovable depths are the same
In powerful expanses as in stormy unrest,
So is the spirit as mighty and clear
In free repose as in passionate desire.
Freedom, bondage, repose, and unrest
Elapse and then appear again,
But it remains, and in elemental striving
Only reveals its power. (Solovyov 1990, 21)

As we transition to the embodiment of All-Unity in the organic world, the difference between the unification and fragmentation vectors that I designated above now comes into play. Solovyov writes, "The overall picture of the organic world is represented by two basic features, without uniform recognition of which we cannot have any understanding of earthly life nor philosophy of nature, and consequently, no aesthetics of nature" (Solovyov 1989, 372). The first feature: the organic world "cannot be *directly derived* from a single absolute creative principle, since in that case it would represent an unconditional perfection, a serenity and harmony not only within the whole, but among all its parts. Reality, meanwhile, is far from corresponding to this kind of optimistic representation" (ibid.). To explain this "non-correspondence" and its sources, Solovyov *relies on the most recent discoveries in the natural sciences* that assert, "Our biological history is a delayed and painful birth" (ibid.). There is an internal confrontation in nature, "jolts and convulsive tremors, a groping around in blindness; the unfinished sketches of unsuccessful creatures: so many monstrous spawn and abortions!" (ibid., 373). Does this mean we must sacrifice Beauty as a fundamental side of All-Unity and a corresponding "aesthetics of nature," along with the image of God the Artist? For the whole essence and style of the concept of All-Unity, this question is every bit as important as it is difficult. Solovyov (as was his wont) does not avoid the difficult question, but instead makes it an additional feature of his tense drama of All-Unity and of his outline of the complex idea of God the Creator, God the Artist. This leads to the second feature of his picture of the organic world: "The life-giving agent abandons his awkward attempts without regret, however (and here we have the second basic feature of organic nature) he cherishes not only the goal of the process, but each of its innumerable stages, as long as each stage has, in its measure and in itself, done well to embody the idea of life" (ibid.). Even what seems to *us* deformed has its own nature of life, including the aesthetic. "Generally if *beauty in nature* (as we argue) is *the real, objective work of a complex and continuous cosmological process*, then the existence of deformed phenomena is entirely understandable and necessary" (Solovyov 1989, 374; italics mine).

Thus, according to Solovyov, organic nature provides "the opportunity for new, more perfect embodiments of the all-uniting idea in beautiful forms, but only the opportunity." At the same time, according to Solovyov's truly dramatic imagination, there is a strengthening of the "opposing ability to resist the ideal principle along with the possibility of carrying out this resistance in more complex and significant material" (Solovyov 1989, 377). The forms that the "cosmic artist" leaves in the organic world are discussed by Solovyov in great detail and, moreover (what at first seems paradoxical for the theological, metaphysical style of his whole argument), with the support of material from then-new natural science, in particular Charles Darwin's theory of natural selection, subject to criticism because its author did not take into account the "self-contained, objective significance of the aesthetic motif (!) in at least its most superficial expressions" (ibid., 384).

3. Solovyov approaches the human world above all with already roughly sketched cosmological-aesthetic, theological, and even teleological premises. He views man as the kind of form whose creation is a "particular goal" of the creator: "along with the greatest corporeal beauty," "the supreme inner potential of light and life, which we call self-consciousness," appears in the world (Solovyov 1989, 389). Thus, the starting point for discovering the idea of All-Unity as embodied in the human world is also *theological* and *teleological cosmologism* (man is interpreted as the achievement of an "overall cosmic idea" through special means), again united with *aesthetic idealism*. However, the issue is not limited by this: "Man not only participates in the action of cosmic principles, but he is capable of *knowing the goal* of this action and, consequently, of laboring toward it intelligently and freely" (ibid.). The discussion of Beauty as a fundamental hypostasis of "universal all-unity" does not end here: on the contrary, it transitions to a new stage by virtue of two other aspects of All-Unity being added to it, Truth and the Good.

The realization of the principle of All-Unity in Solovyov's doctrine of man, that is, in his philosophical anthropology, is of course not divorced from philosophical tradition, but it is marked by the influence of then-new philosophical mindsets and values. The impact of tradition appears, first of all, in the way in which the link between man and some broader unity (the universe, the cosmos, nature, God, society), so characteristic of the multitude of philosophical doctrines stretching from antiquity to the nineteenth century, preserves its paradigmatic significance for Solovyov, and second, in the way in which the simultaneously emphasized freedom, individuality, and inherent worth of man that originated in Modern Era doctrines, particularly the concepts of individual rights and freedoms in Kant, Fichte, Shelling, and Hegel, also remain immutable for Solovyov. Meanwhile, the philosopher's works betray a dissatisfaction with the way traditional philosophy considered it necessary and possible to resolve the difficult antinomies of the cosmic and the human, of the universal and the individual, of necessity and freedom. In this dissatisfaction, Solovyov joins the critics of the Modern Era's classics of philosophy, Schopenhauer and Nietzsche, though he largely disagrees with the conclusions that they and other critics advanced.

In Solovyov's interpretation, how should we view the difficult pairing of the governing All-Unity, its universality, its wholeness, and its necessity with the individuality, freedom, and singularity inherent to man? What is the situation with Truth and the Good, two other hypostases of All-Unity (along with Beauty)?

A passionate partisan of the principle of All-Unity, Solovyov paradoxically begins his argument about the realization of Truth with an even more heavily emphasized individuality and freedom of each individual human being than had been characteristic of the tradition:

> The advantage of man over all of nature's other creatures, his ability to cognize and realize truth, is not just generic but also individual: *each* man is capable of cognizing and realizing truth, and each can become a living reflection of the absolutely whole, conscious, and self-contained organ of universal life. (Solovyov 1989, 504)

That said, the ontological premises of Solovyov's concept of truth appear in his assertion that "There is truth (or the image of the Divine) in the rest of nature, as well." However, All-Unity as truth in a world of individual creatures of nature acts, according to Solovyov, "as a fatal force, as a law unknown to them that they obey unwillingly and unconsciously" (Solovyov 1989, 504), but "for themselves," these creatures experience being "as separate from the *all*, and consequently outside of truth." If truth, the universal, nonetheless continues to force its way forward, Solovyov considers it not by virtue of each individuality, but through "the continuation of the genus and the death of individual life." As for man, the situation is fundamentally different: "Human individuality, precisely because it can contain truth in itself, is not abolished by it, but rather preserved and strengthened through its triumph" (ibid.). In other words, the fundamental bases for unifying individualities, on the one hand, and All-Unity in its true hypostasis on the other, in a metaphysical, substantial relationship are completely different than in the rest of nature. Solovyov decisively elevates the metaphysical, ontological status of this human individuality, assigning it the ability to nonetheless access All-Unity as truth.

However, even here the situation is not without its difficulties and contradictions, nor without its internal drama:

But in order for an individual creature to find its own justification and argument in truth, in all-unity, having consciousness of truth alone is insufficient; it must be in truth, but the individual man, like the animal, is not immediately and directly in truth: he finds himself as an isolated particle of the universal whole, and in his egoism he asserts this partial being as a whole for himself, wanting to be all in separation from the all, outside of truth. (Solovyov 1989, 504)

Solovyov is infinitely far from moralizing about an egoism that hinders individuality from becoming an immediate embodiment of truth and of life in truth. In Solovyov's anthropology, egoism, too, has its own ontological status: egoism is "the real, basic principle of individual life"; it pervades this life, guides it, "concretely defines" it. "*The justification and salvation of individuality through the sacrifice of egoism*" (Solovyov 1989, 505) is nevertheless possible, and possible by virtue of another, opposing egoism of living and life-creating forces. "Truth, like a living force that masters the internal being of man and that really guides him away from false self-assertion, is called love" (ibid.).

Once again, I would emphasize the personal aspect here. Love, both here and later, not only represents for Solovyov one of the central categories of philosophy, one of the manifestations of All-Unity, but his life was also warmed by love: not only love for women, friends, his loved ones, not only for nature, for his country, and ultimately, for humanity, but also the sensation, the experience, the praising of love (*syzygy*, from the Greek for "conjunction") as a truly cosmic, spiritual-creative principle. Solovyov himself would repeatedly return to the theme of love (see his work *The Meaning of Love*), which is why scholars of his work, both then and now (Trubetskoi 1913, Chapter 16; Wenzler 1978, 343ff.) have analyzed the fundamental significance of the category of love in Solovyov's philosophy. It is amazing, by the way, that Solovyov's reverential-personal (and in Evgenii Trubetskoi's opinion, idealized) attitude to love, as a simultaneously human and cosmic principle, allowed him to formulate maxims of human behavior that are relevant even today. Here is one example:

> Nature was thus far either the all-powerful, despotic mother of an infant humanity, or a slave foreign to it, as a thing [...] The establishment of a truly loving, or syzygetic attitude of man not only to his social environment, but also to his natural and universal environment: this purpose is clear in itself.[...] Every conscious human action defined by the idea of universal syzygy and having the goal of embodying the all-uniting ideal in some particular sphere thereby produces or liberates the real, spiritual-corporeal currents that have gradually come to possess the material environment, spiritualizing it and embodying in it some particular image of all-unity, the living and eternal semblance of absolute humanness. (Solovyov 1989, 546–547)

What is this, if not the formulation of a maxim of the sort of savvy humanist and ecological consciousness that we so need today? If this seems too philosophical and elevated to some, one could argue that the philosophy of All-Unity and its apparently purely ideal principles has proven highly productive in anticipating and justifying those truly global, practical rules without which the salvation of human civilization itself would be impossible in our day. For human individuality, participation in All-Unity, in truth, really does represent a special means of relating to other individuals, to nature, to everything "else." *"True individuality is a certain defined image of all-unity,* a certain defined way of perceiving and assimilating everything else. Affirming himself outside of everything else, man thus deprives his own existence of meaning, robs himself of life's true content, and turns his individuality into empty form" (Solovyov 1989, 506–507; italics mine).

Let us turn our attention to two significant details. First, by "truth" I have meant truth more in the ontological, existential sense than in the purely epistemological sense: after all, Solovyov's image of "truth" is above all not cognition of the truth but *individual's meaningful existence in truth.* Second, Solovyov's argumentation in defense of All-Unity is characteristic: this is not at all a consideration of self-sacrifice, altruism, and so forth, but an assertion that individuality's "own" meaningful, substantive, rich "existence," that is, "life's true content," is possible only in the bosom of All-Unity.

Now that I have shed some light on All-Unity as a fundamental basis of unity in the world and as the harmonization of a philosophical system, let me return once again to the concrete aspects of more system-related issues.

(A) Solovyov's Attitude to Philosophical Systematics and to the Disciplinary Division of Philosophical Knowledge: Philosophical Beginnings of Integral Knowledge [Filosofskie nachala tsel'nogo znaniia]

In sketching out his project of "free theosophy, or integral knowledge" in his early work and proclaiming theosophy not as just another angle or type of philosophizing but as "the supreme condition of all philosophy" (Solovyov 1989, 194), Solovyov also defines his attitude to a systematic disciplinary division of philosophy. Free theosophy purports to synthesize "three main areas: mysticism, rationalism, and empiricism." In having the "truly existent" [*das wahrhaft Seiende*] or "the absolute" as its object of study, free theosophy branches off into "three philosophical sciences." The first of these, *logic,* examines the "absolute principle" in its own general and necessary (a priori) definitions. The second science, *metaphysics,* analyzes this absolute principle as one that "produces or considers ultimate reality outside itself." The third science, *ethics,* examines the "reunification" of the absolute principle with this ultimate reality. It is characteristic that Solovyov emphasizes the continuity of his understanding of the connection between philosophical disciplines and the traditional approach to the principle of systematicity:

> This tripartite division of philosophy arising out of its very nature has a very ancient origin and in some form or another is found in all complete and at least

174   N. V. MOTROSHILOVA

> somewhat complex systems, because each separate system, being in fact only a
> one-sided manifestation of some aspect in philosophical knowledge, strives from
> its limited perspective to represent the whole of philosophy. (Solovyov 1989, 195)

To distinguish his division of "free theosophy" from the divisions adopted in other systems, Solovyov calls the three parts, the three disciplines in his system, "organic logic," "organic metaphysics," and "organic ethics," promising to explain their specialized meanings later in *Philosophical Beginnings of Integral Knowledge* [*Filosofskie nachala tsel'nogo znaniia*] (*FNTZ*). To understand the essence of this division, we must first take into consideration the fact that metaphysics, in turn, involves cosmological, ontological, epistemological, and psychological dimensions, so the number of dimensions approaches what I presented above in our outline. Nor is it unimportant that in this work, Solovyov begins his system analysis with logic, as if to remind us of Hegel's mature system. However, the logic that Solovyov depicts, appearing as "organic logic," differs quite substantially from the Hegelian counterpart.

Where Hegel's logic, in its basic content, is an elaborated doctrine of categories (united in the spheres of being–essence–concept), Solovyov's organic logic is dominated more by epistemological topics, like sensory perception, intellectual contemplation, abstract thought, ideas, and artistic contemplation.[5] Hegel, of course, also turned to these issues in his logic, but his analysis of them is strictly subordinate to successive dialectical-categorical analysis (expecting, however, that some aspects of these issues would appear in the *Phenomenology of Spirit* and others would be moved to the philosophy of spirit). Solovyov explicitly defends his departure from the Hegelian categorical example of logic: he declares Hegel's development of the "logic of rationalism" to be untenable, since Hegelian logic, "for all the profound formal truth of its individual deductions and transitions, is devoid of any real significance, of any actual content, overall; it is a kind of thinking in which nothing is thought" (Solovyov 1989, 216). That said, when Solovyov, seemingly following the rhythms of Hegelian logic, turns fairly quickly to the problem of being in his organic logic, this is the result: he does not set out to weave a delicate network of the categories of being, but intends to identify the very essence of the logic-being problem (and thus the epistemological-ontological problem): *the nonidentity of being* [*bytie*] *and the existent* [*sushchee*]. "The empirical and purely logical elements are essentially two possible *modes of being* [*obraza bytiia*], the real and the ideal, and the third absolute principle is not defined by one or the other mode of being, consequently, it is not at all defined as *being*, but as a positive principle of being, or *the existent*" (ibid., 217). Incidentally, Solovyov himself explains why he does not follow Hegel in his analysis of being:

> Hegel understands the *being* with which he begins his logic not as a means or
> modus of self-positing of the super-existent [*sverkhsushchee*] (in which sense being
> is one of the basic and positive definitions), but only as a general concept of
> being, abstracted from any signs and not belonging to any subject; in this sense

being has, evidently, a purely relative and completely negative character, and is consequently equal to the concept of *nothing*. (Solovyov 1989, 277)

Unlike Hegel, Solovyov makes the existent [*das Seiende*] the fundamental concept of his organic logic rather than being, and furthermore, the existent in its form of truly-existent, making a delicate and complex distinction between the two categories. Solovyov's main purpose is to depart from the abstract formalism of Hegelian logic (and from any logic of that kind) and to return to reality, to content, to life. At this point, Solovyov's logic is tightly interwoven with the ontological dimension, to which the philosopher's original theoretical findings are related.

It is worth noting (and taking into account) that *FNTZ* is an unfinished work, not to mention one intended for a specific purpose, namely, defense of a dissertation. Also significant is the fact that, in the historical and substantive sense, it followed *Sofiia* [*The Sophia*] (and even reproduced some of its parts). The question of how much *Sofiia* influenced *FNTZ* and to what extent Solovyov needed to depart from his earlier ideas and texts, both due to external circumstances and to the impact of development and changes in his own philosophical ideas, is an enormously difficult one.[6] In any case, I would like to emphasize that, in *Sofiia*, Soloyov's interest was tied to issues related to absolute principle, to the nature of metaphysical cognition and man's need for it, to monism (or the absolute principle as a unity) and dualism (or the absolute principle as a duality), to the issue of the Spirit, the Mind, and the Soul as principles of the "spheres" of cosmic and historical process, to morality and politics, and to issues of "theological principles."[7] This, in terms of systemization, means that already in *Sofiia* Solovyov was thinking about substantially uniting all those aspects, those dimensions of the philosophical-theological system, that appear in our list. Of course, the nature of their unity was specified to a great extent. For Solovyov himself this means the construction of a philosophical-religious foundation for an integral edifice of "universal doctrine," a new "theosophy," unifying the traditions of Gnosticism and European mysticism, but also certain rationalist traditions (Kozyrev 2007; see also Carlson 1996).

In *FNTZ*, Solovyov puts more emphasis on the philosophical rather than theological aspects of his doctrine; as for mysticism, it is present, but in a more "rationalized" form. Scholars have suggested that this shift was to a significant degree based on his need to prepare a text for his official defense. Whatever the case may be, given all the continuity of individual aspects of the areas of research in question, *FNTZ* differs markedly from *Sofiia* in both philosophical content and style, above all in relation to the fact that his analysis here largely goes back to traditional philosophical systematization. Meanwhile, in distinguishing its logical-epistemological and logical-ontological dimensions, Solovyov essentially no longer continues further construction of his philosophical system. One thing is completely clear, however: his determination to construct his philosophy like an integral system of knowledge, to distinguish and defend the absolute "principle," a principle that both unites and divides, but that ultimately

176 N. V. MOTROSHILOVA

unifies and synthetizes, is a determination he demonstrated both in *Sofiia* and in *Philosophical Principles of Integral Knowledge* [*Filosofskie nachala tsel'nogo znaniia*].

(B) CRITIQUE OF ABSTRACT PRINCIPLES (1880)

The Critique of Abstract Principles [*Kritika otvlechennykh nachal*] was Solovyov's doctoral thesis. In this work, his philosophical systemization is embodied in its fullest form.

The text begins with a defense (in chapters I and II) of the role of "supreme principles and criteria in life, knowledge, and creation." What follows is a whole set of chapters dedicated to ethical issues (chapters III–XI). This transitions to a socio-philosophical and philosophical-legal set (chapters XII–XVII and XVIII–XX), leading to philosophy of religion (XXI–XXIV). After a summary of the previous analysis (chapter XXV), Solovyov transitions to issues of metaphysics, to an overall definition of the existent, and then to issues of epistemology, that is, to determining knowledge and truth.[8] Chapters XXIX–XL are dedicated to traditional metaphysical topics, theory of cognition, historical-philosophical typology, and critiques of empiricism, sensualism, rationalism, and naturalism. In the concluding chapters (XLIV–XLVI), he shifts his analysis to issues of being and the existent, of the existent as the absolute, of man as a "second absolute." In other words, *the basic dimensions of a philosophical system are present: the metaphysical* (mainly in its ontological and epistemological hypostases), *the socio-philosophical, the philosophical-legal, and the ethical.*

A clarification of the issues related to unifying knowledge, of philosophical systematicity, comes in the final chapter (XLVI): "An *All-Unified System of Knowledge*. Its Basic Elements. The Abstract Dogmatism of Theology. Free Theosophy." Above all this refers to the necessary synthesis of "natural scientific" and "mystical" knowledge that serves as a synonym for knowledge about phenomena and knowledge about the essence of things. According to Solovyov, we need "a true synthesis of these elements" (Solovyov 1988, 738; italics mine) that could be undertaken "by means of the rational element" (ibid., 739). But this is only "a *task* for *the mind*" to be addressed. Of course, this was undertaken by humanity in ancient times. "Mystical knowledge" accumulated in theology, "the science of divine things." But a dissatisfaction with theological answers pushed humanity to seek rational answers to questions of reality, which led to the development of rational philosophy, "or speculative science." Meanwhile, positive minds sought "to cognize truth from actual experience, from observations of what exists, from summaries of facts," which "turned out to be a highly productive source for particular areas of cognition" (ibid., 739). Solovyov writes:

> Our age has seen the rapid development both of abstract philosophical principle (in Hegelianism) and of the abstract scientific principle (in positivism); in the former we have a system of knowledge without any reality, and in the latter a

system of facts without any internal connection; pure philosophy provides reason with no content, and pure science renounces reason itself. (Ibid., 740)

Does this mean that we need simply to return to old dogmatic philosophy, as its contemporary defenders insist? From Solovyov's perspective, this would be highly "lamentable." A synthesis of religious-mystical knowledge with rational knowledge is possible only if we reject religious dogmatism and introduce religious truth "in the form of a free, intellectual thought." Then it would be possible "to organize the whole domain of true knowledge *in a complete system* of free and scientific theosophy" (ibid.; italics mine, N.M.).

Translated by Brad Damaré

Notes

1. For a detailed bibliography of publications on Vladimir Solovyov until the end of the last century see Groberg 1998.
2. This does not contradict what Evgenii N. Trubetskoi has rightly noted, that the weakness of Solovyov's early works was their lack of clarity or their contradictory nature regarding the systemic question of where the exposition of philosophy should begin. Solovyov places ethics "at the forefront of his philosophy," but he leaves his underworked theoretical-cognitive and metaphysical premises of philosophy for a later time. Of course, he would later recognize and partially eliminate these weaknesses and gaps, Trubetskoi argues (Trubetskoi 1913, 124–125ff.)
3. Solovyov has the word "all-unity" in lowercase letters. When my study refers to the principle of All-Unity, the central category for Soloyov, I find capital letters appropriate.
4. For a discussion of Solovyov's indebtedness to, as well as his departure from, the tradition, see Sutton 1988.
5. On epistemological (gnostic) elements of Solovyov's philosophy, see Carlson 1996 and especially Kozyrev 2007.
6. See Alexei Kozyrev's notes to the publication and translation of *Sofiia* (Solovyov 2000, 320f.). See also Kravchenko 2006.
7. For a discussion of the origins and the religious significance of the "divine Sophia" in Solovyov's philosophy, see Du Quenoy 2010; Finlan 2006; Kornblatt 2009; Kravchenko 2006.
8. On Solovyov's quest for metaphysics, see Nemeth 2014.

Bibliography

Carlson, Maria. 1996. Gnostic Elements in the Cosmogony of Vladimir Soloviev. In *Russian Religious Thought*, ed. Judith Deutsch Kornblatt and Richard F. Gustafson, 49–67. Madison, WI: University of Wisconsin Press.

Du Quenoy, Paul. 2010. Vladimir Solov'ev in Egypt: The Origins of the 'Divine Sophia' in Russian Religious Philosophy. *Revolutionary Russia* 23 (2): 147–158.

Finlan, Stephen. 2006. The Comedy of Divinization in Soloviev. In *Theosis: Deification in Christian Theology*, ed. Stephen Finlan and Vladimir Kharlamov, 168–183. Cambridge, UK: James Clark & Co. (Series: Princeton Theological Monograph).

Gaidenko, Piama P. 2001. *Vladimir Solovyov i filosofiia Serebriannogo veka*. Moscow: Progress-Traditsiia.

Groberg, Kristi. 1998. Vladimir Sergeevich Solov'ev: A Bibliography. *Modern Greek Studies Yearbook* 1: 14–15.

Kornblatt, Judith D. 2004. Vladimir Sergeevich Solov'ev. In *Dictionary of Literary Biography*. Volume 295: *Russian Writers of the Silver Age, 1890-1925*, eds. Judith E. Kalb and J. Alexander Ogden with the collaboration of I. G. Vishnevetsky, 377-386. Columbia, SC: Layman Poupard Publishing.

———. 2009. *Divine Sophia: The Wisdom Writings of Vladimir Solovyov*. Ithaca, NY: Cornell University Press.

Kostalevsky, Marina. 1997. *Dostoevsky and Soloviev: The Art of Integral Vision*. New Haven, CT: Yale University Press.

Kozyrev, Alexei P. 2007. *Solovyov i gnostiki*. Moscow: Izdatel'stvo Savin S.A.

Kravchenko, Viktoriia V. 2006. *Vladimir Solovyov i Sofiia*. Moscow: Agraf.

Losev, Alexei F. 2009. *Vladimir Solovyov*. Moscow: Molodaia gvardiia.

Motroshilova, Nelly V. 2007. *Mysliteli Rossii i filosofiia zapada. V. Solovyov. N. Berdyaev. S. Frank. L. Shestov*. Moscow: Izdatel'stvo "Respublika"; Izdatel'stvo "Kul'turnaia revoliutsiia.".

Mrówczyński-Van Allen, Artur. 2013. *Between the Icon and the Idol. The Human Person and the Modern State in Russian Literature and Thought—Chaadayev, Soloviev, Grossman*. Trans. Matthew Philipp Whelan. Eugene, OR: Cascade Books. (Series: Theopolitical Visions.)

Nemeth, Thomas. 2014. *The Early Solov'ëv and His Quest for Metaphysics*. Cham: Springer.

Solovyov, Vladimir S. 1988. In *Sochineniia v 2-kh tomakh*, ed. A.F. Losev and A.V. Gulyga, vol. 1. Moscow: Mysl'. (Series: *Filosofskoe Nasledie*).

———. 1989. In *Sochineniia v 2-kh tomakh*, ed. A.F. Losev and A.V. Gulyga, vol. 2. Moscow: Mysl'. (Series: *Filosofskoe Nasledie*)

———. 1990. *Nepodvizhno lish' solntse liubvi... Stik.hotvoreniia. Proza. Pis'ma* edited by A. Nosov. Moscow: Moskovskii rabochii.

———. 2000. In *Polnoe sobranie sochinenii i pisem v dvadtsati tomakh*, ed. A.A. Nosov, vol. 2, 1875–1877. Moscow: Nauka.

Sutton, Jonathan. 1988. *The Religious Philosophy of Vladimir Solovyov: Towards a Reassessment*. Basingstoke, UK: Palgrave Macmillan.

Trubetskoi, Evgenii N. 1913. *Mirosozertsanie Vl. S. Solovyova, v 2-kh tomakh*. Vol. 1, 1. Moscow: Put'.

Valliere, Paul. 2007. Vladimir Soloviev (1853-1900): Commentary. In *The Teachings of Modern Orthodox Christianity on Law, Politics, and Human Nature*, ed. John Jr. Witte and Frank S. Alexander, 33–105. New York, NY: Columbia University Press.

Wenzler, Lüdwig. 1978. *Die Freiheit und das Böse nach Vladimir Solov'ev*. Freiburg/ Munich: Alber.

CHAPTER 9

Natural Sciences and the Radical *Intelligentsia* in the Late Nineteenth and Early Twentieth Centuries

Daniela Steila

In Russia, the natural sciences have alternately been cheered or denounced as a means of modernizing the country, and had a checkered career, depending on whether the government of the Empire adopted a reformist vision, open to Europe, or was inclined toward an anti-Western, exceptionalist view. In the first half of the nineteenth century, during the reign of Nicholas I, they were mostly considered a "necessary evil" for the development of the country, but they were subjected to strict ideological control to avoid challenging the primacy of revealed religion. One example, among many, shows that they were "governed," as was every other intellectual field, according to the particular political concerns of the moment. The 1828 education statute, promoted by Minister of Education Count S.S. Uvarov, centered the gymnasium curriculum on classical languages and mathematics. While it tolerated a rudimentary teaching of physics, it completely banned any study of biology, physiology, chemistry, or geology. However, when the echoes of 1848 reached Russia, the republican spirit of classical studies seemed even more dangerous than scientific notions, which, moreover, might have aided Russian economic development. Therefore, in 1852, following a proposal by the new minister, Prince P.A. Shirinskii-Shikhmatov, the teaching of Greek in the gymnasia was replaced by a general introductory class in "natural science," and by specified classes in zoology,

---

D. Steila (✉)
Department of Philosophy and Education Sciences, University of Turin, Turin, Italy
e-mail: daniela.steila@unito.it

© The Author(s), under exclusive license to Springer Nature
Switzerland AG 2021
M. F. Bykova et al. (eds.), *The Palgrave Handbook of Russian Thought*,
https://doi.org/10.1007/978-3-030-62982-3_9

180   D. STEILA

botany, mineralogy, anatomy, and human physiology (Vucinich 1963, 247–258).

When the government of the "reformer" tsar Alexander II promoted scientific studies with the aim of modernizing the country and reopened contact with European scientists, these new orientations were welcomed with great enthusiasm. In Germany, an entire generation of scholars and researchers had abandoned the metaphysical speculations of idealist *Naturphilosophie* in favor of materialism. Although the Russian government quickly took a stand in favor of the traditional dualist doctrine that envisioned a separation of "spirit" and "matter" by giving chairs of psychology at the universities to theologians, the names of Karl Vogt, Ludwig Büchner, and Jakob Moleschott became very popular (Vucinich 1970, 122; Lossky 1955, 174). In *The Demons*, Dostoevsky pointed out the "most impossible oddities" performed by a young radical sublieutenant with the following words: "For example, he had thrown two icons belonging to his landlord out of his apartment, and chopped one of them up with an axe; and in his room he had placed the works of Vogt, Moleschott, and Büchner on stands like three lecterns, and before each lectern he kept wax church candles burning" (Dostoevsky 2006, 346). When, in 1858, the professor of physiology at the University of Kazan, Wilhelm Bervi, dared to criticize the new materialist trend, an attack by Nikolai Dobrolyubov appeared in the radical journal *The Contemporary* in support of a letter signed by seventy-one students, who categorically refused to continue to attend the professor's lectures, and enjoined him to leave his chair, which was actually given shortly after to another professor (Pustarnakov 2003, 307; Koshtoiants 1946, 156–157).

The success of the natural sciences in pre-revolutionary Russia, even as an epistemological model for knowledge in its entirety, has been investigated by Alexander Vucinich in his monumental works, which remain an essential reference today.[1] Here, I will pause over the ethical and political implications that derived from that model for the large part of the *intelligentsia* that made "science" the center of its comprehensive worldview. In particular, I will consider the confrontation between the Marxists and the Narodniki during the 1890s and the reaction to the so-called bankruptcy of science by the end of the century. The common general background to both of these cases is the relevance of the experimental method of the natural sciences for the "nihilist" generation of the 1860s, as part of their revolt against traditional knowledge. The new generation opposed to the melancholic and tormented "superfluous man" the figure of the doctor and scientist, who only trusted the results of the empirical method. Indeed, the paradigmatic character Bazarov in *Fathers and Children* by Ivan Turgenev recommended reading *Force and Matter* [*Kraft und Stoff*] by Büchner instead of reading Pushkin. Like Bazarov, the "new people" of Chernyshevsky's *What Is to Be Done?* trusted animal physiology as a means of studying human beings and investigated the nervous system by dissecting frogs (Turgenev 1991, 19–24; Chernyshevsky 1986, 60). In fact, the dominant belief was that human beings were essentially physical and corporeal beings like animals and that historical, moral, and political events had to be analyzed with the same methods as in the natural sciences. For Chernyshevsky, the "anthropological principle" of Feuerbach, whom he viewed as his inspiration, considered human beings to be "simple beings having only one nature, so as not to divide human life into two halves, each belonging to a different nature, so as to consider every aspect of human activity as an activity of the whole organism, from head to foot, everything included" (Chernyshevsky 1987, 226). As a consequence, the "natural sciences are both the basis of that part of philosophy that considers the problems of human beings, and the basis of that part of philosophy that studies the problems of external nature" (Chernyshevsky 1987, 166). Physiology was introduced as the key to a "scientific" reading of the human world, and lectures on physiology were actually drawing crowds during the 1860s (Florovsky 1972, 79; Vucinich 1970, 102–103).

In Russia, interest in Feuerbach's "anthropological principle" and the fortunes of German physiological materialism intertwined with Darwin's theory of evolution. Darwin was greeted in the 1860s as the Newton of biology (Rogers 1960; Vucinich 1988). As a witness recalled a few decades later, "Darwin's theory was received in Russia with profound sympathy. While in Western Europe it met firmly established old traditions which it had first to overcome, in Russia its appearance coincided with the awakening of our society after the Crimean War and here it immediately received the status of full citizenship and ever since has enjoyed widespread popularity" (Vucinich 1972, 229–230; Todes 1989, 23).

Dmitrii Pisarev's writings from the 1860s very clearly show the intertwining of different components in the radical ideology of the time. With Moleschott's *Physiological Sketches* [*Physiologisches Skizzenbuch*] he explained human behavior by studying the nervous system; he endorsed the maxim, according to which "man is what he eats," and admired Darwin as "a new type of critical thinker, one who studies facts as they really are, unburdened by metaphysical or religious prejudices" (Graham 1993, 58). In the natural sciences, as in history, the dominant approaches had to be materialism and rationalism, the critique of sources and respect for facts, and, on that basis, this new science would lead humanity to overcome the shame of poverty and hunger through scientific progress (Peace 2010, 131). In the ethical field too, the most coherent and extremely rational egoism had to be established: since honesty is rationally more convenient than dishonesty, according to Pisarev, "Bazarov would not steal a handkerchief for the very same reason that he would not eat a piece of rotting meat" (Pisarev 1894, 376; Peace 2010, 128). It is a utilitarian calculation that leads the heroes of Chernyshevsky's *What Is to Be Done?*, the "gospel" of Russian radicals in the 1860s, to behave as the strictest of ascetics, as this behavior was advantageous to the collective (Paperno 1988, 26–38, 195–198). Superior moral values or the hope for ultra-mundane rewards were not necessary, the narrating voice of the novel declared: "No sacrifices are required; no deprivations are asked; they are not necessary. Desire to be happy! that is all; only this desire is wanted" (Chernyshevsky 1986, 316). For Chernyshevsky, the maximum happiness for the greatest number of people was the fundamental and indisputable criterium of the only possible "scientific" morality, because only a mathematical calculation would provide "an 'all-encompassing' formula that would explain and govern everything," an "instrument capable of an all-inclusive solution to the basic problems of human existence," which, according to Irina Paperno, Chernyshevsky searched for his whole life (Paperno 1988, 168–169).

However, the very idea of a strictly "scientific" ethics implies a deterministic option that ultimately renounces human free will. Only if behavior obeys deterministic laws on the basis of the physiological constitution of the human body and of its consequent rational egoism, is it possible to elaborate a "human science" as sound as the natural sciences. "What's important is that twice two is four and all the rest's nonsense," proclaimed Bazarov in *Fathers and Children* (Turgenev 1991, 44), but, in this way, he reduced the idea of human free will to a trifle. It is these same philosophical implications of utilitarianism and of rational calculation that encountered a major critique from Fyodor Dostoevsky, who observed that a world entirely dominated by deterministic laws would reduce human beings to nothing more than the key of a piano or the pipe of an organ played by someone else's hands (Dostoevsky 1974, 26–27). According to Dostoevsky, the mathematical calculation of usefulness carried out by the positivists did not take into consideration that which human beings hold dear above all else: "One's own free, untrammeled desires, one's own whim, no matter how extravagant, one's own fancy, be it wrought up at times to the point of madness—all of this is precisely that most advantageous of advantages which is omitted, which fits into no classification, and which is constantly knocking all systems and theories to hell" (Dostoevsky 1974, 28). Human beings renounce every rational calculation to do something foolish, irrational, and crazy, by which they even renounce their own well-being to jam the perfect mechanism of the necessary laws of science with just a bit of unpredictable irrationality in the assertion of one's own self (Thompson 2002).

With no space left to choose freely, human beings should also renounce the responsibility of their actions, because everything would be determined chemically and physiologically by the stimuli of the external environment. In *The Brothers Karamazov*, Dostoevsky reports the confused speech that Mitya gives to his brother Alyosha after the former seminarist and radical Rakitin came to visit him in prison in order to write an article about him; in it, the lack of responsibility of the alleged patricidal murderer is evident: "'It was impossible for him not to kill, he was a victim of his environment,' and so on." Our perceptions, desires, and actions—Mitya explains—ultimately depend on physiology:

> Imagine: it's all there in the nerves, in the head, there are these nerves in the brain (devil take them!) [...] there are little sorts of tails, these nerves have little tails, well, and when they start trembling there [...] that is, you see, I look at something with my eyes, like this, and they start trembling, these little tails [...] and when they tremble, an image appears, not at once, but in a moment, it takes a

9 NATURAL SCIENCES AND THE RADICAL *INTELLIGENTSIA* IN THE LATE... 183

second, and then a certain moment appears, as it were that is, not a moment—devil take the moment—but an image, that is, an object or an event, well, devil take it—and that's why I contemplate, and then think [...] because of the little tails, and not at all because I have a soul or am some sort of image and likeness, that's all foolishness. [...] It's magnificent, Alyosha, this science! The new man will come, I quite understand that [...] And yet, I'm sorry for God! (Dostoevsky 2002, 589)

In Mitya's view, with no faith in God or in a future life, the "new people" would become "scoundrels," "Bernards," since Mitya transforms the famous French scientist into the symbol of an entire breed of people with no moral scruples whatsoever (Dostoevsky 2002, 588).

The brutality of the mechanistic application of determinism to the entire human world was a problematic element within the radical milieu, the Narodniki and the anarchists, too, among whom some new positions were developing that contrasted sharply with the social implications of the struggle for existence. When, in 1864, Varfolomei Zaitsev drew explicitly sexist and racist conclusions from a Darwinian premise, a lively controversy developed in the newspapers and journals; among many others, it involved the young Nikolai Nozhin, a biologist by education and a follower of Proudhon. He reproached Darwin for not understanding the specificity of human evolution: "he does not see that the struggle for existence is not helpful for evolution, that by itself it is only the source of pathological phenomena, phenomena diametrically opposed to the laws of physical evolution" (Rogers 1972, 521). According to Nozhin, who had certainly been influenced by the Proudhonian notion of *mutualité*,[2] organisms of the same species did not fight against each other, unless a "sick" society compelled them to by means of the division of labor.

The ideal of a reciprocity where every individual can fully develop significantly influenced Nozhin's friend and roommate in St. Petersburg Nikolai Mikhailovsky, the "ruler of ideas" of the younger generation of Narodniki (Rogers 1972, 517–523). Human beings are indeed natural beings, which can be investigated physiologically and biologically, but they are also a unique product of evolution, capable of distancing themselves from a purely determinist course of events, which they can judge according to values and preferences, and of actively intervening in the flow of history. In open contrast with the objective method glorified by the positivists, the most eminent theoreticians of Populism (along with Mikhailovsky, also Pyotr Lavrov) supported the "subjective method," which has been summarized by Andrzej Walicki in the following words:

First, it was a defense of ethical standards, and implied that men had the right to judge everything from their own point of view and to protest even against the "objective laws of history"—that indeed they were obliged to protest against human suffering even where the situation seemed hopeless. Second, it was an epistemological and methodological standpoint that disputed the possibility of "objective" knowledge in social sciences; "subjectivism" in this sense implied that

> historical and sociological knowledge could never be really objective because they were colored by the scholar's social position, his unconscious emotions, or consciously chosen ideals. Third, it was a philosophy of history that claimed that the "subjective factor"—human will and consciousness (expressed in the activity of a revolutionary party or in deliberate state intervention)—could effectively oppose the spontaneous development trend and influence the course of history. (Walicki 2015, 375)

These new ideas shattered the firm belief of the generation of the 1860s that the natural and social sciences should follow the same method and the belief that the space of human freedom was reducible to the deterministic laws of the universe. The role of Lavrov's "critically thinking" individual and of Mikhailovsky's "subject" was leading history toward its actual telos, which was supposedly not the fragmented division of capitalist labor, but the harmonic cooperation of fully developed individuals. According to Mikhailovsky's famous "formula of progress:" "Progress is the gradual approach to the integral individual, to the fullest possible and most diversified division of labor among the human being's organs and the least possible division of labor among human beings" (Mikhailovsky 1911, 150). By reinterpreting Comte's theory of the "three stages," Mikhailovsky proposed to divide history into three epochs: the first period would be defined as "objectively anthropocentric," because human beings were spontaneously at the center of nature, and anthropomorphically interpreted each of its phenomena. Simple cooperation, which constituted the economic foundation of primitive society, guaranteed survival within homogenous social groups, composed by "differentiated, equal, free, and independent" individuals. The complex cooperation of the second stage, the so-called eccentric period, overturned this situation, thus creating differentiated and heterogeneous societies, whose members were "unequal, not free, unilaterally specialized, and hierarchically subjugated to each other" (Mikhailovsky 1911, 41). This fragmentation of human personality broke every solidarity; by opposing isolated groups of interest to each other, it led to unilateral specialization in singular fields of knowledge; and it idealized an abstract, "objective," and completely dehumanized model of science. The new epoch would restore the central value of the individual: in this "subjectively anthropocentric period" human beings would again be at the center of the universe, however this time they would be aware that this was not an actual fact, but a legitimate point of view by which they would claim the right to evaluate the entire world. For the Narodniki, every single individual always had the possibility to orient their action toward progress, to take the responsibility of moving history in the desired direction. In the case of Russia, this came down to upholding the communal tradition of the peasants to circumvent the painful experience of capitalism.

Nevertheless, the results of the political activity of the Narodniki were rather disappointing, both in the form of the "going to the people" movement of the 1870s—when young and enthusiastic intellectuals tried to pay their debt of gratitude toward the most disadvantaged section of humanity, which, as Lavrov put it, "has paid dearly so that a few thinkers at their desks could discuss its progress" (Lavrov 1967, 135)—and in the form of individual terroristic attacks. Around the mid-1880s, some authoritative Narodniki steered, with growing conviction, toward Marxism, whose philosophy of history, a heritage from Hegel, seemed to guarantee the success of socialism with the same sound firmness as natural "laws." The Narodniki emphasized the free actions of the individual within history; Marxists deemed that there were strictly deterministic and objective historical laws, to which human activities should adapt in order to be successful. To many of its followers, Marxism seemed to be a more satisfactory ideology, thanks to its historical determinism. This meant that the certainty of the 1860s, according to which human society could be studied with the same methods and the same unfaltering soundness as the natural sciences deployed, was returning. Georgii Plekhanov, the most prominent figure among the early Russian Marxists, went as far as to write that Marxism was just "Darwinism in its application to social science": "[Darwin] regarded the origin of man as the origin of *a zoological species.* The supporters of the materialistic view want to explain the *historical* fate of such a species" (Plekhanov 1956–1958, 1: 692; 5: 293).

Numerous witnesses confirm that the success of Marxism as a "materialistic conception of history," as it was named in legal publications to avoid censorship, was due exactly to the supposed indestructibility of its "scientific" determinism. Many years later, Semyon Frank reported: "Marxism attracted me because of its scientific form, specifically as 'scientific' socialism. I was attracted by the idea that the life of human society, if studied in the way natural science studies nature, can be known through natural laws" (Frank 1986, 110–111). As late as 1922, the poet Vladimir Mayakovsky observed: "All my life I have been amazed by how Socialists can disentangle facts and systematize the world" (Mayakovsky 1942, 15). If it is true, as Nikolai Lossky observed while remembering his own youth, that "the young Russia" at the end of the nineteenth century "does nothing but talk about the eternal questions" (Dostoevsky 2002, 234), and looks for "a distinctively formulated worldview" (Lossky 1968, 75), Marxism seemed to provide a very solid one. For a radical *intelligentsia* that had grown up in awe of the natural sciences, the conviction of founding one's historical predictions on a solid scientific base, comparable to that of physics and chemistry, held an indisputable appeal. Even the most controversial point in the debate between the Narodniki and the Marxists, the maintained or denied possibility for Russia to realize socialism without going through the capitalistic phase, was ultimately reduced to a question of historical laws. For both contenders, the Russian economy had taken the road of capitalism, but, while for the Marxists this defined the trajectory of subsequent history, for the Narodniki the subjective will of the individuals was still able to change its course. Plekhanov argued in *On the Development of the Monistic View of History* [*K voprosu o razvitii monisticheskogo vzgliada na istoriiu*] (1894):

186   D. STEILA

Starting from the abolition of serfs, Russia has clearly taken the road of capitalism. The subjectivist gentlemen notice this ceaselessly; for one thing, they all assure us that the relationships of production are developing with astonishing and constant rapidity here. But this does not mean anything, they say: we are leading Russia to the boat of our ideal, and it will sail until the end of the world. (Plekhanov 1956–1958, 1: 713)

Instead of indulging in the subjectivist dreams of the Narodniki, Marxism as a systematic and scientific worldview would guide political practice toward success, because "reason can win over blind necessity only after having learned its internal laws, after having defeated it with its own weapons" (Plekhanov 1956–1958, 1: 692). The only possibility of successful action in history was based on the acknowledgment and the acceptance of necessity, according to the lesson that Plekhanov traced back not only to Hegel, but to Spinoza. He wrote:

My freedom would not be a vain word anymore, only on the condition that the *consciousness* of it can be accompanied by the *understanding of the causes* that produce the *free* actions of my neighbors, which is to say only if I can consider them from the point of view of their *necessity*, and if my neighbors can say the same thing about *my own* actions. What does all this mean? That the *possibility of a free (and conscious) historical activity for every individual is equal to zero if, at the base of free human actions, there is no necessity understandable by the acting subject.* (Plekhanov 1956–1958, 1: 593)

In fact, Marxism promised to capture the intrinsic necessity of history with the same solidity as the natural sciences found for natural laws, thus allowing successful human realization in both fields. Only by obeying the laws of nature can technology create its prodigious instruments; only by discovering "the laws, under which the historical development of humanity takes place" can one "guarantee the chance of a conscious action within the course of such a development, and, from being a powerless toy of 'chance,' one becomes its master" (Plekhanov 1956–1958, 4: 425).

Marxist determinism raised some serious objections, especially on the level of its ethical and political consequences. In *Economy and Law* [*Wirtschaft und Recht*], which was translated into Russian in 1898 and was so successful that it sold three editions in two years (Stammler 1898, 1899), Rudolf Stammler accused Marxism of a fundamental incoherence: by reducing history to the deterministic dynamics of economic laws, Marx was accounting for an ultimately inevitable process, which was independent of human will. But then, Stammler wondered, why push human beings to struggle? The most coherent attitude would be to sit and wait. No one, Stammler observed, would ever think of founding a political party or a revolutionary movement to realize a lunar eclipse, well knowing that this exclusively depends on astronomical laws, which are completely indifferent to human action. For Stammler, the very fact that Marxists incited the people to act was a sign of the fact that they themselves, more or less consciously, considered human effort toward a goal a condition for the realization of the goal itself (Stammler 1896, 432–433). Pavel Novgorodtsev, a liberal philosopher with Neo-Kantian sympathies, who had then just returned to Russia from Germany, commented that

> it is difficult to overstate that combination of fatalism and pragmatism that is peculiar to the doctrine of Marx. The fatalistic certainty in the inevitable affirmation of the perfect condition actually relegates the human action to the level of a simple reflex in the objective course of events. What is the meaning of calls to act and to struggle if everything is decided by the immanent and ineluctable laws of history? (Kolerov 2002, 87)

Plekhanov intervened in these discussions with the essay *K voprosu o roli lichnosti v istorii* [*The Role of the Individual in History*], which was directed mainly against the Narodniki, but also against Stammler. Plekhanov admitted that "only in a madhouse could a party be constituted to bring about a lunar eclipse," because "human action does not and cannot be a part of those conditions whose coincidence is necessary for a lunar eclipse." However, Plekhanov continued:

> For the example of the lunar eclipse not to be absurd [...] it would be necessary to imagine that the moon were given a conscience, and that its position in the universe, the cause of its eclipses, would seem to it to be the product of its own free will, and not only caused it an immense pleasure, but were also absolutely necessary for its moral tranquility, as a consequence of the fact that it would always passionately aspire to maintain that position. While imagining all of this, it would be necessary to wonder what the moon would feel, if it ultimately understood that, in reality, neither its will nor its "ideals" determine its movement in the sky, but, on the contrary, its movement determines its will and its "ideals." (Plekhanov 1956–1958, 2: 303)

If Stammler were right, the moon would be paralyzed. According to Plekhanov, on the contrary, the most energetic practical action can derive from the awareness of the necessity of a certain process. It was a matter of the identity of freedom and necessity, which had already been established by Spinoza: "in my conscience, necessity is identified with freedom, and freedom with necessity, and then I am not free only in the sense that *I cannot violate this identity of freedom and necessity, I cannot oppose one to the other, I cannot feel limited by necessity. But*, at the same time, *a similar lack of freedom is its most complete manifestation*" (Plekhanov 1956–1958, 2: 307). According to Plekhanov, from the point of view of the human subject in history, "the consciousness of the absolute necessity of a given phenomenon cannot but increase the energy of the human being who sympathizes with it, and considers themselves to be one of the forces that provoke said phenomenon" (Plekhanov 1956–1958, 2: 308). According to Plekhanov, the persistent, combative determinism that derived from it restated the scientific foundations of Marxism against the voluntarism of the Narodniki.

Plekhanov fundamentally kept the same model for the natural sciences that had taken root in the 1860s. This is confirmed by his own interest in the epistemology of the French materialists of the eighteenth century, in Feuerbach and Chernyshevsky, in human physiology, and in Darwin (Steila 1991). But the traditional positivist model was already in crisis. In 1876, the authoritative physicist Gustav Kirchhoff had stated that the task of mechanics was "to describe completely and as simply as possible motions occurring in nature," instead of providing an actual understanding of them, as had been the ambition of mechanistic physics up to that point (Frank 1989, 37). Heinrich Hertz, the discoverer of the electromagnetic wave, argued that scientific concepts and laws did not have to claim to be immanent in reality at all, because it was sufficient that they helped to calculate and predict the occurrence of phenomena. Wilhelm Oswald put forth an interpretation of nature based on the concept of energy instead of matter. The "bankruptcy of science," which was being debated in other European countries, especially in regard to the confrontation with metaphysics and religion (MacLeod 1982), caused a profound consternation among those who had founded their whole worldview on the solidity of scientific knowledge in Russia. Now, those same scientists confessed that they did not possess any definitive answers, and the concepts that had guided their research for decades showed an irreducible conventionality. Alexander Bogdanov, one of the leading figures in the philosophical debate within Russian Marxism at the beginning of the century, would define that period as "the epoch of a great and unprecedented revolution in the world of scientific knowledge, when the scientific laws that seemed the most stable and universal staggered and fell and left their place to be filled by new and incredible forms, thus opening unexpected and incommensurable perspectives" (Bogdanov 2012, 25).

In Russian laboratories and universities, the "revolution" praised by Bogdanov was welcomed with less enthusiasm. The most famous and important figures mostly aligned themselves in defense of mechanics. Aleksander Stoletov, a physicist at the University of Moscow, for example, stood against those who abandoned mechanics "under the impression of the fecundity of the principle of energy, from which, as from the horn of plenty, the most varied and unexpected fruits have spread; under the influence of the second law of thermodynamics, which has developed outside mechanics and is not subject to a simple mechanical interpretation; under the awareness of the immense gaps of our information about the molecular and electrical processes." He suggested interpreting energy itself as a "mechanical" concept, whose ultimate function was to reduce phenomena to movement (Stoletov 1950, 567–569). In the journal *Scientific Word* [*Nauchnoe slovo*], Dmitrii Gol'dgammer, a student of Stoletov, stated: "scientific truth is made of the answers to our questions: what is it, why is it so; and, if we have closely connected the scientific truth in physics—and in the natural sciences in general—to the question of the mechanical scheme, the reason is clear: only the mechanical scheme promises to give an

9 NATURAL SCIENCES AND THE RADICAL *INTELLIGENTSIA* IN THE LATE...   189

answer to the questions" (Gol'dgammer 1904, 15). Similarly the outstanding scientist Kliment Timiriazev, in *Russian Thought* [*Russkaia mysl'*], stated that "truth is what is," and the only way to come close to the unreachable ideal of exhaustive knowledge was a scientific inquiry that followed the proven methods of the classical tradition (Timiriazev 1904, 197). From his point of view, the speculations of Mach, Ostwald, Helm, Duhem, and Poincaré all had to be rejected because they admitted the success of contemporary science, but denied the methods with which it had been reached.

However, in the Russian scientific world as well, there were some who approved of the new epistemology. The physicist Nikolai Umov, who was also active as a popularizer within the Psychological Society of Moscow and in the journal *Problems of Philosophy and Psychology*, suggested that physics should abandon the Newtonian empirical tradition to go back to the Cartesian one, to find its center around the importance of the theoretical phase of the elaboration of models for interpreting reality (Umov 1896). In fact, sensations could only provide a frame with gaps that had to be filled by the correct use of hypotheses that could change in time. For example, the discovery and study of energy suggested that the ultimate unities of reality had to be "energetic individualities" and not material atoms, which found their connections in the electromagnetic field and not in a mechanical relationship between forces. In Petersburg as well, Orest Khvol'son supported the relevance of the hypotheses in contemporary physics (Khvol'son 1887, 713) and insisted throughout his whole life on this idea, which he would state in a particularly clear way in his later years: "real science does not consist in a list of phenomena and laws, but in the construction of a theory of phenomena, which is to say in the union of the greatest quantity of facts and laws in a well-constructed whole, which deserves to be called a scientific building; its foundation is a defined hypothesis" (Khvol'son 1916, 13).

Russian scientists were generally aware that the introduction of alternative hypotheses to materialism and mechanics would have ample repercussions outside the mere academic and scientific domain. For Alexei Bachinskii (a student of Umov, an experimenter in molecular physics, and a disseminator of Poincaré in Russia) the rejection of matter as an "ephemeral and illusory idol" would have finally brought scientific thinking back to neutrality in the political and social fields. As a matter of fact, he detected a close link between the materialism that had dominated mechanistic physics and the economical materialism of "scientific socialism." Freeing science from the former would have saved it from the latter as well (Bachinskii 1906, 201–202; Vucinich 1970, 373–374). This was exactly what worried one of the most prominent scientists at the time, the chemist Dmitrii Mendeleev. While placing all his authority in favor of Newtonian physics and mechanics, he described the loss that the "bankruptcy" of science was causing in much of Russia's *intelligentsia*, who had been accustomed, for decades, to trusting scientific results as objective and indisputable. Mendeleev wrote:

The old gods have been overturned, new ones are being looked for, but we are coming to nothing accessible and complete; and skepticism becomes law by being content with aphorisms and denying the possibility of a complete general system. This is quite sadly reflected in philosophy, which follows Schopenhauer and Nietzsche; in natural science, which tries to "embrace the ungraspable" [...]; in the whole of the *intelligentsia*, which is used to adhering to the "latest word of science," but is incapable of understanding anything of what is done now in science; and more sadly than ever the dominant skepticism is reflected on youth, which is losing its way. (Mendeleev 1954, 455–456)

In face of the confusion that came from the uncertainty of the solid scientific model, which many had found to be the basis of their comprehensive world-view, reactions were different. Orthodox Marxists maintained Plekhanov's unshakeable faith in the "objective legality" of nature and of history, borrowed from Hegel and Spinoza, Marx and Engels. According to orthodox Marxists, the contemporary epistemology in Europe, and the critique of the concepts of "matter," "substance," and "object," could dangerously affect the Russian progressive *intelligentsia*, since they ultimately represented a regression to bourgeois thinking. Plekhanov came to recognize that some recent scientific discoveries, such as the second law of thermodynamics, could cause a crisis for the old mechanics, but they still had no consequences against dialectical materialism, which would ultimately be reinforced by them. In fact, "none of these discoveries will undermine the definition of matter as that which (existing 'in itself') acts either mediately or immediately, or under certain conditions can act on our external senses. That is enough for me" (Plekhanov 1956–1958, 3: 469). According to Plekhanov, admitting the objective existence of an external world, independent from the experiencing subject, was the indefeasible presupposition of both the natural and human sciences, which, as such, aimed to analyze, describe, explain objective reality, and to define the objective laws that allow the understanding and prediction of the dynamics of reality.

At the turn of the century, others, who were nonetheless proclaiming themselves "Marxists," tried a "moral" re-foundation of their political ideal by rejecting the determinism of orthodox Marxists. In some cases, Kantianism provided a way to avoid the opposition between idealism, compromised by the reaction, and materialism, discredited by the natural sciences themselves. Among the first to do so, Nikolai Berdyaev declared that "the singsong of positivism, naturalism, and hedonism had been sung to its exhaustion" (Berdyaev 1901, 2), and that, if the claims of positivism continued to have some foundation in natural sciences, they had to be decisively rejected by the philosophy of history and ethics. By tracing the road that had rapidly gone "from Marxism to idealism," Sergei Bulgakov noted that, while he was still trying to defend Marxism against Stammler's critique, he "had to admit beyond any possible disagreement that the ideal of Marxism is not given by science, but by 'life,' and is therefore *extra*-scientific or *a*-scientific. This conclusion is really rather fatal for 'scientific' socialism, which is precisely proud of the scientific nature of its ideal" (Bulgakov 1903, 7). According to Bulgakov, the justification of "progress" in the history of humanity could not derive from positivist science, but only from the ideal identification of values. Therefore, political choices had now to be founded "ethically" rather than "scientifically"—which would also strengthen them, instead of weakening them: "The contemporary social struggle will seem to us to be not only the clash of adversary interests, but also the realization and the development of a moral idea. And our participation in it will not be motivated by selfish class interest, but will become a religious duty, an absolute imperative of moral law, a commandment from God" (Bulgakov et al. 1902, 46).

The impact of contemporary Western epistemology was massive and profound, especially on the radical *intelligentsia*, who had been nurtured by the "scientism" of the Russian revolutionary tradition and were elaborating their beliefs during the decade preceding the revolution. In the words of Victor Serge, "the new theory of energy of Mach and Avenarius, revising the notion of matter, was of cardinal importance for us" (Serge 2012, 30). And it was exactly the empiriocriticism, which had been elaborated independently by the Austrian physicist Ernst Mach and the Zurich philosopher Richard Avenarius, that fascinated the Russian radicals who were looking for a new paradigm that could account for the most recent scientific thinking without corroding the traditional deference to the natural sciences in the process. Unlike Neo-Kantianism, which attempted to find the foundations of the scientific nature of science in the transcendental structures of pure consciousness, empiriocriticism aimed to draw the model of knowledge from the concrete process of existing sciences. Ernst Mach, while he underscored the relativity of scientific discoveries and the conventionality of its principles and concepts, advocated for the fundamental role of scientific knowledge in human life. Richard Avenarius developed his theoretical thinking on the ground of psycho-physiology, which was long familiar to the Russian radicals. What is more, empiriocriticism, in both its versions, echoed the themes of Darwinian evolution: knowledge appeared as an instrument for adapting to the environment; the very development of ideas was subject to the "struggle for survival," which meant that the most effective conception became more and more preponderant in history. The extraordinary Russian career of empiriocriticism can be explained by the particularly favorable combination of the theoretical proposal of Mach and Avenarius with the "horizon of expectations" of those who received it.[3] In Russia, those who turned to empiriocriticism found a confirmation of the traditional "scientific" worldview, which was capable of surviving the crisis of classical positivism, the "dematerialization" of the world put forth by science, and the fall of Newtonian mechanics. It is not a coincidence that the often-repeated accusation of the so-called Russian "Machists" against orthodox materialism was precisely based on the backwardness of the latter's scientific references. In Bogdanov's words, Plekhanov and his followers continued to apply, in an uncritical and unsystematic way, concepts like "matter," "things," "property," "nature," "force," etc., both in a metaphysical sense and in a vaguely physical one. But these very concepts had been profoundly transformed by the science of the nineteenth and beginning of the twentieth centuries. Philosophy can progress only if an indissoluble and lively link with the development of *science as a whole* is maintained, and not by lagging tiredly behind among familiar, but undetermined, concepts. (Bogdanov 2012, 259)

Bogdanov, who was certainly the most authoritative and original of the "Machists," openly asserted the opportunity of "harmonically introducing" into Marxism "everything that is vital in the ideas" of empiriocriticism (Bogdanov 1904, 174). For the "Machists," this did not imply a concession to bourgeois thinking, which would "contaminate" the Marxist orthodoxy, as was claimed by Plekhanov and his followers, but, on the contrary, it was going to re-establish ideas that were already "familiar" to Marxism (Lunacharsky 1906, VI): the "biological" and "pragmatic" conception of knowledge as a way of adaptation to the environment, a strict empiricism stretched until the distinction between subject and object was overcome, and the critique of every metaphysical idea in the face of the essential factuality of experience, which had to be approached without prejudice (Lunacharsky 1905, 368).

The internal dispute within Marxism that these subjects ignited, and that even caused some witnesses to talk about a real "fight around Mach" (a "Machomachy") (Izgoev 1910), is well-known, at least because it occasioned Lenin's "philosophical" work, *Materialism and Empiriocriticism* (Steila 2013). Here, without entering into the specific terms of this conflict, I would like to limit my observations to the fact that both the orthodox Marxists and the "Machists" shared the same faith in the "scientific" value of historical materialism and Marxist political theory. The division came from the idea of "science" that they supported, and the epistemology they embraced. According to Plekhanov's followers, the claim of a reformation of Marxism on the basis of empiriocriticism would destroy any possible materialist conception of history. Liubov' Aksel'rod, who was so faithful to Plekhanov's line that she chose the pseudonym "Orthodox," observed "that *the acknowledgement of the objective laws of history cannot coexist with the denial of the reality of nature and its objective laws in general*" (Aksel'rod 1906, VIII). On the side of the "Machists," the then young historian Mikhail Pokrovsky maintained that:

> science is the means of finding one's way in the chaos of experience, and thus of economizing the energy of consciousness which would otherwise be infinitely dispersed [...] From this point of view, that which is best and will most surely lead to the fundamental goal of science will be the most scientific. The hypothesis that can explain in the most direct way the greatest quantity of phenomena possesses the *record* for scientific nature in a given moment. Naturally, this *record* is relative: in the following moment, an even more scientific hypothesis can appear, but this will be such only in the case in which it comes even closer to the scientific ideal. (Pokrovsky 1904, 125)

The "law" does not reproduce an objective reality at all, nor does it represent the "plan" that reality follows in its development. It is just a formula, reached by way of generalizations, which enfolds all known phenomena that possess a certain characteristic. In this sense, history was no exception, if only for the degree of proximity to the model of scientific knowledge:

> the concepts of natural science are elaborated according to a strictly defined method, which is to say by respecting certain logical conditions. Most historical concepts come from life, where they have been formed with no method at all [...] But this difference is in the degree of perfection, not in substance. The concepts that serve as a basis for the historian refer to the same logical category of the concepts of natural science, but the former are less adapted than the latter to the scientific requirements: this is all the difference there is. (Pokrovsky 1904, 118)

With this, Pokrovsky used empiriocriticism to reject Neo-Kantian and historicist positions in the name of a concept of history as science with the same rights and meaning as natural science.

However, according to the orthodox Marxists, "Machists" rejected the objective criterion of truth, the ultimately "real" foundation of any possible knowledge and judgment, and therefore their political actions were to take the risk of arbitrariness and errors. The great advantage that early Marxism had been able to hold against the Narodniki, which was its reference to an objective "science" of society that interpreted reality and predicted its development with certainty, seemed to have been utterly smashed. If, in 1913, Lenin stated with conviction that "the Marxist doctrine is omnipotent because it is true" (Lenin 1977, 25), it was exactly the strength of that "truth" that the "Machists" seemed to undermine. Plekhanov could put forth against the "Machists" the same arguments that, a decade earlier, he had held against the "subjectivist" Narodniki:

> The criterion of truth does not reside in me, but in existing relationships outside of me. The *true* ideas are those that give an exact representation of these relationships; the *false* ones those that deform them. In the sciences of nature, the theory that faithfully embraces the relationships between natural phenomena is *true*; in history, the description that faithfully accounts for the existing social relationships in the described period is *true*. (Plekhanov 1956–1958, 1: 671)

The possibility of linking Mikhailovsky's "subjective sociology" and empiriocriticism was supported by many, and not simply because one of the latter's most coherent advocates in its applications to the study of history and society was Viktor Chernov, one of the proclaimed heirs of the tradition of the Narodniki (Chernov 1907). The interpretation of Marxism as a "philosophy of action," the revision of the traditional categories of reality and causality, and the foundation of a new historical monism based on the critique of experience were common themes in the thought of the "critical" Marxists and late-Narodniki. This was particularly clear in a polemical piece signed by Anton

194 D. STEILA

Morev, who protested against the presumed originality of the "self-critique" of Russian Marxists, and against their lack of gratitude for their authentic "fore-runners," who were to be found among the Narodniki (Morev 1909, 8–9). In 1909, while the well-known philosophical discussion within the Bolshevik faction was raging, an anonymous reviewer in the journal *The Russian Wealth* [*Russkoe bogatstvo*] commented that, a few years earlier, "the invitation to align with the flag of Mach's and Avenarius' empiriocriticism, the critique of the 'truths' of metaphysical materialism, the references to the early works of Marx in spite of the 'dogmatic' Marxism of the various Misters Plekhanov etc., were branded as 'petty bourgeois ideology,' typical of the followers of Lavrov and Mikhailovsky. But *tempora mutantur*" (Retsenziia 1909, 111–112). Now, among the Marxists, "Machists" seemed to repeat the very same ideas of the Narodniki.[4]

In this perspective, it is interesting to observe that the first reception of empiriocriticism in Russia had occurred a few decades before in the Populist milieu. Vladimir Lesevich, a student of Lavrov, the founder of a school for peasants, a scholar of folklore, a friend of Mikhailovsky, and even a contributor, under the pseudonym of "Ukrainian," to the clandestine *Bulletin of the People's Will* [*Vestnik Narodnoi Voli*], was the first, at the end of the 1870s, to adhere to the program of "scientific philosophy" of Avenarius, and to enthusiastically start its dissemination in Russia. Vladimir Bonch-Bruevich assigned him a direct responsibility for the success of empiriocriticism among the Marxists by recalling that Lesevich had held a lecture on Avenarius in Petersburg in 1898 and some of the attending Marxists had then begun "to bring the philosophy of Avenarius closer to dialectical materialism and to Marx's philosophical opinions" (Bonch-Bruevich 1929, 32–33). According to Bonch-Bruevich, Mikhailovsky was also present at the lecture, and asked Lesevich a direct question about the relationship between the philosophy of Avenarius and the subjectivist method. Lesevich allegedly answered that the new philosophy "was opening doors and windows to subjectivism" (Bonch-Bruevich 1929, 33). Actually, it was not difficult to connect the empiriocriticist attacks on metaphysics, and the claim that the conscience plays a "constitutive" role in the elaboration of experience, with the assertion of the driving function of individuality in history. For Lesevich, scientific knowledge, free from prejudices, was going, prospectively, to allow humanity to transform the world. To this end, "it is necessary to look at nature directly, to desist from its personification, to stop attributing to it goals and tendencies, to resist the seduction of vain expectations. Intentionality and teleology are only present in human activity" (Lesevich 1915, 598). Lesevich's epistemological ideal, the disillusioned knowledge of reality, was thus embracing action as consciously oriented toward the aim of political activity. Lesevich presented the seemingly abstruse and abstract philosophical system of Avenarius to the Russian readers of *Russian Thought* [*Russkaia mysl'*] as the foundation of a project that had to be realized in history. He wrote:

> Richard Avenarius [...] made clear that traditional knowledge only contains casual and unconnected elements of experience, and it is overloaded with a great quantity of fictions; he made it clear that the preservation of life and the strengthening of its stability demand that these fictions be eliminated from experience, that "pure experience" be established, and he irrefutably demonstrated that the stability of social groups [...] is based on the development of social solidarity, which triumphs and distances the threats against itself only on the basis of the complete and systematic elaboration of "pure experience." (Lesevich 1903, 83–84)

An equally committed reading of empiriocriticism, this time with an anti-Narodniki purpose, was put forth a few years later by the journal *Scientific Survey* [*Nauchnoe obozrenie*], which, although it was not openly Marxist, was considered by contemporaries to be "an authentic platform for materialistic thought and for the struggle against Populism" (Strumilin 1969, 3). Filippov, the founder and soul of the journal, a scientist by education, reproached the Narodniki for propounding the subjectivist method "not as the regulator of every scientific research, but as an autonomous method independent from research, which was applicable to the phenomena of the individual and social life of human beings" (Filippov 1895, XVII). To his eyes, on the contrary, the "subjectivist point of view" was not eliminable from any research, and, for this reason, had to be consciously taken into consideration. At the heart of the polemics between the Marxists and the Narodniki about historical determinism, Filippov invoked the principles of "scientific philosophy" that could bring the natural and human sciences closer; he observed that "an unconditional necessity, even in the physical world, is a metaphysical myth, just like chance or unconditional freedom" (Filippov 1897, 114). The natural and historical world is understood as an interconnected web of functional relationships, where "every necessity is conditional, and those who *can* do something to overcome evil, *must* do it. The only question is the *accurate evaluation of our strength*, otherwise, like a bad general, we risk wasting it all where it is not actually needed" (Filippov 1897, 130). From Filippov's point of view, the unavoidability of a strictly "scientific" worldview was again stated as necessary in order to have effective political action.

Russian reception of the European conception of science between the late nineteenth and early twentieth centuries was largely bound to political and social thought, as had been the case for Darwin's theories. In general, this confirms the traditional conception of historiography, according to which, in Russia, "philosophy was not expected to answer the theoretical questions of reason, but rather to provide some indication about a possible way of resolving the questions of life" (Zenkovsky 1991, 120). Even reflections about the epistemological foundations of the natural sciences were loaded with ethical and political implications. More specifically, this whole history shows the relevance of the problem of the "scientific" foundation of different worldviews and of different political and social projects within the Russian revolutionary movements.

Translated by Lucia Pasini

NOTES

1. See Vucinich (1963, 1970, 1988). For a more recent survey, Ellis (2010).
2. The idea of mutuality would be taken up again at the beginning of the century, among the anarchists, by Pyotr Kropotkin (1908).
3. About the concept of "horizon of expectations," see Jauss (1987).
4. Here, the reviewer was referencing Bazarov (1908) in particular.

BIBLIOGRAPHY

Aksel'rod, Liubov' I. 1906. *Filosofskie ocherki. Otvet filosofskim kritikam istoricheskogo materializma*. St. Petersburg: izd. M.M. Druzhininoi i A.N. Maksimovoi.

Bachinskii, Aleksei I. 1906. Pis'ma po filosofii estestvoznaniia. Pis'mo II: O vozmozhnom vliianii matematicheskikh metodov na cherty nauchnogo miroponimaniia. In *Sbornik po filosofii estestvoznaniia*, 183–205. Moscow: Tvorcheskaia mysl'.

Bazarov, Vladimir A. 1908. K voprosu o filosofskikh osnovakh marksizma. In *Pamiati Marksa. K dvadtsatiletiu so dnia ego smerti (1883–1908)* [anonymous eds.], 50–79. St. Petersburg: izdanie O. i M. Kedrovykh.

Berdyaev, Nikolai A. 1901. Bor'ba za idealizm. *Mir bozhii* 6: 1–26.

Bogdanov, Alexander A. 1904. Zamechaniia avtora stat'i 'Filosofskii koshmar'. *Pravda* 8: 173–174.

———. 2012. *Prikliuchenie odnoi filosofskoi shkoly. Polemicheskie zametki o G.V. Plekhanove i ego shkole*. Moscow: Librokom.

Bonch-Bruevich, Vladimir D. 1929. Zhenevskie vospominaniia. *Pod znamenem marksizma* 1: 18–46.

Bulgakov, Sergei N. 1903. *Ot marksizma k idealizmu. Sbornik statei (1896–1903)*. St. Petersburg: Obshchestvennaia pol'za.

Bulgakov, Sergei N., Evgenii N. Trubetskoi, Pyotr B. Struve [P.G.], Nikolai A. Berdyaev, Semyon L. Frank, Sergei A. Askol'dov, Sergei N. Trubetskoi, et al. 1902. *Problemy idealizma. Sbornik statei*. Moscow: Izdanie Moskovskogo Psikhologicheskogo Obshchestva.

Chernov, Viktor M. 1907. *Filosofskie i sotsiologicheskie etiudy*. Moscow: Sotrudnichestvo.

Chernyshevsky, Nikolai G. 1986. *What's To Be Done?* Translated by N. Dole and S.S. Skidelsky. Ann Arbor: Ardis.

———. 1987. Antropologicheskii princip v filosofii. In *Sochineniia v 2-kh tomakh*, ed. N.G. Chernyshevsky, vol. 2, 146–229. Moscow: Mysl'.

Dostoevsky, Fyodor M. 1974. *Notes from Underground*. Translated by Mirra Ginsburg. New York, NY: Bantam Books.

———. 2002. *The Brothers Karamazov. A Novel in Four Parts with Epilogue*. Translated by Richard Pevear and Larissa Volokhonsky. New York, NY: Farrar, Straus and Giroux.

———. 2006. *Demons*. Translated by Richard Pevear and Larissa Volokhonsky. London: Vintage.

Ellis, Charles. 2010. Natural Science. In *A History of Russian Thought*, ed. William Leatherbarrow and Derek Offord, 286–307. Cambridge, UK: Cambridge University Press.

Filippov, Mikhail M. 1895. *Filosofiia deistvitel'nosti*. St. Petersburg: A. Porokhovshchikov.

———. 1897. Sub'ektivizm i narodnichestvo. *Nauchnoe obozrenie* 12: 112–130.

Florovsky, Georges. 1972. *Ways of Russian Theology. Part Two*. In *Collected Works of Georges Florovsky*, vol. 6. Belmont: Nordland Publishing Company.

Frank, Philip. 1989. *Einstein. His Life and Time*. Cambridge: Da Capo Press.

Frank, Semyon L. 1986. Predsmertnoe (Vospominaniia i mysli). *Vestnik Russkogo Khristianskogo Dvizheniia* 1 (146): 103–126.

Gol'dgammer, Dmitrii A. 1904. Nauka i istina. *Nauchnoe slovo* 10: 5–20.

Graham, Loren R. 1993. *Science in Russia and the Soviet Union*. Cambridge, UK: Cambridge University Press.

Izgoev, Aleksander S. 1910. Na perevale. III. Makhomakhiia v lagere marksistov. *Russkaia mysl'* 2: 106–114.

Jauss, Hans Robert. 1987. *Die Theorie der Rezeption. Rückschau auf ihre unerkannte Vorgeschichte*. Konstanz: Konstanzer Universitätsreden.

Khvol'son, Orest D. 1887. Osnovnye gipotezy fiziki. *Vestnik Evropy* 2: 713–740; 3: 197–238.

———. 1916. *Znanie i vera v fizike*. Petrograd: F. K. Fetterlein.

Kolerov, Modest A. 2002. Idealismus militans: istoriia i obshchestvennyi smysl' sbornika 'Problemy idealizma'. In *Problemy idealizma. Sbornik statei*, 61–224. Moscow: Tri kvadrata.

Koshtoiants, Khachatur S. 1946. *Ocherki po istorii fiziologii v Rossii*. Moscow-Leningrad: izd.-vo AN SSSR.

Kropotkin, Pyotr. 1908. *Mutual Aid. A Factor of Evolution*. London: William Heinemann. Accessed February 16, 2019. https://archive.org/details/in.ernet.dli.2015.96351/page/n5.

Lavrov, Pyotr L. 1967. *Historical Letters*. Translated by James P. Scanlan. Berkeley and Los Angeles, CA: University of California Press.

Lenin, Vladimir I. 1977. The Three Sources and Three Component Parts of Marxism. In *Collected Works*, vol. 19, 21–28. Moscow: Progress Publishers.

Lesevich, Vladimir V. 1903. Mezhdunarodnyi iazyk kul'turnykh snoshenii. *Russkaia mysl'* 2: 67–91.

———. 1915. *Sobranie sochinenii*. Vol. 3. Moscow: Knigoizdatel'stvo Pisatelei.

Lossky, Nikolai O. 1955. *Histoire de la philosophie russe des origines à 1950*. Paris: Payot.

———. 1968. *Vospominaniia. Zhizn' i filosofskii put'*. München: Fink.

Lunacharsky, Anatoly V. 1905. *Etiudy kriticheskie i polemicheskie*. Moscow: Pravda.

———. 1906. *Otkliki zhizni*. St. Petersburg: Izdanie O. N. Popova.

MacLeod, Roy. 1982. The 'Bankruptcy of Science' Debate: The Creed of Science and Its Critics, 1885–1900. *Science, Technology, and Human Values* 7 (41): 2–15.

Mayakovsky, Vladimir. 1942. *Mayakovsky and His Poetry*. Translated by H. Marshall. London: The Pilot Press.

Mendeleev, Dmitrii I. 1954. *Sobranie sochinenii v 25 tomakh*. Vol. 24. Moscow: AN SSSR.

Mikhailovsky, Nikolai K. 1911. *Polnoe sobranie sochinenii v 15 tomakh*. Vol. 1. St. Petersburg: N. N. Mikhailovsky.

Morev, Anton. 1909. *Filosofskaia samokritika marksizma*. St. Petersburg: tip. Ia. Balianskogo.

Paperno, Irina. 1988. *Chernyshevsky and the Age of Realism. A Study in the Semiotics of Behavior*. Stanford, CA: Stanford University Press.

Peace, Richard. 2010. Nihilism. In *A History of Russian Thought*, ed. William Leatherbarrow and Derek Offord, 116–140. Cambridge, UK: Cambridge University Press.

Pisarev, I. 1894. Bazarov. (*Ottsy i Deti*, roman I.S. Turgeneva). In *Sochineniia D. I. Pisareva. Polnoe sobranie v 6-ti tomakh*, vol. 2, 373–422. St. Petersburg: Iu. N. Erlikh.

Plekhanov, Georgii V. 1956–1958. *Izbrannye filosofskie proizvedeniia*. Vol. 5. Moscow: Izdatel'stvo social'no-ekonomicheskoi literatury.

Pokrovsky, Mikhail N. 1904. 'Idealizm' i 'zakony istorii'. *Pravda* 3: 112–126.

Pustarnakov, Vladimir F. 2003. *Universitetskaia filosofiia v Rossii. Idei. Personalii, Osnovnye centry*. St. Petersburg: Izdatel'stvo Russkogo Khristianskogo Gumanitarnogo Instituta.

Retsenziia na knigu: V. Bazarov. *Na dva fronta*. 1909. *Russkoe bogatstvo* 12: 111–112.

Rogers, James A. 1960. Darwinism, Scientism and Nihilism. *Russian Review* 19 (1): 10–23.

———. 1972. Proudhon and the Transformation of Russian 'Nihilism'. *Cahiers du Monde Russe et Soviétique* 13 (4): 514–523.

Serge, Victor. 2012. *Memoirs of a Revolutionary*. New York: The New York Review of Books.

Stammler, Rudolf. 1896. *Wirtschaft und Recht, nach der Materialistischen Geschichtsauffassung, eine sozial-philosophische Untersuchung*. Leipzig: Veit.

———. 1898. *Khoziaistvo i pravo s tochki zreniia materialisticheskogo ponimaniia istorii*. St. Petersburg: tip. M. Merkusheva; prilozhenie k *Severnomu Vestniku*. 1 (10/12).

———. 1899. *Khoziaistvo i pravo s tochki zreniia materialisticheskogo ponimaniia istorii*. St. Petersburg: N. Berezin i M. Semenov.

Steila, Daniela. 1991. *Genesis and Development of Plekhanov's Theory of Knowledge. A Marxist Between Anthropological Materialism and Physiology*. Dordrecht: Kluwer Academic Publishers.

———. 2013. *Nauka i revoliuciia. Recepciia ėmpiriokrititsizma v russkoi kul'ture (1877–1910 gg.)*. Translated by Ol'ga Popova. Moscow: Akademicheskii proekt.

Stoletov, Aleksander G. 1950. *Izbrannye sochineniia*. Moscow-Leningrad: Izdatel'stvo tekhniko-teoreticheskoi literatury.

Strumilin, Stanislav G. 1969. Predislovie k pervomu izdaniiu. In *Ternistyi put'. Zhizn' i deiatel'nost' russkogo uchenogo i literatora M.M. Filippova*, ed. Boris M. Filippov, 3–4. Moscow: Nauka.

Thompson, Diane O. 2002. Dostoevsky and Science. In *The Cambridge Companion to Dostoevskii*, ed. William J. Leatherbarrow, 191–211. Cambridge, UK: Cambridge University Press.

Timiriazev, Kliment A. 1904. Nasushchie zadachi sovremennogo estestvoznaniia. *Russkaia mysl'* 4: 196–204.

Todes, Daniel P. 1989. *Darwin without Malthus: The Struggle for Existence in Russian Evolutionary Thought*. Oxford: Oxford University Press.

Turgenev, Ivan S. 1991. *Fathers and Sons*. Translated by Richard Freeborn. Oxford: Oxford University Press.

Umov, Nikolai A. 1896. Znachenie Dekarta v istorii fizicheskikh nauk. *Voprosy filosofii i psikhologii* 4: 489–520.

Vucinich, Alexander. 1963. *Science in Russian Culture: A History to 1860*. Stanford, CA: Stanford University Press.

———. 1970. *Science in Russian Culture 1861–1917*. Stanford, CA: Stanford University Press.

———. 1972. Russia: Biological Sciences. In *The Comparative Reception of Darwinism*, ed. Thomas F. Glick, 227–268. Austin, TX: University of Texas Press.

———. 1988. *Darwin in Russian Thought*. Berkeley, Los Angeles, and Oxford: University of California Press.

Walicki, Andrzej. 2015. *The Flow of Ideas: Russian Thought from the Enlightenment to the Religious-Philosophical Renaissance*. Frankfurt a.M.: Peter Lang.

Zenkovsky, Vladimir V. 1991. *Istoriia russkoi filosofii*. Vol. 1. Leningrad: Ego.

CHAPTER 10

Lev Shestov's Philosophy of Freedom

Yulia V. Sineokaya and Anton M. Khokhlov

For Lev Shestov attaining spiritual freedom means overcoming existential anxiety about fate (to borrow Paul Tillich's term) by way of comprehending God. His philosophy is aimed at liberating man from the power of an extrinsic anonymous objective order that consigns him to suffering here on earth. By correlating the interpretation of existential experience and biblical text, Shestov arrives at his own religious-philosophical concept of freedom. This chapter examines three mythologemes that are fundamental to Shestov's philosophy of freedom: "creation out of nothing" (as the ultimate expression of dispensation), "the Fall" (as the metaphysical ground for irrationalism), and eschatological "annulment of past evil" (as the moral correlate of theistic voluntarism). The central—and essentially the only—problems Shestov grappled with were the search for freedom through overcoming existential anxiety about fate, and personal communion with God as the ground and the goal. The final words of his early work—"One should seek Him who is above compassion and above Good. One should seek God" (Shestov 1993a, 157)—could serve as an epigraph to the philosopher's entire work.

The thinker who had committed his talent to the quest for God not where the Truth is usually sought—among scientists, philosophers, and moralists— but in biblical irrationalism, was driven by the urge to overthrow the

---

An earlier version of this chapter was published under the same title in *Studies in East European Thought* 68: 213–227 (2016); https://doi.org/10.1007/ s11212-016-9257-6. Reused here with permission.

Y. V. Sineokaya (✉)
Department of Philosophy of the History of Western Philosophy, Institute of Philosophy, Russian Academy of Sciences, Moscow, Russia

A. M. Khokhlov
Independent scholar, Moscow, Russia

© The Author(s), under exclusive license to Springer Nature Switzerland AG 2021
M. F. Bykova et al. (eds.), *The Palgrave Handbook of Russian Thought*, https://doi.org/10.1007/978-3-030-62982-3_10

oppression of "eternal truths." He saw in God the liberation of the individual from the power of necessity, that is, "environment," "heredity," "tradition," and "moral ideals." In her study *Russian Thinkers and Western Philosophy*, Nelly Motroshilova pinpointed the attitude that permeates Shestov's work:

> As I see it, L. Shestov's philosophy marks a perfectly legitimate positive pivot toward a new type of philosophizing about man and his spirit, upholding the inalienable rights and freedoms of the human individual in the face of any—be it natural or social—necessity in a very promising search for the kind of freedom and personal self-expression that can hold their own against formidable force in the guise of necessity and are not reduced to conformist rationalizations. Freedom and individuality untrammeled by any necessities and generalities are the main thrust of L. Shestov's thought-passion. (Motroshilova 2006, 394)

Shestov was convinced that faith is the only dimension of thought that is alien to speculative philosophy and can pave man's way to freedom, to the Creator of everything there is in the world, and to the obliteration of any boundaries between what is and what is not possible.

Shestov's philosophy challenges culture as the fateful obstacle on the way to the "true manifestations of the human spirit," and negates morality based on the laws of Reason that is independent of God. He believes that the dilemmas of freedom and culture, philosophy and faith, arose because God has been supplanted by abstraction and faith by knowledge. Culture that dominates faith impedes direct manifestation of feelings and reflection distorts them.

Shestov maintains that philosophical reflection should be put in the service of the entire emotional sphere of man and not only his thirst for knowledge. Many existential philosophers have sought to make "the whole man" the object of philosophical inquiry. Similar ideas have been expressed by Pascal, Kierkegaard, Unamuno, Mounier, and Marcel. With Shestov, the need to overcome existential anxiety takes the form that is commonly referred to in the philosophical literature as the tragic quest.

Intuition of existential anxiety is the starting point of Lev Shestov's philosophy of freedom. Shestov is a writer of philosophical essays, a philosopher without definitions. To analyze the structure of existential anxiety in his work we have chosen the ideas of the philosopher and theologian Paul Tillich, known for his masterful transformation of psychological into ontological description.

Tillich describes existential anxiety as a state in which being is aware of possible non-being:

> anxiety is the existential awareness of non-being. "Existential" in this sentence means that it is not the abstract knowledge of non-being which produces anxiety but the awareness that non-being is a part of one's own being. It is not the realization of universal transitoriness, not even the experience of the death of others, but the impression of these events on the always latent awareness of our own having to die that produces anxiety. Anxiety is finitude, experienced as one's own finitude. (Tillich 2011, 45)

It is the fact that anxiety is embedded in man's very existence that lends it an existential character. The term "anxiety" used by Tillich plays an important role in Existentialism. There are similar concepts in French (*angoisse*), in German (*Angst*), and in English (*anguish*). One may also recall the Latin *anxietas*.

Tillich distinguishes three types of anxiety in accordance with the three realms in which non-being threatens being:

> Non-being threatens man's ontic self-affirmation, relatively in terms of fate, absolutely in terms of death. It threatens man's spiritual self-affirmation, relatively in terms of emptiness, absolutely in terms of meaninglessness. It threatens man's moral self-affirmation, relatively in terms of guilt, absolutely in terms of condemnation. Anxiety is the awareness of this threefold threat. (Tillich 2011, 52)

The three forms of anxiety are not mutually exclusive, on the contrary, they are immanent in one another, though as a rule one of them predominates.

The dominant form of anxiety in Shestov's work is the anxiety of fate inasmuch as it is relatively autonomous from the anxiety of death. The anxiety of condemnation (relatively autonomous from the anxiety of guilt) is also an abiding feature of Shestov's thought. By contrast, the anxiety of meaninglessness and emptiness is relatively muted. It is mainly anxiety of alienation from the fundamental meanings of spiritual culture, above all its religious element.

For the most part Shestov writes about earthly suffering, suffering that is of this world. Death, especially an individual's own death, is on the periphery of Shestov's concerns. The philosopher's main concern is the meaning of life here on earth, something he is prepared to die for. This feature of Shestov's perception of the world is highlighted in the following fragment from his personal correspondence dated 1897:

> I think death is by no means the most absurd or dreadful thing in a person's life. I have no mystical fear of death. If people had no hope that someday they would leave this world life would be impossible. Whether there is life after death or whether man vanishes forever in inanity—all the same death gives him a chance [...] If one is afraid of death life is not worth living. (Baranova-Shestova 1983, 1: 35)

This is an early articulation of Shestov's interpretation of existential anxiety that would be characteristic of Shestov throughout his creative life, as witnessed by another testimony dating to 1938 (shortly before his death) left by Shestov's friend Alexander Lazarev. Lazarev recalls that during his illness the philosopher said: "I had no fear, I felt relief, great relief. There, I thought, the shackles will soon fall off" (Baranova-Shestova 1983, 2: 175).

Fate, according to Shestov, is the realm of accident. For a finite being the source of fate-anxiety is the awareness that there is no ultimate need for its existence and of the accidental nature of being. Shestov's interpretation of the anxiety of fate is consonant with existential concepts of "unreliability" (Jaspers), "insecurity" (Marcel), and "abandonment" (Sartre).

In the early period of his work, seeking to fathom fate and the meaning of life, Shestov drew inspiration from the artistic genius of Shakespeare who could discern order and meaning where others saw nothing but chaos and absurdity. The young philosopher was mesmerized by Shakespeare's gift of seeing "reasonable necessity" where others saw only wanton chance.

In his mature years Shestov challenged necessity in all its manifestations, however "reasonable" and morally justified it may have been. Shestov so detested the concept of "accident" that he considered it to be his mission as a philosopher not only to "interpret" it but to "uproot" it and "turn it to ashes." To this end, Shestov turns to Almighty God, who can at his discretion cancel past misfortune.

In his later period, Shestov showed some sympathy for Kierkegaard's critique of genius as "the greatest sinner" whose sin consisted in being able to "discover fate" everywhere (Shestov 1992, 93–94). Shestov believed that in order to attain existential freedom one had also to overcome the anxiety of guilt and condemnation. On that issue, the biggest influence on him was Kant. One has to note, however, that in Shestov's intellectual drama Kant is more often than not an anti-hero. One of the main reasons for that is his rejection of the Kantian categorical imperative. Shestov's main objection to the categorical imperative is that the imperative is a repressive force that is external to man and that is incapable of pardoning or forgiving someone who has sinned just once, thus dooming him to eternal damnation and, moreover, impelling him to commit more crimes.

Shestov, like Tillich, was convinced that the guilt-anxiety (a relative threat to man's moral being) and the condemnation-anxiety (an absolute threat) arise when a person realizes that he has departed from his mission in his quest for self-actualization. In other words, when a person realizes that he is not what he should be. One can safely say that Shestov considered feelings of guilt to be legitimate, but was categorically opposed to the threat of condemnation.

Tillich considers two methods of transforming the anxiety of guilt into moral action. He described as "anomism" the first method based on the vicissitudes of fate and as "legalism" the second method based on the responsibility of freedom. By choosing the first method a person may end up neglecting any verdict and moral principles underlying it. By choosing the second method, a person risks succumbing to moral rigorism and the arrogance engendered by such rigorism.

In Shestov's work we can readily find manifestations of both methods of moral self-affirmation. In his work *Shakespeare and His Critic Brandes* (1898), one finds Shestov's brand of "legalism" (which, however, is at odds with Kantian legalism). Yet in his next work entitled *Good in the Teachings of Count Tolstoy and Nietzsche* Shestov inveighs heavily against the Tolstoyan version of legalism in line with his new idea of anomism which was particularly apparent in his works of 1905–1910.

The theme of moral guilt looms large in Shestov's major work about Luther, *Sola Fide, Only by Faith* (1914). The philosopher argues that Luther's revolt against Catholicism and the monks was prompted not so much by Rome's abuses and the dissipation of the monks as by their arrogant claim to sanctity and infallibility which went hand-in-hand with the abuses. Luther was a monk and an ascetic, and one day in the monastery it dawned on him that even in holy life he remained inwardly an inveterate sinner. He realized that his will was powerless in the face of sin and that, strictly speaking, he was not even guilty of his own sins. These sins were not simply inherited by him from his sinful progenitor but were part of the inscrutable and unknowable will of God. God "created us as sinners" but he saved us by sacrificing his Son. Luther became aware from his own spiritual experience that man's only salvation is faith and that all that is required of man is repentance and humility and trust in God's inscrutable Providence. Shestov showed a keen interest in the personality of Luther and his legacy and had sympathy for his teaching. Shestov's work about Luther discovers a precedent of moral anomism that he could identify with.

In the works that followed, Shestov brought to bear the power of his irony on the moral guilt. For Shestov, the justice of moral condemnation was phony and a pitiful travesty of a perfect moral order where evil is not only punished but banished from being. For the same reason Shestov rejects traditional forms of theodicy, for to justify God means to condemn man. In his later work, Shestov wants God to be liberated from any rational strictures and, in His omnipotence, to justify the world and man. Anxiety in face of emptiness and lack of meaning, understood as a loss of interest in life and loss of a sense of an existence that lends meaning to all meanings, is marginal to Shestov's interests. However, the loss of the spiritual center brings about a crisis in particular areas of spiritual life. For Tillich, anxiety at life's meaninglessness is a psychological correlate of the threat non-being poses to man's spiritual self-affirmation: "Spiritual self-affirmation occurs when man lives creatively in the various spheres of meaning." As an example of creative life within meanings Tillich cites a scientist who is *au fait* with the scientific discoveries of his time and who even if he himself has not made any discoveries, through meaningful participation in them can "affirm himself spiritually" (Tillich 2011, 59).

Shestov (in his early and middle period) is a vivid example of a thinker endowed with crisis consciousness. Shestov is a man at the intersection of various cultures and worldviews. That position secured him the status of a man of "mixed identity." A Russian Jew, a Judaist who asserted the inner unity of the Old and New Testaments, a religious skeptic, an immoralist, a critic of political violence, a mystical anarchist, and a metaphysical human rights activist—this only begins the list of possible characterizations of Shestov. The difficulty of "placing" him and his constant meanderings between worldviews is a feature repeatedly noted by himself and by those who have studied his work. Commenting in *Good in the Teachings of Count Tolstoy and Nietzsche* (1900) on the spiritual situation of his era (and his own spiritual predicament), Shestov wrote:

We can no longer find without searching. More is required of us. And we have to abdicate. [...] We have to understand the full horror of the situation described by Nietzsche through the mouth of an insane man, hidden beneath Heine's humor, experienced by Dante behind his door, the horror that gave rise to the tragedies of Shakespeare and the novels and sermons of Count Tolstoy. In the days of yore very few people were aware of these tragic secrets of life. The rest had their faith handed down to them. Times have changed. Religious consciousness is attained in a different way. While formerly sermons, threats, and moral authority sufficed, today more is required. (Shestov 1993a, 157)

Hamlet's phrase "the time is out of joint," so cherished by Shestov, might be one way to describe a state of being plucked out of a spiritual tradition capable of investing being with existential meaning. In Tillich's opinion, an element of doubt is "a prerequisite of any spiritual life." It is quite another thing if doubt becomes overwhelming. Then it turns from methodological questioning into existential despair. However, another extreme that is a counterweight to radical skepticism is fanaticism, the self-blinding faith a person acquires by consciously or semi-consciously giving up his own freedom:

He flees from his freedom to pose questions and to answer for himself and ends up in a world in which no further questions can be asked and the answers to previous questions are imposed on him authoritatively. In order to avoid the risk of asking and doubting he surrenders the right to ask and to doubt. He surrenders himself in order to save his spiritual life. [...] Now he is no longer lonely, not in existential doubt or despair. [...] Meaning is saved, but the self is sacrificed. And since the conquest of doubt was a matter of sacrifice, the sacrifice of the freedom of the self, it leaves a mark on the regained certitude: the fanatical assertion of one's own rightness. (Tillich 2011, 62–63)

A fanatic furiously attacks those who do not share his views, for they bring back into his consciousness a sense of anxiety that he has banished.

For Shestov, one of the key spiritual tasks is to keep the delicate balance between skepticism and fanaticism. The vaccine of skepticism is needed to liberate oneself from the power of ingrained stereotypes, prejudice, and rational limitations. The impulse arising from existential anxiety plays a huge role in this process. Shestov describes this way out of limitations by citing the examples of Nietzsche, Dostoevsky, Tolstoy, Luther, and many others. It has to be noted, however, that even these "giants of the spirit" were unable to stay at the heights of the ultimate spiritual freedom that opened up before them and tragically descended into the realm of doctrine, of preaching, or, to use Tillich's term, "of fanaticism."

Shestov's creative evolution was a gradual process of search for a symbolic answer to the question of the meaning of existence. The philosopher finds it through building a religious-philosophical concept based on an existentialist interpretation of the biblical text. The evolution of Shestov's thought can be represented schematically as two successive processes: the gradual liberation of "divine dispensation" from any rational restrictions and the subsequent "taming" of what is basically a useless dispensation with the aid of religious myth.

Three fundamental mythologemes are pivotal for Shestov's philosophy of freedom: "creation out of nothing" (as the ultimate expression of dispensation), "the Fall" (a metaphysical justification of irrationalism), and the future eschatological "annulment of past evil" (a moral correlate of theistic voluntarism). It would be fair to say that these three mythologemes represent the three existential projects of Lev Shestov's philosophy of freedom.

Undoubtedly, Shestov's thought had a religious dimension from the very start. However, until 1910 his religiosity is highly diffuse, with myth practically indistinguishable from literary metaphor.

Shestov introduces the concept of "creation out of nothing" in his work devoted to Chekhov (Shestov 1908). That such creativity is possible and desirable for a despairing human being is one of Shestov's pet themes. It is interesting to note Shestov's unorthodox interpretation of the underlying biblical subtext (reference to the theological notion of the world created out of nothing). The philosopher argues that Chekhov's despairing characters are confronted with the utter meaninglessness of their existence, so that looking for an opportunity to create out of nothing is the only way they can continue living. However, this kind of creation is in reality unattainable for Chekhov's characters.

Shestov's book about Luther was in many ways a turning point in his work. Obviously, the religious component owes much to the tragic events of the World War and the Russian Revolution that plucked him out of the decadence and Nietzscheanism of the Silver Age context and lent his thought a historiosophic, apocalyptic dimension that was in fact previously absent in his work. The philosopher likened the upheavals of the war and the revolution that put an end to the progress-oriented mindset of the previous century to the fall of the Tower of Babel (Shestov 1991, 2001).

Shestov links the concept of truth with the repressiveness of law. To truth, Shestov counterposes mystery as a realm of unlimited freedom, as a space where "divine providence" can manifest itself.

His quest for "divine providence" gradually leads Shestov to religiosity in a more rigorous sense: from Nietzsche and Dostoevsky's "underground man" to the spiritual experience of religious thinkers. He devotes particular attention to the manifestations of mystical ecstasy and the profoundly irrational revelations of ultimate freedom spurred on by the tragic experience of existential anxiety. The philosopher turns to medieval mystics and to the heritage of Luther and Plotinus. This marks a distinct attempt to "tame" providence through religiosity. Chekhov's fictional literary characters (potential "creators out of nothing") are replaced by real historical mystics.

Feeling that the first existential project in the philosophy of freedom is deficient, the philosopher tries to buttress it with two other projects. The transition from the mythologeme of "creation out of nothing" to the second project is clearly discernible in the works of his middle period between his books *Sola Fide, Only by Faith* and *In Job's Balances (Wanderings Among Souls)* (1929).

At that stage, the key problem engaging Shestov is that of the tragic clash of the human individual with anonymous order, which is repressive with regard to the individual. The philosopher identifies two possible strategies to resolve the resulting difficulty in his approach. One strategy is proposed by rationalist philosophers and the other by a host of "prophets" (in which category he includes not only the Old Testament prophets but also St. Paul, Luther, Pascal, Kierkegaard, and even the "godless" Nietzsche).

According to Shestov, the rationalist tradition offers "salvation" through ataraxy. He makes an attempt to trace the continuity of this kind of strategy from Socrates through the Stoics to Spinoza and Hegel. Shestov vehemently opposes this strategy. For him nothing can be more terrible than the dispassionate death of a philosopher inside the Brazen Bull of Phalaris, a path to salvation through total indifference.

The second strategy is embodied in exceptional and often morbid personal mystical experience. Whatever this extreme experience may be, it invariably climaxes in a moment of revelation and ecstasy.

Shestov focuses on the ecstatic experience of ultimate spiritual freedom that is often provoked by a tragic personal situation (Luther's sinfulness, illness in the cases of Pascal and Nietzsche, Dostoevsky's death sentence, etc.). Here we see a gradual development of the line of thought initiated in Shestov's article about Chekhov. The philosopher reverts to the idea of "creation out of nothing" but his perception of the experience of final despair is increasingly tinged with religion. Shestov describes the same scenario: a person who experiences despair discovers the ultimate spiritual freedom, absolute freedom that is outside the laws of reason. But this freedom, to use the language of Nietzsche's hero, Zarathustra, is "freedom from" and not "freedom for," it is negative and cannot lead to "creation out of nothing." Moreover, man discovers it for a brief moment before losing it again. Shestov notes that the very varied authors he discusses all had such experiences: Nietzsche, Dostoevsky, Luther, Augustine, and later on Kierkegaard.

Examining the legacy and biographies of great Western thinkers, Shestov discovered again and again "an idle stroke": the upward movement toward ultimate freedom and "creation out of nothing," followed by a plunge into the dungeon of the laws of reason. Here, more than anywhere else, Shestov thinks like an existentialist.

It is worth noting that the extreme experience discussed by Shestov is not strictly theistic, as witnessed by his reference to Nietzsche's spiritual experience. This displays Shestov's characteristic ability to transform abstract philosophical concepts into mythological images and vice versa. Thus, Shestov identifies Luther's *Deus est creator omnipotens* and Nietzsche's *Wille zur Macht*:

> Luther's *sola fide* led him to Him of whom he says: '*est enim Deus omnipotens ex nihilo omnia creans*' (He is the Almighty God who creates everything out of nothing). But then is not Nietzsche's *Wille zur Macht* just another way to express Luther's *sola fide*? Luther proceeded from the authority of the Scripture, the

prophets and apostles. Nietzsche became drawn to the Sinai heights when the Bible lost all authority in his eyes. (Shestov 1993b, 1: 457–458)

Likewise, elsewhere in the same work Shestov identifies Nietzsche's *amor fati* with Luther's *bellua, qua non accisa, homo non potest vivere* (Shestov 1993b, 1: 470).[1]

It is important to note that Shestov is exceedingly skeptical about the possibility of transmitting strictly personal mystical experience. He does not believe in the power of preaching. Two circumstances need to be pointed out: on the one hand, an individual mystical experience is brief and transitory; on the other hand, it has no factual meaning. In either case, Shestov observes, it fails. It is here, apparently, that one should look for the sources of the interpretation of the Fall which came to characterize Shestov's later works. Why is man doomed to lose again and again the ultimate revelation attained at such a high, tragic price? Because man is haunted by original sin. Thus, a tale from the Book of Life becomes a paradigm-setting event in the spiritual life of every human being. However, it is hard to understand whether Shestov considered the sin of Adam and Eve to be something inherited or simply an archetype of what every person is doomed to accomplish while living on Earth.

It should be admitted that Shestov forcefully articulates the failure of the strategy of the extreme experience whose main content is salvatory freedom and unlimited freedom: man cannot remain in a state of ultimate revelation for long and inevitably sinks back to the level of mundane experience and mundane thinking.

Shestov looks for new paths toward existential freedom. Gradually, he focuses on the story of the Fall. Georgii Fedotov describes the story of the Fall as "the main myth of Shestov's religion" (Shestov's second myth, according to Fedotov, is the Last Judgment).

In 1935, Shestov delivered a lecture devoted to the work of Kierkegaard and Dostoevsky. Formulating the theme of his lecture, he said, "I shall speak only about how Dostoevsky and Kierkegaard understood original sin or—which is the same thing—about speculative and revelatory truth" (Shestov 1992, 7). How did it come about that for Shestov original sin and the contraposition of speculative and revelatory truths are "the same thing"?

The story of the Fall engaged Shestov's mind from the start of his philosophical work. He first turned to this theme in the preface to his book *Good in the Teachings of Count Tolstoy and Nietzsche*. At that time his interpretation of the myth of the Fall was totally devoid of religious implications, in striking contrast to his interpretation of this biblical story in his later period when the Fall came to play the central role. The mention of the Fall in *Good in the Teachings of Count Tolstoy and Nietzsche* is merely a metaphor and a provocative one at that. It has a "Gnostic" undertone since Shestov does not rule out that the tree of knowledge is at the same time the tree of life.

In the volume *The Great Vigils* we find a still more provocatively "unorthodox" interpretation of the story of the Fall which marks a transition in Shestov's work.

> One may wonder what else did Adam need? He lived in paradise close to God from whom he could learn all he needed. But he was not content with that. It was enough for the serpent to make his cunning offer for man to forget about God's wrath and all the dangers that threatened him and to pluck the apple from the forbidden tree. And then the fall into a great, probably infinite variety of truths that were constantly born and constantly dying. That was the seventh day of creation that is not written down in history. Man became a co-worker of God and himself became a creator. (Shestov 1996, 301)

What marks this passage out as a transitional one is the distinct religious implications of the author's interpretation and at the same time the sharp "Gnostic" and titanic overtones that are absent in the philosopher's later works.

In the final period of his work Shestov totally reappraised the story of the Fall. In his speech about Kierkegaard and Dostoevsky Shestov said:

> Man yielded to temptation and tasted the forbidden fruit, his eyes opened and he became knowing. What did he see? What did he learn? He discovered what the Greek philosophers and the Hindu sages had discovered: the divine "supreme good" has not come true: in the created world not everything was good, in the created world precisely because it has been created—here has to be evil, a great deal of evil, unendurable evil. This is amply demonstrated by everything that surrounds us, the direct perceptions of our consciousness; so he who looks at the world with "open eyes," he who "knows" cannot be of a different opinion. Sin, followed by evil, entered the world from the moment man became "knowing," that is, together with "knowledge." This is what the Bible says. (Shestov 1992, 9–10)

Herein lie the roots of Shestov's categorical rejection of "speculative philosophy."

In the event, Shestov's enemy is not science or common sense, but the palliative purporting to liberate man from tragedy that the adherents of speculative philosophy proffer. Speculative "liberation," as seen by Shestov, consists in admitting the existence of individual will, individual desires, and individual emotions to be fundamentally sinful and thus presenting suffering as something deserved. And there can be no question of deliverance from suffering in empirical life, because suffering is metaphysically justified.

Shestov cites Anaximander, the forerunner of Western philosophy, to bolster his view:

> Whence things have their origin,
> Thence also their destruction happens,
> According to necessity;
> For they give to each other justice and recompense

For their injustice
In conformity with the ordinance of Time.
(Shestov 1992, 8)

According to Shestov, this passage implies that individual, private existence is already inherently sinful.

Shestov's tragic questioning is obviously rooted in his reluctance to devalue personal suffering. Without any doubt, Shestov had sympathy for the position that he ascribed to Dostoevsky:

> At last Dostoevsky said the final word. He now openly declares what he first expressed, with reservations and qualifications, in *Notes from Underground*: no amount of harmony, no ideas, no love or forgiveness, in short, none of the things thought up by wise men from ancient to modern times can justify the absurdity in the fate of an individual human being. (Shestov 1993b, 1: 389)

For Shestov the human personality is above all the sum of emotions. That is why he rejects reflection as a means of overcoming suffering. To renounce one's suffering is to betray oneself. Instead of simply sweeping empirical evil and suffering out of being, speculative philosophy says that evil and suffering are woven into the very metaphysical structure of being and could only disappear together with being. Man is prompted to this thought by his reason, which tends to regard the existing state of affairs as eternal. But what is the root of this tendency? Why is reason "eager to make sweeping and binding judgments"? This is Shestov's answer: "if you like, the fruits hanging on the forbidden tree were precisely the synthetic *a priori* judgments which, according to Kant, make possible our knowledge and render it universal and obligatory" (Shestov 1992, 379).

In his last work, *Athens and Jerusalem* (1938), Shestov returns to his favorite themes, which engaged him throughout his life. But the philosopher's gaze is now tempered by a new worldview synthesis:

> [H]aving lost his freedom, having turned from a *res cogitans* into an *asinus turpissimus*, man learns from his own experience about the abyss into which the divine light extolled by the wise men leads him, and begins to make meaningless and downright insane attempts to struggle against the force that entrances him. Being at peace with oneself and the associated bliss, like the virtue that is its own reward, all these "consolations" offered by the fruits from the tree of knowledge—to use a biblical image, or Reason that draws on itself, to use Hegel's philosophical language—suddenly reveal to him their stark essence: all this brings not eternal salvation, but eternal destruction. And the first answer to this is what is taboo for philosophers, i.e., *lugere et deterstari*, which attests above all that there are still vestiges of life in man. (Shestov 1993b, 1: 451)

Shestov sees the story of the Fall as a narrative which, he feels, is capable of undermining the foundations of speculative philosophy.

The ideas of original sin and the annulment of past evil are central to the final period of Lev Shestov's work. Why did he attach such great significance to them? Perhaps Shestov cherishes the biblical story because he perceives it as the most irrational of all narratives. For Shestov the irrational is not the totality of all that cannot be conceptualized, but rather the sum of all the implications for one's worldview of the rejection of "sweeping *a priori* judgments." Maia Neto, who studied Shestov's work, writes:

> Kant's move from the first to the second *Critique* allows Shestov to conceptualize biblical thought by contrast. The first *Critique* demonstrates the insufficiency of logical or metaphysical thinking. Basically, Kant shows that, contrary to a traditional metaphysical assumption, the world is not rational. The focus is then shifted to the realm of practice (second *Critique*): given that the world is not rational, what should the rational agent do about it? Whereas Marburg Neo-Kantians such as Cohen say that the task the first *Critique* poses to the rational agent is to act to rationalize the world, i.e., to undertake an effort to bring the world closer to the ideal rational (the *noumenon*), i.e., to act ethically, Shestov says that the task is to undertake an effort to get rid of rationality: to look for non-rational ways of being. Shestov finds precisely in the Bible the call to irrationality. (Neto 1995, 92)

The story of the Fall as interpreted by Shestov carries the ultimate condemnation of the human theoretical faculty and at the same time a metaphysical justification of the fight against the ineluctability of human suffering.

Shestov interprets the tree of knowledge as the source of speculation and the tree of life as the source of revelation. The tree of knowledge leads to speculative truth (synthetic a priori judgments) which forever deprives us of the opportunity to "get an account" of each individual's suffering. Revelatory truth (contained in the Bible) leads us to the tree of life promised in the Apocalypse. According to Shestov, the fruits from the tree of life should heal the epistemological damage to man's nature caused by the Fall. The philosopher puts it like this: "Man seeks to think in the categories in which he lives, and not to live in the categories he has become accustomed to think in: the tree of knowledge no longer smothers the tree of life" (Shestov 1993a, 328). That is why for Shestov original sin, on the one hand, and the contraposition of speculative and revelatory truth, on the other, are "one and the same thing" (ibid., 329).

The biblical story of the Fall enabled Shestov to lay a solid metaphysical basis for the existential experience he described. However, the final act of the drama, the redemption, cannot yet be derived from the tale of the Fall. The story of the Fall, as interpreted by Shestov, provides an epistemological introduction to his soteriological teaching about the annulment of past evil by a benevolent and omnipotent God. This is the last of the mythologemes in Shestov's doctrine of freedom that became central to the later period of his career (1927–1938).

The impulse that drove Shestov's philosophical work was the question of man's tragic predicament and the desire to attain freedom. Shestov begins his journey toward freedom by curbing and overcoming existential anxiety and "including it in the courage of self-affirmation" (Tillich 2011, 64). His next philosophical task is to attain God. In search of God Shestov renounces the concept of Good.

The philosopher repeatedly criticizes the traditional forms of theodicy:

> "God is to blame. God created evil. Absit," shouted, indeed screamed everyone—both the learned fathers of the church and ordinary monks. If there is evil on Earth, not God but man has created it and is to blame for it: this is the only way to justify and save the all-merciful God. And sure enough: if there are eternal truths before God and above God, if what once was cannot become what was not, there is no choice but to oppose man as the creator of Evil to God the creator of Good. Man too becomes a *creator omnipotens, ex nihilo omnia faciens*. And there is no, and cannot be, redemption, liberation from the sinful past, from the nightmare of death and the horrors of life. (Shestov 1993b, 1: 468–469)

The question of theodicy cannot be self-sufficient for Shestov. Justifying God cannot be an end in itself. For him a God who needs justification does not deserve to be called God. Such is the God of the philosophers and theologians. In his later years Shestov aimed at restoring the omnipotence of the biblical God by releasing him from the prison of rationalist interpretations. Shestov seeks to return to God that same "arbitrariness" divined by Dostoevsky and Chekhov.

As if to renounce his past "titanic" and "epistemological" aspirations, Shestov writes in *Sola Fide:* "God creates out of nothing and man only perceives God when, after a painful and tormenting preliminary process of inner negation, he loses all faith in his own creativity" (Shestov 1966, 254).

The willfulness of the biblical God is no longer the pure and self-destructive whim that Shestov praised in 1905–1910. It is a willfulness that is not indifferent to every concrete individual, the willfulness of a God "who will wipe away every tear."

Shestov borrowed the idea of possible annulment of the past from the eleventh-century theologian Peter Damian. Damian's teaching on God's omnipotence proclaims that God can undo the past. Shestov believes that the idea of annulling the past provides the coveted resolution of the issue of innocent suffering formulated by Belinsky and Dostoevsky. God can undo the evil that has been done, but in order to believe this we must realize that our cognitive ability, which maintains that this is impossible, constantly misleads us because it is the consequence of the Fall instigated by the Devil. The idea of God's omnipotence reflects the yearning for "creation out of nothing" which had for so long tormented Shestov and which man needs in order to rid himself of the "horrors of life," but which in practice is out of his reach.

It is in this context that Shestov interprets the biblical story of Job: God gives him back his dead children. Shestov seems to identify Ivan Karamzov's child tormented to death with Job's children and Abraham's son Isaac, whom these prophets had to sacrifice to God, but whom God, after the trial is over, eventually does not claim and returns to them. There Shestov's philosophical journey is indeed his very personal journey, the journey of a father who lost his only son to war.

In the paradigm of annulment of the evil done Shestov interprets Kierkegaard's thirst for "repetition" and even Nietzsche's teaching of "eternal recurrence." Thus, he writes:

> About the idea of "eternal recurrence" [...] Nietzsche says virtually nothing, but what he does say merely attests that he was not destined to get it across to people, and instead of it he brought them something very different and even opposite. Only once, as far as I can judge—in *Jenseits von Gut und Böse*—does he manage to express it adequately. "I have done this," my memory tells me. "I could not have done this," my pride tells me and it is relentless. In the end memory yields. (Shestov 1993b, 1: 463)

And elsewhere he states:

> I repeat, he failed to find the genuine word to describe what revealed itself to him. But there was here something immeasurably more important and more significant than eternal recurrence. He saw that, contrary to the eternal law—*quod factum est infectum esse nequit* (what is done cannot be undone)—it is not memory which accurately reproduces the past, but a kind of will ("pride," once again for want of a better word) turned what once was into what was not and this will brought him the Truth. (Shestov 1993b, 1: 464)

A little further on Shestov proclaims: "the idea of eternal recurrence, or rather what revealed itself to Nietzsche under that name, can hold only if the highest seat on which necessity sits is destroyed" (Shestov 1993b, 1: 472).

However, in considering Shestov's teaching about annulment of the past a critically important question arises: if God can undo past evil and destroy it *post factum*, what is the point of there being evil at all? If evil can be a conscious and in some sense a great temptation for the human race, called upon to make this race truly free and wise, to temper its will, then obviously it cannot be canceled, otherwise the effect of evil would be lost. If it is meaningless and can be canceled, why allow it in the first place? Philosophers in the more speculative and schematic mold, for example, Vladimir Solovyov, struggled with such questions, thus putting into doubt the logical coherence of their speculative system. Shestov, though, as Czeslaw Milosz aptly put it, is inclined to "give up the chess game and kick the table over" (Milosz 1992, v). Shestov's biggest enigma is his ability to make a "leap of faith," pass on directly from intense desire, from nostalgia, to the coveted salvation, from existential anxiety to its inclusion in the courage of self-affirmation, by invoking the biblical myth.

The word "truth" as used by Shestov has an ambivalent character, taking on alternately positive and negative connotations. It is in his teaching on God's omnipotence that he turns back to the theme of "the truth." Speaking about Luther in his book *Athens and Jerusalem,* he writes:

Luther is not constrained by the "eternal truths" of Reason: on the contrary, he senses that they are a monster without killing which man cannot live. If these truths are to triumph, there is no salvation for man. To translate it into the language of philosophy: by absolutizing truth we relativize being and Luther resolves to surrender truth to the will of the Almighty Creator who creates everything out of nothing. If the truth is in the power of the Creator, the Creator can cancel it. (Shestov 1993b, 1: 468)

This is Lev Shestov's gospel, the coveted overcoming of existential anxiety and attainment of freedom. For Shestov the meaning of life lay in overcoming man's self-alienation and self-rejection and attaining the truth, that is, spiritual freedom. For him, the path to truth led to faith as the embodiment of absolute freedom. Shestov's philosophy is the final great battle for the self to have the right to be itself.

NOTE

1. In his work, *Sola fide* Shestov also compares Luther's experience with that of "the underground man" (Shestov 1966, 247).

BIBLIOGRAPHY

Baranova-Shestova, Natalia L. 1983. *Zhizn' Shestova. Po perepiske i vospominaniiam sovremennikov v 2-kh tomakh*. Vol. 1. Paris: La Presse Libre.

Milosz, Czeslaw. 1992. Shestov, ili O chistote otchaianiia. In *Kierkegaard i existenzial'naia filosofiia*, ed. Lev Shestov, i–xvi. Moscow: Progress–Gnozis.

Motroshilova, Nelly V. 2006. Lev Shestov i filosofiia Zapada. In *Mysliteli Rossii i filosofiia Zapada (V. Solov'ev, N. Berdiaev, S. Frank, L. Shestov)*, ed. N.V. Motroshilova, 382–447. Moscow: Respublica. Kul'turnaia revoluciia.

Neto, Maia. 1995. *The Christianization of Pyrrhonism. Scepticism and Faith in Pascal, Kierkegaard, and Shestov*. Dordrecht, Boston, and London: Kluwer Academic Publishers.

Shestov, Lev. 1908. Tvorchestvo iz Nichego (A.P. Chekhov). In *Nachala i Kontsy*, 8–21. St. Petersburg: Tipografiia M.M. Stasiulevicha.

———. 1966. *Sola Fide. Tol'ko veroiu*. Paris: YMCA PRESS.

———. 1991. Ugroza sovremennykh varvarov. *Vestnik Akademii Nauk SSSR* 5: 181–195.

———. 1992. *Kierkegaard i existenzial'naia filosofiia*. Moscow: Progress-Gnosis.

———. 1993a. Dobro v uchenii grafa Tolstogo i Fridrikha Nietzsche. In *Izbrannye Trudy*, ed. Lev Shestov, 39–157. Moscow: Renessans.

———. 1993b. Afiny i Ierusalim. In *Sochineniia v 2-kh tomakh*, ed. Lev Shestov, vol. 1. Moscow: Nauka.

———. 1996. Velikie kanuny. In *Sochineniia v 2-kh tomakh*, ed. Lev Shestov, vol. 1. Vodoley: Tomsk.

———. 2001. Chto takoe russkii bol'shevizm? *Istoriia Filosofii* 8: 109–120.

Tillich, Paul. 2011. *Muzhestvo byt*. Moscow: Modern.

CHAPTER 11

Nikolai Berdyaev's Philosophy of Creativity as a Revolt Against the Modern Worldview

Vladimir L. Marchenkov

INTRODUCTION

It is revealing to look at modernity as the site of a struggle between what Hegel called "Eternal Powers," when he described the nature of tragedy (Hegel 1975, 2: 1162). On the one hand, there are the old pre-modern—as well as parallel non-modern—holistic worldviews and, on the other hand, there is the new, modern infinitist view of the world. The modern outlook created itself by a series of profound inversions of its pre-modern counterpart: where the pre-modern person perceived the world as an integral whole, the modern mind asserted a non-world, constituted by time and space stretching to infinity in all directions. Where the former saw a world ruled by a transcendent Supreme Power, the latter asserted a human individual as the only living being and, therefore, the only agent in the entire order of things with its own will and purpose. Where the pre-modern community centered itself on the mystery lying at the heart of this order, the modern individual advanced the vision of the infinite progress of science and technology in the service of his own power. Throughout modern history, we see epic collisions of these Eternal Powers; the cultural and political fabric of modern history is woven by their intertwining threads.

The Russian Silver Age was one episode in this four-century-old conflict. There had been the religious-philosophical struggles of the seventeenth century, erupting on the political surface of history as civil wars. There had been

V. L. Marchenkov (✉)
Ohio University, Athens, OH, USA
e-mail: marchenk@ohio.edu

© The Author(s), under exclusive license to Springer Nature
Switzerland AG 2021
M. F. Bykova et al. (eds.), *The Palgrave Handbook of Russian Thought*,
https://doi.org/10.1007/978-3-030-62982-3_11

217

218 V. L. MARCHENKOV

the rise of Romanticism as a reaction to the abstract dogmas of the Enlightenment, erupting as the revolutions and vast military conflicts that we call the Napoleonic Wars. The era of the Russian Silver Age saw yet another attempt by the culture of the modern age to overcome the relentless fragmentation of the world, society, and the human subject, forced by the mythical underpinnings of the immanentist-infinitist outlook sketched above. In the stifling atmosphere of positivism and materialism, the followers of Vladimir Solovyov launched a thorough-going critique of the modern outlook. The names of the brothers Sergei and Evgenii Trubetskoi, Fr. Pavel Florensky, Fr. Sergei Bulgakov, Dmitrii Merezhkovskii, Semyon Frank, and Lev Karsavin, to mention only a few, have come to represent a quest to rediscover the spiritual values that had been marginalized or suppressed altogether in modernity's struggle against religion. The rise of Russian religious-philosophical thought was an act of conscious resistance to the forces of modern progress understood in purely external, quantitative terms. The philosophers who belonged to this school, as well as the artists who were inspired by their ideas and the Symbolist sensibility, envisioned and advocated a historic transformation that would overcome the centrifugal thrust of modern thinking. On the political surface of things, they lost their battle, their opponents won—and went on to establish a thoroughly modern regime that directed Russia's resources and energy to carving its own largely unmodern body, by the merciless violence of massive social engineering, into a modern nation, bent on overtaking the rest of the world in the race of progress. In political history the new collision of these two worldviews manifested itself as the First World War, a series of social revolutions, and the Russian Civil War of 1918–1922, as well as by similar events outside Russia. Those conflicts were marked by unprecedented violence and destruction but, tragically, the violence resolved nothing, and the clash was soon repeated, with even greater destruction and even more merciless violence, now truly on a global scale. All of this violence failed to resolve the basic underlying conflict. And today we find ourselves embroiled in the ongoing struggle of worldviews, and religion is once again at the heart of this struggle, even in the confidently secular societies (or so it would seem) like those of the so-called developed nations of Europe and North America. The ideas, symbols, and myths that brought about the upheavals of the early twentieth century when Nikolai Berdyaev's philosophy of creativity first appeared are part and parcel of today's realities.

In Berdyaev's oeuvre (1874–1948), two books, *The Meaning of the Creative Act: An Essay on Anthropodicy* (1916) and *The New Middle Ages* (1924), frame the experience of the Russian Revolution.[1] Between these two books, each marking a watershed moment in the philosopher's own development, Berdyaev witnessed and experienced the First World War, the February and October revolutions of 1917, the Civil War, and his own forced exile from Russia in 1922.[2] Berdyaev's philosophy of creativity emerges as a rebellion against modernity against this dramatic and turbulent historical background.[3] That it was a rebellion needs no proof: every page of both books screams it. *The*

Meaning of the Creative Act opens with the declaration: "The human spirit is in prison. Prison is what I call this world, the given world of necessity" (*MCA* 11). It closes with the assertion that "truth and beauty cannot triumph on the plane of the [mundane] world," and a call to a "merciless" clearing of the path toward "creative life " (*FTK* 1: 310–311; *MCA* 310–311). The task of the book is Mosaic: to blaze the trail that would lead the human spirit out of captivity. The task of this chapter, therefore, is not so much to prove that Berdyaev was charting an exodus from modernity, as it is to evaluate his philosophy of creativity as a map for such an exodus. From the book's first appearance, its success in this regard was questioned. Sergei Bulgakov, for example, reproached Berdyaev for excessive immanentism, that is, the sin of which Berdyaev himself accused modernity.[4] Vyacheslav Ivanov described *The Meaning of the Creative Act* as "a passionate creation of daring thought soaring on high, of a burning will and *rash willfulness*" (Ivanov 1994, 353, emphasis added). Vasily Zenkovsky stated that "the main design of the book has failed: the religious meaning of creativity has remained obscured because of Berdyaev's basic lack of religious vision."[5] Later, in his mid-century *History of Russian Philosophy*, he criticized Berdyaev for being a Romantic who disdained the world as an insult to his aesthetic sensibility (Zenkovsky 2003, 2: 772). Writing at the end of the twentieth century, Renata Gal'tseva perceived "the stamp of an existentialist recoiling from the world" in Berdyaev's approach and described his attitude as an "anarchist-individualist apotheosis of creativity" (*FTK* 1: 8, 14). These were criticisms by Berdyaev's allies. There is hardly any need to quote the reactions of his enemies, such as the Marxist Anatoly Lunacharsky; they were as predictable as they were uncomprehending (Ermichev 1994).

And yet Berdyaev's defense of man, though clearly a child of its time (the same Zenkovsky called it "a true monument to our restless epoch"), seems to have lost none of its urgency to this day; it encapsulated something essential in the anxious quests of the twentieth century and gave a stirring expression to the dilemmas that continue to generate the pulse of our time (Ermichev 1994, 284). Today, when "the death of art" has been proclaimed by various voices and certain schools of thought have denied the very possibility of creativity, arguing instead that its place has been taken by quotation and interminable repetition, Berdyaev's doctrine is worth revisiting and its successes or failings are worth weighing again. Of particular interest in this regard are the philosophical underpinnings of Berdyaev's critique of modernity. What was the object of this critique? Did he understand the modern worldview correctly, and did his own proposal succeed in surmounting this worldview's shortcomings? What are the implications of his doctrine for today's philosophy of art? These are the questions that guide my reflections in what follows. But first a qualification: Berdyaev was charting a course in opposition not just to the modern worldview, but also to official Christian theology, which he wished to overcome with no less intensity. In other words, Berdyaev's critique of modernity was not driven by an impulse toward restoration, as the notion of the new Middle Ages may suggest. It rather aimed to elaborate a *new* type of worldview

220 V. L. MARCHENKOV

in which the shortcomings of both existing alternatives would be surmounted. In this chapter, I focus on Berdyaev's opposition to the modern frame of mind and largely leave his quarrel with official Christianity aside.

CRITIQUE OF MODERNITY

The tension between the pre-modern and modern worldviews is the live nerve of Berdyaev's thinking; its current passes through his philosophy of history and his philosophy of art. In philosophy of history, Berdyaev wishes to transform progressive time into a sacred one and, conversely, sacred time into a progressive one; in his philosophy of art he wishes to transform a life-shaping ritual into a work of art, and vice versa. This tension is not resolved by Berdyaev but it is perhaps the most interesting, and potentially the most promising, thing in his philosophy of creativity.

Berdyaev's anthropodicy is the defense of a certain concept of the human person, one that radically differs from the typical modern understanding of personhood. The latter is the vital center of the modern outlook in general, where its basic components come to the forefront in a particularly vivid fashion. The first such component is *immanentism*, that is, the conviction that reality is confined to the immanent plane of being and that the transcendent plane is either irrelevant or simply does not exist. At its most generous, this outlook holds that God is a hypothesis, according to the famous quip by Marquis de Laplace, and an unnecessary one at that.[6] Empiricism, materialism, atheism, and naturalism are all manifestations of this basic attitude that had gradually ascended from early modernity and reached its peak in the late nineteenth and early twentieth centuries. The second component is *infinitism*, that is, the belief that the basic forms of existence, space and time, are infinite by nature. Its rise to dominance in the modern outlook is intimately linked to that of immanentism—to the extent that the two form, in fact, an inseparable unity. That is to say, *immanentist infinitism* is one of the essential features of the modern concept of the human person. The latter is, according to this view, something purely immanent, devoid of any transcendent dimension, and at the same time infinite, unlimited by anything in the whole order of things. More precisely, this two-headed construct is at once a part of the definition and a tool in the hands of the modern subject. That is to say, intertwined with the next basic component, *progressivism*, that is, the understanding of human existence as *becoming infinity*, an unlimited expansion in time and space. Furthermore, this person uses the *intellect* (as opposed to the *faith* of her pre-modern counterpart) in order to accomplish her goals. In Hegel's terminology, this intellect is *Verstand*, that is, rigid thinking in abstractions, rather than *Vernunft*, that is, dynamic thinking in dialectically connected categories (Hegel 1991, 128–133, §§81–82). Contrary to a widespread belief, the intellect is not what crowns all these characteristics. Rather, at the top of the hierarchy of human faculties the modern mind places *will* and more specifically *the will to power*. "The Age of Reason" is a misnomer for the Enlightenment; it should be called the age of will, armed with the intellect. This intellect, whose most prominent manifestation is modern science, is merely a tool for the human subject, whose will is directed, as I have already pointed out, toward an infinite expansion of its power. In Max Horkheimer and Theodor Adorno's felicitous phrase, this intellect is described as *instrumental* (Horkheimer and Adorno 2002, 2).

It is this peculiar and, in fact, totally unique configuration of typical features that I call "the modern subject": an immanent human being who is driven by the will to dominate the entire realm of existence and uses its intellect for that purpose. Berdyaev's anthropodicy aims to overcome precisely this type of subject and the world created by it. His thought belongs to that current in modern history which serves as a counterpoint to modern subjectivity. To call this current "conservative" or "reactionary" is to surrender it in advance to the voluntarist, rationalistic, and progressivist point of view that it opposes. The presence of this current in the modern history of ideas suggests a different story than those offered by either the progressivists, who believe in the upward and onward trajectory of events, or the pessimists, who see modern progress as decline, or even the postmodern critics of both, for whom this trajectory disintegrated, to quote my own description, into "an inchoate mass of multiple shifting points" (Marchenkov 2014, 133–134). Instead, the story seems to be one of continuous interaction between the hegemonic modern subject and various avatars of pre- and non-modern human personhood that persist alongside it, usually on the margins of culture.[7] The interaction may take the forms of resistance, partial syntheses, and even recoiling or withdrawal—when, that is, the pre- and non-modern outlooks are not violently destroyed by the march of progress and swept aside as so much debris. But even where, and when, the modern subject manages completely to dominate, the irrationalities inherent in its own conceptual composition give rise to internal fragmentation and result in immanent critique. This happened, for example, with the poststructuralism that became the modern subject's futile attempt to cleanse itself—without, however, giving up its own most treasured essence (Marchenkov 2014, 133–146).

Against immanentism, Berdyaev advances his antinomic-mystical dialectics of the immanent and the transcendent; against infinitism, he pits a similar dialectics of the finite and the infinite; against the abstract intellect, he proposes mystical intuitivism inspired by the Gnostics, German mystics, and German idealism. And, finally, against the will to power, Berdyaev argues for the effort of the human spirit in which *philosophy* plays the key part (the book opens with the chapter on "Philosophy as a Creative Act"). But this is where his approach begins to show inconsistency, for Berdyaev subordinates philosophy to mystical revelation, which compromises his entire argument. Still mysticism is a peculiar stance fraught with several possible outcomes, not all of which are antiphilosophical. Berdyaev's philosophy of creativity is an especially good example of its ambivalence. I shall return to this point later in the chapter. In his defense, such intuitivist mysticism seems to be the distinctive feature of Russian philosophy at large; Victor Bychkov summed up its pervasive presence when he called it "the foundation of our national philosophizing."[8] "Russian philosophy is a

222   V. L. MARCHENKOV

Schellingian," in Arsenii Gulyga's well-known aphorism, and Bychkov's remark echoes this assessment. Berdyaev's approach confirms it, too: the ultimate organ of thought for him is intuition, insight, and spiritual revelation. Berdyaev himself was clearly aware of the peculiar nature of his philosophizing and never tried to present his insights as anything other than what they were. This sincerity is one of the most winning traits in his intellectual persona.

A more detailed consideration of Berdyaev's wrestling with the modern outlook, the individual threads of which modern subjectivity is woven, can be disentangled in Berdyaev's prose only with difficulty and only conditionally. Berdyaev everywhere sees them as closely interconnected and constantly interacting with one another. Still, his treatment of these concepts is remarkably consistent throughout the text. With regard to immanentism, Berdyaev establishes the main parameters of his attitude in the Introduction to *The Meaning of the Creative Act*, where he postulates the mutual immanence of God in man and man in God as the true state of affairs that can only be attained, however, in religious life rather than philosophy (*FTK* 1: 43; *MCA* 15–16). What I termed immanentism above, Berdyaev condemns as false (*FTK* 1: 128; *MCA* 110). True immanentism, by contrast, rests on the realization that "cognition is immanent to being." In other words, by true immanentism, Berdyaev seems to mean that identity of thought and being, the recognition of which Hegel called the gateway into philosophy—except, of course, that for Berdyaev this identity could be ultimately ascertained by mystical intuition alone (Hegel 1969, 45). Kant's immanentism, for example, is false, while Goethe's is true (*FTK* 1: 553n3).[9] "The true Christian transcendentism," Berdyaev continues, "means that man is transcendent to the [mundane] world and that God is immanent in man" (*FTK* 1: 133; *MCA* 115, modified). In the history of the arts, Classicism is marked by "an immanent self-enclosure," whereas Romanticism, by "a transcendent breakthrough into infinity" (*FTK* 1: 130; *MCA* 111, modified). "Realism in art," Berdyaev remarks, "is the extreme form of adaptation to 'this world'" (*FTK* 1: 227–228; *MCA* 220). Pagan art is Classical and immanent; Christian art is Romantic and transcendent (*FTK* 1: 219; *MCA* 211). Traces of Hegel's periodization of the history of fine art from his *Lectures on Aesthetics* are unmistakable here but they lead to an un-Hegelian culmination. The antinomy is to be resolved in *theurgy*, where "Christian transcendence is transformed into immanence" (*FTK* 1: 237; *MCA* 230).

Berdyaev's critique of modern infinitism follows a similar pattern. He attacks it both epistemologically and cosmologically. The false or spurious infinity is, according to him, "the bad multiplicity of truths," the source of inexorable doubt and "doubling of spirit" that are imposed on the human mind by "the given world of necessity." "Doubt," declares Berdyaev, "is slavery to spurious infinity, obedience to spurious multiplicity" (*FTK* 1: 68; *MCA* 46).[10] Anticipating Alexandre Koyré's studies in the history of modern cosmology, he observes that in modernity "[t]he closed heaven of the medieval and ancient worlds became unlocked, revealing an infinity of worlds in which the human being lost itself, along with its pretensions at being the center of the universe"

(*FTK* 1: 93; *MCA* 72; Koyré 1968). Berdyaev sees the effect of this transformation, touted to this day by modern science as one of its own supreme accomplishments, as far from felicitous (*MCA* 73).[11]

The concept of infinity plays a key part in Berdyaev's treatment of anthropocentrism. Commenting on the fall of "naturalistic anthropocentrism," that is, the naïve belief that man is the center of the world, Berdyaev sets it in contrast with "absolute anthropocentrism." "This absolute anthropocentrism," he writes, "which overcomes the spurious infinity of the starry heaven by the eternity inherent in man, cannot be crushed by any science, just as it cannot be validated by any science; it is beyond the reach of science" (*FTK* 1: 94; *MCA* 73–74, modified). Bad infinity is also evident, Berdyaev believes, in sexual life as the endless change of generations. "The sexual act confirms," he writes, "the evil, endless relay of births and deaths" (*FTK* 1: 191; *MCA* 180). This endless repetition is "the inescapable tragedy of sex" that condemns the human person to "the disintegration of personality in the begetting of children, to a bad infinity instead of good eternity" (*FTK* 1: 191; *MCA* 179, modified). In sociopolitical affairs, Berdyaev likewise discerns endless division and hostility. "A bourgeois peace," he remarks, "in the bourgeois world is not cosmic; it is rather a bad infinity of enmity brought under norms and within boundaries for selfish and all-too-human purposes" (*FTK* 1: 273; *MCA* 269). It falls short of the ideal of "eternal divine peace" that can only be attained when the world is lifted into "a cosmic state" and turned into "a divinely beautiful harmony" (ibid.). And, finally, spurious infinity is the element of all logical thinking, which brings us to Berdyaev's critique of the modern abstract intellect (*FTK* 1: 538n10).

Like all the other threads in Berdyaev's argument, this critique is interwoven with that of immanentist infinitism and takes the form of an attack—or, given the sway of positivism at the time, a counterattack—against modern science and especially against the philosophy that seeks to emulate the scientific approach to things. This desire is shared by positivists, materialists, metaphysicians, and critical philosophers alike. "Modern consciousness," states Berdyaev, "is possessed with the idea of a 'scientific' philosophy, it is mesmerized by the *idée fixe* of 'the scientific' [*nauchnosti*]" (ibid.).[12] The proper response to this tendency consists, Berdyaev argues, in approaching philosophy as an art. Sounding a Schellingian note, Berdyaev defines philosophy as "the art of cognition in freedom, through the creation of ideas that resist the given world and its necessity and penetrate into the transcendent essence of the world" (*FTK* 1: 54; *MCA* 30, modified). The problem with science, Berdyaev thinks, is that it is a means of mere adaptation to the given conditions of human existence, whereas genuine philosophy is moved by Sophia to reach beyond them (*FTK* 1: 50–52; *MCA* 27–29). The contrast is between obedience and necessity on the one side and creativity and freedom on the other. "Philosophy," states Berdyaev, "is a cognitive exit from the world as it is given, a vision that surpasses the world's necessity" (*FTK* 1: 53; *MCA* 29). Berdyaev sees the struggle between the genuine, creative philosophy and its scientific perversion as a perennial drama in the history of ideas. One can find it in Western and Eastern thought, in Antiquity and the Middle Ages, as well as today (*FTK* 1: 55; *MCA* 32). The epistemic conflict here is between the creative intuition of true philosophy and the formal logic of discursive thought (*FTK* 1: 57–58; *MCA* 34–35). This, in turn, is rooted, according to Berdyaev, in the conflict between the spirit of *sobornost'*, or human community of faith, and individualism, the conception of the human being as solitary and separate from all others. The shared faith of a conciliar community is the criterion of truth in the former case, while endless skeptical ratiocination relies, Berdyaev believes, on the formal majority vote for deciding what is true and what is false (*FTK* 1: 59; *MCA* 36).

In his *Philosophy of Freedom* [*Filosofiia svobody*], written immediately prior to *The Meaning of the Creative Act*, Berdyaev explained his view regarding the role of *will* in cognition, and this explanation is highly relevant to his critique of modern epistemology in the later work. These thoughts are so important for our theme that they are worth quoting at length.

> The epistemology of endless reflection is the absence of will [*bezvolie*], and will must set a limit to it. Creative will must once again clear the space for ontology, the investigation of the mysteries of being without the constant looking over one's shoulder, indecision, and reflection, without perpetually doubting the possibility of cognition and the reality of being. Our will, our integral spirit from the start must be firm, persistent, and steadfastly confident; it must exclude all skepticism, all reflection, and all corrosive doubt. Skepticism and skeptical reflection cannot be overcome intellectually and rationally, but only reinforced. Skeptical reflection is vanquished by an integral spirit and strong will. [...] The destiny of truth depends not solely on the intellect, but on will as well. By the act of a will that has taken a decision and made its choice, by the fullness of life, we must declare that we reject the very "epistemological" framing of the problem, the very plane on which all this unfolds. May skepticism, reflection, and perpetual looking over one's shoulder be condemned and may they be wiped off the face of the earth by the will toward the new organic epoch. Critical feebleness can be vanquished only by an organic spirit, only by a resolute will. (Berdyaev 1989, 32–33)

We have chosen to believe, Berdyaev inveighs, in the immanent world; our ability to see transcendent reality likewise depends on our choice (ibid., 52). Our failure to connect with the transcendent dimension of the world is the result of the fact that "our will is turned away from those spheres of being" (ibid., 53). In contrast to Nietzsche, whose influence is distinctly felt here, for Berdyaev the act of free choice is one of *faith*; it has already taken place "in the mysterious depth of being" as far as the immanent world is concerned, and we must now make a similar if opposite choice to make the other world the object of our love. "To reveal the world of invisible things," Berdyaev teaches (with some inconsistency), "we need an act of the entire human nature, its overall effort, rather than that of the intellect alone, as is the case with the knowledge of the visible world" (ibid., 52).

Clearly, *will* is the pinnacle of Berdyaev's hierarchy of human faculties, it is at the heart of faith and the cornerstone of the edifice of knowledge. Both Berdyaev's epistemology and his ontology are voluntaristic in the most profound sense of the word: he thinks that will establishes the possibility of knowing and grants access to the object of knowledge. These convictions show Berdyaev firmly following the line that can be traced back, via Nietzsche, to Schelling, who likewise claimed that "[i]n the final and highest instance there is no other being than Will," that "Will is primordial Being," and that "[a]ll philosophy strives only to find this highest expression."[13] When he speaks of critical epistemology as the domain of slavish obedience to necessity and of philosophy as the domain of creative freedom, Berdyaev builds on such a voluntaristic ontology. With this, we approach the most consequential internal contradiction in Berdyaev's philosophy of creativity.

All his vehement criticism of the modern worldview notwithstanding, Berdyaev retained in his own philosophy the basic structure of the very subjectivity he was attacking. The human agent that arises from the pages of Berdyaev's books is a voluntaristic subject, whose abstract intellect must be guided by its will, and even the shape of the world in which the subject realizes its creative potential is determined by it. This aspect of Berdyaev's thinking caused Ivanov to find "rash willfulness" in *The Meaning of the Creative Act*. Zenkovsky, too, hit the mark when he characterized Berdyaev's overall way of thinking as moralistic. "Berdyaev constantly teaches," he wrote, "insists, accuses, and summons; the moralist in him is always evident" (Zenkovsky 2003, 2: 762). What distinguishes Berdyaev's human person from the modern subject is her ardent aspiration toward transcendence and toward the ultimate completion of her journey instead of endless striving. But this aim is fatally compromised by Berdyaev's choice of means, namely, the supremacy of will.

Will is an indispensable moment in the transition from passivity to action; it is the impulse of consciousness that sets the human agent in motion but the impulse as such does not contain the *purpose* of the action; the latter is established by the intellect. If we compare two treatments of volition by philosophers who, in all other respects, could not be more different from each other, we shall be struck by the similarities in their analyses. In Aristotle's *De Anima* the impulse of consciousness that sets the animal in motion figures as appetite [ὄρεξις]. Aristotle distinguishes between the work of the practical mind that "calculates means to an end" and appetite which is, properly speaking, the motive phase of consciousness.[14] But he immediately notes that "appetite is in every form of it relative to an end" and therefore it is "the *object* of appetite [that] starts a movement and as a result *thought gives rise to movement*" (ibid., emphasis added).[15] Similarly, Nietzsche discerns in the act of will, first, two states of affairs, "the state 'away from which'" and "the state 'toward which'" (Nietzsche 1966, 25). He then remarks, second, that "in every act of the will there is *a ruling thought*." "Let us not imagine it possible," he exclaims, "to sever this thought from the 'willing', as if any will would then remain over!" (ibid., emphasis added). Finally, there is also in the act of will "the affect of command," rooted in Nietzsche's larger vision of morality as the domain of "supremacy," that is, of "commanding and obeying," which, like necessity and freedom in Berdyaev's case, underlies Nietzsche's entire vitalist-voluntarist ontology (Nietzsche 1966, 26–27). Aristotle's remarkably perceptive analysis, echoed by Nietzsche millennia later, makes it clear why, when Schopenhauer upholds will as the supreme *archē* of all existence, that is, sets it over and above its object and end, the result is an irrationalistic metaphysics of directionless motion. (It also explains why, when Nietzsche wished to give direction to this will, he filled it with his own, un-Schopenhauerian content.) The peculiar quality of will noted by Aristotle and Nietzsche—to be the motive force of action *only* when it is guided by a *goal* established by either the intellect or the imagination or both of them together—also manifests itself in the infinitist component of modern thinking. By asserting will as the supreme human faculty and subordinating the intellect to it, this thinking launches an irrational project that at once must and cannot have a final goal. This project is called progress.

Berdyaev's own voluntarism prevented him from correctly analyzing the modern subject. He failed to perceive, for example, that this subject's attitude toward the natural world was not one of obedient and will-less adaptation, but, on the contrary, was driven by an insatiable desire to dominate and exploit. Berdyaev did not perceive that immanentist infinitism was a weapon in the hands of the modern subject, by which it sought to pulverize the natural world into a homogeneous mass that could be used as raw material for its maniacal projects. Far from being an imperious necessity shackling the human spirit, the natural world was and remains for the modern subject a mere storage place of such raw materials. Not only the natural world, but human society, too, was and continues to be subjected to a similar homogenizing "atomization [*raspylenie*] of the world's flesh," in Berdyaev's own words, so that it, too, can be used as a resource in the name of progress (*FTK* 1: 225; *MCA* 225). The uncritical acceptance of the primacy of will blinded Berdyaev—as it did Nietzsche, too—to the hegemony of the will to power as the mainspring of the modern world.

Theurgy

Berdyaev's philosophy of history provides the necessary framing for his theory of creativity; his philosophy of art is the beating heart of the entire endeavor. Berdyaev chooses as his point of departure, from whence he then derives all his valuations and interpretations of historical developments, a half-doctrine and half-myth about three periods of sacred history: the era of necessity and law, the era of redemption, and the era of creativity. The first era corresponds to the period from man's fall to the appearance of Jesus Christ; the second, from the appearance of Christ to the present moment; and the third is in store for us—if, that is, we correctly grasp the meaning of this moment. To disclose this meaning is the purpose of Berdyaev's prophecy. This simple scheme does not, of course, exhaust the entire picture, but it is present everywhere in Berdyaev's text, and his entire critique of science, philosophy, religion, and art is correlated with it. It is notable that Berdyaev shows no trace of the concern about the vacuity and formlessness of beginnings that is so strong in Hegel's thought; the Russian philosopher delivers the truth "like a shot from a pistol," as Hegel remarked in the Preface to the *Phenomenology of Spirit* about some of his own contemporaries (Hegel 1977, 16). This casts a peculiar complexion on Berdyaev's entire enterprise; it can be called "philosophy" only with serious qualifications. Berdyaev walks a thin line between philosophy, which does not recognize any limits to its analyses, and theology, which consists in the extraction of rational meanings and implications from a set of dogmas—themselves rooted in a mythology—that provide the ultimate ground for its exercises.[16] More often than not and despite many valuable insights, Berdyaev's thought travels through the territory across the line from philosophy.

The doctrine of theurgy is the culmination of Berdyaev's philosophy of creativity. In fact, Bychkov regards it as central to Berdyaev's philosophy in general. As he puts it, in theurgy "Berdyaev sees the meaning and the ultimate goal of human life, of the whole created world's being; this idea encompasses practically the main meaning of his entire philosophy" (*RTA* 711). The concept of theurgy as the ultimate goal of humanity's creative evolution was introduced by Solovyov at the end of his philosophical career, when he turned, briefly, to aesthetics in the 1890s.[17] It occupies a tiny place in Solovyov's overall output but became one of the most important parts of his legacy for the arts and philosophy of the Silver Age, and Berdyaev's *Meaning of the Creative Act* is one of the most extensive and important elaborations of Solovyov's original idea. "We are standing on the threshold of the global religious epoch of creativity," declares Berdyaev, "at a cosmic watershed" (*FTK* 1: 116; *MCA* 97, modified). There have been two revelations, according to Berdyaev's historical scheme, those of Moses and of Christ, but the third one must come from man himself rather than from God; it will be the "anthropological revelation" by the creative human being (*FTK* 1: 120; *MCA* 101). Once again we hear a note from the young Schelling who believed that, having served as the original "ground of all harmony between the subjective and the objective," mythology will also be the medium "for the return of science to poetry [...] in the course of history to come" (Schelling 1978, 232–233). A similar pattern is at work in these two cases, more than a century apart: what is sought and what is at issue is the synthesis of the pre-modern and modern worldviews. Unlike Schelling, though, who thought of the new myth as the creation of distant future generations, Berdyaev believes that the imminent epoch of theurgic creativity will accomplish this synthesis:

> Theurgy does not create culture, but new being; it is super-cultural. Theurgy is art creating another world, another being, another life; creating beauty as essence, as being. [...] In theurgy the word becomes flesh. In theurgy art becomes power. The beginning of theurgy is the end of literature, the end of all differentiated art, the end of culture, but an end which takes unto itself the world-meaning of cul-

ture and art, a super-cultural end. Theurgy is man working together with God, God-working; it is divine-human creativity. In theurgic creativity the tragic opposition of subject and object is removed, the tragic hiatus between the will to a new world and the attainment of mere cultural values. The theurge creates life in beauty. (*FTK* 1: 236; *MCA* 229, translation modified)

There are two crises that are simultaneously resolved in theurgy: the crisis of modern art and the crisis of religion. Contemporary art as creation of mere cultural values has come to its limit, and traditional Christianity has also reached the nadir in its trajectory of "obedience." There is an echo of Hegel in Berdyaev's remark that, "[a]t its highest, culture arrives at self-negation" (*FTK* 1: 131; *MCA* 113). "Creativity in art," he continues, "in philosophy, in morals, in social life, exceeds the limits of its own sphere, is not to be contained in any classic norm, reveals an impulse toward the transcendent" (ibid., modified). Passing into theurgy, art becomes the creation of being itself, while religious life exchanges obedience for free creativity and thus fulfills its own true destiny.

Berdyaev's essentially dialectical scheme sets him sharply apart from traditionalists, on the one hand, and avant-gardists, on the other. The former in turn included those who, like Bulgakov, Florensky, and Zenkovsky, opposed the progressivist thrust in his doctrine, as well as those who, like Ivanov, disagreed with his dismissal of the cultural tradition and its role in the historical trajectory that leads up to theurgy. For Florensky, religious art—icon-painting and liturgy—is not something that needs to be overcome; he finds in them the perfect symbolism and the perfect synthesis of the arts already attained, as well as the transformation of life in accordance with humanity's spiritual needs. From his point of view, neither icon-painting nor the synthetic "templar act" [*khramovoe deistvo*] has anything to learn from contemporary art; on the contrary, the latter has much to learn from them.[18] Zenkovsky echoes Florensky's attitude when he chides Berdyaev for dismissing the transfigurative impulse both in the Christian tradition and contemporary culture.[19] Just like the icon for Florensky, the Gospel for Zenkovsky "is not yet the past for us, not archeology, but the system of ideal truth and justice [*pravdy*] standing far ahead" (297). Similarly, Ivanov believes that Berdyaev misunderstands the creative aspect of Christianity but he also notes an inconsistency in Berdyaev's treatment of theurgy. On the one hand, Berdyaev insists on contrasting theurgy to cultural production but, on the other hand, he also speaks of theurgic creations as ideal. Will they not, asks Ivanov, be the same as cultural production, which theurgy is supposed to leave behind?[20] But Ivanov's chief objection has to do with Berdyaev's "rash willfulness" (Ivanov 1994, 353), "self-assertion in blind affect" (355), "blind will" (358), and "desire to separate oneself from conciliar [*sobornoi*] unity" (359).

Method, Myth, and Moralism

Whichever of these three threads in Berdyaev's doctrine—method, mythology, or moralism—one takes up first, it will lead to the other two as well. Berdyaev sees all things as locked into antinomies, and the relations among phenomena as the utmost tension between opposing principles that he "resolves" mystically. The free but radically limited *aesthetic* art, for example, is in stark contrast to religious *life*, confined by obedience, and the two are supposed to be united in theurgy, which will become the truly free activity creating a new reality (*FTK* 1: 237; *MCA* 230). Berdyaev's entire argument leads up to this synthesis but at the eleventh hour the synthesis turns out to be a mystical event, a new revelation whereby a new religious epoch comes into being. In this method all that Berdyaev learned from dialectics is thrust aside at the most important moment in the name of a great mystery, and the final *coincidentia oppositorum* remains forever unattainable to reason.[21] The new revelation means new mythology, the most vivid example of which is Berdyaev's own narrative of the three religious epochs. The fabric of the myth is woven of several threads. Its basic pattern is derived from the Bible, but this pattern is then heavily embroidered by medieval and modern Germanic mysticism, from Meister Eckhart to Franz Baader to Rudolf Steiner. Further, this mythology derives much inspiration from *modern* thinking about history and art. Aphorisms such as "The nature of genius is always revolutionary" (*FTK* 1: 176; *MCA* 163) and "Genius is the sainthood of daring, rather than sainthood of obedience," echo throughout the twentieth century and to this day on the pages of catalogues from every exhibition of avant-garde art. And, conversely, the cult of the ground-breaking genius is mixed with pre-modern motifs: "[T]he creative experience of [artistic] genius," writes Berdyaev, "will be acknowledged as religiously equal in value to the ascetic experience of sainthood" (*FTK* 1: 177; *MCA* 164). Why is it necessary for Berdyaev to reformulate the existing sacred history? Because he needs a myth that would satisfy his sense of personal freedom. Everything under the sun and in heaven is defined, for Berdyaev, by progress from unfreedom to freedom. Thus, from the method, and through mythology, one arrives at Berdyaev's sweeping, metaphysical moralism. And if one begins with the latter, one will see that free artistic creativity can by no means satisfy Berdyaev, no matter how highly he may have valued it. All (ludic) art, he argues, must necessarily pass into (serious) theurgy (*FTK* 1: 236; *MCA* 229). A poetry that stops playing, however, and starts enunciating reality is nothing other than *myth*, which is mystical by definition. And thus, we retrace our steps from moralism via myth to mysticism.

The dialectics of mutually connected categories and tiers of thought is the strong aspect of Berdyaev's doctrine. However, he weakens it by assigning so much significance to mysticism and by elevating intuitive insight. Either the transformation of art into theurgy remains beyond human comprehension or theurgy is indeed the free human creation of a new life. For, if the former is true, then the human being is not the master of this transformation and consequently not free in it. A truly free theurgist must master his or her supra-art, leaving no obscurity unaccounted for, that is to say, the human being must *comprehend* it. And here the chief philosophical problem in Berdyaev's doctrine once again comes to light: his thought revolves within the vicious circle created by the opposition between freedom and unfreedom. As long as one stays within the limits of the world defined by this essentially voluntarist system of coordinates, Berdyaev's dilemma remains unresolvable. One needs to transcend such a world in order to solve its contradictions. Let us recall that, according to the New Testament, truth will guide the human person to freedom (John 8: 32). Closer in history, Hegel similarly observed that the contradictions of the moral order itself push us to a higher plane of spirit (Hegel 1975, 1: 50). One must take a critical look at the hierarchy of human faculties adopted by modern consciousness and topple will from the throne it has usurped. But in order to do so Berdyaev would have had to revise his method as well. Instead of intuition he would have had to adopt what Hegel called the speculative mode of thinking, that is, that phase in our comprehension of things where the fully unfolded dialectics of antinomies finds resolution in a *rational* rather than some allegedly supra-rational unity (Hegel 1991, 133 (§82 Addition)). Losev called such a unity "internally articulated whole" [*edinorazdel'noe tseloe*].[22]

Intuition is something like an intellectual conditioned reflex: just as muscles and nerves develop a habit for certain actions, which then become automatic, so is intuition the result of repeated mental operations, which eventually "fold," as it were, into a seemingly instantaneous insight. One can arrive at recognizing, in this manner, some aspects of the object at hand that have so far remained hidden from one's view; this would be the work of distinguishing or analytic intuition. Or one can intuitively recognize some hitherto unnoticed connections among things; this would be the work of integrating intuition. But in both cases the apparently instantaneous cognitive leaps must be prepared by the prolonged deliberate work of the intellect. Hegel's "speculative reason" is marked precisely by its integrating action; it consists, in fact, in the synthesis of dialectical essences that ceaselessly flow into one another. But in Hegel's thought it is comprehended as a rationally necessary stage in our ascent toward knowledge. It is a momentary revelation that is unfolded into a clear picture of thought's movement and the same rational dynamics constitutes the inner spring of synthesizing intuition. "[T]he meaning of the speculative," Hegel observed, "is to be understood as being the same as what used in earlier times be called 'mystical'" (Hegel 1991, 133). But he also added this crucial point: "Thus, everything rational can equally be called 'mystical'; but this only amounts to saying that it transcends the [abstract] understanding. It does not at all imply that what is so spoken of must be considered inaccessible to thinking and incomprehensible" (ibid.). Berdyaev's thought remained mystical-intuitive in the older sense of the word.

Now with regard to myth, Berdyaev openly acknowledged its primacy in his own thought. As he states, "The gracious help of God in philosophic knowledge, without which integral and final truth cannot be attained, cannot be the method of philosophy: it can be only a gift sent in recompense for the creative deed of knowing. But philosophy must re-establish the original truth of the mythological nature of human consciousness" (*FTK* 1: 74; *MCA* 52, modified). However, what Berdyaev takes as his own point of departure can be considered myth only in a highly qualified sense. The apparently indubitable truths attained by immediate insight are, in fact, complex structures that do indeed comprise fragments of old myths and yet these are modified and rearranged by philosophical reflection in order to provide answers—usually to questions that Berdyaev's stark antinomies leave unanswered. I call such constructs, whether in Plato's dialogues or in Solovyov's mystical poetry, *mythosophy*: mythical idiom deployed to complete a philosophical argument or doctrine, to crown a philosophical edifice in such a manner that myth and philosophical reflection are seamlessly joined into an integral totality (see Marchenkov 2009, 34–39). Berdyaev's mythosophy rounds out his entire philosophical approach. The intuitivism with which it begins serves as the ground for extensive philosophical structures that culminate in a return to the mystical intuitivism of mythical consciousness. The obvious weakness of this procedure lies precisely in its mythical-mystical phase: the black box of divine mystery can spew out unpredictable things, which is another way of saying that the mystic *fills* divine mystery with his or her own immediately held beliefs that are uncritically absorbed from a given sociocultural environment.

In sum, as a philosophical program for transcending the modern worldview, Berdyaev's philosophy of creativity has the doubtless virtue of aiming to merge the pre-modern and modern outlooks. Unlike the Russian and Western progressivists, who wished to shake the dust of the past off modernity's feet; and unlike the restorationists, who offered pre-modern remedies to a modern malaise, Berdyaev sought a solution that would bring the two types of worldviews together in an integral unity. Ten years after *The Meaning of the Creative Act* first appeared, he still thought of his project in these terms: "Neither the principles of modern history nor those of the old Middle Ages can overcome the crisis of the world and [the crisis] of Christianity" (*FTK* 1: 363–364). Another virtue of his doctrine is the fact that he focused on the domain of religion, art, and philosophy rather than the socio-political or purely religious aspects of human experience as the site where the truly meaningful transformation, both personal and social, was to take place. Unfortunately, Berdyaev's philosophical approach could not resolve the antinomies that he so keenly saw and so eloquently set forth. One could say that he stopped at the very threshold of speculative thinking and, his rebellious nature notwithstanding, never dared cross that threshold. However, the most basic philosophical shortcoming of Berdyaev's doctrine was that he retained the very metaphysics of the human subject which he set out to overcome, namely, voluntarism in command of the instrumental intellect.

Concluding Thoughts

When Nietzsche is reproached for being an amoralist, it is the result of a misunderstanding. Nietzsche's voluntarism is, perhaps, the most radical absolutization of morality in the history of philosophy. If morality is, as Kant believed, the kingdom of will, then voluntarism is not a breakthrough beyond the bounds of morality, but its purest distillation. One can therefore regard the entire modern culture as moralist through and through. Modern moralism is responsible for such fantastic notions as the aesthetic autonomy of art, *l'art pour l'art*, and the artist's "ivory tower." It is an equally perverse distortion of morality as well. The elevation of the moral principle over and above the principles of beauty and truth is an unjustifiable subjugation of reason to will. To surmount moralism is, therefore, to surmount voluntarism by rethinking the relation between will and reason in order to determine the will's rational place among such categories as teleology, motivation, and agency. Today's widespread notions about art and its relation to morality are dominated by moralism and, if we wish to form an adequate view of the problems raised by Berdyaev in his philosophy of creativity, a thoroughgoing philosophical critique of moralism and voluntarism is a task of the first order. Contemporary thought about art, by contrast, is deeply absorbed in the struggle of one set of moral values against others and views art as a weapon in this struggle. Feminists praise those artworks that expose patriarchy; their opponents praise positive depictions of "the family"; LGBTQ, American patriots, liberal Enlighteners, Social Democrats, Marxists, environmentalists, conservatives, and evangelicals add up to a picture of an art world overpopulated by "issues." Moralism imposes on scholarship the assumption that art directly projects political and ideological meanings and that its most relevant function is political intervention. This assumption is typical of the entire ideological spectrum, from ultra-conservatives to ultra-leftist critics, from religious fundamentalists to gender equality activists, from the Taliban to Pussy Riot. Despite such near-universal acceptance, this attitude is philosophically indefensible. Berdyaev understood that the relation between art and morality was far more complex than this teeming pseudo-dynamism of "issues" allows one to discern. His philosophy of art, by its very contradictions, points to a radically different task, namely, not to offer yet another progressive or traditionalist set of values that would finally satisfy everyone, but to overcome moralism as such.

Berdyaev's philosophy of creativity is suffused with an impatient, fervent, and anxious anticipation of an impending future. Our epoch, by contrast, is captive to the sentiment of finality; "post-" is the most fashionable prefix in our discourse. If Cervantes wrote today, he would probably choose a Steven Pinker-like figure as his hero, a man blinded by the images of a world gone by and trying to live by its rules, deprived of the very organ by which he could perceive what reality has become. Cervantes' Don Quixote was, of course, far from simple, for, although he could not see modernity in his own contemporary moment, he could still see it *sub specie aeternitatis*. The hero of our times would have the converse handicap: he would not be able to see in his contemporary moment anything *other* than modernity. Amidst a world groaning under his brisk step, he would cheerfully sing his song of the never-ending march onward and upward, to ever new heights of his own power. Nietzsche's contemporary, Peter Tchaikovsky, gave us an example of such a march in his Sixth Symphony, and Hitler and Stalin's contemporary, Dmitri Shostakovich, created an even more disturbing cousin in his Seventh. Despite a certain indebtedness to modern progressivism, Berdyaev's anticipation of the future was more Cervantesque. Commenting on Berdyaev's sense of the revolutionary moment, Bychkov notes the tragic motif in it: "[T]he tension between the surface and the underground of culture has finally reached a threatening magnitude and the explosion is imminent, both in society and in culture." He then correctly remarks: "Today, a century later, we know that the entire past century became in fact such an interminable catastrophic explosion of culture, as a result of which culture's 'underground' reigns supreme today where a century ago one found its 'smoothed-out surface'" (*RTA* 643–644). I should add to this that, when we hear at the end of the twentieth century the most varied voices announcing the end of history, whether in art or in politics, we should be aware that they announce the exhaustion of precisely the *moral* horizon of thought, not of all thought in general. Arthur Danto, Francis Fukuyama, and Jean-François Lyotard all think in similar basic categories, and these categories belong in their ultimate depth to practical reason, that is, to the kingdom of will. Such is the logic of the modern outlook from the beginning, and it finally becomes fully evident, that is, it emerges from the cultural "underground," as Bychkov puts it, to the surface and no one is surprised any longer by this baring of the metaphysics of the modern subject, in contrast to earlier, more innocent times when this metaphysics could still shock the consciousness that remained, if only partially, under the spell of pre-modern values. On the contrary, this logic, the logic of metaphysical voluntarism, is now hailed as the truth that has finally been discovered. Is not the essence of Derrida's *deconstruction* that it must uncover in the phenomenon at hand—any phenomenon, all phenomena—the writhing knot of forces wrestling for power? And that once this mortal combat is made evident, analysis must stop as though there were nothing left to discover?

Rather than a breakthrough, whether theurgic or avant-garde, beyond the boundaries of art and toward the creation of some sort of "life," what is needed is, in fact, a *rethinking* of art's relation to religion and morality as it has been understood at least since Plato's time. Plato is an appropriate thinker to evoke at this juncture because one finds in his dialogues a fairly profound understanding of the nature of art—alongside the implacable resolve to enslave it to moral and even political interests and purposes. In Plato, at the very foundation of the European philosophical tradition, one sees the assertion of *will* over reason in matters of art, of moral values over artistic ones, and the root of this peculiar voluntarism lies in a misunderstanding of the value of artistic *play*. This is all the more striking because Plato's entire philosophy is suffused, through and through, with the ludic current; it is truly a *theatrum philosophicum*. But when it comes to determining the place of play in the human person's self-cognition and self-transformation, Plato looks at it through a moralist lens and pronounces the only possible verdict: play is *useless* (*Laws* II 667d–e). In other words, it is irrelevant as such and only the moral content of ludic pursuits matters. One can think whatever one wishes of aesthetics, which was forged in the crucible of the Enlightenment, but one cannot deny it the virtue of directly challenging this millennia-old moralism. Although Kant did not succeed in overcoming it completely; although Nietzsche, whose thought appeared to be deeply aestheticized, likewise remained captive to voluntaristic moralism; and although even Nietzsche's contemporaries, aesthetes and decadents, impotently sought in *l'art pour l'art* refuge from the moralism that was raging all around them—nonetheless, for the first time in the history of ideas aesthetic thinking persistently pushed art into the center of modern culture's concerns and demanded an open recognition of art's unique role. The most vivid example showing that this demand did not remain unheeded is Hegel's philosophical system, where art is lifted into the realm of Absolute Spirit, that is, it is included in the pinnacle of the hierarchy of cultural values.

Berdyaev left art in subordination to morality, for religion, whose new era he prophesied, shares with morality the orientation toward *life*, which they both wish to transform *in earnest*, and looks upon art's *ludus* with the same implacable suspicion as did Plato-the-moralist. This seriousness, however, contains the poison by which sooner or later moral and religious life make themselves moribund. Throughout its existence Russian philosophical thought about art has been under the spell of moralism, and only a handful of thinkers and artists could resist the power of this spell. Berdyaev's philosophy is a battlefield where a genuine understanding of the nature of art struggles to emerge through the layers of moralistic thinking that are pressing it down, and the fires of this battle illuminate the later destiny of art, down to the current moment.

By insisting on the importance of the serious principle alone, one in fact strips this principle of its defining characteristic. Excessive seriousness with regard to life threatens, in other words, to turn this life, negatively, into play. This is precisely what we find in the so-called "democratic" literary and cultural criticism in Russia in the 1860s. When Dmitrii Pisarev, Nikolai Dobrolyubov, and Nikolai Chernyshevsky insist on the primacy of art's social-utilitarian function, they in fact begin to transform, without realizing it, social reality itself into a plaything in the hands of man-the-technologist. Technologist, because in their chosen system of coordinates art as such cannot exist at all; there is only technology as the practical implementation of scientific knowledge. It may seem that Berdyaev's religious outlook has nothing in common with the progressivism of Populist-Democrats and Konstantin Mikhailovskii's "critically thinking individuals." But they do come together in extolling the serious principle over and above its ludic counterpart. Berdyaev is no doubt more sensitive to the uniquely specific nature of art but, in the end, he still wishes that art be transformed into serious, *religious* activity. But here one finds the same dialectics at work as in the case of Populist moralists: When the serious religious attitude to things fully subsumes the ludic one, the former loses its outline precisely as serious. The sacred act fuses with the profane one and the two become indistinguishable. The priest needs the fool just as much as the fool needs the priest; they each lose their essence without each other.[23]

Contrary to what Berdyaev and so many others thought, art is not *beneath* theurgy but is ahead and above it, closer to the philosophical attitude toward being, existence, and reality than morality and religion. At the same time, even such a consummate aesthete as Oscar Wilde understood very well that art cannot replace life and the artistic vision of the world should not displace its moral counterpart; such is the "moral," if you will, of *The Picture of Dorian Gray*, a meditation on art's destiny in the modern world. But art and its *ludus* are not merely linked to morality, religion, and, generally, the *praxis* that aims "to remake actuality," to use Losev's favorite expression. Artistic thinking and *poietic* play are most intimately woven into this *praxis* and constitute, in fact, the driving engine of its evolution. Both morality and religion need the vital stimulus of the artist's free creativity in order to evolve but art needs them no less vitally, for it can exist only as a ludic contrast to their otherwise unrelieved earnestness.

Artistic creativity based on such a foundation—that is, first and foremost, on the recognition of the primacy of reason over will—is infinitely more revolutionary than any avant-garde and far more spiritual than any theurgy.

NOTES

1. *Smysl tvorchestva. Opyt opravdaniia cheloveka* [*The Meaning of Creativity: An Essay on Anthropodicy*]. The Russian *tvorchestvo* can mean "creativity," "creative work," "oeuvre," or "creation" (*Russian-English Dictionary*). For the early history of this term in Russian thought see Mjør (2018). Quotations in this chapter are from the 1994 two-volume Russian edition (further referred to as *FTK*, followed by the Roman volume number and Arabic page number) and from the English translation by Donald A. Lowrie (referred to as *MCA*). Translation from Russian sources is mine unless indicated otherwise.

2. According to L. V. Poliakov, the author of the introduction to the 1989 Pravda edition of the *Smysl tvorchestva*, Berdyaev developed the design and wrote the first pages of *Smysl tvorchestva* in Italy in the winter of 1912–1913 and finished the manuscript by February 1914 ("*Filosofiia tvorchestva Nikolaia Berdiaeva* [*Nikolai Berdyaev's Philosophy of Creativity*]," in Berdiaev 1989, 4). Lowrie likewise mentions 1914 as the year of the completion of the manuscript (*MCA* 7). However, in the preface, dated March 1926, to the 1927 German edition Berdyaev states that the book was written "fifteen years ago" (*FTK* 1: 533 and *MCA* 9).

3. Berdyaev has long had the reputation of a rebel. Lowrie titled his 1960 biography of Berdyaev *Rebellious Prophet*, and Part One of Matthew Spinka's *Nicolas Berdyaev: Captive of Freedom* is titled "The World Berdyaev Revolted Against."

4. *Svet nevechernii* [The Light That Does Not Fade], 279; quoted from Berdyaev 1989, 590 (editor's commentary).

5. Zenkovsky, "*Problema tvorchestva* [The Problem of Creativity]," in Ermichev (1994, 304). See also his verdict against *The Meaning of the Creative Act* as "a flaming apotheosis and an apology for genius" in which Berdyaev's "sincere and profound moral passion degenerated into an 'ethics of creativity', indifferent to reality" (Zenkovsky 2003, 2: 778, 780).

6. R. Harré, "Laplace, Pierre Simon de," in Borchert (2006).

7. By pre-modern subjects, I refer to the dominant conceptions of the human person in Antiquity and the Middle Ages. By non-modern subjects I mean the types of personhood in cultures that existed, both in the West and in other parts of the world, chronologically alongside modernity but were typologically distinct.

8. "Intuitive-aesthetic insight—this is the foundation of our national philosophizing, and Berdyaev was well aware of it from his own personal experience" (*RTA* 632). Igor Evlampiev similarly finds that the primacy of intuitive-mystical insight is "the most typical feature of almost all theories in the Russian philosophy of the early twentieth century" (Evlampiev 2017, 282).

9. Berdyaev's notes are not included in *MCA*.

10. *FTK* 1: 68; *MCA* 46. Lowrie renders the Russian *plokhaia*, "bad," as "evil" in his translation. "Spurious" (along with "bad" sometimes) has become the accepted translation of Hegel's *schlechte Unendlichkeit* (cf. Hegel 1991, 149). In Russian since Berdyaev's time, Hegel's phrase has come to be rendered as *durnaia beskonechnost'*, a wording Berdyaev himself occasionally used, too (cf. "*Beskonechnoe* [the Infinite]," *Filosofskii entsiklopedicheskii slovar'* [*Philosophical Encyclopaedic Dictionary*]; *FTK* 1: 94).

11. Berdyaev's younger contemporary, Aleksei Losev, took up and enlarged this theme in his *Dialectics of Myth* (1930), where he devoted many pages to the pre-modern subject's reaction to the new cosmology.

12. In a note, Berdyaev quotes Edmund Husserl's seminal 1911 essay "Philosophy as Rigorous Science," where the founder of the phenomenological school asserts that, once science has pronounced its verdict, "wisdom must learn from it" (*FTK* 1: 312).

13. *Of Human Freedom*, 24; quoted from Schelling (1978, xxix). In his *Philosophie der Offenbarung*, Schelling calls spirit itself "*Macht, Potenz über das Sein* [might, power over being]" (Schelling 1977, 102).

14. Aristotle, *De Anima*, Bk. III, ch. 10; Aristotle (1941, 598). The language that follows this passage somewhat muddies the waters by ambiguating between the mind and appetite as sources of motion (433a22–433b5). But the inextricable conjunction between the two is not affected by it.

15. The role of the object of appetite in *De Anima* is clearly analogous to the role of the final cause in the *Metaphysics* which sets everything in motion by being loved (Bk. XII, ch. 7, 1072b; Aristotle 1941, 879).

16. This was rather sharply noted by Vasily Rozanov (Ermichev 1994, 262).

17. Solovyov's most important essays on aesthetics were "Beauty in Nature" (1889), "The Universal Meaning of Art" (1890), and "A First Step toward a Positive Aesthetic" (Solovyov 2003, 29–82, 135–144).

18. The sense of liturgy as fully realized *artistic* perfection is evident in Florensky's essay on "The Church Ritual as the Synthesis of the Arts" (*Beyond Vision*, 105–110). For an excellent summary of Florensky's views see the chapter on Florensky and especially the section on "*Ikona kak vershina iskusstva* [*The Icon as the Pinnacle of Art*]," in Bychkov's *RTA*, 242–262.
19. Zenkovsky, "*Problema tvorchestva*," in Ermichev (1994, 293–294).
20. Ivanov, "*Staraia ili novaia vera?*," in Ivanov (1994, 354). In his 1918 article "*Krizis iskusstva*," Berdyaev responded to Ivanov's criticism, saying, "New art will no longer create in the form of images made of physical flesh, but those of another, finer flesh; it will pass from material bodies to psychic [*dushevnym*] ones" (*FTK* 1: 413–414).
21. While criticizing rationalism in *The Meaning of the Creative Act*, Berdyaev remarks that "we need to revise our attitude toward Hegel." The remark was made apropos of Hegel's tenet that categories of thought are not mere tools used by reason, but stages in a complex process which, taken in its entirety, *is* reason (*FTK* 1: 315–316n15). Apparently, Berdyaev never got around to such a revision or at least, if he did, it did not change his mind regarding the limits of rational cognition. He remained convinced that in Kant's philosophy, "reason passed judgment upon reason and recognized its limits" (Berdyaev 1953, 7).
22. Losev's coinage, a centrepiece among his categories, *edinorazdel'noe* (literally "unified-divided") comes close to "universal" (see Losev 2014; Marchenkov 2013, especially 83n29). My translation builds on the Latin *articulāre*, "to divide into distinct parts" (see etymology for "articulate" in the *Oxford English Dictionary*).
23. This is the theme of Giorgio Agamben's short but pregnant book *Profanations* (Agamben 2007; see especially the chapter on "Parody," 37–51).

BIBLIOGRAPHY

Agamben, Giorgio. 2007. *Profanations*. Translated by Jeff Fort. New York, NY: Zone Books.

Aristotle. 1941. *The Basic Works of Aristotle*. Edited by Richard McKeon. New York, NY: Random House.

Berdyaev, Nicolas. 1953. *Truth and Revelation*. Translated by R.M. French. New York, NY: Collier Books.

———. 1962. *The Meaning of the Creative Act*. Translated by Donald A. Lowrie. New York, NY: Collier Books. Abbreviated as *MCA*.

Berdyaev, Nikolai. 1989. *Filosofiia svobody. Smysl tvorchestva*. Moscow: Pravda.

———. 1994. *Filosofiia tvorchestva, kul'tury i iskusstva v 2-kh tomakh*. Moscow: Iskusstvo. Abbreviated as *FTK*.

Borchert, Donald (Editor-in-chief). 2006. *Encyclopedia of Philosophy*. 2nd ed. Detroit, MI: Macmillan Reference.

Ermichev, Alexander A., ed. 1994. *N. A. Berdiaev: pro et contra. Antologiia*. Vol. 1. St. Petersburg: Izdatel'stvo Russkogo khristianskogo gumanitarnogo universiteta.

Evlampiev, Igor I. 2017. *Russkaia filosofiia v evropeiskom kontekste*. St. Petersburg: Izdatel'stvo RKhGA.

Hegel, Georg Wilhelm Friedrich. 1969. *Hegel's Science of Logic*. Translated by A.V. Miller. New York, NY: Humanity Books.

———. 1975. *Aesthetics: Lectures on Fine Art*, in 2 vols. Translated by T.M. Knox. Oxford: Clarendon Press.

———. 1977. *Hegel's Phenomenology of Spirit*. Translated by A.V. Miller. Oxford: Oxford University Press.

———. 1991. *The Encyclopaedia Logic (with the Zusätze)*. Translated by T.F. Gaerets, W.A. Suchting, and H.S. Harris. Indianapolis, IN and Cambridge, UK: Hackett Publishing Company, Inc.

Horkheimer, Max, and Theodor Adorno. 2002. *Dialectic of Enlightenment: Philosophical Fragments*. Translated by Edmund Jephcott. Stanford, CA: Stanford University Press.

Ivanov, Vyacheslav I. 1994. *Rodnoe i vselenskoe*. Moscow: Respublika.

Koyré, Alexandre. 1968. *From the Closed World to the Infinite Universe*. Baltimore, MD: Johns Hopkins Press.

Losev, Aleksei. 2014. *Problema simvola i realisticheskoe iskusstvo*. Edited by A.A. Takho-Godi and V.P. Troitskii. Moscow: Russkii Mir.

Marchenkov, Vladimir. 2009. *The Orpheus Myth and the Powers of Music*. Hillsdale, NY: Pendragon Press.

———. 2013. Prophecy of a Revolution: Aleksey Losev on Wagner's Aesthetic Outlook. In *Wagner in Russia, Poland and the Czech Lands*, ed. Stephen Muir and Anastasia Belina-Johnson, 71–91. Burlington, VT: Ashgate.

———. 2014. *Between Histories: Art's Dilemmas and Trajectories*. New York, NY: Hampton Press.

Mjør, Kåre. 2018. Metaphysics, Aesthetics, or Epistemology? The Conceptual History of *tvorchestvo* in Nineteenth-Century Russian Thought. *Slavic and East European Journal* 62 (1): 4–25.

Nietzsche, Friedrich. 1966. *Beyond Good and Evil: Prelude to a Philosophy of the Future*. Translated by Walter Kaufmann. New York, NY: Vintage Books.

Schelling, Friedrich. 1936. *Of Human Freedom*. Translated by James Gutmann. Chicago, IL: Open Court.

———. 1977. *Philosophie der Offenbarung 1841/42*. Edited by Manfred Frank. Frankfurt am Main: Suhrkamp.

———. 1978. *System of Transcendental Idealism (1800)*. Translated by Peter Heath. Charlottesville, VA: University Press of Virginia.

Solovyov, Vladimir S. 2003. *The Heart of Reality: Essays on Beauty, Love, and Ethics*. Edited and translated by Vladimir Wozniuk. Notre Dame, IN: The University of Notre Dame Press.

Spinka, Matthew. 1950. *Nicolas Berdyaev: Captive of Freedom*. Philadelphia, PA: Westminster Press.

Zenkovsky, Vasilii V. 2003. *A History of Russian Philosophy*, in 2 vols. Translated by George Kline. London and New York, NY: Routledge.

CHAPTER 12

Lenin and His Controversy over Philosophy: On the Philosophical Significance of *Materialism and Empiriocriticism*

Marina F. Bykova

Writing on Lenin and philosophy is not an easy task. The challenges that one encounters by addressing Lenin's philosophical legacy are of both an ideological and a conceptual nature.

Until quite recently, the third largest country in the world lived under a political system that was supposedly initiated by Lenin. The Revolution led by Lenin changed the existing social order of the Russian Empire by transforming the working class into a real socio-economic power, the goal for which Marx actively fought in both theory and practice. Yet the disastrous evolution of the Soviet state led to the emergence of a totalitarian regime that found its realization in the Gulag and in the severe limitation of civil and political rights and freedoms. This state needed an ideology that would justify its policies. The ideological support was found in Lenin, who shortly after his death was

---

An earlier version of this essay appeared under the title "Lenin and Philosophy: On the Philosophical Significance of *Materialism and Empiriocriticism*," in *The Handbook of Leninist Political Philosophy*, edited by Tom Rockmore and Norman Levine, 121–160. London, New York: Palgrave Macmillan, 2018 (Bykova 2018a). Used here with permission of Palgrave Macmillan.

M. F. Bykova (✉)
North Carolina State University, Raleigh, NC, USA
e-mail: mfbykova@ncsu.edu

© The Author(s), under exclusive license to Springer Nature Switzerland AG 2021
M. F. Bykova et al. (eds.), *The Palgrave Handbook of Russian Thought*,
https://doi.org/10.1007/978-3-030-62982-3_12

239

established as a superior authority to which the Soviet state could appeal to confirm its actions. In the early 1930s, the Bolshevik party[1]—now led by Stalin—was quick to declare Leninism, the social and political principles expounded by Lenin, its new ideology. This is how the myth of a special "Leninist stage in Soviet philosophy" was born. Initially formulated in the infamous "article by the three [authors]"—written by three (then) young orthodox-minded philosophers of the Institute of Red Professors, Mark Mitin, V. Ral'tsevich, and Pavel Yudin, and published in the official party newspaper *Pravda*—the thesis of the Leninist stage not only recognized the new epoch in Marxist philosophy that Lenin had initiated, but also insisted on the greatness of Lenin's achievements in philosophy (see Mitin et al. 1930).[2] The authors saw Lenin's chief philosophical contribution as lying in his offering "the richest and most complete understanding of Marxist dialectic" (ibid., sec. 4). Certain later works also deemed Lenin's philosophical ideas novel for their criticism of recent revisionist and anti-Marxist theories, for clearly distinguishing between materialism and idealism, and for introducing the notion of *partiinost'* into Marxist philosophy (see, for example, Mitin 1930). Notwithstanding the general nature of this statement, it served as a theoretical foundation of what soon became the obsession of official Soviet philosophy, namely, "a thorough working out of the Leninist stage in the development of dialectical materialism."[3] Yet, beside the official declaration of the new era Lenin had supposedly introduced, there was barely any serious work in this period that would provide a detailed analysis of Lenin's philosophical insights.[4] All claims about Lenin's contribution to philosophy remained largely unsubstantiated. There was virtually no genuine attempt to justify them. This leads some critics to believe that the true focus of the Leninist stage was not Lenin himself or his own philosophical achievement. The strategy of presenting Lenin as the ultimate authority was nothing but a kind of necessary camouflage for establishing the cult of Stalin,[5] who was openly declared "Lenin [of] today" and who at that time was already well positioned to interpret and employ "Lenin's wisdom" in both theory and practice according to his own political and ideological goals.

While the discussion of the "real goal" of the Leninist stage in Soviet philosophy is beyond the scope of this chapter, it is worth noticing that the agenda of this stage had not been prepared by any genuine philosophical interest. In this sense, the rhetoric of Leninism—which might be interesting as important evidence of the development of Russian intellectual discourse in the early Soviet period—has a very limited philosophical value, especially with respect to the analysis of Lenin's achievement in philosophy.

Yet, it seems to be clear that it is impossible to deny Lenin's serious and more or less consistent engagement with philosophy. During his years as a revolutionary activist and a political practitioner, he published a number of articles, pamphlets, and books on a variety of philosophical topics. If, however, we recall that Lenin was not a philosopher by training or by temperament, then the question of the motivation of his philosophical exploration becomes very important.

I

The theme of Lenin and philosophy has received considerable attention in recent years (Budgen et al. 2007; Lih 2008b). It has proved attractive, and not merely because as a practitioner and the leader of the Russian Revolution, Lenin had won for himself a place in history. He apparently attached great significance to philosophy and philosophical inquiry. Not only did he produce extensive works on the subject, but he also sought answers to many practical questions by turning to philosophy and its historical sources. Lenin's contemporaries and biographers, as well as his admirers and critics, are all puzzled by the fact that in the most difficult and critical moments in Russian history as well as in his own life he would delve into philosophy, putting aside all other practical tasks that had required his urgent attention.

After the failure of the First Russian Revolution of 1905, the rolling back of the revolutionary wave led to panic and confusion not only among those who showed some sympathy toward revolution but also among the Bolsheviks themselves. Philosophy was in crisis. The trap of "one reactionary philosophy" was so strong that even its closest and most loyal proponents—Anatoly Lunacharsky, Maxim Gorky, and Alexander Bogdanov—fall into it. There appeared many philosophical camps, schools, and theories: God-seeking, God-building, empiriocriticism, empiriomonism, empiriosymbolism, and so on. One's reaction to these ideas determined not only how one thought but also how one acted. And in this critical moment, when there was an urgent need to find new revolutionary tactics, Lenin spent weeks and months in the National Library in Geneva and the Library of the British Museum in London, studying philosophical as well as scientific (especially physics) literature and discovering for himself all the peculiarities of philosophical argumentation. He comments on this period: "I am neglecting the newspaper [*Proletarii* [The Proletariat]] because of my hard bout of philosophy," and wanted to talk about the subject matter "*concretely*, in detail, simply, without unnecessarily frightening […] readers with philosophical nuances. And at all costs I shall say it *in my own way*" (*LCW* 34: 387, 388). Philosophy told "in his own way" is depicted in *Materialism and Empiriocriticism*,[6] his first and one of his most important philosophical books.

In the year of 1914, Europe was experiencing the devastating effects of World War I. In a patriotic frenzy, yesterday's comrades in the Second International left the organization and returned to their national quarters. Lenin was in exile in Bern. Here again he spent an enormous amount of time in the library, reading and decrypting the dialectical puzzles of Hegel's *Science of Logic* and studying philosophical writings by such thinkers as Clausewitz, Lassalle, and others. As a result of these efforts, eight notebooks on philosophy (known as *Philosophical Notebooks*)[7] came into being.

In the summer of 1917, only a few months before the October Revolution, Lenin escaped to Razliv, where, living in a tent, he wrote a book about the materialist conception of history, entitled *The State and Revolution*.[8]

The year of 1922 was again a "critical time." The old scheme of "war communism" had been eradicated. The question of the development of socialism, which became urgent, required the consolidation of all sound and democratically oriented intellectual forces. Lenin published an article "On the Significance of Militant Materialism"[9] that called for a resolute "militant atheism." He also set the task of creating "a society of materialist friends of the Hegelian dialectic" and of facilitating closer cooperation between materialist philosophers and natural scientists, who, according to Lenin, were natural allies of philosophical materialism.

What did Lenin's extensive engagement with philosophy and philosophical ideas really mean? How can we fit this concern into a common picture of Lenin as exclusively a revolutionary practitioner, a master of political struggles, and a "hard pragmatist" (see Liebmann 1975), who supposedly never hesitated or doubted in acting and thus had no need to turn to philosophy (or any other sources of new ideas) in search for answers to enduring questions? The above view seems to contradict the historical facts. Instead, the more complex, more acute, and more pressing the present moment of history was, the deeper and more urgent was Lenin's interest in philosophy. Even at the end of his life, the terminally ill Lenin kept on his nightstand and attentively studied *Hegel's Philosophy as the Doctrine of the Concreteness of God and Man* by the Russian émigré philosopher Ivan Ilyin.

Certainly, Lenin is traditionally viewed as a great revolutionary, a witty polemicist, and an organizational man. While this common image of Lenin may be accurate, it omits a vital philosophical dimension. Philosophical inquiry undoubtedly played a crucial role in Lenin's intellectual and political life, and by eliminating this engagement with philosophy from Lenin's legacy, we are in danger of losing sight of something important about Lenin himself. At the same time, we should avoid idolizing Lenin and reading his works as sacred texts. This tendency is typical not only of the Soviet period literature, but also of more recent publications by a variety of political and social movement groups and their theoreticians (see Lih 2008a, Le Blanc 2006, Le Blanc 2015, Boer [blog]). It would also be wrong to try to measure Lenin and the theoretical significance of his work by the standards we usually apply to professional philosophers. We should rather see Lenin for what he really was and assess his philosophical legacy in the historical context in which it emerged.

Lenin was a practitioner of revolution and a man committed to taking decisive political actions; he was also a social and political theoretician. He was not, however, a philosopher in any traditional sense. And even though many believe that he fits well the ideal of the philosopher as envisioned by Marx, who said that "philosophers have only interpreted the world in various ways; the point is to change it" (Marx 1981, 422), it might be hard to argue that the Lenin's kind of engagement with the philosophical field warrants labeling him as a representative of the profession. Moreover, Lenin himself did not have any illusions in this regard either. In his letter to Maxim Gorky, he admitted, "[P]hilosophy. I am fully aware of my unpreparedness in this sphere, which prevents me from speaking about it in public" (Lenin 1908, *LCW* 34: 381). This does not mean, however, that Lenin had nothing genuinely philosophical to say and that his theoretical and practical contributions are philosophically irrelevant. On the contrary, I believe that the philosophical dimension of Lenin's legacy is very significant and that we have something important to learn from his specific form of "philosophizing."[10] However, I believe that it would be a mistake to speak of Lenin's philosophy, which, in my opinion, does not exist, at least not in the same way as Plato's, Kant's, or Hegel's philosophy. Neither is it a matter of what Lenin says *about* philosophy, which would be a kind of metaphilosophical exercise of a rather low value. Rather my topic is the question of Lenin's contribution to philosophy and philosophical enterprise. The aim of this chapter is to explore the philosophical importance of Lenin's thought. It attempts to reevaluate Lenin's philosophical legacy by examining his major and perhaps most controversial and often misinterpreted philosophical work *Materialism and Empiriocriticism*. With that in mind, the emphasis will be on the philosophical significance and originality of key concepts and ideas he formulated.

I would argue that Lenin's philosophical legacy was essentially a specific development of Marxist thought that he developed further both theoretically and practically in the light of the specific historical circumstances and experiences of Russia in the first two decades of the twentieth century. Yet it is important to see that he did not merely "excavate Marxist theory from beneath layers of European social democracy" and mechanically apply it to Russian circumstances. In his effort to find solutions to urgent practical issues and as the leader of the Russian revolution and of the newly established state, he turned to philosophical and other theoretical sources, attempting to bring together and further advance Marxist theory and revolutionary practice. In this process he offered an array of new philosophical, political, and social ideas and thus advanced Marxist thought. While Lenin attentively read Marx and Engels and in his own philosophical exploration largely relied on their guidance,[11] he was never a merely "passive recipient" of Marx and Engels's ideas as some commentators suggest (see, for example, White 2015, 139). Nor did he just attempt to "align his thinking with that of Marx and Engels" (ibid., 140). As an independent thinker who not only highly valued the dialectical content of Marxist doctrine but also used the dialectical method in his theoretical and practical work, he realized the dynamic nature of Marxist doctrine and the necessity of its further development as appropriate in the changing political and social situation. Although he did not create an independent theoretical system, he regenerated, reenergized, and deepened elements of Marxist thought that his ideological and political opponents intended to bury. As an adherent of Marxism, he did not question the truth of Marxist doctrine, but at the same time he never treated it like a sacred source, which merely inspired awe, assuming a passive attitude. Lenin's appreciation for Marxism can rather be described in terms of reverence: Lenin showed a deep respect for Marxist doctrine, which acted as a stimulus for his active engagement with Marx and Engels, an engagement that assumed a further development of the Marxist doctrine. This explains Lenin's genuine interest in philosophical questions, which he displayed throughout his career. He took philosophy to be a vital part of the Marxist doctrine, openly recognizing its importance not only for revolutionary practice but also for a deeper and more accurate understanding of Marxist thought and for the further advancement of Marxism that he championed. It is true that Lenin's legacy is inseparable from Marxism and that many of his philosophical writings have as one of their goals the defense of what he considers authentic Marxism. However, Lenin's commitment to Marxism goes much further than its mere defense and has a more constructive determination than merely the preservation of Marxist doctrine, as Frederick C. Copleston and many other commentators believe (see Copleston 1986, 292ff.). In addition, there is a tendency to interpret Lenin's Marxism exclusively as the theory and practice of revolution and class struggle (Krausz 2015, esp. 357, nn. 7 and 8; Le Blanc 2015), which oversimplifies Lenin's theoretical position and downplays its philosophical significance. It "reduces" Lenin's Marxism to the ideology of political class struggle, and, eventually, merely to party ideology, which is exactly how Leninism was construed in the Stalinist period.

Both these narratives, I would suggest, are flawed because they neglect the great significance of the philosophical dimension of Lenin's particular version of Marxism that largely distinguishes it from other variant forms of Marxism. By emphasizing its philosophical tenets and advancing philosophical methodology, he took Marxist doctrine further theoretically. Lenin not only resisted the vulgar ideology of class, the populist perception of class struggle, and the unjustified abstract appeal to existing positions. His ideas philosophically resist fragmentation by discipline and instead point toward totality and indivisible progress. He eliminates the still existing walls separating theory from practice and science from philosophy. Perhaps the most important among Lenin's philosophical achievements are, first, his sharp and uncompromising differentiation between philosophical materialism and philosophical idealism that clearly demonstrates the dividing line between the two and, second, his defense of the materialist dialectics, which reconfirms it as the core of the Marxist world outlook. Lenin effectively demonstrates both of these results in *Materialism and Empiriocriticism*, which presents the fundamentals not of materialism in general but of *dialectical* materialism (the materialist dialectics), a dimension that some commentators are not ready to acknowledge. Instead, they insist on the idea that Lenin at best develops in the book the position of "naïve materialism" or "realism" (Bakhurst 1991), thus misconstruing not only Lenin's understanding of materialism but also his understanding of the dialectics.

It must be noted that for many critics, the contributions mentioned above do not appear to be Lenin's own accomplishments or at least not his so-called decisive contributions. A largely hostile attitude toward Lenin's philosophical achievement still prevails in the West. Certainly, many of Lenin's philosophical ideas can be traced back to Marx and Engels or even more precisely, especially concerning dialectics, to the Hegelian roots of Marxist doctrine. Yet I would argue that a closer consideration of Lenin's book reveals important new concepts that Lenin produces in addressing important philosophical issues. My attempt in this chapter is to provide a more sympathetic though also critical assessment of Lenin's philosophical thought. The aim is to avoid either, on the one hand, falling back into the narrowly construed confines of Marxist–Leninist (orthodox) canonization or, on the other hand, blindly following largely dismissive Western critiques.

II

There is still no consensus among scholars concerning the theoretical aim and the philosophical significance of Lenin's first book-length contribution, *Materialism and Empiriocriticism*, which was published in Moscow in 1909 under the pseudonym of Vl. Ilyin. While some commentators consider the book a canonical philosophical text by describing it as "a classic of dialectical materialism" (Ilyenkov 1980, 4), others openly question the philosophical character of the work by doubting that it belongs to the history of philosophy at all (Besançon 1981, 206). Many Western critics, even those sympathetic to Lenin and inclined to view the work as philosophical, disagree about its author's main motivations and the extent of his philosophical sophistication. There is a strong belief that the author's "attack on empiriomonism was not motivated by anything approaching lively interest in philosophical problems for their own sake" (Copleston 1986, 292) and that the author has "mainly pragmatic and polemical intentions" (Liebmann 1975, 442). Furthermore, some commentators point to the "amateur" character of the work that is supposedly reflected in the philosophical deficiency of the arguments Lenin presents.

To be sure, the philosophical significance of the work is certainly not an uncontroversial matter. The work is indeed polemical, as is explicitly indicated in its subtitle—*Critical Comments on a Reactionary Philosophy*—something that was not well known to a contemporary reader. The same subtitle clearly indicates the author's intention to provide a criticism of "a reactionary philosophy." Yet the philosophical content of this criticism still requires close analysis. Furthermore, the work is not wholly original. It draws heavily on both Engels and his popularization of Marxist philosophical views, especially in *Anti-Dühring*, and the views of Georgii V. Plekhanov, Lenin's philosophical mentor and the principal Russian Marxist theoretician of that time. Nevertheless, I would suggest that *Materialism and Empiriocriticism* should be read as a distinctive philosophical work, which, despite its polemical nature, can be viewed as an attempt to provide an outline of the fundamentals of a dialectical form of materialism by defending it against philosophical idealism. In this process, it clarifies the fundamental notions, concepts, and principles of dialectical materialism, gives important insights about its theory of knowledge, and shows its relevance to the recent revolution in science, thus further advancing Marxist philosophical doctrine, in particular by reconfirming its instrumental role in the changing historical and social situation. It is worth noticing that the conception of dialectical materialism that Lenin defends in the book is not identical to the infamous *diamat* preached by Soviet orthodox and dogmatic Marxism–Leninism, which was transformed into an ideology that served to justify the political system installed in Russia. Although Lenin, too, associates the work not only with philosophical but "also [with] serious political obligations," dialectical materialism as he conceived it in the book still appears as a philosophical theory, and not as the sort of ideological dogmatism characteristic of philosophy in Russia in the Soviet period. Thus, I intend to take the philosophical content of *Materialism and Empiriocriticism* seriously in order to show that a more sympathetic reading of the work reveals important details about Lenin's version of Marxism as well as his contributions to philosophy. I believe that this work, despite its many weaknesses, plays an essential role in Lenin's larger project of overcoming the self-contradictions of nineteenth-century philosophy. As such, it deserves serious consideration and analysis.

III

Lenin's work is largely a response to the "Machist" controversy, which caused a crisis within Marxism during the first decade of the twentieth century. Thus, before turning to Lenin's philosophical arguments in the work it is necessary to describe, at least in broad outlines, the philosophical context in which these arguments were developed.

The controversy is closely associated with the philosophy developed in the late nineteenth century by Ernst Mach and Richard Avenarius. This philosophy, commonly known as Machism, arose out of the decay of positivism into competing materialist and idealist views.

As one of the first serious attempts to apply the methodology of the natural sciences to the study and reform of modern society (Bottomore 1991, entry "Positivism"), the positivism of the nineteenth century positioned itself as a scientific (as opposed to a metaphysical or idealistic) philosophy. However, it is more accurate to say that science displaced philosophy both theoretically and practically. The role of philosophy was reduced to merely correlating the findings of different scientific disciplines, while all forms of primary research into the nature of the world were assigned to science. This, however, allowed positivism to reject traditional metaphysics and respond (at least to some extent) to associated ontological and especially epistemological issues. By heavily relying on the discoveries and assumptions of contemporary science, positivism, which thus committed itself to empiricism and to an empiricist epistemology, insisted on the limitless ability of human consciousness to know all the aspects of the world without exception. There was a hope that the empiricist approach would enable an overcoming, so to speak, of the ontological dualism of early modern philosophy while at the same time avoiding the agnosticism of Hume and Kant. Extending this anti-metaphysical attitude beyond the physical realm to the social sciences, positivism also proposed to apply the methods of empirical science to social reality and to use them for resolving problems of contemporary society. In an era when the existing philosophical and political movements discredited themselves by their inability to provide answers to urgent theoretical questions and offer solutions to pressing political and social issues, positivism thus appeared as a promising scientific alternative and, for this reason, it was initially received with great enthusiasm.[12]

Although in the rest of Europe positivism served as a major theory that was able to satisfactorily address both intellectual and political concerns, in the German-speaking regions the political goals of positivism received much less notice than its philosophical foundations. Here it was considered as a successor to the idealist and post-idealist systems dominant in the early century. But positivism as an intellectual doctrine could not withstand the philosophical challenges of rigorous analysis and soon the tension between its two main philosophical components, materialism and empiricism, largely suppressed at first by diverting attention to social and political issues, grew into a critical concern.

After the failed revolutions of 1848 and growing nationalism and political reaction, the emptiness of the political hopes of earlier positivism became clear. At this point, positivism's decay was unavoidable. This process culminated in the emergence of two opposite philosophical movements or schools of thought: mechanistic (or vulgar) materialism, which represented the materialistic intuitions of positivism, and idealism, in which the empiricist elements of positivism played out to their logical conclusion. The materialism of this period was represented by such figures as Jacob Moleschott, Karl Vogt, Ernst Haeckel, and others. Although they were not philosophers but instead scientists by training with solid backgrounds in biological sciences and medicine, they attempted to provide a philosophical (and largely ontological) framework for the materialistic assumptions of modern science. Yet they overlooked the epistemological problems raised by science's empirical methods and proved unable to deliver anything resembling a secure epistemic foundation within a materialist framework. Rather, the idealism that emerged in the writings of Ernst Mach (1836–1916) and Richard Avenarius (1843–1896) gave methodological priority to positivist epistemology over positivist ontology. But despite being more philosophically astute than its counterpart, the idealism of Mach and Avenarius was not more successful than mechanistic materialism at resolving the serious philosophical tensions within positivism. A physicist by training, Mach was well versed in philosophy. He was greatly influenced by Hume and Berkeley, especially by their rejections of metaphysical speculation and appeal to sense-perception. Rejecting materialism with its explanation of mental events as functions of the brain, Mach instead attempted to explicate scientific and practical concepts as well as all objects of experience in terms of perceptions and sense-data. Following Hume, he assigned primary epistemic status to the immediately given data of sense experience, while considering physical objects as well as the categories we utilize for the purpose of thinking about them as methodologically posterior. Turning to the German tradition, he also rejected all forms of Kantian apriorism, insisting on its metaphysical and unscientific character. As a result, he overlooked the important fact that some features of the world might be grounded in the cognitive structures of the knowing subject itself, and not in experience. Unable to see the theoretical advantage of Kant's transcendental idealism with its focus on the unity of the knowing subject, Mach's idealism, as Lance B. Richey rightly points out, "resulted in a regression to the pre-critical problems of Hume and Berkeley which Kant believed himself to have overcome" (Richey 2003, 18).

According to his fundamental philosophical assumptions, Mach was a realist. He believed that there was an external world accessible through our experience. However, he was not consistent in his application of this assumption to epistemological problems. For example, he openly denied the existence of atoms and molecules, because we are not able to perceive them, but can instead only infer their existence from our knowledge about the construction of matter (see Mach 1986). As a result of the ambiguity of his views about the status of the external world, Mach's position was interpreted idealistically even among his most loyal supporters, despite the fact that he himself vigorously rejected the charge of idealism. One of these supporters was Richard Avenarius, a German–Swiss philosopher, who had greatly contributed to the development of Mach's radical position of empirical criticism, or "empiriocriticism" as it is commonly called.

In attempting to overcome this skepticism, and especially the subjectivism of earlier philosophical systems (which was a persistent feature for both Hume and Mach), Avenarius introduced the "principle of coordination." According to Avenarius, both the skepticism of Hume and the transcendental idealism of Kant were consequences of a wrong fundamental assumption (which he calls "introjection") that an unknowable world exists beyond our subjective sense experiences. There is thus an unavoidable opposition between "my" experience of the world (the concept of the subject) and the world itself (the concept of the object). Instead, he presupposes the original relationship between the subject and the object. This relationship is rooted in "pure" experience, which is fundamental to both subject and object. In other words, subject and object must be regarded as standing in a relationship from the start. What governs this relation is the "principle of coordination," which allows us to "unify" the world into a single and self-consistent realm of experience. However, Avenarius's attempt to get around the problem of the subject by replacing introjection with the principle of coordination fails. His effort not only relinquished the epistemological aspirations of Mach (and empiriocriticism in general) but also revived the important ontological issues left unsolved by Kant and other early philosophers. While Avenarius's empiriocritical presupposition might appear as a ground for determining the relation of the subject (the "I") to the world (the objective surrounding) in such a way that both are present as common and inseparable elements, in fact, it points to a number of substantial problems. First, it is not clear what determines the "coordination" which the "I" experiences and to what extent the "I's" activity can impact it. Second, the concept and the ontological status of the "I" remain obscure. Avenarius rejects in principle a transcendental subject. At the same time, when he identifies the "I" with the human nervous system, which is for him an equal component of experience as well as of other things, he describes it as "the central term of coordination." Since he eventually makes it into the condition of the appearance of all its other components, he thus falls into subjective idealism. Although Avenarius himself tries to avoid this conclusion in claiming that it contradicts his empiriocritical presupposition, it is difficult to see how it can be avoided if his basic tenets are maintained consistently.

It should at least be clear that Mach and Avenarius did not just have strong idealistic tendencies, but their underlying (empiriocritical) assumptions were idealistic in their very nature and content. This idealism seriously influenced some Russian Marxists in the first decade of the twentieth century, prompting Lenin to address the Machist controversy in his *Materialism and Empiriocriticism*.

Despite some obvious political motivations, Lenin's target in the work was primarily key philosophical questions, which he believed were of central importance not only to Marxist philosophy but also to Marxist revolutionary theory and practice. Working within the Russian context, Lenin responded to Russian Machism, which caused a serious philosophical (and political) struggle within Russian Marxism at the beginning of the twentieth century (see Bykova 2018b). At that time, Machist epistemology was favored and eventually adopted by a large portion of the Russian intelligentsia representing both Bolshevik and Menshevik theorists and including such diverse thinkers as Anatoly Lunacharsky, Viktor Chernov, Nikolai Valentinov, and others. Yet the unofficial "ideological" leader of the movement and the key figure among all of them was Alexander Bogdanov, a Bolshevik, who represented a young generation (as opposed to Plekhanov[13]) of Marxist writers in Russia. Many of Bogdanov's philosophical ideas were already present in embryo in his initially published works, which mainly focused on problems of economy and a historical view of nature (see Bogdanov 1897, Bogdanov 1899, Bogdanov 1901).

Bogdanov not only was familiar with Mach's and Avenarius's main ideas, but also believed that he had found in their philosophy a foundation needed for preserving the objective and scientific character of Marxist political theory. In fact, he was indebted to empiriocriticism for many of his ideas and concepts. In his informative discussion of Bogdanov, David Rowley nicely summarized his approach as follows:

> Following the empiriocriticism of Ernst Mach, Bogdanov espoused a strict empiricism and denied the possibility of a priori knowledge of any sort at all. He explicitly rejected the notion of absolute truth, cause and effect, and absolute time or space—as well as absolute ethical value. Bogdanov defined reality in terms of experience: The real world is identical with human experience of it. (Rowley 1996, 5)

Although Bogdanov agreed with the main philosophical tenets of empiriocriticism pioneered by Mach and Avenarius, he thought that they were not able to overcome the dualism of the "dependent" and the "independent" series and to appropriately show the unity between the events that took place in the mind and those that took place in the external world. According to Bogdanov, Mach and Avenarius failed to develop a monistic explanation because they employed an approach from the point of view of the isolated individual rather than that of society as a whole (Bogdanov 2003, 14). Thus he proposed a philosophical system of Empiriomonism, which he elaborated in a series of articles published as a three-volume collection under that title which appeared between 1904 and 1906.

Lenin viewed Bogdanov as the most important representative of Russian Machism, and many of his critical philosophical arguments developed in *Materialism and Empiriocriticism* were directed against Bogdanov and his "empiriomonism." Some commentators present the clash between Lenin and Bogdanov as a minor theoretical debate within Russian émigré politics (see, for example, Pannekoek 2003). But this misconstrues the real motivation and goals of Lenin's work and underplays its significance. It is hard to believe that Lenin, who was busy with the intrinsically practical revolutionary task, would decide to devote almost the entire year of 1908 to refuting Bogdanov and other Russian Machists just in order to contribute to an inferior theoretical dispute. To Lenin, the appearance of Bogdanov's empiriomonism (and empiriocriticism in general) within the framework of Russian Marxism was as much a political as a philosophical event. The situation was not as easy to resolve as it might initially appear. Indeed, considered in the then current political and ideological context of the Russian Social-Democratic Party, which was split into two opposing factions (of Bolsheviks and Mensheviks),[14] the situation was highly paradoxical. The Bolshevik Lenin sharply argued against his comrade Bogdanov after openly declaring that, in the realm of philosophy, he was himself allied with Plekhanov, the acknowledged leader of the Menshevik fraction. Lenin writes: "It takes physical strength to keep oneself from being carried away by the mood, as Plekhanov does! His tactics are the height of ineptitude and baseness. In philosophy, however, he upholds the right cause. I am for materialism against 'empirio-' etc." He continues: "Can, and should, philosophy be linked with the trend of Party work? With Bolshevism? I think this should not be done at the present time. Let our Party philosophers put in some more work on theory for a while, let them dispute and [...] *seek a meeting of minds.* For the time being, I would stand for *such* philosophical disputes as those between materialists and 'empirios' being separated from integral Party work" (Lenin 1908, *LCW* 34: 381–382).

Why does Lenin declare that the boundary line in the realm of philosophy did not necessarily coincide with the boundary line in the realm of politics and that the differences in political views should not here stand in the way of the philosophical critique? Certainly, there was a very profound connection between his philosophical positions and his political views. This connection cannot simply be ignored, and Lenin had no doubt about it. He was fully aware of the entire complicated, confused context in which he was forced to enter the "philosophical brawl." But he believed that the "most urgent thing" in the existing circumstances was to fight against Bogdanov's Machism, even if to do so required cooperating with Plekhanov, Lenin's political opponent. He considers Bogdanov and other Russian Machists as being "misguided and dangerous," and not just because they threatened to hinder effective political action by redirecting attention to intellectual critique[15] nor because they might destroy Russian Social Democracy.[16] There were much deeper political and philosophical reasons that prompted Lenin to engage in this vital philosophical debate.

It is worth recalling that, at that time, Plekhanov was one of the few Marxists who sharply criticized philosophical revisionism of all kinds, basically focusing on Machism. He showed that Machism in general, and its Russian variety in particular, was nothing more than the subtly refurbished subjective idealism of Berkeley and Hume, disguised by a new name. Recognized as one of the leading Russian Marxist theoreticians in Russia and abroad, Plekhanov masterfully exposed the empty pretentions of Machism to represent the most modern scientific philosophy that was set to become the philosophy of the proletariat. But, since Bogdanov, Lunacharsky, and other Russian Machists, whom Plekhanov criticized, were affiliated with the Bolshevist faction, readers following the debate had an impression that the philosophy these thinkers energetically preached was the official theoretical credo of Bolshevism. And the Menshevik Plekhanov, of course, did not miss a chance to reinforce such an impression by portraying the Bolsheviks as revisionists, who had shifted away from the dialectical materialism of Marx and Engels and toward the controversial philosophy of Machism.[17] When Lenin joined the battle and sided with Plekhanov in the theoretical struggle with Bogdanov and other Russian Machists, he was far from accepting any political compromise. Instead, he was motivated by his understanding that further silence on the matter of Machist philosophy would only strengthen the Mensheviks' tactical line in the revolution. His important political and ideological goal was not only to reinstate authentic Marxist ideas and reject any kind of revisionism but also to clearly demonstrate that Bolshevism, and not the faction of Plekhanov, had its theoretical foundation in the philosophy of Marx and Engels and strongly adhered to Marxist ideas. The task was extremely difficult. It was necessary not only to thoroughly expose the essence of Bogdanov's (and of other Russian Machists') revisions of the philosophical views of Marx and Engels, but also to reestablish and clearly explain the "true" Marxist position in philosophy. This is what Lenin effectively accomplishes in *Materialism and Empiriocriticism*, delving into intricate philosophical questions and problems.

It is worth emphasizing that despite Lenin's active participation in politics, his critique of Russian Machism was driven not only, and certainly not exclusively, by political or ideological considerations. Though this point is often contested, in fact Lenin's objections to Bogdanov and empiriocriticism in

252   M. F. BYKOVA

general have an important philosophical ground that is often overlooked. He was largely concerned with Bogdanov's epistemological presuppositions, such as his radical empiricism and idealism and the implications these tendencies must have both for political activity and for Marxism, especially for understanding history, the external world, and the justification of objective truth claims. Lenin was aware that "If truth is [just] a form of human experience, there can be no truth independent of humanity; there can be no objective truth" (*LCW* 14: 123). Furthermore, by his denial of an independently existing material world, which can ultimately explain the contents of human consciousness and the objective logic behind the development of history, Bogdanov was close to accepting the pre-Marxist belief that history was determined not by objective social laws, but rather by the random actions of individual agents caused by their subjective moral volitions. For Lenin this view appeared to be only one step away from the traditional religious worldview that declared God to be the one supreme agent of the world, who not only determined the purpose and the end of history but also "*produced* nature" (*LCW* 14: 229).

Thus, Lenin saw his goal in *Materialism and Empiriocriticism* as exposing Bogdanov's (and Machism's) "dangerous theoretical mistakes" through an exposition of their implications for revolutionary theory and practice. He equated Machism with idealism and fideism and rejected both as incompatible with the scientific and political character of Marxism. He warned that "behind the epistemological scholasticism of empiriocriticism one must not fail to see the struggle of parties in philosophy, a struggle which in the last analysis reflects the tendencies and ideologies of the antagonistic classes in modern society" (*LCW* 14: 358). The parties in philosophy to which Lenin referred were philosophical materialism and philosophical idealism. He further had in mind the ideological struggle between the two concerning the question of the independently existing material world and the primacy of matter. Lenin's work was the defense of philosophical materialism over philosophical idealism, of the objectivity of the world over its explanation based on individual subjective experience, of supremacy of matter over any idealistic and fideistic approach to reality. Whatever the political motives of Lenin's assault on empiriocriticism, it can hardly be dismissed as a purely political (intra-party) dispute. It illustrated the essential connections which Lenin saw between theory and practice and which were vital for political activity, but also, to an even larger extent, it illuminated the problems confronting any form of Marxist philosophy at the beginning of the twentieth century. For Lenin, the idealism of Mach and his Russian followers was not compatible with Marxist philosophy. Likewise, he realized that the vulgar (mechanistic) materialism that arose out of positivism was also unable to deliver the desired result. It follows that any new attempt at a Marxist philosophy that could adequately justify political praxis would require a complete break with the entire philosophical heritage of positivism, for which idealism and mechanistic materialism appeared as the only possible philosophical options. This radically different philosophical position was eventually named dialectical materialism, which Lenin reinstated and advanced in *Materialism and Empiriocriticism*.

Some commentators claim that in this work Lenin was still far from being able to argue for a dialectical materialist position and that both the author's arguments and the author's own views were indistinguishable from those of the early materialists, who did not employ dialectics (see Copleston 1986; Pannekoek 2003; Anderson 1995; and several of the contributions in Budgen et al. 2007, esp. 101–119, 120–147). The same commentators point to the *Philosophical Notebooks* as the first place in his writings where Lenin introduced the methodology of dialectical materialism. They insist on Lenin's inability to discuss dialectics in his early years, simply because he was not familiar with it at that point and his first exposure to dialectics supposedly only came in 1912 when he started reading Hegel's *Science of Logic*. On this view, there is an essential "gap" between the two works that indicates the philosophical deficiency of *Materialism and Empiriocriticism* and its inability to deliver on what was promised, since its extent was limited to only presenting the fundamentals of materialism in general, and not Marxist materialism or dialectics. This reading is not only erroneous but also inconsistent with Lenin's own philosophical development as well as with ideas he put forward in his writings. It is worth recalling that according to the memoirs of Nadezhda K. Krupskaia, Lenin studied the classics of world philosophy, including Hegel's writings, specifically the *Phenomenology of Spirit*, which he studied while in exile in Shushenskoe from 1897 to 1900. Those who are familiar with Hegel's *Phenomenology* would agree that the essence of Hegelian dialectics comes through in this text much more clearly, vividly, and concretely than in the *Science of Logic*, which requires special philosophical training to be read. Thus, it seems plausible to claim that Lenin was perfectly well acquainted with the Hegelian dialectics and had a good grasp of it much earlier than when writing the conspectus, now known under the title *Philosophical Notebooks*. In the *Notebooks*, he turned to a special, more critical, investigation of Hegelian dialectics based on his study of other Hegelian texts, including not only the *Science of Logic* but also the *Lectures on the History of Philosophy* and the *Lectures on the Philosophy of History*. Yet, as a mature Marxist, Lenin had read these and other texts by Hegel much earlier, long before he was ready to perform a critical analysis of them, the results of which are found in the *Notebooks*. In this sense, I agree with Evald V. Ilyenkov, who argued that there is a clear continuity between *Materialism and Empiriocriticism* and the *Notebooks* in terms of Lenin's understanding of philosophy.[18] While in his earlier work Lenin formulated the *fundamentals* of dialectical materialism, introducing issues central to his understanding of dialectics, which had already been developed, in his later work he further sharpened and refined the details relevant to dialectics, which benefited from a more Hegelian treatment.

But all this time, the single philosophy that Lenin took to be true and authentic was Marxist philosophy, which he equated with dialectical materialism and nothing else. Not simply materialism and not simply dialectics, but only materialism understood dialectically. This organic unity of both was what gave man, understood generally, the necessary means to grasp the external world and to explain the objective tendencies and lawful nature of the development of this world. All other kinds of materialism were for Lenin unable to perform this task and remained merely a wishful desire. Similarly, dialectics without materialism turned into a purely verbal art that often had nothing to do with the real world and its proceeding. In May 1908, in "Ten Questions to a Lecturer," Lenin sought a "straight" answer from Bogdanov: "Does the lecturer acknowledge that the philosophy of Marxism is *dialectical materialism*?" (*LCW* 14: 15). He empathetically stressed the last two words that contained the key to his own understanding of philosophy and also clearly showed where his disagreement with Bogdanov lay. Lenin consistently developed this position in his book, whose significance was not exhausted by the fact that it defeated "one reactionary philosophy" and put an end to its false pretensions to be "the only scientific philosophy" and serve as the philosophy of "all contemporary science." Much more important was that by debating Bogdanov and other Russian (and non-Russian) Machists, Lenin masterfully outlined his own understanding of the problems that philosophy faced in his time in the light of the new economic and political situations as well as of scientific and technological advances that the world endured. He also proposed various solutions to these problems, some of which proved to be successful.

Thus, in his work, Lenin employs two—negative (critical) and positive (constructive)—approaches which generally coincide with the book's two main aims: first, he criticizes and rejects both empiriocriticism (of Bogdanov and his like-minded forerunners) and vulgar materialism (of Vogt, Haeckel, and, ultimately, Dietzgen as well). Yet the temper of his criticism differs from his fierce attack upon Machism, leading to a relatively more gentle treatment of materialists. Second, he argues for dialectical materialism, thus offering a positive philosophical program, which he further explicates and defends against both idealistic and vulgar materialistic philosophical positions. In Lenin's work, both critical and constructive approaches were essentially intertwined, so it is often difficult to separate one from another. This is, in fact, what distinguishes this work from any other. It is not only polemical, but a positive philosophical program was introduced as a result of the necessary conclusion of the criticism and rejection of existing philosophical positions. Instead of starting with the argument for dialectical materialism, Lenin first showed the philosophical limitations and eventual failure of the self-proclaimed philosophical scientists to come up with a philosophical theory suitable for Marxism's theoretical and practical purposes. Lenin applies this methodology throughout the work. If anything, this pointed to Lenin's serious concern with the philosophical crises within Marxism that potentially contained dangerous consequences for Marxist theory and practice. It was this philosophical impasse that Lenin had to confront and that is depicted in *Materialism and Empiriocriticism*. There is no doubt that Lenin's criticism and ultimate dismissal of the philosophical ideas of his opponents required not only perseverance but also philosophical erudition, awareness of the intellectual situation, mastery of philosophical argumentation, and discernment.[19]

IV

Let us now take a closer look at Lenin's "positive program" and discuss some of his key philosophical ideas formulated in *Materialism and Empiriocriticism*. I will focus only on one main feature of Lenin's work: his understanding of materialism. Certainly, this analysis cannot offer an exhaustive discussion of the philosophical ideas Lenin introduced in this book. Yet I believe that the conception under consideration can effectively illustrate philosophical innovations Lenin offered in the book. For it provided a significant philosophical response to and advancement beyond the positivist philosophical systems Lenin criticized, and as such it was a valuable contribution to Marxist philosophy. This should be sufficient to distinguish Lenin from his philosophical predecessors and to demonstrate the philosophical significance of his ideas.

Lenin's understanding of materialism seems to create a problem for commentators. As I mentioned earlier, many observers are disappointed with Lenin's notion of materialism, equating it with naïve materialism, realism, or even believing that

> what we find in *Materialism and Empirio-criticism* is nothing more than a repetition of the biological materialism which Büchner, Moleschott, and others put forward without success half a century earlier, in which it was simply assumed that a physical account of brain processes can be substituted for the concept of the mental without difficulty or remainder. (Pannekoek 2003, 50)

But even those who take the philosophical content of Lenin's materialism seriously still view it as a purely epistemological notion that he used to address a narrow circle of problems that emerged as a result of his polemic with one of the minor schools of subjective idealism. Indeed, what was this materialism Lenin so fiercely and firmly defended in his book?

First, it needs to be made clear that Lenin's materialism, at least as presented in *Materialism and Empiriocriticism*, should not be associated with any kind of reductive materialism of mind (or consciousness). Lenin's interest in materialism in this work was not defined by the traditional mind–body problem or by psychological issues of any kind. Instead, he developed his understanding of materialism in response to idealist and skeptical views about the external world. The strong tendency toward skepticism and idealism was typical of the empiricist tradition, which dominated modern science and prevailed in Machism. Lenin clearly recognized this in his views on Bogdanov and other supporters of Empiriocriticism. Second, Lenin's account of materialism was not associated exclusively with epistemology, and its philosophical significance is not limited to the bounds of a special argument against a specific form of subjective idealism. In fact, having moved beyond the epistemology of the positivist tradition,

Lenin also broke with its understanding of materialism. Contrary to philosophers of previous generations, he did this not by choosing between epistemology and ontology, but rather by attempting to unite them in a new theory that went by the name of dialectical materialism.

Following Engels, Lenin held that all philosophical positions were ultimately either materialist or idealist. Lenin wrote:

> in connection with every problem of epistemology touched upon and in connection with every philosophical question raised by the new physics, we traced the struggle between *materialism* and *idealism*. Behind the mass of new terminological artifices, behind the clutter of erudite scholasticism, we invariably discerned *two* principal alignments, two fundamental trends in the solution of philosophical problems. (*LCW* 14: 335)

The two camps were divided based on their accounts of the reality of the external world, its independence from the thinking subject, and the degree to which knowledge of it was possible. There was no third option, be that either "agnosticism" or "empiriocriticism." All other possibilities were said to collapse into idealism. Lenin's tactic was thus to demonstrate Empiriocriticism's commitment to idealism and to commend the materialist case against it. Yet, Lenin conceived materialism not just as a purely epistemological formula (even though epistemological questions become an integral part of his account of materialism), but as a fundamentally ontological view. His materialism was committed to the strong thesis that matter (the physical) is "primary" with respect to consciousness (the psychical, mental). Furthermore, he declared that the question of the primacy of matter was "the root question" which divided philosophers into materialists and idealists.[20] Lenin's materialism was a form of ontology that claimed that in the first instance the external world was just matter in motion, that is, matter that undergoes constant change. Consciousness was then nothing else but a property of highly developed matter, a function of the brain (see *LCW* 14: 42–57, 14: 351). The content of consciousness was determined through a variety of interactions of the subject with the external world, which existed independently of our experience of it. Idealism, on the other hand, claimed that what was primary was our mental process, our mind, and our thoughts. What was perceived and behaved ordinarily was not an entity in itself, but was created in or by the mind. This was the view that, according to Lenin, emerged in Bogdanov's theory of Empiriocriticism.

Bogdanov attempted to rebut this charge of idealism. For him, "materialism" and "idealism" were just terms that described the old-fashioned dualism of the psychical (mental) and the physical that Empiriocriticism successfully overcame. While idealists were supposed to believe that reality was fundamentally mental or ideal, according to Mach the basic constituents of reality were the "elements" that were given to us in experience. We may refer to some of these elements as "physical" and to others as "mental." This, however, was not a difference in the substance of the elements, but rather a difference in the organization of our perception of them. Bogdanov further clarified how to differentiate between the two. For him the distinction between the mental and the physical was the distinction between individually and socially organized experiences. The mental and the physical were thus not two basic realms of being, but merely the same "elements" under different descriptions. Bogdanov denied that experience was either mental or physical. For him the mental–physical distinction was drawn within experience itself, and only for "technical" purposes. Yet, he did not say anything about the ontological status of experience that in his system became the substance of the world. Moreover, Bogdanov's view of socially organized ("collective") experience was consistent with methodological solipsism. What he understood by collective experience had nothing to do with social or intersubjective experience, as the term may suggest. What was under consideration here was still individual, but shared experience. In addition, Bogdanov appealed to collective experience only in order to explain how, on the basis of individual experience alone, the subject could acquire the concept of objectivity. The answer that he provided was that each subject determined objectivity by appealing to his own experiences of the behavior of others. No doubt, this answer would be (and in fact was [see Russell 2009]) endorsed by many methodological solipsists.

Lenin thus rightly accused Bogdanov of idealism and solipsism. The problem, however, was that he did not go further. Although he effectively showed the idealist essence of Empiriocriticism (including Bogdanov's version of it), he did not convincingly refute it. Even though he offered an account of why Empiriocriticism's idealism was dangerous by pointing to its two disastrous philosophical consequences (it inevitably collapsed into solipsism and eventually led to conceptual relativism) (*LCW* 14: 78–87, 14: 94–97, 14: 134–138, 14: 308–312), the arguments he provided came rather to be of a combative nature, and thus are not conclusive. I do not want to speculate about Lenin's tactical aims here, including whether he was indeed ready to settle "for the weathering effect of incessant criticism in lieu of one solid blow."[21] What, however, should be taken into consideration is the fact that for Lenin the critique of idealism was rather a secondary element of the overall strategy employed in the book. He saw his main goal as reinstating and promoting Marxist materialism, from which he said, "you cannot eliminate one basic premise, one essential part, without departing from objective truth, without falling prey to bourgeois-reactionary falsehood" (*LCW* 14: 326). And he effectively illustrated this idea with his demonstration of how Bogdanov's Empiriocriticism eventually collapses into idealism, thus encroaching on the philosophical foundation of Marxism, specifically on its materialism. This explains why Lenin so vigorously defended materialism.

Let us now return to our original question about Lenin's understanding of materialism. There is one more important issue here that needs clarification. As I mentioned earlier, some commentators equate Lenin's materialism with philosophical realism.[22] How justified is this belief and to what extent does it correctly describe the form of materialism that Lenin proclaimed? Although there are many different forms that realism can take, philosophical realism in general is the belief that there exists an external, objective world that is ontologically independent of thinking subjects. If we accept this definition of realism, then it should be clear that all materialists are realists. This, however, does not mean that the reciprocal statement "all realists are materialists" is true as well. A simple glance at the history of philosophy is enough to see this point. Plato, for example, was a realist. However, he was not a realist because he advocated that only material beings exist, but because he advocated the existence of entities such as the forms and numbers. Similarly, many scholastics were realists not because they advocated that only material beings are real, but because they advocated the thesis that universals are *real*. The same is true of mathematicians. Many of them describe themselves as realists, but not because they advocate that only material beings exist, but because they advocate the thesis that mathematical entities, which are ideal, are real. The point that I am trying to make here is that realism tends to be a much broader position than materialism. While the materialist holds that the world is material and objective reality comprises *only* material beings (since *only* material beings *are*), the realist accepts that a wide variety of different types of entities are equally real. It is thus doubtful that Lenin's position can be equated with realism. Furthermore, Lenin himself was very explicit about his distrust of "realism." He wrote: "Following Engels, I use *only* the term materialism [...] and consider it the sole correct terminology, especially since the term 'realism' has been bedraggled by the positivists and other muddleheads who oscillate between materialism and idealism" (*LCW* 14: 60). And this was for him not just a terminological issue. He insisted that what the philosophy of materialism taught was that "the world is matter in motion, that the external world, the physical world familiar to all, is the sole objective reality" (*LCW* 14: 220; see also 14: 169).

Lenin held that human beings come to know reality through sense perception. The thinking subject was able to build up a conception of the world based on the senses or more exactly on the material of perception as a result of a subject's sense experience. However, his *materialist* position was not just an acknowledgment of "the existence of an external world and its recognizability in our sensations."[23] For him as a materialist, the matter—the objective reality given to us in sensations—was the foundation of the theory of knowledge (epistemology). On the contrary, for idealism of any kind, the basis of epistemology was consciousness that appeared under one or another name, be it the "psychical" or the "system of forms of collectively organized experience." It was also not true that the world was recognized in our sensations. In sensations the external world was only *given* to us, in the same way as it was given to a dog or any other living creature. It was recognized not in sensations, but in the activity of thought, the science of which was, according to Lenin, the materialistic theory of knowledge (epistemology) understood dialectically, as dialectical logic.

A discussion of Marxist dialectical logic is beyond the scope of this chapter. Furthermore, it would be difficult, if not indeed impossible, to offer a more insightful discussion of this topic than was provided by the twentieth-century Russian-Soviet Marxist Evald V. Ilyenkov.[24] I would only like to emphasize that dialectical logic and its application in *Materialism and Empiriocriticism* is where the dialectical essence of Lenin's materialism lies. Contrary to Mach, Bogdanov, and other Empiriocriticists, for whom logic was just a collection of "devices," "methods," and "rules" that regulated our thinking, Lenin, following Marx and Engels, conceived logic as the philosophical theory of cognition. It described the (universal) laws which govern the objective processes of how man (as mankind) was gaining knowledge of the world. These laws were not randomly chosen principles or rules of cognition. They were rather understood as the objective laws of development of the material world, of objective reality itself. These laws were reflected in our consciousness, leading to the building up of conceptions and theories that were portraits, models of the external. It was fundamental to Lenin's position that human beings were capable of constructing theories that adequately reflect the way things are. The adequacy of a concept or theory was verified by practice, which was understood as a social and historical event. This was the on-going practice of mankind that continued through generations of people and through centuries of their joint activity.

It should be clear that Lenin's materialism was not of the same kind as the naïve materialism of previous philosophers. Nor did he just uphold mechanistic materialism. Instead, he defended the position of the materialist dialectics. This was dialectics as the logic and theory of knowledge of contemporary materialism, that is, dialectical materialism, the true legacy of Marxist philosophy.

The materialist epistemology that Lenin developed in *Materialism and Empiriocriticism* also warrants special attention. This epistemology was known as the reflection (often called "copy") theory of knowledge that had been subject to extensive criticism. According to Lenin, the material world was a knowable reality, and we, thinking subjects, were able to form conceptions and theories that reflected reality. The adequacy of our conceptions and theories depended upon the degree to which they resembled, or corresponded to, how things really are. The closer our conceptions resemble the world, the more adequate they are. A true conception is said to be one that corresponds to the world. Thus, we can think of our theories as a series of attempts to "copy" reality. Lenin explained: "The recognition of theory as a copy, as an approximate copy of objective reality, is materialism" (*LCW* 14: 265). Lenin saw his "copy" theory of reflection[25] as the necessary epistemological counterpart of any materialism. Furthermore, he believed that this was the only way out of the idealism and agnosticism of his opponents, among whom he identified not only the Russian Machists but also such philosophers as Berkeley, Hume, and Kant. The similarity that Lenin saw in the representatives of both parties was that all of them adopted an empiricist epistemology, which inevitably led to idealism and agnosticism. The problem that Lenin correctly saw in empiricism was that it understood our knowledge of the world as being constructed out of a collection of sense-data immediately presented to consciousness. Our access to the world was then eternally mediated by the screen of sensations that like a "wall" separated human consciousness from the external world (see *LCW* 14: 51). Many skeptical problems about the existence and nature of the world that preoccupied philosophy in the eighteenth and nineteenth centuries as well as the idealism which penetrated skepticism had their roots in this empiricist belief. Lenin made it clear at the beginning of *Materialism and Empiriocriticism* that the theories of Russian Machists were nothing but a repetition of the same empiricist-idealist mistakes that Berkeley had made two centuries ago. Lenin wrote:

> Berkeley denies [...] the theory of knowledge, which seriously and resolutely takes as the foundation of all its reasoning the recognition of the external world and the reflection thereof in the minds of men. [...] In our further exposition we shall frequently find "recent" "positivists" repeating the same stratagem or counterfeit in a different form and in a different verbal wrapping. (*LCW* 14: 29)

Lenin's attack on empiricism was not just a polemical device used in the book. It was rather an indication of his philosophical judgment about the serious failures of the empiricists' epistemology, both in its classic and contemporary forms. This was why, for him, the reflection theory of knowledge became a sort of materialist epistemological test. He saw the reflection theory of knowledge as a benchmark for Marxist philosophy. Thus, he criticized Plekhanov's theory of knowledge, according to which our ideas were just "symbols" or "hieroglyphs" of the external world. Lenin charged him with not being truthful to Marxism and instead providing support for the empiriocritical position: "our Machist would-be Marxists fastened with glee on Plekhanov's 'hieroglyphs,' that is, on the theory that man's sensations and ideas are not copies of real things and processes of nature, not their images, but conventional signs, symbols, hieroglyphs, and so on" (*LCW* 14: 232). Lenin stated his materialist position about knowledge very clearly. He insisted that our knowledge was in fact a "reflection" or "copy" (sometimes he also uses the term "photograph") of the external world. There existed "the direct connection between consciousness and the external world," and our sensation that empiricists turned into an insuperable barrier between human consciousness and the external world was in fact "only *an image* of the external world" (*LCW* 14: 51, 14: 69). Not only did Lenin find a firm support for this epistemological theory in Engels, who in his works spoke of "mental pictures or images" of things that he traced back to sensations. Furthermore, he maintained that this materialist view of knowledge was consistent with the commonsense assumption of "naïve realism" of an independently existing world that could be known by the mind. He says that "materialism deliberately makes the 'naïve' belief of mankind the foundation of its theory of knowledge" (*LCW* 14: 69–70) and sees in this fact a sort of plausible justification for his reflection theory of knowledge. It is doubtful, however, that this provides a sufficient philosophical explanation, especially since he does not present any detailed discussion of how mental images reflect or reproduce physical objects. Instead, by referring in this context to "naïve realism," he drew his opponents' fire upon himself. Not only was it understood by many critics as his explicit equation of materialism and realism, but it also allowed them to talk about his epistemology as a version of "naïve realism."[26] Ironically, Lenin himself employed the expression "naïve realism" here not as a term of abuse, but as the recognition of a commonsense understanding that, in his opinion, would not require any further explanation. To be sure, the accusation that his philosophy was naïve realism is not completely groundless. The terminology he used to articulate his reflection theory of knowledge was too vague and not very precise. Consider how he talked about our sensations: he claimed that consciousness consists of "copies," "photos," or even "mirror-reflections" of the objective things. Taken literally it did not make any sense, or at least it indeed sounded *very* naïve to believe that my consciousness, which was a product of the psychological activity of my mind, could be a "copy" of the physical thing. As a result, Lenin's copy theory of reflection is often dismissed as "amateurish" and "pre-critical." Furthermore, the fact that Lenin himself failed to raise or answer traditional objections to "naïve realism" did not help his cause either. Yet, the most extensive criticism of Lenin's epistemology was voiced by the Logical Positivism that dominated the Anglo-American philosophical tradition throughout almost the entire twentieth century. It should not come as a surprise, for the empiricist problematics were and still remain central within this tradition. Interestingly, in the Russia of the late Soviet and post-Soviet period, there also emerged a number of critical epistemological studies[27] of Lenin's reflection theory. However, it would be difficult to point to any publication that offers a complete and sophisticated analysis of Lenin's thought. Since I cannot comment here on Lenin's reflection theory in detail, I would like to mention only a few points that are important for our overall discussion of Lenin's materialism.

In my opinion, in considering Lenin's epistemological theory it is important to take into consideration his overall goal in *Materialism and Empiriocriticism* and the specific role that his reflection theory of knowledge plays. It seems to be clear that for Lenin epistemology is not an end in itself and that he employs his reflection theory of knowledge only in order to defend materialism against idealism and agnosticism (which he also eventually links to idealism). Accordingly, Lenin immediately rejects the empiricist view that our knowledge is "of discrete *sensibilia* capable of a variety of different combinations" whose connections are governed by an arbitrary principle determined by some external factors (e.g., science for Mach and ideology for Bogdanov). Lenin's reflection theory offers, on the contrary, a coherent argument for cognition. He maintains that our knowledge is not an approximate construction of ideas out of raw sense-data, but rather knowledge of real objects that exist in nature, which reflects real connections between them. Instead of being drawn into debates about some particular characteristics of specific theories of knowledge, he focuses on "the really important epistemological question that divides the philosophical trends." For him the central question is whether what we know reflects the world as it is, whether our ideas correspond to real features of the external world, or whether our mind is the single source of our knowledge and we just impose our ideas upon the world (see *LCW* 14: 159). It should be abundantly clear that Lenin's most fundamental concern in epistemology is and remains the defense of materialism. His goal in using the "copy" theory is to advance a materialistic theory of knowledge and to remove any ground for raising idealistic, agnostic, and also skeptical objections against knowledge. He argues that while "an image can never wholly compare with the model, [...] [t]he image inevitably and of necessity implies the objective reality of that which it 'images.'" In contrast, the "'[c]onventional sign,' symbol, hieroglyph" or any other notions used to describe sense-data "are concepts which introduce an entirely unnecessary element of agnosticism" (*LCW* 14:235). It is worth emphasizing that Lenin never claims that the reflection theory guarantees the indubitability of knowledge and that our ideas and concepts are immune from error or imprecision. We differentiate between true and false ideas by testing our ideas in our practical activity. Thus, practice is a criterion of truth.

Although he argues for the correspondence theory of truth, this does not mean that the concepts and theories that we have about the world cannot be false. It is rather the case that the falsity of a concept is determined only by its relation to the world and whether it accurately describes (i.e., corresponds with) that world. Furthermore, the correspondence of the concept with the objects of the real world does not mean the identity between the two. In the passage cited above, Lenin openly states that it is "beyond doubt that an image can never wholly compare with the model" (*LCW* 14: 235). In other words, when he sometimes uses confusing terms such as "copy," "photograph," and "image," he communicates the idea that our knowledge is real knowledge of the material world, a reflection of objective reality. There is another important connotation, not often recognized by commentators. This is Lenin's attempt to reconcile a materialist theory of knowledge with a purely materialist ontology. In fact, by saying that an image is a "copy" of the real world, Lenin also states that the mind "reflects" reality. Thus reality, the material world, is primary with respect to consciousness. The obvious commitment to materialism in the text seems to rule out certain misconceptions concerning Lenin's theory of knowledge. I should, however, recognize that even then there still remains a whole host of problems that would require further clarification.[28] Unfortunately, Lenin himself does not provide any guidance on which path to follow. Still, I think the existence of an important philosophical connection between Lenin's reflection theory of knowledge and his commitment to a strict materialistic ontology may provide some help in this regard.

Lenin insists that his materialism is philosophical in its character. Responding to the revolution which occurred in modern physics around the turn of the century and to the challenge it posed to traditional materialism, he separates out the most important conceptual features of matter, retaining only the philosophical content and leaving other more specific features to science. Accordingly, questions of the structure of matter and of the explanation of non-perceived physical entities such as electrons should not be answered by philosophy; they belong to the domain of science. Lenin's materialism is not committed to any substantive account of the nature of matter. He is adamant that the ever-developing story of the structure of matter is the province of natural science, and not of philosophy. Philosophical materialism is committed only to one single property of matter, which is the property of being an objective reality that exists outside of the mind (see *LCW* 14: 260–261). He states: "Matter is a philosophical category denoting the objective reality which is given to man by his sensations, and which is copied, photographed, and reflected by our sensations, while existing independently of them" (*LCW* 14: 130).

From a philosophical perspective this account of materialism seems to be conclusive. Furthermore, Lenin correctly identifies the need for philosophy to properly distinguish between the philosophical function of materialism and its scientific role. Whereas materialism as a philosophical thesis is a commitment to an external world that exists independent of thinking subjects, the scientific role of materialism consists in providing a particular explanatory framework for natural phenomena. Nobody made this distinction prior to Lenin, and it was hardly obvious before his critical analysis of Russian Machism in *Materialism and Empiriocriticism*. Yet Lenin's version of materialism is not without its problems. The most serious one is that if materialism as a philosophical thesis is completely separated from and fully independent of any scientific question about the structure of matter, then it is not clear what role Lenin's materialism can play in everyday scientific practice. Lenin himself proclaimed the union of philosophy and natural science, entrusting philosophy with a function to verify and correct errors in our scientific knowledge. It remains unclear, however, how his materialism can offer this sort of corrective if it has no immediate access to the results of the proposed scientific inquiry. The relation and the principles of interaction between a philosophical and a scientific materialism would require a more detailed explanation, which Lenin does not provide.

Despite these theoretical shortcomings, Lenin's version of materialism is a clear advance over the versions developed by his predecessors, even in the absence of explicit answers to the problems mentioned above.

CONCLUSION

One of my central aims in this chapter was to put Lenin's work in the historical context in which it was written. I believe that it may be possible to adequately understand a theoretical work only if it is read and evaluated from the perspective of the political and social situation to which it responds. When we consider the historical epoch after the first Russian Revolution of 1905, including the political and ideological struggles of the period, Lenin's decision to turn to philosophical questions appears in a different light than the simple intellectual exercise of a philosophical amateur. Lenin's *Materialism and Empiriocriticism*, which was written at the end of a half-century reign of positivism that captivated the most brilliant minds of his time, both in science and philosophy, is a significant philosophical achievement. It was the first philosophical assault on positivism from the position of (dialectical) materialism.

Not only does Lenin see the dangerous consequences of positivism for philosophical inquiry, but he also realizes the damaging effects of the positivistic position for Marxism and Marxist philosophy. In this way, he responds to the crisis of Marxism that emerged at the beginning of the twentieth century and that he sees in Russian Marxism and Empiriocriticism. His answer to the challenge is his defense of the consistent materialist position that he advances in *Materialism and Empiriocriticism*. Despite its problems and combative style, which often stands in the way of the impartial evaluation of the book by distracting attention from its philosophical argument, the book's ability to identify and, to some extent, overcome problems of previous philosophy is a significant theoretical result which secures it an important place in the history of philosophy.

NOTES

1. The official party name was the Russian Communist Party (of Bolsheviks) (RCP[b]), and it was not until 1952 that the party formally dropped the word "Bolsheviks" from its name.
2. It is worth mentioning that the main focus of the article is more general, namely, the discussion of the importance of philosophy for social practice and of the necessity of applications of the philosophical theory to practical problems relevant to building socialism. The authors praised Stalin for showing an example of "deepened understanding of Marxist-Leninist dialectics" and for his fight against deviation from Marxism on both fronts—Left and Right. One such "deviation" was Deborin and his confederates. Although the authors do not openly attack the Deborinists, the article treats them as the real enemy on the philosophical front, those who "undervalue Lenin as a philosopher."
3. Originally published as a journal editorial article in *Pod znamenem marksizma* ([Editorial] 1930) and later reprinted in *Pravda* (26 January 1931).
4. For more details about this period, see Bakhurst 1991, 92–99.
5. See Yakhot 1981, 196–220. David Bakhurst makes this point as well in Bakhurst 1991, 94–96.
6. The full title of Lenin's book is *Materialism and Empiriocriticism. Critical Comments on a Reactionary Philosophy*. It was written in the period from February to October 1908 (with the Supplement to Chapter IV, Section I in March 1909) and published in Moscow in May 1909 by the Zveno Publishers. See Lenin 1909, *LCW* 14: 17–362 (all further references to this book are given to *LCW* 14).
7. *Philosophical Notebooks* consist of a set of notes and book summaries along with Lenin's own critical remarks and evaluations. The work comprises the content of ten notebooks, eight of which (those produced in 1914–1915) were entitled by Lenin himself *Notebooks on Philosophy*. The material in *Philosophical Notebooks* does not constitute a complete work written by Lenin for publication. First published in 1929–1930 as a part of *Lenin Miscellanies IX and XII*, these philosophical writings were only in 1933 organized in a separate book under the title

of *Philosophical Notebooks*, under which the content of the volume is known today. See Lenin 1933, *LCW* 38 (all further references to this book are given to *LCW* 38).

8. The book *The State and Revolution: The Marxist Theory of the State and the Task of the Proletariat in the Revolution* was written in August–September 1917 and first published in 1918. See Lenin 1918, *LCW* 25: 381–492 (all further references to this book are given to *LCW* 25).

9. First published in *Pod Znamenem Marksizma*, 1922, no. 3. See Lenin 1922, *LCW* 33: 227–236 (all further references to this essay are given to *LCW* 33).

10. This chapter was partially influenced by Althusser's *Lenin and Philosophy* (see Althusser 2001). While the conclusions that Althusser draws in this study are substantially different from the ideas I am arguing for in my chapter, I believe that Althusser's approach to Lenin and his philosophical legacy is very productive.

11. A major influence on Lenin was the correspondence between Marx and Engels published in 1913 (see Bebel and Bernstein 1913). Not only did Lenin attentively read the correspondence, providing a series of conceptual annotations and notes on it (see Lenin 1959). In his philosophical studies of 1913 and beyond, he turned to authors mentioned in the correspondence, using it as a kind of "reading guide" and commenting on some of Marx's and Engels's ideas formulated there. On the role of the *Briefwechsel* in Lenin's philosophical evolution, see White 2015, especially 133–137.

12. For a full discussion of the development and influence of positivism in nineteenth-century Europe, see Simon 1963.

13. By that time, Plekhanov had already established himself as the leading Russian Marxist theoretician.

14. A dispute in the Russian Social-Democratic Labour Party (RSDLP) in 1994 between Vladimir Lenin and Julius Martov led to the party splitting into two factions: the Bolsheviks and the Mensheviks.

15. In fact, this was the tendency among the Young Hegelians that Marx and Engels had attacked in *The German Ideology* some sixty years earlier. Lenin was certainly concerned about it as well. However, it was not his chief motivation to respond to Bogdanov and his followers in *Materialism and Empiriocriticism*.

16. This is the justification offered by Copleston 1986, 292.

17. Plekhanov accused the Bolsheviks of revisionism as early as the Third Party Congress in April 1905, and he openly repeated the charge at the Fifth Party Congress that took place two years later. For Lenin it was a signal for action. He must have feared, and not without reason, that the entire Bolshevism would be seen as a revisionism that renounced Marxist ideas.

18. Ilyenkov formulated this position in his 1979 work, which was translated into English and published in an English version in 1982. See Ilyenkov 1983. A similar position is expressed in Bakhurst 1991, 100.

19. It was Louis Althusser who praised Lenin for having good judgment. In his famous essay "Lenin and Philosophy," he empathetically writes: "And Lenin denounces and knocks down all those ephemerally philosophical scientists who thought their time had come. What is left of these characters today? Who still remembers them? We must concede at least that this philosophical ignoramus Lenin had good judgment. And what professional philosopher was capable, as he was, of committing himself without hesitation or delay, so far and so surely,

absolutely alone, against everyone, in an apparently lost cause?" (Althusser 2001, 29).

20. Cf. *LCW* 14: 335–336: "Whether nature, matter, the physical, the external world should be taken as primary, and consciousness, mind, sensation (experience—as the *widespread* terminology of our time has it), the psychical, etc., should be regarded as secondary—that is the root question which in *fact* continues to divide the philosophers into *two great camps.*"

21. This is the approach that David Bakhurst suggests taking. See Bakhurst 1991, 108.

22. One of them is Bakhurst, who explicitly states that "Lenin's materialism is a form of philosophical realism" (Bakhurst 1991, 108). He recognizes that "Lenin himself rejects the term "realism," but still prefers "to keep the term in play" (ibid., 108n8). See also Pannekoek 2003, 51.

23. This is how Mikhail Bulgakov introduces Lenin's position in his review of *Materialism and Empiriocriticism* published as Bulgakov 1909.

24. Ilyenkov 1977. An English trans. by H. Campbell Creighton is available at: https://www.marxists.org/archive/ilyenkov/works/essays/ See also: Ilyenkov 1983.

25. While Lenin's "copy" theory may sound like the traditional correspondence theory of knowledge, there are a number of essential differences between the two. One of the most important is that Lenin focused on the nature of knowledge in a general sense and not truth per se.

26. In fact, one of the first who accused Lenin of naïve realism was Lyubov Axelrod, an admiring pupil of Plekhanov and a fellow Menshevik. She argued that Lenin espoused not materialism but "naïve realism," which identifies objects and our perceptions of them, and is fundamentally akin to Machism. For more contemporary examples, see Joravsky 2009, especially 17–23; Jordan 1963, 35ff.

27. See, for example, Lektorsky 1990 and 2010; Kuvakin 1990.

28. Some of these issues are mentioned and discussed by David Bakhurst, who devotes a special section in his study to ambiguity in Lenin's materialism. See Bakhurst 1991, 111–123.

Bibliography

Althusser, Louis. 2001. *Lenin and Philosophy and Other Essays.* Trans. Ben Browster. New York, NY: Monthly Review Press. [Originally published: New York: Monthly Review Press, 1971].

Anderson, Kevin. 1995. *Lenin, Hegel, and Western Marxism: A Critical Study.* Urbana, IL: University of Illinois Press.

Bakhurst, David. 1991. *Consciousness and Revolution in Soviet Philosophy: From the Bolsheviks to Evald Ilyenkov.* Cambridge, UK and New York, NY: Cambridge University Press.

Bebel, August, and Eduard Bernstein, eds. 1913. *Der Briefwechsel zwischen Friedrich Engels und Karl Marx 1844 bis 1883.* In 4 vols. Vol. 1. Stuttgart: Detz.

Besançon, Alain. 1981. *The Intellectual Origins of Leninism.* Trans. Sarah Matthews. Oxford: Basil Blackwell.

Bogdanov, Alexander A. 1897. *Kratkii kurs ekonomicheskoi nauki.* Moscow: Izd-vo kniznogo sklada A.M. Murinovoi.

12 LENIN AND HIS CONTROVERSY OVER PHILOSOPHY: ON THE PHILOSOPHICAL... 267

———. 1899. *Osnovnye elementy istoricheskogo vzgliada na prirodu.* St. Petersburg: Izdatel'.

———. 1901. *Poznanie s istoricheskoi tochki zreniia.* St. Petersburg: Tipografiia A. Leiferta.

———. 2003. *Empiriomonizm: stat'i po filosofii.* Moscow: Respublka.

Bottomore, Tom. 1991. *A Dictionary of Marxist Thought.* 2nd ed. London: Blackwell.

Budgen, Sebastian, Kouvelakis Stathis, and Slavoj Žižek, eds. 2007. *Lenin Reloaded: Toward a Politics of Truth.* Durham, NC: Duke University Press.

Bulgakov, Mikhail. 1909. Retsenziia na knigu 'Materialism i empiriokrititsism' N. Il'ina. *Kriticheskoe obozrenie* 5: 7–8. [Reprinted in *LCW* 13: 326-328.].

Bykova, Marina F. 2018a. Lenin and Philosophy: On Philosophical Significance of *Materialism and Empiriocriticism.* In *The Handbook of Leninist Political Philosophy,* ed. Tom Rockmore and Norman Levine, 121–160. London and New York, NY: Palgrave Macmillan.

———. 2018b. Lenin and the Crisis of Russian Marxism. *Studies in East European Thought* 70 (4): 235–247.

Copleston, Frederick C. 1986. *Philosophy in Russia: From Herzen to Lenin and Berdyaev.* Notre Dame, IN: University of Notre Dame Press.

Editorial. 1930. O zhurnale "Pod znamenem marksizma." *Pod znamenem marksizma* 10-12: 1-2.

Ilyenkov, Evald V. 1977. *Dialekticheskaia Logika. Ocherki istorii i teorii.* Moscow: Progress Publishers. [An English translation by H.C. Creighton is available at: https://www.marxists.org/archive/ilyenkov/works/essays/]

———. 1980. *Leninskaia dialektika i metafizika pozitivizma.* Moscow: Politizdat.

Ilyenkov, Evald. 1983. *Leninist Dialectics and the Metaphysics of Positivism: Reflections on V.I. Lenin's Book, Materialism and Empirio-Criticism.* Trans. E. Williams. New York: New Park Publications.

Joravsky, David. 2009. *Soviet Marxism and Natural Science: 1917-1932.* New York, NY: Routledge.

Jordan, Zbigniew A. 1963. *Philosophy and Ideology: The Development of Philosophy and Marxism-Leninism in Poland since the Second World War.* Dordrecht, Holland: D. Reidel Publishing Company.

Krausz, Tamás. 2015. *Reconstructing Lenin: An Intellectual Biography.* Trans. Balint Bethlenfalvy with Mario Fenyo. New York: Monthly Review Foundation.

Kuvakin, Valery A. 1990. *Mirovozzrenie Lenina: formirovanie i osnovnye cherty.* Moscow: Nauka.

Le Blanc, Paul. 2006. *Marx, Lenin, and the Revolutionary Experience: Studies of Communism and Radicalism in the Age of Globalization.* New York, NY: Routledge.

———. 2015. *Lenin and the Revolutionary Party.* Chicago, IL: Haymarket Books.

Lektorsky, Vladislav A. 1990. *Deiatel'nost': teoriia, metodologia, problemy.* Moscow: Nauka.

———. 2010. Otrazhenie. In *Novaia filosofskaia entsiklopedia v 4-kh tomakh,* ed. V.S. Stepin and G.Yu. Semigin, vol. 3, 178–180. Moscow: Mysl'.

Lenin, Vladimir I. 1908. Letter (168) to Maxim Gorky, February 7, 1908. In *LCW* 34: 379–382.

———. 1909. *Materialism and Empiriocriticism: Critical Comments on a Reactionary Philosophy.* In *LCW* 14.

———. 1918. *The State and Revolution: The Marxist Theory of the State and the Task of the Proletariat in the Revolution.* In *LCW* 25: 381–492.

———. 1922. On the Significance of Militant Materialism. In *LCW* 33: 227–236.

———. 1933. *Philosophical Notebooks*. In *LCW* 38.

———. 1959. *Konspekt Perepiski K.Marksa i F.Engelsa 1844-1883 gg*. Moscow: Gospolitizdat.

———. 1977. *Lenin Collected Works* in English, 4th ed. Moscow: Progress Publishers. [1st printing 1962.] (All references to this edition are abbreviated in text as *LCW*, following by volume and page numbers in the following form: *LCW* 14: 231)

Liebmann, Marcel. 1975. *Leninism Under Lenin*. Trans. Brian Pearce. London: Merlin Press.

Lih, Lars T. 2008a. *Lenin Rediscovered: What Is to Be Done? in Context*. Chicago, IL: Haymarket Books.

———. 2008b. *Lenin*. London: Reaktion Books.

Mach, Ernst. 1986. In *Principles of the Theory of Heat: Historically and Critically Elucidated*, ed. Brian McGuiness. Dordrecht: B. Reidel.

Marx, Karl. 1981. Theses on Feuerbach. In *Earlier Writings*, ed. K. Marx, 421–422. Harmondsworth: Penguin.

Mitin, Mark B. 1930. K itogam filosofskoi diskussii. *Pod znamenem Marksisma* 10-12: 25–59.

Mitin, Mark B., Vasil Ral'tsevich, and Pavel Yudin. 1930. O novykh zadachakh marksistsko-leninskoi filosofii. *Pravda* (7 June): 5-6.

Pannekoek, Anton. 2003. *Lenin as Philosopher: A Critical Examination of the Philosophical Basis of Leninism*. Milwaukee: Marquette University Press.

Boer Roland. (blog). "Lenin and Religion," Blog *Philosophers for Change* at philosophersforchange.org

Richey, Lance B. 2003. Editor's Introduction: Pannekoek, Lenin, and the Future of Marxist Philosophy. In *Lenin as Philosopher: A Critical Examination of the Philosophical Basis of Leninism*, ed. Anton Pannekoek. Milwaukee, WI: Marquette University Press.

Rowley, David G. 1996. Bogdanov and Lenin: Epistemology and Revolution. *Studies in East European Thought* 48: 1–19.

Russell, Bertrand. 2009. *Human Knowledge: Its Scope and Limits*. New York, NY: Routledge.

Simon, William M. 1963. *European Positivism in the Nineteenth Century*. Ithaca, NY: Cornell University Press.

White, James D. 2015. Lenin and Philosophy: The Historical Context. *Europe-Asia Studies* 67 (1): 123–142.

Yakhot, Jehoshua. 1981. *Podavlenie filosofii v SSSR: 20-30 gody*. New York, NY: Chalidze.

CHAPTER 13

Russian Marxism and Its Philosophy: From Theory to Ideology

Maja Soboleva

The bibliography of works discussing Russian Marxism is huge; therefore, it is very difficult to give a novel interpretation of this phenomenon. To distinguish myself from the interpretative mainstream, the subject matter of my chapter will not be the linear progression of Russian Marxism from its adaptive (since 1880) to its dogmatic stage (since 1930) with a focus on persons and chronology.[1] Instead, I propose a systematic approach and ask whether there was a specific logic in the unfolding of Russian Marxism which led finally to its consolidation in the form of a triad including dialectical materialism, political economy, and scientific communism, and transformed it from a vibrant, pluralistic philosophy into the monolithic official ideology of the Russian Communist Party.

My approach will, then, have a reconstructive character: I focus on some fundamental propositions of Soviet Marxism which are recorded in textbooks on philosophy used in the Soviet Union and try to recover their philosophical genesis. This allows me to restrict myself to the selection of relevant topics. Besides, this allows me—by contrast to the traditional philosophical-historical narrative—to keep the philosophical discussions separate from the political controversies, though I am completely aware that people's philosophical ideas are strongly influenced by their political activity. In my chapter, I try to show that behind Soviet Marxism, dogmatized as the ideology of a party-state, lay a

M. Soboleva (✉)
Philipps-University of Marburg, Marburg, Germany

Institut für Philosophie, Alpen-Adria-Universität, Klagenfurt, Austria
e-mail: soboleva@mailer.uni-marburg.de

© The Author(s), under exclusive license to Springer Nature Switzerland AG 2021
M. F. Bykova et al. (eds.), *The Palgrave Handbook of Russian Thought*,
https://doi.org/10.1007/978-3-030-62982-3_13

269

270 M. SOBOLEVA

number of vital living ideas competitive with and alert to the accomplishments of contemporary philosophical thought. Though the tension between ideology and philosophy that has characterized Marxism in general and Russian Marxism in particular from the outset was resolved in Russia in favor of the former, it is still interesting to investigate the philosophical origin of these orthodox propositions.

DIALECTICAL MATERIALISM: METHODOLOGY OR THEORY?

Marxist philosophy in general represents the unity of theory and method. (Konstantinov and Bogomolov 1979, 185)

We shall consult Georgii Plekhanov (1857–1918) to provide us with the key for understanding Russian Marxism as philosophy. While for many of Plekhanov's contemporaries, Marxism did not possess its own philosophy since its founders did not leave any well-formed philosophical doctrine, he advocated in his seminal work *Fundamental Problems of Marxism* (1907) the opposite view and claimed that Marx and Engels developed their special philosophical theory, namely, dialectical materialism.[2]

In the principle of dialectical materialism he saw, first of all, an effective scientific methodology for social and historical studies.[3] In this respect it may be noted in passing that the end of the nineteenth to the beginning of the twentieth century was a time that distinguished itself by a search for a methodology for conducting historical, human, and social sciences. Dilthey, Windelband, Cohen, Husserl, and many others proposed their methodological strategies for achieving a scientific understanding of human life. However, Plekhanov considered these approaches idealist and therefore without practical relevance. Politically engaged, he saw an effective alternative in Marxist methodology because of its theoretical substantiality and practical applicability, that is, because of the qualities which form the scientific character of its doctrine. In the period of the beginning of the industrial-scientific revolution, science was broadly regarded as the preferred means to solve all possible problems; in this way Plekhanov was aligned with his epoch.

If one accepts dialectical materialism as methodology, then concepts like "unity of thought and being," "materialism," "dialectics," "class," "proletariat," "capital," and "class struggle" should together, as analytic tools, provide a scientific approach with which to study social phenomena. At the same time, such a social science which tells us about the most general laws and driving forces of society should become the "algebra of revolution" (Plekhanov 1929, 30), that is, provide the labor movement with a theoretically and methodologically sound strategy of action.

Vladimir Lenin (1870–1924) followed Plekhanov in this practical-political respect as, in his *Philosophical Notebooks*, he defined dialectical materialism as "socialist materialism" (Lenin 1969, 435). It is socialist since "the socialists Marx and Engels for the first time exactly proved that material, namely, economic relationships of human society build the basis, which, finally, determines the entire superstructure of legal and political institutions as well as religious, philosophical, and other ideas of every epoch" (ibid.). However, in contrast to Plekhanov, Lenin stresses that dialectics is not a methodology, but rather a theory of knowledge: "Dialectics *is* the theory of knowledge of (Hegel and) Marxism. This is the 'aspect' of the matter (it is not 'an aspect' but the *essence* of the matter) to which Plekhanov, not to speak of other Marxists, paid no attention" (Lenin 1976, 360).

Thus, the question has arisen among Russian Marxists of whether dialectical materialism should be regarded as a methodology or theory. It seems to be not a minor consideration because, since methodology is concerned with the so-called *how* questions, it determines the general research strategy that outlines the way in which research is to be undertaken and the methods to be used in it. In contrast, a theory deals with the *what* questions: it is a system of assumptions, principles, and propositions which constitute some specific content. If we use dialectical materialism as methodology, we assume that it serves to prove the theory. In contrast, by applying it as a theory, we determine some specific content, or ontology.

The history of Russian Marxism shows that this alternative was never considered seriously; the method has been simply identified with the theory. This fact is apparent in Soviet textbooks on philosophy. For example, the textbook edited by Fyodor Konstantinov and Alexei Bogomolov stated (1979, 36) that "materialist dialectics was not only method, but also theory, namely, the theory of development." A consequence of such an approach was that *method* did not serve to verify (or falsify) theory, but, instead, constituted it. Owing to this theoretical-methodological synthesis, the epistemological categories distorted their true cognitive functions and it became impossible to practice a truly scientific approach to social-philosophical knowledge.

Soviet philosophy accepted dialectical materialism as materialism based upon self-evident facts and exact reasoning and called it "dialectical" because it emphasized change and development. In turn, dialectics has been accepted as materialist dialectics which is applicable to all natural and cultural processes. This identification of theory and method may be seen as one of the sources for the dogmatic character of Soviet dialectical materialism since it constituted "the point of view of totality" which formed the decisive difference between Soviet scientific Marxism and real science (Lukács 1971, XX). On the other hand, it is for this reason that dialectical materialism has become an effective, though blind and brutal, method of revolutionary action.

Dialectics: Logical or Ontological Category?

Marxist philosophy overcame the gap between ontology and gnoseology [i.e., epistemology] thanks to the theory of reflection on the dialectical-materialistic basis and understanding the dialectics of subject and object as the practical activity of human beings directed toward the creation of a new world of things and relations. (Kopnin 1973, 7)

The term "dialectics" was borrowed from Hegel. A materialist reading of Hegel's *Science of Logic* was introduced into Russian Marxism in works by Plekhanov and later developed by Lenin, according to whom "Hegel ingeniously guessed a dialectics of things (phenomena, world, *and nature*) in a dialectics of concepts" (Lenin 1969, 178). Lenin formulated the new task for Marxist philosophy to "stand Hegel right side up." This means to transition from the dialectics of concepts to the dialectics of real processes by replacing the concept with matter.

In Soviet philosophy, the following triple constellation was established: dialectics as a real process of functioning material and ideal entities, dialectical logic as the theory of knowledge of these processes, and dialectics as the method of practical activity. The understanding of dialectics as an *onto-logic* interpreted in a materialist way is the quintessence of Soviet Marxism. Here, Hegel's speculative identity of being and consciousness is reflected in the identity of empirics and logic. From this perspective, knowledge is explained from the identity of natural causal connections with logical connections in human consciousness. Due to this identification, the Soviet methodological approach appeared as a peculiar kind of logical empiricism: the general laws of materialist dialectics were regarded as the basic *logical* laws of the *real* natural and historical processes. One of the consequences of this assumption is that the difference between reality and its interpretation does not exist anymore; it becomes possible to represent the description as the reality itself.

On the basis of Hegel's speculative logic, some fundamental laws of materialist dialectics were deduced, namely: the law of transition of quantitative changes into qualitative ones and back, the law of the unity and conflict of opposites, and the law of the negation of the negation. These "fictions" (in the words of Alexander Ermichev) were "invented during the codification" (Ermichev 2007, 14) of Marxist-Leninist philosophy and considered universal categories despite, in fact, contradicting Hegel's logic, since they stressed dialectics merely as the "negative-rational" moment of logic and neglected the speculative, "positive-rational," moment.

Thanks to Plekhanov and Lenin, the essence of Hegel's dialectics was seen as lying in the principle of development through contradictions, which was universalized and extended from the ideal sphere of logic to the sphere of real life as well. Thus, in Russian Marxism, dialectics became the principle of the world's development. Konstantin Grebnev's opinion is representative in this regard. According to him, "the core issue is not Hegel's system, but his method—a principle of general movement and general interaction" (Grebnev 1929, 31–32).

Alexander Bogdanov (1873–1928) was one of those who pointed out this one-sided interpretation of development as merely dialectics. In his *Philosophy of Living Experience* (1913), he demonstrates the polyvalence of the term "development," distinguishing between progressive and regressive development (Bogdanov 1913, 201). He argues:

> Thus, the basic concept of Marx's dialectics, as well as of the dialectics of Hegel, did not reach its full clarity and completeness; and thanks to this, the very application of the dialectical method becomes inexact and indistinct; its schemes are contaminated with arbitrariness, and not only the borders of dialectics are uncertain, but its sense is sometimes strongly perverted. (Bogdanov 1913, 210)

The main criticism of Bogdanov is aimed, however, not at Hegel, but at Marx and the interpreters of his theory, Plekhanov and Ilyin (Lenin),[4] for their universalization of the concept of dialectics. According to him, the most significant aspects of history are humankind's fight against nature and class struggle in society. The first of these two aspects can be accounted for as a basic and constant engine of history, while the second aspect is derivative and temporary. Therefore, he concludes, dialectics as an explanatory category for the analysis of passing phenomena can only have restricted application.

He claims that "dialectics is not something universal at all" and it "cannot become a general method of knowledge […] [rather] it is a special case of organizational processes which can also go other ways" (Bogdanov 1913, 216–217). Bogdanov is convinced of the "historical limits" of the concept of dialectics, and of the "necessity of transition to a broader and general point of view" (Bogdanov 1913, 221). He believes that "organizational processes in nature run *not only* through the conflict of opposites, but also in other ways; therefore dialectics is just a special case and its scheme cannot become the universal method" (ibid.). Bogdanov defines dialectics as merely a special type of organizational process (but not as the development as such), which "proceeds due to the fight between opposite tendencies" (Bogdanov 1913, 200), and proposes the alternative: "to investigate the united structure of the world process from the point of view of *all possible ways and kinds of organization*" (Bogdanov 1913, 217). He tried to realize his project by developing a universal organizational science which he called "tectology."

In spite of Bogdanov's criticism, dialectics in Russian Marxism was interpreted as a universal philosophy of negation, contradiction, and conflict, with the focus not only on logical but also real contradictions. Contradiction was evaluated positively as both a necessary moment of movement and a symptom of growth and development. This positive assessment of Plekhanov's and Lenin's understandings of dialectics dominated until the collapse of Soviet philosophy. For example, one of the later so-called critical Marxists, Evald Ilyenkov, still believed that "The correct relation to Hegel's philosophy established by Marx, Engels, and Lenin is an integral part of Marxism; and a critical and materialist assimilation of Hegel's dialectics remains one of the necessary conditions for a really deep and serious Marxist education" (Ilyenkov 1970).

The Theory of Cognition: The Theory of Reflection or the Theory of Active Experience?

[Dialectical materialism] is the scientific and philosophical system, the method of cognition and revolutionary changing of the world, the philosophical basis of the scientific outlook of the working class and other forces fighting for socialism. (Iovchuk et al. 1971, 2)

Interest in the epistemological problems within Russian Marxism was generated by the view that philosophy should become a useful tool for social transformation. In this way, epistemology is expected to shape contingent historical possibilities for a society by determining the norms and constraints of public practice, worldview, and self-awareness. Indeed, epistemology seems to play the role of a non-neutral power in mediating both knowledge production and dissemination, which form the landscape of everyday existence in a society. This understanding of epistemology can explain the heavy struggle of Marxist social-democrats at the turn of the twentieth century for materialism and against idealism, and for materialist dialectics and against metaphysics.

Moreover, the question of what image dialectical materialism, as an accurate Marxist epistemology, ought to have also sparked controversies. For example, Plekhanov criticized the so-called legal Marxists (Struve, Berdyaev, Bulgakov, and others)[5] and the so-called Machists[6] (Bogdanov, Yushkevich, Bazarov, Lunacharsky, and others); Lenin criticized the legal Marxists, the Machists, and Plekhanov; and Bogdanov criticized the legal Marxists, Mach, and the so-called orthodox Marxists[7] (Plekhanov and Lenin).[8] The mutual fight between different philosophical directions within Russian Marxism over what Marxist materialism actually *is* formed the principal content of its philosophical evolution. In what follows, I bring together two fields of the discussion: (a) the notion of materialism, and (b) materialist forms of cognition.

The Notion of Materialism

It is surprising that discussion of the notion of materialism among Russian Marxists was carried out in Kantian terms as concerned with the "thing-in-itself." It was Plekhanov who introduced Kantian terminology into the materialist vocabulary of Russian Marxists. However, as he stressed, he "employ[ed] the term 'thing-in-itself' in a quite different sense from the Kantians and Machists" (Plekhanov 1976, 219). Let us see how Plekhanov interpreted this term. In his work *Materialismus Militans*, he writes:

> In contrast to "spirit," we call "matter" that which *acts on our sense-organs and arouses in us various sensations.* What is it exactly that acts on our sense-organs? To this question I answer with Kant: *things-in-themselves.* Thus, matter is nothing else than the totality of things-in-themselves, in so far as these things constitute the source of our sensations. (Plekhanov 1976, 212)

From this quotation, it follows that Plekhanov's matter is identical with unknowable things-in-themselves. In other words, he uses this Kantian concept as a guarantee of the materiality of the outer world and the objectivity of our sensations. According to him, all things-in-themselves are material. He explains: "We call material objects (bodies) those objects that exist independently of our consciousness and, acting on our senses, arouse in us certain *sensations* which in turn underlie our notions of the external world, that is, of those same material objects as well as of their relationships" (Plekhanov 1976, 214). Otherwise put, matter is an unknowable object of any of our senses and the source of all our ideas, the ideas out of which human knowledge is constructed. Should Marxist materialism be understood as a pseudo-Kantian "sensationalism"?

This perspective has been disputed by those who refute things-in-themselves both as ontological entities and as epistemological-analytical tools. One of these critics was Lenin, who believed that "[t]here is definitely no difference in principle between the phenomenon and the thing-in-itself, and there cannot be any such difference. The only difference is between what is known and what is not yet known" (Lenin 1972, 103). The things-in-themselves have been reduced to material objects, to "things outside our sensations, perceptions, and so forth" (Lenin 1972, 117–118). Thus, the concept "thing-in-itself" has lost its ontological relevance. However, Lenin's famous definition of matter does not differ significantly from that of Plekhanov: "Matter is a philosophical category denoting the objective reality which is given to man by his sensations, and which is copied, photographed, and reflected by our sensations, while existing independently of them" (Lenin 1972, 130).[9]

In contrast to Lenin and Plekhanov, Alexander Bogdanov (1873–1928), Iakov Berman (1868–1933), Viktor Chernov (1873–1952), Pavel Yushkevitch (1873–1945), Vladimir Bazarov (1874–1939), and others developed innovative theories which set experience in the place of things-in-themselves. These authors were erroneously called representatives of empiriocriticism or "Machism," but they considered themselves critical positivists (see Suvorov 1909, 11; Bogdanov 2003, 12).[10] Their theories shared a common origin in Comte's as well as Richard Avenarius's and Ernst Mach's positivism combined with Marxism, Neo-Kantianism, and the achievements of particular sciences. In contrast to Mach's empiriocriticism, which focused on the cognitive subject and pure experience, here experience was broadly interpreted as intersubjective (social) and historical (being dependent on social factors). However, their individual positions are very different within this general framework. For example, Bogdanov's empiriomonism was challenged by Yushkevitch's empiriosymbolism. In general, empiriomonism accounts for the experience of socially organized complexes of psycho-physical elements (Bogdanov 2003, 33). The organizing mechanism is a substitution which transforms subjective psychic phenomena into inter-subjectively valid physical phenomena, that is, into objective reality. In contrast, empiriosymbolism considers experience as sense-perceptions which are spontaneously structured and symbolized through understanding the subject. Human cognition is thus an "inseparable connection of the real and the ideal, the given and the created, the factual and the symbolical" (Yushkevitch 1908, 178). Objective reality is accessible for us only through empiriosymbols, that is, symbolized sensations such as color, temperature, smell, mass, and energy.[11]

It seems to be the consensus among Russian Marxists of different styles that, outside us and independently of us, there exist objects, things, and bodies, and that our perceptions are caused by the external world. Hence, metaphysical idealism has been overcome. Correspondingly, the concept of the thing-in-itself has either been used as a mere metaphor for independently existing material objects or completely renounced. When Lenin, Plekhanov, Bogdanov, and others criticize each other for ontological idealism, they actually talk past each other.

What separates them is their understanding of how the outer world becomes knowable for a human being. What are our perceptions and how are they related to the reality? Are they hieroglyphs (Plekhanov),[12] copies (Lenin), empiriosymbols (Yushkevitch), or models (Bogdanov)? As Lenin put it:

> All knowledge comes from experience, from sensation, from perception. That is true. But the question arises, does objective reality "belong to perception," i.e., is it the source of perception? If you answer yes, you are a materialist. If you answer no, you are inconsistent and will inevitably arrive at subjectivism, or agnosticism. (Lenin 1972, 127–128)

The mutual accusation of idealism has been caused, in fact, not by a doubt *that* the external world is, but by a different understanding of *what* the external world is.

This question can be reformulated as the problem of the character of our perceptions: whether we passively reflect the outer things, or actively form the content of our perceptions. In other words, the question is whether the senses' intuition through which something is given also contains a concept of an object, or whether it is non-conceptual. At least three absolutely different positions can be distinguished in regard to this question.[13]

Lenin represents the most radical intentionalism and non-conceptualism in the sense that mental phenomena could be defined by saying that they contain an object merely intentionally within themselves. Indeed, according to him, sensations are "a true copy of this objective reality" and "images of the sole and ultimate objective reality" (Lenin 1972, 129). Even when, with each step in the development of science, new aspects of reality are discovered, these aspects are nothing else than reflections of this very reality. We can conclude from this that, for Lenin, the meaning of concepts is imposed by objects, and the human being adds nothing subjective to the perceived reality. This position can be interpreted as a pleading for absolute facts and absolute truth. Indeed, "if objective truth exists […], then all fideism is absolutely refuted" (Lenin 1972, 125).

Plekhanov is more moderate in this respect. He believes that perceptual content is intentional (or objectual), and yet, in some sense, conceptual due to the specificity of human mental and psycho-physiological organization. But he warns:

> From this, however, it does not follow that the properties of the external world have only subjective significance. By no means! If a man and a snail move from point A to point B, the straight line will be the shortest distance between those two points for both the man and the snail; if both these organisms went along a broken line *they would have to expend a greater amount of labor for their advance.* (Plekhanov 1976, 230)

From this quotation, it follows that human sensations represent only forms and relations which man finds among the objects he or she perceives, but these forms and relations are real. The other content of our perceptions comprises our conceptions of reality.

Bogdanov and Yushkevitch can be considered conceptualists since they assume that the meaning of the concept lies not in perceived objects, but in human experience. According to them, not only does interpretation as a conscious, deliberate act define the content of perception, but also the impressions, in that there are no active inferences being made that have a conceptual character. Human experience, Bogdanov argues, is individually and socially organized. The individual experience has a subjective character, while the socially organized experience gives us what we call "objective reality" (Bogdanov 2003, 233–234). The key point is that the social experience influences individual perceptions: "Thus, experience is social in its basis, and its progress is the *socio-psychological process of its organization*, to which the organizing individual-psychic process completely adapts itself" (Bogdanov 2003, 234–235).

The physical world, according to Bogdanov, is a "socially-organized experience" (Bogdanov 2003, 234), "the result of the collective organizing labor of all people, in a certain sense a cognitive 'socialism'" (Bogdanov 2003, 235). The objectivity of the physical world we encounter in our experience is "in the last analysis established by the mutual verification and co-ordination of the utterances of various people" (Bogdanov 2003, 21). "Objective" hence means having universal significance. This view opposes the authoritarian metaphysics of the absolute with its idea of only one absolute truth. Bogdanov declares: "As I understand it, Marxism contains a denial of the unconditional objectivity of any truth whatsoever, the denial of all eternal truths" (Bogdanov 2003, 217). Truth, he claims, is merely an organizing form of human cognitive experience.

Yushkevitch argues that perception is an "empiriosymbol" which systematizes our knowledge (Yushkevitch 1908, 163). There are no isolated sensual data; rather, "experiences are given in a certain perspective, in relation and connection to each other, that is, in a mutual dependency" (Yushkevitch 1908, 178). Therefore, a pure, non-conceptualized description is impossible: "Such a natural science is a myth; science is indeed description, but it does not use copies, it uses symbols" (Yushkevitch 1908, 188). Since experience is always a synthesis of immediate sense-perception and spontaneous reasoning, the ultimate reality appears to be an empiriosymbol: "The so-called genuine reality, being-in-itself, is the infinite, complete system of symbols at which our cognition is aimed" (Yushkevitch 1908, 188). The scientific process of cognition is, according to Yushkevitch, the transition from more simple to more complex and abstract empiriosymbols, from symbol-copies to symbols as conventional signs.

This short outline of the theoretical debate on materialism shows by itself how controversial and multifaceted this debate was. We can conclude that, although Marxist materialism supports a materialist understanding of the world, one can represent it without embracing absolute materialism in Lenin's sense. We should then differentiate between "material" and "materialist" approaches in epistemology.

The participants in this epistemological debate did not have any common ground and lacked tolerance and the willingness to understand and accept the arguments of the opposite side. Probably because epistemology was meant to solve not only scientific but social problems as well, Lenin's conception of materialism, with its rigorous concept of objective reality as independent of men, and with only one possible absolute truth enforced by this ultimate reality, prevailed, since it was well-suited for "fundamentalist" polemics. For in this case, one can appeal to the natural or social "objective" law for explaining and justifying one's beliefs and actions. The attempt to search for the basis of objectivity in the sphere of coordinated collective experience, as Bogdanov proposed, looked indeed in the time of social catastrophes like idealism. However, it was not theoretical but practical idealism.[14]

Materialist Forms of Cognition

The quintessence of Plekhanov's theory of knowledge is summarized by his statement that:

> By acting upon us, the thing-in-itself arouses in us a series of sensations on the basis of which we form our conception of it. Once we have this conception, the thing-in-itself takes on a two-fold character: it exists, firstly, in itself, and, secondly, in our conception of it. Its properties—let us say, its structure—exists in exactly the same way: firstly, in itself, and, secondly, in our conception of it. That is all there is to it. (Plekhanov 1976, 231)

By contrast, Lenin's theory of knowledge can be summarized as follows:

> Thus, the materialist theory, the theory of the reflection of objects by our mind, is here presented with absolute clarity: things exist outside us. Our perceptions and ideas are their images. Verification of these images, differentiation between true and false images, is given by practice. (Lenin 1972, 110)

Although Plekhanov posits a break between reality and impression due to the mental and psycho-physiological constitution of the human being and Lenin, on the contrary, argues for the complete identity of reality and image, they share a common point—namely, they consider our experiences as the result of the immediate impact of the external world reaching our consciousness. Their materialist theory of cognition takes the form of a strong naturalism since it asserts that perceptual cognition determines the properties of our concepts and, hence, our theories.

What also seems to be common ground between Plekhanov and Lenin is their commitment to evidence-based explanations, causality, and physicalism. For example, Plekhanov is convinced that "there cannot be a *non*-materialist natural science" (Plekhanov 1976, 244). Lenin's physicalism is clearly expressed in his claim that "objective and subjective belong to the same genus" (Lenin 1969, 409). He repeats: "We consider intellect the same empirical data as the matter. Thought and being, subject and object are equally within the limits of experience" (Lenin 1969, 415). For him, "to regard our sensations as images of the external world, to recognize objective truth, to hold the materialist theory of knowledge—these are all one and the same thing" (Lenin 1972, 130).

One more commonality between Plekhanov and Lenin is that their approach starts from the traditional position of the individual knower who is ultimately concerned with whether his or her beliefs correspond to objects that are presumed to exist independently of his or her own individual or collective activity.

In contrast, the "Marxist positivists" such as Bogdanov, Yushkevitch, and Bazarov have quite a different starting point: they do not begin with an object, but focus on the epistemic properties of individuals that arise from their relations to other members of society, as well as the epistemic properties of social groups. Though Plekhanov and Lenin stressed their Marxist orthodoxy, their theories of knowledge, in fact, underplay the importance of the social dimension for knowledge production. Their models have a tendency to neglect the fundamentally social nature of the contexts in which epistemic activity, knowledge production, and expertise take place. For them, to search for objectivity in collective experience is nothing other than pure idealism. For instance, Lenin addressed the following criticism to Bogdanov:

> But if there is no objective truth, if truth (including scientific truth) is only an organizing form of human experience, then this is in itself an admission of the fundamental premise of clericalism, the door is thrown open for it, and a place is cleared for the "organizing forms" of religious experience. (Lenin 1972, 125–126)

Plekhanov misunderstands Bogdanov's approach and declares that "the 'philosophy' which claims that the physical world was created by men is the most thoroughgoing, though of course very confused, *idealist* philosophy" (Plekhanov 1976, 257).

As Bogdanov set out in his *Empiriomonism*, one of his key questions is about how the pursuit of knowledge ought to be organized. His task is to show

how cognition arises from non-cognitive processes.[15] The underlying thesis is that the production of knowledge is a collective and normative endeavor. Bogdanov stresses that the sphere of knowledge has a logic of its own and describes this logic in terms of "social causality." The category "social causality" must demonstrate the dependence of cognitive processes upon social and labor practices, methods, and relations. In his short historical excursion into epistemology *Cognition from a Historical Point of View* (1902), Bogdanov highlights the correlation between the organization of thinking and that of labor. In the sphere of labor, he differentiates mental and manual labor as well as organizational and executive forms of actions. For him, labor specialization and the separation of organizers from those who carry out orders determined some historical models of cognition, which were based upon epistemological traditionalism, authoritarianism, and individualism (Bogdanov 1914). Correspondingly, knowledge had a fragmented character and could not satisfy the developing society; therefore, such a cognitive situation should be overcome.

I stress that Bogdanov was attentive not only to social structures that have determined the limits of cognition historically, but also to the role that power, subordination, and oppression play in the historical creation of norms, practices, and systems of knowledge. For instance, he made a forceful case for distinguishing groups of "organizers" to reveal the epistemic outcome and epistemic effects of social interactions.

In his analysis, Bogdanov highlights that cognition and knowledge reflect social experience, while organization of labor impacts the structure of knowledge and the entire cultural landscape of historical society. He uses the term "sociomorphism" and introduces the concept of the "social system of cognition" (Bogdanov 1902, 174) to describe this correlation between representations and underlying labor activity. Indeed, it seems to be a fundamental feature of social institutions: they function as instances of the constitution and legitimation of knowledge. This leads to the conclusion that changing forms of cognition and the character of knowledge requires changing the social structures in which knowledge is produced and legitimated.

Bogdanov's universal mechanism of the organization of cognitive experience is "substitution." Substitution can be seen as a complex, stepwise, expanding process of constructing symbolic reality through the subordination of some mental complexes to others or, in other words, by means of the consistent building up of knowledge to an entire picture of the world, proceeding from an initial set of simple statements. In general, psychical phenomena become physical phenomena, that is, objective reality, through substitution—which means that the immediate sense-perceptions of individuals become intersubjectively[16] organized, meaningful things.[17] In contextualized knowledge, a certain sum of elements is selectively combined, corresponding to the cultural and social background, needs, and interests of different social groups according to their pragmatic goals and social order. Therefore, social experience and knowledge are always conditional and relative. On the basis of the different kinds of substitution, Bogdanov distinguishes among different historical epistemic paradigms, such as primitive, authoritarian, individualist, and collectivist, with regard to their specific understandings of knowledge and truth.

Identifying knowledge with forms of collective experience, Bogdanov moves to *social epistemology* which seeks to investigate the epistemic effects of social interactions and social systems. This is a radical departure from classical individualist epistemology. He combines this with a constructivist view of cognition. His epistemological constructivism means that socially structured human activity discovers, causes, and sustains scientific facts and norms, thereby justifying knowledge about the world.

Yushkevitch's empiriosymbolism, by contrast, is social in a different way, by assuming that theories function as "our constructions" and the "products of idealization" (Yushkevitch 1908, 173–175) which specify facts. He claims that science reforms the natural world according to its formal concepts: a fact appears to be derived from a theory; therefore, facts may be seen as contingent historical constructions that reveal our collective process of cognition.

As distinguished from Bogdanov, Yushkevitch's ideas were developed in the direction of anthropology. Starting from the fact that human beings create the "artificial, social—at the same time material and ideal—environment, through which he affects nature and conquers it" (Yushkevitch 1908, 177), he posits "symbol-making" as the ultimate anthropological category. He defines man, long before Ernst Cassirer did, as a "symbol-making animal" (Yushkevitch 1908, 177) who lives in a culture built up of "empiriosymbols" of different grades of complexity. He argues that human experience is essentially symbolic in character: "It is, so to say, a natural artificiality, a conditional conditionality, as strange as these phrases probably sound" (Yushkevitch 1908, 178). Yushkevitch asserts that the distinctive trait of human existence is the symbolic transformation of experience. The entire human experience is translated into symbols, including not only the artificial symbols of science, logic, and mathematics, but also natural linguistic signs. It is embedded in historical and social contexts and is dependent upon the diversity of positions and perspectives, conflicts, and contradictions in social life.

Although Bogdanov and Yushkevitch did not use the expressions "social epistemology" and "social anthropology," the social emphasis of their thought makes these terms appropriate for their work. According to them, there are no material facts *sensu stricto*; matter, or reality, is always socially defined, transformed by and associated with respective collective representations. For them, there are no things-in-themselves at all because of the phenomenal character of human reality. Their insightful approaches, which redefined epistemological concepts according to the experimental character of modern science, its methodological functionalism, and its theoretical dynamism, laid the groundwork for contemporary perspectives in Marxist theory of cognition. Unfortunately, they were not admitted into Russian Marxist orthodoxy and are still relatively unknown in modern Russia.

Historical Materialism Between Base and Superstructure

> The natural historical process is as lawful, necessary, and objective as natural processes; it is not only independent of human will and consciousness, but, on the contrary, it affects human will and consciousness. At the same time, by contrast to natural processes, the natural historical process is the result of human activity. (Konstantinov and Bogomolov 1979, 187)

These basic propositions and principles of Marxist social theory—introduced by Marx and Engels and interpreted differently by different Marxist currents—highlight its two most important characteristics: first, strict historicism, or the view of society as something that is in a state of permanent unilineal progressive development; second, the understanding of history as a law-governed process, conditioned in the final analysis by the development of productive forces. Here, social laws are treated in the same way as laws of nature. This is expressed in the description of social development as a "natural historical process."

On the one hand, this understanding implies that objective and necessary natural historical processes determine people's will and consciousness. On the other hand, it implies that this process is created by people themselves possessing will, purposeful thinking, and desire. Thus, this proposition appears to imply a logical contradiction, which should be resolved if the materialist conception of history is to make sense.

Marxists generally resolve this contradiction by assuming determinism. All versions of this theory have in common the claim that reconciliation is achieved between natural laws and human historical agency since, in pursuing their subjective aims, people live under certain objective conditions that determine the direction and character of their thought and activity. However, individual positions differ considerably within this common theoretical framework.

For example, Plekhanov believes that materialism's task in history is to explain "how environment can be modified by men who are themselves a product of this environment" (Plekhanov 1929, 58). The outline of his explanation goes something like this: first, there are some kinds of states of affairs in society that are exempted from a sphere of human responsibility. Plekhanov upholds a view that:

> the character of the "economic structure" and the direction in which that character undergoes transformation do not depend on the human will, but on the condition of the forces of production, and on the nature of the changes which occur in the relations of production and which become necessary to the society owing to the development of those forces. (Plekhanov 1929, 58)

Second, he does not reject the fact that individuals have free will. However, he accepts determinism in human relations and therefore contends that only some of people's actions are free. According to him, relations of production *between human beings are strongly determined by the character of* productive forces: "Here human activity exhibits itself, not as free activity, but as necessary activity, that is to say in conformity with law and able to be subjected to scientific study" (Plekhanov 1929, 58–59). Third, in Plekhanov, personal individuality relates to social type analogically to the relation between incidence and necessity. The existence of personal individuality is, therefore, compatible with the path of mankind's *intellectual* development which "tends to run parallel to that of economic evolution" (Plekhanov 1929, 69–70).

The hierarchical five-level model proposed by Plekhanov describes the influence of social being on social consciousness with the Marxist terms "base" and "superstructure" (working from the base up) as follows: (1) the state of the productive forces; (2) the economic relations these forces condition; (3) the socio-political system that has developed on the given economic "basis"; (4) the mentality of social man, which is determined in part directly by the economic conditions obtaining, and in part by the entire socio-political system that has arisen on that foundation; (5) the various ideologies that reflect the properties of that mentality (Plekhanov 1929, 72).

Plekhanov's schema of the causal dependency of superstructure on the institutions of material production and reproduction does not seem to be an adequate way to understand the complexity of social phenomena, even though it was widely accepted in Russian Marxism. This schema, while attractive in that it preserves the principle of universal causation, suffers from its abstract character.

It was, in particular, Nikolai Bukharin (1888–1938) who tried to develop the materialist conception of history in more detail in accordance with the "most orthodox, materialist, and revolutionary understanding of Marxism" (Bukharin 1928, 360, 371). This means that, similarly to Plekhanov, he tried to apply the general materialist world outlook to history and society. His starting point is a strong determinism. He acknowledges that human choices and actions can make a difference but holds that these choices and actions are subject to causal laws:

> In a word, man's feeling and will are dependent on the condition of his organism and on the circumstances in which he finds himself. His will, like all the rest of nature, is conditioned by certain causes, and man does not constitute an exception to all the rest of the world. (Bukharin 1925, 36)

He claims that:

> the doctrine of freedom of the will (indeterminism) is at bottom an attenuated form of a semi-religious view which explains nothing at all, contradicts all the facts of life, and constitutes an obstacle to scientific development. The only correct point of view is that of determinism. (Bukharin 1925, 37)

Nevertheless, Bukharin describes historical processes as conducted through the human will. For this purpose, he differentiates between "unorganized" and "organized" society. He puts forward an argument that in an unorganized society, social phenomena do not coincide with the wills of individuals but are independent of them. He explains:

> This "independence of the will of persons" consists not in the fact that the events of social life proceed outside of the persons concerned, but in the fact that in unorganized society, in chaotic, elemental evolution, the social product of this will (or wills) does not coincide with the objects that are proposed by many persons, but is sometimes in direct contradiction with these objects (a man wishing to make profit finds himself ruined). (Bukharin 1925, 39)

By contrast, the state of affairs in an organized (socialist) society is quite different: social phenomena are the result of the guided collective will of men.

At first glance, this innovation of Bukharin seems to contradict the orthodox one-dimensional explanation of the vertical relation between base and superstructure since it acknowledges the relative autonomy of humanity's role in history.[18] However, Bukharin's entire view of historical mechanisms according to which "[t]he mental life of society is a function of the forces of production" (Bukharin 1925, 61) demonstrates his consistent commitment to the principles of historical materialism and determinism. He repeats that:

> hidden behind the law of cause and effect in the evolution of the class will and the various permutations and combinations in the clash of the opposed class wills— differing from each other—is the profounder causality of the objective evolution, a causality that determines the phenomena of the will at every stage in evolution. (Bukharin 1925, 308)

Under this condition, class struggle appears to be not a demonstration of the people's free will, but merely a "transmission apparatus in the transition from one social structure to another" (ibid.).

This position might give a theoretical resolution of the paradox of historical materialism as it was formulated by Plekhanov, but it nevertheless is unable to explain a huge number of historical facts, including the October Revolution in Russia. That the most advanced social revolution occurred in the most backward capitalist country looks, indeed, impossible from the standpoint of the orthodox Marxist historical materialist doctrine. Bukharin's theory of the proletarian revolution reflects this difficulty. He puts forward a hypothesis that:

> A revolution begins when the property relations have become a hindrance to the evolution of the productive forces; revolution has done its work as soon as *new* relations of production have been established, to serve as forms favoring the evolution of the productive forces. Between this beginning and this ending lies the *reverse order in the influence of the superstructures.* (Bukharin 1925, 264)

The first sentence of this phrase is in accord with Marx's thesis, contending that a necessary condition of revolution is the conflict between the material forces of production in society and the existing relations of production. It implies that increasing productive forces have achieved the maximal level of development which is possible under the given relations of production. The last sentence of this quotation negates this necessary condition: superstructural changes can occur earlier in time than the corresponding economic changes.

Moreover, if one accepts the principle of the reverse influence of superstructure, Bukharin's next necessary condition of revolution, namely, "a revolutionizing of the consciousness of the new class, an ideological revolution in the class that is to serve as the grave-digger of the old society" (Bukharin 1925, 255), appears not to be fulfilled due to the lack of an essential conflict between the productive forces and relations of production which alone determines the class consciousness. Ultimately, Bukharin's efforts to support the orthodox version of historical materialism reached an opposite goal, that is, they pointed to its logical inconsistency.[19]

While Bukharin accepts the active role of superstructure in exceptional, revolutionary, situations, Bogdanov insists that superstructure—he uses instead the term "ideology"—is an "organizational tool" and has a significant "organizing function" (Bogdanov 2003, 272) in society. "Ideology" embraces three levels, namely, "the forms of immediate communication" (language, mimic), "the cognitive forms" (concepts, beliefs, religion, science, etc.), and "the normative forms" (tradition, morality, law, patterns of rationality, etc.) (Bogdanov 2003, 268–269). These forms build the cultural-social context for technology, labor, and production relations as well.

The technical sphere is the genetically primary sphere insofar as it is a sphere of direct interactions between man and nature (Bogdanov 2003, 270), that is, the sphere of production and reproduction of life. However, Bogdanov denies the direct causal determination of ideology by base and argues for their functional dependency. Being a genetically secondary and dependent phenomenon, ideology may later become a factor of primary importance. According to Bogdanov, ideology consists of different subsystems, each of which has its own dynamics: some of them (for instance, relations of production) are closely connected with the sphere of social labor and react immediately (positively or negatively) upon its changes; the others are more stable and conservative and can resist or even prohibit technical or economic innovations. Thus, the functional causality implies the mutual, two-way impact of subsystems (or "complexes") on each other. The functional explanation provides a way of recognizing the vital influence of ideology on the material sphere, while still assigning ontological primacy to the latter.

What Marx refers to as "the growth of productive forces" Bogdanov calls "the progress of social technology"; what Marx refers to as "economy" Bogdanov calls "the border area between technical and ideological process"; and what Marx refers to as "the conflict between productive forces and production relations" Bogdanov calls "the disturbing of structural equilibrium in society." This reformulation of fundamental Marxist sociological concepts allowed him to undertake a more flexible and exact analysis of social reality in what he felt was the most up-to-date scientific terms. While the rule remains valid that technological process forms the ground of social phenomena, ideology, by contrast, is their active "forming moment" (Bogdanov 2003, 297). In accordance with Marxist orthodoxy, Bogdanov attempted to explain all ideological phenomena by reference to a basic Marxist category, labor as the mediator of the metabolic interaction between society and nature. However, he expanded Marxist vocabulary by introducing a theory of energetics, a theory of evolution, and a general system theory.

In his book *On the Psychology of Society* (1904), Bogdanov states that ideology constitutes the "social environment" which enables and affects the development of different "social complexes" (Bogdanov 1904, 89; cf. 49). He summarizes his sociological ideas in his later work *The Science of Social Consciousness: A Short Course of Ideological Science in Questions and Answers* (1914). He claims that it is not enough to know that ideology originates from and depends upon social relations of production. It is also necessary to understand its practical role and function. He criticizes the view which, from the derivative character of ideology, concludes that it is a "secondary" and "nonsignificant addition" to economy (Bogdanov 1914, 6). He defines ideology as "an instrument for the organization of society, production, classes, and other social forces and elements; it is an instrument without which this organization is impossible" (Bogdanov 1914, 7). Ideology underlies the "principle of social causality" (Bogdanov 1914, 26) according to which it is only "in the last analysis" determined by conditions of production, although it can also be caused by another ideological phenomenon as well (Bogdanov 1914, 26).

Bogdanov's acknowledgment of the active role of ideology results in a practical maxim that the "work on class consciousness, class ideology, is the most important and historically necessary in our epoch" (Bogdanov 1914, 7). Only class ideology makes possible conscious, purposeful activity by great masses of people. Bogdanov's theory of proletarian culture aimed at the preparation of a modern, industrial, well-organized, and rational working class for its vanguard role in the social transformation from capitalism to socialism appears to be a consequence of this theoretical assumption.

Thanks to Bogdanov, historical materialism had a chance to refuse strong materialist determinism in the social sciences. However, his views contradicted the dominant orthodoxy, which seemed to be better suited for political practice, and became the subject of severe criticism. As a result of ignorance of alternative interpretations of the relationship between base and superstructure, Soviet Marxism became trapped in a vicious cycle of apparent historical necessity and absence of personal freedom.

Concluding Remarks

Western European Marxist studies undertaken during the Soviet era routinely distinguished the Marxist tradition from Marxism-Leninism.[20] They denied the latter any philosophical status at all, considering it as merely the official ideology of the Communist Party and the worldview expected to be adopted by the population of the USSR. Yet despite all the propagandist flavor that Marxism-Leninism undoubtedly had, it did endorse and promote Marxist ideas. Furthermore, the unity of dialectical and historical materialism crucial to Marxist philosophy certainly remained a central part of Marxism-Leninism—even if it appeared in a simplified and distorted form in the official Soviet philosophical doctrine.

Recently, numerous attempts were launched by former Soviet philosophers to demonstrate that there was legitimate philosophical activity in the Soviet Union. However, the main direction of this endeavor is to detect either internal opposition, for instance, non-Marxist and non-Soviet philosophers during the Soviet era (Losev, Bakhtin), or internal criticism (Ilyenkov), or innovative development (Shchedrovitsky, Grushin, Bibler, Batishchev, Mamardashvili). The official Soviet philosophical doctrine remains outside the focus of general interest and is still an unexplored field for the history of philosophy. One does not need to be a Marxist or a sympathizer with the Soviet Union to recognize that whenever we are inclined to see purely ideological content in it, we find, upon closer examination, that this originates in some sort of legitimately philosophical rumination. In the end, it is a necessary part of critical work to discuss whether such a phenomenon as Soviet philosophy existed and whether during the Soviet period there was not some genuine philosophical (and not just politically or ideologically motivated) research that contributed to its development.

Notes

1. Among the many books on the history of Russian Marxism, see, for example, Anderson (1963), Jordan (1967), Harding (1983), Walicki (1979), and Walicki (2010). It is one of the themes in two standard histories of Russian philosophy: Zenkovsky (1953) and Galaktionov and Nikandrov (1970). Another good reference work is Carpi (2016).
2. Plekhanov invented this term. Marx himself called his approach, from which his materialist conception of history would emerge, "the materialistic basis of my method" ("die materialistische Grundlage meiner Methode") (Marx and Engels 1968, 19). He also called it "new materialism" or "modern materialism" in order to distinguish himself from the mechanist and reductive materialism of the eighteenth century. For more on Marx's materialism, see, for example, Jordan (1967) and Graham (1987).
3. Plekhanov writes (1929, 24) that "the value of the materialist conception of history is primarily methodological."
4. Born Vladimir Ilyich Ulyanov, *Lenin* used several *pseudonyms*, including Illyn.
5. The term "legal Marxism," in contrast to the revolutionary wing of Russian Marxism, was derived from the fact that its supporters promoted their ideas in legal publications. Legal Marxists held numerous open debates from the mid-1890s through the early 1900s, notably at the *Free Economic Society* in Saint Petersburg, and published three magazines between 1897 and 1901: *Novoe*

slovo, Nachalo, and *Zhizn'*. Many legal Marxists soon abandoned Marxism and converted to Neo-Kantianism or religious philosophy.

6. Ernst Mach's (1838–1916) positivism called "empiriocriticism" influenced many Russian Marxists. In 1908, Lenin wrote a philosophical work, *Materialism and Empiriocriticism*, in which he criticized Mach, Machism, and the views of "Russian Machists."

7. In the term "orthodox Marxism," the word "orthodox" refers to the body of Marxist thought, namely, dialectical and historical materialism, that emerged after the death of Karl Marx and which became the official philosophy of the socialist movement as represented in the Second International until the First World War in 1914. This term implies adherence to Marx's theory as he intended it.

8. The history of these controversies is very well-researched and documented. See, for example, Baron (1963), Grille (1966), Jensen (1978), Scherrer (1979), Volodin (1982), Williams (1986), Steila (1991), Tiutiukin (1997), Soboleva (2007), and Oittinen (2009).

9. For more about Lenin's theory of cognition see, for instance, Oittinen (2009) and Bakhurst who tried to give "a more sympathetic reading of the work" (1999, 99).

10. Bogdanov pointed out the differences between his and Mach's theories in his *Empiriomonism* (2003, 6 and 22).

11. For a detailed analysis of empiriomonism and empiriosymbolism, see Soboleva (2007).

12. Plekhanov developed the idea that our impressions of objects are conventional signs, or hieroglyphs, for the first time in his paper *Materialism Yet Again* (1899). In his later works *A Critique of Our Critics* (1906) and *Materialism Militans* (1907), he revisited this understanding and believed that our impressions are determined by the properties of the real, existing world. However, he did not refuse the idea that the external world can act upon a subject in a way determined by her or his organization. According to Plekhanov, the properties of objects have objective significance, "although they are 'seen' differently by different organisms at different stages of development" (Plekhanov 1976, 230).

13. Of course, one can name more than three epistemological standpoints. For example, one can mention pragmatism, which was represented by Jakov Berman. However, these other positions did not belong to the ideological core of the polemic between materialism and idealism within Russian Marxism.

14. In their programmatic book *Ocherki realisticheskogo mirovozzreniia [Essays on the Realist Worldview]* (1904, VI), the representatives of so-called critical positivism declared their credo as "theoretical realism" and "practical idealism."

15. Bogdanov explicitly formulates this goal already in his early book *Cognition from a Historical Point of View* (1902, 2) and represents this position later as well.

16. For example, in his work *Empiriomonism*, Bogdanov analysed the concept "objectivity" and argued that objective means a "concordance of experience" ("soglasovannost' opyta") (Bogdanov 2003, 15) and an "intercourse with other people" ("obshchenie s drugimi liud'mi") (Bogdanov 2003, 19).

17. For more on this subject matter, see Soboleva (2007, 111–115) and Steila (2009, 153–158).

13 RUSSIAN MARXISM AND ITS PHILOSOPHY: FROM THEORY TO IDEOLOGY

18. It is true that Bukharin's conception of superstructure "is a complex, differenti-ated conception, including, in addition to the 'social political order, with all its material parts,' social psychology and ideology," as Stephen Cohen has put it (Cohen 1980, 111). However, he remained faithful to the basic tenets of the materialist view of history and social life.

19. In fact, Bukharin conceived of historical materialism as a doctrine of technologi-cal materialism. His innovations made under the influence of Bogdanov were either exceptions to the rule or contradicted his main theoretical position.

20. See, for example, Blakeley (1964) and Somerville (1967). By contrast, James Scanlan shows in his studies (1985) that there was a plurality of intellectual posi-tions under the umbrella of Marxist-Leninist doctrine.

BIBLIOGRAPHY

Anderson, Thornton. 1963. *Masters of Russian Marxism.* New York, NY: Appleton-Century-Crofts.

Bakhurst, David. 1999. *Consciousness and Revolution in Soviet Philosophy: From the Bolsheviks to Evald Ilyenkov.* Cambridge, UK: Cambridge University Press.

Baron, Samuel H. 1963. *Plekhanov, the Father of Russian Marxism.* Stanford, CA: Stanford University Press.

Blakeley, Thomas E. 1964. *Soviet Philosophy: A General Introduction to Contemporary Soviet Thought.* Dordrecht: Reidel Publishing Company.

Bogdanov, Alexander A. 1902. *Poznanie s istoricheskoi tochki zreniia.* St. Petersburg: Tipografiia Leiferta.

———. 1904. *Iz psikhologii obshchestva (Stat'i 1901–1904).* St. Petersburg: Dorovatovskii i Charushnikov.

———. 1913. *Filosofiia zhivogo opyta. Populiarnye ocherki.* St. Petersburg: Izdanie Semenova.

———. 1914. *Nauka ob obshchestvennom soznanii.* Moscow: Kniga.

———. 2003. *Empiriomonizm (1904–1906).* Moscow: Respublika.

Bukharin, Nikolai I. 1925. *Historical Materialism: A System of Sociology.* New York, NY: International Publishers.

———. 1928. *Teoriia istoricheskogo materializma: populiarnyi uchebnik marksistskoi sotsiologii.* 5-e izd. Moscow and Leningrad: Gosudarstvennoe izdatel'stvo.

Carpi, Guido. 2016. *Istoriia russkogo marksizma.* Moscow: Common Place.

Cohen, Stephen. 1980. *Bukharin and the Bolshevik Revolution: A Political Biography, 1888–1938.* New York, NY: Vintage Books.

Ermichev, Alexander A. 2007. Vstupitel'naia stat'ia. In D.I. Chizhevskii, *Gegel' v Rossii,* ed. Alexander Ermichev, 1–17. St. Petersburg: Nauka.

Galaktionov, Anatolii A., and Petr F. Nikandrov. 1970. *Istoriia russkoi filosofii IX–XIX veka.* Moscow: Nauka.

Graham, Loren. 1987. *Science, Philosophy and Human Behavior in the Soviet Union.* New York, NY: Columbia University Press.

Grebnev, Konstantin. 1929. Gegel' v otsenke revizionizma i marksizma. *Revoliutsiia i kul'tura* 4: 25–32.

Grille, Dietrich. 1966. *Lenins Rivale. Bogdanov und seine Philosophie.* Köln: Wissenschaft und Politik.

Harding, Neil. 1983. *Marxism in Russia.* Cambridge, MA: Cambridge University Press.

Ilyenkov, Evald V. 1970. Gegel' i sovremennost. *Pravda*, August 23.

Iovchuk, Mikhail T., Teodor I. Oizerman, and Ivan Ya. Shchipanov. 1971. *Kratkii ocherk istorii filosofii*. 4th ed. Moscow: Mysl'.

Jensen, Kenneth M. 1978. *Beyond Marx and Mach: Alexander Bogdanov's Philosophy of Living Experience*. Dordrecht: Reidel Publishing Company.

Jordan, Zbigniew A. 1967. *The Evolution of Dialectical Materialism: A Philosophical and Sociological Analysis*. New York: St. Martin's Press.

Konstantinov, Fyodor V., and Alexei S. Bogomolov. 1979. *Osnovy marksistsko-leninskoj filosofii (Foundations of Marxist-Leninist Philosophy)*. 4th ed. Moscow: Izdatel'stvo politicheskoi literatury.

Kopnin, Pavel V. 1973. *Dialektika kak logika i teoriia poznaniia*. Moscow: Nauka.

Lenin, Vladimir I. 1969. *Polnoe sobranie sochinenii v 55 tomakh*. Vol. 29, 5th ed. Moscow: Izdatel'stvo politicheskoi literatury.

———. 1972. *Polnoe sobranie sochinenii*. Vol. 14. Moscow: Progress Publishers.

———. 1976. *Polnoe sobranie sochinenii*. Vol. 38. Moscow: Progress Publishers.

Lukács, Georg. 1971. *History and Class Consciousness: Studies in Marxist Dialectics* (1923). Cambridge, MA: The MIT Press.

Marx, Karl and Friedrich Engels. 1968. *Das Kapital*. In Karl Marx and Friedrich Engels, *Werke*, vol. 23. Berlin: Dietz Verlag.

Ocherki realisticheskogo mirovozzreniia. 1904. St Petersburg: Izdatel'stvo Darovackogo i Charushnikova.

Oittinen, Vesa. 2009. Das Ding an sich—Stein des Anstosses der Bolschewiki? Zur philosophischen Polemik von Lenin und Bogdanov. In *Alexander Bogdanov Revisited*, ed. Vesa Oittinen, 297–329. Helsinki: Aleksanteri Series.

Plekhanov, Georgii V. 1929. *Fundamental Problems of Marxism*. London: Martin Lawrence Limited.

———. 1976. Materialismus Militans: Reply to Mr. Bogdanov. In *Izbrannye filosofskie proizvedeniia*, vol. 3, 188–283. Moscow: Progress Publishers.

Scanlan, James P. 1985. *Marxism in the U.S.S.R.: A Critical Survey of Current Soviet Thought*. Ithaca and London: Cornell University Press.

Scherrer, Jutta. 1979. Bogdanov e Lenin: il bolscevism al bivio. In *Storia del marxiosmo*, 493–546. Torino: Giulio Einaudieditore.

Soboleva, Maja. 2007. *Alexander Bogdanov und der philosophische Diskurs in Russland zu Beginn des 20. Jahrhunderts. Zur Geschichte des russischen Positivismus*. Hildesheim: Georg Olms Verlag.

Somerville, John. 1967. *The Philosophy of Marxism*. New York: Random House.

Steila, Daniela. 1991. *Genesis and Development of Plekhanov's Theory of Knowledge*. Dordrecht: Springer.

———. 2009. From Experience to Organisation: Bogdanov's Unpublished Letters to Bazarov. In *Alexander Bogdanov Revisited*, ed. Vesa Oittinen, 151–172. Helsinki: Aleksanteri Series.

Suvorov, Sergei. 1909. Osnovy filosofii zhizni. In *Ocherki filosofii kollektivizma*, ed. anonymous, 3–112. St. Petersburg: Znanie.

Tiutiukin, Stanislav V. 1997. *G. V. Plekhanov. Sud'ba russkogo marksista*. Moscow: ROSSPÉN.

Volodin, Alexander I. 1982. *"Boi absoliutno neizbezhen": Istoriko-filososkie ocherki o knige V.I. Lenina "Materialism i empiriokriticizm" ("The struggle is absolute inevitable": Some Essays on Lenin's Book "Materialism and Empiriocriticism")*. Moscow: Politizdat.

Walicki, Andrzej. 1979. *A History of Russian Thought from Enlightenment to Marxism.* Stanford University Press.

———. 2010. Russian Marxism. In *A History of Russian Philosophy 1830–1930: Faith, Reason and the Defence of Human Dignity*, ed. G.M. Hamburg and Randall A. Poole, 305–325. Cambridge University Press.

Williams, Robert. 1986. *The Other Bolsheviks: Lenin and His Critics 1904–1914.* Indiana University Press.

Yushkevitch, Pavel. 1908. Sovremennia energetika s tochki zreniia empiriosimvolizma. In *Ocherki po filosofii marksizma*, 162–214. Sankt Peterburg: Zerno.

Zenkovsky, Vasilii V. 1953. *History of Russian Philosophy.* New York: Columbia University Press.

CHAPTER 14

Between East and West: Russian Identity in the Émigré Writings of Ilya Fondaminsky and Semyon Portugeis

Alexei A. Kara-Murza

INTRODUCTION

This chapter serves as an introduction to the primary philosophical and socio-logical views of two prominent Russian émigré intellectuals of the first half of the twentieth century: Ilya Isidorovich Fondaminsky (1880–1942), whose political and literary pseudonym was Bunakov, and Semyon Osipovich Portugeis (1880–1944), who wrote under the pseudonyms of Ivanovich and Talin. Having both been born in 1880, they responded to the 1917 Russian Revolution in their prime, with extensive scholarly knowledge and political experience. Fondaminsky-Bunakov was a prominent figure in the right wing of the Socialist Revolutionary Party (SRP), which was close to the moderate liberals. Portugeis-Talin-Ivanovich was a prominent figure of the Menshevik (anti-Leninist) wing of the Russian Social Democratic Labor Party (RSDLP). However, the most important period of their lives was spent in exile after the victory of the one-party Bolshevik regime in Russia. Their scholarly and jour-nalistic talents flourished abroad, and in the Parisian émigré community they became the leading philosophical and sociological authorities concerning the historical development of Russia. In the 1920s and 1930s, Fondaminsky and Portugeis offered original interpretations of Russian history and Bolshevik modernity, and were able to provide valuable insight into Russia's future. Many of their perspicacious insights are gaining new relevance today.

A. A. Kara-Murza (✉)
Department of Philosophy of Russian History, Institute of Philosophy, Russian Academy of Sciences, Moscow, Russian Federation

© The Author(s), under exclusive license to Springer Nature Switzerland AG 2021
M. F. Bykova et al. (eds.), *The Palgrave Handbook of Russian Thought*,
https://doi.org/10.1007/978-3-030-62982-3_14

Fondaminsky and Portugeis: Two Biographies

Ilya Fondaminsky was born in Moscow to a wealthy merchant family who raised him in a fairly typical Moscow-Jewish environment, where, according to his friend and legendary social revolutionary, Vladimir Zenzinov, "the fathers and children belonged not only to different generations, but also to different worlds" (Zenzinov 1948, 300–301). Fondaminsky's oldest brother, Matvei Fondaminsky, left the family early to join the Narodnaya Volya revolutionaries. He was arrested and after two years of incarceration was sentenced to ten years of exile in the Yakut Governate. After participating in the 1889 riot of political exiles, he was sentenced to twenty years of hard labor. In 1895, he was released to settle in Siberia, but a year later, before reaching the age of thirty, he died in Irkutsk of tuberculosis.

Fondaminsky tried to matriculate into the Lazarev Institute of Oriental Languages, but was unable to do so because of restrictions on the admission of Jews, and instead studied at the more democratic private gymnasium of Franz Kreiman in Moscow.[1] From 1900 to 1904, he studied philosophy at the universities of Berlin and Heidelberg, where he joined a circle of young Russian radicals.[2] In the spring of 1902, he was arrested for the first time on the Russian-German border for the illegal transportation of revolutionary literature, and spent two months in prison. Here, Fondaminsky experienced his first "spiritual breakthrough," which his friend Zenzinov later remembered: "It seemed to him that the solitary walls parted, and a new and bright truth was revealed for which alone he could and should live" (Zenzinov 1948, 303–304).

Soon after being released, he married his childhood friend Amalia Gavronsky, who also attended the philosophy seminars of Kuno Fischer and Wilhelm Windelband in Heidelberg. She was the granddaughter of Wolf Wissotzky, who was a millionaire tea merchant (nicknamed the Tea King) and one of the leaders of the Russian Zionist movement. Fondaminsky, who was already well off, received a large dowry which included shares in Wissotzky's tea plantations in Sri Lanka.

After receiving a diploma in Heidelberg at the end of 1904, Fondaminsky returned from Germany to Moscow and entered the leadership of the Socialist Revolutionary Party. Shortly after, he distinguished himself as a brilliant speaker at many rallies and was given the pseudonym Bunakov.[3] In December 1905, he took an active part in organizing an armed uprising in Moscow, spending large sums of his personal wealth on weapons and equipment for combat detachments.

After the suppression of the 1905 Russian Revolution, Fondaminsky and his wife completed their first emigration to France where they lived from 1907 to 1917. Over the years, he gradually became disenchanted with political terror and focused on literary-enlightenment work with a growing interest in religious issues. After the 1917 February Revolution, Fondaminsky returned to Russia, and during the April All-Russian Peasant's Congress, he was elected deputy chairman of the Executive Committee of the Council of Peasant Deputies. Many of his friends from the Socialist Revolutionary Party ran the

Provisional Government, and in the summer of 1917 he was sent as general commissioner to the Black Sea Fleet, where he quickly gained support from sailors and officers, and, for some time, successfully resisted the Bolshevization of the fleet. In fact, it was the Black Sea Fleet sailors that elected Fondaminsky-Bunakov to the All-Russian Constituent Assembly.[4]

After the 1917 October Bolshevik Revolution and the dispersal of the Constituent Assembly, Fondaminsky became a member of the Union of the Renaissance of Russia, which existed underground. From the summer of 1918 until April 1919 he lived in Odessa, after which he emigrated for a second time back to France with his wife by way of Constantinople. In Paris, he was a co-editor for *Sovremennye zapiski*, the most authoritative journal of the Russian émigré community. From 1920 to 1940, the journal published works by Russian philosophers (Berdyaev, Bulgakov, Lossky, Shestov, Frank, Florovsky), fiction writers (Bunin, Merezhkovskii, Nabokov, Remizov, Aldanov, Zaitsev, Osorgin), and politicians (Miliukov, Maklakov, Kerensky), regardless of their political affiliation. In 1931–1939, together with Georgii Fedotov and Fyodor Stepun, Fondaminsky also published the Christian-democratic journal *Novy Grad*. For many years, his Paris apartment on the Avenue de Versailles, 130, in the Passy district was one of the cultural centers of the post-revolutionary Russian émigré community.

Following the death of his wife in 1935, Fondaminsky published a book in her memory which consisted of the recollections of their friends. In those months, his enthusiasm for Christianity intensified, and, along with the philosopher Nikolai Berdyaev and Mother Maria Skobtsova, he became one of the founders of The Orthodox Cause, an Orthodox Christian organization.

In the summer of 1941, after Germany's attack on the USSR, Fondaminsky was arrested by the Nazis and detained in the Compiegne concentration camp along with other Russians. That year, on the night of the feast of the Nativity of the Virgin (September 20), Fondaminsky was secretly baptized in an improvised Orthodox chapel in the camp barracks by Konstantin Zambrzhitsky, a priest who had himself been imprisoned in the camp.

Fondaminsky was given the opportunity to escape from the camp, but chose to stay with his Jewish comrades who had been sentenced to death by the Nazis. Eventually, he was transferred to the Drancy concentration camp and then to the Auschwitz extermination camp, where he died on November 19, 1942. In 2004, the Patriarchate of Constantinople canonized Fondaminsky among five Russian Christian martyrs who died in exile.

Semyon Osipovich Portugeis was also born in 1880 into the large, poor family of a Jewish artisan living in Chisinau, a city known as a place where political exiles were sent.[5] Portugeis' biographer, Boris Nikolayevsky, wrote, "He rose from the bottom up by the only path available to talented young people of his social stratum: through participation in the revolutionary movement" (Nikolaevskii 1944, 394).

Already in his youth, Portugeis fell in with the political circle of one Chisinau exile, D.B. Goldendakh, an educated Marxist who later adopted the pseudonym Riazanov. Since that time, Portugeis himself adopted many pseud-onyms, which confused not only the professional investigative services of his time but also less sophisticated historians and bibliographers who could not fully connect his numerous faces to one personage.

Additionally, Nikolaevskii was not entirely correct when he said that the young Portugeis had no choice but to join the revolution. Talented young people of his circle had another path to establish themselves in life, that of slow professional growth in their immediate domestic and ethno-cultural environ-ment. Later, the relationship between the slow process of culture, the evolu-tion of everyday life, and the violent breaking of history would be the focus of Portugeis-Talin-Ivanovich's writings.

In 1901, the twenty-year-old scholar went to Germany for the first time and entered the technical school in Mannheim; in 1902, he moved to Munich, where he graduated from a brewer's school. It seemed that he made a choice in favor of a profession. However, Europe not only provided him with a profes-sion but also broadened his horizons. The well-known Menshevik, Grigory Aronson, wrote the following in Portugeis' obituary: "At the time, the foreign land changed the plans and fate of young people who were eager for a better life. What was laid in the Riazanov circle was manifest in Munich" (Aronson 1944, 66). The choice in favor of Europe, culture, and enlightenment was still a choice in favor of revolution.

Portugeis' first literary experiments took place in the Odessa journal, *Southern Review* [*Iuzhnoe Obozrenie*], edited by Alexander Izgoev, the future author of the famous philosophical anthologies *Signposts* [*Vekhi*] and *From the Depths* [*Iz glubiny*]. In 1904, after his home was once again searched by the authorities, Portugeis fled abroad, where he had published several striking arti-cles about Russia in revolutionary publications. He became an active partici-pant in Swiss émigré discussions, where he attracted the attention of various socialist leaders who tried to draw the talented speaker and journalist into their party, and, as was customary in that environment, into their clan. However, the signs of revolution back in Russia gravitated Portugeis back to the revolution-ary centers of his homeland.

Believing in his revolutionary and literary calling, he settled in St. Petersburg, collaborated with numerous publications, and quickly established himself as one of Russia's best political journalists. During these years he joined the Mensheviks headed by Alexander Potresov, whose friend and collaborator he remained until the older comrade's death in 1934.

With the outbreak of the First World War, Portugeis sided with the *oborontsy* [defensists] and edited *The Day* [*Den'*], a newspaper where he continued to work after the Bolshevik coup. However, after heightened repression, he was forced to move from Petrograd to Kiev and then to Odessa, where he lived out the Russian Civil War.

In 1921, he left Bolshevik Russia and, with the help of smugglers, illegally moved to Bessarabia and then to Paris, where in the same year he published the widely read pamphlet "Twilight of Russian Social Democracy" (Portugeis

1921) in which he contrasts the monarchist and liberal versions of the revolution as the fault of socialism before Russia, but contrary to the official Menshevik position that alleged there was no socialism in Bolshevism. Instead, Portugeis described Bolshevism as an "acute illness of socialism," which was the inevitable result of socialism's gradual theoretical and political "darkening."

Beginning in the early 1920s, Portugeis actively worked with *Contemporary Notes* [*Sovremennye zapiski*], and in the spring of 1922 began publishing his own monthly, *The Dawn* [*Zaria*]. After Alexander Potresov's arrival in Paris, Portugeis started another journal for Potresov and his group, called *Notes of a Social Democrat* [*Zapiski sotsial-demokrata*].

In parallel, Portugeis worked as a political correspondent for Pavel Miliukov's liberal daily newspaper *Latest News* [*Poslednie novosti*]. However, Portugeis' most important work consisted of a series of monographs: *Five Years of Bolshevism (Beginnings and Ends)* [*Pyat' let bol'shevizma (Nachala i kontsy)*] (1922); *The Russian Communist Party* (1924); *Revolutionary Communist Party* [RKP]; *Ten Years of Communist Monopoly* (1928); *Red Army* (1931). Each of these works was methodically prepared, using extensive documentary and statistical material received from Russia by the Turgenev Library in Paris and the Library of the International Labor Office in Geneva.

The catastrophe of the new world war forced Portugeis to move from Nazi occupied Paris to New York City. Already quite ill, he spent most of his time in hospitals. He died on the night of February 27, 1944, and was buried in New Mount Carmel, a Jewish cemetery in Queens. In *New Journal* [*Novyi zhurnal*] (New York), the historian Boris Nikolaevskii wrote, "With the passing of this man, we have lost one of the most profound journalists of the socialist camp of today's Russian émigré generation" (Nikolaevskii 1944, 394).

Ilya Fondaminsky (I): Russia in the Context of World History—Eastern Theocracy in Northern Eurasia

Starting with the second issue of *Sovremennye zapiski* (January 1921), Fondaminsky-Bunakov (one of its founders, publishers, and co-editors) began to publish a series of essays under the heading "Russian Paths" ["Puti Rossii"].[6] The spatial and geographical framework in which the author analyzed the complex interrelationships of Rus'/Russia and its civilizational neighbors (primarily Western Europe) proved to be extremely unusual for the Russian historiography of the nineteenth and twentieth centuries.

"The great Northern continent of Eurasia," wrote Fondaminsky, "juts into the ocean surrounding it from all sides with deep protrusions [...] In the south are the peninsulas of Indochina, Hindustan, and Arabia; in the west is the peninsula of Western Europe. [...] The struggle between Eastern and Western civilizations, between the East and the West, is the struggle of the great Northern continent with its Western peninsula" (Fondaminsky 1921b, 237).

With regard to Russia, Fondaminsky outlined its geography as follows: "To the east of the Western European peninsula, deep into the continent, unfolds a great Northern plain. […] It stretches for many thousands of miles from west to east until the Yenisei River and from north to south from the White Sea to the Black Sea, and from the shores of the Arctic Ocean to the Hindu Kush Mountains" (Fondaminsky 1921b, 238).[7]

Speaking about the geo-cultural and geo-political identity of Russia, Fondaminsky departs from traditional West-East coordinates, and prefers to talk about Russia as the North: "The Great Northern Plain lies on the shores of the Arctic Ocean […] The tragedy of Russia is that its coastal perimeter is bound by the ice of the Arctic Ocean, that the great Russian rivers carry their waters to this 'dead' ocean" (Fondaminsky 1921b, 239).

But if geographically, and even geopolitically, Russia is *the North*, then culturally it is *the East*, one of the great Asian theocracies: "The Russian Empire resembles the architecture of the East. […] The Tsarist cupola crowns the entire structure of the state" (Fondaminsky 1933, 310).

Fondaminsky believed that historians had been for a long time mistakenly "restoring the state structures of the Russian Empire according to Western models"—laying the foundations for class and estate, and erecting state institutions over them. However, such constructions are "just the illusion of a Western gleam over the imperial structure" (Fondaminsky 1933, 310). Fondaminsky considered the main shortcoming of Russian historical science as follows: "Russian historical science is a child of the West […] It builds Russia against the backdrop of the West. […] The East remains hidden in the fog and almost merges with 'nature.' Therefore, the context of Moscow Tsardom is artificially limited" (Fondaminsky 1927, 230), but modern historical science requires a completely different structure:

> We must push Russia into world history. It is necessary to restore the image of Moscow Tsardom not only in relation to the West, but also in relation to the East. It is necessary to compare Moscow Tsardom with the great Eastern theocracies […] The essence of the people's soul of Moscow Tsardom is Eastern. […] As in all Eastern theocracies, the entire existence of Moscow Tsardom is permeated with religion and faith in God […] Serving God and his earthly consul, the Tsar, is the basic beginning of Moscow life. (Fondaminsky 1927, 230)

Until the reforms of Peter the Great, Muscovy was practically undifferentiated from other Asian countries:

> As in the states of the East—India, China, Japan—Muscovite Russia developed a proud national self-confidence, and an unshakable awareness of its superiority over all other peoples […] Relations between Russia and the West […] did not differ much from the relations that existed between the West and China and Japan until the nineteenth century. (Fondaminsky 1921a, 277)

It is therefore not surprising that European influence in Russia was still very weak and barely noticeable in the sixteenth and seventeenth centuries. The Russian state did adopt some of the West's military and technical knowledge in the interests of the army and industry; however, while Russian "higher society adopted European fashions and entertainment, it barely adopted its ideas" (Fondaminsky 1921a, 277).

Only beginning with the epoch of Peter the Great was Muscovy subjected to intensive Western influence: "With the pivot West, a new—Western—light was cast over the face of Russian statehood and its bearer—the Russian sovereign" (Fondaminsky 1932a, 304). However, according to Fondaminsky, the new trends were "only a Western reflection on the old Eastern face of Muscovite Russia [...] Its true facial features changed little" (Fondaminsky 1932a, 304). This is why the power of Emperor Peter I seemed to contemporaries even more limitless than the power of Tsar Ivan the Terrible: "In the old state machine, some of the gears were replaced, but the engine remained the same" (Fondaminsky 1933, 322).

Even during the reign of Catherine II, Russia had not changed its theocratic nature, similar to that of some Asian countries:

> Catherine the Great was a person of the West [...] Like most enlightened Westerners of her time, she was indifferent to religion and, if she admitted the existence of God, it was in the form of Voltaire's Creator of the universe. (Fondaminsky 1932a, 313)

However, the Russian Empress was an intelligent woman and had

> A talent for rule [...] Having ascended to the all-Russian throne on the bayonets of her guards, she knew perfectly well that it was impossible to preserve her power on bayonets alone [...] The souls of the Russian people in her time were strongly Orthodox. (Fondaminsky 1932a, 313–314)

That is why, long before her accession to the throne, Catherine "audaciously overcame her religious indifference and zealously began to study Orthodox law," and when she ascended to the throne, "firmly rose to the defense of the Orthodox faith and behaved in strict accordance with that faith throughout her entire reign as befits a pious and Orthodox empress" (Fondaminsky 1932a, 314). Therefore, notes Fondaminsky, in the sphere of state building, Catherine faithfully repeated the methods of Peter the Great "to build a new Western state without touching its old Eastern foundations" (Fondaminsky 1934, 281).

After Alexander I's unsuccessful attempts to reform Russia, his brother Nicholas I established strict Orthodox order in the empire: "Autocracy and Orthodoxy almost merged into a single confession of imperial faith" (Fondaminsky 1932a, 315). Emperor Nicholas, although externally clothed in a European military uniform:

was permeated with the Byzantine-Orthodox understanding of tsarist power that was characteristic of the Muscovite Tsars [...] He treated his religious duties as reverently as his royal duties. The tsar's calling is a heavy burden imposed by God on his chosen messenger, a sacrificial service to God and Russia. [...] He worked without rest, led a simple and Spartan life, sacrificed everything for the sake of duty, and died with the terrible awareness of his heavy responsibility before God for the devasted Russia. (Fondaminsky 1932a, 316)

Fondaminsky believed that the divine right of Russia's rulers and the awareness of their sacred duty

did not leave the Russian sovereigns until the very end of the Romanov dynasty [...] One cannot understand the tragic life and death of the last emperor without understanding the decisive role this characteristic played in his personality. [...] In his difficult life, he was guided not by arguments of reason and not by the advice of state officials, but by a voice from above [...] The Tsar is only an instrument of the Most High, a submissive performer of His will. (Fondaminsky 1932a, 317–318)

What else, according to Fondaminsky, distinguishes Western monarchies from Eastern theocracies?

Eastern despotism is governed by the will and caprice of individuals—the monarch and his servants. Western Monarchy is governed on the solid basis of law [...] The Russian emperors rebuilt Moscow Tsardom into a European Empire, took all the forms of the Western state [...] But they adamantly refused to take that *form* which determines all the others. [This *determining form* consists of] the state institutions that are independent of the monarch's will, made up of the representatives of the estates or the people. For they [the Orthodox monarchs] correctly believed that these independent representatives of the institutions limit the will of the monarch. (Fondaminsky 1933, 316–317)

Indeed, how can an unlimited autocrat limit himself? Can unlimited power be combined with law, or autocracy with freedom? The practice of the West, according to Fondaminsky, convincingly shows that this is absolutely impossible: "For an unlimited autocrat to limit himself is as impossible as for a wingless man to fly in the air [...] The Russian Empire remained an Eastern despotism in Western form" (Fondaminsky 1933, 317–318).

The real Europeanization of Russia began only after the monumental reforms of Emperor Alexander II in the 1860s:

Western civilization begins to slowly but steadily disperse into the lower classes of the people. The Muscovite foundations of the life of the people—serfdom and conscription—began to fall away. Western views of the world, the state, and the individual gradually penetrated popular consciousness. [However, we should not deceive ourselves.] The transition from sacred Eastern theocracy to Western rule of law is a descent through cliffs and abysses. [...] The flow of Western culture into Eastern folk consciousness is an excruciating and dangerous operation [...]

The mask of slavery slowly comes off, revealing horrible traces [...] Western ideas, having penetrated Eastern consciousness, created an unprecedented, volatile combination. (Fondaminsky 1932a, 324, 331)

Western consciousness took possession of the lower classes in the era of the first Russian revolution of 1905–1907:

Only in the years between the first revolution and the war did it conquer the village [...] Even on the eve of the Great War and the Revolution, the Eastern layers remained at the foundations of people's lives—in their being, economy, and consciousness. It was as if Europe had yet to touch this. [...] When revolution broke through to the people's depths, these layers rose to the top. [...] That is why the Great Russian Revolution with its many features was so surprisingly reminiscent of the old Moscow revolt. (Fondaminsky 1932a, 324–325)

At the end of his sagacious historical analysis, Fondaminsky draws an important conclusion (and these words were written in 1932):

That is why the modern Soviet state, emerging from the revolution, so strangely resembles the old serfdom of Muscovy Tsardom. Both the revolution and the Soviet state are only conceived in a Western way; they are knit together in the Eastern way and from Eastern materials. (Fondaminsky 1932a, 325)

Ilya Fondaminsky (II): Death of an Empire—The Order of the Intelligentsia Against the State

In his 1920s essays published in *Sovremennye zapiski*, Fondaminsky drew attention to a phenomenon of Russian history, which, in his opinion, fundamentally distinguished the paths of Russia from the paths of classical Eastern theocracy. This phenomenon is the *Russian intelligentsia*, which he referred to as the Order, and the fate of which he made the focus of his research and practical efforts.

The main idea of Fondaminsky was that the Russian Empire, as a sacred realm, was an *exceptionally stable form of statehood*. Although sometimes quite radical, all the popular movements in Russia, all the so-called Times of Trouble were phenomena that occurred exclusively within the imperial paradigm. "Troubles and popular unrest are usually cited as evidence of the instability of the Moscow state system. But, in fact, they prove the opposite. For what is 'trouble' in the eyes of Muscovites? Why did the Muscovites rise up? Trouble came when Muscovites were 'stateless.' And they always rose up in the name of God and the sovereign" (Fondaminsky 1927, 231).

Fondaminsky poses the question: What explains the riots and insurrections that continued throughout the entire imperial period? Of course, the position of the Russian people has always been difficult, and this burden has repeatedly engendered open discontent. But this popular unrest, according to

Fondaminsky, was never directed against the autocratic authorities, and even less so against the supreme bearer of autocratic power: "On the contrary, when the people rebelled, they rose in defense of legitimate power against that power's enemies, or in defense of the legitimate tsar against his substitute. The state ideology of the insurgents and those who suppressed the insurrection was always identical" (Fondaminsky 1931, 33).

Consider, for instance, the Pugachev Rebellion. *Against* whom and *in support of* whom did the followers of the most famous peasant leader, Emel'ian Pugachev, rise up? "Against Catherine II's usurpation of imperial power and in support of the legitimate Emperor Peter III" (Fondaminsky 1931, 33, 1932b, 289). This was also the nature of the Decembrist revolt of December 14, 1825.

> For our left-wing public, the December revolt is the beginning of the open struggle of the Russian people against autocracy, but this is a historical illusion [...] In order to get the people and the army on their side, the conspirators took advantage of the interregnum. No one knew exactly who the lawful tsar was [...] There were two tsars, two oaths. This was a tragedy of allegiance to the tsar and the oath, and not the shadow of protest and outrage against authority. (Fondaminsky 1931, 33)

However, the initial unobtrusive *awakening* that began in Russia at the turn of the eighteenth and nineteenth centuries truly was dangerous for the autocratic-theocratic Empire:

> The 'fermenting germ' of the West began to spread. [...] This was the beginning of the amazing 'spiritual-knightly order' of the Russian intelligentsia, whose significance for the Russian public was invaluable and whose exploits would be included in the 'golden book' of history. (Fondaminsky 1921a, 279)

In his journalistic essays and scholarly articles, Fondaminsky-Bunakov repeatedly drew attention to the following paradox: "The empire expanded, grew economically powerful, had great international prestige, and relied on the love and devotion of its people, and, nevertheless, it crumbled to dust" (Fondaminsky 1931, 35). Why? "Because *consciousness split from being*. Because the soul of the people separated from the Empire" (Fondaminsky 1931, 35). The cause of this separation was the Order of the Russian intelligentsia.

Fondaminsky names Alexander Radishchev the founder of this Order. During the reign of Catherine, "in the era of Imperial Russia's greatest prosperity," an almost imperceptible event occurred that would determine the fate of the Empire:

> A group of young noblemen was sent to Europe to study Western science [...] Radishchev returned to Russia, burning with the ideas of the Western Enlightenment—the law, the individual, and freedom [...] And having returned with the light of this new truth, Radishchev's soul left the Empire. The 'reflection

of this light' became Radishchev's famous book, *Journey from St. Petersburg to Moscow*. (Fondaminsky 1931, 36–37)

Radishchev's work made a great impression on Catherine II. "She was an intelligent woman and immediately understood the true significance of this event," writes Fondaminsky, commenting on the diary entries of the Empress's secretary, Khrapovitsky: "This is the spread of the French contagion, disgust with the authorities. The author is a rebel worse than Pugachev" (cited in Fondaminsky 1931, 37).

"Catherine was right. Radishchev was more dangerous for the Empire than Pugachev" (Fondaminsky 1931, 37). As Alexander S. Pushkin had noted, Pugachev "merely" caused a revolt, which was "senseless and merciless" and, therefore, sterile.

[But Radishchev] initiated a liberation movement that ended in the collapse of the Empire; his book was the first crack in the grand structure of imperial Russia. [Beginning with Radishchev] the liberation movement grew uncontrollably [...] one soul lit the next, like one candle lighting another, and burning with the light of the new truth, these souls left the Empire. At first, these were the lonely souls who wandered the grandiose Empire like a desert. Then they came together in small groups and circles and, finally, united in the spiritual Order of the Russian Intelligentsia. [...] [On the surface] nothing changed in the Empire. The knights of this Order led peaceful lives that from the outside seemed perfectly ordinary [...] The vast majority of the Order's members came from the upper classes [...] But, nevertheless, the change was immense: a new alien body began to grow in the body of the Empire; a spiritual core of freedom had been created in the theocratic kingdom of serfs. (Fondaminsky 1931, 37)

The author goes on to draw attention to the image of the Russian intelligentsia:

Before us are people with the well-born faces of noblemen, dressed in the uniforms of officers and clerks—the brothers of those on whom the Empire stands. [At the same time] these new people are not at all like their brothers [...] Sad-thoughtful eyes scintillating in narrow animated faces. [...] And around them everything is also changing—new love, new family, new attitudes toward the serfs and service, new morality, science, and literature. [...] The imperial tradition of serfdom melts away where these people appear. [...] And the Empire, sensing the danger of this threat, wages a ruthless struggle against them. (Fondaminsky 1931, 37)

But the Empire's struggle against this Order was already hopeless because every blow it dealt translated into a new victory for the intelligentsia: "By restricting the free expression of the word, the Empire raised creative and spiritual tensions to heights that would have been impossible under other circumstances" (Fondaminsky 1931, 37). By pursuing the people of the Order, the

304 A. A. KARA-MURZA

Russian authorities only turned them into heroes and martyrs; by sending them into exile, it only spread the spiritual contagion deeper into the country. By sending them to the gallows, the Empire "self-inflicted irreparable harm [...] Five hanged Decembrists melted the ice of the Empire more than a thousand conspirators left at large" (Fondaminsky 1931, 37).

Already during the reign of Nicholas I, when the whole of the Empire seemed to be made of granite and "every free breath was ruthlessly suppressed," the organization of the Order of the Intelligentsia was, in Fondaminsky's paradoxical assessment, already over and its victory was assured:

> All the spiritual peaks of educated Russian society had been taken by the Order, and all living, talented people were in its ranks. To complete its victory, the Order had one more mission: to take the soul of the people from the Empire. [...] [This was accomplished over] the last three Tsardoms. [...] At the beginning of the Great War, the mission was over: the souls were taken away. The grandiose Empire was soulless. The desiccated shell was empty. At the first collision, it crumbled to dust. (Fondaminsky 1931, 37–38)

According to Fondaminsky, the people's devotion to the monarchy began to deteriorate especially rapidly during the Russian-Japanese War and the 1905 Revolution, and "finally disappeared during the Great World War" (Fondaminsky 1931, 33). Referring back to the testimonies of socialist agitators, Fondaminsky writes, "Back in 1905, it was necessary to speak about the tsar in the village with the utmost caution. The people still loved the tsar, although they were beginning to doubt him" (Fondaminsky 1932a, 333). In the period between the first revolution and the world war, "the melting of the love for the tsar was uncontrollable [...] During the war the soul of the people left the tsar for good. As the love of the tsar fell, so did the main foundation of imperial power. The Russian Empire stood helpless before the impending revolution" (Fondaminsky 1932a, 333).

Semyon Portugeis (I): The Riddle of the Bolshevik Coup

The main idea of Portugeis' socio-political worldview was the *democratization of history*. History is stable and forward-moving only when it is based on the steady progress of the average individual who makes up an average citizen. This democratic presumption (which crystallized in the early years under the influence of Goldendakh-Riazanov, and then Plekhanov and Potresov) caused Portugeis to dissociate himself from, on the one hand, all manners of political sectarianism and conspiratorialism, and, on the other hand, the Narodnik complex of worshiping the people. Portugeis is a democrat-evolutionist who talks not about *the people* but of *the citizens* who can only exist within the legal culture of the modern city and within the developed forms of production.

Portugeis' beginnings can be traced back to a rare type of liberal-democratic socialism. He did not like the liberalism of his time because of its supercilious elitism, insensitivity to the problems of the majority, popularity with the bourgeois, and commitment to the primacy of economic calculation over cultural creativity. It is rare to meet an author who considers himself a socialist, but also so actively criticizes the problems of socialist doctrine from the standpoint of protecting the civil rights of the individual.

Portugeis saw the main problem of modern socialism as *the dictatorship of economics*; when it formulated solutions to social problems, it absolutized material factors to the detriment of cultural factors. He believed that although the economic forms of human existence are the basis of social development, the progress of humankind is carried out mainly at the tops of superstructures and consists of the gradual release of the individual from the bonds of economic dependence. The catastrophic spasms of the First World War led to the collapse of culture down to "the basis of an elementary struggle for elementary economic needs." At this foundation, or base, social (especially socialist) thought is completely reduced to those aspects of being where the economic function of humanity is primary: "The dictatorship of economics was just the result of the unprecedented impoverishment of humankind. The replacement of the citizen by the worker was only an ideological expression of this impoverishment" (Portugeis 1922b, 77). For Portugeis, the dictatorship of economics was the result of the collapse of culture, which set Russia far back and long delayed the realization of public harmony.

The degradation of socialist consciousness, Portugeis noted, lies in the fact that "the citizen is knocked from his place, won in the blood of the great workers' revolutions." Instead of resisting cultural degradation, the Russian socialists try to turn this process to their own advantage and lead it. The Bolsheviks brought this twilight trend of socialism to its logical conclusion by denigrating the "principle of the citizen" and exalting the "principle of the worker," but "as soon as the criterion of the citizen disappears, so does the criterion of freedom" (Portugeis 1922b, 74).

Portugeis formulates the main contradiction between the culture-centric (civil) idea of socialism (which he upheld his entire life) and the anti-culture attitude of the Bolsheviks, who seemed to posit "the poorer, the better" as their guiding principle:

> Socialism will come from wealth. [...] For socialism to succeed, society must be in its prime. [...] Revolution always comes from poverty. [...] For a revolution to break out (and revolutions only break out), society must be in a state of extreme decline. (Portugeis 1922c, 238)

Portugeis believed the Bolshevik catastrophe was caused by the long-identified gap between the culture of the pre-revolutionary Russian elite, which reached great heights in art, literature, and social theory and the rest of the masses: "A few rare eagles circled the mountain peaks, while masses of frogs populated the enormous swamps" (Portugeis 1927b, 378). However, if in literature and art this asymmetry can be considered normal and natural, the elite maximalism of the socio-political sphere was dangerously divorced from the general civic maturity of the people. This, in Portugeis' opinion, was the main problem of Russia's historical development: "With enormous leaps and bounds, we ascended to great heights, and when in the Great War and then in the Great Revolution we needed the people, the masses, the national will, and state intelligence, we only found empty space" (Portugeis 1927b, 378).

Ultimately, those who won out in Russia believed that capitalism was not the *precondition* of socialism, but a *hindrance* to it. A dangerous logic prevailed: "What is bad for capitalism, is good for socialism. When capitalism is sick, it is necessary to finish it, so that socialism becomes possible." Portugeis' point was that between the idea that *capitalism is impossible* and the idea that *socialism is possible* there is a fundamental logical and political difference. The bourgeoisie can be overthrown (which is not so difficult if it is criminal, stupid, talentless, and egotistical to the point of blindness), but this will have progressive meaning only if "the thing it did badly is done well by those who replace the bourgeoisie" (Portugeis 1921, 13). Reversing Jean Jaurès' well-known formula "revolution is a barbaric form of progress," Portugeis believed that the Bolshevik coup was "a barbarous form of regression." Only progress (above all the expansion of the possibilities of cultural creativity) can justify the radicalism of the revolutionary method. While dealing a blow to culture, Bolshevism meant "the triumph of regression in the cycle of events that began in the spring of 1917" (Portugeis 1922a, 25–26).

During the 1920s–1930s, Portugeis carefully analyzed the factors that contributed to the Bolshevik victory in Russia, and argued that Bolshevism caused the rising revolution to descend into chaos, defeating culture and its bearers. A major role was played by the First World War, which was the apotheosis of anti-cultural trends. For, despite the superficiality and fragility of the Europeanization of Russia (which, according to Portugeis, was a "fragile glaze on our barbarism"), only the war was able to break through the shell of culture and expose the national chaos.

Unfortunately for Russia, there was a political force that made a conscious bet on the escalation of Russian barbarism. According to Portugeis, the leaders of the Bolsheviks understood what their opponents did not, or did not want to, understand. It was the Bolsheviks, particularly Vladimir Lenin, who realized that the coming years would pass in Russia under the reign of chaos and the collapse of the most elementary foundations of society: "Lenin foresaw that while the war would impoverish some peoples, it would mutilate the Russian people, physically and mentally mutilate, breaking the spine of the people" (Portugeis 1922a, 25). The political tactics of the Bolshevik-Leninists proceeded from this cynical but accurate calculation:

> Only the Bolsheviks decided to make the spirit of war, its poison, its immoral, brutal, and chaotic elements the spirit of their party. [...] Those who argued with them at rallies, who saw them in action prior to their victory, could not help but

get the impression that they were betting shamelessly and frankly on chaos. (Portugeis 1922a, 26)

The immediate driving force behind the Bolshevik coup was the groups of people who had been *declassed* in the course of the First World War and the breakdown of culture:

The world disintegrated, and on the bare scorched earth stood a naked, mutilated man who valued nothing. The Bolsheviks looked for this man at the front, among the deserters, among the declassed masses of the village and the city, among the motley crowds drawn by the military-industrial bacchanalia into the hot heat of industrialization. (Portugeis 1922a, 14)

It was precisely this person that the Bolsheviks "found in sufficient quantities to form an avalanche of elemental chaos that suffocated the scattered specimens of the human-citizen" (Portugeis 1922a, 15). The "Jesuit genius" of Lenin consisted in his fearless embrace of this chaotic rebellion, in his intuitive belief that "rebellion is not opposite to power, but a convulsive jerk away from a power that no longer instilled fear toward a power that would restore that fear" (Portugeis 1924b, 9). Lenin turned out to be the only one in Russia who shrewdly understood that

he would gain absolute power, similar to divine power, by unleashing the elements of a rebellion. [...] [He felt that] only an enraged mass that had lost all traces of social consciousness can be turned into the obedient herd of the dictator. He knew that rebellion would bring this mass to an exhausted and devastated state, which would serve as the most expedient foundation for his stardom. (Portugeis 1924b, 9)

The tragedy of the democratic opponents of the Bolsheviks was that they dangerously underestimated the forces of corruption and anarchy that had accumulated in Russia by that time. However, genuine democracy could not have found those elements necessary to overcome the chaotic forces of the necessarily brutal struggle:

Democracy, which was unable to follow the chaos, had to look for a *balancing power* between the forces of chaos and the ideals of democracy. But it was not able to find a force powerful enough to *counteract* the chaos. (Portugeis 1922a, 16)

Russian democracy proved powerless in the face of Bolshevism also because it was faced with a completely new historical phenomenon—*the democratization of reaction* (which Portugeis believed was also adopted by German Nazism):

What happened was what the democratic consciousness of the nineteenth and twentieth centuries was least prepared for. Political reaction turned from that of the noble and the lordly into the popular and the plebeian. The social democratization of reaction gave it its grandiose scope and extraordinary power [...] [And in popular form] it easily absorbed some of the ideas of socialist anti-capitalism, and it was clearly revealed how a socialism deprived of the ideas and ideals of political democracy is barbaric and destructive for human individuality. (Portugeis 1936, 399)

How could a regime, the genesis of which was based on antisocial elements and the destruction of all order, survive for so long? Is there a way out of this destructive state of civilization? These questions were central to Portugeis' scholarly research.

SEMYON PORTUGEIS (II): IS THERE A WAY OUT OF BOLSHEVISM?

The originality of Portugeis' conception of social history consists in examining the chain of historical events from two opposing sides, or, more precisely, at the intersection of two different analytical strategies. On the one hand, every event enters history one way or another. In this sense, the bizarre chain of early twentieth-century Russian revolutions has already occupied its place in history. There is, however, another principle of history, which, Portugeis notes, is applied far less often: "Not only do events enter history, but *history also enters events*. [...] In other words, the forces of 'dialectics' pass into the event; thus, the forces of sociological development transform the initial meaning of an event, often into its opposite" (Portugeis 1927b, 356).

According to Portugeis, not only did Bolshevism enter history, but history entered Bolshevism; these historical forces gave it life, but this life developed along paths the Bolsheviks could not control:

> Russian history entered Bolshevism, but Bolshevism was different, which is why it resorted and continues to resort to terrorism, because it fanatically intended to isolate Russia and itself so that Russian history never entered it. Russian Bolshevism wanted to be anti-historical, extra-historical, and super-historical and in this consisted its extreme "revolutionariness"—to enter history without letting history enter it. (Portugeis 1927b, 356)

Hence, the terrorist hysteria of the Bolsheviks, who were constantly trying "to ensure that history did not penetrate their organism" (Portugeis 1927b, 356). Related to this, while Russian historiography of a Slavophile bent drew parallels between the historical role of the Bolsheviks and that of Peter the Great, Portugeis always insisted on their fundamental difference. Having cut a window to Europe, Peter I let history enter Russia, while Lenin and Stalin tried to isolate Russia from history.

Portugeis introduces another pair of concepts: *History* and *Historical Accident*. The Bolsheviks knew perfectly well that their victory was the product of Historical Accident (a military catastrophe, spontaneous militarization of consciousness, moral and cultural collapse), but against them was History—the basic laws of modern development. The war imposed a temporary moratorium on these objective historical laws, but even war cannot completely destroy them. The meaninglessness of communist utopia lay in the fact that "it wanted to turn accident into history, and history, at least the thousand year old history of Russia, into a discretionary accident" (Portugeis 1927b, 356–358).[8]

Portugeis' merit as a Sovietologist is his multifaceted analysis of the relationship between the organic nature of history and the Bolshevik violence against history. Another paradox formulated by the author is that all the anti-historical plans of the Bolsheviks, as they were theoretically conceived, inevitably devolved into fiascos. However, it was precisely because these plans failed on a regular basis, and precisely to the extent that they failed, that the Bolsheviks could retain their dominance over Russia:

> Only by carefully jettisoning their program, only at the cost of shameless opportunism, unheard of in the history of the revolution, could the Bolsheviks stay in power. Only by enduring defeat as a regular principle could Bolshevism remain a fact. They declared a sacred campaign against history, but history entered them, gave them life, and took away *their* meaning. (Portugeis 1927b, 357)

After all, the consistent jettisoning of basic communist principles by the Bolsheviks (especially, the rejection of the state as a machine of violence, the liquidation of property inequality, and world revolution) is the chronicle of Russian Bolshevism.

In contrast to abstract claims that Bolshevism was "a relapse to Russian barbarism," "a reversion to Asiatic savagery," and "the restoration of Eastern despotism" so familiar from many anti-Bolshevik émigré authors, Portugeis sought to identify the specific social forces that produced what he called "the Istanbulization of Russia." He was interested not only in questions like "Who took the lead?" or "Who realized the coup?" but also "Whom did it benefit?"

An interesting part of his analysis was the conclusion that the middle stratum and the petite-bourgeoisie played a decisive role in the Bolshevik coup (i.e., precisely those social forces that had previously been relegated to the periphery of Russian life). The objective content of the Bolshevik coup, according to Portugeis, was the spontaneous breakthrough of trends triggered by extraordinary circumstances, which had been secretly brewing in Russia for decades, and were catalyzed by the world war.

Indeed, the degradation of major civilized forms of economic life had already been noticed at the beginning of the war. Thus, the process of destroying capitalism did not benefit the proletariat (which quickly disappears due to the paralysis of industry), but primarily the *petite bourgeoisie*. In this sense, the 1917 Russian Revolutions (both February and October) were, in Portugeis' opinion, not socialist or bourgeois: "Not the proletariat and the bourgeoisie, but the conglomerate of the middle elements of the city and the countryside— the 'petits bourgeois' (whom we did not notice or despised in every possible way) announced their existence and their claim to history" (Portugeis 1927b, 364–365). A necessary condition for the plebeian petit bourgeois to enter the historical arena was the socio-cultural catastrophe of the nation, "the collapse of centuries of pre-revolutionary development, of economic, cultural, and spiritual levels [...] Everything had to fall apart so that these late-born social elements could rise up [...] Otherwise, they could not rise up" (Portugeis 1927b, 360).

In other words, the middle stratum broke to the forefront of history only thanks to Bolshevism, which provided the nutrients for its rapid growth. This concerned not only socio-economics but also cultural and psychological revenge: "It was necessary to break the spiritual hegemony of the Russian intelligentsia, to dislodge its anti-petit-bourgeois pathos, to humiliate it not only socially, but also psychologically" (Portugeis 1927b, 368).

Thus, Bolshevik power established itself under the demagogic veil of the dictatorship of the proletariat and facilitated the emergence of the middle stratum of society. However, Bolshevism inevitably and immediately entered into a long-term and irreconcilable conflict with this stratum because it represented a new subject of history. Striving for its own consolidation, Bolshevism diligently created mechanisms of influence and control over various social groups, but these groups used the same mechanisms for the historical reproduction of themselves and, in this sense, against the anti-historical Bolshevik dictatorship.

Behind the process of destruction through redistribution (a phenomenon characteristic of all revolutionary epochs, according to Portugeis), more far-reaching trends are conjured up, which explains the deeply concealed logic of the system's evolution. Here, the phenomenon of the total criminalization of Soviet society is explained:

> After all the property, all the valuables were redistributed under the leadership of the Soviet government, after everything was taken and there was no one left to rob, then the state itself began to be robbed. [...] Communist property, the property of the state was no more sacred than the property against which Soviet power had organized its campaign. (Portugeis 1927b, 371)

When the regime grew decrepit, the property of the communist state became the object of barbarous plunder, and this was the direct consequence of the barbaric psychology of redistribution engendered by Bolshevism. Portugeis' fundamental idea was that everyday life developed in spite of Bolshevism, gradually regenerating the objective logic of the development of human relations, the logic of the development of culture and history. The key institutions of the Bolshevik regime—the party, the Komsomol, and the army—had been conceived as reliable instruments of domination, but eventually they became the focal points of acute internal struggle. Because these institutions were so important, they were where the contradictions of the system manifested themselves in the culture of everyday life that began to flourish, a culture that was contrary to the paroxysms of revolutionary extremism.

As a Sovietologist, Portugeis closely studied the internal metamorphosis of the main institution of Bolshevism—the Party. Of course, the very term *party* as applied to the phenomenon of the Russian Communist Party (RCP) and All-Union Communist Party (AUCP) can be subjected to critical analysis:

> Whether a party is large or small, it is always only a part of the political forces of a given country […] Places where all parties are destroyed, where a single group of people acts, destroying with fire and sword not only those who act but those who think differently, this dominant group becomes the whole. And, having become a whole, ceases to be a part, and consequently ceases to be a party. (Portugeis 1924a, 3)

The point here is not about false self-appellation, but about the fact that by establishing a monopoly on power, the "Party" did not eliminate social and political contradictions, but drove them deeper inside itself: "The party was able to prevent and suppress the emergence of a second party in the country, but it suffered a severe defeat at home, because its home turned into an arena of grandiose feuds" (Portugeis 1928, 415).

Thus, history "played a cruel joke on the RCP." Indeed, the Party monopoly set itself the task of destroying all activities that contradicted its goals. Under these circumstances, many of the forces that were persecuted and evicted from everywhere else found their refuge in the Party itself:

> If one is allowed to rule only through the RCP, then the entire diverse world of interests, passions, and clashes connected with economic activity [and] class struggle […] all this must find some reflection in the huge sponge of the RCP […] The struggle of the population with the monopoly of the legality of the RCP was transferred to the RCP itself. (Portugeis 1924a, 8–9)

The Communist Party of the Soviet Union became a kind of Noah's Ark, where diverse groups of people, often with sharply differing interests, rescued themselves from the flow of lawlessness raging across the country:

> This is the legal part of the country, united only in this—the title of legality […] "Outsiders" continue to hole up inside the party itself, and not only do they watch and listen, but they also vote. Because they are party members. They have put on the party hat of invisibility, and their role in the political development of the country represents the most dangerous force for the political dictatorship. (Portugeis 1928, 405–406)

Already in the early 1930s, Portugeis wrote that "The Party is losing its 'social capacity' for those elements of the population who want to become a part of the socio-political and economic leadership" (Portugeis 1932c, 6). He finishes by making a prediction about the deadlock and ultimate insolvability of this contradiction: "When the AUCP fails to organize more and more hundreds of thousands of people in command positions, one of the most powerful supports of its dictatorship will begin to deteriorate" (Portugeis 1932b, 6–7).

Thus, the main contradiction of the Bolshevik system is the inevitable clash of the regenerative culture of everyday life within the doctrinally limited communist framework. When the regime was conceived during the years of the revolution and the civil war (when, as Portugeis puts it, "the country burned in the flames of the civil war and the elementary fear of death, hunger, bullets, and disease suppressed the human in humanity"), the Bolshevik brand was not so vulnerable and exasperating. But once those times passed and the needs of individuals grew infinitely in all directions, the "Soviet party brand became intolerable, which was the basis for a deep rift between the population and the ruling class" (Portugeis 1927a, 510).

For its part, the Bolshevik regime intuitively understood the source of its secret power, and with all its might countered the regenerative power of human nature: "We must continue the revolution at all costs. Otherwise, we die." One of the most effective ways of artificially prolonging the revolutionary youth of the Bolshevik government was by constantly conjuring up the image of a common enemy:

> The autocracy of the Romanovs saved itself by giving the crowd, as if on loan, violence against the Jews. The autocracy of the Communists saved itself by giving over to the full disposal of the working people violence against the bourgeoisie. [...] Bolshevik demagogy desperately needed an assailable bourgeoisie that could be energetically strangled, but never completely annihilated. (Portugeis 1922a, 64–65)

This led to the perpetual show trials of real and imaginary enemies of the people, periodic party purges, and so forth.

But as the regime steadily aged, the active forms of self-rejuvenation (terror, purges, trials of the enemies of the people) were replaced by increasingly perfunctory forms, which were mostly ritualistic and, ultimately, meaningless. The regime was no longer able to ban history, but was still capable of sabotaging the regenerative process of everyday life.

Meanwhile, notes Portugeis, the irreversible process of senile degeneration was already affecting the very top of the communist elite. Bright-eyed revolutionary enthusiasts were gradually replaced by gray-haired officials who considered the stability of their position to be their top priority. This is what Portugeis colorfully called "the ersatz of the communist catalogue." "These elements [...] want the revolution not to continue, but to end. But this is death for a dictatorship" (Portugeis 1929, 2). The end of the revolution would be the work of the communist elite, and the collapse of the Soviet system would begin from within its main institution—the monopoly Party—which is what Portugeis analytically predicted in the 1920–1930s.

Unlike most emigrants of the first post-revolutionary wave, Portugeis was convinced that "Bolshevism can be overcome not by those who initially rejected it, but by those who left it from within" (Portugeis 1936, 390). Thus, a new regime is never overthrown:

> It must grow old to concentrate in itself the enmity of the majority in order to shatter all illusions associated with its birth and early years [...] The regime must cool, bend, and grow old, to lose the luster of great events [...] so that in the psyche of the people the elements of objective orientation of their own position can be accumulated. (Portugeis 1936, 390–392)

Portugeis wrote cautiously about the future of the anti-Bolshevik coup. Some of his works show that he preferred the most bloodless outcome: operating in the shell of the Bolshevik regime, history would gradually "hollow out this temporary political container" and then "the overthrow will occur with a small push, that is, not in the style of the 'great revolution'" (Portugeis 1927b, 378).

As for the future character of Russia freed from Bolshevism, Portugeis was never a great optimist. He had no doubt that even after the fall of the Bolsheviks, the path of Russia would not be strewn with roses—it seems that the choice is "not between good and evil, but between a bigger and lesser evil" (Portugeis 1922b, 105). To think that beneath the rubble of the dictatorship is concealed a blessed society that requires only liberation from its shackles is to repeat once again the tragic mistake already made by Russia's revolutionary dreamers (Portugeis 1931, 15).

The point is not to work toward anti-Bolshevism, but toward cultural, enlightened post-Bolshevism. Even if this strategy cannot be perfectly implemented, the principal task remains: if the anti-Bolshevik revolution spontaneously occurs in Russia, one should take all measures to "protect it from possible reactionary and revanchist distortions." And this, in turn, assumes not passivity, but "an active political and cultural struggle against the Soviet dictatorship and for future Russia, even when the revolutionary situation seems to be completely absent" (Portugeis 1932a, 13).

According to Portugeis, another important historical lesson of Russian Bolshevism is that this historical obscuration comes to history not only in the form of great violence but also in the form of great temptation. Back in the early 1920s, Portugeis foresaw that after the collapse of Bolshevism in Russia, its appeal would likely continue in mass consciousness: "After being defeated as a fact, Bolshevism will quite possibly be even more tempting as an idea and illusion [...] After Bolshevism 'passes away' and no longer 'beats one over the head,' its extraordinarily real and really extraordinary manifestations, its ideological influences, may become very strong." He concludes with a comment that seems particularly relevant to our time. This will be especially true "if Bolshevism descends to the realm of shadows in the aura of martyrdom, and its victors are incapable of quickly establishing tolerable conditions for life in Russia" (Portugeis 1921, 113).

Conclusion

The remarkable life trajectories of these two talented Russians, the socialist-revolutionary Ilya Fondaminsky and the social-democrat Semyon Portugeis, crossed in the expatriate community of 1920s Paris. Each in his own way belonged to the predominant left spectrum of Russian political life and with the same ardor dreamed of the collapse of the "prison of nations" that was the Russian Empire, and both worked hard to achieve this noble, as it then seemed, goal. Life forced them to reconsider their views regarding the Empire, which sank into History, and, more broadly, to reconsider the main historical trends of Russia. In place of the reviled Russian Empire came the Empire of Lenin and Stalin, which turned out to be a much more repressive and totalitarian monster, which maimed the destinies of both Fondaminsky and Portugeis, and which eventually gave rise to the monster of German Nazism—the empire that killed them both. However, through their intense intellectual work (and in the case of Ilya Fondaminsky through his own life!), they managed to atone for their youthful, revolutionary mistakes. If Russia is destined to eventually abandon its totalitarian past, these two illustrious intellectuals will undoubtedly deserve some of the credit.

Translated by Peter Golub

Notes

1. According to the law of 1887, the proportion of Jewish students in Moscow was not to exceed 3 percent. More fortunate than Fondaminsky in this respect was another descendant of the old Moscow Jewish community, the future outstanding philosopher of the Russian Silver Age, Semyon Frank (also then an emigrant), who did manage to matriculate in the Lazarev Institute. As a side note, my grandfather, Sergei Georgievich Kara-Murza (1878–1956), had no problem matriculating in the prestigious Lazarev Institute, and studied alongside Semyon Frank. He went on to become an attorney, journalist, and theorist of drama, and remained in Soviet Russia after the revolution.
2. In the Russian circle in Heidelberg, Fondaminsky met another student from Moscow, the famous philosopher and sociologist Fyodor Stepun, who in his memoirs commented about the erudition and oratory talent of the young socialist revolutionary (Stepun 2000, 90–91).
3. Fondaminsky once admitted that he chose the pseudonym Bunakov absolutely by accident. At one of the mass rallies where he was to speak, he saw a bright sign on the Moscow street bearing the name of the owner.
4. During the only meeting of the Constituent Assembly on the night of January 5, 1918, one of the Bolshevik sailors in the Taurida Palace in Petrograd tried to shoot Fondaminsky in the meeting room after recognizing the then Deputy Fondaminsky as the former Socialist-Revolutionary Commissioner of the Black Sea Fleet.
5. For more on the biography of Semyon O. Portugeis, see Kara-Murza (2006).
6. The publication of "Puti Rossii" lasted until the final issue (no. 70) of *Sovremennye zapiski*, published in 1940 during the chaos of the Second World War. From

14 BETWEEN EAST AND WEST: RUSSIAN IDENTITY IN THE ÉMIGRÉ WRITINGS... 315

1921 to 1940, he published seventeen of these philosophical-historical essays with their unprecedented conception and depth.

7. In recent years, interest in the history of the concept of the Nordic identity of Russia has reappeared in contemporary Russia. I refer to several of my recent works on this topic: Kara-Murza (2017b, 2017c, 2018).

8. See also Kara-Murza (2017a).

BIBLIOGRAPHY

Aronson, Georgii. 1944. S.O. Portugeis. 1880–1944. *Socialisticheskii vestnik* 5–6: 66.

Fondaminsky, Ilya I. (pseudonym Bunakov I.). 1921a. Puti Rossii. Stat'ia 3. *Sovremennye zapiski* 7: 237–260.

———. 1921b. Puti Rossii. Stat'ia 2. *Sovremennye zapiski* 4: 228–284.

———. 1927. Puti Rossii. Stat'ia 7. *Sovremennye zapiski* 32: 216–278.

———. 1931. Puti osvobozhdeniia. *Novyi grad* 1: 31–48.

———. 1932a. Puti Rossii. Imperiia 1. *Sovremennye zapiski* 48: 304–333.

———. 1932b. Puti Rossii. Imperiia 2. *Sovremennye zapiski* 49: 289–317.

———. 1933. Puti Rossii. Imperiia 4. *Sovremennye zapiski* 52: 310–338.

———. 1934. Puti Rossii. Imperiia 5. *Sovremennye zapiski* 54: 281–316.

Kara-Murza, Alexei A. 2006. *Pervyi sovetolog russkoi emigratsii. Semyon Osipovich Portugeis (1880–1944)*. Moscow: Izdatel'stvo Genezis.

———. 2017a. Istoriia' i 'istoricheskii sluchai' v sotsial'noi kontseptsii russkogo bol'shevizma V.I. Talina. *Voprosy filosofii* 11: 112–115.

———. 2017b. Rossiia kak Sever. Metamorfozy natsional'noi identichnosti v XVIII–XIX vv. *Filosofskie nauki* 8: 121–134.

———. 2017c. Kontseptsiia 'russkogo severianstva' v geroicheskikh odakh G.R. Derzhavina (k voprosu o rossiiskoi identichnosti). In *Politicheskaia kontseptologiia* 3: 187–194.

———. 2018. Russkoe severianstvo' kniazei Viazemskikh (k voprosu o natsional'noi identichnosti). *Voprosy filosofii* 3: 40–50.

Nikolaevskii, Boris. 1944. Pamiati S.O. Portugeisa (St. Ivanovicha). *Novyi zhurnal* 8: 399–400.

Portugeis, Semyon O. (pseudonym St. Ivanovich). 1921. *Sumerki russkoi sotsialdemokratii*. Paris.

———. 1922a. *Piat' let bol'shevizma*. Berlin, 64–65, 84.

———. 1922b. Demokratiia i sotsializm. In *Sovremennye problemy*. Paris, 71–81.

———. 1922c. O diktature. *Sovremennye zapiski* 10: 234–256.

———. 1924a. *Rossiiskaia kommunisticheskaia partiia*. Berlin.

———. (pseudonym V.I. Talin). 1924b. U groba Velikogo Diktatora. *Zaria* 1: 7–10.

———. 1927a. Nasledniki revoliutsii. *Sovremennye zapiski* 30: 479–513.

———. (Ivanovich). 1927b. Ob istoricheskom massive (Iz razmyshlenii o russkoi revoliutsii). *Sovremennye zapiski* 32: 356–379.

———. (Talin). 1928. Pobezhdennye i pobediteli. *Sovremennye zapiski* 39: 401–423.

———. 1929. Kuter'ma i revoliutsiia. *Poslednie novosti* 2: 2.

———. (Ivanovich). 1931. Piatiletka, sotsializm i Otto Bauer. *Zapiski sotsialdemokrata* 3: 10–16.

———. 1932a. Dobrye sovety khoroshikh druzei. *Zapiski sotsial-demokrata* 10: 10–16.

———. 1932b. Iubileinye zametki o VKP(b). *Zapiski sotsial-demokrata* 17: 5–9.

———. 1936. Puti russkoi svobody. *Sovremennye zapiski* 60: 383–403.

Stepun, Fyodor A. 2000. *Byvshee i nesbyvsheesia*. St. Petersburg: izdatel'stvo Aleteiia.

Zenzinov, Vladimir M. 1948. I.I. Fondaminsky-Bunakov. *Novyi zhurnal* 18: 299–317.

CHAPTER 15

Ivan A. Ilyin: Russia's "Non-Hegelian" Hegelian

Philip T. Grier

THE MAKING OF A PHILOSOPHER, LAWYER, AND POLITICAL THEORIST

The life and influence of Ivan Aleksandrovich Ilyin (1883–1954) must be approached in three distinct phases: (1) from youth to middle age, during which he emerged as a prominent philosopher and political theorist in his native Moscow; (2) the period of exile in Germany and Switzerland stretching from his enforced exile in 1922 until his death in 1954, during which he played a prominent role in the intellectual and political life of the Russian emigration in Western Europe, but was largely forgotten (and his works suppressed) in his homeland; and (3) the period beginning around the collapse of the Soviet system in 1991, following which awareness in Russia of his legacy of political, philosophical, and spiritual writings began to grow rapidly.

In this chapter I will focus attention primarily upon two of his main philosophical works—the two-volume commentary on Hegel published in 1918, and the posthumously published work in political and legal philosophy entitled *On the Essence of Legal Consciousness* (1956)—because these are the only ones currently available in English translation. At the same time I will briefly sketch a few of the most significant events in his life because without them it is more difficult to comprehend the man or significant portions of his writings.

Ilyin came of age and began to play a prominent role in the intellectual life of Moscow during the years just prior to and during the Bolshevik Revolution

P. T. Grier (✉)
Dickinson College, Carlisle, PA, USA
e-mail: grier@dickinson.edu

© The Author(s), under exclusive license to Springer Nature Switzerland AG 2021
M. F. Bykova et al. (eds.), *The Palgrave Handbook of Russian Thought*,
https://doi.org/10.1007/978-3-030-62982-3_15

317

and the ensuing Civil War. For example, in 1920, upon the death of Lev Lopatin, the long-time president of the Moscow Psychological Society, the most prominent association for philosophers and psychologists in Russia, Ilyin was elected to replace him. In addition to his philosophical work during those years, primarily on Hegel, he also revealed himself to be a combative, strongly opinionated political commentator and theorist, thoroughly engaged with contemporary events. From quite early on he revealed a strong antipathy to the Bolsheviks, a dominant aspect of his persona that would persist to the very end of his life.

As a sympathizer (and suspected collaborator) of the defeated Whites, Ilyin was arrested, tried, and forcibly exiled by the Red victors in the immediate aftermath of the Civil War. He was among those intellectuals rounded up and judged to be "irreconcilable," that is, implacable foes of Soviet Russia, and exiled aboard the so-called philosophers' ship in the fall of 1922, accompanied by his wife Natalia Nikolaevna (neé Vokach). This was the fate suffered primarily by a group of approximately sixty Russian philosophers, historians, and other intellectuals who had already achieved sufficient prominence outside the borders of Russia that their simple "disappearance" might have created awkward questions for the new authorities.

From late 1922, after being permanently exiled from Soviet Russia, he played a similar, equally prominent and no less combative role in the intellectual life of the Russian emigration in Western Europe, first in Germany and then in Switzerland, where he eventually died.[1] Proving the accuracy of the Bolsheviks' judgment, he became one of the most consistent, adamant, uncompromising foes of Communism, Stalinism, and the Soviet system in the entire Russian emigration, never wavering from his determined opposition to them right up to his death in late 1954 (having outlived Stalin by the better part of two years). In the early years of his exile in Germany, at the request of General Wrangel, he wrote extensively in defense of some of the objectives of the White movement in exile, eventually becoming known as the "Theorist of the White Idea."

He also never wavered from his certainty that the entire Soviet system would eventually collapse of its own internal contradictions and its failure to achieve the necessary characteristics of a genuine state—meaning above all, commitment to the rule of law. During the last few years of his life (1948–1954) he authored some 220 "bulletins," making detailed projections of what Russia would experience in the immediate aftermath of the collapse of the Soviet system, and outlining the steps that would need to be taken in order to resurrect the Russian nation, politically, morally, and spiritually. It was these writings, gathered together under the title *Our Tasks*, that first attracted widespread attention during the years just before and after the collapse of the Soviet "state" in December 1991 and brought Ilyin's long-suppressed name into prominence once more in his homeland.[2]

Ilyin was known for his eloquence, his exceedingly strong opinions, and a general refusal to compromise on any issue that he considered vital, even facing threats of incarceration or the possibility of execution.[3] As a writer he was celebrated by some of his contemporaries such as his friend Petr Struve as one of the greatest masters of language in the history of Russian culture. Archimandrite Konstantin thought he could be compared only to Pushkin and Metropolitan Filaret of Moscow, the great nineteenth-century ecclesiastical writer (Ilyin 2010, lxiii).

In 1918, Ilyin achieved intellectual prominence in Moscow, and eventually abroad, with his first major philosophical publication, a two-volume exposition, interpretation, and critique of the philosophy of Hegel. That work was produced as his thesis for the Magister degree in the Faculty of Law at Moscow University. His undergraduate studies for the Diploma had taken place in that same faculty between 1901 and 1906, under the mentorship of Pavel I. Novgorodtsev, generally known as the informal head of the "Moscow School" of jurisprudence. The other most prominent influence upon the young Ilyin was Prince Evgenii N. Trubetskoi, who joined the Faculty of Law six months prior to Ilyin's completion of the Diploma, and helped to guide his graduate studies between 1906 and 1909, by the end of which period Ilyin had completed his formal studies and examinations for the Magister degree, lacking only a thesis. Upon giving some trial lectures in 1909, Ilyin was granted the status of *docent* and commenced teaching at three Moscow institutions of higher education, including Moscow University.

Beginning in 1908 Ilyin had undertaken a close study of Hegel's philosophy, which continued for the next eight years. It is worth noting that even as an undergraduate Ilyin had been quite comfortable with literary German, as his mother had grown up in a German-speaking household in Moscow, and started teaching Ilyin German from the age of five. Initially he supposed that he might write a dissertation involving Hegel's legal and political thought, in the context of German "Rationalist" philosophy of law in the nineteenth century. But at some point he began to focus on Hegel's legal philosophy alone and, finally, broadened his thesis into a study of, and commentary on, Hegel's philosophy as a whole.

As was the usual tradition for Russian graduate students in those days, Ilyin expected to be sent abroad for six months or a year in order to pursue research for his thesis, as well as to learn the latest methods and approaches of university teaching in Western Europe. Departing for Germany at the end of 1910, over the next nearly eighteen months Ilyin spent time studying with Jellinek, Husserl, Nelson, Rickert, and Simmel at their respective universities. Of all of these experiences, the time spent with Husserl seems to have made the greatest intellectual impact upon him, as revealed especially by his insistence in the commentary on Hegel that Hegel's and Husserl's philosophical methods should be considered together as versions of intuitionism.

Ilyin was hopeful that his work on Hegel would make some impact on philosophical discussion in Germany. At one point he confessed to a close confidant his hope to quickly produce a German translation of his commentary, immediately following his defense of the thesis in Russian, anticipating that

320   P. T. GRIER

there would be greater interest in his work in Germany than in his homeland (notwithstanding the recent history of critical German attitudes toward Hegel).[4]

Ilyin was encouraged to think that such a contribution to German discussion might be well received, because he was aware of the early stirrings of a "renaissance" of German interest in Hegel in the very early years of the twentieth century. In 1905, Georg Lasson had begun publishing the *Sämtliche Werke*, a revised and enhanced edition of Hegel's collected works, and in 1907 Herman Nohl had published his collection of Hegel's early theological works.

Against this background of a renewal of at least some favorable German interest in Hegel, Ilyin privately announced an ambition to produce a "synthesizing constructive exposition" of Hegel's thought (Ilyin 2010, xxiii). It was "synthesizing" and "constructive" because Ilyin undertook to identify all the most distinctive terms, concepts, and elements of thought characteristic of Hegel's work, noting every occurrence and re-occurrence of each one across the entire range of Hegel's published works, and then "re-constructing" Hegel's system, as it were, by reassembling all of these elements he had identified in such a way as to exhibit what he took to be the essential structure of Hegel's thought. The most visible mark of Ilyin's intellectual procedure is the presence at the bottom of most pages of his commentary of a listing of *every* occurrence of the term or concept under discussion, drawn from the whole of Hegel's *Collected Works* as well as additional sources, in an extremely compressed system of citations, amounting almost to a complete concordance for Hegel's works.[5]

The result was entitled *The Philosophy of Hegel as a Doctrine of the Concreteness of God and Humanity*, in two volumes.[6] The first volume was *The Doctrine of God* (Ilyin 1918a); the second, *The Doctrine of Humanity* (Ilyin 1918b). Part one of volume one, "The Doctrine of the Essence of Divinity," provided in seven chapters a complete account of Hegel's doctrine of "speculative concreteness" as "the criterion of all reality and all value" (Il'in 2010, 135). These first seven chapters drew upon more or less the entire range of Hegel's works. However, Ilyin organized the exposition in his own quite distinctive way, building the account through four levels, beginning with (1) the concrete-empirical, next proceeding to (2) the abstract-formal, and thence to (3) the abstract-speculative, culminating in (4) the concrete-speculative. This reconstruction arrived at the conclusion that the central idea of the whole of Hegel's philosophy was the claim that "Everything real is subordinate to the law of speculative concreteness" (Il'in 2010, 134).

In volume one as a whole Ilyin undertook to show how this conception of concreteness pertained to the being of God and, in volume two, to the being of humanity in the world and in history. The second volume explicated Hegel's doctrine of the concreteness of humanity, focusing upon the system of ethical life (*Sittlichkeit*) as the form in which humanity becomes fully actual (concrete). Accordingly, the organizing principle for volume two is the explication of each of the successive moments of *Sittlichkeit*, culminating in the doctrine of the state as the highest manifestation of human actuality (the concreteness of humanity) in the realm of objective spirit.

Ilyin's focus on the theme of the concrete versus the abstract represented a major advance in the history of Hegel studies. While Ilyin did not claim to be the first to have recognized the centrality and importance of this theme in Hegel's thought, he did claim to be the first to have produced a complete commentary on the whole of Hegel's philosophical system from this point of view, a claim that appears to be fully justified. The crucial point is that Hegel's usage of the terms "concrete" and "abstract" departs radically from the traditional empiricist usage in which "concrete" usually refers to some existing particular, and "abstract" to some abstract universal or other category of thought. On the contrary, a bare particular in Hegel's vocabulary would be *abstract*, while a fully differentiated and developed existing whole of thought would be *concrete*, more or less reversing the traditional seventeenth- to eighteenth-century empiricist conception.[7] Thus, when Hegel proclaims that "The truth is the whole" he is referring to a fully developed, wholly differentiated *actuality* as what is *concrete*—hence the justification for Ilyin's claim that "speculative concreteness" is the criterion of all reality and all value. To further emphasize the point, Ilyin insisted that "We can recognize as Hegelian only one who consciously professes that *the dialectical actualization of speculative concreteness by real thought is the essence of any being and any value*" (Il'in 2010, 135).

The historical significance of Ilyin's achievement can be judged from the perspective of a number of other commentaries on Hegel's philosophy from much later in the twentieth century. In 1964 George Kline published a review of eight recently published (mid-century) commentaries on Hegel in a variety of European languages (Kline 1964). Of the eight prominent authors he surveyed, only two appeared to grasp the significance of Hegel's distinctive use of the term "concrete." And only one of them, a work by Wilhelm Seeberger, was entirely reliable on this point. It turned out that Seeberger (alone) had closely studied Ilyin's 1946 German translation of his commentary on Hegel (Seeberger 1961).

A further unmistakable achievement of Ilyin's commentary was his focus on the centrality of Hegel's philosophical theology for his system as a whole. Ilyin's contribution in this respect represented a recovery from a notable defect of much nineteenth-century commentary on Hegel. In the aftermath of Hegel's sudden death, his followers soon began to quarrel among themselves over the significance of the prominent use of theological vocabulary throughout his work. The specific *casus belli* was the question of what meaning could be ascribed to the "personhood" of God and the immortality of the soul. Two camps soon emerged, which became known as the "Right" and "Left" wings of Hegel interpretation. The commentators on the Right tended to read Hegel's theological vocabulary as an endorsement of traditional Christian theological doctrine, and worked to subordinate Hegel's system (specifically, Absolute Spirit) to a conception of God as supreme being, existing independently of the creation and ruling over it as transcendent monarch. The Left, on the other hand, rejected any literal reading of the theological vocabulary, and attempted to explain it away as merely an elliptically expressed anthropology or a methodological conception.

In retrospect, neither of these tendencies can be accepted as a sound reading of the texts, despite having dominated much of the history of Hegel commentary. There was also an attempt in those early years to develop what might have succeeded as a "centrist" reading of Hegel, principally by Karl Ludwig Michelet, which however proved to be abortive in historical terms. Nevertheless, Michelet attempted a much more defensible interpretation of Hegel's project from a theological point of view. He argued that Hegel was entirely serious about his theological vocabulary (contra the Left), but that Hegel's own theology was grounded in his doctrine of the Concept, and that only those elements of traditional theology that could be reconciled with the Concept could claim a place in the system (contra the Right). Hegel thus reinterpreted Christian doctrine in terms of the Concept, rather than "molding" the Concept to fit traditional Christian doctrine.

On a particularly crucial theological point, Hegel rejected the traditional Christian doctrine of the impassibility of God, and instead argued that God must be conceived as susceptible of tragedy, suffering, and death. Setting aside the history of largely failed interpretations of Hegel's theological language in the nineteenth century, Ilyin accurately depicted the centrality of Hegel's theology for his entire project, and also clearly recognized the respects in which Hegel overturned elements of traditional Christian doctrine. In particular, he rightly focused attention upon Hegel's rejection of the doctrine of divine impassibility, accurately delineating the fundamental role of this rejection of the tradition in Hegel's theology as a whole.[8] Had Ilyin's commentary been widely available to scholars through the twentieth century, it is entirely possible that the Left-Right struggle of Hegel interpreters over the theological element might have been abandoned sooner than it in fact was.

Only relatively recently has there been a concerted effort to resurrect something like the "centrist" perspective of Michelet in the treatment of these theological dimensions of Hegel's thought. One of the most prominent advocates of this development was Robert Williams, whose two final books are major contributions to the re-interpretation of Hegel along these lines.[9] He engaged with Ilyin's work in a substantial way in both of them, viewing Ilyin as the first important Hegel interpreter of the twentieth century to have recognized the central importance of theology for Hegel, while simultaneously setting aside both the Left- and Right-wing traditions of interpretation. Williams explicitly presented his own interpretation as a renewal of the "centrist" tradition where Michelet had left off in 1842, while at the same time identifying and rectifying a fundamental defect that undermined Michelet's interpretive effort.

Yet another illustration of the distinctiveness of Ilyin's commentary as well as his uncommon insight into Hegel's system was his recognition that, strictly speaking, Hegel *did not* possess a so-called dialectical method of thinking. He joined this conclusion to his claim that Hegel was an *intuitivist* in terms of method, comparing Hegel's method to the *eidetic intuitionism* practiced by Husserl:

> Thus, according to the method *of his philosophizing*, Hegel must be recognized not as a "dialectician," but as an intuitivist, or, more precisely, as an intuitively thinking clairvoyant. If by "method" is meant the "type and mode" of cognizing subjectively practiced by the philosopher, then one may regard Hegel as a "dialectician" only given a completely superficial, abstractly rational approach. He neither "searches" for contradictions in concepts nor "strives" to reconcile them afterward; [...] It is *not he* who practices "dialectic" but *the object*. (Il'in 2010, 115–116)

Precisely what Ilyin intended by his comparison of Hegel's "intuitionism" and Husserl's "eidetic intuitionism" is not entirely clear. However, a number of contemporary Hegel scholars would agree with the opinion that Hegel does not have a dialectical method in the sense of engaging in a special type of "dialectical" thinking which could be (arbitrarily) applied to a variety of subject matters.[10] More precisely, if we take seriously Hegel's claim that the *Science of Logic* is engaged in a *presuppositionless* thinking, then it follows that no fundamental distinction can be drawn between the *content* and the *method* of that thinking. In that sense, then, it would be true that Hegel had no distinctive "dialectical" method of thinking which could be contrasted with the content of what is being thought.

Beyond these specific features of Ilyin's commentary on Hegel, the overall impression created by it upon first reading is of an extraordinarily comprehensive and exhaustive exposition of Hegel's philosophical system. It seems to offer exceptional insights into the inner structure of that system, and into its fundamental motives and principles of construction. There appear to be almost no distinctive features of Hegel's thought that are not presented and commented on somewhere in Ilyin's commentary. These impressions have undoubtedly contributed to the enduring interest in Ilyin's work.

Ilyin presented his voluminous thesis (totaling 657 published pages in two volumes) to the Faculty of Law for a formal defense in May 1918. The designated first and second official opponents were his chief mentors, Professors Novgorodtsev and Trubetskoi. In the event, the defense was touched by drama, as the day before, the Cheka had placed Novgorodtsev's name on a list of individuals to be arrested immediately, and had indeed attempted to arrest him at his home in the middle of the night. Novgorodtsev had managed to elude them, and to appear at the defense the next afternoon, if somewhat delayed. Following the presentations by Novgorodtsev and Trubetskoi, and Ilyin's responses to both, the assembled Faculty took the highly unusual step of immediately awarding Ilyin *two* degrees: the Magister and the Doctorate. The first degree was awarded for volume one, and the second for volume two, in recognition of the extraordinary philosophical depth as well as the extent of his work (Il'in 2010, xxii).

The Russian Civil War was commencing even as this academic defense took place, and the chaos unleashed affected the lives of all the principals involved in the defense. All three of them had made their political opposition to the Bolsheviks public knowledge, and were generally supposed to be supporters of the White armies beginning to form through the opening skirmishes of a bloody conflict that would not end for four years. Ilyin's commentary on Hegel was in its own way a victim of the conflict, in that most of those who would have formed the appropriate audience for it had been scattered across the countries of Central and Western Europe by the end of the war, if they had not perished, and were now living as refugees. Only a limited number of copies of the work had been printed, and thus it all but vanished in the ensuing maelstrom of conflict and dislocation.[11]

A CRITIQUE OF ILYIN'S CRITIQUE OF HEGEL

Notwithstanding the indisputable achievements of Ilyin's commentary, including his many learned insights into Hegel's thought, it must be acknowledged that, deeply woven into his exposition of that same thought, there are the threads of a systematic critique that must finally be judged a conspicuous failure.[12]

The most significant source of these problems can be traced to part two of volume one. In part one he concluded his exposition of Hegel's doctrine of the speculative concreteness of the Concept by referring to "absolute" concreteness as "the final and highest stage of the speculative process," declaring that "this self-produced *absolute organism of meaning* is the nature of Divinity itself" (Il'in 2010, 158–159). Picking up the same theme at the beginning of part two, he declares that "Hegel's doctrine consists in the claim that the *Concept*, revealing itself to speculative thought, *is the Divinity itself*, and that this Concept is the *sole reality*" (ibid., 163). He adds that "The absolute Concept, as 'universal Substance' and at the same time as 'subject,' is 'Spirit'" (ibid., 167).

Having characterized the Concept as "divine," he then proceeds to characterize it in terms of "absolute perfection":

> The Concept is divine because it contains in itself absolute reality and absolute perfection. It possesses absolute reality still more when it reaches the heights and reveals all its potential content. It possesses absolute perfection even when it mysteriously conceals this perfection in its depths. It possesses absolute perfection still more when organic concreteness becomes its actualized form. (ibid., 169)

Continuing this line of thought, Ilyin asserts that the Concept is nothing other than "knowledge of itself" and knowledge of "everything as itself" (ibid., 170). Thus Hegel's Absolute Idea is the Divinity itself, God in his essence as thought thinking itself (ibid., 170). Quoting Hegel to the effect that "The absolute idea [...] is the sole object and content of philosophy," he concludes that "true philosophy professes *pantheism*" (Il'in 2010, 171).

From *pantheism*, Ilyin moved to *panepistemism*: "But the life of the absolute Concept unfolds itself into a system, and this system is nothing other than [philosophical] *Science*" (ibid., 175). In short, the Real is ultimately thought thinking itself, or rather, knowledge knowing itself, and hence the Real is *Philosophical Science*; thus the system is a panepistemism. Given that Hegelian Science is simply the unfolding of the logical Concept, it also follows that the entire system is committed to *panlogism* in his view: "Therefore, philosophy affirms that *besides Science there is nothing*, and in this way transforms pantheism into *panlogism* or into a distinctive *panepistemism*" (ibid., 178). Thus, by the conclusion of his rather extraordinary Chapter Eight, "The Concept and Science," Ilyin has firmly cast Hegel's system as *monistic, pantheistic, panepistemic, panlogistic,* and also *theogonic* (i.e., as a *theogony*)—*but only in its original aspiration*, according to him.

Only in aspiration, because in the following chapter Ilyin proceeds to argue that none of these aims can actually be realized in the way Hegel attempts, and in tacit (*but never explicit*) recognition of this unhappy truth, Hegel will be forced to introduce a series of *compromises* of his original aspirations. These compromises will be effected by a subtle *bifurcation* of the argument affecting every aspect of his thought. Explicit acknowledgment of such a bifurcation would have condemned the system to an openly confessed *dualism*; hence in order to maintain the appearance of a monism, Hegel had to continuously divert the reader's attention from the fact of the bifurcation. In a sense, the remainder of Ilyin's commentary consists of struggling to expose the subtle bifurcation in each of its guises, while simultaneously pointing out Hegel's strategies for maintaining the appearance of a successfully monistic system.

The crux of Ilyin's argument is developed in the middle of Chapter Nine, on "Logic." There he points out that "all the states of the world and all the stages of the philosophical sciences are saturated and permeated by the categories of logic, which form their essence" (Il'in 2010, 189). "Thus, before Hegel there arises the iron necessity not only of *recognizing the logical categories as the living substance of the subordinate spheres, but also of including the content of these spheres in the organism of the logical process*" (ibid., 190). Ilyin grants that the first part of this task, "recognizing the logical categories as the living substance of the subordinate spheres," is accomplished "directly and unambiguously" by Hegel (ibid., 190).

However, according to Ilyin, the second part of the task could not be achieved. "Here before Hegel arose a significant difficulty: the path bifurcated, and he had to compromise" (ibid., 190). He claimed that there were two possible paths open to Hegel, neither of which would have permitted him to succeed in the original aspiration for his system. The first path would have involved including the entire content of the subordinate sphere, the philosophy of nature and the philosophy of spirit, in the Logic. But this was completely unacceptable, because it would have destroyed "Hegel's entire conception of the

Absolute in its essential foundations" (Il'in 2010, 191). It "*would have meant depriving the Logic of its pure, originally divine character*" (ibid., 191). The essence of Ilyin's critique is given in the following paragraph:

> [I]n this case it remains merely to recognize that the speculative mode of life intrinsic to the Concept *is not realized* in the relation of the Logic to the subordinate spheres, or realized only one-sidedly. To be specific, the universal *enters* with its content into the particular and singular as their living essence. But the particular and singular *do not* enter with their content into the universal, and *do not* achieve identity with the universal in an organic unity. In other words, *Logic is the substance of "nature" and "spirit," but "nature" and "spirit" remain unassimilated to the pure Concept.* (ibid., 191–192)

This claim constitutes the heart of Ilyin's critique, in the sense that most of the remainder can ultimately be unfolded from it. The first problem to be noticed concerns Ilyin's understanding of the structure of Hegel's Concept (the concept of the Concept).[13] Ilyin claims that "the universal enters with its content into the particular and singular as their living essence." However, the *content* of the universal according to Hegel *just is* the particular and singular, that is, the self-particularizing universal which thereby exhibits singularity. These *are* the moments of the "pure" Concept. Thus, it simply could not be the case that "the particular and singular do not enter with their content into the universal." A "universal" without the moments of particularity and singularity would not be concrete, and could play no role in Hegel's *Subjective Logic*.

Thus, Ilyin leaves the impression that he might be supposing that the particular and singular belong to the "empirical" world, while the universal (alone?) belongs to the realm of pure logic. Otherwise, he may suppose that there are "pure" moments of particularity and singularity belonging to the "pure" universal (supplying its "content") *plus* duplicate or corresponding "empirical" particularities and singularities belonging to the subordinate sphere, which might not be capable of identification with the former. Neither of these possibilities could comport with Hegel's *Logic*.

I would argue that in reality Ilyin believed this first path to be "blocked" only due to his repeated but mistaken insistence in part one of this first volume on the "purity" and "perfection" of the Concept as the absolute Divinity itself, joined with an entirely traditional Christian conception of the Divine: "The Concept is divine because it contains in itself absolute reality and absolute perfection" (ibid., 169). For Ilyin, the absolute "purity" and "perfection" of the Divinity seemingly entailed that no admixture of the content of the subordinate spheres was conceivable.

Given that this first path was blocked, according to Ilyin, he concluded that Hegel necessarily had to take the *second* path: tacitly distinguishing between a *logical* process and a *cosmogonic* process (i.e., the alleged bifurcation), while nevertheless treating the two separate processes as though they formed a single coherent development emerging from the *Logic* (Il'in 2010, 192). Summarizing these arguments, Ilyin claims that Hegel operated with *two conceptions* of the logical series, one of which Ilyin labeled the *formal-logical* or the *formal-rational* series, and the other, the *cosmic-historical* or the *concretely-empirical* series (ibid., 196–197).

The first narrative consists of the *Logic* read as a science, systematically connected with the *philosophy* of nature and the *philosophy* of spirit (i.e., the "logical" process). The second narrative consists of the *Logic* read as the process of Divine Life proceeding before the creation of the world, but connected with *real Nature* and the *real life* of the human spirit (i.e., the "cosmogonic" process) (ibid., 198).[14]

Perhaps the most authoritative response to Ilyin's characterization of Hegel's "original aspirations" for his system was provided long ago by the well-known German Hegel scholar Richard Kroner in a review of Ilyin's 1946 German translation of his commentary. In 1949 Kroner published this little-noted review in an informally published journal emanating from the German Department of the University of Chicago (Kroner 1949).[15] Kroner observed there that "'the logic' is not as 'Parmenidean' as Ilyin deems it to be," and further that:

> Historically it is not true that Hegel first developed a panlogistic scheme of thought which he later on transformed so that the irrational data of secular experience could find their place in it. Rather the very first published form of his system, the "Phenomenology of Mind," contains already all these contents [of the finite, empirical world] and gives them meaning within the whole of experience, though a relative meaning only. (Kroner 1949, 50)

Thus Kroner would dismiss the claim that Hegel actually faced any such dilemma as the one Ilyin formulated as the center-piece of his critique.

The most significant remaining problem with Ilyin's critique of Hegel, in my view, stems from his insistence that the finite, contingent, empirical world possesses its own fully independent being, not derived from that of the true infinite. Although Ilyin commented on Hegel's conception of the true infinite in passing, he nowhere explicitly came to terms with Hegel's unambiguous assertion that the *ideality* of the finite was "the most important proposition of philosophy." The being of the finite, in Hegel's view, could only be *derivative* from that of absolute being, or the true infinite, that is, the being of the whole: hence the *ideality* of the finite.

Instead, Ilyin came close to ridiculing Hegel's doctrine of the ideality of the finite:

> The philosophical negation of the world does not affect the object, but only "judgments about it." Nature as an infinite multiplicity of spatiotemporal appearances and events continues to exist regardless of this speculative ostracism.

It continues *to be* in accordance with its own laws and its own order. (Il'in 2011, 235)

Hegel could never deal with the easy and natural, naively realistic recognition that empirical things exist in actual fact; he would always have been glad of a new and reliable proof of their illusoriness and nonbeing. (ibid., 237)

Ilyin's claim here is at bottom a rejection of the most fundamental ground of Hegel's idealism itself, and exhibits a thinking that remains at the level of the understanding rather than of reason. From the standpoint of reason, as opposed to the understanding, the being of each finite can only ultimately be derived from that of the true infinite—hence the "ideality" of the finite. "The truth of the finite is rather its *ideality*. [...] This ideality of the finite is the most important proposition of philosophy, and for that reason every genuine philosophy is *Idealism*" (Hegel 1991, 152 [§95, Remark]).

To take the being of the finite as separate, and to conceive it as existing *alongside* the infinite, is to think both of them merely at the level of the understanding. The infinite, so conceived, turns out to be merely another finite alongside the first. From this standpoint every attempt to conceive the relation of the finite to the infinite (or the infinite to the finite) produces a kind of metaphysical train wreck. If the being of the finite is fully given, independently of the infinite, then the relation of the infinite to the finite can only be of one independent being to another. But in that case, the infinite (the Divine?) is always confronted by a being which is other than itself, and therefore is not truly infinite (not "that which is confronted by nothing other than itself"). Not being truly infinite, then, this "infinite" is in fact only another *finite*, or a "spurious infinite." Thus, attempting to conceive the relation of the finite to the infinite (or vice versa) from the standpoint of the understanding inevitably fails to result in a concept of the genuine or true infinite. And in consequence the understanding is genuinely unable to grasp the nature of the ultimately real, or the Divine; it remains anchored in an inevitably dualistic conception of God and the world as distinct. And this appears to be the fate that befell Ilyin's interpretation of Hegel, one which in some sense he seems to have welcomed, insisting that Hegel himself could not avoid it either.

Upon reflection, it appears that Ilyin's critique of Hegel is essentially grounded in a thoroughly Neo-Kantian philosophical framework, one characterized by multiple, ineliminable dualisms. Such a perspective upon Ilyin's commentary has been painstakingly explored in an extraordinarily detailed investigation by Giacomo Rinaldi (see Rinaldi 2020). Even as he rejects Ilyin's *critique* of Hegel, however, he notes the paradoxical brilliance and insight of much of Ilyin's *exposition* of Hegel:

The entire critical setting and the radically negative results of Ilyin's Commentary are perplexing, if only because of the plain incongruity between the chapters in which he expounds the Hegelian doctrines, conferring on them an undeniable persuasiveness which makes it impossible to doubt their truth, and those in which he instead sets out his critique, which mostly avoids taking into consideration those very Hegelian arguments he had previously expounded, which, in truth, offer in advance a convincing reply to his objections. (Rinaldi 2020, 18–19)

This same paradox is likely to strike most readers already reasonably well-versed in Hegel's thought prior to approaching Ilyin's commentary. Ilyin's exposition of Hegel appears to be so insightful concerning so many aspects of his thought, and so successful in advocating and defending its claims to truth, that one is then startled by the sweeping and seemingly uncomprehending negation of that same truth, launched from bases that have already been swept away previously in Hegel's name by the same writer. It seems at times that Ilyin was firmly in the grip of two quite distinct truths, ultimately irreconcilable, and failed to grasp the intensity of the conflict between them that was on display in his very own work.[16]

One other perspective on the root of Ilyin's failed critique of Hegel was offered by Errol Harris, and is very much worth quoting:

> The mistake clearly is to undervalue the importance of difference in unity (and/or identity). These critics all forget Hegel's protest against "the night in which all cows are black." His absolute is never a bland (abstract) unity. So how can Ilyin, after so admirably grasping the nature of speculative concreteness, complain that the Absolute fails to abolish the reality (*not* ultimate) of tragedy, death, etc.? The Absolute just would not be concrete if the Other were lost in it without trace. Surely the whole point of Hegel's argument is that the Self, God, the Idea is at home with itself in the Other. The identity of the One and the Other in the Absolute preserves death, and neither is totally submerged even if and when transcended [*übergriffen* or *aufgehoben*].[17]

In my own view, the ultimate irony of this outcome is that despite having potentially educated the entire future community of Hegel scholars to the crucial role of *concreteness* in Hegel's philosophical thinking, Ilyin himself failed to grasp the relevance of his own insight into the role of concreteness at the very highest level of the system, that is, the Absolute, and thus left himself receptive to a thoroughly dualistic dismissal of it.

Later Writings in Political and Legal Theory: The Collected Works

Following his forced exile from Soviet Russia, Ilyin and his wife settled in Berlin, where Ilyin joined the faculty of the Russian Academic Institute, in effect an institution of higher education for the sons and daughters of the Russian emigration. He continued in that role until 1934, when he was fired from his position by the Nazis for refusing to cooperate with their ideological demands in his teaching (Grier 1994, 165 and 182–183). They remained in Germany until 1938, at which point the constraints imposed upon Ilyin by the

Gestapo had made it essentially impossible to live. He was forbidden to engage in any form of political activity, including lectures in public venues, and denied the right of employment in any form. Despite the order from the Gestapo that Ilyin was not to be given an exit visa, a sympathetic local police official issued one anyway, which permitted them to travel peacefully to Switzerland with all of Ilyin's papers and their personal possessions in mid-1938.[18]

Altogether during the three phases of his adult life in Russia, Germany, and Switzerland, Ilyin published approximately forty books and shorter works (including political brochures), in both Russian and German. He published and edited his own journal from 1927 to 1930, and published several hundred essays on topics ranging from Russian culture to political conditions and economic developments, to military campaigns, to philosophy and literature—the entire range of topics likely to be of interest to the Russian emigration as well as other European intellectuals.

Most of that material is now accessible for scholarly research in the form of Ilyin's *Sobranie sochinenii*, a collected works currently extending to thirty-one volumes. The existence of this resource is due to the solitary persistence and dedication of the mathematician and scholar Yuri T. Lisitsa, who first began assembling these materials in the 1980s. The first volume was published in 1993 (Ilyin 1993), and the thirty-first volume appeared in 2019 (Ilyin 2019). No less than three separate publishing houses have been involved in the project at various points. The contents of every volume published to date have been assembled and edited through the efforts of Professor Lisitsa and his wife Olga, one of the more remarkable feats of scholarly activity in post-Soviet Russian letters.[19]

The only other major work to have been translated into English at this point is Ilyin's *On the Essence of Legal Consciousness* [*O sushchnosti pravosoznaniia*] (Il'in 1956). The history of that text is complex.[20] The work contains twenty-two chapters, of which the first ten were composed between 1916 and 1918, each one of which was apparently delivered as a public lecture in the Faculty of Law at Moscow University. Moreover, all ten of them were typeset for publication as a book in 1919, the galleys for which are located in the archive at MGU. However, it does not appear that the book was ever published at that point. The remaining twelve chapters were apparently composed only in the final years of Ilyin's life, in Switzerland.

The work as a whole is an impassioned argument for the necessity of a shared "consciousness" of the law and a recognition of its essential role in society and state. Such consciousness needed to be shared by the general population, by the ruling authorities, and by the body of jurists responsible for administering as well as justifying and defending the rationality of the law. The general framework of Ilyin's discussion is taken from von Savigny's nineteenth-century Historical School of jurisprudence, of which Ilyin's work could be viewed as a late extension.

The aim of such a shared legal consciousness was to produce a well-ordered state, the chief defining mark of which would be the realization of the rule of law. As did the ancient Greeks, Ilyin presumed that such a well-ordered state could be achieved only on the basis of the well-ordered souls of its individual citizens. Failure to develop such a consciousness, or the corruption of it on the part of any of the three groups mentioned, would inevitably bring the state to ruin. By the time he was composing the later chapters of the book, in the immediate post-war years, Ilyin believed that recent history offered all too many examples of such failed states. It is worth noting that, without actually citing Hegel explicitly, Ilyin made constant use of distinctively Hegelian themes to formulate his central thesis, above all defining the necessary spiritual unity required by the well-ordered state as "The We that is I, and the I that is We"—a well-known formula explicating Hegel's concept of 'spirit' borrowed from *The Phenomenology of Spirit*.[21]

Ilyin's own personal life experience prior to his period of residence in Switzerland was shaped by a succession of just such failed states and political misadventures. He first lived through the declining years of an enfeebled Tsarist autocracy, then experienced the revolution of 1905, the February revolution of 1917, and, finally, the Bolshevik revolution—followed by four years of exceptionally bloody military conflict and the consolidation of power by a fanatic Bolshevik dictatorship. Expelled from Soviet Russia, he landed in Weimar Germany and lived through the spectacular economic collapse of that society. From 1933 to 1938 he was an immediate witness to the development of the Nazi regime in Germany.

In a well-informed and thoughtful essay, Andrei G. Sytin has recently argued that the experience of living in Switzerland during the final sixteen years of his life made a discernable impact upon Ilyin's political thinking (Sytin, in Evlampiev 2014). Up until his Swiss experience, Ilyin had never directly experienced a functioning democratic political system. The evidence of Ilyin's writings from those years suggests that he was continually pondering the necessary preconditions for the realization of democratic forms of government.

He rejected out of hand the idea that democracy consisted in some universally applicable formula. Instead he believed that it could only emerge in specific nations whose individual citizens were possessed of sufficiently high standards of legal consciousness and self-discipline (i.e., a certain level of spiritual development), civic education, a strongly developed sense of social solidarity, and a belief that the government was a genuine expression of their own national unity. During the years in Switzerland he repeatedly returned to the issue of the necessary conditions for the emergence of a "genuine," "organic," or "healthy" democracy among particular populations, also discussing it as the challenge of "creative" democracy. Sytin points out that these same themes were also a preoccupation of John Dewey's writings on democracy in the same time frame, as well as those of several other mid-twentieth-century American and British political theorists.

As is frequently noted, Ilyin argued that in the immediate aftermath of the collapse of the Soviet system, the Russian population would not constitute appropriate ground for the development of democratic institutions, and that some "national dictatorship *of the best people*" would be necessary. What is far less frequently pointed out is that he also clearly argued that such a form of politics could only be justified as a *temporary* measure. He thought that in the long run the only appropriate goal should be some form of creative democratic political institutions exhibiting the requisite spiritual basis in *pravosoznanie* [legal consciousness—the rule of law], regardless of whether they bore the outward forms of monarchy or republicanism. He suspected that the former would ultimately prove more congenial to the Russian people, but insisted that the issue could not be "pre-judged" by him or anyone else.[22]

NOTES

1. Some aspects of that "combativeness" are discussed in Grier (1994).
2. That volume (sometimes published in two tomes), *Nashi Zadachi*, has not been translated into English. However, the flavor of one of the most quoted ones can be grasped from some excerpts translated in the early 1990s in an article of mine (Grier 1994).
3. Between the years 1918 and 1922 he was arrested six times by the Cheka on suspicion of counter-revolutionary activities, repeatedly held and interrogated in the cellar of the Lubianka, and, finally, following the sixth arrest, sentenced to permanent exile abroad on pain of execution should he ever return. The records of all six interrogations were recovered from the KGB archives by Yuri T. Lisitsa, and showed that Ilyin refused to misrepresent himself even under these circumstances. These documents and all associated official orders and records were published in 1999 in the Appendix to a supplementary volume to the *Collected Works* in Russian (Ilyin 1999, 373–438). Later, during the 1930s in Nazi Germany, he was also regularly interrogated by the Gestapo, who regarded him with suspicion following his refusal in 1934 to accede to their demands for his cooperation with their anti-Semitic and anti-Russian propaganda campaigns. Ominously, the Gestapo eventually placed his name on a list of aliens who were not to be granted exit visas from Nazi Germany.
4. This hope, first articulated in a letter from Germany in 1911 during his period of study abroad, was to be at least partially realized, though not until 1946 (see Iljin 1946), and in a world he could not have imagined in 1911, while he lived out a personal fate he also could not have imagined as a young man. Several of his fellow émigré friends had urged him repeatedly over the years to produce a German translation of his Hegel commentary. They feared that his great work, published in a very small printing in Russia on the eve of the Civil War, would otherwise be entirely forgotten. Finally, during World War II, he produced a translation of all of volume one, supplemented by the two concluding chapters (only) from volume two, omitting eight chapters from the latter. He explained that he lacked the time and strength to translate the remainder. This single volume was published in Switzerland in 1946 under a new title: *Die Philosophie Hegels als Kontemplative Gotteslehre* (A. Francke AG: Bern) by Professor Dr. Iwan Iljin, "früher an der Universität Moskau."
5. There are not a few individual pages with upwards of 50 to 100 such citations.

6. Both volumes are available in English translation: Il'in (2010, 2011). Both volumes have recently been issued in paperback. Volume One contains an extensive "Translator's Introduction" (73 pp.), and Volume Two contains a somewhat shorter one as well.
7. A discussion of these issues can be found in Grier (1990, 59–84).
8. However, Ilyin decisively rejected Hegel's view on divine impassibility at the end of his commentary, giving no real argument for his own position. He seemed rather to view the impassibility of the divine as a self-evident truth, implying perhaps that Hegel's view could not be taken seriously by any believing Christian.
9. See Williams (2012, 2017).
10. See, for example, Kenley Dove (1971, 35), William Maker (1994, 99–100), Stephen Houlgate (2006, 32–35), Richard Dien Winfield (2012, 18).
11. Ilyin's own life between 1918 and 1922 was anything but peaceful. He was arrested by the Cheka a total of six times, and at certain points was forced into hiding to avoid further arrests. On two of these occasions the Cheka was apparently moving to execute him. In an utterly improbable sequence of events, his life was spared twice by the intervention of Vladimir Lenin, who was incidentally known among other Bolshevik leaders to be quite interested in Hegel. The first intervention occurred at the request of an older mutual acquaintance of Ilyin and Lenin, Aleksei I. Yakovlev, who cited the fact that Ilyin had authored the commentary on Hegel as one of the reasons Lenin should take an interest in the matter. During the second episode, Lenin was given a copy of the work itself, and afterward proceeded to read it, concluding that although the author was "not one of us," "his were good books, all the same." In the event, however, upon being informed that the Cheka had arrested Ilyin again, he was reported to have picked up the telephone and angrily ordered the head of the prison, Agranov, to release him immediately and leave him in peace. In his memoirs Ilyin later related an encounter he had had with one of his jailers, who had referred to him as a "Hegelian." Ilyin, who always insisted that he was not a Hegelian, replied that that was a misunderstanding: he had *never* been a Hegelian, and moreover, Marx had nothing in common with Hegel. The jailer apparently replied, "Shut up and don't object! When we have disappeared, then you can announce that you are not a Hegelian; but until then, that's your protection." At some point there was also said to have been a notation in the Cheka files that he was a "Hegelian"—meaning that he had to be dealt with very carefully. See the account in Tomsinov (2012, 76–94, esp. 88–89).
12. The following critique is developed at greater length and more detail in Grier (2020).
13. See Hegel's *Science of Logic*, Volume Two, "Subjective Logic," Chapter 1 of Section One: "The Concept."
14. One could argue that with his talk of a tacit "bifurcation" in the argument of Hegel's *Logic*, Ilyin was dimly sensing a genuine issue concerning the status of Hegel *Logic*, one that has been properly presented only in quite recent commentary on the *Science of Logic*. I am referring to the view, defended, for example, by George di Giovanni in the Introduction to his translation of that work, according to which one must view the *Logic* as both the *first* and the *final* stages of the circular system consisting of the *Logic*, the *Philosophy of Nature*, and the *Philosophy of Spirit*. In the first reading one is tracing the development of the

Concept in the sphere of thought, culminating in the Absolute Idea, in which thought and being are revealed as an identity-in-difference. Next one traces the development of the *Realphilosophie* through the successive stages of nature and spirit, revealing their consonance with the Concept, and finally one *re-reads* the *Logic*, this time as a "recapitulation" of the *Realphilosophie*, in which (to use Ilyin's vocabulary) one "recognizes the logical categories as the living substance of the subordinate spheres" while simultaneously "including the content of these spheres in the organism of the logical process"—precisely what Ilyin denied that Hegel could do. But his talk of the "bifurcation" could be seen as a failed attempt to get at something quite important about the structure of Hegel's system. See Hegel (2010), "Introduction," xxi–xxii, xxvii, and liii.

15. The journal in question was not typeset, but typed, and apparently circulated in the form of mimeographed copies. (Many thanks to James Devin for bringing this document to my attention.)

16. I would argue that signs of this fundamental ambiguity in his attitude toward Hegel can be detected in subsequent writings of Ilyin as well. His "break" with Hegel never appeared to be either decisive or complete.

17. Errol Harris, personal communication. Quoted with permission.

18. Having reached safety in Switzerland, the Ilyins were soon alarmed to discover that the Swiss authorities did not view them as being entitled to permanent residence and threatened to return them shortly to Nazi Germany (and very likely to Ilyin's death). After numerous fraught appeals, Ilyin was finally informed that the Swiss authorities would grant him permission to stay, but only on the condition that he pay a "caution" of 4000 Swiss Francs, a sum utterly beyond their means. In desperation Ilyin approached the composer Rachmaninoff, then resident in Switzerland, with whom he had been acquainted in Moscow before the revolution. Ilyin was an accomplished amateur pianist, and the two of them had been joined in mutual admiration of the composer Nikolai Medtner, with whom Ilyin was very close. In view of Ilyin's extreme peril, Rachmaninoff paid the caution, in all probability saving his life. At this point the Ilyins were able to settle in the village of Zollikon, on the outskirts of Zurich, where they remained until his death in 1954, and hers in 1963. However, Ilyin's right of permanent residence was initially conditioned on a prohibition of political activity of any sort— a situation that sometimes led him to complain that he was living as a "slave in a democracy." During this initial period, in order to publish in Swiss papers (earning small sums toward subsistence) Ilyin wrote under pseudonyms, posing as a Swiss citizen, and only in German. Finally, after the end of the war, that prohibition was lifted, at which point Ilyin resumed publishing in Russian as well as German.

19. Due to challenging economic circumstances in the immediate aftermath of the collapse of the Soviet system, the *Collected Works* wound up being published in a somewhat odd fashion. The first twelve tomes were published as ten numbered volumes, at which point no further *numbered* tomes or volumes were published. All subsequent volumes (tomes) were published as unnumbered "supplementary" volumes, in the same black bindings with gilt lettering as the first twelve. To identify each of these supplementary volumes, one can only cite its published title and date of publication, which, among

other things, makes it quite difficult to know whether one has a complete collection. This difficulty was ameliorated in what was in effect the thirtieth volume (tome) in the series, an unnumbered supplementary volume entitled *Nemetskii idealizm. Istoriia eticheskikh uchenii. Istoriia drevnei filosofii* [German Idealism. History of Ethical Doctrines. History of Ancient Philosophy] published in 2015, by the *Pravoslavnii sviato-Tikhonovskii gumanitarnii universitet* [*Izd. PSTGU*]. In an Appendix, on pp. 539–603, that volume contains a complete table of contents, in order, of every volume from 1 through 30. It also explains that the first 26 tomes (of which only the first 12 were numbered) were all published by *Izd. Russkaia kniga*, while the 27th through the 30th (unnumbered) tomes were published by *Izd. PSTGU* (Ilyin 2015). It must be noted that the 31st (unnumbered) tome, *Novaia natsional'naia rossiia, Publitsistika 1924–1952 godov* [New National Rossia. Journalistic Writing, 1924–1952] was published by yet another publishing house: *Institut naslediia: Rossiiskii nauchno-issledovatel'skii institut kul'turnogo i prirodnogo naslediia imeni D. S. Likhacheva*. Perhaps it is worth adding that the publishing quality of the most recent five volumes is significantly improved over that of the preceding ones.

20. For a full account of that history, see Il'in (2014, 92–94).
21. I will not devote more attention to this work here, as the published translation contains a substantial amount of introductory material setting out the framework of presuppositions and the major themes of the book.
22. In an unexpected coda to the story of Ilyin's life, in 2005, at the request of the Russian government, the remains of Ilyin and his wife, as well as of General Denikin and his wife, were disinterred, brought to Moscow, and reburied with honor on the grounds of Donskoi Monastery in a service conducted by the Russian Patriarach Alexei II. Thus, a White general and the Theorist of the White Idea were returned to Russia, in a symbolic gesture of reconciliation.

Bibliography

Dove, Kenley. 1971. Hegel's Phenomenological Method. In *New Studies in Hegel's Philosophy*, ed. Warren E. Steinkraus, 34–56. New York, NY: Holt, Rinehart and Winston.

Evlampiev, Igor I., ed. 2014. *Ivan Aleksandrovich Ilyin*. Moscow: ROSSPEN.

Grier, Philip T. 1990. "Abstract and Concrete in Hegel's Logic," including a "Reply" by Errol E. Harris. In *Essays on Hegel's Logic*, ed. George di Giovanni, 59–84. Albany, NY: State University of New York Press.

———. 1994. The Complex Legacy of Ivan Il'in. In *Russian Thought After Communism: The Recovery of a Philosophical Heritage*, ed. James P. Scanlan, 165–186. Armonk, NY: M. E. Sharpe.

———. 2020. I. A. Il'in as an Interpreter of Hegel. In *Etica, Politica, Storia universale: Atti del Congresso (Urbino, 24–27 October, 2018)*, ed. Giacomo Rinaldi and Giacomo Cerretani, 159–183. Rome: Aracne Editrice.

Hegel, Georg Wilhelm Friedrich. 1991. *Encyclopedia Logic*. Trans. Theodore F. Geraets, W. A. Suchting, H.S. Harris. Indianapolis, IN: Hackett.

336   P. T. GRIER

———. 2010. *The Science of Logic.* Trans. George di Giovanni. Cambridge, UK: Cambridge University Press.

Houlgate, Stephen. 2006. *The Opening of Hegel's Logic: From Being to Infinity.* West Lafayette, IN: Purdue University Press.

Iljin, Iwan. 1946. *Die Philosophie Hegels als Kontemplative Gotteslehre.* Bern: A. Francke AG.

Ilyin, Ivan A. 1918a. *Filosofiia Gegelia kak uchenie o konkretnosti Boga i cheloveka. Vol.1. Uchenie o Boge.* Moscow: Izd. G. A. Lemana i S. I. Sakharova.

———. 1918b. *Filosofiia Gegelia kak uchenie o konkretnosti Boga i cheloveka. Vol.2. Uchenie o cheloveke.* Moscow: Izd. G. A. Lemana i S. I. Sakharova.

———. 1956. *O sushchnosti pravosoznaniia.* Munich: Tip. Obiteli prep. Iova Pochaevskago.

———. 1993–. *I. A. Ilyin: Sobranie sochinenii.* Ed. Yuri. T. Lisitsa. Moscow: Russkaia kniga.

———. 1999. *Dnevnik, pis'ma, dokumenty (1903–1938).* Supplementary volume in *I. A. Ilyin: Sobranie sochinenii.*

———. 2015. *Nemetskii idealizm. Istoriia eticheskikh uchenii. Istoriia drevnei filosofii.* A supplementary volume to *I. A. Ilyin: Sobranie sochinenii.* Ed. Yuri. T. Lisitsa. Moscow: Pravoslavnii sviato-Tikhonovskii gumanitarnii universitet.

——— 2019. *Novaia natsional'naia Rossiia, Publitsistika 1924–1952 godov.* A supplementary volume in *I. A. Ilyin: Sobranie sochinenii.* Ed. Yuri. T. Lisitsa. Moscow: *Institut naslediia: Rossiiskii nauchno-issledovatel'skii institute kul'turnogo i prirodnogo naslediia imeni D. S. Likhacheva.*

Il'in, Ivan A. 2010. *The Philosophy of Hegel as a Doctrine of the Concreteness of God and Humanity. 1. The Doctrine of God.* Trans. and ed. Philip T. Grier. Evanston, IL: Northwestern University Press.

———. 2011. *The Philosophy of Hegel as a Doctrine of the Concreteness of God and Humanity. Vol. 2. The Doctrine of Humanity.* Trans. and ed. Philip T. Grier. Evanston, IL: Northwestern University Press.

———. 2014. *On the Essence of Legal Consciousness.* Edited, introduced and translated by William E. Butler, Philip T. Grier, and Vladimir A. Tomsinov. Bristol: Wildy, Simmonds & Hill Publishing.

Kline, George L. 1964. Some Recent Reinterpretations of Hegel's Philosophy. *Monist* 48 (1): 34–75.

Kroner, Richard. 1949. Review of Iljin, Iwan, *Die Philosophie Hegels als kontemplative Gotteslehre.* In *German Books: A Selective Critical Bibliography of Publications in German,* II (2): 49–51. Chicago, IL: Department of Germanic Languages and Literatures at the University of Chicago.

Maker, William. 1994. *Philosophy without Foundations: Rethinking Hegel.* Albany, NY: State University of New York Press.

Rinaldi, Giacomo. 2020. Neo-Kantianism versus Hegelianism: Ivan Aleksandrovich Il'in's Interpretation and Critique of Hegel's Philosophy. *Jahrbuch für Hegelforschung* 21: 11–100.

Seeberger, Wilhelm. 1961. *Hegel, oder die Entwicklung des Geistes zur Freiheit.* Stuttgart: Ernst Klett Verlag.

Sytin, Andrei G. 2014. Genezis idei 'tvorcheskoi demokratii' v shveitsarskii period tvorchestva I. A. Ilyina. In *Ivan Aleksandrovich Ilyin,* ed. Igor' I. Evlampiev, 299–327. Moscow: ROSSPEN.

Tomsinov, Vladimir A. 2012. *Myslitel' s poiushchim serdtsem: Ivan Aleksandrovich Ilyin – russkii ideolog epokhi revoliutsii*. Moscow: Izd. "Zertsalo.".

Williams, Robert R. 2012. *Tragedy, Recognition, and the Death of God: Studies in Hegel and Nietzsche*. Oxford: Oxford University Press.

———. 2017. *Hegel on the Proofs and the Personhood of God: Studies in Hegel's Logic and Philosophy of Religion*. Oxford: Oxford University Press.

Winfield, Richard Dien. 2012. *Hegel's Science of Logic: A Critical Rethinking in Thirty Lectures*. Lanham, MD: Rowman & Littlefield.

CHAPTER 16

Gustav Shpet's Path Through Phenomenology to Philosophy of Language

Thomas Nemeth

Early Hints of a Phenomenological Philosophy of Language

Although Shpet was neither the first to introduce Husserl's thought in general into Russia nor the first to study with Husserl in Germany, he was the first to expound, interpret, and offer to the Russian intellectual community a critique of the latter's only recently (1913) published *Ideen I*.[1] Shpet's 1914 work *Appearance and Sense* [*Iavlenie i smysl*] was chiefly a highly compressed exposition of Husserl's newly formulated philosophical position as seen, of course, through Shpet's eyes. But apart from that, it is remembered today largely for its claim that Husserl's dichotomy between two sorts of intuition—experiencing and eidetic—is insufficient. Husserl had, in Shpet's eyes, omitted a third sort of intuition, viz., intelligible intuition (Shpet 1991, 158, 2005, 170). Husserl was correct in requiring each species of being to have its own cognitive method. However, since he only recognized physical being and psychic, or ideal, being, he saw only the two mentioned sorts of intuition. Against this, Shpet charged Husserl with failing to recognize "a peculiar species of empirical being," viz., social being, and its associated distinctive mode of cognition, viz., intelligible intuition. Empathy is one particular form of such intuition (Shpet 1991, 100, 2005, 120).

Shpet discerned, in the history of philosophy, only the two intuitions Husserl mentioned, but each time a philosopher had sought to bridge the two, as a way of proceeding from one to the other, difficulties arose. For Husserl, we obtain

T. Nemeth (✉)
Independent Scholar, Manchester, NJ, USA

© The Author(s), under exclusive license to Springer Nature Switzerland AG 2021
M. F. Bykova et al. (eds.), *The Palgrave Handbook of Russian Thought*, https://doi.org/10.1007/978-3-030-62982-3_16

339

the empirical through experiencing intuition in what he called the natural attitude. Likewise, we obtain the ideal through essential, or eidetic, intuition in the phenomenological attitude (Shpet 1991, 27–28, 2005, 62).[2] Shpet clearly is quite reticent to criticize, let alone abjure, Husserl. But is Husserl's proposal adequate to resolve philosophical problems? Husserl has not disclosed how it is that there is a continuous and necessary correlation between the two intuitions he mentioned. The only possible solution is that there must be some third "thing" that is a representation for both intuitions. Such a possibility must be grounded in the same thing as the correlativity of the intuitions. Being ever so cautious here in 1914, Shpet states only that the phenomenological task confronting us is to elucidate how a concept (an ideal) presents itself in terms of an intuitive expression (something intersubjective). He is quite reluctant to "show his cards" at this time, but we know in retrospect where he will find the answer.

To be sure, Shpet's main concern in *Appearance and Sense* is not at this stage with the philosophy of language. Here, he is principally concerned with thinking through *Ideen I* and its importance for ontology, particularly as it relates to the "being" of consciousness, or how it is.[3] To help resolve critical problems in accounting for the essential characteristic of consciousness, viz., its intentionality, Husserl introduced such concepts as "noema" and "positum." Shpet is certainly willing to proceed along with Husserl, although neither of them gives an unambiguous definition of the former, which has led to considerable controversy in the secondary literature, at least with respect to Husserl.[4] Shpet, however, at one point calls the "content of the noema" its sense, leaving us in the dark as to what else for him constitutes the noema besides the intentional act's sense. But even with the designation of the noematic content as an intentional act's sense, we cannot be sure we have correctly grasped what a "sense" is. Shpet, in one instance, calls it a "sign" of an object's "internal something" (Shpet 1991, 149, 2005, 162). And the "internal something" of an ax, to take his own example, is that it is used for "chopping." A mental act that "sees" signs in the object indicating the "internal something" of that object is a hermeneutical or sense-bestowing act. Thus, in Shpet's 1914 understanding of Husserl, a hermeneutical act need not be a linguistic expression; recognizing that a relatively hard, flat surface with at least three roughly perpendicular "legs" intended to be sat upon *is* a stool is a hermeneutic act. We can also look at a printed text and, reading it, strive for the "sense" of the text, that is, what the text means. This also is a hermeneutical act. However, Shpet tells us that he, following Husserl, prefers the term "sense" [*smysl*] when speaking of hermeneutical acts in general and "signification" or "meaning" [*znachenie*] when speaking of verbal expressions or statements (Shpet 1991, 154, 2005, 166).[5] We can speak of a text as having a particular meaning, even though the text physically consists of dried ink on a piece of paper. Similarly, some people speak of an alignment of stars in the sky as predicting good (or bad) fortune, all the while not doubting that the stars are far away suns comparable to our own. Each hermeneutical act is an interpretation or construal.[6]

How do we know the purpose, the "entelechy," of an object, that, for example, a kitchen knife is to be used for cutting food? If that purpose were "originarily given," to use Husserlian terminology, we could speak of an "intelligible intuition" alongside experiencing and ideal intuition. However, if I were to describe the physical appearance of a knife to someone somehow unfamiliar with knives, would it be immediately obvious what its purpose is? In looking at a knife what tells us that it is a tool for cutting food? What is the source of our "hermeneutical act"? In the case of a knife, we might say our parents showed us its use when we were children. Nevertheless, this does not stop someone from using it in a pinch as, say, a substitute for a screwdriver or to pry out a small object from a crevice. Clearly, we can "see" these other uses of a knife without being instructed by another person. However, in the cases where we learned something from someone else, the communication *itself* was the object of our attention. The communication was the intentional object. In order to learn from someone, we must understand or comprehend. Shpet holds that the ability to comprehend belongs to the essence of consciousness. Writing in 1914, he sees comprehension as the faculty of intelligible intuition. Were we to forgo it but remain with only the other two sorts of intuition, we would face a "solitary confinement." Only with it can we be social beings. The very nature of reason lies in establishing the purpose or entelechy of an object. Shpet was not yet ready to expound on what communication is.

Shpet concludes *Appearance and Sense* not with a statement of his departure from Husserlian phenomenology, but rather with a declaration of his allegiance to its own understanding of itself as fundamental philosophy. What he finds of particular value is not its solutions to problems, but its constant quest for new problems—and this quest is precisely where Shpet sets out to go.

From the Being of Consciousness to the Logic of History

In January 1916, Shpet published his only contribution to a traditional technical philosophical issue in a *Festschrift* for the Moscow University professor, G. I. Chelpanov. Shpet's concern in his essay "Consciousness and Its Owner" [*"Soznanie i ego sobstvennik"*] is not explicitly with the philosophy of language, but with an egological conception of consciousness advocated by, among others, the Marburg neo-Kantian Paul Natorp and Husserl himself, who, in *Ideen I*, had abandoned his own earlier stance in the 1900/1901 *Logische Untersuchungen*. The question in short is how the "I" in such a proposition as, for example, "I think, therefore I am" stands to the "I" in such a proposition as "I have shoes." In the latter, the "I" is a particular physical being with a proper name alive at a specific time and place. But what is the "I" in the former proposition? Clearly, in both cases we find the same word "I," but do they have the same meaning? Shpet recognizes that, although some find an analogy between the two meanings, employing the same word in two quite different contexts introduces problems. In the latter case, we can undoubtedly speak of a distinct psychophysical organism possessing and existing independently of the shoes, which in turn exist independently of my legal or physical possession of them. Can we, however, also understand the "I" in the Cartesian proposition as existing independently of the thought processes had, and can those processes be conceived as existing independently of their possession by the "I"? For our purpose at present, we need not linger on the details of Shpet's presentation. His view, in brief, is that although we use the same word "I" in both cases, a philosophical problem arises when we conceive the "I" in the Cartesian proposition as a distinct something that *possesses* psychic states and abilities. In doing so, we misuse language. Shpet writes, "Our thinking not infrequently gets us into trouble. Our enemy is our language. [...] Errors arise when we initiate a search for the *general* meaning or the *common* origin of homonyms" (Shpet 2006, 264, 2019, 158).

Certainly, we have no basis for thinking that Shpet believed *all* traditional philosophical problems were simply the result of a misuse of language and that once we use language correctly these problems would disappear. Another young philosopher writing in Vienna just two years later would, admittedly, make such a sweeping claim, stating that the reason such problems arise in the first place "is that the logic of our language is misunderstood" (Wittgenstein 1961, 3). Wittgenstein too relied heavily on examples from ordinary speech in his various writings, including his discussion of the "I" in his somewhat later *Philosophical Remarks*. Admittedly, his concern in those "remarks" was quite different from Shpet's, but he also recognized that "one of the most misleading representational techniques in our language is the use of the word 'I'" (Wittgenstein 1975, 88). Thus, both Shpet and Wittgenstein relied heavily on an analysis of ordinary language, that is, on an analysis of how we actually use the word "I" in our everyday speech to uncover both the source of the problem, viz., our misuse of "I," and its solution. Shpet believes his examples, of which he gives several others, raise the possibility of meaningfully speaking of a communal consciousness that cannot be characterized as the possession of single individuals alone. For Shpet in early 1916, ordinary-language analysis may not be the means to solve all philosophical problems, but it can in specific instances prove to be a useful device by means of which we can clarify misunderstandings.

As was customary, Shpet gave a short talk in May 1916 before the defense of his enormous thesis *History as a Problem of Logic* [*Istoriia kak problema logiki*]. The reworked text of his remarks was quickly published in the leading Russian philosophy journal of the Imperial era, *Questions of Philosophy and Psychology* [*Voprosy filosofii i psikhologii*]. It appeared under the title "Philosophy and History: An Address" ["*Filosofiia i istoriia: Rech*"] and had little to do with the philosophy of language, but its reiteration of themes from earlier publications demonstrated his continuing preoccupation with them, an attempted resolution of which would lead him to language.

In reflecting on the cognitive process, contemporary philosophy seemingly arrived at the paradox that the further away we distance ourselves from concrete experience, the closer we come to the truth. We have here the dichotomy between reason and the immediately given. Yet, he asked, can these two sources alone account for historical cognition? Or do we need another, a third source along with reason and sense intuition (Shpet 2005, 198–199, 2019, 275–276)? If we concede a traditional strict dichotomy between the two, do we not have to accede to the existence of a third source as well, the primary function of which is interpretive or hermeneutic? What do we need in order to understand and interpret historical events and the actions of individuals, not just those in the present, but particularly those in the past? In early 1916, Shpet gave every indication he still sought an answer.

In light of Shpet's brief and general address before his thesis defense, we can hardly be surprised that he did not present his conclusive and definitive position on the means of mediating experience and reason, or whether there is a third intuition in addition to experiencing intuition and eidetic intuition. He did reaffirm, however, in the "Introduction" of his thesis, his 1914 claim that "an analysis of the originary given in social and historical phenomena is by way of an analysis of understanding or *comprehension* [*urazumenie*]" (Shpet 2002, 63). Implicit here is the question as to what is the technique or device behind comprehension. Just how do we achieve—or attempt to achieve—comprehension? If it is not, as Shpet avers, a matter of simple inference, which, after all, would involve reason alone, then comprehension must relate to all that we call "social." In terms of his concern at that time, viz., the study of history, our source material is neither external appearances as such, as in the natural sciences, nor inner mental processes, as in introspective psychology, but documents and artifacts from the past taken as signs. Such signs demand comprehension in order to account for actions in the past. Thus, history as a discipline is *essentially* a hermeneutic science. It is only natural, then, that Shpet would follow up his exploration in the history of historical methodology with a work on the history of hermeneutics.[7] But for Shpet there is a greater significance to the study of historical methodology than just another concern to keep investigators busy. As essentially a hermeneutic science, it has a unique philosophical significance. It shows that *all* studies of the concrete require interpretation for an understanding of their subject matter. All scientific knowledge is expressed conceptually (Shpet 2002, 80).

Shpet remarks that concepts can be conveyed in other forms than through words, for example, through gestures and drawings, but a linguistic expression is the most general form. All scientific knowledge is expressed ultimately in words.[8] With such statements, Shpet draws ever closer to seeing language as the needed bridge between the external and the internal, the empirical and the ideal, but for now he refrains from embarking on a full-scale inquiry into language. Instead, Shpet returns in the second part of his study to the topic of an additional source of knowledge over and above the two intuitions Husserl had indicated. He holds that the understanding (*rassudok*) can indeed form concepts independently in response to intuitions that may be both non-sensible and non-eidetic. And we have every right to call such intuitions "intellectual." The non-sensible part of the intuitive content of a perception is this intellectual intuition. In the case of a social object, we see sense qualities but also something else along with them. Shpet's own example is that of an ashtray. Looking at it, we can see certain qualities, for example, its shape, color, size, but we can also see something else "in" the object that establishes it as an ashtray. We can immediately see its purpose, the function it serves in society, and we can see this purpose without paying any attention to the other qualities mentioned. This, to Shpet's mind, is the justification behind calling the immediate recognition of its function an "intellectual intuition" [*intellektual'naia intuiciia*] or "intelligible intuition" [*intelligibel'naia intuiciia*] (Shpet 1991, 158, 2005, 170).[9]

In January 1917, Shpet wrote a long article entitled "Wisdom or Reason?" and published it in an unfortunately short-lived yearbook that he himself edited. Among the wide range of issues discussed, he returned once again to the sorts of intuition and their respective roles. Surprisingly, he affirmed that although we speak of just the two sorts, experiencing and eidetic, they are actually one—merely two different degrees of seeing with essentially different intended objects. In one case, our gaze is fixed on the contingent and in the other on the essential or eidetic. We can also speak of two corresponding attitudes of consciousness. One attitude is that associated with a concern for the contingent and the other with the essential or eidetic. All of this is reminiscent of Husserl, particularly in the opening chapters of *Ideen I*. Shpet recognized, though, that in every case our experiences are always verbally expressed or presented in some other way that can still be called a linguistic or verbal expression. Any attempt to convey what is involved in a cognizing consciousness will take the form of words. Words are concepts, and "word-concepts" have meaning.[10] We understand these meanings through an act of "intelligible intuition."[11] Whether this is the same intuition that we saw earlier in *Appearance and Sense* is far from clear, for now in 1917 its function is different in being tied to the overall expression of words rather than to the purpose of physical objects. In any case, Shpet holds that intelligible intuition provides us with an understanding of the word-concept's meaning. Although Shpet is not explicit on this point and states that meaning "demands interpretation," we must therefore conclude that in his mind intelligible intuition is not a completely transparent process, that is, one that gives us that meaning as it truly is "in itself" (Shpet 2006, 353, 2019, 251). For otherwise, there would be no need of "interpretation." In order that experience become knowledge, it must be expressed in words. If words could be transmitted ideally, the truth they seek to convey might be received error-free. However, that there is a need for interpretation of the word-concepts shows that we cannot exclude the possibility of error in our understanding. Curiously, Shpet summarizes his position by a Latin expression: "*nihil est in intellectu, quod non fuerit in historia, et omne, quod fuit in historia, deberet esse in intellectu*" (Shpet 2006, 353, 2019, 351–352). Do we not, then, face a relapse into a form of relativism, a "historicistic Kantianism" with objectivity and truth fading from view? To complicate matters further, Shpet remarks that in looking at the eidetic content of a word-concept we find the concept's meaning. But if we obtain that meaning through intelligible intuition and that meaning is an eidos, an essence, precisely what is the difference between intelligible intuition and eidetic intuition, since both have essences as their object—or is it merely a shift in our conscious attitude thereby affirming the fundamental identity of these two sorts of intuition?

Certainly, to some degree our questions above may be a result of Shpet's desire to keep his essay "Wisdom or Reason?" on what he explicitly considered a "popular" level (Shpet 2006, 357, 2019, 255). However, he could not have believed the next essay to which we turn to be of a popular nature. It bears the date 25 February 1917. Thus, Shpet must have written it immediately upon finishing the former even though the latter was not published until 1922 in the obscure journal *Scientific News* [*Nauchnye izvestiia*]. Shpet reaffirmed in this essay "History as an Object of Logic" [*"Istoriia kak predmet logiki"*] many of the themes we have already seen: the intentionality of consciousness as its essential characteristic, the strict correlativity of the object and consciousness as the genuine fundamental principle of knowledge, the dichotomy between a world of contingent facts and a correlative one of ideal, necessary essences. Even consciousness itself in terms of its ideal, objective forms can be the object of study. All of this is again distinctly reminiscent of "Husserlian" themes found in *Ideen I*.[12]

Instead of his earlier concern primarily with consciousness, Shpet turned in the 1917/1922 essay to scientific methodology in general but with a particular emphasis on historical methodology. He remarks that if we were to evaluate science from the standpoint of the ideal of a pure cognition of reality, we would have to accord first place among the empirical "sciences" to the one that represents the model of the most perfect cognition of the concrete, viz., history (Shpet 2005, 223)! This is a most curious observation, and we have every reason to ask whether his conclusion is as obvious as he appears to think. Is it inconceivable that Shpet has simply defined his terms, for example, "concrete" and "perfect cognition," so that history as a "science," in his mind, fits the model best? Would a contemporary physicist, even a contemporary economist, assent to Shpet's contention? Would they too agree that the logic of all the empirical sciences is the logic of history?[13] In any case, Shpet held that the choice of mathematical physics as the paradigmatic science, which emerged in the nineteenth century, was misguided and that our understanding of the empirical sciences themselves and of their methodology must be reexamined and reworked. Such a task would amount to a science of the sciences.

Shpet pursued, though, the much more limited task of examining the logic of historical methodology alone. Although he reiterates his earlier observation that history as a science has only words as source material, he speaks of them in 1917 as not just signs, but also the logical "forms" in which the historian's material is clothed. Certainly, the other empirical sciences also rely on words, but this is not as obvious and direct as in history. Cognition logically begins, and only begins, at the moment we invest experience in linguistic form. And since history as a science—unlike the natural sciences and such social sciences as psychology—deals directly with words, its logical primacy among the empirical sciences is clear. Shpet pithily expresses the thought: "Logic, for its part, knows only one true *principium cognoscendi—words*" (Shpet 2005, 229; see also Shpet 2006, 245).

Shpet's turn from the being of consciousness to the logic of historical methodology may not appear surprising to us, who know of his factual interest in the latter as predating his acquaintance with Husserl. But it surely would have appeared peculiar to the early phenomenologists who knew nothing of that early interest. Even from the ahistorical standpoint of *Ideen I*, Shpet's concern with history appears anomalous. Although arguably less discussed today, various disciplines have thought that theirs is more "fundamental" than others, for example, that all of chemistry could be "reduced" to physics, that sociology could be "reduced" to psychology, and even that mathematics could be "reduced" to logic. As we have just seen, some have thought that philosophical problems could be "reduced" to issues in the use, or misuse, of language. Although Shpet does not seek to "reduce" any other discipline to history—in fact he railed against all such attempts (Shpet 1991, 3–4, 2005, 41–42)—the latter's methodology must serve as the guide for the others. Moreover, since hermeneutics, in turn, plays such a fundamental role in history as a discipline, it must also serve a crucial role in all empirical sciences.

With his initial concern in 1914 being the further development of "positive philosophy" as against Kant's "negativism," Shpet's concern with hermeneutics and language represents a convoluted path. Given his explicit project to study the being of consciousness, we would expect from Shpet an ontological counterpart to Kant's epistemological investigation into the structure of consciousness. Just as the early Husserl and his disciples proclaimed "*Zu den Sachen selbst!*" we would expect Shpet; if true to his original concern, to proclaim albeit in Russian, the equivalent of "*Zum Bewusstsein selbst!*" That he did not pursue this project further as an eidetic, ahistorical study shows that between 1914 and 1917 at the latest, he either realized that project's untenability except by way of taking a detour through historical methodology and shortly afterward by taking into account the fundamental importance of language and semiotics, or at least downgraded the project's importance.

Shpet's invocation of our use of language, of words and signs, is, arguably, less striking to us today than that of history. Husserl himself devoted considerable attention to them in his *Logical Investigations*, particularly the first "investigation," and Shpet himself remarked in a letter to Husserl dated 14 December 1914 that he had radically reworked his entire presentation in *Appearance and Sense*, particularly the theory of meaning (*die Lehre über "Bedeutung"*), as given in the fifth chapter, in light of the new edition of Husserl's *Investigations* from the prior year (Husserl 1994, 529–530). Shpet neither ever mentions Husserl in the text of "History as an Object of Logic" nor does he provide German words for the apparent technical terms that he employs. Yet, his message is Husserlian in spirit, even though he departs into the sphere of history.

Shpet holds that if we direct our attention to an expression, consisting of words, with respect to its signifying function, we find that it is given to us as sense-informed, that is, that it has a sense or meaning as a certain given content (Shpet 2005, 231).[14] We "see" this content, as it were, through the transparent form of the expression. The forms of organized speech include, of course, grammatical ones, but also ideal, properly logical forms that to Shpet's mind are analogous to Humboldt's inner form of language and which he proposes to call "ideal inner forms" (Shpet 2005, 231). The introduction *here* of Wilhelm Humboldt is surprising as well as unhelpful and foreshadows a later more detailed reflection on Humboldt. Shpet clearly believed that the reference would serve as an aid to help the reader understand his own conception. In this he utterly failed, since Humboldt's conception of the "inner form of language" is not obvious and is still today very much a topic of controversy. Just what is part of an "inner form"?

Shpet tells us that the ideal *inner* forms are *logical* forms, but they are not *grammatical* forms. He also mentions that they are independent of the forms of purely linguistic expression. Our access to them is exclusively by some "intellectual" or "mental" [*umstvennyi*] means. Fortunately, Shpet's previously mentioned essay "Wisdom or Reason?" helps us to understand his discussion now in "History as an Object of Logic." In fact, in the former too he distinguished various forms, including the grammatical and the logical, saying that the latter are "neither fortuitous nor empirical, but essential and necessary, as stable and uniform as the formative object is identical in itself." And Shpet again there called these logical forms "the ideal inner forms of language" (Shpet 2006, 346, 2019, 244). These forms are present in every cognitive process, for thought requires words.[15] Furthermore, they directly indicate the cognitive object's unity, rendering unnecessary an immanent object in consciousness as the representative of a transcendent object. For example, I can know much about a person or a place, referring to it by name, without ever meeting the person or having gone to that place. The logical forms must be "inner" forms for the simple reason that they are not "stamped" into any of its external signs. Let us take Shpet's own example here of the proposition "A person thinks." It can also be written as "A person is thinking." This re-writing, however, does not aid in a logical analysis of the forms. If we follow the usual practice and say that in this case the subject is the thinking person, then the predicate is the person thinking. But however we may analyze such a proposition, where do we direct our intellectual gaze [*vzor*] in order to notice the logical forms? Shpet holds that the logical forms of a proposition can be tied only to the predicate. After all, the predicative function of the words composing the grammatical predicate is precisely their logical function. However, an expression of predicativity, as we see, requires a repetition of the entire expression. Of course, there are many predicative forms just as there are many different objects, and the object of each scientific discipline will have its own distinctive forms, though

348   T. NEMETH

they may allow for specific generalizations. Indeed, on their basis we accept not only generalizations of types of sciences but also relations between them. Shpet remarks that what we have just seen is the logical justification for his claim concerning the fundamental character of the historical discipline with respect to all other concrete studies of reality (Shpet 2005, 232). Of course, whether Shpet has truly made his case is for the reader to decide.

We already know that the historian, as an investigator, works, above all, with words, which, as signs, demand understanding from us. For our purposes here, though, we are concerned not with the content of history, that is, with what it specifically says, but with the *logic* of history as a discipline. No doubt we can trace the approach the historian's work takes, but unless we direct our consciousness specifically toward the *ideal* foundations of thinking itself, we will not be able to establish any ideal relations either in terms of content or of form. We can obtain at most only certain psychological generalizations, which may be interesting for those concerned with such matters, but we would only be deceiving ourselves in thinking we have deduced the logic of historical science. We seek the "science" of the techniques and methods of scientific exposition, and so our immediate question concerns where we can derive judgments about the *logical* forms—not ontological or empirical forms—of history from. Furthermore, "these forms are the ideal, inner forms of a linguistic expression of the historical, or, to put it another way, *the forms of historical concepts*" (Shpet 2005, 238).

We cannot find all empirically realized forms of history through the mere analysis of history's logic, but we can determine those that are ideally *possible*. Logic, being an ideal science, is concerned with the ideal or essential, which is a necessary correlate in each contingent givenness. We obtain the essential through what Shpet now in 1917 terms the "exemplificative" method, that is, Husserl's eidetic reduction, though thinly disguised. This method is not a matter of abstraction from what is alike across a number of examples. One example can suffice.[16] If more examples are, for whatever reason, deemed necessary, they can be produced through phantasizing.[17]

This apparent digression into exemplification shows both that Shpet retained his earlier conception of essences as ideal and necessary forms and that for him their "detection" is the central concern in the philosophy of history. We would make a fatal error, however, if we were to assume at the start that the methodological characteristics of one science are the same in all. Hermeneutics functions as the epistemology of history as a scientific discipline. It serves as the connecting link between a theory of investigative methods into history and the methods of pure presentation. For history is a communication about the past via records from a time prior to the historian and then from the historian to his/her reading public. Thus, by its logical methods history is the foundation of all empirical knowledge, but philology by its investigative methods must be considered the foundation of history.

In light of Shpet's concern with the role of communication and understanding, it can hardly be surprising that he turned to a systematic study of hermeneutics. Moreover, given his approach to the philosophy of historiography by way of a majestic sketch of its history, we can hardly be surprised that in approaching hermeneutics he did so again by way of a systematic historical study. Shpet's only posthumously published *Hermeneutics and Its Problems* [*Germenevtika i ee problemy*] was composed in 1918 and thus shortly after the completion of the other works discussed above.[18] He initially intended to make this sketch of the history of hermeneutics the projected third volume of *History as a Problem of Logic*. However, by the next year or so he decided that the work could stand on its own and wanted to have it appear as a separate monograph. Although he was apparently sufficiently satisfied to submit it for publication, the *Hermeneutics* remained unpublished during Shpet's lifetime.[19] A detailed look into its contents is considerably beyond the scope of the present study. It should suffice that Shpet found the defect of previous forays into hermeneutics to lie fundamentally in their failure to connect problems of language closely with methodological concerns in the human sciences and history. That failure prevented progress from being made with respect to all other methodological problems (Shpet 2005, 412, 2019, 148).

ONWARD TO THE LOGIC OF LANGUAGE

During the years immediately following the Bolshevik Revolution, Shpet wrote a number of long studies devoted to the history of Russian thought and philosophy, but for our purposes here the completion of his *Aesthetic Fragments* [*Esteticheskie fragmenty*] in early 1922 is particularly notable, given the increasing repression of critical thought and Shpet's personal isolation. We could not possibly provide here an adequate summary of all that Shpet had to say in the *Fragments* regarding verbal communication, and so we must limit ourselves to some brief highlights in line with our focus on Shpet's turn from his initial concern with consciousness to the logic and philosophy of language.

The second of these *Fragments* is devoted to the structure of the word "in its aesthetic usage" (Shpet 2007, 253). It is not an easy text to understand, especially given Shpet's writing style, which incorporates both literary allusions and a flair for abstraction without examples. Nevertheless, what is unique in it is that Shpet, for the first time in his publications, thematizes words and their role in human culture. Particularly striking is his Husserlian contention that not all signs are words, but among signs they are in a class by themselves.[20] This is the result of Shpet's additional contention that words, properly understood, are the manifest conveyers of sense. Although this may seem absurd—after all, the sense or "meaning" of a particular word can be found in a dictionary— Shpet writes that words have a sense, but "the isolated word, strictly speaking, lacks a sense [*smysl*]" (Shpet 2007, 215).[21] Presumably, we are to understand this in much the way we understand Frege's "context principle."[22] The isolated word does not communicate, but is a means for doing so. In the absence of the complete "word," any attempt on our part to ascribe a sense to the isolated word would entail invoking a subjective mental image and thus lead us into psychologism.

Of course, the connection between a word and its sense is not something detectable by our corporeal faculties, that is, by our five senses [*chuvstv*]. The specific nature of the connection is determined, rather, by the word's sense [*smysl*], which is itself also a peculiar object (Shpet 2007, 208).[23] That Shpet singles out an analysis of sense as against the word, as a sound or physical thing, is of importance in order to avoid any relapse into a psychologism resulting from a misunderstanding of just what the former is.[24] Thus, consistent with this concern to avoid any reductionism, Shpet writes that there is in the structure of a word an objective moment or element, which is not sensibly, but mentally or intellectually, perceived. Through this "objective moment" the word refers to something presented, not by some sense intuition but by intellectual intuition. The word indicates or *intimates* something.[25] But, Shpet continues, we must not confuse intimation and what is intimated with comprehension and what is comprehended, which already refers to sense and semantic functions (Shpet 2007, 218). A statement, for example, may refer to an objective state of affairs, whereas it may intimate to someone who hears it something about the condition of the individual expressing it.

Shpet holds that the act of apprehending the sense of a word, of its pure and inner forms, is a matter of intellectual givenness in intuition. The sole activity of the intellect is conceptualization. Its possibility is just as inconceivable without intellectual intuition as sense perception is without sense intuition. The fundamental mistake of Kant's idealism is that it sees the content of cognition as being supplied exclusively through the material of the senses. Too often in history reason has been contrasted with understanding, as an intuitive faculty in opposition to discourse. Shpet, thus, sees reason as directly tied to discourse and to its understanding. Reason is the faculty directed toward the seeing of sense. "Its acts are acts of understanding, of intelligible intuition, directed toward the very content of the word expressed" (Shpet 2007, 239).[26] However, in saying that the apprehension of a word's sense is via some intuitive process Shpet runs the very real risk of diminishing the role of language, as though we could intuit these senses apart from language. To be sure, his talk does allow us to connect his earlier thoughts in *Appearance and Sense* with his present concerns, but he expects his readers to associate, even identify, this intelligible or intellectual intuition with our everyday mastery of a language. We need not invoke Schellingian terminology to explain simple requests from a child to a parent. Rather, the child has simply mastered the everyday usage of language at the requisite level.

No doubt Shpet is correct in recognizing that the sense, the content in the structure of the word, has a fundamentally special place in comparison to the other elements within the structure. Owing to this, we cannot realistically discuss sense abstractly or separately from the word. Just as there is no pure sense manifold, there is no pure sense, no pure content of thought. However, if sense and word are indeed inseparable, the talk above of an intelligible thought seizing senses is untenable unless we identify, in some manner, that intuition with language mastery. Of course, the act of seizing the sense is a temporal event, and Shpet reminds us that to understand a word, we must place it in a "sphere of conversation," that is, in a context. This applies, certainly, to indexical expressions, such as "I," "here," and "now," but Shpet makes no such qualification. A sense, being ideal, does not depend for its existence on our existence. This much is clear. However, Shpet continues, "A sense is also historical, more precisely, a dialectical accumulator of thoughts, always prepared to transfer its mental charge [*myslitel'nyi zariad*] to a proper receiver. Every sense harbors a long 'history' of changes in meanings [*Bedeutungswandel*]" (Shpet 2007, 240). Since a sense is ideal, it is extratemporal and, therefore, cannot change as can a physical object. On pain of contradiction, then, Shpet must view the senses themselves as intrinsically changing, that is, as being replaced temporally. In Shpet's terminology, a meaningful act precisely relates a word to the object of the moment. The sense or meaning itself can change, and even the mode of reference, while the object remains constant. That is, the meaning at t_1 may not be identical with the meaning at t_2. Thus, psychologism is averted. To claim otherwise would be to claim that only the inessential components of the meaning change in that interval.

Shpet's concern with language and sense percolated through his various writings in the 1920s but became the focus in two of them, to which we must turn, regrettably in brief. The first of these, an only posthumously published manuscript, is dated by its editors as being written between 1921 and 1925 and, thus, from the same time period as the *Aesthetic Fragments*. "Language and Sense" ["Iazyk i smysl"] is a surprisingly long document written in connection with Shpet's plan for a third volume of his *History as a Problem of Logic*. However, despite the apparent polished finality of many of the manuscript's statements, we should be cautious, as with all such unpublished writings, in what we take to be Shpet's considered position. For example, he writes that it is impossible to investigate understanding alone without concomitantly investigating sense and expression, just as it is impossible to investigate either of the latter two in isolation from the others. Such a promising start, albeit from a Fregean-Wittgensteinian perspective, is then seemingly qualified, if not contradicted, by his claim that only *after* resolving the fundamental problem of understanding can we pass to the "logically ontological forms of its expression in a term, a sentence, a science, as a whole" (Shpet 2005, 475). In keeping with the former statement, we would expect Shpet to undertake a logical analysis of expressions *as* revealing what understanding is without venturing into any account of thought. But does he resolutely adhere to this restriction, a restriction that such analytic philosophers as Dummett believed Husserl disregarded and that as a result led the latter to an idealism?

Despite its title, Shpet's primary concern in this manuscript is not with the philosophy of language as such, but rather with "the logical forms of knowledge, where 'logical forms' is taken to mean the relation of a sign to its meaning" (Shpet 2005, 519). Shpet's statement is vague, but we can be sure that despite his talk of "knowledge" his is not an epistemological inquiry. For if it were, then he would attempt to provide the criteria for determining whether the meaning refers to the sign. Again, this is not what he does. Instead, he focuses on the sign-meaning relationship, particularly on its ontological forms. He writes at one point that empiricism cannot reconcile itself to the fact that a referential relation is essentially ideal. Even when we point to a physical object, the referentiality is conceived and, as such, is ideal. For the analytically minded philosopher such talk of the ideality of reference is patently out of place. The understanding of the reference never leaves the real world and is simply a matter of knowing the "game" involved, whether it be a spoken language or pointing one's finger. For the phenomenologist, however, meanings must emanate from the mind, all the while avoiding any hint of psychologism, on the one hand, yet be intersubjectively communicable, on the other. Shpet seeks to reconcile these horns of the dilemma by writing that referentiality "as an immediately apparent relation, necessarily presupposes within itself an ideal moment. Relations, consequently, are *objects*—using Meinong's terminology—*of a higher order*" (Shpet 2005, 520). Are these relations "objects" inhabiting a distinct, inalterable Platonic realm, located perhaps within, say, Frege's third realm? Or is Shpet simply mistaken in depicting referentiality as a relation, it is, as Brentano suggested, relation-like [*etwas Relativliches*]?

Shpet in 1927 published his last work before his arrest. Although *The Inner Form of the Word* is subtitled *Studies and Variations on Themes in Humboldt*, this, as we saw, was not his first encounter with Humboldt. Shpet remarked in "Language and Sense" that we must not forget that the form of a word is not like a Kantian form; it is also a product of a certain activity. In *The Inner Form*, he stresses a dynamic model, commenting that the forms can appear as content with respect to other forms (Shpet 2007, 393). Surely, though, we must also be careful not to ascribe this activity to the human individual, lest we fall into subjectivism and empirical skepticism. The sole guarantee that the forms are fixed and common to all would be the assumption of a psychophysical uniformity across the human race. But for Humboldt the "creator of forms" is the nation or, more precisely, the "spirit of the nation" (Shpet 2005, 621). Whereas this appears as though Humboldt has substituted the nation for the Kantian subject and would suffer from the weaknesses of a sociologistic interpretation of the latter, Shpet reminds us first that the Humboldtian conception is more Romantic than Kantian. But, in particular, Shpet rejects the relativistic consequence of its prevalent interpretation, saying that the unity of the word is an originary givenness that is determined by a specific act of consciousness: "Humboldt's impartiality and his independence from psychological hypotheses is best reflected in the fact that he insists on the originary nature of the corresponding act" (Shpet 2007, 355). Having avoided a simple lapse into psychologism, Humboldt, nevertheless, errs with an overly Kantian interpretation of his own conclusion. The categories he established have, in his eyes, objective significance only for the subjective individual.

16 GUSTAV SHPET'S PATH THROUGH PHENOMENOLOGY TO PHILOSOPHY... 353

Although Shpet adopts a particular interpretation of Humboldt's position, finding much that is congenial, we see that he finds much in it that is wrong or, at least, needs correction. Both intimately linked thought and language so that one without the other is impossible. To be sure, in 1927, the traditional phenomenological focus on sense is not in the foreground. Instead, Shpet adopts Humboldt's terminology of "inner form." Unlike the sounds of the word's "external form," the inner forms have no constant sensory indices, for they are the forms of what is thought or understood, viz., what is communicated in some fashion (Shpet 2007, 393–394). The sense expressed in a word, as the object or state of affairs, is that to which our attention is directed. The constitution of the content of the discourse's sense demands a special creative act, which is the condition of communication. Without it, there is no genuine understanding and comprehension. Unfortunately, Shpet's attempted clarification and elaboration of this point leaves much to be desired. Although we have an immediate intuition of a "thing,"[27] we ordinarily also speak of an active grasping of the thing's conceivable [*myslimyi*], not sensible, content. For example, we can speak of "grasping" or comprehending a difficult point in a discussion. Such "grasping" of an object is thought to be entirely objective.

Conclusion

There is, of course, much more that can be said concerning Shpet's reflections on Humboldt and even concerning the inner form of a word. They deserve an in-depth investigation in light not just of our current understanding of Humboldt's thought itself, but also of the current state of the linguistic enterprise. Hopefully, though, we have sketched the path that *led* Shpet to a phenomenological philosophy of language. We have seen that from a concern with determining how we grasp the "sense" of a social object, be it a physical thing or some action, Shpet followed Husserl's intricate account of the logical structure of intentionality. This account included sense as the central component of the noema within an intentional act. It is because of the noema that an intentional act may have an object. Shpet applied this basic idea to language, detailing its structure, and in this way explaining how it serves the purpose of communication. With the tenet that language is, on the one hand, a social activity and, on the other, inseparable from thought, Shpet recast phenomenology by interpreting the Husserlian noematic sense of an intentional act as the sense of the inner form of a word. The Husserlian hylé, thereby, becomes a word's sound. There can be no doubt that the sheer variety of languages reflects the wide diversity of their structural composition, but their mutual intelligibility reflects a constancy within each that escapes the clutches of any form of relativism. What sets Shpet's phenomenologically oriented philosophy of language apart from analytic accounts is that unlike them Shpet never disconnects his analyses from consciousness. Whereas analytic accounts *equate* or *identify* language with thought, regarding the examination of the former *as* an examination of the latter, Shpet views language itself as an intentional act of consciousness. In this way, Shpet, more consistently than many of his contemporaries and even late analytic philosophers, fought the temptation of reductionism. They, unlike him, sought to eliminate philosophical problems by linguistic analysis or saw them as linguistic obfuscations. What sets Shpet's account apart from Husserl's is that for the former consciousness is not merely individual, but also social. Shpet saw this as his correction of Husserl's phenomenology, which he otherwise held in the highest esteem. Even in what may have been his final philosophical pronouncement, an encyclopedia entry on himself written during the early Stalinist era, Shpet wrote, "Husserl pointed to the correct solution to the problem through his introduction of the concept of 'ideation' [*Wesenserschauung*]" ([Shpet] 1929, 380; Shpet 2019, 296).

NOTES

1. Among those who offered early assessments of Husserl's *Logische Untersuchungen* was Henry Lanz, who was born in Moscow in 1886 to American parents. He graduated from Moscow University and then studied in Germany before returning to Russia in 1914. He "immigrated" to the United States with the Bolshevik Revolution. Unlike many at the time, Lanz found the omission of a transcendental viewpoint in the *Logische Untersuchungen* to be its principal *deficiency*.
2. Such, at least, is how Shpet read Husserl at this time. Whether this is precisely correct is not our concern here.
3. At this stage, Shpet viewed Husserl's philosophical contribution to "positive philosophy" to be just this turn to the "being" of consciousness, whereas Kantian Criticism, as a "negative" philosophy, was concerned with the *limitations* of consciousness.
4. For an introduction to this controversy, see Drummond and Embree (1992). The editors themselves concede, "Husserl's own statements regarding the noema are somewhat ambiguous" (Drummond and Embree 1992, 3).
5. For Husserl's distinction, see Husserl (1976, 285 (§124)). Kersten in his English-language translation of *Ideen I* renders *Bedeutung* as "signification," whereas the more recent translation by Dahlstrom renders it as "meaning."
6. Seifrid correctly recognizes "that 'hermeneutics' for Shpet means an eidetic operation, interpretation as an eidetic seeing or reading" (Seifrid 2009, 184).
7. He purposely limited the scope of his immense thesis, writing "In this first part of our investigations we gather only material" (Shpet 2002, 87). He did write a second part, but it remained unpublished for decades after his murder.
8. In light of, on the one hand, the ever-increasing mathematization of the sciences, including the "human" or social sciences, and, on the other hand, the increasing opacity of physics since Shpet's day, it is doubtful that his claim stands scrutiny. However, for Shpet's own somewhat extended and qualified discussion of this matter, see Shpet (2002, 1065–1066).
9. The former expression with its long history in German and Russian idealism may reflect Shpet's desire both to remain within that philosophical tradition while also finding a solution to a problem that is compatible with the spirit of phenomenology.

16 GUSTAV SHPET'S PATH THROUGH PHENOMENOLOGY TO PHILOSOPHY... 355

10. We must bear in mind throughout our discussion that, as Haardt correctly points out, Shpet's frequent usage of "word" is to be understood "in the broad sense of the Russian expression for 'word,' namely, *slovo*. *Slovo* can refer not only to words but also to clauses and complex sentences, even to literary texts and the totality of a natural language" (Haardt 2009, 172). For confirmation of this, see Shpet (2007, 208).

11. Presumably, "intelligible intuition" differs from the other two sorts only with respect to its associated attitude of consciousness and, therefore, its intended object. However, Shpet does not explicitly say that here.

12. Unless we assume Shpet allowed this essay to appear despite no longer sharing these ideas *and* at a time (1922) when in light of the political situation it would have been more advantageous not to have the essay published, we must grant that he was still deeply indebted to phenomenology.

13. See Shpet (2005, 224).

14. Cf. "The word 'expression' is normally understood [...] as the sense-informed expression" (Husserl 1970, 281). We write "sense or meaning" here, since in drawing a parallel between Shpet and the early Husserl, the latter writes, "'Meaning' is further used by us as synonymous with 'sense'" (Husserl 1970, 292).

15. In his not unusual metaphorical style, Shpet further on in the essay wrote, "*A dumb thought without words is a beast*" (Shpet 2006, 349, 2019, 247). Shpet will reiterate this idea in 1922. See Shpet (2007, 222).

16. "One and the same example can serve as the source of originary and of corrected judgments. Other examples can aid in cases where certain features appear more vividly and more clearly" (Shpet 2005, 240).

17. Cf. "The Eidos, the *pure essence*, can be exemplified for intuition in experiential data—in data of perception, memory, and so forth; but it can equally well be exemplified in *data of mere phantasy*" (Husserl 1982, 11 (§4); also Husserl 2014, 14). Note Husserl's own usage of the words "exemplified" [*exemplifizieren*] and "phantasy" [*Phantasie*] in writing here of "eidetic seeing."

18. Nevertheless, Shpet apparently intended to write something on the problems associated with hermeneutics already in 1913 as evidenced by a recording in his notebook: "An article on Hermeneutics to conclude with a reference to Husserl (Investigation IV)—the idea of a pure hermeneutics (general, philosophical!)—and then especially: Humboldt—Steinthal—Marty—Husserl (and others)" (Shpet 2005, 416).

19. The basis for this claim that Shpet was satisfied with the manuscript is his 1919 official report of his scholarly activities for Moscow University. See the "Einleitung" to the German translation of the *Hermeneutics*, Špet (1993, 16).

20. Husserl writes, "Every sign is a sign for something, but not every sign has 'meaning,' a 'sense' that the sign 'expresses'" (Husserl 1970, 269 (Investigation 1, §1)).

21. Unlike earlier, Shpet, apparently, does not distinguish here between meaning [*znachenie*] and sense [*smysl*].

22. Cf.: "never to ask for the meaning of a word in isolation, but only in the context of a proposition" (Frege 1980, x).

23. Haardt correctly remarks, "Shpet's central thesis that the sense of a proposition is given only pursuant to predication and eludes an isolating objectification is strongly reminiscent of Frege's theory of predication" (Haardt 1993, 145f.).

24. Cf. in particular Husserl (1970, 276 (Investigation I, §6)), where Husserl distinguishes "the expression physically regarded" from "a certain sequence of mental states [...] which make it the expression of something. These mental states are generally called the 'sense' or the 'meaning' of the expression."
25. Likewise, Husserl wrote, "This function of verbal expressions we shall call their intimating function" (Husserl 1970, 277 (Investigation 1, §7)).
26. It is unclear why Shpet writes here "intelligible" instead of "intellectual." Surely, he did not hold that there is an "intelligible intuition" in addition to an "intellectual intuition."
27. Providing one of his few definitions, he says, "By 'thing' (*ens*), we understand [...] anything that can be named, consequently not only material things and substances, but also psychic acts, actions, and human behavior" (Shpet 2007, 398f.).

Bibliography

Drummond, John J., and Lester Embree. 1992. *The Phenomenology of the Noema*. Dordrecht: Springer Science+ Business Media.

Frege, Gottlob. 1980. *The Foundations of Arithmetic*. Trans. J. L. Austin. Evanston, IL: Northwestern University Press.

Haardt, Alexander. 1993. *Husserl in Russland: Phänomenologie der Sprache und Kunst bei Gustav Špet und Aleksej Losev*. München: Wilhelm Fink Verlag.

———. 2009. Shpet's Aesthetic Fragments and Sartre's Literary Theory. In Tihanov, 169–178.

Husserl, Edmund. 1970. *Logical Investigations*. Trans. J. N. Findlay. New York: Humanities Press.

———. 1976. *Ideen zu einer reinen Phänomenologie und phänomenologischen Philosophie, I. Buch: Allgemeine Einführung in die reine Phänomenologie*, ed. Karl Schuhmann. Den Haag: Martinus Nijhoff.

———. 1982. *Ideas Pertaining to a Pure Phenomenology and to a Phenomenological Philosophy*. Trans. F. Kersten. The Hague: Martinus Nijhoff.

———. 1994. *Briefwechsel. Band III, Die Göttinger Schule*, ed. Karl Schuhmann. Dordrecht: Kluwer Academic Publishers.

———. 2014. *Ideas for a Pure Phenomenology and Phenomenological Philosophy*. Trans. Daniel O. Dahlstrom. Indianapolis, IN: Hackett Publishing Company.

Seifrid, Thomas. 2009. Sign and/vs. Essence in Shpet. In *Gustav Shpet's Contribution to Philosophy and Cultural Theory*, ed. Galin Tihanov, 181–191. West Lafayette, IN: Purdue University Press.

[Shpet], G. G-n. Shpet. 1929. *Enciklopedicheskii slovar' Granat*. (In 58 vols.) 50: 378–380. Moscow and Leningrad: Granat.

Shpet, Gustav. 1991. *Appearance and Sense*. Trans. Thomas Nemeth. Dordrecht: Kluwer Academic Publishers.

———. 2002. *Istoriia kak problema logiki. Kriticheskie i metodologicheskie issledovaniia*, ed. V.S. Miasnikov. Moscow: Pamiatniki istoricheskoi mysli.

———. 2005. *Mysl' i slovo. Izbrannye Trudy*, ed. T.G. Shchedrina. Moscow: ROSSPEN.

———. 2006. *Philosophia Natalis. Izbrannye psikhologo-pedagogicheskie Trudy*, ed. T.G. Shchedrina. Moscow: ROSSPEN.

———. 2007. *Iskusstvo kak vid znaniia. Izbrannye trudy po filosofii kul'tury*, ed. T.G. Shchedrina. Moscow: ROSSPEN.

———. 2019. *Hermeneutics and Its Problems. With Selected Essays in Phenomenology*. Ed. and Trans. Thomas Nemeth. Cham: Springer.

Špet, Gustav. 1993. *Die Hermeneutik und ihre Probleme*. Trans. Erika Freiberger und Alexander Haardt. Freiburg/München: Karl Alber.

Tihanov, Galin, ed. 2009. *Gustav Shpet's Contribution to Philosophy and Culture Theory*. West Lafayette: Purdue University Press.

Wittgenstein, Ludwig. 1961. *Tractatus Logico-Philosophicus*. Trans. D. F. Pears and B. F. McGuinness. London: Routledge & Kegan Paul.

———. 1975. *Philosophical Remarks*. Ed. R. Rhees and Trans. R. Hargreaves and R. White. Oxford: Basil Blackwell.

CHAPTER 17

Evald Ilyenkov: Philosophy as the Science of Thought

David Bakhurst

INTRODUCTION

This chapter is devoted to Evald Vasil'evich Ilyenkov, the most brilliant Soviet Marxist philosopher and the most influential voice in Russian philosophy during the post-Stalin thaw. From the mid-1950s to the early 1960s, Ilyenkov's writings and speeches had a transformative effect, inspiring a new generation of philosophers to see beyond the dogmatic orthodoxy of "official Soviet philosophy." Whether they agreed or disagreed with him, no Soviet philosopher working at the time could ignore the phenomenon of Ilyenkov.

However, since most of the Stalinist old guard retained their positions of power in the philosophical establishment, Ilyenkov was constantly in trouble, and his career lurched from one crisis to the next. There were a number of triumphs, but there were many vexations. Though he received the Chernyshevsky Prize in 1965, he was never made a professor, let alone an academician. Though he published in the Party journal *Kommunist* (e.g., Rozental' and Ilyenkov 1969, Altaiskii and Ilyenkov 1973, Vasil'ev and Naumenko 1973, Ilyenkov 1979), and saw his writings appear in translation (e.g., Ilyenkov 1977a, b),[1] he often experienced difficulty publishing, and his opportunities to travel abroad were limited.[2] The effect of many such frustrations, combined with disappointment over the path the Soviet Union was taking, wore Ilyenkov down. He committed suicide in 1979 at the age of 55.

D. Bakhurst (✉)
Queen's University, Kingston, ON, Canada
e-mail: david.bakhurst@queensu.ca

© The Author(s), under exclusive license to Springer Nature Switzerland AG 2021
M. F. Bykova et al. (eds.), *The Palgrave Handbook of Russian Thought*,
https://doi.org/10.1007/978-3-030-62982-3_17

359

When I began my research on Soviet philosophy in the early 1980s, I focused on Ilyenkov both because of the significance of his role in Soviet thought and because of the intrinsic interest of his ideas. The outcome was my book *Consciousness and Revolution in Soviet Philosophy* (1991). After the Soviet Union collapsed, I assumed that Ilyenkov and my book about him were destined to be forgotten. Who now, in Russia or the West, would be drawn to a Soviet Marxist who styled himself a dialectical materialist and a Leninist? Surprisingly, however, interest in Ilyenkov's legacy did not wane. Posthumous editions of his works have steadily appeared in Russia (e.g., Ilyenkov 1984, 1991, 1997, 2002, 2009a), culminating in the recent publication of three striking volumes of archival materials and formerly unpublished writings, edited by his daughter Elena Illesh (Ilyenkov and Korovikov 2016; Ilyenkov 2017, 2018a). Andrey Maidansky, who collaborated with Illesh on the two most recent of these volumes, runs a website which makes available many of Ilyenkov's writings, including his candidate's and doctoral dissertations.[3] A further archival website is in preparation.[4] An annual conference, the "Ilyenkov readings" (*Il'enkovskie chteniia*), is held in Moscow every spring, and a documentary film, *Ilyenkov*, has recently been made by Alexander Rozhkov. An authoritative *Collected Works*, comprising some ten volumes, is in production. In the West, his works continue to appear in translation (e.g., 2009b, 2014, 2016, 2018b). This interest is far from purely retrospective. His ideas are being taken up in novel ways, most notably by followers of Vygotsky's cultural-historical psychology and the activity theory of A. N. Leontiev, and in the Queer Communism of Georgii Mamedov and Oksana Shatalova (Mamedov and Shatalov 2017).

In what follows, I explore the main contours of Ilyenkov's ideas, placing them alongside events of his life. I hope it will become clear why Ilyenkov continues to fascinate.

Beginnings: The Ilyenkov-Korovikov Theses

Evald Ilyenkov was born in Smolensk on 18 February 1924. His father Vasilii Pavlovich Ilyenkov (1897–1967) was a writer and journalist who later achieved fame for his socialist realist novels, *Driving Axle* (1931), *Sunny Town* (1935), and *The Great Road* (1949), and for tales of war published in the Red Army newspaper, *Krasnaya Zvezda*. Ilyenkov's mother, Elizaveta Il'inichna Ilyenkova (née Zykova) (1888–1974), was a teacher, though she did not work after the birth of her children. Ilyenkov had one sister, Aida, two years his junior.[5] In 1928, the Ilyenkov family relocated to Moscow, and from 1933 they lived in a writer's cooperative behind the Moscow Art Theatre on the corner of what is now Tverskaia ulit'sa and Kamergerskii pereulok. The cooperative seems to have provided a congenial environment (notwithstanding the fact that the apartments initially had no kitchens to encourage the writers to converse in the building's cafeteria). The family also had access to the famous retreat at Peredelkino. Evald and Aida spent a happy childhood in the company of authors, poets, and artists. The family emerged unscathed from the terror of the late 1930s.

In 1941, Ilyenkov completed his education at Moscow School No. 170 and was admitted to the Moscow Institute for History, Philosophy, and Literature (MIFLI). However, in October of that year, war forced the evacuation of the Institute and its students to Ashkhabad, where it was absorbed into Moscow State University (MGU), before a further evacuation proved necessary in July 1942, this time to Sverdlovsk. A month later, Ilyenkov was called up for military training. From October 1943, he served on the Western and then the Belorussian fronts. As a junior lieutenant, he commanded an artillery platoon at the Sandomierz offensive and was part of the force that liberated Berlin (there is a remarkable photograph of Ilyenkov standing on the ruins of the Reichstag). He was decorated for heroic deeds.

In August 1945, Ilyenkov returned to Moscow on secondment to the newspaper *Krasnaya Zvezda*, before being demobbed in January 1946. He then recommenced his philosophical studies, finishing his degree in 1950. He became a member of the Communist Party in the same year. He then entered MGU as a graduate student, defending his candidate's dissertation in 1953, under the supervision of Teodor I. Oizerman. In December of that year, he joined the Sector of Dialectical Materialism at Moscow's Institute of Philosophy as a "scientific worker," a position he held until his death.

Ilyenkov also had a teaching position at MGU, and it was here that he made his first, dramatic contribution to Soviet philosophy. In May 1954, Ilyenkov and his friend and colleague Valentin Korovikov presented their "Theses on Philosophy" to an open meeting of their department, the Kafedra of the History of Foreign Philosophy, attended by some 200 people. Although the text was lost for many years, resurfacing only in 2016, the key message of the theses lingered long in the memory of Soviet philosophers.[6] This was the rejection of the orthodox Soviet view that philosophy was a meta-science describing the most general laws and principles governing "the world as a whole" or "nature, society, and thought." If there are such laws (and Ilyenkov, certainly, is skeptical), it would be for science to discover them.[7] Similarly, the project of synthesizing the findings of particular sciences cannot be offloaded to philosophy. Such an undertaking would require genuine expertise in the relevant sciences, something philosophers typically do not possess. For Ilyenkov and Korovikov, philosophy is one science among others and its distinctive subject-matter is *thought* [*myshlenie*].

The philosopher does not approach thought as the psychologist, cognitive scientist, or neurophysiologist does. Philosophy studies thought's forms and its movement. This is not an empirical inquiry: philosophy is only incidentally concerned with how we actually do think. Its subject is thinking in its relation to being; that is, how thinking must be if it is to be true to reality. Since it is in the nature of thought to think reality—the very act of judgment is thinking *this is so*—philosophy studies how thinking must be if it is to be true to itself. Philosophy is thus an exercise in self-consciousness. It is thought thinking itself, thought making explicit its own nature. So although philosophy is not a meta-science of the kind Soviet *diamat* envisages, its distinctive subject-matter does place it in a special relation to other disciplines, for philosophy, by elucidating thought, brings those other disciplines to self-consciousness. In this sense, philosophy enters all other sciences.

Ilyenkov follows Lenin (1976, 319) in endorsing the unity of logic, dialectics, and the theory of knowledge. He calls this unity "Logic with a capital L" or "dialectical logic." This is a discipline quite different in ambition from formal symbolic logic. When Ilyenkov speaks of the forms and the movement of thought, he has in mind, not formal structures of inference and argument, but the fundamental concepts or categories by which we think the world, the ways in which we bring the world into view and hold it there, and the ways thought finds to transcend its own limits at any given time. This is a logic of content, concerned with elucidating the essence or heart of the matter, to disclose the nature of the object of inquiry in all its multidimensionality, and to understand that understanding in all *its* multidimensionality.

But before we consider Ilyenkov's contributions to logic thus understood, we must first visit an early paper which provides unprecedented insight into Ilyenkov's philosophical vision.

Cosmological Phantasmagoria

"Kosmologiia dukha" ["Cosmology of Spirit"] was written sometime between 1950 and 1953, as "an attempt to establish, in general terms, the *objective* role of thinking matter in the system of universal interaction." Ilyenkov playfully subtitles the essay "a philosophico-poetic phantasmagoria based on the principles of dialectical materialism" (Ilyenkov 2016, 164; 2017, 127). The work draws on Ilyenkov's familiar heroes, Engels, Spinoza, and Hegel, but it is also influenced by Pobisk Georgievich Kuznetsov, who was inspired in turn by the Russian Cosmists Vladimir Vernadsky, Alexander Chizhevsky, and Nikolai Fedorov.[8] The essay is bold, ingenious, written with style and panache, and utterly different from standard Soviet texts of dialectical materialism.

Ilyenkov's position is especially noteworthy for two reasons. The first is his assertion that, "Just as there is no thought without matter, so there is no matter without thought" (Ilyenkov 2016, 167; 2017, 131). Ilyenkov does not deny that thought emerges from and supervenes upon matter. His claim is that if matter is the universal substance, thought is one of its necessary attributes. The development of matter necessarily entails the development of thinking matter; indeed, thought is "the highest product of universal development" (ibid.). This challenges orthodox readings of the "primacy" of matter and contradicts the mechanistic materialist view (which Ilyenkov took to have infected Soviet *diamat*) that thought is a merely contingent product of the organization of matter.

Also noteworthy is the argument at the centerpiece of the essay. Ilyenkov maintains that it is thought's destiny to negate the thermal death of the universe. At some point, millions of years hence, when the universe is close to entropic collapse, human beings (or some other community of thinkers) will draw on their now-massive technological power to engineer a new "big bang" that will launch a new cycle of cosmic development. The new world that results will in turn create further thinking beings that will eventually save it from thermal death by sacrificing themselves, and so on. The "cosmic and grand [...] sublime and wonderful," "highest and final" end of thought (Ilyenkov 2016, 188; 2017, 163) is to bring about:

> a process that will transform dying, freezing worlds into the fiery-incandescent hurricane of emerging nebula.
> In these conditions, thinking spirit sacrifices itself. [...] But its sacrifice is made out of a duty to mother nature. Humanity, thinking spirit, pays back its debt to nature. At some point, in its youth, nature gave birth to thinking spirit. Now, in return, thinking spirit, at the cost of its own existence, gives back to mother nature, now dying a "thermal death," a new flame of youth—a state from which great cycles of development may begin anew, and which will at some point, at a different region of space and time, lead to the emergence [...] of a new thinking brain, a new thinking spirit. (2016, 184 [translation amended]; 2017, 156)

Such cosmological reflections are hard to evaluate, being a mélange of metaphysical postulation, popular-scientific synthesis, and teleological assumption. However, the true significance of Ilyenkov's essay lies not in the plausibility, or lack of it, of his argument. In my view, the real point of this work is to express *reverence for thought*, indeed, to express the reverence for thought befitting a philosopher. For this reason, though the article remained unpublished in Ilyenkov's lifetime (it was almost certainly written for its own sake with no expectation of publication), it is essential background to the better-known elements of his contribution.

Dialectics of the Abstract and the Concrete

According to Ilyenkov's conception of Logic, to understand the forms and movement of thought, we must understand the nature of scientific knowledge and its methods. This is the subject-matter of much of his early writing, including his candidate's thesis, *Some Questions of Materialist Dialectics in Marx's "Contribution to a Critique of Political Economy"* (1953), his first book, *The Dialectics of the Abstract and the Concrete in Marx's "Capital"* (1960a, 1982), and numerous articles (e.g., Ilyenkov 1955, 1957, 1960b, 1967). In these writings, Ilyenkov presents cognition as a movement—an ascent—from the abstract to the concrete.

It is perhaps easiest to understand Ilyenkov's position by contrasting it with views he rejects: empiricist accounts of concept formation and positivist philosophy of science. Such approaches, he maintains, represent cognition as a movement from the concrete to the abstract. For them, the concrete is what we apprehend in experience—sensory particulars. We then proceed to form concepts of things and their qualities by a process of abstraction. For example, we form the concept *white* by abstracting a particular property (in this case a shade of color) exhibited by certain sensory particulars, thereby isolating the common properties essential to all and only white things. Similarly, we form the concept *four-legged* by abstracting the properties shared by all and only four-legged things. Equipped with such concepts, we can then identify relations between the entities they characterize. Some of those relations will be logical (e.g., nothing can be white and black all over), some will be contingent (e.g., an angry dog barks). Science ultimately establishes empirical laws governing the behavior of things or, perhaps we might say more strictly, the instantiation of properties. Such general causal laws ultimately express regularities (if an event of type A occurs, an event of type B occurs) and enable us to explain and predict events (event B occurred because event A occurred; if A occurs, B will occur, and so on). The more general the explanatory principles, the better. So, thought moves from confrontation with the concrete in experience to ever more abstract representations of reality.

Ilyenkov dislikes everything about this picture and proposes an entirely different approach. He argues that the paradigm of an object of cognition is a complex whole, consisting of interrelated parts, a "unity in diversity" in interaction with other objects of cognition in a wider context. This is the concrete totality we seek to understand: an object of inquiry that has a reality, a nature, independent of our attempts to understand it.[9] Our task, then, is to countenance the nature of this object in all its complex interrelatedness, "to reproduce the object in thought as a 'living whole'." To attain this is to achieve "concreteness of thought" [*konkretnost' myshleniia*] (Ilyenkov 2017, 228).

In contrast to this ideal of concrete thinking, the understanding from which inquiry begins is abstract; that is, partial and one-sided.[10] We see aspects but do not understand how they are essential to the object's being what it is. Of course, the ability to deploy the mental power of abstraction—to hold qualities apart in thought, to construct "ideal" representations, and so on— is an essential precondition for the possibility of knowledge. But such abstraction is not an end in itself. It is a means to the proper end of cognition: grasping the essential nature of the object as a concrete totality by capturing both the internal interrelationships of its constituent elements and the relations it bears to other objects.

To achieve the desired understanding, we must alight upon that feature of the object which is essential to the evolution of the whole. Tracing the development of that "cell" will disclose to us the nature of the whole as a unity in diversity. This factor Ilyenkov calls a "concrete universal." He argues that such an approach is exemplified by Marx's method in *Capital*, where Marx shows how understanding the nature and evolution of the value form of the commodity is the key to comprehending capitalism as a whole.

Capitalism is a system of universal commodity production and the commodity form represents its basic form of value. It is the fundamental unit from which capitalist society develops. The commodity seems relatively simple and transparent: its value must be a function of what it can be exchanged for (which in turn reflects its use value). But though exchange value is the visible manifestation of the commodity's value, its real source, Marx argues, resides ultimately in the labor required to produce it. Exploring the complex dialectical relations within this value form enables us to understand the emergence and transformation of other forms of value (money, capital, profit, etc.) until we can grasp capitalism as a complex self-reproducing system, the manifestation of which at any time is an expression of the necessary path of its development.

Such an account is historical in character. But, of course, this is not a matter of cataloguing readily apparent historical facts. The categories necessary to understand the evolution of the object will be available to us only once the object has attained its developed form, and our logical reconstruction of its development is unlikely to reproduce the temporal order of empirical history. The logical order of explanation discloses the necessary core of the object's historical development; it doesn't just tell a temporal story.[11]

Although Ilyenkov portrays "the ascent from the abstract to the concrete" as "the only possible and correct procedure for the solution by thought of the specific task of theoretical cognition of the world" (Ilyenkov 1982, 135), Marx's political economy remains his primary focus and he rarely mentions concrete universals in other domains. However, the Soviet literature does contain other examples of this style of explanation. Perhaps most notable is Vygotsky's account of consciousness in *Thinking and Speech*, which casts "word meaning" [*znachenie slova*] as the concrete universal underlying the development of the higher mental functions constitutive of the human mind. Vygotsky's terminology may be different, but the parallels between his approach and Ilyenkov's are plain to see.

Ilyenkov's account raises many questions. How, for example, are we to determine which feature of the object is the concrete universal? And how are we to decide what account to give of the system's evolution? For Ilyenkov, no general answers can be given to such questions. There is no acid test for concrete universals and no general methodological principles that dictate the path of inquiry. The question can be settled only by sustained investigation aspiring to follow the "logic of the object" and take us to the "essence of the matter." The ultimate test of theory is practice, not because a belief's truth consists in its consequences for action, but because a satisfying theory enables us to act on beliefs in harmony with the world, a harmony explained by the fact that the world is as our theory represents it to be.

Another point of contention is Ilyenkov's treatment of dialectical contradiction. The ascent from the abstract to the concrete is supposedly achieved through the identification and resolution of contradictions. In this, contradiction is said to be a real feature of things, not merely a characteristic of aberrant thought. Indeed, for Ilyenkov, the reverse is true: sometimes we find ourselves compelled to represent the object of inquiry in contradictory ways precisely because there are contradictions within it. The latter are the source of the object's transformation and development, and so thought will be adequate to its object only if it captures the object's contradictory nature. The evolution of the value form, for example, is understood by Marx as the outcome of the contradictory character of its manifestations (see Ilyenkov's discussion (1960a, 244 ff.; 1982, 254 ff.) of the commodity as a contradictory unity of use and exchange value).

While there are undoubtedly ways of reading Ilyenkov which make sense of the idea of objective contradiction, Ilyenkov is sometimes unnecessarily belligerent in his affirmation of the view, casting doubt on the laws of non-contradiction and identity, and dismissing formal logic as allied to a metaphysical, anti-dialectical vision of reality (see Ilyenkov 1974, chapter 10; 2009b, 195–213; 2018b, 373–381). However, the law of non-contradiction is implicitly affirmed in every act of judgment. When I judge *this is so*, my judgment rules out its contrary. To deny this is to deny the very possibility of judgment itself. It is another matter that, having judged *this is so* for good reasons, I may find myself with compelling reasons to make a contrary judgment. And those warring reasons may reflect features of the real nature of that about which I judge. But we can make sense of this without impugning the law of non-contradiction, and without reifying contradiction itself.

Yet, however we might question the cogency of Ilyenkov's account, there is no doubting the intellectual integrity of this work, which shows a subtlety of philosophical sensibility and an intensity of philosophical vision in stark contrast to most Soviet writing of the time. Ilyenkov was determined to encourage a critical reading of Marx's texts informed by high standards of scholarship. But more than this, he sought to read Marx's text as a contribution to philosophy's greatest task: thought's understanding of its own nature. In light of this, it is no surprise that Ilyenkov's work in this area influenced and inspired the emerging generation of Soviet philosophers.[12]

THE IDEAL

Ilyenkov's work on scientific method undoubtedly inspired the emerging generation of Soviet philosophers, but his most thrilling contribution was his article "The Ideal" (1962), which appeared in volume two of the *Philosophical Encyclopedia*, a landmark publication of the "thaw." Ilyenkov maintained that there was nothing original in his approach to this topic, affirming that he was simply setting out a position found in Marx and the German classical tradition. But in this, he was unduly modest. Ilyenkov was unique among Marxists at this time for seeing the importance of this issue, and for approaching it in the distinctive way he did. While others, inside and outside the USSR, wrote on Marxist method (e.g., Alexander Zinoviev, Jindrich Zelený), only Ilyenkov addressed the problem of the ideal.

The problem, at its broadest, concerns the status of non-material phenomena in the material world. As we have seen, Soviet *diamat* was committed to the primacy of matter over thought, spirit, consciousness, and mind. Accordingly, "the ideal" was used as a catch-all term embracing the realm of the non-material as such, though the term was sometimes used to refer more narrowly to, for example, "abstract representations," "ideal objects," and "universals"—entities that can be contrasted with "real" material particulars. At any rate, most Soviet philosophers made quick work of the ideal. They identified the ideal and the mental, asserting that ideal phenomena were a merely subjective reality. Mental goings-on were then represented as functions of the brain. In this way, the ideal was confined to the human head and the ontological primacy of the material was upheld.

Ilyenkov, in contrast, denies that all ideal phenomena can be reduced to mental phenomena. Some, at least, have an objective existence. This is true of economic value, as analyzed by Marx, for whom value is a genuine property of certain material entities and not merely a subjective projection of individuals' mental states. Similarly, Ilyenkov contends, artifacts are material entities in which significance and purpose have been objectified. This objectification constitutes the artifact as such and precedes the object's relation to any particular individual. Indeed, we only understand what such an object is in so far as we relate to it as embodying that significance and purpose.

Ilyenkov argues that each human individual is born into an environment replete with objectively existing ideal phenomena—meanings, values, reasons, concepts, and so on—instantiated in the practices of the community, and in the form the world has taken on as a result of those practices. This is a fact of enormous philosophical significance. *Contra* epistemic individualism, so typical of empiricism (but of many other schools too, historical and contemporary), it is not the case that each human child fashions for herself a conceptual scheme out of materials provided by the subjective deliverances of experience. Rather, we inherit ideal forms of thinking and reasoning by internalizing the community's practices—including, of course, natural language—and by learning to navigate the ideal forms our environment lays before us. As we enter "humanity's spiritual culture," so too we acquire the conceptual resources to express our emerging powers of mind. Initiation into the realm of the ideal is thus the very source of our mindedness. We are not minded beings at all prior to and independently of our commerce with the ideal. Thus, Ilyenkov reverses the traditional direction of explanation. For him, there is no possibility of explaining the nature of individual human minds without appeal to the objectively existing realm of the ideal, hence no reduction of the latter to the former is possible.

Activity [*deiatel'nost'*] is the concept central in Ilyenkov's account. Objectively existing ideal forms are not supernatural in kind. They are instantiated in the material world by human activity. In some cases, such as the Marxian analysis of economic value, we might hope to provide a theory that explains exactly how activity creates the ideal properties under scrutiny.[13] In other cases, the relation to activity will resist sharp theoretical articulation. But the ultimate source and substance of the ideal is activity.

Activity is also central to understanding the character of the individual mind. In a way reminiscent of Gilbert Ryle (1949), Ilyenkov denies that mental representations should be seen as static, quasi-pictorial states hovering before the mind's eye in some ghostly theater generated by the brain. A mental representation is ultimately related to action, to the power to do. To know the layout of a room is to know how to navigate it, and perhaps how to reproduce its contours in a model or map.[14] This is no crass behaviorism. It is rather an insistence that we break away from the contemplative model attacked by Marx in the *Theses on Feuerbach*, and take seriously the unity of mind and action. Activity, therefore, represents the concrete universal that enables us to understand the origins of the ideal as an objective phenomenon and the individual human mind in its essential relation to the life activity of the minded individual.

Ilyenkov's position is extraordinarily thought-provoking. It also provoked many objections. His Soviet opponents saw, in his bold endorsement of the objectivity of the ideal, an apology for idealism. Moreover, if, as Ilyenkov suggests, we always relate to reality idealized by human activity how can we ever know things as they are in themselves? Doesn't Ilyenkov face the same problem thought to beset Kantians; namely, that we are trapped in a phenomenal world of our own creation? Ilyenkov would have little patience with such objections. Of course, he would say, we encounter reality in thought in virtue of the mediation of ideal forms, "concepts," for example. But those forms are the means by which reality is disclosed to us, not a barrier that comes between us and things as they really are. After all, thought is a mode of activity manifest in our bodily engagement with the world, an engagement that will go awry if thought does not respect reality as it really is. Once we liberate ourselves from misleading philosophical pictures of being trapped "inside" our minds, confined to representations rather than reality, we can recognize that there is no general skeptical predicament to overcome. Of course, healthy skepticism is always desirable, because we are fallible creatures, prone to deceive ourselves about the nature of things, but that is a familiar epistemic problem that does not require philosophical solution. Rather, it must be dealt with by careful application of appropriate methods of inquiry aimed at discovering the truth. And every truth we discover implicitly affirms that we are material beings, rational animals, living in a material world.[15]

IDOLS AND IDEALS

The issues Ilyenkov boldly defined in his early writings continued to preoccupy him for the rest of his career. Much of his scholarly writing in the 1960s focused on the history of philosophy, specifically on conceptions of thought in the German classical tradition. This was the focus of his doctoral dissertation, *On the Question of the Nature of Thought*, which he defended in 1968 (Ilyenkov 1968a). The work explores the philosophies of Kant, Fichte, Schelling, and

Hegel. Much of this material appears, in revised form, in Ilyenkov's 1974 book, *Dialectical Logic*, which included further historical essays—on Descartes and Leibniz, Spinoza and Feuerbach—together with five substantial papers on Marxist dialectics, including a version of the 1962 paper on the ideal, and reflections on logic and dialectical method.

In addition to his more scholarly writing, Ilyenkov penned many popular and polemical pieces, which he published in a wide variety of venues, including *Literaturnaia gazeta* and the Party journal *Kommunist* (e.g., Ilyenkov 1964, 1968d, 1972). Most of these writings bring his philosophical perspective to bear on issues of immediate practical importance. Above all, Ilyenkov sought to affirm a humanistic vision in opposition to the positivistic ideology he took to have gripped Soviet political and intellectual culture, as evidenced by its fascination with the "scientific-technological revolution" (Gvishiani and Mikulinski 1978, 681–685). He also argued passionately for a conception of education as the cultivation of the power of thought in the service of universal human flourishing. These themes come together in the engagingly written *Of Idols and Ideals* (1968b).

Ilyenkov's skepticism about the scientific-technological revolution is expressed in his writings on cybernetics. Initially dismissed as a "bourgeois science," cybernetics had become an object of growing interest, and admiration, in the USSR since the late-1950s. Ilyenkov makes clear he has nothing against cybernetics itself. How could he? He is a philosopher, not a computer scientist. But, what he questions is its power, first, to illuminate human thought and, second, to transform Soviet socio-economic reality.

In harmony with his work on the ideal, Ilyenkov denies that human thinking can be reduced to computational processes going on in the brain. Of course, the brain is the "organ of thought" in the sense that a properly functioning brain is a precondition of an individual's thinking.[16] But we should not say that the brain itself thinks. Thought is not a process occurring in some "inner" space, but a mode of activity of the entire body ("the thinking body," as Ilyenkov liked to say) in unity with its social environment; that is, in interaction with other subjects inhabiting a world idealized by human agency. Therefore, the person, not the brain, is the subject of thought.[17]

The power of thought is a universal power—the power to grasp reality as such, to think the world as a totality. But it is also a power to think whatever reality offers to be thought. Hence the power of thought cannot be merely given, for it must include the power to transcend its own limits. In this sense, the thinking body is unlike a machine. A machine is an artifact, designed for some purpose. Its ability to realize that purpose is determined by its given nature. It can change under external circumstances; it may even be able to "learn" in some sense. But it cannot transform itself in self-conscious recognition of its own constraints. Ilyenkov sometimes puts this point by invoking the notion of contradiction. The logic of human thinking is dialectical—in the face of genuine contradiction, the thinking being changes the world and itself. It grows through contradiction. In contrast, the machine, built in accord with

370   D. BAKHURST

formal logic, is broken by contradiction. The power of thought is therefore not something that can be codified, captured in algorithms, inherited genetically. It cannot be built into the human individual at all. It can be acquired only through initiation into the conceptual powers objectified in humanity's spiritual culture (see Ilyenkov 1968b, 287–288).

Cybernetic speculation about the creation of machines more intelligent than human beings therefore rests on a mistake. Machines may be able to fulfill specific functions more quickly and more efficiently than human beings, but they are not strictly speaking intelligent at all. They lack the universal power of thought. It is ironic when socialists fetishize machines, fantasizing artificial intelligence organizing the economy efficiently. They forget that capitalism is a system that turns human beings into machines, by creating people who live to fulfill specific economic functions. Moreover, the whole capitalist system can be seen as nothing but a highly "intelligent" machine. This is not cause for celebration, but revolution—revolution in the service, not of mechanism, but human flourishing, which requires the cultivation of the power of thought in all its universal, self-transcending creativity. Communism is the social order in which human beings must take responsibility for creating the social conditions which enable the all-round flourishing of everyone. Technology is essential to this, but it is only a means to realize human ends. Those who aspire to offload socio-economic problems to machines forget that the relation of person to machine is just the relation of person to person mediated by machines. We remain responsible for our ends and the means we take to solve them.

Such views naturally drew Ilyenkov to questions of education. He took the ideal of universal flourishing to be incompatible with the division of labor, and accordingly he was adamant that all children should be equipped with a broad general education. Of course, human beings are finite creatures with specific talents, aptitudes, and interests, so individuals will be drawn to some activities and not others. But specialization should always be the outcome of their informed choice, rather than a consequence of a narrow education, or, even worse, of social engineering designed to fulfill economic needs. In the conclusion to *Of Idols and Ideals*, Ilyenkov writes:

> The real task posed to humanity by the development of civilization in the last centuries, and scientifically formulated by Karl Marx, is not to intensify the professional limitations of each living individual, not to deepen the difference between humanity's concept and its real existence, but the reverse—to create the social conditions, on the basis of which each living individual will "coincide with his own concept" not in fantasy, but in reality. To put it simply, society has become sufficiently rich to permit the development of culture, not at the price of turning individuals into professionally-limited, partial people, but on the basis of the maximal possibilities nature has given them.
>
> This doesn't mean of course that each individual will dissolve in the ether of "pure universality," dispersing into a state of blissful and inept dilettantism. No. To concentrate one's individuality in some or other chosen direction is a condition without which it is impossible to do anything worthwhile at all. But it is one

thing when a mature individual "imposes limits upon him- or herself" ("Those who would achieve greatness must collect themselves—the master reveals himself through his limits," said Goethe), but quite another, when a human being from childhood, as a result of her helplessness, is driven into a cage of narrow professionalism, and turned into a limited specialist, chained for life to the same profession and doomed to life-long limitedness.

In the first case, the person is a master who voluntarily imposes upon herself limits, thereby individualizing the universal power of her nature. In the second, her natural powers are limited externally, moreover extremely one-sidedly. From the very beginning she is formed as a limited being, as a "partial person." She is not first made a person as such, but immediately a violinist, sales clerk, ballerina, or mathematician. That is, without concern to develop in her, at the level of contemporary culture, universal human virtues—intellect, morality, physical well-being.

In the first case, in every limited form of her activity she acts as a full-blown representative of the "human kind," understanding the sense and significance of her actions in the context of culture. In the second case—she acts as a representative of only that limited form of activity into which she has been "trained." There's a huge difference. (Ilyenkov 1968b, 291–293)

Of course, technology can liberate human beings from meaningless labor—Ilyenkov is only too keen to recruit cybernetics to that end. But if human beings are to be enabled to act in ways that express their universal nature, they will require education appropriate to that ideal. To educate for personhood requires, above all, an education in how to think creatively and independently. Ilyenkov argues that students must develop a critical disposition that will enable them to challenge received wisdom, and they must be empowered with the confidence to confront intellectual discord and contradiction. For Ilyenkov, such intellectual virtues are a *sine qua non*.

Ilyenkov's commitment to the power of education and his interest in the social preconditions of mind come together in his writings on Alexander Meshcheryakov's work with blind-deaf individuals at the now famous Zagorsk boarding school, founded in 1963 (see Gurgenidze and Ilyenkov 1975; Ilyenkov 2018b, 240–254; Bakhurst and Padden 1991; Maidansky 2018). Ilyenkov met Meshcheryakov in 1967 and became much involved in his work, especially with the education of four young adult students, who, despite their disabilities, were eventually able to enter Moscow University, graduating in 1977. Ilyenkov was passionate about this endeavour. He argued that the education of blind-deaf children provided invaluable insight into the development of mind, refuting simple-minded empiricist views of concept acquisition, and revealing the significance of enculturation into basic human activities—such as eating with a spoon—as the foundation of the emergence of psychological capacities. Such basic activities represent the child's first entrance into culture, into the domain of the ideal, where they learn to engage with objects embodying meaning and purpose.

Ilyenkov extolled the importance of Meshcheryakov's work not just for its significance in psychology. He also saw it as embodying a moral ideal at the heart of communism: the idea that society must be organized to ensure the all-round flourishing of all citizens, whatever their "natural" abilities and disabilities. Meshcheryakov's pupils should not be seen as defective machines, to be cast aside or trained to fulfill some menial tasks. They too could, through initiation to human culture, express the universal power that is the power to think.

Trials and Tribulations

Let us now turn to the controversies that beset Ilyenkov over the course of his career. The first major incident concerned the Ilyenkov-Korovikov theses. For months after their initial presentation in April 1954, the theses were the subject of intense debate. Just as the younger generation of philosophers found Ilyenkov and Korovikov inspiring, so the philosophical establishment saw them as threatening. Not only did they challenge the standard Soviet interpretations of Marxism, they advanced a conception of philosophy which was beyond most of the old guard, who had neither the education nor the ability to do philosophy in this way. On 29 March 1955, eleven months after the theses were first presented, Ilyenkov and Korovikov were condemned at a meeting of the Scientific Council of the MGU Faculty of Philosophy, their work denounced as a neo-positivist, "menshevizing idealist," anti-Marxist deviation. A few days later, Ilyenkov endured a similar trial at the Institute of Philosophy, where a large audience met to discuss "The Theoretical Mistakes of Comrade Ilyenkov." Again, he was denounced for his revisionism and criticized for his hubris and arrogance. In May, Ilyenkov and Korovikov were removed from their teaching appointments at MGU. Ilyenkov managed to hold on to his research position at the Institute, though even that was in jeopardy as controversy continued through the autumn and winter, abating only in February 1956, when the 20th Party Congress sent shock waves through Soviet society.

The ensuing thaw created a climate of optimism among the creative Marxist intelligentsia. They were all too aware, however, that progress would depend upon the removal of the old guard from positions of administrative and political power within the Soviet academic world. This did not happen and soon Ilyenkov was once again in trouble. In 1956, he was approached by the Italian communist Sergio d'Angelo, who worked for Radio Moscow as an editor and reporter. D'Angelo also served as a literary agent for the communist publisher Giangiacomo Feltrinelli. D'Angelo asked Ilyenkov if he had material he would consider publishing with Feltrinelli. In the summer of 1957, Ilyenkov gave d'Angelo the manuscript of his recently completed book, *The Dialectics of the Abstract and the Concrete in Scientific-Theoretical Thought* [*Dialektika abstraktnogo i konkretnogo v naucho-teoreticheckogo myshleniia*].

Unbeknownst to Ilyenkov, Boris Pasternak was among the writers d'Angelo had approached, and in November 1957, Feltrinelli published the first edition of *Doctor Zhivago*. When Ilyenkov's involvement with the same publisher became known, all hell broke loose. He had to attend numerous Party meetings exploring his misdemeanors, at which he was accused of revisionism, and of lacking patriotism and *partiinost*.[18] Ilyenkov was forced to confess his errors, agree to "reckon with the opinion of the collective," and pledge "to become more circumspect in theory and in life" (Ilyenkov 2017, 49).

As an illustration of the character of these proceedings, consider the words of M. Sh. Bakhitov at a closed Party meeting at the Institute of Philosophy on 27 November 1958. They show how little things had changed:

> Everyone praises Ilyenkov as talented. But what's his talent? He did bad work, remote from life. And being remote from life is one of the worst dogmas of the Second International and a characteristic mark of revisionism. There is a lot of interest in us from abroad. Our enemies try to use our failings and mistakes against Marxism. The enemy took Ilyenkov's work in order to use it against Marxism, against Soviet Philosophy. Recently, the Institute has established very wide contacts with people from abroad. We need to be vigilant, we need to be careful. We need to curtail unauthorized meetings between party members and foreigners. We need to put a stop to communication with foreigners. We need to protect our secrets. Comrade Ilyenkov admitted his mistakes, but he needs to continue working on himself. Ilyenkov must become closer to life, he must decisively re-make himself. (Ilyenkov 2017, 71)

The Bureau felt that Ilyenkov's errors warranted expulsion from the Party, but in view of his sincere self-criticism, the penalty was commuted to a severe reprimand,[19] a narrow escape. A much-edited and reorganized version of his manuscript was eventually published as *Dialectics of the Abstract and the Concrete in Marx's "Capital"* (1960a). The complete text was not published under its original title until 1997.

The early 1960s passed relatively calmly. His article on the ideal provoked much discussion, but there was no official condemnation despite its conflict with Soviet orthodoxy. In May 1964, Ilyenkov did resign angrily from the editorial team of the *Philosophical Encyclopedia*, while at work on the third of the project's five volumes, over what he took to be the privileging of formal over dialectical logic.[20] But this was largely an academic rather than political matter (so far as that distinction can be drawn in the Soviet context).

The late 1960s, however, saw further controversy. On 8 December 1967, *Komsomol'skaya pravda* ran an engaging article, "The Courage of Thought," reporting a philosophical roundtable, in which Ilyenkov participated along with Felix T. Mikhailov, Anatolii S. Arsen'ev, Vladimir S. Bibler, Genrikh S. Batishchev, and others (Klyamkin and Tsipko 1967). The discussion focused on the value of studying philosophy, and the message conveyed by Ilyenkov and his likeminded colleagues was that philosophy should not be taught as a kind of general commentary on the methods and achievements of the other sciences. Rather, philosophy is the science of thought and to study its history is to engage with human intellectual culture in its highest manifestation. The article provoked an uproar. By implying that philosophy was badly taught in the Soviet Union, and portraying the history of philosophy as a font of intellectual riches while making no mention of the obligation to provide a class-based critique of pre-Marxist philosophy, the participants opened themselves to inevitable denunciations (see Ilyenkov 2018a, 340). The situation quickly became uncomfortable. Ilyenkov, however, emerged relatively unscathed. Arsen'ev and Mikhailov took the brunt of the abuse.

The year 1968 was pivotal for Ilyenkov. On the one hand, much went well. *Of Idols and Ideals* was published, "Mind and Brain," Ilyenkov's well-known reply to David Dubrovsky, appeared in *Voprosy filosofii* (Ilyenkov 1968c), and in December, Ilyenkov successfully defended his doctoral dissertation, after an intense nine-hour-long defense.[21] However, the year was blighted by the Warsaw Pact invasion of Czechoslovakia in August. This had a devastating effect on Ilyenkov, and profoundly influenced the rest of his life.

The Prague Spring stood for the creation of "socialism with a human face" (or "humanized socialism," as the Russian has it), a trope equally fitting to describe the ethos of Ilyenkov's philosophy. Although his reflections on the scientific method and on the objectivity of the ideal might seem to imply a rather impersonal vision, it is evident from his corpus as a whole that Ilyenkov is focused on human flourishing, which he measures, not merely by the achievements of humanity's spiritual culture, but by the flourishing of people—of real human individuals—enabled by their appropriation of culture. Hence, Ilyenkov, who stood for critical and creative inquiry and for openness and honesty, could not but have been sympathetic with Dubcek's reforms. He therefore found the Soviet response utterly demoralizing. V. A. Lektorsky comments, "In the oppressive ideological atmosphere following the suppression of the 'Prague Spring,' the hope of the creation of a 'humanized socialism' collapsed. All of us found this hard to endure, but for Ilyenkov, as a convinced Marxist, it was especially painful" (Lektorsky 2018, 445).

Prague also provided the Soviet authorities with a pretext to clamp down on "revisionism" and dissent. An immediate target was the Institute's renowned "wall newspaper," to which Ilyenkov regularly contributed irreverent caricatures, sometimes affectionate portraits of respected colleagues, sometimes mocking cartoons of the Institute's leadership. Early in 1969, Ilyenkov and the rest of the editorial team were severely rebuked and a new editor appointed, charged with reforming the paper.

As time went on, the climate worsened and Ilyenkov was constantly under suspicion and subjected to persecution. As Lektorsky reports (2018), instrumental in this was Elena Modrzhinskaya, a former KGB operative under Beria, who was now (incredibly) a faculty member at the Institute of Philosophy. Modrzhinskaya wasted no opportunity to attack Ilyenkov, criticizing him, for example, for publishing in a Western book alongside Czech philosopher Karel Kosic, as well as members of the Yugoslav Praxis group.[22] The then-Director, P. V. Kopnin, protected Ilyenkov. In response, Modrzhinskaya wrote a denunciation to the KGB, listing ten "anti-communists" at the Institute. The list included Kopnin, Ilyenkov, and Lektorsky, now the Head of Ilyenkov's Sector.

The Sector somehow survived, but not Kopnin, who died before he reached 50. The Institute then lingered without a permanent director until B. M. Kedrov took over in 1973. Kedrov was a fine philosopher and a decent person, and he too protected Ilyenkov. However, hopes of a better future were dashed when Kedrov, finding conditions intolerable, resigned after only a year.

Kedrov's replacement was B. S. Ukrainstev, who was explicitly charged with "eradicating the revisionist infection" in the sectors of dialectical materialism (led by Lektorsky) and historical materialism (led by V. Zh. Kelle) (Lektorsky 2018, 440). The result was several years of petty but debilitating abuse. A typical instance was the protracted debate about the publication of *Dialectics as Logic in the Theory of Knowledge* [*Dialektika kak logika v teorii poznaniia*], a collection of essays written by members of Lektorsky's sector, in accord with the sector's five-year plan. Notwithstanding the fact that the text had undergone numerous reviews, the Institute's Scientific Council would not approve publication unless Ilyenkov's contribution was excised. This was his article, "Dialectics of the Ideal," which revisited the themes of his 1962 classic and brought them into dialogue with contemporary developments in Soviet philosophy, including his debate with Dubrovsky.

Vexations like this were nothing new. In 1974, Ilyenkov complained that none of the planned work he had produced over the past eight years had seen the light of day (Ilyenkov 2018a, 373). But the drama over "Dialectics of the Ideal," which began in 1976 and continued for years, must have been particularly galling, as the intention was to deny Ilyenkov a voice on a subject he had made his own. Ilyenkov was also disparaged for his involvement in Meshcheryakov's project. It was not until 1977—a decade after his interest began—that he was permitted to give a paper on this topic to the Institute's Scientific Council. The reaction was at best disinterest, and at worst hostility. V. V. Bykov, for example, commented that, although Meshcheryakov's achievements were "interesting," "none of the philosophical conclusions Evald Vasil'evich draws are warranted. And the language in which he presents all this gives no basis for a scientific discussion" (Ilyenkov 2018a, 396). Ilyenkov, whose commitment to Meshcheryakov's project was profound, was dismayed by this dismissive reception. He never attended the Scientific Council again.[23]

Such ordeals eventually broke Ilyenkov. One might wonder how he could be brought down by the petty machinations of Ukrainstev and Modrzhinskaya when he had survived far worse in the 1950s. This is not a matter on which it is easy, or even appropriate, to speculate. I will only observe that, as Lektorsky puts it, during the thaw:

> all of us living at that time had a sense of the future, a confidence that barriers would be overcome, that philosophy would be set free, that we would be able to create a meaningful and human life. (Lektorsky 2017, 16)

After Prague, that optimism, and the fortitude it engendered, was gone. And that loss, above all, destroyed Ilyenkov.

CONCLUSION

At a critical meeting of the Scientific Council at MGU, the Dean of the Faculty of Philosophy, V. S. Molodstov, exclaimed that "the theses of Ilyenkov and Korovikov are dragging us into the realm of thought" (Ilyenkov and Korovikov 2016, 59). The protocol of the meeting records "Laughter in the hall," though not the response reputedly shouted from the floor: "Don't worry, no-one could drag *you* there, not even with a lasso!" Of course, however ludicrous his remark, Molodstov had hit the nail on the head. Ilyenkov *was* above all a philosopher of *thought*.

Ilyenkov would likely have found that description no less comical than "Diadia" Molodstov's. Since thought is philosophy's true subject, any genuine philosopher must be a philosopher of thought. But the epithet does make sense in the Soviet context, not just because the ideal of philosophy as the science of thinking guides everything Ilyenkov did, but because it was also the cause of everything that was done to him. The establishment hated Ilyenkov's emphasis on thought because it represented a vision of philosophy distinct from the orthodoxy, one that rode a fine line along the boundary between materialism and idealism. But more than this, they disliked the way Ilyenkov put philosophy in the service of thought—of free, critical, creative thinking, questioning, challenging, transcending. As we have seen, Ilyenkov saw the power of free creative thought as a constituent of communism's only ultimate end: human flourishing. In this, Ilyenkov was the herald and the conscience of Soviet Marxism.

No wonder, then, that he was destroyed. But no wonder also that his legacy lives on.

NOTES

1. During his lifetime translations of his writings appeared in Chinese, German, English, French, Greek, Italian, Japanese, Polish, Serbo-Croat, Slovakian, and Spanish. Posthumous translations have appeared in many of these languages, as well as Bulgarian, Czech, Finish, Korean, and Punjabi. A list of Ilyenkov's translated works can be found at: http://amaid.tk/ilyenkov/aln.html.

2. It is important to understand the character of Soviet academic censorship. It is not that Ilyenkov's writings were subjected to the blue pencil of an official censor. Rather, the work of members of the Institute of Philosophy, especially collective work specified in the Institute's five-year plan, was usually submitted to (not entirely disinterested) peer review and required the approval of the Institute's Scientific Council before it could be published. The system was open to many abuses (see the discussion of the controversy around Ilyenkov's paper "Dialektika ideal'nogo" below and in Ilyenkov 2018a, 354–373). Between 1964 and 1970, Ilyenkov made five trips abroad to Austria (1964), GDR (1965, 1970), Czechoslovakia (1966), and Bulgaria (1967) (Ilyenkov 2018a, 294–295). At least one other trip, in 1967 to a conference at the University of Notre Dame, USA, was canceled, ostensibly because he was hospitalized (see Bakhurst 1991, 7). After 1970, his requests to travel abroad were denied.

3. http://amaid.tk/ilyenkov/index.html.
4. http://iljenkov.ru.
5. Aida Vasil'evna Ilyenkova (1926–2002) became an architect, specializing in the restoration of historic buildings. She married architect Evgenii Grigor'evich Rozanov (1925–2006), who became a renowned exponent of Soviet "brutalism."
6. In presenting Ilyenkov's position, I draw not just on the text of the theses (which is actually rather obscure), but also on other writings from this period, and relevant commentary, as presented in Ilyenkov and Korovikov 2016. That book was prepared prior to the discovery of the complete manuscript of the theses, and so contains only Illesh's partial reconstruction thereof. The full text is included in Ilyenkov 2017. See Bakhurst 2019 for a detailed discussion, which includes an English translation of the theses.
7. It is important that by "science" Ilyenkov and Korovikov mean any discipline engaged in systematic and rigorous inquiry aimed at knowledge, not just natural science; the Russian *nauka* has affinities with the German *Wissenschaft*.
8. There is a 1975 photograph of Ilyenkov with Kuznetsov. It is reproduced in Ilyenkov 2018a, facing p. 305.
9. Of course, if the object of inquiry is a mental phenomenon, its nature may be constituted, at least in part, by our understanding of it in the sense that some mental states are essentially self-conscious. However, we may still fail to understand how this is so: even if self-consciousness is a necessary feature of judgment, we can still misunderstand the nature of judgment and the nature of self-consciousness.
10. This notion of abstraction is derived from Hegel, whose essay "Who Thinks Abstractly?" was a favorite of Ilyenkov's.
11. Ilyenkov seems to think all objects of cognition must be understood in their historical evolution. This makes sense for social and economic systems, but what of the objects of the natural sciences? I think Ilyenkov would say that the ultimate objects of scientific inquiry do have a history: the universe, the solar system, the Earth, life, and so on. These are the objects that the physical and life sciences ultimately seek to explain *in their development*. Mathematical objects are not historical entities, but they are ideal, and the ideal in turn has a history, as we shall see in the next section.
12. For further discussion, see Bakhurst 1991, chapter 5.
13. Note, however, that this will not be a reductive account of the ideal, since much of the activity in question is intelligent and purposeful and hence infused with ideality.
14. In a 1968 lecture on the ideal, recently published for the first time, Ilyenkov refers to Ivan Sokolyansky's blind-deaf pupil Iulia Vinogradova, who returned from a walk in a ravine and made a plasticine model of the shape of the ravine (Ilyenkov 2018a, 102). Her mental image of the ravine could hardly be the kind of thing philosophers typically take it to be, but what she had was the power actively to reproduce by the movements of her body and her hands, the objective form of the object.
15. I defend Ilyenkov from such objections in Bakhurst 1991, chapter 6 (which provides a comprehensive account of his views on the ideal), 1997, and 2011, 112–114. Ilyenkov certainly gave them shorter shrift than I do.

16. There is a hilarious discussion in Ilyenkov's lecture, "Historicism in Psychology," where Ilyenkov says that the fact that people think with their brains and not their arses is admitted by all, and given experimental confirmation by Dr. Guillotine, who not for nothing designed his machine to cut off heads and not buttocks (Ilyenkov 2018a, 229). A tape of this lecture exists, the only known recording of Ilyenkov in action.
17. This line of argument is explored in Bakhurst 2008.
18. *Partiinost'* [literally "partyness"] is hard to translate. "Commitment to the Party" probably comes closest to its meaning.
19. The self-criticism may not in fact have been so sincere. The typescript of Ilyenkov's remarks suggests that not everything he said was written by him (see Ilyenkov 2017, 50).
20. Ilyenkov protested that dialectical logic had been assigned only two entries ("Logic (dialectical)" and "Logical and historical"), compared to 22 devoted to aspects of formal logic. This gave the misleading impression that dialectical logic was a sub-branch of logic, instead of a comprehensive approach to thought that subsumed and transcended formal approaches. Ilyenkov also complained that the editorial work he had so far undertaken had been redone and "hopelessly spoiled" by A. G. Spirkin. Ilyenkov asked that his name be removed from the list of editors of volume three, asserting that he hadn't "the slightest desire to put his name to Spirkin's work" (Ilyenkov 2018a, 306).
21. At the defense, Ilyenkov was harshly criticized by two colleagues, I. Elez and G. A. Davydova. Davydova, who had formerly been Ilyenkov's follower, was the ex-wife of Ilyenkov's friend, the psychologist V. V. Davydov. She was now married to Elez. Illesh comments, "I am not saying that her theoretical change of mind was directly connected to the change in her personal life, but neither can we entirely ignore this circumstance" (Ilyenkov 2018a, 328). The dissertation passed by 26 votes to 3 (the third negative vote was likely B. S. Ukraintsev's, see below). Notwithstanding this massive majority, VAK (the "Higher Attestation Committee"—the principal degree-awarding body of the USSR) insisted on sending the dissertation to a further referee before finally granting Ilyenkov the degree in April 1969.
22. This was Ilyenkov's paper for the Notre Dame conference, "Marx and the Western World," which Ilyenkov was unable to attend in person (see note 2 above).
23. Ilyenkov was genuinely convinced that Meshcheryakov's work was of deep philosophical significance. There is no doubt, however, that he is often incautious in the way he states his case, portraying the work as an *experimentum crusis* vindicating his Marxist account of the social construction of mind. However, such claims need to be understood in context. Many of these writings were designed to celebrate and popularize Meshcheryakov's work in an effort to convince the authorities to provide the resources that would allow the work to continue. This was particularly crucial after Meshcheryakov's sudden death in 1974. Naturally, such writings tended to simplify the issues and it was no surprise that they provoked a negative response from thinkers who favored more naturalistic conceptions of mind. However, it was one thing to get an uncomprehending response from a geneticist, such as A. A. Malinovskii (1970) (son of Lenin's rival A. A. Bogdanov), another to find one's own colleagues utterly uncomprehending of the philosophical depth of Meshcheryakov's project. (Ukrainstev's

reflections, in response to Ilyenkov, on the sense of smell as a channel of communication are astonishing in their stupidity.) Hostility to Ilyenkov's work in this area continued after his death, when his old adversary David Dubrovsky and others mounted "a battle for truth in blind-deaf pedagogy," accusing Ilyenkov of falsifying data and other failures of academic integrity. Carol Padden and I came to Ilyenkov's defense in Bakhurst and Padden 1991. Some of Ilyenkov's best writing on Meshcheryakov was published only recently in Ilyenkov 2018a, 240–254.

BIBLIOGRAPHY

Altaiskii, Mikhail A., and Evald V. Ilyenkov. 1973. Fal'sifikatsiya marksistskoi dialektiki v ugodu maoistskoi politike. *Kommunist* 18: 93–105.

Bakhurst, David. 1991. *Consciousness and Revolution in Soviet Philosophy: From the Bolsheviks to Evald Ilyenkov*. Cambridge, UK: Cambridge University Press.

———. 1997. Meaning, Normativity and the Life of the Mind. *Language and Communication* 17 (1): 33–51.

———. 2008. Minds, Brains and Education. *Journal of Philosophy of Education* 42 (3–4): 415–432.

———. 2011. *The Formation of Reason*. Oxford: Wiley-Blackwell.

———. 2019. Punks Versus Zombies: Evald Ilyenkov and the Battle for Soviet Philosophy. In *Philosophical Thought in Russia in the Second Half of the Twentieth Century*, ed. Vladislav A. Lektorsky and Marina F. Bykova, 53–78. London: Bloomsbury Academic.

Bakhurst, David, and Carol Padden. 1991. The Meshcheryakov Experiment: Soviet Work on the Education of Blind-Deaf Children. *Learning and Instruction* 1: 201–215.

Gurgenidze, G. S., and Evald V. Ilyenkov. 1975. Vydaiushcheesia dostizhenie sovetskoi nauki. *Voprosy filosofii* 6: 63–73.

Gvishiani, Dzharmen M., and Semen R. Mikulinski. 1978. Scientific and Technological Revolution. In *Great Soviet Encyclopedia*, vol. 17, 681–685. New York: Macmillan Inc.

Ilyenkov, Evald V. 1953. *Nekotorie voprosy materialisticheskoi dialektiki v rabote K. Marksa "K kritike politicheskoi ekonomiki"*. Candidate's thesis, Moscow State University.

———. 1955. O dialektike abstraknogo i konkretnogo v nauchno-teoreticheskom poznanii. *Voprosy filosofii* 1: 42–56.

———. 1957. K voprosu o protivorechii v myshlenii. *Voprosy filosofii* 4: 63–72.

———. 1960a. *Dialektika abstraknogo i konkretnogo v "Kapitale" Marksa*. Moscow: Izdatelstvo Akademii nauk. (English translation Ilyenkov 1982).

———. 1960b. Logicheskoe i istoricheskoe. In *Elementy dialektiki*, 310–343. Moscow: Nauka.

———. 1962. Ideal'noe. *In Filosofskaia entsiklopediia*. vol. 2, 219–227. Moscow: Sovetskaia entsiklopediia.

———. 1964. Mnogoznanie umu ne nauchaet. *Literaturnaia gazeta*, 22 September.

———. 1967. Problema abstraknogo i konkretnogo. *Voprosy filosofii* 9: 55–65.

———. 1968a. *K voprosu o prirode myshleniya (na materialax analiza nemetskoi klassicheskoi dialektiki)*. Doctoral dissertation, Akademiia nauk, Moscow.

———. 1968b. *Ob idolakh i idealakh*. Moscow: Politizdat.

380   D. BAKHURST

———. 1968c. Psikhika i mozg. *Voprosy filosofii* 11: 145–155.

———. 1968d. O voobrazhenii. *Narodnoe obrazovanie* 3: 33–42.

———. 1972. Proidena li tablitsa umnozheniia? *Literaturnaia gazeta*, March 1.

———. 1974. *Dialekticheskaia logika: ocherki istorii i teorii*. Moscow: Politizdat. (English translation Ilyenkov 1977a).

———. 1977a. *Dialectical Logic: Essays in its History and Theory*. Translated by H. Campbell Creighton. Moscow: Progress. (Reprinted in Ilyenkov 2009b, 1–214).

———. 1977b. The Concept of the Ideal. In *Philosophy in the USSR: Problems of Dialectical Materialism*, 71–99. Moscow: Progress. (Reprinted in Ilyenkov 2009b, 253–284).

———. 1979. Materializm voinstvuiushchii — znachit dialekticheskii. *Kommunist* 6: 47–60. (English translation in Ilyenkov 2018b, 229–247).

———. 1982. *The Dialectics of the Abstract and the Concrete in Marx's* Capital. Translated by S. Syrovatkin. Moscow: Progress.

———. 1984. *Iskusstvo i kommunisticheskii ideal*. Moscow: Isskustvo.

———. 1991. *Filosofiia i kul'tura*. Moscow: Politizdat.

———. 1997. *Dialektika abstraknogo i konkretnogo v nauchno-teoreticheskom myshlenii*. Moscow: ROSSPEN.

———. 2002. *Shkola dolzhna uchit' myslit'*. Moscow-Voronezh: Modek.

———. 2009a. Dialektika ideal'nogo. *Logos* 1: 6–62. English translation by A. Levant in Ilyenkov 2014, 25–78.

———. 2009b. *The Ideal in Human Activity*. Pacifica, CA: Marxist Internet Archive.

Ilyenkov Evald V. 2014. *Dialectics of the Ideal: Evald Ilyenkov and Creative Soviet Marxism*. Edited by A. Levant and V. Oittinen. Leiden: Brill.

Ilyenkov, Evald V. 2016. Cosmology of the Spirit. Translated by G. Vivaldi. *Stasis* 5 (2): 164–190.

Ilyenkov Evald V. 2017. *Ot abstraknogo k konkretnomu. Krutoi marshrut. 1950–1960*. Compiled and edited by Elena E. Illesh. With contributions by Vladislav A. Lektorsky, Ilya A. Raskin, and Andrey D. Maidansky. Moscow: Kanon+.

———. 2018a. *Ideal'noe i realnost'. 1960–1979*. Compiled and edited by Elena E. Illesh. With contributions by Vladislav A. Lektorsky and Andrey D. Maidansky. Moscow: Kanon+.

Ilyenkov, Evald V. 2018b. *Intelligent Materialism: Essays on Hegel and Dialectics*. Edited and translated by Evgeni V. Pavlov. Leiden: Brill.

Ilyenkov Evald V., and Valentin I. Korovikov. 2016. *Strasti no tezisam o predmete filosofii 1954–1955*. Complied and edited by E. Illesh. With contributions by Vladislav A. Lektorsky and Ilya A. Raskin. Moscow: Kanon+.

Klyamkin, Igor', and Aleksandr Tsipko. 1967. Myzhestvo mysli. *Komsomolskaia pravda* 8 (December 2).

Lektorsky, Vladislav A. 2017. Vmesto vvedeniia. Vospominaniia i razmyshleniia. In Ilyenkov 2017, 5–24.

———. 2018. Vmesto zakliucheniia. 'Chto pomniu, o chem dumaiu. In Ilyenkov 2018a, 435–448.

Lenin, Vladimir I. 1976. *Philosophical Notebooks*. In *Collected Works*, vol. 38, 4th English ed. Translated by Clemence Dutt. Edited by Stewart Smith. Moscow: Progress Publishers.

Maidansky, Andrey D. 2018. Uroki zagorskogo ekperimenta. In Ilyenkov 2018a, 413–434.

Malinovskii, Aleksandr A. 1970. Nekotorye vozrazheniia E.V. Il'enkovu i A. I. Meshcheriakovu. *Priroda* 1: 92–95.

Mamedov, Georgii, and Oksana Shatalov. 2017. Against Simple Answers: The Queer Communist Theory of Evald Ilyenkov and Alexander Suvorov. http://artseverywhere.ca/2017/08/17/against-simple-answers/.

Rozental', Mark M., and Evald V. Ilyenkov. 1969. Lenin i aktual'nye problemy dialekticheskoi logiki. *Kommunist* 12: 24–35.

Ryle, Gilbert. 1949. *The Concept of Mind*. London: Hutchinson's University Library.

Vasil'ev, I. (Evald V. Ilyenkov), and Lev K. Naumenko. 1973. Tri veka bessmertiia. *Kommunist* 5: 63–73.

CHAPTER 18

The "Men of the Sixties": Philosophy as a Social Phenomenon

Abdusalam A. Guseynov

The philosophy of the "men of the sixties" refers temporally to Russian philosophy in the second half of the twentieth century, though they do not fully overlap. It denotes a qualitative shift that occurred in Soviet philosophy of that period in terms of its fully official (subject to censors) manifestations. The following text is an attempt to analyze this shift and to answer these questions: (1) Why was it designated by the term "men of the sixties"? (2) What caused it and what was it, in essence? (3) How was it inscribed in the overall portrait of philosophical life, nationally and globally? (4) Whose works served as its fullest representation?

WHO WERE THESE "MEN OF THE SIXTIES"?

The term "men of the sixties" spread naturally and became a concept, a kind of meme, in Soviet public consciousness and humanist vocabulary after literary critic Stanislav B. Rassadin (1960) published an article of that name dedicated to new literary works about young contemporaries. It has no strictly fixed meaning, but characterizes a broad cultural movement tied to a particular generation, those born primarily in the 1920s and 1930s, as well as the time period (the late 1950s and early 1960s) during which this generation began engaging in robust public activity. Membership in this particular generation and time period alone is an insufficient reason for someone to be considered a "man of the sixties." One's system of values and civic position, which we might

A. A. Guseynov (✉)
Institute of Philosophy, Russian Academy of Sciences, Moscow, Russia

© The Author(s), under exclusive license to Springer Nature
Switzerland AG 2021
M. F. Bykova et al. (eds.), *The Palgrave Handbook of Russian Thought*,
https://doi.org/10.1007/978-3-030-62982-3_18

383

generalize as the struggle against Stalinism and for a humanistic renewal of public life, is also of great importance. I believe the question of whether they drifted away from socialism or stayed within its parameters remains an open one. At the very least, they stayed within the system of Soviet values in terms of their subjective attitudes; they were committed to the ideal of socialism with a human face. It is precisely this movement toward humane social relationships, toward creative freedom and individual self-expression, that allows us to identify the "men of the sixties." The problem they faced was whether it was possible to have faith in communism without fanaticism and in a collectively oriented way of life without asceticism, as were characteristic of the generations who lived through the Civil War and first Five-Year Plans. This is also important for defining the timeframe of their activities.

We might consider 1956 the beginning of the "men of the sixties" generation: they loved to call themselves the children of that year's 20th Soviet Party Congress. This congress and the criticisms of Stalin's cult of personality that were heard there, the subsequent weakening of the party-ideological press, and the policy of peaceful coexistence with the capitalist West became a lawful source and political stimulus for this generation's social activity and creative inspiration. Its end stretched from the 1968 invasion of Czechoslovakia by Soviet troops, which gave rise to a sobering disillusionment and their first schisms over beliefs, to Perestroika, which became the de facto era of dismantling Soviet socialism in its historically existing forms.

The "men of the sixties" created their own public image, and it was generally a positive one, though accompanied from the very beginning by critical remarks that particularly intensified in post-Soviet Russia. The "men of the sixties" were not dissidents. The relationship between these two forms and stages of civic resistance in the Soviet Union requires a specialized study, but it seems obvious overall that, in terms of time period and in essence, the "men of the sixties" preceded the dissidents, and some of them even became dissidents, though they themselves as a cultural phenomenon were not dissidents. They remained humanism-oriented communists, Romantic communists, and practicing idealists. Dissidence was the next, markedly liberal stage of civic activity that followed the "men of the sixties" and served as the starting point for a critical attitude toward the latter. It was associated with human rights work, while the "men of the sixties" were ideologically oriented toward a humanistic renewal of socialism.

As a significant cultural phenomenon of Soviet history, the "men of the sixties" were represented in the world of film, visual arts, and music, but most widely in literature, and especially so in poetry. They did not create any formal associations. If we take the most famous names personifying the "men of the sixties," its idols, they were all separate and clearly expressed creative individualities. What united them was in fact their difference from one another, namely, that each of them was equal to himself and asserted an anti-totalitarian pathos in his work. They were like stars, each unique in itself, united by a sky of soaring aspirations. For examples, it may suffice to mention such well-known figures as the poet Evgenii Yevtushenko, the writer Yuri Trifonov, the director Andrei Tarkovsky, the artist Ernst Neizvestny, and the composer Alfred Schnittke.

There is no formally established tradition of using the "men of the sixties" concept to understand what was happening in Russian philosophy in the second half of the twentieth century, nor for everything related to the "men of the sixties" as a social phenomenon (Lektorsky and Bykova 2019). Nevertheless, it would not be artificial to do this. The point is not only that young researchers who marked an era of change in philosophy inhaled the same atmosphere of hope, or that these young cultural figures and their circles of personal contacts often crisscrossed (e.g., Alexander Zinoviev and Merab Mamardashvili were frequent guests of sculptor Ernst Neizvestny, while future well-known director Grigorii Chukhrai attended Zinoviev's doctoral defense). Something else was even more significant. The philosophy of Marxism held the status of state ideology in Russia, so whatever happened in the philosophy environment, however philosophy itself and its place in human life was understood, was no narrowly professional issue, but represented a direct, broadly public interest. Looking at changes in philosophy as an integral part of the "men of the sixties" movement allows us to distinguish which qualitative changes occurred at precisely that moment in time, as well to clarify more precisely their historical context and social-moral pathos. In addition, applying terms that describe literary processes to the field of philosophy is fully in line with Russian cultural traditions. There are many examples of this: one of the most recent and clearest is the widely accepted characterization of early twentieth-century philosophy as "Silver Age philosophy," where the term "Silver Age" was originally introduced to designate twentieth-century poetry in contrast to nineteenth-century (Golden Age) poetry.

How did this Renewal of Philosophy Begin, and What did it Include?

We should regard philosophy as it was in Soviet society, as well as this society itself, as something unique in kind. The usual criteria and assessments are not suitable in this case. If the history of European culture provides any experiences that could serve as a support or at least starting point for analysis of the Soviet experiment, these were purely intellectual utopias at best. The only real historical foothold that Marxism's founders could locate was the 72-day experience of the Paris Commune, which could just as well be considered a historical accident. Here, they were trying to elevate an enormous country, one sixth of all terrestrial land, and the whole planet after it, to a Marxist utopia, a space for realizing the communist ideal. In full accordance with Marx's famous eleventh thesis, they wanted not to interpret the world, but to change it, to transform and cleanse it through Marxist truth.

They had no doubts that the world—and society, and man, and even nature—must be changed in line with Marx. The socialist revolution was started for this reason. The only question was whether any space remained for philosophy in a Marxist system. This very issue became the subject of controversy in the 1920s (the first decade of the new social order) after the forcible termination of activities at traditional philosophy institutes and non-Marxist philosophy schools. Two opposing points of view arose, one of which believed that the new proletarian culture was based on purely scientific knowledge and was overcoming (discarding) philosophy as a form of false consciousness, while the other proceeded from the idea that philosophy itself could be scientific, as it would be under Marxism. The viewpoint Lenin expressed before the revolution, that philosophy is one of Marxism's constituent parts and has its roots in German classical philosophy, ended up prevailing.

As Soviet society was considered a Marxist project, the philosophy of Marxism was to become an integral part of this project in the form of a universally obligatory state ideology. Several problems needed to be solved before any transformation could occur and philosophy be given its ideological form. First, it had to be declared uniquely and indisputably true. Second, it had to be reduced to some visible and easily digestible amount of dogma that could serve as a kind of secular symbol of faith. Third, there needed to be a corresponding infrastructure for organizational propaganda designed to introduce this philosophy to the masses. Given this framework for understanding the essence of philosophy and its place in society, the work of philosophers themselves consisted of defending the doctrine's purity and standing guard over it, reducing its content to a limited set of clear, easily digestible dogmas, and accepting philosophy's place in these social mechanisms by introducing these dogmas into public consciousness. Defending the unconditional truth of Marxist philosophy caused some difficulty related to interpretation of the classic texts, which were far from being explicit and provoked a great deal of controversy. Even more difficulties arose in relation to aligning them with dogma, since a number of statements directly contradicted this, particularly Friedrich Engels' well-known comment, later repeated by Lenin, that Marxism was not a dogma but a guide to action. A way past these meaningful discussions was eventually discovered: the issue of philosophy was deemed too serious to entrust to philosophers, so it was transferred from academic auditoria to the sphere of public policy. The first two problems listed above were solved by creating a short Stalinist summary of Marxist philosophy entitled "On Dialectical and Historical Materialism" ("O dialekticheskom i istoricheskom materializme"), which proclaimed dialectical materialism as the official worldview of the Communist Party and reduced the dialectical method to four features, philosophical materialism to three, and the social application of philosophical materialism to three. To address the latter, they created the corresponding departments, institutes, journals, enlightenment societies, and an extensive, mass network for political education. In all its manifestations (as a field of knowledge, as an academic subject, and as a form of social consciousness engaging researchers, cultural figures, and ordinary people), philosophy came under the direct control of the ruling party and was directly subordinated to political exigencies.

The most complete, we might even say "model," reduction of philosophy to ideology was carried out in the 1930s and 1940s. In those years, philosophy in any meaningful sense of the word was in fact dead. We see only a few flickers of life, such as the three-volume history of philosophy (Aleksandrov et al. 1941–1943). Specific philosophical topics, discussions, and books were generally dictated by party authorities and decisions; they defended the necessity and wisdom of a succession of tasks such as collectivization, industrialization, the struggle against enemies of the people, and other issues unrelated to the scope of philosophical questions. The very language of philosophical works changed: philosophers no longer researched, examined, or disputed, but fought, battled, exposed, and praised. The *Short Course on the History of the All-Union Communist Party of Bolsheviks (AUCPB) (Kratkii kurs istorii VKP[b])*, one of whose sections consisted of Stalin's philosophical text mentioned above, was declared by a November 14, 1938 resolution of the Central Committee of the AUCPB to be "an encyclopedia of philosophical knowledge in the field of Marxism-Leninism," forbidding "any frivolous interpretations" (KPSS 1954, 316). If "Soviet philosophy" could be called a unique ideological construct (as opposed to philosophy of the Soviet years of Russian history), then its most vivid manifestation was the official philosophy of the 1930s and 1940s. If it bears a single most characteristic feature, it is this consistent dogmatism that excluded any independent or individually responsible judgment.

The experience of Soviet philosophy during this period was undoubtedly a negative one, indicative of what can happen to philosophy when it is transformed into an ideology, regardless of the ideology in question. The very fact of subordination to ideology is enough to kill philosophy. This is a clear example of pseudomorphism: philosophers remain philosophers, but without the right to think independently, without the right to philosophize. By the late 1940s and early 1950s, Russian philosophy had ossified to such an extent that it could not generate a single vibrant thought. The appearance of two new theoretical works by Stalin, "Marxism and the Problem of Linguistics" ("Marksizm i voprosy iazikoznaniia") in 1950 and "Economic Problems of Socialism in the USSR" ("Ekonomicheskie problemy sotsializma v SSSR") in 1952, as well as the instantaneous, all-encompassing reaction from the print and oral industries that focused entirely on unrestrained praise, including a comprehensive redrawing of all educational programs, showed clearly that philosophers themselves and their institutions had been completely deprived of their right to theorize. If any further movement within the framework of philosophy was possible, it could consist only in restoring philosophy's right to be philosophy. It could not be a continuation of what philosophy had become in those years, but a complete and decisive break with that. This is what actually happened. The fact that philosophy had reached rock bottom turned out to be a blessing, providing the conditions for its movement in the opposite direction.

The turning point came with two events at the Lomonosov Moscow State University (MSU) Faculty of Philosophy involving two of its graduates, Evald Vasil'evich Ilyenkov (1924–1979), who was at that time an assistant in the

Department of Foreign Philosophy, and Alexander Aleksandrovich Zinoviev (1922–2006), who was a postgraduate student in the Department of Logic. Both events occurred in 1954. When considering why these two young people became heroes of Russian philosophy, we should of course note their personal qualities: the vital force and gift of genius that each possessed. However, the fact that both of them served as combat officers (Ilyenkov as an artilleryman, Zinoviev as a pilot) and took part in a terrible war all the way to Berlin seems even more important. They knew the value of life, and they knew that life was at stake: both life itself and its human characteristics required a courageous struggle. As their behavior showed in these years and beyond, they had come to understand the extraordinary seriousness of their mission, which involved taking part in great affairs like philosophy. Their seriousness was the seriousness of Atlas supporting the heavens. They proceeded from the belief that a correct ordering of society depends on a correct understanding of philosophy. Their individual qualities and experiences at the front do not, of course, explain the later events that occurred in their historical significance (individual human deeds cannot, in principle, be explained as inevitabilities), but they do constitute important touches in the overall portrait.

In a theory seminar led by Professor Teodor I. Oizerman (1914–2017), Evald Ilyenkov, along with his colleague Valentin Korovikov (who retired from philosophy and became well-known in Russia as a journalist and international relations expert), delivered a paper, "The Interrelationship of Philosophy and Knowledge of Nature and Society in the Process of Their Historical Development" ("K voprosu o vzaimosviazi filosofii i znanii o prirode i obshchestve v protsesse ikh istoricheskogo razvitiia"). They defended the thesis that, according to the overall experience of history of philosophy, philosophy deals with thought, and its objective content and real subject matter are the study of logical categories that establish our scientifically theoretical knowledge of the world. The authors' main conclusion, for which they were subjected to scathing critique from the department's professors and branded as "gnoseologists," was as follows:

> Only philosophy can isolate and study in their purity and abstractness the laws of dialectics as logical categories, as a law of dialectical thinking. Only by making theoretical thought, the process of cognition, its subject matter can philosophy bring the most common features of life under its consideration, and not the reverse, as is often assumed. Philosophy is the science of scientific thought, of its laws and its forms. (Ilyenkov and Korovikov 2016, 146)

Debate over these conclusions lasted several weeks. It initially proceeded calmly, if not sluggishly. However, an unexpected and unofficial order came from the highest Party authority to halt the discussion. The head of the seminar prudently decided to do so. The young participants opposed this and firmly demanded further discussion. The lines of confrontation here were vivid. On one side was a department professoriate that did not accept their conclusions,

18 THE "MEN OF THE SIXTIES": PHILOSOPHY AS A SOCIAL PHENOMENON   389

denounced them, went far beyond the boundaries of academic decency, and did not shy away from ideological labels: it wanted to exclude the whole situation from discussion. On the other side was a group of young graduate students and researchers who fervently supported the ideas expressed and demanded open debate. The latter also included Alexander Zinoviev who, as Georgii Shchedrovitsky testified, uttered a phrase at the end of his own presentation that later became folkloric in philosophy circles in those years as a broadly popular aphorism: "If Marx were alive today, he would add a twelfth thesis to his earlier eleven: bourgeois philosophers used to interpret the world, while Soviet philosophers do not even do that" (Shchedrovitsky 2001, 28). The most immediate formal outcomes of this discussion were Ilyenkov's expulsion from the university and a decision by the faculty's Academic Council that included an obligation for the dean's office "to take decisive measures against further dissemination among the faculty of this paper's anti-Marxist ideas" (Ilyenkov and Korovikov 2016, 63). The longer-term and more substantial result was the beginning of a new era in Soviet philosophy.

The second event took place four months later, in September of that year. This was Alexander Zinoviev's defense of his candidate-level dissertation, *An Ascent from the Abstract to the Concrete (using K. Marx's Kapital as material)* (*Voskhozhdenie ot abstraktnomu k konkretnomu (na materiale "Kapitala" K. Marksa)*) (see Zinoviev 2002). The defense was repeatedly postponed and eventually took place over several days in front of a crowded auditorium packed with a large number of students. The dissertation was an extensive monograph, much lengthier than the usual works, and it devoted its main emphasis to the structure and specific mechanisms of the dialectical method. The author identified the logical structure of Marx's work and viewed ascension as a complex and differentiated research technique that was nothing at all like a great syllogism that could be extended to various individual fields of knowledge: on the contrary, it always assumes we account for the totality of development of the corresponding science. The defense turned into a sharp polemic (see *Tekst stenogrammy* 2014), repeating both in general tone and personal content the confrontation so evident in the discussion of Ilyenkov and Korovikov's arguments. Zinoviev received support from his young advocates, in particular the later well-known philosophers Merab Mamardashvili, Georgii Shchedrovitsky, and Boris Grushin, according to one testimony (Lektorsky 2016, 9), as well as from Evald Ilyenkov. Zinoviev's critics were the venerable proponents of dogmatic philosophy who understood it as a set of general provisions that were not only universally significant, but possessed explanatory potential in relation to specific areas of knowledge. The very style of Zinoviev's analytical thinking unsettled them. In his speech, the chair of the Department of Logic, V. Cherkesov, said outright, "The style of the dissertation is not good. This is not a 'Marxian' style but a 'Zinovievian' style." Zinoviev's thesis was eventually approved,[1] but he himself was forced to leave the university.

Thus, the philosophy of "men of the sixties," a kind of renaissance, a new beginning for Russian philosophy, originated even before the 1960s. To characterize its features, some of which were already observable at the source, we should take note of the following points.

Above all, the appeal to the issues of thought and of understanding philosophy as a doctrine of thought was essential. The testimonies of two famous philosophy professors whose student years coincided with the events described above speak to this. Vladislav Lektorsky writes that Ilyenkov and Zinoviev "opened up a field of philosophical research that was new for that time: the logic of the construction and development of scientific theory, the methods of this development, the interrelationship between theoretical and empirical knowledge, the logic of research and the logic of presentation, etc. In other words, theory of scientific knowledge" (Lektorsky 2017, 326). Vyacheslav Shestakov noted that Evald Ilyenkov and Alexander Zinoviev led a "revolution" against "dogmatic Marxism-Leninism," stressing, "they opened the path to a new range of philosophical questions related to the methodology of thought and of scientific knowledge" (Shestakov 2017, 206). The issue is not just that these young philosophers used this new range of questions and the nature of its production to dissociate themselves thematically from what came before them, although this was in itself significant. More importantly, they returned philosophy to its own origins, reopening issues that were thought to have been finally solved by Marxism: an understanding of philosophy's subject matter and methods. They demonstrated the kind of analytical technique and soundness of argument that reduced the citation-based method and the polemical method of incrimination to nothing, one that required a detailed knowledge of the history of philosophy and solid preparation in logic. This was a fundamentally different level of professional self-awareness and academic culture.

In terms of research priorities, the philosophy of the "men of the sixties" was liberated from direct ideological dictatorship and reinstated its own subject areas for philosophical argument and criteria for evaluating its quality. It also contained a highly charged social liberationism that dovetailed directly with the process of public de-Stalinization, which had flowed naturally into various areas of culture until it was adopted in its already defined state and consciously expressed at the 20th Party Congress. It also dovetailed with the anti-totalitarian social context not apart from its own philosophical research, but by virtue of the character of these studies themselves. Focusing primarily on issues of methodology and scientific thought, on issues of epistemology and philosophy of science, philosophers pursued a highly relevant task related to an individual's being in the world: they defended reason's sovereign right to truth, its possibilities, and its role as a universal (democratic) path to truth. A more detailed analysis would require addressing issues such as the extent to which researchers adapted the achievements of European philosophy to Russian reality, the extent to which they developed these issues independently, and what the merits of each of these were.[2] As I offer this general historical description, I would like to note that, on the whole, this was an Enlightenment-style philosophical movement. We might formulate its motto as follows: "Man can live according to his own mind, and must live by it." The task of philosophy is to defend this. We should emphasize in particular that the philosophy of the "men of the sixties" was simultaneously an intellectual movement and a social position that had to be fought for and paid for, as both thinkers who stood at its origins and at its very center did indeed pay: Zinoviev was expelled from the country, and Ilyenkov was driven to suicide.

After Stalin's death, a process eventually called the "Thaw" began in Soviet society. "Thaw" in the original and most direct sense of the word indicates a particular condition of the weather, a rise in temperature during winter or early spring that is accompanied by the melting of snow and ice. Describing these emerging changes in life, the writer and sensitive social commenter Ilya Ehrenburg had called his short 1954 novel *The Thaw* (*Ottepel*). The term appeared as naturally and, in fact, in the very same way as "men of the sixties" did. It became widespread in public consciousness and represented the "popular," so to speak, designation for the process of de-Stalinization. It is usually associated with the name of the then-head of both party and country, Nikita Khrushchev, and is thus often called the Khrushchev Thaw. This referred to a deliberate weakening of political, administrative, and, above all, repressive mechanisms in every sphere of life, a condemnation of mass repressions, including the discrediting of the cult of Stalin himself as the one responsible for them, a relative liberalization of public behavior, relative freedom of creative activity, and the transition to a foreign policy of peaceful coexistence. In short, these were changes that covered all aspects of life and concerned the very ideology of social order. Its essence consisted of the following. The Soviet model that ultimately took shape in the 1930s and 1940s was based on an ideology of unconditionally prioritizing public interests over personal or group interests. At the same time, the highest-ranking party and government officials were supposed to be the spokesmen for and bearers of the public interest. Individual people were viewed as elements (cogs) of a single state mechanism, and their place in it determined by those who controlled this mechanism. De-Stalinization (Thaw) meant the liberation of the individual, his private life, and his forms of social expression from total external control by repressive politics. This meant a situation not unlike the words of a certain popular song, that one could breathe freely in one's country.[3] The "men of the sixties" philosophers, who had laid the foundation for a new intellectual movement, responded to this challenge. They expanded their criticism of Stalin's cult of personality to include the necessity of restoring each individual's personal dignity and status, an assumption of his intellectual and moral maturity, of his independence in thought and action. By focusing on serious and thorough research into the problems of cognition, thought, and scientific methodology, these philosophical thinkers essentially began with a criticism of cults of any kind, the necessity of a resolute abandonment of paternalism in the intellectual sphere. They fought for freedom of thought, arguing that the criteria of reason, truth, scientificity, and evidence were more thorough, more elevated, and worthier than the ideological criteria of class struggle, partisanship, and political expediency.

They defended an individual's right to independent and responsible judgment, his right to live according to his own mind.

At first glance, issues of logic and epistemology and questions of philosophy of science seemed like a relatively safe area of philosophical research. They were, in part, as this field of topics and issues was far from the most immediate political-ideological concerns and party propaganda. What also protected this area of philosophy was the fact that it required specialized training and was therefore inaccessible to the ideologically motivated criticism of party demagogues, who were more often than not poorly educated. These considerations had, of course, some subjectively motivating significance. In fact, it was this area of logical methodology that contained philosophy's colossally charged social critique, one more powerful than direct polemical attacks, which were, of course, also important in themselves. This pertains to defending the autonomy of the human mind, the authority and power of reason to oppose the authority and power of rulers. The "men of the sixties" philosophers did understand the social significance of what they were doing. In that sense, they recreated in their own country the path and logic of modern European philosophy's development, which began its struggle for the emancipation of reason and the individually responsible existence of man with a foundation for the scientific method of thought—with Bacon's *Novum Organum*, with Descartes' *Discourse on Method*, and with Kant's *Critique of Pure Reason*.

The "Hamburg Score" of Philosophy

The "men of the sixties" philosophy did not represent the entirety of Russian philosophy in the second half of the twentieth century. It was only a part of it; the most productive and worthy part, but a part. In terms of volume, it was even an insignificant part, something like the warm Gulf Stream in the cold ocean. However, because I do not limit the notion of "men of the sixties" philosophy to a single generation or specific time period but tie it to Russian philosophy's anti-dogmatic, humanistic shift and the new research prospects this shift produced, all corresponding philosophical achievements essentially fall under this label. This meant a new vector and level of philosophical research, but not an overall change in philosophical life and environment. The mechanisms for managing the mind that had been developed in the previous generation were weakened, but they persisted. As academician Vyacheslav Stepin, himself a prominent representative of the "men of the sixties," once testified, "ideological control over philosophy was preserved, but it was associated with a much-reduced level of repressiveness and often limited to requiring only an external ideological formulation of philosophical affairs" (2011, 288). Philosophy continued to be taught according to uniform, centrally approved programs and textbooks, to be under a party control that continued over that time and even strengthened (e.g., a rule was even introduced during the Brezhnev era to admit students to philosophy faculties only on recommendations from party organs). The heads of philosophy institutes and even of

18 THE "MEN OF THE SIXTIES": PHILOSOPHY AS A SOCIAL PHENOMENON 393

science departments were either appointed by party organs or directly under their control. Party institutions also intervened in the subject areas of research. Philosophical life on the whole remained within the boundaries of party ideology and party control, and the "men of the sixties" philosophers and their idea of sovereign reason and developed sense of professional dignity represented only a small fraction of the overall mass of philosophy. As Nelly Motroshilova, herself an active participant of the "men of the sixties" philosophical movement, once wrote, "a bizarre and unhealthy coexistence, a confrontation between the official, ideologically orthodox and the unofficial, unorthodox communities that had been in place since the 1950s, stretched across entire decades" within Soviet philosophy (Motroshilova 2017, 311).

This duality is of great significance if we wish to understand the topic of this chapter and to read the texts of the "men of the sixties" adequately, texts written in the framework of the Marxist tradition or, at the very least, under that label. This means a coexistence of two levels (registers) of appreciation: the official and the unofficial. The unofficial level was not illegal, but it existed within the framework of state-sanctioned philosophical activity as a kind of internal dimension, a sort of "Hamburg score,"[4] that is, a real body of knowledge, not a sham, not a façade, but actual achievements by philosophers that the professional community itself possessed and in many cases really used. As a rule, this was also expressed in the discrepancy between the official hierarchy of philosophical authorities established as such by various social privileges and the actual authorities in the world of philosophy itself. We should particularly emphasize that this kind of duality is not identical to the difference between esoteric and exoteric philosophy. The latter derives from philosophy's unique place in culture and is determined by whether the philosopher writes (speaks) in his own conceptually and terminologically fine-tuned language or in the generally available natural language, whether he remains within the framework of his school and narrowly professional environment or appeals to the broader public. As for that duality within the framework of Soviet philosophy, it was conditioned not by the features of philosophy, but by the features of the social conditions in which it existed. We could assume that this is inevitable for any ideologically controlled philosophy. This duality existed in a very weak form within the Soviet philosophy of the 1930s and 1940s when it fell not only under the ideological press, but also under fear of physical repressions, yet certain philosophers managed to conduct their professional activities in the same way that certain plants manage to break through asphalt. There were certain experts in those years, such as Valentin F. Asmus, who stood out from the other philosophers because of the general quality of their work and the level they set, and their real authority within the professional sphere was incomparably higher than their public status. However, this philosophical Hamburg score existed only in a very weak form in the 1930s and 1940s.

The situation changed significantly in the next period, when the alternative philosophy of the "men of the sixties," a philosophy constructed in the style of the Hamburg score, became a relatively broad and conspicuous trend in the philosophical community; it was in fact legalized and acquired a semi-official status. The philosophy of the "men of the sixties" was not represented by specific individuals, but by a large group of authors (primarily scholars) scattered throughout the country and in either open or covert opposition to the official party philosophy. The lines dividing these two levels (divisions) of philosophical life were evident enough. They represented different generations: the older generation that personified official philosophy opposed the philosophical youth who graduated from universities in the early 1950s, though there were, of course, representatives of the older generation who were actively involved in the new movement, not to mention young philosophers who adhered to the officially prescribed positions. They were also somewhat institutionally divided: official, ideologically oriented philosophy was centered at party institutions for science and education, and to a great extent at those university departments subject to a rigid party press.[5] The alternative philosophy was predominantly concentrated at academic institutions, primarily the Institute of Philosophy at the Academy of Sciences of the USSR, where Ilyenkov and Zinoviev were taken on as rank-and-file researchers after their expulsion from the university. The creative potential and professional horizons also differed between those belonging to "official" philosophy and those advocating its renewal: official philosophy did not extend far beyond the kinds of philosophical generalizations found in the works of Friedrich Engels and Vladimir Lenin, while the "men of the sixties" philosophers began with a new reading of Karl Marx, including his early works, climbing from there to Hegel, Kant, Spinoza, and other classics of philosophy, and relying broadly on twentieth-century achievements in science and Western philosophy. The "men of the sixties" philosophers were distinguished from the general population of fellow instructors and researchers by their level of research culture and professionalism. They brought with them not only a new range of topics, but also a new, higher level of academic work. They undoubtedly stood out from their colleagues by virtue of their very attitude toward philosophy as an exceptionally serious and responsible affair. They were conscious of, and in a certain sense even cultivated, their intellectual elitism. Official party philosophy and the semi-official "men of the sixties" philosophy represented two different circles of communication, parallel worlds in fact, whose intersections often resulted in social conflict and human destruction.

The ideological constraints on philosophical life that inevitably led to its bifurcation meant that honest professional work in the field of philosophy demanded certain additional qualities of its workers: an accentuated human decency forbidding the use of arguments fraught with bureaucratic reprisals, not to mention more severe ones; a developed sense of professional dignity; an absence of excessive career ambitions that exceeded their actual opportunity to engage in philosophical work; and a supportive and reliable camaraderie that extended directly from professional solidarity and collaboration. The "men of the sixties" philosophers created a special environment, an unspoken community, a kind of "parallel polis," to use Václav Havel's term. Their professional ties were supplemented by and interwoven with friendly personal relationships, and they perceived the occupation of philosophy itself as a mission, a viewpoint on life. In addition to purely professional goals, they were united by their desire to support and defend one another.

Like all creative people, they were of course professionally jealous of one another; like all normal people, they had complex relationships at the personal level. The force unifying them was not some constructive mutual understanding and cooperation (in that respect they remained individualists and in many cases competitive with one another), but their overall critical attitude toward the social order, an attitude centered in opposition to official, dogmatized philosophy, a struggle against it, and, in particular, against the administrative conditions through which this world of philosophy flowed. In order to persevere, to defend their right to free intellectual activity, to engage in philosophy according to the criteria of philosophy itself, to wrest philosophy from the grasp of the administrative system of ideology, these "men of the sixties" philosophers had to support one another, to create a new environment that could serve as the center of gravity for all those who wished to engage honestly in philosophy. The life of philosophy from the 1950s to the 1980s was full of episodes in which these people united in solidarity to oppose administrative party-related infighting and to support one another, finding creativity not only in their academic pursuits, but also in their life struggles. A great deal has already been said about this (see Mamchur et al. 1997; Mitrokhin 1997; Gulyga 2000; Lektorsky 1998). This style was originally established by those first "men of the sixties" Ilyenkov and Zinoviev. Shchedrovitsky, himself an active participant in these events, tells us that in the Faculty of Philosophy in the early 1950s,

> two groups clearly conscious of themselves as such had already formed and were present there. These were the group around Evald Ilyenkov, a generally neo-Hegelian type of group whose work was based on the principle of identifying being with thought and the idea that everything was defined through this, and the group around Alexander Zinoviev, which rejected the principle of identifying being with thought and proceeded from a rather rigid and clear opposition between the world of being on the one hand, and the world of thought on the other. [...] At the same time, however, both groups lived a single, very tight-knit life, that is, entirely unlike two collectives that took shape in opposition to each other. (Shchedrovitsky 2001, 18)

THE PROMINENT "MEN OF THE SIXTIES" PHILOSOPHERS

The two initiators of this philosophical movement, Evald Ilyenkov and Alexander Zinoviev, also became its central figures. They identified and used their work to advance two mutually contrary vectors of philosophical research that could generally and overall be correlated with what twentieth-century Western philosophy calls the difference between continental and analytic philosophy (West 2015). If we allow that continental philosophy can be defined more by the set of names associated with it than by its collection of ideas, and that neo-Marxists are included among them, that it is distinguished by methods that are not in the analytic tradition and (more or less pointedly) oppose it, and that its sources go back to Hegel's speculative philosophy, then Ilyenkov can undoubtedly be classified under this style of philosophizing. Zinoviev, on the other hand, represented a different style, one oriented toward verifiably precise and unambiguous philosophical statements; he considered methodology and logic not simply a form of occupation, but as near synonyms for philosophy itself. Among modern Western philosophers, his sympathies were on the side of those representing the analytic tradition. Ilyenkov was a Marxist philosopher, and it was in that capacity that he subjected the various kinds of limitations set by officialdom to criticism (Tolstykh 2009). His "crime" was not only the fact that he projected his own understanding of Marxism, but also the fact that he therefore challenged existing practices in the communist movement, practices in which party leaders alone held the monopoly on interpretations of Marxism. "He basically declared war on their own territory and challenged their right to his territory, which was more dangerous at that time than any non-Marxist sedition" (Mezhuev 2017, 270). He developed philosophy as a theory of dialectics, and he considered its basis to be an ascent to the concrete, which he understood as the world of culture. The idea, derived from Spinoza and Hegel, of identifying being with thought played an important role in his doctrine, along with a materialist interpretation of the ideal, which is objectified in social forms of human existence and cannot be explained on the basis of an individual's psychophysiological nature. He was a pointed and scathing critic of positivism. Given the sources, ideas, and titles of his main works— *Dialectics of the Abstract and the Concrete in Scientific-Theoretical Thought* (*Dialektika abstraknotogo i konkretnogo v nauchno-teoreticheskom myshlenii*), *Dialectical Logic: Essays on History and Theory* (*Dialekticheskaya logika. Ocherki istorii i teorii*), "Dialectics of the Ideal (Dialektika ideal'nogo)"—it may seem that Ilyenkov was a traditional academic philosopher, that there is nothing Marxist or Soviet in him, and that he could even, for example, be called a Hegelian, as we sometimes see argued in the literature. Of course, this was not the case in reality. He directly linked dialectics with the doctrine of communism, with man's overcoming of his alienation from the results of his activity. He saw in positivism the theoretical expression of bourgeois narrow-mindedness. Ilyenkov was a Marxist, and as a thinker he could appear exactly in this Soviet society. His entire philosophy is essentially a theory-based criticism of Soviet society from the perspective of the communist ideal, and it is no accident that he paid so much attention to the issues of pedagogy, ethics, and aesthetics.

Ilyenkov had his own students, but his role and significance in modern Russian philosophy was much broader. He influenced the entire philosophical atmosphere in the country, becoming a kind of cult figure. He laid out a tradition of dialectical philosophy in whose framework such original thinkers as Genrikh Batishchev, Vladislav Lektorsky, and Zhabaikhan Abdil'din would appear. Russian interest in him has not faded with time, and has even increased in recent years. His work has even achieved fame abroad. However, the more time has passed, the more he has been perceived both domestically and abroad as a philosopher in the classical sense, isolated from the communist pathos that inspired him.

The other pole of research activity was represented by Ilyenkov's friend and opponent, Alexander Zinoviev, whose banner was the scientificity of philosophy. Zinoviev focused on issues related to modern logic and scientific methodologies (Guseynov 2009; Guseynov et al. 2002). The first of his six monographs on this subject, *The Philosophical Foundations of Many-Valued Logic* (*Filosofskie osnovy mnogoznachnoi logiki*) from 1960, was published in many countries, including the United States, making him an internationally significant expert. He created his own concept of logic that he called "complex logic." Given an understanding of logic whose laws are universal in nature, he showed that there should be no problems in science that are unsolvable due to shortcomings in logic itself. He rejected speculative philosophy that allowed for many-valued interpretations of concepts and arguments, and he even stated that he was not a philosopher, identifying instead as a logician. One important feature of his complex logic is its expansion of the field of logic by including the development of the conceptual apparatus of the empirical sciences. In particular, this includes logical geometry, logical physics, and, as he would later argue, logical sociology.

Zinoviev had his own school of logic with his own students. More importantly, he demonstrated in a highly productive and successful way a different model for understanding philosophy than that of Ilyenkov and his school, narrowing it to logic as the science of language rules.

Within the framework of "men of the sixties" philosophy, these tendencies were in no way, not even informally, divided by academic schools or communities; furthermore, even their circles of personal relationships did not coincide with these theoretical priorities. The "men of the sixties" philosophers really did function as respectful thinkers, professionally recognizing one another, even objectively influencing one another given the internal polemics among them, but nevertheless remaining independent in their own work. Each of them deserves his own separate and particular discussion. In this chapter, which treats the "men of the sixties" philosophy as a social phenomenon, we will briefly mention three more names: Georgii Shchedrovitsky, Merab Mamardashvili, and Ivan Frolov. All three were bright "men of the sixties" philosophers, well-known throughout the country, and their influence on the public has continued to the present day.

Georgii Petrovich Shchedrovitsky (1929–1994) left his mark on a number of the human sciences (psychology, pedagogy, philosophy of science and technology, and linguistics), but above all on the one he himself created, which might be called a universal methodology of thought and action (Shchedrovitsky 2010). In his understanding of being and consciousness, he began by prioritizing the activity-focused approach over the naturalistic, and to some extent even over the epistemological. For him, the world of thought and action represents the primary world. He believed that people's thoughts and actions in all their variations are based on a single methodology, a common and unified theory, which he, too, was attempting to create. He considered methodology to be the highest form of so organizing the world of thought and action, a form that creates one's holistic image in a way that, in his opinion, neither science nor any traditional philosophy associated with it is capable of doing. He introduced the notion of a systemic "thought-activity" and studied a special form of its collective organization, organizational-activity games, which became his own research laboratory and at the same time a way of optimizing management practice in those areas of activity to which it was devoted. Shchedrovitsky himself conducted more than ninety such games. He was creator and director of the Moscow Methodological Circle, through which thousands of people passed over the years and whose work continues through the efforts of his students; it became the basis for Russia's methodological movement, which clearly resonated with the public. Shchedrovitsky was inspired by the idea of creating an intellectual elite and tried to create one himself, first by considering himself one of that elite (the only such figure in the world) and then by developing a theory for a kind of mental engineering and management of the process of creating a class of similar such experts, called methodologists. We could consider his experiment successful, given that many of those who were forged in the fire of his seminars and games became influential managers in contemporary Russia.

Merab Konstantinovich Mamardashvili (1930–1990) was, we might say, a pure philosopher (Motroshilova 2009). What he studied, and how he studied, was the exclusive matter of philosophy, of philosophy alone, such that, even though it is connected to the whole expanse of culture, it nevertheless stands alone. He understood philosophy as an individually formative issue, as thinking aloud, and he gathered large audiences of listeners at his lectures (whose posthumous records constitute the greater part of his heritage). He is sometimes referred to as a Socratic-style philosopher.

Mamardashvili shared both the fate and the privilege of great philosophers to remain only partly understood, the subject of the widest variety of interpretations and even evaluations. As a philosopher, he used natural, generally understandable Russian language, at least in the sense that he avoided resorting to any kind of specialized formal apparatus. At the same time, however, he discussed issues that were completely unobvious, and in order to convey just how unobvious they were, he used words in their less typical meanings and resorted to completely unexpected word combinations and sentence constructions. As a result, his speech was fundamentally polysemic—so polysemic, in fact, that he could say of any interpretation that he was not arguing that at all.

Thinking was also his special topic of interest. He understood that thinking can only be grasped by thought, so his philosophical pathos was to reach the very source of thinking, how thought is generated, to understand thought as an event. Mamardashvili tried to interpret the very generation of thought as an act of freedom. The idea of connecting freedom with man's rational essence, with his thought, was not, of course, a new one; it could be considered the mainstream of European philosophy. Researching thinking and justifying its sovereignty was also, as I have tried to show, at the center of the "men of the sixties" philosophy. What was new for Russian philosophy connected with Mamardarshvili's name was the interpretation of the act of thought as an act of freedom. His development of this thesis also philosophically sanctions the individual's complete spiritual and intellectual emancipation, with this individual as the basic foundation of society. The idea of an individual freedom found in the event of thought, the pathos of autonomy of thought and of intellectual self-legislation, remains valuable to this day and explains the public relevance of Mamardashvili as a philosopher.

Ivan Timofeevich Frolov (1929–1999) was one of the central figures of "men of the sixties" philosophy not just in terms of the scale of his achievements, but also from the point of view of his place relative to the extremes represented by Zinoviev and Ilyenkov. This also applies to his theoretical priorities and socialist convictions. Frolov's reflections began with the Marxist idea of culture as the inorganic body of man, his second nature. Studying the methodological issues of biological research, he arrived at the conclusion that human biology itself has largely become his second nature due to the rapid progress of scientific research and technology. From this he concludes that anthropo-sociogenesis is incomplete and requires an "ethical-epistemological synthesis" (Korsakov 2014, 5), a kind of union of humanism and science, whenever it becomes an internal requirement (and limitation) of knowledge itself. Analyzing the scientific-technological prospects for human improvement, he formulated the paradox that we who undertake those improvements must be better today than the future we want to create (Frolov 1987, 21). That said, he saw a future for humanity in which man remains rational but also becomes a humane being. This changing mode of cognition and action is related to a change in the object, which acts as a complex and multifaceted network of interactions between nature and man that takes the form of global issues. As a pioneer in research on these issues in Russia, Frolov introduced the concept of globalization to argue that all global issues center around man and could be grouped around the main vectors of his relationships: man—nature, man—society, and man—man. Global issues require an appropriate methodology, one which he defined as the complex study of man. They require a global approach to mankind's future, the essence of which consists of establishing humanity itself as an integrated social community. He saw democratic socialism based on prioritizing universal values as the path to this.

Frolov occupied a unique position among the "men of the sixties" in that he combined his academic work with active and, just as important, highly successful scientific organizational and sociopolitical activities. As he was already engaged in the problems of biology, he actively joined the struggle against belligerent retrogrades in science. He was later made editor-in-chief of the pivotal philosophy journal *Voprosy filosofii* and the theoretical journal of the Communist Party *Kommunist*, assistant to the General Secretary of the Communist Party Central Committee, Mikhail Gorbachev, and a member of the Communist Party Politburo. He made major contributions to collaborative work between philosophers and naturalists, initiated and served as first director of the scientific research center The Institute of Man, increased the level of international cooperation among Russian philosophers, and successfully launched and managed the organization of the 1993 World Congress of Philosophy in Russia. We should note in particular his project bringing together the "men of the sixties" philosophers to create the collective textbook *Introduction to Philosophy* (*Vvedenie v filosofiiu*), a project he himself was able to conceive and bring about by virtue of his position. Frolov's public activities were defined by his convictions, convictions based on the idea that socialism was capable of becoming humane and democratic. We must not, therefore, passively hope for the future or stay mired in an unacceptably difficult past: we must improve real society, the basically healthy and viable socialist society in which we live. He worked consistently with this in mind. As Sergei N. Korsakov, who studies Frolov's legacy, says,

> having entered the field of philosophical activity alongside the 'men of the sixties' generation of philosophers, and among that generation's most advanced cohort at that, Ivan T. Frolov remained the sole philosopher in Russia who retained the 'men of the sixties' ideals in their primeval sense. (Korsakov 2014, 9)

Let us return to the works and fate of Zinoviev, which are important for understanding the societal context of the "men of the sixties" philosophy and its conclusion. First, however, we must insert a quick note. Ilyenkov and Zinoviev indicated two vectors not only for understanding philosophy, but also its ability to be a force for transforming the world. In other words, their attitude toward Marxism and toward socialist society as its practical continuation also differed. We have already emphasized that loyalty to Marxism and socialism was an important feature of philosophy's "men of the sixties" sensibility as a social phenomenon, but there was a wide degree of amplitude to this loyalty, with its extreme points at the positions of Ilyenkov and Zinoviev. Ilyenkov was a staunch Marxist, and he lived by that conviction. He considered the socialist society as it really existed in the Soviet Union as a first step: an imperfect one, but a necessary stop on the road to communism as a collectivized humanity. From his perspective, Soviet society, whatever it limitations historically, was fundamentally superior to the capitalist West. His critique of socialism as it existed was a critique from socialism's own future, that is, from the perspective of the communist ideal. One of Ilyenkov's closest students and friends, Sergei N. Mareev, says that he once found him at home weeping (Mareev 2015, 14). The apparent reason for this was a report on the military conflict between China and Vietnam. At the time, the prevailing belief was that socialism was essentially peace-loving, and war between socialist countries was therefore impossible. Zinoviev's attitude to Marxism and socialism was different. He considered Marxism a secular ideology, albeit a high-quality one, if perhaps too complex for an ideology, while the socialist society whose nature he analyzed and maliciously ridiculed could not have been more different. Of course, this does not mean that he considered capitalist society better: it was also

18 THE "MEN OF THE SIXTIES": PHILOSOPHY AS A SOCIAL PHENOMENON 401

monstrous in its own way. He believed that ideal social structures, whether in Marxism or in any other similar version of social equality, could not exist in principle. Zinoviev made no effort to conceal these views among friends, but in his work and for the time being, he limited himself to not identifying as a Marxist, and he limited his own research to formal logic.

Zinoviev emphasizes that he does not consider logic an end in itself, just as it was not simply a quiet academic harbor where one could maintain professional dignity without risk to one's life under conditions of Soviet ideology (we should note, by the way, that he later described this brilliantly and in detail in the novel *The Yellow House* [*Zheltyi dom*]). This was a necessary stage for developing his methodological toolkit for studying the society in which he happened to be born and to live. He had no doubt about what he needed to research, since it was fairly evident to him: how Soviet society understood itself, the official explanation of its nature, was far from what it actually was. The glaring discrepancy with the communist ideal that announced itself as a vital goal, was taught in schools, was proclaimed from every podium, and served as the everyday reality of Soviet society became, by Zinoviev's own admission, his main experience and impetus for research. This contradiction between the ideal and the real was the main, to a great extent conscious, and to the extent possible pronounced social motif of the intellectual preoccupations and scientific inquiries of all the "men of the sixties." Zinoviev made this phenomenon the focus of his scientific analysis: he dedicated himself to the study of Soviet society as a unique empirical object, which not only shifted the focus of his academic work (he transitioned from logic to sociology), but also changed his life's trajectory.

His study of Soviet society inevitably turned into criticism. It could not have been otherwise: even though he began his experiments in logic with an analysis of Marx's *Kapital*, highly valued it as a scientific work, and used it as a text for reconstructing the logic of scientific theory, Zinoviev was never a Marxist in terms of his own personal convictions. His need for a scientific analysis of Soviet society necessitated that Marxist theory, which was in fact the basis for official Soviet ideology, be ill-suited for that role. From the very beginning, Zinoviev rejected the favorite bit of sophistry from critically inclined Marxists that Soviet socialism as it existed was not really socialism and did not correspond to the Marxist plan, that if it had not diverged from theory, it would be a completely different, almost ideal society. He decisively rejected this kind of purely ideological line of thought and approached the issue as a scientist, proceeding from what the object of our research really is, not from what we think about it. He concluded that Soviet society in the actual form in which it was established in Russia, as it was and not as some intention or philosophical plan in the minds of thinkers, regardless of their brilliance, was the real communism, and there was no other communism. Furthermore, any other communism is impossible in principle. He first expressed this understanding, his expanded theory of Soviet communism, in artistic form, creating a new literary genre of "sociological novel" in his book *The Yawning Heights* (*Ziiaiushchie vysoty*) (Zinoviev 1979), and then later in his systemic study *The Reality of Communism*

(*Kommunizm kak realnost'*) (Zinoviev 1984). The novel was published in 1976 by a Western (Swiss) publisher, which, in itself and regardless of the book's content, was considered a completely unacceptable act, virtually equal to treason against the homeland.

He was then expelled from the party, ousted from his job, stripped of all ranks and awards, including those earned in combat, and deported along with his family in 1978, spending twenty-one years of forced emigration in Germany. His expulsion from the party and ouster from his job were carried out with the personalized support (i.e., by votes at both a party meeting and on the academic council) of his "men of the sixties" colleagues at the Institute of Philosophy where he worked. The sincerity of their support was relative at best. They understood that Zinoviev had, by his own deeds, crossed the boundary separating the "men of the sixties" from the dissidents and violated the unspoken rules by which the former played: they were allowed their freedom of argument and action, except for those obviously hostile or disloyal to the Soviet system and to the higher party leadership. Zinoviev did not consider himself a dissident, nor was he one, although that was of no interest to anyone. Zinoviev dissociated himself from the dissidents, although in many respects he was a deeper and more pointed critic of the Soviet regime than they. Afterwards, he rejected Gorbachev's Perestroika, calling it "Catastroika," predicting its collapse and its likely disastrous consequences even when all the other "men of the sixties" were completely ecstatic about it. He later rebelled against the destruction of the Soviet state and became an implacable critic of Russia's post-Soviet system. He subjected the new social system, which had been established in the West, to incriminating sociological analysis, calling it "Westernism." All this put Zinoviev as a thinker and citizen into a special position all his own. This, however, is another story, one beyond the boundaries of our topic, but it explains, among other things, why the late Zinoviev, a rebel, found himself outside the "men of the sixties" circles.

Conclusion

We can establish the beginning of the "men of the sixties" philosophy by time and location accurately enough. The end is harder to establish for two reasons. First, it is blurred by time and events, though it ultimately occurred in the second half of the 1980s during Gorbachev's Perestroika and Glasnost, when the "men of the sixties" to a great extent openly expressed solidarity with the dissidents. Second, the end of the "men of the sixties" philosophy as a social phenomenon did not mean the end of the individual men of the sixties, many of whom still continue their work actively and even more successfully than before. Be that as it may, the "men of the sixties" philosophy ended with the collapse of the Soviet system, which naturally raises the question of its role in that collapse. Leaving this question open, I would simply note that a tree falls not only when it is cut down from the outside, but also when it is weakened from within.

Translated by Brad Damaré

NOTES

1. It was published only in 2002 as an eightieth birthday gift from the Institute of Philosophy at the Russian Academy of Sciences to its already internationally famous researcher (see Zinoviev 2002).

2. This kind of analysis, as applied to the most prominent examples of this particular stage, was conducted in a collaborative, multivolume academic publishing project by the Russian Academy of Sciences Institute of Philosophy and the nonprofit Georgii P. Shchedrovitsky Institute for Development: *Russian Philosophy of the Second Half of the Twentieth Century* (*Filosofiia Rossii vtoroi poloviny 20-go veka*) (Lektorsky 2009–2010). The volumes in this series have their own editors, and are devoted to considering the ideas expressed by Alexei F. Losev, Mikhail M. Bakhtin, Valentin F. Asmus, Sergei L. Rubinstein, Bonifatii M. Kedrov, Evald V. Ilyenkov, Alexander A. Zinoviev, Merab K. Mamardashvili, Ivan T. Frolov, Pavel V. Kopnin, Vladimir S. Bibler, Georgii P. Shchedrovitsky, Mikhail A. Lifshits, Genrikh S. Batishchev, Mikhail K. Petrov, Vladimir A. Smirnov, Erik G. Yudin, Yuri M. Lotman, and Lev N. Mitrokhin.

3. This refers to a popular Soviet song, "Song of the Motherland" ("Pesnia o Rodine") by the composer Isaak Dunaevsky and poet Vasilii Lebedev-Kumach, whose first words ("Vast is my motherland") became an unofficial second title. The song includes the lyrics, "I know of no other country where a man breathes so freely."

4. A term popularized by Viktor Shklovsky for a closed-door wrestling match in which athletes tested their "real" worth, which was not always reflected in rigged public matches. —Ed.

5. Erikh Yu. Soloviev, a lively and active member of this moment, accurately pinpointed the location of "men of the sixties" philosophy: "The project to renew philosophy was miraculously birthed at 11 Mokhovaia (the street address of the Moscow State University Faculty of Philosophy). It was like an island of healthy greens had suddenly taken shape in a damp cellar, surrounded by mold; it had taken shape, but could only die in such a hopeless place. The greenhouses where this project survived and began to be realized included, for example, the Ministry of Education's Institute of Psychology, the newest edition of *The Philosophical Encyclopedia* [*Filosofskaia entsiklopediia*], the Rostov University Faculty of Philosophy, and beginning in the early 1960s, the editorial staff of the Prague-based international journal *Problems of Peace and Socialism*. But the main patch of green, protected from spring frosts, was of course at 14 Volkhonka, in the building where the Soviet Academy of Sciences Institute of Philosophy was located, along with the editorial office of its publishing organ, the journal *Voprosy filosofii*" (Soloviev 2017, 92–93).

BIBLIOGRAPHY

Aleksandrov, Georgii F., Bernard E. Bykhovskii, Mark B. Mitin, and Pavel F. Yudin. 1941–1943. *Istoriia filosofii*. Vol. 1: *Filosofiia antichnogo i feodal'nogo obshchestva*. Vol. 2: *Filosofiia XV–XVIII vekov*. Vol. 3: *Filosofiia pervoi poloviny XIX veka*. Moscow: Politizdat.

404 A. A. GUSEYNOV

Frolov, Ivan T. 1987. Chelovek budushchego: ideal i real'nost'. In *Razdum'ia o budushchem. Dialogi v preddverii tret'ego tysiacheletiia*, 21–26. Moscow: Politisdat.

Gulyga, Arsenii V. 2000. Polveka na Volkhonke. In *Estetika v svete aksiologii. Piat'desiat let na Volkhonke*. St. Petersburg: Aleteiia.

Guseynov, Abdusalam A., ed. 2009. *Aleksandr Aleksandrovich Zinoviev*. Moscow: ROSSPEN.

Guseynov, Abdusalam A., Ol'ga M. Zinovieva, and Karl M. Kantor. 2002. *Fenomen Zinovieva*. Moscow: Sovremennye tetradi.

Ilyenkov, Evald, and Valentin Korovikov. 2016. *Strasti po tezisam o predmete filosofii (1954–1955)*. Compiled by Elena Illesh. Moscow: "Kanon+" ROON "Reabilitatsiia".

Korsakov, Sergei N. 2014. Filosof gumanizma. *Filosofskie nauki* 8: 7–19.

KPSS v resoliutsiiakh…. 1954. 7th ed., part 3. Moscow.

Lektorsky, Vladislav A., ed. 1998. *Filosofiia ne konchaetsia… Iz istorii otechestvennoi filosifii. XX veka: v 2-kh kn*. Moscow: ROSSPEN.

———., ed. 2009–2010. *Filosofiia Rossii vtoroi poloviny XX veka*. Moscow: ROSSPEN.

———. 2016. Glazami ochevidtsa. In *Strasti po tezisam o predmete filosofii (1954–1955)*, ed. Evald Ilyenkov and Vladimir Korovikov, compiled by Elena E. Ilesh, 6–13. Moscow: "Kanon+" ROON "Reabilitatsiia".

———. 2017. Kak ia byl gnoseologom? In *Filosofskaia ottepel' i padenie dogmaticheskogo marksizma v Rossii*, 322–336. Moscow: Nestor-Istoriia.

Lektorsky, Vladislav A., and Marina F. Bykova, eds. 2019. *Philosophical Thought in Russia in the Second Half of the Twentieth Century. A Contemporary View from Russia and Abroad*. London: Bloomsbury Academics.

Mamchur, Elena A., Nikolai F. Ovchinnikov, and Aleksandr P. Ogurtsov. 1997. *Otechestvennaia filosofiia nauki: predvaritel'nye itogi*. Moscow: ROSSPEN.

Mareev, Sergei N. 2015. *E.V. Ilyenkov: zhit' filosofiei*. Akademicheskii proekt; Triksta: Moscow.

Mezhuev, Vadim M. 2017. Evald Ilyenkov i konets v Rossii klassicheskoi marksistskoi filosofii. In *Filosofskaia ottepel' i padenie dogmaticheskogo marksizma v Rossii*, 269–278. Moscow: Nestor-Istoriia.

Mitrokhin, Lev N. 1997. *Moi filosofskie sobesedniki*. Moscow: ROSSPEN.

Motroshilova, Nelly V., ed. 2009. *Merab Konstantinovich Mamardashvili*. Moscow: ROSSPEN.

———. 2017. Sotsiokul'turnyi kontekst 50-80-kh gg. XX v. i fenomen M. Mamardashvili. In *Filosofskaia ottepel' i padenie dogmaticheskogo marksizma v Rossii*, 298–321. Nestor-Istoriia: Moscow; St. Petersburg.

Rassadin, Stanislav B. 1960. Shestidesiatniki. Knigi o molodom sovremennike. *Iunost'* 12: 58–62.

Shchedrovitsky, Georgii P. 2001. *Ia vsegda byl idealistom…*. Moscow: Put'.

Shchedrovitsky, Petr G., ed. 2010. *Georgii Petrovich Shchedrovitsky*. Moscow: ROSSPEN.

Shestakov, Viacheslav P. 2017. Filosofiia, estetika i iskusstvoznanie v MGU: 60-ie gody. In *Filosofskaia ottepel' i padenie dogmaticheskogo marksizma v Rossii*, 197–218. Moscow: Nestor-Istoriia.

Soloviev, Erikh Yu. 2017. Mokhovaia, 11—Volkhonka, 14 (iz istorii moskovskoi filosofskoi ottepeli). In *Filosofskaia ottepel' i padenie dogmaticheskogo marksizma v Rossii*, 84–109. Moscow: Nestor-Istoriia.

Stepin, Vyacheslav S. 2011. *Tsivilizatsiia i kul'tura*. St. Petersburg: SPbGUP.

Tekst stenogrammy zashchity kandidatskoi dissertatsii A.A. Zinoi'eva. 2014. www.ergojournal.ru/?p=2613.

Tolstykh, Valentin I., ed. 2009. *Evald Vasil'evich Ilyenkov*. Moscow: ROSSPEN.

West, David. 2015. *Kontinental'naia filosofiia. Vvedenie*. Delo: Moscow.

Zinoviev, Alexander A. 1979. *The Yawning Heights*. Translated by Gordon Clough. London: Bodley Head.

———. 1984. *The Reality of Communism*. Translated by Charles Janson. London: V. Gollancz.

———. 2002. *Voskhozhdenie ot abstraktnogo k konkretnomu (na materiale "Kapitala" Karla Marksa)*. Moscow: IF RAN.

CHAPTER 19

The Activity Approach in Late Soviet Philosophy

Vladislav A. Lektorsky

The activity approach was popular in Soviet philosophy of the second half of the twentieth century, as well as in some human sciences, especially psychology. In this context, Russian philosophers contributed a series of interesting ideas. Since activity theory is again gaining popularity in the understanding of cognition and consciousness in cognitive science (Varela et al. 1992; Clark 1997; Engeström 2005) and in constructivist theories (Gergen 1994), it makes sense to consider what achievements in this area were accomplished in Russian philosophy of the Soviet era and how relevant these ideas are in the present day. The productivity of several activity theory ideas and concepts expressed in Soviet philosophy becomes evident in light of ongoing discussions in philosophy, cognitive science, and the human sciences.

S.L. Rubinstein: An Early Version of Activity Theory in Soviet Philosophy and Psychology

The Soviet philosopher and psychologist Sergei L. Rubinstein (1889–1960) formulated the principle of the unity of consciousness and activity in his seminal article, "Problems of Psychology in the Works of Karl Marx"(1934). In this text, Rubinstein references the early works of Karl Marx and argues against the idea of an introspective psychology of immediate consciousness (immediate experience as an object of psychology) and in favor of the objective mediation of consciousness. The point here is that activity mediates consciousness: "there is a genuine possibility of illuminating the consciousness of

V. A. Lektorsky (✉)
Institute of Philosophy, Russian Academy of Sciences, Moscow, Russia

© The Author(s), under exclusive license to Springer Nature Switzerland AG 2021
M. F. Bykova et al. (eds.), *The Palgrave Handbook of Russian Thought*,
https://doi.org/10.1007/978-3-030-62982-3_19

407

a person through his activity, in which consciousness is formed and revealed" (Rubinstein 1934, 8).

Rubinstein draws attention to a fundamental idea developed in Marx's early work according to which a person does not merely multiply himself in the object-oriented world he creates, he does not just set a mirror in which he is reflected, but creates himself for the first time. This is what Marx means when he writes that practice must be understood as "the coincidence of the changing of circumstances and of human activity or self-changing" (Marx and Engels 1974, 262). Proceeding from these philosophical principles, Rubinstein develops a psychological conception according to which a psychological subject is formed in the process of his own activity, and mental processes are mediated by cultural objectifications. This conception became the basis for specific psychological and experimental research.

Rubinstein's little-known article "The Principle of Creative Self-activity" ["Printsip tvorcheskoi samodeiatel'nosti"], first published in 1922 in Odessa, was rediscovered in 1969. It contains no references to Marx and Marxism, but it does present Rubinstein's critique of philosophical realism in general and materialism in particular (as well as subjective idealism) and, at the same time, posits what would become his main conception of activity. In this 1922 article, his thesis is formulated as the principle of creative self-activity.

Rubinstein criticizes the idea according to which the subject is conceived of as the agent or source of his deeds in which he is revealed and manifested. (He attributes this idea to Kant's doctrine of intelligible character.) According to this idea, "deeds are thought of as related to a particular subject. They are *his* deeds. But since their content does not contribute to his construction, his composition, they do not define him as a subject" (Rubinstein 1989, 93). Rubenstein agrees that there are deeds that do not determine the character of the individual, the subject. But there must also be those that build the subject. Otherwise, the former could not exist.

According to Rubinstein, in reality "the subject in his deeds, in the acts of his creative self-activity, is not only revealed and manifested, but is created and defined. Thus, we can determine what he is by what he does" (ibid.). By creating his work, the artist creates his own individuality. A moral person is made in creating an ethical, social whole from the debris and fragments of humankind, which alone are given to us. The thinking person is formed from the organization of the world of thoughts. Spiritual identity grows from spiritual creativity. "The creator is created in creativity […] There is only one way—if there is a way—to create a great identity: great work on a great creation" (ibid., 95).

The striking similarity between this article's thesis and what Rubinstein later formulated as the principle of the unity of consciousness and activity, and the fact that in it he criticizes Kant and subjective idealism, has led many to interpret the article as marking Rubinstein's sharp departure from his former neo-Kantianism and toward the independent development of ideas that were very close to Marx. We might conclude that this is what allowed Rubinstein to subsequently assimilate Marxism and lay the foundations for his psychological theory of activity. However, in the early 1920s, Rubinstein had yet to depart from Marburg neo-Kantianism.

In fact, the 1922 article criticizes realism and objectivism as a philosophically naive position. Rubinstein stressed that to believe that existence is independent of cognition leads to the conclusion that knowledge must be nothing other than the perception of existence. In reality, "objective existence necessarily includes an element of creative self-activity" (ibid., 93). This is precisely the understanding of objectivity shared by the Marburg neo-Kantians and Hegel. Rubinstein provides a characteristic example of this. He compares the relation of creative self-activity to the objective world with the relation of the artist-creator to his work. "The more perfect the work of art, the more complete the whole, the more independent the 'world' it represents. Therefore, the more substantial the creative activity of the artist, the more independent and whole is his creation" (ibid., 92). I want to stress that Rubinstein is concerned not only with the objectivity of knowledge but with the objectivity of existence itself, which does not exist outside of creative self-activity.

The key to understanding the 1922 article may be an even earlier article (likely written in 1917–1918) first published in 1994 under the title "On the Philosophical System of Hermann Cohen" ["O filosofskoi sisteme G. Kogena"]. In this article, Rubinstein focuses on the ethical subject, because without an ethical dimension the individual cannot exist as a subject (and the subject as an individual). First and foremost, the deed must be understood as ethical. The freedom of an ethical subject is nothing more than his autonomous deed, that is, the deed in accordance with what he himself is. But this selfhood is meaningfully expressed in moral law and is conditioned by it. The subject who is the source of his deeds and for whom deeds are merely the manifestation of his preformed essence is not an ethical subject but only a type of psychological formation. The ethical subject is a goal, not a preformed source of deeds: "the ethical subject is not a given and does not exist before its ethical deeds, and, thus, in its ethical deeds, it is not simply revealed and manifested—in fact, *it does not exist until it is manifested*: therefore, it is not revealed and expressed in deeds, but *originates* and *emerges* from them" (ibid., 154). Being identical with and determined by its deeds, the subject is self-determined.

When a person commits an ethical deed, he always presumes another person as another ethical subject. The ethical deed exists only in relation to a person as an individual. In relation to the thing, there is only activity, only a physical or mental act, but not the deed, Rubinstein emphasizes. Therefore, "I do not exist without the other; I and the other are complementary" (ibid.).

We must remember that the principle of the unity of consciousness and activity was never clearly formulated by Rubinstein as a philosophical principle, and in his later work *Man and the World* [*Chelovek i Mir*], he criticized the universalization of activity theory and stressed that activity cannot supersede contemplation, which he believed was just as important for the relation of the individual and the world (Rubinstein 1976, 339–340). (Some researchers even believe that Rubinstein abandoned activity theory in his later years.)

ACTIVITY THEORY IN SOVIET PSYCHOLOGY

Other versions of activity theory were developed in Soviet psychology. The most widespread was the theory of psychological activity proposed by the renowned Soviet psychologist Alexei N. Leontiev (1903–1979), who developed Lev S. Vygotsky's ideas about the cultural-historical genesis of higher mental functions. According to Leontiev, mental life can be understood as the result of the inclusion of individual human activity into collective activity. Activity is aimed at realizing motives, which can be understood as objectified needs. The components of activity are actions that are aimed at the actualization of goals. The components of actions are operations that are ways of solving problems. Leontiev criticized Rubinstein's principle of the unity of consciousness and activity since it indicated only how consciousness was mediated by activity but not how consciousness arose. According to Leontiev's psychological theory of activity, specifically human mental entities can be understood as the result of the internalization of external object-oriented actions—their transfer to the "internal plane" (Leontiev 1977).[1] Similarly to Leontiev, the psychologist P. Ya. Gal'perin (1902–1988) used the idea of internalization to develop the theory of "the formation of mental actions" (Gal'perin 1976).

Leontiev's conceptualization was criticized by Rubinstein and other psychologists. The main objection was that it focused too much on individual activity and individual actions and operations, rather than the collective activity from which individual activity, especially individual action, is derived. The idea of internalization was also criticized. Rubinstein and others pointed out that within this framework it is unclear what gives rise to the internal plane. In addition, these critics believed that reducing internal mental processes to transformed external actions was an oversimplification.

The new stage in the development of the psychological theory of activity was formulated in the last works of Gal'perin's pupil, Vasilii V. Davydov (1930–1988), and his research group. Davydov began to build a psychological theory of collective activity. He proceeded from the assumption that collective activity is not an extension of individual activity, or the simple transfer of the characteristics of individual activity (with its interrelations of activities, actions, and operations) to the collective one. Collective activity includes reciprocal activity and reciprocal actions. The interaction of its participants can be understood as communication. In this case, participants must constantly discuss specific problems with each other, engage in dialogues and polylogues, in order to understand the positions of others, and simultaneously learn to see themselves through the eyes of others—to develop the quality of self-reflexivity. In studies of collective activity, it was shown that the process of internalization must be understood differently: not simply as the "transfer" of external activity to the "internal plane," but as the individual appropriation of the forms of collective activity.

Actions that are part of interacting with another person are not the same as actions that produce an object or that change an objective situation, because interacting with another suggests that he too is an independent subject. Thus, the result of my actions is not entirely up to me—I cannot fully control it (Davydov 1986, 2008).

THE MEANING OF ACTIVITY THEORY IN SOVIET PHILOSOPHY

Philosophers who worked with activity theory thought of it as a bridge across the trench dug by Descartes separating the subjective world from the objective world. The Cartesian understanding of the subjective world of the individual significantly influenced European philosophy and human sciences, particularly classical psychology, which cultivated introspection as a specific way of cognizing mental phenomena. Attempts to remove the sharp opposition of the subjective and the objective are typical in twentieth-century philosophy. Various attempts were made by reinterpreting activity within the frameworks of pragmatism, the phenomenology of Sartre and Merleau-Ponty, and Wittgenstein's later work. In Soviet philosophy, the understanding of the individual and of activity was developed in the traditions of Marx, Fichte, and Hegel.

In the Soviet Union, activity theory provoked the suspicions of official ideologues. It seemed to them that it marked a departure from the theory of reflection and philosophical materialism. Soviet ideologues believed that the emphasis on human activity and its freedom contradicted the principal role of the Communist Party in the life of society.

Soviet supporters of activity theory were also suspected of sympathizing with the Yugoslavian philosophical group Praxis (established in the 1960s), which called for a return to Marx's authentic views and to the humanistic treatment of Marxism, while focusing on issues of alienation, practical activity, and creativity. The members of Praxis were primarily engaged in the social criticism of alienation, international consumerism, the bureaucratic socialism of the Soviet Union, and authoritarian phenomena in Yugoslavia. With good reason, official Soviet ideologues felt threatened by the views of this group and could not allow Soviet philosophers to converge with its members.

Many Soviet philosophers did sympathize with the activities of Praxis and had personal contacts with its members, particularly with M. Markovich, who repeatedly visited the Soviet Union. However, Russian philosophers did not have practical opportunities for open social criticism, although many were critical of Soviet social reality. Russian philosophers also studied the problems of alienation (e.g., Evald V. Ilyenkov's influential 1967 article (Ilyenkov 1967)) and analyzed the problems of humanism (Genrikh S. Batishchev wrote about this extensively (1969)), but their interest was primarily concerned with the study of the structure of activity itself and with the methodological problems of the human sciences, and science in general. Hence, there was a close

412   V. A. LEKTORSKY

association of activity theorists with psychology (Evald V. Ilyenkov, Georgii P. Shchedrovitsky, Eric G. Yudin, Vladislav A. Lektorsky), pedagogy (Batishchev, Shchedrovitsky), and the philosophy and history of science (Vyacheslav S. Stepin, Igor S. Alekseev, Mikhail A. Rozov, Vladimir S. Shvyryov).

Another important difference between the Soviet development of activity theory from what was done in the Praxis group is that the Yugoslavian philosophers believed that adopting (as an initial philosophical position) the thesis of the practical relation of the individual to the world eliminates the opposition of materialism and idealism. No Russian adherents of activity theory rejected materialism. And although they were criticized for this, their understanding of materialism did differ from its simplistic interpretation in official philosophy.

ACTIVITY AS A PHILOSOPHICAL PROBLEM

At the beginning of the 1960s, activity and activity theory became one of the central themes for a new wave of Soviet philosophy. This was primarily the result of Ilyenkov's work, especially his article "The ideal" ["Ideal'noe"] (Ilyenkov 1962) and the article "The problem of the ideal" ["Problema ideal'nogo"], published posthumously in two issues of the Russian journal *Problems of Philosophy* (1979). Official Soviet philosophy perceived these articles as a great heresy. Ilyenkov argued that the ideal exists primarily in the forms of collective human activity, that is, outside the mind of a single individual as an active form of a thing outside the thing itself. The subjective world arises from the inclusion of the individual into this activity. External reality is presented to the individual through activity and in the forms of this activity. Human freedom and the norms of life arise precisely in and through activity.

The ideal form is the form of the thing, though outside this thing, specifically inside the individual in the form of his active life-activity, in the form of his goals and needs. Or vice versa, it is a form of active human life-activity, but outside the individual, namely, in the form of the thing he creates. "Ideality" in itself only exists in the constant interchange of these two forms of its "external embodiment," not coinciding with either of them taken separately. It exists only through the perpetual process of transforming the form of activity into the form of the thing and back—the form of the thing into the form of activity (of the social individual) (Ilyenkov 2008, 212–213):

> From the very beginning [the individual] looks to "nature" (to matter) as a material where his goals are "incarnated," and as a "means" for the realization of his goals. That is why he initially sees in nature what "fits" for this role, what is and can be a means of realizing his goals, that is, something already involved in the process of goal oriented activity.
>   Thus, in the beginning, he turns his attention to the starry heavens as "a natural clock, a calendar, and a compass," as the instruments and tools of his life-activity and notices their "natural" properties and regularities only insofar as these

19 THE ACTIVITY APPROACH IN LATE SOVIET PHILOSOPHY   413

natural properties and regularities are the properties and regularities of the material in which his activities are realized, which is why he must consider it as a completely objective (in no way dependent on his will and consciousness) component of his activity.

But this is also the reason why he accepts the results of his transformative activity (the creation of self-imposed forms and relations of things) for the forms and relations of things-in-themselves. (Ibid., 211)

Issues relating to consciousness, the subjective world, the world of norms, linguistic meanings, and categories of thinking were understood by Ilyenkov in terms of human activity.

The Russian psychologists who continued in the tradition of Vygotsky's cultural-historical school (Leontiev, Davydov, etc.) took the position of Ilyenkov. Moreover, I believe that Ilyenkov's development of the problematic of activity led Leontiev to develop his psychological theory of activity in the early 1970s.

In connection with this, I want to draw attention to the way Ilyenkov's idea of activity influenced not only the theory of Russian psychologists but also their experimental practice.

Here, I am referring to the celebrated work of Russian psychologists relating to the education of deaf-blind children and their efforts in helping these children develop complete human minds. Ilyenkov began this work as a way of testing his philosophical ideas. In the experimental-practical work of psychologists, it was shown that the mastering of the object-oriented meaning of words can occur in such a child only if the corresponding object is included in collective activity. Originally, this is the "co-divided" activity of the child and the adult, since the fixed ways of handling an object in collective activity identify that object's relevant objective properties. Object-oriented activity depends on the objective characteristics of the object. At the same time, it identifies in the object what is important and necessary for the activity. This is why attempts to teach the child language by simply correlating linguistic signs with objects alone did not produce results. In this case, it is clear that interaction is included in activity and is its integral component: outside of relations with another person, activity is impossible. A special role in this process is played by special objects. These are manufactured objects: spoons, cups, shoes, clothes, and so forth. These are not just things, but ways of inter-human communication. For Ilyenkov, the case of deaf-blind children is not special (although there is enough specificity), but a kind of "cruel experiment" of nature, allowing us to observe the characteristics of human activity and its role in the formation of the mind, consciousness, and identity in "pure form" (Ilyenkov 1975, 82).

The work of Genrikh S. Batishchev made an important contribution to the philosophical-anthropological development of activity theory. In the 1970s, many Soviet authors saw in Batishchev's work the most striking articulation of the philosophy of activity theory. In his article "The Active Essence of the Individual" ["Deiatel'naia sushchnost' cheloveka"] (Batishchev 1969), he presented an extensive study of the structure of activity, the relation between objectification and deobjectification (since, as he stressed at the time, their unity is what creates activity), the relation of objectification and alienation, the transformation of external reality (subject-object relations), and inter-human (subject-subject) relations. Batishchev specifically analyzed the creative nature of activity, its openness, transcending the limits of existing stereotypes, its connection with a critical social attitude, the freedom inherent in it,[2] and the specific features of the cultural objectivization of activity ("works of art"):

> Human reality, which is also the reality of the individual as subject, arises only when the boundaries of nature are transcended—it is a special kingdom, *where fundamentally new possibilities are created* that seem *impossible* to immediate nature, that is, the place where *creation* occurs. Human object-oriented activity is precisely the process in which the substantiality of nature is *creatively* "completed" to the impossibility in nature itself and is simultaneously assimilated as natural. (Batishchev 1969, 89)

Batishchev wrote extensively about the object-oriented nature of activity:

> Activity is the ability of a person to behave not in accordance with the organization of his body, not as a slave of the "specificity" of his organism, but in accordance with the specific logic of each specific object; in other words, to be "faithful" not to "oneself," but to the world of objects as they are in themselves, and in this faith immanent to objects, to their own logic, for the first time to be truly *oneself*; to not be a body among other bodies, not a finite thing among other finite things, but a "being" of object-oriented activity, an agent. [...] The activity intrinsic to object-oriented activity occurs and develops not from the "species" specificity of the organism as a finite thing, but from the mastering of objects such as they are in themselves, as they are in their measures and essences. (Ibid., 82)

Later, Batishchev's attitude toward activity theory changed significantly. If at first he emphasized the unity of activity and communication (e.g., "The essence of the individual is activity as the identity of activity and communication" (ibid., 96)), then later he began to contrast two components of activity— subject-object relations versus subject-subject relations—and prioritized the latter. In the 1980s, he began to write about the boundaries of activity theory, the existence of non-activity layers of consciousness (intuition, empathy, unconsciousness, etc.), and the need to complement activity with "deep communication" as a more adequate relation to the Universal: "activity is not an only possible universal way of human, cultural, or social existence; it is not the only and all-encompassing way of linking the individual to the world" (Batishchev 1990, 24–25).

The above shows Batishchev's departure from Marxism. (He even wrote an unpublished work criticizing Marx's "Theses on Feuerbach" (Khamidov 2009, 75–76).) Another unique development of activity theory was in scientific methodology. In these works, activity was studied primarily in its subject-object aspect.

In the 1970s, Vyacheslav S. Stepin developed an original philosophical concept of scientific theory by studying the structure and dynamics of theory in physics. In particular, he studied the distinct activity of scientific experimentation and described the interrelation of experimental actions with formal and informal operations in the process of building and developing a scientific theory, the connection of models of the world, and scientific ontologies with these operations. Stepin's originality was in demonstrating how in the natural sciences theory is not built in a hypothetical-deductive way (as many in the Soviet Union and the West had assumed), but through a genetically-constructive method that involves mental experimentation with ideal objects. Stepin defended the idea about the operational sense and constructive corroboration of theoretical schemes (Stepin 2003).

In relation to this, Stepin considered how human activity relates to the observation of objects that cannot be directly influenced (e.g., the moon, planets, stars in astronomy). First, he began with the premise that astronomical observation is analogous to instrumentation, when the interaction of one object with another is used as a kind of natural experiment (Stepin 1998, 662). Second, he noted that activity selects from an object's infinite set of actual and potential features only a limited subclass of features (ibid., 663).

Stepin debated this issue with another Russian philosopher of science—Igor S. Alekseev. According to the latter, any observable objects outside of activity do not exist, and the world does not consist of stationary objects that have actual properties. It is rather a set of potential opportunities, only a part of which can be realized. Activity realizes those possibilities that cannot arise in nature itself. In this sense, activity creates its own objects, and it can be considered a primary substance (ibid.).

Proceeding from his conception of activity as a substance, Alekseev called his position "subjective materialism." Today, we can rightly consider it constructivist.

A special role in the development of Russian activity theory was played by the ideas of the philosopher and methodologist Georgii P. Shchedrovitsky. In the 1960s, he began work on the activity theory of thinking, which proceeded from the premise that thought was an activity that occurred on two planes: the generation of content and movement in symbolic form. The generation of content begins with the operation of object-oriented practical comparison, which is followed by operations with the form itself. All operations were divided into their components, while the set of operations was assumed to be finite (Shchedrovitsky 1995, 34–49; 590–630). Shchedrovitsky and his adherents studied specific patterns of thinking; they also worked with psychologists and pedagogues and offered specific recommendations. In the 1970s, Shchedrovitsky put forward a general theory of collective activity according to which activity is a collective system that includes the goals of the activity, the means of its actualization, norms, and the division of the participants' positions. For

Shchedrovitsky, the task of the methodologist is to design various kinds of organizations in the form of different systems of activity: in science, in education, and in society. In this connection, cognition is understood as entirely derivative of design.[3] The tasks created by Shchedrovitsky's theory of activity were understood very ambitiously: "The theory of activity raises the question of the global or total design and planning of the entire society, of its organization on a scientific basis" (Shchedrovitsky 1995, 320).[4]

Shchedrovitsky and his group established close ties with a number of areas that related to everyday life. This understanding of activity gave rise to the "organizational-activity games," which have been successfully developed to the present day.

Shchedrovitsky was influenced by Marx, Hegel, and the organizational theory of Alexander A. Bogdanov and created a kind of technocratic version of activity theory (which is fundamentally different from Ilyenkov and Batishchev). For Shchedrovitsky, activity is a self-developing substance. The individual is captured by this substance, and only to the extent that he occupies a certain functional place in activity can he become a person. Shchedrovitsky is not interested in the individual's subjectivity and identity. His understanding of activity is fundamentally non-subjective. Activity is a kind of self-developing substance, which is only parasitic on the individual just as it is on machines and sign systems. The human individual is a kind of fiction that exists only insofar as it is included in activity.

At the core of the development of Shchedrovitsky's understanding of activity and methodology lie two seemingly incompatible ideas: first is Hegel's idea of the self-development of thinking (coinciding with activity) as an autonomous and self-contained process (Shchedrovitsky repeatedly refers to Hegel); second is the idea that activity (including thinking) can be understood as a technological process based on the strict correspondence of goals, resources, procedures, and the input and output of product. The combination of Hegel with technological design seems impossible. However, Shchedrovitsky was not the first theorist to go down this path. Long before him, the idea that a person is a product of his own activity based on the development of technology was expressed by Marx, who is sometimes referred to as the "philosopher of technology." Marx, of course, had a different understanding of practice and activity, and his philosophy is much broader and more diverse. Shchedrovitsky's theory is his own invention. But, in principle, his understanding of activity can be interpreted as the development of Marx's ideas. In his development of activity and methodology, Shchedrovitsky constantly refers to Marx and his understanding of activity. However, this is not a mere tribute to the official attitudes of his time, especially since Marx is mentioned in practically all of the Shchedrovitsky's oral lectures published only after his death. In fact, Shchedrovitsky was very critical of the social reality that surrounded him and was expelled from the Communist Party. The very idea of total design, planning, and the creation of ideal organization lies at the heart of the Soviet social project. Shchedrovitsky entertained this deep belief his entire life, despite his sharp rejection of the real social life of the Soviet era.

ACTIVITY IN THE CONTEXT OF EPISTEMOLOGY

In the Soviet philosophy of the 1960s–1980s, there were other influential concepts of activity. Here are several.

Eric Yudin singled out four functions of activity: (1) activity as an explanatory principle in the human sciences (psychology, linguistics, social sciences), (2) activity as a subject of study (psychology, in particular, in the theories of Rubinstein and Leontiev), (3) activity as the subject of design (ergonomics), and (4) activity as a cultural value. In connection with the fourth of these, Yudin noted that activity was not a revered cultural value in all cultures and at all times. In some cultures it was accepted as a necessary condition of human life, but was not particularly valued in its own right. This applies to antiquity (e.g., in ancient philosophy the word "theory" originally referred not to a type of ideal construction, but a special kind of contemplation), to the European Middle Ages, and to Eastern cultures. Activity, as the creation of the new, began to be revered only in Modern Europe (Yudin 1978).

Vladimir S. Shvyryov emphasized that human activity exists in two different modes. It can be performed using the available methods and norms—being inscribed in a certain closed system. In this case, activity runs parallel to established traditions. And it can mean the creation of new norms, orientations, and socio-cultural paradigms—the change of existing programs of activity, their "reprogramming," and transcending existing ways of including the individual in the world. The last form of activity demonstrates its open, creative character and manifests human freedom, which broadens the horizon of the individual's relation to the world and himself. On the historical scale, tradition that determines the closed nature of activity functions as a derivative of the open nature of activity and its ability to form new socio-cultural paradigms (Shvyryov 1984, 2001).

Mikhail A. Rozov proceeded from the fact that the objects of knowledge are not objects in and of themselves, but objects of action, and that during the process of cognition, a person doesn't "read" the book of nature so much as he "writes" it. In this regard, he did not see a significant difference between cognitive and engineering activity, emphasizing that just as an engineer creates technological constructions, a scientist creates a world of ideal objects with which he works. (Thus, Rozov was inclined to epistemological constructivism.) He interpreted the history of collective epistemic activity as the history of "social relay races" and in this framework tried to understand activity as a wavelike process [a *kumatoid*]. This led him to analyze the role of reflection in scientific knowledge and single out various types of scientific research programs (Rozov 1977, 2008).

Vladislav A. Lektorsky investigated the role of artificial objects that function as intermediaries in the epistemic process, beginning with linguistic signs and tools of labor and ending with laboratory instruments and theories in science. He also noted that as an artificial process, human activity enters into a complex relation with natural processes and that questions concerning the artificial

418 V. A. LEKTORSKY

remaking of the world and humanity itself become acute in connection with the new possibilities of science and technology. The issue of the interrelation between the "given" and the "made," and the possibility of replacing the first with the second, is not just an academic philosophical problem, but concerns the future of humanity and culture (Lektorsky 1980, 1990, 2001).

ACTIVITY THEORY IN CONTEMPORARY PHILOSOPHY AND COGNITIVE SCIENCE

The disagreements among Soviet philosophers and psychologists concerning the conception and evaluation of activity theory were not accidental. They relate to real theoretical problems and today are at the center of contemporary discussions relating to epistemology, philosophy of mind, and cognitive science.

First, this relates to the basic thesis of activity theory: the world is given to the human individual in the forms of his activity. Does this mean that the objective world is something like a Kantian thing in itself and that a person can only deal with what he himself creates and builds (the idea of philosophical constructivism)?

Yes, comes the response from those siding with Alekseev, Shchedrovitsky, and Rozov. The opposition to this affirmative response is represented by Ilyenkov and the early Batishchev, who support their counter-argument with reference to Marx: human activity is always object-oriented and is not performed in accordance with the particular organization of the human body, but in accordance with the specific logic of each specific object—this is the human "universality" that distinguishes the human from all other living beings.

The "Embodiment Cognition Approach," which is popular today in cognitive science, resists philosophical constructivism since it proceeds from the premise that any cognitive and active being deals with the real world. This approach implies that activity identifies those features of the world that are essential for a specific type of cognitive being: this identification depends on the size and other characteristics of the body of the cognitive being and its needs. Moreover, it is necessary to distinguish between the physical world and the surrounding world, and, within the latter, one should distinguish different sub-worlds or realities. This is one of James Gibson's main ideas and has significantly influenced the formation of the Embodied Cognition Approach (Gibson 1979). At the same time, a person's relation to the world is not limited to the particularities of his body and needs: he "exits" beyond his bodily boundaries, creates the world of artificial objects, and tries to understand the relation of different worlds and sub-worlds in terms of their own specifics. This is the idea of the currently popular "extended" understanding of cognition (Clark and Chalmers 1998; Wilson 2004).

Another problem concerns the interrelation between contemplation and activity. Earlier in this chapter, I wrote that some of the founders of activity theory in Soviet philosophy, such as Sergei L. Rubinstein and the late Batishchev, opposed activity and contemplation, emphasizing the irreducibility of the second to the first. This is indeed a difficult problem. If activity is the transformation of reality, then cognition is the comprehension of reality as it is. Thus, one cannot identify activity and cognition (although this is what some cognitive scientists, in particular F. Varela, are trying to do). However, it is important to bear in mind that cognition is intrinsically woven into activity, since activity connects the cognizing subject and the cognized object, and distinguishes the essential features of the latter. Within the framework of the activity approach, a new concept of perception arises that resists many ideas of the classical interpretation of perception in philosophy and psychology. This particularly concerns the idea that perception is not a simple processing of information but is the continual process of extracting information from the world; this means that perception is not "given" and not constructed but is "extracted" with the help of object-oriented action (Gibson 1979; Neisser 1976; Noë 2004).

Finally, another problem is the interrelation of activity and communication. The fact that communication is not an activity (and that it is impossible to reduce subject-subject relations to subject-object relations) was addressed by the opponents of activity theory in psychology (B.F. Lomov) and philosophy (Rubinstein and Batishchev). It seems obvious that relating to another subject is not the same as relating to an inanimate object. If I perceive another as an external reality, I assume that this subject perceives me the same way. And this means that the very perception of another person includes the awareness of being perceived by another. But why should activity be understood only as the transformation of inanimate things? Activity is the change of different types of realities, including the reality of inter-human relations. This can clearly be achieved through communication, which is, of course, an activity, although of a special kind. One must remember that the epistemic and activity-oriented relation of the human individual to the world inherently implies communication, for we deal with the world via the mediation of a special set of objects made by other people. The use of such objects must include communication with others (as in the case of deaf-blind children). And, finally, any act of communication is meaningful only within the framework of a broader system of activities. The concepts of "extended knowledge" and "extended consciousness" that are being developed today deal with precisely this set of issues (Clark and Chalmers 1998).

Today, there are philosophers, psychologists, and specialists in culture studies who adhere to various constructivist conceptions, especially to those of social constructivism (Gergen 1994 et al.) and to the narrative approach (Sarbin 1986). Some Russian philosophers believe that constructivism best articulates what remains of value from activity theory. Social constructionism, however, is opposed to activity theory.

Social constructionism holds that when we study the mind, consciousness, and human identity, we are dealing not with real objects, but only with two kinds of constructions. First, these are the products of social interactions and different kinds of communications that have a cultural-historical character. Second, the researcher and the human subject build the studied subject, which does not exist outside this process. Thus, what is taken for knowledge does not exist in reality. According to this model, the psychologist or sociologist is in reality not a researcher or a scientist, but only a participant in the creation of certain social relations, of an ephemeral social reality, which can only be spoken of conditionally, because it exists only in the framework of constructive activity. According to this position an experiment in social psychology cannot be a method of obtaining objective knowledge because the experimenter and the object of experimentation (the human being) enter into communicative interaction during which the object of research fundamentally changes. Thus, these authors think, it is meaningless to talk about scientific theory in the study of human individuals.

But this position cannot be accepted. There is something in social constructionism that is similar to cultural-historical activity theory, it is the idea that the mind, consciousness, and identity are the products of social interactions and communications, and have a cultural-historical character. Adherents of this view refer to Lev Vygotsky and Mikhail Bakhtin and state that social constructionism is the contemporary development of their ideas. However, the thesis that the researcher is dealing not with something that really exists, but creates the reality in the process of studying it, is fundamentally different from activity theory as it was understood in Soviet philosophy and psychology. In fact, any construction presupposes the reality in which it is realized and which it identifies and attempts to transform. On the other hand, reality is revealed and actualized for the subject only through his constructive activity.

It is not necessary that what is constructed not be real. If the "I," personality, and identity are social constructions, it does not follow that they are not real. The table I am sitting behind is also constructed, but this does not mean that it ceases to exist. It can be said that all social institutions are the products of human activity and are constructions, yet this does not imply their unreality. People often create things (both material and ideal) that become independent and take on a real life of their own. This includes social institutions, which is why their structure can and should be studied, and theories be formulated about them. This also includes the subjective human world—the subject of psychological research, both theoretical and experimental. This is the world of the ideal products of human creativity, which develop according to their own specific laws within the framework of human activity, as described by Ilyenkov. These ideal objects are so separated from their creators that today many consider it meaningless to raise the question of their authorship (Lektorsky 2009, 2017).

The elaboration of the activity approach is relevant today in light of current developments in philosophy, psychology, and cognitive science. The achievements of Russian philosophy can be stimulating in these discussions.

Translated by Peter Golub

19 THE ACTIVITY APPROACH IN LATE SOVIET PHILOSOPHY   421

NOTES

1. The well-known contemporary American-Finnish psychologist Yrjö Engeström uses a number of Leontiev's ideas in his theory of expanding activity (Engeström 2005).
2. Batishchev's analysis of "revolutionary-critical activities" particularly displeased Soviet official ideologues (especially Mikhail A. Suslov).
3. The separation of cognition and practice must be done away with. Shchedrovitsky emphasized that cognition is a kind of practice (Shchedrovitsky 1995, 508).
4. We must "develop methods for designing the human being of future society" (Shchedrovitsky 1995, 227).

BIBLIOGRAPHY

Batishchev, Genrikh S. 1969. Deiatel'nostnaia sushchnost' cheloveka kak filosofskii printsip. In *Problema cheloveka v sovremennoi filosofii*, 73–144. Moscow: Nauka.
———. 1990. Neischerpannye vozmozhnosti i granitsy primenimosti kategorii deiatel'nosti. In *Deiatel'nost': teorii, metodologiia, problem*, ed. Vladislav A. Lektorsky, 7–14. Moscow: Politizdat.
Clark, Andy. 1997. *Being There: Putting Brain, Body and World Together Again*. Cambridge, MA: The MIT Press.
Clark, Andy, and David Chalmers. 1998. The Extended Mind. *Analysis* 58 (1): 7–19.
Davydov, Vasilii V. 1986. *Problemy razvivaiushchego obucheniia*. Moscow: Pedagogika.
———. 2008. *Problems of Developmental Instruction*. Edited by V. Lektorsky and D. Robbins. New York, NY: Nova Science Publishers.
Engeström, Yrjö. 2005. *Developmental Work Research: Expanding Activity Theory in Practice*. Berlin: Lehmanns Media.
Gal'perin, Pyotr Ya. 1976. *Vvedenie v psikhologiiu*. Moscow: Izdatel'stvo Moskovskogo gosudarstvennogo universiteta.
Gergen, Kenneth. 1994. *Realities and Relationships: Soundings in Social Constructionism*. Cambridge, MA: Harvard University Press.
Gibson, James J. 1979. *The Ecological Approach to Visual Perception*. Boston: Houghton Mufflin.
Ilyenkov, Evald V. 1962. Ideal'noe. In *Philosopshkaia Encyclopedia v 5 tomakh*, vol. 2, 219–227. Moscow: Izdatel'stvo Sovetskaia Encyclopedia.
———. 1967. From the Marxist Point of View. In *Marx and the Western World*, ed. N. Lobkovich. Notre Dame: University of Notre Dame Press.
———. 1975. A.I. Meshcheriakov i ego pedagogika. *Molodoi kommunist* 2: 212–230.
———. 2008. *Problema ideal'nogo*. Moscow: ROSSPEN.
Khamidov, Alexander A. 2009. Put' otkrytii kak otkrytie puti: filosofskie iskaniia G.S. Batishcheva. In *Genrich Sterpaniovich Batishchev*. Series "Filosofiia Rossii vtoroi poloviny 20-go veka," 11–242. Moscow: ROSSPEN.
Lektorsky, Vladislav A. 1980. *Sub'ekt. Ob'ekt. Poznanie*. Moscow: Izdatel'stvo Nauka.
———., ed. 1990. *Activity: Theories, Methodology, and Problems*. Orlando: Paul Deutsch.

—. 2001. Deiatel'nostnyi podkhod: smert' ili vozrozhdenie? *Voprosy filosofii* 2: 64–76.

—. 2009. Realizm, anti-realizm, konstruktivizm i konstruktivnyi realizm v epistemologii i nauke. In *Konstruktivistskii podkhod v epistemologii i naukakh o cheloveke*, 5–40. Moscow: Kanon.

—. 2017. Realism as the Methodological Strategy in Cognitive Science: In *Varieties of Scientific Realism: Objectivity and Truth in Science*, ed. E. Agazzi, 353–366. Cham: Springer.

Leontiev, Alexei N. 1977. *Deiatel'nost', soznanie, lichnost'*. Moscow: Politizdat.

Marx, Karl, and Friedrich Engels. 1974. Tezisy o Feyerbakhe. In *Sochineniie v 50 tomakh*, vol. 42, 2nd ed., 262–263. Politizdat: Moscow.

Neisser, Ulric G. 1976. *Cognition and Reality: Principles and Implications of Cognitive Psychology*. San Francisco: Freeman.

Noë, Alva. 2004. *Action in Perception*. Cambridge, MA: The MIT Press.

Rozov, Mikhail A. 1977. *Problema empiricheskogo analiza nauchnykh znanii*. Novosibirsk: Nauka. Sibirskoe otdelenie.

—. 2008. *Teoriia sotsial'nykh estafet i problemy epistemologii*. Moscow: Novyi khronograf.

Rubinstein, Sergei L. 1934. Problemy psikhologii v trudakh Karla Marksa. *Sovetskaia psikhotekhnika* 1: 8–15.

—. 1976. *Problemy obshchei psikhologii*. Moscow: Pedagogika.

—. 1989. Printsip tvorcheskoi samodeiatel'nosti. K filosofskim osnovam sovremennoi pedagogiki. *Voprosy filosofii* 4: 88–109.

Sarbin, Theodor R., ed. 1986. *Narrative Psychology*. New York: Praeger.

Shchedrovitsky, Georgii P. 1995. *Izbrannye Trudy*. Moscow: Shkola kul'turnoi politiki.

Shvyryov, Vladimir C. 1984. *Nauchnoe poznanie kak deiatel 'nost'*. Moscow: Izdatel'stvo Nauka.

—. 2001. O deiatel'nostnom podkhode k istolkovaniiu "fenomena cheloveka" (popytka sovremennoi otsenki). *Voprosy filosofii* 2: 108–110.

Stepin, Vyacheslav S. 1998. V mire teoreticheskikh idei. In *Filosofiia ne konchaetsia. Iz istorii otechestvennoi filosofii. 20 vek. 1960–80 gody*, ed. Vladislav A. Lektorsky, vol. 2, 653–669. Moscow: ROSSPEN.

—. 2003. *Teoreticheskoe znanie*. Moscow: Izdatel'stvo Progress–Traditsiia.

Varela, Francisco, Evan Thomson, and Eleanor Rosh. 1992. *The Embodied Mind: Cognitive Science and Human Experience*. Cambridge, MA: MIT Press.

Wilson, Robert. 2004. *Boundaries of the Mind: The Individual in the Fragile Sciences. Cognition*. Cambridge: Cambridge University Press.

Yudin, Eric G. 1978. *Sistemnyi podkhod i printsip deiatel'nosti*. Moscow: Nauka.

CHAPTER 20

A Return to Tradition: The Epistemological Style in Russia's Post-Soviet Philosophy

Boris I. Pruzhinin and Tatiana G. Shchedrina

INTRODUCTION

The title of this chapter articulates the dichotomous situation in Russian philosophy today. Russian philosophy is largely still post-Soviet, but it is also striving vigorously to acquire its own contours, both thematic and conceptual, at least in some areas of philosophical research. We argue that the conceptual significance and prospects of efforts by those Russian epistemologists who are introducing original perspectives into contemporary philosophical issues and launching discussions that are new for this plan of research can be largely attributed to their appeals to the ideas and themes of the Russian philosophical tradition. We will attempt to defend this thesis below by demonstrating how the epistemological style of late nineteenth- and early twentieth-century Russian philosophy manifests in the modern philosophical analysis of cognition and how the modern epistemological (and not only epistemological) cluster of themes is being transformed by the ideas highlighted in this style.

Our decision to address epistemological issues in an article about returning to the Russian philosophical tradition is not at all accidental. Epistemology is a fundamental, that is, foundational, area of philosophical research, and if our goal is to identify trends in modern post-Soviet philosophy, we must trace the

---

B. I. Pruzhinin (✉)
Institute of Philosophy, Russian Academy of Sciences, Moscow, Russia

T. G. Shchedrina
Moscow State Pedagogical University, Moscow, Russia

© The Author(s), under exclusive license to Springer Nature
Switzerland AG 2021
M. F. Bykova et al. (eds.), *The Palgrave Handbook of Russian Thought*,
https://doi.org/10.1007/978-3-030-62982-3_20

423

shifts in ideas that are taking place in this area today. At the same time, addressing epistemology is also important in this case because our argument about the return to Russian philosophical traditions in the sphere of theory of knowledge sounds dissonant in relation to the currently prevailing opinion in both Western and Russian historical-philosophical literature that the Russian philosophical tradition is anti-methodological. Instead, the artistic-existential structure of these philosophical texts and the confessional orientation of their ideas are usually emphasized as their particular features. Let us stress that we do not at all deny the existence of a strongly expressed emotional-artistic form in the Russian philosophical tradition, nor of the religious attitudes that particularize that form. However, we also believe that these dimensions of Russian philosophy that give it its inherent color by no means exhaust its essence as a holistic phenomenon of Russian culture. There is at least one more set of ideas constituting Russian philosophy that has remained in the shadows until now, and through the epistemological stylistics in the work of Russian philosophers, that component will come to the fore as the most important factor determining the prospects of modern Russian philosophy as a whole. We have in mind the tradition of "positive philosophy on Russian soil" and its underlying idea of conversation as the highest cultural value.

Bringing "Positive Philosophy on Russian Soil" Up to Date for Modern Epistemology

In an essentially programmatic article published in the first issue of *Questions of Philosophy and Psychology* [*Voprosy filosofii i psikhologii*] (1899), Nikolai Ya. Grot uncovered the general thrust of ideas in Russian philosophy in the context of Western European thought of the nineteenth and early twentieth centuries, defining its main task as "building a holistic doctrine of the world and of life, one alien to any logical contradictions and capable of satisfying not only the intellect's demands but also the heart's needs" (1889, ix). A large number of Russian philosophers who were enormously different in other respects adopted this philosophical project, which was known as "positive philosophy." "I understand this unity as the tradition of positive philosophy," wrote Gustav G. Shpet, who clarified a great deal in the understanding of this philosophical project:

> And I dare say that I feel this tradition not as a distant, general, and indirect connection, but as a vibrant, near, and immediate spiritual unity. Let us take only *our own* and those closest to us: who would deny that the philosophical doctrines of P. Yurkevich, Vl. Solovyov, Prince S. Trubetskoi, and L. Lopatin participate in precisely this tradition of positive philosophy stretching back, as I have indicated, to Plato? We see that Yurkevich understood philosophy as *complete* and *holistic* knowledge;[1] philosophy for him is a holistic worldview, dealing not with the individual but with mankind. Solovyov begins with a critique of abstract philosophy and is already offering a genuine concrete-historical philosophy in *Filosofskie*

nachala tsel'nogo znaniia [*Philosophical Principles of Integral Knowledge*]; Prince Trubetskoi calls his doctrine "*concrete* idealism"; Lopatin's system is "a system of *concrete* spiritualism" [...] All of this should suffice to see the unity toward which our "positive philosophy" should continue to tend. Our aspirations should concentrate in this direction, and our powers be applied accordingly. (Shpet 2005, 199–200)

The authors of this article also see their task as bringing this particular trend in Russian philosophical thought up to date.

To understand the essence and sources of "positive philosophy," we must begin with two features that played a significant role in shaping this idea: on the one hand, the critical attitude of its founders (Pamfil D. Yurkevich and Vladimir S. Solovyov, in particular) toward European Enlightenment rationalism and, on the other hand, their respectful (so to speak) attitude toward science, toward rational knowledge, that allowed them to avoid anti-rationalism and highlight the value of scientific knowledge. Russian philosophers saw no particular need to reject Enlightenment ideas, including the idea of cognition based on reason, but Russian philosophy obtained its positive sense from a different idea: the idea of a "holistic knowledge" that unites "the intellect and the heart," the idea of knowledge that bears universally significant meaning and thereby contributes to mutual understanding among people.

There have already been quite a large number of publications in post-Soviet philosophy devoted to discussing the epistemological ideas of various Russian philosophers (Gustav G. Shpet, Nikolai A. Berdyaev, Lev I. Shestov, Pavel A. Florensky, Vladimir Solovyov, etc.) in this very vein (see Popova 2015; Motroshilova 2013; Shchedrina and Pruzhnin 2017; Parshin 2013; Gaidenko 2002). We will discuss below the main standpoints in "positive philosophy" as realized in its epistemological program, but we must begin with a historical-philosophical digression whose necessity is due to the presence of a highly significant "intellectual inertia" in interpretations of "Russian philosophy" as a phenomenon, an inertia that substantially hinders the clarification of positive philosophy's epistemological potential. The publication of works by Russian philosophers that began in *Voprosy filosofii* in 1989 was greeted with enthusiasm, as it coincided with the search for Russia's national roots. At almost the same time, intense debates opened up around this very vein of interpreting Russian philosophy's heritage of ideas. The issue was that the core of relevant ideas related to Russia's cultural self-identification had changed over time. It sounded in one way from the mouth of Pyotr Chaadaev in the nineteenth century, then in another way in the Slavophile and Westernizer debates, then in an entirely different way in émigré literature of the first half of the twentieth century. Finding a harmonious historical form for this topic was necessary, and the socio-intellectual post-Soviet atmosphere influenced the means both of assimilating and of interpreting the theme of Russian philosophy's characteristic features: a significant portion of the Russian intelligentsia of the 1990s viewed the unique feature of national Russian philosophy as its religiosity.

However, it soon became clear that developing a modern philosophy based solely on a religious interpretation of the Russian philosophical tradition would not suffice. The ideas of Russian philosophers were encapsulated in the separate, specialized area of "history of domestic philosophy," while the topical issues in theory of cognition, philosophy and methodology of human knowledge, ethics, aesthetics, and so forth continued to be debated separately from the Russian philosophical tradition, supported primarily by European philosophy and cultural-historical experience, which had become widely available during those years. This "isolationist" mindset in research on the Russian philosophical tradition created an increasingly tense intellectual situation across Russian philosophy as a whole, given that it had become clear since the end of the 1990s that understanding even the most pressing sociocultural problems of modern Russia, not to mention any specialized issues in philosophy, turned out to be outside any of Russian philosophy's specific heritage of ideas. Whenever attempts are made to bring this kind of mindset up to date, mental constructs of the most universal (or rather: Utopian) nature come to the fore.

In addition, introducing the ideas of Russian philosophers, especially those of the emigration era, into discussion of the most topical issues has been no easy task, not to mention the fact that the émigré thinkers were located in a different social environment and used a different Russian philosophical language for their reflections. Their works were written in a specific time and in a specific context, which undoubtedly influenced their priorities in terms of ideas and their assessments of key figures and basic trends in Russian intellectual history. *The History of Russian Philosophy* [*Istoriia russkoi filosofii*] by Nikolai O. Lossky, Vasily V. Zenkovsky, and Sergey A. Levitsky; *The Russian Idea* [*Russkaia ideia*] by Nikolai A. Berdyaev; and *Ways of Russian Theology* [*Puti russkogo bogosloviia*] by Georges V. Florovsky were less exhaustive, objective descriptions of the history of Russian intellectual reality than attempts by philosophers in the Russian diaspora to understand themselves in their real-life situation (their "Russianness" was limited to their Orthodox faith and artificially created structural enclaves). In that vein, all other "non-religious" content in Russian philosophy represented the result of outside and therefore uncharacteristic Western European influence.

Gradually, however, both the nature and the vector of research on the Russian philosophical tradition have been changing significantly both in scale and in conceptual foundations. Above all, we see an increasingly substantial belief that these attempts to characterize Russian philosophy as exclusively religious unjustly narrow the circle of personalities, ideas, and themes that actually shape the phenomenon we call the Russian philosophical tradition and thereby limit our understanding of Russian culture as a whole, both in terms of the ideas and in terms of the existential sources of this tradition. These attempts neglect dozens of original thinkers and entire subject areas: Russian philosophy of psychology (Georgii I. Chelpanov, Lev S. Vygotsky, Sergei L. Rubinstein, and others), original logico-gnoseological (logico-epistemological) research (Mikhail I. Karlinsky, Nikolai A. Vasil'ev, Vladimir N. Ivanovsky), phenomenological and hermeneutical ideas (Gustav G. Shpet), semiotics and structuralism (Shpet, Roman O. Jakobson), and more. Even the ideas of predominantly religious philosophers are impoverished by the narrowly confessional interpretation of Russian philosophy (e.g., Pavel Florensky's semiotic ideas seem to retreat into the background and become secondary), not to mention such areas as Russian Neo-Kantianism, Russian philosophy of law, the development of Russian anarchist ideas, and others. In particular, areas of philosophy that could be brought up to date in the context of modern epistemology's most pressing concerns (among them: communicative breaks in scientific cognition and the sociocultural status of knowledge, as well as the semiotic interpretation of knowledge) lie outside the field of vision. It is striking how much these themes harmonize with the epistemological ideas of "positive philosophy on Russian soil."

Shpet distinguished between negative philosophy (Kant) and positive philosophy deriving from Plato, suggesting we seek philosophical guideposts, including those in cognition, where universally significant issues come to the fore. Furthermore, given the backdrop of processes taking place in modern science, this intention of Russian philosophy acquires a special urgency today that is reflected in modern epistemological debates. Russian philosophy sought to overcome the narrowness of Enlightenment rationalism, but we would emphasize that this was about overcoming narrowness without rejecting the very idea of *ratio* as the most important element of European culture. Obviously, this position has become especially pressing for epistemology given the background of the relativistic interpretations of scientific knowledge that are popular today.

RESEARCH TRENDS IN CONTEMPORARY RUSSIAN EPISTEMOLOGY

We should emphasize that we are employing the concept of "epistemology" in a broader sense, that is, not only as a particular philosophical discipline ("theory of cognition") but also as an intellectual practice (the historical experience of cognition). After all, the relevance of modern epistemology is expressed not in the external standardization of cognition, nor in the creation of universal schematics for the abstract process of cognition, but in the methodological support for concrete scientific research. This broader view allows us to include the methodology of science in the field of epistemology. We believe that experts will not raise serious objections to our assertion that epistemology has found itself in a state of profound crisis today (as has the entire field of philosophical reflection on science). The goals of epistemology have been reduced to descriptions of individual episodes in the history of science, episodes which have no methodological significance for the ongoing practice of cognition. Epistemological arguments are thereby deprived of the proper status of a science, and epistemology itself thus loses its status as philosophical knowledge. The naturally arising consciousness of modern science cannot in itself confront the literally universally accepted belief that science as a phenomenon is no cognitively different from everyday opinion, social utopia, myth, and so forth.

Most modern Russian research on epistemological issues focuses on analyzing the cognitive role of the sociocultural dimensions of cognition. We should note that research in these areas of Russian philosophy has been reasonably successful and attracts interest from foreign experts in epistemology and philosophy of science, leading to active cooperation with prominent Western philosophers such as Evandro Agazzi, Richard Rorty, Tom Rockmore, Hans Lenk, Steve Fuller, Rom Harre, and Chris Hübner. Three main areas of research have emerged in modern Russian epistemology, and their overlap constitutes the field of epistemological debate. A particular epistemological style (sociological, cognitive, cultural-historical) is characteristic of each of these areas.

The first area presents knowledge, including scientific knowledge, as an exclusively social construction. This radical epistemological perspective (with elements of postmodernism) has been developed within the Russian version of social epistemology (Ilya T. Kasavin, Alexander Yu. Antonovskii, and others). From this point of view, science is not so much associated with cultural and historical contexts as it is one of the social forms of assimilating the world, along with everyday, pragmatic, ideological, and political forms, among others (see Kasavin 2017; Goldman 1999).

The second area of research attempts to overcome the sociocultural relativism of modern philosophy of science by relying on philosophical analysis of the most cutting-edge cognitive sciences and other sciences dealing with cognition (including analysis of artificial intelligence). This area posits a new (non-classical) situation in modern science and cognition overall, relying on reinterpreted traditions of classical epistemology based on the subject-object relationship. This applies above all to the concept of "constructive realism" (Vladislav A. Lektorsky), which invokes the activity approach in its modern interpretation. This framework highlights the sociocultural interpretation of cognition and consciousness, overcoming the choice between psychology and anti-psychology (see Lektorsky 2010).

Cultural-historical epistemology, which is based on the tradition of "positive philosophy on Russian soil" (see Pruzhinin and Shchedrina 2017a), offers another way of opposing the social relativization of knowledge. In order to present this area in the respect that interests us, we must provide a clarification that is small but important for our topic, one that relies on the history of translating the concept of *Allgemeingültigkeit* into Russian. This term has at least two interpretations in Russian conceptual language: (1) the interpretation deriving from I. Kant and the Baden Neo-Kantians, and (2) the one deriving from Rudolf Hermann Lotze and phenomenology. In the former case, this term was passed down as "universally binding" [*obshcheobiazatel'nost'*] or "universality" [*vseobshchnost'*], while the latter emphasized the significance of the content of knowledge in itself. By virtue of intertwining these traditional uses of the term in German philosophy, Russian translations acquired not only the two aforementioned meanings ("universally binding" and "universality"), but also a third, "universal validity" [*obshchegodnost'*]. This is the word most often used by Shpet, following in Yurkevich's footsteps (see Shpet 2014, 30).

The basis of the concept *Gültigkeit* (from *gelten*) indicates both a reality and a norm, which is why the term *Allgemeingültigkeit* was so appealing to Russian philosophers, but also so difficult to translate, since normative and ontological concepts are generally distinguished in the Russian language. As a result, Russian philosophical language adopted the neologism we find in Vladimir Solovyov: "universal significance" [*obshcheznachimost'*]. This concept emphasizes the gnoseological aspects of knowledge while capturing not only its universality, but also its involvement of conversation [*obshchenie*]: the general [*obshchee*] is understood as "the universal" [*obshchnoe*], which emerges in conversation and is intended for conversation. In that context, the concept of "the self-integrity of knowledge" becomes a kind of correlate of *Allgemeingültigkeit*, given that it emphasizes not only the practical usefulness of knowledge, that is, its applicability, and not only its compulsory normativity, but also its value for human conversation.

The Epistemological Debate over "the Self-Integrity of Knowledge"

It was in the pages of the journal *Voprosy filosofii* that an intense polemic over the ontological status of knowledge arose (see Pruzhinin et al. 2016). Some participants (e.g., Vladimir P. Filatov and Vladimir N. Porus) argued that the concept of "self-integrity" characterizes only the social dimensions of knowledge and has no relation to its cognitive parameters. Others, including the authors of this chapter, argued that knowledge (as a cultural-historical phenomenon) must have a certain form of being within the framework of cultural-historical consciousness. Knowledge must be expressed in order to be "comprehended," that is, it must acquire a verbal density, a corporeality, and therefore a semantic determinacy, a concreteness, while also retaining the qualitative features of knowledge about the world. It is this correlation of the ontological and epistemological status of knowledge that is captured by the word "self-integrity," allowing us to specify the human sciences today in a way that preserves their scienticity and universal significance. Furthermore, the self-integrity is inextricably linked with the idea of recognition [*Anerkennung*], which has become widespread in epistemological interpretations of hermeneutics (see Mikeshina 2016; Shul'ga 2002). After all, in conversations and discussions, understanding becomes possible only when meaning is implied, comprehended, and recognized by all communicating parties, whether the context be a scientific debate, a philosophical conversation, or a translation of meaning from language to language.

Posing the issue by initiating an appeal to the Russian philosophical tradition opens up additional opportunities for epistemological research on the changes that activities related to science and cognition are currently undergoing. From the point of view that we have presented, scientists who aim at obtaining concrete results achieve a level of universal significance only when their conversation itself obtains the status of a self-sufficing cultural value, only when it is deployed for its own sake (see Reed 2010). This kind of methodological pivot allows us to bring those existential aspects of cognition that relate to personal motivation (which, incidentally, correlate with anthropological issues as presented by Sergei S. Horujy, who relies on the Russian philosophical tradition [see Horujy 2015]) into modern epistemology's field of vision. After all, it is precisely the fact that conversation obtained the status of a recognized cultural value in the Greek polis that created the conditions for the emergence of European science as a phenomenon.

BASIC SCIENCE AND APPLIED RESEARCH: BETWEEN CONVERSATION AND COMMUNICATIONS (ON "TRADING ZONES" AND "SPHERE OF CONVERSATION" ["SFERA RAZGOVORA"])

Meanwhile, in modern commodified science (both natural and social/human sciences), where science is transformed into commerce, conversation incurs a cost while simultaneously losing its cultural value. One consequence of this process is the transformation, and sometimes even the destruction, of intra-science communications,[2] which stimulates attempts to comprehend the changes taking place, including those located within the framework of epistemology. Peter Galison's introduction of the concept of "trading zones" (Galison 1999) provided the opportunity for a recent discussion (see Pruzhinin et al. 2017) that attempted an epistemological analysis of scientific communications relevant to the topic of this article. During this discussion, reference to the Russian philosophical tradition demonstrated a very high degree of conceptual effectiveness. The appeal to Russian philosophy's epistemological style indeed allowed for making clear distinctions between conversation among scientists and communicative contacts, the latter as an *informational trade* that is always subject to applicable goals.

The immediate occasion for this discussion was the ambivalence of this concept of "trading zones" in Galison's work. In his research on interdisciplinary communications, Galison had to face the fact that the cognitive process could not be viewed as the result of any individual experience, be it sensory or rational, and he states that communications literally permeate the content of cognitive processes. Describing the scientific-cognitive situation that emerges here, he introduces the metaphor "trading zone," where experts who speak and think in different languages are able to communicate. Relying on this metaphor, he attempted to answer a very concrete question about scientific research: how and to what extent do communications define the content of knowledge?

This question, however, also has a more universally applicable philosophical sense. Classical epistemology assessed the role of communications critically, believing that they disrupt the cognitive process as it takes place in a particular subject. Consequently, the classical (mostly positivist) philosophy of science saw its task as elaborating the standards that, among other things, would be able to inhibit the influence of communications on the process of cognition. This way of viewing knowledge has simply lost its meaning in regard to modern science, with its system of interdisciplinary interactions, its enormous laboratories, its flows of information exchange, and so forth. It is for precisely this reason that philosophical comprehension of the issues that arise here, including those in Russian philosophy, today belongs to the context of notions of neo-classical epistemology (see Lektorsky 2001). At the same time, the most popular view both in Russia and abroad is that of communications' role in cognition, based once again on ideas from social epistemology. This view proposes a sociologized treatment of scientific communications as a natural element in what is essentially the social phenomenon of cognition. However, a different interpretation of the nature of intra-science communications is possible, one that accounts for the cultural status of knowledge in addition to its social status. In that case, the fundamental factor in interpreting the cognitive role of communications is the scientist's value orientation, one that provides communications with an additional status, the status of cultural value, that is, represents them as a form of conversation that is valuable in itself. The themes of "positive philosophy on Russian soil" resound clearly in that interpretation.

The problem is that sociocultural contexts force modern epistemologists to turn their attention to the issues of scientific communications that essentially synthesize all the changes taking place in science from an angle that is highly relevant for modern science. In the course of scientific research and the social use of its results, the communicative gaps between scientists of different specializations must be overcome, not to mention those between scientists and engineers, businessmen, government officials, politicians, and various social strata. Collective forms of cognitive scientific work, the structure of science as a social institution, the role of science in society, and the relationship of society to science, that is, its sociocultural status, are all changing intensively today. One way or another, all of these changes are being projected onto scientific communications. Embroiled in addressing concrete social tasks, science is increasingly acquiring the features of applied research. As a result, the notion of an obtained result's truth is being supplanted in the minds of scientists by the notion of its practical effectiveness. The bulk of basic research has, for obvious reasons, been relegated to the margins of science as a socioeconomic system. Philosophy, which, incidentally, emerged in the same (Greek) cultural atmosphere as science, now faces the question of how to combine truth with effectiveness. The philosophical subtext of this question is whether science can abandon truth and remain science, the most important component of European culture.

Any philosopher of cognition today would agree with this assessment of the situation. The divergences begin with choosing an epistemological strategy for addressing it, and these divergences already appear very clearly in interpretations of Galison's proposed metaphor of "trading zones." Galison offers an analogy to an ancient type of trade that used cowry shells, which were widespread in the Mediterranean. How are these shells exchanged when each tribe projects its own meaning into what they represent? One group considers them to be simply money. The second group considers them an ornamental element. The third views them as repositories of their ancestors' souls. However, they all use these shells for trade. The question is how the communicative zone that provides for this trade takes shape.

The strategy provided by social epistemology for answering this question suggests that mutual understanding arises during the communicative interaction of various languages based not on theoretical considerations but on purely practical ones. Hence, the supporters of social epistemology suggest the term "trading zone," that is, a literal zone of trade. Accordingly, the focus of epistemology, which seeks to be practically effective, should be issues related to the social and human science technologies of scientific communicability. These technologies do not provide for an expansion of the sphere of knowledge nor of the content of knowledge itself, but, given collaborative cognitive acts, they only contribute to an external mutual understanding sufficient for addressing the applicable goals.

Should we adopt this interpretation of Galison's metaphor, however, we find ourselves faced with the question of who, precisely, represents the subject of conversation in this "trading zone," whether it be a Mediterranean market or modern science. From the perspective of social epistemology, we find that communicative contact occurs among the goods themselves or among fragments from the body of available knowledge that use people for their interactions and sometimes even do without them by virtue of the achievements of modern information technology. From the perspective of cultural-historical epistemology, communicative contact occurs among persons who cognize the world, experts from different fields of knowledge, with different languages and different images of the world, but nevertheless *people* who consider conversation to be, among other things, valued in itself. It is thanks to this mindset that they achieve a mutual understanding on whose basis they can address even the more practical tasks. Incidentally, it is Galison himself who constructs this metaphor invoking a cultural situation, and that invocation is not just an analogy, but also an attempt to comprehend the practice of interdisciplinary interactions in science. These interactions require an understanding of the Other, and the cultural interpretation of the trading zone is an attempt to show forms of conversation that are built on certain pragmatic goals, that is, they assume the cultural value of knowledge, not just its cost. This, among other things, is a condition for the existence of science as the foundational element of European culture.

Unlike social epistemology, cultural-historical epistemology views science not as a "structure of governance" requiring external legal regulation, but as a "civil society" shaping its own levers from within (see Shchedrina 2014, 263). Here, prescriptive methodology gives way to a self-organizing community of experts based on historical experience (including its own personal experience) of methodological comprehension of concrete scientific research that regulates the activity of scholars from within. Cultural-historical epistemology's interpretation of the "trading zone" emphasizes the values of scientific-cognitive activity that ensure that cognition aims at comprehending the world rather than at developing its technologies. In the "trading zone" of interdisciplinary research, this focus is made relevant through the contact of meanings and the contact of languages. In that regard, practical interests by no means exhaust the essence of the issue, since this is more about cognition of the world. Ultimately, science took shape as a kind of universal language, as a means of universally significant utterance about the world, as a language focused on the self-sufficing value of conversation. The cultural-historical interpretation of the "trading zone" suggested here thus returns us to ideas that have already developed in Russian philosophy and demonstrates the effectiveness of bringing them up to date.

Undoubtedly, the sociology of science can demonstrate how we can effectively organize the market of knowledge. Today, however, it is already evident that the most important condition for successful functioning of science (and of the education system associated with it) is whether scientific-cognitive activity has a cultural dimension built on sociality. As we have already noted, this dimension in Russian philosophy is associated with a particular attitude toward conversation that differs from sociologized communications. Understanding the intrinsic value of conversation opens up new opportunities for research on scientific communications, particularly the prospect of studying the forms of knowledge associated with its semiotic nature. This approach was in fact developed in early twentieth-century Russian humanist thought (in the works of Shpet, Florensky, Jakobson, and Vygotsky). The semiotic understanding of knowledge served as a basis for developing methods of structural analysis in linguistics, literary criticism, and anthropology. By the mid-twentieth century, structuralist approaches in the human sciences came under increasing criticism. The main object of that criticism was the formalism in structuralist methodology, which excluded the historical dimension when examining human phenomena: synchrony at the expense of diachrony, statics at the expense of dynamics. However, a return to the philosophical sources of Russian structuralism and semiotics (i.e., to the tradition of "positive philosophy on Russian soil") shows that not all of the Russian epistemological style's methodological potential was exhausted within the framework of structuralism.

The Cognitive Status of the "Epistemological Style"

In his time, G. Shpet developed the semiotic theme in Russian philosophy in a substantially gnoseological way. His philosophical-phenomenological concept realizes the idea of "holistic knowledge" in its treatment of scientific knowledge as an open semiotic system. According to Roman Jakobson, who developed the ideas of structuralism and semiotics in the human sciences, the most important part of Shpet's concept was the idea of the structure and semiotic nature of an object (see Pruzhinin and Shchedrin 2013, 252–280). Jakobson later applied Shpet's ideas effectively in scientific research on the phenomenon of language (Jakobson 1996), with special interest in precisely this transformation of the idea of semiotics as Jakobson saw it (see Avtonomova 2009). Examining language as a systemic structure, Jakobson presents "the word" only as a formal segment of a language system, which is how he projects Shpet's philosophical ideas into linguistics and introduces the prospect of a specific area of structural research on language and culture. Shpet, incidentally, understood the word as a meaningful element of a holistic system of language and centered his research around the "inner form of the word," that is, the idea of meaning and its reflexively grasped historical evolution in the course of conversation. This methodological course is especially relevant today in the sphere of human cognition, where scientific research on phenomena in the human sciences proves promising only to the extent that the element of formal scienticity does not exclude historicism. The ideas of historical dynamics of meaning have proven particularly productive today in the development of cultural-historical psychology (Lev Vygotsky, Michael D. Cole, Vladimir P. Zinchenko) and in research on the history of concepts (e.g., Koselleck 2006; Bödeker 2002; Timofeev 2016). At the same time, we should note that the first Russian works on the history of concepts came from Shpet's colleague at the State Academy of Artistic Sciences, V.N. Ivanovsky, who began collaborating with André Lalande, editor-in-chief of the *Vocabulaire technique et critique de la philosophie* (1902–1923) in the early 1900s (Shchedrina 2012).

At this point in our discussion of the reasons for the methodological effectiveness of the idea of the historical evolution of meaning as one of the central themes in the Russian philosophical tradition, we would like to draw attention to one of the core ideas of "positive philosophy," that of "holistic knowledge." It is important to remember that the notion of "wholeness" so often used to designate the characteristic feature of Russian philosophy has an established English tradition of being rendered as "integrity" in translations of Russian religious philosophy (Sergeev 2017). We believe that this English word does not entirely express what Russian philosophers have in mind. The issue is that the English word "integrity" and its Russian calque "*integrativnyi*" are based on the Latin *integratio* (restoration, replenishment), which signifies "unification" or "interpenetration" in Russian. Thus, the original state of integral knowledge is "separate" and only later "restored" or "replenished," which takes for granted the unification of separately existing elements into a whole. However, the "whole, holistic knowledge" of the Russian philosophical tradition is not knowledge "restored" from its parts, but an indivisible knowledge, a knowledge indissoluble into separate elements, a self-evident knowledge that requires "grasping," "understanding" in conversation, in the "*sphere of conversation*" (see Pruzhinin and Shchedrina 2017b). This is the only kind of knowledge that has a concrete nature within the framework of "positive philosophy," the only kind that, as we noted above, is directed toward conversation. At the same time, we feel it is important to emphasize that this direction began to take shape in the religious-philosophical works of Ivan Kireevskii, Vladimir Solovyov, and Yurkevich, acquiring its concrete-logical and phenomenological-hermeneutic features in the works of M.I. Karinskii, Shpet, and others.

In principle, this was the general mindset of Russian philosophers from Yurkevich to Vl. Solovyov, who combined their critique of positivism with the idea of the self-integrity of knowledge (see Nemeth 2013, 2015), both before the expulsion of Russian thinkers from the country in 1922 and later, through the Soviet "men of the sixties" and to the present day (see Pruzhinin et al. 2016). For our purposes, it is important to note that the development of this mindset was accompanied by the emergence of a special type of philosophical-methodological comprehension of cognition, a special form of representing it and successively translating it. This is the form that we have designated a "style," the special epistemological style of Russian philosophy. To give a more precise understanding of the meaning of this concept as it applies to our topic, we will turn to Shpet's reasoning on this issue.

When discussing the dynamics of thought, Shpet argued,

> [T]he *style* of a given era or a given generation is predetermined by the spiritual life of the previous generation; the new one attempts to use existing forms to convey its new spiritual content, but as its expression is new, it destroys and transforms the inherited forms […] until it reaches new ones, which are destined for destruction by succeeding generations. Style, therefore, is not about constructive forms, nor about purely expressive ones, but about their relationship, that is, their internal expressive forms. (Shpet n.d.)

In the context of modern philosophical-methodological questions, we can further clarify this description of style. In both the cultural-historical interpretation of the processes of scientific cognition and the semiotic characteristics of its results, Shpet directs us to the Word, to a linguistic reality filled with meaning. Only in the former case does he mean knowledge as a true opinion expressed for the Other in the process of conversation (what Shpet understood as "expression"). In the latter case, he means the continuous semantic overflow of the expression of knowledge, which by its very essence is intended as a message to the Other, but which in the dynamics of cognition always extends beyond established linguistic forms and their already defined meanings. The sense of knowledge that we wish to communicate never fits within the existing linguistic forms. The word is able to extend beyond developed meaning and symbolically point toward something greater in its content. This "greater" within the word is revealed through style as the feature of an additional semantic layer of conversation, as the level of conversation that actually requires understanding.

With this clarification in mind, the expression "the epistemological style of Russian philosophy," or more broadly "the epistemological style in Russian intellectual culture," thus means that the cultural-historical approach to modern Russian epistemological thought views knowledge and cognition primarily in their semantic dimension. Moreover, it means that the epistemological approach itself expresses the results of its research according to this style, which extends beyond the theoretical constructions of traditional normative epistemology. These features require us to understand that this is the means by which epistemology comprehends dynamics in science, overcoming the relativistic dead ends of sociologized theories of cognition and the limitations of normative structures in traditional philosophy of science.

We should note that the concept of "styles of scientific thought" had already been introduced into the epistemological current in the early twentieth century by researchers themselves (M. Born and L. Fleck) to comprehend (so to speak) their place in the dynamics of science, to clarify their own cultural-historical coordinates. Eventually, however, this concept was usurped in philosophy of science by the notion of "paradigms." This arrived alongside a loss of attention in philosophy of science to the most important dimension of scientific-cognitive activity, the scientists' own comprehension of the unity of the semantic field in which they work in a particular historical period. One aspect of the notion of paradigm that replenished that loss of a semantic foundation for the historical unity of the scientific community was the sociologization of mechanisms that provide for consensus among members of that community. However, the limitless relativization of knowledge that accompanies this kind of idea makes any methodological claims by philosophy of science meaningless. Unlike sociologization, the concept of a style of scientific thought contained, from the very beginning: first, an idea that cognition has an internal semantic wholeness (its historicity) that is realized in its style, a set of specific features of language in various periods of scientific development; and second, the idea of polyvariance, a stylistic diversity of expression in the scientific language of knowledge concerning the same fragment of the world. Today, these ideas are opening up new horizons for philosophical-methodological reflection on science, and it is this idea of turning to the history of the formation of these ideas that allows us to discover the methodological potential contained in them.

Born used the expression "the style of scientific thought" primarily for the integrated set of features he saw in what was then a new phase of development in physics (related to the theory of relativity and quantum mechanics). At the same time, he interpreted a universal methodological and scientific meaning into this concept:

> I do not suggest that, apart from mathematics, there are any principles which are unchangeable, a priori in the strictest sense. But I think that there are general attitudes of the mind which change very slowly and constitute definite philosophical periods with characteristic ideas in all branches of human activities, science included. Pauli, in a recent letter to me, has used the expression "styles," styles of thinking, styles not only in art, but also in science. Adopting this term, I maintain that physical theory has its styles and that its principles derive from this fact a kind of stability. They are, so to speak, relatively a priori with respect to that

period. If you are aware of the style of your own time you can make some cautious predictions. You can at least reject ideas which are foreign to the style of your time. (Born 1966, 113–114 [1956, 123–124])

HISTORICISM AS THE FOUNDATIONAL PRINCIPLE OF COGNITION: A DISCUSSION OF RECONSTRUCTIONS

As we have tried to show, the epistemological style of "positive philosophy on Russian soil" returns us to ideas whose conceptual potential and methodological applicability open up new horizons for research. Another area in human sciences research where this style has been demonstrating its effectiveness is history (in all its aspects, from historical science to history of philosophy) (see Kitcher 2011; Stroud 2011). Our discussion about reconstructions (see Pruzhinin et al. 2018) opens up interesting methodological possibilities here. The focus of modern Russian researchers has been the nexus of issues related to the epistemological status of methods for reconstructing historical knowledge. What are the features of using these methods in fields of knowledge related to the human sciences, such as history, sociology, philology, or textology? In terms of reconstructive strategies, features that mainly relate to the processes of pragmatization of modern science have come to the forefront today. The goals of reconstruction were set beyond the scope of actual cognitive activity, while the formal aspects of using reconstructive methods receded into the background. Modern methodological debate centered on whether reconstruction was appropriate for technological, social, or ideological purposes (i.e., external to cognition as such). As a result, historical reconstructions began to be treated as constructs that fundamentally relativize knowledge.

It is especially notable that this trend of "relativizing" reconstruction manifested itself in the field of methodology of social-human sciences, and in the field of methodology of historical cognition in particular, and as a result, interpretations of reconstructive strategies have acquired shades of postmodernism. At the same time, against the backdrop of pragmatizing interpretations of reconstruction, another feature of reconstructive procedures that was previously evident but not very important from an instrumental point of view has come to the fore: their interpretative nature (see Pruzhinin and Shchedrina 2014). This has put their focus on understanding the meaning of past events at the forefront of reconstructive strategies.

On the one hand, treating the reconstruction of a given event as an interpretation situates reconstructive procedures within the tradition of hermeneutical methodology, and on the other hand, it emphasizes the possibility of cultural-historical reflection on the grounds for their specific use. Reconstructing past events does not, in this case, represent constructing images of reality under certain pragmatic goals (goals somewhat external to cognition), but as a purposeful interpretive strategy included in the history of cognition of a given historical event. In other words, it provides for the possibility of historicizing the consciousness of the researcher himself, by virtue of which the researcher who consciously applies the methods of reconstruction necessarily relates himself to the history of cognition of the reconstructed event and to the history of scientific cognition as a whole (i.e., to the third millennium of confronting various versions of relativized knowledge about the world). Most importantly, however, a focus toward understanding the meaning of the event allows the researcher to avoid psychologism; by immersing himself in the reconstructed reality, he reflexively records his ideas, aspirations, intuitions, and methodological convictions and compares them with interpretations that exist in history as expressed either by those who participated in the events themselves or by historians. This approach opens up additional opportunities for identifying an event's significant context and includes the researcher himself in the living history of cognition.

What we in fact propose is to examine historical reconstruction as a tool necessary for historicizing the consciousness of the researcher, who realizes during the act of reconstruction that he is attempting to understand reality and bears responsibility for that before science, before its history, before the preceding generations of scholars, and before the future, ultimately before culture. At the same time, this "historicizing" expansion of the methodological treatment of reconstruction contains a means (so to speak) for opposing various kinds of arbitrary, "relativizing" factors. This methodological "means" was once described with great accuracy by Shpet in his works on hermeneutics: the "closure" of context in which one views a reconstructed reality and selects what is significant for the event within that context. Modern reconstructive methodological strategies in textology and translation studies provide a vivid example of this kind of "closure." The researcher must clearly indicate the range of evidence on which he relies, constructing his conscious reality and indicating what makes our interpretive reconstruction defensible. This does not mean that other interpretations are impossible, but the creation of other interpretive reconstructions requires an equally conscious change in the contextual configuration in which the other research is examining the given text. Obviously, this leads to a great number of epistemological issues related to determining and defending the choice of contexts, but this is what scholarly work entails, and these problems are solved not abstractly and for all time, but through, shall we say, the historical movement of our knowledge: the author's competence and his ability to grasp the meaning of the event.

We believe it is necessary to reemphasize something here. By "historical reconstruction," we understand not only the recreation of a past reality and all of its details in "our era," not only the copying of it down to the most insignificant detail, and definitely not role-play with past events (in the social, psychological, or "material" versions of assimilating or "living through" the past). Obviously, this all plays an auxiliary, supportive role when shaping knowledge about the past. By referring to historical reconstruction, we mean the use of reconstruction to clarify the meaning of verbal matter that represents the sole means by which the past is given to us. We therefore emphasize the role of reflection on the part of the researchers, as reflection provides an

20 A RETURN TO TRADITION: THE EPISTEMOLOGICAL STYLE IN RUSSIA'S... 439

understanding of the language through which the past speaks to us. In history, we are primarily interested in the particular verbal fabric that we are trying to understand today from the perspective of our own contemporaneity. We are aware of the limitations of our ability to understand the past "as it was" in all its fullness, but we refine our idea of it, expanding it and documenting the cultural-historical context in which a given event took place, essentially reconstructing it as intelligible. We understand language in precisely the same way: we must have "conversation" with the past.

There is one more epistemological aspect to this topic. Strangely enough, if you tell someone today that he supports the Leninist theory of reflection, he will likely protest and react with forceful denial. When it comes to reconstruction as a method of historical cognition, however, there are objections suggesting that the historical past should only be "copied" or "photographed" in full accordance with precisely this Leninist theory of reflection. This understanding of knowledge, much less of history, was abandoned in the 1960s even within the literature of Marxist philosophy. Nevertheless, this position continues to reappear from time to time, most often among philologists, particularly when it comes to publishing manuscripts, drafts, or epistolary materials. In our own experience with publication, preparing handwritten materials for the press always involves a reconstruction, sometimes a radical one, for which the person working with the texts is ultimately responsible. Even then, instead of discussions and critiques of the reconstruction itself, we hear that it is necessary simply to take the original text and copy it as is. In the first place, this would still not be a mere copy of the original: it would be a reconstruction. It is not the original document, let alone all its details, like the state of the manuscript, the handwriting itself, editing by the author or by someone other than the author, the quotation marks, and other editors' intrusions. In the second place, we would ask: why bother publishing something under the pretense that it is a copy? Clarifying deciphered "non-texts" (i.e. not complete texts) means working with the original or, in extreme cases, a facsimile. If the philosopher aims to understand the meaning, then the ideas represented in the reconstruction are sufficient for him, and a readable text is necessary if he is to evaluate that meaning.

This is of fundamental importance to philosophy because it is focused on meaning. It is not even the word that is reproduced per se, but the meaning that is reproduced. We understand why, for example, we devote special attention to the marginal edits, drawings, and working details in Pushkin's manuscripts, because they illustrate the poet's creative process, his precise selections of rhymes, his words. It is the published copy that allows the illustration of this process: a reconstruction focused on making the work relevant, that is, a reconstruction intended for certain purposes, whether academic, educational, or other purposes. If the goal in this particular case is historical knowledge as such, then one must turn to the original, to the archive, but because this is a question of meaning, it must always be identified in the text with the aid of interpretative strategies of reconstruction. The same applies to translations:

translation is always a reconstruction. This is why there are new translations every 50 years or so that bring the original works of interest up to date. Reconstruction is continuous work by generations of human scientists. It is historical work, and it is through this historicism that it stands in opposition to arbitrariness.

The reconstruction method has acquired particular relevance and effectiveness in studies on the history of Russian philosophy (see Janzen 2002). After all, the nature of that history has been vividly expressed as "an interrupted flight." Today, there is an enormous array of archives, epistolary materials, drafts, and much more that is changing our understanding of works published by Russian philosophers in the first half of the twentieth century. The creation of a new viewpoint on our philosophical heritage has been facilitated by the project *Russian Philosophy of the 20th Century* [*Filosofiia Rossii XX veka*],[3] which has, since 2010, issued 49 volumes: 22 volumes in the series *Russian Philosophy of the First Half of the 20th Century* [*Filosfiia Rossii vtoroi poloviny XX veka*] (edited by Vladislav A. Lektorsky) and 27 volumes on Russian philosophy from 1900 to 1950 (edited by Boris I. Pruzhinin). Several hundred philosophers (epistemologists, ethicists, philosophers of religion, methodologists, historians of philosophy, phenomenologists, etc.) have taken part in these publications. They emphasize the modern resonance of ideas of Russian philosophers, on the one hand, by inscribing them into present-day philosophical issues and, on the other, by disclosing their real historical meaning with the aid of archival research. In the process of modern historical-philosophical reflection on the existential origins of Russian philosophers' theoretical ideas, the authors involved in this project have carried out epistemological analysis of archival materials and contemporaneous responses to these philosophers' works. This pivot allows a rethinking of the methodological status of archival work. In any case, it has illustrated the inevitability of rejecting the rigid boundaries between the individual archives of Russian philosophers (the archives of Florensky, Losev, Shpet, and others) and demonstrated the effectiveness of an "Archive of Epoch" for research, that is, a holistic archive in which the meaning of the era and the voice of each participant in the philosophical "*sphere of conversation*" is considered in the context of historical-philosophical reconstructions of the thematic preferences of those participants.[4]

CONCLUSION

This chapter's discussion of contemporary issues in epistemology shows that knowledge and cognition remain the foundation of the European philosophical tradition (which includes the voice of "positive philosophy on Russian soil"). Modern epistemologists are seeking new opportunities for a specific standardization of cognition, given that the existence of rational norms represents at least a necessary condition for the existence of science, if not a sufficient one. This is why we consider it extremely important to seek out those means of uniting reason with broader sociocultural contexts that would allow us to preserve the status of reason in culture, society, and science. We believe this is the central positive task of Russian philosophy today. It is precisely for experience with that kind of reflection that we return to the epistemological style of the Russian intellectual tradition.

Translated by Brad Damaré

NOTES

1. The English word "holistic" was not coined until the 1920s, so earlier English translations of philosophers like Shpet and Vladimir Solovyov used "integral," which has become the traditional rendering of *tsel'nyi* in these works. However, as the authors discuss later in the chapter, "integral" fails to capture the essence of *tsel'nyi*, so, by editing this text, we have opted for "holistic" as the more accurate, better "reconstructed" option available today.—Ed.
2. In this section, the authors use two words that mean "communication": *obshchenie*, which can also suggest a more generally associative activity, and *kommunikatsiia*, a loanword describing the process of transmitting information. Both could be translated as "communication" in the context of this article, but to keep the ideas distinct without resorting to imprecise synonyms, *obshchenie* has been rendered as singular "communication" to emphasize the former's more general concept, and *kommunikatsiia* as plural "communications" to emphasize the latter's nature as transmissions.—Ed.
3. More than 200 Russian and foreign scholars of Russian philosophy took part in this project.
4. We find this kind of experiment in historical-philosophical reconstruction of archival materials in the book by Tatiana G. Shchedrina (2008) that demonstrates new possibilities of applying Shpet's methodology to historical-philosophical research.

BIBLIOGRAPHY

Avtonomova, Natalia S. 2009. *Otkrytaia struktura: Jakobson-Bakhtin-Lotman-Gasparov*. Moscow: ROSSPEN.

Bödeker, Hans Erich, ed. 2002. *Begriffsgeschichte, Diskursgeschichte, Metapherngeschichte*. Göttingen: Wallstein Verlag.

Born, Max. 1966. Die begriffliche Situation in der Physik. In *Physik im Wandel meiner Zeit*, 113–131 [Russian Translation: 1963. Sostoianie idei v fizike. In *Fizika v zhizni moego pokoleniia*. Moscow: Inostrannaia literatura.] [English Translation: 1956. The Conceptual Situation in Physics and the Prospects of Its Future Development. In *Physics in My Generation*, 123–139. London: Pergamon Press.]

Gaidenko, Piama P. 2002. *Vladimir Solovyov i filosofiia Serebrianogo veka*. Moscow: Progress-Traditsiia.

Galison, Peter. 1999. Trading Zone: Coordinating Action and Belief. In *The Science Studies Reader*, ed. Mario Biagioli, 137–160. New York: Routledge.

Goldman, Alvin. 1999. *Knowledge in a Social World*. New York: Oxford University Press.

Grot, Nikolai Ya. 1889. O zadachakh zhurnala. *Voprosy filosofii i psikhologii* 1: v–xx.

Horujy, Sergei S. 2015. *Practices of the Self and Spiritual Practices: Michel Foucault and the Eastern Christian Discourse*. Edited and with an Introduction by Christina Stoeckl. Translated by Boris Jakim. Grand Rapids, MI: W. B. Eerdmans Publ. Co.

Janzen, Vladimir. 2002. Pis'ma russkikh myslitelei v bazel'skom archive Fritsa Liba. In *Isseldovaniia po istorii russkoi mysli: Ezhegodnik za 2001–2002 gody*, 227–563. Tri kvadrata: Moscow.

Kasavin, Ilya. 2017. Towards a Social Philosophy of Science: Russian Prospects. *Social Epistemology* 31 (1): 1–15.

Kitcher, Philip. 2011. Epistemology Without History Is Blind. *Erkenntnis* 75 (3): 505–524. (Special Issue: "What (Good) Is Historical Epistemology?")

Koselleck, Reinhart. 2006. *Begriffsgeschichten. Studien zur Semantik und Pragmatik der politischen und sozialen Sprache*. Frankfurt am Main: Suhrkamp Verlag.

Lektorsky, Vladislav A. 2001. *Epistemologiia klassicheskaia i neklassicheskaia*. Moscow: Editorial URSS.

———. 2010. Realism, Antirealism, Constructivism, and Constructive Realism in Contemporary Epistemology and Science. *Journal of Russian and East European Psychology* 48: 5–44.

Mikeshina, Liudmila A. 2016. *Sovremennaia epistemologiia gumanitarnogo znaniia: mezhdistsiplinarnye sintezy*. Moscow: ROSSPEN.

Motroshilova, Nelly V. 2013. Nikolai Berdyaev: filosofiia zhizni kak filosofiia dukkha i zapadnaia mysl' XX v. In *Nikolai Aleksandrovich Berdyaev*, ed. Vladimir N. Porus, 331–366. (Serial "Filosofiia Rossii pervoi poloviny XX veka.") Moscow: ROSSPEN.

Nemeth, Thomas. 2013. *The Early Solov'ëv and His Quest for Metaphysics*. Archives Internationales d'Histoire des Idées. Cham: Springer.

———, ed. 2015. *Vladimir Solov'ëv's Justification of the Moral Good*. Translated by Thomas Nemeth. Cham: Springer.

Parshin, Alexei N. 2013. Lesnitsa otrazhenii (ot gnoseologii k antropologii). In *Pavel Aleksandrovich Florenskii*, ed. A.N. Parshin and O.M. Sedykh, 156–178. (Serial "Filosofiia Rossii pervoi poloviny XX veka.") Moscow: ROSSPEN.

Popova, Varvara S. 2015. Logicheskie issledovaniia Gustav Shpeta v kontekste sovremennykh filosofsko-metodologicheskikh diskussii (razmyshleniia nad knigoi 'Istoriia kak problema logiki'). *Voprosy filosofii* 9: 162–170.

Pruzhinin, Boris I., and Tatiana G. Shchedrina, eds. 2013. *Epistemologicheskii stil' v russkoi intellektual'noi kul'ture XIX–XX vekov: Ot lichnosti k traditsii*. Moscow: ROSSPEN.

———, eds. 2014. *Sovremennye metodologichestkie strategii: Interpretatsiia. Konventsiia. Perevod*. Moscow: Politicheskaia entsiklopediia.

———. 2017a. The Ideas of Cultural–Historical Epistemology in Russian Philosophy of the Twentieth Century. *Social Epistemology* 31 (1): 16–24.

———. 2017b. On the Specifics of Russian Philosophy: A Reply to Mikhail Sergeev. *Social Epistemology Review and Reply Collective* 6 (8): 37–41.

Pruzhinin, Boris I., N.S. Avtonomova, V.A. Bazhanov, I.N. Griftsova, I.T. Kasavin, V.N. Kniazev, V.A. Lektorsky, V.L. Makhlin, L.A. Mikeshina, P.A. Olkhov, V.N. Porus, G.V. Sorina, V.P. Filatov, and T.G. Shchedrina. 2016. Dostoinstvo znaniia kak problema sovremennoi epistemologii. Roundtable Discussion. *Voprosy filosofii* 8: 20–56.

20 A RETURN TO TRADITION: THE EPISTEMOLOGICAL STYLE IN RUSSIA'S... 443

Pruzhinin, Boris I., A.Yu. Antonovskii, N.N. Voronina, I.I. Griftsova, A.M. Dorozhkin, I.T. Kasavin, E.V. Maslanov, I.D. Nevvazhai, S.V. Pirozhkova, T.D. Sokolova, G.V. Sorina, O.E. Stoliarova, T.G. Shchedrina, and B.G. Yudin. 2017. Kommunikatsii v nauke: epistemologicheskie, sotsiokul'turnye, infrastrukturnye aspekty. Roundtable Discussion. *Voprosy filosofii* 11: 23–52.

Pruzhinin, Boris I., F.E. Azhimov, I.I. Bendersky, P.A. Datsenko, A.V. Zagumennov, N. .A. Kazhaeva, L. .A. Mikeshina, E. .N. Motovnikova, P.A. Olkhov, D. .V. Ratushina, R.Iu. Sabancheev, A. .G. Shushkina, I.O. Shchedrina, and T.G. Shchedrina. 2018. Istoricheskaia rekonstruktsiia v gumanitarnykh issledovaniiakh: metodologicheskie vozmozhnosti i problemy. Roundtable Discussion. *Voprosy filosofii* 5: 5–42.

Reed, Isaac Ariail. 2010. Epistemology Contextualized: Social-Scientific Knowledge in a Postpositivist Era. *Sociological Theory* 28 (1): 20–39.

Sergeev, Mikhail. 2017. 'Integral Knowledge' and Enlightenment Rationalism: A Reply to Pruzhinin and Shchedrina. *Social Epistemology Review and Reply Collective* 6 (4): 1–3.

Shchedrina, Tatiana G. 2008. *Arkhiv epokhi: tematicheskoe edinstvo russkoi filosofii*. Moscow: ROSSPEN.

———. 2012. Vladimir Ivanovskii i Gustav Shpet: metodologicheskii proekt 'istorii poniatii. *Voprosy filosofii* 11: 10–18.

———. 2014. Kul'turno-istoricheskaia epistemologiia i sotsial'naia epistemologiia: Dva puti k real'nosti. In *Kul'turno-istoricheskaia epistemologiia: problemy i perspektivy. K 70-letiiu Borisa Isaevicha Pruzhinina*, ed. N.S. Avtonomova and T.G. Shchedrina, 262–272. Moscow: Politicheskaia entsiklopediia.

Shchedrina, T.G., and B.I. Pruzhinin. 2017. The Historicism of Lev Shestov and Gustav Shpet. *Russian Studies in Philosophy* 55 (5): 336–349.

Shpet, Gustav G. 2005. Filosofiia i istoriia. In *Mysl' i Slovo. Izbrannye trudy*, ed. T.G. Shchedrina, 191–200. Moscow: ROSSPEN.

———. 2014. *Istoriia kak problema logiki. Kriticheskie i metodologicheskie issledovaniia. Chast' pervaya. Materialy*. Moscow: Universitetskaia kniga.

———. n.d. *Konspekty rabot raznykh avtorov*. OR RGB, f. 718, k. 7, ed. khr. 10.

Shul'ga, Elena N. 2002. *Kognitivnaia germenevtika*. Moscow: IF RAN.

Stroud, Barry. 2011. Epistemology, the History of Epistemology, Historical Epistemology. *Erkenntnis* 75 (3): 495–503. (Special Issue: What (Good) Is Historical Epistemology?).

Timofeev, Dmitrii V. 2016. Metodologiia 'istorii poniatii': ot teorii k praktike issledovanii istorii obshchestvennoi mysli Rossii pervoi chetverti XIX veka. *Novoe proshloe* 4: 155–168.

Yakobson (Jakobson), Roman O. 1996. Moskovskii lingvisticheskii kruzhok. Edited by M.I. Shapir. *Philologica* 3 (5/7): 361–379.

PART II

Philosophy in Dialogue with Literature and Art

CHAPTER 21

The Russian Novel as a Medium of Moral Reflection in the Long Nineteenth Century

Lina Steiner

THE EDUCATION OF THE RUSSIAN NOVEL

Russian novels have long enjoyed the reputation of being serious "novels of ideas," whose primary goal is not to provide pleasant distraction, but to impel their readers to reflect on moral and social questions. Already in the first Western monograph on the Russian novel, E.M. de Vogüé remarked about Gogol, Turgenev, Tolstoy, and Dostoevsky: "None of these novelists sets himself a purely literary goal. All of their work is governed by a double concern: for truth and for justice" (de Vogüé 1913, 341). Those familiar with twentieth-century Russian novels would agree that the same observation could apply to Boris Pasternak, Alexander Solzhenitsyn, Vasilii Grossman, and many other Soviet novelists. As contemporary critics point out, although Russian literature has long caught up with West European literature in terms of formal inventiveness, it has retained its comparatively archaic sociocultural function as the medium of *paideia*.

> Literature was predominantly understood as something of a "textbook of life" or a "theory of life," and the process of autonomization of the literary-aesthetic field from those of politics, society, and the broader culture that was in evidence in Western Europe throughout the nineteenth century seems to have never—nei-

For Peter Roussanov

L. Steiner (✉)
University of Bonn, Bonn, Germany
e-mail: lsteiner@uni-bonn.de

© The Author(s), under exclusive license to Springer Nature Switzerland AG 2021
M. F. Bykova et al. (eds.), *The Palgrave Handbook of Russian Thought*,
https://doi.org/10.1007/978-3-030-62982-3_21

447

ther in the nineteenth nor in the twentieth century—quite gotten off the ground in Russia. As a result, whereas the evolution of form-oriented approaches to art and literature finds parallels in the West, the specific conditions of Russian historical development stimulated an understanding of literature as intricately woven into the fabric of socio-political life. (Kliger and Maslov 2016, 9)

To understand the pedagogical ambitions of Russian authors one should consider the precipitous character of the country's modernization. Unlike Western Europe, where the Enlightenment emerged out of the Renaissance and Reformation, the Russian Enlightenment in the eighteenth century was imposed by autocratic rulers upon a country whose population consisted mostly of illiterate serfs. Even the gentry, especially in the provinces, remained semiliterate well into the eighteenth century.[1] Russia's first professional writers belonged to court society and were essentially recruited by the state to disseminate the new cultural norms borrowed from Western Europe. Thus the first phase of Russia's modernization unfolded under the sign of neo-classicism.[2] Although a few eighteenth-century thinkers raised their voices against foreign cultural domination, it was not until Napoleon's invasion that an actual nationalist awakening began to occur.[3]

Russia's intellectual mobilization during the first three decades of the nineteenth century unfolded in constant dialogue with German thought. Political alliance with Prussia throughout the Napoleonic wars and the restoration period facilitated cultural exchange, making Russian intellectuals party to both progressive and conservative trends in German thought.[4] Nonetheless, one should be careful not to project intellectual historical categories developed by the students of German thought onto Russia, which had a rather different cultural landscape. In contrast to Germany, where secularization and the Enlightenment had begun before the Wars of the Reformation and were rooted in the European humanistic movement, Russia had no such traditions.[5] Russia's newly emerged professional literature, disseminated through the so-called thick journals, had to make up for both the lack of a native humanistic tradition and the weakness of philosophy, whose status remained fragile until the 1860s.[6]

The novel, which German Romantic criticism established as the leading modern genre, captivated the Russian literary public sphere in the 1830s when historically minded writers set out to align or, rather, realign Russian culture with European modernity. They saw the novel not only as the medium of unencumbered artistic imagination but also as a crucial instrument of identity formation.[7] Neo-classical and sentimental authors, such as Mikhail Kheraskov and Nikolai Karamzin, had already made forays into the genre of the pedagogical narrative (Serman 1959, 1962; Hammamberg 1991). Radishchev, whose radical Enlightenment attack on serfdom, *The Journey from Petersburg to Moscow*, was disguised as a sentimental travelogue à la Sterne, was another important predecessor of nineteenth-century social critical novelists (Lotman 2005, 239–249). He was one of the first Russian authors to secularize devotional literature, transforming hagiography into a vehicle for subjective moral reflection.[8] His banishment to Siberia, however, meant that his work was virtually lost to the public until the 1860s.[9]

The reactionary atmosphere in the wake of the French Revolution made the dissemination of the popular philosophical ideas very difficult, impeding the kind of liberalization of self-consciousness that we observe in Radishchev and in the autobiographical writings of the Masons.[10] Thus during the first quarter of the nineteenth century the literary public sphere was confined to the aristocratic salon society and was dominated by lyric poetry. Divided by the "archaists" versus "innovators" quarrel over literary language and genre, poetry became covertly political.[11] The rapprochement between these factions and their competing visions of cultivated Russianness began in the pages of *The Polar Star*, a Romantic almanac co-edited by the poet Kondratii Ryleev (one of the five executed Decembrists) and the prose writer Alexander Bestuzhev-Marlinskii (another Decembrist, who was sent as a private to the Caucasus where he perished). Addressed to a broader public interested in self-education, this journal included essays, historical works, poetry, Romantic prose fiction, literary and art criticism. However, this publication was too short-lived to fully articulate and transmit its liberal agenda to a wider audience. After the Decembrists' fiasco, the secret society of the *Wisdom Lovers*, the first Russian intellectual circle to engage in a properly philosophical inquiry, did not try to reach out to the broader public (Frede 21–53; Zenkovsky 1953, 1: 132–48). However, the leader of the circle Prince Vladimir Odoevskii did offer a glimpse into the *Wisdom Lovers'* world in his novel *Russian Nights*, a multi-genre Romantic text framed as a dialogue between several friends engaged in a project which early German Romantics would have described as *symphilosophy*.[12]

The idea that literary works should not only improve the readers' taste and offer a pleasant distraction but also promote Russian subjects' conscious quest for enlightenment and self-realization (what German thinkers called *Selbstbildung*) was first cogently articulated by Vissarion Belinsky in his 1834 essay *Literary Reveries* [*Literaturnye mechtaniia*] (Belinsky 1953–1959, 1: 20–104). Taking a cue from Chaadaev's critique of the superficiality of Russian culture, Belinsky argued that despite the existence of quite a few authors and works, contemporary Russia still lacked a genuine national literature. Even the most talented authors, he argued, were culturally dependent on foreign ideas and tastes and therefore could not come into their own (ibid., 87). What Russia still needed was a real, rather than a merely bookish enlightenment, which could be obtained only by facing the unvarnished reality of Russian life (ibid., 101).

It is important to distinguish Belinsky's conception of literature as the medium of self-consciousness immersed in reality from the cruder positivistic versions of realism and naturalism advocated by Nikolai Chernyshevsky, Nikolai Dobrolyubov, and Dmitrii Pisarev in the 1860s. As Lydia Ginzburg has demonstrated, Belinsky's investment in "realism" as a method was bound up with his quest for individual self-realization. Along with other Moscow idealists, he

450   L. STEINER

struggled to transcend the confines of the inward-looking Romantic *Schöneseeligkeit.*[13] The most impoverished among the members of the Stankevich circle, Belinsky was motivated to seek professional success, transforming philosophical studies and philosophically inspired criticism from a private spiritual exercise into a way of life as well as a way to make a living. Having moved to Petersburg, Belinsky quickly achieved prominence as one of the most outspoken contributors to the topical debate on literary nationalism or *narodnost'*. The meaning he attributed to this controversial term, however, was quite different from the one accepted by the official culture. The term *narodnost'* was part of the official ideology promoted by the Minister of Education Count Uvarov, whose "triad" linked it to autocracy and Orthodoxy. Belinsky, on the contrary, understood *narodnost'* not as a nebulous spirit enshrined in religious customs and political institutions, but as poetic creativity expressed through language. Unlike Uvarov's, Belinsky's vision was faithful to the original conception of *Volksgeist* in Wilhelm von Humboldt and Herder, who were also Uvarov's sources.[14] According to Belinsky, to produce works imbued with *narodnost'*, writers had to become less dependent on their European predecessors' opinions and tastes, better informed about Russian history and everyday life, and more willing to trust their own judgement and intuition. In short, they had to become more mature in Kant's sense of the term.[15] Belinsky argued that Pushkin was able to reach this maturity in *Eugene Onegin*, which he hailed as the "encyclopaedia of Russian life," and welcomed Pushkin's Shakespeare-inspired turn to historical drama and prose. Thus, he applied Herder's idea of the historicity of language and literature to the Russian context, suggesting that Russian culture after Pushkin had reached the "manly" age when poetry should give way to prose.[16]

After Pushkin's death, the critic invested his hopes in Lermontov and Gogol. But Lermontov was killed in 1841 at the age of twenty-seven, and Gogol succumbed to a spiritual crisis after the publication of the first part of *Dead Souls*. The only work he was able to complete and publish before his death in 1852 was *Selected Passages from Correspondence with Friends*. These archconservative sermons provoked Belinsky's indignant *Letter to N.V. Gogol*, which was destined to play a fateful role in the life of another author, Dostoevsky.[17]

The 1840s witnessed the emergence of a new cohort of novelists, including Herzen, Goncharov, Dostoevsky, Pisemskii, and other exponents of the "natural" school,[18] whom Belinsky valued highly. Despite this, the mortally ill critic argued in his last annual review of contemporary Russian literature written in 1847 that Russian literature was still in the process of becoming, thus returning to the idea he had expressed in *Literary Reveries*.[19] This was certainly a comment not just on the quality of literature but also on the socio-political drawbacks of a country that had not yet emerged as a nation. While Belinsky's vision of literary history was continuous with the early German Romantic conception of modernity as a new stage in the history of art attained by liberated creative individuality, his political vision was shaped by Hegel's philosophy of right. What grieved him most of all was lawlessness and the abuse of power throughout Russia. Belinsky saw the literary enlightenment as crucial for preparing Russian subjects to become citizens in a rational state based on a constitution. Literary prose was supposed to change Russian readers' mental habits by demystifying their consciousness, teaching them to doubt the narratives handed down by the authorities and look for rational solutions to life's eternal questions.

It would be a mistake, however, to think that the majority of novels that appeared in the wake of Belinsky's intervention, which Soviet-era critics classified as "realistic," were actually products of a rational "civilized humanity," whose coming Belinsky sought to hasten. When one considers popular usages of the term "realism" in the mid- to late nineteenth century, one might even wonder whether this term should continue to be applied as a standard marker for a class of prose novels produced by Russian writers in the 1840s–1870s.[20] When characterizing the Russian novel as a distinctive cultural phenomenon, Bakhtin's neologism *romannost'* ["novelness"],[21] which cuts across categories such as "romanticism" and "realism," as well as across centuries and national traditions, appears to be more helpful.[22]

The reason realism caused so much scandal in Europe had to do not only with the violation of decorum, but, more importantly, with a putative ethical transgression. As Peter Brooks points out, verisimilitude and attention to the minutest details of everyday life were not a complete novelty in either European literature or painting, where picaresque and novelistic genres, as well as realistic genre painting, had been ascendant at least since the sixteenth century (Brooks 2005). Seventeenth-century French moralists and eighteenth-century comic writers such as Marivaux and Choderlos de Laclos also made forays into realistic moral psychology, which their nineteenth-century followers Balzac, Stendhal, and Flaubert only deepened and broadened by including in their purview not only the aristocratic *beau monde* but the whole spectrum of French society. Leaving the history of visual art aside, I suggest that literary realism came to be perceived as provocative due to its coldly analytical approach to morals, which bourgeois critics perceived as a sign of the author's putative immorality. Thus real scandals began when novels, which shed light on less than exemplary human behaviour, withheld ethical judgement.[23]

In Russian prose fiction, Lermontov broached this kind of psychological realism, a stepping-stone to a nihilistic value crisis, in *A Hero of Our Time*. But while depicting his autopsychological hero as a dispassionate psychologist, who applies his quasi-scientific approach to himself and to others, Lermontov did not break with the conventions of the old moralist novel, where the sense of right and wrong is embodied in marginal characters portrayed as simpletons or children. In Lermontov's novel, it is the unassuming captain Maxim Maximych who functions as such a moral anchor. It is telling that when Tolstoy began to experiment with psychological realism in *The Sebastopol Stories* and in *War and Peace*, he also tried to balance his self-obsessed, nihilistically inclined main heroes with the help of "honest souls" like Maxim Maximych.[24] Nevertheless, Tolstoy's contemporaries frequently mistook his "soul dialectics" (*dialektika dushi*, a term introduced by Nikolai Chernyshevsky) for nihilism. That Tolstoy was not just a cynic, but, rather, a thoroughgoing moral thinker and reformer, only became clear in the 1880s, after his *Confession* and other religious tracts became known to Russian readers. Tolstoy's "coming out" as a writer-cum-philosopher and religious reformer throws into relief nineteenth-century Russian literature's persistent quest for the absolute ground of truth,[25] which contrasts sharply with Western novels of the time, whose heroes are more interested in worldly success.

As I have argued elsewhere, despite their preoccupation with the theme of education, only a few Russian novels can be directly compared to the nineteenth-century European *Bildungsroman* (Steiner 2019). This genre, which Franco Moretti has characterized as the leading symbolic form of Western modernity, cultivates a pragmatic individualism within the boundaries of social contract (Moretti 1987, 3–13, 2013). The most influential Russian novelists, on the contrary, tended to cultivate a highly perfectionistic and idealistic moral consciousness. Repelled by the egoistic bourgeois civilization they saw in contemporary Europe, they yearned for another, more wholesome reality, one which could only be expressed through recourse to ancient or archaic forms. Hence their formal experimentations, which transformed the realist novel and paved the way for modernism.[26]

Of course, not all nineteenth-century Russian authors were Promethean rebels and bold genre experimenters. Ivan Turgenev and Ivan Goncharov, for example, looked at contemporary Russian reality through Hegel's philosophical lens and tried to represent it by using the Goethean *Bildungsroman* framework. And yet, finding a niche in contemporary Russia proved impossible for Turgenev's heroes, whereas Goncharov's novels usually end in bitter disappointment with the very ideal of happiness.[27] Thus, upon closer examination, Goncharov's reader discovers that the types of happiness one can attain in this life are either artificial or banal, whereas human beings are too inert to look for another world. The stories of Alexander Aduev from *The Same Old Story* and Olga Il'inskaia from *Oblomov*, who build lives that only a shallow observer might see as happy, as well as those of Oblomov and Raisky from *The Ravine*, who are sensitive dreamers incapable of breaking out of their shell, convey deep frustration with both reality and human nature. In contrast to Romantic ironists, Goncharov stays completely outside of his work. Thus, the senselessness of the world he depicts is not balanced by the presence of the creative artist, which could inspire hope. *The Same Old Story* and *Oblomov* bring us to the point of realizing that a quest for self-realization is spurred by illusions. To avoid disillusionment one should return to pre-modern ways of life. But where in this world could one lead such an unhistoric life? Even Oblomov's passivity is somewhat utopian, because, as *The Ravine* makes clear, even the most idyllic corners of provincial Russia teem with passions and conflicts.[28]

Unlike Goncharov, Turgenev (who served as Russia's self-appointed ambassador to the "world republic of letters" beginning in the 1850s) could never disavow Belinsky's vision of Russian modernity as a quest to join the

European enlightenment.[29] He did realize, though, that Belinsky's quest for maturity and realism implied a quest for a new society that had not yet emerged in either Russia or Europe. The friendly circles and associations that appeared in Russia during the Decembrist period and in the 1830s and 1840s foreshadowed this coming community, but the idealist ethos they cultivated was at odds with the social norms of Nicholas I's oppressively bureaucratic and militaristic state. To translate their aspirations and dreams into action, Herzen and Bakunin emigrated and got involved in political activism. Turgenev also moved to Europe but did not abandon fiction. In fact, he became the "last minstrel" of the gentry revolution and the ultimate representative of the novelistic tradition which Thomas Pavel describes as "modern idealism."[30]

Both ancient and modern idealistic fictions portray heroes who staunchly defend moral norms in a disorderly world. But whereas ancient heroes believe in their divine election, the heroes of modern idealistic fiction see their own moral sense, or conscience, as the only force that can bring beauty and nobility to this world. This moral psychology, first expressed by the authors of chivalric romances and pastorals, survived Cervantes' parodic critique of romance in *Don Quixote* and received a new impetus in the seventeenth- and eighteenth-century French and English moralist and sentimental novel, which in turn stimulated the development of Romanticism.[31] For early Romantic critics, Don Quixote was no longer a fool, but the noblest novelistic hero.[32] However, by the late 1850s, when Turgenev defended Cervantes' hero as the archetypal idealist in "Hamlet and Don Quixote," reviving this ethos was itself a quixotic endeavour (Turgenev 1954–1958, 11: 168–187). Socially useful activity was now associated with science and popular positivistic philosophy. After a thorough re-evaluation of his values throughout the 1850s, however, Turgenev arrived at the conclusion that the idealism of his youth was the ideology that a Russian writer ought to defend.[33]

Novelistically, Turgenev reaffirmed his idealism in *Punin and Baburin*, a short autobiographical *Bildungsroman* whose hero grows up under the influence of an admirable person, Baburin, who resembles both Don Quixote and Belinsky.[34] This compact narrative can be read as an allegory of the Russian literary and revolutionary movements, which are closely intertwined. The first title hero, Punin, is a former serf and a great lover of Russian literature. He is an innocent who would not have survived without Baburin's support. The heroine, called Muza, is a dreamy young woman who resembles Pushkin's Tatyana. Her name suggests that she might be an echo of the poet's Muse from *Eugene Onegin* who represents both poetic inspiration and the *beau idéal*. Unlike Tatyana, Muza becomes a victim of seduction, but she is rescued by Baburin who gradually turns from a lonely defender of human dignity into a professional revolutionary and builds her into a revolutionary as well. The narrator's own role is to serve as the life-long confidant and biographer of these beautiful souls.

In his speech at the Pushkin Festival, which accompanied the unveiling of the Pushkin monument in Moscow in June of 1880, Turgenev once made it

454   L. STEINER

clear that he still saw Russian literary history in the same vein as Belinsky, who had argued that Pushkin's art was the first sign of Russia's emergence as a European nation (ibid., 12: 212–224). However, it was not Turgenev, but Dostoevsky who got the most passionate applause at the Pushkin Festival. In his speech Dostoevsky announced the end of the epoch when Russians looked up to Europe as a superior civilization from which they were obliged to learn.[35] Taking his cue from Apollon Grigor'ev, who saw Pushkin's exceptional intellectual breadth and ability to enter into the mentalities of many different cultures as a token of his panhuman "universal responsiveness" [*vsemirnaia otzyvchivost'*], Dostoevsky presented Russia's national poet as a Promethean mangod, a *Vsechelovek*, who creates a new humanity.[36]

Dostoevsky's summary of Pushkin's career was shaped as a kind of *Bildungsroman* which described the poet's development from youth to maturity: the period from 1826 to 1837 during which Pushkin became an imperial historiographer and began editing his own journal, *The Contemporary*.[37] Dostoevsky argued that Pushkin's ideological transformation was caused by his disillusionment with Romanticism as reflected in his narrative poem *The Gypsies*. Its quasi-autobiographical hero, Aleko, is a nobleman who escapes from home and falls in love with a young gypsy, Zemphira. Unable to adopt the gypsies' values, he murders Zemphira when she falls in love with someone else and is, in turn, ostracized by the tabor. Turning to *Eugene Onegin*, Dostoevsky describes Onegin as a similar kind of wanderer, a "stranger to himself," who hides behind the mask of a disenchanted and bored dandy. Onegin's skepticism prevents him from appreciating the pure-hearted Tatyana when he first meets her in the country. Tatyana, who never left her native land but derived her knowledge of life from novels, is praised for her ability to penetrate into Onegin's fragmented psyche after perusing the books in his library. Having glimpsed his disenchantment, she becomes wary of him and eventually marries an old general and becomes a loyal wife. While Grigor'ev had already praised Tatyana's innate common sense, which he equated with her *narodnost'*, Dostoevsky praises her for transforming from a naïve dreamer into a critical reader of novels and people. Thus Tatyana becomes a symbol of Russian virtuousness and wisdom destined to conquer the world.[38]

In the last two decades of the nineteenth century, Russian culture was moving from the periphery to the centre of the "literary world system," so that, by the turn of the twentieth century, Dostoevsky's idea of a Russian-speaking world literature was not a chimera, but an ambitious bid for global cultural domination. However, the far-reaching implications of Dostoevsky's own novelistic experiments, as well as those of other daring Russian authors, like Gogol and Tolstoy, became evident when modernism came to the fore. Like Romanticism, modernism was not merely a radical change of taste and style, but involved a rethinking of the fundamental philosophical assumptions underlying Western civilization. While German thinkers blazed a new trail at the turn of the nineteenth century, Russian novelists became the leaders of the new modernist turn a hundred years later. The formal aspects of this cultural revolution have been well researched, so that today nobody doubts that Henry James, Virginia Woolf, Thomas Mann, French existentialism, surrealism, and a number of other literary movements—not to mention visual art and cinema—would not have been able to develop their unique languages without exposure to Russian literature and art. The impact of the Russian novel on Western philosophy, however, is a topic that still awaits new researchers.

One of the few thinkers whose interface with Russian ideas has already received considerable attention is Nietzsche. While most scholars point to Turgenev and Dostoevsky as important precursors to Nietzsche's battle against pessimism, I would also stress his familiarity with Herzen's memoirs.[39] Having read *My Past and Thoughts* and then Dostoevsky's works, Nietzsche recognized that the spirit of relentless negation pervading these works was symptomatic of a value crisis that could become a starting-point for a new renaissance of the entire European civilization.[40] Unsurprisingly, Nietzsche's works quickly reached Russia and had huge resonance there. Even the Pushkin cult received new meanings in the wake of Russian Nietzscheanism. Thus, in his essay written for Pushkin's Centennial in 1899, the leading symbolist Dmitrii Merezhkovskii—doubtlessly inspired by Dostoevsky's speech—argued that Pushkin was "the Russian solution to the tragedy of dualism dramatized by Nietzsche and symbolized by the Apollonian-Dionysian polarity" (Paperno 213). While the symbolists, such as Merezhkovskii and Vyacheslav Ivanov, tried to synthesize Nietzsche's ideas with Solovyov's mystical idea of Godmanhood (Ivanov 1999), a different approach was offered by the cultural historian Mikhail Gershenzon (mostly known in the Anglophone world as the editor of *The Signposts*). In *Pushkin's Wisdom*, written and published during the 1917 Revolution, he offered a Nietzschean interpretation of Pushkin that I find most faithful to Nietzsche.

Gershenzon's Pushkin is neither the modern enlightener portrayed by Belinsky and Turgenev nor the Messianic panhuman [*vsechelovek*] portrayed by Dostoevsky and the symbolists, but a pagan who consistently juxtaposes instrumental reason to the insight of the inspired poet. Invoking Nietzsche's discussion of Heraclitus in *Philosophy in the Tragic Age of the Greeks* (but not citing this work), Gershenzon compares Pushkin's wisdom to Heraclitus' teaching about life as the eternal flux and the unity of opposites (Gershenzon 2000, 1: 9–37). *Eugene Onegin* emerges as a philosophical allegory, where Tatyana represents stasis, completion, and unity and Eugene perpetual movement, incompletion, and fragmentation.

In retrospect, however, the differences between the religiously minded symbolists and the post-religious Gershenzon appear less significant than their shared belief in art's ability to endow life with a meaning, as well as their faith in Russian culture, in which Pushkin's creative spirit was enshrined. Thus, it is not surprising that many writers welcomed the Revolution as an opportunity to extend their horizons, reinvent artistic media, and debate again the eternal questions of life. As Evgenii Zamyatin wrote in his 1923 essay "On Literature, Revolution, Entropy, and Other Matters":

456   L. STEINER

> A literature that is alive does not live by yesterday's clock, nor by today's, but by tomorrow's. It is a sailor sent aloft: from the masthead he can see foundering ships, icebergs, and maelstroms still invisible from the deck. [...] In a storm, you must have a man aloft. We are in the midst of a storm today, and SOS signals come from every side. Only yesterday a writer could calmly stroll along the deck, clicking his Kodak (genre); but who will want to look at landscapes and genre scenes when the world is listing at a forty-five-degree angle, the green maws are gaping, the hull is creaking? Today we can look and think only as men do in the face of death: we are about to die—and what did it all mean? How have we lived? If we could start over again, from the beginning, what would we live by? And for what? What we need in literature today are vast philosophic horizons—horizons seen from mastheads, from airplanes; we need the most ultimate, the most fearsome, the most fearless "Why?" and "What next?" (Zamyatin 1970, 107)

Sadly, instead of a new Renaissance whose approach the modernists were trying to hasten, the Revolution led to a prolonged rule of terror, which forced many intellectuals into exile, with those who stayed behind forced to submit to the dictatorship of the proletariat. Soviet novels approved for publication became increasingly more didactic to the point of transforming into hagiography, whereas the artistically and ideologically daring works lay in their authors' drawers awaiting posterity. (Zamyatin's own anti-Utopian novel *We*, composed in 1921, was published in Russia only in 1988.) Boris Pasternak's *Doctor Zhivago*, most of Alexander Solzhenitsyn's novels, and Vasily Grossman's *Life and Fate* were comparable in scope to *War and Peace* and presented new attempts to portray the emergence of morally responsible individuals against the background of a chaotic, or even utterly senseless and horrifying reality.

Many creative writers also used the ideological strictures of Marxism-Leninism as the opportunity to sharpen their satirical and ironic skills. Mikhail Bulgakov's *Master and Margarita*, Andrei Platonov's *The Foundation Pit*, and Vladimir Voinovich's *The Life and Extraordinary Adventures of Private Ivan Chonkin* are among the most brilliant products of this intellectual dissidence. In connection with this, the fact that Bakhtin never published his book about the novel of education, in which he traced the genre's development from European humanism and Goethe to Maxim Gorky, seems revealing. According to the official story, the manuscript of this book, which Bakhtin submitted to a publisher shortly before the outbreak of World War II, was destroyed together with the publishing house during a German air raid.[41] Bakhtin confessed in the 1970s that he had only one extra copy, which he had used to make cigarettes. While this story is not incredible, I doubt Bakhtin would have failed to recreate his book from memory had he truly wished to publish it. Therefore, I suspect that this work, from which only a brief fragment survived, was either too controversial for the Stalinist academy or did not satisfy the author himself. As a teleological narrative about the novel of education, it was supposed to bring the reader to the creative world of Maxim Gorky, who had been a Nietzschean God-builder before becoming the godfather of socialist realism.[42] But which Gorky did Bakhtin's book reflect?[43] The scholar's decision to concentrate on the theoretical implications of the *heteroglossia* he had discovered in his 1928 work on Dostoevsky, and then to spend much of his career studying the medieval and Renaissance culture of laughter manifest an unwillingness to engage with thinkers and genres that convey monolithic visions of humanity. Thus, instead of focusing on the humanistic *Bildungsroman* tradition, he ultimately chose to concentrate his efforts on uncovering the sceptical anti-tradition.

To outline the goals of this chapter more precisely, I limit my present inquiry to the "long nineteenth century," because it was during this period that Russian educated society, the *intelligentsia*, developed its self-consciousness as an independent moral and cultural force and proceeded to cultivate its unique *ethos*. My chapter is structured as a series of "critical fragments" centred on several works that could be seen as the core of the Russian tradition of the philosophical novel. I want to stress that my analyses are not intended as a historical morphology of the entire Russian novel. I will not, for example, discuss the adventure and picaresque novels by Fyodor Emin, Mikhail Chulkov, and Matvei Komarov, which were technically the earliest Russian novels (see Todd 2006, 403).[44] Although these works do shed important light on eighteenth-century Russia, where literacy was already spreading beyond the upper classes and traditional culture was becoming receptive to Western ideas, this chapter is limited to novels designed to foster serious moral reflection and ponder life's eternal questions.

Karamzin will be the starting-point for my reflections because his career is in many ways emblematic of that of a member of the Russian intelligentsia: a traveller and transmitter of Western ideas to the Russian public and of Russian culture to the West, an enlightener and a Russian patriot, whose ideas provoked heated debates among his followers, leading to the development of both historical and political science in nineteenth-century Russia. A careful re-examination of Karamzin's wide-ranging legacy is beyond my present scope. I will be concerned only with Karamzin as the author of the moralist fictions designed to set readers on the path of self-perfection.

While Karamzin wrote only for the gentry, Pushkin arguably attempted to use Karamzin's educational ideals as the basis for a national education. I say "arguably," because Pushkin's political credo still remains under discussion.[45] The only fact that can be asserted with some certainty is that the last decade of his life (more precisely, from the time when he learned of the failed Decembrist coup until his tragic death in 1837) he adopted "a Shakespearean perspective," which enabled him to empathize not only with foreign poets of different epochs but also with different social strata within Russian society. In his later works Pushkin tried to straddle the divide between the educated elite and the people.[46] However, his attempts to extend cultural self-consciousness beyond the aristocratic salon not only failed to preclude a conflict between individualism and autocracy but, according to many, precipitated the poet's tragic duel, a private and public tragedy, with which Russian culture has tried to come to grips ever since.[47]

458 L. STEINER

In the 1840s, 1850s, and 1860s, the democrats and the populists from the middle ranks of society, as well as many aristocrats (including Turgenev, Herzen, and Tolstoy, whom I will also discuss in this chapter) firmly rejected the Karamzinian ethos of chivalry and began looking for the more democratic ideal of the "beautiful soul." At the same time, the emergence of the Slavophile movement gave impetus to the revival of the Christian ideal of personality. Thus, for both Gogol and Dostoevsky, the quest for truth turned into an attempt to revive Christology. In my view, however, neither of them managed to transcend their Romantic perspective, which implied a rift between the individual thinker and the cosmic order. In "The Gaps in Christology"[48] I demonstrate how Gogol's, and then Dostoevsky's own, failure to create an edifying epic in the manner of Dante called forth the emergence of a multi-genre, tragi-comic narrative which became Dostoevsky's signature genre. Concentrating on *The Idiot*, I show how the writer's attempt to imagine the appearance of a perfectly beautiful Christlike hero amidst modern society intensified the novelist's propensity for irony and self-irony. Dostoevsky's repeated attempts to revive the myth of universal humanity and graft it onto Russian national identity show that the monolithic ethical vision he sought to achieve was no longer achievable without sacrificing the realist novel's commitment to objectivity and verisimilitude.

In the 1880s and 1890s authors from marginalized social groups—workers, peasants (including non-aristocratic female writers), representatives of ethnic and religious minorities—entered the public sphere. During this period the novel lost its former pre-eminence, whereas journalism was in its heyday. Smaller prose forms related to journalism, such as the short story, the feuilleton, and the sketch, enjoyed a renaissance. Like their ancestor, the Italian Renaissance novella, these prose forms typically eschewed idealism and conveyed a rather disenchanted view of humanity. At the other end of the spectrum, however, symbolist and decadent aestheticist movements revived lyric poetry and drama. Tolstoy had anticipated this radical expansion of the public sphere, as well as the socio-political and value crises, back in the 1850s (when he first opened a school for peasant children and immersed himself in the study of European history and education), and tried to negotiate a pathway between high and mass culture through turning to biblical translation and exegesis and didactic storytelling. Having studied the history of world religions, Tolstoy sought to transcend the confines of both nationalism, which he saw as the source of imperialism, and European humanistic culture as a whole, which he saw as too hierarchical and parochial. Due to spatial constraints, I will not be able to do full justice to this thinker's bold ideas. Nevertheless, I will devote my penultimate "fragment" "Revolution as the Resurrection" to Tolstoy's *The Resurrection*, his riposte to eighteenth-century theories of moral-sentimental self-perfection. The most curious aspect of this work is that it throws into relief the limits of a self-guided quest for perfection through conscience alone. To succeed in his struggle for spiritual resurrection, Tolstoy's hero needs both intellectual autonomy and beautiful examples. Often accused of populism and contrasted with Nietzsche, Tolstoy actually overlaps with his German contemporary on many points, including reaffirming the importance of self-elected exemplary individuals.[49]

Drawing on the lessons of the nineteenth-century masters, the symbolists and the modernists proceeded to reinvent the novel, which they saw as the medium of cultural memory and self-fashioning in the Nietzschean sense. The poets and thinkers of the Russian Silver Age thought about literature in cosmopolitan and "planetary" terms,[50] as a vehicle of values that transcend the demands of the day and can be appreciated only as part of a longue durée. I demonstrate this by turning to Vladimir Nabokov, the ultimate legatee of the Silver Age, who managed to escape from both Russian and German totalitarian regimes and develop his individuality to the utmost.[51] Vast erudition and awareness of cultural "deep time" enabled Nabokov to transcend social, political, religious, and linguistic boundaries and assert himself as an Anglophone master of world literature. Although Nabokov's successful career in the West was to some extent due to "moral luck," he worked very hard to become who he became. Born to be an aristocratic dilettante, he fashioned himself into a consummate literary professional, accomplishing the dream of many Russian writers since Karamzin and Pushkin whose quests for beauty, nobility, and moral independence were so often thwarted by political adversity or poverty.

THE PRISONERS OF HONOUR

The ideal of *kalokagathia* first entered Russian literature in the 1790s.[52] It was Nikolai Karamzin, generally regarded as the pioneer of Russian sentimentalism, who tried to awaken in his readers a desire to become not only cultivated members of cosmopolitan polite society but also better human beings. Karamzin's reputation is based on his influential travelogue, *Letters of a Russian Traveller*, a number of sentimental, Gothic, and historical novellas, numerous translations of European authors, editorship of several important journals, and the monumental *History of the Russian State* (Cross 1971; Lotman 1987; Hammamberg 1991). Karamzin's early work testifies to the influence of Rousseau. After the French Revolution, however, Rousseau's influence waned. Karamzin's mature ideology is more in line with Scottish Enlightenment philosophers, who replaced a normative approach to ethics and aesthetics with the notion of beauty based on intuitive moral sense. As a historian Karamzin was opposed the universalism of the French Enlightenment and believed that a vast polity like the Russian Empire could not subsist without autocracy, which alone could guarantee a gradual cultural and moral progress. It was through the cultivation of sensibility, rather than through theoretical knowledge, that the Enlightenment was supposed to unfold. Like many Western contemporaries, Karamzin saw prose fiction as the vehicle of sensibility and thought that good prose should resemble a conversation in polite society (Karamzin 1964, 2: 183–187). Writing well was deemed crucial to moral education because it instilled a sense of propriety in the expression of feelings, which Karamzin linked to sympathy.

Karamzin's most influential fictional work is *Poor Liza*, which tells a story of a peasant girl Liza seduced by a nobleman Erast.[53] Karamzin softens the class conflict somewhat by making the heroine a free countrywoman, rather than a serf. When Erast first meets Liza, he is attracted by her purity. Tired of his dissipated life in Moscow, he comes daily to visit Liza in her bucolic suburb. Gradually, their innocent caresses turn into passion. Once his desires are satisfied, Erast tires of Liza and decides to leave her. He tells her that he must go to war. However, one day Liza comes to Moscow to sell flowers and spots Erast inside a fancy carriage. She runs after the carriage and as soon as Erast steps out manages to catch him in her embrace. Erast brings her inside his mansion and explains that his circumstances have changed and that they must part. He puts one hundred roubles in her pocket and shows her the door. At this point the narrator steps in to explain that Erast did not lie when he had said that he was going to war. He was indeed in the army, but instead of fighting the enemy he spent his time playing cards and accrued debts that he could only repay by marrying a wealthy gentlewoman. From the point of view of high society, Erast acts correctly, since he does not simply abandon Liza but gives her a large sum of money. However, Erast drastically underestimates Liza's sensitive soul. Unable to survive her disillusionment, she drowns herself in a pond. In the story's final lines the narrator informs us that he learned this story, which occurred thirty years earlier, from Erast himself, who had died a year before the story was composed. Erast never stopped thinking about Liza and believed himself to have been her murderer.[54]

This simple tale had a rich reception history (Toporov 1995; Hammamberg 1991; Lotman 1987; Cross 1971). The pure-hearted Liza became the prototype for a whole row of compromised yet inwardly pure heroines in the sentimental social novels and realist novels of the 1840s–1870s, whereas Erast, who develops from a frivolous young man into a melancholy older man racked with guilt, could be seen as one of the first psychological case studies which engendered a rich tradition of psychological realism in Russian literature. As I show later in this chapter, one of the last examples of this type of hero is Prince Nekhliudov in Tolstoy's *The Resurrection*. Like the Tolstoyan hero, Erast is not a confirmed rake like Richardson's Lovelace or like Count NN from Karamzin's (1803) "My Confession."[55] Erast is a basically good person who lacks moral sensitivity because he had been brought up in an unjust society, whose conscience Karamzin sought to awaken. His works were addressed to the social elite whom he wished to transform into characters like Richardson's Sir Charles Grandison, a good man and gentleman.

Having accepted the position of the imperial historiographer left vacant after Karamzin's death, Pushkin tried to fill Karamzin's shoes as a historian and a public enlightener. At this juncture, Pushkin also became interested in Karamzin's legacy as a reformer of Russian prose. Emulating Karamzin, he began to deploy sentimental prose genres and couch his chronicles as fictions of poetic justice. This new direction is most evident in *The Captain's Daughter*, a historical novel written alongside the *History of Pugachev's Rebellion*. A precursor to this novel is *Dubrovsky*, a tale about a young nobleman who turns into a "noble robber" after the death of his father, a righteous man who had been ruined by his rich neighbour. Dubrovsky's peasants rebel against the injustices committed against their old master and push his son to organize a band of robbers. As an officer, the son hesitates to violate his pledge of allegiance, but the duty he feels toward his father and his serfs eventually outweighs his sense of military honour. Early drafts of the novel that would later become *The Captain's Daughter* focus on a historical figure who resembles Dubrovsky: a nobleman Shvanvich who joined Pugachev's army. But in the end Pushkin reworked this plot by adding a new hero, Grinev, and turning Shvanvich into an opportunistic Shvabrin. At the beginning of the story Grinev accidentally meets Pugachev in the midst of a snowstorm. Pugachev guides him and his servant to a tavern and Grinev rewards this mysterious *muzhik* by giving him his old hareskin coat. Pugachev repays his debt by sparing Grinev and his old servant when they are captured along with other defenders of the Belogorskaya Fortress. Pugachev tempts Grinev to join him. But Pushkin's chivalric hero would rather risk death than betray his liege (Catherine II), his family, or his servants. Thus the ultimate test of Grinev's nobility is the way he treats his old Savel'ich.[56]

When Pugachev is captured, Grinev is also arrested and charged with treason. It is his fiancée Masha, the daughter of the captain Mironov executed by Pugachev, who saves him by making a journey to Petersburg, where she finds access to the Empress and convinces her of Grinev's innocence. Stylized as a family chronicle narrated by Grinev, *The Captain's Daughter* presents a liberal conservative view of history as driven by gradual moral progress. As the narrator confesses in Chap. 6, "when I reflect that this happened in my own lifetime and that since then I have lived to see Emperor Alexander's mild reign, I cannot help marvelling at the rapid progress of enlightenment and the spread of humane principles" (Pushkin 1937–1959, 6: 30; Pushkin 1983, 305). Only at the very end does the author disguised as the "editor" of Grinev's chronicle step in to provide an ironic commentary on Grinev's memoir. He tells us that he has visited the estate Grinev received as a gift from Catherine II. It is divided between ten owners who are currently "thriving" there. In other words, Grinev's impoverished grandchildren are as vulnerable as the Dubrovskys (Pushkin 1937–1959, 6: 360). This was, of course, a critical comment addressed to Catherine II and her descendants, who failed to properly reward their loyal servitors, which was tantamount to treating them tyrannically, rather than aristocratically (Steiner 2011, 57–90).

The fact that Pushkin's prose tales usually end with an ironic *pointe* did not escape the attention of de Vogüé, who recognized the imprint of Voltaire's scepticism on Pushkin's mind (de Vogüé 1913, 67). But many nineteenth-century critics overlooked Pushkin's irony. Belinsky was disappointed by *Dubrovsky* and *The Captain's Daughter*, calling them examples of "landowners' literature," which he deemed inferior to Pushkin's dramas and historiography

(Belinsky 1953–1959, 7: 535–582). Apollon Grigor'ev, on the other hand, interpreted *The Captain's Daughter* as an objective family chronicle of the Grinevs, whose idea of honour, which combined fidelity to a father with fidelity to the Tsar, expressed the people's organic values.[57] Eager to see Pushkin not merely as a leader of the gentry intelligentsia but as a national educator, he interpreted Pushkin's exemplary characters not as idealized models of aristo-cratic virtue but as national types (Grigor'ev 2008, 71).

Among Pushkin's younger contemporaries, Lermontov was the only one disturbed by the poet's cooperation with the state and dared to call attention to the gap between Pushkin's actual ethical character and his official persona as court poet and historiographer. In "The Death of the Poet" Lermontov sug-gested that the poet's fatal duel was organized by a cabal of courtiers resentful of his genius and his independence (Lermontov 1961–1962, 1: 412–414). But the younger poet also blamed Pushkin for "giving his hand" to those who were not worthy to shake it. Lermontov, who frequented high society, was undoubt-edly aware of the rumours that circulated there. He certainly knew that the pasquinade, "The Certificate of a Cuckold," which provoked Pushkin to chal-lenge the French-born Guards officer d'Anthès to a duel, hinted at the poten-tial affair between Pushkin's wife and the Tsar, with the Frenchman merely acting as a "screen."[58] From this we can conclude that Lermontov addressed his poetic indictment not only to d'Anthès and the courtiers who backed him but also to Russia's supreme ruler who was above the law and could not be challenged to a duel.

This poem caused such an uproar in society that Lermontov was arrested and, after a short imprisonment, transferred from a prestigious Hussar regi-ment in Petersburg to active service in the Caucasus. There he wrote his novel *A Hero of Our Time*. Like his fictional alter ego Pechorin, a lonely Byronic hero who defies God and distrusts human beings, Lermontov never swerved from the path of negativity, which left him with no friends. He was killed in a duel by his former friend Nikolai Martynov whom he apparently alienated the way Pechorin alienates Grushnitskii.[59] The continuities between Lermontov's literary masks and his behaviour in real life offers one of the first examples of what the symbolists would call life-creation [*zhiznetvorchestvo*].[60] To transform chaotic reality into a meaningful life story, an artist must follow some sort of a rule. For Lermontov's hero, self-worship, which passes in society for demonic pride, serves as a quasi-religious principle that imparts order to the chaotic universe.[61]

Although duels were strictly forbidden since the early eighteenth century, the members of the gentry continued to regard duelling as an instrument by which to assert their moral independence from the state.[62] Only Herzen realized that *point d'honneur* did not actually recognize the inner worth of the individual, but only defended an abstract ideal of Personality. Having declined Georg Herwegh's challenge provoked by the revelation of the German poet's affair with Herzen's wife, he wrote letters to his European "friends in democracy," explaining that the drama in his private life should not impede his public career as an intellectual revolutionary (Paperno 2007, 12). Simultaneously, he began composing a confession about his family drama, which grew into *My Past and Thoughts*. Although Herzen's autobiography was based on real facts, it has been compared to the *Bildungsroman*, which describes the maturation of a "man of the new world" (Ginzburg 1991; Paperno 2007). In contrast to the Romantics, Herzen does not see himself as an "elect personality," but as "the best representative of the 'educated minority' that has been called upon to lead the Russian liberation movement" (Ginzburg 1991, 212). The ethical pathos of his memoirs consists in the two-fold denunciation of the superficial decorum, scrupulously observed by the aristocracy, and the fake civility of the bourgeoisie, whom Herzen refused to see as progressive and humane.

Although Herzen's critique of bourgeois morals was grist to the mill of Russian nationalists, his behaviour puzzled and angered some of his contemporaries, including Dostoevsky, for whom a refusal to fight a duel could be comprehensible only from a religious point of view. Thus Prince Myshkin in *The Idiot* does not challenge Ganya Ivolgin who slaps him in the face because he is something of a holy fool. Meanwhile, in *The Adolescent* Versilov's failure to duel with a man who slaps him in the face is part of his negative character. Versilov, who describes himself as a former follower of Herzen, is areligious and completely self-absorbed. Therefore, in the eyes of his illegitimate son Arkadii, Versilov's decision not to invoke *point d'honneur* does not appear as a rational decision, but rather as a sign of weakness (Steiner 2011, 211).

In fiction, duels continued to function as a moral test, and often as the rites of passage that safeguarded aristocratic identity, all the way to Nabokov.[63] This motif began to fade away when the "woman question" emerged as a central theme, urging writers to reconceive gender roles along with the masculine chivalric ethics of honour. In Herzen's *My Past and Thoughts* the author's avoidance of ritual violence is clearly related to his feminist views. As I will show, the theme of ritual violence as a test of masculinity also looms large in *The Idiot*, where Myshkin's "weak messianic power" is contrasted with the psychic resilience of two strong women. But as for Turgenev, who was also committed to women's emancipation, duelling remains an obligation for any self-respecting male, even a "nihilist." He does, however, infuse the scene of Bazarov's duel with Pavel Kirsanov in *Fathers and Children* with irony.

The Gaps in Christology

The 1830s and 1840s witnessed the advent of Russia's first indigenous philosophical school which sought to recapture the spirit of pre-Petrine Muscovy. The Slavophiles looked for the vestiges of this authentic culture in the patriarchal customs that survived in the countryside and in Orthodoxy. At the centre of the Slavophile social and ethical theory stood the ideal of the organic community, or *sobornost'*, which they juxtaposed with the egoistic individualism of Western culture (Walicki 1975). Throughout the 1840s and 1850s Slavophile salons in Moscow exercised a major influence over the public sphere, drawing

464   L. STEINER

a number of writers and critics into their orbit. After his return from Europe, Gogol also befriended the Slavophiles. But their hopes of transforming this satirist into a national genius, that is to say, a visionary whose poetry expressed the innermost spirit of his people and his age, were dashed when Gogol succumbed to a spiritual crisis and died as a result of zealous fasting during the Lent of 1852. Shortly before his death Gogol burnt his manuscripts, which probably included the second part of *Dead Souls*.

When Dostoevsky received an amnesty in 1859, he began planning a return to literature, which had to be as brilliant as his literary debut in the 1840s. Before his arrest in 1849, Dostoevsky had been a follower of Gogol, whose idiosyncratic mixture of German Romanticism and naturalistic aesthetics Dostoevsky adopted in *Poor People*, *Netochka Nezvanova*, and other early works. His experience as a convict deepened his psychological insight, as well as his knowledge of the Russian people. As a result of this experience, Dostoevsky broke with the rationalistic humanism of the Belinsky circle and began to develop a new existential humanism, which called for a new poetics. The intense dialogues about faith at the heart of *Crime and Punishment* were the first step toward future innovations through which Dostoevsky hoped to transform literature into a medium of moral reform and resurrection. His trips to Europe, whose mercantile rationalism repulsed Dostoevsky, strengthened the writer's resolve to set himself against the dominant naturalistic method and develop his own brand of realism. In his letter to Apollon Maikov from December 11, 1868, Dostoevsky equated his realism with idealism.[64] Thus, Dostoevsky no longer saw himself only as a realistic observer and chronicler of Russian life, but as a prophet.

The novel Dostoevsky was drafting at the time when he wrote to Maikov was *The Idiot*. Like Romantic visionaries, Dostoevsky harnessed his imagination to the idea of apocalypse. His goal was to conjure up the image of a "perfectly beautiful person" reappearing amidst the disorder and *bezobrazie* [ugliness, imagelessness] of modern life (Steiner 2011, 157). Like Wagner's Parsifal, Dostoevsky's Prince Myshkin seems to have been conceived as a sublime fool whose innocence is supposed to transform the world.

At the heart of the story Dostoevsky placed Myshkin's encounter with a "fallen" woman named Nastasya [Anastasia, "resurrection"] Filippovna Barashkova ["Lamb"], whom he tries to save. As the story unfolds, however, Myshkin's altruism begins to look more and more like solipsism and an inability to understand others. According to Nina Pelikan-Strauss, "Myshkin's identity as a failed saviour dedicated to the beautiful *image*, but not to the efficacy or dialogic potential of Christ suggests that Dostoevsky might be moving at this late point in the novel toward the redemptive laughter of carnival described by Bakhtin" (1998, 124). But why and how did *The Idiot*'s religious conception get transformed? Or was Dostoevsky doubtful about his ability to portray a second coming from the start, and therefore gave his hero an oxymoronic name, Lev (Leo) Myshkin (Mouse)?

The novelistic intrigue is centred on the rivalry between two heroines, Nastasya Filippovna and Aglaia, and their competing interpretations of Myshkin as the hero of their own "novels." Nastasya Filippovna's efforts to control life through narrative are quite obvious from the moment she tries to turn her name day party in Chap. 13 of Part One into a collective confession, inviting her guests to share their most shameful memories. This "game" provides her with an opportunity to engage in a Rousseau-like self-dramatization. Of course, her guests already know her story. Nastasya is an orphan of noble lineage whom her guardian Totsky had turned into his concubine when she was a teenager. Her biography harks back to Dostoevsky's *The Hostess*, a tale inspired by Gogol's *Terrible Vengeance*. Like Nastasya, Katerina in *The Hostess* loses her parents and her home in a fire. A demonic man rescues her and then gains full control over her conscience. Nastasya Filippovna is also foreshadowed in *Netochka Nezvanova*. Netochka's mad stepfather is a failed musical genius whose uncanny power over Netochka reminds us of Gogol's magician's power over Katerina's soul.

Unlike Katerina, Nastasya does rebel against Totsky, but in a passive-aggressive way, by delaying her acceptance of the marriage offer from Ganya, a young careerist whom Totsky buys off so that he can marry the oldest daughter of General Epanchin. Once Myshkin catches wind of this plan he also proposes to Nastasya. Suddenly, the merchant Rogozhin also bursts in with his marriage offer. By marrying this millionaire Nastasya can escape from a world controlled by debauched aristocrats. But would this proud beauty, whose genealogy resembles those of Pushkin's impoverished old gentry, stoop down to marry a tradesman? Presented with these options, Nastasya spends the rest of the novel indulging in masochism and tormenting various men whose fortunes depend on her decision.

Nastasya is a *femme fatale*, whose suffering gives her depth. As Molly Brunson has argued, Dostoevsky uses an ingenious mixture of ekphrastic and narrative means to create a Medusa-like image that spellbinds other characters and even readers (see Brunson 2016, Ch. 5). Thus Myshkin feels Nastasya's demonic power when he stares at her photographic portrait. While Brunson compares her to *Rusalka* from Alexander Dargomyzhsky's opera (based on Pushkin's dramatic fragment), I would also link her to the figure of Undine. A great admirer of E.T.A. Hoffmann, Dostoevsky must have been familiar with his opera *Undine* based on a famous novella by Friedrich de La Motte Fouqué, which Vasilii Zhukovsky translated in 1837. As I shall argue, the Romantic triangle that develops between Prince Myshkin, Nastasya, and Aglaia seems to have been inspired by this popular work.[65]

In La Motte Fouqué's novella, a knight named Huldebrand is in love with a lady named Berthalda, who tests his love by sending him to a forest in the midst of a thunderstorm.[66] The knight finds refuge in a fisherman's cottage where he meets Undine, a water spirit in a human form. Struck by her beauty, the knight forgets Berthalda and marries Undine. The couple set off on a journey to the knight's castle. On the way, they go to pay homage to the Duke. In his castle, they meet Berthalda, one of his courtiers. Undine takes Berthalda to her bosom and announces that she has a surprise for her. She had already told her husband that she was a water spirit who could live on earth as long as he loved her. Now she explains to Berthalda that her uncle, a water spirit named Kühleborn, had stolen Berthalda from her parents, the fisherman and his wife, and replaced her with Undine. The courtly society immediately rejects Berthalda, and she travels together with Huldebrand and Undine to their castle on the Danube. One day the trio sets off on a boat trip down the Danube. Kühleborn sends a storm and all humans on board develop terrible seasickness. At this juncture the knight expresses a regret that he married Undine instead of Berthalda. These words shatter Undine's heart and she slips over the side of the boat into the Danube. The knight marries Berthalda and lives happily with her until one night a water nymph rises from the bottom of the well and comes to their bedchamber. She kisses the knight, and he dies.

The parallel between *The Idiot*'s plot and this popular Romantic story reveals Dostoevsky's hesitation between the "fantastic" and naturalistic explanations of the human psyche. Thus, Nastasya is not simply a victim of her milieu, depressed and deranged to the point of not being able to calculate her advantages, but a human who has "slipped over the board of the ship" and turned into a demon. Throughout the novel, Nastasya tries to control and manipulate everyone around her. According to Olga Matich, she "falls in love with Aglaia, constructing a highly-charged erotic threesome consisting of herself, Aglaia, and Myshkin" (Matich 2005, 179). This suggestion is not too far-fetched, considering that Dostoevsky had already depicted homoerotic passion in *Netochka Nezvanova*.[67]

But Aglaia is also a forceful personality. She develops from an ingénue into a modern woman who wants to understand and rationalize the world. She wants Myshkin to become a modern Don Quixote, that is, a liberal along the lines of Turgenev. Caught between two wilful women—one who is mired in myth and believes in her demonism and the other who looks for opportunities to escape from her patriarchal family and become an emancipated woman— Myshkin develops an identity crisis. Thus, at the Epanchins' party in Chap. 7 of Part Four, where he is introduced to society as Aglaia's potential fiancé, he suddenly delivers an inappropriately long speech in defence of hereditary aristocracy (Dostoevsky 1972–1990, 8: 456–458). Princess Belokonskaya, who embodies the values of high society, calls him a "sick man" and urges Lizaveta Prokof'evna to cut him off (ibid., 459). But Aglaia continues to struggle for Myshkin. She even comes to a meeting at Nastasya's house, to which her rival summons her. She tells Nastasya that she comes to talk to her as a human being to a human being ("ia prishla k Vam s chelovechskoiu rech'iu") (ibid., 471). She accuses Nastasya of being manipulative and tells her to leave Myshkin alone (ibid., 471–473). At this juncture the symbolism of Aglaia's name becomes obvious. She is most likely named after Karamzin's influential journal. Thus Aglaia is the spokeswoman of the Enlightenment and her struggle with the demonic Nastasya over Myshkin's soul drives home to us that Lev Myshkin is not a transcendent being but an everyman.

In response to Aglaia's accusation, Nastasya collapses in a hysterical fit (ibid., 474). Her rival runs away, but Myshkin, totally lost, stays behind, reverting to his Christlike role. Nastasya starts making arrangements for her wedding with the Prince. The morning of the wedding, however, she runs away with Rogozhin, who murders her at dawn. When the Prince finally reaches Rogozhin's house and sees Nastasya' dead body, he guesses that Rogozhin has stabbed her with the garden knife which he had earlier seen on Rogozhin's desk—a metonymy of defloration, which might signify the ultimate desacralization of "Anastasia Barashkova." Critics have written a lot about the fact that Nastasya's dead body resembles Hans Holbein's "Dead Christ in his Tomb," a copy of which hangs in Rogozhin's house.[68] Dostoevsky saw this painting in Basel, the city where Prince Myshkin experiences a sudden awakening from mute idiocy. Profoundly disturbed by Holbein's realism, which drove home the idea of human finitude, Dostoevsky depicts Nastasya's dead body with a spellbinding realism. Her destruction, which she had predicted when she met Rogozhin, signals the victory of tragic fatalism over reason. In the epilogue of the novel we learn that Myshkin has suffered a mental collapse and was shipped back to the asylum in Switzerland whence he came, whereas Aglaia has escaped to Europe by marrying a Polish count.

But this tragicomic ending was not Dostoevsky's last word in his debate with the positivists. In the *Brothers Karamazov* he made another attempt at theodicy by assigning the role of a saviour to Zosima and his spiritual son Alyosha. Their ethic of "active love" is similar to Myshkin's love-pity. But Zosima and Alyosha are more self-aware and attuned to reality, which makes them better listeners. As Dostoevsky's speech at the Pushkin Festival makes clear, he continued to think of love as the main Christian value and to hope that even if love does not completely overturn all natural laws, it can add a new dimension to reality, one that allows human beings to escape the Darwinian struggle for survival and partake of what the Slavophiles called *sobornost'*.

REVOLUTION AS THE RESURRECTION

Dostoevsky died on March 13, 1881, nine months after the Pushkin Festival (which occurred on June 20, 1880). On February 8, 1881, the assassination of Tsar Alexander II plunged the country into a new crisis, which only short-sighted conservatives saw as a temporary problem, solvable by police measures. Throughout the reigns of Alexander III and Nicholas II terrorism became part of the underground revolutionaries' tactics. It was in this atmosphere that Tolstoy, who had not published any large-scale fictional works since *Anna Karenina*, resumed his activity as a novelist by publishing *The Resurrection*, which embodied his new expressive theory of art as a medium that creates affective connections among individuals. An offspring of sentimentalism, Tolstoy's expressionism foreshadows both avant-garde expressionism and socialist realism. At the same time, however, Tolstoy did not abandon his commitment to self-critical philosophical reflection. Thus at the heart of *The Resurrection* we find the same tension between old-school didacticism and the critical consciousness of the philosophical *Bildungsroman* which undercut the entire Russian novelistic tradition.

As is well-known, after Dostoevsky's death Tolstoy recognized his rival's significance for Russian culture and began to draw on his characteristic themes and ideas in his works. While Dostoevsky had seen their relationship as an *agon*, which he initiated by attacking the aristocratic author's elitist worldview in *The Adolescent* and by reassessing Anna Karenina in *The Diary of the Writer*, Tolstoy wished to close this debate in a brotherly way, emphasizing the similarities between his and Dostoevsky's viewpoints. Tolstoy's novelistic journey to the underworld of the penal colony, whence the mature Dostoevsky emerged, also signals the beginning of a new life for both the woman who had been victimized by an unjust society and the repentant aristocrat who had caused her ruin.

At the beginning of the story Nekhliudov, a typical young Prince, does what many other Russian aristocrats routinely did: he seduces his aunts' ward Katiusha Maslova and then abandons her. Years later, when serving as a member of a jury he suddenly recognizes Katiusha in the prostitute (now called Liubov', "Love") who is falsely charged with a premeditated murder of a client. Nekhliudov is shocked by the outcome of his youthful dalliance. As a man of honour, he wants to make amends by marrying Katiusha and, once she is convicted, following her to Siberia. She rejects his offer.[69] He nevertheless follows her to Siberia, where he gradually comes to realize that what keeps Katiusha from accepting his proposal is not only pride but also the difference in their life experience, which creates an insurmountable spiritual distance between them. The humiliations she has endured have made her into a strong person who does not see herself as a "fallen woman" waiting to be saved by the magnanimous Prince. Rather, it is Nekhliudov who needs to be saved from his unhappy consciousness. But Katiusha does not wish to play the role of a Gretchen who helps Faust attain salvation. She wants to begin a new life. Katiusha's rejection forces Nekhliudov to re-examine his values. He gradually begins to realize that both his outward life and his self-consciousness have been utterly false and that he must restart his *Bildungsroman* from scratch.

In Siberia, they meet political prisoners many of whom, like Dostoevsky, did not commit any crimes, but were sentenced for distributing propaganda advocating democratic ideas. Tolstoy does not idealize all revolutionaries. He does, however, single out two characters whom he promotes as the new examples of *kalokagathia*: a Jewish intellectual named Simonson and a beautiful young lady Maria Pavlovna, a general's daughter whose portrait reminds us of Aglaia Epanchina. Both characters are quixotic in the noblest sense of the term. Maria Pavlovna is arrested for assuming responsibility for a terrorist act committed by her comrade. Simonson is arrested for pacifist propaganda that echoes the ideas expressed in Tolstoy's religious tracts. He also resembles Turgenev's Baburin from *Punin and Baburin*, and in marrying him Katiusha acts like Muza. Next to these heroic individuals who have broken ties with the old world, Nekhliudov realizes how vain his attempts at self-sacrifice have been and begins dreaming of a new life.

Nekhliudov's narrative concludes with another significant encounter. Shortly before the end of the novel, in Chap. 21 of Book Three, while crossing a river on a ferry, he sees an old schismatic. This man, who looks and speaks like a peasant, is an allusion to two characters: the old schismatic from Dostoevsky's *Notes from the House of the Dead* and the protagonist of Tolstoy's *Father Sergius* at the end of his journey. The schismatic refuses to give his name, calling himself a Human [*Chelovek*], and claims that he believes in no authority beyond his own conscience (PSS 32: 418). When after his final meeting with Katiusha, Nekhliudov realizes that his dream of returning to their shared idyllic past was an illusion, he opens the New Testament, which he received from an English missionary, and for the first time in his life immerses himself in this text. At this juncture, the voice of the hero reading the text to himself merges with that of Tolstoy, the Russian translator of the Gospel (PSS 32: 442–445). The emotional pitch is so intense that we as readers are also compelled to co-experience this powerful moment, which infects us with a belief in the possibility of finding a new life. Given the powerful impression made on Nekhliudov by the schismatic, we can be certain that Nekhliudov's interpretation of the Gospel will not adhere to the canon, but will bring his moral consciousness to a wholly new level. As a religious reformer-cum-writer Tolstoy wishes to reach out to the whole educated public and to push his traditional Orthodox readers to recognize the inauthenticity of their beliefs, while simultaneously rekindling the feelings of hope and love in the nihilists. By merging a typical *Bildungsroman* articulation of individual self-consciousness with emotionally charged religious language, Tolstoy overcomes the dualism of the mind and the heart, Western rationality and Russian faith. He also provides the last in the long line of Russian polemics about the strengths and limitations of high and popular literature.

When the architects of the new Soviet culture began to reform the national literary canon in the late 1920s, they largely rejected Tolstoy's ethical-political teachings, but adopted his didactic methods.[70] Moving stories with clear moral messages became a staple of Soviet literature, which was forced to succumb to the rigorous ideological control of the state. The country's prolonged political isolation and its perpetual struggle to ensure the loyalty of its subjects, whose voluntary daily self-sacrifice was essential to the success or even the survival of the state, led to intellectual stagnation. Although emotionally powerful prose continued to be produced throughout the Soviet period, both its content and its genre system grew increasingly more restricted. The public denunciation campaigns against writers, artists, and even musicians throughout the Stalinist period forced those with the most innovative ideas underground, whereas those in the limelight were forced to create works that corresponded to the current vision of Communist party leaders.

470   L. STEINER

As the crucial form of human self-understanding, the Soviet novel was closely scrutinized by the party cultural authorities. Katerina Clark has demonstrated how this ideological regime caused the novel's devolution from a medium of critical reflection back to such pre-modern forms as hagiography, legend, and the fairy tale (Clark 1981). However, in addition to heroic tales about military commanders, aviators, explorers, and other awe-inspiring heroes analysed by Clark, Soviet literature also included many prose narratives about ordinary people. Every year thick journals like *Oktiabr'*, *Roman-Gazeta*, *Neva*, and *Moskva* published new novels, many of which were written by talented authors. In the post-World War II period the heroism of ordinary people during the war became the richest source for Soviet storytellers.

Another important genre was science fiction. Capitalizing on the ideas of visionaries like Nikolai Fedorov and Konstantin Tsiolkovsky, Soviet writers created optimistic visions of space exploration and/or conquest of new territories. These works were typically full of allusions to classical literature and philosophy and were designed to provoke reflection. For example, *The Roadside Picnic* by Arkady and Boris Strugatsky (which Andrei Tarkovsky transformed into *Stalker*) dramatizes Soviet culture's obsession with humanity's infinite quest for new worlds and ideas. Stalker, a Promethean hero, boldly transgresses the boundaries of familiar reality by entering the mysterious "Zone" and taking possession of strange objects he finds there. But whether his daring behaviour is constructive or potentially destructive is the question the reader/spectator should ponder herself.

Nabokov's Meta-Utopias

Making Russian literature central to world literature was the main ambition of the Silver Age, which conceived of itself not merely as a Russian poetic renaissance, but as the dawn of a new world, which was to become the world of art. A legatee of this epoch, Nabokov was fortunate enough to escape from both post-Revolutionary Russia and Nazi Germany, where his freedom of speech would have been curtailed. Drawing on the works of Andrei Bely and other modernists, he created his own brand of the philosophical novel, which preserves and creatively transforms a number of previous philosophical and artistic systems. While being averse to overt didacticism, Nabokov crafted his works in such a way that they set in motion the readers' own moral consciousness. This strategy, which contrasts sharply with the overt moralizing of many other twentieth-century legatees of the classic Russian novel, makes Nabokov's philosophical novel a particularly interesting example of literary transmission.

Nabokov's magnum opus, *Ada or Ardor*, transcends linguistic and national boundaries and synthesizes nearly all genres of Western fiction from ancient Greece to twentieth-century America. Subtitled "A Family Chronicle," it is a modern riposte to Sergei Aksakov's epic memorialization of the old Russian gentry life that also bears a resemblance to Proust's works.[71] Notwithstanding his declarations of artistic freedom and his belief that works of art are analogous to the natural world, Nabokov is not a solipsistic aesthete like Flaubert or Proust (who were among his favourite authors). As Vladimir Alexandrov has justly argued, Nabokov's philosophical sensibility betrays a debt to Romantic meditations on the rift between human finitude and the infinite (Alexandrov 1991, 18). In my view, however, Nabokov's interest in the "Otherworld" does not necessarily make him a Platonist who firmly believes in the existence of an ideal realm. Constructed as a meta-Utopia, *Ada* demonstrates that consciousness can hardly guarantee salvation. It can, however, add new dimensions to our experience, introducing beauty to the otherwise painful human condition.

Before we can begin unravelling *Ada*, a palimpsest containing records of Nabokov's entire intellectual life, it is helpful to make an excursus into the last novel he wrote in Russian, *The Gift* [*Dar*]. Published in Berlin in 1938, this work is a modernist *Künstlerroman*, whose protagonist, a young poet Fyodor Godunov-Cherdyntsev, completes his apprenticeship as a Russian émigré author in Germany in the 1930s by writing a novelistic biography of Nikolai Chernyshevsky. The very fact that a young aristocrat whose poetic sensibilities are shaped by post-symbolism immerses himself in the life of the author of *What Is to Be Done?* is puzzling. The author provides psychological motivation for his hero's decision by naming the middle-aged couple who act as Fyodor's surrogate parents in Berlin "Chernyshevski."[72] The poet's own father is a natural scientist who disappears during his last expeditions to China and Tibet on the eve of the Russian Revolution. Although Fyodor's desire to write a longer prose work is fuelled by his longing to reconnect with his lost father, instead of composing a family chronicle, he starts working on the biography of the most polarizing nineteenth-century intellectual star. Given that the middle-rank intelligentsia who revere Chernyshevsky outnumber the highbrow intellectuals who dislike him in the émigré community where the novel is set, Fyodor's choice appears imprudent. In the end he delivers a non-canonical work, which mocks Chernyshevsky's flat-footed aesthetic theory, while at the same time acknowledging the strength of his character, which makes Chernyshevsky a much worthier person than the Kirsanovs and the Rakhmetovs he invented.[73] Rife with ambiguities, Fyodor's *Life of Chernyshevski* provokes a critical debate, but the only person whose opinion really matters to Fyodor, his surrogate father-figure Alexander Yakovlevich—who turns out to be a Jewish convert who took the last name "Chernyshevski" out of respect for the radical critic's memory—dies before Fyodor has a chance to talk to him. Thus, Fyodor's polemic with the Chernyshevskys remains unfinalized. From the conventional figure of a young aristocrat displaced by the Revolution Fyodor transforms into a polyphonic character with a complex interiority. We can be sure that Fyodor will not become yet another epigone of symbolism like his favourite poet Koncheyev, whose last name is cognate with the words *konchat'* (to finish, to consummate) and *konchina* (death) (Nabokov 1991, 338–341). But how will his style and trajectory evolve? It is tempting to think that Nabokov's hero, unlike his namesake from Pushkin's *Boris Godunov*, has

472   L. STEINER

inherited a realm from which no pretender can oust him: Russian literature. But safeguarding this fragile patrimony in emigration no less challenging than saving the Tsardom.

While Fyodor completes his apprenticeship by writing a parodic *Life of Chernyshevski*, *The Gift* as a whole is a metaparody, which ironizes the genres of literary biography and apprenticeship novel. According to Gary Saul Morson, "as there are genres and parodic genres, there are also metaparodic genres— that is, genres of works that are designed to be interpreted as a dialogue of parody and counterparody" (Morson 1989, 82). For Morson, Dostoevsky's *Diary of the Writer* is an example of metaparody, which casts ironic light on many pivotal literary genres and traditions, if not on the entire modern institution of literature and literary criticism. Although Nabokov never championed Dostoevsky the way he championed Pushkin and Gogol, I think that his experimentations with parody and other polyphonic genres and devices are indebted to Dostoevsky. A fantasy novel set on a planet called Antiterra, *Ada* is also thematically linked to Dostoevsky's "Dream of the Ridiculous Man."[74] Both works pose the same philosophical question: can a world free from all struggles and suffering be represented in a novel? At the end of his career, the author of *The Idiot* came to realize that any paradise or Arcadia would inevitably lose its innocence once a self-obsessed modern intellectual set foot on it. Thus, the hero of *The Dream of a Ridiculous Man*, who is both a new avatar of Prince Myshkin and Dostoevsky's alter ego, corrupts the ideal planet he visits in the afterlife through some unnamed sin. Dostoevsky's fantastic tale parodies both his own novels and the preceding sentimental tradition that strove to bridge the gap between the real and the ideal by means of fiction. But perhaps Dostoevsky's inability to conjure up Utopia was due to his special accursedness? Or perhaps it was due to the disorderliness of the nineteenth-century Russia that fed his imagination?

At first sight, the vast Anglophone country, where Russian is only a heritage language of a minority in the American provinces of Estoty and Canady and where the Russian-Irish upper-class families of the Veens and the Durmanovs enjoy luxurious lives, is precisely the kind of Utopia that the "paradoxalist" from *Notes from the Underground* would denounce as a fake and his Ridiculous Man would have defiled. For Dostoevsky's narrators, a Utopia free from religious conflicts, economic and natural catastrophes, as well as interpersonal struggles for domination, is a childish fantasy. The first part of Nabokov's novel, which is as long as the other four parts combined, represents this kind of fantasy. But *The Dream of a Ridiculous Man* is only one among many intertexts that should be taken into account when interpreting *Ada*. This work reuses motifs from Nabokov's earlier works, such as nostalgia for the idyllic world of childhood, a quest for self-realization, infantile sexuality, and incest, creating the effect of a *mise en abyme*, and echoes a great many European and Russian classics. This dense allusiveness makes *Ada* irreducible to a single interpretation. However, among all possible interpretations, the one that alludes to Dostoevsky's philosophical parable, as well as to the larger project of his *Diary*, with its complex intersections of parody and self-parody, seems to me to be particularly pertinent insofar as it helps us to recognize the moral dimension of Nabokov's irony. Indeed, despite his aversion to direct moralizing, Nabokov was not an "extra-moral" author. This is quite obvious in *Lolita*, a work that should be interpreted as part of the "confessional" tradition, alongside Karamzin's "My Confession" and Stavrogin's "Confession" from *The Demons*.[75]

The crucial intertext we must know in order to be able to interpret *Ada* is François-René de Chateaubriand's *Mémoires d'outre-tombe* [*Memoirs from Beyond the Grave*], which includes his autobiographical novella *René*. Chateaubriand's work is itself a palimpsest where autobiographical confessions are interspersed with fictions. In it, René's and his sister Amélie's incestual desire, which causes the former's departure to the new world and his sister's escape to a convent, is mirrored by Chateaubriand's recollections of his passionate friendship with his sister Lucille, which does not, however, cross the boundaries of propriety.[76] Byron's *Child Harold's Pilgrimage* and Pushkin's *The Gypsies* were inspired by Chateaubriand's descriptions of his hero's wanderings in North America. Byron's *Manfred* was probably also inspired by René. Unlike Chateaubriand's hero, however, Manfred transgresses the boundary between good and evil by actually raping his half-sister Astarte. Both Chateaubriand's and Byron's heroes suffer, but Manfred's sufferings are those of a nihilist who defies heaven, whereas René suffers from religious nostalgia that prefigures a conversion. Dostoevsky's Raskolnikov also begins his career as a defiant Romantic hero, but ends up feeling as dejected as René. His inability to follow the Christlike example demonstrated by the self-sacrificial Sonya and to "humble himself down" in order to be reborn for a new life is indicative of Dostoevsky's deep-seated fascination with the image of the heroic criminal. And yet, at the end of the epilogue, Raskolnikov finally becomes a Christian.

The post-World War II Western civilization, where Nabokov built his career as an Anglophone novelist, was unromantic and looked askance at the Russian "religion of suffering." So why did the Western readers react with such enthusiasm to his *Lolita* whose plot was inspired by Dostoevsky? Were they only titillated by its frank discussion of sexuality or were they moved by the novel's deep analysis of a criminal's psyche? Having reached fame and financial security after publishing *Lolita*, Nabokov spent the next decade of his life working on *Ada*, whose filiations with the Russian moralist tradition are announced in its very first sentence, which parodies the first line of *Anna Karenina* and inverts its meaning. Although Tolstoy asserts that all happy families are alike, but each unhappy family is unhappy in its own way, Nabokov's first line suggests that unhappiness is the common lot, whereas happiness is the achievement of unique individuals.

This assertion reminds us of Stendhal's "beylism." Stendhal's autobiography, *La vie d'Henry Brulard*, describes the most memorable day of his youth, which occurred at the very beginning of Napoleon's Italian campaign. In anticipation of his trip to Vevey (situated only a few kilometres away from Montreux, where

Ada was written), which was to take place on the following day, the future novelist daydreams about the world of sublime passions described in Rousseau's novel. In his later career as a writer, Stendhal would try to recapture this experience of *bonheur parfait* (Stendhal 1969, 407). Stendhal's pursuit of happiness is close to Nabokov's sensibility. Stendhal's attempts to recapture the feelings he experienced listening to opera and looking at paintings through the act of writing literary prose has much in common with Nabokov's synaesthesia. Like Stendhal, Nabokov wrote for the "happy few" endowed with a refined sensibility. Thus even Humbert's agonizing attempt to portray himself as an aesthete seduced by the nymphet can arouse our sympathy if we find his literary style engaging enough to enter into his perspective.

From the ethical point of view, *Ada* is even more ambiguous than *Lolita*, because it is not a confession of a criminal who acknowledges his guilt, but a memoir of a couple whose sins (if they are sins) remained unpunished, and who are so self-obsessed that they do not consider their misdeeds criminal. But does the author act as a *deus absconditus* or does he actually judge his characters?[77] In my opinion, he judges them, but does it in very subtle ways. For example, their names suggest that the immoral streak runs through the entire Dourmanov-Veen family. Van's father, Dementii, is commonly referred to as Demon. Ada's mother explains that the Russian "a" sounds different from the English "a" and her daughter's name should be pronounced like the English word "ardor." But a Russian reader would certainly make different associations. As Ada herself points out, her name calls to mind the Russian word *ad*, "Hell" (ibid., 457). Her younger sister is named Lucinda, or Lucette. Her name invites associations not only with Chateaubriand's Memoirs, but also with Friedrich Schlegel's novel *Lucinde*, which caused as much scandal by its eroticism and emphasis on free love as by its idiosyncratic play with genres, which ushered in a Romantic revolution in poetics.

The inter-generic dialogue with which Schlegel replaced the Aristotelian plot is a precursor of Nabokov's narrative experiment. To bring out the whole gamut of ideas that emerge through the juxtaposition of these two intricate works requires a separate study. What is essential for interpreting *Ada* as a text with Romantic filiations is the fact that both works are supposed to present their love stories from the point of view of a happy couple whose horizons have almost merged but who nevertheless retain separate voices. Unlike *Lucinde*, however, Ada is not a fragment, but a "family chronicle" that begins with the prehistory, portraying the parents and even grandparents of the main characters, covers their entire lives, and ends with a somewhat disjointed conversation between Van and Ada, who have grown very old and are preparing to die. At the very end of the story their voices finally fade away and the publisher of their memoirs steps in to provide his summary, intended as the backcover blurb (ibid., 460). The editor's blurb reduces Van's and Ada's memoir to an anecdote fit for the readers of *Vanity Fair* or some other fashionable lifestyle magazine. It contrasts with the poetic prose of the main narrative, which Van and Ada design as a monument to their singular love affair, which began when they were barely past childhood and lasted their entire lives. But the editor is, of

21 THE RUSSIAN NOVEL AS A MEDIUM OF MORAL REFLECTION IN THE LONG... 475

course, a "device," which the readers trained on Pushkin would recognize as an invitation for a deep reflection.

In contrast to the characters of Tolstoy and Dostoevsky, Van and Ada are free from sexual inhibitions and do not hesitate to consummate their passion. It is not that Antiterra knows no taboos and social constraints, but Van and Ada seem to be unconscious of them until they realize that they are not completely alone in their paradise. Ada's younger sister frequently observes their love-making and becomes jealous. Irritated by Lucette's intrusions, Ada teases her. However, neither she nor the servants who must have caught wind of the affair between Van and Ada betray their secret. Thus the affair continues, on and off, until the day when Van's (and probably Ada's) father Demon makes it clear that Ada should get married. Once she marries a rich businessman Andrey and goes with him to Arizona—and thence to Hollywood, where she tries to become an actress—Van embarks on a scholarly career. He studies philosophy, becoming a specialist on Terra, a mysterious twin of Antiterra, which poets and madmen see in their dreams. Van's claim to fame is a philosophical novel entitled *Letters from Terra* published under the pseudonym Voltemand (perhaps an allusion to Voltaire). As the reader finds out in Part Five, while researching his project on Terra, Van also began collecting materials for an autobiography. At the same time, he appears to be utterly guilt-free about the incest he and Ada have committed and, while longing to be one day reunited with her, leads a dissolute life, visiting posh bordellos, having meaningless love affairs, and even fighting a duel. The chronicle of his adventures during this period sounds like a second-rate boulevard novel. The only incident that interrupts this banal narrative is Van's encounter with a grown-up Lucette, whose unrequited passion for him leads to her suicide.

Shortly after the death of Marina, Lucette, now a wealthy and independent young woman, accosts Van in his New York penthouse. Although he finds Lucette attractive, he refuses to sleep with her, citing two reasons: firstly, he does not want to have another incestuous affair, and secondly, he loves Ada and not her. But Lucette does not give up, offering a solution that harks back to the story of Undine, Huldebrand, and Bertholda. Van can marry her, the new owner of Ardis Hall, and they can invite Ada to spend summers with them. When Ada comes to visit, Lucette will "fade into the background" (perhaps returning to her role as a voyeur, which she played as a child). Shocked by her suggestion, Van calls her "a loosest Lucinda imaginable," scolds her for her vulgar language and manners, and sends her away (Nabokov 1969, 363). But Lucette continues to pursue him. Some months later she finds out that he is in Europe and plans to return to New York. She also comes to Europe, buys a ticket for the same ocean liner, and stalks Van on board, where they can be seen together by acquaintances. In the evening they go together to see a movie, *Don Juan's Last Fling*, in which Ada plays the role of a seductive Gypsy Dolores.[78] A parody of both Pushkin's *Stone Guest* and Alexander Korda's *The Private Life of Don Juan*, this film includes a scene where Don Juan suddenly behaves like Don Quixote saving Dolores from a miller who accuses her of stealing flour. She embraces Don Juan, but he runs away from her to Donna Anna's castle.

476 L. STEINER

But Dolores reappears there and dances a passionate Spanish Gypsy dance (ibid., 384). While Van cannot tear his eyes away from Ada, Lucette burns with jealousy. The reappearance of Dolores rejected by Don Juan duplicates Lucette's reappearance before Van. Don Juan's sudden metamorphosis into Don Quixote invites a comparison with Van's metamorphosis from a foppish "gentleman scholar" who leads the life of a libertine into a morally responsible older brother who is shocked by Lucette's proposition and concerned about her depravity. Disturbed by his conflicting impulses and emotions, Van loses his calm and abandons the movie theatre, leaving Lucette to wander along the deck as the storm approaches. Abandoned by Van, she gets drunk and then takes an overdose of the pills prescribed for motion sickness, the same sickness that reveals human frailty and hastens the denouement in *Undine*. Predictably, Lucette slips overboard and is swallowed by the ocean.

After Lucette's death Van, who hardly ever talks to his father, writes several different drafts of a letter in which he attempts to explain this incident and make clear that he had never tried to seduce the poor girl. The old Demon responds by saying that he does not give a damn whether Van slept with his youngest sister and goes on to chatter about "Don Juan's Last Fling" (ibid., 390). The "society" of Antiterra does not care all that much about the Veens' family drama. In contrast to the social elites described in nineteenth-century novels, *Ada*'s aristocracy, which has become intermarried with and indistinguishable from bourgeoisie, is too diffuse, too knowledgeable about sexuality, and perhaps too self-obsessed to care about the morals of others. But Van is also too self-obsessed to fixate on Lucette's death. He resumes his luxurious life, which to outside observers appears utterly purposeless, until Ada becomes a widow and they finally decide to spend the rest of their lives together. At this juncture, they embark on their Proustian memoir, which will become their only issue. The Veens are childless and completely isolated from any kind of professional community. Thus the Veens cannot be sure that anyone will care to find out about their inner lives. For whom are they writing their book?

The problem of transmitting values is intertwined with the ethical problems that loom large in Parts Three to Five, which describe the heroes' transition to adulthood in a world that imposes no demands and creates no boundaries for their narcissistic desire. Poets from the Earth have long dreamed about a world where necessity no longer oppresses human beings, allowing them to engage in a perpetual pursuit of happiness. Nabokov designed a realistic model of this paradise, which readers, especially those less spoilt than Van and Ada, might find delightful. Although Nabokov disliked Freud, Ada is written in a kind of ironic competition with his psychoanalytic theory. Readers will be charmed by *Ada*'s sensual prose and, projecting themselves into the lives of Nabokov's guiltless heroes, experience a *jouissance* that eludes them in their daily lives. But even those accustomed to merely voyeuristic pleasures might eventually become bored with Van and Ada's incessant love-making, which neither society nor God cares to punish. As the characters age, their romance loses its novelty and intensity, and readers who are accustomed to reading novels "for the plot"—that is, for the sake of the romantic story driven by desire—will tire of Van and Ada, unless they manage to develop a deeper interest in their souls and wish to trace their moral progress. These readers will have to work hard to understand Van's and Ada's interiority. Like a college course designed in such a way that the students who do not drop out during the "shopping period" later get intellectually rewarded for their assiduousness, Nabokov's novel is designed in such a way that the more patient readers will glimpse a deeper human story beyond a fantasy fiction only when they get to the point where narrative progress slows down and the story becomes retrospective and meditative.

One first notices the change in the narrative style in Chap. 5 of Part Three, where the narrators struggle to account for Lucette's death. The intrusion of the stream-of-consciousness in the midst of a traditional narrative reminds us of Tolstoy's *Anna Karenina*, where the same technique is used in the sequence of scenes that describe Anna's last journey to the train station and her suicide. As a narrative technique, stream-of-consciousness creates the illusion of a shared subjectivity, which implicates both Van and Ada, as well as the readers, in Lucette's suicide. However, they insist that Lucette's last thoughts were different from Anna's. Instead of seeing her entire life as an open book, Lucette's imagination is bombarded with disconnected memories (ibid., 388).

Having represented death from inside a dying girl's mind, the narrative returns to the world of the living. Chapter 6 of Part Three consist of six letters, which Van, his father, Ada, and Van's mistress Cordula exchange in the wake of Lucette's death. In Parts Three to Five, the narrators become painfully self-aware, at times almost scholarly, at times deliberately nonchalant and superficial. Many stories are not even narrated but mentioned drily, as if nothing interesting can be said about them. The deaths of Ada's husband, of Demon, and even Marina (which precedes Lucette's) fail to elicit any emotional response. The sins and secrets of the older generation seem to have no moral import for their children, who claim to be proud of their noble ancestry but prove utterly devoid of filial attachments. Childless and utterly self-sufficient, have they ever known love or was their passion merely an escapist delusion that kept them from developing real attachments, suffering disappointments and heartbreaks—in short, from growing up? As Van and Ada reach the point when they face their imminent deaths, the question about the meaning of life presents itself with utmost urgency. As a result, Nabokov's narrators start arguing about the genre and meaning of their work. Van wants to turn it into a philosophical meditation about Time (with a capital "T"), but Ada questions the meaning of this abstract term (ibid., 420).

Ada begins to be haunted by her sister's ghost. At the end of Part Four, shortly after her husband's death, she spends some time with Van, but then prepares to go back to Arizona. Suddenly, she returns. "I told him [the driver] to turn," she said, "somewhere near Morzhey ('morses' or 'walruses,' a Russian pun on 'Morges'—maybe a mermaid's message)" (ibid., 442). A few pages later, we stumble on the following stream-of-consciousness, which seems to be Van's interior monologue: "('Ursus,' Lucette in glistening green. 'Subside,

478   L. STEINER

agitation of passion.' 'Flora's bracelets and breasts, the whelk of Time')" (ibid., 450). A sea-shell is a fitting metaphor for Time as a receptacle of human utterances. But are the original meanings also preserved in the echoes that resound for thousands of years? Is the Whelk of Time Van's image of the afterlife where he and Lucette can resume their unfinished conversation and perhaps be reconciled, or will Lucette's cries, preserved in the actual whelks that one could theoretically fish out of the Atlantic, remain forever inscrutable and chaotic? Van remembers that when Lucette was fished out, "her body, her head, and particularly those damned thirsty trousers, felt clogged with Oceanus Nox, n,o,x," (ibid., 387).

The allusion to "Oceano Nox," a poem by Victor Hugo that describes death by drowning, along with the allusion to Ursus, the philosopher from Hugo's *Man Who Laughs*, suggests that Van considers Lucette's death in the context of their family chronicle. Perhaps he has come to see his privileged family the way Hugo's Ursus saw English court and aristocracy: as a bunch of depraved imps.[79] Whatever associations Nabokov's hero is making, he never articulates them logically, leaving the reader to wonder whether he actually suffers any remorse. His official ethical code is that of an aristocratic "Voltairian" of Pushkin's generation. A non-believer who sneers at sexual taboos, deep down he still thinks like a "man of honour" along the lines of Onegin. Thus despite being a son of Demon, he is not a cynical nihilist like Pechorin or Stavrogin who deliberately inflict pain on other people. Since he never had any deep feelings for Lucette and was always honest with her, he does not feel responsible for her demise (or even if he does feel some pangs of conscience, his reason represses them). Ada, on the other hand, does express remorse for not loving Lucette and "teasing her to death" (ibid., 459). Echoing Lucette's idea, she says that Van should have married her, so that the three of them could have lived happily together (ibid., 459). This vision of happiness *à trois* is hardly a sexual fantasy, but rather a nostalgic wish to recreate the idyllic life they had enjoyed as children. However, the gods of Antiterra are so kind to these heroes that in the twilight of their life Van and Ada have an opportunity to hire a live-in secretary who resembles Lucette and helps them to transcribe their memoirs. Whatever erotic fantasies might still pass through their minds, the Veens are too old to act on them. Violet's companionship compensates the Veens for the lack of children and grandchildren, making us once again wonder whether the author meant to congratulate his heroes for their ability to be completely aloof from the crowd and its slave morality or to pity them.

Finally, pain and suffering do catch up with them. Thinking about the future, Ada wonders whether after death their souls will go to Nirvana, to Hades, or to their own Otherworld, Vaniada (ibid., 456). Her last whispers sound like ritual incantations, contrasting sharply with the prosaic voice of Van, who complains about his physical pain and dismisses the idea that he should now be racked with guilt over Lucette's death. This strange dialogue in the last pages of the book reminds us of the dialogue of the dead in Dostoevsky's "Bobok" (Dostoevsky 1972–1990, 21: 41–54). This intertextual association with Dostoevsky's Menippean satire becomes even more obvious once both voices are interrupted by the "editor," who wraps up the story by providing his own summary, which might be seen as a parody of various genres and cultural perspectives brought into play by the main narrators, and of the very medium of modern print culture. The intrusion of the publisher reminds us that in today's world even highbrow literature's moral efficacy no longer goes without saying because the market constantly tries to transform it from a medium of independent reflection into a commodity. But most readers who have actually read Nabokov's novel to the end have already been unsettled and puzzled enough not to be able to put this book away with a solemn conviction that they have accrued some cultural capital. Although *Ada* does have a traditional *fabula*, to grasp the actual meaning of this work readers must enter into the endless labyrinth of intertextuality, from which no benevolent narrator will rescue them. Nabokov designed his fictions for those who dare to know. In his ocean one can either sink or learn to swim.

Notes

1. The exact rates of literacy in the eighteenth-century Russia are disputable. Eighteenth-century comedies, most notably Denis Fonvizin's *The Minor* [*Nedorosl'*], satirize the unenlightened and ill-mannered members of the gentry. Eighteenth-century memoirs suggest that home education, especially for women, varied, depending on the socioeconomic level of the family and proximity to court. As evidenced by *The Memoirs of Anna Labzina*, provincial gentry education emphasized piety. See Labzina (2001). On the other hand, *The Memoirs of Princess Dashkova* show that eighteenth-century courtly society valued good manners and cultural erudition above piety. See Dashkova (1995).
2. Luba Golburt offers a fascinating account of eighteenth-century Russian culture as the first phase of Russian modernization and its impact on the cultural imagination of the Golden Age (the age of Pushkin), as well as subsequent periods in nineteenth-century culture (Golburt 2014).
3. Perhaps the most outspoken Russian critic of Westernization was Catherine II's court historian, Prince Mikhail Shcherbatov, who also happened to be Petr Chaadaev's maternal grandfather. On Scherbatov's views, see Walicki (1979, 26–30).
4. The circle of Andrei Turgenev in the 1800s and the literary society *Arzamas* (to which the young Pushkin belonged) were important vehicles for early Romantic liberalism in Russia. See, for example, Maria Maiofis' study of *Arzamas* (Maiofis 2008). For an in-depth intellectual history of this period that stresses the influence of German conservative thought, see Martin (1997).
5. Bakhtin's conception of European modernity, enshrined in his theory of the novel, presents a form of the secularization thesis.
6. This question has been discussed in Chap. 1 of the present volume. See also Frede (2011).
7. As William Todd has argued, the history of the Russian novel cannot be divorced from the institutional history of literature. Thus he analyses the evolution of

novelistic forms in conjunction with the development of print culture. See Todd (2006).

8. Radishchev's extant semi-hagiographic works are *The Life of Fyodor Vassil'evich Ushakov* and *The Life of Filaret the Merciful*. See Steiner (2019).

9. Although Radishchev was recalled from exile by Paul I in 1796, most of his works remained banned. The manuscript of *The Journey* circulated among the liberal intellectuals in the 1800s and 1810s and was known to Pushkin. It is doubtful that his other works were known to anyone beyond the narrow liberal circle that clustered around Radishchev's patron Count Alexander Romanovich Vorontsov and his sister Princess Ekaterina Romanovna Dashkova. *The Journey* became widely known after Herzen published it in his Free Russian Press in London.

10. Like the German Bildungsroman, the Russian novel of education is indebted to the Masonic conceptions of self-purification and self-perfection. Schmid devotes a chapter to the Masons' autobiographies, which he sees as a pathway between the Christian and the enlightened conceptions of personality. See Schmid (2000). In addition to the male autobiographies he discusses, one should also consider the *Memoirs of Anna Labzina*, the wife of a Mason and a participant in the Masonic Enlightenment. See Labzina (2001).

11. For a classic study of this period, see Ginzburg (1969).

12. Vladimir F. Odoevskij (1967). (In this edition Odoevskii's name is transliterated according to the German convention.) In my opinion, the genre of *Russian Nights* could be best understood in comparison to Friedrich Schlegel's *Dialogue on Poetry*. For a different interpretation of this enigmatic work, see Zenkovsky (1953, 1: 143–144).

13. See Ginzburg (1991, 789). For Belinsky, the most intense phase of this self-search began after he moved from Moscow to Petersburg, whence he wrote to V.P. Botkin, a confrere from the Stankevich circle: "For me there is only one way out—you know what it is; it is not in *Jenseits* or in mysticism or in anything that provides a way out for half-endowed natures and half-disillusioned souls […] Only one thing is left—either to make something real of myself or, as long as breath remains in my body, to sing this little ditty: 'I have wasted my life, and now it is gone forever.'" See Belinsky (1953–1959, 11: 416). In his chapter for this handbook Vadim Shkolnikov also discusses Belinsky's quest for self-realization and discovery of the "sociality of Reason."

14. For a detailed discussion of the emergence of the Uvarov triad, see Zorin (2001).

15. In his essay for this *Handbook* Alexei Krouglov discusses the history of Kant's reception in nineteenth-century Russia. Indeed, it was Kant's approach to morality as a domain of independent judgement that explains his popularity among the Russian *intelligentsia*.

16. See Michael Forster's analysis of Herder's influential study of Shakespeare (Forster 2018, 74–116). Kristin Gjesdal discusses Herder's idea of the historical development of language as the vehicle of *Bildung*, by which Herder means both self-consciousness and culture, or self-consciousness achieved through culture in Chap. 2 of her study (Gjesdal 2017, 55–58).

17. The English translation of Belinsky's *Letter to N.V. Gogol* is found in Matlaw (1962, 83–94). When Dostoevsky was arrested along with other members of the Petrashevsky circle in 1849, his charge was that he read Belinsky's forbidden letter at Petrashevsky's gatherings on several occasions.

18. Debates on how to understand Gogol's aesthetics (i.e., whether he should be seen as a Romantic, a realist, a naturalist, or whether his idiosyncratic style cuts across all these categories) began in 1830 and never came to an end. A snapshot of these debates can be found in Maguire (1974).
19. Belinsky was one of the first Russian critics to compose annual critical surveys of the entire literary public sphere. The review in question is V.G. Belinsky, "Vzgliad na russkuiu literaturu 1847 goda" (Belinsky 1953–1959, 10: 279–359).
20. Molly Brunson illuminates different meanings and usages of the term "realism" in Russian literature and art. See Brunson (2016).
21. For a helpful discussion of the Bakhtinian conception of "novelness," see Bruhn and Lundquist (2001). "Introduction: A Novelness of Bakhtin?" The category of "prosaics" introduced by Morson and Emerson has a broader philosophical meaning than "novelness." It is, however, also an illuminating neologism that reveals the full extent of Bakhtin's divergence from Aristotle. See Morson and Emerson (1990).
22. In suggesting that a linear conception of literary historicity be replaced with a more pluralistic and multi-directed one, I am not making a new argument, but echoing Bakhtin and his school, as well as their predecessors Alexander N. Veselovskii and his school of "historical poetics," all of whom have offered different versions of this argument. See Veselovskii (2011). Veselovskii's filiations with Bakhtin can also be gleaned through a comparison of his historical poetics with Dostoevsky's contemporaneous genre experimentations, which inspired Bakhtin's theory of polyphonic discourse. See Holland (2016).
23. The most famous scandal was, of course, the one caused by the publication of *Madame Bovary*. See LaCapra (1982).
24. Bakunin, Stankevich and other members of the Stankevich circle came close to writing in this vein, but their epistolary exchanges remained private. In his "Hamlet of Shchigrov District" and "Diary of a Superfluous Man" Turgenev came close to writing in this vein too, but he carefully drew a line between himself as the author and the heroes whose "divided souls" he explored. Herzen's self-analysis in *My Past and Thoughts* is also extremely self-apologetic. Ginzburg discusses this aspect of *My Past and Thoughts* in detail in Part Three of her study.
25. As George Kline reminds us, even as an officer in Sevastopol Tolstoy already wanted to found a new religion (Kline 1968, 24). See also Ginzburg (1991), as well as the essay by Henry Pickford in this *Handbook*.
26. Kate Holland (2013) discusses Dostoevsky's recourse to the hagiographic and archaic folk genres. See also Kliger (2012).
27. The happy ending of Arkadii Kirsanov's *Bildungsroman* is undermined by Evgenii Bazarov's tragic demise.
28. Ilya Kliger has demonstrated the tragic dimension of *The Ravine* in Kliger (2012).
29. For an illuminating discussion of Turgenev's cosmopolitanism, see Feiges (2020).
30. See especially the Introduction and Chap. 6 in Thomas Pavel's *The Lives of the Novel* (Pavel 2013).
31. For an illuminating discussion of the "beautiful soul" as represented by the chivalric romances and *Don Quixote*, see Pavel (2013), especially Chaps. 1 and 5.
32. Ilya Kliger brings out the Hegelian framework of *The Same Old Story* in Kliger (2011).

33. After the publication of *Rudin* (whose quixotic title hero was most likely modelled on Bakunin), *On the Eve* (which portrayed a female Quixote), and *Fathers and Children* (where he portrayed a nihilist whom unrequited love transforms into a Romantic), Turgenev also struggled with bouts of doubt and pessimism. Turgenev's self-doubt was in part due to the harsh criticism he received from younger radical critics, but also to the shock that he, along with Herzen and other Russian friends, experienced during the 1848 Paris Revolution, and to the influence of the pessimistic philosophers Hartmann and Schopenhauer.

34. "Punin and Baburin" is published in *Sobranie sochinenii v dvenadtsati tomakh*, 8: 185–244.

35. See Dostoevsky, "Pushkin" (Ocherk), in Dostoevsky (1972–1990, 26: 136–148).

36. I discuss Dostoevsky's debt to Grigor'ev's Herderian conception of Russian culture in Steiner (2011) (see especially Chap. 7). As Irina Paperno has shown, Dostoevsky's speech contains in a nutshell the symbolists' Nietzschean interpretations of Pushkin (Paperno 1994).

37. Karamzin had been made the Historian Laureate by Alexander I in 1803 and remained in this position until his death in 1826. Pushkin was invited by Nicholas I to be a historiographer of the Russian state in 1826, but only in 1831 was he promoted to the rank of titular councillor (rank Nine in the Table of Ranks) and given access to the archives. As a sign of special distinction Pushkin was appointed a junior chamberlain at Nicholas I's court. However, the poet was deeply humiliated by this "favour."

38. See Dostoevsky, "Pushkin" (cited in note 35), 141–143. Many Anglophone critics have also looked at Tatyana as an ideal of Russian femininity. See, for example, Hasty (1999).

39. On Turgenev and Dostoevsky as precursors of Nietzsche's nihilism, see, for example, Gillespie (1995, 135–173). Nietzsche's correspondence with his and Herzen's friend Malwida von Meysenbug shows how carefully he read *My Past and Thoughts* and how highly he esteemed it. See especially Nietzsche's letter dated August 27, 1872 (Nietzsche 2005, 40–41).

40. Nietzsche's reflections on Dostoevsky and the "Petersburg nihilism" are scattered throughout his works and letters, beginning with his letter to Franz Overbeck from February 12, 1887, where he first mentions Dostoevsky. Paulo Stellino offers a helpful overview of the Dostoevsky-Nietzsche connection in Stellino (2015).

41. According to Holquist and Clark, Bakhtin's book, titled *The Novel of Education and Its Significance in the History of Realism*, was accepted by the publishing house Soviet Writer. See Holquist and Clark (1984, 273).

42. Bakhtin's plans for this book have recently been published. See Bakhtin (1996, 3: 181–217). Gorky's Nietzscheanism has been thoroughly researched. For a helpful Anglophone study of this topic, see Clowes (1988).

43. On Bakhtin and Nietzsche, see Curtis (1986).

44. In Anglophone criticism, the history of the novelistic genre in the eighteenth-century Russia is sketched out by Hammamberg in Chap. 1 of her study. See Hammamberg (1991). In Russian, see Serman (1959, 1962) and Lotman (2005).

45. In my opinion, one of the best recent works on Pushkin as both a poet and a thinker is Kahn (2008). For an in-depth discussion of Pushkin's politics, see Proskurin (2006).

46. I discuss this phase in Pushkin's career in detail in Steiner (2009).
47. I discuss this phase in Pushkin's life in the next section of this chapter.
48. I borrow this title from Michael Holquist's *Dostoevsky and the Novel*, where he also examines *The Idiot*. My interpretation overlaps with his only insofar as I also see Myshkin as a character in the midst of an identity crisis (Holquist 1977, 102–122).
49. Comparing Tolstoy to Nietzsche became a popular philosophical *topos* from the 1900s to the 1920s. See, for example, Shestov (1969) and Davis and Dewey (1929).
50. I borrow this term from Wai Chee Dimock (2006).
51. As Vladimir Alexandrov points out, Nabokov acknowledged that he was a product of the *Silver Age*. See Alexandrov (1995, 358–359).
52. Among thinkers who influenced Karamzin directly, Johann Gottfried Herder devoted much effort to reviving the Greek notion of *kaloi k'agathoi* (beautiful and noble personalities) and the quality of *kalokagathia*. See Herder (2002).
53. See Karamzin, "Bednaia Liza," in Karamzin (1803, 6: 225–264).
54. Friedrich and August Wilhelm Schlegel, as well as Ludwig Tieck, Cervantes' German translator, and other critics have written about Don Quixote. August Wilhelm Schlegel even penned a poetic encomium addressed to Cervantes' hero. See Schlegel (1846, 1: 341–342).
55. This intriguing work attests to Karamzin's lasting interest in the problem of evil. As Tanya Page points out, Count NN is undoubtedly a precursor of Dostoevsky's Stavrogin. See Page (1985, 154). Whether this "Confession" was intended as a Socratic-Platonic pedagogical tale (as Tanya Pages interprets it), as a proto-naturalist character sketch, or as a parodic "trifle" (as Gitta Hammamberg interprets it) remains debatable. See Hammamberg (1991, 250).
56. This important element of Grinev's characteristic is thrown into relief in Chap. 11, where Grinev almost forgets about his old servant as he rushes to see Masha, imprisoned by Shvabrin. When he hears Savel'ich's voice, however, he stops and waits for him, to make sure that the old man does not remain behind in the rebels' camp. See Pushkin (1937–1959, 6: 335).
57. The idea that "Grinev's chronicle" expresses the naïve spirit of genuine *narodnost'* is developed in Grigor'ev's essay "Razvitie idei narodnosti v russkoi literature so smerti Pushkina" (Grigor'ev 2008, 184–607).
58. There is a vast literature on this topic. One of the most reliable accounts based on the thorough analysis of archival materials is found in Abramovich (1991).
59. David Powelstock discusses Lermontov's Romantic poetry and life in Powelstock (2005). For an in-depth analysis of the Russian duelling culture and its socio-political ramifications, see Reyfman (1999).
60. For a thorough examination of self-creation or life-creation in Russian modernism, see Paperno and Grossman (1994).
61. The last chapter of *A Hero of Our Time*, "The Fatalist," demonstrates Pechorin's utter wilfulness. Intellectually he may be an agnostic who plays with the idea of predestination, but deep down he believes only in his own physical and mental strength.
62. Irina Reyfman sheds light on this essentially Russian understanding of the duel in Reyfman (1999). Although Western scholars often perceive this irrational take on the duel as outlandish, I completely agree with Reyfman's analysis of the Russian aristocracy's moral psychology.

63. One of Nabokov's stories, "A Vile Creature" ["*Podlets*"] describes a Russian émigré in Berlin in the 1920s who challenges his wife's lover to a duel and then fails to appear at the site of the duel.

64. "I have a completely different notion of actuality and realism than our realists and critics. My idealism is more real than theirs" (Dostoevsky 1972–1990, 751).

65. To the best of my knowledge, this connection has never been discussed by the scholars. However, given Dostoevsky's well-known fascination with Hoffmann's work, I find it extremely plausible.

66. I base my summary on V.A. Zhukovsky's translation. See La Motte Foqué (1990).

67. The adolescent heroine of that unfinished novel also falls in love with Princess Katya, the daughter of a princely family that takes Netochka in after the death of her mother and the mysterious disappearance of her stepfather.

68. See Molly Brunson's analysis of this image in Chap. 5 of her book (Brunson 2016).

69. *The Resurrection* is published in Tolstoy, *Polnoe sobranie sochinenii* (1929–1958, 32). The scene I am referring to is described on pages 194–195.

70. For a helpful overview of Tolstoy's reception after the revolution, see Denner (2010). On the Stalinist-period revision and re-adaptation of the classical tradition, including Tolstoy, see Platt and Brandenberger (2006).

71. D.S. Mirsky draws a parallel between Aksakov's *Family Chronicle* and *In Search of Lost Time*. See Mirsky (1999, 186). It is not too far-fetched to suggest that Nabokov might have taken Mirsky's insight into account when designing his magnum opus, originally entitled, "The Texture of Time."

72. Nabokov uses this anglicized spelling.

73. The narrator's tone changes throughout Chap. 4. The chapter begins and ends with a "mediocre but curious sonnet," attributed to an anonymous poet who published it in *Century* in 1909. It is an ironic way to celebrate a life of a thinker who "equated genius with common sense" (Nabokov 1991, 256). In the course of the story, Fyodor's irony gradually becomes more biting until he comes to the point where his heroes' long years of exile, filled with endless work and physical suffering, are described. Gradually irony becomes less diminishing and imbued with sadness. In the end, the mediocre sonnet sounds quite touching. To grasp these modulations of the narrator's voice, one should pay attention to various lyric and rhetorical genres deployed in this text, which would require a separate article.

74. *The Dream of a Ridiculous Man* [*Son smeshnogo cheloveka*] was published in *The Diary of a Writer*. See Dostoevsky (1972–1990, 25: 104–119).

75. See note 52 above. That Nabokov "borrowed" the plot of *Lolita* from Dostoevsky can be gleaned from *The Gift*, where Zina's stepfather Schegolev (an unpleasant character) reveals that he too would like to write a novel. He goes on to describe what is basically the plot of *Lolita*. "D'you feel here a kind of Dostoevskian tragedy?" he asks Fyodor. See Nabokov (1991, 186).

76. For a somewhat different interpretation of the Chateaubriand connection, see Annapaola Cancogni, "Nabokov and Chateaubriand," in Alexandrov (1995, 382–388).

77. Brian Boyd (if I understand him correctly) thinks that Nabokov is too much of a postmodern ironist to be a moralist (see Boyd 1985).

78. Chapter 2 of Part One describes the big picnic on Ada's twelfth birthday, where "the child was permitted to wear her Lolita (thus dubbed after the little Andalusian gipsy of that name in Osberg's novel [...])" (Nabokov 1969).

79. Russian readers would also associate "Oceano Nox" with the saddest chapter from Herzen's autobiography, which describes the deaths of the author's mother and son in a shipwreck on the way to Nice, where they were to be reunited with the rest of the family. In Herzen's narrative, this misfortune, which occurred immediately after Herzen's reconciliation with his wife, signals the destruction of all hopes for a restoration of happiness in Herzen's private life. Interestingly, Herzen's daughter by Natalia Tuchkova-Ogareva, like Lucette, committed suicide out of despair caused by unrequited love. Dostoevsky interprets her suicide as a symptom of nihilism in his *Diary of a Writer*. See "O samoubiistve i vysokomerii," in Dostoevsky (1972–1990, 24: 52–54).

BIBLIOGRAPHY

Abramovich, Stella L. 1991. *Pushkin. Poslednii god.* Moscow: Sovetskii pisatel'.

Alexandrov, Vladimir E. 1991. *Nabokov's Otherworld.* Princeton, NJ: Princeton University Press.

———., ed. 1995. *The Garland Companion to Vladimir Nabokov.* New York, NY: Routledge.

Bakhtin, Mikhail M. 1996. *Sobranie sochinenii v 7 tomakh.* Moscow: Iazyki slavianskikh kul'tur.

Belinsky, Vissarion G. 1953–1959. *Polnoe sobranie sochinenii v 13 tomakh.* Moscow: Akademia Nauk SSSR.

Boyd, Brian. 1985. *Nabokov's Ada: The Place of Consciousness.* Ann Arbor, MI: Ardis.

Brooks, Peter. 2005. *Realist Vision.* New Haven, CT and London: Yale University Press.

Bruhn, Jorgen, and Jan Lundquist. 2001. Introduction: A Novelness of Bakhtin? In *The Novelness of Bakhtin: Perspectives and Possibilities*, ed. Jorgen Bruhn and Jan Lundquist, with a Preface by Michael Holquist, 11–52. Copenhagen: Museum Tusculanum, University of Copenhagen Press.

Brunson, Molly. 2016. *Russian Realisms: Literature and Painting, 1840–1980.* DeKalb, IL: Northern Illinois University Press.

Clark, Katerina. 1981. *The Soviet Novel: History as a Ritual.* Chicago, IL: University of Chicago Press.

Clowes, Edith W. 1988. *The Revolution of Moral Consciousness: Nietzsche in Russian Literature, 1890–1914.* DeKalb, IL: Northern Illinois University Press.

Cross, Anthony. 1971. *N.M. Karamzin: A Study of his Literary Career 1783–1803.* Carbondale, IL: Southern Illinois University Press.

Curtis, James M. 1986. Mikhail Bakhtin and Nietzsche. In *Nietzsche in Russia*, ed. Bernice Glatzer Rosenthal, 251–273. Princeton, NJ: Princeton University Press.

Dashkova, Ekaterina R. Princess. 1995. *The Memoirs of Princess Dashkova.* Translated by Kiril Fitzlyon, with an Introduction by Jehanne M. Gheith. Durham, NC: Duke University Press.

Davis, Helen E., and John Dewey. 1929. *Tolstoy and Nietzsche: A Problem in Biographical Ethics.* New York: New Republic.

Denner, Michael A. 2010. "The proletarian lord": Leo Tolstoy's image during the Russian revolutionary period. In *Anniversary Essays on Tolstoy*, ed. Donna Tussing Orwin, 219–244. Cambridge, UK: Cambridge University Press.

Dimock, Wai Chee. 2006. *Through Other Continents: American Literature Across Deep Time.* Princeton, NJ: Princeton University Press.

Dostoevsky, Fyodor M. 1972–1990. *Sobranie sochinenii v 30 tomakh*, ed. G. Fridlender et al. Leningrad: Nauka.

Feiges, Orlando. 2020. *The Europeans: Three Lives and the Making of a Cosmopolitan Culture*. London: Penguin.

Forster, Michael N. 2018. *Herder's Philosophy*. Oxford: Oxford University Press.

Frede, Victoria. 2011. *Doubt, Atheism, and the Nineteenth-Century Russian Intelligentsia*. Madison, WI: University of Wisconsin Press.

Gershenzon, Mikhail O. 2000. *Izbrannoe*. Moscow and Jerusalem: Universitetskaia kniga, Gesharim.

Gillespie, Michael Allen. 1995. *Nihilism before Nietzsche*. Chicago, IL: University of Chicago Press.

Ginzburg, Lydia Ya. 1969. *O lirike*. Leningrad: Sovetskii pisatel'.

Ginzburg, Lydia. 1991. *On Psychological Prose*. Translated by Judson Rosengrant. Princeton, NJ: Princeton University Press.

Gjesdal, Kristin. 2017. *Herder's Hermeneutics: History, Poetry, Enlightenment*. Cambridge, UK: Cambridge University Press.

Golburt, Luba. 2014. *The First Epoch: The Eighteenth Century and the Russian Cultural Imagination*. Madison, WI: University of Wisconsin Press.

Grigor'ev, Apollon A. 2008. *Apologia pochvennichestva*. Moscow: Izyki slavian-skikh kul'tur.

Hammamberg, Gitta. 1991. *From the Idyll to the Novel: Karamzin's Sentimental Prose*. Cambridge, UK: Cambridge University Press.

Hasty, Olga Peters. 1999. *Pushkin's Tatiana*. Madison, WI: University of Wisconsin Press.

Herder, Johann Gottfried. 2002. Fragments on Recent German Literature (1767–1768) [excerpts on language]. In *Philosophical Writings*, trans. and ed. Michael N. Forster, 33–64. Cambridge, UK: Cambridge University Press.

Holland, Kate. 2013. *The Novel in the Age of Disintegration: Dostoevsky and the Problem of Genre in the 1870s*. Evanston, IL: Northwestern University Press.

———. 2016. From the Prehistory of Russian Novel Theory: Alexander Veselovsky and Fyodor Dostoevsky on the Modern Novel's Roots in Folklore and Legend. In *Persistent Forms: Explorations in Historical Poetics*, ed. Ilya Kliger and Boris Maslov, 340–365. New York, NY: Fordham University Press.

Holquist, Michael. 1977. *Dostoevsky and the Novel*. Princeton, NJ: Princeton University Press.

Holquist, Michael, and Katerina Clark. 1984. *Mikhail Bakhtin*. Cambridge, MA: The Belknap Press of Harvard University Press.

Ivanov, Vyacheslav. 1999. O 'Tsyganakh' Pushkina. In *Pushkin v russkoi filosofskoi kritike. Konez XIX-XX vek*, 218–241. Moscow and St. Petersburg: Universitetskaia kniga.

Kahn, Andrew. 2008. *Pushkin's Lyric Intelligence*. Oxford: Oxford University Press.

Karamzin, Nikolai M. 1803. *Bednaia Liza*. In *Moskovskii Zhurnal*, vol. 6, 2nd ed., 225–264. Moscow: v tipografii Silivanovskogo.

Karamzin, Nikolai M. 1964. *Izbrannye sochineniia v dvukh tomakh*, ed. P. Berkov. Moscow and Leningrad: Khudozhestvennaia literatura.

Kliger, Ilya. 2011. Genre and Actuality in Belinskii, Herzen, and Goncharov: Toward a Genealogy of the Tragic Pattern in Russian Realism. *Slavic Review* 70 (1): 45–66.

———. 2012. Resurgent Forms in Ivan Goncharov and Alexander Veselovsky: Toward a Historical Poetics of Russian Realism. *Russian Review* 71 (4): 2–19.

Kliger, Ilya, and Boris Maslov, eds. 2016. *Persistent Forms: Explorations in Historical Poetics*. New York, NY: Fordham University Press.

Kline, George. 1968. *Religious and Antireligious Thought in Russia*. Chicago, IL: University of Chicago Press.

La Motte Foqué, Friedrich de. 1990. *Undina*. Translated by V.A. Zhukovsky. Moscow: Nauka.

Labzina, Anna. 2001. *Days of a Russian Noblewoman: The Memories of Anna Labzina 1758–1821*. Translated by Gary Marker and Rachel May. DeKalb, IL: Northern Illinois University Press.

LaCapra, Dominick. 1982. *Madame Bovary on Trial*. Ithaca, NY, and London: Cornell University Press.

Lermontov, M.Iu. 1961–1962. *Sobranie sochinenii v 4 tomakh*. Moscow and Leningrad: Akademia Nauk.

Lotman, Yuri M. 1987. *Sotvorenie Karamzina*. Moscow: Kniga.

———. 2005. *Stat'ii o russkoi literature*. St. Petersburg: Iskusstvo SPb.

Maguire, Robert. 1974. *Gogol from the Twentieth Century*. Princeton, NJ: Princeton University Press.

Maiofis, Maria. 2008. *Vozzvanie k Evrope: Literaturnoe obschestvo 'Arzamas' i rossiskii modernizationnyi proekt 1815–1818 godov*. Moscow: Novoe literaturnoe obozrenie.

Martin, Alexander. 1997. *Romantics, Reformers, Reactionaries: Russian Conservative Thought and Politics in the Reign of Alexander I*. DeKalb, IL: Northern Illinois Press.

Matich, Olga. 2005. *Erotic Utopia: The Decadent Imagination in Russia's Fin de Siècle*. Madison, WI: The University of Wisconsin Press.

Matlaw, Ralph E., ed. 1962. *Belinsky, Chernyshevsky, and Dobrolyubov: Selected Criticism*. New York: E.P. Dutton and Co.

Mirsky (Sviatopolk-Mirsky), Dmitrii P. Prince. 1999. *A History of Russian Literature from its Beginnings to 1900*. Edited by Francis J. Whitfield. Evanston, IL: Northwestern University Press.

Moretti, Franco. 1987. *The Way of the World: The Bildungsroman in European Culture*. London: Verso.

———. 2013. *The Bourgeois Between History and Literature*. London: Verso.

Morson, Gary Saul. 1989. Parody, History, Metaparody. In *Rethinking Bakhtin: Extensions and Challenges*, edited by Gary Saul Morson and Caryl Emerson, 63–86. Evanston, IL: Northwestern University Press.

Morson, Gary Saul, and Caryl Emerson. 1990. *Mikhail Bakhtin: Creation of a Prosaics*. Stanford, CA: Stanford University Press.

Nabokov, Vladimir. 1969. *Ada or Ardor*. New York: Penguin.

———. 1991. *The Gift*. New York: Vintage.

Nietzsche, Friedrich. 2005. *Correspondence avec Malwida von Meysenbug*. Translated and edited by Ludovic Frère. Paris: Allia.

Odoevskij, Vladimir F. Prince. 1967. *Russkie nochi/Russische Nächte*. Munich: Wilhelm Fink Verlag.

Page, Tanya. 1985. Karamzin's Immoralist Count NN or Three Hermeneutical Games of 'Chinese Shadows'. *Slavic and East European Journal* 29 (2): 144–156.

Paperno, Irina. 1994. Nietzscheanism and the Return of Pushkin in Twentieth-Century Russian Culture (1899–1937). In *Nietzsche and Soviet Culture: Ally and Adversary*, ed. Bernice Glatzer Rosenthal, 211–232. Cambridge, UK: Cambridge University Press.

———. 2007. Introduction: Intimacy and History. The Gercen Family Drama Reconsidered. Special Issue. *Russian Literature* LXI-I/II: 1–66.

488 L. STEINER

Paperno, Irina, and Joan Delaney Grossman, eds. 1994. *Creating Life: The Aesthetic Utopia of Russian Modernism*. Stanford, CA: Stanford University Press.

Pavel, Thomas. 2013. *The Lives of the Novel*. Princeton, NJ and Oxford: Princeton University Press.

Pelikan-Strauss, Nina. 1998. Flights from *The Idiot*'s Womanhood. In *Dostoevsky's The Idiot*, ed. Liza Knapp, 105–129. Evanston, IL: Northwestern University Press.

Platt, Kevin M.F., and David Brandenberger. 2006. *Epic Revisionism: Russian History and Literature and Stalinist Propaganda*. Madison, WI: University of Wisconsin Press.

Powelstock, David. 2005. *Becoming Mikhail Lermontov: The Ironies of Romantic Individualism in Nicholas I's Russia*. Evanston, IL: Northwestern University Press.

Proskurin, Oleg. 2006. Pushkin and Politics. In *The Cambridge Companion to Pushkin*, ed. Andrew Kahn, 105–117. Cambridge, UK: Cambridge University Press.

Pushkin, Alexander S. 1937–1959. *Polnoe sobranie sochinenii v 16 tomakh*. Moscow and Leningrad: Akademia Nauk SSSR.

Pushkin, Aleksandr S. 1983. *Complete Prose Fiction*. Translated and with an Introduction by Paul Debreszeny. Stanford, CA: Stanford University Press.

Reyfman, Irina. 1999. *Ritualized Violence Russian Style: The Duel in Russian Culture and Literature*. Stanford, CA: Stanford University Press.

Schlegel, August Wilhelm. 1846. *Sämtliche Werke in 10 Bände*. Leipzig: Weidmann.

Schmid, Ulrich. 2000. *Ichentwürfe: Russische Autobiographien zwishen Avvakum und Gercen*. Basel: Pano Verlag.

Serman, Ilya Z. 1959. Stanovlenie i razvitie romana v russkoi literature serediny XVIII veka. In *Iz istorii russkikh literaturnykh otnoshenii XVIII–XX vekov*, 82–95. Moscow: Izdatel'stvo Akademii Nauk SSSR.

———. 1962. Zarozhdenie romana v russkoi literature XVIII veka. In *Istoria russkogo romana v dvukh tomakh*, ed. A.S. Bushmin et al., 40–64. Moscow: Izdatel'stvo Akademii Nauk SSSR.

Shestov, Lev. 1969. *The Good in the Teaching of Tolstoy and Nietzsche: Philosophy and Preaching*. Translated by Bernard Martin. In Lev Shestov, *Dostoevsky, Tolstoy and Nietzsche*, 11–140. Columbus, OH: Ohio University Press.

Steiner, Lina. 2009. 'My most mature poèma': Pushkin's *Poltava* and the Irony of Russian National Culture. *Comparative Literature* 61 (1): 1–45.

———. 2011. *For Humanity's Sake: The Bildungsroman in Russian Culture*. Toronto and London: University of Toronto Press.

———. 2019. The *Bildungsroman* in Imperial Russia and the Soviet Union. In *A History of the Bildungsroman*, ed. Sarah Graham, 84–116. Cambridge, UK: Cambridge University Press.

Stellino, Paolo. 2015. *Nietzsche and Dostoevsky: On the Verge of Nihilism*. Bern: Peter Lang.

Stendhal. (Marie Henri Beyle). 1969. *La vie de Henry Brulard*. Edited Victor Del Litto. 2 vols. In *Oeuvres complètes de Stendhal*, 2. Levallois-Peret: Cercle du bibliophile.

Todd, William Mills. 2006. The Ruse of the Russian Novel. In *The Novel: History, Geography and Culture*, ed. Franco Moretti, 2 vols., 2: 401–423. Princeton, NJ: Princeton University Press.

Tolstoy, Lev N. 1929–1958. *Polnoe sobranie sochinenii v 90 tomakh*. The Jubilee Edition. Moscow: Gosudarstvennoe izdatel'stvo 'Khudozhestvennaia literatura.' (Abbreviated in text as *PSS*.)

Toporov, Vladimir N. 1995. *Bednaia Liza Karamzina: opyt prochteniia*. Moscow: izdatel'skii tsentr RGGU.

Turgenev, Ivan S. 1954–1958. *Sobranie sochinenii v 12 tomakh.* Moscow: Khudozhestvennaia literatura.

Veselovskii, Alexander N. 2011. Iz vvedenia v istoricheskuiu poetiku. In *Izbrannoe: istoricheskaia poetika,* ed. I.O. Shaitanov, 57–170. St. Petersburg: Universitetskaia kniga.

de Vogüé, Viscount Eugene-Melchior. 1913. *The Russian Novel.* Translated by H.A. Sawyer. London: Chapman and Hall.

Walicki, Andrzej. 1975. *The Slavophile Controversy: History of a Conservative Utopia in Nineteenth-Century Russian Thought.* Oxford: Clarendon Press.

Walicki, Adrzej. 1979. *A History of Russian Thought from Enlightenment to Marxism.* Translated by Hilda Andrews-Rusiecka. Stanford, CA: Stanford University Press.

Zamyatin, Evgeny. 1970. On Literature, Revolution, Entropy, and Other Matters. In *A Soviet Heretic: Essays by Evgeny Zamyatin,* ed. and trans. Mirra Ginsburg, 107–112. Chicago: University of Chicago Press.

Zenkovsky, Vasily V. 1953. *A History of Russian Philosophy.* Translated by George L. Kline, 2 vols. London: Routledge and Kegan Paul.

Zorin, Andrei L. 2001. *Kormia dvuglavogo orla: literatura i gosudarstvennaia ideologia v Rossii v poslednei treti XVIII- pervoi treti XIX veka.* Moscow: Novoe literaturnoe obozrenie.

CHAPTER 22

Nikolai Gogol, Symbolic Geography, and the Invention of the Russian Provinces

Anne Lounsbery

Anyone who reads Russian literature has visited the "Town of N," that is, one of those unnamed, unlocated, undistinguished, and indistinguishable provincial places that have been recurring in literary texts since the beginning of the nineteenth century.[1] Works as diverse as Herzen's *Who Is to Blame?*, Turgenev's *Fathers and Sons*, Khvoshchinskaia's *Boarding School Girl*, Dostoevsky's *Demons*, Chekhov's "Ward No. 6," Sologub's *Petty Demon*, and Dobychin's *Town of N* not only make use of the shorthand designation "Town of N" but also draw on the assumptions built into it. Above all, they tend to assume that Russian provincial places—that is, virtually all places outside of the "capitals," Petersburg and Moscow—are characterized solely by anonymity, repetition, and chaos. In place of the highly developed literary regionalism we encounter in other traditions (e.g., British, American), in canonical Russian literature we find instead the tropes of *provintsiia* and *provintsial'nost'*, which insist that all provincial places always are, have been, and will be the same.

Stasis is built into the idea of *provintsiia*. Indeed, according to the imaginary schema that literature has reinforced, *provintsiia* is fundamentally ahistorical (as Bakhtin put it, the chronotope of the provinces is event-less, mired in what he calls a "viscous and sticky time that drags itself slowly through space"; Bakhtin 1981, 247–248). Even as Russian society was undergoing radical transformation over the course of the nineteenth and twentieth centuries, the provinces continued to be depicted in almost identical terms, as if changes as

A. Lounsbery (✉)
New York University, New York, NY, USA
e-mail: anne.lounsbery@nyu.edu

© The Author(s), under exclusive license to Springer Nature
Switzerland AG 2021
M. F. Bykova et al. (eds.), *The Palgrave Handbook of Russian Thought*,
https://doi.org/10.1007/978-3-030-62982-3_22

491

momentous as the end of serfdom, the rise of a market economy, revolutions in transportation and literacy, the gentry's decline, and so on were powerless to affect the country's provincial core. The image of stagnant, homogeneous *provintsiia* proved so tenacious that even those authors who contested it (such as Tolstoy, Leskov, women writers who embraced the label *provintsialki*, and a few others) were nonetheless obliged to engage with it in their works.

It is of course counterfactual to describe all of Russia as Vladimir Sollogub did in the 1840s with the words "everything the same, the same, the same" (Sollogub 1978, 170), or as Chekhov did in a letter of 1890: "In Russia, all towns are the same. Ekaterinburg is exactly like Perm or Tula, or like Sumy and Gadyach" (Chekhov 1974–1983, 11:72). Yet we have become so accustomed to such statements that we perhaps fail to recognize how puzzling they should be. How, then, did we come to accept them? This essay argues that the trope of provincial anonymity took on its enduring power thanks to the writings of Nikolai Gogol, after whom any Russian provincial town risked being characterized by the adjective "Gogolian." It analyzes Gogol's work with an eye to elucidating both the texts themselves and how they have helped shape Russia's symbolic geography—that is, geography not as empirical reality but as "a powerful symbol conveniently located outside of historical time" (to borrow Maria Todorova's characterization of "the Balkans"; Todorova 1997, 7). Gogol's interest in *provintsiia* permeates much of his oeuvre, and in texts like *Dead Souls, The Inspector General,* and *Selected Passages from Correspondence with Friends,* writing about the provinces and provinciality becomes for him a way to raise questions about Russian identity more broadly.

GOGOL: BIOGRAPHY AND GEOGRAPHY

Even though Gogol's works became touchstones of a certain version of Russianness, the writer himself was of course born and raised in Ukraine. In fact it has been maintained that Ukrainian national, or folk, identity represented for him a standard of organic culture against which Russia, an imperial power thought to be plagued by a fundamental lack of *narodnost'* [national character] could be judged and found lacking (see Bojanowska 2007).[2] The status of both Ukrainianness and Russianness is unstable in Gogol's oeuvre, a fact that should not be surprising given the complexity of the Russia-Ukraine relationship both in his time and ours. Gogol's life spanned a period when Ukraine was almost universally seen as an integral part of the Russian Empire, when it was unproblematically referred to as "Little Russia" (*Malorossiia,* a term that "Great Russian" nationalists still use on occasion, but that Ukrainians now find offensive). His family had the kind of mixed background that was not unusual for the Ukrainian gentry: their heritage was partly Polish; they usually spoke Russian at home but at times they spoke Ukrainian; they corresponded in Russian but read in Russian, Ukrainian, and Polish; Gogol's father wrote comedies in Ukrainian, but Gogol himself wrote only in Russian. The family did not experience their Ukrainianness as being in conflict with their status as loyal subjects and at times servitors of the Russian Empire.

In Gogol's day, "Great" Russians (or those who identified with an imperial version of Russian culture, including some Ukrainian elites) could choose to see "Little" Russian identity as simply, and benignly, a variant of Russianness, or even as a quaint version of the Ur-Slavic soul. (For instance, the critic Faddei Bulgarin could interpret *Evenings on a Farm Near Dikan'ka* as a reflection of the national—i.e., Russian—spirit, thanks to the fact that Ukrainians had supposedly preserved a pure form of Slavic-ness; Debreczeny 1966, 5.) Certainly it makes perfect sense that, when Gogol wanted to make a name for himself, he set off for the Russian imperial capital of St. Petersburg because that was where you went to make a career, any career. His departure did not suggest a renunciation of Ukrainianness; rather, it signaled ambition (and Gogol was nothing if not ambitious).[3] Though the analogy is imperfect, think of an Indian writer today who chooses to write in English: because the English language is backed by an empire (or by multiple empires), it promises a more direct pathway to membership in "Great Literature" than would a "less spoken" language. It was in Petersburg that Gogol became famous as a Russian writer. He did so, initially, by making canny use of his "Little Russian" identity at a moment when many things Ukrainian happened to be in vogue, publishing stories set in a "Little Russian" village (the collections *Evenings on a Farm Near Dikan'ka* and *Mirgorod*), written in Russian but full of folksy Ukrainianisms and bits of local color.

For the rest of his life—including his most famous works, which are set not in Ukraine but in Russia—Gogol's perspective was informed by his Ukrainian origins. But exactly *how* these origins shaped his views of Russian culture, the empire, and language is not straightforward. Some of his Russian contemporaries took offense at works like *Dead Souls, The Government Inspector,* and "The Overcoat" in which they discerned an anti-Russian bias that they attributed to his Ukrainianness; others read his work as a sincere, if anguished, paean to the "Russian soul." Both readings are plausible, and each satisfies a constituency; hence "the Gogol wars," which started in his time and are still going on today. One version of the ongoing fight pits Gogol against his more uncompromisingly Ukrainian contemporary Taras Shevchenko, who not only wrote in Ukrainian at a time when the tsarist authorities had forbidden it, but even suffered exile for his impassioned defense of Ukrainian language and culture. In this reading—Gogol as the anti-Shevchenko—Gogol becomes a sell-out to the imperial overlords. But on the other side, there are ongoing attempts to represent Gogol as a passionate Ukrainian nationalist, even as rabidly anti-Russian. In this interpretation, Gogol becomes a sort of fifth-column presence in the literature of the Russian Empire, subverting imperial culture from within (and here the analogy would be Kafka, a Czech Jew writing in and thereby "infiltrating" German).

Perhaps Gogol saw Ukraine as symbolically opposed to Russia proper in which case the symbolic fullness of Ukraine might be seen as a condition of the symbolic emptiness of Russia. If so, the opposition seems only to have encouraged him to collapse the diverse regions of Russia into the category of "the provinces," thereby freighting this ill-defined label with even more significance than it carries in the work of his contemporaries. The Russian provinces—their slippery meaning, their suggestive emptiness—are virtually an obsession for Gogol, who returns to them again and again, often in an interrogative mode, asking questions that will never be answered.

MAKING THE PROVINCES VISIBLE

Gogol devoted a great deal of time to reading and thinking about provincial places, as evidenced not only by his own published works but also by various book reviews, notes, unfinished projects, and so on, which span decades. As early as 1830 he was writing a geography textbook for children; in the late 1840s he composed for himself a long, detailed summary of an eighteenth-century travelogue about the Russian provinces; at the end of his life he was working on what he projected would be "a living geography of Russia" (Gogol 1952, 9: 277–415, 642).[4] And he was not the only one asking questions about provincial Russia at this time: his contemporaries shared his belief that it was necessary to *know* the provinces in order to know Russia, and that such knowledge was necessary to being a true patriot.

Just as his 1828 arrival in Petersburg had coincided fortuitously with a moment of "Great Russian" enthusiasm for all things "Little Russian," so his writings about *provintsiia* in the 1830s and 1840s dovetailed with, and were likely encouraged by, a period of intense official engagement with the question of how best to understand the provinces. In the decades following the Pugachev rebellion, the autocracy had turned its gaze outward, dispatching to Russia's various regions not just military forces but also researchers who were charged with transforming these far-off places into objects of knowledge. Such efforts took on even more urgency in the 1830s and 1840s, as the need for economic modernization motivated the central authorities to create "provincial statistical committees" and other tools for learning about provincial places.

Thus, Gogol's imaginative excursions into the provinces formed part of a trend among elites in the capitals. Like Gogol, the state's information-seeking bureaucrats were motivated by a belief that knowledge of provincial life was essential to helping Russia understand itself. In the words of the civil servant Konstantin Arsen'ev, commenting on information-gathering efforts in the same year that *Dead Souls* was published (1842), "knowledge of one's homeland […] in view of our general striving for *narodnost'* […] ought to be required of every statesman, civil servant, soldier, estate owner, industrialist, merchant, and, in general, every educated patriot" (quoted in: Lincoln 1982, 117). The provincial statistical committees had much work to do, or at least much work to appear to do, if they were to fulfill Petersburg's order to "discover and catalogue the Russian people" (Smith-Peter 2007, 7).

Implicit in the state's project was the assumption that only the capital—the center—could interpret the mass of raw data to be unearthed in the provinces. Representatives of the capital's intellectual authority were being called upon not just to collect facts but to bestow order on what was assumed to be the chaos of *provintsiia*, an order that provincials themselves could supposedly neither perceive nor construct. These bureaucrat-researchers being dispatched to provincial cities were liable to meet a reception nearly as bizarre as Khlestakov's in *The Inspector General* or Chichikov's in *Dead Souls*, since their diligent efforts to compile statistical pictures of various places and institutions were met by equally diligent efforts to thwart them. (Herzen's account of the absurdity and grotesquery he encountered among local officials during his internal exile in the 1830s, for example, reads like an excerpt from *The Inspector General*.)

The state's goal was to "make the local visible to the center" (Smith-Peter 2007, 7; cf. Lincoln 1982, 109–125). Gogol's texts, too, are often concerned with the effort of *looking correctly* at the provinces. At one point in the 1835 essay "On Present-Day Architecture," for instance, he remarks that tall buildings ("huge, colossal towers") are essential in a capital city—because how else will the capital be able to keep watch over the surrounding areas? The capital needs to be able "to see at least a verst and a half in all directions," he asserts, so as always to be "surveying the provinces [*obozrevaia provintsii*], foreseeing everything in advance" (Gogol 1952, 8: 62). The center directs its probing gaze toward the periphery, and the periphery returns this gaze. This relationship between the center and the periphery structures not just "On Present-Day Architecture," but a whole series of Gogol's texts.

The Inspector General (1836) returns again and again to the behavior of provincials who suddenly become aware that the capital has turned its eyes upon them, an awareness that leaves them feeling both gratified and deeply anxious. Petty malefactors in the anonymous provincial city fear the accusatory and unmasking gaze of Petersburg, but they long for it as well—because, it seems, their inconsequential lives might become *meaningful* when seen through the capital's powerful lens. Gogol's provincials dream of the capital not only because of its associations with power and material rewards but also because of its ability to confer significance. One character sums up this view of the capital's signifying power when he begs Khlestakov to inform Petersburg that *he exists*: "In Petersburg tell all the various bigwigs [...] that in such-and-such a town there lives Peter Ivanovich Bobchinksy" (the provincial place— "such-and-such a town"—goes unnamed even by its own inhabitants, 4: 67). Thus in *The Inspector General* the capital looks (occasionally, and unpredictably) at the provinces in order to inspect, indict, and control; the provinces look back in order to imitate, to see themselves reflected in the eyes of the powers-that-be (thereby confirming that they actually exist), and to formulate alibis as needed.

A similar preoccupation with looking and studying is evident right up to the last work Gogol published in his lifetime, *Selected Passages from Correspondence with Friends* (1847). *Selected Passages* is a bizarre mix of religious homily and

496   A. LOUNSBERY

reactionary diatribe posing as a series of personal letters. The letters imagine the provinces as the object of the capital's gaze and as a field of inquiry, a blank space yet to be filled in on Russia's conceptual map. Like the provincial statistical committees, the text quite clearly takes part in the effort to "make the local visible to the center." Gogol counsels his readers to approach provincial Russia "as a new land, hitherto unknown to you," with the explicit goal of collecting information about provincial life. He returns again and again to the idea that "we"—that is, presumably, we residents of the capitals—know nothing of Russia: "Great is the ignorance of Russia within Russia, since everyone lives in foreign journals and newspapers, not in his own land" (Gogol 1952, 8: 303, 308). Gogol counts himself as part of the problem—"I know absolutely nothing of what is inside [Russia]," he laments (Gogol 1952, 8: 311).

According to *Selected Passages*, the solution lies in the assiduous compiling of data: "In the same way that a Russian traveler arriving in some celebrated European city hurries to see all the antiquities and famous sights, in exactly the same way, and with even greater curiosity, after you have arrived in the chief town of a [Russian] district or province, strive to get to know the sights. They are not in architectural works or antiquities but in people" (Gogol 1952, 8: 303). Again and again Gogol insists upon the need to gather information directly from the provincial source, as when he addresses the wife of a provincial governor who must become acquainted with the town where her husband is posted: "In the brief time you have spent in the town of K__ you have come to know Russia better than in all your previous life" (Gogol 1952, 8: 311). One chapter of *Selected Passages* bears the title "It Is Necessary to Travel Around Russia" [*Nuzhno proezdit'sia po Rossii*] (Gogol 1952, 8: 301), an exhortation that is constantly repeated over the course of the letter and throughout *Selected Passages* as a whole. Gogol urges his audience to travel around the country with the goal of bringing back intelligence that will reveal "Russia in its true aspect" [*v istinnom vide Rossiiu*] (Gogol 1952, 8: 302). Having previously suggested (in *Dead Souls*) that people in the provinces are all more or less the same, conforming to a few basic types, here he seems to try to convince himself that if one looks hard enough, essential truths will be revealed.

But looking at provincial Russia will not be easy. For one thing, if you are from the capitals, then convincing yourself that the locals are anything like you is going to require a heroic act of imagination. A striking example of the elite outsider's alienation in *provintsiia* occurs in the letter "The Russian Landowner" [*Russkoi pomeshchik*]. In this letter's opening line, Gogol assumes that the first challenge facing the Russian *pomeshchik* recently arrived in the countryside is, in effect, to believe himself to be a Russian *pomeshchik*. Rather bizarrely, he asserts that "the most important thing is that you have arrived in the countryside and that you *set yourself to being a pomeshchik*" (Gogol 1952, 8: 321, emphasis mine). Here the relationship to what should be one's native place is represented as anything but natural: one cannot imagine, say, an English baronet arriving at his ancestral home and having to convince himself that he really is an English baronet who really does live and belong in this particular place.

(The same holds true for the provincial governor and his wife: Gogol urges them to *try* to think of the provincial city in which they have just arrived as their "native town," thereby conceding that it may be a rough go.)

As this advice suggests, for the richest and most sophisticated Russian landowners, it was a formidable challenge to feel *at home* while living on one's own provincial estate and fulfilling one's duties as a *pomeshchik*. In this sense *Selected Passages*, as bizarre as the text is, actually reflects the historical situation of the landowning class: the ties binding wealthy Russian noblemen to their provincial estates were often weak (compared to those that bound European nobles or American planters to theirs), and Russia's most cultured noblemen were unlikely to view provincial regions as their "native" places. As Peter Kolchin writes, the wealthiest Russian noblemen, far from feeling at home on their estates, "typically felt trapped or isolated" when they were there (Kolchin 1987, 59).[5] Thus, in *Selected Passages* when Gogol assumes that a highbrow nobleman who lands in the provinces will feel deracinated, even bewildered, his assumption reflects certain realities.

Gogol offers the following helpful suggestion to the provincial governor's wife: look at your whole town, he advises, as a doctor looks at an infirmary [*kak lekar' gliadit na lazaret*], and try to "convince yourself that all the sick people in the infirmary are in fact your kinsmen [...] then everything will change before you: you will be reconciled with people and will be at war only with their illnesses" (Gogol 1952, 8: 310). The image of provincial city as sick ward is repeated and developed a few pages later, when Gogol urges the governor's wife to lay out all the town's problems for the bishop: "Show him your entire infirmary [*lazaret*] and display before him all the illnesses of your patients. [...] Inform him constantly of all the fits, symptoms, and manifestations of the illness" (Gogol 1952, 8: 316).

As these lines reveal, in Gogol's day, the provinces could be depicted both as horror show and as repository for true Russianness, their inhabitants both as freaks and as representative Russian types. In keeping with this tendency, *Selected Passages* represents the life of the provincial city as a collection of symptoms so horrific that an outsider must work to convince herself that the city's inhabitants have anything to do with her at all, that they are in fact her "kinsmen" [*vashi rodnye i blizkie k vashemu serdtsu liudi*] (Gogol 1952, 8: 310); the town is so loathsome that she must be counseled on how not to avert her eyes. Compare Herzen's description of an infamous Vyatka official as "a peculiar sort of beast that is met with in the forest, in the wild, a beast that *ought to have been studied*" (Herzen 1954, 7: 247). Gogol shares Herzen's assumption: even if what one sees in *provintsiia* is repellent, one is morally obligated to look, with the goal of putting together an ethnography of the *lazaret* that is provincial Russia.

Where and What Are the Provinces?

Where exactly are Gogol's provinces supposed to be located on the map of Russia? His texts offer little in the way of geographic specificity. *Dead Souls* begins by introducing and describing the Town of N, but of course the town will never be identified. Always a nameless backwater, it is reduced almost to placelessness as well when it is said to be "not far from both capitals" (Gogol 1952, 6: 206): one glance at a map reveals that it is impossible to be simultaneously "not far" from Petersburg and Moscow, two cities that are 400 miles apart. Perhaps the most intelligible geographic message we can discern here is that N is located in European Russia, maybe somewhere in between Moscow and Petersburg: that is, it is *not* located in Ukraine or on the steppes or in any of the other border regions. "Not far from Petersburg and Moscow," then, actually evokes both "no place" and "in the very middle of the undifferentiated space that is (European) Russia." In *The Inspector General*, too, we are never told where the play is set, though the mayor scoffs at another character's surmise that the central authorities might be trying to sniff out traitors "in a little district town": "What is this, the borderlands or something? From here you could gallop three years and not get to a border" (Gogol 1952, 4: 12). Again, we do not know exactly where we are, but we know we are far from any border, that is, in the heart of European Russia.

About half of *Dead Souls* recounts events that take place in the town itself; the rest of the narrative traces the hero's movements through five outlying provincial estates. All these estates are close to N, and we see all the landowners but one in town, as well as in their homes: clearly, in *Dead Souls* provincial estate and provincial city occupy the same symbolic space. Such is not always the case for gentry estates, which in Russian literature, as in life, could be either provincial or cosmopolitan: a huge, lavish estate like the Sheremetevs', complete with its own opera company, was clearly not provincial because it could successfully and self-confidently reproduce the culture of the capital. But the estates in *Dead Souls* are as unambiguously provincial as the town.

In the end it matters little that we cannot locate these places on a map, because in Gogol's world any one of them can stand in for any other. In *Dead Souls*, for instance, no trait is attributed to the Town of N that is not also attributed to "all provincial cities." Chichikov's room at the inn is familiar [*izvestnogo roda*], the inn itself is also familiar [again *izvestnogo roda*, and *kak byvaiut gostinitsy v gubernskikh gorodakh*], the town's architecture is familiar [*izvestnoi*], the men in the town are "like they are everywhere, of two types" (i.e., fat and thin), the paint on the buildings is "that eternal yellow color"—the examples could easily be multiplied (Gogol 1952, 6: 8, 14). In a paragraph describing the inn's common room, forms of the construction *to zhe* (the same) recur six times, summed up with the words, "in a word, everything the same as everywhere" [*slovom, vse to zhe, chto i vezde*] (Gogol 1952, 6: 9). The outlying landscape is described with a similar emphasis on familiarity and sameness: the landscape unfolds "as always with us" [*po nashemu obychaiu*]; a few peasants are said to be yawning "as usual" [*po obyknoveniiu*]; and finally the narrator sums it all up, "in a word, the familiar sights" [*slovom, vidy izvestnye*] (Gogol 1952, 6: 21–22).

This seemingly implausible degree of uniformity points to social and historical realities of which Gogol was well aware. Russia's provincial towns generally *did* look the same, a regularity that was the intentional result of urban planning practices that had been in effect since the time of Peter and especially Catherine. The autocratic state sought to ensure that Russian cities were—or rather, looked—rational, orderly, regular, symmetrical, and permanent, with an emphasis on façades and *paradnost'* [grandeur] (Brower 1990, 15). Hence the real-life standardization Gogol describes in "On Present-Day Architecture," which notes that provincial cities feature avenues "so regular, so straight, so monotonous, that having crossed a street, one feels such boredom that one lacks all desire to look at another one" (Gogol 1952, 8: 61–62).

We do know something about the *types* of towns that figure in *Dead Souls* and *The Inspector General*. Perhaps most important, these places are neither "village" nor "countryside": such locations would be rendered by the word *derevnia*, and *derevnia* is quite distinct from *provintsiia*, the provinces. The label "provincial" does not refer to things rural (and as I have noted, only sometimes does it refer to the life of the gentry estate); rural life is denoted by *derevnia, derevenskii* [village, rural]. *Provintsiia*, and its cognates, typically refer to provincial cities and towns, and sometimes to estates that fall short of an acceptable level of civilization. In Gogol's time the adjective *gubernskii*— from *guberniia*, administrative region—could at times be used almost interchangeably with *provintsial'nyi* to mean provincial, with the exception that *gubernskii* was required for official government designations (*gubernskii gorod* for "provincial capital," *gubernskii sekretar'* for "provincial secretary," etc.).

Forms of *guberniia* appear more often in Gogol's works than do forms of *provintsiia*, but his usage observes no marked difference between the two. In *Dead Souls* the adjective *provintsial'nyi* never occurs (though the construction *v nashikh provintsiiakh* is used twice; Gogol 1952, 6: 18, 577),[6] while forms of *guberniia* and *gubernskii* appear over and over because the novel is set in a *gubernskii gorod* [regional capital]. *The Inspector General* is set in a smaller "district town" (perhaps the very rough equivalent of an American county seat), designated by *gorod* [town] and its diminutive form *gorodok* [sometimes modified by *uezdnyi* and *malen'kii*, district and small]. Here various forms of *provintsiia* recur alongside the occasional *guberniia*, as when stage notes describe the mayor's wife as a *provintsial'naia koketka* [provincial coquette] (Gogol 1952, 4: 9) and Khlestakov disparages yokels as *provintsial'nye gusi* [provincial geese] (Gogol 1952, 4: 61).

In Gogol's world, far more important than these lexical distinctions is the provincial characters' acute awareness of the fact that Russian towns were ranked by law. Under Catherine every city was assigned a place in an official hierarchy, and every town center, depending on its place in the hierarchy, was supposed to contain the same combination of public buildings (Kirichenko and

Shcheboleva 1997, 62–63, 123). Such regulations reflected not only an Enlightenment desire for symmetry and the state's determination to manifest its power in the provinces but also the imperative to look like Petersburg, which in turn looked, or aimed to look, like Europe: ideally, every Russian city was to model itself on cities the next level up.

Just as Gogol's bureaucrats in the Petersburg tales are ever aware of the Table of Ranks that determines their possibilities in life, so everyone in the world of *Dead Souls* is implicitly aware of their town's place on the hierarchy, and as a result, there is nothing in this world that does not aspire to be something else, something on the next level "up" (see Reyfman 2016). The young son of the landowner Manilov ("Themistoclius," a name suggesting acute cultural confusion) has already internalized the system. To the question "which is the finest city in France?" little Themistoclius answers, Paris; and then to the questions "What is our finest city?" and "What's another fine city?" he answers readily, St. Petersburg and Moscow (Gogol 1952, 6: 30). As a *gubernskii gorod*, N itself functions as a kind of capital in relationship to the smaller towns lower down on the hierarchy (e.g., the *bednyi uezdnyi gorodishko* with its *uezdnaia skuka* that is mentioned in passing; Gogol 1952, 6: 110). And for the governor's ball, everyone from miles around (district towns, villages, estates) converges on N, thus reinforcing its place as *gubernskii gorod* [provincial capital] in the ranking system (provinces → capitals → Europe) that structures provincial lives.

"Such Is the Nature of the Provincial City"

In Gogol's world, "provincial" is not a strictly geographic designation: that is, the provinces are not the only locus of provinciality. Indeed his more didactic texts insist openly on the similarities between province and capital: in "Leaving the Theater After the Performance of a New Comedy" (written in response to the reception of *The Inspector General*), one character declares that the vices just exposed on stage are not typical of life only "in a provincial town, but rather here, all around us" in the capital (Gogol 1952, 5: 155). And Gogol's description of the capital in "Petersburg Notes of 1836" recalls nothing if not the provincial town of *Dead Souls*: Petersburg is likened to an inn full of transients where everyone mindlessly apes European ways, a place with virtually no native culture [*malo korennoi national'nosti*] and much that is alien and unassimilated [*mnogo inostrannogo smesheniia, eshche ne slivshegosia v plotnuiu massu*] (Gogol 1952, 8: 177–180). The same similarities between province and capital are also evident in the Petersburg tales, with their repeated evocations of empty, death-in-life existences recalling the characterization of N in the working notes to *Dead Souls* ("the highest degree of Emptiness," "the dead insensibility of life").

Even *Dead Souls*, though set in a provincial town, at times implies and at times states explicitly that there is *no difference* between provinces and capital, no matter how much the characters and even the narrator may insist that there is. The narrator concedes that nothing distinguishes the provincial landowner Korobochka from her imaginary "aristocratic sister" in the capital and that the bear-like landowner Sobakevich, seemingly the incarnation of provinciality, would have been no different had he been born in Petersburg. Sobakevich would be just the same, Chichikov muses, even if he had received a modish education and lived in the social whirl (Gogol 1952, 6: 106). And finally, in the novel's last chapter, the author (by this point seemingly distinct from the narrator, and possessing greater authority) reflects significantly that one feels the same melancholy upon entering *any* town, "even if it's a capital" [*khot' dazhe v stolitsu*] (Gogol 1952, 6: 241).

We are reminded of the claim that N is "not far from both capitals": geographically this remains baffling, but conceptually it becomes suggestive in yet another way, hinting as it does that the differences between Russian province and Russian capital are not as essential as many think, perhaps even that both are equally "provincial." For Gogol this mysteriously "portable" version of provinciality seems to be part of Russians' essence, an essence that will inevitably expose itself. At the governor's ball in *Dead Souls*—the very moment when everyone in N is saying "No, this is not the provinces, this is the capital, this is Paris itself!" [*net, eto ne guberniia, eto stolitsa, eto sam Parizh!*] (Gogol 1952, 6: 163)—we are told that there *must* appear, say, a strange hat that violates every rule of fashion. There is no getting around it: "This is unavoidable, such is the nature of the provincial city: somewhere it will inevitably reveal itself" [*no uzh bez etogo nel'zia, takovo svoistvo gubernskogo goroda: gde-nibud' on nepremenno oborvetsia*] (Gogol 1952, 6: 163–164).

In Gogol's version of *provintsiia*, all attempts to be unprovincial are doomed, even if they are perfectly executed. When Gogol's contemporaries mocked provincial failures of taste, they typically did so because provincials *were* failing (their dance moves were ridiculous, their fashions were behind the times, etc.).[7] But Gogol's indictment of provinciality is somewhat different: his Town of N can never be anything but an attempt to be something else, *even when it gets everything right*; the townspeople's attempts at fashion will remain fruitless *even when they are successful.* The narrator concedes, for example, that the ladies of N really do rival those of Petersburg and Moscow when it comes to observing proprieties and following fashions: "When it came to such things as knowing how to behave, how to maintain good tone and conform to etiquette, as well as a great number of the most subtle proprieties, and especially how to observe the dictates of fashion down to the tiniest details—in all this they surpassed even the ladies of Petersburg and Moscow" (Gogol 1952, 6: 158). But in the end, it makes no difference; they can do nothing but try to catch up, and even their most perfect efforts will be marked by the fact that they are efforts. Similarly, when the narrator insists twice in the space of five lines that the dandies of N do everything—shave, flirt, speak French—"just like they do in Petersburg" (Gogol 1952, 6: 14), the reference to the capital only draws attention to some ineffable but fundamental problem.

And what precisely is the fundamental problem, the fatal cultural deficit, that *Dead Souls* is describing in the Town of N and the surrounding estates? Take N itself: the town is made up of a few random structures (a sentry box, some cabstands, the Administrative Office) scattered throughout an unintelligible pseudo-public space (Gogol 1952, 6: 141). The shop signs are mysteriously garbled (one reads "And This Is the Establishment," another "Vasilii Fedorov, Foreigner"); the stores sell a strange jumble of goods ("nuts, soap, and gingerbread that resembles soap"). Likewise, the estates are filled with vestigial and fragmentary bits of imported "culture," seemingly the flotsam and jetsam of a distant civilization. Manilov's garden, for instance, reveals inept attempts at English landscape design: a ramshackle arbor, dubbed the "Temple for Solitary Meditation," is surrounded by peasants' log huts. And inside his house, what is described as "an exceedingly elegant candlestick of darkened bronze, with the three Graces of antiquity and an elegant mother-of-pearl escutcheon" stands alongside another candlestick, one that is broken, ugly, home-made, jerry-rigged (Gogol 1952, 6: 22, 25).

The point is that what passes for culture in the provinces is both derivative and incoherent—the Three Graces alongside tallow-covered rags. Incongruity and jarring juxtaposition are everywhere. Take the prints that adorn the landowner's walls: they depict everything from watermelons and a boar's head (at Pliushkin's house) to Greek military leaders (at Sobakevich's), and none of them seems to bear a coherent relationship to its current location (Gogol 1952, 6: 95, 115). As the narrator says of one such picture, "there was no way of knowing how or why [it] had gotten there" (Gogol 1952, 6: 95). The estates' furnishings attest to both the meagerness and the illegibility of provincial culture. The same goes for the vulgar painting of unknown provenance that has somehow ended up on the wall of the town inn: the narrator speculates that this image of "a nymph with breasts so large that the reader has probably never seen the like" was "brought back to us in Russia" by "one of our grandees, art lovers who buy [such things] in Italy on the advice of their couriers" (Gogol 1952, 6: 9).

Such passages draw attention to the threat of meaninglessness that haunts a syncretic culture like that of nineteenth-century Russia, a culture that borrowed freely and conspicuously. In Manilov's estate and Sobakevich's paintings, we see Gogol's intensely self-conscious version of a phenomenon that recurs in literary texts of these decades: in Sollogub's "Serezha" (1838), for instance, we encounter a provincial mansion rendered grotesque by decades of discordant embellishments; in Herzen's *Who Is to Blame?* (1846), a provincial church combines Byzantine, classical, and Gothic elements in an entirely incongruous fashion; at an inn described in Sollogub's *Tarantas*, "the ceiling is painted with various little flowers, peaches, and Cupids," everything is marred by "pretensions to filthy foppery," and the menu is so distorted by francophone affectation as to be incomprehensible (Sollogub 1978, 180, 182). In each case, what is being highlighted are objects and styles that have been shorn of context and promiscuously mixed together—thus signaling a fear that

Russian culture had not yet done the work of imbuing these objects with significance.

Of course, Russia's cultural syncretism was a source of great creativity and strength for artists, as Monika Greenleaf and many others have noted (Greenleaf 1994, 15–16).[8] But this syncretism and cultural borrowing also generated anxiety—a fact that helps explain not only Russian literature's preoccupation with *provintsiia* and *provintsial'nost'* but also Gogol's frequent hints that in Russia *provinciality cannot be confined to the provinces*. In *Dead Souls* and *The Inspector General*, in which characters insist tirelessly on the essential and absolute difference between capitals and provinces, such assertions are often cast into doubt by the works as a whole, both of which open up the possibility that there is in fact *no* genuine standard of *stolichnost'* [metropolitanism] against which the provincial might be judged.

For instance, Khlestakov and the townspeople in *The Inspector General* expatiate at length on the wonders of the capital that are lacking in the provincial town, but in the end what Khlestakov tells the locals about the capital is what they themselves already "know." He simply responds to their pre-existing image of Petersburg, an image that is quite capable of accommodating the idea of, say, a 700-ruble melon. Khlestakov tells stories of being "taken for" an important official in Petersburg, and the mayor's wife is duly impressed (Gogol 1952, 4: 48): in a world where being "taken for" a VIP is just as good as being one, a belief in the capital's essential superiority is merely what we might call these characters' foundational mirage, the delusion that generates all their other delusions. There is nothing to suggest that this conviction has any more basis in reality than does Khlestakov's fantastic melon.

Thus, Petersburg and the very idea of *stolichnost'*, along with the absolute standard that this idea implies, begin to resemble floating signifiers. Khlestakov's ecstatic riff to the postmaster suggests as much: "Of course there aren't many people here [in this little town], but why should there be? After all it's not the capital [*ved' eto ne stolitsa*]. Am I right—after all, it's not the capital? [...] After all only in the capital is there real *bon ton*, none of your provincial boors" (Gogol 1952, 4: 60–61). *Ved' eto ne stolitsa*: just as forms of the word "province" [*guberniia*] recur constantly in *Dead Souls* and *Selected Passages*, in *The Inspector General* "capital" and "Petersburg" are so often repeated that they stop sounding like geographic labels and start sounding more like talismanic invocations. Petersburg is a quasi-magical, animating idea behind both Khlestakov and the townspeople's response to him; Petersburg as "conferring power," "seat of authority, ground of judgment." But finally, it is an *empty* idea, functioning only as "a powerful absence in the play" (Fanger 1979, 135, 133).

In the end, despite the characters' insistence on the absolute difference between capital and province, for Gogol the capital too is implicated in provinciality. Rather than sharing his characters' belief—and the belief of his contemporaries—in this absolute difference and in the capital's incontestable primacy, Gogol comes close to imagining a world without *any* cultural or geographic locus of authenticity. The meanings of province and capital begin to run together, a blurring of conceptual boundaries hinting once again that more is at stake in these texts than merely the provinciality of provincials.

Provinces and capitals—seemingly opposed to each other and even appearing to derive their significance from this opposition—are ultimately the same. This is what renders Gogol's vision especially complex, even paradoxical. When writers like Sollogub and Herzen are indicting provincial failings, we know exactly where the author *and we ourselves* stand in relation to this material: its provinciality serves to confirm our sophistication. But in a book like *Dead Souls*, our pleasure must derive from very different sources because here we can never quite define our relationship to the provincial dissonances that are put on display, both in the objects the text depicts and in the language it uses to depict them.

If we are not allowed to feel complacently un-implicated in Gogolian provinciality—if we are not granted permission to regard it with the self-satisfied eye of the aesthete—this is largely because the author refuses to clarify his own stance toward his material. The myriad details that pack *Dead Souls* are laid out with a "flat miscellaneousness" that defies hierarchies of judgment and significance (Fanger 1979, 174). Not only are we presented with the kind of incoherence which, as I have noted, so often characterizes provincial culture, we are also denied any standard, any point of view, from which we might judge its incongruities. Gogol's refusal to clarify his stance toward the bizarre world he creates causes the dissonance of *provintsiia* to become *our* problem, an indictment of *our* failures, aesthetic, intellectual, and moral.

Finally, Gogol's own language is marked by the same kind of unnaturalness and distortion that afflict the provincials of *Dead Souls*—but his art makes conscious and highly sophisticated *use* of such disproportions. In fact, Andrei Sinyavsky asserts that Gogol's genius arose precisely from his provinciality. Gogol was far too "provincial" [*provintsialen*], Sinyavsky says, to strive for anything like the naturalness and ease of a poet like Pushkin, who "whispered verses in his cradle" because poetry was his "native language." Instead Gogol created prose that was constantly "aware of its own formation," perpetually, and often awkwardly, self-conscious [*eto rech', besprestanno pamiatuiushchaia o svoem oformlenii, preispolnennaia soznaniia sobstvennogo sloga*], with its artistry arising out of this very awkwardness and self-consciousness (Terts [Sinyanvsky] 2003, 242–243).

If Sinyavsky can say that "art is provincial in principle" (Terts [Sinyanvsky] 2003, 328), then in Russia perhaps the "provincial" has come to mean something different than it does for someone like T. S. Eliot, whose essay "What Is a Classic?" defines "the provincial point of view" as wholly inimical to high cultural achievement. For Eliot, provinciality is aesthetically damaging because it "confounds the contingent with the essential, the ephemeral with the permanent" (Eliot 1975, 129). But Gogol built an entire oeuvre on "confounding the contingent with the essential, the ephemeral with the permanent," managing to make conscious and highly sophisticated use of the disproportions that attend provinciality while being in no way culturally provincial himself.[9] In doing so, he created resources on which later Russians were able to draw; a French writer, it seems, would be unlikely to echo Sinyavsky's assertion that art is "provincial in principle, preserving for itself a naïve, external, astonished, and envious look" (Terts [Sinyavsky] 2003, 328). Gogol made claims like Sinyavsky's possible; he is the exhilarating exception to the rules as the central authorities wish to define them.

Notes

1. Typically, these places are designated by the term *Gorod N*, a formula perhaps better translated as "Town X," given that in Russian the letter N, from Latin *nomen*, name, functions as a placeholder much as X does in English.
2. Bojanowska claims, for instance, that Ukraine as depicted in *Evenings on a Farm Near Dikan'ka* can be read as "an organic national community that struggles against dissolution in the imperial Russian state" (Bojanowska 2007, 37).
3. In any case, such a renunciation probably would not have been possible: unlike his contemporary Pushkin, who could choose to play up his own African descent as an exotic component of his authorial identity, Gogol was pretty much stuck with Ukrainianness. It was non-negotiable.
4. Hereafter all Gogol citations are from this edition and appear parenthetically in the main text.
5. Recent scholarship has argued that middling landowners who spent virtually all their time on their estates—as opposed to the vastly wealthy and more itinerant few on whom Kolchin tends to focus—had stronger ties to their localities. See, for instance, Katherine Pickering Antonova (2012) and Catherine Evtuhov (2011).
6. Here the noun *provintsiia* appears in the locative plural, though today in this case and meaning it is used almost exclusively in the singular [*v provintsii*].
7. Stories of the 1830s and 1840s provide many examples of awkward provincials and their inept attempts at dancing, dressing fashionably, decorating their houses, and so on. See, for example, Orest Somov's *A Novel in Two Letters*, Aleksei Pleshcheev's *Everyday Scenes*, Vladimir Sollogub's "Serezha" and *The Apothecary's Wife*.
8. Greenleaf's focus is the Romantic period, but her insights shed light on the tradition as a whole.
9. It is important to note that while Gogol played up his own outsider (*Khokhol* or "Uke") status in the capitals' literary circles, he never allowed himself to be figured as an *object* by this society. Compare here Bourdieu's analysis of the "primitive" painter Henri Rousseau, an outsider who had to be constituted as a "real" artist by powerful supporters like Duchamp. Though Gogol was perhaps initially treated as a curiosity who had been discovered and made available for display in elite literary circles, he seized control of the situation for himself. He was never (as was Rousseau, according to Bourdieu) the artist "as object, who does something other than what he thinks he is doing, does not know what he does, because he knows nothing of the field he stumbles into, of which he is the plaything" (Bourdieu 1993, 61).

BIBLIOGRAPHY

Bakhtin, Mikhail M. 1981. Forms of Time and Chronotope in the Novel. In *The Dialogic Imagination*, ed. Michael Holquist. Trans. Caryl Emerson and Michael Holquist. Austin, TX: University of Texas Press.

Bojanowska, Edyta M. 2007. *Nikolai Gogol: Between Ukrainian and Russian Nationalism*. Cambridge, MA: Harvard University Press.

Bourdieu, Pierre. 1993. *The Field of Cultural Production: Essays on Art and Literature*. New York, NY: Columbia University Press.

Brower, Daniel R. 1990. *The Russian City between Tradition and Modernity, 1850–1900*. Berkeley, CA: University of California Press.

Chekhov, Anton P. 1974–1983. *Polnoe sobranie sochinenii i pisem v 30 tomakh*. Moscow: Nauka.

Debreczeny, Paul. 1966. Nikolay Gogol and his Contemporary Critics. *Transactions of the American Philosophical Society* 56 (3): 1–68.

Eliot, Thomas Stearns. 1975. What is a Classic? In *Selected Prose of T. S. Eliot*, ed. Frank Kermode, 115–131. New York, NY: Farrar, Straus, and Giroux.

Evtuhov, Catherine. 2011. *Portrait of a Russian Province: Economy, Society, and Civilization in Nineteenth-Century Nizhnii Novgorod*. Pittsburgh, PA: University of Pittsburgh Press.

Fanger, Donald. 1979. *The Creation of Nikolai Gogol*. Cambridge, MA: Harvard University Press.

Gogol, Nikolai V. 1952. *Polnoe sobranie sochinenii v 14 tomakh*. Moscow: Akademiia Nauk SSSR.

Greenleaf, Monika. 1994. *Pushkin and Romantic Fashion*. Stanford, CA: Stanford University Press.

Herzen, Alexander I. 1954. *Sobranie sochinenii v 30 tomakh*. Moscow: Izd. Akademii Nauk SSSR.

Kirichenko, Yevgenia, and Yelena Shcheboleva. 1997. *Russkaia provintsiia*. Moscow: Nash dom.

Kolchin, Peter. 1987. *Unfree Labor: American Slavery and Russian Serfdom*. Cambridge, MA: Harvard University Press.

Lincoln, W. Bruce. 1982. *In the Vanguard of Reform: Russia's Enlightened Bureaucrats 1825–1861*. DeKalb, IL: Northern Illinois University Press.

Pickering Antonova, Katherine. 2012. *An Ordinary Marriage: The World of a Gentry Family in Provincial Russia*. Oxford: Oxford University Press.

Reyfman, Irina. 2016. *How Russia Learned to Write: Literature and the Imperial Table of Ranks*. Madison, MI: University of Wisconsin Press.

Smith-Peter, Susan. 2007. Defining the Russian People: Konstantin Arsen'ev and Russian Statistics Before 1861. *History of Science* (45) 1: 47–64.

Sollogub, Vladimir A. 1978. Tarantas. In *Tri povesti*, ed. V.A. Sollogub. Moscow: Izd. Sovietskaia Rossiia.

Terts, Abram [pseud. of Andrei Sinyanvsky]. [1981]. 2003. *V teni Gogolia*. Moscow: Agraf.

Todorova, Maria. 1997. *Imagining the Balkans*. Oxford: Oxford University Press.

CHAPTER 23

Belinsky and the Sociality of Reason

Vadim Shkolnikov

Belinsky's Literary and Social Impact

As a literary critic who published in the popular thick journals, Vissarion "the Furious" Belinsky (1811–1848) championed and greatly influenced the early development of realist prose in the 1830s and 1840s—at the time when Russian literature "came of age" and took on a greater *social* role. Belinsky stood at the forefront of this far-reaching cultural transformation, inasmuch as he exemplified something like a new form of social consciousness. Because of this, his very persona took on enormous socio-political significance. He has been widely regarded as the quintessential prototype for what would later become known as "the intelligentsia," and throughout the Soviet period he was canonized as one of the first heroes of the socialist liberation movement.

Belinsky developed intellectually, moreover, at the height of German philosophical influence in Russia. Thus, his manifold and controversial cultural legacy, both in its literary-aesthetic and in its socio-political dimensions, was predicated on the philosophical perspectives he introduced into the understanding of Russian literature and, before that, the formation of his own sense of identity. We can say this because Belinsky was prolific in his private correspondence: his letters themselves hold significant literary and historical value, particularly as a highly expressive record of his inner life and the progression of his thinking. Accordingly, the analysis of Belinsky's correspondence in conjunction with his published articles reveals how his influence on realism *as a literary style* derived from a complex process of personal and philosophical development, through which he first attained the standpoint of realism *as a socio-historical sense of self* (see Ginzburg 1991).

V. Shkolnikov (✉)
National Research University Higher School of Economics, Russian Federation,
St. Petersburg, Russia

© The Author(s), under exclusive license to Springer Nature
Switzerland AG 2021
M. F. Bykova et al. (eds.), *The Palgrave Handbook of Russian Thought*,
https://doi.org/10.1007/978-3-030-62982-3_23

This crucial formative experience began for Belinsky in Moscow in the 1830s, through his involvement in the philosophical circle led by Nicholas Stankevich. Although Stankevich himself died suddenly at 27, without having published a single significant work, the circle became well known as the center of early Hegelian influence in Russia, and a number of its members became important cultural figures, including Mikhail Bakunin, the future anarchist and revolutionary, who was Belinsky's primary influence, as well as his greatest antagonist.

Memoiristic accounts of the Stankevich circle and others like it invariably conjure up an atmosphere of youthful exuberance and an improbable zeal for German up idealist philosophy. At a time when the institutionalized, academic practice of philosophy in Russia was stagnant, the philosophical circle comprised a private, self-enclosed world, in which philosophy served fundamentally as a basis for personal relationships. The result was a unique intellectual culture, which included the quirky practice of applying newly acquired philosophical conceptions to analyze one's own everyday predicaments. This seemingly naïve practice of philosophical self-analysis, however, eventually evolved into a nuanced self-understanding. Thus, the historical importance of the Stankevich circle was predicated on the idiosyncratic way in which German philosophical ideas, especially Hegel, were assimilated, *lived*.

Ivan Turgenev wrote famously that the philosophical circles were seeking "everything in the world, except pure thought" (Turgenev 1978–2014, 11: 27), and Gustav Shpet echoes this premise in his scholarly assessment of Belinsky as a philosopher. Shpet emphasizes that the Hegelianism practiced by Belinsky and his fellow members of the Stankevich circle continuously displayed an inability to sustain a purely philosophical position—as a result of attempting to *use* philosophy to solve problems of personal life. On the other hand, Shpet's argument implies that this inability to remain within the field of philosophy accounts precisely for the characteristic form of "philosophizing" that would come to define the intelligentsia. Belinsky (together with Bakunin) "set a lasting tone for Russian philosophizing," inasmuch as the primary intellectual currents within Russian society became characterized by "the propensity to transform abstract systems borrowed from abroad into a purely Russian *catechism of practical life*" (Shpet 2009, 137, 178, 183).

Always controversial, Belinsky began his career as a critic by declaring that Russia had no literature, in the true sense ("Literary Reveries," 1834). Yes, there were works of literature, even great ones, but there was still no essential, organic connection between Russian literature and Russian life: the two seemed to coexist independently—they did not need each other. Yet over the course of Belinsky's relatively short career, the situation changed dramatically, and by 1846 he would write: "Whatever our literature may be, in any case its significance for us is much more important than it may appear: it [literature] alone constitutes our entire intellectual life and all the poetry of our life" (Belinsky 1953–1959, 9: 430).

Belinsky recognized a new beginning for Russian literature with the appearance of Gogol's stories, which he hailed immediately for epitomizing the growing tendency toward the representation of "reality" [*deistvitel'nost'*]. Later, Belinsky's conviction that this literature of reality constituted the authentic self-consciousness of the modern age, together with his efforts to promote it, made him the de facto theorist and leader of the "Natural School," a group of young writers following in Gogol's footsteps—which included Dostoevsky, Turgenev, Herzen, and Goncharov (as well as the poet Nekrasov). Moreover, under Belinsky's guidance this early stage in the evolution of Russian realism came to manifest an unprecedented new level of social consciousness: as in Dostoevsky's *Poor Folk* and Turgenev's *Hunter's Sketches*, the works of the Natural School were characterized by urban landscapes dominated by poverty, concern for the plight of the peasantry, the powerless, the unfortunate.

Thus, although Belinsky never articulated a clear political agenda, the literature he championed came to be known for its protest against social injustice. Significantly, this *politicized* dimension, first fostered by Belinsky, would continue to inform the realist tradition in Russia—from the radical critics of the 1860s (Chernyshevsky, Dobrolyubov, Pisarev) to socialist realism in the Soviet Union.

Belinsky's class background also played a significant role. As a *raznochinets*, one of the first non-aristocrats to rise to prominence within a literary establishment still dominated by the aristocracy, Belinsky naturally incarnated the democratizing movement within Russian culture, and he remained an undisputed ideological authority for the "marginalized" younger generation of the 1860s, when *raznochintsy* came to dominate the intellectual scene and the term "*intelligentsia*" first became widespread.

On the other hand, commentators have noted the negative consequences of Belinsky's politicization of Russian literature. Some blame him for initiating the artistically fatal impetus to subordinate literature to political ideology, which would culminate in the Soviet period with the repressive, government-controlled institution of socialist realism. As Belinsky's cultural authority grew, he was not always tolerant toward literary forms that did not meet his preferred aesthetic criteria (e.g., the lyric poetry of Afanasy Fet).

Yet even those who opposed the revolutionary movement have attested to Belinsky's undeniable moral integrity and force: the "moral passion" that would come to define "the intelligentsia." In this sense, Isaiah Berlin describes Belinsky as "the original prototype of these sincere, sometimes childish, at other times angry, champions of persecuted humanity [...] the actual, historical embodiment of this most Russian type of moral and intellectual heroism" (Berlin 1979, 152).

Belinsky's moral passion manifested itself, most of all, in the "furious," confrontational nature of his articles and the continuous polemics they engendered. Essentially, Belinsky's career spans an unending series of battles, which gave serious intellectual issues a constant public presence and created the intense ideological atmosphere that would often serve as the setting for the realist novel of the second half of the century.

Meanwhile, within a broader European context Belinsky's moral-intellectual development essentially reflects the prevailing post-Hegelian impetus toward "action," articulated most famously by Marx: "The philosophers have only interpreted the world, in various ways; the point is to change it" (Tucker 1978, 145). Yet Belinsky arrived at analogous conclusions more or less independently. He developed his own distinct conception of *activism* over the course of his psychologically tortuous period of immersion in Hegel's philosophy, highlighted by his remarkable polemic with Bakunin.

As far as what Belinsky actually sought to "change," the one constant is that throughout his entire career he remained focused on overcoming Russia's acknowledged cultural inadequacy vis-à-vis the most advanced Western nations. Consequently, Belinsky's literary endeavors as a whole took the form of a civilizing mission—consciously following in the footsteps of Peter the Great. Belinsky thus became known as one of the foremost "Westernizers" of the 1840s. Yet the ultimate goal was always an autonomous, "organic" Russian culture, not one based on "imitation." In the Hegelian language Belinsky eventually adopted, the objective was for Russia to awaken from its "unconscious," "immediate" condition *outside* "world history" and to assert itself, make its own original statement, on the world-historical stage, among the select group of "world-historical nations." In fact, from this perspective the "prototype" established by Belinsky takes on even more far-reaching global significance. In essence, he prefigures the difficulties facing all intellectuals of "underdeveloped" nations—a situation especially prevalent in the post-colonial context—who must first assimilate the ideas of the dominant Western powers, in order to foster the emergence of an original national culture.

In addition to all this, Chernyshevsky made the crucial observation that Belinsky was the first *historian* of Russian literature (Chernyshevsky 1939–1953, 3:191). To become the first historian it was necessary to perceive a logical evolution in Russian literature and to construct a *narrative*, which, among other things, would explain the emergence of realism as a rational necessity, based on the principle that literature and society must evolve together. Thus, the many aspects of Belinsky's literary and social impact were predicated on his construction of this philosophical narrative—one which, in fact, derived from his own personal experience, his own striving for philosophical self-realization.

The perception that Belinsky lacked logical consistency, that he characteristically renounced his own former convictions, was actually fueled by Belinsky himself. Certainly, there are cases when he reverses individual judgments. Yet looking back over his entire career, we can perceive a single, prevailing line of intellectual development, which informs both his impact on Russian literature and the socio-political significance of his persona. From his early days in the Stankevich circle and his crucial period of immersion in Hegel's philosophy, Belinsky's personal and conceptual evolution follows a predominant trajectory that corresponds to the discovery and affirmation of one of Hegel's most important principles: the sociality of reason (see Pinkard 1994). In other words, it was essential for Belinsky to discover, through his own tortuous experience of Hegelian philosophy, that reality can only be a social reality.

BEFORE HEGEL: MOSCOW UNIVERSITY, THE PHILOSOPHICAL CIRCLE, AND THE TELESCOPE

The young Belinsky gushed with pride when he was accepted to study philology [*slovesnost'*] at Moscow University in 1829, allowing him to leave his small provincial hometown of Chembar, where his father worked as a medical doctor. His time at the university, however, did not go well. He endured difficult living conditions as a poor, state-funded student, and his health began to deteriorate. In 1832 he spent four months in the hospital, suffering from the respiratory illness that would eventually lead to his untimely death. Then, later that year, he was expelled from the university. Although the official reason was "because of weak health" and "limited abilities," it is often assumed that Belinsky was actually expelled for composing a Schilleresque tragedy, *Dmitrii Kalinin*, in which the protagonist lashes out against the "fate" that made him a serf (see Belinsky 1950, 303–416). The fact that Belinsky naively attempted to publish the play suggests that he did not consider it politically subversive. In any case, he did not have a high opinion of his own artistic talent and subsequently all but abandoned creative writing.

In other ways, though, Belinsky's time at Moscow University had a significant impact on his future. Although courses specifically on philosophy were not even taught at the time, many students were first exposed to German idealism by professors such as M. G. Pavlov, who famously incorporated the ideas of Schelling's *Naturphilosophie* into his lectures on physics, mineralogy, and agriculture (see Herzen 1954–1965, 9: 17–18). Another professor devoted to Schelling, N. I. Nadezhdin, hired Belinsky to edit and write for his journal *The Telescope*. Moreover, the circumstances of Belinsky's expulsion brought him together with fellow Moscow University student Nikolai Stankevich and his circle of friends. Like other members of the circle, Belinsky would subsequently speak of Stankevich (who first gave him the nickname "Furious" Vissarion) with the utmost reverence, as one of his greatest influences.

Presumably this influence pertained most to the way Belinsky's experience in the philosophical circle first shaped his intellectual identity. Guided by Stankevich's highly aestheticized vision, the circle's philosophical pursuits, which initially focused on Schelling and Fichte, aimed at moral self-perfection, through a somewhat nebulous notion of union with "the universal" (Stankevich 1890, 154). An individual could not accomplish this alone. Within the circle each member's individual striving for the universal united him with all the others. Mutual recognition gave reality to one's inner intuition of the infinite, and a sense of belonging became the basis for the individual's sense of self. Hence, in a moment of respite from his perpetual torments, Belinsky proclaimed,

"Friendship!—through it, life smiled at me so invitingly and so warmly, and very likely, in friendship, and only in friendship, will my life continue to know itself until the very end" (Belinsky 1953–1959, 11: 190).

The philosophical themes that intrigued the circle are, in turn, reflected in Belinsky's early *Telescope* articles. Significantly, the claim "We have no literature" was initially predicated on a specifically philosophical definition of art as the representation of the eternal, *universal idea*, which animates the world, manifesting itself as unity amid infinite diversity (Belinsky 1953–1959, 1: 30). The problem of imitation, the lack of originality, in Russian literature also related to this universality, understood in terms of Herder's romantic nationalism: literature must express the unique "spirit of a people," which, in turn, represents one particular aspect of universal humanity. The history of such a literature must develop naturally, *organically*: there cannot be any "forced or violent ruptures, caused by some kind of alien influence" (Belinsky 1953–1959, 1: 24). These are the criteria that Russian literary history had failed to meet, despite the already acknowledged greatness of Pushkin and the promising newcomer Gogol. Belinsky noted that the demand for "national character" (*narodnost'*) was already ubiquitous in Russian literary criticism, yet he rejected all shortcuts or superficial solutions to this problem. Moreover, he was especially critical of the artificial, "rhetorical" tendency of prominent eighteenth-century poets. Elaborating this position in later articles, he maintained: "A literature emerged, initially without readers, without a public, a thunderous literature, triumphant, puffed-up, scholastic, pedantic, bookish, without any vital relation to life and society [...] consisting of random works, not connected to one another, which therefore did not yet have a history." Literature was not yet "the consciousness of a people, the expression of its worldview" (Belinsky 1953–1959, 9: 383, 4: 423).

Belinsky's long *Telescope* article on the short stories of Gogol (1835)—in which he hailed Gogol as "the poet of real life"—represents his first major statement on realism in literature. Conceptually, the most significant nuance was that Belinsky interpreted the advent of this new literary style as the result of a transnational historical process and the demands of contemporary life. Yet aside from the vague insistence that Gogol's works were "true to life," Belinsky's theoretical definition of realism and reality was still highly underdeveloped. In fact, he continued to associate the new realist literature with the quintessentially romantic notions of poetic genius, inspiration, and a "mysterious" creative act, which (in accordance with Kant and Schelling's *Transcendental Idealism*) paradoxically combined purposelessness and purpose, consciousness and unconsciousness, freedom and unfreedom (Belinsky 1953–1959, 1: 285). Essentially, Belinsky still conceptualized the realist artist as a "poet-seer" in the romantic tradition.

In sum, Belinsky's *Telescope* articles raised some of the key questions and established the general conceptual framework for virtually all of his subsequent writings on Russian literature. But the specific elaboration of these general ideas would continue to evolve as Belinsky's philosophical acumen deepened—particularly with his immersion in Hegel.

Belinsky's collaboration with *The Telescope* ended abruptly in October 1836, when the journal was shut down for publishing the first of Chaadayev's "Philosophical Letters"—with its scathing critique of Russia's cultural deficiencies. It should be noted that the general ideological direction adopted by Belinsky in *The Telescope* was quite resonant with Chaadayev's position, his claims that Russia lacked a history and that "We are [...] strangers to our own selves" (Edie et al. 1976, 1: 112). Furthermore, the fate of *The Telescope* underscores the fact that, throughout his career, Belinsky had to walk a tightrope in regard to tsarist censorship. Of course, the closing of the journal created considerable material difficulties for Belinsky, and he was still struggling with the resulting hardships when the Stankevich circle turned their attention to Hegel.

Hegel and a New Sense of Self

Belinsky's tumultuous period of preoccupation with Hegel's philosophy as a member of the Stankevich circle represents his most important formative experience, which would leave its mark on all his subsequent cultural contributions. Since Belinsky did not know German, he relied to some extent on the second-hand accounts of his friends (especially Bakunin), for his initial understanding of Hegel. Nevertheless, Belinsky was always determined to grasp these ideas as his own, the basis for his own sense of self:

> I accepted ready-made ideas as a gift, but things did not end there, and from this alone I would have gained nothing. Through my own life, at the price of my tears, the cries of my soul, I absorbed these ideas, and they entered into the depths of my being. (Belinsky 1953–1959, 11: 281)

The decisive shift to Hegel as the intellectual focal point in the life of the Stankevich circle corresponded to a fundamental moment of re-assessment and self-criticism. It all began in early 1837, in the aftermath of Stankevich's ill-fated engagement to Bakunin's sister Liubov—when he acknowledged that he could not love her and, as an explanation, began comparing himself to the suffering, ineffectual "beautiful soul" depicted by Hegel in the *Phenomenology of Spirit*. Hegel's ironic, critical take on the long-standing European ideal of the beautiful soul reveals the problematic, double-edged nature of *conscience*, as an infallible "inner" moral voice. That is, the beautiful soul in the *Phenomenology* represents the perfected form of conscience, the "moral genius" that knows its inner voice to be "divine," but, as a result, eventually shrinks back from all contact with the inevitably dirty realm of practical relations, which could only tarnish its inner purity. Unable to externalize itself, unable to become anything more than potential, the beautiful soul is reduced to a tormented, abstract existence; it becomes "*wirklichkeitslos*"—devoid of reality (Hegel 1977, 397, 400, 407).

514   V. SHKOLNIKOV

This specific conceptual framework marked the starting point for the circle's immersion in Hegel's philosophy and the beginning of their obsession with the concept of reality [*Wirklichkeit, deistvitel'nost'*]. Stankevich was the first to perceive the negative, hypocritical side of the "moral self-perfection" to which the circle had aspired, and following his lead, all the members embraced Hegel's paradigm of the beautiful soul as a compelling psychological portrait, in which each (for different reasons) perceived a criticism of himself.

For Belinsky, who was now struggling to find a livelihood after the closing of the *Telescope*, the beautiful soul represented "one of those people open to everything true, but lacking the strength of will to attain the highest truth" (Belinsky 1953–1959, 11: 188). He even intended to compose a philosophical dialogue between two friends, one of whom would represent the beautiful soul, the other—Hegelian spirit: "In short, I will represent myself as this beautiful soul, and I hope quite accurately." A new agenda was set: it became imperative to emerge from the anguished abstractness of the beautiful soul and *to become real* [*stat' deistvitel'nym*]. This theme soon began to inundate Belinsky's literary interpretations, as in his major article on Shakespeare's *Hamlet*: "Hamlet […] is only a collection of beautiful elements, from which something determinate and real must eventually emerge; he is only a beautiful soul, but not yet real" (Belinsky 1953–1959, 2: 291–292). Within this context, Hegel's philosophy was treated as a practical guide for achieving self-realization.

After Stankevich left for Europe (where he would die three years later), Bakunin and Belinsky took over the lead in expounding the Hegelian line of thinking he had initiated. The result was the notorious phase of "reconciliation with reality," which has often been interpreted as a Hegelian apology for political conservatism, an unquestioning acceptance of Russia's existing social order. Herzen reinforced this point of view in his memoirs, depicting Belinsky's period of "reconciliation" as a kind of passing illness and a baffling betrayal of his true nature (Herzen 1954–1965, 9: 27). Yet having just met Belinsky for the first time, Herzen could not have understood how the reconciliation with reality was a response to the crisis of the beautiful soul.

Belinsky himself identified a fateful turning point with Bakunin's reading of the *Philosophy of Right* (Hegel's theory of the modern state), which shifted their understanding of "reality" to the structures of social power:

> A new world opened up. Power is right, and right is power—I cannot describe what I felt when I heard these words—it was a liberation […] At this time our attacks on beautiful-soulness in the name of reality began. […] The word "reality" for me took on the same meaning as the word "God." (Belinsky 1953–1959, 11: 386–387)

In turn, Bakunin adopted Hegel's *Doppelsatz* from the preface to the *Philosophy of Right* (only inverted)—"What is real is rational [razumno, *vernünftig*], and what is rational is real"—as the motto for his doctrine of reconciliation with reality, which he outlined in the March 1838 issue of the

Moscow Observer, after Belinsky had been given the de facto editorship of the struggling journal. Bakunin's article—which first introduced the circle's neologism *prekrasnodushie* to the Russian public—informs much of Belinsky's subsequent thinking.

Although Bakunin did refer to "the strong and real Russian person, devoted to the Tsar and the fatherland," and depicted the beautiful soul's alienation from reality as a kind of misguided rebellion, this underdeveloped political dimension should not obscure the article's primary thrust, as a lesson on how to emerge from the psychological torment that Belinsky and the others were experiencing (Bakunin 1934, 2: 166–178). Moreover, Bakunin's conception of the beautiful soul's rebellion entailed a question of philosophical methodology: unable to adopt the standpoint of *razum* [reason, *Vernunft*]—the true faculty of philosophical cognition for Hegel—the beautiful soul relies on the lower faculty of *rassudok* [understanding, *Verstand*], which is incapable of grasping the infinite. This hierarchy of *razum* and *rassudok* would remain axiomatic for Belinsky. In proper Hegelian fashion Bakunin identified the work of reason [*razum*] with mediation, the overcoming of spontaneity, immediacy. Accordingly, his call for reconciliation was never really a call for political quietism, but rather a challenge to his friends—to move beyond the circle's original, unconscious, spontaneous condition and to reunite with the infinite on a mediated, self-conscious level.

It is also significant that much of Bakunin's article is devoted to conceptualizing the problem of beautiful-soulness, which had befallen his circle of friends, as an unavoidable logical consequence of the entire development of European philosophy and culture since the Reformation. This merging of the personal and the historical, a perspective that Belinsky proceeded to develop more fully, represents a crucial step toward the emerging intelligentsia's sense of identity.

Belinsky repeatedly acknowledged the importance of Bakunin's influence, and he basically adhered to the same theoretical definition of reality. Yet his persistent goal (which he was unable to achieve at once) was a kind of self-realization, based on the knowledge of reality, which would manifest itself not just theoretically, but in action (Belinsky 1953–1959, 11: 317). And so, a remarkable polemical correspondence with Bakunin ensued, an exchange of "dissertations on reality." Throughout the polemic the two relied on virtually the same Hegelian concepts—which Belinsky had initially learned from Bakunin. Each continuously berated the other's beautiful-soulness and simultaneously lamented the beautiful-soulness from which he himself could not escape. In the end, Belinsky insisted that Bakunin's ineptitude in personal relationships undermined his philosophical position, and eventually Belinsky became convinced that the realization he sought was simply not possible within a self-enclosed circle of friends: "I'm sick of the beautiful soul's circling around in empty circles [*prekrasnodushnoe kruzhenie v pustykh krugakh*] of false relations, false friendships, false love, and false hatred" (Belinsky 1953–1959, 11: 368).

In his competing version of reconciliation with reality, Belinsky placed even greater emphasis on the social element of reality, which had been latent in Bakunin's article: "The foundation [*pochva*] of all reality is society" (Belinsky 1953–1959, 11: 479). Accordingly, Belinsky re-envisioned the philosophical circle's notion of "getting closer to the life of the infinite," which now demanded perceiving unity, universality, a rational order, and rational development in the manifold particularities of the everyday social sphere: "With insatiable curiosity I look into these springs, these instruments, outwardly so crude, vulgar, and prosaic. [...] I look at reality, so disdained by me previously, and I tremble with secret delight, knowing its rationality" (Belinsky 1953–1959, 11: 284, 282). Yet all along Belinsky's preoccupation with deciphering the mechanisms of social reality was driven by the need to formulate a new sense of self, after the demise of his former identity as a member of the philosophical circle. The goal was to be able to declare: "I am no longer a candidate for membership in society but a member; I feel myself in society and society in me; I have grafted myself to its interests, penetrated into its life, [...] given myself to it in tribute" (Belinsky 1953–1959, 11: 316). Significantly, Belinsky's understanding of reality would always retain a sense of membership and belonging.

Belinsky's final break with the life of the philosophical circle came in November 1839, when he relocated from Moscow to St. Petersburg. *The Moscow Observer* was simply not working out financially, particularly since the journal's overly abstract, overly philosophical direction was not attracting enough readers. Belinsky therefore decided to try his luck in the more thriving literary market of Petersburg, where he was hired to edit the criticism section of A. A. Kraevsky's journal *Notes of the Fatherland*. (He moved to the *Contemporary* in 1847.)

Belinsky's first articles in *Notes of the Fatherland* actually represented the fruition of his polemic with Bakunin and his own fully developed take on reconciliation with reality. A pair of articles occasioned by the 1839 commemoration of the battle of Borodino (in which Napoleon was defeated in 1812) provoked outrage from Herzen and others, who only saw a defense of Russian autocracy, based on an alleged misinterpretation of Hegel. In actuality, Belinsky was clearly seeking a more rigorous philosophical understanding of the historical dynamics of social power. He was attempting a theoretical analysis of Russia's biggest moment on the global stage as a prelude to the nation's rise to full-fledged "world-historical" status (Belinsky 1953–1959, 3: 240). In fact, founding Russian Marxist Georgii Plekhanov recognized that Belinsky's thinking marked a critical *positive* contribution to the development of revolutionary ideology: "For us it is important that Belinsky arrived at the doctrine of reconciliation with *Russian reality* by way of *an analysis of Russia's historical development*, albeit an inaccurate and highly superficial analysis" (Plekhanov 1956–1958, 4: 437). For Plekhanov this was the first logical step toward the "scientificity" that would separate Marxism from "idealistic" socialism.

Two subsequent articles of "reconciliation"—"Menzel, Critic of Goethe" and "Griboedov's *Woe from Wit*"—seem to contradict the very values for which

Belinsky ultimately became famous. Belinsky rebukes Menzel for criticizing Goethe's apolitical attitude and scorns the social criticism of Griboedov's protagonist Chatsky, who appears to be a forerunner of the oppositional intelligentsia. Nevertheless, Belinsky was not rejecting protest and social activism per se. In effect, he was struggling to conceptualize a form of protest and activism consistent with his conception of reality. Thus, Menzel is derided because he merely expresses the limited standpoint of the understanding (*rassudok*), while Chatsky is not depicted in Griboedov's play as belonging to any social constituency, and so his protest amounts to "a storm in a glass of water" (Belinsky 1953–1959, 3: 449). In fact, this problem goes back to the polemic with Bakunin and the debunking of "abstract heroism"—a vague ethos of protest armed with nothing more than an "abstract ideal of society, torn away from the conditions of historical development" (Belinsky 1953–1959, 11: 385). In this sense, Belinsky's period of Hegelian reconciliation represents a crucial moment of self-criticism and self-negation in the history of the emerging intelligentsia, which helped to transform elemental, unreflective dissent into a socially and historically grounded theory of revolution.

The striving for reconciliation in the *Phenomenology*, however, fails repeatedly, and this is what happened to Belinsky in Petersburg, when his newfound sense of belonging to society proved unstable. As a result, Belinsky ostensibly renounced Hegel and his "philosophical cap" in a famous letter to Vasily Botkin: "I have suspected for a long time now that the philosophy of Hegel is only a moment, although a great one" (Belinsky 1953–1959, 12: 22). Yet the impact of Hegel's philosophy on Belinsky's thinking did not end when he renounced his own "vile" reconciliation with "vile reality" (Belinsky 1953–1959, 11: 556). Rather, the change in his attitude reflected the continued expansion of his conceptual gaze: world history, rather than simply "society," now took over as the ultimate measure of reality.

Writing to Botkin, Belinsky actually disputed the Hegelian notion of rationality in history, demanding that Hegel "account for all the victims of the conditions of life and history, all the victims of accident, of superstition, of inquisitions, of Philip II, and so on" (Belinsky 1953–1959, 12: 23). Yet virtually at the same time in an article on Peter the Great he wrote:

> Only rational necessity constitutes the essence of history. [...] Despite all the motleyness, all the bright colors, all the diversity of clashing elements, the history of Europe constitutes a graceful and grandiose picture of rational and great events; the gaze of the thinker perceives in the form of this multifaceted picture a unity of dialectically developing thought. (Belinsky 1953–1959, 5: 95–96)

Essentially, Belinsky conceptualized the prodigious achievement of Peter the Great in terms of Hegel's philosophy of history, based on the distinction between the few, privileged world-historical nations and the un-historical nation: the eternal China, where time stands still. Peter, according to Belinsky, initiated the historical process by which Russia will eventually attain self-consciousness and its destined status as a world-historical nation. But for now Russia remained somewhere in between. Thus, in the article Belinsky praises Peter for setting the process in motion and expresses confidence in the eventual attainment of the goal. Meanwhile, Belinsky's letters to Botkin express the frustration and despair of an individual who realizes that the goal is still far away and will probably not be achieved in his lifetime.

Within this context, the "vile" Petersburg reality Belinsky now rejected was characterized by "Chinaism," the pervasive manifestations of obdurate historical immobility, and he now insisted, "Chinaism is worse than beautiful-soulness" (Belinsky 1953–1959, 11: 348). These judgments pertained most of all to the Petersburg literary establishment, and thus, in an invective against his "forced reconciliation with vile Russian reality, that Chinese kingdom of brute, material force," Belinsky listed a litany of evils culminating with: "where Pushkin lived in poverty and died a victim of baseness, while Grech and Bulgarin control all literature" (Belinsky 1953–1959, 11: 577). At one point, Belinsky referred to Grech as "the apotheosis of Russian reality" (Belinsky 1953–1959, 12: 9).

Along these lines, Belinsky finally concluded that his Petersburg world did not even belong to reality, as understood in Hegelian terms. Based on the conception of a socially grounded reality, every failure to attain self-realization that he had experienced or witnessed since his days in the Stankevich circle could now be attributed to the absence of a developed social structure and unifying social bonds:

> Without society there can be no friendship, no love, no spiritual interests, but only a longing for all this. [...] Our entire life and our relationships serve as the best proof of this bitter truth. You do not feel yourself in society, because it does not exist. (Belinsky 1953–1959, 12: 49–50)

In turn, Belinsky proclaimed his new mantra of "sociality" [*sozialnost'*] as a proposed solution: "Sociality, sociality or death. [...] There is nothing more noble than to promote its development" (Belinsky 1953–1959, 12: 69, 71). Although the term *sozialnost'* presumably derives from the French *socialité*, and Belinsky's wording clearly alludes to the French revolutionary tradition, which began to fascinate him at the time, we should not simply equate sociality with what later became known as French utopian socialism (after the *Communist Manifesto* of 1848). The context of Belinsky's ongoing intellectual development shows that this notion emerged, simultaneously, as the culmination of his Hegelian thinking on reality. Belinsky even insisted that sociality did not entail rejecting Hegelian historicity, the rationality of historical development, or the primacy of reason [*razum*] over understanding [*rassudok*]. Essentially, sociality entailed replacing a merely traditional sense of duty, imposed "from outside," with *rational*, "inner" unifying bonds. Fundamentally, this called for the creation of a new institutional form of collectivity—and the negation of the old.

We can say that Belinsky's self-realization culminated when this line of thinking merged with his notion of *historical agency* as the true measure of understanding reality: "Peter the Great (who was a very bad philosopher) understood reality better and more fully than Fichte" (Belinsky 1953–1959, 11: 315). Logically, Belinsky could only point to Peter I and the institution of the Tsar as the best examples from Russia's past of the kind of historical agency he envisioned. In turn, it was essential for Belinsky to project his own sense of self onto the world-historical stage, before he could finally define his role as the historical *negation* of traditional social and moral forms not yet based on self-conscious reason: "Negation is my God" (Belinsky 1953–1959, 11: 70).

Thus, the distinct sense of self that emerged over the course of Belinsky's struggles with Hegel exemplified what Irina Paperno has called "the historicization of private life and the privatization of history" (Paperno 2004). Moreover, Belinsky's determination to devote himself to serving sociality marks the culmination of the philosophical process described by Shpet: the transformation of abstract systems into a "purely Russian *catechism of practical life.*"

Literature and Sociality

The experience of living the philosophical ideas he acquired carried over to Belinsky's thinking about literature and his practice of literary criticism. This is in fact what Isaiah Berlin observed when he spoke of "The kind of social criticism [...] virtually invented by the great Russian essayist Belinsky—the kind of criticism in which the line between life and art is of set purpose not too clearly drawn" (Berlin 1979, 116). Belinsky himself spoke of the *difficult* role of a critic "suffused with conviction, who does not separate questions of art and literature from questions of his own personal life" (Belinsky 1953–1959, 8: 74).

Belinsky's projection of his own emotional experiences onto his interpretation of Pushkin was particularly significant, because it became the cornerstone of his developing understanding of Russian literary history—that is, a confirmation that Russian literature does indeed have a history. Belinsky had already integrated Pushkin into his ongoing Hegelian drama when he declared that Pushkin's posthumously published works can be comprehended only by one who has "passed from the struggle of beautiful-soulness [*bor'by prekrasnodushiia*] to the harmony of an enlightened spirit reconciled with reality" (Belinsky 1953–1959, 2: 348–349). Then, in a monumental 11-part series of articles, Belinsky's most fully developed analysis of Pushkin as Russia's first poet-artist again invoked the Hegelian thematics of reconciliation: "He posited the emergence from the dissonances of life and reconciliation with the tragic laws of fate not in otherworldly dreams, but in the self-grounding strength of spirit" (Belinsky 1953–1959, 7: 354). The element of personal, emotional identification explained why Gogol was

> not a Russian poet in the same sense as Pushkin, who, through his own self, expressed and drained all the depths of Russian life and in whose wounds we may

lay our fingers, to feel the pain of our own wounds and treat them. (Belinsky 1953–1959, 11: 534)

In turn, Belinsky's culminating statement as a critic of Pushkin—"To write about Pushkin means to write about all Russian literature"—also marked another crucial turning point, inasmuch as Belinsky was finally able to declare, "despite the poverty of our literature, within it there is vital movement and organic development; consequently, it has a history" (Belinsky 1953–1959, 7: 106).

From 1840 to 1847 Belinsky published a series of annual overviews of Russian literature, in which we can observe a steady change in his overall assessment: from pessimism to hope and enthusiastic approval, as the realist agenda he had envisioned began to assert itself. He began by returning to his claim that Russia had no literature, but he now argued that the very posing of this question marked the starting point for Russian literature's true development. Belinsky continued to adhere to the general German philosophical conception of literature as a means of collective self-consciousness, an expression of an epoch's underlying socio-historical meaning, but he emphasized that art must first be art, before it can express the spirit of the age (Belinsky 1953–1959, 10: 303).

Within this framework, the historical movement of literature drawing "closer to reality" became a sign of maturation, a coming of age, the possibility of finally attaining self-consciousness (Belinsky 1953–1959, 6: 526). Earlier in "Literary Reveries," noting that Russian literature had already passed through periods of classicism and sentimentalism and that the age of lyrical poetry had been succeeded by novels, short stories, and drama, Belinsky insisted, "And all this has been for no reason [*bez prichiny*], it is all a product of imitation: when will we have an age of true art?" (Belinsky 1953–1959, 1: 101). Yet over the course of the 1840s, he began to perceive that all these phases and even the necessity of imitation itself belonged to a single metanarrative—a movement toward "naturalness" and *samobytnost'*, literally "being-self"—which defined the trajectory of Russian literary history and endowed it with meaning (Belinsky 1953–1959, 10: 15, 294). As in the case of Belinsky's own personal history, this was essentially a narrative of self-realization.

The narrative culminated with the rise of the "Natural School," a group of young, talented authors, who developed under the influence of Gogol. By 1847—after the appearance of *The Physiology of Petersburg* almanac (edited by Nekrasov), Dostoevsky's *Poor Folk*, Turgenev's "Khor and Kalinych," Herzen's *Who Is to Blame*, Goncharov's *An Ordinary Story*—Belinsky could proclaim that the Natural School stood at the forefront of Russian literature, having turned to Russian life itself, the life of the common "crowd," as the source of its inspiration (Belinsky 1953–1959, 10: 287, 314). Thus, although the basic aesthetic characteristics of the Natural School—the predilection for depicting the mundane, the lowly, the impoverished, the marginalized—can be found in other national literatures of the period (in Dickens or Balzac, for instance), these aesthetic tendencies took on a different, localized significance within the context of Russian cultural history. For, as Belinsky insisted, the realism of the Natural School represented the first pervasive moment in Russian literature that arose (following in the footsteps of Pushkin and Gogol) purely as an "organic" product of Russian life, truly as the result of Russian society contemplating itself. Russia finally had an original national literature.

Although Belinsky continued to conceptualize the "naturalness" of the Natural School as the antipode of rhetoricism in literature, the issue of depicting the society's lower strata—peasants, menial workers, the debased—provoked the most controversy. This choice of subject matter clearly entailed an egalitarian ideology, although in his published articles Belinsky never went as far as translating this egalitarianism into political terms, as a liberationist agenda. Instead, he defended it as a form of objective scientific observation: for the "anatomist" or "physiologist," any human being is a worthy subject of study, regardless of class standing (Belinsky 1953–1959, 10: 300). This comparison to the natural sciences underscores why the so-called *physiological sketch* (such as those by Vladimir Dal') was central to Belinsky's conception of a realist literature. The modest goal was to conceptualize distinct societal *types*, as part of the larger social *organism*. These were the essential building blocks of Russian literary realism, before it turned in the second half of the nineteenth century to more complex psychological dramas. Belinsky's inclination toward scientificity was also significant in itself for the future political opposition, especially the radicals of the 1860s (in addition to Plekhanov, as already mentioned). Thus, the above-quoted references to the observation of nature clearly foreshadow the frog-dissecting nihilist Bazarov from Turgenev's *Fathers and Children* (which was dedicated to the memory of Belinsky). Yet Belinsky never reduced realism simply to empirical observation: "in order to copy nature faithfully," a realist work must capture "the entire soul of the original" (Belinsky 1953–1959, 10: 304).

Fundamentally, however, Belinsky's realism was predicated not only on subject matter and the style of representation, but also on the functioning of literature within society, and, ultimately, a symbiotic relationship between the development of literature and the development of society was required. In response to criticism that this entailed subordinating art to social interests, Belinsky insisted: "To take away art's right to serve social interests is to lower, rather than elevate it, because this deprives art of its most vital strength" (Belinsky 1953–1959, 10: 311).

Accordingly, in the early 1840s Belinsky shifted his agenda from "we have no literature" to "we have no reading public." Literature must arise "like a flower" from the soil of a reading public, in order to exert its influence back on the life of this cohesive mass (Belinsky 1953–1959, 8: 71). A reading public in this sense would comprise a single, evolving, collective self, which would recognize "its own spirit, its own life" in the works of literature. Belinsky was well aware of the inherent paradox: without a public there can be no true literature, but without a true literature there can be no public.

An important moment for Russia's developing intellectual community was the appearance of antagonistic "literary parties": Belinsky's side, the Westernizers [*poborniki evropeizma*], and their opponents, the Slavophiles, who idealized pre-Petrine Russia and condemned Peter's reforms. An early journalistic battle pitted Belinsky against Konstantin Aksakov, who had been a fellow member of the Stankevich circle. The question was whether Gogol's *Dead Souls* should be considered Russia's national epic (see Aksakov 1981, 141–150; Belinsky 1953–1959, 6: 253–260). Belinsky insisted that the epic genre was simply not possible in modern society, and in general he saw the Slavophiles as romantics, incapable of understanding contemporary reality. Yet it was essential for Belinsky to conceptualize the rational historical necessity underlying the appearance of such romantics: "Their history is closely connected to the history of our literature, which is also closely connected to the history of our society's education" (Belinsky 1953–1959, 9: 382). Belinsky's ongoing polemic against the Slavophiles served as the subtext for his highly critical analysis of Aleksandr Aduev, the protagonist of Goncharov's *An Ordinary Story*: "It would have been better and more natural had [Goncharov] made him a Slavophile" (Belinsky 1953–1959, 10: 343). In Goncharov's novel the young romantic Aduev must reconcile himself to the harsh reality of Petersburg, much like Belinsky himself had to do. Belinsky's point was that "this experience and practical logic of life" forced strong natures to develop and mature, whereas weaker natures perished from it—perhaps a reference to the fragile psyche of the gifted Slavophile Ivan Kireevsky (Belinsky 1953–1959, 10: 343). Thus, Slavophilism is explained in terms of stalled personal development: the Slavophiles underwent the same formative experiences as Belinsky, they were a product of the same forces at work in the development of Russian society, but they never made it through a crucial stage in their conceptual evolution, and consequently they were not the people to guide Russia's further social development.

Ultimately, Belinsky's realist agenda—propagating both a literary aesthetic and a distinct sense of self—aimed at establishing the unifying spiritual bonds and the mutual recognition of each individual's "human dignity" that Russian society lacked. The notion that contemporary literature could create such bonds (rather than the economic interdependence of capitalism) made Belinsky's enterprise perhaps unprecedented. He still conceptualized the intellectual circle of friends, who ignored class distinctions as a grassroots source for the new social consciousness which he saw emerging: "This is the true beginning of educated sociality, created through literature" (Belinsky 1953–1959, 9: 436). But the problem was how this consciousness could extend beyond an intimate circle: could individuals in different parts of the country who never met feel themselves a part of a single community, and could a realist literature, together with a shared understanding of reality, establish social bonds more stable than the tenuous, subjective, emotional bond of "philosophical friendship"? Although the word "intelligentsia" had not yet entered common usage, Belinsky seemed to be referring precisely to a future intelligentsia, when he observed, "Our literature [...] has produced something like a particular class in society," a new social grouping that did not fit any existing socioeconomic categories, a group brought together by purely intellectual bonds (Belinsky 1953–1959, 9: 432). Literature both reflected and served as the catalyst for this social transformation.

Herzen's portrayal of Belinsky as a "warrior" in *My Past and Thoughts* helped to immortalize him as the quintessential model for the oppositional intelligentsia. Yet prior to that, the image of Herzen constructed by Belinsky in his analysis of *Who Is to Blame?* represented an important early formulation of the intelligentsia's unifying ethos. (Belinsky and Herzen had joined forces after their short-lived dispute over "reconciliation with reality.") The notion of Herzen (Iskander) as a "poet of humanity" [*gumannost'*] served to elaborate the nebulous notion of recognizing each individual's "human dignity." Herzen's novel exemplified "concern for human dignity," debased by prejudice, ignorance, injustice, and the individual's "own disfiguring of himself" (Belinsky 1953–1959, 10: 319–320). Thus, concern for human dignity meant opposing all that stands in the way of the individual's free self-realization: "The human heart acts according to its own laws; it does not want to and cannot acknowledge other [laws]" (Belinsky 1953–1959, 10: 324). This sense of absolutely free self-determination was consequently the crucial precondition for the intelligentsia's turn to *activism*, transmuting one's inner convictions into life, and as Belinsky confirmed: "Only recently have we begun to notice a certain number of people, striving to realize their moral convictions through action" (Belinsky 1953–1959, 9: 435).

Belinsky's dramatic, culminating statement turned out to be his furious private letter to Gogol (July 1847)—after Gogol had published *Selected Passages from Correspondence with Friends*, which revealed his actual, shockingly reactionary social views. The letter, which was copied and circulated clandestinely, would play a prominent role in the founding mythology of the intelligentsia. When Dostoevsky was arrested for his involvement in the Petrashevsky circle, he was officially charged with reading Belinsky's letter aloud at one of their meetings.

The letter represents Belinsky's most direct demand for political change: the abolition of serfdom and control over the pervasive brutality and lawlessness engendered by the Russian social system. Yet the distinct *form of consciousness* that underlies these demands is what defines Belinsky. In response to Gogol's religious obscurantism as an affront to "human dignity" (perpetrated so unexpectedly by the writer who had had the greatest influence on the current progressive direction in Russian literature), Belinsky affirmed his own stance as a civilizer, the awakener of a new sense of self:

> Russia sees her salvation not in mysticism, not in asceticism, not in pietism, but in the success of civilization, enlightenment, humanity. She does not need prophecies [...] or prayers [...] but the awakening of a sense of human dignity in the people. (Belinsky 1953–1959, 10: 212–220)

He could confidently feel himself part of a larger social constituency, no longer based on personal acquaintances, "a multitude of people, whom neither you nor I have seen" (Belinsky 1953–1959, 10: 212). Moreover, the existence of this new social grouping reflects "the condition of Russian society, in which fresh forces are seething and struggling to emerge" (ibid., 217). Literature serves (and has the responsibility of serving) as the unifying focal point for the group's consciousness, because it *moves*, follows a logic of historical development: "Only in literature, despite the Tatar censorship, is there life and movement forward" (ibid., 217). Thus, Russian literature, which was formerly scorned as disconnected from Russian life, was now recognized as an unquestioned, vital, driving force.

Bibliography

Aksakov, Konstantin A. 1981. *Literaturnaia kritika*. Moscow: Sovremennik.

Bakunin, Mikhail A. 1934. *Sobranie sochinenii i pisem v 4 tomakh (1828–1876)*. Moscow: Izdatel'stvo vsesoiuznogo obshchestva politkatorzhan i ssyl'no-poselentsev.

Belinsky, Vissarion G. 1950. *Literaturnoe nasledstvo II*, 56. Edited by A.M. Egolin, Y.A. Bel'chikov, et al. Moscow: Akademia Nauk SSSR.

———. 1953–1959. *Polnoe sobranie sochinenii v trinadtsati tomakh*. Moscow: Akademiia nauk SSSR.

Berlin, Isaiah. 1979. *Russian Thinkers*. Edited by Henry Hardy and Aileen Kelly. London: Penguin Books.

Chernyshevsky, Nikolai G. 1939–1953. *Polnoe sobranie sochinenii v 15 tomakh*. Moscow: Goslitizdat.

Edie, James M., et al., eds. 1976. *Russian Philosophy*. 3 vols. Knoxville, TN: University of Tennessee Press.

Ginzburg, Lydia. 1991. *On Psychological Prose*. Translated by Judson Rosengrant. Princeton, NJ: Princeton University Press.

Hegel, G.F.W. 1977. *Hegel's Phenomenology of Spirit*. Translated by A.V. Miller. With Analysis of the Text and Foreword by J.N. Findlay. Oxford: Oxford University Press.

Herzen, A.I. 1954–1965. *Sobranie sochinenii v 30 tomakh*. Moscow: Akademiia nauk.

Paperno, Irina. 2004. Sovetskii opyt, avtobiograficheskoe pis'mo i istoricheskoe soznanie. *Novoe literaturnoe obozrenie*, 68. http://magazines.russ.ru/nlo/2004/68/pap5.html.

Pinkard, Terry. 1994. *Hegel's Phenomenology: The Sociality of Reason*. Cambridge: Cambridge University Press.

Plekhanov, Georgii V. 1956–1958. *Izbrannye filosofskie proizvedeniia v 5 tomakh*. Moskva: Gos. izd-vo polit. lit-ry.

Shpet, Gustav G. 2009. *Ocherki razvitiia russkoi filosofii. II. Materialy*. Moscow: ROSSPEN.

Stankevich, Nikolai V. 1890. *Stikhotvoreniia, tragediia, proza*. Moscow.

Tucker, Robert C. 1978. *The Marx-Engels Reader*. New York, NY: W. W. Norton & Company.

Turgenev, Ivan S. 1978–2014. *Polnoe sobranie sochinenii i pisem v 30 tomakh*. Moscow: Akademiia nauk.

CHAPTER 24

The Vocations of Nikolai Grot and the Tasks of Russian Philosophy

Inessa Medzhibovskaya

THE ENIGMA OF GROT'S PHILOSOPHY

Grot died on May 23, 1899, thirty-five days after turning forty-seven. His death was shockingly sudden. His students, his many friends, his colleagues at the Moscow Psychological Society[1] (he had been its Chairman from 1888 almost until his death), and his fellow professoriate at Moscow University all mourned him deeply and sincerely. In the outpouring of obituaries and commemorations, these authors spoke in unison about Grot's remarkable character, his selflessness, integrity, his honest, enterprising spirit, and, of course, his devotion to the philosophical profession and its pedagogy. Everyone acknowledged his unique role as the longtime Chairman of the Society and the founder in 1889 of its internationally respected journal, *Questions of Philosophy and Psychology* [*Voprosy Filosofii i Psikhologii*].[2] Despite the effusive grief, very little was said about Grot's philosophy as such or of his philosophical contributions proper. In fact, every eulogy sounded reserved notes on this score, as if trying to disguise an awkward perplexity behind sobs and exclamation marks. Alexander Vvedensky—a committed Kantian, who considered the life of the soul (the unknown) to be available to psychology only in its phenomenal expressions, and to philosophy only in the reality of a sense of moral obligation, and who was therefore a frequent critic of Grot—acknowledged only Grot's talent for philosophical proselytism (Vvedensky 1911, 135–147).[3] Vladimir Solovyov, a member of Grot's innermost circle, praised him for being a voracious thinker,

---

I. Medzhibovskaya (✉)
The New School for Social Research, New York, NY, USA
e-mail: inessam@newschool.edu

© The Author(s), under exclusive license to Springer Nature   525
Switzerland AG 2021
M. F. Bykova et al. (eds.), *The Palgrave Handbook of Russian Thought*,
https://doi.org/10.1007/978-3-030-62982-3_24

a rarified "poly-wit" [*mnogodum*] among the more common specialist "mono-wits" [*odnodumy*] (Solovyov 1911, 149–156). Another friend, Lev Lopatin, who would succeed Grot at the MPS and edit *VFP* until the closure of the journal by the Bolsheviks, observed that Grot never built a system: his most steadfast philosophical theme—that of the freedom of the will—had been "under a noticeable influence of the ideas of Count L. N. Tolstoy" (Lopatin 1911, 96). To Tolstoy himself, Grot was interesting for his evolution from "a zealous positivist and a devotee of Spencer, who denied abstract philosophy," to "an abstract metaphysician."[4]

There are occasional mentions of Grot in books on the history of philoso-phy and psychology in Russia. An editor or publisher of several of the later Tolstoy's tracts (one thinks of *On Life* and *What Is Art?*, primarily), Grot is more or less cursorily mentioned in the context of Tolstoy's life from 1885 onward.[5] References to Grot are mandatory in studies focused on the MPS and on the history of Russian idealism.[6] But the scope of Grot's work as a philoso-pher remains incidental and tangential in these discussions. If there is any truth in Bertrand Russell's words about the experience of truth against the possibility of falsehood—that by means of the study of syntax we may "arrive at consider-able knowledge concerning the structure of the world" (Russell 1996, 347)—we may do Grot justice by spending more time with his own words, in the inner world of his work, in order to reconstruct his worldview and system of thought.

While on a retreat in Riga to reverse the onset of his developing health prob-lems, on April 24, 1894, Grot composed the following description of this pro-file in a brief autobiography requested for a planned encyclopedic dictionary by a Czech colleague of his. The entry contained expected information on his solid schooling, major works and appointments, and several lines in conclusion that listed a smattering of his honorary memberships and academic distinc-tions.[7] Referring to himself in the third-person, Grot gives less attention to the description of his credentials and provides a rather discursive formulation of his philosophical creed.[8] *In his own words*, these are the key points of Grot's philosophy:

1. Grot insists on the open-ended character of his philosophizing: "In the development of the philosophical views of N. Ia. Grot, which are far from complete, one ought to notice a gradual transition from realism to idealism, from empiricism to a metaphysical point of view" (Grot 1911, 342).

2. Grot claims that he has developed an original epistemology, "the meta-physics of inner experience, of self-cognition," as the sole and immedi-ate source of our ideas about the world and ourselves in the life of our spiritual I:

   The whole of external experience is only a form and particular region of the internal. All conditions of consciousness—ideas, feelings, strivings—are potentially contained in our spiritual *I*. The world merely prompts, through agitations, the discharge and purging of a contingent psychic energy in the form of perceptions, feelings, and strivings. This energy is revealed as will in self-consciousness, on one side of the equation, and as perception on the other side. (Grot 1911, 342)

3. Grot's epistemology is a form of spiritual anthropology in which thought and feeling are signaling expressions of psychic content: "For thought and feeling are but different forms of perception of the psychic content per se—objective and subjective ones, respectively" (Grot 1911, 342).

4. Grot insists that we know nothing but our spirit, which is both the object and subject of cognitive activity. And we know it dually: in its universal and immutable quality, and subjectively. Consequently, we are also dual-natured: as instantiations of eternal reason and will, and as instances of being (in Grot's usage of *byvanie* [being or occurring], we can recognize a precursor to Heideggerian facticity):

In other words, we find within our individuality the unity of a duality: 1) of the eternal substantial being (reason = will), which is revealed to us immediately through psychological, logical, aesthetic, and ethical laws, and, mediately in the reason-begotten physical, mathematical, biological, and social (laws); and 2) the temporal-spatial "being" [*byvanie*] or movement, for the explanation of which it is necessary to posit an element of all changes that is alien and hostile to spirit—matter. (Grot 1911, 342)

5. Grot's metaphysics corrects Schopenhauer and postulates matter from the double ground of reason and will: "Matter is the necessary postulate of 'the reason of will' [*razuma voli*], the sole thing known to us and immediately verifiable in its substantive being and in the phenomena of the spiritual element" (Grot 1911, 342).

6. Grot notes that the idea of God is not simply *our* idea of abstract and absolute ideality, but is rather our *mediate* experiential link to ideas:

In the supra-individual and yet empirically-cognizable laws of spiritual being, we find the foundations not only for recognizing the being of our soul as the immutable and eternal substance but also of the being of God, or the supra-individual spiritual foundation of all [*vsego*] that is within us and without (as the postulate of our *I*). (Grot 1911, 342)

7. Grot's next point is Kantian, but he studiously forgoes Kant's *aporias*: "All of our *ideals* of truth, beauty, and the good follow from cognizing within the self the most universal laws of supreme reason, of creative freedom, and of moral duty. As immanent to us, they are quite accessible to our cognition and expression" (Grot 1911, 342).

8. This point is a reminder about the distance traveled by nineteenth-century science and psychology (and in the philosophies of Schelling, Fechner, Lotze, Teichmüller, Helmholtz, and Wundt) away from the dogmatism of German idealism in which feelings are separated from rational experience. This we can see vividly in Grot's wording of the idea that we know through feelings and that the transcendent—and not the transcendental—is immanent to us: "Self-knowing is the knowing within one's self [*v sebe*], through the prism of experience, of the universal substance of the world and the laws of its being" (Grot 1911, 343).

9. Moreover, in our experience of self-cognition, we are not merely intelligent and sensory organs of the microcosm, but immanent co-occurrences of the eternal: "The transcendent is immanent to us [*transtsendentnoe nam immanentno*] and is revealed to us in our own immediate psychic experience, in self-cognition, in the revelation that arrives by means of feeling and thought of that which is true and exists eternally, that which is possible and mutable, and that which is necessary and must be" (Grot 1911, 343).

10. The flux of the states of our consciousness is not a hindrance to our epistemic reliability or thinking identity, this flux is in fact our key to appreciating dialectical changes in the world and even their causes: "Through the states of our very own consciousness we cognize in the world only the phenomena, but we deduce their laws from these phenomena, the laws governing the mechanisms for the change of phenomena" (Grot 1911, 343).

11. But we also find out more about everything, including the cause of causes, from within: "Within ourselves, we discover not only the phenomena, but also the being that creates them, which extracts them out of itself and pours them forth eternally" (Grot 1911, 343).

12. Summarizing his eclectic mosaic is a shifting statement based largely on Tolstoy's ideas in his tract *On Life* (1887), which proves only that Grot's own philosophy is still in flux:

> This reason or will, which is limited in our person by the material organization postulated by our own selves, but which, excepting everything individual and subjective, is revealed to us in its absolute, eternal, and immutable contents, in its absolute laws as the supra-individual and the supra-temporal substance, but not as the supra-personal one, because "a reasonable and free spiritual person," is exactly the concept expressing the inner nature of this absolute substance. (Grot 1911, 343)

Instead of a finished positivist system of *psychological associationism*, which Grot had aimed to establish at the beginning of his career, the logical-positivist analysis of the syntax of Grot's mid-career philosophy of flux reveals instead *an associative mind* excited by the challenges of finishing a terminological mosaic, the mind of an editor who is trying to realign through language the puzzle

24 THE VOCATIONS OF NIKOLAI GROT AND THE TASKS OF RUSSIAN PHILOSOPHY 529

pieces of the reigning philosophical disagreements into a readable narrative. We should be careful not to read into this interpretation, *petitio principii*, the open-ended method of investigation characteristic of Heidegger's teacher, Edmund Husserl, or Russell's student, Ludwig Wittgenstein. Indeed, let me warn in advance that Grot's paratactic predilection for flux—which was believed to be an essential ingredient in the customs of Russian thought and is perennially a matter of disagreement as to whether it should be regarded as a cause for pride over the utilitarian logic and paradoxical aphorism of the West or as its Byzantine bane—was sharply objected to by Grot's role models and teachers at the dawn of his career, including a friend of the family, Konstantin Kavein, and Grot's dissertation advisor at St. Petersburg University, Mikhail Vladislavlev, who was the translator into Russian of Kant's *Critique of Pure Reason* (which provided a buttress for Vladislavlev against psychological materialism).[9] Grot's departure into empirical psychology in the 1870s was a moment of enormous chagrin for Vladislavlev, who could never quite forgive Grot for it. Up until his death in 1885, Kavelin had been trying to excise the dilettantism from Russian science and philosophy, of which the deficit of discipline and clear ethical conviction, he argued, had an adverse impact on their meaning to society. It was time, according to Kavelin, to put the tasks of philosophy and science in Russia into clear terms.[10] For Tolstoy, whose terms and style Grot attempts to imitate in the passages quoted above, these were examples of Grot's "scribe" mentality, preventing him from writing lucidly, imaginatively, and precisely. Tolstoy wondered how Grot could be friends and actively correspond with Archbishop Nikanor of Kherson and Odessa, the very paragon of the Pharisee elucubration, who maneuvered his Church-Slavonic word-weaving to pronounce an anathema on Kant (Medzhibovskaya 2019b, 15–17).[11] Grot's definitions of the tasks of his own philosophy, true philosophy, and Russian philosophy, in conversation with the great tradition and his contemporaries, will be the subject of the six sections that follow.

THE PHILOSOPHY OF FLUX AND ITS METHODS, 1877–1885

On the heels of his post-graduate German training in the history of philosophy, psychology, and positivism, Grot rejected the idea that philosophy could be the gatherer of every disparate bit of knowledge, a host to "facts," and a force of synthesis; he rejected the idea that philosophy could be the science of the sciences:

> As a special science about the world as a whole, which proceeds from the general foundations of other sciences, philosophy is not only not needed but is also impossible, both from a theoretical and a practical point of view [...] Until individual branches of knowledge have arrived in the process of their natural evolution at a satisfactory synthesis of laws governing the world—until then, in our view, every developed human being must—by any means, and of his own devices

[*sam pro sebia*]—sum up his knowledge and take account of his relationship toward [*otnoshenie k*] the surrounding sphere of phenomena. (Grot 1904, 10–11)[12]

In this picture, a thinking and experiencing person is his own philosopher; he is a whole discipline of faculties at work. In the period spent finishing his master's thesis (defended in 1880) on the identity and role of feelings, Grot changed his mind. At this stage, Grot came to consider philosophy indispensable, given "the variety of tasks on which the human mind is at work"—not as a science, however, but as a form of art-making. In "Philosophy as a Branch of Art" ["Filosofiia kak vetv' iskusstva," 1880], from which the words above are taken (Grot 1904, 27), Grot unites art and philosophy in their capacity to create images of ideal existence, quite independent of scientific "facts." And while learned poetry might look ridiculous, the philosophical predilection for abstraction may be rectified by admitting sensuous and emotional forms of cognition and interpretation derived from poetry into the enactments of its open perspective toward the world (Grot 1904, 27–31).

Grot begins as a naïve Heraclitus with the question: why can't people who know the laws of logic explain the flux of reality? Logic must exercise a "turn" [*povorot*] toward psychology and the life sciences. This was the scope of his doctoral dissertation, which he completed in Tübingen in 1882 and published in Leipzig the same year.[13] In the dissertation, Grot calls for a "psychic turn" in logic, a revolution similar to Kant's transcendental turn. New scientific findings concerning the psychology of emotions and feelings [*psikhologiia chuvstvovanii*] tried to combine the study of thinking with evolutionary theory, but the connections understood by then-contemporary science between associative and conscious thought, between psychic urges and deliberate mental acts that produce individual and cultural thought methodologies, did not satisfy Grot.[14] The very concept of "the rules" of thinking derived from the old logic fares poorly with the daily realities of empirical and psychological interpretation (Grot 1882, 270–272; 285–287). Grot was very interested in finding the nexus between individual inner feeling and "the universal mind" [*vseobshchem ume*] of a thinking culture (Grot 1882, 249–250).

Grot's solutions for combatting the errors of the older logic by means of the "mobilization of cognitive actions" (Grot 1882, 338–339) for the achievement of palpable goals that complemented personal satisfaction with social benefit suggest that he was no armchair dreamer or technocrat. Even his youthful fascination with translating the terminology of British empiricism and German and French positivism into Russian speaks of his active and reformist attitude. With the practice of philosophy, he truly wanted to transform the world. And from the earliest years of his philosophical practice, he believed it was absolutely possible.

Grot's prefatory remarks to the audience during his doctoral defense may seem to be a conciliatory step when he sums up his position as follows:[15]

The cooperation of science and philosophy is eternal and one cannot say that there used to be a time when there was one and not the other, or that there will be such a time. In his nature, man has always sought and will seek the simultaneous satisfaction of the needs of his personal life and his communication with the world. At present, the moment has come when he will serve these twin needs quite consciously, that is, by way of will and methodically. (Grot 1904, 41)

At the same time, in a point made earlier in the presentation, Grot speaks forcefully about the role Russian artists played for Russian thought and culture. And he recommends that art as the *superior* faculty (and discipline) should consider serving the needs of a "lower" one (he means the nascent philosophy in Russia) (Grot 1904, 37).

Grot moved to Odessa for a tenured professorship in philosophy at the University of Novorossiisk in 1883. This move reinforced Grot's desire to find a proper philosophical precedent for the equation of the conservation of energy principle with that of predestined harmony that would allow for immanent parallelism between noumena and phenomena, even though Grot did not believe in psychological parallelism.[16] The situation in the Russian academe was worsening. In 1884, a new "university regulation" [*universitetskoe ulozhenie*] went into effect on the territory of the Russian Empire that severely restricted the range of philosophical subjects on the curricula.[17] While the ministry treated psychology as a science rather than a humanities discipline, it vetted and scrutinized with suspicion the philosophy of the modern period, and Kantian philosophy in particular. Amid the thickening doom, which resulted in massive faculty resignations and transfers, Grot composed an optimistic plan of teaching philosophy under the new regulations.[18]

Grot begins his note with a promise that, if planned thoughtfully, the pedagogical system of Russian philosophy could vouchsafe the firmness of its foundations [*tverdost' osnov*] against the shakiness of the mind [*shatkost' umov*] (Grot 1884, leaf 1) brought on by years of reform. The replacement of modern philosophy built on critical methods with classical curricula alone, which was what was advocated by the government, had not proven itself successful in making the youth more ethically responsible, Grot argues. On the university level where, in addition to an interest in acquiring a specialization, Grot observed a real "thirst for the universal" [*zhazhda k obshchemu*] in the young (Grot 1884, leaf 8), the acquaintance through philosophical surveys and history of philosophy lectures with the truths that never age may be just the thing to provide a guiding principle to satisfy the conditions of adaptation to modernity, and to allow the inoculation and channeling in the right direction of the "fermentation of thought" [*brozhenie mysli*] and "malignant urges" [*zlokachestvennye pobuzhdeniia*] (Grot 1884, leaf 8) in Russian youth. Grot calls attention to the fact that most incoming students are materialists by conviction forced instead to limit their acquisition of the discipline through coursework in history and philology. The ignoring of human biology and physiology in the study of psychological phenomena would have costly consequences for Russian psychology, Grot warned (Grot 1884, leaf 13).

And here are his radical recommendations: Grot calls for moving psychology to the natural sciences because it is more dependent on knowledge of the integrity of the human organism and thus on advances in experimental studies in biology and physiology. With regard to philosophy, because it covers the idealistic aspects of the life of the soul, Grot recommends taking the lead from Plato, Descartes, and Malebranche, who were all aware of the organic connection in their philosophizing on the soul with their own human physiology (Grot 1884, leaf 16). Grot is convinced that preparation in mathematics, chemistry, physics, zoology, and the conduct of natural scientific experiments, together with the clear and firm consciousness [*iasnoe i prochnoe soznanie*] that they foster, will cleanse the researchers' minds of any erroneous ideas, deter them from committing themselves to anything intellectually perverse [*prevratnoe*], while their ongoing study of the historic life of the human soul through the avenues of the history of philosophy, logic, ethics, criminal law, the philosophy of right, and theology would enrich their potential for creativity (Grot 1884, leaf 17).

At this point, what was initially a defensive document drawn out of tactical and strategic considerations for keeping philosophy on the curricular books spreads its wings of fantasy, becoming, toward the end, a proud apology for the right to be a philosopher in Russia and to be useful to Russia in that capacity (Grot 1884, leaf 21).

Grot's note on the reform of Russian philosophy discussed above is much bolder than a summary of related thoughts, with regard to the classification of the sciences that he published, also in 1884.[19] The note immerses itself in politically controversial issues of involving philosophy in matters of humanistic-scientific enlightenment, and pushes back on the degree of interference it will suffer from the government in sorting out what is an old dispute among humanistic faculties as to their institutional setup and disciplinary divisions. At a time when Solovyov withdrew from university teaching after a similar condemnation of positivism and the abstract philosophy of the West,[20] what was at stake for Grot during the writing of both the note and the classification essay was a rather Nietzschean question: what is honest philosophy? Moreover, how could philosophy be taught with integrity? Should he stay in the academe or should he leave it? In this regard, the question of method was still important to Grot. For the sake of integrity, there needed to be parallelism in the concordance of inner and external experience [*vnutrennego i vneshnego opyta*] (Grot 1904, 116).

In the classification essay, Grot makes his final attempt to vindicate positivism as *the* scientific method of choice, for psychology and philosophy, by creating an elective fusion of Comte's and Spencer's war on intellectual anarchy with idealism (Grot 1904, 90–103). And although he does not utter the name, the ghost of Kant—peacemaker of the faculties—hovers as an inspiring angel above the handshake between Comte and Spencer that Grot hopes to broker. Kant is mentioned later as an antipode to Locke's denial to the intellect of that which has never been in the senses (Grot 1904, 119), and then again when Grot looks in the direction of the newest trends in German "psychophysicists" and "psychophysiologists"—namely Helmholtz and Wundt, who, as we know, and even though Grot does not say as much, were the very thinkers who tried to practice science with Kant's unproven posits (God, the soul, freedom, and immortality) subjected to doubt and yet posited with hope (Grot 1904, 120). Grot pauses at the end of this essay on the thought that philosophy should focus on studying the "incessant evolution" [*nepreryvnoe razvitie*] inherent in nature and man, and that it is impossible to draw hard and fast lines between one's philosophizing on either (Grot 1904, 121–122).

THE SOUL AND THE TASKS OF MONODUALISM

Grot's encounters in Odessa with Bruno's pantheism and, separately, with Tolstoy's banned religious writings of the early 1880s, during Grot's teaching of the mandated surveys of premodern philosophy, changed Grot's life. In these thought systems, Grot finally discovered the patterns for "naïve realism" that he had been looking for. Bruno's inspired pantheism rested on the conviction that in the whole of the animate universe, which combines the cooperation of more developed organisms with the constantly separating and merging simpler monads of material and psychic nature, we should live according to the universal laws of this magnificent order called life. Bruno's trust in the science that he used to glorify God's universe through new discoveries never questioned the importance of the enlightened enjoyment of wise knowing. Grot finds other formulas of wise knowing illumined by the awareness of Christ as logos [*razumenie*] incarnate in Tolstoy's desire to recreate the routes of logos so understood through philosophy and science as to find satisfactory answers about the questions of life that could rectify the imbalances created by skepticism that plague modern minds. Kavelin had just died in May 1885 in St. Petersburg. Had he arrived in Odessa a few years earlier, his colleague at the university would have been the author of the world-famous *Reflexes of the Brain* (1863) and Kavelin's critic, Ivan Sechenov. But Grote spoke often with the antipode of the father of Russian physiology, Archbishop Nikanor—an aspiring father of Russian spirituality. Sechenov arrived in Odessa from St. Petersburg to escape from the government's draconian university policies, which were much worse in the capitals, giving up on the polemical and combative edge he had taken in his younger years against Kavelin's suspicion of physiology. Sechenov would remain in Odessa until 1876 and Ilya Mechnikov, his great disciple, also at Odessa until 1886, discussed optimistic scientific projects to uncover the secrets of conserving and recycling vital energy, projects to guarantee individual people and all of humanity a life of longevity free of disease and decrepitude. Although Grot did not overlap with Sechenov in Odessa, and did so only with Mechnikov, such pursuits resonated with Grot's interests after his readings of Bruno (Medzhibovskaya 2019b, 1–41 and 229–232).

534   I. MEDZHIBOVSKAYA

The mid-1880s was a decisive time for the future of Russian philosophy and psychology.[21] It was a decade of intensive debate about the presence of a *Russian spirit* in new academic and scientific professions. These contradictory influences were in the background during Grot's contemplation of the professional relevance of such old concepts as soul, will, and spirit, and his choice concerning these terms in 1886, before his transfer to Moscow University from Odessa, is therefore of paramount importance. Grot's appointment in Moscow was supported by the positivist Matvei Troitsky (chair of the department of philosophy from 1875),[22] who was also a key force behind the foundation and incorporation of the MPS within the university on the permission of its trustees in 1885, and a most ardent follower of English and Scottish empiricism in Russia (from Locke to Huxley). Troitsky was an energetic supporter of secular philosophy, and was keen on hiring Grot out of Odessa, but Nikanor, meanwhile, was very fond of Grot's public lectures in Odessa and wanted him to stay there, seeing in Grot a perfect ally for proving the existence of God and the immortality of the soul with the help of the positivist method.

Although Grot would take Troitsky up on his offer, philosophically he had already made his choice in favor of Kantian ethics (or, rather, Tolstoy's explication of Kant's categorical imperative and Schopenhauer's notion of empathy). After reading the clandestinely circulated *A Confession* (finished in 1882) and *My Religion* [*V Chem moia vera*], finished in 1884, Grot wrote to Tolstoy from Odessa in 1885 sending him by way of recommendation the brochure with one of his recent public lectures, which stated: "Moral responsibility is the idea that arises on the soil of moral striving for the happiness and well-being of the whole […] The idea of moral responsibility transferred from the consciousness of an individual to the consciousnesses of society cannot justify the idea of retribution" (Grot 1885, 46; Medzhibovskaya 2008, 264, 276, 291). Grot thinks that the idea of moral autonomy should form the foundation of a philosopher's worldview.

But Grot finds that Kant's ethics is an insignificant annex to his abstract philosophy. In the early stages of his transitions from positivism, Grot preferred working with nineteenth-century adjustments of Kant, for example with Friedrich Lange's *History of Materialism*, of which the third volume in particular Grot considered to be the "work of an unredeemed Kantian," but one who does not approach the topic of the body and soul from the extremely transcendentalist vantage point.[23] Grot shifts to a modified Kantianism, modified not only by nineteenth-century developments in science and philosophy, but also by Leibniz's notions of *vis sensitiva* (the sensory force) and *vis appetitiva* (the force of striving) and by Schopenhauer's notion of will. Grot notes, however, that Schopenhauer's interest in spirit [*dukh*] is insufficient and that his distinction between reason and will is altogether unsatisfactory. This displeasure is most evident in one of Grot's final lectures delivered in Odessa, *On the Soul in Connection with Contemporary Teachings about Force*, from which a comment on Lange is quoted.[24] One phrase in Grot's talk must have appealed to Troitsky especially:

We thus believe that there are not only no obstacles lying hidden in the contemporary scientific-positivist tendency for a new and broader resolution of the question about the nature of the spiritual element of life [*prirode dukhovnogo nachala*], but more generally, that this very tendency is a bridge of sorts for the construction of a new philosophical teaching outside of the exact specialized natural sciences that study the phenomena of 'objective' experience. (Grot 1886, 19)

Grot comes up with the idea of monodualism, or the teaching about the "the supreme unity of the dual existence" [*vysshshee edinstvo dvoistvennogo bytiia*] of force and spirit, orchestrated by a "supreme third element" [*tret'ie vysshshee nachalo*], the cause of causes (Grot 1886, 22–23).

And, moreover, force is not determined as material:

The very force is cognized from within, and because what is known by man (at the highest point of development) is known from within, if consciousness is the sum of purely spiritual phenomena [*dukhovnye iavleniia*], then would we not be right to say, in contradistinction to materialists, that it is not spirit that is force but that force is spirit, and that for us first of all, force is our own soul with all of its psychic states. (Grot 1886, 76)

IN SEARCH OF THE DISCIPLINE AND THE TASKS OF TRUE PHILOSOPHY (1886–1892)

As he was leaving Odessa, Grot sent the brochure of the lecture on the soul to Tolstoy, who was finishing "The Death of Ivan Ilyich." Tolstoy's description of Ivan's flight toward liberation [*osvobozhdenie*] from morbid materiality into the realms of the supra-temporal and supra-sensory may have been promoted by Grot's brochure.[25] Although toward the end of the brochure, Grot references Nikanor's anti-Kantian *Pozitivnaia filosofiia i sverkhchuvstvennoe bytie* [*Positive Philosophy and Supersensible Being*],[26] he crushes Nikanor's hopes for an alliance by finishing, while already in Moscow, a public response to Nikanor in the form of a quasi-penitent confession: "As of late, I have made a new step in developing my teaching concerning the tasks of philosophy, having identified philosophy wholly with the concept of ethical or moral teaching."[27] In this open letter to Nikanor, Grot defines philosophy as "his" philosophy, his personal rightful profession of faith, and as his right to err:

A philosopher is looking for truth, but in keeping with the very tasks of philosophy, which is to sum up the entire knowledge of man, it can never find it (the truth) once and for all, for there is no limit for the expansion of the elements of its construction. [...] A philosopher advancing along his path is subject to the general law of movement in nature. (Grot 1904, 148)

And he adds, almost heretically in the context of the exchange set up by him on purpose as a conversation of a prodigal son of religion with his former shepherd, that he had come to the idea of God and beauty not by way of Nikanor's or the Church's graces and benedictions, or by the fear of retribution, but through Bruno's pantheism, Kant's subjectivity, and Mill's and Lange's "subjective induction" (Grot 1904, 148, 156–158).

Grot's inaugural lecture at Moscow University on October 6, 1886, was a seminal opportunity for him to articulate his philosophy.[28] Leaving them flabbergasted at first, Grot advised his students not to despise the mandated classical curriculum: from the Greek definition of philosophy, through the history of its every thinker and school, we learn to respect wisdom, this highest virtue that comes with authentic philosophizing. The main task of all true philosophy is the recovery of the ethical concept of wisdom as an intellectual virtue, and of the character of the wise man as an ideal philosopher:

> We call wise a man who has worked out a distinctively highest view of life, which the mass of humanity do not possess […] and which sometimes does not even depend on one's quantity of knowledge—that is, the degree of learning— although knowledge is the way toward achieving "conscious" wisdom. (Grot 1904, 132)

But the wisdom of old should not despise the tasks of the scientific and empirical exploration of life. Consequently, the new Russian philosophy must comprehend that its ideal is, firstly, "not comprehensive theoretical knowledge [*vsevedenie*], but only a reasonable, commonsensical [*zdravoe*] explanation of the meaning and moral elements of life"; and, secondly, that instead of metaphysics, it achieves this comprehension "by way of an attentive study of the foundations of life" (Grot 1904, 144) in our own self-consciousness and in the life of society, and by integrating the conclusions of "special sciences about nature and man" (Grot 1904, 144) into our worldview.

Grot's career after he became chairman of the MPS is one of the better-known stages of his life's work. But there are still lacunae in the essential details of Grot's understanding of philosophical tasks after he unofficially took the helm of the MPS in February, 1887 (before his official installation in the role in 1888) and after he became the editor of its two periodicals, *VFP* and *Trudy Moskovskogo Psikhologicheskogo Obshchestva*—appointments that meant that, in essence, he became the institutional leader of Russian philosophy.[29] In the space remaining, I shall concentrate on these defining details.

It must have come as a surprise to the listeners at his inaugural talk in Moscow that Grot excluded metaphysics from the tasks of true philosophy. The explanation for this is that he did not consider the metaphysics that was known by that name in his time to be an avenue for true philosophy, which he necessarily associates with freedom. In his first years in Moscow (around 1887–1890), Grot conducts this search for philosophical freedom through his study of feelings and emotions, on the one hand, and freedom of the will on the other. His work on the freedom of the will became known through a series of talks he gave at the MPS in February and March, 1887, which were covered widely in the press and later published in the third issue of *Trudy*, in 1889, as

Critique of the Concept of the Freedom of the Will [*Kritika poniatiia svobody voli*].[30]

In his study on the meaning of feelings and emotions in cognition, Grot criticizes Kant's etiology of feelings, which Kant treated narrowly as functions and intuitions of the mind, as dispositions, or as very abstract forms of perception involved in the process of forming judgments (Grot 1904, 174–176).[31] Grot thinks that Kant made a grave underestimation concerning how artistic and moral creativity can lead to breakthroughs in understanding (which Grot terms "grasping" [*postizhenie*] in contrast to Kant-inspired *Verstand* "understanding" [*rassudochnoe ponimanie*]). One of the goals he thus sets for himself in establishing the discipline of philosophy in Russia is a defense of the principle of creativity that makes philosophy not simply important for a well-rounded education, or for the formation of a strong Russian worldview, but *humanly* necessary: "Philosophy is not only a science, but first of all an internal process of the subjective growth of a human being, a process of creativity, an irrational development of feeling and will, and their cleansing off of the individual and accidental elements" (Grot 1904, 177–178).

Whereas his work on feeling was a putative correction of Kant, Grot's work on the freedom of the will was, mutatis mutandis, a correction of Schopenhauer's metaphysics. For Grot, control and mastery of the will are not things to be achieved through a pessimistic extinguishing of the *principium individuationis* so as to achieve Nirvana. On the contrary, "Our true spiritual subject is manifested in the acts of our personal will that suppress into inactivity the external wills and forces and whatever contradicts the strivings of our true spiritual I" (Grot 1889b, 82). It is at this point that Grot develops a strong interest in Nietzsche, of whom more will be said shortly.

One of Grot's strengths in his position of leadership at the MPS and *VFP* was his keen knowledge of the potentials of philosophy as a part of the public sphere, and his deep commitment to the necessity of an interdisciplinary dialogue, with a tolerant and respectful exchange of opinions, devoid both of professional or national self-conceit, and of a sense of Russian inferiority due to the fledgling nature of its philosophy. After becoming Editor of *VFP*, Grot made three milestone statements on the shaping of philosophy as the discipline by its periodicals: two in 1889, and then one in 1891 when taking stock of the great substantive success of the journal, even though it was facing financial perils. This was, to use Kantian language, Grot's opinion on the tasks of the public employment of reason in philosophy.

Grot wrote the following in his editorial preface to the *On the Freedom of Will* [*O svobode voli*] volume of *Works* [*Trudy*]: "But the Moscow Psychological Society will not—as we hope—fixate itself completely on the sphere of tasks that are being discussed by psychologists of authority from other countries. It shall, as it did in the past, follow its own course and will search for truth and be guided by its own inner drives and intellectual interests according to which the entire Russian society lives."[32] And he wrote in the first preface to *VFP*: "As a result of the collective work of minds that are disciplined enough, one can hope to attain what all of us dream about: new fulcra for correct teaching about the world and about life" (Grot 1889a, xv). He further predicted that the Russian "national perception of the world is destined to advance *the ethical interests of life* [*nravstvennye interesy zhizni*] to the forefront," because the "major interests of human life lie in the *activity* of man, and the activity of man has as its source his *will and its aims*" (ibid., xviii). In 1891, Grot spoke in much stronger terms on the ethics of philosophizing, blending Nietzsche with Plato: "Any exclusive defense of one's individuality, of one's one-sided personal truth is crude self-conceit, and an imitation of a foreign, alien spirit. Every mockery of truth simply because it is not *my* truth is an insult to the truth eternal and the all-human" (Grot 1891, "Eshche o zadachakh," vi). Grot's definition of the metaphysics of the future, both as a science of the collective conscious and as the reasonable activity [*soznatel'no-razumnoi deiatel'nosti*] of a nation dependent on tradition-building and continuity, and on the relationship of "systematic conformity" between ideals and the factual data of experience, brokers a conversation between Comte and Kant.[33] New notes sound in this article, toward the conclusion of the meandering piece, with an elusively Heideggerian title[34] that shows Grot's indebtedness to Solovyov's theory of the justification of the good, in both the practical and ideal reality of the "all-unity" (*vseedinstvo*):

> The subjective element in philosophy, the element of feeling and personal creativity involves linking it inseparably with the psychic architecture of a personality and a nation. Man is the carrier of universal elements [*vselenskikh nachal*], one of the incarnations of universal reason. At the same time, man is a person, a peculiar and subjectively-integral individual. As a particular manifestation of universal reason, he is a metaphysician, mathematician, astronomer, physicist, chemist, etc., who—ideally—knows no nationality. As a subjectively integral individual, he is an artist and a philosopher, the carrier of the subjective-ideal worldview, and he is one of the incarnations of the national peculiarities of the spirit. (Grot 1904, 211)

On Moral Ideals and the Ethical Tasks of Philosophy (Kant, Nietzsche, and Tolstoy)

Grot's fascination in the mid-1880s with Bruno's *eroici furori* found expression in the 1890s in his close study of the heroic enthusiasm of Tolstoy and Nietzsche. Grot wrote two essential texts comparing these thinkers, arguably his clearest and best-written works, but before he could do that, he needed to reappraise the importance of the tasks and obligations posed by Kant's ethics, treating Kant's definition of happiness and the good life more critically than he had previously. Kant's categorical imperative falls short of the mark, in Grot's view, as it is basically uninformed by the psychology of evil, and uninterested in the question of what allows radical evil to endure. Grot criticizes Kant in 1893, and he simultaneously assigns a new task for the philosophy of the future: discovering a potential for heroism in the will of man.

24 THE VOCATIONS OF NIKOLAI GROT AND THE TASKS OF RUSSIAN PHILOSOPHY   539

For us personally, the best addendum and correction to Kant's system is the teaching of Schopenhauer on the will. In spite of its extremes, it is precisely this teaching that has best pointed to the means of transition from the absolute forms of self-cognition [*samopoznaniie*] to the idea of "the absolute beginning of being" of the will, even though this teaching requires radical transformation and reworking in its own right. For us, it therefore appears certain that *the most immediate task of the philosophy of the future* must be the removal of the cardinal contradiction within Kantian philosophy.[35]

In scrutinizing the importance of Tolstoy's, and Nietzsche's, moral heroism in a work on the moral ideals of his time, Grot brings up in the same year (Grot 1893b) his former question about the dialectics of mastery and obedience in the activity of the will. Tolstoy and Nietzsche, who both often stand accused of nihilism and anarchism, represent extreme cases of either obedience to the highest law (Tolstoy) or disobedience to it (Nietzsche). For Tolstoy, the heroic obedience of self-restraint that he calls Christian is an enlightened form of humility, a supreme bondage that leads to increase of the good. For Nietzsche, the disobedience goaded by the will to power and a thirst to revalue values leads to the mastery of a free rein, to absolute unrestraint that does good. Both examples of heroism have their strengths and shortcomings: being obedient to spirit, Tolstoy neglects the cravings of the body and soul; being disobedient to it, Nietzsche's Overman is still no more than a "tamed beast" [*vydressirovannyi zver'*] (Grot 1893b, 145–146). Grot is not the first to have indicated these contradictions, but he is the first to try to derive fruitful implications for philosophy from the juxtaposition of Tolstoy and Nietzsche:

The question is about the kind of method, or the kind of *sphere* in which this compromise can be resolved. This method and sphere have long been known to the *philosopher*. The extremes of the ethical worldviews of our times pose *a new question for philosophy*—that peacemaking "science of the sciences" that reviews and verifies the foundation of all knowledge, generalizations, and syntheses. The task of the philosophy of our time is to comprehend all the great lessons of recent history, to understand Tolstoy and Nietzsche and many other mouthpieces of the unstable and fluctuating moral consciousness of humanity today, and, by appropriating what is true and good in their teachings, to rework all of this into a new integral worldview that is both theoretical and practical. (Grot 1893b, 153–154; emphasis mine)

With this designation of philosophy as the science of morality (ethics), Grot completed the definition of philosophical tasks in the realm of ethics in 1895 in a work called "*Ustoi nravstvennoi deiatel'nosti*" ("The Foundations of Moral Activity"):

[I]f ethics were to prove that the main foundations of morality consist of human striving for spiritual perfection, self-control, and selfless work for the benefit of the world, then man would have to reject as amoral the ideal and criterion of

540   I. MEDZHIBOVSKAYA

personal happiness, and instead arrange his moral life and activity in an entirely different way. (Grot 1895, 146)

In this work, Grot discovers philosophical happiness by other means, in between Bruno's exaltation, a Kantian relativization of the concept of happiness (because, as a state of mind or a state of satisfaction, it cannot be of one piece with absolute good), and positivist and utilitarian readings of eudaimonia.

PLATO AND THE TASKS OF RUSSIAN PHILOSOPHY

In the last years of his life, Grot leans increasingly toward Platonism. His vocations carry him forward, and more surely than before, through the classic stages of philosophizing with an ultimate cause in mind, an approach emblematized by Fichte. Grot reverses Comte's account of philosophical evolution, according to which philosophy begins as religion, evolves into metaphysics, and then into positivism. Following Fichte, who in 1794–1800 set out to correct Kant's metaphysics, Grot starts with skepticism of the mind's I (in the Cartesian vein), then moves on to the stage of "knowledge" (represented by positivism and psychology), and toward the end, becomes more and more involved in thinking about faith as a philosophical issue for ethics, pedagogy, and cultural politics.[36]

In the huge work that he finished in 1894, to which he gave an Augustinian title, "On Time" ["*O vremeni*"], Grot expresses the largest ambition of his career so far: "to establish a correct concept about a supra-sensory or spiritual experience and its forms" (Grot 1904, 274), with the aim of proving "the timelessness of the forms of self-consciousness" [*osnovnaia mysl' o bezvremennosti form samosoznaniia*] (Grot 1904, 310). According to Grot in 1894, ideas are eternal:

1. If proven wrong or eventually rejected, ideas still remain "real and unchangeable facts, such as the ideas of Kant, Aristotle, or Descartes, or of any other human mind" (Grot 1904, 241);
2. although born in a certain historical and geographical context, "an idea is an act of the free creative work of spirit, which is subordinate only to the laws of thought or to logical rather than physical, temporal, or spatial causes and connections" (Grot 1904, 241); and
3. "the eternal inner identity of the idea can be espied everywhere, even in the facts of perception" (Grot 1904, 242); even perceptions that are tied to a place or to a certain point in time give rise to images and ideas that become "portable" such that one's impression of the green color of the foliage of an oak tree growing near one's parental home seen years earlier would be perfectly identical to one's current perceptions of it (Grot 1904, 243).

24 THE VOCATIONS OF NIKOLAI GROT AND THE TASKS OF RUSSIAN PHILOSOPHY   541

We live in a perceptual cave, confronting the walls of "the all," which is not exhausted by all-animate life, for if it were, there would be no freedom. Liberation from the cave is the aim of *psychological perception* "in the form of a known state of consciousness, of a certain potential psychic energy, which occurs under two conditions, as a push from without and an inner endeavor" (Grot 1904, 262). To achieve approximation with the "unified substance of the world," or "God" (Grot 1904, 313), one will need to correct Kant's and Schopenhauer's errors in maintaining a transcendental and voluntarist dualism. Kant made the mistake of not asking himself about the relationship between *reine Anschauung* (pure intuition/viewing) and perception, and the reality of psychic life itself (Grot 1904, 243). And Schopenhauer shared Kant's prejudice to the extent that he thought that time is a form of inner intuition, "although he also finely clarified that by way of inner intuition we get to cognize our own being immediately" (Grot 1904, 279–280). Fichte, Schelling, and Schopenhauer all improved on Kant by showing that the inner intuition of self-consciousness has an immediate and suprasensual character. Grot claims that it is the task of Russian philosophy to complete the correction, as had been done in the volume on the freedom of the will in the works of Lev Lopatin, Petr Astafiev (Grot 1904, 308), and, later by Nikolai Lange, Grot's protégé from 1888 and his successor at Novorossiisk University in Odessa.[37]

Only the self-consciousness of the subject intending contact with God in the supra-spatial and supra-temporal environment of his willing, or the unitary substance of the world [*Bog, edinaia substantsiia mira*] (Grot 1904, 313), will recognize our true authentic will [*podlinnuiu nashu voliu*] and—in our thinking on the intuition of the divine—our true thinking [*podlinnuiu mysl'*] (Grot 1904, 312–313). And thus, the philosophical task formulated by Grot toward the end of this work is the deep comprehension [*urazumenie*] of the timeless nature of the spirit [*bezvremennoi prirody dukkha*] in our thinking and willing. And contemporary psychology should direct its effort toward this deep comprehension [*urazumenie*], as it is the discipline for the study of it, and the "foundation of a future, new metaphysics" (Grot 1904, 313). With this final synthesis of the positive tasks of philosophy with God-seeking in our intuition and thinking, and with the work done in contemporary psychological explorations of psychic reality, Grot is at last brought to the destination for which he was searching: Plato.

Grot portrayed Plato as tragically misunderstood, but not in the same way Solovyov did. Solovyov saw hubris in Plato's pagan failure to achieve the all-unity of being [*vseedinstvo*] in his un-Hegelian lack of interest in tracing through history the destinies of "the organism of all-humanity" [*vsechelovecheskii organizm*].[38] Grot saw the tragedy of Plato differently: precisely because of his tragic misunderstanding by the later Western tradition, which failed to take the correct lessons from his mighty impact, Plato's philosophical science needed to find its true inheritor in Russian philosophy, which would correctly adopt Plato's method: "In the history of philosophy, Plato claims ownership of the discernment of the truth about spiritual unity and the

542   I. MEDZHIBOVSKAYA

spiritual origin of the world, the truth that is provable by the scientific method of philosophy [*nauchno-filosofskim metodom*]" (Grot 1896, 188). Grot prepares for this striking conclusion by a no-less-striking sequence of reasoning: only Russia appreciates Plato's insight that the soul of man has a divine nature and that therefore "nothing divine is alien to it" (Grot 1896, 177), and that the cultivation of human virtues based on this divinity by means of correct scientific methods requires the environment provided by the conditions of an ideal state (Grot 1896, 181). In order to accomplish the path of self-knowing by directing it to ever-newer spheres of this intellection that is divine in origin, Russian philosophy would continue to recreate ideas—and the world itself—in His image. The essay concludes on a declaration that to remember one's human function is to remember one's vocation. By making this declaration, Grot essentially deletes the distinction between the tasks and aspirations of human and professional vocation introduced by Aristotle in the *Nicomachean Ethics* (1096a), between individual and national quests for the divine.

The Duty of Philosophical Vocation

Grot was destined for success as an academic. The son of an academic—Yakov Karlovich Grot, a famous philologist—Grot Jr. was born into an academic dynasty and achieved unparalleled distinction in this previously unknown category of hereditary academic meritocracy in Russia.[39] As one of the first recipients of a doctoral degree from a philosophical department at a Russian university (St. Petersburg), Grot trained in Germany with Eduard Gottlob Zeller, became a corresponding member of the Paris Society of Physiological Psychology and an honoree of the psychological societies of Berlin and Munich, and represented Russia at international congresses of psychology, to the extent that he was universally mourned after his death. Grot certainly "made it." His role in the making of the discipline, its curricula, and the functioning of its venues and institutions in Russia in his capacity as administrative and academic leader can never be called into question. As a progressive innovator, he won the battle to establish a philosophy "*novo methodo*," as Fichte called it in the *Wissenschaftslehre*, by overcoming coercion and its effects upon cognition, against the resistance of the famed and well-worn Leviathan of the bureaucratic-autocratic disabling of the most capable Russians.

Although they do reflect the hesitations and hankerings after a hopeful future of the young tradition of philosophy in the final quarter of the nineteenth century in Russia, after having considered Grot's persistent re-examination of the duties and tasks of philosophy, his original philosophical contributions, expressed in the form of disparate insights, are difficult to gauge. On the very rare occasions when he is discussed, Grot's evolutionary flux is blamed on the inconsistency of his career as a positivist. Lossky and Walicki both note that, after 1885, allegedly after recognizing how untenable his work in logic and psychology had been, Grot called off his projects in these areas in favor of idealism (Lossky 1991, 173; Walicki 1979, 362). Lossky goes so far as to suggest that Grot's final arrival at Platonism is tantamount to a degradation by fall (Lossky 1991, 172). Both these critics note that in his work on the interaction of psychic and material processes, Grot was influenced by Wilhelm Ostwald's ideas (Lossky 1991, 173; Walicki 1979, 362). However, this is an inaccurate point because Ostwald's renowned discoveries in the realm of catalysis, which were crowned with the Nobel Prize, were made much later than Grot's short-term preoccupation with these topics. Grot, in fact, had a large number of influences and interests. In his work on time, he compared the human body to a book that doubles itself as a self-recharging battery, an imprint of the great book of nature with inexhaustible supplies of energy, a book with sorted and printed pages, "bound into the corpus of a known organism" (Grot 1904, 257). One can tear away and disperse its leaves, but they do not disappear. This is the boastful claim of many a dilettante, nourished by a self-loving and self-flattering sensibility, which was completely at odds with, among others, Kant's reservation about calling such conduct an act of pure duty.

Nobody but Tolstoy could pronounce a more exact epitaph on this onto-logical and professional error of Grot's—not so much in terms of the definition of his task, but in terms of the dereliction of his vocation by spreading it too far and too fast:

> Grot was a very good and sincere person, but he had many avocations and few stable views. His philosophy was not deep, but I valued in him the fact that his erudition and learning did not muffle the freshness of thought in him and did not deprive him of a simple and clear view on life. Had he not needed to expend himself too much on the externals of life he might well have thought up his way onto something good. But live he did not; rather, he was constantly "boiling in a cauldron," as he himself used to put it. And so he boiled out prematurely. However, some of his writings I used to read with pleasure, especially good was his short book on Plato. (Everling 1923, 791)[40]

Grot's is *minor philosophy*,[41] but in the "the turbulence of a more original questioning" (Heidegger 2008, 110), it sought to reach after big tasks in pioneering a great tradition. And in this regard, Grot's activity—"literally ablaze with love for wisdom" (Vvedensky 1911, 135)—and its final funeral pyre had a major impact on the future of Russian philosophy.

Notes

1. The Moscow Psychological Society will be henceforth abbreviated "the MPS," or referred to as the "Society" in appropriate contexts.
2. The journal *Voprosy Filosofii i Psikhologii* will be henceforth abbreviated *VFP.*
3. Here and elsewhere in the essay, for complete bibliographic details, see the Bibliography section at the end of this essay.
4. The remark was recorded by Dushan Makovitsky on September 12, 1910. See Makovitsky (1979, 4:347).

5. All of these dictionary-style briefs discuss Grot's work in psychology more than in philosophy and borrow heavily or even entirely from P. P. Sokolov 1904 (see Bibliography), which was reprinted in 1911 in *Grot v ocherkakh* (99–135). For short descriptions of Grot's thought, see Lossky (1991, 172–173), who discusses Grot in a paragraph under the banner of Russian gnoseology; Walicki (1979, 360–362) offers a very garbled portrait of Grot, mentioning a spiritualist twist in his evolution and the short-lived meaning of his activity. Walicki uses Lossky's entry, and both base their judgments on secondary literature and not on Grot's own writings. Joravsky, by contrast, is mostly fair (Joravsky 1989; 95–96; 102–107; 116–118).

6. See especially Chernikov (2008) passim and Poole (1995) passim.

7. See Grot's "An Autobiographic Sketch" ["Avtobiografcheskii ocherk"] in *Grot v ocherkakh*, (Grot 1911, 339–343).

8. As much as possible, I will try to reproduce Grot's emphases and internal quotes. The quotes stand for his method of drawing attention to his highly quixotic terminology. All translations of Grot's work in this essay are mine.

9. In the mid-1870s, Vladislavlev had attempted to upgrade Kant's transcendental psychology and its study of intuition with Fechner's study of emotions. See Vladislavlev (1881).

10. See Kavelin's "The Tasks of Psychology" ["Zadachi psikhologii"] written in 1871 and first published in 1872 in Kavelin (1897–1900, esp. 3: 382–383, 418, 633).

11. Nikanor dabbled in philosophy and entertained ambitions of blending Orthodoxy with positivism for the creation of a Christian science of the soul for the Russian nation. See esp. Episkop Nikanor (1875–1876; 1888). The latter volume 3 (1888) is a critique of Kant's first *Critique*.

12. These words, from the twenty-five-year-old Grot forming part of his attack on Leibniz in defense of Comte, were delivered in an article-long rebuke to his committed opponent Aleksey Kozlov (1831–1901), a vivid representative of the personalist approach in Russian thought. See Grot's review of Kozlov's *Etudes*, "Filosofskie etiudy (A.A. Kozlova)" in Grot (1904, 1–26). Grot's and Solovyov's Master's defenses are poles apart. Unlike Grot's subscription to science (Comte's religion of the future), at his Master's defense in 1874 Solovyov identifies the reunion of philosophy and religion as the chief task of the day (Solovyov 1908–1911, 3: 221–225).

13. Grot, N. Ya., Concerning the Question of Reforming Logic: An Experiment in a New Theory of Mental Processes: A Treatise by N. Ya. Grot, Master of Philosophy, Full Professor of the Historico-Philological Institute at Nezhin. [K voprosu o reforme logiki. Opyt novoi teorii umstvennykh protsessov. Rassuzhdenie N.Ia Grota]. See Bibliography.

14. See especially the opening sections of the book in which Grot elaborates the state of the discipline and tries to predict the future of logic evacuated of the old rules (Grot 1882, 1–46).

15. The talk was published separately in 1883 as "The Relationship of Philosophy to Science and Art" ["*Otnoshenie Filosofii k Nauke i Iskusstvu*"] (Grot 1904, 32–43).

16. See especially Grot's "To the Question on the Criteria of Truth, Concerning the Possibility of a Scientific Justification of Naive Realism" ["K voprosu o kriteri-

24 THE VOCATIONS OF NIKOLAI GROT AND THE TASKS OF RUSSIAN PHILOSOPHY   545

iakh istiny. Vozmozhnost' nauchnogo opravdaniia naivnogo realizma"] (1883) in Grot (1904, 43–64).

17. Alongside the general loss of freedom in curricular planning, other restrictions concerned the forming of academic associations, faculty and student governance, quotas on the categories of matriculation, hiring, and faculty retention. See Schchetinina (1976).

18. I am drawing here on what can be translated as Grot's "A Note on Organization of Philosophy Teaching under the New Regulation: Summary by the Author" (1884) (Grot, "Zapiska ob ustroistve," see Bibliography). To my knowledge, this document has not only remained unpublished, but has never been discussed or mentioned in the existing scholarship.

19. "On the Classification of the Sciences" (Grot 1904, 65–121).

20. See especially *The Crisis of Western Philosophy* [*Krizis zapadnoi filosofii*, 1874] and *The Critique of Abstract Foundations* [*Kritika otvlechennykh nachal*, 1880]; *Lectures on Divine Humanity* [*Chteniia o Bogochelovechestve*, 1877–1881] and *The Spiritual Foundations of Life* [*Dukhovnye osnovy zhizni*, 1883].

21. For a general survey of the trends of this period, see Budilova (1960), Porter and Ross (2003), and Shkurinov (1980).

22. By 1885, Troitsky's major works had already been published: *Nemetskaia psikhologiia v tekushchem stoletii. Istoricheskoe i kriticheskoe issledovanie, s predvaritel'nym ocherkom uspekhov psikhologii so vremen Bekona i Lokka* (first publ. 1867, reissued in a two-volume edition in 1883) and *Nauka o dukhe. Obshchie svoistva i zakony chelovecheskogo dukha*, 2 vols. (1882).

23. The three volumes of Friedrich Albert Lange's *Geschichte des Materialismus und Kritik seiner Bedeutung in der Gegenwart* [*History of Materialism and Criticism of Its Present Importance*, 1866] were translated into major European languages throughout the 1870s. The Russian translation appeared in 1881–1888.

24. On Leibniz and Schopenhauer, see Grot, *O Dushe* (1886, 19, 28); on Lange, see p. 28. Lange died in 1875 when Grot was still a convinced positivist. Lange's work continued to play a pivotal role in Grot's idealistic reinterpretation of materialism and the creation of his system of *monodualism*.

25. Medzhibovskaya (2008, 333–335; 353–354). As follows from Tolstoy's marginalia on the copy of the brochure preserved in his library, which I was able to examine in 2000, and then reexamined in 2010, he only supported the idea of liberation of the spirit and of the soul from the body.

26. See note 11 in this chapter.

27. Grot, "On the Directions and Tasks of My Philosophy (Regarding the Article by Archbishop Nikanor)" [*"O napravleniiakh i zadachakh moei filosofii (po povodu stat'i arkhiepiskopa Nikanora)"* 1886], in Grot (1904, 160).

28. "To the question about the true tasks of philosophy" [*"K voprosu ob istinnykh zadachakh filosofii*," 1886], in Grot (1904, 122–145). The talk was initially published in the November issue of the journal *Russkaia Mysl'* in the same year.

29. *Trudy Moskovskogo Psikhologicheskogo Obshchestva* (hereafter, *Trudy*) were serially published volumes of the transactions of the Society dedicated to special topics or gathering discussion forums of talks and responses delivered at the various sessions of the MPS.

30. For the full citation, see Bibliography.

546   I. MEDZHIBOVSKAYA

31. I am quoting from Grot's talk delivered in Moscow, "*Znachenie chuvstva v poznanii i deiatel'nosti cheloveka*" ["The Significance of Feeling in Human Understanding and Activity"] (1889), in Grot (1904, 174–176, 177–178).
32. "Nikolai Grot's Introduction" ["*Predislovie N. Ya. Grota*"] (v–x), in *On the Freedom of Will* [*O svobode voli*], ix.
33. "What is Metaphysics?" ["*Chto takoe metafizika?*" 1890], in Grot (1904; see especially 195, 207–208, 210).
34. I mean of course Heidegger's "What is Metaphysics?" his inaugural address at Freiburg on July 29, 1929.
35. Grot, "The Significance of Kant" ["*Znachenie Kanta*," (Grot 1893a, 91)]. Grot's chapter on Kant is a conclusion of his longer essay, "Major Moments in the Development of Modern Philosophy" ["*Osnovnye momenty v razvitii novoi filosofii*"] that *VFP* published in installments.
36. Of Fichte's many writings on the topic, see primarily his *The Vocation of Man*, finished in 1799 and published in 1800.
37. In mentioning Lange's work on the collation of impressions in a perceptive cycle (Grot, "O vremeni," in Grot 1904, 286), Grot must mean especially N. N. Lange (1893), passim.
38. These are Solovyov's frequently made points in "The Life Drama of Plato" ["*Zhiznennaia drama Platona*" 1898], the long essay he wrote as a preface to the translation of Plato's dialogues. The essay first appeared in issues three and four of the journal *The Messenger of Europe* [*Vestnik Evropy*], in 1898.
39. Grot's brother Konstantin (1853–1934) was a noted literary historian and a specialist in Slavic philology and linguistics.
40. The irregular and erroneous quote on page 791 of the above passage is provided here in my modified and corrected translation. For a fuller discussion of Tolstoy and Grot, see Medzhibovskaya (2008, 2019b).
41. I am here paraphrasing Deleuze and Guattari (1986). I expand on this notion of minor philosophy in Medzhibovskaya's *Tolstoy's On Life: From the Archival History of Russian Philosophy* (2019a), 221–229.

Bibliography

Budilova, Elena A. 1960. *Bor'ba materializma i idealizma v russkoi psikhologicheskoi nauke: vtoraia polovina XIX-nachalo XX v.* Moscow: Akademiia Nauk SSSR.

Chernikov, Dmitrii Yu. 2008. *Moskovskoe Psikhologicheskoe Obshchestvo v istorii russkoi filosofii.* Moscow: Moskovskii Gosudarstvennyi universitet im. M.V. Lomonosova.

Deleuze, Gilles, and Félix Guattari. 1986. *Kafka: Toward a Minor Literature.* Translated by Dana Polan. Foreword by Réda Bensmaïa. Minneapolis, MN: University of Minnesota Press.

Episkop Nikanor. 1875–1876. *Pozitivnaia filosofiia i sverkhchuvstvennoe bytie.* Vols. 1-2. St. Petersburg: Izdatel'stvo tovarishchestva Obshchestvennaia Polz'a.

———. 1888. *Pozitivnaia filosofiia i sverkhchuvstvennoe bytie.* Vol. 3. St. Petersburg: Tip. F. Eleonskago.

Everling, Sergey N. 1923. Three Evenings with Count Leo Tolstoi. *The Nineteenth Century and After. XIX–XX. A Monthly Review* 93 (January–June): 786–792, 841–849.

24 THE VOCATIONS OF NIKOLAI GROT AND THE TASKS OF RUSSIAN PHILOSOPHY   547

Grot, Nikolai Ya. 1882. *K voprosu o reforme logiki. Opyt novoi teorii umstvennykh protsessov*. Leipzig: F.A. Brokgauz [Izdanie Instituta].

———. 1884. *Zapiska ob ustroistve prepodavaniia filosofii v universitetakh pri novom ustave. Avtoreferat*. RGALI fond 123, opis' 1, delo 1115, 22 leaves, no obverse.

———. 1885. *O nravstvennoi otvetstvennosti i iuridicheskoi vmeniaemosti*. Odessa: Tip. Odesskogo vestnika.

———. 1886. *O dushe v sviazi s sovremennymi ucheniiami o sile. Opyt filosofskogo postroeniia*. Odessa: Tipografiia Odesskogo vestnika.

———. 1889a. O zadachakh zhurnala *Voprosy Filosofii i Psikhologii. Voprosy Filosofii i Psikhologii* 1 (1): v–xx.

———. 1889b. Kritika poniatiia svobody voli v sviazi s poniatiem prichinnosti. In *O svobode voli. Opyty Postanovki i Resheniia Voprosa. Referaty i Stat'i Chlenov Psikhologicheskogo Obshchestva. Trudy Moskovskogo Psikhologicheskogo Obshchestva*, Vypusk III, XIV–XXVIII and 1–96. Moscow: Tipografiia A. Gatsuka.

———. 1891. Eshche o zadachakh zhurnala. *Voprosy Filosofii i Psikhologii* 6 (3): i–vi.

———. 1893a. Znachenie Kanta. *Voprosy Filosofii i Psikhologii* 20 (5): 77–93.

———. 1893b. Nravstvennye idealy nashego vremeni (Friedrich Nietzsche i Lev Tolstoy). *Voprosy Filosofii i Psikhologii* 16 (4): 129–154.

———. 1895. Ustoi nravstvennoi deiatel'nosti. *Voprosy Filosofii i Psikhologii* 27 (6): 145–168.

———. 1896. *Ocherki filosofii Platona*. Moscow: Posrednik.

———, ed. 1904. *Filosofiia i eia obshchie zadachi. Sbornik statei*, Moscow Psychological Society. St. Petersburg: A.S. Suvorin.

———. 1911. Avtobiografcheskii ocherk. In *Nikolai Yakovlevich Grot v ocherkakh, vospominaniiakh i pis'makh tovarishchei i uchenikov, druzei i pochitatelei*, 339–343. St. Petersburg: Tipografiia Ministerstva Putei Soobshcheniia/Tovarishchestvo I.N. Kushnerev & Co.

Heidegger, Martin. 2008. What Is Metaphysics? In *Heidegger's Basic Writings*, ed. David Farrell Krell, 89–110. Revised and expanded edition. London: Harper Perennial.

Joravsky, David. 1989. *Russian Psychology. A Critical History*. Oxford: Basil Blackwell.

Kavelin, Konstantin D. 1897–1900. Zadachi psikhologii. In *Sobranie sochinenii v chetyrekh tomakh*, ed. M.M. Stasiulevich, A.F. Koni, D.A. Korsakov, et al., vol. 3, 375–648. St. Petersburg: Tipografiia N. Glagoleva.

Lange, Nikolai N. 1893. *Psikhologicheskiia izsledovaniia*. Odessa: Tip. Sht. Odesskago voennogo okruga.

Lopatin, Lev M. 1911. N. Ya. Grot. In *Grot v ocherkakh, vospominaniiakh i pis'makh tovarishchei i uchenikov, druzei i pochitatelei*, 88–98. St. Petersburg: Tipografiia Ministerstva Putei Soobshcheniia/Tovarishchestvo I.N. Kushnerev & Co.

Lossky, Nikolai O. 1991. *Istoriia Russkoi Filosofii*. Moscow: Sovetskii Pisatel.

Makovitsky, Dushan P. 1979. In *U Tolstogo, 1904–1910. "Iasnopolianskie zapiski" D.P. Makovitskogo*, Literaturnoe nasledstvo 90, ed. S.A. Makashina, M.B. Khrapchenko, and V.R. Shubina. Moscow: Nauka.

Medzhibovskaya, Inessa. 2008. *Tolstoy and the Religious Culture of His Time, a Biography of a Long Conversion, 1845–1887*. Lanham, MD: Lexington Books.

———. 2019a. *Tolstoy's On Life: From the Archival History of Russian Philosophy*. DeLand, FL: The Tolstoy Society of North America and *Tolstoy Studies Journal* 2019.

548   I. MEDZHIBOVSKAYA

———. 2019b. Tolstoy's *On Life and Its Times*. In Leo Tolstoy, *On Life. A Critical Edition*, ed. Inessa Medzhibovskaya, 1–41. Translated by Michael Denner and Inessa Medzhibovskaya. Evanston, IL: Northwestern University Press.

Poole, Randall A. 1995. *The Moscow Psychological Society and the Neo-Idealist Development of Russian Liberalism*. PhD. Diss., Notre Dame University.

Porter, Theodore M., and Dorothy Ross. 2003. Psychology in Russia and Central and Eastern Europe. In *The Cambridge History of Science*, vol. 7, 431–449. Cambridge: Cambridge University Press.

Russell, Bertrand. 1996. *An Inquiry into Meaning and Truth*. New York: Routledge.

Shchetinina, Galina I. 1976. *Universitety v Rossii i ustav 1884 goda*. Moscow: Nauka.

Shkurinov, Pavel S. 1980. *Pozitivizm v Rossii XIX veka*. Moscow: Izd-vo Moskovskogo universiteta.

Sokolov, P.P. 1904. Filosofskie vzgliady i nauchnaia deiatelnost N. Ya. Grota. In *Filosofiia i eia obshchie zadachi, Sbornik statei*, Moscow Psychological Society, ed. N.Ya. Grot, lxvii–ci. St. Petersburg: A.S. Suvorin.

Solovyov, Vladimir S. 1908–1911. Neskol'ko slov o nastoiashchei zadache filosofii. In V.S. Solovyov, *Pis'ma Vladimira Sergeevicha Solovyova v trekh tomakh*, ed. E.L. Radlov, vol. 3, 221–225. St. Petersburg: Tip. Izd. Obshchestvennaia Pol'za.

———. 1911. Stat'i V.S. Solovyova (Pominka—Iz st. "Tri kharakteristiki"). In *Nikolai Yakovlevich Grot v ocherkakh, vospominaniiakh i pis'makh tovarishchei i uchenikov, druzei i pochitatelei*, 149–156. St. Petersburg: Tipografiia Ministerstva putei soobshcheniia/Tovarishchestvo I.N. Kushnerev & Co.

Vladislavlev, Mkhail I. 1881. Psikhologiia. In *Izsledovanie osnovnykh iavlenii dushevnoi zhizni v dvukh tomakh*. St.-Petersburg: Tip. V. Bezobrazov i Komp.

Vvedensky, Alexander I. 1911. Pamiatii Nikolaia Yakovlevicha Grota. In *Nikolai Yakovlevich Grot v ocherkakh, vospominaniiakh i pis'makh tovarishchei i uchenikov, druzei i pochitatelei*, 135–147. St. Petersburg: Tipografiia Ministerstva Putei Soobshcheniia/Tovarishchestvo I.N. Kushnerev & Co.

Walicki, Andrzej. 1979. *A History of Russian Thought from the Enlightenment to Marxism*. Translated by Hilda Andrews Rusiecka. Stanford, CA: Stanford University Press.

CHAPTER 25

Chernyshevsky and Dostoevsky: Together in Opposition

Vladimir K. Kantor

If any cultural-historical justice exists, it has no statute of limitations. Shakespeare was forgotten for almost 200 years. Within living memory, Mikhail Bulgakov and Andrei Platonov, not to mention Russian religious philosophy, resurfaced from oblivion. There are, however, more complex, even inconceivably complex cases where a writer and thinker is seemingly well-known, but his name has acquired such extreme connotations and interpretations that he might as well be in a lead coffin. I am referring here to Nikolai Chernyshevsky, whose language I want to present to the modern reader in what I hope is an undistorted form. I have written about this more than once, but Plutarch is perhaps right that only twinned portraits provide real illumination. Thus, I will consider Nikolai Chernyshevsky alongside Fyodor Dostoevsky.[1]

Fyodor Mikhailovich Dostoevsky was born in Moscow in 1821, and Nikolai Gavrilovich Chernyshevsky was born in Saratov in 1828. Thus, Dostoevsky was seven years older than Chernyshevsky. Both writers would go through phases of fascination with Gogol, Pushkin, and Schiller (who was long an idol of both), both read Belinsky, and both were concerned with religious issues that led to the question of Russia choosing its spiritual path.[2] I would add that there were also clergy in both families. Dostoevsky's grandfather was a priest in the town of Bratslav in the Podol'skaia province [*guberniia*], although his father

---

This study has been funded by the Russian Academic Excellence Project "5-100."

V. K. Kantor (✉)
National Research University Higher School of Economics in Moscow (Russian Federation), Moscow, Russia

© The Author(s), under exclusive license to Springer Nature Switzerland AG 2021
M. F. Bykova et al. (eds.), *The Palgrave Handbook of Russian Thought*,
https://doi.org/10.1007/978-3-030-62982-3_25

549

550   V. K. KANTOR

became a physician in the Mariinskii Hospital for the Poor in Moscow. Chernyshevsky also came from a clerical family: his father was an Archpriest in Saratov. In order to attain priesthood, however, young people needed a good education; education was also required to enter other respected professions, such as medicine. In either case, these were versions of a class that had no wealth or property and whose representatives had to earn their living by their own labor. In fact, Dostoevsky's first heroes were from this stratum of petty officials with small salaries. *Poor Folk*, Dostoevsky's first novel and the story of the tragic love of a petty official, brought him fame, and one might even say glory. However, we should immediately note that aristocratic writers, even famous authors of Russian classics (like Ivan S. Turgenev) who set the literary tone, did not approve of Dostoevsky's work (especially after his innovative novel *The Double*). Interestingly enough, the young Chernyshevsky, who was a university student at the time, read Dostoevsky's early tales with great enthusiasm and would recount them to classmates. He retold them with such feeling that his classmates sometimes believed he was telling his own stories. A diary entry from 1849 reads, "March 12. With a trembling voice, I retold *The Double* to him [a friend] and he initially thought that I had written it" (1939–1953, 1: 363).

It is nonetheless necessary to note that they both received a higher education, another indispensable condition for later life, in order to earn a living. Dostoevsky entered the School of Mining Engineers in St. Petersburg in 1838 and graduated in 1843 with the title of military engineer. He immediately sat down to write his first novel, starving but stubbornly giving himself over to his work. *Poor Folk* was published in 1846, and his life as a writer began. That same year, Chernyshevsky entered St. Petersburg University. He wrote his first work on the Ipat'ev Chronicle under Izmail Sreznevskii, the great Slavist and expert on ancient Russian culture. All these years, Chernyshevsky read Dostoevsky's novels and wrote about them in his personal diary; the young author's prose was very much to his liking, including *The Jealous Husband*, *Netochka Nezvanova*, and *White Nights* (which taught him self-sacrifice in relation to one's beloved, something he later practiced in his own relationship with Ol'ga Sokratovna). He attempted to do some writing himself but found the results unsatisfactory.

In 1849, Dostoevsky was arrested as a participant in the Petrashevskii Circle, whose namesake preached the utopian socialist ideas of Fourier, Cabet, and Owen. A short trial followed, but the government believed the crime to be more serious. The academic edition of the great writer's complete collected works has published archival materials related to the "Petrashevskii Case," including the text of Dostoevsky's verdict:

> The military court finds the defendant Dostoevsky guilty of having received from the nobleman Pleshcheev (defendant) in Moscow in March of this year a copy of a criminal letter by the author Belinsky and of reading this letter in his meetings. [...] The military court therefore sentences him, retired engineer-lieutenant Dostoevsky, for failing to inform about the dissemination of the author Belinsky's

letter about religion and government [...] to be stripped on the basis of the Code of Military Decrees. [...] of his ranks and all the rights of his status, and to execution by firing squad. (Dostoevsky 1972–1990, 18: 189)

The issue of the Russian people's religious consciousness had first become the subject of open consideration in Russian literature and aesthetics after the publication of Gogol's *Selected Passages from Correspondence with Friends.* Belinsky's letter was a reply to that book. Gogol was firmly convinced of the Russian people's Orthodoxy and the Russian church's vitality. I should note that his relationship with Belinsky was a tragic story of rapture, schism, and finally overcoming. When Belinsky died in 1848, it was a great shock to Dostoevsky, and his reading of the letter by Gogol's critic was a sort of intellectual farewell to Belinsky. The Russian philosopher Lev Shestov believed that Dostoevsky had a choice: to remain true to his intuitions and ideas, or to break with them and submit to Belinsky's enchanting and energetic personality:

As a result, and without "great reason," the student abandoned the teacher who had already grown bored of *Poor Folk* and who considered Dostoevsky's following work to be "nervous nonsense." This is not, as you can see, a joyful history. But the beast flees into the trap. [...] The break with Belinsky was the first trial that Dostoevsky had to endure, and he endured it with honor. (Shestov 1995, 36)

Belinsky observed changing spiritual attitudes in public consciousness and also declared that the Russian people were deeply atheistic. They still held to numerous superstitions, but there was no trace of religiosity. Before Gogol's book, it had never occurred to anyone to declare, publicly and in the secular press, their sincere devotion to Orthodoxy, to discuss the great calling of the Russian clergy, or, even more unusually, to assure the world of the Russian people's Orthodoxy. The Orthodox Church and the faith it defended were protected by administrative methods, and the autocracy saw no need to protect it with the help of writers, nor were there any such writers until the early nineteenth century, until the Slavophiles and Gogol, Belinsky, and Dostoevsky. Through the military court's verdict, Dostoevsky was forever linked to the dispute between Belinsky and Gogol, having been convicted for his interest in it. From then on, that dispute became a fact not only of his personal biography, but also of his creative biography, while the issues in dispute became the subject of his most intense reflections. In other words, Dostoevsky was sentenced to death for his independent search for a religious solution to Russian problems.

Today we can see that *the fate of Chernyshevsky was foreshadowed* in that of the Petrashevskii circle. They were sentenced to death *for nothing!* More precisely, they were convicted of *ideological crime*, the kind of conviction the Bolsheviks would inherit from the autocracy. For having thought independently, Chernyshevsky too would be sentenced to penal servitude. An enormous amount has been written about Nabokov's famous novel *Invitation to a Beheading*, but only in recent years have scholars seen an echo of Chernyshevsky's fate in the fate of Nabokov's protagonist Cincinnatus, who is sentenced to death for *thought crime* ("gnoseological turpitude").[3] Later, the monarchist and great religious thinker Sergei N. Bulgakov would write much about how the autocracy was preparing its own demise by destroying all attempts at independence, even the most well-intentioned. Looking ahead, I would note that Chernyshevsky's main political idea was constitutional monarchy, not rebellion, or more precisely, in opposition to rebellion. Yet it was for this thought, not even expressed in a very politically clear way, that he was sentenced to a practically unlimited term in Siberia.

Russia had begun to face the problem of actualizing Orthodoxy, which, according to general opinion, had long been inoperative. Many wrote about the Russian Church's necrosis, Gogol pondered it, and Belinsky was sure of it. Years later, the Elder Zosima in Dostoevsky's great novel sends Alyosha out into the world, thereby making a gesture that thinkers like Lev Tikhomirov would reproach as Catholic. Attempting to energize the old religious texts, the son of a Saratov archpriest Chernyshevsky considered it a question of Orthodoxy's efficacy in the world. His thoughts always circle around Christian issues, which he wants to protect with all his might, and he seeks new approaches in modern thought that allow for this. On September 24, 1848, he writes down in his diary:

> I will write something about my religious convictions. I must say that I am, in essence, resolutely Christian, if we understand that to mean a belief in the divine virtue of Jesus Christ, that is, just as the Orthodox believe that he was God and suffered, and rose again, and worked miracles, in general, I believe all this. But this is united with the idea that Christianity must improve with time, and therefore I do not reject the rationalists at all. (Chernyshevsky 1939–1953, 1: 132)

Dostoevsky was removed from the polemics, but the issue remained. When Dostoevsky ended his sentence in 1856 and remained a soldier in Semipalatinsk, Chernyshevsky was already an influential critic writing in *Sovremennik*. For Chernyshevsky, then as before, Christianity remained the basis of European civilization. In 1856, the prominent journalist writes, "Christianity has begun to reach these savages [meaning the unbaptized Svans and Khevsurs]; our government has already built several churches in their land" (Chernyshevsky 1939–1953, 3: 487).

For Chernyshevsky, Christ was the Enlightener, and we must appreciate this, because this concept is usually only applied to a certain literary-philosophical current of the eighteenth and nineteenth centuries. Enlightenment for the Christian is light itself, the light of reason. As the Gospel says, "In Him was life, and that life was the light of mankind" (John 1: 4).

In 1853, Chernyshevsky defended his dissertation on aesthetics, which was rejected by his aristocratic contemporaries, who found the phrase "beauty is life" confusing. Alexei F. Losev would later claim that this phrase is ancient ontology, stating that Russia had only two true aestheticians, Chernyshevsky and Vladimir Solovyov. In his dissertation, Chernyshevsky constructs a kind of triad when discussing the perception of beauty among different strata of the Russian population.

He lays the notion of beauty among "common people" at the foundation: "In descriptions of beauty in folk songs there is not a single sign of beauty not expressed as blossoming health and balanced forces in the organism, the everyday consequence of a contented life under constant and serious but not excessive labor" (Chernyshevsky 1939–1953, 2: 10). Rejecting this simple life so aligned with natural processes is the life of the upper crust, which is characterized by a "fascination with pale, sickly beauty, a sign of the artificial corruption of taste" (ibid., 2: 11). However, what he then calls a synthesis, for him the highest point, is the life and notion of beauty among "educated people," people who are able to distinguish the "face," the personality:

> Every *truly educated person* feels that *the true life is the life of the mind and the heart*. It is imprinted in the expression of the *face*, most clearly *in the eyes*, the *facial expression*, about which so little is said in folk song, thus obtains great significance in the concepts of beauty that prevail among educated people, and it often happens that a person seems beautiful to us only because he has *beautiful, expressive eyes*. (Chernyshevsky 1939–1953, 2: 11; italics mine)

We should recall here the words of the Gospel that give essential context to Chernyshevsky's statement: "The eye is the lamp of the body" (Luke 11: 34). Is this not obviously the source? It is also the first appearance of the *face/image* theme in non-religious Russian literature.

At the time, young radicals were already appearing and demanding that literature (following Herzen's example) transform into revolutionary propaganda. Dostoevsky would vehemently oppose this suggestion. Meanwhile, Chernyshevsky penned a clear formulation of *Sovremennik*'s credo in an 1857 editorial:

> Man's aspirations and man's needs exist independently of literature. Literature can neither arouse, nor lull, nor strengthen, nor weaken them. It cannot set new goals for man to which he did not already aspire without its aid. Its authority over all this is powerless; all this is solely under the dominion of events that act equally upon those who remain silent, those who do not chatter, those who do not read, and those who do not read journals. But to take these aspirations that are independent of literature and to introduce circumspection and prudence into them: only literature can do this. Only the habit of consulting the printed sheet can guard society against impulsiveness. The whole question thus comes down to which is better, impulsiveness or judiciousness, given one and the same aspiration. Given identical events, a difference in force cannot be produced or it will not involve literature. Only whether the idea is impulsive or prudent, anxious or calm, depends on that circumstance. (Chernyshevsky 1939–1953, 4: 769)

Thus, a *warning against impulsiveness*. This statement could not avoid being noticed by conservative opponents who expected only turpitude from yesterday's seminarian, but the signal was meant for Herzen, not for them.

554 V. K. KANTOR

In his treatise *On the Development of Revolutionary Ideas in Russia*, published abroad, Herzen argued that it was Russian literature itself (Pushkin, Gogol, etc.) that contained the revolutionary principle. From that moment, the two young leaders became evident though secret enemies. Herzen used the journal *The Bell* to call for rebellion; Chernyshevsky wrote in his *Unaddressed Letters* that peasant revolt would be the worst thing possible for Russia. Dostoevsky and Herzen likewise turned out to be fierce antagonists. On returning from penal servitude, Dostoevsky even went to London and handed Herzen his *Notes from the House of the Dead* on prison labor. Incidentally, this happened the same day Chernyshevsky was arrested and began his own journey to the House of the Dead. Dostoevsky later portrayed Herzen in *Demons* as Stavrogin, bearer of diabolical intentions, and he wrote in his *The Diary of a Writer* that Herzen had not emigrated nor set the terms for Russian emigration, but was simply born an emigrant.

Here, we should probably highlight the balance of power involved in order to understand why the *raznochintsy* ["mixed rank"] Chernyshevsky and Dostoevsky seemed to be on one side, while authors from the nobility (Turgenev, Herzen, etc.) were on the other. After the publication of *Poor Folk*, Dostoevsky's first printed work, and the temporary fame and success of the young writer (who was apparently of "mixed rank" despite a noble-born father), Turgenev and his friends began to abuse Dostoevsky, calling him "the Finn." Moreover, Turgenev committed an act of literary tactlessness (to put it mildly) by writing a poetic libel in 1846 in the voice of Belinsky:

> Belinsky's Address to Dostoevsky: ("Knight of Woeful Countenance ...")
>
> Knight of woeful countenance,
> My dear, pompous Dostoevsky,
> On the nose of literature
> You glow red, a new pimple.
> (Turgenev 1978, 332)[4]

The only person who supported the young, poor, and self-absorbed genius was Nekrasov's lover Avdot'ia Panaeva. I believe it was no coincidence that Dostoevsky gave her name to one of his most beautiful heroines, Avdot'ia, the sister of Rodion Raskol'nikov. Dostoevsky later delivered a sweeping reply to Turgenev by portraying him in *The Demons* as the writer Karmazinov, who adapts himself to Russian devilry.

Beginning in the mid-1850s, the former seminarian and "mixed class" Chernyshevsky also came under attack, some of which included very harsh mockery. Grigorovich (*the poet of the poor*) attempted to humiliate Chernyshevsky with the strangest, most inane epithet evoking the critic's non-noble, seminarian origins: "reeking of bedbugs." This was amusing to the nobility. However, it was not only his origins that offended them, but also his independence and his so-called disrespect for authorities (as Chernyshevsky himself later titled one of his articles).[5] Leo Tolstoy called him "a gentleman reeking of bedbugs." As Lidiia M. Lotman writes,

In the summer of 1855, Druzhinin, Turgenev, and Grigorovich composed a farce in which they presented Turgenev, Nekrasov, Panaev, and Chernyshevsky in a comic light. Soon afterwards, Grigorovich apparently took inspiration from Druzhinin and reshaped this farce into his story "Shkola gosterpiimstva" [The School of Hospitality], which offers libelous portraits of Chernyshevsky (Chernushkin), Nekrasov (Bodasov), and Panaev (Tarataev). Druzhinin printed "The School of Hospitality" in *Biblioteka dlia chteniia*, hoping to thereby aggravate the relationship between Grigorovich and the editorial board of *Sovremmenik*, perhaps even leading to the writer's break with the journal and his move to *Biblioteka dlia chteniia*. (Lotman 1955, 514–515)

Nekrasov managed to quash the scandal. Chernyshevsky fully understood the journalistic politics involved and did not object.

The young thinker was criticized for his artistic insensitivity, his inability to experience and understand a genuine work of art (which contemporary literary critics assert, as well), even though everyone has since adopted his formulation for Leo Tolstoy's work, "a dialectic of the soul," which applies equally to both Tolstoy's early and late work, namely to his artistic method. It is curious, however, how much personal vanity affected their estimations of the man. From the very beginning of his literary activity, he wrote much about and praised Tolstoy, but the phrase "a dialectic of the soul," which Chernyshevsky expressed in 1856 in the twelfth issue of *Sovremennik*, clarified Tolstoy even to himself and became the standard definition everyone applied from then on. Tolstoy's impression of Chernyshevsky immediately changed. He writes in a diary entry dated January 11, 1857, "Chernyshevsky arrived, clever and heated" (Tolstoy 1955, 40).

Chernyshevsky lived a Christian life, if not a Life in the hagiographic sense. In the house he rented and maintained with his own money, he himself occupied only a small room, to which the mischief-making housekeeper below and the guests who visited would at times carry up his meals. He wrote frantically, as if praying from morning to night as a hermit. A list of texts he wrote from his dissertation to his arrest would take up several printer's sheets. I will therefore focus on his central works, the ones that provoked loud and public literary responses. Immediately after his 1855 dissertation defense, the first article in his cycle *The Essays on the Gogolian Period of Russian Literature* [*Ocherki gogolevskogo perioda russkoi literatury*] appeared in the December issue of *Sovremennik* (1855, no. 12).[6] He used these to trace the shape of Russian literature and criticism from N. Polevoi to V. Belinsky.

The response was far from unanimous. As if by inertia, the aristocratic literati were irritated, especially since it was clear from the first article that he was seizing on the idea of Russian culture's literature-centric nature and saw Belinsky as the leading critic of the period. He begins almost immediately with a veiled reference to Belinsky's work as the apex of Russian literary thought:

Criticism generally develops on the basis of facts presented by literature, whose works serve as the necessary data for criticism's conclusions. For example, Pushkin, with his Byronically inflected poems and *Evgenii Onegin*, was followed by criticism in *Telegraf*, and when Gogol acquired dominion over the development of our self-consciousness, the so-called criticism of the 1840s followed. (Chernyshevsky 1939–1953, 3: 8)

Clearly recognizing that he would be reproached for a lack of independent thought, he responds with an almost Biblical formulation:

Readers may sense an echo of powerless indecision in our words, one that Russian literature has acquired in recent years [...] These readers would be correct, in part. But nor are we entirely wrong. Any support is good to a falling man, even if only to right him on his feet; and what should we do if our era does not prove itself capable of standing on its own? And what is to be done if this falling man can support himself only on coffins? *We must ask ourselves, is it really the dead lying in these coffins? Are those lying in them not the living?* At the very least, is there not far more life in these dearly departed than in many of those we consider alive? After all, if the writer's word is animated by the idea of truth, by the striving for a beneficial effect on the mental life of society, then his word contains in itself the seed of life, and it will never be dead. (Chernyshevsky 1939–1953, 3: 9; italics mine)[7]

As we see, his message is defined by the evangelical theme of life generating the meaning of existence. Of course, this is a reliance on evangelical thought necessary to fulfill the will of the Heavenly Father rather than one's own will: "The Son can do nothing by Himself or of Himself, but what he sees his Father the Creator do: for what He does, the Son also does" (John 5: 19).

Furthermore, the issue of whether the men lying in these coffins are dead was echoed much later in the conversation between the brothers Ivan and Alyosha in *Brat'ia Karamazovy* [*The Brothers Karamazov*], when Ivan sighs that European culture is already a graveyard:

The precious are lying there, and each stone above them tells of such an ardent past life, of such passionate faith in their deeds, in their truth, in their struggles, and in their science that I, I know full well beforehand, will fall to the ground and kiss these very stones and weep over them. At the same time, I am convinced with all my heart that it has long been a graveyard, and nothing more. (Dostoevsky 1972–1990, 14: 210)

Alyosha responds, "We must resurrect your dead, who maybe never really died" (14: 210). This pertains not just for Western culture, but also for literature, which alone, according to Chernyshevsky, preserves the spiritual life of a culture.

The year 1861 was not only the year of the serf emancipation, but also the year of what are perhaps Chernyshevsky's most significant articles, as well as the year in which some of those closest to him died. These articles that so impressed his contemporaries and are important for understanding his position were "The Apology of a Madman" (his commentary on a Chaadaev text with the same title), "The Russian Reformer" (about Count Mikhail Speranskii), "On the Causes of Rome's Fall (An Imitation of Montesquieu)," his most important historiographical work and a dispute with Herzen about the possible death of Western Europe, and *Polemical Beauties*, his most biting text on the contemporary state of Russian intellectual life.

He was, in some ways, forced to write the last of these. He and other authors of *Sovremennik* were accused by their enemies of being ignorant charlatans. It was, in fact, a declaration of war by their enemies. As Heraclitus (whose work he knew well) once said, "war (Polemos) is the father of all, the king of all: he declares some gods and others humans, makes some slaves and others free" (Lebedev 1989, 202). Chernyshevsky considered himself free and not at all a charlatan, as *Russkii vestnik* had labeled him and his colleagues (Dobrolyubov and Pypin). In response, Chernyshevsky launched a sweeping attack aimed at the critic Dudyshkin, the theologian Yurkevich, the poet Vyazemsky, the journalist Katkov, the printer Kraevskii, the critic Gromeka, and even the great philologist Buslaev (who had written against *Sovremennik* in *Otechestvennye zapiski*).

Chernyshevsky fought with everyone and formulated a generalization that offended them all, constructing a spiritual hierarchy in which he located himself in a rather high position:

> Are you pleased to know that they have used the word "ignorant" to describe, well, not to mention me, but for example Hegel? Do you know why they called him ignorant? Because he had a certain way of thinking that some scholars disliked. [...] Do you know why they called Kant ignorant? [...] Men of routine accuse any kind of innovator of ignorance due to his being an innovator. (Chernyshevsky 1939–1953, 7: 770)

Later, he adds, "You might blame me for calling attention to progress in science. [...] As you wish. Perhaps you believe the old is better than the new. But allow yourself the possibility of thinking otherwise" (Chernyshevsky 1939–1953, 7: 771).

No one wanted to admit this possibility. In his article, he therefore strikes broadly at his literary enemies, and with such contempt that it was less his position that elicited so much irritation, but the sense of superiority that his words so obviously conveyed, like a teacher berating a classroom full of children who do not want to learn the most elementary things.

The aristocrat Pyotr Vyazemsky, a former friend of Pushkin who vainly attempted to woo the poet's widow Natal'ia Nikolaevna, published a poetic response to Chernyshevsky's article in *Russkii vestnik*. The style of his response recalls Turgenev's verse on Dostoevsky, "Knight of Woeful Countenance." Vyazemsky's text was a paraphrase of Druzhinin's lampoon and Grigorovich's

558 V. K. KANTOR

"The School of Hospitality," where Chernyshevsky was presented under the name "Chernushkin":

> A hate-filled note to enemies and friends
> Sometimes masks the bile of evil envy.
> What they profess as proud freedom
> Is often hatred at those above.
> (Vyazemsky 1887–1896, 387)

In a remarkable article, Valerii L. Serdiuchenko very elegantly and bluntly explains that the reason these aristocratic writers were so irritated was in fact Chernyshevsky's intellectual superiority:

> Chernyshevsky knew his own worth. He fought his way into great literature and took his place as its leading light at the price of an almost unheard-of productivity, multiplied by a university education, which even the best minds of the aristocratic intelligentsia often abandoned. For this reason alone he could already afford no special sympathy for those who found themselves on the literary Olympus on their first attempt, no matter how talented that attempt may have been. (Serdiuchenko 2003)

There was no journal, no critic, that would not strike back against this insolent seminarian's *Polemical Beauties*. Except for Dostoevsky!

In general, their affinity is surprising, possibly explained by their similar fates. That similarity would also manifest later in life, after Chernyshevsky's arrest and during his time in penal servitude. For now, I would explain it by juxtaposing the "mixed class" writers (after all, Dostoevsky was essentially "mixed class" in his financial and social position) with the nobility, as well as the level at which they perceived each other. Here is what Dostoevsky said:

> Do you know what we would say in conclusion? After all, it was you that Mr. Chernyshevsky recently offended with his "polemical beauties," as you sighed with your elegiac tears. We, at the very least, are certain of this much. He did not even deign to speak to you using respectable language. Such insolence! We can discuss Mr. Chernyshevsky without fearing that they will take us for his sayyids or arrant partisans. We have very often touched on our capricious polemicist, and very often disagreed with him. And Mr. Chernyshevsky's fate in Russian literature is in fact extraordinary! They are scrambling to convince each and every one that he is ignorant, even impudent; that there is nothing, absolutely nothing to him, just empty chatter and empty color, and nothing more. Suddenly Mr. Chernyshevsky publishes, say, something like his "polemical beauties." [...] Good Lord, the gnashing of teeth and the elegiac howl that follows. [...] After these beauties, *Otechestvennye zapiski* dedicated nearly six articles in a single volume (yes, it seems it really was six) entirely to Mr. Chernyshevsky, and precisely in order to prove his insignificance to the whole world. One joker even said that "Ten Italian Women" ["Desiat' Ital'anok"] was the only article in *Otechestvennye zapiski* that did not mention Mr. Chernyshevsky's name. But if he is so insignificant

and ridiculous, why are there six articles in such a serious and scholarly journal, much less at the same time, and in a single volume? The situation is the same in Moscow: there was something like a small earthquake there. There were even some leaflets written about Mr. Chernyshevsky. Why does everyone seem so worried? What a strange, truly strange fate for this strange writer! (Dostoevsky 1972–1990, 19: 177)

His fate was strange, indeed: strange and tragic, in the style of Dostoevsky's own fate.

I should repeat that 1861 was a difficult year for Chernyshevsky. His father, who was his friend and teacher, died, as did the person closest to him in spirit, the brilliant young Nikolai Dobrolyubov, who had taken over the literary criticism department of *Sovremennik*, freeing Chernyshevsky to write articles on philosophy and political economics. Dobrolyubov's final article, "The Downtrodden Folk," focused on Dostoevsky's *The Insulted and the Injured*.[8] We can say with some certainty that everything written by Dobrolyubov was approved by Chernyshevsky. Dobrolyubov firmly placed Dostoevsky among the first ranks of Russian literature: "Mr. Dostoevsky's novel is quite good, so good in fact that we read it almost entirely with pleasure and talked about it almost entirely with complete praise. [...] In a word, Dostoevsky's novel represents the best literary phenomenon so far this year" (Dobrolyubov 1961–1964, 7: 249). We can only regret that he did not live long enough to see Dostoevsky display the full measure of his talent.

Even worse days would follow for those who were trying to bring an element of freedom into society. Their autocratic rulers did not know how to behave in situations where free-thinking people were appearing in public, so they preferred to punish them, condemning them to prison and penal servitude. On the other hand, the radicals did not understand that one could live freely without entering into organized struggle against the regime.

If we consider that Chernyshevsky attempted to prevent young people from taking radical actions, what happened later seems almost surreal. The most striking part is that Chernyshevsky was accused and tried for being a revolutionary, the leader of an approaching rebellion, *while in fact he tried to resist rebellion with all his might*. In *Unaddressed Letters* [*Pis'ma bez adresa*] written in March 1862, he discusses the possibility of popular uprising:

All individuals and social strata who are separated from the people tremble at this unexpected denouement. Nor are you alone: we, too, would like to avoid it. After all, the idea has also spread among us that our interests would be affected by it, [...] even [...] the interests of enlightenment. We think the people are ignorant, full of coarse prejudices and blind hatred of all who have abandoned their wild habits. It makes no distinction between people dressed as Europeans; it would treat them all the same. It will spare neither our science, nor our poetry, nor our arts; it will destroy all of civilization. (Chernyshevsky 1939–1953, 10: 92)

560 V. K. KANTOR

These letters represented a desperate attempt to appeal to the reason of tsar and government: "My contemptible writer's habit of placing my hopes in the power of the word overshadows me" (ibid.). The article was banned.

That May, the terrible fires began in St. Petersburg. Fires were not actually uncommon in the capital, which was full of wooden and dilapidated houses. It is fitting and somehow symbolic (apparently someone told him what to expect) that he would witness the terrible St. Petersburg fires during his first year after arriving there with his wife, fires that would later, in 1862, be attributed to him as the nihilists' inspiration; that is, he was not accused of arson, but of having inspired arsonists. The early 1860s were, to put it mildly, somewhat tense, given the manifesto announcing the serf emancipation, the temperance movement riots, the revolt in the village of Bezdna, the newspaper *The Bell*'s calls for revolutionary struggle, the arrest of students and a number of professors, and the temporary closure of the university. Then there were proclamations of a kind never before heard in Russia. The *Young Russia* proclamation used utterly Herzenian language to call for violence against the regime. We know that the fires lasted for more than two weeks and occurred in different areas of the city: on Bol'shaia Okhta, Iamskaia Street, in the Moskovskaia, Karetnaia, and 3rd Admiraltesikaia districts, and on Malaia Okhta, where the entire Soldatskaia outskirts burned down. The reason was unusually hot and dry weather that had settled over St. Petersburg. The "Apraksin" fire was especially strong, destroying several thousand shops in the Apraksin Yard on May 28 (see Kantor 2016, 261–266; Demchenko 2019, 181–190).

Of course, the students were accused of both the proclamation and the fires, and the proclamation itself was understandably linked to the fires. Newspapers (official, semi-liberal, and liberal) printed theories, rumors, and gossip. Both the proclamation and the fires greatly concerned Dostoevsky. We have his 1873 reminiscences of a visit to Chernyshevsky during this time, as well as Chernyshevsky's reminiscences of the same episode. Dostoevsky begins his version by expressing his sympathy for Chernyshevsky:

> I met Nikolai Gravilovich Chernyshevsky for the first time in 1859, the first year after my return from Siberia, but I do not remember where or how. After that, we met on occasion, but very infrequently, and chatted a bit, but very little. However, we always shook hands. Herzen told me that Chernyshevsky made an unpleasant impression on him, that is, his appearance, his manner. I liked Chernyshevsky's appearance and manner. (Dostoevsky 1972–1990, 21: 24–25)

It is interesting that Herzen told everyone how much he disliked Chernyshevsky. Dostoevsky considered the copy of the proclamation attached to his door an example of Chernyshevsky's influence among the radicals, though he did not think he was involved in composing it.

I remember it was about five o'clock in the afternoon. I found Nikolai Gavrilovich completely alone, not even the servants were home, and he answered the door himself. He greeted me extremely cordially and led me to his office.

"Nikolai Gavrilovich, what is this?" I pulled out the proclamation. He took it as if it were a completely unfamiliar object and read through it. There were only ten lines or so.

"Well, what about it?" he asked with a slight smile.

"Surely they aren't so stupid and ridiculous? Surely you can stop them and put an end to this abomination?"

His reply was extremely authoritative and impressive:

"Surely you don't suppose that I'm in solidarity with them, nor think that I could have participated in composing this scrap of paper?"

"I wasn't suggesting that," I replied, "and didn't even think it necessary to assure you of that. But in any case, it must be stopped at all costs. Your word is authoritative for them, and of course they fear your opinion."

"I don't know any of them."

"I am certain of that, too. But you don't need to know or talk to them personally. All you need to do is express your censure out loud somewhere, and it will reach them."

"It may, yet produce no effect." (Dostoevsky 1972–1990, 21: 24–25)

The last line was apparently decisive. Dostoevsky himself realized that the people who composed these kinds of texts could not be the close associates of an armchair scholar. Chernyshevsky's version, written in response to Dostoevsky's reminiscences, differs. He directly links the latter's visit with the first. Evidently, Dostoevsky had changed his reason for the visit later, after considering everything that had happened, although the general point of his request was to stop the revolutionaries. Chernyshevsky described the writer's visit as follows:

A few days after the fire that wiped out the Tolkuchii Market, a servant handed me a visitor's card with the name F.M. Dostoevsky and told me that this visitor wanted to see me. I immediately entered the drawing room; it was a man of medium height or a bit shorter than average, and whose face was somewhat familiar to me from his portraits. Approaching him, I asked him to have a seat on the couch, and I sat beside him with words to the effect that I was pleased to see the author of *Poor Folk*. After a few seconds of hesitation, he responded to my greeting with an immediate explanation of the purpose of his visit in short, simple, and direct words, more or less as follows: "I have come to you with an urgent request related to an important matter. You are a close associate of those who burned the Tolkuchii Market, and you have influence over them. I beg you to keep them from repeating what they have done." (Chernyshevsky 1939–1953, 1: 777)

Chernyshevsky, amazed that the public "could combine ideas about me with notions of arson at the Tolkuchii Market," nevertheless promised to use his influence in order to reassure Dostoevsky. All the same, Dostoevsky's

562 V. K. KANTOR

experience as an innocently condemned convict allowed him to take a different view of the situation.

He penned an article titled "The Fires" ["*Pozhary*"] for his journal *Vremia*, but this only became known in the early 1970s. The article was not only censored, but the Emperor himself asked who the author was, and its publication was forbidden. Among other things, Dostoevsky wrote:

> Quite a few speculations travel through the people. One that we wouldn't say is quite widespread but is at least reliably present concerns our young generation, our poor students. We hope we can be allowed candor in this case: the matter is too important and touches on the most urgent issues. We cannot be silent whenever the most terrible reproaches land on our Russian youth who are dedicated to learning and on whom all of thinking Russia's hopes are rightly placed. Here we must fully clarify the matter and bring everything out into the open. Among other things, the students are accused of the fires. And this is not only speculation by the common folk, but also by others in different spheres. We even believe that this speculation did not appear among the people on its own, or that the people came to it themselves, but that they perhaps heard it from the outside. It is very difficult to imagine that the people would suddenly and for no apparent reason suspect the students of such a terrible crime. Where, we wonder, did this suspicion come from? [...] Where are these facts uncovered by the investigation that would clearly prove the students' actual solidarity with phenomena like this? (Dostoevsky 1973, 49)

Perhaps it was impossible to write more candidly that young people had nothing to do with it, that it would generally be necessary to look for other powers capable of provocation for achieving government goals, but as we all know, the people in charge never leave traces of their crimes. That said, no one else could have ordered a provocation like this, and after spending time in the Petrashevskii Circle and being arrested, Dostoevsky could understand better than most how provocation worked. "The Petrashevskii Circle [...] had been watched for a long time already, and in the evenings, a certain young man from the Ministry of Internal Affairs would come [...] a man who carefully attended the gatherings, who *himself incited others to radical discussions* and then wrote down everything said at the meetings and conveyed it to the authorities," recalled another member of the group, the writer A.P. Miliukov (Tiun'kin 1990, 266; italics mine). This young man was a certain P.D. Antonelli, son of a Russian art scholar. He even acquainted the Petrashevskii Circle with "ferocious Circassians" who were supposedly ready "for a coup," but were in reality Nicholas' former palace guards. Members of the circle were arrested and convicted, but no revolutionary plots were uncovered. They were condemned anyway. Something similar happened after the May fires.

Sovremennik was immediately suspended after the May fires for eight months. Suspended, but not shuttered! The state's games with the public were astounding. They let everyone know they were unhappy with the journal, and that perhaps it might suffer financially, if not collapse, during its eight months without publication. I think a financial rationale was also behind it. In July, Chernyshevsky's wife Ol'ga Sokratovna departed with the children for Saratov. What was to be done when rumors were already labeling him the initiator, the radicals' chieftain, a mysterious one behind the fire's initiators, a kind of Russian Nero? Nero, at least, was an *emperor*, while Chernyshevsky was a mere *litterateur*.

What was to be done? The answer was already clear: Chernyshevsky knew that he bore no responsibility under Russian law, though it is amazing that such a sober man could believe that Russia had already entered the legal fold. The regime tried to push him into emigration to silence him, even while understanding that he was not at fault, though he did contribute to a societal desire for independence. In a May 5, 1863, report by an agent of the Third Department (i.e. the secret police), we find this relevant passage: "On April 23, some sort of courier from the military governor-general came to Chernyshevsky's. He first asked the doorman whether it was Chernyshevsky's home, then went inside when he received an affirmative answer. After a few minutes, the courier exited, accompanied by Chernyshevsky, who thanked him very much for something" (Chernyshevskaia 1968, 102–103).

We find an explanation for this visit, and a highly interesting one at that, in the memoirs of Sergei G. Stakhevich, a fellow political convict who was with Chernyshevsky at the Aleksandrovskii Factory from 1868 to 1870, where he held detailed conversations with the famous convict, whom the other prisoners had given the respectful nickname "core of virtue." Stakhevich recalls the episode with the courier from the St. Petersburg governor-general, albeit confusing the title by referring to the prince as a count:

> Shortly before Nikolay Gavrilovich's arrest, he was visited by an adjutant of the St. Petersburg governor-general, a Count Suvorov; this count was a personal friend of Emperor Alexander II. On behalf of his superior, the adjutant advised Nikolai Gavrilovich to go abroad, and that he would soon be arrested if he did not leave. "How can I leave? It's such a hassle! [...] the foreign passport [...] The police may already prevent issuing me a passport." "Don't worry about that: we'll bring you a passport, and we'll bring you to the border ourselves, that way you won't face any obstacles from anyone." "Why is the count so concerned on my behalf? Well, they'll arrest me; what's it to him?" "If they arrest you, it means, essentially, that they'll be banishing you, without any wrongdoing, for your articles, even though they were rejected by the censors. The count prefers that the sovereign, his personal friend, not bear the stain of banishing an innocent writer." The conversation ended with Nikolay Gavrilovich's refusal to follow Suvorov's advice: "whatever happens, I will not go abroad." (Stakhevich 1982, 75)

It was, of course, a fateful choice, though some little hope remained: he had not written or done anything illegal. It is amazing how much the "philosophers' ships" are part of the Russian tradition, one of the archetypes of the Russian government's attitude toward dissenting voices. There has always been destruction, prison, or penal servitude, but as early as Alexander II, the Great

Liberator, attempts were made to expel disagreeable figures abroad when their activities did not run afoul of Russian criminal law. Lenin remained within this Russian administrative tradition and Chernyshevsky within the circle of thinkers who refused to take their seats on "philosophers' ships" and whose persecution continued.

Advocating freedom within an authoritarian regime is difficult. When there exists an insane fear that a free man, even posthumously, can revive the notion of freedom in the minds of his people, there will be an attempt to remove him from society. The tsar forbade burying Pushkin in St. Petersburg, sending his body by cart to Mikhailovskoe at night, the coffin wrapped in bast matting, accompanied by the police captain F.S. Rakeev, the very same man who, as a colonel twenty-five years later, would arrest Chernyshevsky. Chernyshevsky was arrested and imprisoned in Peter and Paul Fortress on July 7, 1862 (Demchenko 2019, 205–208).

It is curious that the extreme radicals Bakunin and Nechaev were, like the regime, also against Chernyshevsky. Dostoevsky came out of his meeting with Chernyshevsky firmly convinced that he had nothing to do with the blood-soaked proclamations of Young Russia. Nor is it a coincidence that, in the drafts of *Demons*, the character Petr Verkhovenskii (Nechaev) labels Chernyshevsky a "reactionary," juxtaposing his ideas with total destruction: "I really don't care; it doesn't interest me in the least whether the serfs are free or not, whether this business is good or ruined. Let the Serno-Solov'evichs worry about the reactionary Chernyshevskys! We have something else. You know: the worse, the better (in my opinion, tear it all up by the roots!)" (Dostoevsky 1972–1990, 11: 159). Relations between these two Russian thinkers were not amiable, but we also have the word of Marx and Engels on this very subject. Like Dostoevsky, they also defended Chernyshevsky against Bakunin and Nechaev, who had written that Chernyshevsky was obviously serving the regime when he protested against radicalism, that he was dreaming of a cushy position:

> The *cushy position* Chernyshevsky received from the Russian government was a cell in a Siberian prison, while Bakunin, free of that danger by virtue of his work on European revolutions, limited himself to demonstrations *from abroad*. And just when the government strictly forbade any mention of Chernyshevsky's name in the press, Mr. Bakunin and Mr. Nechaev attacked him. (Marx and Engels 1961, 397)

Above all, Marx liked Chernyshevsky's notes in *Essays on Political Economy (According to Mill)* and called him "a great Russian scientist and critic" for this work. Interestingly enough, Chernyshevsky also considered this his best work. As Nikolai Reingardt recalled, "Nikolai Gavrilovich objected that his novel *What Is to Be Done?* could not be considered his most outstanding work because he, Chernyshevsky, has no literary talent whatsoever. He considers his most outstanding, serious work to be his commentaries on Mill's political economy" (Reingardt 1959, 274).

For most Russian readers, however, he was the author of *What Is to Be Done?* How exactly and where was this novel written? He wrote it while confined in the Alekseev Ravelin, where he sat alone from early July to late October, spending four months in total isolation from the world, deprived of books, paper, and ink. He was not even summoned for interrogation. Time passed, nonetheless, and with no explanation of why he was arrested, nor on what grounds. Why were they keeping him in the Ravelin? Finally, October 30 arrived. There were no questions asked. It was clear that they had no evidence against him, nor anything to accuse him of. As he would later write to the emperor, he waited another two weeks. He asked to be summoned to the Commission of Inquiry. He received no summons, so he asked the commandant of Peter and Paul Fortress for permission to write the emperor. They permitted this, and the letter has been preserved. I will discuss it, but first we require some context. Very often, Russian writers who found themselves disgraced, in prison, in exile, or in penal servitude wrote letters to the emperor in which they repented and begged for mercy. Let us take a moment, for example, to consider the letter from Mikhail Bakunin, who was also considered the "ringleader" of each and every European liberal (like those who led the Dresden uprising in 1849). The Germans arrested him and handed him over to Emperor Nicholas, who imprisoned him in the Fortress. A couple of years later, he wrote his *Confession* to the emperor. Here we might suggest that one can only really confess to members of the clergy, but Bakunin was not interested in subtleties: "Your Majesty! I am a great criminal and undeserving of your clemency!" (Bakunin 2010, 183). Another interesting detail: at the beginning of Bakunin's "Confession," Nicholas scribbled a note for his heir, Alexander II. "This is worth your reading; it is highly interesting and instructive" (Bakunin 2010, 239). The Tsar-Liberator knew perfectly well from his father's lessons how prisoners in the fortress were expected to write their ruler. Incidentally, Alexander II released Bakunin from prison. This, however, is what Chernyshevsky wrote:

> Your All-Merciful Majesty. Over the course of this case, I have concluded that there are no charges against me. I knew this and said so at the time of my arrest... Your Majesty, I have reason to address your highness as a man innocent of all guilt, and if you find that I am, then be kind, I beseech you, and grant me justice by ordering my release from arrest. Your majesty's subject, N. Chernyshevsky. November 20, 1862. (Chernyshevskaia 1968, 268–269)

Consider what is so unexpected in this letter to the emperor. Note the total lack of exclamation points, as well as the *demand for justice* ("be kind, I beseech you, and grant me justice by ordering my release from arrest"). Of course, the pinnacle of his disrespect is the signature. The usual signature line is "*Your loyal subject.*" Chernyshevsky writes simply "*Your subject,*" a bare factual statement of the relationship between the subject of the empire and his suzerain. Compare

566   V. K. KANTOR

this to Bakunin's closing line: "Having lost the right to call myself a loyal subject of Your Imperial Majesty, I sign this with a sincere heart: the penitent sinner, Mikhail Bakunin" (2010, 184).

Bakunin groveled for exile, fleeing to Europe, where he continued trying to destroy Russia, created the horrifying *Catechism of a Revolutionary* with Nechaev, scolded Chernyshevsky's *What Is to Be Done?* for being reactionary, and argued that Chernyshevsky was only using his novel to secure himself a "cushy position." The Chernyshevsky case certainly brought out all the best and worst aspects of human nature.

Vasilii F. Antonov called Chernyshevsky a "gradualist reformer" (Antonov 2010, 174), and this is a very important observation. He was not calculating enough for revolution. Few of his contemporaries acknowledged his originality, but it is worth mentioning what the most observant conservative writer, A.S. Suvorin, said about Chernyshevsky: "He is the equal of the best figures of the past," and furthermore, he managed to do what the Slavophiles only dreamed of: he dared to "free himself from the cradle of Western thought and [...] to speak for himself [...] using his own words, not those of strangers" (Lanskoi 1973, 380).

He wanted to build Russia, not destroy it.

What about this novel that he composed in almost one copy, and with such incredible speed? I would first add another note about the author's productivity. From the moment he was finally allowed to read and write, he read authors available in the Ravelin, including Dickens, Georges Sand, Sterne, Gogol, Lermontov, Kol'tsov, Tiutchev, Fet, Béranger, Heine, Pomialovskii, Horace, Ovid, Reybaud, Currer Bell (Charlotte Brontë), Montaigne, Flaubert, Lesage, Smollett, Freytag, Darwin, Vogt, Thomas Huxley, Lyell, and Owen. At the same time, he continued his translation work, for example, translating the fifteenth and sixteenth volumes of Schlosser's *Universal History* and twenty pages of Gervinus' *History of the Nineteenth Century*, and on July 9 and 24 he sent *Sovremennik* his translations of volumes seven and eight of Macaulay's *History of England* (ninety-one pages). He also began to translate Rousseau's *Confessions*. Pavel Shchegolev has calculated that, over his entire term in the fortress, Chernyshevsky wrote enough to fill 250 printer's sheets (4000 regular pages plus!) if not a bit more. On average, he left his signature on 11.5 printer's sheets (or more than 200 pages) per month (Shchegolev 1989, 33–34). He was a fantastic worker, but why did he choose the novel over more academic genres? First, he had made attempts at literary works since his youth, and second, he wanted to begin his own Encyclopedia in the form of a captivating novel, as the French Enlightenment writers had done.

On December 12, 1862, Chernyshevsky completed his translation of the two Schlosser volumes. He then appealed to the authorities for permission to purchase and translate the seventeenth volume, and also reported that he "had begun to write a fictional story whose content, of course, is completely innocent. It is taken from family life and has nothing at all to do with political issues, but if there is any kind of objection to busying himself with fiction, then, of course Chernyshevsky," as he described himself in the third person in his note on December 15, 1862, "would abandon it" (Chernyshevsky 1939–1953, 16: 364). He is referring to his novel *What Is to Be Done?*, which he began to write on December 14, 1862, and completed on April 4, 1863.

The novel became a public event. Young people read it as a call to resist the authorities, but the idea behind *What Is to Be Done?* was a simple one: we must believe in one another and help one another, relying on the idea of a rational egoism that the author derived from Christ's golden rule, to love your neighbor as yourself. To love another, you must first love yourself. As nearly everyone notes, the primary literary opponent of Chernyshevsky's novel was Dostoevsky. Indeed, he seems to be polemicizing with Chernyshevsky himself: not with his ideas, but with his belief that man is a free and good creature in an anthropological sense. Here, Dostoevsky is closer to Kant, who wrote about the "innate evil" in human nature, but there is an evident affinity to Chernyshevsky himself, too:

> Chernyshevsky's convictions never offended me. It is possible to hold great respect for a person while vehemently disagreeing with his opinions. Here, however, I can say something that is not entirely unfounded, and even offer a small bit of evidence. One of the last issues (if not the very last issue) of the journal *Epokha*, which was shuttered around that time, published a long critique of Chernyshevsky's "famous" novel *What Is to Be Done?* The article is remarkable and came from a well-known pen. And guess what? The article credits everything to the mind and talent of Chernyshevsky. This was said about his novel, even very passionately so. No one has ever doubted his remarkable mind. We said so in our own article on the qualities and evasions of his mind, but the very seriousness of that article testified to our critic's due respect for the merits of the author he was examining. Now you must agree: if I hated him because of his convictions, of course I would not have allowed an article in my journal to discuss Chernyshevsky with due respect; after all, I was in fact the editor of *Epokha*, and no one else. (Dostoevsky 1972–1990, 21: 29–30)

Dostoevsky was somewhat mistaken. He was referring to an article by Nikolai Strakhov, but this article was not published in *Epokha*: the journal was closed by then. Strakhov's article was first published in 1865 in *Biblioteka dlia chteniia*, but Dostoevsky obviously knew its content. Strakhov's text somehow reminded him of Belinsky's reaction to his own first novel, *Poor Folk*. Strakhov had written:

> There is one phenomenon among this multitude that seems highly durable. It is the novel *What Is to Be Done?*, which, I believe, will endure in literature, because the impression it produces it not at all a ridiculous one. Even if one is inclined to laugh, one will lose that inclination to laughter upon rereading these thirty printer's sheets. The novel is written with such enthusiasm that it is impossible to treat it coolly and objectively, which good-natured and sincere laughter requires. Hence, it elicits indignation, or an overall uneasy feeling, one that readers will perhaps notice. And should that be the case, I will say that it nevertheless requires a lot for that. (Strakhov 2008, [1890], 558)

568   V. K. KANTOR

It is astonishing that Lenin gave the identical title *What Is to Be Done?* to his book about creating a revolutionary organization completely subordinate to its leader, given that Chernyshevsky's novel argues for a lack of any kind of centralization and the freedom of individuals within the association. Clear-headed readers with no partisanship toward one political group or another clearly saw this, recognizing that Lenin was instead following in the footsteps of Bakunin, Nechaev, and Tkachev. "Need we demonstrate," wrote Fyodor Stepun, "the traces of Bakunin's passion for destruction and the fascist theories of Tkachev and Nechaev that can only be found in the programs and tactics of Bolshevism?" (Stepun 2000, 635). Stepun's thoughts on Chernyshevsky were just as distinct: "It was clear to Chernyshevsky that everything was premature, moving at a completely senseless pace" (ibid., 351). Nevertheless, I would repeat that treating Chernyshevsky as a martyr to Tsarism was significant for those planning for revolution against the autocracy. Why, however, did Strakhov call his analysis of the novel "Happy People"? Strange as it may seem, the title derives from the novel's Christian pathos. After all, Christianity values both suffering and happiness, and even happiness in suffering. "The novel teaches us how to be happy." For a believer, the world is designed in such a way that we can construct the right relationships within it. There is only one reply to Herzen's question "*Who is to blame?*": the world's design itself is guilty, or if you prefer, God. This makes rational positive activity impossible. There is a different reply to Chernyshevsky's question "*What is to be done?*": we can build the right relationships within God's world. The heroes overcome their suffering through the words of the Gospel, where happiness is found in suffering: "Blessed are those persecuted for the truth, for theirs is the Kingdom of Heaven. Blessed are you when they reproach you and persecute you and slander you in every way because of Me. Rejoice and be glad, for great is your reward in heaven, for they also persecuted the prophets who came before you" (Mathew 5: 10–12).

Speaking of the novel's influence, we should not forget that this was the author's sole complete and, most importantly, published artistic work during his lifetime. All the more staggering is the fact that his readership lasted for nearly a century, as well as his influence on the content and level of Russian literature in what we might call the "post-Chernyshevsky era." To understand its success, we should look for evidence of how it was perceived by the public in those years. As a contemporary and enemy of Chernyshevsky, Professor Tsion, quipped ironically, a European "will ask you, who is this Chernyshevsky? You will respond and say that Chernyshevsky wrote a bad novel, even in the opinion of the nihilists themselves […] the novel *What Is to Be Done?*, which nevertheless became the nihilists' gospel" (Tsion 1886, 776–777). That word "gospel" explains a lot, though we should take it seriously rather than sarcastically. In his novel, the thinker actualized the New Testament, since his "new people" had to herald a better life. It is worth noting that he practically knew the Holy Scripture by heart. For example, Chernyshevsky suggested using Christ's sermons to study foreign languages: "As a practical device for learning the language, Nikolai Gavrilovich recommended reading books *with a well-known text, above all the*

Gospels" (Demchenko 1982, 26; italics mine). Here is how he described new people studying a foreign language: "Kirsanov did otherwise: he learned German from various books with lexicons, just as Lopukhov did French, though he himself learned French differently, from one book, without a lexicon: *the Gospels, a very familiar book*. So he grabbed the Geneva version of the New Testament and read it eight times; by the ninth, he already understood everything, that is, he was ready" (Chernyshevsky 1975, 147; italics mine). Chernyshevsky's novel is permeated with memories of the Gospel.

Curiously, Chernyshevsky's heroes never transfer responsibility for their own actions onto others. The main condition of the Christian life, after all, is responsibility for oneself. "By making man responsible," Dostoevsky wrote, "Christianity thereby recognizes his freedom" (Dostoevsky 1972–1990, 21: 16). Freedom defines Dostoevsky's way of life, as well. Obeying the will of God, he was free from subordination to the authorities. Like Dostoevsky, Chernyshevsky—and this bears repeating—despite his doubts, carried his hosannas "through the crucible of doubt," but he carried them nonetheless. It is astonishing that he was always accompanied by two devotional icons, personal icons that he took with him from his father's home, as his spiritual legacy. These were an icon of the Mother of God and, of course, an icon of Christ set in a decorative covering. It was no coincidence that people compared him to the latter.

We should add to these argumentative responses Dostoevsky's brilliant novella *Notes from the Underground*, a very unique polemical answer to *What Is to Be Done?* in which the antihero argues the impossibility of doing good. The author's idea is clear, despite the gossip and the anti-Chernyshevsky message: Chernyshevsky is correct that it is necessary to do good, but he thinks too highly of man; man is so vile and disgusting that even Christ could not repair him. I do not quite understand why this unnamed antihero's maxim is cited by so many scholars as a wise objection to the idea of reason as preached by Chernyshevsky (see Voge 2003; Shestov 1995; Dzhekson 1998; Budanova 2016). The idea of reason as the basis of the Christian message is a classical one, expressed by the apostle John: "We know that we are from God and that the whole world lies in evil. We also know that the Son of God came and gave us light and reason" (1 Jn 5: 19–20). Naturally, the theomachist/paradoxicalist opposes reason. The underground man is essentially the original version of the Grand Inquisitor, who tells Christ that man is weaker and baser than He imagined him to be! Here, the antihero begins with himself, showing that generosity of spirit is impossible for him. He understands that he is a wrongdoer and comes to the same conclusion as the Grand Inquisitor: "Well, try, give us, for example, more independence, untie our hands, expand our range of activity, relax your guardianship, and we, I assure you, we will immediately ask you to return that guardianship to us" (Dostoevsky 1972–1990, 5: 178). Dostoevsky understood quite well that the evil was inside the hero himself, and not in his surroundings. As we know, he generally thought little of the "environmental" theory, that a man's crimes could be blamed on his environment. Chernyshevsky wrote in his novel that people could overcome the filth surrounding them, but not ordinary people. It is interesting that the average man was so terrified of the kind of women's liberation that Chernyshevsky's heroine Vera Pavlovna proclaimed.

Dostoevsky mocked this kind of fear. Below is an 1866 record by Maria Aleksandrovna Ivanova, a niece of Dostoevsky. To clarify the context, the protagonist of this real-life vaudeville was Aleksandr Petrovich Karepin, a relative of his brother-in-law, the husband of Dostoevsky's sister, Varvara Mikhailovna (Karepina by marriage).

> When he came to visit us at the dacha in Lyublino (the summer of 1866), Karepin was not yet married, but he constantly dreamed of his ideal bride, whom he drew as necessarily short-haired and no older than sixteen. He jealously guarded his bride ahead of time. "My children," he would say, "will be pure-blooded Karepins!" [...] He very much disliked emancipated women and said his wife would stay far away from any modern ideas about women's equality and employment. At that time, nearly everyone had read Chernyshevsky's novel *What Is to Be Done?* and teased Karepin, predicting his wife would have the same fate as the novel's heroine. Dostoevsky once told him that the government was encouraging wives to flee their husbands to St. Petersburg to train at sewing machines, and there were even special trains organized for runaway wives. Karepin believed him, grew angry, lost his temper, and was nearly ready to fight over his future bride. One day, Dostoevsky proposed arranging an improvised play, a trial between Karepin and his future wife. Fyodor Mikhailovich portrayed the magistrate, wearing one of the Ivanov sister's red sweaters, a bucket on his head, and paper glasses. Next to him was the court secretary, Sof'ia Aleksandrovna Ivanova, and the Karepins, husband and wife, as defendants. Fyodor Mikhailovich delivered a brilliant speech in defense of the wife, who wanted to flee to St. Petersburg and learn how to sew at a sewing machine. In the end, he accuses the husband and sentences him to exile at the North Pole. Karepin angrily rushes at Dostoevsky. The curtain falls on Act One. (Volgin 2013, 284–285)

As we see, both the novel and Chernyshevsky himself were well within the range of both serious meditation and the culture of humor in nineteenth-century Russia.

There is also an important point of affinity between these two thinkers, since his novel's influence on all of subsequent Russian literature is far more interesting than its impact on Chernyshevsky himself. Mikhail Bakhtin wrote that Chernyshevsky had posed the problem of creating ideological novels in Russian literature. Chernyshevsky's novel not only demanded responses, both polemical and positive, but also created a certain level of debate about the universe and about Russia. The questions that resound in his work had never been posed before him and offered a paradigm that all reasoning henceforth had to employ. If we make no concessions, then Dostoevsky was the only one among his contemporaries not overwhelmed by this subject matter and set of issues. Moreover, as Bakhtin indicated, Chernyshevsky came very close to the idea of the polyphonic novel that Dostoevsky would develop:

The new "objective" authorial position (whose realization Chernyshevsky finds only in Shakespeare) permits the characters' points of view to unfold to their maximal fullness and independence. (Chernyshevsky finds this only in Shakespeare.) This allows the protagonists' point of view to be revealed in all its fullness and independence. Each character *freely* (without the author's interference) reveals and substantiates the rightness of his position: "each says for himself: 'the full right is on my side'—you judge these conflicting claims. I do not judge." Precisely in this freedom for other points of view to reveal themselves without any finalizing evaluations from the author does Chernyshevsky see the chief advantage of the new "objective" form of novel. We emphasize that Chernyshevsky saw in this no betrayal of his strong and fixed convictions. Thus we can only say that Chernyshevsky came very close indeed to the idea of polyphony. [...] Such is the interesting conception of new novelistic structure by one of Dostoevsky's contemporaries, who keenly sensed, as Dostoevsky himself did, the extraordinary multi-voicedness of his epoch [...] Chernyshevsky clearly felt the need to go beyond the prevailing monologic form of the novel. (Bakhtin 1984, 67)

If we discussed both thinkers' attitudes toward Christianity's situation in Russia, we would need to say the following. It was Christianity that Chernyshevsky tried to revive at the new historical turning point, though he also knew of failed attempts of this kind: Lutheranism, the Old Believers, and so forth. He understood, of course, how incredibly difficult this transformation would be, but he believed it was possible. Dostoevsky, another Russian genius who also dreamed of reviving and strengthening Christianity in Russia, nevertheless showed that this kind of victory was impossible in this world, for the world lies in evil and the devil rules as its prince. As the Kingdom of Christ is not of this world, Christ must yield to the Grand Inquisitor, who, as Alyosha Karamazov says, "does not believe in God; that's his whole secret!" (Dostoevsky 1972–1990, 14: 238). Believers are bound for prison, the pillory, penal servitude, in short, Golgotha, which neither Dostoevsky nor Chernyshevsky was able to avoid. Each of them in turn bore his own cross, but neither was broken, which is why they remain spiritual leaders of Russian society.

Translated by Brad Damaré

Notes

1. For a detailed discussion of Chernyshevsky, see in particular Kantor (2016). See also Kantor (2001, 2018).
2. At the beginning of his career Dostoevsky met Belinsky, who was defaming Christ. Later, in his *Diary of a Writer*, Dostoevsky wrote about Belinsky: "Whenever I mentioned Christ, his face changed as if he was going to cry" (Dostoevsky 1980, 11). When the adolescent Chernyshevsky was leaving for the University, the seminary inspector said to his mother: "It is a shame that you are depriving the clergy of this star" (Zakharova 2012, 128).
3. See Alexander Dolinin (1995, 136–137) and Brian Boyd (1990, 416–417).

572 V. K. KANTOR

4. In the Russian original:
Vitiaz' gorestnoi figury,
Dostoevsky, milyi pyshch,
Na nosu literatury
Rdeesh' ty, kak novyi pryshch.
5. Chernyshevsky's article "Nepochtitel'nost' k avtoritetam" was published in 1861 in *Sovremennik* no. 6. It offers a review of A. Tocqueville's book *Democracy in America* (Kiev, 1860, vols. 1 and 2).
6. The next eight articles (articles 2–9) appeared in *Sovremennik* the following year (1856). See also Chernyshevsky (1947).
7. This first appeared—heavily affected by censorship—in *Sovremennik* 1861, no. 9.
8. *Sovremennik* 1861, no. 9 (division III, pp. 99–149), signed as N.-bov (on the cover: N.A.-bov).

BIBLIOGRAPHY

Antonov, Vasilii F. 2010. *N.G. Chernyshevsky: Obshchestvennyi ideal anarkhista*. Moscow: Editorial URSS.

Bakhtin, Mikhail. 1984. *Problems of Dostoevsky's Poetics*. Edited and translated by Caryl Emerson. Introduction by Wayne C. Booth. Minneapolis, MN: University of Minnesota Press.

Bakunin, Mikhail A. 2010. *Ispoved'*. St. Petersburg: Azbuka-klassika.

Boyd, Brian. 1990. *Vladimir Nabokov: The Russian Years*. Princeton, NJ: Princeton University Press.

Budanova, Nina F. 2016. 'Zapiski iz podpol'ia.' Zagadki tsenzurnoi istorii povesti. In *Dostoevsky. Materialy i issledovaniia*, vol. 21, 236–245. St. Petersburg: Nestor-istoriia.

Chernyshevskaia, Nina M. 1968. *Delo Chernyshevskogo. Sbornik dokumentov*. Saratov: Privolshskoe knizhnoe izdatel'stvo.

Chernyshevsky, Nikolay G. 1939–1953. *Polnoe sobranie sochinenii v 16 tomakh*. Moscow: GIKhL.

———. 1947. Ocherki gogolevskogo perioda russkoi literatury. In *Polnoe sobranie sochinenii v 16 tomakh*, ed. N.G. Chernushevsky, vol. 3, 5–309. Moscow: GIKhL.

———. 1975. *Chto delat'?* Leningrad: Nauka.

Demchenko, Adol'f A. 1982. *N.G. Chernyshevsky v vospominaniiakh sovremennikov*. Moscow: Khudozhestvennaia literatura.

———. 2019. *N.G. Chernyshevsky. Nauchnaia biografiia (1859–1889)*. Moscow: ROSSPEN.

Dobrolyubov, Nikolai A. 1961–1964. Zabitye liudi. In *Sobranie sochinenii v 9 tomakh*. Moscow: Goslitizdat.

Dolinin, Alexander. 1995. The Gift. In *The Garland Companion to Vladimir Nabokov*, ed. Vladimir E. Alexandrov, 135–168. New York, NY: Routledge.

Dostoevsky, Fyodor M. 1972–1990. *Polnoe sobranie sochinenii v 30 tomakh*. Leningrad: Nauka.

———. 1973. Peterburgskie pozhary 1862 g. i Dostoevsky. 'Pozhary.' Stat'ia pervaia. In *Novye materialy i issledovaniia. Literaturnoe nasledstvo*, ed. F.M. Dostoevsky, vol. 86, 16–54. Moscow: Nauka.

————. 1980. Dnevnik pisatelia. In *Polnoe sobranie sochinenii v 30 tomakh*. Vol. 21. Leningrad: Nauka.

Dzhekson, Robert Luis [Robert Louis Jackson]. 1998. *Iskusstvo Dostoevskogo. Bredy i noktiurny*. Moscow: RADIKS.

Kantor, Vladimir. 2001. Pavel Smerdyakov and Ivan Karamazov. In *Dostoevsky and the Christian Tradition*, ed. George Pattison and Diane Oenning Thompson, 189–220. Cambridge, UK: Cambridge University Press.

Kantor, Vladimir K. 2016. *Srublennoe drevo zhizni. Sud'ba Nikolaia Chernyshevskogo*. Moscow and St. Petersburg: Tsentr gumanitarnykh initsiativ.

Kantor, Vladimir. 2018. Chernyshevsky and Dostoevsky: paralleli. In *Literatura rosyjska: idee, poetyki, interpretacje*, ed. P. Fasta, 101–131. Katovice: Stowarzyszenie Inicjatyw Wydawniczych.

Lanskoi, Leonid R. (ed.). 1973. Dostoevsky v neizdannoi perepiske sovremennikov. In *F.M. Dostoevsky. Novye materialy i issledovaniia*. Literaturnoe Nasledstvo vol. 86, 349–566. Moscow: Nauka.

Lebedev, Andrei V. 1989. *Fragmenty rannikh grecheskikh filosofov*. Part 1. Moscow: Nauka.

Lotman, Lidiia M. 1955. Grigorovich. In *Istoriia russkoi literatury v 10 tomakh*. Vol. 7. Moscow, Leningrad: AN SSSR. Institut russkaia literatura (Pushkinskii Dom).

Marx, Karl, and Friedrich Engels. 1961. Al'ians sotsialisticheskoi demokratii i mezhdunarodnoe t-vo rabochikh. In *Sochineniia*, 2nd ed. Vol. 18. Moscow: Gospolitizdat.

Reingardt, Nikolai V. 1959. Vstrechi v Astrakhani. In *N.G. Chernyshevsky v vospominaniiakh sovremennikov v 2 tomakh*. Vol. 2. Saratov: Saratovskoe knizhnoe izdatel'stvo.

Serdiuchenko, Valerii L. 2003. Chitaia Nabokova. Chernyshevsky. *Neva* (8). http://magazines.russ.ru/neva/2003/8/serd-pr.html.

Shchegolev, Pavel E. 1989. *Alekseevskii ravelin*. Moscow: Kniga.

Shestov, Lev. 1995. *Dostoevsky i Nitshe (filosofiia tragedii)*. In *Sochineniia*, 15–175. Moscow: Raritet.

Stakhevich, Sergei G. (ed.). 1982. Sredi politicheskikh prestupnikov. In *N.G. Chernyshevsky v vospominaniiakh sovremennikov*. Moscow: Khudozhestvennaia literatura.

Stepun, Fyodor A. 2000. *Sochineniia*. Edited by Vladimir K. Kantor. Moscow: ROSSPEN.

Strakhov, Nikolai N. 2008 [1890]. Schastlivye liudi. In *N.G. Chernyshevsky: pro et contra. Antalogiia*. Edited by Adol'f A. Demchenko, 555–576. St. Petersburg: RKhGA.

Tiun'kin, Konstantin I. (ed.). 1990. *F.M. Dostoevsky v vospominaniiakh sovremennikov, v 2 tomakh*, 1. Moscow: Khudozhestvennaia literatura.

Tolstoy, Lev N. 1955. *O literature*. Moscow: GIKhL.

Tsion, Il'ia F. 1886. Nigilisty i nigilizm. *Russkii vestnik* 6: 776–777.

Turgenev, Ivan S. 1978. *Polnoe sobranie sochinenii i pisem v 30-tomakh*. Moscow: Nauka.

Vyazemsky, Pyotr A. Prince. 1887–1896. Zametki. 'Svobodoi dorozhu...' In *P.A. Vyazemsky. Polnoe sobranie sochinenii kniazia P.A. Viazemskogo*. 11. St. Petersburg: izd. grafa S.D. Sheremeteva.

Voge, Peter Norman. 2003. *Dostoevsky: sverzhenie idolov*. St. Petersburg: Vsemirnoe slovo.

Volgin, Igor' L., ed. 2013. *Khronika roda Dostoevskikh*. Moscow: Fond Dostoevskogo.

Zakharova, Inna E. 2012. Materialy k biographii G. I. Chernyshevskogo. In *Stat'i, issledovaniia, materialy. Sbornik nauchnykh trudov*, ed. N.G. Chernyshevsky, Issue 18. Saratov: Izd-vo Saratovskogo universiteta.

CHAPTER 26

Tolstoy's Philosophy of Life

Lina Steiner

I

The last three decades have witnessed a remarkable resurgence of interest in Tolstoy's philosophical legacy both in Russia and in the West. Although Tolstoy was one of the most outspoken public intellectuals of the late nineteenth and early twentieth centuries, whose impassioned critique of authoritarianism, militarism, and religious obscurantism resonated with audiences throughout the world, his philosophical and political writings have not yet received the attention they deserve.[1] This was partly due to censorship, which kept some of Tolstoy's most incisive writings under a ban, while forcing the writer to cut, revise, and dampen the rhetoric in many of his published works. After Tolstoy's death in 1910, his controversial legacy as an idiosyncratic philosopher and religious thinker occasioned a heated debate among Russian intellectuals, including radicals, liberals, and representatives of the school of Russian religious philosophy.[2] However, after the Bolshevik victory in 1917 this debate gradually subsided as the ruling party assumed ideological control over the humanities and set out to revise the national canon. Throughout the Soviet period Tolstoy's legacy was handled with great caution. Certain topics, such as Tolstoy's translation and philosophical critique of the New Testament, his comparative study of world religions, and his political philosophy, were practically forbidden.[3] Thus even such outstanding scholars as Boris Eikhenbaum and Viktor Shklovskii, both of whom were in the vanguard of the Russian Formalist movement in the

---

For my brother Nikolai Roussanov

L. Steiner (✉)
University of Bonn, Bonn, Germany
e-mail: lsteiner@uni-bonn.de

© The Author(s), under exclusive license to Springer Nature   575
Switzerland AG 2021
M. F. Bykova et al. (eds.), *The Palgrave Handbook of Russian Thought*,
https://doi.org/10.1007/978-3-030-62982-3_26

1910s and 1920s and subsequently turned to the study of Tolstoy, contributed now-canonic biographies which presented Tolstoy as first and foremost a literary artist.[4] Soviet critics' efforts to carve out a niche for formal literary studies as a field relatively uncontaminated by the ideological struggles and to inscribe Tolstoy into this niche is historically understandable and even commendable in so far as it helped seal off Tolstoy scholarship from contemporary political debates and minimized the damage done by dogmatic Marxist interpreters. At the same time, one has to admit that a purely literary approach that prioritizes aesthetic and formal issues over Tolstoy's moral, social, and political concerns cannot be satisfying in the long term and that the time is ripe for reevaluating the legacy of this idiosyncratic philosopher-poet.

Fortunately, in recent years there appeared a whole array of innovative studies which assign greater significance to Tolstoy's philosophical works, Biblical translations, and diaries.[5] Thus both the ideologically skewed Soviet-era representations of Tolstoy's art and thought and the old clichéd Western image of the Russian author as a naïve genius with quirky ideas are quickly fading into the past, making room for an alternative image of Tolstoy as an intellectual of great learning and acumen, whose unique combination of poetic and philosophical gifts made him both a major cultural force in his homeland and an active contributor to global cultural, religious, and political debates.[6]

This chapter will focus on Tolstoy's contribution to one of the most topical European debates of the second half of the nineteenth century: the debate on the meaning and value of life. In Germany, where this debate was stirred (or reignited) by Schopenhauer and Hartmann, it was symptomatic of the growing tension between the scientific and religious worldviews, as well as between positive science and classical German philosophy, whose optimistic faith in Humanity was shattered by the political cataclysms and the socioeconomic challenges of the 1840s and 1850s (see Beiser 2016). In Russia, the same period was likewise marked by great hardships, including the lost Crimean war and the economic crisis which spurred the Great Reforms. However, the prevalent mood was quite different from the pessimistic atmosphere of Germany and much of continental Europe. The abolition of serfdom, liberalization of the press and the judiciary system, as well as other liberal improvements inspired hope and ushered in Utopian fantasies, including Utopian socialism, spiritualism, and various permutations of the "Russian Idea."[7] It is telling that even an inveterate Westernizer enraptured by Schopenhauer, Ivan Turgenev, let himself be so carried away by the optimistic spirit of the moment that he found a way to end *Fathers and Children* (1862) not on a tragic note, but rather by striking a compromise between a Schopenhauerian worldview represented by the story of the "nihilist" Bazarov and a hopeful liberal scenario represented by the Kirsanov family.

Fathers and Children remains one of the most powerful literary representations of the Great Reforms era which sheds light on the intellectual atmosphere of the age of Tolstoy's youth and early adulthood.[8] At this time professional philosophy was only beginning to revive after having been suppressed for over a decade.[9] In the meantime, natural science and popular philosophical movements derived from positivism held sway, producing a whole generation of young "nihilists" with radical political views, fatalistically-minded positivists, or cynics devoid of convictions. A reaction against the scientific materialism of Feuerbach, Moleschott, Büchner, and other thinkers popular among the *intelligentsia* began as early as the mid-1850s, during the crisis caused by the Crimean fiasco. Interestingly, one of the pioneers of the emergent idealistic current in Russian philosophy was a renowned physician and public educator Nikolai Pirogov (Zenkovsky 1953, 376–392). In his 1856 essay "Questions of Life," published in the prestigious *Naval Journal*, Pirogov meditated on the problems of modern education, whose utilitarian bent encourages young people to adopt a purely pragmatic attitude to life, which cannot save one from an existential crisis bound to occur in every life (Pirogov 1985). Pirogov's experience as a military surgeon in Sevastopol lent credibility and authority to his pronouncements about the meaning of life and death, raising the Russian public's awareness of the contemporary value crisis. Having rejected religious dogmas and traditional folk beliefs, the educated part of society found itself face-to-face with rampant materialism. The soullessness of modern life could drive one to despair, argued Pirogov. Echoing Kant's injunction to embrace autonomy, he called on his readers to develop their own moral compass (Pirogov 1985, 45). A representative of the same generation, albeit from a different sociopolitical background, Alexander Herzen also argued, still more radically, that it was incumbent on modern intellectuals (including both the members of the Russian intelligentsia and their European counterparts) to reject the dogmas purveyed by the established religious and political orders and seek "rational maturity" (*razumnoe soznanie*, a term that encompasses both *Vernunft* and individual self-consciousness) by their own means.[10] Thus the ideal of self-guided Humanity which lay at the heart of the German Enlightenment and was known to the most educated Russians purely theoretically, as an ideal propounded by German philosophers they studied, had finally dawned on them as an intrinsically Russian problem.[11]

Among Pirogov's and Herzen's younger contemporaries, Tolstoy was particularly enthusiastic about their appeal to moral individualism. A former defender of Sevastopol, he entered literature at the point when Pirogov had just fired the opening salvo in a battle of idealists and materialists that shaped Russia's intellectual life in the 1860s and 1870s. But Tolstoy, having quickly earned acclaim as a writer of fiction, took another decade to develop his intellectual perspective. The first inklings of Tolstoy's inordinate philosophical propensity were revealed by *War and Peace*. However, many readers, who perceived and valued Tolstoy as a realistic novelist, were perplexed and some were even annoyed by his philosophical digressions.[12] It was not until Tolstoy's emergence (nearly thirty years after his first appearance as the author of *Childhood*) as the author of moral and religious tracts that the full extent of his philosophical commitment started to become obvious to a broader public.[13]

Tolstoy's first public encounter with an audience consisting almost entirely of professional philosophers occurred under the auspices of the newly-founded Moscow Psychological Society. The founder of this society, Nikolai Grot, invited Tolstoy to give a lecture alongside his own presentation, titled auspiciously "On the Freedom of the Will," on March 14, 1887.[14] Tolstoy's lecture, "On the Concept of Life," became the basis for his treatise *On Life* (Medzhibovskaya 2019, 25). Tolstoy's lecture was not very well received by philosophers, most of whom were budding neo-Kantians.[15] Tolstoy (who never joined any movements) presented an idiosyncratic position that emerged out of his life-long quest for self-understanding and a good life. If one reads this work attentively, one can discern in it Tolstoy's ongoing dialogues with many Western thinkers, from Plato, Epicurus, Aristotle, Montaigne, Pascal, and Leibniz to Rousseau, Kant, Herder, Hegel, and Schopenhauer (to name only the most obvious interlocutors). His work also reveals Tolstoy's more recent interests in the comparative history of religion and eastern philosophical and religious traditions, especially Confucianism and Buddhism. Finally, as my analysis will reveal, *On Life* also contains multiple allusions to Tolstoy's fictional and other philosophical and didactic works, some of which were still in progress. Part treatise, part spiritual meditation, *On Life* captures Tolstoy's innermost self as he battles with the encroaching fear of old age and death. However, these feelings, which, as Tolstoy would argue, are natural to any living being, have little in common with the existential dread that seizes the hero of *The Notes of a Madman*, a story that fictionalizes Tolstoy's own existential crisis of 1869.[16] A product of a later, genuinely philosophical Tolstoy, *On Life* is not an arresting confession, but a work that offers counsel.

II

Tolstoy opens the "Introduction" to his treatise by comparing life to a river and a man—to a miller who inherited a water mill. As long as the miller concerns himself with the quality of the grain he produces and does not inquire into the mechanism of the mill, his life goes smoothly. If he starts worrying too much about how the mill is made, what causes the river to flow, and other theoretical questions, his output will be diminished and the mill might fall into disrepair (Tolstoy 2019, 51).[17] Thus, Tolstoy emphasizes the primacy of practical reason over theoretical expositions of "life." By the latter Tolstoy means not the old-fashioned scholasticism that had been consigned to the dustbins of intellectual history by the Enlightenment, but rather contemporary scientific theories that describe life in physical, chemical, and biological terms. According to Tolstoy, the danger of these theories consists in alienating man from his actual existence. As a miller who forgets his work while engaging in speculations about the chemical and physical properties of the river and the mechanism of the mill, people get distracted and alienated from their own selves as soon as they start pondering abstract scientific questions (Tolstoy 2019, 51–60). And yet, human beings, endowed with language and memory, cannot help but reflect on their experience. Once they learn the word "life," they get obsessed with its meaning (ibid., 56).

In Chap. 1 Tolstoy suggests that the question of life should be posed differently from the way the scientific community poses it. Instead of pondering the phenomenon of life everyone should ask himself: "Why do I live?" Everyone intuitively knows the answer to this question. Human beings seek happiness and desire what is good for them [*blago*]. However, all conscious beings are self-conscious[18] and as such they cannot help realizing that their individual lives are intertwined with the lives of others and that their happiness depends on these other beings (ibid., 61). Intuitively, one wishes harmony with other beings who appear to be kindred. But in reality, life is a battlefield. Therefore, the real question is how to transform or rearrange life so that it leads to happiness. For centuries the answers to this question, known to ancient wisdom teachers, had been concealed from humanity by "scribes" and "Pharisees," because people armed with this wisdom would no longer need any cultural authorities (ibid., 64–66). To find a road to happiness, people should free themselves from the illusions of already possessing a knowledge that makes them masters of nature and shift their attention to their inner psychological well-being. In this respect, the teachings of old sages and enlighteners of humanity, which science has eclipsed, could prove invaluable.

In Chap. 4, with a cumbersome title, "The Teaching of the Scribes Substitutes the Visible Phenomena of Man's Animal Existence for the Notion of the Whole of Human Life and Thus Derives Conclusions about the Aim of His Life," Tolstoy finally begins to explain how man's properly human life differs from animal life.[19] While all animals are subject to what Schopenhauer had called the *principium individuationis*, only human beings can realize that this individualized existence represents only part of their real life. Unfortunately, only the most evolved humans recognize their true vocation. The majority, however, sees life only as a series of more or less pleasurable activities that occupy our time from birth to death. Tolstoy writes:

> New people are conceived, born, and grow up, and as they gaze into this crush of existence called life—in which old, dignified people, upon whom respect is lavished, also take part—and also become convinced that this insane ruckus is life itself, and that there is no other, they retreat after clamoring a bit at its door. Thus a man who has never before been to an assembly, upon seeing a pushy, loud, and animated crowd at the entrance, decides that this must be the assembly itself, and having tussled a bit at the door, returns home with bruised ribs, fully convinced that he has been to the assembly. (Tolstoy 2019, 76)

Tolstoy goes on to argue that the more a human being evolves, that is to say, the more he reflects on his life, the less satisfied he is with an existence that resembles a "busy entrance room" (ibid., 76). Even religious skeptics and agnostics yearn for another life. Echoing Strakhov's description of the midlife crisis, as well as his own autobiographical *Confession*,[20] Tolstoy points out that what distinguishes human beings from other animals is that they can become restless and satiated precisely at the point when the demands of their animal individuality are completely satisfied (ibid., 77). As Tolstoy and Strakhov had already mutually acknowledged in their correspondence, all utilitarian schemes of happiness are ultimately pointless. While the satisfaction of individual desires appears to be the animals' utmost goal, for human beings realization of desires constitutes a new challenge.[21] The agnostic Strakhov's position was not to seek any remedies for a psychological crisis occasioned by the realization of man's finitude. *The World as a Whole* suggests that our only consolation might come from science with its promise to extend our earthly life or find other worlds we can colonize, or else from science fiction.[22]

Tolstoy, with his sentimental cast of mind, could not be satisfied by a theory of life that did not lead to happiness. Rejecting the tough-mindedness of his agnostic friends, he reached back to eighteenth-century thinkers, whose ideas he had imbibed in his youth, seeking to redeem their teleological vision of Humanity.[23] As I will argue, in composing these chapters Tolstoy once again drew on his eighteenth-century teachers, including not only Kant, from whom he borrows the second epigraph to his treatise and against whom he polemicizes throughout the text, but also Herder and a number of other thinkers whose ideas shaped the intellectual atmosphere of the time and provided impetus for the debate between Herder and Kant.[24]

Moreover, when approaching *On Life* we should bear in mind that Kant, unlike Herder, was a relatively new intellectual interest for Tolstoy. Although his name appears in the drafts to *War and Peace*, Tolstoy seems to have been only superficially acquainted with Kant's ideas until he read Schopenhauer in the wake of his 1869 crisis. This belated reencounter with Kant's philosophy is well-known and sufficiently documented (Krouglov 2010, 2012; Paperno 2014). Herder, on the other hand, was part of Tolstoy's intellectual life since the 1850s (if not earlier) and richly contributed to the philosophical framework of *War and Peace*.[25] Therefore, when analyzing *On Life* we should not get overly fixated on obvious allusions to Kant's first and second *Critiques* and *Religion Within the Limits of Reason Alone*. Because Kant was undoubtedly the most fashionable philosopher in the contemporary anti-positivistic circles, including Grot's Moscow Psychological Society, references to his work could help establish common ground between Tolstoy and the philosophical audience and raise Tolstoy's professional credibility. But the problems he was addressing were by no means new to him. For example, the topic of *perfectibility* was one of Tolstoy's most fundamental concerns since the 1850s, when he first tackled the question of education.[26]

Moreover, it is doubtful that Tolstoy's anti-theoretical turn, announced on the first pages of *On Life*, was an immediate consequence of studying Kant's practical philosophy in the 1870s. As every reader of Tolstoy's novels knows, poking fun at theories and theorists is Tolstoy's favorite occupation as a satirist, one that sometimes drove him to dangerous extremes: in *War and Peace* he indulged his wit at the expense of German military strategists, whereas in *Anna*

Karenina he gently but decisively mocked Lyovin's half-brother Koznyshev, a professional philosopher.[27] It is only logical to assume that upon receiving an invitation from Koznyshev's "colleague" Grot (to whom Tolstoy was well-disposed), he would do his best to prepare a presentation that would not embarrass himself or his host, reading up on trendy philosophical issues and finding ways to link them back to the problems that had always been crucial to his art and thought. Therefore, Tolstoy's numerous invocations of the *Critique of Practical Reason* might be interpreted as a tribute to the then-fashionable turn "back to Kant" as the anchor for a newly revived idealism in its battle against vulgar positivism and pessimism. Deep down, however, Tolstoy had always identified with the moral and political goals of the *Aufklärung*. A pupil of Rousseau, Herder, and Karamzin, he had always viewed human beings as educable rational agents.[28] In *On Life* he takes a fresh look at these longstanding issues, offering arguably his most articulate exposition of what he means by wholly evolved Humanity, or "rational consciousness."[29] But before moving on, I shall briefly recapitulate the debate on Humanity that Tolstoy had first read about while researching *War and Peace*, where the name "Herder" serves as a shorthand for an entire chapter in German intellectual history—one that had a massive influence on the Russian intellectual elite of the 1800s–1820s.[30]

Herder's conception of Humanity emerged gradually through a debate he had first entered as a young thinker. This debate was occasioned by the publication of Johann Joachim Spalding's treatise on the vocation of humanity.[31] Spalding's argument begins with claim that the life of the senses, or the epicurean pleasure principle, could not be fulfilling for a wholly rational human subject (Spalding 2006, 11). A thinking person would sooner or later feel bored and start wondering whether there is a higher point to life. This reflection would lead to a recognition of an ethical dimension, involving obligations to others whom one sees as worthy of respect. At this stage a person becomes acutely aware of his moral sentiments. As Zammito points out, on this issue, Spalding is quite similar to Kant in the *Critique of Practical Reason* who also suggests that the awakening of moral self-consciousness and meditations on the injustices of this life inevitably lead us to speculate about the afterlife (Zammito 2002, 170).

Spalding's theodicy was enthusiastically received by the first German translator of Plato's *Phaedo*, Moses Mendelssohn, who found in it a corroboration of Plato's theory of Ideas. However, some of the younger representatives of the German Enlightenment, most notably Thomas Abbt and Herder, attacked a vision of humanity that posited a rupture between the natural and the supersensible realms (Printy 2013; Zammito 2002, 167–77; see also Steiner 2020). In a series of essays on philosophy of language and mind Herder went on to formulate completely new naturalized conceptions of the human soul, reason, and history that would free them from their dependence on the supernatural. Although the *Ideas* is usually regarded as a less radical work, here too Herder abstains from positing the existence of another world in which human beings could awaken to a new life.[32] Rather, he argues that the vocation of a human being consists in realizing her[33] uniqueness among other living creatures and reflecting on the significance of this exceptional stature. According to Herder, the upright position of the human body bespeaks our predisposition for upward striving. A human being attains her end as a creature of perfectibility once she comes to see herself as an upward striving being. Thus, a properly human being is for Herder one who perpetually strives toward or "awaits immortality."[34]

Likewise, Tolstoy insists that our "rational consciousness" is aimed at self-transcendence. Moreover, he even insists on the existence of the invisible spiritual realm. At the same time, to the great disappointment of many of his contemporaries, including most notably Vladimir Solovyov, Tolstoy argues against the possibility of resurrection. Tolstoy's vision of immortality actually anticipates that of Georg Simmel and other modernists who substituted for the myth of personal salvation the idea of spiritual self-transcendence and afterlife through cultural memory.[35] This vision rests on the organic understanding of human formation that harkens back to eighteenth-century debates on epigenesis.[36]

The body is the crucial juncture between animal and human individuality. However, unlike animals who suffer from their physical ailments and desire to escape them, a human being understands that physical individuality is given in order to help develop an individualized moral character. Thus, according to Tolstoy, a properly human life, one aimed at the awakening of "rational consciousness," begins when a human being realizes that the body (and its enjoyments) is not the end of life, but merely a tool with which one builds another spiritual life:

> It is clear to us that all matter and its laws against which the animal struggles and that it overcomes for the existence of its animal individuality are not in fact obstacles but instead are the means for the animal to attain its goals. An animal lives only by processing matter and by means of matter's laws. The same is true of a person's life. The animal individuality in which he finds himself, and that he is called upon to make obedient to his rational consciousness, is not an obstacle but a means to attain the goals of his happiness: The animal individuality is the tool a person uses to work. The animal individuality is a person's spade, given to a rational person so that he can dig and, in digging, first make it blunt, then sharpen it; use it up, rather than keep it clean and stored away. This is his talent to nurture, and not to hoard. "Those who find their life will lose it, and those who lose their life for my sake will find it." (Tolstoy 2019, 108)

The metaphor of digging the earth calls to mind both the life-affirming process of agricultural labor and the images of death and burial. Thus, Tolstoy creates the image of life as a perpetual cycle of creativity and destruction. It is worth bearing in mind that Tolstoy started working on his lecture "On Life and Death" (that became the basis for his treatise) during a difficult convalescence from a hunting accident (Medzhibovskaya 2019, 3). But notwithstanding its slightly masochistic tenor, Tolstoy's depiction of life as an unremitting struggle that yields more wisdom the harder one works and the more one suffers is wholly in line with Tolstoy's earlier depictions of his heroes' spiritual growth through morally and physically trying experiences. In Tolstoy's fictional world wisdom is often inversely proportional to physical well-being. As long as Tolstoy's heroes enjoy bodily health, they remain egocentric and focused only on their own happiness. Only painful experiences can interrupt their blind egoistic striving and turn them into wisdom seekers. Those endowed with supreme vitality, intelligence, and physical attractiveness experience these *peripateias* most intensely. Thus both Andrei Bolkonskii and Anna Karenina overcome their egoism and truly forgive and love others (if only in temporarily) only when they are in mortal agony, whereas less dashing characters like Konstantin Lyovin and Alexei Karenin can forget their own sufferings and develop genuine love and humility while observing the agonies of others.

However, as Tolstoy argues in Chap. 17, an awakening from ordinary consciousness and a spiritual resurrection as participants in "rational consciousness" can occur not only to those who have lived their lives with intense self-enjoyment. All people experience this liberating transformation of consciousness once they confront the limit of their purely physiological development (Tolstoy 2019, 109). Chapters 18, 19, 20, 21, 22, 23, 24, 25, 26, 27, 28, 29, and 30 describe (or rather, try to describe) the conversion that transforms a self-centered seeker after wealth, glory, sexual fulfillment, and other mundane, transitory goals into a being completely indifferent to these earthly goals who already partakes of immortality.

Here we are reminded of the image of Platon Karataev from *War and Peace*, whose loving kindness toward his fellow prisoners as well as the French guards taught Pierre Bezukhov how to forget his own miseries and experience an ecstatic joy of life in the midst of imprisonment. However, Tolstoy's most eloquent treatment of the theme of ultimate self-perfection as a liberation from both the false consciousness of animal life and the concomitant fear of death can be found in *The Death of Ivan Il'ich*, a work contemporaneous with *On Life*. This story (which Heidegger credits as an inspiration behind his idea of Being-toward-death) provides a vivid illustration for Chaps. 16 and 17, where Tolstoy describes the awakening of a qualitatively new self-consciousness, one no longer concerned with suffering and death.[37] But if Heidegger's point is to rid a *Dasein* of the illusions that sustained *das Man*, Tolstoy's goal, on the contrary, is to liberate a human individual from death. The author of *Ivan Il'ich* and *On Life* is hardly an existentialist in the twentieth-century sense of the term. Thus both works end with a passionate denial of death and what I take to be a reaffirmation of a Romantic view of an infinitely expanding organic "world as a whole." According to Tolstoy, we come into our own as full-fledged personalities not through an anti-idealistic denial of transcendence and a radical reorientation toward finite existence, but rather when we stop fearing and thinking about death as an existential limit and about ourselves as intrinsically limited beings, concentrating our rational efforts on loving our brothers (as does Ivan Il'ich when he acknowledges his servant Gerasim as a kindred being). When the thought of physical extinction no longer occupies the center of our consciousness and is replaced by love, our consciousness can naturally expand beyond self-consciousness.[38]

And yet, Tolstoy is not satisfied with the phenomenology of consciousness he has described, but keeps groping for a more convincing definition of immortality. Chapter 31, "Life of the Deceased Does Not End in This World," suggests that our deeds and the sentiments they aroused in the hearts of others will produce a spiritual residue that will outlive us. Exemplary individuals do not disappear completely, says Tolstoy, because the feelings that they stirred in us and their unique "attitude to the world" become part of our lives (Tolstoy 2019, 154–155).[39] Curiously enough, Tolstoy does not say anything about villains whose evil deeds also leave an imprint in our memories. This omission can be explained by his life-long refusal to acknowledge radical evil. Indeed, in Tolstoy's fiction most sinners sooner or later repent. Those who do not repent are regarded either as pompous fools whose punishment is mockery (such as Napoleon in *War and Peace*) or as perverse, beastly creatures (such as Nicholas I in *Hadji Murat*). The spiritual realm of "immortality" is reserved for those like Jesus or Platon Karataev, whose charitable deeds live on in the memories of their disciples, exercising a continual influence over their lives.

In the middle of the chapter Tolstoy suddenly breaks into a confessional tone and tells us that his deceased brother has never left his mind:

> This recollection is not merely an idea, it is something that has an effect on me, the same effect my brother's life had on me during his lifetime on earth. This recollection is his invisible and immaterial atmosphere that surrounded his life and affected me and others during his existence in the flesh, and it continues to affect me now, after his death. (Ibid., 157)

This sudden eruption of intimate memories into the abstract philosophical prose fleshes out the point Tolstoy is trying to make. At this juncture it becomes clear that his whole work is not merely a treatise, but a meditation provoked by autobiographical circumstances. This spiritual exercise is a sequel to Tolstoy's unfinished *Confession*, which reveals the transformation not just of his theoretically held convictions, but of his whole being as it gets illumined by the transcendent "rational consciousness." Moreover, echoing Montaigne, Tolstoy shows that such a profound transformation of one's character can only occur through a dialogue with a friend, "my other self," whose loveable image inspires us to seek perfection. Tolstoy admits that his brother has never been far from his thoughts and, most importantly, from his heart. This lyrical tribute to a brother who has become invisible yet omnipresent in his life throws into relief the sentimental framework of Tolstoy's moral philosophy and anthropology. Brotherly love and the good [*blago*] are synonyms for Tolstoy, because only one who benefits from love can love others and truly desire to better the world. By drawing on his own experience as an orphan for whom his siblings' love made up for the lack of parental care, Tolstoy explains how concrete loving individuals begin to shape our personalities before we are even able to account for ourselves. This discussion shows that Tolstoy's view of the origin of moral self-consciousness is different from Kant's, for he does not recognize a gap between "nature" and "freedom." For Tolstoy, moral reason is rooted in our nature, in our earliest memories of being part of a loving family or community of siblings.[40] Our cognitive understanding of the good grows along with our self-consciousness, shaped by memories.[41]

In retrospect it is clear why Tolstoy is so adamant in his rejection of modern science with its predilection for mathematical and statistical approaches to nature. A disembodied Cartesian perspective from which a scientist observes phenomena makes him uninterested in their human idiosyncrasies and impervious to their unique moral appeal. A participant in the increasingly important hermeneutic tradition, Tolstoy believes that human beings and their interactions cannot be cognized the way mathematical laws are cognized. Only a flesh-and-blood individual can appreciate another individual, with all his or her foibles. This is why Tolstoy insists that everyone should use his individualized existence as a tool with which he builds his immortal life, that is, everyone should pass through all stages of life—from childish innocence to youth, with all its passions and illusions, to adulthood, with all its animal pleasures, ambitions, and mistakes—before arriving at the moment of illumination that will reveal the vanity of individuality and shift our attention to other individualities.[42] Indeed, for the mature Tolstoy the ultimate goal of *Bildung* is not just to die without fear (although this Stoic note can be heard throughout Tolstoy's oeuvre), but to improve this world as much as one can by living well and becoming a model to others. As Tolstoy would repeat throughout the 1890s and into the 1900s, the Kingdom of God is within us. It need not be postponed until some hypothetical end of History, because everyone who seeks it can find it already in this life. It is not a heavenly, but an earthly kingdom, which is built the way fields and gardens are cultivated—with sweat, frustration, perseverance, and hope. Nobody can enter this kingdom as a naïve beautiful soul,[43] for even the simplest and the crudest life has its temptations and moral challenges. If Tolstoy in the 1850s and even 1860s still believed in the moral superiority of the country folk, whose conflicts and rivalries supposedly resolved themselves idyllically, in his mature work Tolstoy no longer entertained such illusions.[44] Selfishness and vice were found at all levels of society and in all kinds of civilization and the only cure for them was enlightenment.

III

To conclude, I want to turn to a tale that I consider a fitting illustration for Tolstoy's vision of life as a quest for "rational consciousness": *Father Sergius*.[45] Written at the point when Tolstoy's disagreements with the official Church teachings turned into an open conflict between the writer and the Russian Orthodox Church, this story outwardly resembles a Saint's Life. Upon a closer look, however, this didactic tale presents a parody of a vita, one that mocks ascetic virtues and exposes the hypocrisy of institutionalized religion. But the main point is not to mock Church institutions, but to show how one can reach enlightenment without dogmas and superstitions. This story is a more fitting illustration to *On Life* than *The Death of Ivan Il'ich*, famous for its masterful description of the phenomenology of death from within the point of view of a dying man's self-consciousness, because it tries to represent conversion and life within "rational consciousness" over a period lasting some years. The emphasis is not on liberating oneself from existential angst, but on living an ethically perfect life.

Like many Tolstoyan heroes, the protagonist of this tale, Prince Stepan Kasatskii, is vaguely autobiographical. He is well-born, intelligent, ambitious, and exceedingly proud. An idol of his family, he spends his childhood in the idyllic atmosphere of a country estate and is thrown into the world only as a teenager, after the death of his father. He is sent to Petersburg where he enters a prestigious military school under the patronage of Nicholas I. The young Prince, his soul burning with a childish faith and love of everything noble and beautiful, adores the Emperor, who seems to favor him. Encouraged by Nicholas's favor, Kasatskii strives toward perfection and preeminence in every aspect of his life. Thus he decides to advance himself as far as possible in courtly society. With this goal in mind he gets engaged to a beautiful court lady and becomes so carried away by this infatuation that he does not realize that he is being used. A typical naïf, he does not know what is known to the whole *beau monde*, namely that a year ago his fiancée was the Emperor's mistress.

When shortly before the wedding Kasatskii's bride reveals her past to him, he feels betrayed both by her, whom he had perceived as an ideal of purity and virtue, and by his beloved Tsar (whom he cannot challenge to a duel). Hurt and disgusted, he breaks off the engagement, quits military service, and enters a monastery. But the transition from court society to the monastery is only a prelude to the real drama, for the hero's torments do not cease when he sheds his noble name and title and assumes a new identity as Monk Sergius. Sergius's new father figure, an Orthodox Elder, recognizes that his pupil suffers from pride and urges him to develop humility. Sergius, accustomed as he is to excel in everything he does, embraces ritualized piety with the same zeal he had once showed in the guards' school and in drawing rooms. However, one day an encounter with a former regimental commander who comes to visit the monastery reveals to him the similarity of the worldly and monastic spheres. Aware of Sergius's past, the ambitious Abbot invites him to join himself and General in a social gathering. And when the General tells Kasatskii that he is glad to see him in his new "angelic state," the Prince explodes (forgetting that his vows forbid him to experience rage). Recognizing his wretchedness, Sergius asks for permission to be transferred to a remote hermitage, where he lives for another six years as a recluse.

Even in the hermitage he is tormented by an inner conflict caused by two problems: his persistent religious doubt and lust. But lust is the weaker of the two temptations and one day Sergius has a chance to prove that he can withstand it. When an attractive society lady, Makovkina, who had heard about

Sergius's holiness, tries to seduce him, he hacks off his own finger and burns it, causing a moral crisis in his temptress. The narrator tells us that a year later she too enters a convent. Meanwhile, Sergius's drama reaches an apogee, as his reputation as a holy man begins to spread. Pilgrims from around the world flock to his monastery. A voice within his soul tells Sergius that the monastery is using his fame to attract more visitors and that by cooperating with the holy fathers' scheme he sinks deeper and deeper into sin. He procures a peasant dress and keeps thinking of escape without acting until fate suddenly gives him a chance to experience an utter fall. One day a merchant brings his neurasthenic daughter to Sergius asking him to cure her. This time the girl, who is described as a sensual creature utterly devoid of reason, manages to seduce Sergius. In some of the drafts he kills his seductress. In the finished version, Sergius dons his peasant garb and leaves the monastery at daybreak.

Once outside the monastery walls, he falls into a trancelike sleep and has a strange dream. He recalls an episode from his childhood when a girl named Pashen'ka comes to visit his parents' home. She seems to be a simpleton and the boys make fun of her, asking her to show how she swims on dry land.[46] Waking up, he remembers that he had heard of her recently. He knew that she had been married to a petty official in a provincial town and was now utterly destitute. Suddenly, he resolves to go to that town. The narrator does not say whether Sergius feels ashamed of his behavior as a child and wants to apologize or whether he is drawn to a childhood friend on whose compassion he can count. This explanation would be redundant, because at this juncture the hero's emotional and rational instincts coincide. After walking as a pilgrim for days Kasatskii finds his way to a shabby provincial town where Praskovia Mikhailovna, as the lady is now called, lives with her daughter, a sickly son-in-law, and five grandchildren. After the death of her husband, who had squandered her inheritance, she is reduced to poverty and supports her family by giving music lessons.

Pashen'ka barely recognizes the handsome young Prince or the legendary Elder in the old beggar. She is shocked to hear Kasatskii confess (without giving her any details) that he is not a saint but a terrible sinner. But she is even more surprised when he urges her to tell him how she spent her life. Haltingly at first, she tells him her life story. Filled with prosaic misfortunes (an unhappy marriage, loss of fortune, the deaths of her husband and son, her daughter's unsuccessful marriage), this life, nonetheless, seems meaningful to Sergius: while living only for her family and never going to the church, this unassuming woman actually lives for God.

Kasatskii leaves as he came, on foot and dressed as a pilgrim. He turns into a wanderer who lives from alms. At the end of the story the narrator describes the episode where a group of rich travelers including a Frenchman distribute the alms among the pilgrims. The Frenchman notices Kasatskii's dignified appearance and asks a Russian who accompanies him to inquire after the vagabond's identity: "A slave of God," answers Tolstoy's hero and humbly takes twenty kopecks that he immediately gives to another pilgrim (*PSS* 31: 45).

588   L. STEINER

But this is not quite the end of the story. Having ultimately shed his identities as Prince Kasatskii and Sergius, Tolstoy's hero has not yet escaped from the predicament of *principium individuationis*. As much as he repents his past and wishes to imitate and even outdo his new role model, a meek and hardworking gentlewoman who has lost the trappings of her rank but not her soul, finding a framework in which one could live an utterly selfless and useful life is harder in Tolstoy's Russia than one might think, for the state persecutes vagrants without a stable abode and identity documents. Finally, Tolstoy's hero gets arrested for vagrancy, sentenced, and exiled to Siberia, where he ends up living on a rich peasant's farmstead, working in the garden, teaching children, and caring for the sick (ibid., 46).

This ending, narrated in the present tense, recalls another famous literary ending—that of Voltaire's *Candide*. This fable mocks Leibniz's theodicy, represented by Candide's teacher Pangloss, by demonstrating the role of chance in life and the limitations of our reason. Full of the most fantastic adventures, Candide's story concludes with an idyllic retreat from the world. But Candide refuses to interpret his newfound peace in teleological terms. His injunction, "we must cultivate our garden," is usually interpreted as a riposte to Pangloss's tireless attempts to rationalize experience and sum it up as a theodicy.[47] Thus Candide's hard won wisdom, which consists in keeping idleness, vice, and poverty at bay, is a critique of the overly intellectualized view of happiness, which implies that it cannot be complete unless it is rationally defensible. In choosing a simple-minded Pashen'ka, who is as indifferent to religion as Candide, as his exemplum, the hero of *Father Sergius* seems to agree with Candide's view of life.

And yet, Tolstoy's tale lends itself to another reading as well, one that redeems an optimistic worldview and further secularizes the Leibnizian theodicy. Unlike Candide, Kasatskii/Sergius is not incurably naïve and is not being propelled through life by sheer chance and accident. On the contrary, he is the author of his own life. As he keeps making mistakes, his self-consciousness accrues. He comes to realize the falseness of his attempts to escape from his earthly, merely human self by becoming a monk. But having acknowledged, and even indulged in, his human weaknesses, he does not turn into a skeptic. Leaving the monastery, Kasatskii/Sergius seeks a new framework for his quest for perfection. Although his earlier belief in the superhuman purity and virtue which he had falsely attributed to his fiancée and tried to pursue in his own life gets debunked, a new way to make life meaningful is revealed to him by Pashen'ka's prosaic this-worldly saintliness. This woman, whose friendship he spurned as a child, now becomes his most intimate confidant. He continues to toil in the garden of his life, finding a new reservoir of life-sustaining force. But unlike Candide, Tolstoy's hero finds happiness by working in the garden belonging to a peasant, rather than in his own garden. Thus ends a secular Vita that drives home to us the redundancy of the supernatural in our daily struggles to improve ourselves and the world.

We are reminded of Rousseau's letter to Voltaire, in which he defends Alexander Pope's poetic theodicy against Voltaire's mockery. Surely, a belief in divine Providence cannot withstand rational critique. Nevertheless, says Rousseau, "I feel it, I believe it, I desire it, I hope for it, and I will defend it to my last breath" (quoted in Stewart 2009, 146). For Tolstoy goodness [*blago*] is also something we start feeling and desiring before we can fully articulate it. It does not require rational proof. However, its continual presence and growth in this world cannot be secured without the help of "rational consciousness." A pupil of both Rousseau, together with the sentimental tradition he inspired, and the rationalists, Tolstoy rewrites the narrative of the Enlightenment in such a way that the progress of reason in harmony with inner feeling appears to be both natural and unavoidable.

NOTES

1. This observation requires a qualification. Certainly, Tolstoy specialists cannot be accused of neglecting this side of his oeuvre. However, Soviet-era scholars suffering from ideological control had limited opportunities to discuss Tolstoy's ideas. Émigré Russian philosophers in the first half of the nineteenth century and Slavic scholars in the West were in a much better position. However, linguistic and institutional boundaries reduced their impact on Slavic studies. Among non-Slavic scholars, only American pragmatists paid considerable attention to Tolstoy and acknowledged his influence. For a more detailed discussion of the American reception of Tolstoy, see Orwin 2003 and Menand 2001.
2. For an in-depth discussion of the reception of Tolstoy by Russian critics between the two Russian revolutions, see Denner 2010.
3. As Georgii Plekhanov suggested in 1928, the emergent Soviet culture could only accept Tolstoy "from here and to here" [*otsiuda i dosiuda*]. See Nickell 2006. This restrictive approach led to an overexploitation of *War and Peace* as a source of patriotic propaganda as well as to the canonization of late Tolstoy (as the author of *The Resurrection*) as a forebear of socialist realism. Only the most courageous critics could resist these pressures. For an example of a particularly daring non-dogmatic approach to Tolstoy as a psychologist, see Ginzburg 1971.
4. Eikhenbaum's *Molodoi Tolstoy* was written as early as 1922. See Eikhenbaum 1974; see also Eikhenbaum 1972, 1982, as well as Shklovskii 1963.
5. See, in particular, Medzhibovskaya 2008; Paperno 2014; Kokobobo 2008; Klimova 2018. Contemporary philosophers have also been paying attention to Tolstoy. See, in particular, Pickford 2016, Goldie 2000.
6. This outdated image of Tolstoy has already been criticized by Berlin, whose essay "Tolstoy and Enlightenment" was one of the original inspirations behind my work on Tolstoy. See Berlin 1978; Steiner 2011b.
7. Ilya Vinitsky discusses the spiritual atmosphere of the epoch that shaped Tolstoy's mindset and aroused his interest in the issue of the "soul" in "The Warm of Doubt: Prince Andrei's Death and the Russian Spiritual Awakening." See Vinitsky 2010.

590   L. STEINER

8. Among more recent works on this topic, see, for example, Justin Weir's essay "Turgenev as Institution: Notes of a Hunter in Tolstoy's Early Aesthetics." See Weir 2010a.
9. See the "Introduction" to the present *Handbook.*
10. Herzen adopts the term *razumnoe soznanie* in his essay on Robert Owen, which had a big influence on Tolstoy's intellectual development. I adopt Constance Garnett's translation of *razumnoe soznanie* as "rational consciousness" and use it throughout this chapter, not only because I consider it more elegant than the "reasonable consciousness" preferred by some Tolstoy scholars, but also because I wish to point out the philosophical continuity between Herzen and Tolstoy. See Herzen 1982; Steiner 2019. Aileen Kelly offers an illuminating analysis of Herzen's intellectual path, which involved an immersion in German idealism, as well as an in-depth study of natural science under the famous physiologist Ivan Pavlov. See Kelly 2016.
11. For a more in-depth discussion of the incipient tradition of *Bildung* in Russia, see Steiner 2013.
12. In *The Craft of Fiction* Percy Lubbock summarized the charges against Tolstoy presented by nineteenth-century Western critics, starting with Henry James and Gustave Flaubert. "The well-made book is the book where the subject and the form coincide and are indistinguishable. […] In *War and Peace* the story suffers twice over for the imperfection of the form. […] Whether the story was to be the drama of youth and age, or the drama of war and peace, in either case it would have been incomparably more impressive if all the great wealth of the material had been used for its purpose, all brought into one design." See Lubbock 1963, 40–41. Nikolai Mikhailovskii has both summarized and rebuffed similar aesthetic charges coming from Tolstoy's Russian critics. See Mikhailovskii 1957.
13. For an illuminating discussion of Tolstoy's emergence as the author of moral and religious tracts, see Chap. 2 of Irina Paperno's recent book, Paperno 2014.
14. Inessa Medzhibovskaya discusses the genesis of Tolstoy's treatise *On Life* in great detail in a book-length commentary to her and Michael Denner's translation of Tolstoy's treatise (Medzhibovskaya 2019). A shorter version of this text is published alongside the new translation: Tolstoy 2019.
15. Medzhibovskaya and Scanlan discuss the reception of *On Life* by contemporary Russian philosophers, covering practically the whole spectrum of contemporary philosophical opinion. See Medzhibovskaya 2019; Scanlan 2006.
16. An unfinished text from 1884, "Notes of a Madman" ["Zapiski sumashedshego"], is usually interpreted as an autobiographical work describing the experience that Tolstoy had dubbed his "Arzamas nightmare." For an alternative interpretation of this work as a fiction, see Parthé 1985. I also discuss this text in Steiner 2011b.
17. The text of *On Life* appears in volume 26 of Tolstoy's *Polnoe sobranie sochinenii.* The Jubilee Edition. However, throughout this chapter I will cite the English translation by Denner and Medzhibovskaya.
18. For Tolstoy (as for Herder on whom he evidently drew) consciousness is inner sense, self-consciousness. Thus, many animals are conscious, including Kholstomer in the eponymous story or the dog who befriends Platon Karataev in *War and Peace* and barks anxiously after his execution. As I will go on to explain, what animals lack is the wisdom of *razumnoe soznanie*, a product of

reflection on lived experience over the course of one's life that would enable them to change their instinctive behavior and gradually build the Kingdom of God on earth.

19. At this juncture, I should note that the gendered language I use corresponds not only to the nineteenth-century conventions, but also reflects Tolstoy's own gender bias. As is well-known, for a long time Tolstoy did not believe in women's political and economic emancipation. A change in his views can be detected in "Father Sergius," *The Resurrection*, and a few other late fiction works where spiritually strong and independent (but not wholly emancipated) women are heroicized. Nevertheless, throughout my chapter I will stick to the gendered language Tolstoy used in his tracts.

20. Tolstoy's friend and philosophical interlocutor Nikolai Strakhov describes the process of physiological growth and maturation as the beginning of what we would call a midlife crisis in Chap. 7 of *The World as a Whole*. As Strakhov puts it, a fully grown-up human being begins to "thirst after" a higher life (Strakhov 2007, 260). On Tolstoy's *Confession* as a testimony to both an existential crisis caused by the fear of death and a value crisis spurred by Tolstoy's activities as a social worker, see Shestov 1978, 20–72.

21. On the significance of Tolstoy's epistolary dialogue with Strakhov, see Paperno 2014, 39–60.

22. Chapter II of Part One of Strakhov's book, "The Denizens of (Other) Planets," harkens back to the Enlightenment speculations on life on other planets and anticipates Russian Cosmism, as well as the actual scientific experiments of Konstantin Tsiolkovsky.

23. Eikhenbaum has written extensively on the significance of Karamzin for the then young Tolstoy. According to Eikhenbaum, it is through Karamzin that Tolstoy encountered Herder. I would add that Tolstoy might have first learned about Wieland, Kant, and other German and Swiss luminaries Karamzin had met and mentioned by reading his *Letters of a Russian Traveller*. The French philosophers were also known to Tolstoy since childhood and his student years. However, I agree with Eikhenbaum that through all his skeptical crises Tolstoy preserved a sentimental proclivity originally developed under the tutelage of Karamzin (and as I would like to add, Herder). See Eikhenbaum 1972; Steiner 2020. The significance of Karamzin for the entire tradition of Russian psychological prose has been recapitulated by Donna Orwin. See Orwin 2007.

24. Tolstoy's epigraph is derived from the *Conclusion* to the *Critique of Practical Reason*. He quotes only the first paragraph.

25. Tolstoy's indebtedness to Herder's anthropology and philosophy of history has been discussed by several scholars, including, most recently, Vinitsky 2010, Steiner 2011a, Steiner 2013, and Steiner 2020.

26. See Berlin 1978. I also discussed Tolstoy's forays into philosophy of education and their connections with *War and Peace* in Steiner 2011a and 2013.

27. Gary Saul Morson brilliantly demonstrates Tolstoy's distrust of theory, which he attributes to the influence of Aristotle's ethics. See Morson 1987.

28. The allusions to *Bildung* [*obrazovanie*] throughout his pedagogical articles offer ample testimony to this. See Berlin 1978, 258; Steiner 2013.

29. In this work Tolstoy does not use Karamzin's term *gumannost'* (obviously borrowed from Herder), because he has consciously chosen a more recent term *razumnoe soznanie* (with its Hegelian baggage).

30. I have in mind, first of all, the impact of secret societies and literary associations of the pre-Decembrist period on Russian literary and political history. Scholarly literature on this topic is very rich. I would like to point especially to Yuri Lotman's numerous essays and Karamzin's intellectual biography, as well as to the monographs by Andrei Zorin and Maria Maiofis. See Lotman 1992, 1997, Zorin 2001, Maiofis 2008. For additional bibliography, see my essay, "The Russian Novel as a Medium of Moral Reflection," in this *Handbook*.

31. In summarizing this discussion I draw on the original texts as well as on Chap. 4 of John Zammito's *Kant, Herder, and the Birth of Anthropology* (Zammito 2002).

32. As Vinitsky has pointed out, this is not how Tolstoy understood Herder in *War and Peace*, where he seems to subscribe to the idea of *palingenesis* (see Vinitsky 2010, 131). However, as I will show, in later writings Tolstoy gets increasingly skeptical about the ideas fashionable among contemporary spiritualists and seeks to confine his "pious hopes" to this-worldly life.

33. Tolstoy, for most of his life, was a staunch conservative when it came to the "woman question" (at least until the 1880s and 1890s).

34. My understanding of Herder's philosophy is indebted to Michael Forster. See Forster 2018. It is also indebted to Adler 1968, Heintz 1994, Zammito 2002 (among others).

35. The Tolstoy-Solovyov polemic is covered in detail in Medzhibovskaya 2019, 180–219.

36. For a discussion of *epigenesis* versus evolution (preformation), see Richards 2002, 416. Tolstoy probably first glimpsed the Romantic epigenetic view of nature in Goethe's works, which he read in his youth. On Goethe's role in Tolstoy's development, especially with regard to his interest in nature, see Orwin 1993.

37. For an insightful discussion of *The Death of Ivan Il'ich* and Heidegger, see Repin 2002.

38. *The Death of Ivan Il'ich*, first published in 1886, was written within less than a year. See *Polnoe Sobranie sochinenii* 26: 69–111.

39. Tolstoy's discussion of his brother's undying "predisposition" or "attitude to life" recalls Kant's discussion of the *Anlage* or *Keime* as the "birth place" of "pure concepts." It is noteworthy that the term "seed" is also used by Tolstoy in chapter 9, which begins as follows: "Contemplating the passing of time, observing the manifestation of life in the human creature, we notice that true life is always preserved in man as it is preserved in a seed: the time arrives, and life is revealed. The manifestation of true life occurs when the animal individuality draws man toward its own happiness, while reasonable (or rational) consciousness demonstrates to him, on the other hand, the impossibility of individual happiness and identifies another kind of happiness" (Tolstoy 2019, 85). In recent years, scholars have suggested that the theory of epigenesis played a big role in Kant's understanding of grounding and self-generating. See Helbig and Nassar 2016. Given these Kantian echoes, I think we could see Tolstoy's treatise as an attempt to reconcile transcendental idealist and sentimentalist approaches to morality. Nevertheless, I still believe that Tolstoy's ethics is at base a sentimentalist ethics and that his best explanation for the "origins" of his "rational consciousness" is one that involves his earliest memories of a brotherly bond he had enjoyed as a child.

26 TOLSTOY'S PHILOSOPHY OF LIFE 593

40. In a longer version of this chapter I discuss Tolstoy's *Memoirs* recorded by Pavel Biriukov, in which he reveals his earliest and happiest memories in which his late brother Nikolai plays the key role. Anna Berman has discussed the role of brotherly love in Tolstoy's ethics and politics in her recent book, Berman 2015.

41. On the role of early memories and memory in general in Tolstoy, see Ginzburg 1971 and Paperno 2014. Although I have no proof that Tolstoy had firsthand familiarity with Herder's "On the Cognition and Sensation of the Human Soul," their views of selfhood strike me as kindred. Given that the two thinkers had a number of intermediaries (Karamzin, Radishchev, Hegel, and other German philosophers) insisting on historical/textological evidence seems arbitrary.

42. In a longer version of this work I discuss the differences between Tolstoy's and Schopenhauer's ethics. In a nutshell, the former envisions the overcoming of individuality and the development of a compassionate attitude to other beings as a gradual process which all people (even women, who are more enslaved to the species than men) can potentially undergo, whereas the latter reserves ethical life for exceptional people, ascetic "saints."

43. Tolstoy was familiar with the details of the French and German debates on the "beautiful soul." In brief, this debate revolved around the question whether the beautiful soul was an innate or acquired virtue. While Rousseau and some German Enlightenment thinkers, including Mendelssohn, attributed the beauty of the soul to innocence, some others, for example, Schiller, saw it as a product of self-consciousness, or *Bildung*.

44. In contrast to Tolstoy's early stories about peasant life, such as "Idillia" (1861) and "Tikhon and Malania" (1862), Tolstoy's later works set in the peasant milieu are increasingly naturalistic and dark, culminating with the *Power of Darkness* (1902). For an insightful interpretation of Tolstoy's drama, see Justin Weir 2010b.

45. See Tolstoy 1929–1958, 31: 6–46.

46. I thank Victoria Juharyan for reminding me that Hegel uses the metaphor of "swimming on dry land" in the Introduction to the *Logic* to emphasize the difference between scholasticism (which attempts to philosophize outside of experience) and his own method (which he compares to real swimming). One could speculate why this metaphor resurfaces in Tolstoy's text precisely at this juncture. Having escaped from the world and even from the monastic community by becoming a hermit (like the Desert Fathers who were venerated by Orthodoxy as the ultimate model of Christian piety), Kasatskii himself was trying to "swim on dry land." Meanwhile, Pashen'ka was living an ordinary human life, full of mistakes and trials that helped her develop true wisdom.

47. See Philip Stewart's illuminating interpretation of *Candide*'s philosophy, Stewart 2009.

BIBLIOGRAPHY

Adler, Emil. 1968. *Herder und die deutsche Aufklaerung*. Wien, Frankfurt, Zürich: Europa.

Beiser, Frederick C. 2016. *Weltschmerz: Pessimism in German Philosophy, 1860–1900*. Oxford, UK: Oxford University Press.

Berlin, Isaiah. 1978. Tolstoy and Enlightenment. In *Russian Thinkers*, ed. Henry Hardy and Aileen Kelly, 238–260. London: Penguin.

Berman, Anna. 2015. *Siblings in Tolstoy and Dostoevsky: The Path to Universal Brotherhood*. Evanston, IL: Northwestern University Press.

Denner, Michael A. 2010. The 'Proletarian Lord': Leo Tolstoy's Image During the Russian Revolutionary Period. In *Anniversary Essays on Tolstoy*, ed. Donna Tussing Orwin, 219–244. Cambridge: Cambridge University Press.

Eikhenbaum, Boris M. 1972. *The Young Tolstoy*. Trans. Gary Kern. Ann Arbor, MI: Ardis.

———. 1974. *Lev Tolstoy: semidesiatye gody*. Leningrad: Khudozhestvennaia literatura.

Eikhenbaum, Boris. 1982. *Tolstoy in the Sixties*. Trans. Duffiled White. Ann Arbor, MI: Ardis.

Forster, Michael N. 2018. *Herder's Philosophy*. Oxford: Oxford University Press.

Ginzburg, Lydia Ya. 1971. *O psikhologicheskoi proze*. Leningrad: Sovetskii pisatel.

Goldie, Peter. 2000. *The Emotions: A Philosophical Exploration*. Oxford: Oxford University Press.

Herzen, Alexander. 1982. *My Past and Thoughts: The Memoirs of Alexander Herzen*. Berkeley and Los Angeles: The University of California Press.

Heinz, Marion. 1994. *Sensualistischer Idealismus. Untersuchungen zur Erkenntnistheorie und Metaphysik des jungen Herder (1763–1778)*. Hamburg: Meiner Verlag.

Helbig, Daniela, and Dalia Nassar. 2016. The Metaphor of *epigenesis*: Kant, Blumenbach and Herder. *Studies in History and Philosophy of Science* 58: 98–107.

Kelly, Aileen. 2016. *The Discovery of Chance: The Life and Thought of Alexander Herzen*. Cambridge, MA: Harvard University Press.

Klimova, Svetlana M. 2018. *Intelligentsia v poiskakh identichnosti. Dostoevsky. Tolstoy*. Aletheia: St. Petersburg.

Kokobobo, Ani. 2008. Authoring Christ: Novelistic Echoes in James Tolstoy's Harmonization and Translation of the Four Gospels. *Tolstoy Studies Journal* 20: 1–13.

Krouglov, Alexei N. 2010. Das Problem des Friedens bei I. Kant und L.N. Tolstoj. In *War and Peace: The Role of Sciences and Arts*, ed. Sonja Nour and Olivier Remaud, 99–130. Berlin: Dinker und Humboldt.

———. 2012. *Kant i kantovskaia filosofia v russkoi khudozhestvennoi literature*. Moscow: Kanon.

Lotman, Yuri M. 1992. *Izbrannye stat'ii v 3 tomakh*. Tallinn: Alexandra.

———. 1997. *Karamzin*. St. Petersburg: Iskusstvo.

Lubbock, Percy. 1963. *The Craft of Fiction*. London: Jonathan Cape.

Maiofis, Maria. 2008. *Vozzvanie k Evrope: Literaturnoe obshchestvo 'Arzamas' i rossiskii modernizationnyi proekt 1815–1818 godov*. Moscow: Novoe literaturnoe obozrenie.

Medzhibovskaya, Inessa. 2008. Tolstoy and the Religious Culture of his Time: A Biography of a Long Conversion, 1845–1887. Lanham, MD: Lexington Books.

Medzhibovskaya, Inessa. 2019. *Tolstoy's On Life: From the Archival History of Russian Philosophy*. DeLand, FL, and Toronto: Tolstoy Studies Journal.

Menand, Louis. 2001. *The Metaphysical Club: A History of Ideas in America*. New York, NY: Farrar, Strauss and Giroux.

Mikhailovskii, Nikolai K. 1957. Desnitsa i shuitsa L'va Tolstogo. In *Literaturno-kriticheskie stat'ii*, ed. V. Vorovskii, 59–180. Moscow: Khudozhestvennaia literatura.

Morson, Gary Saul. 1987. *Hidden in Plain View: Narrative and Creative Potentials in 'War and Peace'*. Stanford, CA: Stanford University Press.

Nickell, William. 2006. Tolstoi in 1828: In the Mirror of the Revolution. In *Epic Revisionism: Russian Literature and History as Stalinist Propaganda*, ed. Kevin M.F. Platt and David Brandenberger, 17–43. Madison, WI: University of Wisconsin Press.

Orwin, Donna. 1993. *Tolstoy's Art and Thought 1847–1880*. Princeton, NJ: Princeton University Press.

———. 2003. What Men Live By. In *William James in Russian Culture*, ed. Joan Delaney Grossman, Ruth Rischin, et al., 59–79. Lanham, NY: Lexington Books.

———. 2007. *Consequences of Consciousness: Turgenev, Dostoevsky and Tolstoy*. Stanford, CA: Stanford University Press.

Paperno, Irina. 2014. *Who, What am I?' Tolstoy Struggles to Narrate the Self*. Ithaca, NY, and London: Cornell University Press.

Parthé, Kathleen. 1985. Tolstoy and the Geometry of Fear. *Modern Language Studies* 15 (4): 80–94.

Pickford, Henry W. 2016. *Thinking with Tolstoy and Wittgenstein: Expression, Emotion, and Art*. Evanston, IL: Northwestern University Press.

Pirogov, N.I. 1985. Voprosy zhizni. In *Izbrannye pedagogicheskie sochineniia*, 29–51. Moscow: Pedagogika.

Printy, Michael. 2013. The Determination of Man: Johann Joachim Spalding and the Protestant Enlightenment. *Journal of the History of Ideas* 74 (2): 189–212.

Repin, Natalie. 2002. Being-toward-Death in Tolstoy's 'The Death of Ivan Il'ich': Tolstoy and Heidegger. *Canadian-American Slavic Studies* 36 (1–2): 101–132.

Richards, Robert J. 2002. *The Romantic Conception of Life: Science and Philosophy in the Age of Goethe*. Chicago and London: The University of Chicago Press.

Scanlan, James P. 2006. Tolstoy among the Philosophers: His Book On Life and its Critical Reception. *Tolstoy Studies Journal* 18: 52–69.

Shestov, Lev. 1978. The Good in the Teachings of Tolstoy and Nietzsche: Philosophy and Preaching. Trans. and Ed. Bernard Martin. *Dostoevsky, Tolstoy and Nietzsche*, ed. Lev Shestov, 1–140. Columbus, OH: Ohio University Press.

Shklovskii, Viktor B. 1963. *Lev Tolstoy*. Seria "Zhizn' zamechatel'nykh liudei." Moscow: Khudozhestvennaia literatura. (Series: *Zhizn' zamechatel'nykh liudei* [The Lives of Remarkable People].)

Steiner, Lina. 2011a. *For Humanity's Sake: The Bildungsroman in Russian Culture*. Toronto and London: University of Toronto Press.

———. 2011b. The Russian *Aufklärer*: Tolstoy in Search of Truth, Wisdom and Immortality. *Slavic Review* 70 (4): 773–794.

———. 2013. A Vital Question: The Quest for *Bildung* in Russia, 1860s–80s. In *Die Bildung der Moderne*, ed. Michael Dreyer, Michael Forster, Kai-Uwe Hoffmann, and Klaus Vieweg, 197–201. Tübingen: Finke.

———. 2019. A Revolutionary as a Beautiful Soul: Lev Tolstoy's Path to Ethical Anarchism. *Studies in East European Thought* 71 (1): 43–62.

———. 2020. Herder's Russian Advocate: Tolstoy on the Vocation of Humanity. In *Herder and the 19th Century*, ed. Liisa Steinby, 427–443. Heidelberg: Synchron Press.

Stewart, Philip. 2009. Candide. In *The Cambridge Companion to Voltaire*, ed. Nicholas Cronk, 125–138. Cambridge: Cambridge University Press.

Strakhov, Nikolai N. 2007. *Mir kak tseloe*. Moscow: Airis.

Tolstoy, Lev N. 1929–1958. *Polnoe sobranie sochinenii v 90 tomakh*. (Jubilee Edition). Moscow: Gosudarstvennoe izdatel'stvo "Khudozhestvennaia literatura."

Tolstoy, Leo. 2019. *On Life: A Critical Edition*. Trans. Michael Denner and Inessa Medzhibovskaya. Edited by Inessa Medzhibovskaya. Evanston, IL: Northwestern University Press.

Vinitsky, Ilya. 2010. The Warm of Doubt: Prince Andrei's Death and the Russian Spiritual Awakening. In *Anniversary Essays on Tolstoy*, ed. Donna Tussing Orwin, 120–137. Cambridge, Cambridge University Press.

Weir, Justin. 2010a. Turgenev as Institution: Notes of a Hunter in Tolstoy's Early Aesthetics. In *Turgenev: Art, Ideology, and Legacy*, ed. Joe Andrew and Robert Reid, 217–236. Amsterdam/New York: Rodopi.

———. 2010b. Violence and the Role of Drama in the Late Tolstoy: *The Realm of Darkness*. In *Anniversary Essays on Tolstoy*, ed. Donna Tussing Orwin, 183–198. Cambridge: Cambridge University Press.

Zammito, John H. 2002. *Kant, Herder, and the Birth of Anthropology*. Chicago: University of Chicago Press.

Zenkovsky, Vasily V. 1953. *A History of Russian Philosophy*. Trans. George L. Kline, 2 vols. London: Routledge and Kegan Paul.

Zorin, Andrei L. 2001. *Kormia dvuglavogo orla: literatura i gosudarstvennaia ideologia v Rossii v poslednei treti XVIII- pervoi treti XIX veka*. Moscow: Novoe literaturnoe obozrenie.

CHAPTER 27

"Teaching of Life": Tolstoy's Moral-Philosophical Aesthetics

Henry W. Pickford

Throughout his long, prolific writing career, Tolstoy reflected on the nature and societal significance of art. Embedded within literary works, diary entries, and letters, and developed in published essays and unpublished drafts, these reflections chronicle Tolstoy's evolving struggle to clarify for himself and present to others a normative theory of art in which aesthetics and politics are jointly grounded in a moral-religious orientation. Tolstoy's most accomplished, and most influential, account, written by his own admission over fifteen years, is his treatise *What is Art?*, completed in 1898, although earlier and later essays augment the central arguments to be found in it. As he wrote in the opening of the treatise's final chapter, "when I began writing about art fifteen years ago, I thought the task I had undertaken would be finished without interruption; but it turned out that my thoughts on this subject were still unclear, that I could not expound them in a way that would satisfy me. Since then, I have thought this subject over incessantly, and have started writing six or seven times, but each time, after writing quite a lot, I felt unable to bring the thing to a conclusion and abandoned work on it" (Tolstoy 1995, 157; hereafter WiA). The present essay first presents an overview of Tolstoy's normative philosophical aesthetics, narrowly construed; then the view is widened to include the moral-political framework within which proper artworks should fulfill their vital function. It concludes with some brief remarks on the influence of Tolstoy's ideas on later thinkers.

H. W. Pickford (✉)
Department of German Studies, Duke University, Durham, NC, USA
e-mail: henry.pickford@duke.edu

© The Author(s), under exclusive license to Springer Nature
Switzerland AG 2021
M. F. Bykova et al. (eds.), *The Palgrave Handbook of Russian Thought*,
https://doi.org/10.1007/978-3-030-62982-3_27

597

The Narrow Context: Philosophy of Art

Tolstoy's treatise *What is Art?* is one of the founding texts of what is now called the *expression theory of art*. Precursors can be found in the iron ring analogy in Plato's *Ion* and his suspicion of the baleful influence of poets in the *Republic*, in Longinus's study *On the Sublime* of how elevated language yields not persuasion but "transport," and in Nietzsche's account in *The Birth of Tragedy* of how Dionysian art can momentarily suspend each consciousness's *principium individuationis* in communal ecstasy.[1] But Tolstoy's treatise presents the first elaborate account and defense of art as the expression and transmission of a feeling.

Tolstoy's argument proceeds first by adducing reasons to reject the orthodox, traditional view that "art is the manifestation of beauty" (WiA, 12). His first argument proceeds by claiming that authentically for "a Russian man of the people who knows no foreign languages, the Russian word for 'beauty' [*krasota*] means merely that which is pleasing to the sight," and that the contemporary practice of ascribing beauty to actions and to music are misuses of the term. Rather, Tolstoy asserts, the concept *good* [*dobryi, khoroshii*] includes within its intension the concept *beautiful*, so that saying of an object valued for its appearance that it is "good" implies that we are also saying it is "beautiful"; but to attribute beauty to an object by no means implies that it is also good. Only the importation of Western European aesthetic theories, which Tolstoy canvasses with impressive completeness and understanding, has perniciously conflated beauty of form with goodness, including moral goodness.

Tolstoy's second, more elaborate argument proceeds from his review of prevailing Western European theories of art as beauty. He first divides the theories into two broad categories: those "objective," "metaphysical" theories according to which beauty is some intrinsic property or a sensuous manifestation of an "absolute" such as spirit, will, or God; and those "subjective," "physiological" theories according to which beauty is a certain kind of pleasure which one experiences. He then claims that even the objective theories imply that one recognizes the objective property or intimation of the "absolute" because one subjectively experiences aesthetic pleasure, and so both groups of theories collapse into the single view that beautiful art is recognized by the pleasure it produces in its recipient. But, Tolstoy argues, when aestheticians shift the inquiry from the nature of art to the nature of what is pleasing, relativism and subjectivism result, and most often, conclusions that in fact are merely reports of the preference in taste of the tiny minority composed of the educated and privileged upper class. In short, these theories assert that the aim of art is beauty, that beauty is known by the pleasure it gives, and that the pleasure given by art is good, so that ultimately for these theorists art is grounded in hedonism, whereby the "egoistic pleasure and immorality of existing art" is justified (WiA, 36).

Having in this way dispatched conventional Western European theories of art, Tolstoy expands the scope of his question, drawing on an analogy that partially organizes his entire treatise, namely, that art is like food or nourishment:

> To see the aim and purpose of art in the pleasure we derive from it is the same as to ascribe the aim and significance of food to the pleasure we derive from eating it [...]
>
> Just as people who think that the aim and purpose of food is pleasure cannot perceive the true meaning of eating, so people who think that the aim of art is pleasure cannot know its meaning and purpose, because they ascribe to an activity which has meaning in connection with other phenomena of life the false and exclusive aim of pleasure. People will understand that the meaning of eating is the nourishment of the body only when they cease to consider pleasure the aim of this activity. So it is with art. People will understand the meaning of art only when they cease to regard beauty—that is, pleasure—as the aim of this activity. (WiA, 35; cf. 88, 114, 138)

Thus Tolstoy looks to the wider context within which art is a human activity, to consider "its purpose in the life of man and of mankind," a kind of "spiritual nourishment" [*dukhovnoe pitanie*] no less vital to human thriving than bodily sustenance, "as one of the conditions of human life. Considering it in this way, we cannot fail to see that art is a means of union among people" (WiA, 37), where the Russian term for "union" [*obshchenie*] also connotes sacramental "communion" (Mandelker 1996). We shall explore this wider context in the second part of this essay.

As a means, the activity of art, for Tolstoy, must be that of transmitting a feeling by which the artistic creator(s) and all recipients are united, just as words are a means to convey thoughts from one to another, thereby uniting them in knowledge. The master image Tolstoy deploys throughout his belletristic and essayistic writings to capture this idea of conveying a feeling is that of "infection" [*zarazhenie*], and in *What is Art?* he stipulates the definition of art as follows:

> *To call up in oneself a feeling once experienced and, having called it up, to convey it by means of movements, lines, colors, sounds, images, expressed in words, so that others experience the same feeling—in this consists the activity of art. Art is that human activity which consists in one man's consciously conveying to others, by certain external signs, the feelings he has experienced, and in others being infected by those feelings and also experiencing them.* (WiA, 39–40, italics in original)

We can slightly modify Noël Carroll's definition of the "transmission theory" to gloss Tolstoy's definition in the following way:

> x is a genuine work of art if and only if x is (1) an intended (2) transmission to an audience (3) of the self-same (type-identical) (4) individualized (5) feeling state

(emotion) (6) that the artist experienced (himself/herself) (7) and clarified (8) by means of lines, shapes, colors, sounds, actions and/or words. (Cf. Carroll 1999, 65)

Tolstoy makes clear that his stipulative definition is normative, not merely descriptive: the capacity to transmit a feeling is the criterion of adequacy for what he calls "genuine" [*istinnoe*] art. This definition entails that many artifacts and activities which conventional aesthetic theories would dismiss here fall within the scope of art as "the entire human activity that conveys feelings":

> The whole of human life is filled with works of art of various kinds, from lullabies, jokes, mimicry, home decoration, clothing, utensils, to church services and solemn processions. All this is the activity of art. (WiA, 41)

> [S]o-called genre painting and statues, portrayals of animals, landscapes, caricatures of a content understandable to all, and various sorts of ornaments […] works in painting and sculpture (porcelain dolls) […] [are not considered art, but] in reality, all such objects, if they sincerely convey the feeling of the artist (however insignificant it may seem to us) and are understandable to all people, are works of genuine good Christian art. (WiA, 135)

> In just the same way there is not a narrowing but a broadening of the area of content for the art of the future which will convey the most simple, everyday feelings, accessible to all. In our former art, what was considered worthy of being conveyed in art was only the expression of feelings proper to a certain exclusive position, and that only on condition that they be conveyed in a most refined way, inaccessible to the majority of people; but the whole enormous realm of popular children's art—jokes, proverbs, riddles, songs, dances, children's games, mimicry—was not considered worthy object of art.
> The artist of the future will understand that to invent a little tale, a touching song, a ditty, an amusing riddle, a funny joke, to make a drawing that will give joy to dozens of generations, or to millions of children and adults, is incomparably more important and fruitful than to write a novel or a symphony or paint a picture that will for a short time divert a few members of the wealthy classes and then be forgotten forever. The realm of this art of simple feelings accessible to all is enormous and as yet almost untouched. (WiA, 154-155)

These passages indicate just how truly radical Tolstoy's expressivist theory of art is. It is not an *ontological* theory, as on this account an artwork can be an instance of high art (Tolstoy acknowledges some novels, for instance), a folk tradition, a ritualized activity, an ornament evoking admiration, household utensils, etc. The work of art can be authored or not, a perduring object or an ephemeral event. It is not an *institutional* theory, as Tolstoy rejects all recognitional institutions as ultimately reflecting and serving elitist ends, nor is it an *historical* theory, since the normative criterion is transcultural and transhistorical. It might perhaps best be termed an *anthropological pragmatic* theory, in the sense that the nature of art for Tolstoy is grounded wholly in its demonstrable, human capacity to convey universally a feeling, that is, in the artwork's infectiousness.

Infectiousness, in turn, relies on three normative criteria that provide a scalar measure of an artwork's success. Perhaps invoking Descartes, Tolstoy holds that the greater the particularity or distinctiveness [*osobennost'*]—one might say the individuation—of the feeling conveyed, and the greater the clarity [*iasnost'*] of the transmission of the feeling, the more successful the artwork's infectiousness.[2] The third criterion is the sincerity [*iskrennost'*] of the artist, "that is, the greater or lesser force with which the artist himself experiences the feelings he conveys" (WiA, 121).[3] The fulfillment of these criteria ensures, Tolstoy seems to suggest, that the feeling will be universally conveyed, which he claims is the necessary and sufficient condition for genuine art: "Great works of art are great *only* because they are accessible and comprehensible to everyone" (WiA, 81).

An artwork that fails to fulfill one or more of these criteria is "counterfeit" [*poddel'noe iskusstvo*], a mere simulacrum of genuine art. Tolstoy provides a short genetic argument for the emergence and prevalence of counterfeit art that is grounded in both the societal conditions of nineteenth-century Europe and Russia and the expressivist internal relation between work and author in Tolstoy's aesthetic theory. The *societal premise* claims that the upper classes, because they lead a life of idle luxury, demand a continuous production of pleasing, amusing works. The *expressivist premise* claims that it is impossible to produce any art at will, for "it must be born of itself in the artist" (WiA, 84), what he calls "an inner need" and equates to the artist's "sincerity" (Emerson 1996, 105). From these two premises Tolstoy concludes that so-called artists must therefore invent methods or devices by which they can continuously and mechanically produce objects simulating artworks, and he identifies and describes four such devices. The first device is "borrowing" [*zaimstvovanie*], that is, finding or adopting artistic subject matter from external sources (the tradition, generic or stylistic conventions, other artists, etc.). Borrowing fails, firstly, because it negates the sincerity condition: "an artistic impression is an infection, it works only when the author has himself experienced some feeling and conveys it in his own way, not when he conveys someone else's feeling as it was conveyed to him" (WiA, 85). A work based on borrowing fails secondarily, in that it "cannot produce a true artistic impression, because it lacks the chief property of a work of art—wholeness, organicity, in which form and content constitute an inseparable whole expressing the feeling experienced by the artist" (WiA, 88; cf. Emerson 2000). The second device is "imitativeness" [*podrazhatel'nost'*] by which Tolstoy means intricate, extraneous details added to the work that ultimately undermine its infectiousness: "the attention of the one receiving the artistic impression is distracted by all these well-observed details, and this prevents the author's feeling, if indeed there is any, from being conveyed" (WiA, 88). The third device is the use of "striking effects" [*porazitel'nost'*]: either artistic devices that stimulate physiological reactions such as sensual lust, horror, and so on, or one artistic medium portraying something usually or properly portrayed by another (such as program music being used to describe a scene), the novelty of which affects the recipient. This device fails because such works "do not convey any feeling, but only affect the nerves" (WiA, 89), and such short-lived, merely physiological effects are insufficient presumably because in themselves they are simply causal excitations, rather than a semantically meaningful content as part of the feeling that is conveyed by a genuine artwork. The final device of counterfeit art in turn qualifies from the other direction the semantic or cognitive component of the feeling conveyed, for "diversion" [*zanimatel'nost'*] is intellectual interest that is superadded to the work to engage the recipient's curiosity and render the work not completely comprehensible but thereby undermines its infectiousness: "the mental effort required of a spectator, listener, or reader to satisfy their aroused curiosity, or to master the new information imparted by the work, or to grasp its meaning, absorbs the reader's, spectator's, or listener's attention, thereby interfering with the infection" (WiA, 90).[4]

In demarcating genuine art—in which a feeling is conveyed—from counterfeit art, Tolstoy explicitly concedes that the content of artworks plays no criterial role, writing that "[sincerity of the artist, particularity, and clarity of the feeling] are the three conditions the presence of which distinguishes art from artistic counterfeits and at the same time determines the worth of any work of art regardless of content" (WiA, 122).[5] That is, the criteria of genuine art for Tolstoy are categorically amoral: it is quite conceivable that a genuine artwork would excel in conveying a morally vicious feeling.

Clearly the theory so far is insufficient to evaluate and exhort the production of specific artworks, and so Tolstoy in a second move provides the normative criterion for demarcating the content of an artwork, namely, whether the feeling it conveys is "good" [*khoroshee*] or "bad" [*durnoe*]. The feeling conveyed by an artwork "depends on people's understanding of the meaning of life, on what they see as good and evil in life. Good and evil in life are determined by what are called religions" (WiA ,42). We shall return in the second part of this essay to consider the sense and larger context of Tolstoy's invocation of "the meaning of life," but in the context of his aesthetic theory he identifies good content with "Christian religious consciousness" [*religioznoe khristanskoe soznanie*] as embodied in the Gospels: "the consciousness of the fact that our good, material and spiritual, individual and general, temporal and eternal, consists in the brotherly life of all people, in our union of love with each other" (WiA, 126); "the essence of Christian consciousness consists in each man's recognition of his sonship to God, and their consequent union with God and with each other, as it stands in the Gospel, and therefore the content of Christian art is such feelings as contribute to the union of men with God and with each other" (WiA, 129). According to Tolstoy, only two types of feelings are able to contribute to uniting all people, and therefore there are only two types of good art: "religious art, which conveys feelings coming from a religious consciousness of man's position in the world with regard to God and his neighbor," and "universal art, which conveys the simplest everyday feelings of life, such as are accessible to everyone in the world. Only these two kinds of art can be considered good art in our time" (WiA, 131–132). This is, in broad strokes, the argumentative armature of Tolstoy's definitive, now canonical philosophical aesthetics as presented in his treatise *What is Art?*

However, aspects of his other aesthetic writings are worth brief consideration here, because they demonstrate his extensive sources and examples of failed and successful artworks as well as developments and variations in his thinking that in turn may indicate fundamental commitments and potential challenges within his final, established theory.[6] For instance, in his 1894 forward to the Russian translation of the works of Maupassant, he claims that a "true work of art" must fulfill three conditions: "(1) a correct, that is a moral, relation of the author to his subject; (2) clearness of expression, or beauty of form—the two are identical; and (3) sincerity, that is, a sincere feeling of love or hatred of what the artist depicts" (Tolstoy 1969, 21). While Maupassant enjoys abundant literary talent and meets the second and third conditions, he fails the first, and for Tolstoy foremost, condition, a condition that runs throughout all his writings on art, even as his understanding of concepts such as feeling, beauty, and sincerity undergo development. Central to Tolstoy's thinking is that the artwork, regardless of its content, is expressive of its creator, manifests his moral, evaluative perception and understanding of the world:

> The cement which binds any artistic production into one whole, and therefore produces the illusion of being a reflection of life, is not the unity of persons and situations, but the unity of the author's independent moral relation to his subject. In reality, when we read or look at the artistic production of a new author, the fundamental question that arises in our soul is always of this kind: "Well, what sort of a man are you? Wherein are you different from all the people I know, and what can you tell me that is new about how we must look at this life of ours?" Whatever the artist depicts—saints, robbers, kings, or lackeys—we seek and see only the artist's own soul. (Tolstoy 1969, 38; cf. Gershkovich 2013)

In his earlier fragment "On Truth in Art" from 1887 Tolstoy makes clear that this moral understanding of the world is not to be located principally in the content of the artwork, in what is narrated or depicted, and the truth of an artwork is not to be equated to the factual, probable, or even plausible verisimilitude of its contents. Rather, invoking Christ's "I am the way, the truth, and the life" along with the Platonic image of the sun as the Good by which we should orient ourselves, Tolstoy claims that artworks are true "when they show what ought to be [...] when they set a value on what is good and evil—when they show men the narrow path of God's will, which leads to life" (Tolstoy 1969, 11).[7] In his preparatory writings on aesthetics Tolstoy varies and rebalances definitions and accentuations, while remaining committed to the general theory, as when he writes in one of the fragments entitled "On Art" (ca. 1895–1897): "A perfect work of art will be one in which the content is important and significant to all men, and therefore [*sic*] it will be *moral*. The

604 H. W. PICKFORD

expression will be quite clear, intelligible to all, and therefore *beautiful*; the author's relation to his work will be altogether sincere and heartfelt, and therefore true" (ibid., 56).

Examples of failed and successful artworks shed further light on Tolstoy's morally inflected expression theory of art. Examples of failed or counterfeit art for Tolstoy are largely tantamount to the orthodox canon of Western masterpieces. Frequently deploying the technique Viktor Shklovsky would later call "defamiliarization" [*ostranenie*], Tolstoy alienates these well-known works from his readers' familiarity with them by describing their inherited generic conventions and contrived mechanisms from an outsider's—sometimes personified as a "simple laborer's"—perspective. This defamiliarizing technique reaches back to the narrator's description of Natasha Rostova's experience of the opera in *War and Peace* (Part Five, section IX; cf. Lowe 1990), written 1865–1867, and includes Tolstoy's descriptions of productions of Wagner's *Ring* cycle and of *Hamlet* in *What is Art?* (sections XIII and XIV) and of *Lear* in his 1906 essay "On Shakespeare and his Drama." Alienating his reader from any possible identification with or absorption in these works' characters and actions, Tolstoy emphasizes precisely the qualities that characterize "counterfeit" art and obstruct the immediate conveyance of a clear feeling, instead likening the effect to that produced by hypnosis, wine, or opium: "These poetical, imitative, striking, and diverting qualities, owing both to Wagner's peculiar talent and to his advantageous position, are brought to the highest degree of perfection in these works, and affect the spectator by hypnotizing him, as a man who listens for several hours to the ravings of a madman uttered with great oratorical skill will also become hypnotized" (WiA, 111). Such analogies imply that Western high art *qua* counterfeit art fosters addictive pleasures and solipsistic stupor, undermining the potentiality of human nature for community and moral development.

In *What is Art?* Tolstoy adduces multiple positive examples of genuine art, consideration of which will help to elaborate his theory. In the first example, peasant women singing a song to greet his recently married daughter infectiously and imperceptibly raise his and his household's spirits (WiA, 115–116; cf. a related scene in *Anna Karenina*, Part Three, chapter XII), in contrast to his experience of a Beethoven sonata that evening: "the women's song was true art, conveying a definite, strong feeling. While the 101st sonata of Beethoven was only an unsuccessful attempt at art, containing no definite feeling and therefore not infecting one with anything" (WiA, 116). In the second example Tolstoy recounts the plot of a story by a peasant writer for a children's magazine. A poor widow obtains hard-to-find white flour to bake an Easter bread, and asks her children to watch over it briefly. The children are distracted and the mother returns to find a mother hen feeding it to her chicks. Having scolded the children, she then feels sorry for them and bakes them bread from rye flour, comforting them by reciting a proverb that "rye is the grandpa of white": "the children suddenly go from despair to joyful rapture, each time repeating the proverb, and they look forward to the [bread] with all the more merriment" (WiA, 117). The third example is a genre painting by the English artist Langley "depicting a wandering beggar boy who has apparently been asked in by a woman who feels sorry for him"; while she feeds him a little girl intently watches the boy, "obviously realizing for the first time what poverty is, what inequality among people is, and for the first time asking herself questions: why is it that she has everything, while this boy is barefoot and hungry? She feels both pity and joy. And she loves the boy and the good. [...] And one feels that the artist loved this girl and what she loved" (WiA, 118). The fourth and final example is the folk theater of a "savage people," the nomadic Siberian tribe of the Voguls, in which a bow hunter cautiously stalks a mother reindeer and her calf as the natural world (in the persona of a tribe member playing a bird) warns the deer. Eventually the hunter strikes the calf, which clings to its mother as she licks its wound. "The hunter sets another arrow to his bow. The spectators, according to the narrator's account, sit stock still; one hears deep sighs and even weeping" (WiA, 119).

While these works appear to exemplify the jointly sufficient conditions Tolstoy requires of genuine and good art, namely, the transmission of clearly individualized feelings—joy, pity, compassion—they also indicate open questions and possible objections. In some cases a feeling is *conveyed* (e.g., in the first example), while in others a portrayed scene *arouses* an appropriate feeling from the audience (e.g., vulnerability and innocence presumably elicit compassion and solicitude in the fourth example). Tolstoy seems to identify and accept this bifurcation, when he writes of a contemporary play that "the author wishes to convey to the public his compassion for a girl tormented to death. To call up this emotion in the spectators by means of art, the author ought to have made one of his characters express this compassion in such a way as to infect everyone [thereby conveying compassion to the audience], or to have given a true description of the girl's sensations [thereby arousing compassion in the audience]" (WiA, 89). The first disjunct fulfills the conditions laid out by Tolstoy's (and Carroll 1999) expression theory, strictly understood as a "transmission theory"; the second disjunct does not, but can be accommodated by an expression theory that also includes an "arousal theory" of emotion in art (e.g., Matravers 1998).

However, the first and fourth examples raise another question: if Tolstoy's theory presupposes an artist who calls up a feeling previously experienced, what of artworks that appear to have no artist-creator, such as a folk song or a folk play? If one concedes that in such and other cases, it is the performer who calls up a past feeling in order to artistically transmit it to her audience, other questions ensue. Either actors need not have experienced, or even currently experience, the feeling they are simulating (as Denis Diderot famously argued in his essay "Paradox of the Actor"), or an actor's range is delimited by her factual experiences, which presumably leaves few actors prepared to play murderers or saints. Subsequent proponents of the expression theory of art have tried to address this concern by uncoupling the artwork from the causal history of its production by differentiating expression from expressiveness, arguing that an

606   H. W. PICKFORD

artwork does not express an emotion but rather is expressive of an emotion, in that it exhibits or exemplifies some quality that is suggestive, metaphorical, or similar to an expressive human gesture (Carroll 1999, 83–84; Pickford 2016, Chapter 8).

Tolstoy himself wrestled with another problem confronting his theory. In an as-yet-untranslated draft on aesthetics from 1896 entitled "On What is Called Art" ["O tom, chto nazyvaiut iskusstvom"] he speculated that art arises from play [*zabava*], both being forms of relaxation necessary for the working person's life. Whereas play is actively engaged in by its participants, and therefore particularly good for the young, art is passively received by its audience, and therefore particularly good for the old. However, the special virtue of art is that it conveys new feelings to people who have not yet experienced, and might not be able to experience, them in their actual domains of activity:

> Therefore art is play [*zabava*], which occurs when a person consciously subjects himself to the infection of that feeling which the artist experienced. The pleasure of this play consists in the fact that the person, not making efforts (not living), not bearing all the vital consequences of feelings, experiences the most diverse feelings, becoming infected with them immediately [*neposredstvenno*] from the artist, lives and experiences the joy of life without the labor of life. The pleasure consists almost in the same thing in which the pleasure of dreams consists, only with greater consistency; and precisely in the fact that the person does not experience all the friction of life [*vesgo togo treniia zhizni*] that poisons and lessens the enjoyment of actual life, and meanwhile receives all the excitements [*volneniia*] of life, which make up the essence and charm of life, and receives them with greater intensity since nothing impedes them. Thanks to art a person without legs or a decrepit [old man] experiences the enjoyment of folk-dancing, looking at a dancing artist-*skomorokh* [a Medieval wandering harlequin or minstrel-clown]; a person, not exiting his northern home, experiences the enjoyment of southern nature, looking at a painting; a meek, weak person experiences the enjoyment of strength and power, looking at a painting, reading, or watching a poetic work in the theater, or listening to heroic music; a cold, austere [*sukhoi*] person, never having felt pity, never having loved, experiences the enjoyment of love, of compassion.
>
> The play of art lies in this.
>
> A game is a necessary condition for the life of children, the young, or those organizing a celebration of people's life, when there is an excess of physical strength, not directed to material work; and art is the necessary condition of life of adults and elderly people, when physical powers are all directed to labor or these powers have weakened, as happens with disease and old age. Both [game and art] are necessary to a person for relaxation from that circle of labor, sleep, and nourishment, in which he moves from the day of his birth to his death, like every animal. And thus since man has been living, he has always had and will always have both forms of play—games and art, and art, not being that mystical devotion to beauty as which it is described in aesthetics, nevertheless remains a necessary condition for people's lives. (Tolstoy 1929–1958, vol. 30, 252–253 [hereafter PSS]; my translation)

What Tolstoy lauds here—that art as a form of playful pretense can convey feelings without the recipient experiencing their accompanying "friction of life" or "bearing all the vital consequences" of those feelings—he comes to perceive as a danger, perhaps as a result of reading Schopenhauer, according to whom music conveys intense feelings without the reasons or motives justifying them. For Schopenhauer this decontextualization of emotion in music entails that how the emotion will be taken up, and ultimately even individualized as one emotion rather than another, will depend on the moral character of the recipient. One can view the problem from another vantage point. Tolstoy's theory seems to accommodate a wide, undifferentiated spectrum of sensations, moods, feelings, and emotions (Jahn 1975). At times he likens the transmission of a feeling by art to the physiological contagiousness of laughter or yawning: the recipient will laugh or yawn without feeling amused or tired (cf. Robinson 2008). But genuine emotions, it is often argued, also have a cognitive, judg-mental, or appropriateness dimension. Tolstoy implies this cognitively richer dimension of human emotional life most directly in his exposition of the third example, in which the viewer of the painting sees that the girl feeling pity is also realizing its context of elicitation: poverty, undeserved suffering, and human dignity. The tension between the merely causal, physiological notion of sensa-tion and the normative, cognitive dimension of emotion, and the dependence of the emotion experienced upon the moral character of its recipient is enacted in Tolstoy's 1899 novella "The Kreutzer Sonata," in which the narrator, who had killed his wife in a jealous rage after hearing the eponymous Beethoven sonata, confesses, "under the influence of music I have the illusion of feeling things I don't really feel, of understanding things I don't understand, being able to do things I'm not able to do" (Tolstoy 1985, 96; cf. WiA, Chapter V, Emerson 2010, Pickford 2016).

Tolstoy's general strategy to evade this problem is to anchor feelings in the context of nature. The union of human beings that good art can achieve relies on the universality of human nature, suggestive of the theories of moral senti-ments current in Tolstoy's time (Orwin 1993). On this reading, Tolstoy's examples emphasize basic universal human emotional responses such as pity, compassion, joy, and sadness, so "usually, when a person receives a truly artistic impression, it seems to him that he knew it all along, only he was unable to express it" (WiA, 81). For Tolstoy this context of human nature is essentially gendered and familial, paradigmatically embodied in the mother-child relation, as are all the positive examples discussed above: the singing peasant women celebrate a recent marriage and presumably the start of a new family, while the other three explicitly portray human and animal mother figures caring for a child. In these emblematic examples, the individual artworks illustrate the fruitful and nurturing role Tolstoy defines for good art, as those in the upper classes who no longer can be infected with such emotions "live without the softening, fertilizing effect of art" (WiA, 139). This gendered naturalizing stratagem reaches its culmination in an extended simile in which good art is itself likened to the "proper" procreative function of womanhood:

608 H. W. PICKFORD

> Terrible as it may be to say it, what has happened to the art of our circle and time is the same as happens with a woman who sells her feminine attractions, destined for motherhood, for the pleasure of those who are tempted by such pleasures.
>
> The art of our time and circle has become a harlot [*bludnitsa*]. And this comparison holds true in the smallest details. It is, in the same way, not limited in time, is always in fancy dress, is always for sale; it is just as alluring and pernicious.
>
> The genuine work of art can manifest itself in an artist's soul only rarely, as a fruit of all his previous life, just as a child is conceived by its mother. [...]
>
> Genuine art has no need for dressing up, like the wife of a loving husband. Counterfeit art, like a prostitute, must always be decked out.
>
> The cause of the appearance of genuine art is an inner need to express a stored-up feeling, as love is the cause of sexual conception for a mother. The cause of counterfeit art is mercenary, just as with prostitution.
>
> The consequence of true art is the introduction of a new feeling into everyday life, as the consequence of a wife's love is the birth of a new person into life. The consequence of counterfeit art is the corruption of man, the insatiability of pleasures, the weakness of man's spiritual force. (WiA, 149–150)

The simile is grounded in the stipulated normative force of naturalized—and socialized (through marriage)—gender relations, by which Tolstoy can liken the artist, production, artwork, and its effect to the "proper" nature and activity of a young wife. This commitment to such a normative conception of woman runs deep in Tolstoy's thought, as in his reactionary stance to the "woman question" at the turn of the century, and in his critical essays. For instance, in a 1902 review of a novel he highlights a scene in which, after being beaten by her drunken husband for having taken money from him to feed their children, the wife makes him comfortable as he lies passed out in bed: "here at once the reader is shown the consciousness of conjugal duty educated by tradition, and the triumph of a decision maintained—not to give up the money, needed, not for herself but for the family—here also is the offense, forgiveness of the beating, pity, and if not love, at least the memory of love for her husband, the father of her children" (Tolstoy 1969, 316). And in his 1905 introduction to Chekhov's story "Darling" Tolstoy notes that Chekhov wanted to mock the simple-minded devotion of the female protagonist, but despite himself in his portrayal of her love for a man and her self-sacrifice he exalted her: "he blessed, and involuntarily clothed that sweet creature in such a wonderful radiance that she will always remain a type of what woman can be in order to be happy herself and to cause the happiness of those with whom her fate is united" (Tolstoy 1969, 327).[8] Gendered vital activities, therefore, provide Tolstoy a normative background and grounding of universal feelings by which people are united. This normatively "naturalized" background has received less attention from scholars of Tolstoy's aesthetic theory, but it provides central insights into his understanding of what role art ought to play in society.

The Wider Context: Philosophy of Life

We have already seen at least two ways in which vitalist concepts inform Tolstoy's aesthetic theory: first, in that the organic unity of author, form, and content best assures the infectiousness constitutive of a genuine artwork; and second, in the invocation of nature and gendered relations to ground and anchor potentially underdetermined feelings that a genuine artwork transmits. However, Tolstoy's vitalism reaches far beyond these two aspects, for Tolstoy holds that such artworks express the proper "meaning of life" and thereby unify people and fulfill unique functions in the life of society, such that only this wider context of what could be called Tolstoy's "philosophy of life" accurately and adequately explains Tolstoy's philosophy of art narrowly construed.

As noted above, throughout *What is Art?* Tolstoy considers art to be "spiritual nourishment," ascribing it an essential life function for the individual. He writes: "The appreciation of the merits of art—that is, of the feelings it conveys—depends on people's understanding of the meaning of life, on what they see as good and evil in life. Good and evil in life are determined by what are called religions" (WiA, 42). This "religious consciousness" is an orientation toward the Good and God as ultimately a theistic-moral value realism, which as it were conditions the artist's worldview:

> The good is the eternal, the highest aim of our life. No matter how we understand that good, our life is nothing else than a striving toward the good—that is, toward God.
>
> The good is indeed a fundamental understanding, which metaphysically constitutes the essence of our consciousness, an understanding undefinable by reason.
>
> The good is that which no one can define, but which defines everything else. (WiA, 52)

A key thought here is that morality is not an independent or separable domain of human experience, thought, or rational philosophical inquiry, not a value or set of values different in kind from an independent, objective world of facts; rather for Tolstoy one's value orientation pervades and colors one's world, including how one defines and determines factuality, how one views the world. As he wrote in the 1893 text "Religion and Morality": "Neither philosophy nor science is able to establish man's relationship to the universe, because this relationship must be established before any kind of philosophy or science can begin [...] a man's relationship to the world is determined not just by his intellect but by his feelings and by his whole aggregate of spiritual forces" (Tolstoy 1987, 139). So the meaning of life, religious consciousness, is not the independent or separable (doctrinal) content of an artwork, but rather pervades its every aspect, as he asserts in "On Shakespeare and on Drama" (1906):

> By religious content of art I do not mean the external preaching of some religious truths in artistic form and not the allegorical representation of these truths, but rather a definite worldview [*mirovozzrenie*] corresponding to the highest religious

610   H. W. PICKFORD

> understanding of our time, which, serving as the incentive for the creation of the play, unconsciously for the author penetrates his entire work. This has always been the case for a true artist and especially for a dramatist [...] only that person can write a drama who has something to say to people, and something that is of the greatest importance for people: about a person's relationship to God, to the universe, to everything eternal, unending. (Tolstoy PSS 35: 267, my translation)

Moreover, recalling the previous quotation from *What is Art?*, religious consciousness qua fundamental understanding is not defined or captured by reason, but rather by feeling.

Here Tolstoy combines with the Platonic realism of the Good—as the light in which all should be perceived—the communal sentimentalism of Rousseau and above all the Christian Gospels, according to which the fundamental feeling—a value-affect in analogy to Max Weber's value rationality [*Wertrationalität*]—is love. As he wrote in "The Law of Love and the Law of Violence" from 1908: "It is becoming more and more evident in our age that the true significance of the Christian doctrine [as opposed to Church doctrine, which Tolstoy came to reject as empty, formalized ritual in his 1882 *A Confession*] is that the essence of human life is the ever-growing manifestation of the source of everything, indicated in us through love; therefore that the essence of human life and the highest law governing it is love," which is now recognized not only by following Christ's teaching, but "through spontaneous awareness" (Tolstoy 1987, 172, 194). Hence in *What is Art?* he describes the current religious consciousness as "the consciousness of the fact that our good, material and spiritual, individual and general, temporal and eternal, consists in the brotherly life of all people, in our union of love with each other" (WiA 126; cf. 167). The resulting picture of Tolstoy's "meaning of life" corresponds to "religious consciousness," as does the awareness, attitude, and sentimental attunement to living in the truth of one's relationship to the divine in the sense of the universal, egalitarian love—pity, compassion, solicitude, care, and so on—by which humanity is united (cf. Kyriacou 2019; Gustafson 1986; Medzhibovskaya 2009). Because understanding the "meaning of life" means practically understanding how to live, good artworks which induce this understanding are vital, constitute "spiritual nourishment."

To this picture of religious consciousness Tolstoy adds an historical and social-critical account that likely originated in his adherence to Rousseau's writings. As he wrote in a letter in 1905, "Rousseau has been my master since I was fifteen. Rousseau and the Gospels have been the two great and beneficent influences of my life" (quoted in Meyer 2007). While Rousseau's *On the Social Contract* (1762) informs Tolstoy's utopian conception of an egalitarian community grounded first and foremost in transparently shared, universal natural sentiments, that—so Tolstoy—can be cultivated through the union of artist and recipients produced by affective infection, Tolstoy's account in *What is Art?* of the moral depravity of aestheticism among the upper classes clearly echoes the French philosopher's *First Discourse* (1750) and *Discourse on*

Inequality (1755). In the former work Rousseau argued that the original and inherent potential for art and the sciences to improve humanity materially and spiritually has been repressed through ideological distortions of their practices in order to reinforce class privilege, political and material power. And in the *Discourse on Inequality* Rousseau proffers a speculative genetic account of the emergence from the naturally egalitarian state of nature of the social inequality and its consolidation and perpetuation in modern society's economic, political, and legal structures that Tolstoy categorically condemns in his writings (Barran 1992; Orwin 1993). Like Rousseau, Tolstoy views moral-social progress as the historical advance in recuperating the natural sentiments as a basis for community. While the capacity for these natural sentiments is present *in potentia* in all people, in any age there will be specific figures, as a spiritual vanguard, who express the most advanced stage of "religious consciousness" and knowledge of "the meaning of life" most clearly. In this sense history is the continual, never ending clarification of these natural social capacities as attunements to a continually more definite, morally colored world: "the explanation of the meaning of life and the resulting guidance for conduct is never finalized but becomes continually clearer":

> Compared to all the ancient [religious] teachings Christianity is neither new nor different; it is simply a more clear and precise expression of the basis of human life that was felt and vaguely expounded by previous religions. In this respect the peculiarity of the Christian teaching lies only in the fact that, being the last, it uses greater precision and clarity to express the essence of the law of love and the guidance for conduct that must follow from it. And thus the Christian teaching on love is not, as in former doctrines, merely a teaching about a certain virtue, but it is a definition of the supreme law of human life and the guidance for conduct that inevitably follows from it. Christ's teaching clarifies why this is the highest law in life, and at the same time it indicates a series of actions which men must either commit or not commit as a consequence of accepting this teaching as the truth. (Tolstoy 1987, 155, 172–173)

This wider context for Tolstoy's aesthetic theory is articulated in the final chapters of *What is Art?* Developing a parallel he had established early in the treatise between reason, thoughts, and their transmission in words on the one hand, and sensibility, feelings, and their transmission in artworks on the other, Tolstoy calls science and art the two "organs of communication" (ibid., 139), likening them to the lungs and heart "so that if one organ is perverted, the other cannot function properly" (ibid., 157). Here the naturalized framework for Tolstoy's aesthetic theory is fully expressed, as art alongside science is troped as an organ within the body politic whose vital function serves the spiritual and material growth of humanity. He diagnoses two distinct ways in which these organs, say, the organ of art, can fail. In the first case, namely, "the absence in that society of the activity which should be accomplished by the organ," the majority of society's members will lack the capacity to be infected by true works of art, being merely stimulated by counterfeit art, and so will live "without the softening, fertilizing effects of art," becoming more crude and coarse (ibid., 139). In the second case, namely that of "harmful activity of the corrupted organ," an aesthetic of beauty unconnected to the good will induce the upper classes to "free themselves from the demands of morality," and will produce confusion in children and simple working people. Given this diagnosis, Tolstoy endorses Plato's recommendation: "better that there be no art than that the depraved art, or simulacrum of it, which exists now should continue" (WiA, 146).

In the final chapter of the treatise, however, Tolstoy elaborates his ideal social-moral polity, which integrates several of the influences and lines of reasoning already outlined above. Both science and art are spiritual activities that require the correct axiological worldview, in the sense of value rationality, in order to fulfill their life functions as organs of the body politic: "True science studies and introduces into human consciousness the truths and knowledge which are regarded as most important by the people of a certain period and society. Art transfers these truths from the realm of knowledge to the realm of feeling. Therefore, if the path that science follows is false, so, too, will the path of art be false" (WiA, 157–158). Deploying an extended simile of how a river-barge is operated, Tolstoy appears to be claiming that religious consciousness of the meaning of life, that is, the correct values by which humanity at a given time should flourish, provides the fundamental value orientation, recognizing what is important, salient, morally significant in the world. Science, in turn, produces knowledge that illuminates how these values can be actualized in the world, and art provides an affective impetus and engagement in people for this actualization. True science, then, should study "how human life should be arranged—the questions of religion, morality, social life, without resolving which all our knowledge of nature is harmless and worthless. [...] [True science lies] in discovering what ought or ought not to be believed; in discovering how the overall life of mankind ought or ought not to be arranged: how to arrange sexual relations, how to bring up children, how to use the land, how to cultivate it without oppressing others, how to relate to foreigners, how to relate to animals, and many other things important to human life" (WiA, 160, 161). When thus oriented toward the proper axiological worldview, science will "become a harmonious, organic whole with a definite and reasonable purpose, understandable to all people—namely, the introducing into people's consciousness of the truths that come from the religious consciousness of our time. And only then will art, which always depends on science, be what it can and should be—an organ of the life and progress of mankind as important as science" (WiA, 165).

Tolstoy's vision of true science is as conservative-revolutionary as is his vision of true art. Present science, in his view, is corrupted in ways similar to Rousseau's critical diagnosis in his *First Discourse*. Science either serves the ideological needs of the upper classes to maintain and justify the unjust order: this is the perverted function of fields such as theology, philosophy, history, and political economy. Or science is pursued for its own sake, in analogy to aestheticism, serving to satisfy idle curiosity or the profit interests of the upper class: hence Tolstoy condemns fields such as mathematics, astronomy, chemistry, and the other natural sciences. Counterfeit art and an empty aesthetics of beauty and pleasure correspond and supervene on such sciences and their knowledge production. It is important to note that rather than claim that technological progress would usher in social-political structural changes, as so many utopian movements of the time espoused, Tolstoy saw the dependency relation running in the opposite direction: so long as the basic value orientation of society continued unchanged, science would be misdirected in its focus and goals, and its products would tend to reinforce the present order. Instead, Tolstoy acknowledges science's potential to abolish coerced labor, the division of labor, distribution of property, and class struggle (in language reminiscent of Marxist theorists[9]), but laments that "according to [contemporary] science, the existing order of things is immutable, like the movement of the heavenly bodies, and therefore the task of [contemporary] science lies not in elucidating the falseness of this order and establishing a new, reasonable system of life, but in feeding all the people while maintaining the existing order, and giving them all the opportunity to be as idle as the ruling classes are now, living their depraved life" (WiA, 163).

But should science find its true path and devote itself to its proper task of discovering and developing the rational arrangement of human life in accordance with the present age's religious consciousness, this change, while necessary, is still not sufficient for bringing such arrangements into being: for that, true art is required, which Tolstoy ultimately expands beyond simple feelings to include virtue-theoretic responsiveness: habituated dispositions, attunements that properly respond to the morally colored world's affect- and action-inducing affordances. Just as traditional religious art can instill reverence and convey rituals and customs, for Tolstoy true art "can evoke reverence for each man's dignity, for every animal's life; it can evoke the shame of luxury, of violence, of revenge, of using for one's pleasure objects that are a necessity for other people; it can make people sacrifice themselves to serve others freely and joyfully, without noticing it [...] will show them, not in reasoning but in life alone, the joy of general union beyond the barriers set up by life"—where "without noticing it" echoes Tolstoy's own reaction to the peasant women's song earlier in the treatise (WiA, 166; cf. 115f.). It thus becomes clear that Tolstoy's expression theory of art, beyond its intrinsic philosophical-aesthetic interest, presupposes a wider naturalized, moral-political framework in order to be fully appreciated.

LEGACY

The influence of Tolstoy's thoughts on artistic expression and its place in society has been immense; here only a few chief instances can be mentioned. The presence of Tolstoy in Ludwig Wittgenstein's thought can be seen, for instance, in his views on value as transcendental and inexpressible in his *Tractatus*

Logico-Philosophicus (1922) and his later views on style, expression, and aspect-seeing in his *Philosophical Investigations* (1953). R. C. Collingwood in his *Principles of Art* (1938) develops an alternative theory of aesthetic expression indebted to the Idealist philosopher Benedetto Croce; whereas in central passages of *What is Art?* Tolstoy indicates that the artist consciously seeks the best expressive means to manifest an emotion she wishes to transmit, for Collingwood the artist first inchoately senses a feeling, the individuation and conscious recognition of which is only achieved through its externalization in the artwork; in this way his version of an expression theory of art has been deemed "Romantic" (Mounce 2001, 82–93). On the other hand, John Dewey's *Art as Experience* (1934) explicitly acknowledges its debt to Tolstoy's theory of aesthetic expression—for example, for valuably complicating the temporal and qualitative phenomenology of emotion in aesthetic experience—but also to Tolstoy's vision of art's function within a harmonious, organic arrangement of society, as indicated in this passage:

> We live in a world in which there is an immense amount of organization, but it is an external organization, not one of the ordering of a growing experience, one that involves, moreover, the whole of the live creature, toward a fulfilling conclusion. Works of art that are not remote from common life, that are widely enjoyed in a community, are signs of a unified collective life. But they are also marvelous aids in the creation of such a life. The remaking of the material of experience in the act of expression is not an isolated event confined to the artist and to a person here and there who happens to enjoy the work. In the degree in which art exercises its office, it is also a remaking of the experience of the community in the direction of greater order and unity. (Dewey 1934, 84)

Perhaps the most pervasive and compelling presence of Tolstoy in contemporary philosophy is to be found in the works of the philosopher and novelist Iris Murdoch and those influenced by her thought in turn. Tolstoy the novelist of psychological realism inhabits her earliest essays (e.g., her 1959 "The Sublime and the Beautiful Revisited") as an exemplar of the loving attention to the infinitely rich reality of other people that progressively reveals moral character (e.g., Murdoch 1999, 280).[10] It is not implausible that this early orientation to Tolstoy at least partially informed her picture of morality and moral philosophy, beginning as early as her 1956 paper "Vision and Choice in Morality." There and in subsequent papers she argued for a form of moral realism, in which a suitably trained person can with "a just and loving gaze" (Murdoch 1999, 327) discern moral facts and properties such as courage, humility, and generosity.[11] For such a person these facts can themselves be intrinsically motivating affordances, calling forth responses, so that freedom consists ideally in acting in accordance with the moral reality that one correctly perceives (ibid., 329–331). Such a picture of morality rejects a scientistic view of the world as containing only independent "objective" facts upon which a "subjective" evaluative point of view supervenes or to which it is reducible.

Rather, the world is pervasively imbued with evaluative properties, such that morality pervades thought, and all consciousness has a moral character: "It seems to me that one cannot 'philosophize' adequately upon the subject [of ethics] unless one takes it as fundamental that consciousness is a form of moral activity: what we attend to, how we attend, whether we attend" (Murdoch 1993, 167, 1999, 301, 321; cf. Diamond 2010). Morality, and moral philosophy, is not a separate and isolatable compartment of people's lives and our thinking; rather their understanding of "the meaning of life," to use Tolstoy's locution, informs the world they inhabit and how they inhabit it: "total vision of life, as shown in their mode of speech, their choice of words, their assessment of others, their conception of their own lives, what they think attractive or praise-worthy, what they think funny: in short, the configurations of their thought which show continually in their reactions and conversations" (Murdoch 1956, 39).

Murdoch's view of moral perception entails that individually and historically one's view of the world can change. Her paradigmatic example is how a mother comes to reappraise her daughter-in-law's behavior and character, first seeing her as vulgar, undignified, and noisy, and later, after further observation, interaction, introspection, and contemplation, seeing her as "not vulgar but refreshingly simple, not undignified but spontaneous, not noisy but gay, not tiresomely juvenile but delightfully youthful, and so on" (Murdoch 1999, 311–313). Individually and collectively, therefore, human beings have the ability "to 'deepen' or 'reorganize' the concept or change it for another one" (Murdoch 1956, 55). Hence "as moral beings we are immersed in a reality which transcends us and [...] moral progress consists in awareness of this reality and submission to its purposes" (ibid., 56). The virtues that promote a just and loving discernment of the moral "fabric of being" of a person—virtues such as justice, truthfulness, humility, respect for a reality beyond oneself and one's self—are trained in artistic and intellectual production and reception as well (Murdoch's example is learning Russian). The attention we devote to moral reality and goodness is similar to the attention we devote to God, for the Good is indefinable: "it is in its nature that we cannot get it taped [measured or defined]. This is the true sense of the indefinability of the good, [...] it lies beyond and it is from this beyond that it exercises its authority" (Murdoch 1999, 350; cf. 344, and Murdoch 1956, 46). The echoes of Tolstoy's understanding of aesthetic reception in the narrow context, and of the role of "religious consciousness" and awareness of "the meaning of life" in the wider context of his moral-political thought, are unmistakable in Murdoch's rich and suggestive writings.

Murdoch's unique vision of the moral life, informed by Tolstoy, Wittgenstein, as well as Simone Weil, has in turn influenced contemporary moral philosophers, including John McDowell (1979), Bernard Williams (1985), Martha Nussbaum (1990), Cora Diamond (1996, 2010), and Alice Crary (2007), among others (cf. Broackes 2012). Together they attest to the continued presence of Tolstoy's views on art, morality, and the meaning of life.

NOTES

1. Contrary to some commentators, who see no relation between Tolstoy's theory and the Western tradition in aesthetics other than negation. For instance, Morson (1987) and Silbajoris (1990), who in the conclusion to his book-length study of Tolstoy's aesthetics claims that *What is Art?* should be read as a "withdrawal from all conventional standards and concepts of art carried onwards through history by the rising tide of civilization" and "the entire enormous structure of aesthetics that was built through long centuries" (Silbajoris 1990, 263; cf. Morson 1987, 37).

2. It is worth noting that what could be called the pleasure principle returns here in Tolstoy's aesthetics, despite his rejection of all theories grounded in beauty as pleasure-inducing. "The more particular the feeling conveyed, the more strongly does it affect the perceiver. The perceiver experiences the greater pleasure the more particular the state of mind into which he is transferred, and therefore the more willingly and strongly does he merge with it" (WiA, 121). Tolstoy appears to be suggesting that it is the particularity—and not the specific content—of the feeling that induces pleasure; in earlier texts such as his essay on Maupassant he explicitly identifies "clearness of expression" with "beauty of form" (Tolstoy 1969, 21), thereby complicating the general and fundamental contrast he draws in *What is Art?*.

3. Caryl Emerson (2002, 244) notes that "sincerity" [*iskrennost'*] "is built off *iskra*, a 'spark': that which flashes momentarily and either catches fire or dies. The artistic effect either takes, or fails to take," and Tolstoy likens the effect of genuine art to that of a spark: "It sometimes happens that people, while together, are, if not hostile, at least alien to each other in their moods and feelings, and suddenly a story, a performance, a painting, even a building or, most frequently, music, will unite them all with an electric spark [*kak elektricheskoi iskroi*], and instead of their former separateness, often even hostility, they all feel unity and mutual love" (WiA, 130–131).

4. Compare in *Anna Karenina* the painter Mikhailov, who rejects the notion of mechanical technique in favor of the intuitive perception of an essence to be conveyed by the work: "If what he saw had also been revealed to a little child or to his kitchen-maid, they too would have been able to lay bare what they saw. But the most experienced and skilful painter-technician would be unable, for all his mechanical ability, to paint anything unless the boundaries of the content were first revealed to him" (Tolstoy 2000, 474).

5. Similar claims: "Thus art is distinguished from non-art, and the worth of art is determined, regardless of its content, that is, independently of whether it conveys good or bad feelings" (WiA, 123); "*The stronger the infection, the better that art is as art, regardless of its content—that is, independently of the worth of the feelings it conveys*" (WiA, 121; italics in original).

6. Many—but not all—of these essays are collected in volume 30 of Tolstoy's complete works (1929–1958) and are summarized in Zurek (1996) and systematically investigated in Lomunov (1972).

7. Compare in *Anna Karenina* the muzhik Platon's words to Levin about a peasant who "lives for the soul. He remembers God. [...] Everybody knows how—by the truth, by God's way" (Tolstoy 2000, 794).

8. For an interpretation that questionably makes artistic unintentionality intrinsic to Tolstoy's expression theory of art, see Denner (2003).
9. In "The Law of Love and the Law of Violence" (1908) he wrote: "And today this process [the "ever-increasing elucidations of the true meaning" of the teaching of the Gospels and the "ever-increasing alienation of man from the possibility of a good and reasonable life"] has reached the point where the Christian truth, formerly only recognized by a few, endowed with a keen religious sentiment, has been made accessible, in some of its aspects, to even the simplest people, through the doctrines of the Socialists; and yet life contradicts this truth at every step in the most crude and obvious way [...] It is neither resolutions, nor the subtle, clever Socialist and Communist structures of unions, arbitrations, etc. that will serve mankind, but only when this spiritual awareness becomes general" (Tolstoy 1987, 202–203).
10. Murdoch rejects the later Tolstoy's emphasis on simplicity and folk tales, however, both in his aesthetic theory and in his literary practice, because such genres appear to deny the psychological depth required of art and morality to understand another individual. Cf. Murdoch (1993, Chapter 5) and Murdoch (1999 [originally 1959], 212). More work needs to be done here, however, as she also writes: "Certain parables or stories undoubtedly owe their power to the fact that they incarnate a moral truth which is paradoxical, infinitely suggestive and open to continual reinterpretation," adducing the parable of the prodigal son as an example (Murdoch 1956, 50); thus there is conceptual space to differentiate kinds of forms and guidance within these genres.
11. What Murdoch calls "normative-descriptive words" (1999, 324) Bernard Williams will famously call "thick" ethical concepts in his *Ethics and the Limits of Philosophy* (1985).

BIBLIOGRAPHY

Barran, Thomas. 1992. Rousseau's Political Vision and Tolstoy's *What is Art? Tolstoy Studies Journal* 5: 1–13.
Broackes, Justin, ed. 2012. *Iris Murdoch, Philosopher.* Oxford: Oxford University Press.
Carroll, Noël. 1999. *Philosophy of Art: A Contemporary Introduction.* New York, NY: Routledge.
Collingwood, R. C. 1938. *The Principles of Art.* London: Oxford University Press.
Crary, Alice. 2007. *Beyond Moral Judgment.* Cambridge, MA: Harvard University Press.
Denner, Michael A. 2003. Accidental Art: Tolstoy's Poetics of Unintentionality. *Philosophy and Literature* 27 (2003): 284–303.
Dewey, John. 1934. *Art as Experience.* Reprinted in 1980, New York, NY: Perigree Books.
Diamond, Cora. 1996. 'We Are Perpetually Moralists': Iris Murdoch, Fact and Value. In *Iris Murdoch and the Search for Human Goodness,* ed. Maria Antonaccio and W. Schweiker, 79–109. Chicago, IL: University of Chicago Press.
———. 2010. Murdoch the Explorer. *Philosophical Topics* 38 (1): 51–85.
Emerson, Caryl. 1996. What Is Infection and What Is Expression in *What Is Art?* In *Lev Tolstoy and the Concept of Brotherhood,* ed. Andrew Donskov and John Woodsworth, 102–115. Brooklyn, NY: Legas.
———. 2000. Tolstoy's Aesthetics: A Harmony and Translation of the Five Senses. *Tolstoy Studies Journal* 12: 9–17.

618   H. W. PICKFORD

———. 2002. Tolstoy's Aesthetics. In *The Cambridge Companion to Tolstoy*, ed. Donna Tussing Orwin, 237–258. Cambridge, UK: Cambridge University Press.

———. 2010. Tolstoy and Music. In *Anniversary Essays on Tolstoy*, ed. Donna Tussing Orwin, 8–32. Cambridge, UK: Cambridge University Press.

Gershkovich, Tatyana. 2013. Infecting, Simulating, Judging: Tolstoy's Search for an Aesthetic Standard. *Journal of the History of Ideas* 74 (1): 115–137.

Gustafson, Richard F. 1986. *Leo Tolstoy: Resident and Stranger*. Princeton, NJ: Princeton University Press.

Jahn, Gary R. 1975. The Aesthetic Theory of Leo Tolstoy's *What is Art? Journal of Aesthetics and Art Criticism* 34: 59–65.

Kyriacou, Christos. 2019. Tolstoy's Implicit Moral Theory: An Interpretation and Appraisal. *Russian Literature* 106: 117–138.

Lomunov, Konstantin. 1972. *Estetika L'va Tolstogo*. Moscow: Sovremennik.

Lowe, David. 1990. Natasha Rostova Goes to the Opera. *Opera Quarterly* 7 (3): 74–81.

Mandelker, Amy. 1996. Tolstoy's Eucharistic Aesthetics. In *Lev Tolstoy and the Concept of Brotherhood*, ed. Andrew Donskov and John Woodsworth, 116–127. Brooklyn, NY: Legas.

Matravers, Derek. 1998. *Art and Emotion*. Oxford: Oxford University Press.

McDowell, John. 1979. Virtue and Reason. *The Monist* 62: 331–350. Reprinted in *Mind, Value, and Reality*, 50–73. Cambridge, MA: Harvard University Press, 1998.

Medzhibovskaya, Inessa. 2009. *Tolstoy and the Religious Culture of His Time: A Biography of a Long Conversion, 1845–1887*. Lanham, MD: Lexington Books.

Meyer, Priscilla. 2007. *Anna Karenina*, Rousseau, and the Gospels. *The Russian Review* 66: 204–219.

Morson, Gary Saul. 1987. *Hidden in Plain View: Narrative and Creative Potentials in 'War and Peace'*. Stanford, CA: Stanford University Press.

Mounce, Howard O. 2001. *Tolstoy on Aesthetics: What Is Art?* Aldershot: Ashgate.

Murdoch, Iris. 1956. Vision and Choice in Morality. *Proceedings of the Aristotelian Society, Supplementary Volumes* 30: 32–58.

———. 1993. *Metaphysics as a Guide to Morals*. New York, NY: Penguin.

———. 1999. *Existentialists and Mystics. Writings on Philosophy and Literature*. New York, NY: Penguin.

Nussbaum, Martha. 1990. *Love's Knowledge: Essays on Philosophy and Literature*. New York, NY: Oxford University Press.

Orwin, Donna T. 1993. *Tolstoy's Art and Thought 1847–1880*. Princeton, NJ: Princeton University Press.

Pickford, Henry W. 2016. *Thinking with Tolstoy and Wittgenstein: Expression, Emotion and Art*. Evanston, IL: Northwestern University Press.

Robinson, Douglas. 2008. *Estrangement and the Somatics of Literature: Tolstoy, Shklovsky, Brecht*. Baltimore, MD: Johns Hopkins University Press.

Silbajoris, Rimvydas. 1990. *Tolstoy's Aesthetics and His Art*. Columbus, OH: Slavica.

Tolstoy, Lev N. 1929–1958. *Polnoe sobranie sochinenii v 90 tomakh*. Moscow: Gosudarstvennoe izdatel'stvo "Khudozhestvennaia literatura." (Abbreviated as *PSS* in text.)

Tolstoy, Leo. 1969. *What Is Art? and Essays on Art*. Translated and Introduced by Aylmer Maude. Oxford and London: Oxford University Press.

———. 1985. *The Kreutzer Sonata and Other Stories*. Trans. David McDuff. New York, NY: Penguin.

———. 1987. *A Confession and Other Religious Writings*. Trans. Jane Kentish. New York, NY: Penguin.

———. 1995. *What Is Art?* Trans. Richard Pevear and Larissa Volokhonsky. London: Penguin. (Abbreviated as WiA in text.).

———. 2000. *Anna Karenina*. Trans. Richard Pevear and Larissa Volokhonsky. New York, NY: Penguin.

Williams, Bernard. 1985. *Ethics and the Limits of Philosophy*. Cambridge, MA: Harvard University Press.

Wittgenstein, Ludwig. 1922. *Tractatus Logico-Philosophicus*. Trans. C. K. Ogden. London: Routledge & Kegan Paul.

———. 1953. *Philosophical Investigations*. [4th edition, 2009.] Edited and translated by P.M.S. Hacker and Joachim Schulte. Oxford: Wiley-Blackwell.

Zurek, Magdalene. 1996. *Tolstojs Philosophie der Kunst*. Heidelberg: Universitätsverlag C. Winter.

CHAPTER 28

Osip Mandelstam's Poetic Practice and Theory and Pavel Florensky's Philosophical Contexts

Sofya Khagi

It has been well established in Mandelstam scholarship that the poet's oeuvre is over-saturated with cultural (literary, philosophical, historical, painterly, scientific, etc.) allusions. Among other subtexts, his lyrics reverberate with the philosophical notions of Arthur Schopenhauer, Friedrich Nietzsche, Vladimir Solovyov, Pavel Florensky, and Lev Shestov. Nadezhda Mandelstam has in particular stressed Mandelstam's dedication to Florensky. As she points out, *The Pillar and Ground of the Truth* was the book Mandelstam always kept by his side.[1]

This chapter places Mandelstam in dialogue with Russian idealist philosophy of the Silver Age—primarily, Florensky's seminal work *The Pillar and Ground of the Truth* [*Stolp i utverzhdenie istiny*] (1914) and his essay "Common Human Roots of Idealism" ["obshchechelovecheskie korni idealizma"] (1909)—and branches off into other works by Florensky and the notions of (Neo)-Platonists, Schopenhauer, Nietzsche, Saussure, Solovyov, and Lotman.[2] I focus on Mandelstam's lyrics "Silentium" (1910) and "The Horseshoe Finder (A Pindaric Fragment)" ["Nashedshii podkovu (Pindaricheskii otryvok)]" (1923), and trace the ways his poetry resonates with Florensky's problematic, imaginatively intertwining and reworking philosophical ingredients.

S. Khagi (✉)
Department of Slavic Languages and Literatures, University of Michigan,
Ann Arbor, MI, USA
e-mail: skhagi@umich.edu

© The Author(s), under exclusive license to Springer Nature
Switzerland AG 2021
M. F. Bykova et al. (eds.), *The Palgrave Handbook of Russian Thought*,
https://doi.org/10.1007/978-3-030-62982-3_28

621

622   S. KHAGI

"Common Human Roots of Idealism"

Florensky's essay privileges the ideals of "all-unity" and integral knowledge [*tsel'noe znanie*] over the fragmentation of the modern subject:

> In the moment of the poet's singular vision the boundaries of worldly separateness are removed. [...] There is nothing farther from the people's unmediated consciousness than that spiritual atomization [*dukhovnyi atomizm*] that has eaten up the modern soul like a cancer. The ideal of *integral* knowledge that Plato outlined so clearly no longer guides science. [...] Are there many for whom nature does not disintegrate into the ground, the forest, the field, the river, etc., disconnected among themselves? [...] People of the present have no soul, only psychic currents, associative ties, psychic dust [*psikhicheskaia pyl'*]. [...] Life flows slowly and solemnly—broad, light, and fresh as the Volga River, and its separate currents interweave among themselves, move amiably, and fuse together. [...] Energies of things flow into other things [*vtekaiut v drugie veshchi*], and everyone lives in all, and all—in everyone. [...] The world is a constantly moving, unfolding, trembling half-being, [...] and beyond its wavering and watery outlines the keen eye discerns *another* reality. [...] One becomes a part of nature, and nature a part of one. One marries nature [*vstupaet v brak s prirodoi*]. [...] The magician's thoughts flow into words of their accord. His words are already beginning actions. Thought and word, word and action become inseparable. (Florensky 2003, 10–17)

Florensky differentiates between knowledge of the world (from-without) and mystical insight (from-within) in which the division of the subject from the object is removed in one's fusion with the world. To yield richer insights about life, the mystic unites all psychic forces into one whole and attains the unity of inner being with the source of all existence.

"Common Human Roots of Idealism" draws on Plato's understanding of true knowledge as forms or ideas, transcendent patterns of the physical world in which humans live. In the (neo)-Platonic argument, the Absolute rules over the multitude of things and is the source of everything in the world. In the *Cratylus* the Absolute is unitary and all-inclusive, calling things back to their origin, "an intangible essence visible to the mind" (Plato 1970, 247). In our writing and telling "we are but urging toward it; out of discussion we call to vision; to those desiring to see, we point the way" (Plotinus 1962, 617–618). It is in sympathetic agreement with the world, not via abstract conceptual knowledge, that its divine essence is revealed: "If anyone sees it, what passion will he feel, what longing in his desire to be united with it. [...] There is no longer one thing outside which he is looking at, but the keen sighted has what is seen within" (Plotinus 1962, 27, 212).

For Florensky Plato's integral knowledge is a key notion—because in Russian Orthodoxy, influenced by Hesychasm, a version of apophatic theology, the ultimate goal is also an unmediated union with the divine through a path of mystical exercise. Even if the visions of the mystic are not believed to be deceptive (St. Gregory in *The Philocalia*), one has to push beyond them, "to withdraw the intellect from sensory things" (Palmer et al. 1979, 269), and achieve an awareness of unity with the divine.

Such notions remained central in Russian idealist philosophy of the Silver Age, including Solovyov's work, which was foundational for Florensky. In "The Meaning of Art" ["Obshchii smysl iskusstva"] (1890) Solovyov advocates a synthesis of diverse approaches, rational, empirical, and mystical, that permits one to discern the unity of mankind, nature, and God. There are two ways of knowing, "externally, from the side of our phenomenal awareness," and "internally, from the side of our absolute being, intrinsically linked with the being of what is known—unconditional, mystical knowledge" (Solovyov 1966–1970, 2: 331). Humans, though each appears as an Other to his fellows, should strive to restore all-unity. As Solovyov formulates it in "Beauty in Nature" ["Krasota v prirode"] (1889), "Life in its most general sense is the free play or movement of particular forces and positions united into an individual whole." The aesthetic significance of this living movement "is enhanced by its boundlessness, which seems to express the insatiable longing of finite beings separated from the absolute all-inclusive unity." Therefore the boundless sea "acquires new beauty as the symbol of the gigantic struggle of elemental forces which cannot break the universal connectedness of the cosmos or destroy its unity" (Solovyov 1991, 48–49).

If modern cerebral knowledge and language are artificial and burdensome (for Florensky and Solovyov), the kind of language that enables integral knowledge is not a mere "flagellum aeris—beater of the air" (Florensky 2003, 18). Florensky refers to nominalism in linguistics, including the ideas of Wilhelm von Humboldt and Alexander Potebnia, envisioning thought and action as inseparable from, and realized in, words. The magical (theurgic) word "is the emanation of one's will, one's soul, an independent center of forces—as if a living entity with a body made of air and the inner structure that is the form of the sound wave" (Florensky 2003, 19). It is "the thing itself. It is therefore always a name. The magic of actions is the magic of words and the magic of words—that of names. The name of the thing is its essence" (Florensky 2003, 21). The name is an entity relatively independent of its bearer, and both a representing and an influencing one. The right kind of insight and word, moreover, equates with love: in erotic ecstasy "the magician cognizes the essence of nature and takes its higher reality into himself" (Florensky 2003, 27).

As in many linguistic discussions, theological issues are also at stake here. The magical word, like the divine Word, not only reveals but also influences the nature of things. In Florensky's reference, evidently colored by the Hebraic tradition, he cites "the omnipotent Name of God giving complete power over all of nature because in that *Name* His divine energy and assistance are revealed" (Florensky 2003, 25). Otherwise words are but empty disturbances of the air; so, when a twentieth-century intellectual wants to underscore the illusory nature of some being, he says: "This is but a name."

624 S. KHAGI

It is on the issue of verbal iconicity versus non-iconicity that Florensky's discussion of theology cum language importantly hinges:

> Names express the nature of things. Names are but conditional signs of things. Cognizing names gives insights into things; things have names by their essence. Cognizing things allows us to give them names, the latter are given by human will. [...] "By nature" and "by authority" [*po prirode i po avtoritetu*], long ago contrasted by Plato (in his *Cratylus*) on the question of the essence and origin of names, briefly encapsulate later debates on the subject. (Florensky 2003, 23)

Florensky outlines a key dichotomy between words taken to be organically bound to things and words produced by arbitrary formation. Signs and signifieds may stand in a necessary relationship, or signs may be pasted onto signifieds by random human will. It is only in the former case that the knowledge of names allows genuine insights into and impact on the named.[3]

Simultaneously verbal iconicity manifests one's connection to others and the cosmos. The right kind of language transmutes mystical insight into an organ of collective thought on account of its supra-personal nature. Florensky's essay "The Term" ["Termin"] (1917) engages Humboldt and Potebnia to claim words' organic connection to their referents and, therefore, their ability to merge the individual self with the collective: "Through the word I leave the boundaries of my limitedness and fuse with the historically expressed will of the people that has collectively manifested itself by forming this particular sememe of the word" (Florensky 1990, 263).[4]

For Florensky the relationship between the signifier and the signified is a central ontological and theological question—as in Schopenhauer's *The World as Will and Representation* (1819), where the wrong kind of symbolism provides "absolutely no connection between what is depicted and the concept indicated by it," or again, "the sign and the thing signified are connected quite conventionally by a positive fixed rule casually introduced" (Schopenhauer 1969, 1: 239).[5]

The dichotomy between sign and signified carries similar significance in later semiotic discussions, for instance, in Yuri Lotman's and Boris Uspensky's "Agreement" and 'Self-Giving' as Archetypal Models of Culture" ["'Dogovor' i 'vruchenie sebia' kak arkhetipicheskie modeli kul'tury"] (1981). This essay identifies a dichotomy between the ethics of contract characteristic of the West and the ethics of unconditional self-giving characteristic of Russia. Self-giving pertains to one's relation with the divine, and the means of communication between humans and God are symbols that preclude the possibility of expression being alienated from content and consequently of deception. By contrast, a transaction with the powers of darkness is obtained through the production of arbitrary signs, and the conventionality of signification offers opportunities for cheating: "It is in dealing with such forces [the powers of darkness] that the fact that communication through verbal signs is based on convention and that this enables words to be used for deception is made apparent. The possibility of variously interpreting a word (casuistry) was likewise understood as the wish to deceive rather than an attempt to explain its true meaning" (Lotman and Uspensky 1985, 128). Lotman-Uspensky thus couch the problem of symbol/ iconicity versus sign/conventionality in divine versus demonic terms.

"Letter Two: Doubt"

The introductory section of *The Pillar and Ground of the Truth*, "To the Reader," praises Orthodox spirituality on anti-rationalist, anti-conceptual grounds: it cannot be encompassed by "the narrow coffin of logical definitions" (Florensky 2003, 35). "Letter One: Two Worlds" challenges conventional logical axioms such as the law of identity and non-contradiction on the grounds that they betray humanity's alienation from the world and itself, and identifies Christ as the single "pillar of truth" amidst worldly transience and illusions:

> Everything whirls. Everything slides into death's abyss [*vse kruzhitsia, vse skol'zit v mertvennuiu bezdnu*]. Only One abides, only in Him are constancy, life, and peace. "To Him is drawn the whole course of events, as the periphery to the center. Toward Him converge all the radii of the circle of the ages [*k nemu skhodiatsia vse radiusy kruga vremen*]." [...] Outside of this One Center, "the only certain thing is that nothing is certain and there is nothing more miserable or arrogant than man." That was said by Pliny the Elder. [...] In life everything is in a state of unrest, everything is unstable, is a mirage. And out of these depths of the soul there arises an unbearable need to find support in the "Pillar and Ground of the Truth" [...]—not just one of the truths, not in one of the particular and fragmented human truths, which are unstable and blown about like dust chased by the wind over mountains, but in total and Eternal Truth. (Florensky 1997, 12)[6]

"Letter Two: Doubt" contains Florensky's own forceful articulation of skepticism. The letter opens with an etymological disquisition on the word "truth" in multiple languages including Russian, Greek, Latin, and Hebrew. As Florensky claims, the Russian word *istina* means the genuinely existent as opposed to the illusory. The Greek ἀλήθεια, on the other hand, stresses memory over destructive temporality. As Florensky traces the etymology of ἀλήθεια, he holds that the Greek word consists of the negative particle *a* and *lethos* (I lose for memory, i.e., for consciousness in general, I forget):

> The ancient idea of death as a transition to an illusory existence, almost to self-forgetting and unconsciousness, and, in any case, to the forgetting of everything earthly, finds its symbol in the image of the shades' drinking of water from the underground river of Forgetfulness. [...] Forgetting [...] was not merely a state of the absence of memory, but a special act of the annihilation of a part of the consciousness [*spetsial'nym aktom unichtozheniia chasti soznaniia*]. [...] This power of forgetting is the power of all-devouring time [*eta sila zabveniia—sila vsepozhiraiushchego vremeni*]. [...] To say "exists" is to say "in time," for time is

the form of the flux of phenomena [*forma tekuchesti sobytii*]. […] Time, chronos, produces phenomena, but, like its mythological image, Chronos, it devours its children. […] Truth overcomes time, does not flow but is fixed, eternally remembered. (Florensky 1997, 16–17)

The Latin *veritas* is juridical, and, finally, the Hebrew *emet* means "supported, propped up," as in the domain of architecture. That is, Florensky infers, for Jews and for Russians Truth is primarily reliable [*dostovernaia*] and transcendental, while Greeks and Romans attend to its human form.

How may one, when affirming something, guarantee its truthfulness? Florensky points to the problem that change, external and inner, is ever-present in the world, so that the present opposes itself to its past and its future in time just as in space a thing is opposed to all things positioned outside it. Consciousness is ever self-disharmonious. If in the idealistic tradition worldly flux [*tekuchest'*] indicates the Symbolist "*A realibus ad realiora*" ("Common Human Roots of Idealism"), in more skeptical readings such as Nietzsche's "On Truth and Lying in an Extra-Moral Sense" (1873) the world-as-becoming is ruptured and unknowable. While concepts delude humans into thinking that there exist certain entities (e.g., the bed, the leaf), nature possesses no forms, concepts, or species, only an indefinable X.[7]

As Semyon Frank describes this in his own contribution to the idealist corpus, *The Unknowable: An Ontological Introduction to the Philosophy of Religion* [*Nepostizhimoe: Ontologicheskoe vvedenie v filosofiiu religii*] (1939), to practically orient ourselves in the world, we must be capable of apprehending familiar elements in the new and changing. This is the foundation of conceptual knowledge which subsumes "everything that is fluid and diverse in the world under 'concepts,' i.e., finds in the world identical 'essences' […] on the basis of which we can apprehend the new and altered as the repetition of the familiar" (Frank 1983, xiii).

Nietzsche's critique of language is simultaneously an assault on religious ontology. While the Bible claims words' necessary relation to things, he responds, "The origin of language from the nature of things cannot be proven" (Nietzsche 1989, 210). In *Thus Spoke Zarathustra* (1885) language provides a comforting illusion of all-unity, one's connection to fellow humans and the world: "Are not words and sounds rainbows and elusive bridges between things which are eternally apart? […] Speaking is a beautiful folly: with that man dances over all things" (Nietzsche 1954, 329).[8] The subject is solipsistically imprisoned within the self, yet words cover (deceptively) the cleft between the subject and the external world.

Adopting for the moment a skeptical Nietzsche-esque stance, Florensky describes language-mediated knowledge and the world-as-becoming as mutually exclusive, and the world-in-flux as incommensurate with all-unity. The "previous A" is not equal to the "present A," and the "future A" differs from the "present A." But whereas Nietzsche champions epistemological and ontological skepticism, Florensky paints absolute skepticism as extreme suffering:

Molten lava flows in the veins [*rasplavlennaia lava techet to zhilam*], and a dark flame penetrates the marrow of the bones. At the same time, the deadening cold of absolute solitude and perdition turns the consciousness into a block of ice. [...] It is uncertain whether I yearn for Truth. Perhaps that too only seems. But perhaps this very seeming is not seeming? In asking myself this last question, I enter the last circle of the skeptical hell, the place where the very meaning of words is lost. Words cease to be fixed; they fly out of their nests. Everything turns into everything else. Every word-combination is completely equivalent to every other [*vse prevrashchaetsia vo vse, kazhdoe slovosochetanie sovershenno ravnosil'no kazhdomu drugomu*], and any word can change places with any other. Here, the mind loses itself. It is lost in a formless, chaotic abyss. (Florensky 1997, 29–30)

Absolute doubt means the impossibility of affirming anything at all, even— in the Cretan Liar paradox—its own non-affirmation. Truth is not encompassable by its signifier—something complete, containing everything, akin to the Neo-Platonic idea of the Absolute, and, therefore, only conditionally expressed by its name. Since neither "objective" evidence of the senses nor "subjective" reason can provide definite proof of Truth, one falls into doubt and despair that express themselves as language losing all meaning. Absolute doubt ultimately means refraining from all statement.

Having taken this skeptical detour, Florensky concludes "Letter Two: Doubt" with re-affirmation of (neo)-Platonic and Orthodox all-unity. Spatialtemporal multiplicity does not violate the law of identity if all the multitudinous elements are synthesized in the Truth of Christ:

"The other"—both in the order of coexistence and in the order of succession [*v poriadke sosushchestvovaniia i v poriadke posledovaniia*]—is at the same time "not other." [...] If "another" moment of time does not destroy or devour "this" moment, but, being "another," it is "this" at the same time, if the "new," revealed *as the new*, is the "old" in its eternity; if the *inner structure* of the eternal "this" and "other," the "new" and the "old" in their real unity is such that "this" must appear *outside* the "other" and the "old" must appear *before the* "new"; if the "other" and the "new" is such not through itself but through "this" and *the* "old," and "this" and the "old" is such not through itself but through the "other" and the "new"; if, finally, each element of being is only a term of a substantial relationship, a relationship-substance [*otnosheniia-substantsii*], then the law of identity, eternally violated, is eternally restored by its very violation. (Florensky 1997, 35)

Florensky's conceptualization of this ontological-religious all-unity is tied to his thinking about language. The "inner structure of the eternal" echoes the inner structure of the word—as in the "inner structure that is the form of the sound wave" and Florensky's sememe in "The Structure of the Word" ["Stroenie slova"] (1922).[9] Simultaneously, his conception of each element of being as a term of a substantial relationship resembles Saussure's taking the value of elements in a linguistic system as generated by their difference from

628   S. KHAGI

other elements (*Course in General Linguistics*, 1906–1911)—to be given a further skeptical twist in Derrida's concept of *différance* ("The Difference," 1968). Yet far from espousing epistemological and ontological skepticism à la Derridean deconstruction, Florensky understands such a relationship-substance as an aesthetic unity of being in God, even if with too many "ifs."

"Silentium" and All-Unity

Mandelstam's essay "The Word and Culture" ["Slovo i kul'tura"] (1921) imagines language much the same way Florensky does, informed by the post-Saussurean consciousness of the split between signifier and signified and Potebnia's ideas on the inner form of the word. The word is a living entity that is not subsumed by the object it denotes, it is a Psyche that "wanders around the thing freely, like the soul around a body it has cast off but not forgotten" (Mandel'shtam 1993, 1: 215). His "On The Nature of the Word" ["O prirode slova"] (1922) takes nominalism to be the reality of "the word as such" and of its independence.[10]

Mandelstam's early lyric "Silentium" (1910) poeticizes the ideals of all-unity and the magical word. The poem, clearly inspired by a host of Silver Age idealist philosophy motifs, venerates singing nature: "Word, return to music" ["I slovo, v muzyku vernis'"] (Mandel'shtam 1993, 1: 51).[11] It urges one to go mute, and equates music and silence in the traditional apophatic/Hesychast manner: "May my lips / Find primary muteness, / Like a crystalline note / That is pure from birth!" ["Da obretut moi usta / Pervonachal'nuiu nemotu, / Kak kristallicheskuiu notu, / Chto ot rozhdeniia chista"] (Mandel'shtam 1993, 1: 50). Such a paradoxical sounding silence is the necessary condition for intimating the transcendental.[12]

The urge to merge with the kernel of being—"with the fundamental principle of life" ["s pervoosnovoi zhizni"] (Mandel'shtam 1993, 1: 51)—resembles Florensky's "when the boundaries of worldly separateness are removed" and loss of the self in the Absolute in Neo-Platonic and Hesychast terms.[13] The subject (the poet) and the object (nature, the world) become one. Or, to be more precise, Mandelstam expresses longing for the primeval state in which such a fusion was possible: "May my lips find…" ["Da obretut moi usta…"] (Mandel'shtam 1993, 1: 50).

Ecstatic mystical experience is often likened to the ecstasy of love—as in Florensky's marriage of the magician and nature and the erotic ecstasy of the magician when he takes the higher reality of nature into himself. Mandelstam's mythological referent is Aphrodite's birth from sea-foam, and his painterly referent is Botticelli's "Birth of Venus" (1482) (Brown 1973, 166). In Hesiod's description of Aphrodite's birth in *Theogony*, the goddess is born following Uranus's castration by his son Chronos. Uranus, Heaven, perpetually embraces the Earth, his wife Gaia, and Aphrodite is born of an act that separates Heaven and Earth. Chronos throws Uranus's genitals into the sea, and a maiden emerges from the foam spreading around them.

The birth of the goddess of love marks the creation of the world and the beginning of time. Botticelli's painting has Aphrodite blown to the shore on a seashell and showered with roses.[14] On reaching shore she is clothed by the Hours—and, accordingly, Mandelstam portrays entrance into time when one is "formed" and the magical feeling of suspended temporality prior to creation. The rising of Aphrodite from the foam marks the transformation of the ineffable conception in the poet's soul into the body of the poem, a spirit (or a symbol) into an image.[15] So long as Aphrodite remains a symbol (Greek: "to join together"), she represents "the indestructible connection of everything living" ["vsego zhivogo nenarushaemaia sviaz'"] (Mandel'shtam 1993, 1: 50).

Water—Florensky's "separate currents interweaving among themselves and fusing together" and Solovyov's "struggle of elemental forces which cannot break the universal connectedness of the cosmos"—conveys the all-unity at the heart of things. The sea is a place where the first living forms arose, and beauty, as the material embodiment of the idea of total unity, is seen best in those aspects of nature that highlight the movement of discordant elements and simultaneously stress their concord. Therefore, it is in the calmly breathing sea that Mandelstam observes the "indestructible connection of everything living."

Aphrodite, more than an anthropomorphic goddess of love, figures a transcendental principle of origination. "Silentium" focuses on the moment before Aphrodite has emerged from the foam of the Aegean. As the ineffable Absolute, it cannot be incarnated in the finite form of the goddess lest its intangible essence be misrepresented. Aphrodite ("born of sea-foam") pre-exists as a supra-temporal potential. As an incorporeal spirit, the unborn goddess exists out of time and space and can be anything, whereas the divinity of the Greek pantheon is more of a finite being.

The state in which one attends to the music of nature but has not yet translated it into the realized actuality of a poem is one of arrested time and of the soul's complete identification with the external world. The moment prior to creation is one when the poem is already alive, though no words have yet been strung together. In the terms of "Word and Culture," a poem is alive "because of its inner image, because of that sounding mold of form that anticipates the written work. There is not a single word yet, but the poem already sounds. What sounds is its inner image, which is perceived by the poet's ear" (Mandel'shtam 1993, 1: 215).

Mandelstam's *vnutrennii obraz* ["inner image"] and Florensky's *vnutrenniaia struktura* ["inner structure"] resonate, likely via Potebnia's notion of the inner form of the word (Freidin 1987, 162; Paperno 1991, 32). However, Mandelstam's sounding mold of form that exists prior to the writing down of a single word is more akin to Florensky's "inner structure that is the form of the sound wave" than to Potebnia's etymological meaning of the word as the basis of poetry.[16] "Silentium" celebrates the state before a single word has been written but the poem already sounds. The moment prior to verbalization is sheer spirit (hidden abstraction, unbodied Aphrodite, Plato's/Florensky's/the

630   S. KHAGI

Symbolists's *realiora*), while the actual poem is language and form (visible beauty, "embodied" Aphrodite, *realibus*).

According to Schopenhauer, music relates to the word as spirit (Mandelstam's unbodied eros) to form (Aphrodite after her birth), and the poet "gains the consciousness of the identity of one's own inner being with that of all things" (Schopenhauer 1994, 98, xii). In Nadezhda Mandelstam's recollection of the way her husband composed verse, poetry is not made up but, rather, extracted from a pre-existing unity: "I had an impression that all the process of creation consists of a strained capturing and manifestation of the harmonic and semantic unity that is already extant, and that is being transmitted from an unknown place, gradually getting embodied in words" (Mandel'shtam 1970, 74). The poet wants to prolong the moment when the lyric is already intimated but its music has not yet been transcribed. Aphrodite as a poem-in-waiting is music and language, a pre-existing harmony that awaits its articulation in the poem. Music provides a universal means of communication, uniting the self and the other, and the loss of the self allows one "to merge with the fundamental principle of life."

Florensky's conceptualization of verbal iconicity versus non-iconicity as a theological issue is also important to Mandelstam. "Silentium" does not merely say that Aphrodite is "music and the word and the undisrupted connection of everything living"—rather, it says that Aphrodite is "*both* music and the word and *therefore* the undisrupted connection of everything living." If signifier, music as the word's euphonic properties, and signified, the word as logos, are organically connected, or if the means of communication are, in Lotman's terms, symbolic, divine harmony is present in the world.

"Silentium" imagines poetry's theurgist capacity to divulge the soul of phenomena—even though the rapport of external reality and the poetic self is more of a wish than an actual state. The lyric emerges from a special spiritual and musical experience. It desires that the word return to music because language cannot be equal either to the melodiousness of the soul or to universal harmony.[17] Are these: "And word, return to music, / And heart, merged with the fundamental principle of life, / Grow ashamed of heart,"—words, thoughts, or actions? Perhaps they are "magician's words" proper (as in Florensky's description), inseparable from thoughts and actions as well as love.

"The Horseshoe Finder" and "Doubt"

The verbal reduction "Silentium" represents is balanced by a sense of cosmic harmony between nature and man even though this harmony may be but a utopia of the past.[18] Florensky's problematic of all-unity versus fragmentariness, space-time as the form of the flux of phenomena, and the magical word versus language as a mere air beater are replayed in a more skeptical key in "The Horseshoe Finder."

Stephen Broyde has interpreted "The Horseshoe Finder" as advancing the notion of poetry's timelessness in a transient world: "Mandelstam and Pindar share an essentially similar view toward poetry's ability to remain timeless in a transitory, often disorderly world. The poem is uniquely able to remain intact while all else changes, and hence to contact an unknown future recipient of an unexpected gift in which is preserved also a part of the poet" (Broyde 1975, 175). While such an interpretation is possible, Clare Cavanagh's reading of the poem as "exhibiting a crisis in language, more specifically in poetic language" (Cavanagh 1995, 188) seems more compelling to me. I would likewise agree with Lada Panova that "The Horseshoe Finder" "illustrates both the thesis of the deadliness of linear time" and the thesis that "nothing disappears entirely" (Panova 2003, 621), save that I see the former as prevailing.[19]

"The Horseshoe Finder" overflows with metamorphoses, portraying the world-in-flux.[20] Most of the poem's images involve multiple spatial and temporal perspectives presented simultaneously. At the poem's start, pine trees prospectively glimpse into and yearn for their future as ship's planks, "Offering vainly that the skies exchange / Their noble burden for a pinch of salt" ["Bezuspeshno predlagaia nebu vymeniat' na shchepotku soli / Svoi blagorodnyi gruz"] (Mandel'shtam 1993, 2: 43). Reciprocally, the ship's planks retrospectively preserve the identity (carry the memory) of pine trees: "Inhaling the scent of resinous tears / That have oozed through the ship's planks [...] We say: They too stood upon an earth" ["Vdykhaia zapakh smolistykh slez, prostupivshikh skvoz' obshivku korablia [...] Govorim: / I oni stoiali na zemle"] (Mandel'shtam 1993, 2: 43).[21] Similarly, "The sharp turn of [a horse's] neck [that] still retains the memory of racing" ["Krutoi povorot ego shei / Eshche sokhraniaet vospominanie o bege"] and "A horseshoe [that] will no more strike sparks from flint" ["I bol'she uzh ei ne pridetsia vysekat' iskry iz kremnia"] (Mandel'shtam 1993, 2: 44–45) capture spatial-temporal shifts, multiple moments within a single image.[22]

"Everything turns into everything else," as in Florensky, albeit in a reductive manner. Time is the form of the flux of phenomena, but this fluidity is less the benign world-as-becoming we see in "Common Human Roots of Idealism," where "energies of things flow into other things, and everyone lives in all, and all in everyone." It is instead the disturbing "time, chronos, producing phenomena, but, like its mythological image, Chronos, devouring its children" (*The Pillar and Ground of the Truth*). The reductive or even destructive aspect of its metamorphoses, moreover, grows from the poem's beginning to its finale: pine trees—>ship planks, horse—>horseshoe, poet's words—>petrified wheat, poet—>buried coins. The trace—the horseshoe—may not be totally valueless but it is the reduction of a living and breathing entity.

"The Horseshoe Finder" is subtitled "fragment" and ends on an ellipsis. All that remains of the racehorse portrayed in the ode—that is, of the language of the past, and the poet himself—is a fragment, a horseshoe.[23] The poem moves through a series of disjointed images, exposing the disintegration of the poet's word, his past, and his very self: "With what to begin? / Everything cracks and sways" ["S chego nachat'? Vse treshchit i kachaetsia"]; "What I am saying now is not said by me" ["To, chto ia seichas govoriu, govoriu ne ia"] (Mandel'shtam

1993, 2: 43–45). "What I am saying now is not said by me" and "There is no longer enough of me for me" ["I mne uzhe ne khvataet menia samogo"] (Mandel'shtam 1993, 2: 45) convey the atomization and fragmentation of the lyrical subject akin to Florensky's critical portrayal of modernity's spiritual malaise.

The main thrust of the poem's skepticism is directed at the lyrical self. The obsolete lyricist fails to perform on a par with modern (presumably, revolutionary) odists: his lightweight carts of poetry, "In a flamboyant harness of flocks of birds, / Dense with strain, burst to pieces / To compete with the snorting favorites of the races" ["V broskoi upriazhi gustykh ot natugi ptich'ikh stai / Razryvaiutsia na chasti, / Sopernichaia s khrapiashchimi liubimtsami ristalishch"] (Mandel'shtam 1993, 2: 43).[24] The poet is bankrupt, "has fluffed, botched his reckoning" ["sbilsia, zaputalsia v schete"] (Mandel'shtam 1993, 2: 44). He lives in accordance with an outdated calendar: "The frail chronology of our era comes to a close" ["Khrupkoe letoischeslenie nashei ery podkhodit k kontsu"] (Mandel'shtam 1993, 2: 44). Time is out of joint for him: "Children play knucklebones with the vertebrae of dead animals" ["Deti igraiut v babki pozvonkami umershikh zhivotnykh"], which evokes Heraclitus's "eternity is a child playing dice—a child's kingdom" (Freidin 1987, 112) as well as Mandelstam's own image of a broken spine that also appears in "The Age" ["Vek"] (1922). The poet no longer knows how to write, all words have lost their meaning.

As Gregory Freidin has pointed out, Florensky's "Second Letter: Doubt" in *The Pillar and Ground of the Truth* contains a passage that Mandelstam follows virtually word for word (Freidin 1987, 369): "I enter the last circle of the skeptical hell, the place where the very meaning of words is lost. Words cease to be fixed; they fly out of their nests. Everything turns into everything else. Every word-combination is completely equivalent to every other." Mandelstam echoes this with "Everything cracks and sways. / The air shakes from similes. / Not a single word is better than another, / The earth buzzes with metaphor" ["Vse treshchit i kachaetsia. / Vozdukh drozhit or sravnenii. / Ni odno slovo ne luchshe drugogo. / Zemlia gudit metaforoi"] (Mandel'shtam 1993, 2: 43). The disintegration of language interweaves the loss of meaning in the world and the dissolution of selfhood: "There is no longer enough of me for me."

The disintegration of the world, the word, and the self also expresses itself as the danger of amnesia—as in Florensky's disquisition on the ancient Greek "truth," with death being a transition to an illusory experience, almost to self-forgetting and unconsciousness. "The Horseshoe Finder" also points at the threat of memory loss. The poem abounds in tropes, yet has few proper names. Therefore, on its own, and on Florensky's terms, it is *not* "singled out among its friends with a headband / Curing unconsciousness" ["otmechena sredi podrug poviazkoi na lbu, / Istseliaiushchei ot bespamiatstva"] (Mandel'shtam 1993, 2: 43).

Memory and Mnemosyne-poetry that embody the past may be strategies to compensate for existential losses, but this kind of compensation can hardly be adequate. For Florensky memory desires to stop movement, to freeze the motion of fleeting phenomena, and forgetting is not just a state of the absence of memory but an active annihilation of a part of consciousness. "The Horseshoe Finder" closely follows this scenario: "And there is no longer enough of me for me." Language does not preserve the poet's living essence but remains only as lifeless fragments—"grains of petrified wheat" ["zernam okameneloi pshenitsy"] (Mandel'shtam 1993, 2: 45). Like *The Pillar and Ground of the Truth*, "The Horseshoe Finder" employs the bird-word simile to convey the loss of poetic power. The lightweight cart of poetry, harnessed to birds, bursts into pieces from over-exertion.[25]

"Letter Two: Doubt" and "The Horseshoe Finder" alike portray a concurrent verbal, spiritual, and physical collapse via a vertiginous seismographic (earthquake) imagery. In Florensky "molten lava flows in the veins, and a dark flame penetrates the marrow of the bones," as if a volcanic eruption is internalized within the subject; his fragmenting human truth is restless and fluttering "like ashes driven by the breath of the wind on the mountains," and the skeptical mind gets lost in a formless abyss. In Mandelstam, too, the breakup of language and cognition finds its correspondence in a physical collapse of the poet's world: "Everything cracks and sways," "the air shakes," it "can be dark as water" ["Vozdukh byvaet temnym, kak voda"]; it is "mixed as densely as the earth" ["Vozdukh zameshen tak zhe gusto, kak zemlia"] (Mandel'shtam 1993, 2: 44). As the facts of language acquire physicality, they disrupt the earth. The confusion of elements (air like water, like crystal, like earth) is eschatological. Verbal apocalypse is an analogy, an enactment, and a cause of a greater cosmic apocalypse.

Once more Mandelstam is preoccupied with the problem of verbal iconicity versus conventionality. A necessary connection of signifier to signified is testimony to ontological harmony, including humans' harmonious connection to others and to the cosmos, as in "Silentium." The obverse is the unmotivated, deceitful sign, at its furthest reach—an utter disruption of the connection between the referring term and the referent, the hypertrophy of an empty signifier (Lotman). In popular consciousness unmotivated signs are regarded as coming from the devil, and in "The Horseshoe Finder" the earth is furrowed by "pitchforks, tridents" ["vilami, trezubtsami"] (Mandel'shtam 1993, 2: 42). The pitchfork, related to working on the land, is paired with Poseidon's trident, belonging to the water realm, to indicate the confusion of elements. Tools are erroneously linked through their formal similarity, their multiple prongs. Like language, these implements have lost semantic value. The world has grown demonic (tools no longer obey man), just as language has grown devilish through the proliferation of meaningless verbiage ("Not a single word is better than another").

Florensky's "everything turns into everything else" indicates the loss of meaning in the world and simultaneously the metaphor. In "The Horseshoe Finder," "the air shakes from similes," "the earth buzzes with metaphor." Rhetoric (figurative language) subverts the idea (rejection of figuration). The multiple metaphors of the poem, oriented toward the ancient tradition, are striking in light of the poem's wariness of tropes. The lines renounce figurative language yet the poem employs one simile after another: "The air can be dark as water"; it is like "a crystal in which wheels move and horses dash aside" [*"khrustal', v kotorom dvizhutsia kolesa i sharakhaiutsia loshadi"*]; it is like "the moist black earth of Neaira" ["vlazhnyi chernozem Neery"] (Mandel'shtam 1993, 2: 43). A particularly ironic disjointedness occurs when Mandelstam uses "metaphor" as his term of comparison.

If Botticelli's "Birth of Venus" is the painterly referent for "Silentium," Karl Briullov's "The Last Day of Pompeii" ["Poslednii den' Pompeii"] (1830–1833) is an apocalyptic painterly analogy to both Florensky's "Second Letter: Doubt" and Mandelstam's "The Horseshoe Finder." In Pliny the Younger's description (which clearly influenced Briullov), "The buildings were now shaking with frequent large-scale tremors; as though dislodged from their foundations, they seemed to shift now one way and now another" (Pliny 2009, 144). Meanwhile "from Mount Vesuvius widespread flames and fires rising high blazed forth in several places, their gleaming brightness accentuated by the darkness of the night" (Pliny 2009, 144). Florensky's hell-scape of absolute doubt evokes a volcanic eruption where absolute skepticism is depicted as molten lava and vertigo without "a pillar of truth"—as in Briullov's canvas where spurts of flame shoot from Vesuvius against the unnatural darkness and falling columns.

No less importantly, Briullov's dynamic canvas captures temporal movement—providing an illusion of four-dimensionality (three-dimensional space plus the fourth dimension of time). That is, "The Last Day of Pompeii" deals, by painterly means, with space-time as the form of the flux of phenomena—Florensky's and Mandelstam's core problematic in *The Pillar and Ground of the Truth* and "The Horseshoe Finder."[26] The eschatological confusion of elements in Mandelstam also invokes Pompeii and Herculaneum: "The air is mixed as densely as earth."

The excavated ancient cities of Pompeii and Herculaneum have captured the imagination of on-lookers with their effects of "arrested time." As for "The Horseshoe Finder," it unfolds with the dynamic world (ships, horses, wheels) of the poem's first half fossilized in the latter section. A "crystal in which wheels move and horses dash aside" indicates stopped time, like a piece of amber with a pre-historic insect inside. Yet the past is hardly brought back to life in its living fullness. Rather, the poem captures the transformation of its vibrant reality into an archaeological residual. Movement is arrested into *nature morte*—"vertebrae of dead animals," "the sharp turn of [a horse's] neck [that] still retains the memory of racing," a "horseshoe [that] will no more strike sparks from flint." Many relics of the past are reductive remnants of poetic selfhood: the horseshoe, the poet's lips stiffened into the shape of their final utterance, words as grains of petrified wheat, or devalued coins. If this is eternal recurrence à la Nietzsche, post-existence (or another existence) is a damaged and gloomy one.

Briullov's "The Last Day of Pompeii" features pagan and Christian priests, and has been interpreted as an allegory of the start of Christianity.[27] "The Horseshoe Finder" marks the opposing temporal point, the closure of the Christian era: "The era rang like a golden sphere, / Hollow, molded, supported by none" ["Era zvenela, kak shar zolotoi, / Polaia, litaia, nikem ne podderzhivaemaia"] (Mandel'shtam 1993, 2: 44). The departing era used to give brief and honest childlike replies: "At every touch it responded 'yes' and 'no'" ["Na vsiakoe prikosnovenie otvechala 'da' i 'net'"] (Mandel'shtam 1993, 2: 43).[28] Now everything swings to and fro with epistemological and ontological vertigo. Language is inflated, nature chokes with words.

In Florensky's reading, reason cannot move past nihilistic despair and doubt and loss of the value of words but can be transcended by faith. In a whirling world, "only One abides" and "toward Him converge all the radii of the circle of the ages." Spatial-temporal multiplicity, of coexistence (otherness) and succession (transience), is synthesized in all-unity, the Truth, or Christ. This is why the differentness, the alienness of "the other" becomes an expression and disclosure of the identity of "this one."

While "Letter Two: Doubt" proceeds from skepticism to faith, "The Horseshoe Finder" possesses no such certitude with which to counter skepticism. The golden Christian sphere is no longer the center of gravity toward which history and humankind gravitate (hollow, supported by no one). If the pine trees of the poem's opening gravitate teleologically, as it were, toward their future condition as shipboards (even if the living unity of the forest is transformed into artifice, this artifice is human and meaningful), the final metamorphosis, "Time cuts me like a coin" ["Vremia srezaet menia, kak monetu"], and "There is no longer enough of me for me" (Mandel'shtam 1993, 2: 45), conveys a clearly destructive connotation.

The motif of money points to the collapse of meaning in another sense. Currency is an apt metaphor for an arbitrarily fixed signification. Not only is language subject to economic laws but in everyday usage words communicate by acting as a medium of exchange; that is, they are like money used to buy things (objects, ideas) in the marketplace. The arbitrary nature of the relation between the signifier and the signified can be likened to the exchange of money in the marketplace. The problem is that words may casually represent their referents with no inherent connection between signifier and signified (Saussure's arbitrariness of signs).

Saussure himself in *Course in General Linguistics* uses the analogy between linguistic and monetary forms of exchange to elucidate his claim of the arbitrariness of the sign along with the central notion that each sign in the system that makes up a language gets its meaning only because of its difference with other signs:

> To determine the value of a five-franc coin, for instance, what must be known is:
> (1) that the coin can be exchanged for a certain quantity of something different,
> e.g., bread, and (2) that its value can be compared with another value in the same

636   S. KHAGI

system, e.g., a one-franc coin, or a coin belonging to another system (e.g., a dollar). Similarly, a word can be substituted for something dissimilar: an idea. At the same time, it can be compared to something of like nature: another word. Its value is therefore not determined merely by that concept or meaning for which it is a token. It must also be assessed against comparable values, by contrast with other words. The content of a word is determined in the final analysis not by what it contains but by what exists outside of it. (Saussure 1986, 113)

From Florensky's perspective, if each element of existence constitutes a term of a relationship-substance, the law of identity is restored, and spatial-temporal multiplicity is united (in Christ). For Saussure, in marked contrast, signs (like money) are constituted by something different, which is liable to be exchanged with a thing whose value is determined (signification) as well as by similar things that can be compared with the thing whose value is in question (other signs). Money, like the sign, can be iconic if a coin is worth its weight in precious metal or arbitrary if its value is conventionally assigned.[29] Mandelstam's cut coins are deceptive demonic signs since the signifier (the appearance of the slivered coin, the text) misleads one with respect to the signified (monetary value, poetic interiority). If figurative language is rejected ("the earth buzzes with metaphor"), then "time cuts me like a coin" is doubly vacuous as a figuration of figuration.

Previous poetic utterances, like coins, lie buried in the earth. Seemingly able to resist the assault of time, they are actually disfigured by it, bearing imprints of the age's teeth over their original patterns: "The age, trying to gnaw them through, / Has imprinted its teeth on them" ["Vek, probuia ikh peregryzt', ottisnul na nikh svoi zuby"] (Mandel'shtam 1993, 2: 45). One may say the coins are newly minted through disfiguration; their defacement becomes their identity. Poetic interiority is compromised in the case of older poets, and yet more extremely so in the case of the poem's protagonist who is "cut like a coin by time" (Gasparov 2001, 642).[30] The cut coin echoes contrastively the hollow yet molded golden sphere of the dying Christian era. Mandelstam's poet finds himself insolvent and disfigured in the new post-Christian age.

"The Horseshoe Finder" proceeds from a comfortable expression of all-unity (marked on the level of grammar), "We say" ["Govorim"], to the damaged self under the assault of reality and time, "I say" ["Govoriu"] (Mandel'shtam 2: 41–45). But even this lonely "I say" is illusory, for the text is no longer under the author's control, cut from his consciousness and existence: "What I am saying now is not said by me."[31] The poet will speak no more: "Human lips, / Which have nothing more to say, / Preserve the shape of the last word spoken" ["Chelovecheskie guby, / Kotorym bol'she nechego skazat', / Sokhraniaiut formu poslednego skazannogo slova"] (Mandel'shtam 1993, 2: 45). Like a distant star shining in the skies though it died out long ago, the poem sounds after its author is gone: "The sound still rings, though its reason is gone" ["Zvuk eshche zvenit, khotia prichina zvuka ischezla"] (Mandel'shtam 1993, 2: 44). "The Horseshoe Finder" is not a museum of the past, not even a funereal urn of the poetic self. It is a geological stratum in which a frail fossil of the poet is buried. The fossil may be exhumed but the poet can hardly be resurrected.

CONCLUSION

Mandelstam's "Silentium" and "The Horseshoe Finder" distill, in concentrated form, the major motifs and principles of his art from the pre-Acmeist period and the 1920s, respectively. As I have sought to show, these poems resonate with the core philosophical problems in Florensky's oeuvre. Florensky weaves idealist and skeptical strands of thought side by side—while clearly privileging the former. In the idealistic view in the act of verbal expression one transcends the dualism between the subject and the world and gains an intimation of cosmic unity. Whereas Mandelstam's early "Silentium" imagines the poet's mystical fusion with the cosmos, and the signifier and the signified as organically connected, his later "The Horseshoe Finder" is a great deal more doubtful about the possibility of all-unity as well as the capabilities of the word. The relationship between poetry and philosophical arguments thus emerges as a dynamic interplay.

NOTES

1. On Florensky and Mandelstam, see Nadezhda Mandel'shtam (1990, 71, 90). For previous comparative studies of Mandelstam and Florensky, see, for example, Uzharevich (1995) and Sedykh (2010).
2. The intellectual interest in Schopenhauer in Russia "was not to flag until the outbreak of the First World War, as Grusenberg's (rather incomplete) Schopenhauer bibliography of 1914 demonstrates" (Stammler 1979, 36). The principle of existential uncertainty "has been absorbed from Annenskii, Shestov, and, ultimately, Nietzsche" (Freidin 1987, 185).
3. To name "is not to assign an arbitrary sound to some perception but [...] to approach in one's thoughts the thoughts of the human race, with the result that the word now appears to embody a consistent, inwardly necessary link between external expression and internal content. [...] This inwardly necessary link makes of the word or name a 'symbol'" (Seifrid 2005, 104).
4. Cf. Vyacheslav Ivanov: "In realistic symbolism, the symbol [...] links separate consciousnesses, but their ecumenical unity is achieved through a common mystical contemplation of the objective essence that is one for all" (Ivanov 1971–1987, 2: 552).
5. Florensky's symbol "has a phenomenal (real, earthly) and noumenal (seeming, heavenly) components" (Sedykh 2010, 300).
6. I am using Florensky (1997) with modifications for accuracy.
7. In "On Truth and Lying in an Extra-Moral Sense" concepts are arbitrary and artificial phenomena since sounds get invented and randomly fixed to images (Nietzsche 1989, 210–211).
8. Cf. the word as a bridge connecting "I" and "not-I" (Florensky 1997, 48).

9. In the process of speech "the speaker joins up with a trans-individual, collective (*sobornoe*) unity, and the energy of an individual spirit and that of the collective mutually grow into one another" (Seifrid 2005, 100).

10. On Mandelstam's philosophy of language, see Broyde (1975), Przybylski (1987, esp. 46–78), Toddes (1974), Taranovsky (1976), Terras (1998, 184–218) and Terras (1973), Paperno (1991, 31), Surat (2004, 156), Surat (2009, 97–100), and Ronen (1983, 202–203).

11. According to Dmitrii Segal, Mandelstam "actually talks not about silence but about the soul's return to the world before its birth" (Segal 1998, 89). For Victor Terras, Mandelstam's poem "suggests that the acoustic—or musical form of the word is valuable and meaningful" (Terras 1998, 191). Mikhail Gasparov reads "Silentium" as a Verlaine-like response to Tiutchev—a denial of words, a return to pre-linguistic music (Gasparov 1997, 8). Kirill Taranovsky emphasizes the uselessness of poetry as opposed to its impossibility (Taranovsky 1976, 122). Clare Cavanagh argues that Mandelstam exceeds both Tiutchev and the Symbolists in his appeal: "Word, return to music" (Cavanagh 1995, 41). John Malmstad provides an analysis of Mandelstam-Ivanov connections (Malmstad 1986, 237).

12. The poem asks "to be made one with the unformed source of all being" (Cavanagh 1995, 42). It imagines "the primeval harmony of the universe" (Taranovsky 1976, 122), and longs for a pre-historic existence "when there was no duality to overcome, no opposition of Music and Word, no chaos or Cosmos" (Malmstad 1986, 243).

13. "There is no doubt that Mandelstam has ties to the Platonic tradition, and one may assume that Florensky, a big expert and fan of Plato, played the role of mediator here" (Uzharevich 1995, 33).

14. In "The Sea-Shell" ("Rakovina") (1911) the poet is likened to a seashell filled with the whispers of foam.

15. True realism is for Florensky "a 'theory of two worlds,' namely two discontinuous worlds that can be grasped and kept together only by means of a third element, i.e., a symbol consisting of both concrete and abstract elements, which finally provides a wider paradigm for the 'whole,' as well as a feasible access to it" (Oppo 2018, 52).

16. The sound speaks to consciousness, "carrying out an old appeal, 'word, return to music'" (Gasparov 1997, 31–32).

17. "And Still on Mount Athos" ["I ponyne na Afone"] (1915) endorses name worshipping [*imiaslavie*] but also posits that, together with the name, we kill unnamed love. "Your image, tormenting and elusive" ["Obraz tvoi, muchitel'nyi i zybkii"] (1912) develops around the conceit of God's name as his spirit, represented by a bird. The divine, as in Hebrew apophasis, is unknowable and unnamable. God's name, the living force for *imiaslavie* advocates, cannot be articulated without dire consequences. For Florensky on the *imiaslavie* debate, see "Imiaslavie as a Philosophical Premise" ["Imiaslavie kak filosofskaia predposylka"] (1922) (Florensky 1990).

18. On "reversed time" [*obrashchennoe vremia*], see Florensky (1996).

19. In more hopeful readings, "a horse dies, but the horseshoe becomes a talisman which protects the human home" (Ronen 1983, 84), or becomes a sign of Nietzschean "eternal recurrence" (Panova 2003, 577). For analyses of this poem, see Brown (1973, 287–295), Broyde (1975, 169–199); Cavanagh

(1995, 157–192), Freidin (1987, 112–113, 215–216), Myers (1991), Panova (2003, 607–715), and Smoliarova (2003).

20. The poem "is built thematically as a chain—in terms of its plot and metaphors—of creation, destruction, modification" (Panova 2003, 692).

21. The "ship of poetry" metaphor is at work in "The Horseshoe Finder." In "On the Nature of the Word," Mandelstam likens poems to Egyptian boats of the dead.

22. Florensky's reverse perspective "involves multiple spatial and temporal viewpoints presented simultaneously in a work of art" (Oppo 2018, 49–50). Reverse perspective is "the possibility of depicting objects from multiple viewpoints and, indeed, of showing various moments of time within the framework of a single picture" (Pyman 2015, 36).

23. "The word 'fragment' of the subtitle was especially suitable [...] for the dominant theme of the second part, where all the operative images are residua" (Brown 1973, 292). "The verbal fragment [the poem] echoes the physical fragment [the horseshoe], and both are metonyms for a cultural unity that is, perhaps, lost forever" (Cavanagh 1995, 165).

24. Cf. "We have bound swallows / Into battle legions" ["My v legiony boevye / Sviazali lastochek"] (Mandel'shtam 1993, 1: 135) of "The Twilight of Freedom" ["Sumerki svobody"] (1918).

25. Cf. "January 1st 1924" ["1 ianvaria 1924"] (Mandel'shtam 1993, 2: 51) and "The Swallow" ["Lastochka"] (1920) (Mandel'shtam 1993, 1: 146). On petrified wheat, see "The Human Wheat" ["Pshenitsa chelovecheskaia"] (1922) (Mandel'shtam 1993, 2: 248).

26. Cf. Mandelstam's "When arrested in the warm night" ("Kogda v teploi nochi zamiraet"). On space and time in the visual arts, see Florensky (2000).

27. For "The Last Day of Pompeii" as an allegory of the start of Christianity, see Lotman (1995, 294).

28. Cf. Sermon on the Mount: "But let your communication be, Yea, yea; Nay, nay: for whatsoever is more than these cometh of evil" (Matthew 5: 37). On this Biblical subtext, see Panova (2003, 661). On the golden Christian sphere, see Gasparov (1997, 566). Cf. the essays "The Nineteenth Century" ["Deviatnadtsatyi vek"] (1922) and "Scriabin and Christianity" ["Scriabin in khristianstvo"] (1917).

29. In Nietzsche's "On Truth and Lying in an Extra-Moral Sense" worn-out metaphors are compared to coins turned into metal since their markings have been erased (Nietzsche 1989, 250)—an image akin to Mandelstam's "assorted copper, gold, and bronze cakes [that] lie with equal honor in the ground."

30. A cheat might have "cut slivers from the coin while pawning off the coin at its face value, which no longer corresponded to its weight" (Cavanagh 1995, 87).

31. Personal pronouns "vanish entirely in stanzas 3 through 5: there is already apparently 'not enough of me for me,' and the past passive form of 'dug up' ('vyryto') shows that it is not the poet himself performing exhumation" (Cavanagh 1995, 173–186). Florensky's sememe "constantly wavers, it breathes, it is iridescent, and has no independent meaning that exists separately from *this* speech of mine, spoken right *here* and now, in the whole context of lived experience and also in the *present* place of this speech" (Cassedy 1991, 545).

640 S. KHAGI

BIBLIOGRAPHY

Brown, Clarence. 1973. *Mandelstam.* Cambridge, MA: Harvard University Press.

Broyde, Steven. 1975. *Osip Mandelstam and His Age: A Commentary on the Themes of War and Revolution in the Poetry 1913–1923.* Cambridge, MA: Harvard University Press.

Cassedy, Steven. 1991. Pavel Florensky's Philosophy of Language: Its Contextuality and Its Context. *Slavic and East European Journal* 35 (4): 537–552.

Cavanagh, Clare. 1995. *Osip Mandelstam and the Modernist Creation of Tradition.* Princeton, NJ: Princeton University Press.

Florensky, Pavel A. 1990. *U vodorazdelov mysli.* Moscow: Pravda.

———. 1996. *Ikonostas. Sochineniia v 4 tomakh.* Moscow: Mysl'.

———. 1997. *The Pillar and Ground of the Truth.* Trans. Boris Jakim and introduction by Richard F. Gustafson. Princeton, NJ: Princeton University Press.

———. 2000. Analiz prostranstvennosti i vremeni v khudozhestvenno-izobrazitel'nykh proizvedeniiakh. In *Stat'i i issledovaniia po istorii i filosofii iskusstva i arkheologii,* 79–421. Moscow: Mysl'.

———. 2003. *Stolp i utverzhdenie istiny. Opyt pravoslavnoi teoditseii.* Moscow: AST.

Frank, Semyon. 1983. *The Unknowable: An Ontological Introduction to the Philosophy of Religion.* Trans. Boris Jakim. Athens, OH: Ohio University Press.

Freidin, Gregory. 1987. *A Coat of Many Colors: Osip Mandelstam and His Mythologies of Self-Presentation.* Berkeley, CA: Berkeley University Press.

Gasparov, Mikhail L. 1997. Poet i kul'tura. Tri poetiki Osipa Mandel'shtama. In *Polnoe sobranie stikhotvorenii,* ed. Osip Mandel'shtam, 5–64. St. Petersburg: Novaia biblioteka poeta.

———. 2001. Kommentarii. In *Stikhotvoreniia. Proza,* ed. Osip Mandel'shtam. Moscow: Folio.

Ivanov, Vyacheslav I. 1971–1987. In *Sobranie sochinenii v 4 tomakh,* ed. D.V. Ivanov and O. Deshart. Brussels: Foyer Oriental Chrétien.

Lotman, Yuri M. 1995. Zamysel stikhotovoreniia o poslednem dne Pompei. In *Pushkin,* 293–299. Saint Petersburg: Iskusstvo-SpB.

Lotman, Yuri M., and Boris A. Uspensky. 1985. "Agreement" and "Self-Giving" as Archetypal Models of Culture. In *The Semiotics of Russian Cultural History: Essays by Iurii M. Lotman, Lidiia Ia. Ginsburg, Boris A. Uspenskii,* ed. Alexander Nakhimovsky and Alice Stone Nakhmovsky, 125–140. Ithaca, NY: Cornell University Press.

Malmstad, John. 1986. Mandelstam's "Silentium": A Poet's Response to Ivanov. In *Vyacheslav Ivanov: Poet, Critic and Philosopher,* ed. Robert L. Jackson and Lowry Nelson Jr., 236–252. New Haven, CT: Yale University Press.

Mandel'shtam, Nadezhda Ya. 1970. *Vtoraia kniga.* Moscow: Moskovskii rabochii.

———. 1990. *Vospominaniia.* New York: Chekhov.

Mandel'shtam, Osip E. 1993. In *Sobranie sochinenii v 4 tomakh,* ed. P. Nerler and A. Nikitaev. Moscow: Art-Biznes-Tsentr.

Myers, Diana. 1991. The Hum of Metaphor and the Cast of Voice: Observations on Mandel'shtam' "The Horseshoe Finder." *The Slavonic and East European Review* 69 (1): 1–39.

Nietzsche, Friedrich. 1954. *Thus Spoke Zarathustra: A Book for All and None.* Trans. Walter Kaufmann. New York: Modern Library.

―――. 1989. *Friedrich Nietzsche on Rhetoric and Language.* Ed., trans., and introduction by Sander Gilman, Carole Blair, and David Parent. Oxford: Oxford University Press.

Oppo, Andrea. 2018. Overturning Naturalism: Pavel Florenskii's Aesthetic Realism. *Slavic and East European Journal* 62 (1): 42–59.

Palmer, Gerald E. H., Philip Shepard, and Kallistos T. Ware, eds. and trans. 1979. *Philocalia: The Complete Text.* Compiled by St. Nikodimos of the Holy Mountain and St. Makarios of Corinth. London: Faber and Faber.

Panova, Lada. 2003. *"Mir," "prostranstvo," "vremia" v poezii Osipa Mandel'shtama.* Moscow: Iazyki Slavianskoi Kul'tury.

Paperno, Irina. 1991. O prirode poeticheskogo slova. Bogoslovskie istochniki spora Mandel'shtama s simvolizmom. *Literaturnoe obozrenie* 1: 29–36.

Plato. 1970. *Cratylus.* Trans. J. Sanders. Harmondsworth and London: Penguin.

Pliny the Younger. 2009. *Complete Letters.* Oxford: Oxford University Press.

Plotinus. 1962. *The Enneads.* Trans. Stephen MacKenna. London: Faber and Faber.

Przybylski, Ryszard. 1987. *An Essay on the Poetry of Mandelstam: God's Grateful Guest.* Trans. Madeline G. Levine. Ann Arbor, MI: Ardis.

Pyman, Avril. 2015. Afterthoughts to a Biography. In *Pavel Florenskij tra icone e avanguardia,* ed. Matteo Bertele, 29–39. Trevison: Terraferma edizioni.

Ronen, Omry. 1983. *An Approach to Mandelstam.* Jerusalem: Bibliotheca Slavica.

Saussure, Ferdinand. 1986. *Course in General Linguistics.* Trans. and ed. Roy Harris. Chicago, IL: LaSalle.

Schopenhauer, Arthur. 1969. *The World as Will and Representation.* 2 vols. Trans. E. Payne. New York, NY: Dover.

―――. 1994. In *Philosophical Writings,* ed. Wolfgang Schirmacher. New York, NY: Continuum.

Sedykh, Oksana. 2010. 'Med, vino i moloko': motiv obrashchennogo vremeni v tvorchestve P. A. Florenskogo i O. E. Mandel'shtama. In *Antichnost' i kul'tura Serebrianogo veka,* 299–305. Moscow: Nauka.

Segal, Dmitrii. 1998. *Osip Mandel'shtam: istoriia i poetika.* Berkeley, CA and Jerusalem: Berkeley University Press.

Seifrid, Thomas. 2005. *The Word Made Self: Russian Writings on Language, 1860–1930.* Ithaca, NY: Cornell University Press.

Smoliarova, Tatyana. 2003. Pindar i Mandel'shtam. *Toronto Slavic Quarterly* 31. http://www.utoronto.ca.proxy.lib.umich.edu/tsq/13/smolyarova13.shtml. Accessed May 1, 2018.

Solovyov, Vladimir S. 1966–1970. *Sobranie sochinenii v 10 tomakh.* Brussels: Zhizn' s Bogom.

―――. 1991. *Filosofiia iskusstva i literaturnaia kritika.* Moscow: "Iskusstvo".

Stammler, Heinrich. 1979. Metamorphoses of the Will: Schopenhauer and Feth. In *Western Philosophical Systems in Russian Literature: A Collection of Critical Studies,* ed. Anthony Mikotin, 35–58. University of Southern California Series in Slavic Humanities. 3. Los Angeles, CA: University of Southern California Press.

Surat, Irina Z. 2004. Prevrashcheniia imeni. *Novyi mir* 9: 151–168.

―――. 2009. *Mandel'shtam i Pushkin.* Moscow: IMLI RAN.

Taranovsky, Kirill. 1976. *Essays on Mandelstam.* Cambridge, MA: Harvard University Press.

Terras, Victor. 1973. Osip Mandel'shtam i ego filosofiia slova. In *Slavic Poetics: Essays in Honour of Kirill Taranovsky*, ed. Jakobson Roman, C.H. Van Schooneveld, and Dean S. Worth, 455–460. The Hague: Mouton.

———. 1998. *Poetry of the Silver Age: The Various Voices of Russian Modernism*. Dresden: Dresden University Press.

Toddes, Evgenii A. 1974. Mandel'shtam i Tiutchev. *International Journal of Slavic Linguistics and Poetics* 17: 59–85.

Uzharevich, Iosip. 1995. Pavel Florensky i Osip Mandel'shtam. In *Postsimvolizm kak iavlenie kul'tu ry*, 28–39. Moscow: RGGU.

CHAPTER 29

Future-in-the-Past: Mikhail Bakhtin's Thought Between Heritage and Reception

Vitaly L. Makhlin

THE PROBLEM

In a book on Russian thought, it seems relevant to come to terms with one of the issues central to work of Mikhail Bakhtin (1895–1975). This is the problem that could be expressed in the form of the following question: What was the *event (or the events) of thinking*, in twentieth-century philosophy and humanities, in which this Russian philosopher and scholar participated and to which he responded, according to his own concepts of "participative thinking" and an "actively responsive understanding" (Bakhtin 1986, 69, 1993, 8)?

What follows is an attempt to answer this question by providing access to these major Bakhtinian concepts, with the help of the category of "historicity" (*Geschichtlichkeit* in German, *istorichnost'* in Russian)—a term used here in its hermeneutical or "dialogic" sense of open-endedness of both some cultural past and an interpretive "outsideness" to that past (or *vnenakhodimost'* to use Bakhtin's well-known term). Within the contexts of so-called Bakhtin studies, Eastern and Western, the subject matter of the present essay would be the "in-between," that is, some meaningful distance between this author's heritage and the "first hundred years" of Bakhtin's reception history (Emerson 1997).

V. L. Makhlin (✉)
Moscow State Pedagogical University, Moscow, Russia

© The Author(s), under exclusive license to Springer Nature Switzerland AG 2021
M. F. Bykova et al. (eds.), *The Palgrave Handbook of Russian Thought*,
https://doi.org/10.1007/978-3-030-62982-3_29

643

644   V. L. MAKHLIN

THE ABYSS

In Bakhtin's private lectures on Russian literature from the 1920s, there is a methodologically relevant remark (in connection with the Symbolist reception of ancient myths): "Between heritage and reception there is an *abyss*" [*bezdna*] (Bakhtin 2000, 377). In Bakhtin's own case, I argue, the "abyss" has turned out to be much wider and deeper than in the case of any other important Russian thinker of his age. Right now, it should be sufficient to say that we do not know even today "where Bakhtin came from" and how to "locate" his thought and work in Russian, as well as in Western, intellectual history. Critical literature on Bakhtin had become extensive already by the end of the previous century, and it continues to grow nowadays, so one cannot avoid referring to it (see, e.g., Iurchenko 1995; Adlam and Shepherd 2000). However, it seems that the reception still lacks a methodologically adequate approach to a specific dimension of Bakhtin's "own" time and thought, its "historicity" (in contrast to so-called historicism). Bakhtin himself called such a dimension, in his 1921/1922 programmatic text, "the whole concrete historicalness," or "being-as-event" as an "ontologically eventful" pre-condition of any individual act or thought (Bakhtin 1993, 3, 57, 10–11, 15–19, etc.). What is meant by these terms seems to be a historically common or communal experience which Bakhtin is known to have always opposed to any "official" consciousness and ideology, as well as to any "rhetoric to the extent of its mendacity."[1]

Indeed, the time in which Bakhtin lived, thought, and wrote has usually been viewed by his "belated" readers and commentators, against their own "postmodern" background and horizon of understanding and expectation, and not from the viewpoint of Bakhtin's concrete historical situation with its own objective challenges and problems, and the participants who responded to that common situation and experience. In one of his so-called disputed texts from the 1920s Bakhtin defined (and briefly described) the theoretical aspect of that situation as the "constellation of problems" [*problemnaia konstelliatsiia*] in philosophy and the humanities during the first decades of the twentieth century (Bakhtin and Medvedev 1978, 4). That "constellation," I argue, "came from" a mobile feast of revolutions in the fields of philosophy and humanities, in which the Russian thinker was an active participant, "though only one among the many," as he was wisely called half a century later by an outstanding compatriot (Averintsev 2010, 93).[2]

So much has been said about the "disputed texts," and so little about the texts themselves—a paradox which is more or less evident in the interpretations of Bakhtin's later, most famous writings as well. In fact, everybody is likely to know today what "dialogue," or "polyphony," or "carnival" and "carnivalization" mean; but it is rather unlikely that the critics and commentators would know (if they care to know) what Bakhtin *the author* implied by these (and other) concepts and terms he introduced (or re-introduced) into contemporary thought. Moreover, since the 1960s Bakhtin's texts and concepts have often been interpreted (particularly in the West) from the philosophical and scholarly positions which this Russian thinker had *criticized* already in the 1920s; what a fascinating material for research in the genre of "serio-comic" that Bakhtin himself (re)introduced into contemporary literary theory and so-called cultural studies! However, even those serio-comic misinterpretations and disorientations have revealed a keen interest in something not at all false or naïve.

One can designate this "something" as the creative potential of Bakhtin's thought, which is, I believe, not a riddle or a mystery, but rather a specific problem of historical thinking, of which the "abyss" is not the cause, but the consequence.

Methodologically, one thing seems clear at the moment: it is within concrete historicity—not within those modernized and "theorized" notions or images of the creative past that Thomas Kuhn called, in his famous book about scientific revolutions, the "ideology of science as profession" with its "temptation to re-write history backward" (Kuhn 1970, 137)—that one should look for access to Bakhtin's thought and its unusual, discontinuous continuity in the history of twentieth-century philosophy and humanities.

FUTURE-IN-THE-PAST

No wonder, then, that a specific quality of Bakhtin's heritage as a whole, his idea that "nothing is absolutely dead: every meaning will have its homecoming festival" (Bakhtin 1986, 170)—let us call this idea an ontologically eventful *"future-in-the-past"*—seems to have been lost or absent in Bakhtin studies from almost the beginning. For, that very dimension of temporality, while having always been *experienced* by many of Bakhtin's readers, nevertheless fell apart, during the decades of the "death of the author," into two mutually alienated temporalities: Bakhtin's heritage with its "whole concrete historicalness," on the one hand, and Bakhtin's reception history since the 1960s, on the other. That is to say, Bakhtin's creative potential was, at first, enthusiastically but mistakenly taken up by his postmodern readers (irrespective of their "ideology" or "rhetoric") for a possible creative future of postmodernity itself *minus* the other's historicity and "open-ended" thinking. "We are the real thing," that was (and still is) a kind of unofficial and non-rhetorical slogan of so-called postmodernity (Cassedy 1990, 1–6). Indeed, in almost all the attempts, up to the present, to perceive and grasp the ontologically eventful figure of temporality Bakhtin called "great time" (Bakhtin 1986, 5), past and future have been, as it were, divorced from each other, and this dissociation of sensibility and of historical continuity has actually resulted in a radical rupture or break of communication, that is, the "abyss."

THE AMBIVALENCE

At the same time, however, the recent collapse of both modernity and postmodernity, East and West, seems to be *ambivalent* in a specifically Bakhtinian sense of the word. For, on the one hand, we are experiencing, in the new century, a cultural and intellectual dead-end, to the extent that creative

646 V. L. MAKHLIN

future-in-the-past itself has almost left all the so-called disciplines of interpretation; even the idea and ideal of the "university" seems to be "in ruins" (Readings 1997). In this new context of the "end of history," Bakhtin's overwhelming idea of the "homecoming festival," as well as his conception of an open-ended "dialogue," have almost ceased to be attractive or relevant in recent decades, both in scientific communities and in the public realm. Yet our present temporal and semantic "outsideness" to the four or five hundred years of what Bakhtin called, in his 1929/1963 Dostoevsky book, "the entire ideological culture of modernity" [*novogo vremeni*] (Bakhtin 1984a, 80), is rather productive in a new way, because it has revealed the narrowness, as well as sustaining meaningfulness, of all the previous views and ideologies, and has opened up new perspectives and possibilities of vision and research. In other words, in modernity [New Time, *v novom vremeni*] productive perspectives for future philosophy and the humanities seem to be found not in the so-called "new word" [a breakthrough], but, rather, in an ability to show the relevance of what has already been said in the past for the present potential of the "future-in-the past" meanings of that past.

In any case, the contemporary dimension of historicity, devoid of its own "horizons of expectations," appears to become more and more sensitive to the ontologically eventful "otherness" of histories and authors of the past. In this new context a question arises: What, actually, has been there "between" Bakhtin's thought and its reception, mostly from the 1960s on?

The In-Between(s)

"Between the word and its object, between the word and the speaking subject," Bakhtin wrote in his "Discourse in the Novel" (1934/1935), "there exists an elastic environment of other, alien words about the same object, the same theme, and this is an environment that is often difficult to penetrate" (Bakhtin 1981, 276). Why, then, is the "environment" *between* Bakhtin's heritage and its reception so difficult to penetrate? The difficulties are more or less known, but they have rarely been analyzed as a meaningful whole, that is, the *in-between(s)*. What, then, are the objective difficulties of the reception?

First and foremost: in contrast to his famous European contemporaries, Bakhtin, like so many in his Russian generation, was unable to develop and publish his ideas normally, that is, *institutionally and timely*; he therefore did not have an authentic "biography" (a public form of self-accounting). Just imagine, for a moment, that Heidegger's *Sein und Zeit* (1927), or Buber's *Ich und Du* (1923), was to have been published and discussed fifty or eighty years later; but that was, in fact, Bakhtin's case.[3] And not only his, of course: "The history of Russian thought," a well-known scholar and critic wrote recently comparing the Soviet reception of Shakespeare with Bakhtin's interpretation, "is a history with missing or omitted chapters" (Shaitanov 2011, 233).

As a result, and this is the second difficulty for penetrating and "locating" Bakhtin's thought: a reader or an interpreter has to deal not with Bakhtin's work as a whole, but, actually, with innumerable fragments, sometimes without a beginning and end, even without the author's title (not to mention the "disputed" books and articles published under his friends' names). Even Bakhtin's famous monographs on Dostoevsky and Rabelais are, in a way, fragments, particularly difficult to penetrate in their philosophical and religious roots hidden under the rubric of literary criticism and cultural history.

Moreover, and this is the third difficulty of the "in-between," there is a seeming contradiction between what Bakhtin himself characterized, not long before his death, as a "unity of the emerging (developing) idea" of his thought and what he also described in the same unfinished preface to his posthumously published collection of essays (1975) as "[m]y love for variations and for a diversity of terms for a single phenomenon," as well as "a certain internal open-endedness of my ideas" (Bakhtin 1986, 155). Paradoxically, this external contradiction refers to the internal continuity of *the development* of Bakhtinian thought. In fact, Bakhtin was so alien to the official culture he had to live in most of his life ("on this graceless soil, beneath this unfree sky," as he told Sergey Bocharov on June 6, 1970 [Bocharov and Liapunov 1994, 1012]), that his texts, since the mid-twenties, have always assumed a specific official context and audience, a kind of "adressivity"—without real address.[4]

In Bakhtin's reception history there have been more or less interesting attempts by scholars to find and define an overarching concept that would provide some meaningful continuity to the textual and chronological discontinuity of what Bakhtin called the "unity of the emerging (developing) idea." The most compelling among them are to be found in the chapter entitled "The Architectonics of Answerability" (see Holquist and Clark 1984, 63–94), *Mikhail Bakhtin: Creation of a Prosaics* (Morson and Emerson 1990), and *Dialogism: Bakhtin and his World* (Holquist 1990). However, even in these most valuable attempts, the problem of concrete historicity as a pre-condition of Bakhtin's individual thinking remains, at best, an open question.

The next difficulty is a consequence of the previous three, that is, the "ontologically eventful" gap or "abyss" between Bakhtin's thought and his "belated" audiences, in Bakhtin's own land in particular. In 1995, when Bakhtin's posthumous and post-totalitarian "boom" seemed to be at its height, both in the East and in the West, Sergei G. Bocharov asked rather rhetorically: "where are the continuers of his course [...], those who are thinking out his thoughts and represent his tradition, [where is] his trend, his training?" (Bocharov 1999, 508). In the same year, a historian of Russian philosophy, Konstantin Osipov, gave quite a sober response in his spectacular essay "The Death of the 'Other'" (Osipov 1999). This response did not, actually, challenge Bakhtin's thought or work but it perceptively and aptly described, I should say, the end of the romantic relationship with Bakhtin in Russia after the end of the official ideology. For a mostly unofficial and sincere enthusiasm of the reception in the USSR had been historically motivated, yet blind and theoretically helpless; the "abyss," as it were, came to the surface *after* the collapse of the Soviet state and its ideology (Makhlin 2019).

648   V. L. MAKHLIN

In the post-Stalinist decades, Bakhtin's ideas could find no historical background for understanding except either the traditional quasi-Hegelian historicism of the nineteenth century, or the formalist alternative to it at the beginning and at the end of the Soviet century; while Bakhtin himself, as is well known today, had opposed, from the 1920s on, these very paradigms of thinking. In other words, his philosophical and scholarly roots had left no historical traces at the time when the "homecoming festival" of his ideas began.

Still another difficulty we face when approaching and trying to understand Bakhtin is the paradox that was hinted at by Sergei Bocharov, Bakhtin's most important and most informative interlocutor and commentator, in his invaluable memoirs (Bocharov and Liapunov 1994).[5] Indeed, the philosopher for whom official philosophical activities and career were in fact impossible had nevertheless managed to *remain* a philosopher *outside* philosophy *as an academic discipline*, that is, in the fields of the humanities (literary theory, linguistics, cultural history, and the like). It is this, let us say, "enriching impoverishment" of the initial philosophical project that decades later made Bakhtin a sensation (particularly in the West) as a most relevant thinker and theorist comparable to many leading figures in twentieth-century philosophy and other humanities (see, for instance, Jachia and Ponzio 1993; Bialostosky 1989; Holquist 1990; Jefferson 2001; Mandelker 1995; Tihanov 2006; Haardt 2009; Steinby 2011; Steinby and Klapuri 2013; Wyman 2016). In other words, not only did Bakhtin retain, but he also *developed* his initial authorial intent and philosophical position (the "unity of the emerging (developing) idea") by transforming it in the direction of future perspectives of the humanities and modern philosophy as well.

For the relevant function of philosophy today, as Michael Theunissen among others argued (Theunissen 1992, 21–25), is not so much to build up new systems or constructions, but, rather, to critically reflect and correct historically existing academic disciplines where they seem blind, as it were, to their own philosophical roots and cognitive limits outside or beyond the disciplines themselves. Thus, it is philosophy as critical practice that may protect the disciplines from what Kuhn called the "ideology of science as profession."[6]

Still another difficulty of the "in-between" is Bakhtin's very rare ability to study socio-cultural phenomena and texts *between or, better, across the disciplines*, in his own words, "to move in the frontier spheres, that is, on the borders of all [...] disciplines, at their junctures and points of intersection [*na ikh stykakh i peresecheniiakh*]" (Bakhtin 1986, 103; translation revised). Like many motifs and traits in Bakhtin's thought, this *intra*disciplinary mode of textual analysis is a later "variation" of the method developed in his early philosophical texts, where "the ethics of artistic creation" is presented in phenomenological descriptions "around the basic architectonic points of the actual world of the performed act or deed" (Bakhtin 1993, 54). This method seems as relevant to the situation in the humanities today as it is difficult to penetrate and follow, because the borders of the academic disciplines have become too institutionalized and reified to see and use their inner interrelations, that is, their in-betweens after the end of modernity (New Times). The "walls" between the university disciplines no doubt reflect the "in-between" that Hannah Arendt (among others) described in the 1960s in her existential hermeneutics of "politics."[7]

In fact, for many philologists and historians Bakhtin's thinking is "too philosophical" to penetrate, whereas for many philosophers Bakhtin is "too philological" in his later writings and rather obscure in his early fragments. It is this seemingly obscure quality, I believe, that is really at issue today, from the point of view of the history of thinking, particularly in relations *between* Russian and Western philosophy in the twentieth century. Why so?

THE TRANSITION

With this question we return to our initial and crucial problem of Bakhtin's concrete historicity as the immediate intellectual and socio-cultural precondition, or "otherness," of his thought. In trying to find an excess to his *formative* historical context, it seems natural to *share* Bakhtin's permanent intention to defend the so-called existential personality of both the "I" and the "other" *by their own in-between(s)*, thus confronting "all the decadent and idealistic (individualistic) culture, the culture of essential and inescapable solitude" (Bakhtin 1984a, 287). This tendency, I believe, was an essential part of the "radically new authorial position" (ibid., 57) Bakhtin *shared* with Dostoevsky, not, of course, in the sphere of literary creation but in the sphere of philosophy and scholarship. Indeed, Bakhtin was the only one among the many in his philosophical generation who sprang into existence in the period which the Russian writer Evgenii Zamiatin called (in his 1924 review article) "the decade of one hundred years" [*stoletnee desiateletie*] between 1914 and 1923 (Zamyatin 1999, 101).[8]

That was, actually, the time when the concepts of "historical facticity" and the "ongoing event" [*mir kak sobytiie*] (Bakhtin 1993, 28), as well as the concept of the "hermeneutical facticity" of history and *Dasein* (Heidegger 1988) became (and remained in the twentieth century) the center of philosophical thinking as opposed to the "entire ideological culture of recent times." As we have tried to show above, this event of being in philosophy itself (*das Neue Denken*, the "new thinking" as they called it in the 1920s in Germany) did not and could not take place in the Soviet Russia "officially," that is, timely and institutionally, though the "constellation of problems" was the same, East and West, before and after the "Great War."[9]

As a preliminary step to identifying Bakhtin's participation in the paradigmatic revolution of twentieth-century philosophy, let us comment on one passage from Bakhtin's war time notes (c. 1943). The passage runs as follows (in Caryl Emerson's translation): "The position occupied by consciousness while creating an image of the other and while creating an image of one's own self. At the present time this is the central problem of all philosophy" (Emerson 1994, 211).

650 V. L. MAKHLIN

By "all philosophy" Bakhtin means here, to be sure, neither the Soviet "materialist," nor the Russian "idealist" philosophy (before and after the Revolution). On the other hand, he refers here not to so-called continental philosophy in general, with its "parting of the ways" between, say, Carnap, Heidegger, and Cassirer (Friedman 2000). Rather, the Russian thinker implies, in this context, a particular movement or trend in European philosophy initiated, in his view, mostly by Kierkegaard and Husserl, Dilthey and Scheler, not to mention Nietzsche and the others who constituted the historical constellation of problems that spurred Bakhtin's thought.[10]

That is why, I believe, Bakhtin could develop his early existential phenomenology and social ontology without "reading" similar projects of his contemporaries who represented the same line of thought, which combined the idea of "strict science" with the idea of "experience" (German *Erleben*) in a concrete historical world. To put it differently: during the "decade of one hundred years" Bakhtin developed, quite originally, a new paradigm of thinking similar to that represented by his European contemporaries (Jaspers and Heidegger, Buber and Rosenzweig, Marcel and Rosenstock-Huessy, Ferdinand Ebner and Romano Guardini, as well as many others more or less well known today), without even knowing most of them. For, the historical condition, the constellation of problems, and the "sources" were more or less common or communal at that time, in-between Russia and the West.[11]

What matters here, I argue, is a more or less common *transition* from "mere" philosophy to the critical exploration of the concrete disciplines of interpretation in their relation to the world of life, to reality or *Wirklichkeit*. In this sense, while studying Bakhtin's heritage today, "the former grounds the latter" (Denischenko 2017, 255), that is, Bakhtin's early philosophical project may give some orientation to the later writings without, however, giving a *direct* access to them—not the other way round. Perhaps for this reason, the center of gravity in recent Bakhtin studies is being transferred, in the East as well as in the West, from philology and literary criticism to the history of philosophy (Tihanov 2000; Schitsova 2002; Nikiforov 2006, Haardt 2009, Steinby 2011; Makhlin 2015; Guseynov 2017a; 2017b; The Bakhtin Forum 2017).

Thus, Bakhtin's thought, in the objective-historical perspective (or, rather, in retrospect), belongs to the revolutionary turn in twentieth-century philosophy that the above-mentioned Michael Theunissen (1932–2015) analyzed scrupulously in his well-known 1965 book *Der Andere* [*The Other*] (Theunissen 1984).[12]

In a broader historical context, what Bakhtin meant in the forties by "all philosophy" Gadamer would call half a century later, in his appeal to "Russian readers" after the collapse of the Berlin Wall, the *"transition from the world of science to the world of life."* Gadamer meant by this the line of thought of those who, like himself, had studied the philosophy of Husserl and Heidegger in the 1920s and developed it in the subsequent decades of the previous century (Gadamer 1991, 7).

THE REVERSAL

A full-scale analysis of the "transition" Gadamer meant lies beyond the scope of this article; but at least two aspects of it should be mentioned here in connection with the "unity of the emerging (developing) idea" in Bakhtin's thought.

The first aspect might be defined as "hermeneutical": The philosophical revolution during and after the "decade of one hundred years" *reversed* the traditional metaphysical subordination of temporality or *Zeitlichkeit* to the sphere of meanings and eternal truths. It is not so-called eternity that grounds the temporality of the historical world, but vice versa: any concrete historical facticity or temporality grounds eternal notions and meanings. In Bakhtin's formulation: "every entry into the sphere of meanings is accomplished only through the gates of the chronotope" (Bakhtin 1981, 258). In this sense Bakhtinian "great time" is closely connected (as in the philosophical hermeneutics of the twentieth century) with "the great cause of liberating" open-ended meanings, in the history of philosophy and culture "from the captivity of time" (Bakhtin 1986, 6). This idea of liberating time through and by time itself, that is, through *another* time (Bakhtin's "homecoming festival") can also be expressed by the English grammatical metaphor of the "future-in-the-past."

The second aspect of the "transition from the world of science to the world of life" belongs to what is known as the "linguistic turn." In the hermeneutical ontology of the twentieth century, in particular, the "transition" was (and still is) a shift from "pure" thinking and reason to a concrete historicity of utterances responding to other utterances, specifically, from the concept of *theoria* to that of *phronesis*, that is, to the analysis of "everyday" discourse. Against the background of the history of philosophy, "the linguistic turn" meant a paradigm shift from the Aristotelian *apophansis* to the "social" or historical character of any logos or speech (Gadamer 1977, 13–15).[13] In Bakhtin's classification of discourse (in the fifth chapter of his Dostoevsky book) alongside "direct and unmediated object-oriented" utterances there exists the "reflected discourse of another." This is a kind of "carnivalesque" reversal of any "monologic" utterance: the latter is not at all negated (as in some "postmodern" theories) but turns out to be relative or addressed to "others" outside or inside itself (Bakhtin 1984a, 185–203).[14]

Thus, the transition from *pure* reason, from apophantic ("monologic") discourse to concrete historical utterances in the world of life, constitutes what Bakhtin called (modifying Husserl) the "dialogic background" [*dialogiziruis-chii fon*] of his own thinking. He could no doubt have approved (if he had known it) the young Heidegger's evaluation of the previous philosophy (up to his immediate predecessors like Rickert) as the *Platonism of barbarians* [*Platonismus der Barbaren*] (Heidegger 1988, 42), or Rosenstock-Hussy's motto "I am not a pure thinker" (Rosenstock-Huessy 1969). In this sense, it was not an exaggeration when, comparing Bakhtin's and Heidegger's versions of social ontology, a historian of philosophy, Erikh Soloviev, wrote that

> if *Towards a Philosophy of the Act* had been published in the 1920s (and not in 1986 as was actually the case), it might perhaps already have come to an intensive development of the whole hermeneutical trend in Western Europe in the pre-war period. (Soloviev 1991, 388)

Now, Bakhtin's connection to the philosophical revolution in the West has, it seems, become clearer. Yet, the question remains: What was (and still is) Bakhtin's connection to *Russian* philosophy?

The Decisive Fact

An extensive work on a constellation of philosophical, practical, and religious issues was one of the key features of the development of Russian philosophical thought during the first decades of the twentieth century. Thus, it was only natural that Bakhtin's attitude to Russian philosophy was part of his early project to rethink the Western metaphysical tradition from Plato and Aristotle to the Neo-Kantians and Husserl—a project very similar and yet not identical to those of his elder and younger contemporaries in the West. For it would be naïve to think that the Russian philosophy of the nineteenth and twentieth centuries was immune to European idealism and utopian socialism, as well as the utopian character of philosophy itself. The real problem here, I believe, is the fact that the radical turn in Western thinking that one of Heidegger's later disciples called a "farewell to utopian thinking" (Marten 1988) did not occur either in Soviet or in so-called Russian religious philosophy. Hence, Bakhtin's relative loneliness in Russian thought "after Communism" appeared even greater and deeper than before. In any case, his "place" in the nation's traditions seems to be rather problematic.

Bakhtin usually criticized those philosophical traditions and trends that he was close to, and, conversely, he used to underscore positive and relevant traits in the traditions which were rather alien to him; this seems to be rather unusual (if not "fantastic"). So-called philosophy of religion, as we know today, was an integral part of Bakhtin's overall authorship, and for this very reason his critical target was, among other things, the neo-idealist tradition based on the ideas of Vladimir Solovyov. "While inheriting the tradition's problematics," writes Sergei Bocharov, "Bakhtin changed the language of philosophizing. One could collect more than a few parallels between Bakhtin's early treatises and the propositions of Berdyaev or Karsavin, but I insist on *one decisive fact*: Bakhtin diverged from the fundamental course of Russian philosophy at the beginning of the century" (Bocharov and Liapunov 1994, 1018). But this divergence, as I have tried to show in this article, cannot be understood without taking into consideration the radical turn in "all philosophy," in relation to which Bakhtin's thought was neither alone nor an exclusion.

NOTES

1. See the 1943 fragment under this title in vol. 5 of Bakhtin's *Collected Works* (Bakhtin 1996, 63–71). The emphasis on the methodological differentiation between "official" and "unofficial" culture and consciousness culminating on the last page of the Rabelais book, appears for the first time, to my knowledge, as early as the 1927 book about Freudianism, where the "content" of consciousness is differentiated into "ontological" (i.e., "unofficial") and "ideological" (i.e., official or rhetoric) motifs. See Voloshinov 1976, 85.

2. In his later philosophy of literature and the novel Bakhtin described the "constellation of problems" in the ideological and literary culture of the Renaissance (Rabelais) and of the German renaissance of the eighteenth century (Lessing, Herder, Goethe). He showed that in both epochs new forms of time and temporal representation arose in response to a common or communal crisis: "A new chronotope was needed that would permit one to link real life (history) to the real earth. It was necessary to oppose to eschatology a creative and generative time, a time measured by creative acts, by growth and not by destruction" (Bakhtin 1981, 204, 206). Bakhtin's own epoch was, no doubt, characteristic of a similar crisis and response to it in philosophy and the humanities.

3. In his 1973 conversations with the philologist Victor Duvakin, Bakhtin said that the Soviet century had meant for him a falling out, as it were, from his own biography, a life-long catastrophe "beginning, of course, not from childhood, not from the youth on, but from the October Revolution on" (Bakhtin 2002, 219). One may find a phenomenological description of the biography/autobiography in Bakhtin 1990, 150–166.

4. The ultimate case of this "heteroglossia" [*raznorechie*] was (and sometimes still is, mostly in the West) Bakhtin's "Marxism," that is, his ability as a non-Marxist to express his "developing idea," under the concrete circumstances of the times, in the language of the official discourse.

5. Bocharov wrote in his invaluable essay about Bakhtin's Dostoevsky book: "Above all, I believed (and still believe) that the turn from the philosophical criticism of Dostoevsky practiced at the beginning of the century toward a structural-eidetic examination of his works, such as Bakhtin achieved in his book, was highly productive and was what enabled him to say that 'new word'" (Bocharov and Liapunov 1994, 1013).

6. Bakhtin initiated this kind of philosophical criticism of the humanities in his 1924 treatise on the aesthetics and literary studies of his day, and continued it, more or less explicitly, in subsequent decades. The best example is, perhaps, his "Discourse in the Novel," where he criticized philologists who, with their traditional empirical methods, failed to come to terms with novelistic discourse: "Many do not even see or recognize *the philosophical roots* of the stylistics (and linguistics) in which they work and shy away from any fundamental philosophical issues. [...] Others—more principled—make a case for consistent individualism in their understanding of language and style" (Bakhtin 1981, 267).

7. Hannah Arendt writes: "The world lies between people, and this *in-between*— much more (than is often thought) men and even man—is today the object of the greatest concern and the most obvious upheaval in almost all the countries of the globe" (Arendt 1993, 4). Compare this to Bakhtin: "We are most inclined to imagine ideological creation as some inner process of understanding,

comprehension, and perception, and do not notice that it in fact unfolds externally, for the eye, the ear, the hand. It is not within us, but between us" (Bakhtin and Medvedev 1978, 8). However, Bakhtin's theory of ideological creation is represented in his *Author and Hero* from the early 1920s. See Bakhtin 1990.

8. That article was published in the journal *The Russian Contemporary* edited by Gorky and Zamiatin. Bakhtin wrote his essay on the transformation of traditional aesthetics and literary studies for that journal (1924), but the latter was prohibited by the Bolsheviks, and Bakhtin, as usual, simply gave up the work. The written part of it (Bakhtin 1990, 257–318) was published fifty years later without an actual response, and not for political reasons. Today his 1924 essay is particularly difficult to penetrate for both philosophers and philologists.

9. This was brilliantly demonstrated in Vladimir Nikiforov's monograph *The Collapse of Philosophy and Its Rebirth*, the first full-scale philosophical study in English, to my knowledge, that analyzes Bakhtin's dialogues in connection with pre-war philosophy (mostly German and Russian). See Nikiforov 2006. However, the decisive event of the "paradigm shift" in philosophy during and after World War I is not principally taken into consideration in this study.

10. In a 1962 letter to a literary critic Vadim Kozhinov, in response to the latter's question about Heidegger (cf. the journal *Moskva* 1992, issue November/ December, 180), Bakhtin wrote that the "determining influence" [*opredeliaiuschee vliianie*] on him came from Husserl, and that among Husserl's disciples he was particularly impressed by Max Scheler and his personalism. Any "influence" on Bakhtin, however, should not be exaggerated: "Even when Bakhtin accepted and appropriated others' ideas," a recent scholar writes in connection with Scheler, "he reshaped them to his own purposes" (Denischenko 2017, 257, n. 5). Indeed, Bakhtin as philosopher cannot be *seen* without *his* concrete intellectual background; yet his thought cannot be understood with the help of the "sources" he "read."

11. In his 1954 article on "The History of the Dialogical Principle" Martin Buber recollected how struck he had been by the similarities between his own thoughts and the ideas of his contemporaries, who, like himself, did not know each other during the Great War. While preparing for publication of his *I and Thou* (1923) he read Ferdinand Ebner' s *Das Wort und die geistigen Realitäten* (1921) and experienced a shock: so close to him was that unknown "dialogic" Catholic thinker. "His book," Buber wrote *decades* later, "showed to me, as no other book since then (for, sometimes the text seemed to be almost unbelievably akin to my thoughts), that in such times as ours, men of different molds and traditions were all in search of the common heritage in its upheaval" (Buber 1962, 298).

12. According to Michael Theunissen, the line of thought he called the "contemporary social ontology," with the concept of the "other" at its center, was developed, *between 1917 and 1923*, in two principled directions: the "transcendental" one (Husserl, Heidegger, and Sartre), and the "dialogic" one (Buber, Scheler, Rosenstock-Huessy, Guardini, and many others). What is today called Bakhtin's "dialogism" is, I believe, a specific (and specifically Russian) unity of *both* directions later transformed into some sort of metaphilosophy, that is, "on the borders of all [...] disciplines, at their junctures and points of intersection" (Bakhtin 1986, 103).

13. In Bakhtin's programmatic fragment from 1921 to 1922 (thus, long before his "disputed" 1929 book on the philosophy of language) the very motif of the "linguistic turn" in philosophy is clarified: "I think that language is much more adapted to giving utterance precisely to that truth, and not to the abstract moment of the logical in its purity. That which is abstract, in its purity, is indeed unutterable: any expression is much too concrete for pure meaning—it distorts and dulls the purity and validity-in-itself of meaning. That is why in abstract thinking we never understand an expression in its full sense" (Bakhtin 1993, 31).

14. It seems that Sergei Averintsev was the first to identify, in his 1976 review article, Aristotle as Bakhtin's "true and greatest" adversary or opponent, with the whole intellectual tradition he had established in the history of scientific philosophy (Averintsev 2010, 99–100). Yet Averintsev stressed, within the Soviet chronotope, Bakhtin's opposition to the Aristotelian *poetics*. The alternative idea of "prosaics" introduced by the American scholars Morson and Emerson in their well-known book stressed Aristotle's ethics in relation to the early Bakhtin, not, however, in relation to the "unity of the emerging (developing) idea" (Morson and Emerson 1990).

Bibliography

Adlam, Carol, and David Shepherd, eds. 2000. *The Annotated Bakhtin Bibliography*. Leeds: The Modern Humanities Research Association.

Arendt, Hannah. 1993. *Men in Dark Times*. New York: Harcourt Brace.

Averintsev, Sergei. 2010. Lichnost' i talant uchenogo (1976). In *M.M. Bakhtin: Kriticheskaia Antologiia. Russkaia Filosofiia Vtoroi Poloviny 20-go Veka*, ed. Vitalii Makhlin, 93–101. Moscow: ROSSPEN.

Bakhtin, Mikhail. 1981. *The Dialogic Imagination: Four Essays by M.M. Bakhtin*, ed. Michael Holquist. Trans. Caryl Emerson and Michael Holquist. Austin, TX: University of Texas Press.

———. 1984a. *Mikhail Bakhtin. Problems of Dostoevsky's Poetics*. Trans. and ed. Caryl Emerson. Minneapolis, MN: Minnesota University Press.

———. 1986. *Speech Genres and Other Late Essays*. Trans. Vern W. McGee, ed. Caryl Emerson and Michael Holquist. Austin, TX: University of Texas Press.

———. 1990. *Art and Answerability: Early Philosophical Essays by M.M. Bakhtin*. Trans. and Notes Vadim Liapunov. Ed. Michael Holquist and Vadim Liapunov. Supplement Trans. Kenneth Brostrom. Austin, TX: University of Texas Press.

———. 1993. *Toward a Philosophy of the Act*. Trans. and Notes Vadim Liapunov. Eds. Vadim Liapunov and Michael Holquist. Austin, TX: University of Texas Press.

———. 1996. *Sobranie sochinenii v semi tomakh*. Ed. Sergei Bocharov and Leontina Melikhova. Moscow: Iazyki slavianskikh kultur.

———. 2000. Lekzii o russkoi literature. In *Sobranie sochinenii v 7 tomakh*, ed. Sergei Bocharov, Leontina Melikhova, and M.M. Bakhtin. Vol. 2: 213–427. Moscow: Iazyki slavianskikh kultur.

Bakhtin, Mikhail. 2002. *Besedy s V.D. Duvakinym*. 2nd ed. Moscow: Soglasie.

Bakhtin Forum. 2017. Bakhtin Forum: The Dark and Radiant Bakhtin. Wartime Notes. *Slavic and East European Journal* 61 (2): 233–310.

Bakhtin, Mikhail M., and Pavel N. Medvedev. 1978. *The Formal Method in Literary Scholarship*. Trans. Albert J. Wehrle. Baltimore, MD and London: John Hopkins University Press.

Bialostosky, Don H. 1989. Dialogic, Pragmatic, and Hermeneutic Conversation: Bakhtin, Rorty, and Gadamer. *Critical Studies: A Journal of Critical Theory, Literature and Culture* 1 (2): 107–119.

Bocharov, Sergei. 1999. *Siuzhety russkoi literatury*. Moscow: Iazyki russkoi kul'tury.

Bocharov, Sergei, and Vadim Liapunov. 1994. Conversations with Bakhtin. *PMLA* 109 (5): 1009–1024.

Buber, Martin. 1962. "Zur Geschichte des dialogischen Prinzips" (1954). In Martin Buber. *Werke*. Bd. 1: Schriften zur Philosophie, 291–305. München/Heidelberg.

Cassedy, Stephen. 1990. *Flight from Eden: The Origins of Modern Literary Criticism and Theory*. Berkeley, CA: University of California Press.

Denischenko, Irina. 2017. Beyond Reification: Mikhail Bakhtin's Critique of Violence in Cognition and Representation. *Slavic and East European Journal* 61 (2): 255–277.

Emerson, Caryl. 1994. The Making of M.M. Bakhtin as Philosopher. In *Russian Thought after Communism: The Recovery of a Philosophical Heritage*, ed. James P. Scanlan, 206–226. New York and London: M.E. Sharpe.

———. 1997. *The First Hundred Years of Mikhail Bakhtin*. Princeton, NJ: Princeton University Press.

Friedman, Michael. 2000. *A Parting of the Ways: Carnap, Cassirer, and Heidegger*. Chicago and La Salle, IL: Open Court.

Gadamer, Hans-Georg. 1977. Philosophical Foundations of the Twentieth Century. In *Philosophical Hermeneutics*, ed. H.-G. Gadamer, 107–129. Berkeley, CA: University of California Press.

———. 1991. *Aktual'nost' prekrasnogo*. Moscow: The Art Publishers.

Guseynov, Abdusalam. 2017a. Filosofiia postupka kak pervaia filosofiia. *Voprosy filosofii* 6: 5–15.

———. 2017b. Pervaia filosofiia kak nravsvennaia filosofiia. *Voprosy filosofii* 7: 65–74.

Haardt, Alexander. 2009. Ethische und Aesthetische Persönlichkeit bei Sören Kierkegaard und Michail Bachtin. *Studies in East European Thought* 61 (2/3): 326–342.

Heidegger, Martin. 1988. *Ontologie (Hermeneutik der Faktizität)* (1923 SS lecture course). In *Gesamtausgabe*, ed. Martin Heidegger, Bd. 63. Frankfurt a. Main: Vittorio Klostermann.

Holquist, Michael. 1990. *Dialogism: Bakhtin and His World*. London and New York: Routledge.

Holquist, Michael, and Katerina Clark. 1984. *Mikhail Bakhtin*. Cambridge, MA: Harvard University Press.

Iurchenko, Tatiana G. 1995. *M.M. Bakhtin v Zerkale Kritiki*. Moscow: INION.

Jachia, Paolo, and Augusto Ponzio, eds. 1993. *Bachtin e …Averincev, Benjamin, Freud, Greimas, Levinas, Marx, Peirce, Valéry, Welby, Yourcenar* [unpublished Bakhtin]. Roma; Bari: Laterza.

Jefferson, Ann. 2001. Bodymatters: Self and Other in Bakhtin, Sartre and Barthes. In *Bakhtin and Cultural Theory*. Revised and expanded second edition, ed. Ken Hirschkop and David Shepherd, 201–228. Manchester and New York: Manchester University Press.

Kuhn, Thomas. 1970. *The Structure of Scientific Revolutions*. Chicago, IL: The University of Chicago Press.

Makhlin, Vitalii. 2015. *Bol'shoie vremia: Podstupy k myshleniiu M.M. Bakhtina*. Siedlice (Poland): Uniwersytet Przyrodniczo-Humanistyczny.

———. 2019. A Belated Conversation. In *Philosophical Thought in Russia in the Second Half of the 20th Century*, ed. Vladislav A. Lektorsky and Marina F. Bykova, 277–284. New York and London: Bloomsbury.

Mandelker, Amy, ed. 1995. *Bakhtin in Contexts: Across the Disciplines*. Evanston, IL: Northwestern University Press.

Marten, Rainer. 1988. *Der menschliche Mensch: Abschied vom utopischen Denken*. Padeborn: Schoeningh.

Morson, Gary Saul, and Caryl Emerson. 1990. *Mikhail Bakhtin: Creation of a Prosaics*. Stanford, CA: Stanford University Press.

Nikiforov, Vladimir. 2006. *The Collapse of Philosophy and Its Rebirth: An Intellectual History with Special Attention to Husserl, Rickert and Bakhtin*. Ontario, CA: The Edwin Mellen Press.

Osipov, Konstanin G. 1999. The Death of the Other. In *Critical Essays on Mikhail Bakhtin*, ed. Caryl Emerson, 153–167. New York, NY: G.K. Hall and Co.

Readings, Bill. 1997. *The University in Ruins*. Cambridge, MA and London: Harvard University Press.

Rosenstock-Huessy, Eugen. 1969. *I am Not a Pure Thinker*. Four Walls: Argo Books.

Schitsova, Tatiana V. 2002. *Sobytie v filosofii M.M. Bakhtina*. Minsk: The I.P. Logvinov Publishers.

Shaitanov, Igor. 2011. Istoriia s opyschennymi glavami: Bakhtin i Pinskii v kontekste sovetskogo shekspirovedeniia. *Voprosy Literatury* 3: 233–274.

Soloviev, Erikh I. 1991. *Proshloie Tolkuiet Nas*. Moscow: Poliizdat.

Steinby, Liisa. 2011. Hermann Cohen and Bakhtin's early Aesthetics. *Studies in East European Thought* 63: 227–249.

Steinby, Liisa, and Tinti Klapuri, eds. 2013. *Bakhtin and His Others: (Inter)subjectivity, Chronotope, Dialogism*. London/New York/Dehli: Anthem Press.

Theunissen, Michael. 1984. *The Other: Studies in the Social Ontology of Husserl, Heidegger, Sartre, and Buber*. Trans. Christopher Macann, with Introduction by Fred R. Dallmayr. Cambridge, MA and London: The MIT Press.

———. 1992. *Negative Theologie der Zeit*. Frankfurt a. M: Suhrkamp.

Tihanov, Galin. 2000. *The Master and the Slave: Lukács, Bakhtin, and the Ideas of their Time*. Oxford and New York: Oxford University Press.

Voloshinov, Valentin N. 1976. *Freudianism: A Marxist Critique*. Ed. Neil H. Brass and Trans. I.R. Titunik. New York, NY: Academic Studies Press.

Wyman, Alina. 2016. *The Gift of Active Empathy: Scheler, Bakhtin, and Dostoevsky*. Evanston, IL: Northwestern University Press.

Zamyatin, Evgenii. 1999. *Ia bius'*. Moscow: Nasledie.

CHAPTER 30

Bakhtin, Translation, World Literature

Galin Tihanov

This chapter is an attempt to understand how the work of a thinker exists across time, and what journeying through languages and cultures has to do with these peregrinations. There is more at stake in this process than the certainty of canonization would suggest. Building on my previous work, I want to examine the principal trajectories of appropriating Bakhtin in the West since the 1960s; this will allow me to revisit the question of Bakhtin's longevity, and the potential of his work to gain traction in current debates on world literature. Bakhtin's work can serve as a litmus test of appropriation that involves constant meta-reflexion on what constitutes translation in different cultural zones.

My approach to Bakhtin's legacy is sustained by a wider theory of translation which comprehends translation both more globally and more historically; at the end of this article, I also discuss the problem of translation vis-à-vis recent debates specifically on world literature, again in the context of Bakhtin's work. Let me begin with a historical excursus. Translation, in the modern sense in which we understand the term, is a fairly recent phenomenon. Its emergence is concomitant with the rising sense of intellectual property—and of the significance originality and imagination have in literature and in scholarship— that appears in the late eighteenth century. Before that, translation lives other lives: those of imitation, transposition, rendition, emulation, and re-creation of the text. This is true of the West, as much as it is true of the wider cultural region formed by the Middle East, the Caucasus, Central Asia, and the Indian Subcontinent. In the European context, we are aware of poetic contests that

---

G. Tihanov (✉)
Queen Mary University of London, London, UK
e-mail: g.tihanov@qmul.ac.uk

© The Author(s), under exclusive license to Springer Nature
Switzerland AG 2021
M. F. Bykova et al. (eds.), *The Palgrave Handbook of Russian Thought*,
https://doi.org/10.1007/978-3-030-62982-3_30

659

660   G. TIHANOV

sought to emulate, rhetorically, examples of Greek and Roman poetry; these competitions were forms of translation; the resulting texts do not insist on originality, nor—importantly—do they insist on complete faithfulness. They present a mode of creativity that is beyond the binary expectations of either originality or loyalty. For centuries on end, helping oneself to someone else's plot or figure of speech, or range of similes, or metaphors, often suitably updated, was a way of ferrying an earlier discourse into a new zone of contemporaneity. This wider meaning of "translation" which highlights both the passive following and the co-creative departure from the example continues—at least to some extent—to be constitutive of our seemingly more advanced, but perhaps also more one-sided, understanding of translation today. As late as the twentieth century, we can still observe this mode of consciously unfaithful translation in what, in the German tradition, is known as *Nachdichtung*, the making of poetry following another text, a process grounded in a deliberate refusal of copying or rendering that text with precision. Of course, there lurks behind all this the question of the canon, for it is the assumption of the rhetorical force and beauty of the canonical text that often enables these acts of permissible transgression. In Central Asia and Persia, as well as in the Arab-speaking world, for a very long time the practice of translation remains alien to our *modern* notion of it. When Nizami, in the second half of the twelfth century, creates his five epic poems in Persian, all through to the eighteenth century we have nothing but forms of rendition that are based on emulation, adaptation, and conversation with the canonical pieces—but not on the literal reproduction our norms of translation would require. This emulation through conversation with the source text is a genre of its own at the time, known as *nazire*: a work in its own right that responds to an earlier work by plunging today's reader into uncertainty as to where the line between translation, re-creation, and original writing is to be drawn—if such a line exists at all before the late eighteenth century.[1] I would thus venture a hypothesis: for as long as the canon—based on the certainty flowing from adherence to a relatively stable combination of rhythm, plot, composition, and rhetorical figures—remains in place, there is no imperative for literal repetition or precision. It is with the shift towards originality, the premium value placed on novelty, and the sense of property that emerges as a by-product of this shift, late in the eighteenth and in the first half of the nineteenth century, that tradition is put under strain and ceases to be self-evident (in Europe, the practice of translation as identifying "ownership" begins gradually already in the sixteenth century). We know that it is precisely at that time—late in the eighteenth and early in the nineteenth century—that the European canon of "great literature" is constructed, in which Shakespeare takes his pride of place. But no longer as the borrower of circulating plots, but rather as the originally irregular, chaotic, and disorderly potent genius that the German Romantics saw in him. Similarly, Calderon is unearthed from oblivion. But not the Calderon who was stealing plots, lifting in one of his plays an entire act from Tirso de Molina. Rather, it is his Baroque vacillation between dream and reality, the quality of un-folding, to invoke

Deleuze (1993), that underwrites his place in this new canon that reshuffles the previous order and signals the virtues of instability, not least the unmooring of literature from a long-standing pool of recurring plots, metres, compositional patterns, and rhetorical devices.

This is when translation as we know it becomes important, fitting into a new situation in which novelty and originality require to be captured with reliable precision of nuance. What is more, this is a process that—historically speaking—seems to me to be nothing but the culmination and logical end to the protracted transition from powerful cosmopolitan *koines*—Greek, Latin, Persian, Sanskrit—to a multitude of vernaculars, each of which insists on its own inimitable vocabulary, sensitivity, and plasticity, in the way advocated by the many supporters of a presumably organic bond between language and thinking, from Humboldt to Georgii Gachev. Although this is true of translation of profane rather than sacred texts (the history of the translation of the Bible would reveal other patterns and trends), what I am contending here is not just true of the way *literary* texts have been treated until the early nineteenth century. The translation of philosophical and political texts would be marked by the same relaxed interpretation of fidelity, by co-creation and adaptation, sometimes amounting to co-writing. One of my favourite examples is the first German translation of Edmund Burke's "Reflections on the Revolution in France" by that inveterate conservative, Friedrich Gentz. Gentz published his translation of Burke's important book in 1793, only three years after its appearance. The translation is marred not just by inaccuracies, but by numerous insertions of Gentz's own thoughts and interpretations of Burke's work.[2] By our standards today this is not a reliable translation, and yet it is this translation that penetrated German and Austrian conservative debates and participated in them for more than a century and a half until a new German edition was published, not long before the eventful year 1968, that eventually revealed the less than conventional ways in which Gentz approached his task as translator (Burke 1967). The moral of the story here is one we may wish to keep in mind: the texture of ideas is discursive, and translations—even before the time our stricter notions of loyalty to the source text were introduced—have always been very much part of this texture. Once a translation begins its circulation, it begins its work through this discursive universe, from which it becomes inseparable. The effects of a translation, once planted in the discursive body of culture, cannot be undone, the clock can never be turned back completely.

This, of course, bears on how we see the task of the translator, to echo the title of Benjamin's famous essay (Benjamin 1969). I should begin, perhaps, by saying that Bakhtin's position in this battle within modernity over the limits of dynamic originality, on the one hand, and stability based on recurrence, on the other, a battle which we see enacted in the transition from a looser to a stricter notion of translation, reflects his own wider understanding of literature and culture. In a sense, Bakhtin performs the opposite transition. He begins by sharing a belief in the uniqueness and originality of the writer only to end up endorsing the overbearing power of tradition imprinted in what he calls "the memory of genre." The entire intellectual evolution of Bakhtin can be described as a struggle against psychologism and an ever more powerful negation of subjectivity (in its classical identitarian version). He admitted to Vadim Kozhinov that Edmund Husserl and Max Scheler played a vital role in his re-education into a thinker who mistrusts psychologism (Kozhinov 1993, 124–125). Beginning with a celebration of Dostoevsky as a unique and inimitable writer of singular achievement, Bakhtin ended up in the 1930s (in his essays on the novel) and in 1963 (in the reworked version of his Dostoevsky book) focusing on the impersonal memory of genre, leaving little room for creativity as such and examining instead the inherent laws of poetics (note the change in the title of the 1963 book, *Problemy poetiki Dostoevskogo*). Bakhtin's entire work and intellectual agenda, indeed the most important questions he sought to answer, are shaped by his resistance to traditionally conceived, stable subjectivity: from the question of the body (which we gradually cease to possess and be in control of, as the book on Rabelais maintains) to the question of language (which, as the essays on the novel would have it, reaches us through established generic patterns and is never quite our own—as it has always already been in someone else's mouth). The fortunes of the novel embody this rejection of classical subjectivity in full measure: the individual writer is virtually irrelevant, he or she is no more than an instrument through which the genre materializes itself, no more than a mouthpiece that enunciates the calls of generic memory. Bakhtin, in other words, despite his apparent attraction to canonical figures such as Goethe, Dostoevsky, and Rabelais, would ideally have liked to be able to write a history of literature without names (the formula "history without names" was, of course, derived from the work of art historian Heinrich Wölfflin and had drawn approval from the Russian formalist Boris Eikhenbaum and also from Pavel Medvedev, who, together with Matvei Kagan, was the most important transmitter of art-historical and art-theoretical knowledge in the Bakhtin Circle).[3] Bakhtin's trajectory is thus the trajectory of a thinker who returns from a more modern notion of individual originality and creativity to the notion of a nameless tradition, in which stable discursive formations recur and suck in, in a manner that is as fascinating as it is unstoppable, the work of individual writers who are deprived of their individualities to become servants of tradition. Of course, Bakhtin remains modern as he performs this move, for tradition to him is not a soothing force; it is disruptive in the way the archaic is both disruptive, but also enduringly constitutive, of the modern.

Bakhtin, then, is a thinker who de-emphasizes originality and property, those underlying features attached to our modern understanding of literature and its translation. If a pun be allowed, he retranslates literature away from the endeavour of individuals, and towards the work of anonymous verbal masses that support the *typomachia* of dialogue and monologue, of the centripetal and the centrifugal. His most important book, in my no doubt biased judgement, the monograph on Rabelais, is a case in point. Admittedly, one of the seven chapters of the book is dedicated to Rabelais' language. But even there, Bakhtin does not approach Rabelais from a philological perspective. Most of what he has to say on Rabelais' use of language is borrowed—and readily acknowledged—from Leo Spitzer and the work of other contemporaries. Nor are the principles of interpretation exclusively pertinent to, or derived solely from, literature. The reason for all this is that Bakhtin is trying to think, in this book, as a philosopher of culture in its totality; language as such takes a back seat, it is only one amongst many different manifestations of culture. In fact, language is here drowned by sweeping manifestations of culture produced by the body in simultaneous acts of laughter, eating, copulation, etc. One might even argue that Bakhtin's Rabelais book has *non-verbal* communication and creativity at its heart.

Whether all this endows and licenses an approach towards Bakhtin's work that applies a charitable and more flexible understanding of translation away from the—often unproductive—obsession with terminological fixity is a difficult question. To begin to formulate an answer to it, we have to be able to survey Bakhtin's intellectual career as a whole and discern that which its different stages have in common. Bakhtin's work falls, roughly speaking, into three distinct periods. The first one, I think, is the time up until the first version of his Dostoevsky book, when Bakhtin is primarily preoccupied with ethics and aesthetics; the second phase encompasses the 1930s, the time when he thinks as a philosopher of culture, most pre-eminently in the essays on the novel and in the Rabelais book. Again, we should not be misled into considering these texts examples of philology or literary theory. Both Bakhtin and the Formalists came of age by pushing away from preoccupations with aesthetics. Aesthetics was their shared starting point; but from there, the Formalists developed into literary theorists, Bakhtin—into a philosopher of culture who employs literary examples, but often (as in the book on Rabelais) also examples drawn from other domains, always in order to ponder larger issues that have to do with the deeper mechanisms of culture, its inner make-up and typology, and its evolution. The last stage in Bakhtin's intellectual career begins already in the early 1940s; this is the time when his attention is gradually claimed by the methodology of the humanities. The late appearance of the Rabelais book and the republication of the reworked Dostoevsky book have skewed our perspective on what is the longest period in Bakhtin's work, from the 1940s through to the early 1970s. What genuinely interests him here is a range of *new* questions that have a meta-dimension: what is an utterance; what is meaning and how is it produced and communicated; what is the role of dialogue in how we understand the world we are immersed in? Yet different as these three periods might arguably be, they have something very important in common: the way in which Bakhtin handles language in his own writing. Whether preoccupied with philosophy of culture, or with the nexus of moral philosophy and aesthetics (which he seeks to resolve in the first version of the Dostoevsky book by putting forward and valorizing a non-finalizing and non-objectifying *polyphonic* writing), Bakhtin's proper realm as thinker was the in-between territory that is confined to no particular discipline and that he inhabited with such non-negotiable sovereignty. It is in this space between the disciplines that he crafted his own metaphors that enabled him to move freely between different levels of argumentation and address issues located above and beyond particular fields of knowledge. Often elusively, but always extremely stimulatingly, Bakhtin lifts the categories he employs above the conceptual constraints of their home disciplines and instils in them new life by obliterating their previous conceptual identity. One brief example, the way in which he formulates the idea of dialogue, should suffice. We hear in Bakhtin's use of dialogue a linguistic substratum, which can probably be attributed to Lev Yakubinsky and a host of other early Soviet linguists, and yet Bakhtin's specific interpretation of this category is so much wider, applicable to entire narratives and whole domains of culture, that focusing exclusively on its linguistic origins, even when these are attestable, would not explain the power and fascination of Bakhtin's dialogism. By way of illustration we could reference here Jan Mukařovský's important essay "Dialogue and Monologue," written in 1940 (Mukařovský 1977). Terminologically, Mukařovský's text is much more disciplined and rigorous, and yet in scope and inventiveness it lags behind Bakhtin's version of dialogue. Mukařovský (who knew and was highly appreciative of some of Voloshinov's writings) works within a narrowly linguistic juxtaposition of dialogue and monologue; Bakhtin transcends this limitation, he refreshes our understanding of dialogue by inviting us to hear the dialogue within a single uttered word, or the dialogue embodied in voices that convey conflicting outlooks and perspectives on the world, or indeed dialogue as the foundation for a wide-ranging typology of cultural forms. This transformation, which subjects the term to inner growth (sometimes at the expense of exactitude), a transformation whereby the term expands its scope of relevance to the point of turning into a broader metaphor, is the most important feature informing Bakhtin's prose, the hallmark of his writings, especially those of the 1930s. It is this transformative energy that sets him apart from his likely, or even demonstrable, antecedents hailing from various specializations, be they linguistic, sociological, theological, or art-historical for that matter. It is not difficult, for example, to demonstrate how several of Bakhtin's concepts— architectonics, space, gothic realism—were derived, at least to a significant degree, from the German art-historical tradition.[4] This, however, would tell us very little about the significant transformation of these concepts when thrown into the melting pot of Bakhtin's argumentation. Bakhtin's originality as thinker is actually the originality of the great synthesizer who took, at liberty, from various specialized discourses—linguistics, art history, theology—and then reshaped, extended, and augmented the scope of the respective concepts.

Bakhtin is thus a thinker who handles language in a way that protects him from falling prey to terminological fetishism. His often-metaphoric deployment of terminology from different domains of knowledge gives volume and breadth to his writing that cannot be matched by a translation that shies away from preserving this potential metaphoricity. The failure to accept this hallmark of Bakhtin's writing has been responsible, at least in part, for the vicissitudes of his reception in the West since the 1960s. Bakhtin's discoveries have been articulated differently at different historical junctures and in different cultural settings; the Bakhtin we see today is a fluctuating image, resulting from superimposed perspectives involving growth, modification, loss, and a complex adjustment of meaning, as his body of writing travels across time, languages, and discursive traditions and meets inherited patterns of reasoning. Bakhtin's work is thus not a reliable supply of knowledge or wisdom; it rather derives from the elusive, sometimes blurred, and never quite finished work of mediation and translation. Thus, Bakhtin's legacy is the function of multiple historical articulations, a patrimony in transit, and subject to translation and dialogue.

We have to recall that Bakhtin's appropriation in the West commences under the sign of Structuralism and its belief in scientific rigour. While in Russia Bakhtin was thought to be a foe of Formalism and Structuralism—and by extension, in the eyes of his future opponents (such as Mikhail Gasparov), a denier of "exact" literary science—his career in the West, particularly in the Anglophone world, began and evolved for about two decades under the auspices of Formalism and Structuralism. Ladislav Matejka, an émigré scholar from Prague who had reached the United States via Sweden, published, in 1962, a slender anthology titled *Readings in Russian Poetics*, incorporating texts in Russian by, amongst others, both Voloshinov and Bakhtin. The second edition (1971), which was considerably expanded and published in English, carried the telling subtitle "Formalist and Structuralist Views"; it became the first major collection in the West to include translated work by Bakhtin and Voloshinov. Bakhtin was here introduced with a portion of his 1929 Dostoevsky book, which Matejka had first read in a class offered at Harvard by the truly ubiquitous Dmitro [Dmitrii] Chizhevsky (Steiner 2007, 735). Matejka was very clear about Bakhtin's status as a critic, rather than a proponent, of Formalism, and yet he described both Bakhtin and Voloshinov in his postscript as "followers of the Russian Formal method" (Matejka 1971, 290).[5] The trend of packaging Bakhtin together with the Formalists continued all through the 1970s, often on the grounds that his Dostoevsky book put the study of the *ideas* of Dostoevsky's novels second to the exploration of categories that originated in aesthetics, such as voice, author, or hero.

This trend persisted for two decades until Caryl Emerson and Michael Holquist began translating and editing Bakhtin's essays on the novel, whose appearance marked a new stage in his discovery in the West during the 1980s and beyond. But let me also briefly point to the more difficult fortunes of Bakhtin's writings in two continental environments with strong domestic philosophical traditions, where Bakhtin's lax ways with terminology would not earn him much sympathy. In 2008 and 2011, Bakhtin's early texts "Author and Hero in Aesthetic Activity" and "Towards a Philosophy of the Act" were finally translated into German, thus rounding off the canon of his works available in that language. To be fair, an important text of Bakhtin's, "Epos i roman" ("Epic and Novel"), had first appeared in German translation—at the end of 1968, with a publication date of 1969—in a collective volume in the GDR, before appearing anywhere else in any other language, including Russian (Kowalski 2008, 353–354). As Edward Kowalski reveals in his essayistic epilogue to the 2008 German translation of "Author and Hero in Aesthetic Activity," the typescript of Bakhtin's article "Epic and Novel" was smuggled out of the Soviet Union following encouragement from Kozhinov. The Russian text was published only in 1970, in the journal *Voprosy literatury*. Bakhtin's Dostoevsky and Rabelais books, as well as his other essays on the novel, were also translated into German without much delay. Yet in Germany his discovery seems to have been hampered by the resistance of a rich and elaborate domestic philosophical tradition which found it difficult to relate to Bakhtin's evocative but—by the standards of that tradition—largely loose and floating style of reasoning. Bakhtin's impact in Germany hardly went beyond Slavic Studies, with the exception of some Bakhtinian presence in art and film theory.[6]

In France, Bakhtin's discovery faced similar barriers. In a 1998 interview with Clive Thomson, Julia Kristeva complained that Bakhtin's style was alien to the Cartesian spirit of the French humanities (Kristeva 1998).[7] Bakhtin's writing seemed to generate too many ambiguities and too little terminology. As if to placate these concerns, in her own work Kristeva had taken Bakhtin's unstable, fluid, yet extremely productive notion of dialogue and had rather controversially "upgraded" it to intertextuality, a shift which, she believed, not only made Bakhtin her contemporary but also added that indispensable degree of lucidity (arguably also "objectivity") which the French public appears to have missed in his works.[8] Kristeva is acutely aware of Bakhtin's precarious status as a thinker: measured by the requirements of the various fields of specialized knowledge, he doesn't quite fit anywhere. The central categories of his mature writings, body and discourse, were perceived as either too vague or too obsolete by the French psychologists, anthropologists, and linguists.

We thus see that Bakhtin's peregrinations across linguistic and disciplinary borders have had everything to do with his own mode of handling language and terminology. The lifting of the Structuralist curtain that had been obscuring the ultimate impossibility of thinking about literature and culture by deploying a disinterested metalanguage has revealed a Bakhtin who gains in acts of translation which do not seek to reify his prose in a string of one-dimensional concepts.

Of course, the case for translating—and interpreting—Bakhtin with due sensitivity for his capacious and often unfixed terminology should not be pushed too far. The early Bakhtin, for example, was serious about phenomenology, as *Towards a Phenomenology of the Act*, *Author and Hero in Aesthetic Activity*, but also "The Problem of Content, Material, and Form in Verbal Art" abundantly demonstrate. As late as the early 1940s, in a fragment titled "Toward the Philosophical Foundations of the Humanities" ("K filosofskim osnovam gumanitarnykh nauk"), in which he takes his leave from phenomenology, Bakhtin confronts his readers with a piece of philosophical prose that poses multiple challenges (here, with insignificant adjustments, in Irina Denischenko's excellent translation, as yet unpublished):

The problem of understanding. Understanding as seeing the meaning. Yet this seeing is not a phenomenal one but is rather a seeing of the living meaning of lived experience and expression, a seeing of the internally comprehended, so to speak, self-comprehended phenomenon.

Expression as comprehended matter or as materialized meaning, an element of freedom that has pierced through necessity. Outer and *inner* flesh awaiting mercy. Different layers of the soul lend themselves to externalization to varying degrees. The artistic core of the soul (I for myself) cannot be externalized. The counter activity of the object of cognition. (Bakhtin 1996, 9)

Clearly Bakhtin here activates a vocabulary that is as recognizably Hegelian ("an element of freedom that had shot through necessity"; "externalisation" = "*Entäußerung*"), as it is Platonic and phenomenological "*videnie smysla*," even as he rejects the phenomenological perspective. A translator will have no choice but to heed these fixed layers of terminology. Yet even here the fragment carries an almost untranslatable potentiality inscribed in the noun "*милование*," to be rendered most certainly as "caressing," but to a reader of Russian, if read out with a different accentuation ("*mílovanie*" instead of "*milovánie*"), also triggering associations with "forgiveness" and "absolution." This example is only one illustration of the rewarding, perhaps also daunting, task of translating Bakhtin's philosophical prose at the confluence of equivalences shaped by, and indicative of, different philosophical and cultural traditions.

Before I proceed to my conclusion, I feel compelled to dwell on a particular aspect of Bakhtin's work in which the significance of translation and Bakhtin's renewed relevance for current discussions in literary studies intersect in a most telling manner. We seem to have been facing, in recent years, the rise (or, historically speaking, I should say, "return") of "world literature" as a prism through which to spectate and study literature. A lot of this hinges, as is well-known, on the question of the legitimacy of working in translation. The main positions are not difficult to adumbrate by now: there are those like David Damrosch who believe this legitimacy to be beyond doubt, and those like Emily Apter who fear that the failure to accept that certain things are untranslatable fuels the practice of harnessing translation for the production of misleading (and ideologically consequential) equivalences. One should state here that today the legacy of modern literary theory is not available in a pure and concentrated fashion; instead, it is dispersed, dissipated, often fittingly elusive. The reason for this is that this inheritance is now performing its work in a climate already dominated by a different regime of relevance, which it faces directly and which it must negotiate. The patrimony of literary theory is currently active within a regime of relevance that thinks literature through its market and entertainment value, with only residual recall of its previously highly treasured autonomy. It is this regime of relevance that has engendered the interpretative framework of "world literature" that has recently grown and gained enormous popularity, also in the classroom. I take the words "world literature" in quotation marks, for they refer to a particular liberal Anglo-Saxon discourse grounded in assumptions of mobility, transparency, and re-contextualizing (but also de-contextualizing) circulation that supports free consumption and unrestricted comparison of literary artefacts (see Tihanov 2017).

If we look at Russian literary theory during the interwar decades, we would be struck to see that many of its major trends were, obliquely or more directly, relevant to this new framework of understanding and valorizing literature in the regime of its global production and consumption. Bakhtin begins his book on Rabelais with a reference precisely to world literature: "Of all great writers of world literature, Rabelais is the least popular, the least understood and appreciated" (Bakhtin 1984, 1). Bakhtin, however, pays lip service to the then powerful notion of world literature as a body of canonical writing: he ostensibly compares Rabelais to Cervantes, Shakespeare, and Voltaire. But this understanding of world literature does not really interest him. Instead, he takes a different route, re-conceptualizing the study of world literature as a study of the process that shapes the novel into a world genre, a global discursive power that, in Bakhtin's words, "colonizes all other genres." Of course, Bakhtin is here indebted to the Russian Formalists: for him, too, the novel is the underdog of world literature, whose discursive energies are at first feeble and scattered, unnamed for a long time, until they begin to coalesce and rise to prominence.

Bakhtin's engagement with world literature holds a distinctly non-Eurocentric and, let me repeat this, non-philological charge. He works with the novels he lists mostly in translation, as does Shklovsky before him. Bakhtin appears to be relying on a Western canon to validate his theses. But, in truth, he is more interested in the literature and culture of pre-modernity, the time when Europe is not yet a dominant force, long before the continent begins to see itself as the centre of the world. Bakhtin is thus actually a thinker much more fascinated by the subterranean cultural deposits of folklore, of minor discourses, of ancient genres, of anonymous verbal masses—all of which long predates European culture of the age of modernity (beginning roughly with the Renaissance, but especially since the eighteenth century when the doctrine of cultural Eurocentrism is worked out by the French *philosophes*, only to witness its first major crisis in the years around World War One), which is the only *dominant* (Eurocentric) European culture we know. Even Rabelais' novel interests him above all for its traditional, pre-modern, folklore-based layers. Bakhtin performs a flight away from Eurocentrism not by writing on non-European cultures, but by writing on pre-European cultures, on cultures that thrive on the shared property of folklore, rites, rituals, and epic narratives, before Europe even begins to emerge as an entity on the cultural and political map of the world: his is an anti-Eurocentric journey not in space, but in time. His contemporaries, the semantic palaeontologists Nikolai Marr and Olga Freidenberg, whose writings Bakhtin knew, did something similar in their work on myth and pre-literary discourses (see Tihanov 2012). All of this casts

Bakhtin's work in a new light and allows us to enlist him as an early predecessor of the non-Eurocentric and translation-friendly drive of today's Anglo-Saxon academic programmes in literature.

In 2000, Caryl Emerson published her article "The Next Hundred Years of Mikhail Bakhtin" (Emerson 2000), itself a reference to her well-known book *The First Hundred Years of Mikhail Bakhtin* (1997). Eighty more years to go until the end of the century. The excitement—and the anxiety—here stem from the fact that we cannot possibly know which *longue durée* this century, in retrospect, will have turned out to be part of, or, to speak in Bakhtinian terms, how this century will have positioned itself vis-à-vis "great time." We know by now that "great literature" is a historically attestable category that has both a birth and an expiry date. Will there be "great thinkers" by the end of the century, or will this, too, have proved to be a construct that disintegrates once the foil of a universal humanity is withdrawn? Bakhtin's work cannot answer these questions, but it can infuse trust in the eventual returns of meaning, celebrated for its ability to cross borders, to exude invigorating and challenging multiplicity, and to resist monopolizing appropriation. Ferrying a thinker across time and language, translation is the platform that can transform these returns into departures.

NOTES

1. On *nazire* in the context of translations-responses to Nizami's five poems, see, above all, Aliev (1985).
2. For a recent study of this translation, see Green (2014).
3. See Medvedev (1978, 50–52; with a quote from Eikhenbaum's earlier endorsement of Wölfflin on page 52). On the idea of "history without names" in the Bakhtin Circle, see also Pereda (2003).
4. For an excellent study of the origins of the term *gothic realism* in Bakhtin, see Pan'kov (2008, 237–239 on Max Dvořak's impact, and 241–248 on [neo-]classical aesthetics in *Literaturnyi kritik* and Bakhtin's implicit polemic with it in the Rabelais book).
5. Cf. also Pomorska's statement that the anthology wanted to "present theoreticians who 'rounded up' and transformed the work of the *Opojaz*" (Pomorska 1971, 273).
6. For Bakhtin's appropriation in Germany, see Anthony Wall's articles (Wall 1996, 1998).
7. The interview appeared in *Recherches sémiotiques/Semiotic inquiry* (Kristeva 1998). See also Kristeva's earlier interview about Bakhtin (Kristeva 1995).
8. Todorov later followed this move from "dialogue" to "intertextuality," thus continuing the process of domesticating (or rather enfeebling) Bakhtin's key concept (see Todorov 1981, 95, where he adopts Kristeva's terminological change).

670 G. TIHANOV

Bibliography

Aliev, G. 1985. *Temy i siuzhety Nizami v literaturakh narodov Vostoka*. Moscow: Nauka.

Bakhtin, Mikhail. 1984. *Rabelais and His World*. Translated by Hélène Iswolsky. Bloomington, IN: Indiana University Press.

———. 1996. K filosofskim osnovam gumanitarnykh nauk. In *Sobranie sochinenii v 7 tomakh*. Vol. 5, 7–10. Moscow: Russkie slovari.

Benjamin, Walter. 1969. The Storyteller. *Illuminations*. Translated by Harry Zohn. Edited and with an introduction by Hannah Arendt, 83–109. New York: Schocken Books.

Burke, Edmund. 1967. *Betrachtungen über die französische Revolution*. Frankfurt am Main: Suhrkamp.

Deleuze, Gilles. 1993. *The Fold: Leibniz and the Baroque*. Minneapolis, MN: University of Minnesota Press.

Emerson, Caryl. 2000. The Next Hundred Years of Mikhail Bakhtin (The View from the Classroom). *Rhetoric Review* 19 (1–2): 12–27.

Green, Jonathan. 2014. Friedrich Gentz's Translation of Burke's *Reflections*. *The Historical Journal* 57 (3): 639–659.

Kowalski, Edward. 2008. Bachtins langer Weg zum deutschen Leser. In Bakhtin, Mikhail M. *Autor und Held in der ästhetischen Tätigkeit*, 353–356. Frankfurt am Main: Suhrkamp.

Kozhinov, Vadim. 1993. Bakhtin i ego chitateli: Razmyshleniia i otchasti vospominaniia. *Dialog. Karnaval. Khronotop* 2–3: 120–134.

Kristeva, Julia. 1995. Beseda s Iuliei Kristevoi. *Dialog. Karnaval. Khronotop* 2: 5–17.

———. 1998. Dialogisme, carnavalesque et psychanalyse: entretien avec Julia Kristeva sur la reception de l'oeuvre de Mikhail Bakhtine en France. *Recherches sémiotiques/ Semiotic Inquiry* 18 (1–2): 15–29. (Special issue "Bakhtine et l'avenir des signes/ Bakhtin and the future of signs," edited by Anthony Wall).

Matejka, Ladislav. 1971. The Formal Method and Linguistics. In *Readings in Russian Poetics: Formalist and Structuralist Views*, ed. L. Matejka and K. Pomorska, 281–295. Cambridge, MA: MIT Press.

Medvedev, Pavel N. 1978. *The Formal Method in Literary Scholarship: A Critical Introduction to Sociological Poetics*. Translated by Albert J. Wehrle. Baltimore and London: The Johns Hopkins University Press.

Mukařovský, Jan. 1977. Dialogue and Monologue. In *The Word and Verbal Art: Selected Essays*, trans. J. Burbank and P. Steiner, 81–112. New Haven, CT and London: Yale University Press.

Pan'kov, N. 2008. Smysl i proiskhozhdenie termina 'goticheskii realizm'. *Voprosy literatury* 1: 227–248.

Pereda, Felipe. 2003. Mijail Bajtín y la historia del arte sin nombres. In *Mijail Bajtín en la encrucijada de la hermenéutica y las ciencias humanas*, ed. B. Vauthier and P.M. Cátedra, 93–118. Salamanca: SEMYR.

Pomorska, Krystyna. 1971. Russian Formalism in Retrospect. In *Readings in Russian Poetics: Formalist and Structuralist Views*, ed. L. Matejka and K. Pomorska, 273–280. Cambridge, MA: MIT Press.

Steiner, Peter. 2007. Interview s Ladislavem Matějkou. *Česká literatura* 55 (5): 733–738.

Tihanov, Galin. 2012. Framing Semantic Paleontology: The 1930s and Beyond. *Russian Literature* 72 (3-4): 361–384.

———. 2017. The Location of World Literature. *Canadian Review of Comparative Literature* 44 (3): 468–481.

Todorov, Tzvetan. 1981. *Mikhail Bakhtine: Le principe dialogique*. Paris: Seuil.

Wall, Anthony. 1996. On the Look-Out for Bachtin in German. *Le Bulletin Bakhtine/ The Bakhtin Newsletter* 5: 117–141. (Special issue "Bakhtin Around the World," edited by Scott Lee and Clive Thomson).

———. 1998. How to Do Things with Bakhtin (in German)? *Recherches sémiotiques/ Semiotic Inquiry* 18 (1–2): 267–294. (Special issue "Bakhtine et l'avenir des signes/ Bakhtin and the future of signs," edited by Anthony Wall).

CHAPTER 31

Alexei F. Losev's Mythology of Music as a Development of the Hermeneutics and Sociology of Music

Elena A. Takho-Godi and Konstantin V. Zenkin

INTRODUCTION

Alexei Losev was born in 1893 in the town of Novocherkassk in southern Russia.[1] While studying in the gymnasium or (high school), he became interested in music, ancient languages, and the philosophy of Plato and Vladimir Solovyov. In 1911, he entered the Department of Classical Philology and Philosophy at Moscow University. The same year he joined the *Vladimir Solovyov Religious-Philosophical Society*. From 1918 to 1922, he also attended Nikolai Berdyaev's *Free Academy of Spiritual Culture*.

Losev's first published papers devoted to philosophy ("Eros in Plato") and music (Giuseppe Verdi's *La Traviata* and Nikolai A. Rimsky-Korsakov's *The Snow Maiden*) appeared in 1916. He was fascinated by Husserl's phenomenology (Haardt 1993; Dennes 1998, 181–188), but named Plato, Neoplatonists (Plotinus, Proclus) (Bychkov 2002, 163–179), Pseudo-Dionysius the Areopagite (sixth century A.D.), Nicholas of Cusa, Schelling and Hegel as his

---

Research for this chapter was carried out by Elena Takho-Godi at the A.M. Gorky Institute of World Literature, the Russian Academy of Sciences, with financial support of the Russian Science Foundation (RSF, the project № 17-18-01432-П).

E. A. Takho-Godi (✉)
Lomonosov Moscow State University, Moscow, Russia

K. V. Zenkin
P.I. Tchaikovsky Moscow State Conservatory, Moscow, Russia

© The Author(s), under exclusive license to Springer Nature Switzerland AG 2021
M. F. Bykova et al. (eds.), *The Palgrave Handbook of Russian Thought*,
https://doi.org/10.1007/978-3-030-62982-3_31

673

greatest influences, though the last of these was "equally a teacher and an opponent" for him (Losev 1995, 332; Tchizhevskij (or Chizhevsky) 1934, 368–370; Grier 2010, 326–345). In 1918, Losev attempted to publish a series of religious-philosophical books comprising the works of Nikolai Berdyaev, Sergei Bulgakov, and Vyacheslav Ivanov, which later were included in *Out of the Depths*, a collection of articles edited by Petr Struve (Takho-Godi 2013, 214–241, 2014a). In 1922, Pavel Florensky officiated Losev's wedding to Valentina Sokolova (a student of mathematics and astronomy). After Patriarch Sergius issued his *Declaration*, where he professed the loyalty of the Russian Orthodox Church to the Soviet government, Losev and his wife took secret vows in 1929 and received their monastic names of Andronik and Afanasiia. This was a symbol of their revolt against the Sovietization of the Church.

During the 1920s, Losev published eight monograph volumes. In 1927, he published *The Ancient Cosmos and Modern Science*, *The Philosophy of Name*, *The Dialectics of Artistic Form* (Losev 2013a), *Music as a Subject of Logic*: *The Dialectics of Number in Plotinus* appeared in 1928; *Criticism of Platonism by Aristotle* in 1929; *Essays on Classical Symbolism and Mythology* (Losev 1993a, 2018) and *The Dialectics of Myth* in 1930 (Losev 2001, 2003, 2021). The basic concepts of Losev's system are "name," "number," and "myth." Advocating "materialistic idealism," positing the unity of thought with being and mind with matter, Losev studies the *Universum* as a single whole in its various manifestations: verbal (the world as a verb of different tenses), logical (in forms of notions), aesthetic (in the ultimate expressiveness of its ideas), mathematical (analysis of infinitely small quantities, theory of sets, theory of functions of a complex variable, and different kinds of spaces), musical (the correlation between number and time), and, finally, mythological-symbolical, since the whole world is myth and miracle. Semyon Frank believed that Losev's finesse in dealing with abstract thought in *The Philosophy of Name* can be compared only to Hegel's *Phenomenology of Spirit* (Frank 1928, 89; see also Takho-Godi 2008c, 219–237) and welcomed the book's publication as both the *naissance* of a new philosophical system and evidence of spirit being alive and well against the background of Soviet dictatorship.

For his anti-Marxist and religious beliefs, Losev was declared a "class enemy" at the Sixteenth All-Union Communist Party Congress. In 1930, he and his wife Valentina were arrested and sent to labor camps (Lossev and V. Lossev 2014). Upon the completion of the White Sea-Baltic Canal in 1933, a half-blind Losev was among 500 prisoners who were released with a restitution of civil rights (while full rehabilitation came no sooner than on March 22, 1994, after the collapse of the Soviet Union and six years after the scholar's death). Deprived of the opportunity to publish his works, Losev plunged into mathematics, writing the book *Dialectical Foundations of Mathematics* (1936) (see Losev 2013b), which incorporates the thought of ancient and medieval thinkers (including Plotinus, Sextus Empiricus, Proclus, and Nicholas of Cusa) (Losev 2016; Takho-Godi 2008b, 255–279). He also delved into the study of ancient mythology (Losev 2005; the first edition of the book was published posthumously) and aesthetics. Without any hope of getting them published, he wrote both purely philosophical texts and musical-philosophical prose[2] which reflected the basic ideas of his 1920s books and also the classical Russian literary tradition, especially Fyodor M. Dostoevsky. During this period he also wrote an autobiographical novel *The Encounter* and a story *From Conversations at the Belomor Construction* both of which dealt with his Gulag experience, as well a novel *The Woman Thinker*, whose heroine was modeled on a pianist and member of the Bakhtin circle, Maria Veniaminovna Yudina (whom Losev knew personally).[3] Not earlier than 1944 was Losev allowed to take a position at the Department of Philology of the Moscow State Pedagogical Institute, where he taught the Greek language and comparative linguistics until the end of his life (he died on May 24, 1988).

Throughout the 1960–1980s, Losev was immersed in philosophy of language, publishing *Introduction to the General Theory of Language Models* (1968), *Sign. Symbol. Myth* (1982), and *Language Structure* (1983). He was particularly concerned with the semantic structure of language, highlighting the "law of polysemy" and its implications for communicative and interpretive acts (Kusse 2004). He was also involved in the historical study of theories of style from the eighteenth century until the 1920s.[4] Trying to retrieve the concept of symbol forbidden in Soviet scholarship, he wrote *The Problem of Symbol and Realistic Art* (1976),[5] where he discussed structural and semantic characteristics of the symbol, its typology and its general logic, the differences between symbol and sign, artistic image, personification, and metaphor. It is noteworthy that Losev disagrees with the Moscow-Tartu School of Semiotics and Yuri Lotman, criticizing them for "anti-realism" and for bringing sign, rather than symbol and myth, to the forefront (see Takho-Godi 2014b; Bird 2019).

A large series of entries on ancient philosophy for the *Philosophical Encyclopedia*, his articles on Greek and Roman mythology for the *Encyclopedia of Myths of the Nations of the World*, an edition of Plato's collected works published under his editorship, and his papers on the history of aesthetics caused a massive stir in the Russian academic milieu. Another book, *Ancient Mythology in Its Historical Development* (1957), became a prologue to the description of antiquity as an integral cultural type. Losev's ideas received their ultimate expression in the eight-volume *History of Ancient Aesthetics* (1963–1994), which ranged from Homer and the pre-Platonic authors to the Neoplatonists of the last centuries of the Roman Empire, who witnessed the rise of Christianity (Takho-Godi 1984; Davidson 2009; Takho-Godi and Rezvykh 2018). Losev's monographs *Hellenistic-Roman Aesthetics of the First and Second Centuries A.D.* (1979) (reissued with supplements as Losev 2002b), *Aesthetics of the Renaissance* (1978) (the latest edition: Losev 2017; see also Platov 2011; Takho-Godi 2018a), and *A Summary of Lectures on the History of Modern Aesthetics: Renaissance. Classicism. Romanticism* are logically connected with the *History of Ancient Aesthetics* and constitute an impressive summary of the history of aesthetics from antiquity to the nineteenth century. The first book on Vladimir Solovyov ever published during the Soviet era was written by Losev,[6] manifesting his role as a link between pre-revolutionary and post-Soviet Russian thought.[7]

Absolute Dialectics = Absolute Mythology

After Losev's death, hundreds of works analyzing his aesthetic and philological views, the doctrine of the Name, Myth, and Symbol, as well as some touching upon the influence of different philosophical traditions on his thought were published.[8] However, the connection of Losev's theory of myth with the semiotic and epistemological investigations of the twentieth century, including social epistemology (Takho-Godi 2018b), as well the sociological component of texts that analyze musical phenomena, has remained outside researchers' purview. Consideration of how Losev's musical mythology gradually grows into the understanding of sociological problems contributes to the understanding of Losev's doctrine of myth as the quintessence of both the naming of entities and historical reality itself.

Losev's doctrine of myth is closely related to his interest in onomatodoxy [*imiaslavie*], a religious and philosophical school of thought that was developed by the early twentieth century, while being rooted in the Eastern Orthodox thought of Byzantium, namely, in the fourteenth-century doctrine of energy (knowledge of the essence of God through its energy), formulated by St. Gregory Palamas (see Zenkin 2005; Gurko 2009; Graham and Kantor 2009; Reznichenko 2010, 591–592; Kenworthy 2014; Obolevitch 2011, 2019a, 139–144, 2019b, 2020). Onomatodoxy with its central thesis—"The name of God is God, but God is not a name"—forms the basis of Losev's epistemology. According to Losev, the word (name) is "a certain *meeting place* of the two energies: objective (the said objectivity) and subjective (human consciousness)" (Losev 2013a, 172). This "intimate unity of the spheres of life put asunder" within the name clearly distinguishes Losev's approach from the idea of Mikhail Bakhtin about the juxtaposition of different forms of consciousness within a "two-voiced word" (Gogotishvili 2014).

For Losev, philosophy is "the language that had been analyzed" (Losev 1993a, 90), as existence is "a living organism given as a Concept," as "Thought and Word in the form of *flesh*" (ibid., 134). The meaningful nature of name "pushes the indistinguishable Abyss toward Numbers, Number toward Eidos, Eidos toward Symbol and Myth" (Losev 1993b, 745). Dialectics turns out to be the logical skeleton of the myth's body, the philosophy of "mystical symbolism and, consequently, *mythology*," which has "the manifestation of Meaning and the degree of meaningful interpenetration and transparency of Being-Myth" (Losev 1993a, 134) as its main principle. Hence, the task of philosophy is "in the mindful realization of this myth and in the translation of it into the realm of thought" (ibid., 674).

By revealing "profound intuitions and thoughts embedded in language," philosophy simultaneously discloses the "inner content of words and names revealed to a given people and created by it" (ibid., 90). This becomes a stimulus for studying not only "absolute" mythology (the Christian "sacred history" with its central image of the God-man Jesus Christ, the Absolute Person), but also individual, "relative" mythologies and their *sociology*. "Relative" mythology is the result of the historically conditioned mythologization of various spheres of life: science, philosophy, literature, art, economics, and collective consciousness (e.g., the deification of matter, the idea of building socialism, exacerbating the class struggle, etc.). Losev sets himself the task of providing history with philosophy in its separate real faces ("the face of the nation" [ibid., 7]) that constitute the living body of a common historical process. In *The Dialectics of Artistic Form* (1927) he suggests that

> now compared to the social sphere of being, any other sphere of being is pure abstraction: natural, scientific, artistic, or philosophical—not to mention physical, physiological, psychological, naturalist causal-sociological, and even any individually-human sphere of being. (Losev 2013a, 243)

Losev regards myth not as a fabrication but as a substantial reality and corporeality; it is an essence of the person and personal life represented in another way—in a word, picture, or sculpture. Myth is a person's energetic self-assertion, a personal countenance, a "person's miraculous story put into words," "*the unfolded magical name taken in its absolute being*" (Losev 2003, 201). Thus, Losev regards philosophy, mythology, and aesthetics as a single whole. Artistic form, according to Losev, has a personal being and lives through and changes the course of history; music as art is not an exception here. A philosopher striving to approach "the idea of existence with his thought" (Losev 1994, 760) needs dialectics, which is both "the rhythm of reality itself" (Losev 1993b, 617) and "the eyes that help a philosopher to see life" (ibid., 625). This is perfectly evident from the section of *The Supplement* to *The Dialectics of Myth* that focuses on the unity of absolute dialectics and absolute mythology (Losev 2001, 350–364). Dialectics allows one not "to write about being, but to write the being itself" (Losev 1999, 16) and becomes the basis of artistic symbolic-mythological discourse.

MUSICAL MYTH AS A HERMENEUTIC METHOD

The structure of Losev's philosophy of music[9] in the 1920s can be divided into the following parts: (1) the phenomenology of music, (2) the psychology of music, (3) musical aesthetics, and (4) musical criticism aimed at presenting each particular work or composer impressionistically and mythologically. In fact, the last of these points is about hermeneutics and the interpretation of the music's meaning. Mythology and science speak about this from different standpoints: mythology enters where science [*ratio*] is powerless. Mythology and philosophy of music coexist, interacting in a complex and diverse way, creating different types of discourse: sometimes scientific and aloof, sometimes personal and engaged, as if being given "from within" the myth itself.

Losev's philosophical work began in 1916 with musical criticism and bears all its signs: perception of the essence of music not as such, but through its otherness (words about music). In his article on Nikolai Rimsky-Korsakov's *The Snow Maiden*, he suggests that from the religious and mythological point of view the opera "*does not know the boundary between the cosmic and the real human*," as "there total-unity and transformation are achieved" (Losev 1995, 620).

In his article on Verdi's *La Traviata* Losev emphasizes the opposition of two types of worldviews that the author (taking into account the tradition that stretches from the Romantic Movement, through Wagner,[10] to Nietzsche and to the symbolist Vyacheslav Ivanov) defines as "Apollonian" and "Dionysian," as "contemplation" and "action," as "optimism" and "pessimism." According to Losev, music basically represents the second type, that is, "pessimism, irrationality, and cosmism" (Losev 1995, 625–626). Prominent representatives of the "cosmist" (Dionysian) worldview are Beethoven, Wagner, and Scriabin. Against the background of these titans, whose work he regarded as "the pinnacle of modern music," and applying the highest religious measure of values to *La Traviata*, Losev comes to the paradoxical conclusion that the childish simplicity and innocence of Verdi's Italian *melos* is worthy of the Kingdom of Heaven (ibid., 634). He is convinced that the world will eventually find a way to combine two worldviews: Scriabin's "dark, irrational contemplation of sounds with the lightsome and tender melody of the Italian and Slavic musical tradition," but that this will be accomplished in "not a human artistic way, but a God-man transforming one" (ibid., 636).

As for the music of Scriabin, Losev regards it as the ultimate expression of the spirit of the modern era, which prompts him to criticize the composer in his article "On Scriabin's Philosophical Worldview" (1921). Scriabin's philosophizing is characterized as a unique synthesis of pagan cosmism (with its typical immanence of God and the world), Christian historicism (the apocalyptic dimension of history, the design of the Mystery as an act of universal transfiguration), and the new European individualism in its most extreme form (solipsism, lapsing into the deification of self). For Losev, Scriabin's music is the pinnacle of the whole of Western European culture and "the end of it" (Losev 1995, 779).

The analysis of Verdi's, Rimsky-Korsakov's, and Scriabin's works in the context of a religiously perceived being shows the maximalist character of Losev's thought. It is written as a philosophical and poetic essay which synthesizes emotionally intuitive-figurative and abstract-logical thinking. This synthesis makes Losev's analysis nearly seamless.

All of this allows us to draw the following conclusions about the early stage in the development of Losev's musical mythology:

- His mythology of music had not yet separated from his philosophy of music; they coexisted and interpenetrated each other in the space of musical criticism, saturated with hermeneutics and axiology.
- In the evaluation of any musical phenomenon, this mythology was emphatically oriented toward Christianity with its absolute value system. Hence, the "Kingdom of Heaven" in the article on *La Traviata*, the image of the transformed and resurrected earth in the work about *The Snow Maiden*, and the anathema against Scriabin.

Losev's mythology of music not only drew on musical critique, but also had strictly philosophical (aesthetic) origins. The most salient and insightful example is an essay titled "The Structure of the Artistic Worldview," an unfinished manuscript by Losev dating back to 1915–1916. The essay suggests the following aesthetic premise: there is a "primary being" underlying music as well as all other arts, "which might be described 1) as indiscrete creative fluidity; and 2) as purely epistemological unshaped quality or meaning" (Losev 1995, 300). It is

> the primary being, untouched by thought, yet bears the stamp of dawning transformation that occurs here as the transformation of rigid matter into the genuine form of beauty; and this very matter is paramount for art. However, it presents itself in art as transformed and redeemed, as an indeed religious thing. True aesthetics is an aesthetics of religious materialism. Therein the form, as the art's inherent constituent, is being conceived. (Losev 1995, 300)

In other words, art in general is a symbolic transformation (under the influence of Divine energy) of rigid matter, and music is art in its purest form.

In the 1920s, everyday work in the State Institute of Music Sciences (1921–1930), the Moscow Conservatory (1922–1929), and the State Academy of Art Sciences (1923–1929), where Losev delivered about fifty academic reports, including some directly related to aesthetics and music, pushed the thinker to reflect on the problems of musical aesthetics (see Dunayev 1991; Plotnikov et al. 2017). The remaining abstracts demonstrate how in the 1920s the conceptual apparatus of Losev's philosophy of music was formed.

In his work *Music as a Subject of Logic*, Losev states this in an emphatically rigorous form. The issue is the essence of music, the phenomenology of number, time, and expression, as well as the central musical and theoretical concepts: tone, rhythm, melody, harmony, tone quality, tempo, tonality, and so on. Separate large sections present the comparison of music and mathematics, the logic of musical form, and the basic mathematical laws of musical form, including the law of golden proportion. By Losev's "phenomenological dialectical formula," music is "a purely alogically expressed thingness of the life of numbers, given in the aspect of pure *intelligentia*" (Losev 1995, 512).

Refusing to settle for "phenomenology of music," Losev considers the essence of music, drawing on already essentially different, "namely purely *mythological* points of view" (ibid, 470), as music "speaks" not at all about the objects of our physical world and not about logical concepts. Thus, using the mythological-symbolic method, he introduces a fragment entitled "Music Myth" into his strictly philosophical treatise. In this text, his own methodology is represented by the following phrase: "Beholding the essence of music through the nature of the feminine and the madness of the artistic [...]" (ibid., 471). His romantic symbolist style, which reminds one of the philosophical and musical prose of the German Romantics (first of all, Novalis and Hoffmann[11]), Vladimir Odoevsky's *Russian Nights*, and Andrei Bely's "symphonies," as well as the Wagnerian[12] and Nietzschean understanding of the essence of art, is necessary for Losev to create the image of the Eternal Feminine, Eternal Music, and at the same time a musical worldview as "the madness of the artistic." "Music Myth" for the first time presents the heroes that became an indispensable part of Losev's prose in the 1930s: the female artist and her listener, who with her help becomes able to look into the mysteries of the nature of music:

> When She was sitting, exhausted and blessed, at the piano, giving birth to blazing lights and mysterious noises; when through Her subtle body scarlet and pink sounds were heard, making her being tremble; when sitting next to Her, Immeasurable and Exultant, I lost consciousness and even Her; and all was enveloped in a fiery fog through which I could see the white and delicate fingers dancing their agonizingly sweet dance and that trembling body of Hers glorifying her God with zeal and enthusiasm, at that very moment the music opened to my prophetic ears as a special, independent, eternal (the only possible?) form of world perception. (Losev 1995, 470)

Hoaxing the reader, Losev presents this text as a translation "from a little-known German writer" (ibid., 470). Though the "German writer" sought to present a "universal musical myth" adequate to the music of any composer and era, *Losev himself* states that the author's excessive "propensity to a certain line (Beethoven, Wagner, Liszt, Scriabin)" (ibid., 587) prevented the fulfillment of the task.

Despite its distant attitude and symbolic poetics, many key ideas of the "Music Myth" directly coincide with the ideas of the main part of the book. The essence of music appears in "Music Myth" as follows:

- Music is a manifestation of the higher, divine world.
- Music is a chaos and continuous formation, the fusion of meanings and opposites in general.
- Music is inseparable from love and from the image of an ideal lover.
- Music is ambiguous in its impact on a person, as it can be positive (participatory in the Divine principle) or negative (participatory in a chaotic, demonic origin).

Losev presents the mythological pattern of music's self-awareness from the standpoint of the very worldview that inspired its absolutization: European culture fully realized music's self-containment during the Romantic era with the concept of "absolute music" as the most salient example. However, this "madness of the artist" is resolutely separated from the *sober* Losev's view: on closer examination, it turns out to be analogous to Scriabin's self-deification!

Similarities between Scriabin's personal "myth" and those of the famous nineteenth-century Romantic composers are no coincidence. According to Losev, Scriabin is the heir to the Romanticism of Chopin, Liszt, and Wagner (Losev 1995, his essay "On Scriabin's Philosophical Worldview"). This parallelism of personal myths emphasizes that such myths are concerned not with the individual shape of a particular composer, but rather with the music in general. The genius of Scriabin brought to the logical limit (and therefore, according to the laws of dialectics, to self-denial) the principles of a Romantic worldview and creativity. Exaltation and even deification of art in Romanticism was as stable a tendency as the absolutization of human individuality. Both tendencies had the fragile boundary between the artistic and the ordinary as their basis. The three marked features brought to the *limit* and combined led Scriabin, a Romantic artist, to think "I am God"[13] with an inexorable logical *consistency*—hence, his musical-mysterious messianism, self-deification, paganism, and demonism. If the deification of the world is a way of salvation and transfiguration, then another way, namely the immanence of God and the world, is a "profanation" of God and "*an essential and unparalleled paganism on the new European ground*" (Losev 1995, 767).

Reconstructing Scriabin's music myth, Losev thereby disavows anthropocentrism and individualism, which lie at the foundation of a Romantic worldview as "the highest tension of Western European creative thought" (ibid., 779). For Losev, the absolutization of music is the relative myth that reflects the spiritual quintessence of the era and stems from the mind of a Romantic creator, who perceives earthly art as absolute and the only possible worldview, whereas this worldview does not know the true absolutist way out of the earthly horizon from the dead ends of earthly history.

Not abandoning the idea of creating music myths of particular works or individual composers (which may be considered hermeneutical), Losev in the 1920s focused on recreating the mythology of music in general, logically developing ideas implicit in the musical critique of the 1910s. In the works of the 1910s, the religious attitude as a criterion and principle of evaluation was directly postulated. It resulted in the fact that music "myths" of *La Traviata* and *The Snow Maiden* were organically inscribed in the Christian context, to which the "Scriabin myth" is obviously antithetical. Thus, stating the existence of "two worldviews," the author directly approached the problem of correlating these two mythologies: absolute (Christianity) and relative (in this case, the Romantic myth of music). This antithesis would become central in the book *The Dialectics of Myth*, although without special discussion of musical issues and without the name of Scriabin as the central symbol of the era that marks the spiritual and historical crisis of the beginning of the twentieth century.

FROM HERMENEUTICS TO HISTORICAL SOCIOLOGY

In prose fiction written by Losev in the 1930s and 1940s, especially in the story *I Was Nineteen Years Old* and the short novels *Tchaikovsky Trio*, *The Meteor*, and *The Encounter*, as well as the novel *The Woman Thinker*, Losev's musical mythology acquires the most multifaceted and elaborated form. In this case, Losev needs certain constants:

- The focus of attention is the encounter of the hero, embodying thought (most often the alter ego of the author is the philosopher Nikolai Vladimirovich Vershinin), and the female musician-artist, personifying music itself in its antinomic essence.
- There is a love affair between a thinker and an actress.
- Heroes are doomed to tragedy, separation, sudden death, violence, insanity, camp barracks, and so on.
- Music reveals the mystical roots of the heroes' experiences, demonstrating their connection with the main world-perception types.
- A true understanding of life and music is revealed in these intense dialogues.

Music and the question of its compatibility with life and love become a touchstone of Losev's prose, testing the inner essence of man. That is why his characters wish to destroy art in general (a hero from the story *Theatre-goer* burns the theater); abandon art (as is the desire of the brilliant pianist Radina in *The Woman Thinker*) and leave it for the world of the fleshly life (symbolized by Radina's three husbands—Pupochka [Belly-button], Beethovenchik, and Bachianchik); transform ordinary life into a unity of art and life (like Vorobyov from *The Woman Thinker* who kills Radina); part forever in order to preserve spiritual purity (as with the beloved Vershinin and pianist Yelena Doriak from the short novel *The Meteor*); and replace art with contemplation and prayer (as Vershinin from *Tchaikovsky Trio* or Telegin from *The Woman Thinker* plan to). Only after the death of the pianist Tomilina does Vershinin from *Tchaikovsky Trio* begin to see that his "own theory of the incompatibility of life and music […] [is] a dead end" (I, 214). Ultimately, music is already a synthesis, "opening an essential and concrete All-unity or path toward it" (Losev 1995, 476). The world of music "is utterly a being and a consciousness, the primordial basis and essence that form the ground for postlapsarian individual consciousness and intellect, and on the other hand, a formalized and mechanical world of natural being and matter" (ibid., 476–477). Vershinin from *The Woman Thinker* is already sure that music is "normal," natural, and non-hysterical in itself: it is being that is hysterical and erratic; life with its "infamy and nonsense" causes the folly of man and his music.

For Losev reproduction of the same storyline (a philosophizing man encountering a female artist) has a symbolic meaning: is the flesh able to embody the idea and under what conditions? Can the genius of female flesh perceive the masculinity of the idea? Losev-the-novelist solves this philosophical problem using purely literary means, such as his plot, system of characters, and so on.

Questions about music and love are central to *The Woman Thinker*. Hence the plot of the novel: the struggle of Vershinin and his friends for the spiritual salvation of the brilliant pianist Radina. Who or what will finally possess Radina is a matter of crucial importance for the author: the soulless team of three husbands—Pupochka, Beethovenchik, and Bachianchik—who are living by their instincts (hence the image of Radina as a harlot in Vershinin's dreams), the new socialist order (hence another dream's image of Radina as a *chekist* [national security official] who together with her three husbands executes Vershinin), or true art, blessed by prayer and faith (hence Vershinin's dreams, where Radina is portrayed as heavenly Mary, as Mother and Bride, as a nun and a pianist, whose performance pleases angels' ears). For Vershinin the wisdom of a woman is "to be the living, but fearless flesh of truth, wherein truth itself seems to be ready to move and hesitate" (II, 18). That is why "the philosopher-monk" Vershinin dreams of fulfilling his "Great Synthesis" of the total-unity of faith, knowledge, and life with the brilliant pianist Radina. However, in the prevailing socio-historical conditions she cannot achieve a "synthesis" and ascend to Heaven. Her "synthesis" is the darkness of non-being: physical and spiritual death. The very "social being re-embodies logic, symbolism, and mythology and makes their abstract contours completely unrecognizable" (Losev 1993a, 707). Radina is no longer a Mother, nor a beautiful Nun, but a chekist who condemns Vershinin to death.

Condemning his heroes to the "world of nightmare" (separation, sudden death, violence, madness, prison, and camp barracks), the author pursues several goals:

- This would accurately convey the spirit of the very culture of the early twentieth century; one of the leading critics of this period Korney Chukovsky wrote that the "nightmare" became the main motive of Russian literature during the so-called Silver Age (Chukovsky 2017, 7: 386).
- The horrors of "relative mythology" makes them recall the lost bliss of "absolute being" so that "the deep memory" (Losev 2003, 167) blossoms as an absolute myth, which is nothing but the highest form of "*self-consciousness*" (ibid., 144).
- The epoch of Russian modernism seems to be the same "spiritual adventurism" as was described by Hegel in relation to the era of Romanticism. This "adventurism" became one of the prerequisites for the revolutionary catastrophe of 1917.

Losev's philosophy of art is related to his cultural and historical morphology, which does not erect boundaries between different types of cultures (in Spengler's sense) but builds "a row of human cultures as a whole, as the life of a single human organism" (Losev 1993a, 63). Thus, only a philosopher can understand music in its entirety, as one who reflected on "each and every world-perception type that belonged to humankind": it is impossible "to understand Bach without Leibniz; to understand Beethoven without Kant, Fichte, and Hegel; to understand Wagner without Schopenhauer; to understand Debussy and Ravel without Bergson; to understand Scriabin without Fichte and solipsism; and to understand Prokofiev without modern phenomenological morphologism" (II, 128).

In the 1930s, Losev regards Prokofiev's music as the symbol of "the dictatorship of the proletariat," exactly as Scriabin used to be the symbol of the anthropocentrism and individualism of the past in the 1910s.

In the short novel *The Encounter* Losev gives a detailed comparison of the two composers and emphasizes that Prokofiev gradually separates from Scriabin and "slowly but surely approaches the modern foxtrot culture" (I, 364). As Victor P. Troitskii noted in 2001, the introduction of foxtrot and jazz in Losev's *The Encounter, From Conversations at the Belomor Construction, The Woman Thinker*, as well as in his 1960s paper "The Downfall of Bourgeois Culture and Its Philosophy," is directly connected with the way he wished to portray his time in the first (predominantly "sociological") part of *The Supplement* to *The Dialectics of Myth* that only partially survived (Troitskii 2001, 583–592).

Not only human existence, but also human music is a "social phenomenon," and therefore, Losev suggests, "it is hardly possible to discuss it without philosophy and without sociology" (I, 371). In that social existence where Vershinin and Radina have to live, Bach's music is an obsolete past, while foxtrot and martial music are prevalent. That is why, mocking Radina's desire to participate in modernity, Vershinin advises her to play Prokofiev, whose music is "the pure materiality of the spirit" (II, 115). Free "from any ideology, from the problems of the individual and being, from feelings and emotions" (I, 363), it is a stepping-stone on the path to foxtrot and jazz.

Foxtrot in Losev is a genuine symbol as it combines in itself the two levels of being: the internal one ("the sphere of the human subject with his 'anarchic bluff,' with [...] a cynical and lustful joy of complete expediency") and the external one ("the sphere of objective expression, where 'visible vigor and clarity' reign") (Troitskii 2001, 591). The music that embraces voluptuously anarchic, nihilistically optimistic impersonality, spiritual emptiness, and substantially catchy, almost mechanical, repetition becomes the mythological expression of modernity (I, 397).

An individual from the era of the dictatorship of the proletariat and collectivism should not love a woman, nor music, but production and technology. Deprived of anything after the revolutionary upheavals, he is forced to portray "the enthusiasm of construction in conditions of internal devastation of the spirit" (I, 458); that is why the foxtrot with its internal nihilism and external optimism can become a symbol of time and convey its spirit. After all, "socialism itself is based on an extra-personal community" and "the absolute of impersonality" (I, 469), while from a musical-mythological point of view it is based "on the foxtrot" (I, 469) (this is a *From Conversations on Belomorstroi* character's paradoxical statement). At the same time, Belomorstroi, a concentration labor camp that was the proletariat dictatorship society's ground for the mastery of nature and the re-creation of man, is likened to "intellectually and technically expressive, productive, and social foxtrot" (I, 456). "Foxtrot is our romanticism," the romanticism of the victorious proletariat, because "romanticism is where all objective values are destroyed, and only their psychological restoration remains," says Vershinin from *The Encounter* (I, 398; I, 456).

For Losev, "Romanticism is above all a special kind of individualism and consideration of the human person as the basis of all being" (Losev 1995, 363). According to Losev, a religious man remains a man of the Middle Ages even in the era of Soviet revolutionary romanticism. No matter how hard Losev criticized the "old" Romanticism with its anthropocentrism (originally, that of the Renaissance) instead of theocentrism and its absolute music instead of religion, he is perfectly aware of its superiority over Soviet "Romanticism" and over the new era of aesthetic, ethical, and religious disintegration.

Foxtrot and jazz constitute the common style of the era in both the Western and Soviet worlds. The peculiarity of this style is evident in modern Western philosophy, which is "very energetic, powerful, showing some kind of flowering" and can be compared to the "apparent cheerfulness" of jazz, which "is built on very brisk, almost march-like rhythms, but is pierced with depraved, melting, and slack melody, in which everything that possesses form drowns nihilistically, while leaping and sharp *syncopes* together with tiresomely and tenderly whining and hovering *glissandos* transform the whole into some kind of immoral, alogical unbelief that does not value human well-being" (Losev 1962, 353). Foxtrot and jazz are the musical face of the era in which philosophy preaches nihilistic optimism.

According to Losev, jazz is the result and the end of old European music, and at the same time, the starting point for "proletarian music to develop" (I, 365), as it is the only musical form "equally intelligible for both hardened capitalist and Soviet revolutionary proletarians [...] for as long as the musical depths of the bourgeois subject reigned, as long as there were Beethoven and Wagner, it was needless to think about proletarian music" (I, 365–366). The impersonal, objective-material world of the proletariat dictatorship arms itself with foxtrot and jazz as "technologies and machine culture," subjecting them to "a new, already socialist, evolution" (I, 366). The attitude to music that will prevail in the coming communist society will be determined by "party and class feeling" and "proletarian instinct" (I, 366). As a character from *The Encounter* says, one does not have to "prejudge our future decrees": we will see tomorrow if the Central Committee decides to ban Bach, Beethoven, or jazz (I, 366).

The rejection of the personal, the prevalence of the material over the spiritual, the inner anarchy, the emptiness, and the external energetic aspiration push, according to Losev, modern liberal Western culture and Soviet culture closer together as the two faces of the same post-anthropocentric, post-humanist era, promising only disasters and nightmares. Peering into this apocalyptic "tomorrow," the author shows various utopian experiments on the reorganization of the world and their catastrophic consequences (Takho-Godi 2004). Violent social changes envisioned by political philosophers since Plato's *Republic,* and especially by Marxist-Leninist theory, are aimed at destroying the person in all its manifestations, be it faith, art, or love. Losev foresees that the White Sea-Baltic Canal will be a staging ground for testing the model of future society (shared barracks, injustice, the regulation of life by the punitive bodies of the OGPU [Special State Security Service of the USSR], etc.), that personal violence in the name of Communist ideas and central planning will continue to grow: soon marriage, love, and thought will be rationed by the government (I, 394). It will also invent a "means of instilling thoughts in a certain dose" (I, 394) to finally conquer nature not only around humans (as it does during the construction of the White Sea-Baltic Canal) but also inside them. Moreover, the subordination of nature (love) and spiritual restrictions (prohibition of thought and art) will open the way to the main goal, that is, the destruction of the soul. In Vershinin's visions from the novel *The Woman Thinker*, the struggle with the human soul has already been put on a serious medical basis: doctors in the hospitals do the "same operations" and instill "inability to think," "inability for art," while "the excess of thought and feeling is punished with the death penalty" (II, 134).

Obviously, the idea of a third type of civilization, based on the totalitarianism of production and technology, is already outlined in *The Encounter* and *The Woman Thinker*. This idea will be developed in a later text, in the story *From Conversations on Belomorstroi*, where talk about music symptomatically fades away, as mechanism replaces person and technology replaces art, while the revolution itself is referred to as "the formless and passionate music of history" (I, 481).

Losev's criticism of the Renaissance and post-Renaissance (New European) humanism from the idealist positions of medieval Christianity, present in his 1910–1920s works, is quite common for Russian philosophy, as it is also inherent in both Pavel Florensky and Nikolai Berdyaev. However, Losev's prose is a new variation on this: the author provocatively forces his heroes to criticize humanism from the standpoint of a new socialist collectivism. For example, Vershinin argues that the Soviet authorities should have banned art and music in its former, bourgeois variant and that preserving them is a violation of the revolution's logic. Provocation like that allows Losev to reveal the absurdities of socialism and at the same time prophetically predict the future: half a century later in Cambodia, Pol Pot, the leader of the Khmer Rouge, ordered public executions of numerous artists. The question of the fate of music as an intrinsically valuable art, formulated in Losev's *The Encounter*, is now more acutely posed by history itself. The musical face of the epoch depicted by Losev in the 1930s is still timely. One can only "make an adjustment for the fast-flowing time and substitute for foxtrot (or jazz band) new hard rock, rap, hit parade (or whatever) sounds in Losev's equation" (Troitskii 2001, 591). Apparently, Losev's predictions are also valid as they actually apply not only to a totalitarian society, but also to modernity as a whole, which is permeated with postmodern relativism and nihilism, perceived as the only possible outcomes.

Thus, the music myth in Losev's fictional prose becomes historically and sociologically concrete. The musical mythology develops

- in comparing two types of enthusiasm, corresponding to two understandings of the Absolute (religious Christian and immanently human), which are the praying, religious one and the musical one;
- in affirming the extreme ambivalence of musical existence: approximation to the Divine ideal, higher beauty, harmony, formation, chaos, general relativity, fictitiousness, frustrated expectations, "emptiness," and depravity;
- in comparing three epochs: the era when music was subordinated to the religious Absolute (the Middle Ages), the era of the absolutizing of the human subject (Renaissance—Romanticism—neo-Romanticism), and modernity (from the catastrophic historical events of the 1910s, such as First World War, the October Revolution, the dictatorship of the proletariat, and beyond);
- as a central symbol of the era and its aesthetic attitude: Losev brings to the forefront the mechanical and soulless music of the marches, while the place formerly occupied in his symbolic mythological framework by Scriabin is now occupied by none other than Prokofiev, followed by foxtrot and jazz, which are deprived of a strongly pronounced, personal authorship;
- in apocalyptically colored thoughts about the end of the era of "absolute music," the absolutized personality and freedom of thought: *Tchaikovsky Trio* as the eve of the First World War, which is destroying the entire former way of manorial life with its sophisticated culture and musical leisure; *The Encounter*, *The Woman Thinker*, and *From Conversations at the Belomor Construction* as the establishment of the totalitarianism of production and technology, which is destroying personality and all its free creative manifestations.

Thus, the conversations about music that take place between characters in Losev's prose boil down to a mythological and sociological analysis of the Russian Revolution,[14] including its prerequisites and consequences, and of all human history as a whole.

Translated by Valentin Frolov

NOTES

1. For Losev's biography, see [Aza] Takho-Godi 2007; Borchert 2005, 573–576; Lesourd 2010, 506–510; Dennes 2010.
2. Losev 2002a. Hereafter the volume and the page numbers of this edition will be given in brackets in the body of the text.
3. For details on Losev's prose, see Clowes 2004; [Elena] Takho-Godi 2007b; Takho-Godi 2008a, 131–139; Rimondi 2019.
4. His papers "The History of the Theories of Style: the Central Issues" and "Theories of Artistic Style" were first published in 1994. See Losev 2019.
5. The recent supplemented edition with extended bibliography on the problem of symbolism appeared in 2014 (Losev 2014). See also Obolevitch 2011, 569.
6. On the banning of the book by the Soviet authorities, see A. Takho-Godi's foreword to Losev 2009.
7. As a gesture toward an official recognition of this role, in 2000, by state decree, the building where Alexei F. Losev lived in Moscow was turned into the Losev House, a museum and scholarly library that focus on the history of Russian philosophy and culture. Today, the Losev House is a study and research center, which keeps the museum dust from settling on books, manuscripts, and other artifacts. To commemorate Alexei F. Losev's contributions to the Russian intellectual tradition, in 2006 his monument was erected near the House.
8. For a list of Losev's works, as well as papers about him published in the time period from 1916 to 2013, see Losev 2013c.
9. For Losev's views on music, see Haardt 1994; Cholopow 1994; Bristiger 1996; Uzelac 2007, 228–261; Zenkin 2018a.
10. Two works focus specially on Wagner. The first one, which belongs to the end of the 1910s, is entitled *Filosofskii kommentarii k dramam Rikharda Vagnera* [*Philosophical Commentary on Richard Wagner's Dramas*] (Losev 2015, 741–808). The second one appears much later (Losev 1968). See also Zenkin 2018b.
11. Concerning the connections between "Music Myth" and Hoffmann's texts, see Gamaiunov 1993.
12. Here, as well as in Losev's article on *The Snow Maiden*, the influence of Wagner's *Opera and Drama* is evident: music is regarded as the natural element, the feminine womb, giving birth to "structural formations, condensed in images and words" (Losev 1995, 604).
13. Scriabin's solipsism plainly reveals its artistic origin: the creator of the artistic world is a creator of the Universe as well.
14. As he says through his mouthpiece Vershinin, all the abstract talk about philosophy or music is but "an analysis of the Russian revolution" (I, 392).

BIBLIOGRAPHY

Bird, Robert. 2019. Poniatie "model'" v pozdnikh rabotakh A.F. Loseva. In *Ucheniie o stile*, ed. Aza A. Takho-Godi and Elena A. Takho-Godi, 438–444. Moscow: Nestor-Istoriia.

Borchert, Donald, ed. 2005. *The Encyclopedia of Philosophy in 10 volumes*. 2nd ed, 5. New York: Macmillan Reference USA.

31 ALEXEI F. LOSEV'S MYTHOLOGY OF MUSIC AS A DEVELOPMENT... 689

Bristiger, Michał. 1996. La questione principale delle filosofia della musica secondo Aleksej F. Losev (1893-1988). In *Il pensiero musicale degli anniventi e trenta: Atti del Convegno Arcavacata di Rende 1–4 April 1993*, 259–272. Calabria: Centro Editoriale F. Librario, Universita degli Studi della Calabria.

Bychkov, Oleg V. 2002. Alexej Losev: A Neoplatonic View of the Dialectic of Absence and Presence in the Nature of Artistic Form. In *Neoplatonism and Contemporary Thought*, ed. R. Baine Harris, 163–179. Albany: State University of New York Press.

Cholopow, Yuri N. 1994. Über die Philosophie der Musik von Aleksej F. Lossew. *Acta musicologica*. 66 (1): 31–40.

Chukovsky, Kornei I. 2017. Russkaia literatura v 1908 godu. In *Polnoe Sobranie Sochinenii v 15 tomakh*, Vol. 7: 386. Moscow: Terra-Knizhnyi Club.

Clowes, Edith W. 2004. *Fiction's Overcoat: Russian Literary Culture and the Question of Philosophy*. Ithaca, NY and London: Cornell University Press.

Davidson, Pamela. 2009. *Cultural Memory and Survival: The Russian Renaissance of Classical Antiquity in the Twentieth Century*. Loughborough (Leicestershire): UCL. School of Slavonic and East European Studies.

Dennes, Maryse. 1998. *Husserl—Heidegger: influence de leur œuvre en Russie*. Paris: Éd. L'Harmattan.

———, ed. 2010. *L'œuvre d'Alekseï Losev dans le context de la culture européenne*. Toulouse: Slavica Occitania 31.

Dunaev, Alexei G. 1991. Losev i GAHN. In *A.F. Losev i kul'tura XX veka*, 197–205. Moscow: Nauka.

Frank, Semyon L. 1928. Novaia russkaia filosofskaia sistema. *Put'* 9: 89–90.

Gamaiunov, Michail M. 1993. *Kreisleriana* professora Loseva. *Nachala* 2: 151–165.

Gogotishvili, Liudmila A. 2014. Vklad postsimvolistov Loseva i Bakhtina v teoriiu postroeniia diskursa. *Filologiia: nauchnye issledovaniia* 4: 354–368.

Graham, Loren R., and Jean-Michel Kantor. 2009. *Naming Infinity: A True Story of Religious Mysticism and Mathematical Creativity*. Cambridge, MA and London: The Belknap Press of Harvard University Press.

Grier, Philip T. 2010. Adventures in Dialectic and Intuition: Shpet, Il'in, Losev. In *A History of Russian Philosophy 1830–1930*, ed. G.M. Hamburg and Randall A. Poole, 326–345. Cambridge: Cambridge University Press.

Gurko, Helena. 2009. *Divine Onomatology: Naming God in Imiaslavie, Symbolism, and Deconstruction*. Saarbrucken: VDM Verlag.

Haardt, Alexander. 1993. *Husserl in Russland: Phänomenologie der Sprache und Kunst bei G. Shpet und Aleksej Losev*. München: Fink.

———. 1994. Aleksei Losev and the Phenomenology of Musik. In *Russian Thought After Communism. The Recovery of a Philosophical Heritage*, ed. James Scanlan, 197–205. Armonk, NY: Routledge.

Kenworthy, Scott. 2014. Debating the Theology of the Name in Post-Soviet Russia: Metropolitan Ilarion Alfeev and Sergei Khoruzhii. In *Orthodox Paradoxes: Heterogeneities and Complexities in Contemporary Russian Orthodoxy*, ed. Katya Tolstaya, 250–264. Leiden, Boston: Brill.

Kusse, Holger. 2004. *Metadiskursive Argumentation: Linguistische Untersuchungen zum russischen philosophischen Diskurs von Lomonosov bis Losev*. München: Otto Sagner.

Lesourd, Françoise, ed. 2010. *Dictionnaire de la philosophie russe*. Lausanne: L'Age d'Homme.

690   E. A. TAKHO-GODI AND K. V. ZENKIN

Losev, Alexei F. 1962. Gibel' burzhuaznoi kul'tury i ee filosofii. In *Mysliteli nashego vremeni (62 portreta)*, ed. Hubscher, Arthur, 310–354. Moscow: Izdatel'stvo inostrannoi literatury.

———. 1968. Problema Rikharda Vagnera v proshlom i nastoiashchem. *Voprosy estetiki* 8: 67–196.

———. 1993a. *Ocherki antichnogo simvolizma i mifologii*. Moscow: Mysl.

———. 1993b. Filosofia imeni. In *Bytie. Imia. Kosmos*, ed. A. A. Takho-Godi, 613–801. Moscow: Mysl.

———. 1994. *Mif. Chislo. Sushchnost*. Moscow: Mysl.

———. 1995. *Forma. Stil'. Vyrazhenie*. ed. A. A. Takho-Godi, Moscow: Mysl'.

———. 1999. *Lichnost' i Absoliut*. ed. A. A. Takho-Godi, Moscow: Mysl'.

———. 2001. *Dialektika Mifa. Dopolnenie k 'Dialektike Mifa'*. Moscow: Mysl'.

———. 2002a. In *Ia soslan v XX vek*, ed. A.A. Takho-Godi, E.A. Takho-Godi, and V.P. Troitskii vol. 1–2. Moscow: Vremia.

———. 2002b. *Ellinisticheski-rimskaya estetika I—II vv. n. e.*, ed. A.A Takho-Godi and V.P. Troitskii. Moscow: Mysl'.

———. 2003. *The Dialectics of Myth*. Trans. and Introd. Vladimir Marchenkov. New York, NY: Routledge.

———. 2005. *Antichnaia mifologiia s antichnymi kommentariaami k nei*. Moscow: Eksmo.

———. 2009. *Vladimir Solovyov i ego vremia*. Moscow: Molodaia gvardiia.

———. 2013a. *The Dialectic of Artistic Form*. Trans., annot., and Introd. O.V. Bychkov. Ed. D.L. Tate. München, Berlin, Washington: Verl. Otto Sagner (Arbeiten und Texte zur Slavistik. Bd. 96).

———. 2013b. *Dialekticheskie osnovy matematiki*, ed. V.P. Troitskii. Moscow: Academia.

———. 2013c. *Aleksei Fyodorovich Losev. Bibibliograficheskii ukazatel*. Moscow: Dizain i poligrafiia.

———. 2014. *Problema simvola i realisticheskoe iskusstvo*, ed. A.A Takho-Godi and V.P. Troitskii. Moscow: Russkii mir.

———. 2015. *Na rubezhe epoch. Raboty 1910-kh—nachala 1920-kh godov*. Moscow: Progress-Traditsiia.

———. 2016. *Nikolai Kuzanskii v perevodakh i kommentariiakh*. ed. A.A. Takho-Godi, E.A. Takho-Godi, and V.P. Troitskii. Vol. 1–2. Moscow: Iazyki slavianskoi kul'tury.

———. 2017. *Estetika Vozrozhdeniia*, ed. A.A Takho-Godi. Moscow: Akademicheskii proekt.

Losev, A.F. 2018. "Plato's Doctrine of Ideas: Conclusion (The Summing-up and the Next Steps)" [from Essays on Ancient Symbolism and Mythology]. *Russian Studies in Philosophy* 56 (6): 515–537.

———. 2019. *Ucheniie o stile*, ed. A.A Takho-Godi and E.A Takho-Godi. Moscow: Nestor-Istoriia.

———. 2020. *The Woman Thinker*. Transl., Introduction by Vladimir Marchenkov. Studies in East European Thought, 2020, 72 (3-4) special issue "A Symbiosis of Russian Literature and Philosophy", ed. by E.A.Takho-Godi.

———. 2021. *Dialektika mifa*. Dopolneniie k «Dialektike mifa» (novoye akademicheskoye izdaniye ispravlennoye i dopolnennoye), ed. A. A. Takho-Godi, V. P. Troitskii. Moscow: Izdatel'skiy dom YASK.

Lossev, Alexeï, and Valentina Lossev. 2014. *"La Joie pour l'éternité": Correspondance du Goulag (1931–1933)*. Trad. par L. Jurgenson. Ouvrage publié les conseils du prof. G. Nivat. Préface E. Takho-Godi. Genève: Edition des Syrtes.

Obolevitch, Teresa. 2011. *Od onomatodoksji do estetyki. Aleksego Łosiewa koncepcja symbolu: Studium historyczno-filozoficzne.* Kraków: Wyd-wo WAM.

———. 2019a. *Faith and Science in Russian Religious Thought.* 565–579. Oxford: Oxford University Press.

———. 2019b. Christian Philosophy and the Name of God: Aesthetics as a Way of Life according to Alexei Losev. *The Journal of Eastern Christian Studies* 71 (1–2): 93–106.

———. 2020. Alexei Losev—"The Last Russian Philosopher" of the Silver Age. In *The Oxford Handbook of Russian Religious Thought,* ed. G. Pattison, R. Poole, and C. Emerson. Oxford: Oxford University Press.

Platov, Ilya. 2011. Le mythe de la Renaissance dans l'œuvre d'Aleksej Losev. In *Modernités russes.* Lyon: Centre d'Études Slaves André Lirondelle 12: 171–188. Lyon: Université Jean Moulin.

Plotnikov, Nikolai S., Nadezhda P. Podsemskaia, et al., eds. 2017. *Iskusstvo kak iazyk—iazyki iskusstva. Gosudarstvennaya akademiia khudozhestvennyh nauk i esteticheskaia teoriia 1920-h godov. 2: Publikatsii [Publications].* Moscow: Novoe literaturnoe obozrenie.

Reznichenko, Anna I. 2010. Philosophie du Nom. In *Dictionnaire de la philosophie russe,* 591–592. Lausanne: L'Age d'Homme.

Rimondi, Georgia. 2019. *Filosofskie i mirovozzrencheskie osnovy khudozhestvennoi prozy A.F. Loseva (Simvolicheskoie i muzykal'noie vyrazheniii smysla).* Moscow: Vodolei.

Takho-Godi, Aza A. 1984. A.F. Losev as a Historian of Classical Culture. *Soviet Studies in Literature.* 20 (2–3): 145–166.

Takho-Godi, Elena A. 2004. Aleksei Losev's Antiutopia. Transl. Robert Bird. *Studies in East European Thought.* 56 (2–3): 225–241.

Takho-Godi, Aza A. 2007a. *Losev.* Moscow: Molodaia gvardia.

Takho-Godi, Elena A. 2007b. *The Artistic World of A.F. Losev's Fiction.* Moscow: Bolshaia Rossiskaia Enciklopedia.

———. 2008a. Alexey Losev's Philosophical Novel "The Woman Thinker" and the Problem of the Eternal Feminine. *In Transcultural Studies. A Series in Interdisciplinary Research. Special Issue on Sophia Across Culture: From the Old Testament to Postmodernity* 4: 131–139.

Takho-Godi, Elena A. 2008b. Nicolaus Cusanus in the perception of A.F. Losev. In *"Nicolaus Cusanus: ein bewundernswerter historischer Brennpunkt."* In *Philosophische Tradition und wissenschaftliche Rezeption. Akten des Cusanus-Kongresses vom 20. bis 22. September 2006 in St. Petersburg.* Ed. Klaus Reinhardt und Harald Schwaetzer in Verbindung mit Oleg Dushin, 255–279. Regensburg: Roderer-Verlag.

Takho-Godi, Elena A. 2008c. Zum gegenseitigen Verhältnis von A. F. Losev und S. L. Frank. In *Kultur als Dialog und Meinung. Beiträge zu Fedor A. Stepun (1884-1965) und Semen L. Frank: Specimina philologiae slavicae,* ed. H. Kuße. Band 153: 219–237. München: Verlag Otto Sagner.

Takho-Godi, Elena A. 2013. Aleksei Losev and Vekhi: Strategic Traditions in Social Philosophy. In *Landmarks Revisited: The Vekhi Symposium 100 Years,* ed. Robin Aizlewood and Ruth Coates, 214–241. Boston: Academic Studies Press.

Takho-Godi, Elena A. 2014a. *Alexei Losev v epokhu russkoi revoliutsii: 1917–1919.* Moscow: Modest Kolerov.

Takho-Godi, Elena A. 2014b. Istoriia odnogo razocharovaniia: pis'ma A.F. Loseva k Yu.M. Lotmanu. In *The Problem of Style and the Art of Realism*, 356–373. Moscow: Russkii mir.

Takho-Godi, Elena A. 2018a. Alexei F. Losev's Impressions of Renaissance Literature and Philosophy. *Russian Studies in Philosophy* 56 (6): 459–466.

———. 2018b. A.F. Losev: mezhdu publtsistikoi i sotsial'noi epistemologiei. *Voprosy filosofii* 10: 140–149.

Takho-Godi, Elena A., and Petr V. Rezvych. 2018. From the History of Classical Philology: A.F. Losev and Bruno Snell. *Russian Studies in Philosophy* 56 (6): 449–458.

Tchizhevskij (Chizhevsky) Dmitrij (Dmitry). 1934. *Hegel bei den Slaven*. Reichnber: Stiepel Verlag.

Troitskii, Victor P. 2001. Tipologiia kul'tur A.F. Loseva i simvol fokstrota. In *Kul'tura v epokhu tsivilizatsionnogo sloma. Materialy mezhdunarodnoi nauchnoi konferentsii*, 583–592. Moscow: Sovet po Istorii Mirovoi Kultury RAN.

Uzelaz, Milan. 2007. *Filozofia Muzike*. Novi Sad: Stylos.

Zenkin, Konstantin V. 2005. Gregory Palama's Teachings on Entities and Energies in Losev's Philosophy of Music. In *Aesthetics as a Religious Factor in Eastern and Western Christianity*, 417–436. Leuven/Paris: Peeters.

———. 2018a. *Music—Eidos—Time. A.F. Losev and Scope of Contemporary Discipline of Music*. Moscow: Progress-Tradition.

———. 2018b. Losev's Interpretations of Richard Wagner. *Russian Studies in Philosophy* 56 (6): 491–497.

———. 2020. "Music as a Subject of Discussion in A.F. Losev's Philosophical Prose." *Studies in East European Thought*, 2020, 72 (3-4). Special issue «A Symbiosis of Russian Literature and Philosophy», ed. by E.A.Takho-Godi.

CHAPTER 32

The Young Marx and the Tribulations of Soviet Marxist-Leninist Aesthetics

Edward M. Świderski

INTRODUCTION

The focus of this chapter is a period in Soviet post-Stalinist Marxist-Leninist philosophy: the rise of investigations in philosophical aesthetics in the mid-1950s and continuing through to the mid-1960s. This salient issue had to do with the *foundations* of philosophical aesthetics in the context of the Marxist-Leninist worldview. That this became an issue was due in large part to the appearance, in 1956, of the first Russian translation of Marx's *Economic and Philosophical Manuscripts of 1844*. Marx's emphasis in these writings on the self-constituting, transformative potential of labor suggested possibilities for an aesthetic that did not sit comfortably with the dogmatic principles of dialectical and historical materialism. In effect, the foundational question for a Soviet aesthetics went to the heart of Marxism-Leninism: could young Marx's anthropocentrism be reconciled with the established Soviet doctrine beholden to, on the one hand, Engels' metaphysics of "matter-in-motion" and, on the other, Lenin's copy theory of knowledge? Among the aestheticians, the issue surfaced in a debate about the nature of beauty: is beauty relative to man or is it an objectively cognizable material property? To the degree that the parties to this debate addressed the underlying issue, they tended to remain ambivalent toward the result that neither side—those favoring creative expression versus the defenders of objective beauty—simply conceded nor rejected the views of the other. A systematic philosophical aesthetics within the scope of Soviet

---

E. M. Świderski (✉)
University of Fribourg, Fribourg, Switzerland
e-mail: edward.swiderski@unifr.ch

© The Author(s), under exclusive license to Springer Nature
Switzerland AG 2021
M. F. Bykova et al. (eds.), *The Palgrave Handbook of Russian Thought*,
https://doi.org/10.1007/978-3-030-62982-3_32

693

694   E. M. ŚWIDERSKI

philosophy never saw the light of day. By the mid-1960s, research was ramify-
ing into a variety of adjacent considerations, for example, value theory, theories
of culture and cultural artifacts, the history of aesthetic categories, the social
and pedagogical functions of art, art and morality in relation to the "socialist
way of life," art in the era of the "scientific-technological revolution," and so
on, of which only some recalled the spirit, rarely the letter, of the initial "aesthetics" discussion.

It will be instructive to juxtapose the aesthetics discussion with an earlier
attempt in the Soviet Union to identify the core of a Marxist aesthetics. In a
study published in 1933 (Lifshits 1933), the literary theorist and critic Mikhail
Lifshits purported to demonstrate that Marx's doctrine as a whole—not only
his youthful writings—is a paean to human creative potential once labor is
freed from alienation, exploitation, false consciousness, and fetishism. What, if
anything, remained of this earlier conception as discussions arose anew in mid-
century Soviet philosophy?

THE DAWNING OF AESTHETICS IN SOVIET PHILOSOPHY

Dates had a meaning in Soviet philosophy not typically encountered elsewhere
within academic philosophy: they mark stress points and turnings. I suggest the
following: 1931, 1938, 1947, 1950, 1956, then (somewhat less precisely)
1987, but also, of course, 1991.[1] The first three comprise the struggles in the
formation of Marxism-Leninism; the fourth, the limited but significant loosen-
ing of ideological strictures; the last three, the injection of a potentially corrosive element into orthodox Soviet doctrine, the effects of which stalled during
the "stagnation" only to peter out (as of 1987) as Marxism-Leninism ran into
the ground (1991).

The "corrosive element" was the aforementioned publication of the first
Russian translation of Marx's (and Engels') early texts, including the 1844
Paris manuscripts, known under the title *Economic and Philosophical Manuscripts
of 1844* (Marx and Engels 1956). They were "corrosive" for two related reasons: on the one hand, those who sought inspiration from these early texts
risked conflict with the keepers of orthodoxy; on the other hand, this potential
for conflict acted as a brake on the unambiguous formulation of positions
drawing on these texts. The upshot was an absence of clarity on the foundational issue.

Did Khrushchev's denunciation of Stalin in 1956 act as a stimulus to publish
Marx's youthful writings that same year? Whatever the answer, their appearance in the context of the ensuing "thaw" certainly opened a window on a
possible "renewal" in Soviet philosophy. Younger philosophers who seized the
opportunity to implement Marx's early writings introduced *nolens volens* a current that basically ran contrary to the doctrinal mainstream in place ever since
Stalin's pronouncements about "*diamat*" and "*istmat*" in 1938.[2] The underlying tension had to do with whether Marx's youthful "philosophy" was consistent with the much-touted monolithic consensus among the "classics of

Marxism-Leninism" (i.e., Marx-Engels-Lenin-Stalin [prior to 1956]). A brief sketch of the salient line of development of Marxism-Leninism is needed here.

Marxism-Leninism took its start not directly from Marx but from Engels' materialist reading of Hegel flavored by his positivist take on the science of his day. Engels set Marx's materialist conception of history within this framework: the progressive movement of social formations was governed by universal laws of change and development steering all "matter in motion." The Russian social democrats (first Georgii Plekhanov, later Lenin) followed suit, beholden to Engels as Marx's spiritual heir. Nevertheless, philosophical free-thinking within the ranks of the Bolsheviks (Alexander Bogdanov and Anatoly Lunacharsky) persisted at least until the Revolution (notwithstanding Lenin's efforts to vilify the idealism with which he charged Bogdanov[3]).

In the wake of the Revolution, following fractious discussion about the character of Marxist philosophy—is it an elaboration of the Hegelian dialectics or is it a "science"?—the creeping "bolshevization" of philosophy in the late 1920s entrenched the Engelsian view supplemented by the "Leninist stage" (the reflection or copy theory of knowledge). The outcome was capped by Stalin's chapter on *diamat* and *istmat* in the 1938 "Short Course."[4] The foundations of Marxism-Leninism were laid, and the myth of monolithic consensus among the "classics" acquired doctrinal as well as political status.[5]

However, well before this monolith was erected voices had been heard, in Europe as well as among Russian socialists (e.g., Bogdanov) before 1917, raising doubts about Engels' "dialectics of nature" as an adequate representation of Marx's "philosophical" views.[6] Although Marx's *Theses on Feuerbach* appeared in 1888 in an appendix to Engels' Feuerbach pamphlet, it was not until 1932 that the "Paris manuscripts"—better known as the *Economic and Philosophic Manuscripts of 1844*—appeared (in German), in Moscow. By that time philosophical debate in the Soviet Union was under the control of party stalwarts, and their Marx was inseparable from Engels.

Virtually nothing had been published in the Soviet Union about young Marx before the end of the 1940s. While more appeared following Stalin's death, reticence was the tone.[7] The "mature" Marx, it was said, gave up his youthful, somewhat "idealist" vision of man once he turned to the study of political economy, due in part to Engels' insistence. Thereafter, traces of Hegelian idealism and Feuerbachian naturalism gave way to the "scientific socialism" that brought to light "iron laws" governing class conflict, the impending crisis of capitalism, and the inevitability of communism. The alleged absence in the mature work of the notion of alienation was considered especially telling of the fact that Marx had put behind him the humanism of his youthful incarnation, replacing it with a decidedly determinist vision of socioeconomic history consistent with Engelsian dialectical materialism.

Seen in this light, the post-1956 entry of Marx's early writings into Soviet philosophical resources was an event. However, it came in through the back door, so to speak, viz., *via* aesthetics, at the time a sub-discipline at the margins of Soviet philosophy. In 1956, *philosophical* aesthetics was only just beginning

696   E. M. ŚWIDERSKI

to stake out its terrain and find its voice.[8] Until then, discourse about art, and the function of art in a socialist society, had been the prerogative of the keepers of socialist realism, the theory which consisted of a mix of themes drawn mostly from nineteenth-century German (Hegel) and Russian (the Revolutionary Democrats) thinkers, rounded off with Lenin's observations about party literature. While Marx and Engels were not absent from the mix, none of this yet amounted to *philosophical* aesthetics. There was a reason for this: socialist realist theory offered no clear answer to the questions that had been around since the Scottish Enlightenment and refined by Kant (with help from Alexander Baumgarten): "What is the nature of the aesthetic as such?"; "What do phenomena classified as aesthetic have in common?"; and more specifically, "What makes art 'art'?" Appeals to *narodnost'* [nationality], *klassovost'* [the class nature of art], *partiinost'* [the party-minded character of art], progressive versus reactionary art, art as "thinking in images," the depiction of (social) types, all staples of the socialist realist canon, provided no clear insight into the aesthetic nature of art.[9]

No sooner had aspiring aestheticians set to work on this question than the tensions to which I alluded came into the open, pitting, on the one hand, potential innovators eager to exploit Marx's youthful writings against, on the other, traditionalists mindful of orthodoxy and wary of young Marx. This tension is the origin of the so-called discussion about the aesthetic[10] which, as it turned out, became an arena for debating the merits of Marx's youthful philosophy. As stated, the import of these discussions was not—at least not on the surface—to advance or to resist views that could be judged revisionist in character.[11] Rather, among Soviet philosophers of the period, Marx's early texts became means to point out lacunae in the established doctrine. For example, the doctrine placed no premium on statements such as "It can be said that in any practical activity of man the object [of the activity] becomes beautiful only insofar as man recognizes himself, his creative possibilities, the richness of his human essence in it" (Burov 1956, 222). Once it became possible to go into print with such statements—on the newly minted authority of Marx's early writings—questions sprang up about the concepts behind the terms in such statements, as well as their implications beyond the narrow aesthetic context. How does one square the talk of human creative potential with that of the laws of matter-in-motion believed to underpin effective practical activity? Are we to understand that "beauty" is not a quality in the things themselves, but a quality ascribed to them, thanks to man's "aesthetic relation" to reality? How do the objects of man's activity relate to material objects independent of his activity? Ready answers to such questions were largely unavailable among the resources in use at the time in Soviet philosophical discourse. A significant part of the discussions, into the mid-1960s at least, had to do with whether a statement of the kind quoted had a legitimate place in Marxism-Leninism.

MARX—THE AESTHETICIAN?

I begin by examining the reception of young Marx *qua* aesthetician *well in advance* of the period of primary interest here. I noted in the introduction that, in 1933, Mikhail Lifshits published a study, the first of its kind in Russian, entitled *On the Question of Marx's Views on Art*.[12] In the same year, an anthology of Marx's and Engels' writings on matters both aesthetic and artistic—jottings, musings, off-hand observations, scraps of literary criticism, and so on, scattered throughout their writings—appeared, prepared and edited by Lifshits (among others). It went through several editions thereafter, growing into two volumes.[13] Lifshits' study appeared five years in advance of Stalin's dogmatic codification of the Marxist-Leninist worldview and is largely free of the stilted jargon and tone that marred philosophical tracts long thereafter.[14] It also characterized a Marxist aesthetic in an original way.

Throughout the 1920s, there had been much debate as to the proper aims and methods of a Marxist (mostly literary) aesthetic at the heart of which realism was (and remained) the central issue.[15] The general tenor was that of a sociology of art, for which the Marx of such passages as the Preface to the 1859 *Critique of Political Economy* served as the primary resource: art is a superstructural phenomenon determined by, and "reflecting," socio-economic relations. Lifshits, without entirely distancing himself from this doctrine, presented a far more nuanced account of a Marxist aesthetic, due in large measure to his appreciation of Marx's early philosophical views and their roots.

Lifshits makes the case that attention to aesthetic issues—such as art, the history of art, the aesthetic sense, the close connection between labor as human expression and art, the evils of commodifying art, and so on—is central to Marx's concerns prior to, but also following, the composition of the 1844 Manuscripts. Lifshits did not claim that there is a systematic aesthetics in Marx nor was it his ambition to fill in the blanks. His purpose had been to underscore how fundamentally aesthetic in character Marx's *overall* vision is.[16] This he did by exploring the influences acting on the young Marx—influences both philosophical (German aesthetics from Kant and Schiller to Hegel, and Marx's reading of Friedrich T. Vischer) and artistic (from the Greeks to Shakespeare, Goethe, Heine, et al., together with the Romanticism he nevertheless eschewed)—as well as Marx's conception of labor. As Lifshits read him, the aesthetic sense underpins the connections Marx drew between the evils of alienation and its dénouement once the communist ideal finds full expression in unfettered, creative human personality.

The labor process is multifaceted; through it, man actively relates to nature and to the collective in which each and all are embedded. Among these relations, the quintessentially human is the aesthetic relation. Lifshits explains:

> An aesthetic relation to reality is one of inner organic unity with the object, equally remote from abstract, contemplative harmony with it as from arbitrary distortion of its own dialectics. In such form, this unity by no means contradicts

698   E. M. ŚWIDERSKI

the progressive development of social production; quite the contrary, it is its highest spiritual development. (Lifshits 1973, 82)

This passage is highly reminiscent of Marx's first and second *Theses on Feuerbach*: "contemplative harmony" would be the one-sided passive "materialism" that Marx decries in the first thesis; the "arbitrary distortion" could well be assimilated to equally one-sided "idealism," whose emphasis on activity likewise violates the "object." It is tempting to read Lifshits' reference to "organic unity" as equivalent to the *praxis* that Marx extols in the first two theses, a *praxis* equated by Lifshits with the "aesthetic relation" of the inner organic unity of object and activity.

In another passage Lifshits underscores Marx's excerpts from Vischer's *Ästhetik* (1846) calling attention to his paraphrase of Vischer's contention that beauty is no real property of things:

> The beautiful exists only for consciousness, paraphrased Marx. […] Hence beauty is a property of man even though it seems to be a property of things, of the "beautiful in nature." […] This does not mean, however, that the 'aesthetic' is purely subjective. (Lifshits 1973, 95–96)

Little could Lifshits know that he was here addressing the question that, as we will see shortly, became the major point of contention within the aesthetics discussion post-1956. Calling on his readers to appreciate the "role which the subjective-objective productive activity plays in Marx's economic and philosophical views," Lifshits subscribes Marx via Vischer to Schiller's aesthetic:

> Beauty is simultaneously an object, and a subjective state. It is at once form, when we judge it, and also life, when we feel it. It is at once our state of being and our creation. (Lifshits 1973, 96)

Now, taking these considerations together with the previous passage about the "aesthetic relation," and allowing for his poetic language, it appears that although Lifshits does not quote the following passage from Marx's 1844 manuscripts, he could well have had it in mind:

> It is only when the objective world everywhere becomes for man in society the world of man's essential powers—human reality and for that reason the reality of his *own* essential powers—that all *objects* become for him the *objectification of himself*, become objects which confirm and realize his individuality, become his objects: that is *man himself* becomes the object. (Tucker 1979, 74)

The context in the *Manuscripts* in which this passage occurs has nothing to do with aesthetics. Nevertheless, bearing in mind Lifshits' remarks cited above, it is plausible to assume that had he cited this passage, he could have concluded that it bears directly on "man's aesthetic relation to reality" as the "highest spiritual development" of social production.

But why might he have restricted the import of this passage to aesthetics when Marx appears to have considerably more in mind, nothing less indeed than human reality in its entirety? One conjecture has to do with the ideological context at the time Lifshits prepared his study: around 1930 the "bolshevization" of philosophy in the hands of Mark Mitin, Pavel Judin, and others, to the detriment of Abram Deborin and his followers, raised Lenin's reflection theory to canonical status.[17] Room for Leninist-style reflection is absent in the above passage from the *Manuscripts*; far from advancing the cause of reflection, Marx embraces a kind of "expressivist" conception of human activity (consistent with the German idealist tradition). That may have been reason enough not to cite it when composing a treatise about Marx's aesthetics in 1933.

That said, nowhere in Lifshits' 1933 book is Lenin's "copy theory" an issue one way or another.[18] Though the potentially conflicting passage from the *Manuscripts* was absent, Lifshits was not reticent in depicting the aesthetic character of Marx's enterprise in terms close to the spirit of that passage. He states:

> By means of the class struggle [the proletariat] shows the way to a classless culture; by means of the development of an art inspired by the [...] proletariat, it leads to *the abolition of the disparity between social and artistic development*, an unprecedented growth of art upon a wide mass basis. This is the ultimate meaning of all of Marx's comments upon literature and art; this is his historical bequest. (Lifshits 1973, 106, italics mine)

This passage makes of Marx the great cultural emancipator, an idea that reinforces the conclusion reached in the first quotation from Lifshits above: the apotheosis of the history of social production is the aesthetic relation. Moreover, as young Marx subscribed to the idea that "beauty is form and a subjective state," we can surmise that he endorsed—at least on Lifshits' reading—the Kantian-Schillerian aesthetic: the pursuit of pure form for its own sake, free from utilitarian considerations. For Lifshits, it was an endorsement with an added twist: access to the "pure form" supposes a primary relation of the subject to the object via social production (praxis), such that the contemplation of "pure form" is tantamount to the witness Man pays to his powers, those through which Man "humanizes" the world.[19] Thus, although Lifshits does not cite the passage previously quoted from the *Manuscripts*, on this reading he would concur with its message: man instills his human essence into the object of his labor. The form to which the aesthetic sense grows sensitive captures Man's creative capacity in relation to the objects of his labor, and that experience is the apotheosis of all of Man's relations—to himself and for himself; it is his self-affirmation.

How much of this was still in the offing as Soviet philosophical aesthetics started to emerge in the mid-1950s, once Marx's early philosophical writings were admitted into the discussion?

700   E. M. ŚWIDERSKI

The Societalists [obshchestvenniki] Versus the Naturists [prirodniki]

As the "aesthetics" discussion heated up post-1956, the passage from the *Manuscripts* that Lifshits omitted nowhere figured prominently in the writings of those who enlisted young Marx in their pursuit of a philosophical aesthetic. Nonetheless, they did aspire to pass off its spirit as compatible with the object, then under consideration, of Marxist-Leninist aesthetics. The trouble was that their ploy did not escape the critical gaze of the friends of reflection who held them accountable. Thus, the stage was set for the controversy alluded to, that between the societalists [*obshchestvenniki*] and the naturists [*prirodniki*][20] over the nature of the aesthetic in light of the Marxist-Leninist worldview.[21] The matter for debate came down to arguments for or against realism about aesthetic properties/qualities, where "against" did not mean embracing antirealism in some guise, least of all its extreme variety, subjectivism. No one was—no one at that time could dare to be—antirealist and still lay claim to be a Marxist-Leninist; everyone agreed that there are aesthetic properties/qualities. Instead, the question came down to deciding what kind of aesthetic realism was consistent with the Marxist-Leninist worldview.[22]

All comers to the debate at least paid lip service, through a variety of formulations, to the following "axiomatic" principles. For instance,

> Aesthetic qualities belong to the phenomena of reality itself, existing objectively outside and independently of man's perception of them. Their reflection in human consciousness [...] is called man's aesthetic relation to reality. (Vanslov 1957, 26)

Conceiving man's aesthetic relation to reality as realism about aesthetic properties yields a truth-maker conception of aesthetic descriptions:

> The importance of the question about the objectivity of aesthetic properties consists in the fact that it is a question about the criteria of the truth of one aesthetic perception and the falsehood of another. (ibid.)

The naturists, committed to the mainstays of Soviet theory—the Leninist reflection theory, *diamat*'s leading role vis-à-vis *istmat*, and the ideological (class content of) art—came down on the side of a robust (property) realism: the concept of the aesthetic ranges over terms tethered to referents in the material world beyond the human epidermis. While there was some room for nuance—not a little of which is better characterized as ambiguity, hedging, and downright unclarities—the naturists argued that aesthetic qualities/properties either exist as such in the material world beyond Man or at the very least have their primary ground in material properties, that is, in nature.

Occasionally, naturists wrote as if they were alive to the concept of supervenient properties, viz., properties an object has that depend on the kind, and arrangement of, underlying, basic properties (e.g., a jagged, broken trace would hardly be perceived, rightly characterized, as delicate). For instance,

> [T]he expression "aesthetic qualities" is fully justified if these qualities (properties) are considered as aesthetic particularities of objects and phenomena of the entire objective world and not as a choice of narrowly conceived traits or separate elements. (Egorov 1959, 91)

This is meant as a claim, specifically, that there are no aesthetic properties without a grounding in material properties; free-floating aesthetic properties are nowhere to be found. Some commentators alluded to levels of properties in an object; others warned against identifying whatever justifies the use of aesthetic descriptions "with a determinate physical phenomenon in the form of air waves perceived by our hearing organs as sound or the combinations of lights perceived by the retina of the eye" (Dmitrieva 1960, 61).

For the naturists, care was required here: toying with supervenience risks giving aesthetic properties the status of response-dependent properties, viz., an object has a property in virtue of which it elicits a relevant (perceptual and conceptual) response on the part of a perceiver. It is a disposition the object has, one requiring a perceiver in order to be "awakened." The difficulty with this solution, for the naturists, was that response-dependency is ruled out if Lenin's copy theory is understood to be direct realism, as was generally the case. Lenin applied the theory directly to the sensations that he says copy matter ("Matter is that which, acting upon our sense organs, produces sensation"). Any alternative suggesting that aesthetic qualities are response-dependent would be risky to a fault, a step toward rank idealism!

Those, on the other hand, who took their cues from Marx's early texts sought to build a case for a relational (or subject-object) realism. Beyond satisfying concrete needs, labor always and everywhere imparts the creative spark of the human essence to its objects; the aesthetic relation to these objects consists in surpassing the merely utilitarian, functional attitude. While this appears to coincide with Lifshits' formulations thirty years in advance of the aesthetics discussion, there was a difference in emphasis. Lifshits did not worry at all about properties, underscoring instead pure expression and its spiritual benefits once societal conditions permitted giving it free reign.[23] By contrast, the societalists, like their opponents, persisted in speaking of aesthetic qualities or properties, or the objective outcome in the objects of labor. The former advocated a kind of response-dependency thesis, though mitigated by including socio-cultural conditions of individual experience. For instance,

> Aesthetic properties of objects are the capacity of concrete sensible things to call forth in man determinate ideative-emotional relations to them thanks to the role these things play in the concrete system of social relations. (Stolovich 1961, 166)

Again,

> Aesthetic qualities are natural according to their immediate being [*nalichnomu bytiiu*], in that they are material, sensible, dependent on the stuff [*veshchestvu*] of nature, its properties, and laws. But they are social according to their essence, for they express man, the traits and properties formed by his society, they objectively correspond to one side or another of this life activity. (Vanslov 1957, 59)

The term mediating between the stuff of nature and aesthetic qualities is life activity, which could perhaps be understood as man's expression. But our writer blocks that possibility by injecting the all-important term "objectively," clearly meant to obviate any danger of subjectivism that the unqualified use of "expression" might convey.

This last consideration remained a nagging doubt about the societalists: were they staunch realists, as the naturists certainly claimed to be, in keeping with Leninist reflection theory? What the societalists were attempting to communicate can be construed as follows: Marx had stated grandly in the *Manuscripts* that the history of production is the open book of man's essential powers, a testimony to the construction of a socially mediated human world. In the *Theses on Feuerbach*, Marx, still in thrall to the autotelic thrust, if not the idealism, of the Hegelian spirit-in-process, historicizes Feuerbach's *Gattungswesen*, giving it the form of the self-determining, self-productive species rising above nature. Stated in contemporary terms, Marx was groping for an ontology of the humanly made world: the human (institutional, interpersonal, and cultural) reality we share is ontologically subjective in that it depends for its existence on the ongoing organization of human productive activity relative to the raw materials of nature with which social being is in constant intercourse. On the other hand, the ontologically subjective nature of social being is fully compatible with its objective character, epistemologically. What any individual or group believes and claims about social reality is truth-functionally constrained by what it itself is, that is, what it has become in the course of humanity's social production.[24]

In short, the picture drawn by the societalists in pursuit of their goal of a philosophical aesthetic was this: any given individual finds himself/herself in a world that is always already "humanized" (to some degree), that bears myriad traces of the "human essence" instilled by the labor of preceding generations, testifying to the cumulative power of society (hence the label "societalists"). An individual who grows sensitive to its human content *qua human* will experience it as beautiful (using the term as shorthand for aesthetic qualities or properties). It is worth adding here that the individual herself is no abstraction over and against the "humanized world" in which she finds herself: after all, what she is essentially, what she incarnates, is the historically relative "ensemble of the social relations" (discordant in class societies, harmonious in the kingdom of freedom). Indeed, her relational historical essence is the key to her capacity to recognize the corresponding socially mediated aesthetic qualities of the human world.[25]

The naturists were not persuaded, however, for at least two reasons. First, as noted, Lenin's reflection theory has it that knowledge is whatever is objectively given to the senses in contact with material objects beyond the senses.[26] If so, so-called humanized objects are just material objects given sensually to man in relation to his needs, which are fulfilled based on what they, the objects, by nature are. Second, human activity, practice, is effective only when based on the (objective) knowledge of the laws of nature governing objects and human needs. Far from being expressive, practice is primarily adaptive, although in due course, as humans accumulate knowledge, they take nature's forces into their own hands, and in so doing discover nature's aesthetic features.[27]

In this last regard, there is a passage in the *Manuscripts* that gave the societalists headaches, but brought smiles to the faces of the naturists:

> man knows how to produce in accordance with the standard of every species and knows how to apply everywhere the inherent standard to the object. Man, therefore, also forms things in accordance with laws of beauty. (Tucker 1979, 62)

Is this not the knock-down argument against the societalists? The very Marx whom they extoll for his supposed insight that beauty is relative to the practices that construct a human world appears to affirm, to the contrary, that there are laws of beauty inherent in the things on which man operates! For their part, the societalists could take refuge in Marx's claim, likewise in the *Manuscripts*, that the human senses have a history[28] and that sense contact with material objects is mediated by the very same socio-historical reality heretofore humanized by labor, a conception seemingly alien to Lenin's direct sensory realism.

Let it be recalled, by way of partial summary, why all this clamor took place: such strained efforts had been designed to resolve an issue left dangling by the socialist realist theory of art—what makes art *art*? Aleksandr Burov, a central figure throughout these discussions, pointed out, in *The Aesthetic Essence of Art* (1956), that no Soviet theoretician had satisfactorily shown in what the *aesthetic nature* of art consists or, essentially, how the reflection proper to art is aesthetic in character rather than, as was usually stipulated, cognitive (e.g., Vissarion Belinsky's appropriation of Hegel's "thinking in images"). At the time Burov raised his objection, it had become virtually embarrassing to repeat that art's primary function is to reflect reality, since the obvious retort was, "How then does art differ from science and any other specifically cognitive undertaking?" As we have seen, the objection itself became controversial, for it assumed that "we know just what the aesthetic is"!

The challenge Burov—and in rapid succession other societalists—posed was centered on the pillar of Soviet doctrine, generally, Leninist reflection theory. How rigid or flexible was this canonical principle? The societalists sought to render it pliable: art *specifically* reflects the human qualities imparted to nature in the course of mankind's labor. The naturists held to the rigid reading of Lenin's realism: alongside the physical, and so on, properties of things, there

704   E. M. ŚWIDERSKI

are qualities such as harmony, symmetry, proportion, and so on—natural beauty—that art *specifically* reflects.

On balance, the societalist position had the upper hand. Because the aesthetic is relational in character, it comprises a "subjective" as well as an "objective" side, the former understood as activity, labor, the latter as the object stamped by labor. (Recall here Lifshits' account of the aesthetic as an "organic unity" of the subjective and the objective.) The naturists' objection was that labor is not simply human self-expression, if that is all the societalists meant by the aesthetic; after all, labor is activity increasingly in tune with the objective properties of the things, which is why the primary criterion should not be self-expression but effectiveness, practical success, underwritten by the laws of nature. By the same token, however, the naturists threw no light on just what the aesthetic qualitatively is. For instance, the societalists pointed out to the naturists that they failed to explain why the redness of blood and the redness of a rose do not elicit the same aesthetic appreciation despite both being the object of sensory reflection.[29] Something beyond sensory reflection is required to explain the difference where the same sensory qualities are involved, that something being the mediation of human practice appropriating nature, all the while growing in awareness of its powers. There may well be objective aesthetic properties, but as aesthetic, they manifest an essential, constitutive relation to Man.[30]

James Scanlan, in his 1985 study, *Marxism in the USSR: A Critical Survey of Current Soviet Thought*, included a chapter on the philosophy of art. In his review, he notes that, among the societalists, there was a distinction between those who advanced a conception of the aesthetic as "practical-*productive* appropriation" and those who favored what he terms the "practical-*spiritual*" conception, both put forward as answers to the question "In what does the aesthetic essence of art consist?" (Scanlan 1985, 306f.) The first group, mostly in the majority, insisted that the aesthetic relation requires there to be objective aesthetic properties—humanly produced and accessible to reflection. The second group, more in the minority, minimized this condition; for them, the aesthetic is expressive of the human essence. It is not the qualities or properties relative to reflection that are paramount, but what they reveal about their source. Scanlan quotes Burov's account of the latter position:

> [T]he aesthetic is here the self-expression of the creative wealth of the individual in all his life activity. [...] the nature of the aesthetic [...] is wholly determined by the essential powers of man, for it is just these powers that make any object aesthetic. In other words, on this theory the subjective principle is presented as absolutely active, and the objective as absolutely passive. (Scanlon 1985, 310)[31]

Lifshits is not mentioned in Scanlan's survey of Soviet philosophy of art. However, Lifshits' reading of young Marx amounts precisely to the practical-spiritual conception that Scanlan was careful to distinguish. As we have seen, Lifshits ascribed to Marx an expressionist aesthetic of human productive powers in which the latter become self-directed, so to speak, an idea relying on Kantian-Schillerian "free play." The aesthetic relation is the "highest spiritual development of social production," the implication being that, in ideal circumstances, that is, in communist society, all production acquires an aesthetic dimension.

No less an authority than Alexei Losev subscribed to this conception in the entry on "Aesthetics" written for the fifth volume of the *Filosofskaia Enciklopediia* [Encyclopedia of Philosophy], published in 1970. Reviewing the stages of the *aesthetics* discussion, Losev writes:

> To the extent that these ideas of Marx are basic to the understanding of the aesthetic by contemporary Soviet aestheticians, the aesthetic or the object of aesthetics could be characterized as follows: It is the immediately given or the externally sensuous expressiveness of the internal life of the object which includes in itself the two-level process of the 'objectification' of the social essence of man and the 'humanization' of nature, and which is perceived as an independent and disinterestedly contemplatable value of life. (Losev 1975, 214)

Although convoluted, this statement contains the striking phrase "the externally sensuous expressiveness of the internal life of the object" that turns out to consist in humanization rendered objective. Losev explains, "The very term 'expression' indicates an active process of self-conversion of the internal into the external, man's self-revelation in the external world" (Losev 1975, 215f.). On the one hand, there is a "sensible-objective existence" possessing "a complex physical-psychological-physiological-social structure." On the other hand, this existence is infused with an "ideal, meaningful element," thanks to which it becomes "expressive." The aesthetic stands somewhere between the real and the ideal, an insight Losev credits chiefly to Kant, Schelling, and Hegel. All of this is redolent of Lifshits' remark referenced above that the aesthetic involves "inner organic unity" of the object, with the subject who neither merely contemplates nor distorts the object. Losev concluded that the *aesthetics* discussion succeeded in "overcoming [...] the naturalistic understanding of the aesthetic" (ibid.), nothing less than a put-down of the naturist position.

For his part, writing in 1985, Scanlan came to the more plausible conclusion that the dispute about the foundations of Soviet aesthetics could have no unequivocal solution,

> because there is in Marxist-Leninist philosophy no logical way to resolve it, since it straddles a deep rift in Soviet philosophy—the rift between a focus on physical nature and its reflection in the human mind and a focus on the social world as shaped by human labor practice. (Scanlan 1985, 303)

706   E. M. ŚWIDERSKI

What Went Missing During the Aesthetics Discussion

Lifshits' interpretation of the overall aesthetic cast of Marx's thinking included three further themes, altogether absent from the *aesthetic* discussion: the alienation of labor, false consciousness, and commodity fetishism (and the interrelations of these). The first is central to the *Manuscripts*—alienated man, Marx insists, is estranged from the product of his labor, and therefore from the value of his labor, and consequently from his fellows (from his "species-essence"). The alienated object of labor—reproducing the conditions that sustain private property—mediates, indeed reifies, human relations. Overcoming alienation is therefore tantamount to recovering the human essence in the unmediated interchange of every individual with his or her fellows collectively giving expression to their potential.

It is tempting to wonder whether, had Marx's central concern with alienation been injected into the aesthetics discussion of the 1950s, the practical-spiritual, expressivist conception of the aesthetic would have ruled the day as the genuinely Marxist solution. It is a thought that gains plausibility as soon as false consciousness and fetishism are brought into the picture.

The commodity fetishism Marx explored in his *Capital* is usually regarded as the continuation of the alienation problems, restated by means of economic categories that young Marx did not yet have at his disposal. Significant, in this regard, is Marx's description of the experience of the commodity as a fetish, the "fantastic form" of which obscures sight of the underlying reality. The commodity can exist only in a society in which men labor under the false consciousness—the inversion of consciousness that takes illusion for reality—that pervades the superstructure of class societies. This inversion in turn reinforces the division of labor that is its underlying cause, makes it appear natural, inscribed into the very nature of labor, its forms, and the social relations framing production. The upshot is that the object—the commodity—rules. As Marx phrases it in *Capital*, "there is a definite social relation between men that assumes, in their eyes, the fantastic form of a relation between things" (Jordan 1971, 243).

Now, in case the inversion is righted, the illusion revealed, and the alienation recognized for what it is—putting the object before the activity that has been reified in obtuse materials—what remains? The activity alone, so to speak, that is, the practical-spiritual, expressive essence of unmediated human social activity that is henceforth always more than any current form of expression. It is significant, I think, that Lifshits ends his study quoting a passage from the *German Ideology* in which Marx rails against the consequences for art of the division of labor and promises: "In a communist society, there are no painters, but at most men who, among other things, also paint." Accordingly, Lifshits' last line reads: "Art is dead! Long live art! This is the slogan of Marx's aesthetics" (Lifshits 1973, 116).

One looks in vain within the reams of text produced during the aesthetics discussion (at its high point from roughly 1957 to 1962) for more than passing allusions to the topic of alienation. This is not difficult to understand: it is, in the end, a critical tool wielded to expose and condemn dehumanizing forces within a society. At a stretch, it could be said that the denunciation of Stalin and the initiation of the "thaw" was *de facto* recognition that the vaunted construction of communism had violated the communist ideal of a humane society, though neither the term alienation nor its cognates figured in the discourse critical of Stalin's crimes. But what about ferreting out the causes of this failure and condemning them? It hardly needs to be said that neither Khrushchev nor his successors before Gorbachev betrayed any intention to dismantle the real source of the alienation in Soviet society—the self-replicating party-state machine that Stalin utilized to eradicate an independent society. More time needed to pass before personalities such as philosopher and novelist Alexander Zinoviev, the sociologist Yuri Levada, the novelist-historian Alexander Solzhenitsyn, to name perhaps the most prominent, each found the words to characterize, not without becoming the targets of vehement opprobrium, the outcome of this eradication: Soviet reality had produced a mutant—"*homo sovieticus*," the polar opposite of the triumphant image of the "new Soviet man," the *telos* of the communist ideal (flaunted *ad nauseum* in socialist realist art).

Whatever the merits of this interpretation, there was also a factual reason for the absence of the topic of alienation in the aesthetics discussion, namely, the rise of "revisionism" and what came to be known as "neo-Marxism" (including Western Marxism) even as the aesthetics discussion in Soviet philosophy was getting under way. As of 1957/1958, within and outside the Soviet bloc, in Poland, East Germany, Hungary, France, and Italy, the writings of young Marx were inspiring revisionist programs critical not solely of Marxist-Leninist doctrine but especially of the moral, existential consequences of Soviet reality. In response, Soviet theoreticians adopted a defensive posture and went on the attack. In his review of the ensuing situation, Murray Yanowitch wrote:

> Both the tone and analytical content of the Soviet discussions of the young Marx and alienation which began to appear in this period bore the imprint of the "struggle against revisionism." Marx the dialectical materialist had to be defended against his roots in Hegelian idealism and Feuerbachian materialism. Marx the theoretician of surplus value had to be defended against Marx the philosopher of alienation. And Soviet society had to be defended against the criticisms that could be made of it in the spirit of Marx's own writings. (Yanowitch 1967, 36)

There is a cruel irony here: even as they were beginning to assimilate young Marx into the newly emerging aesthetics, Soviet philosophers were aware that they were obliged to curtail their enthusiasm in view of how this same Marx was being read by their non-Soviet brethren. With hindsight, I note again that the aesthetics discussion might have tended toward a solution of sorts, had the topic of alienation acquired a legitimate role in the discussion. Ideological and political constraints blocked this path, the result being the unbridgeable gulf

708   E. M. ŚWIDERSKI

separating the parties to the largely sterile debate about how to account for the objective ("realist") status of the aesthetic.

Afterword

Since the collapse of the Soviet Union, the descriptor "Soviet aesthetics," if used at all, covers writings by, to mention the more prominent, Bakhtin, Losev, early Soviet theoreticians still under the influence of formalism and suprematism, the research carried on at GAkhN[32] until 1931, Lev Vygotsky, Evald Ilyenkov, Yuri Lotman and Uspenskii, and even Moscow conceptualism during the waning years of the Soviet experience. Except perhaps for the last named, the diversity of these personalities and currents does not obscure a common trait: there was nothing dogmatically *Marxist-Leninist* about them, though some (e.g., Vygotsky, Ilyenkov certainly, even Losev to a degree) did not abjure Marxist themes. Thus, the descriptor "Soviet aesthetics" lacks an unequivocal doctrinal reference. Even the case of socialist realism is ambiguous, the emergence of a Marxist-Leninist philosophical aesthetics post-dated the formulation of the doctrine in the early 1930s.

The aesthetics discussed in this chapter began to peter out by the mid-1960s: if Soviet aesthetics is restricted to the period in Marxist-Leninist philosophy canvassed in this chapter, then it had a short lifespan indeed. Whatever remained of it as the Soviet Union slipped into the abyss in the late 1980s knew the same fate that Marxist-Leninist philosophy as a whole ultimately experienced. Unlike the other "representatives" of Soviet aesthetics listed, Marxist-Leninist aesthetics has ceased being an object of investigation and a resource for current research.[33] That said, the list above of what today falls under the rubric of Soviet aesthetics is not complete without noting that Lifshits continues to have a following in Russia, as evidenced by recent events at the Garage Museum of Contemporary Art in Moscow.[34] However, his notoriety today seems to have nothing to do with his early Marx book, but with his relentless anti-modernism directed against the principal currents of twentieth-century art and aesthetics. Indeed, his Marx book could well be read rather in the context of Western or neo-Marxist aesthetics (I have in mind Adorno, Benjamin, Marcuse, and later adepts of the "Frankfurt School").[35]

In the end, the significance of the discussions canvassed in this chapter lies not perhaps in their "scholarly" contributions to academic aesthetics but in the insight that they provide into the dynamics of Soviet philosophy once it could start moving beyond the pale of Stalinist orthodoxy (cf. Świderski 1993a, b). In fact, questions left dangling during the period circa 1956–1963 prompted the development of a range of research issues more or less centered on man, notably ethics and value theory (Vasilii Tugarinov, Oleg Drobnitski, Oleg Dzioev, and Genrikh Batishchev) as well as historical-cultural theory associated with the concept of activity (Evald Ilyenkov and Felix Mikhailov) and drawing on social and developmental psychological theory (Lev Vygotsky, Alexei Leontiev, and Sergei Rubinstein)—themes repressed or absent during high

Stalinism.[36] To assert that the aesthetics discussion, and in particular young Marx's anthropocentrism, influenced such developments directly goes beyond the evidence, but I suggest that they owe more than a little to the spirit of those initial encounters with young Marx.

NOTES

1. 1931: the condemnation of the "mechanists" and Deborinists alike; 1938: Stalin's chapter "On Dialectical and Historical Materialism" in the *History of the Communist Party (Short course)*; 1947: Zhdanov's intervention in discussions on the history of philosophy; 1950: Stalin's letters on linguistics; 1956: Khrushchev's secret speech condemning Stalin, the start of the liberalization known as the "thaw," including the publication of the first Russian edition of Marx's early writings; 1987: the decision to drop the label "Marxist" and "Marxist-Leninist" from the names of disciplines in the human and social sciences in the Soviet Union; 1991: in December, the dissolution of the USSR and the Communist Party of the Soviet Union (CPSU).

2. In my conversation years ago on this subject with the sociologist-philosopher Yuri Davydov, he declared that it was the translation of Lukács' book on the young Hegel that stimulated interest in the early Marx. That suggests a line from Lifshits to Lukács to Ilyenkov, and beyond. I found no clear link to the aesthetics discussion, however.

3. The reference here is to Lenin's 1908 polemical tract, *Materialism and Empiriocriticism.*

4. The reference here is to the history of the party, promulgated by Stalin, under the title *Istoriia Vsesoiuznoi Kommunisticheskoi Partii (Bol'shevikov): Kratkii Kurs*, 1938, translated as *History of the Communist Party of the Soviet Union (Bolsheviks): Short Course*, 1939. It was translated into virtually all languages and continually republished until Krushchev denounced Stalin in 1956.

5. Of the numerous studies that have retraced this line of development, I single out Kołakowski (1978–1979). It should not be concluded, however, that thereafter Soviet philosophy became a dogmatic wasteland (a view to which Kołakowski is prone). One example of a more nuanced approach to the real state of philosophy following Stalin's incursion is Batygin and Deviatko 1994.

6. Among the earliest voices critical of Engels was that of Stanisław Brzozowski, a Pole, who in 1910 published a text, written earlier, entitled "Anti-Engels." Cf. Walicki 1989.

7. There is a paucity of Western literature on the subject. Cf. Yanowitch 1967.

8. "Soviet aesthetics" refers here to aesthetics conducted by Marxist-Leninist philosophers as of the mid-1950s. Whether luminaries such as Bakhtin and the members of the later Tartu semiotic-structuralist school do or do not fit into this picture is not a question pursued here. The case of Losev is perhaps more ambiguous: he did take a position on the debates canvassed in this chapter (see below).

9. The basic principles of socialist realist aesthetics—*narodnost', klassovost',* and *partiinost'*—were distilled from a variety of sources, including Belinsky, Herzen, Dobrolyubov—the "revolutionary democrats"—as well as Lenin, together with thoughts from the likes of Rousseau, Schiller, and Hegel, even though the latter

710   E. M. ŚWIDERSKI

fell short of the "correct" view. A useful presentation has been and remains C. Vaughan James 1973.

10. What is meant is not aesthetics as a philosophical discipline but the nature of the aesthetic, as in the query: "*Chto takoe esteticheskoe*?" ("What is the aesthetic?"). The corresponding German substantive is *das Ästhetische*. It is a meta-category ranging over all the items within the purview of aesthetics.

11. As the debate got under way among Soviet philosophers, interest in the "young Marx" came to prominence in Poland and later in other socialist states, an interest that turned "revisionist" and was condemned as such by the Party authorities. Leading names here included Leszek Kołakowski and Bronisław Baczko. More about this in the last section.

12. The abridged version of the work was translated into English and published under the title *The Philosophy of Art of Karl Marx* in 1938 (New York: Critics Group). It was republished in 1973 (London: Pluto Press).

13. See Marx and Engels 1933. The same edition expanded to two volumes was published in 1957, 1967, 1976, and 1983.

14. A personality with a long and controversial career in the Soviet Union (including a close relationship with Lukács and a period during which he was out of the public eye having been banned from publishing), Lifshits is held in high esteem among Russians today, especially those who, like him, abhor "modernism." Recent research on Lifshits includes an issue of *Studies in East European Thought*: "Lifshits: An Enigmatic Marxist," edited by A. Maidansky and V. Oittinen (Volume 68, Issue 4, December 2016). Included is an interview with Gutov.

15. Ermolaev 1963; Robin 1987. An entirely different account of socialist realism is offered in Dobrenko 2007 and Groys 1992.

16. Robert Tucker (1961) argued that Marx's original vision amounted to the transformation of economics into aesthetics, with communism as the reign of the free creative human being. In a wide-ranging review of the aesthetic views of Marx and Engels, Stefan Morawski (1970) contested this interpretation. James Scanlan (1976) threw cold water on the entire matter. However, there is more than a hint of the general aesthetic tenor of Marx's thinking in the article Aleksei Losev prepared for the fifth volume of the *Filosofskaia enciklopediia* (Losev 1975). Finally, in the preface Terry Eagleton wrote for the second English edition (1973) of Lifshits' book, he underscores how central aesthetic matters were for Marx, without however going so far as Tucker (and perhaps Losev).

17. For thorough but differing discussions of this critical episode in the formation of Soviet philosophy, cf. Bakhurst 1991; and Kołakowski 1978, vol. 3.

18. Following the publication of his Marx study, Lifshits was active in renouncing "vulgar sociologism" to the benefit of realism, with Lenin very much at the forefront. In addition to his Marx study, the Critics Group in New York published in the same year, 1938, a short volume of his entitled *Literature and Marxism*.

19. Kant's paradigm of "beauty" is natural beauty. Cf. Scruton 2007 who digs out some of the motivation at the heart of a Kantian-style aesthetic.

20. Leading "societalists" were: L.N. Stolovich, V.V. Vanslov, Yu. Borev, A. Burov, and S.S. Gol'dentrikht; the "naturists" were represented by, among others, N.A. Dmitrieva, V.S. Kornienko, G.N. Pospelov, and I.B. Astakhov.

32 THE YOUNG MARX AND THE TRIBULATIONS OF SOVIET MARXIST-LENINIST... 711

21. Research on the theme in Western Sovietological literature has been sparse. The only extant book-length monograph is by the present writer. See Świderski 1979a and 1979b. A brief but finely written survey is in James Scanlan's chapter on Soviet aesthetics in Scanlan 1985. An initial report on the rising "*estetiches-koe*" discussion came from John Fizer. See Fizer 1974. An extensive Polish treatment of the discussion is Morawski 1964.
22. Though terms such as "realism" and "antirealism" with respect to aesthetic attributions were largely absent in the Soviet literature at that time, much of the debate focussed on this question.
23. References to his 1933 study on the Marxist aesthetic are present in the writings of the "societalists," though confined to footnotes. I have come across passages in which his writings are so closely paraphrased as to be virtually indistinguishable from the original, due credit however having been withheld.
24. The foregoing reconstruction implements terminology borrowed from John Searle's work (Searle 1995) on social ontology—institutional facts are ontologically subjective but epistemologically objective. A conception of this kind, ranging widely over Marx's writings, was present among Western Marxists and their East European revisionist counterparts (e.g., Kołakowski who wrote of Marx's "social subjectivism"). An elegant statement of a "Western Marxist" is by Alfred Schmidt (Schmidt 1971). Carol Gould's work (Gould 1978) offers another, Aristotelian, optic on the question.
25. Ideas of this sort were to reappear by the mid-1960s in Soviet theory among proponents of the "cultural-historical approach" to human reality (partly under the influence of Lev Vygotsky) as well as the closely related "activity theory" of which Evald Ilyenkov became a prominent proponent. The rise of value theory (the father of which in Soviet philosophy was V.P. Tugarinov) occasioned yet another controversy about the foundations of Soviet philosophy. Oleg G. Drobnitski discounted axiology in favor of a "transformationist" conception of human labor that amounted to a "compromise" between the earlier views of the naturists and the societalists (Drobnitski 1967, the last chapter of which raises the question of the status of aesthetic properties).
26. Lenin opines, "The sole 'property' of matter [...] is the property of being an objective reality, of existing outside the mind." More to point here: "Matter is that which, acting upon our sense organs, produces sensation."
27. A pointed presentation of the fundamental opposition—between Marx and Engels, in fact—is Kołakowski 1978(b).
28. "Just as music alone awakens in man the sense of music and just as the most beautiful music has *no* sense for the unmusical ear—is no object for it, because *my object can only be confirmation of my essential powers and can therefore only be so for me as my essential power is present for itself as a subjective capacity*, because the sense of an object for me goes only so far as my senses go" (Tucker 1979, 74; italics mine).
29. The example, from L. Stolovich, is cited by Scanlan, op. cit., p. 302.
30. If I may interject a comment: missing entirely in the discussion at this time was any idea of intentionality, that is, the aesthetic *meaning* at the core of the "aesthetic relation." This lack is explained by the incessant need to focus on "realism," be it "natural" or "socially subjective."
31. The reference is to Burov, A.I., *Estetika: problemy i spory. Metodologicheskie osnovy diskussii v estetike.* M., 1975, 23–24. Scanlan quotes another critic of this

conception—Avner Zis—for whom it is but a version of the idea put forward by, among others, Alexander Bogdanov in the 1920s: the aesthetic is tantamount to "life-building" [*zhiznestroenie*].

32. GAkhN, the standard abbreviation for Gosudarstvennaia academia khudozhestvennych nauk (The State Academy of Artistic Sciences) that was founded in 1921 and disbanded in 1930. For a time, it was directed by the philosopher Gustav Shpet, a Husserlian hermeneuticist sympathetic to Russian religious philosophy. He was executed in 1937.

33. For an overview of the state of the discussion in aesthetics today, see Petrovsky and Volodina (2014).

34. https://www.artsy.net/show/garage-museum-of-contemporary-art-if-our-soup-can-could-speak-mikhail-lifshitz-and-the-soviet-sixties

35. Current Russian historians of Soviet philosophy include Lifshits as a pivotal figure. Cf. Mareev 2008.

36. This is but a partial listing of developments starting prior to Brezhnev's renewed assault on innovative thinking. The period is known as the period of the "men of the sixties"—*shestidesiatniki*.

Bibliography

Batygin, Gennady, and Inna Deviatko. 1994. The Soviet Philosophical Community and Power: Some Episodes from the Late Forties. *Studies in East European Thought* 46: 223–245.

Bakhurst, David. 1991. *Consciousness and Revolution in Soviet Philosophy: From the Bolsheviks to Eval'd Il'enkov*. Cambridge, UK: Cambridge University Press.

Burov, Aleksandr I. 1956. *Esteticheskaia sushchnost' iskusstva*. Moscow: Iskusstvo.

Dobrenko, Evgeny. 2007. *Political Economy of Socialist Realism*. New Haven, CT: Yale University Press.

Dimitrieva, Nina A. 1960. *O prekrasnom*. Moscow: Iskusstvo.

Drobnitski, Oleg G. 1967. *Mir ozhivshikh predmetov. Problema tsennosti i marksistskaia filosofiia*. Moscow: Politizdat.

Egorov, Anatoly G. 1959. *Iskusstvo i obshchestvennaia zhizn'*. Moscow: Sovetskii pisatel'.

Ermolaev, Herman. 1963. *Soviet Literary Theories, 1917-1934: The Genesis of Socialist Realism*. Berkeley, CA: University of California Press.

Fizer, John. 1974. The Theory of Objective Beauty in Soviet Aesthetics. *Studies in Soviet Thought* 4: 102–114.

Gould, Carol. 1978. *Marx's Social Ontology: Individuality and Community in Marx's Theory of Social Reality*. Cambridge, MA: MIT Press.

Groys, Boris. 1992. *The Total Art of Stalinism*. Princeton, NJ: Princeton University Press.

History of the Communist Party of the Soviet Union (Bolsheviks): Short Course. (Authors not named.) 1939. Moscow: OGIZ-Gosizdat

James, C. Vaughan. 1973. *Soviet Socialist Realism: Origins and Theory*. London and Basingstoke: Macmillan.

Kołakowski, Leszek. 1978. Le marxisme de Marx, le marxisme d'Engels. In *Leszek Kołakowski. L'esprit révolutionnaire, suivi de Marxisme: utopie et anti-utopie*, 133–157. Paris: PUF.

———. 1978-1979. *Main Currents of Marxism—The Golden Age—The Breakdown*. Oxford: Oxford University Press.

Lenin, Vladimir. 1967. *Materialism and Empirio-criticism*. Moscow: Progress.

Lifshits, Mikhail. 1933. *Karl Marks i Fridrich Engels ob iskusstve*. Moscow: Sovetskaia literatura. (The English version is Lifshits 1938/1973.)

———. 1973. *The Philosophy of Art of Karl Marx*. London: Pluto Press Ltd.

Losev, Alexei. 1975. Aesthetics. In *Themes in Soviet Marxist Philosophy. Selected Articles from the Philosophical Encyclopaedia*, Ed. and trans. T.J. Blakeley, 200-219. Dordrecht: D. Reidel.

Maidansky, Andrey, and Vesa Oittinen, eds. 2016. Lifshits: An Enigmatic Marxist. *Studies in East European Thought* 68 (4): 1.

Mareev, Sergei N. 2008. *Iz Istorii Sovetskoj Filosofii: Lukach—Vygotsky—Il'enkov*. Moscow: Kul'turnaia revoliutsiia.

Marx, Karl, and Friedrich Engels. 1933. *Ob iskusstve*. Moscow: Sovetskaia literatura.

———. 1956. *Iz rannykh proizvedenii*. Moscow: Progress.

Morawski, Stefan. 1964. *Między tradycją a wizją przyszłości*. Warszawa: KiW.

———. 1970. The Aesthetic Views of Marx and Engels. *The Journal of Aesthetics and Art Criticism* 28 (3): 301–314.

Petrovsky, Alexandra, and Valentina Volodina. 2014. Aesthetics in Russia: Looking Toward the Twenty-first Century. *Studies in East European Thought* 66 (3-4): 165–179.

Robin, Régine. 1987. *Le réalisme socialiste: une esthétique impossible*. Paris: Payot.

Scanlan, James. 1976. The Impossibility of a Uniquely Authentic Marxist Aesthetics. *The British Journal of Aesthetics* 16 (2): 128–136.

———. 1985. *Marxism in the USSR. A Critical Survey of Current Soviet Thought*. Ithaca, NY and London: Cornell University Press.

Scruton, Roger. 2007. In Search of the Aesthetic. *British Journal of Aesthetics* 47 (3): 232–250.

Tucker, Robert. 1961. *Philosophy and Myth in Karl Marx*. Cambridge, UK: Cambridge University Press.

———, ed. 1979. *The Marx-Engels Reader*. New York: Norton.

Schmidt, Alfred. 1971. *The Concept of Nature in Marx*. London: NLB.

Searle, John. 1995. *The Construction of Social Reality*. London/New York: The Free Press.

Stolovich, Leonid. 1961. Problema ob'ekta esteticheskogo otnosheniia. *Filosofskie nauki* 4: 164–172.

Świderski, Edward M. 1979a. *The Philosophical Foundations of Soviet Aesthetics: Theories and Controversies in the Post-war Years. Sovietica 42*. Dordrecht: D. Reidel.

———. 1979b. Options for a Marxist-Leninist Aesthetics. *Studies in Soviet Thought* 20 (2): 127–143.

———. 1993a. From Social Subject to the 'Person'. The Belated Transformation in Latter-Day Soviet Philosophy. *Philosophy of the Social Sciences* 23 (4): 199–227.

———. 1993b. The Crisis of Continuity in Post-Soviet Russian Philosophy. In *Philosophy and Political Change in Eastern Europe*, ed. Barry Smith, 135–164. Lasalle, IL: The Hegeler Institute. (Series: "The Monist Library of Philosophy.").

Vanslov, Viktor V. 1957. *Problema prekrasnogo*. Moscow: Politizdat.

Walicki, Andrzej. 1989. *Stanisław Brzozowski and the Polish Beginnings of "Western Marxism."*. Oxford: Clarendon.

Yanowitch, Murry. 1967. Alienation and the Young Marx in Soviet Thought. *Slavic Review* 26 (1): 29–53.

CHAPTER 33

Mikhail Sholokhov, Andrei Platonov, and Varlam Shalamov: The Road to Hell in Twentieth-Century Russian Literature

Sergei A. Nikolsky

By radical turns, the Russian twentieth century created several new conditions for its historical-philosophical understanding. However, in Russia, there has yet to be a concerted scholarly effort in this direction. In the Soviet Union, one reason for this was the major prevalence of Marxist theory in the social sciences. Although Marxist philosophy of history (a materialistic framework) provided a form of the philosophy of history, its role as the only legitimate theory of society excluded other historical-philosophical concepts. Only in the last three decades have Russian philosophers been given the opportunity to go beyond the limits established by the adherents of Marxism.[1]

The philosophy of Russian history of the Leninist-Stalinist period (1917–1953) cannot be considered without a philosophical and artistic analysis of public consciousness and the self-consciousness of the people and the state—the makers of history. In order to answer the historical-philosophical question concerning the patterns and spiritual-moral meaning of the historical process, it is necessary (in addition to sources) to turn to the philosophy of art. Having selected the main works of three seminal Russian authors of this period, I will focus on a singular set of concepts written in different genres—the epic documentary of Mikhail Sholokhov (1905–1984), the realistic phantasmagoria of Andrei Platonov (1899–1951), and the witness genre of Varlam Shalamov

---

S. A. Nikolsky (✉)
Department of Philosophy of Culture at the Institute of Philosophy, Russian Academy of Sciences, Moscow, Russia

© The Author(s), under exclusive license to Springer Nature 715
Switzerland AG 2021
M. F. Bykova et al. (eds.), *The Palgrave Handbook of Russian Thought*,
https://doi.org/10.1007/978-3-030-62982-3_33

(1907–1982). What historical patterns did they identify? What spiritual-moral meanings did they observe? How did they reflect these observations in their work?

During the first years of the October Revolution, many thinkers recognized the goal of "storming the heavens" and the inevitable but necessary deaths that would occur so that paradise could be established on earth (Nikolsky 2017), which produced unprecedented victims and the destruction of the foundations of human existence. Previously unthinkable human conditions became the norm. Commenting on this state of affairs, Shalamov wrote, "all human feelings of love, friendship, envy, compassion, mercy, ambition, and honesty left us."

What caused this catastrophe that enraptured so many different people—people who were forced into this paradise, those who dreamed of a bright future, and those who were not only ready to force others, but also ready to sacrifice themselves? What changed in the world and in the people? No less significant is the question: What historical background produced the slogans of the October Revolution, among which were peace, the abolition of autocracy, and the fair distribution of property? I will begin my analysis with this big question, while acknowledging the fact that the presented ideas apply to more than just the past. Without them, one cannot understand the nature of contemporary Russian society, which has yet to comprehend all that has occurred in the previous century.

As a scholarly investigation of the past, an essential feature of the philosophy of history (as opposed to history per se) is its inherent futurological aspect. By analyzing the past, the philosophy of history seeks to provide a picture of the desired future. Its main subject—humanity's place in the historical process—includes an analysis of the past, the present, and the desired future. Since the understanding of humanity in all three spheres must inevitably be indicated by value, the result is value laden.

THE PHILOSOPHY OF RUSSIAN HISTORY AND THE CONSTANTS OF SOCIAL CONSCIOUSNESS

The revolutionary-democratic impulse of the February Revolution and its successor—the dictatorial October Revolution—only ostensibly violated the continuity of the times and spurred the construction of the "world from the beginning." With a more discrete view of Russian history, not only the two revolutions of 1917, but the entire revolutionary process of 1905–1922 can be understood as marking another (unsuccessful) attempt to change the foundations and conditions of Russian life. In the philosophy of Russian history, I have identified three constants: empire, autocracy, and property/propertilessness.[2] According to my conception, these constants are used to organize the functioning of society; they constitute the core of tradition and are repeated throughout history. They are also mental structures of individual and public consciousness that build (or limit) the directives of economic, socio-political, and cultural development, and make possible the emergence of individual or collective actors that are appropriate to them.[3]

Since the second half of the sixteenth century, from the reign of Ivan IV, the Terrible, to the present day, Russian history can be adequately described in terms of these constants. They help us understand the phenomenon of Leninism-Stalinism, which was the background for the works of Sholokhov, Platonov, and Shalamov. This analysis shows that the Russian empire—first in the form of the Russian Federation and later the Soviet Union (1922–1991)—continued its former existence and, following the outcome of the Second World War, not only expanded but reached its apex; this also applies to the force and quality of the imperial consciousness of the Russian population. The idea of an international USSR was deeply rooted in public consciousness and was the product of, if not world revolution (hopes for which disappeared by the mid-1930s), then the inevitable military victory of the USSR over the most powerful countries in the world.

In the USSR, the constant of autocracy was developed even more than in tsarist Russia. Autocracy as a form and method of government was theoretically formulated by Sergei Uvarov in his 1833 Triad, "Orthodoxy, Autocracy, and Nationality," which argued for the sacred unity of the Tsar (consecrated by God) and his subjects (Khomiakov 1983). Under Stalin, the unity of the Soviet people with their "teacher and leader" became synonymous with the unity and power of the state.[4]

The constant of property/propertilessness arguably evolved the most. According to Vasilii Kliuchevskii, Ivan the Terrible's philosophy of autocracy can be reduced to a simple formula: "We are free to reward our servants and to execute them."[5] During Stalin's rule, this formula was implemented on a colossal scale. According to the major Russian historian O.V. Khlevniuk, from 1922 to 1953 Stalin's repression caused the deaths of up to 60 million people.[6] This is an average of two million per year, which includes up to a million people who were shot, imprisoned, or exiled. No less than half the adult Soviet population was deprived not merely of property but of self-ownership (i.e., life and activity). In 1921–1922, 1931–1932, and 1946–1947, from 11 to 13 million people died of hunger, over a million of whom died as a result of collectivization and evictions. Also, although official classified reports put the number of executed prisoners from 1930 to 1952 at approximately 800,000, "the number of people actually liquidated was much greater, since torture was widely used in Stalin's state security agencies, and the camps were periodically turned into mass extermination operations" (Khlevniuk 2015, 67). This scale was never achieved by Russia's most ruthless rulers, Ivan the Terrible and Peter the Great, nor was it approached by the initiators and organizers of the seventeenth-century church schism, which led to the mass resettlement and death of the Old Believers.

718 S. A. NIKOLSKY

Mikhail Sholokhov, Andrei Platonov, and Varlam Shalamov as the Creators of the Philosophy of Russian History

What unites these authors and why should we consider them the creators of the philosophy of Russian history?

One important similarity is the scale and philosophical nature of the problems they raise. Thus, the imperial nature of Russia (implied by Sholokhov) is exposed in *And Quiet Flows the Don*. This nature is revealed in the very phenomenon of the Cossacks as a service class. As a unique part of society, in accordance with the historical reality of the novel, the Cossacks are the vanguard and protective apparatus of the empire. Due to imperial expansion, the best southern lands were given to the Cossacks as a reward for their conquests and their protection, which was the basis of their power and success. Their consciousness organically includes the idea of their territory as a self-contained political, economic, and social system that is closed to the outside world. They are conscious of their special mission and the sacred nature of their leader as both a Cossack and a Russian ataman. Citizenship is secondary to nationality (state-ownership trumps self-ownership), and its economic, political, legal, and cultural foundations are canceled if they contradict the nationality of the ataman and sovereign. (These characteristics of Cossack imperialism mirror the Russian imperialism I identified in my book, *Empire and Culture* [*Imperiia i kul'tura*] [Nikolsky 2017, 9–10].)

In his main work, Andrei Platonov depicted Russian imperialism and the imperialist quality of individual and public consciousness through the prism of the Cossacks. Platonov's heroes are metaphorical, which elevates them to the level of philosophical analysis and abstraction. The hero of *The Foundation Pit*—the all-Russian wanderer and truth seeker, Voshchev—is a perpetual asker of questions and a tireless observer of existence. He is surrounded by the diggers (the builders of a common proletarian house) and the peasants (the eternal transformers of the world). Similar to the real historical explorers, they roam the boundless Russian "desert of ice" and dig wherever the authorities indicate. In the novel, even the hammer-wielding bear is presented as an eternal, natural Russian principle, a partner and confederate of humanity.[7] In Platonov's novel, *Chevengur*, Bolsheviks wander in search of the town of Chevengur and are consumed by the idea of imperial world domination (universal Communism). These are the warrior Kopenkin, who dreams of reaching the German grave of Rosa Luxembourg, and the proletarian intellectual Sasha Dvanov, who searches for new life at the bottom of a lake. Since Communism will inevitably saturate all the lands of Earth, the Bolsheviks send the peasant-kulaks down a river that runs into the borders of other lands or send them even further (to the other world) by shooting them in the yard of the collective farm.

In Platonov's world, the ubiquitous Autocrat is visible and invisible. He is in the letter home written by William Perry—an English engineer invited by Peter the Great to work in Russia.[8] He is in the imperious speeches that pour from the loudspeakers installed in the barracks. He is in the nightly directives sent to the collective farms explaining how to speed up dekulakization.[9] He is in the vigilant stoicism of the old woman Federatovna[10] and in the revolutionary dreams of Kopenkin.[11] He exists as a corporeal person and as an abstract idea. Even when Chestnova skydives or descends below ground to a subway construction site, the image of the father-leader is always with her.[12] With rare exceptions, all of Platonov's heroes are deprived not only of property but of self-ownership. All are commanded by an external and implacable will. When the heroes temporarily gain self-ownership, this external will kills them.[13]

The unrestricted right of one person to kill another (based on abstract ideas and revolutionary authority) is magnified in Platonov's depiction of Stalinism. In Sholokhov's war stories, one person kills another because the other belongs to an outside group. In Platonov's work, people kill each other because their beliefs about the world and themselves are incompatible.

Shalamov's gulag narratives operate on the same scale and cover both the terrestrial space of the USSR and the mental space of the human mind. More than 20 million people were exiled and imprisoned in Stalin's camps. This is close to the population of an average European country (e.g., the 17 million inhabitants of Holland). The lives of these prisoners are the subject of Shalamov's work. Of course, the study of prisoner consciousness and that of the people around them is not determined by any single discipline to which philosophers of Russian history may turn. As for historical depth, Shalamov's work is grounded in pre-Soviet Russia and extends into the post-Stalin period.

What Does a Philosopher Do When Working with a Philosophical Literary Text?

How does an author create the worldviews of his heroes? What does he reveal to the reader? In the work, we deal with impressions and representations on the basis of which we discover (master) the author's ideas, or use the composition of images to produce our own impressions. According to M.M. Bakhtin, the authorial word is an expression of "axiological activity that penetrates the content and transforms it. Thus, when I read or listen to a poetic work, I do not leave it outside myself as the utterance of another, which I merely need to hear and whose meaning [...] I merely need to understand; instead, it becomes my own statement about another [...]" (Bakhtin 1975, 58–59). The contemporary scholars S.S. Neretina and A.P. Ogurtsov concretize Bakhtin's position regarding another's speech: "any utterance (unit of speech) is, in fact, aimed at provoking an answer or question from the person who hears the statement. It is the boundary of a distinct utterance." To produce this kind of speech, "it is necessary to become immersed simultaneously in the text and one's own depths, one's self-consciousness, that is, not to think about culture, but to think and live within a culture" (Neretina and Ogurtsov 2000, 253). When we immerse ourselves in the philosophical artistic text, we are changed and transformed. "To understand, isn't it [...] to overcome something essential in ourselves?" (Gefter 1995, 14).

The classic author (unlike the society writer, the journalist, the historian-chronicler, or the historian-researcher, i.e., unlike other kinds of registrars of reality) creates images that are universal, characteristic, and representative. The author is distinguished not only by what he *gives* via artistic images, but also by what he *withholds*. On the basis of what is necessary or what we already know (e.g., because it could not be otherwise), we can judge what he considers important. These properties of literature function according to the desired future. Even if a literary work is neither utopian nor anti-utopian, it reveals its futurological properties, but in a different, original way. The author of a philosophical artistic text gives us his idea of what should remain in the past—he acts as a futurological negativist. In the philosophy of history, the author's subjective fantasy is valuable and the philosopher-scholar of literature should be thoroughly familiar with the subject to understand what the author considers primary and secondary, what he emphasizes and downplays, and what important content he leaves undeclared.

The literary philosopher works with the author's ideas and consciously transcends their limits. If possible, she understands and recreates the author's personal worldview and the general worldview of his contemporaries. Semyon Frank wrote about how this undeclared text might be comprehended: "The national spirit exists as a real concrete spiritual essence and [...] by investigating its manifestation in art we can nevertheless understand and sympathetically comprehend its internal tendencies and distinctions" (Frank 1996, 163). And in his study of the philosophical content of Anton Chekhov's work, Sergei Bulgakov proposed a method for analyzing the seemingly strange worldviews of Chekov's heroes: "summarize the thoughts and impressions invoked by these works" (Bulgakov 1996, 592).

Sholokhov's *And Quiet Flows the Don* is built around the main ideological foundation of the hero, Grigorii Melekhov, who personifies a certain *type, community, and people*. "I'm not leaving the farm," Grigorii tells Aksin'ia, and by implication, he tells this to the whole world.[14] Why? What makes him follow this internal command? And where does the command come from? It acts as an inexorable force that ultimately drives him toward death, although back on his native soil. In Kant's "Idea for a Universal History with a Cosmopolitan Aim," he writes:

> Here there is no other way out for the philosopher—who, regarding human beings and their play in the large, cannot at all presuppose any rational *aim of theirs*—than to try whether he can discover an *aim in nature* in this nonsensical course of things human, from which aim a history in accordance with a determinate plan of nature might nevertheless be possible. (Kant 2009, 11; Kant 1966, 6: 5–6)

Let us assume that there exists something external to and more powerful than human will, similar to what Kant calls the "plan of nature." In the context of the novel, could this external will be something like Kant's plan of nature? M.K. Petrov provides a possible answer:

Each society at every historical moment is characterized by the totality of its practical relations with the world (technology)—this is a "technological matrix." [...] This is not an unusual proposition: at any moment of historical development, society must satisfy its aggregate demand by actively appropriating material from the environment, and this aggregate demand has always been entered into one or another final list of the means of appropriation, practical relations to the environment, which, in fact, constitutes the "world" or "cosmos" of a given society. (Petrov 1995, 67)

The substantive-practical relation of the Cossacks to the world (as it existed and was portrayed by Sholokhov) constitutes a unique universe comprising the worldviews of its inhabitants and their specific mode of relations with other worlds. With respect to the individual, this world operates according to a kind of Kantian natural aim. The tragedy of the novel's heroes, however, is produced by a different external force that seeks to replace their traditional way of life with haphazard Bolshevik reformation.

The world of the Cossacks existed on certain contractual terms as part of the Russian imperial whole. Thus, when the Bolsheviks began to transform and break down the former empire, they inevitably ran up against the Cossacks. Their prominent economic and living conditions (compared with the rest of Russia) became the target of Bolshevik efforts to equalize the Cossacks with other subjects of the new state. When this proved too difficult, the Bolsheviks sought to eradicate them. The following is a striking example from "The Trade Commissar," an early Sholokhov story published in 1925.

While out on a food requisition assignment, a young Cossack wanders into his native village where he encounters his father:

"So you're with the Reds now, son?"
"That's right father."
"I see," he said looking away.
For a moment, they were silent.
"Look father, we haven't seen each other for six years, but what is there to say?"
The old man wrinkled his nose in an irritated gesture.
"Almost nothing. We've drawn different lots. They want to shoot me for what is mine, for not letting them into my barn. I'm a counter-revolutionary, but the thieves ransacking other people's coffers are law abiding citizens? So rob me, it's your right."
The skin that stretched over the trade commissar's sharp cheekbones went gray.
"We don't rob poor peasants, but mow down those who profited from them. All your life, you've squeezed every last drop from your workers!"

"I've worked day and night my entire life. I didn't waste my time drifting god knows where like you!"

"Those who work side with the power of the workers and the peasants, but you met us with a club [...] Didn't even let anyone past the fence [...] For that you'll be shot!" (Sholokhov 1975a, 247)

Sholokhov's falsehood was as evident to his contemporaries as it is to us today. Food requisitions were the result of the First World War, but also the Bolsheviks' attempt to launch a quick transition to Communism without "intermediary links" (Lenin), and the civil war they instigated in the villages (Nikolsky 1990), which was not met with sympathy or support. Food was never given away voluntarily, and special armed detachments (up to 50,000) had to confiscate it by force. The tragedy was that both sides were right—the side that collected food for urban residents and workers and the side that owned the food and did not want to give it away. However, there was more to this historical dispute. The Bolsheviks strove to destroy not only the Cossacks' economic practices, but also their way of life. Sholokhov portrayed this in several of his works, including the love story between Grigorii and Aksin'ia in *And Quiet Flows the Don*.

Aksin'ia follows Grigorii without hesitation and is ready to die. She is inspired by her lover's rootedness in being. Grigorii is inspired by his experience—his senseless murder of an unarmed Austrian and witnessing the rape of a Polish girl by a regiment of Cossacks. However, his ideology is usually manifest indirectly, impulsively, and through intermediary associations. This is his spontaneous and shameful fear of the Red Army who have the power to shoot anyone on a whim and his fear upon visiting the Cheka's politburo. This also includes his sense of powerlessness when confronted with the chaotic force of the civil war. Sholokhov's hero is deeply human, fated to die, and, therefore, tragic. Unlike the Bolshevik hero, who is adamant and resolute,[15] Grigorii vacillates between the Reds and the Whites. What is the author saying with this wavering and luckless hero?

For obvious reasons, the author's judgments and conclusions are not openly revealed. However, a good author has many ways of communicating his beliefs to the reader, and this includes Sholokhov's ideas concerning the road to Stalin's hell laid by the Communists and Leninists.

The main clashes that expose the worldviews of the heroes occur against the background of the post-revolutionary civil war. Here, the author shows us his worldview, as well as his attitude toward his characters. Sholokhov's unhesitating Bolsheviks possess little not only in material terms, but also in terms of human dignity. In an unsympathetic and acrimonious light, Sholokhov portrays certain indolent day laborers (who are rare among the Cossacks), such as the "slobbering" Valet with his "hedgehog face" that goes "smoky and woolly" in times of danger, or the cowardly and duplicitous Davydka.

Similar insights can be gained from characters who are accidental or completely alien to the Cossacks, such as the revolutionary agitator Osip Shtokman, whom Sholokhov describes ironically: "Shtokman was central and stubbornly moved toward a single goal known to him alone. He drilled simple thoughts and ideas like a wood-boring insect, instilling disgust and hatred for the existing system. Initially, he was met with the cool steel of distrust, but he did not falter and gnawed through it" (Sholokhov 2011, 99).

How are we to react to descriptions like "drilled like a wood-boring insect," "gnawed through steel," and "instilled disgust"? Or that he alone knew the goal unknown to others? Are such qualities and actions evidence of a dignified character deserving respect? In his description of Shtokman's conversation with the Cossacks, Sholokhov consciously uses the language of propaganda clichés, which he went on to develop in the novel *Virgin Soil Upturned*, especially in the self-righteous party speeches of Makar Nagul'nov and Semyon Davydov.

The past social environment of Sholokhov's heroes determines their new role. After the death of his comrades, Mishka Koshevoi (a former day laborer turned Red Army revolutionary) takes merciless revenge against everything he condemns to death in his "revolutionary consciousness" (Sholokhov 1975b, 98):[16]

He no longer stopped to think or listen to the faint voice of pity when a captured Cossack insurgent fell into his hands. He had no compassion for any of them. With eyes as blue and cold as ice he would look at the man and ask, "Did you fight against the government?" and without waiting for an answer, without looking at the prisoner's death-shadowed face, he wielded his sabre. He wielded it ruthlessly. And not only did he wield the sabre, he also sent the "red cock" under the roofs of the houses in the villages abandoned by the insurgents. And when the fear-maddened bullocks and cows broke through the fences of the burning farmyards and charged out into the street, Mishka shot them down pointblank with his rifle.

He waged an implacable, ruthless war upon Cossack affluence, Cossack treachery, upon the whole inviolable and stagnant way of life that had endured for centuries beneath the roofs of the solid Cossack houses. His hatred was fed by the death of Shtokman and Ivan Alekseevich and the words of the order were no more than a vivid expression of what Mishka felt but did not know how to tell. That day he and three of his comrades burned about a hundred and fifty farmsteads in Karginskaia. Somewhere in the storeroom of a merchant's shop he found a can of kerosene and went round the square with a box of matches in his grimy fist, and behind him acrid smoke and flame rose from the smart weather-boarded and painted merchants' and priest' houses, the roomy dwellings of the well-to-do Cossacks, and all those whose scheming instigated the ignorant Cossack masses to rebel. (Sholokhov 1996, 962–963; Sholokhov 1975b, 398)

On the Cossack side, the figure of Mishka is mirrored by Natalia's brother, Mit'ka Korshunov. When Sholokhov introduces Mit'ka, he uses several

724   S. A. NIKOLSKY

negative epithets: "His brazen yellow eyes protruded from two slender slits. His pupils were feline and narrow, which gave his gaze a fluid, elusive quality" (Sholokhov 1975b, 19). While working for the White Army, Mit'ka exercises his natural talent for cruelty:

> When the punitive troops had no right to shoot an arrested person but did not want to let him go alive, he would be sentenced to corporal punishment and Mit'ka would be entrusted with carrying out the sentence. He would perform the task with such zeal that after fifty strokes the victim would begin to vomit blood and after a hundred could safely be wrapped in sackcloth without even listening for his heartbeat. No man thus sentenced had yet been known to survive Mit'ka's ministrations. He himself would say with a chuckle, "If I took all the trousers and skirts off the Reds I've got rid of, I could clothe the whole village of Tatarskii!" (Sholokhov 1996, 1045–1046)

To convey his own worldview, Sholokhov juxtaposes the disparate actions of different characters. Melekhov enters the Cossack occupied Tatarsk to save Koshevoi and Ivan Alekseevich, while Koshevoi returns to Tatarsk and kills Grishka (an irascible but unarmed old man) before burning the Korshunov's home. Or consider the senseless brutality of the Reds who capture the Listnitskii estate, kill a colt, and then kill an old man they accuse of harboring the animal for his Polish masters.

Sholokhov's judgment of the two opposing sides is unequivocal: both are murderous. However, they are distinguished by their conception of the future. If Grigorii (and with him Sholokhov) wants to correct the past without indiscriminate destruction, the Bolsheviks and lower-class Cossacks strive for complete annihilation. What happens as a result? The relentless Soviet program exterminates the Don Cossacks. Grigorii's desire of working the earth goes unfulfilled, but Koshevoi's Bolshevik dream of violently restoring "order" became a reality.

In the Melekhov family, few are left to experience this order. Of the nine members, only Grigorii, his son Mishatka, and his sister Duniashka (who married Koshevoi) are left alive, and Grigorii dies soon after. "He was standing at the gate of his own home and holding his son in his arms. This was all he had left, all that still made him kin with the earth and with the whole huge world around him, glittering under the cold sun" (Sholokhov 1975, 958; translation: Sholokhov 1996, 1335). Before him looms the Bolshevik Koshevoi and the pervasive network of the Cheka that had spread across the Don.

The tragedy of Grigorii Melekhov, and the Cossacks as a special social group, is that he is destroyed, because he is incommensurate with the social body of the Bolsheviks, the new hierarchy of a new world created by a new state. Russia's enormous, gray, faceless mass of hungry peasants, half-savage Kalmyks, militant sailors, and ideological fanatics outweighs everything that Grigorii personifies. His personality is manifest in his independent character, independent love, and independent life; and in this calamitous environment, his self-ownership is targeted and destroyed. His fate is connected to the tragic dismantling of the old world and way of life, which the old regime slowly undid with its historical incompetence and unnecessary war, and the new regime hastened with its incomparably bloodier reformation. Thus, the novel judges both the decrepit autocracy and the violent Soviet system that replaced it. Like Platonov and Shalamov, Sholokhov depicted the first steps on the road to hell and showed that there was no going back.

Sholokhov, Platonov, and Shalamov are the three most profound philosopher-artists of the Leninist-Stalinist epoch; however, Sholokhov is unique. Platonov and Shalamov are unwavering and unambiguous in their depiction and philosophical analysis of the Bolsheviks' ideas and actions. Sholokhov is not. Here, I am referring to his second major work of the 1930s, *Virgin Soil Upturned*. If *And Quiet Flows the Don* is characterized by epic realism, then *Virgin Soil Upturned* was praised by Stalin as a paragon of socialist realism. It is an artistic attempt to argue for the political necessity of collectivization and to conceal the real tragedy of the Don region.

There are many complex reasons behind this shift away from a truthful and deep representation of reality. The Bolshevik-friendly text may have been a way of befriending Soviet power in order to receive hard-to-get help and to save his countrymen from starvation. In other words, it was a pragmatic reaction to the violence and murder of collectivization. He no doubt understood the difficulty of this task. Stalin called Melekhov a "renegade" and direct "enemy" of Soviet power. This reprimand had its desired effect. Sholokhov completed *Virgin Soil Upturned* and became a favorite of Stalin.

In 1932, at the height of the famine and collectivization, he sent a letter to Stalin detailing the methods of collectivization:

> At the Vashaevskii collective farm, the female farmers' feet and skirts were dowsed with kerosene, lit on fire, and then extinguished: "Tell us where you are hiding the grain [...]" Collective farmers are stripped bare and locked in a barn or shed during January and February [...] At the Lebiazhenskii farm, farmers were put to the wall while shotgun shells were fired over their heads [...] At the Zatonskii farm, a propagandist used a sabre to interrogate the farmers. At the same farm, Red Army families were mocked, roofs and stoves were broken, and women were forced into cohabitation [...] At the Solontsevskii farm, a human corpse was brought into the commission building and laid on the table. The farmers were questioned in the same room and threatened with execution. (Osipov 2005, 170–171)

In the same letter, Sholokhov wrote that a collective farmer who met his quota received 400 grams of bread per workday which he had to share with his family, while a worker who did not meet his quota received 200 grams. (For comparison, Shalamov later reported that a prisoner who met his quota in the Kolymsky camp received 1 kilogram, while one who did not meet his quota received 500 grams.)

726   S. A. NIKOLSKY

"If everything I have described," concludes Sholokhov, "deserves the attention of the Central Committee, send to the Veshensky District additional Communists who have the courage to expose without prejudice all those who are fatally wrecking the collective farm economy, who will investigate and root out not only those who used the abominable 'methods' of torture, beatings, and abuse, but also those who encouraged them" (Osipov 2005, 172).

The final words of this letter support the idea that *Virgin Soil Upturned* was written to save the farmers: "I have decided that it is better to write you this in a letter than to write it in my final book, *Virgin Soil Upturned*" (Osipov 2005, 172-173).

Thus, Sholokhov cannot be blamed for covering up the methods of collectivization. In light of the letter's addressee (the initiator and organizer of collectivization), it was impossible to write any other way, while attempting to save his countrymen and his family. Thus, he lied. Moreover, he wisely defined his obligatory role as the Soviet writer/regime-chronicler who worked with the state—"better to write you than include it in my book." This verges on blackmail. This is a courageous act.

Recognizing a man who is ready for anything, Stalin appreciated his desperate courage, took heed, and responded. He initially ordered half the grain needed to stop the famine. When Sholokhov responded "Not enough!" Stalin sent more. In a note to Molotov, Stalin wrote, "This matter has apparently become 'public,' and after such a mess, we can only win politically. A few extra 40-50 thousand poods mean nothing to us" (Osipov 2005, 174). Soon after, the following editorial appeared in *Pravda*, "The Idea That Millions of Soviet Citizens Are Starving in the Volga, Ukraine, and North Caucasus Is Vulgar Slander, a Dirty Smear Campaign" (Osipov 2005, 177).

Today, we might think that Sholokhov's duplicity undermines his reputation as an honest writer and philosopher. However, if he had not sacrificed his reputation, hundreds and even thousands of people would have lost their lives.

"...MY HEART HAS DRIED UP AND MY MIND IS FADING."
—ANDREI PLATONOV

The strength of Sholokhov's epic style is determined, among other things, by the fact that in *And Quiet Flows the Don* it is historically, geographically, and sociologically concrete. Every turn of the plot and every image in the novel has a historical basis. Andrei Platonov's prose philosophically rises above geography, history, and sociology. We see the picture on a grand scale, and although we recognize that the fantasies are mutated versions of reality and that some of the heroes (like the hammer bearing bear who participates in dekulakization) are completely invented, this fantastic world coheres and we believe the author. In the context of history, our faith in Sholokhov's epic realism and Platonov's realistic phantasmagoria leads to the conviction that the two authors are complementary.

Like Sholokhov, Platonov uses the epic form, but in his own way. Platonov's *The Locks of Epifan* opens with the letter of William Perry written to his brother Bertrand, a British engineer: "How remarkable are the wonders of nature, my dear brother Bertrand! The mystery of space is so profound that it is incomprehensible even to the noblest heart! I have lived for four years in the backwoods, and my heart has dried up, and my mind is fading." The Russian Tsar, Peter I, wants to build a channel connecting the Don and Oka rivers, "in order to overcome the vast expanses of the continent and gain access to India, the Mediterranean kingdoms, and Europe" (Platonov 2011d, 86).[17] The work is done by swarms of peasants who either flee (to settle the new territories of the empire) or perish by the thousands. As with the Cossacks, we are presented with the constants of empire, autocracy, and property/propertilessness. The ownership of one group turns others into the property of another.

We encounter these constants of Russian history in Platonov's *The Foundation Pit*. In the novel, propertiless peasants live in straw huts. Cut off from the world, they build a new life; however, their future consists of the coffins they have carefully prepared. The only hope resides with the diggers. However, even though they "knew the meaning of life, which is tantamount to eternal happiness, their faces were sullen and thin, and instead of peace they possessed exhaustion" (Platonov 2011a, 420). Not even the meaning of life can provide them with the strength to live. What is this meaning?

By constructing his philosophy of Russian history in *The Foundation Pit*, Platonov surpasses Sholokhov. While the latter proceeds from historical events as a given, Platonov asks the fundamental question: why did the whole world turn upside down?

This question is presented in different ways as the novel progresses. It arises in connection with the global activities of power, which unites all universal labor without a clear goal; it is connected with the unproductive communes that consume the abandoned resources of the landowners or the resources of the state; and it relates to the destruction of different social groups—the urban bourgeoisie, the intelligentsia, and the prosperous peasantry. It continuously emerges from the text, but is not explicitly formulated by the author. The headpiece of the "revolutionary preserve" is symbolic—a medieval knight's helmet with a red star in the center.

Had the savagery returned or had it never left? Though never articulated, the question is constantly in the background. It is indicated by the frenetic, yet monotonous and meaningless, action of the novel. The foundation pit is being dug for "a single building for the entire local class of the proletariat, while the small single-family houses will remain empty and in them the faint-hearted people of forgotten time will stop breathing." However, what exactly is this building? "Having eliminated the old, natural structure, Chilikin could not understand it." He eliminates without understanding. What for? Voshchev complains: "I'm ashamed to live without truth," and Chilikin consoles him, "We all live in empty space." But why, in the absence of truth, should one be consoled by fact that everyone lives like this? Here is an idea about the future:

"Everything is boring—abolish it, then we will establish life and rest" (Platonov 2011a, 426). But what do "abolish" and "rest" mean in this context?

The time that could be attributed to this anticipated "rest" is represented by Platonov in his unfinished novel *Happy Moscow*: the action takes place in the second half of the 1930s. His heroine, Moskva [Moscow] Chestnova, is a product of the new state. She lives and is brought up in a government orphanage and school. Her curiosity and ebullient energy reveal not only the space of the Soviet country, but also its sky and the earth beneath its capital. She is surrounded by scientists, philosophers, pilots, economic theorists, and, in general, all who can be thought of as the engineers and creators of the brilliant present and future. But Moskva does not understand why

> people cling to the cooperative, to the office, to letters of reference, to the local needs of a fleeting happiness. Why do they exhaust themselves with empty trivialities, when the city had world-class theaters, while there were still so many enigmas to be solved in life, and when, no farther than the main door, a fiddler, unheard by anyone, was playing splendid music? (Platonov 2011c, 27–28)

In the character of Moscow, we recognize Voshchev—a philosopher of earlier times whose questions about the creation of the world remained unanswered.

In *The Foundation Pit*, the source of hope should be the forward-thinking engineer, Prushevsky:

> It was he who had thought up a single all-proletarian home in place of the old town where to this day people lived by fencing themselves off into households; in a year's time the entire local class of the proletariat would leave the petty-proprietorial town and take possession for life of this monumental home. And after ten or twenty years another engineer would construct a tower in the middle of the world, and the laborers of the entire terrestrial globe would be settled there for a happy eternity. (Platonov 2012, 19; Platonov 2011a, 428)

However, confusion about the meaning of life and doubt about its necessity exacerbate this cultural citizen: "Could a superstructure develop from any base? Was the soul within man an inevitable by-product of vital material?" (ibid., 428–429).

Prushevsky's questions remain unanswered and he even decides to kill himself, while Voshchev, reflecting on the lack of meaning in current life, consoles himself with the thought that there will come a time "when everything will become known and placed inside a simple sense of happiness." However, his peace of mind is short-lived. The victim of imperialism, the ugly and disabled Zhachev, reprimands him, stating that Voshchev's desire is "insane, since hostile propertied forces were once more originating and blocking off the light of life; what mattered was to preserve the children—the tenderness of the Revolution—and leave them a testament" (ibid., 449). Does this mean that the meaning of life is to lie down on the ground, believing that the bright future will arrive of its own accord?

Along with these implicit issues, we should note the main preoccupation of Platonov's heroes: the earth. But this is not the earth that yields crops and supports life. Platonov's earth is hard, consisting of clay and rocks (slabs). It has to be broken with a crowbar or cut with an ax. In *The Foundation Pit*, the earth is a solid dense mass that resists human labor. Although it yields slightly to the diggers, it takes revenge by sapping their strength. It does man's bidding only when it protects the hidden coffins of the peasants.

It should be noted that Shalamov's characters are likewise confronted with an unyielding earth, to which is added hostile -50°C weather. After working in air so cold that saliva freezes in midair, a person is ruined after two to three weeks or simply dies.

In general, the earth carries a great semantic load in artistic philosophical work. This is the original, first principle, the last reason for everything, "mother—raw earth." In Platonov's texts, the earth is hostile to man not only because of its nature, but because it is a response to humanity's use of it. Hence, the Chevengurians do not work the earth and do not take care of it. They grow nothing. They do not plow or sow. They scoff at the earth. To "reorganize life in a new way," they drag their houses from place to place and dig up their gardens to plant them elsewhere. Platonov's earth is a symbol of humanity's frenzied labor and death. Chilikin covers the room of Nastya's dead mother with dirt. He digs Nastya's final home in the ground, covering the pit with a slab so that the girl can finally have a place of her own. Earlier in the novel, the little girl lived in the diggers' barracks and slept in a coffin borrowed from the peasants, while keeping her toys in another coffin.

In the Russian worldview, the earth is synonymous with life and death. In Ivan Turgenev's work, it is the fields, meadows, and forests of *A Sportsman's Sketches*. In Leo Tolstoy's work, it is the dugouts and trenches that protect the soldiers in *Sevastopol Stories*, but it is also synonymous with death, as in Tolstoy's "Three Deaths," where a noblewoman falls fatally ill. The woman dies resenting the whole world—deaf to both God and nature: "Her chest was tight and raw; and in the sky, fields, road everything remained gray and deadened. The same monotonous autumn haze poured over the mud of the road" (Tolstoy 1979, 63). Mud covers hands, clothes, porches, wheels, and thoughts themselves. On a page describing her impending death, the word "mud" appears five times.

What are Platonov's diggers doing? Why are they so close to death? Images of earth and death represent Platonov's multifaceted worldview in *The Foundation Pit*. As in Sholokhov, this worldview refers to real historical events, especially collectivization. This tragedy is conveyed to us through pictures of universal suicide and murder. The people most invested in the colossal event, endowing the senseless enterprise with meaning, are its organizers—the powers that be. To guide local activists, they continuously send directives to the villages.

However, the mass delusion was also sustained at the grassroots level by people who had been alienated in their former lives. These lower classes are no less determined and decisive: "'It is high time we put an end to these happy parasites,' said Safronov. 'We no longer feel the heat of the fire of class struggle, but this fire must burn: where else will the active personnel warm themselves!'" (Platonov 2011a, 468–469).

Who are these "active personnel"? The activists? The party? Comrade Stalin? The famous 25,000 communist workers sent to the village to create collective farms, including Liubushka Davydov from *Virgin Soil Upturned*?

The Foundation Pit was Platonov's answer to Sholokhov—the paragon of the Soviet author. What is Platonov's relation to the new world, the "imaginary realm" as he called it? One answer is presented by the central figure of *The Foundation Pit*: "Voshchev quietly walked into the field and lay down so as not to be seen by anyone, pleased that he was no longer participating in the insane circumstances" (Platonov 2011a, 466).

"ALL THE EXCUSES SOUGHT BY THE BRAIN WERE FALSE AND HOLLOW." —VARLAM SHALAMOV

If Platonov's earth still bears shallow trenches where one can lie down for the night, then Shalamov's post-Platonov earth is utterly malevolent. There is little that does not torture and, ultimately, kill the individual. Shalamov's chief work, *The Kolyma Tales*, is preoccupied with one thing: the variety of ways a person is stripped of their humanity and sense of self.

Of the three constants discussed in this article, Shalamov's primary focus is on the constant of property/propertilessness—the ownership of a person by an external power. Shalamov does not consider it necessary to discuss the nature of autocracy. Autocracy, which in the past represented the sacred unity of the sovereign and his subjects, had degenerated into a perpetual bloody tyranny. Stalin's totalitarian state—the dictatorship of the proletariat—represented neither the proletariat nor the Bolshevik Communists who had pledged their allegiance to it. It was a completely individual dictatorship relying on repressive organizations. The latter pervaded the entire society and were themselves subjected to periodic reprisals in order to prevent the emergence of a rival center of power. The authorities strove to fully utilize the instruments of physical repression against certain social groups in order to achieve the political and military expansionist goals of the Communist Party. To achieve these goals a number of problems had to be solved. To create a powerful and technically equipped military, factory machinery had to be purchased from developed capitalist countries, which necessitated the production of products that could be sold abroad (e.g., grain, gold, timber, etc.) and the support of the factories that had to produce them. This problem was solved using cheap human labor, which was provided by transforming human beings into prisoner-slaves. The lower the cost of maintaining a prisoner, the higher the profit. Shalamov wrote about the lives of these prisoner-slaves and how the dictatorial state owned people while depriving them of their right to self-ownership.

A person living in the camps was reduced to an animalistic, even plantlike state. "A person exists for the same reasons as trees, rocks, and dogs" and to survive "only the animal instinct that had been awakened in the mines could suggest and suggested a way out" (Shalamov 2013, 183). Contemplating his survival, one of Shalamov's heroes reaches the following conclusion: "he would be smarter, and have more faith in his body. His body would not deceive him. He had been deceived by his family, his country. Love, energy, talent—everything had been trampled, broken. All the justifications sought by the brain were false, hollow" (ibid., 183). And further: "Did he think about his family? No. About freedom? No. Did he remember poetry? No. Did he remember the past? No. He lived through a simple, apathetic enmity" (ibid., 187).

Few managed to survive while preserving the remnants of their humanity, although they too often inadvertently resembled primitive life forms. To survive, many knowingly stripped themselves of their humanity. Consider, for example, this chance encounter between Shalamov's hero and a prisoner with whom he had once shared a cell:

> Captain Schneider was a German communist who had been active in the Comintern, spoke beautiful Russian, was an expert on Goethe, and an educated Marxist theoretician. Andreev's memory had preserved conversations with Schneider, intense conversations that took place during the long prison nights. A naturally cheerful person, this former sea captain kept the entire cell in good spirits.
>
> Andreev could not believe his eyes.
>
> "Schneider!"
>
> "What do you want?" the captain turned around. His dull blue eyes showed no recognition of Andreev.
>
> "Schneider!"
>
> "So what do you want? You'll wake up Senechka."
>
> But already the edge of the blanket had been lifted, and the light revealed a pale, unhealthy face.
>
> "Ah, captain," came Senechka's tenor voice with a languid tone. "I can't fall asleep without you..."
>
> "Right away, I'm coming," Schneider said hurriedly.
>
> He climbed up on the shelf, folded back the edge of the blanket, sat down, and put his hand under the blanket to scratch Senechka's heels.
>
> Andreev walked slowly to his place. He had no desire to go on living. Even though this was a trivial event by comparison with that which he had seen and was still destined to witness, he never forgot Captain Schneider. (Shalamov 1994, 189; Shalamov 2013, 188)[18]

People's belongings were confiscated regularly by the authorities. Even beggars, Shalamov observes, have some trifle that belongs only to them, and since this logic applies to prisoners, requisition searches were a common occurrence:

> We had no books, no knives, no felt pens, no newspapers, no paper. What then were they searching for? They took away clothes that many had acquired from the

civilian workers […] Were they preventing escapes? Fulfilling orders? Perhaps, some administrative change had occurred?

Everything was confiscated without reports or records. They simply took away! There was no end to the outrage. I remembered how, two years ago in Magadan, hundreds of thousands of fur coats were confiscated from hundreds of prisoner transports headed to the Far North. These warm coats, sweaters, and expensive suits were meant to be used as bribes when there was nothing left. But this last chance at salvation was ended at the Magadan bathhouse. Mountains of clothes piled in the courtyard, and rose above the water tower and the bathhouse roof. Mountains of warm clothes, mountains of tragedies, mountains of human lives were cut abruptly and sharply—all exited the bathhouse fated to die. Oh, how these people had fought to protect their things from the thieves, from the rampant piracy of the barracks, wagons, and transit cars. Now, everything they had managed to save was confiscated by the state in the bathhouse. How simple! (Shalamov 1994, 234; Shalamov 2013, 313–314)

The story "Esperanto" presents us with an alternative definition of the "world language." It signifies the ubiquitous Soviet phenomenon of the unlimited domination of state power over the individual, and not only the state. This story is followed by "A Piece of Meat," a narrative about the unchallenged power of gangs, which, like the rule of the state, is just as terrible and ruthless. After an appendectomy, the hero is convalescing in a hospital when to his horror he encounters a serial killer:

> It was Kononenko, a criminal who had been in the same transit prison with Golubev several months earlier. A murderer with multiple sentences, he played a prominent role among the camp criminals and had been "braking" for several years in pre-trial prisons. As soon as he was about to be sent off to a forced-labor camp, he would kill someone in the transit prison. He didn't care whom he killed as long as it was not a fellow-criminal. He strangled his victims with a towel. A towel, a regulation-issue towel was his favorite murder instrument, his authorial style. They would arrest him, start up a new case, try him again, and add a new twenty-five-year term to the hundreds of years he already had to serve. After the trial Kononenko would try to be hospitalized to "rest up," and then he would kill again. And everything would begin from the beginning. (Shalamov 1994, 224; Shalamov 2013, 297)

The ownership of things, life, and personhood is a constant that during Stalin's time reached a state rarely seen in Russian history.

Conclusion

The philosophy of Russian history, which began in the sixteenth century and is characterized by the constants of empire, autocracy, and property/propertilessness, found fertile ground in the twentieth century during the Leninist-Stalinist period. Although historians still lack all the sources necessary for a complete picture of the events of 1917–1953, this gap is compensated by the philosophy of art. Mikhail Sholokhov, Andrei Platonov, and Varlam Shalamov provide answers regarding the content, regularities, and spiritual-moral meaning of past historical phenomena that are yet to be fully understood. With their depiction of Russia's descent into hell, they provide us with a clear signal: this path is off limits.

Translated by Peter Golub

Notes

1. In 1990–2010, a number of Russian books were published on the subject. Novikova and Sizemskaya 1999; Panarin 2001; Gulyga 2003; Akhiezer et al. 2005.
2. The term *constants* already exists in historical-philosophical scholarship. See Popkov 2010, where among the constants of the Eurasian world, the author identifies centrality, rhythmic symphonism, and western anthropic drift.
3. For more, see Nikolsky 2017a.
4. In their analysis of the unity of power and the people, Yu. S. Pivovarov and A.I. Fursov talk about the *power-centeredness* of the Russian world (Pivovarov and Fursov 2001).
5. "Zhalovat' svoikh kholopei vol'ny my i kaznit' ikh tozhe." See in Kliuchevskii 2002, 236.
6. In 1937, for instance, the adult population was approximately 100 million.
7. In other books, (e.g., *Juvenile Sea* and *Chevengur*) instead of a bear, it is represented by the steppe wind, underground water, self-sowing wheat, and the sun as natural electricity. Platonov establishes the universal scale of imperial (international) Bolshevik expansion—from a channel that crosses the country ("The Locks of Epifan") to the heights of the stratosphere and the underground metro (*Happy Moscow*).
8. "The Locks of Epifan" (Platonov 2016).
9. *The Foundation Pit* (Platonov 2011a).
10. *Juvenile Sea* (Platonov 2011b).
11. *Chevengur* (Platonov 2011a).
12. *Happy Moscow* (Platonov 2011c).
13. Thus, relying on his own curiosity, Sasha Dvanov's father drowns in the lake. The bachelor dies freely associating with nature, subordinate to and connected with nobody. The inhabitants of Chevengur die propertiless, but, most importantly, without an external will over themselves. The girl's bourgeois mother dies, next to the foundation pit, deprived of all her possessions and rejected by the external imperious will. Nastya dies without ever finding anything of her own in the new world.
14. The novel convinces us that Grigorii Melekhov will also never leave this spot because of his understanding of life and his desire to confirm it precisely in this form and in the context of spreading Bolshevism—to preserve it. His inability to live as he had before is a tragedy.
15. This is evidenced by Sholokhov's *Virgin Soil Upturned*, where the author omits the tragedy he witnessed in his native Veshenskaia, including the human-caused famine of 1932–1933 (Sholokhov 2011).

16. The author also gives an example of Mishka's "revolutionary consciousness" in his conversation with Grigorii's mother, when Koshevoi comes to their house to see Duniashka:

> "Aren't you ashamed to come here, you brazen creature?" she said. "You dare to ask me that? You're a murderer …"

> "How do you make out that I'm a murderer?"

> "Indeed, you are! Who killed Petro? Wasn't it you?"

> "Yes."

> "Well, then! Think what that means! And you come here … and sit down as if …" Ilyinichna broke off choking, but quickly recovered her breath and went on, "Am I his mother or what? How can you look me in the face?"

> Mikhail paled noticeably. (Sholokhov 1996, 1201; Sholokhov 2011, 854)

17. The historical John Perry, on whom Platonov's William Perry is based, was hired by Peter the Great to oversee construction of a canal between the Black and Caspian Seas—Ed.
18. Senechka is one of the owners of the barracks—a thief and racketeer (Shalamov 2013, 188).

BIBLIOGRAPHY

Akhiezer, Alexander S., Igor M. Kliamkin, and Igor G. Yakovenko. 2005. *Istoriia Rossii: konets ili novoe nachalo*. Moscow: Novoe izdatel'stvo.

Bakhtin, Mikhail M. 1975. *Voprosy literatury i estetiki*. Moscow: Khudozhestvennaia literatura.

Bulgakov, Sergei N. 1996. Chekhov As a Thinker. In *Puteshestvie k Chekhovu*. Moscow: Shkola-Press.

Frank, Semyon L. 1996. *Russkoe mirovozzrenie*. St. Petersburg: Nauka.

Gefter, Mikhail Ya. 1995. Pamiat' o gibeli evreev nuzhna Rossii. Uroki Kholokosta i sovremennaia Rossiia. 8-16. In *Materials prepared for an international symposium held in Moscow April 6-8, 1994*. Moscow: Utopos.

Gulyga, Arsenii V. 2003. *Russkaia ideia i ee tvortsy*. Moscow: Eksmo.

Kant, Immanuel. 1966. Ideia vseobshchei istorii vo vsemirno-grazhdanskom plane. In *Sochinenia v 6 tomakh*. Moscow: Mysl'.

———. 2009. Idea for a Universal History with a Cosmopolitan Aim. In *Kant's Idea for a Universal History with a Cosmopolitan Aim*. Trans. Allen Wood. Cambridge, UK: Cambridge University Press.

Khlevnyuk, Oleg V. 2015. *Stalin. Zhizn' odnogo vozhdia [Stalin: the life of one leader]*. Moscow: AST.

Khomiakov, Dmitrii. 1983. *Pravoslavie. Samoderzhavie. Narodnost'*. Montreal: Izdatel'stvo Bratstva prep. Iova Pochaevsky.

Kliuchevskii, Vasilii O. 2002. *Kurs russkoi istorii*, 2 vols. Vol. 1, Lecture XXX. Moscow: ACT.

Neretina, Svetlana S., and Alexander P. Ogurtsov. 2000. *Vremia kul'tury*. St. Petersburg: Izdatel'stvo Russkogo Khristianskogo gumanitarnogo instituta.

Nikolsky, Sergei A. 1990. *Vlast' i zemlia. Khronika utverzhdeniia biurokratii v derevne posle Oktiabria*. Moscow: Agropromizdat.

———. 2017a. The October Revolution and the Constants of Russian Being. *Russian Studies in Philosophy* 55 (5): 177–193.

———. 2017b. *Imperiia i kul'tura. Filosofsko-literaturnoe osmyslenie Oktiabria*. Moscow: Institute of Philosophy, Russian Academy of Sciences.

Novikova, Lidiia N., and Irina N. Sizemskaya. 1999. *Russkaia filosofiia istorii*. Moscow: Apent Press.

Osipov, Valentin. 2005. *Sholokhov*. Moscow: Molodaia gvardiia. (Series: *Zhizn' zamechatel'nykh liudei* [The lives of remarkable people].)

Panarin, Alexander S., ed. 2001. *Filosofiia istorii*. Moscow: Gardiriki.

Petrov, Mikhail K. 1995. *Iskusstvo i nauka. Piraty Egeiskogo moria i lichnost'*. Moscow: ROSSPEN.

Pivovarov, Yuri S., and Alexei I. Fursov. 2001. 'Russkaia sistema' kak popytka ponimaniia russkoi istorii. *Polis* 4: 37–48.

Platonov, Andrei P. 2011a. *Kotlovan. Sochineniia v 8 tomakh*. Vol. 3. Moscow: Vremia.

———. 2011b. *Kotlovan. Iuvenilnoe more: povesti*. Moscow: AST.

———. 2011c. *Schastlivaia Moskva. Sochineniia v 8 tomakh*. Vol. 4. Moscow: Vremia.

———. 2011d. *Epifanskie shliuzy. Sochineniia v 8 tomakh*. Vol. 3. Moscow: Vremia.

Popkov, Yuri V. 2010. *Evraziiskii mir: tsennosti, konstanty, samoorganizatsiia*. Novosibirsk: Nonparel.

Shalamov, Varlam T. 1994. *Kolyma Tales*. Translated by John Glad. New York: Penguin Books.

———. 2013. *Sobranie sochinenie v 6 tomakh + 1 tom*. Moscow: Terra-Knizhnyi klub.

Sholokhov, Mikhail A. 1975a. Prodkommissar. In *Sobranie sochinenii v 8 tomakh*. Vol. 7. Moscow: Pravda.

———. 1975b. *Tikhii Don. In Sobranie sochinenii v 8 tomakh*. Vol. 8. Moscow: Pravda.

———. 1996. *Quiet Flows the Don*. Translated by Robert Daglish. New York, NY: Carroll & Graf Publishers, Inc.

———. 2011. *Podniataia tselina*. Moscow: Eksmo.

Tolstoy, Lev N. 1979. *Sobranie sochinenii v 22 tomakh*. Moscow: Khudozhestvennaia literatura.

CHAPTER 34

Yuri Lotman and the Moscow-Tartu School of Semiotics: Contemporary Epistemic and Social Contexts

Natalia S. Avtonomova

Yuri Mikhailovich Lotman (1922–1993) was arguably the most influential and wide-ranging Soviet scholar of the twentieth century. Trained as a philologist specializing in Russian literary history, over the course of his career Lotman applied his mind to a wide range of disciplines, including literary theory, intellectual history, linguistics, semiotics, history of science, cybernetics, cinema studies, and cultural studies (being in fact one of the pioneers of the latter two fields). He was a co-founder of the Moscow-Tartu school of semiotics which became the most exciting intellectual forum in the Soviet Union in the 1960s and 1970s. This dynamic interdisciplinary milieu richly contributed to the development of Lotman's individuality as a scholar. Therefore, it would be appropriate to begin this chapter with a brief excursus into the history of this school (hereinafter *the School*).

THE SCHOOL: ITS STRUCTURE AND MAIN PRINCIPLES

I would like first to make a comment on terminology. The School has been referred to by different names: Tartu, Moscow-Tartu, Tartu-Moscow, and the Moscow-Tartu/Tartu-Moscow school of semiotics.[1] Its members often referred to their subject as *secondary modeling systems*. This euphemism was invented in an attempt to mask the suspiciousness of semiotics—a science that emerged in the 1950s at the intersection of structural linguistics, cybernetics,

---

N. S. Avtonomova (✉)
Institute of Philosophy, Russian Academy of Sciences, Moscow, Russia

© The Author(s), under exclusive license to Springer Nature
Switzerland AG 2021
M. F. Bykova et al. (eds.), *The Palgrave Handbook of Russian Thought*,
https://doi.org/10.1007/978-3-030-62982-3_34

and information theory (Lotman 1998, 195)—from the eyes of the Soviet authorities. In the jargon of *the School*, "primary signifying system" indicates instances in which language models life, while all others sign systems based on a natural language are secondary (e.g., the languages of myth, ritual, art, prohibition, prescription, etc.). In Soviet Russia, the ideas of structure/structurality (initially applied to structural linguistics) and semiotics were introduced into intellectual discourse (with considerable ideological complication) almost simultaneously in the late 1950s and early 1960s, which is why the range of problems discussed by the School includes the two terms: *structural-semiotic method* and *structural-semiotic studies*. In contrast, western scholars, such as Clifford Geertz or the *Tel Quel* group, used the term "semiotics" to refer to a revolutionary method directed against the structuralism that emerged in the wake of Saussurean linguistics with its conception of language as an inert structure. This terminological distinction can be explained by the fact that Lotman and other members to the School saw themselves as the legatees of Russian Formalism and the Prague Linguistic Circle, who already in the 1920s and 1930s started injecting historicity and dynamism into the notions of linguistic structure and literary form.[2]

In the 1950s and 1960s, the period of the Thaw that witnessed the first attempt to lift the iron curtain, Soviet society was swayed by a hope that science could help solve social and political problems. The advances in physics, information theory, cybernetics, and self-governing systems had a major impact on thought across the academy. At the end of his life, Lotman described the emergence of *the School* as a demand of the time, a task of culture, and at the same time a miracle:

> Dead seasons exist (like Pasternak's dead season), and, suddenly, talented people came on the scene [...] When the Tartu-Moscow school was being created, a whole wave of brilliant people had arrived. Many of whom are no longer with us. Of course, it is not always the case that brilliant opportunities produce brilliant results; it is a complex process. But at that time it was precisely in this sphere that the pulse of culture found its rhythm. (Lotman 2003d, 299)

In terms of the bare historical facts, *the School* originated in the early 1960s as an informal association of linguists, literary scholars, and cultural researchers who took up the study of the structure and functioning of sign systems. There were two groups of researchers who were initially independent of one another. In Moscow, there was a group working with the structural typology of Slavic languages (later the Department of Slavic and Balkan Languages at the Institute of Slavic and Balkan Studies of the USSR Academy of Sciences). In Tartu, there was the Department of Russian Literature at Tartu State University. In Moscow, the interdisciplinary group included not only linguists, but also mathematicians, philosophers, and machine translation specialists. Among its most prominent members were Vyacheslav V. Ivanov, Vladimir N. Toporov, Isaak I. Revzin, Boris A. Uspensky, Alexander K. Zholkovskii, Yuri K. Shcheglov, Alexander

M. Piatigorsky, and Iosif I. Levin.[3] Almost simultaneously, in Tartu, a group of researchers focused on the ideas of the OPOIAZ and worked on St. Petersburg/Leningrad literary history (Yuri M. Lotman, Zara G. Mints, Boris F. Egorov, Alexander I. Chernov, and others).[4] In December 1962, the Moscow group organized "The Symposium on the Structural Study of Sign Systems," which generated endless criticism from high-ranking officials. To avoid further harassment, action had to be transferred to another setting.

The next crucial step in the history of *the School* was made by Lotman. A decorated World War II veteran, this young Tartu University professor (and a star graduate of Leningrad University's Philology Department) established contacts with his Moscow colleagues and organized a summer seminar on secondary modeling systems in Kääriku, Estonia, in August 19–29, 1964.[5] While all discussions revolved around the general issues of semiotics, the Tartu scholars focused more on literary criticism, while the Muscovites focused more on art (e.g., icon painting, music, and primitive art). The main themes were divided into days: modeling systems; models of folklore texts; modeling systems in behavior, ritual, and ceremony; style as sign; art and semiotics; the specificity of poetry. Lotman's own presentation was devoted to "Art in a Variety of Modeling Systems." During the following decade (until 1974), five more summer schools took place in Tartu. In 1964, the proceedings of the summer school seminars began to appear under the aegis of the Tartu State University. In the first issue of *Trudy po znakovym sistemam* [*Works in Sign Systems*], Lotman published his first major work, *Lectures on Structural Poetics* (Lotman 1964).[6] Initially published only in Russian, in 1998 *Trudy* began to come out in three languages: English, Russian, and Estonian. Since 1998 it has been edited by Kalevi Kull, Mikhail Lotman, and Peeter Torop.

The school passed through several periods. At first, the dominant paradigm was the application of linguistic methodology to other cultural objects. Later, the attention shifted away from natural human language to the category of culture, its composition, and the correlation of its parts, including those reducible and those irreducible to linguistic models. Thus, the semiotics of culture emerges as the central concern. At this juncture, the difference between *the School* and some other trends in semiotics (e.g., Polish, French, and American) came to the fore. While the latter movements regarded "culture" as a system of languages or codes accrued by humanity over a long period of time, for the members of the Moscow-Tartu *School* "culture" was a system of dynamic relations that human beings establish with the world, as they try make sense of it. Different languages or semiotic codes were only the means of human meaning-making, and as such were subject to change.

In the mid-1970s and even more so in the 1980s the ideological climate in the Soviet Union became uncongenial to the anti-dogmatic, experimentally minded humanists, pushing many members of *the School* into emigration. This, however, did not signal the end of the Moscow-Tartu adventure. Those who remained (and several who emigrated but continued to regard themselves as members of *the School* in diaspora) continued to develop the projects they had started under the aegis of *the School*: Vyacheslav Ivanov and Vladimir Toporov continued their work on reconstruction of cultural archetypes, Yuri Shcheglov and Alexander Zholkovskii focused on the construction of generative poetics, Eleazar Meletinskii continued his study of folklore plots, while Yuri Lotman and Boris Uspensky focused their energies on the development of the new semiotically informed history of culture.[7]

LOTMAN'S INTELLECTUAL TRAJECTORY: CONSTANTS AND CHANGES

Before going any further, I would like to point out that my understanding of Lotman is in some ways different from the standard contemporary interpretation. Today, it is widely believed that structuralism in the humanities is a thing of the past. Consequently, Lotman is considered relevant only to the extent that he was able to overcome his structuralist phase and in his later works embrace the postmodernist ethos that emphasizes uncertainty and openness. The representatives of this position are so many that I will refrain from listing them all. Suffice it to mention Victor Zhivov, one of the most influential contemporary scholars, who interpreted the earlier Lotman in terms of *scientism* and the later Lotman in terms of post-structuralism, freed from scientistic prejudices (Zhivov 2009).[8] However, as I would argue, it is wrong to describe the early Lotman as a structuralist dogmatist focused on closed and static structures, and it is equally wrong to construe the later Lotman as a decided post-structuralist. An organic thinker who frequently described human intellect as a self-accruing Logos (alluding to Heraclitus of Ephesus' conception of rationality),[9] Lotman always sought ways to broaden his methodological perspective with the help of other methodologies and paradigms. He became the most active organizer and contributor to *the School* because he thrived on dialogue, which enabled him to find new approaches to a set of problems that he began to ponder in his youth, when he was working on his Candidate [*kandidatskaia*] dissertation focused on the ideological and literary strife between two crucial eighteenth-century Enlightenment figures: the radical Alexander Radishchev and the conservative liberal Nikolai Karamzin (1951). The problems of traditional versus innovative worldviews, aristocracy versus democracy, gradualism versus revolutionary change in both culture and society were also at the center of Lotman's attention in his doctoral dissertation, *The Development of Russian Literature of the Pre-Decembrist Period* (1961). Unlike many other dissertations from the same period, Lotman's works were relatively free from the Marxist-Leninist commonplaces[10] and rife in fresh philological insights supported by rigorous archival research. When in the early 1960s structuralist methodology rooted in the ideas of Russian Formalism, whose intellectual legacy has never been completely wiped out, despite the repressions that formalists suffered under Stalinism, made a glorious comeback, Lotman embraced it as a more rigorous and scientifically objective approach to the historical data.

"Literary criticism should be a science" became his new motto (Lotman 1967; Pilshchikov 2012).

At the same time, he never abandoned literary-historical research but continued to expand his philological erudition throughout his life. While in the 1960s–1980s his research agenda broadened to include many fields, not excluding those beyond the humanities, he never lost interest in the eighteenth- and nineteenth-century Russian writers he began to study at the outset of his career. For example, in 1987 he published an intellectual biography of Karamzin, in which he presented this aristocratic enlightener and conservative historian of the Russian State in a wholly new light: as a Stoic and liberal who retreated from contemporary political strife to historical study in order to engage in philosophical self-education and self-fashioning.[11] Recently Andreas Schönle has discussed Lotman's life in similar terms, arguing that at the end of his life the scholar finally built an inner citadel where he could enjoy freedom and happiness.[12] To continue this train of thought, Lotman's Stoicism, just like the Stoicism of Radishchev and Karamzin, was not only a strategy devised to resist encroachments by tyrants and other oppressors, but also a way of reinforcing one's identity as a scholar in a perpetually transforming and unpredictable universe. Like Heraclitus, whom he cites on several occasions,[13] Lotman conceived of humanity in dynamic terms, as a perpetual striving for rational mastery of the world. But given that this world, unlike the Platonic cosmos, had no definite form, in order not to lose oneself in the infinite search for truth one had to cultivate self-mastery. The discovery of structuralism and semiotics provided the thinker with a set of methodological principles that helped to strengthen his scholarly self-consciousness without turning him into a dogmatist. Thus, for Lotman, structuralism and semiotics never replaced historical and philological methodologies, but enabled him to better comprehend these disciplines vis-à-vis other sciences or, to use the semiotic terminology, other meta-languages through which human reason seeks to understand and describe itself.[14]

The most cogent expression of Lotman's ideas at the height of his career, which coincided with the heyday of the Moscow-Tartu *School,* can be found in his essay "On the Semiopshere" (Lotman 1992, 1: 11–24). As Lotman confessed, the notion of the "semiosphere" was coined by analogy with the notions of "biosphere" and "noosphere" proposed in the 1940s by the geo- and biochemist Vladimir Vernadsky (Lotman 1992, 1: 12). This visionary scientist was one of the pioneers of the biochemical approach to geology, which led to the discovery of what is now called the "deep time" of the Earth. Vernadsky's interest in history and philosophy propelled him to apply his knowledge of geological and biological evolution of the Earth to the history of science. Thus, by "noosphere" he meant the new organic layer constituted by rational agents inhabiting the Earth. Vernadsky was the first scientist to warn the world about the self-destructive potential of a contemporary science that has gained control over atomic energy. As a humanist confronted with the nuclear arms race, Lotman rediscovered Vernadsky's idea of the "noosphere" as an intelligible reality that was a result of stochastic processes, and yet lent itself to rational control. He went on to develop his own notion of the "semiosphere" as an organic "universe of the mind" (Lotman 1992, 1: 17). It consists of texts, languages, and other man-made sign-systems (ibid., 1: 13). Some of these individualities were conceived as individual human beings, whereas others were collective individualities, such as tribes and other premodern collectivities. Taking a cue from Vernadsky, Lotman realized that not only human languages and man-made codes were involved in semiosis. Thus, his "semiosphere" is not reducible to the traditional notion of "culture" which opposes itself to "nature," but rather represents a more complex view of meaning-making that involves both the interactions among self-conscious semiotic individualities and those between human consciousness and other layers of nature (both organic and inorganic).[15]

According to Lotman, a "semiosphere" has a center and a periphery (a "boundary" zone where dynamic dialogic encounters with other "semiospheres" occur). Lotman emphasizes that the dialogue occurring on what he calls the semiotic "boundary" is not a simple act of communication that passes a discrete amount of information from one "semiosphere" to another, but a real exchange (Lotman 1992, 1: 18).[16] Depending on their frequency and intensity, these boundary-crossings could either gradually transform the "semiosphere" or provoke an "explosion" which destroys it, causing the emergence of a new "semiosphere" (or "semiospheres").

It is often claimed that Lotman's later research mostly revolved around the question of the processes of explosion.[17] However, a careful reader of his 1992 book *Culture and Explosion* would recognize that Lotman did not disregard gradual processes. Rather, he believed that discontinuous and continuous processes either alternate or coexist (which occurs when different cultural strata develop at different rates). Lotman believed that explosive processes are primarily related to art and science, where true "paradigm shifts" can occur, while predictable processes are related to technology, where, as a rule, we are dealing with expected results. The main area from which Lotman draws his examples of explosion and gradualness and their complex interaction in the history of civilization is Russian literary history. He argues that what to us seems accidental is the result of the interaction of different types of causes. Thus, in *The Bronze Horseman*, the natural regularity of the St. Petersburg floods becomes the embodiment of an irregular, retaliatory element that is opposed to the order of Peter the Great's nation-building project.[18] Lotman's other works on the semiotics of culture juxtapose "binary" and "tertiary" cultural systems. In the culture of the former, axiological self-consciousness is based on rigid oppositions: "self" versus "other," "holy" versus "profane," "heaven" versus "hell," the "old" versus the "new," and so on. In these systems, where the boundary lies right next to the center, change occurs only through a radical reversal of values. "Tertiary" systems, on the other hand, have very wide middle areas. Thus, they make room for negotiation between old and new, foreign and local values. Western European culture has traveled a long path from a binary to a tertiary self-conceptualization, whose first glimpses we find in Dante's *Divine Comedy*.[19] The literature of Old Rus' shows that medieval Russia tended more toward the binary model. Russia's westernization was also an "explosion." The same processes that spanned centuries in Europe occurred in a condensed spatial and temporal form in Russia. It was Lotman's hope, however, that the continued dialogue with the West was gradually transforming Russian cultural self-consciousness and shifting its boundaries further away from the center.

Lotman wrote his last articles in the 1990s, at a time when the country in which he grew up and spent most of his life was collapsing and a new sociopolitical reality was beginning to emerge.[20] After Estonia declared independence, the atmosphere in Tartu and in his home University (the former Russian Imperial Dorpat University, where German had been one of the official languages until the Soviet annexation of Estonia in 1940) began to change. One of the most knowledgeable specialists in Russian and German Enlightenment, Lotman observed these changes with philosophical calm and optimism. He believed that the cataclysmic processes his culture was undergoing differed from the earlier revolutionary upheavals. At the same time, he hoped that the binary opposition of the "old" and the "new" (which in the past made it necessary to rebuild the Russian world from scratch) would, in the future, give way to less disastrous scenarios more aligned with Western culture.

In the last years of his life Lotman recorded a series of lectures on the history of Russian culture that were televised across the former Soviet Union. In these lectures the scholar's prodigious erudition and theoretical sophistication were harnessed to serve public enlightenment. Free from the scientific jargon of the 1960s and 1970s, as well as from Marxist or any other ideological presumptions, the lectures acquaint the audience with their cultural past not as a linear narrative that transmits a Tradition (in Gadamer's sense of the term), but rather as a manifold. The only constant value in Lotman's multi-plot narrative is his own unflinching commitment to his task as a scholar of the humanities conceived as a medium of reflection on the successes and failures of reason.

Two Models of Communication and the Idea of Translation

Studying the connections between the textual and non-textual, the rules of languages and metalanguages, and the means of describing norms and prohibitions, Lotman analyzed the impact of texts on behavior and the formation of the ethical regulators of behavior, such as shame, fear, and honor, and outlined new forms of social semiotics.

He wrote about explosion and eruption with regard to intense scientific creativity (e.g., the Renaissance or the Enlightenment), including the surge of creative energy that marked the early period of the Tartu-Moscow school; he also associated explosion with individual inspiration (e.g., Pushkin), which occurs when maximum receptivity coincides with maximum ability for expression. Nearly all instances of explosion also involve fundamental, gradual processes, which are less explored and more difficult to understand than explosions because they do not entail a dramatic change of qualities and, in some cases, even look like cultural stagnation. If this is the case, can we really talk about radical changes in a program or, rather, shifts in the focus of its research? As a historian of literature, Lotman had from the beginning focused on development, dynamics, and explosion. In his early articles, there are elements that could be interpreted as poststructuralist, but they refer back to distant historical periods. For example, in "On the Semiotic Mechanism of Culture" (co-authored with Boris Uspensky) we read:

> [O]ne can assume that humankind went through a long prehistoric period in which the length of time had no role whatsoever because there was no development, and only at a certain moment was there an *explosion* that gave rise to a *dynamic structure* and laid the foundation for the history of humankind. (Lotman and Uspensky 1993, 341; italics mine)

In this case, Russian culture occupies a special place is Lotman's late research.

In one of his later works, "Theses Toward a Semiotics of Russian Culture," Lotman argues that studying the material of Russian culture in light of the ideas of a dynamic structure "can provide new impetuses for the general methodology and semiotics of culture. The dynamism, instability, and constant internal contradictions of Russian culture make it a historical and theoretical testing ground" (Koshelev 1994, 407). The polygon (repeatedly used by Lotman as an image from the lexicon of the brave artilleryman) is nothing but a field for the experiments and research necessary for work with complex objects:

> [N]ow we will test our instruments on complex, unclear, and very diffuse mechanisms, such as Russian culture. It again acquires a new, general, and scientific meaning due to its quality of remaining itself while becoming something else, due to its non-rigidity and its constant self-perception of existing at the boundary of two worlds. [...] in a general scientific sense this makes this material very difficult and very indicative. (Lotman 2003a, 152)

The point here does not relate to the specific nature of the object as such, but to its position on the boundary, and therefore, we are invited to learn as much as possible about the transitional epochs and the dynamic stages of other cultures when they have yet to become static and when they were (or are) in the process of active semiotic activity.

Let us consider the conceptual unity of explosion and dynamic structure. This will introduce a new epistemological feature of Lotman's conceptual program connected with the introduction of "unpredictability in the field of science," and the interlacing of the random and the nonrandom (Lotman 2003a, 156). We could say that in Lotman's work the structuralist spirit is combined with the poststructuralist intuition. Here structuralism and poststructuralism are not two incompatible methodologies, but different research orientations, different ways of adjusting the scholar's inner tuning fork. Structuralism is looking for order in chaos, and poststructuralism is looking for chaos in order. The systemic and the non-systemic are present in both methodologies, but the emphasis of structuralism is on the systemic, while the emphasis of poststructuralism is on the non-systemic. Ideologically, poststructuralism presupposes a turn away from science, away from seeking truth as value, and toward reliance on feeling, experience, and pleasure; methodologically, it uses a set of techniques that replace structure with history, desire, imagination, and eventfulness. And yet, it seems to me that the point is not to deny these shifts, but to follow the path of Lotman's thinking: he does not abandon structure, but understands it as *open* (on my interpretation; see Avtonomova 2009; 2014) and *dynamic* (on his own interpretation; see Lotman 2003a, 156).

While many students of philology and history of culture continue to value Lotman's virtuoso analyses of concrete literary texts, what is important for philosophers is his presumption of structurality introduced into human existence by the universal principles of linguistic communication. In the scholar's own words: "culture as a generator of structurality creates a social sphere around the human individual, which similarly to the biosphere makes life possible; however, it is not organic, but social" (Lotman and Uspensky 1993, 328). It is precisely this presumption of structurality that "has a powerful organizing effect on the entire range of communicative methods" used by people and society (ibid.).

In one of Lotman's final interviews, Peeter Torop asked him about his current ideas, the fate of *the School*, semiotics, and science. Lotman responded with a biblical parable that Leo Tolstoy often repeated: "The grain that does not perish will not grow or bear fruit." The meaning being that to give life, one must perish; "death is rebirth in a new form that will not survive" (Lotman 2003a, 151). Throughout its existence, *the School* went through different stages of euphoria and incredulity, and now we are "on the verge of complete uncertainty" (Lotman 2003c, 302). However, Lotman also noted that when people say that structure is outdated or semiotics is outdated or the orientation toward mathematical methods is outdated or something else is outdated, "I think, it is not serious. We do not know the next discovery" (Lotman 2003a, 148) and we cannot even imagine how it will illumine everything we are thinking about now.

Lotman believed that semiotics "as a method [...] is greatly transforming and during the process of the evolution of consciousness will change into something that is quite different and unpredictable from its starting point" (Lotman 2003a, 150). Shortly before his death, Lotman wanted to believe that instead of having reached an endpoint, we were on the verge of a new big bang, a new threshold on the other side of which new models would appear founded on a broader scientific basis. As noted above, Lotman put forth the idea that art introduces the issues of uncertainty and unpredictability into the sphere of knowledge in the humanities (with its complex objects), and that, therefore, the overall relation of science and art in the world will somehow change.

Translation and Untranslatability

In the early 1960s, even prior to meeting the Moscow linguists and semioticians, Lotman sought methods for making the history of literature more rigorous and objective, and found these methods in the application of linguistic methodology to objects that were not specifically linguistic (Jakobson 1985). Against the background of Jakobson's model of communication, Lotman (speaking on behalf of *the School*) proposed a different view of the communicative act, one that presumes the plurality of languages:

> If the traditional semiotic process focused on the space of one language and represented a closed model, now, apparently, the time has come for a fundamentally open model. The window of the cultural world is never closed. (Lotman 1994, 416)

According to Lotman, multilingualism is one of the fundamental conceptual premises of the Tartu school. At its base is "the insight that the world cannot have one language and that reality is not described by one language. As a minimum there are many languages. It can even be assumed that this number is *open*" (Lotman 2003b, 288, my italics). The next step in the development of this theme emphasizes the need for plurality and difference: "A system that has one language can be a theoretical model, but it cannot exist in reality. What initially seemed the abundance of nature, its extravagance—that it endowed each with a different appearance, different fate, and different language—turned out to be a necessity" (Lotman 2003b, 288).

Lotman injects into Jakobson's abstract structuralist model—one in which the sender and the receiver use the same code and have the same cultural memory—a genuine historicity. This ultimately leads him to reject the viability of the structuralist notion of a "code." A "code" is equal to itself. Yet it is impossible to understand the mechanisms of human communication without taking into account the interpretive activity, which inevitably transform the "code." "Language is code plus its history" becomes one of the fundamental principles of the Moscow-Tartu *School* of semiotics (Lotman 2010a, 15).

As we delve deeper into these problems, we are confronted with what seem like a number of paradoxical conclusions. First is Lotman's belief that "we require incomprehension as much as comprehension" (Lotman, 2003b, 290). This implies that we require the other as well as ourselves; we require "constant tension in the transition from the comprehensible to the incomprehensible, the ingenious to the insignificant. [...] We need the entire diverse, multilingual world. Multilingual—this is the crux of the matter" (Lotman 2003b, 290). This produces another problem that is fundamentally important in linguistic, cultural, and philosophical terms—the problem of translation and untranslatability (or incomplete translatability). Lotman's analysis of this problem forces us to face the paradox of communication and its mechanisms: the more difficult the communication, the more informative it is; the simpler it is, the more primitive and useless it is.

This insight is related to many other ideas concerning cultural dynamics and the complexity of semiosis discussed by Lotman and other members of *the School*. According to Lotman, incomprehension, and even inadequate translation, can change from something that obstructs comprehension into something that stimulates it, turning it into the engine of meaning-generating mechanisms. In previous work, I referred to this turn of thought as Lotman's *productive untranslatability*—productive precisely because certain instances of cultural misunderstanding are involved in the development of new meanings and new opportunities for culture (Avtonomova 2011, 2013).

Lotman consistently emphasizes the significance of translation for the theory of knowledge (Avtonomova 2008; 2016). He insists that it functions as a basic cultural mechanism and argues that "the very existence of a culture involves the construction of the system, rules for *translating direct experience into the text*" (Lotman and Uspensky 1993, 329, my italics). Furthermore, he insists that collective memory "reveals all the signs of *translation from one language to another*; in this case, into the 'language of culture'" (Lotman and Uspensky 1993, 329, my italics).

LOTMAN IN THE TWENTY-FIRST CENTURY

Today, we still lack a general intellectual history of the key concepts introduced into the humanities in the twentieth century. A century has passed since the publication of Ferdinand de Saussure's *Course of General Linguistics* (1916) or Roman Jakobson's organization of the Moscow linguistic circle (1915). During this time, ideas and concepts have traveled between countries, languages, and cultures—and the concepts of "formalism," "structuralism," and "semiotics" have been extensively borrowed and reinterpreted. A thorough intellectual history that would analyze *the School* and its key ideas and concepts alongside other movements and their concepts still remains to be written. As this history is now being researched and written (e.g., Grishakova and Salupere 2015), I think it would be valuable to reconsider the habitual view of structuralism and its Saussurean model as the only possible alternatives beyond the scope of post-structuralism.[21] Lotman's conception of dynamic structure was built using an alternative, in many ways non-Saussurean, model. He referred to Jakobson and Tynyanov ("late formalists" or "early structuralists") and their manifesto of the Prague Theses of 1928 (Tynyanov and Jakobson 1928), as well as to Jakobson's later works. However, as in the case of translation, Lotman disagrees with Jakobson on many issues.

In the past thirty years the ideas developed by Lotman and *the School* have been extended to a variety of contexts and fields, including visual and cinema studies,[22] neurosemiotics and cognitive science (Andrews 2003; Andrews

2012), bio-semiotics, eco-semiotics, and zoo-semiotics (which constitute major scholarly trends in Estonia). There have also appeared several new studies that attempt to apply Lotman's semiotic and philosophical legacy to political science (Makarychev and Yatsyk 2017). Scholars have also staged speculative encounters between Lotman and authors or fields that he never studied. Thus, we come across books and articles that describe Lotman's "encounters" with Dante and Kipling, Florensky and Fassbinder, Gramsci and Greenblatt, Foucault and de Certeau. The idea of the "semiosphere" is being actively compared with the conceptual constructions of contemporary political philosophers, such as Ernesto Laclau and Chantal Mouff (Selg and Ventsel 2012), Agamben, Badiou, and Rancière (Monticelli 2012; 2016). Of course, in order for these extensions and constructivist interpretations of Lotman's thought to be productive, one should never lose sight of the original. We should continue to read and translate Lotman's works and reflect on his ideas.

Translated by Peter Golub

Notes

1. There are currently no complete bibliographies of this material; Eimermacher provides a reliable bibliography up to 1977 (Eimermacher and Shishkoff 1977); Lotman's works in English are collected in Kull 2011; Kull and Gramigna 2014; another useful source is the fiftieth anniversary issue of *Sign Systems Studies—50 Years of Sign Systems Studies* (2014, 429–434). Useful bibliographic and biographical information is also available at www.ruthenia.ru/lotman/. This page is part of the project *Lotmaniana Tartuensia* created by the non-profit organization MTÜ Ruthenia Ühing with the support of Ruthenia.ru, the publishing house O.G.I. (Moscow), and the Department of Russian Literature and Department of Semiotics at the University of Tartu. The project was founded in 2004.
2. The School never created a general program like that of the mathematicians of the Bourbaki group, who worked in a strict axiomatic manner. Thus, we do not have unambiguous definitions of concepts such as structure, model, sign, sign systems, and semiotics. A good step toward defining these concepts was made in *Materials for a Dictionary of the Tartu-Moscow School of Semiotics* [*Materialy k slovariu tartusko-moskovskoi semioticheskoi shkoly*] (Levchenko and Salupere 1999). In this case, the dictionary entries are constructed from collections of quotations, including terms that were introduced or reinterpreted by the members of the School (Koshelev 1994; Nekliudov 1998; Velmezova 2015).
3. For more details, see Nikolaeva 1997 and Poselyagin 2011.
4. OPOIAZ (1910s–1930s) stands for the Society for the Study of Poetic Language. This was a group of St. Petersburg formalist linguists and literary critics that included Viktor Shklovsky, Boris Eikhenbaum, and Yuri Tynyanov.
5. The seminar took the form of an open forum: there were several scheduled talks, but the majority of the time was spent in informal and inclusive discussions in which novice and expert scholars learned from each other.

34 YURI LOTMAN AND THE MOSCOW-TARTU SCHOOL... 749

6. The first twenty-five issues of *Sign System Studies* [*Trudy po znakovym sistemam*] were published in Russian, and since 1998, an English version of the journal, *Sign Systems Studies*, has been published with Kalevi Kull as editor.

7. In the Soviet Union, *the School* was criticized for being reductionist, mechanical, apolitical, and anti-humanist. In essence, Lotman and the School attempted to eschew official ideology and to develop a scientific approach to the humanities within the limits of what could be clearly and openly formulated at the time, resorting to an abstract and specialized metalanguage. In the post-Soviet era, some Russian and Western critics have ideologized this position. Lotman and *the School* were construed either as embodiments of "Soviet-corporate" consciousness and knowledge (e.g., Podoroga 1996, 89) or, on the contrary, as resistance heroes. Thus, in Lotman's obituary, Kristeva drew a vivid image of the "colony of Tartuants" invisible to New York and Paris, but noticed in the Kremlin (Kristeva 1994, 375). Few contemporary critics are ready to investigate the complex drama of communicating with the authorities in the Soviet era. In fact, Lotman and the School were neither dissidents nor sycophants to Soviet power. In all their endeavors, they constantly moved along the slippery, unstable border separating science and ideology which is fundamental to knowledge in the humanities. In the language of the time, the school aspired to be "at the forefront of the scientific revolution," and this slogan contained a powerful anti-ideological charge, which opposed the dogma of Marxism with scientific knowledge in the humanities. However, the perception of Western critics was different. They were not entirely clear as to how a strategy of emancipation can exist without active politics or how objective scientific research can be ascribed revolutionary potential. See Avtonomova 2001, 121; Landolt 2011; Sériot 2016.

8. I have argued against this position from several angles in Avtonomova 2009, 2014; also Avtonomova 2009a.

9. See, for example, Lotman's essay "Mozg-tekst-kul'tura—iskusstvennyi intellekt," in Lotman 1992, 1: 25–33.

10. On Lotman's fresh and non-dogmatic approach to some of the commonplaces of Marxist theory, see M.L. Gasparov, "Yu. M. Lotman: Nauka i ideologiia," in Lotman 2001, 9–17.

11. For a similar interpretation of Lotman's view of Karamzin, see Andrei Zorin's essay "Lotman's Karamzin and the Late Soviet Liberal Intelligentsia," in Schönle 2006, 208–228.

12. Andreas Schönle, "The Self, Its Bubbles, and Its Illusions," Schönle 2006, 183–207, 211.

13. See footnote 9 above.

14. As Lotman confessed, for him historical and structural semiotic methods were organically interconnected: "Personally, I cannot say exactly where historical description ends and semiotics begins. There is no opposition, no break. For me, these spheres are organically connected. This is important to bear in mind since the semiotic approach began with the negation of historical study. It was necessary to move away from historical research in order to *return* to it. It was necessary to break ties with tradition in order to restore them on a completely different basis" (Koshelev 1994, 296; Frank et al. 2012).

15. Vernadsky's legacy has been analyzed from diverse points of view in Yanshin et al. 2000.

16. Much has been written about Lotman's debt to Bakhtin's conception of dialogue, to which Lotman's conception of "semiotic boundary" bears a resemblance. Bakhtin was read and deeply respected by the School. Moreover, Lotman met him personally in 1970. On the details of this encounter and the Bakhtin-Lotman connection, see Egorov 1999, 243–258

17. Ilya Prigogine and Isabelle Stengers' book *Order Out of Chaos: Man's New Dialogue with Nature* (1984) and Thomas Kuhn's concept of the *paradigm shift* have often been invoked in recent discussions of the meaning of *explosion* in Lotman's later work. However, one should bear in mind that Lotman uses this term as a metaphor, rather than as a precise philosophical concept.

18. Lotman brings up this image most explicitly in "Obrazy prirodnykh stikhii v russkoi literature: Pushkin-Dostoevsky-Blok" (written together with Z.G. Mints). See Lotman 1995, 814–820. However, his other discussions of Peter the Great's epoch and its symbol, the city of Petersburg, allude to the image of the "Bronze Horseman" from this narrative poem as well. See, for example, "Simvolika Peterburga i problemy semiotiki goroda," Lotman 1992, 2: 9–21.

19. In Dante's epic symbolic space is conceived not only as a binary opposition ("top" vs. "bottom"), but also as a continuum that allows the pilgrim to move gradually between the two axiological poles of the world while undergoing an inner growth. Lotman offers a sophisticated and complex discussion of Dante's geometrical and cosmological symbolism in *Zametki o khudozhestvennom prostranstve*, Lotman 1992, 1: 448–463.

20. Lotman's last articles include "Iz'iavlenie Gospodne ili azartnaia igra? Zakonomernoe i sluchainoe v istoricheskom protsesse)"; "Russkaia kult'ura poslepetrovskoi epokhi i khristianskaia traditsiia"; "O russkoi literature klassicheskogo perioda"; "Dve 'Oseni"; "Tezisy k semiotike russkoi kul'tury"; and "Smert' kak problema siuzheta."

21. In my opinion, one of the best descriptions of Lotman as a representative of the structuralist-semiotic paradigm (although atypically represented) is provided in the work of the Polish researcher Bogusław Żyłko (2015).

22. The topic of Lotman's contribution to the development of contemporary cultural study is vast and exceeds the scope of this chapter. For an overview, see Paert 2017 and Burini 2015. In recent years Lotman's ideas have been extensively used by advocates of digital humanities (see Ibrus and Torop 2015).

Bibliography

Alexandrov, Vladimir E. 2000. Biology, Semiosis, and Cultural Difference in Lotman's Semiosphere. *Comparative Literature* 52 (4): 339–362.

Andrews, Edna. 2003. *Conversations with Lotman: Cultural Semiotics in Language, Literature, and Cognition.* Toronto and London: University of Toronto Press.

———. 2012. Lotman and the Epistemic Sciences: The Role of Autocommunication in Language. In *Explosion und Peripherie. Jurij Lotmans Semiotik der kulturellen Dynamik revisited*, ed. Susi K. Frank, Cornelia Ruhe, and Alexander Schmitz, 175–190. Bielefeld: Transcript.

———. 2001. L'héritage de Lotman. *Critique* 57 644–645: 120–132.

———. 2008. *Poznanie i perevod: Opyty filosofii iazyka.* Moscow: ROSSPEN. (2nd ed. revised and enlarged. 2016. Moscow and St. Petersburg: Tsentr gumanitarnykh initsiativ.).

———. 2009; 2014. *Otkrytaia struktura: Jakobson, Bakhtin, Lotman, Gasparov* Moscow: Rosspen; Moscow and St. Petersburg: Tsentr gumanitarnykh initsiativ, 2nd ed. revised and enlarged.

———. 2009a. Lotman, perekhodiashchii v pamiat. In *Yuri Mikhailovich Lotman*, ed. Vladimir K. Kantor, 338–369. Moscow: ROSSPEN.

———. 2011. Problema perevoda v svete idei produktivnoi neperevodimosti (po stranitsam rabot Iu. M. Lotmana). In *Pogranichnye fenomeny kul'tury: Perevod. Dialog. Semiosfera: Materialy Pervykh Lotmanovskikh dnei v Tallinnskom universitete, June 4–7, 2009*, 19–35. Tallinn: Tallinn University Press.

———. 2015. Le Lotman des derniers travaux: à l'arrière, au front ou tout simplement 'en route'. In *L'école sémiotique de Moscou-Tartu /Tartu-Moscou, "Slavica Occitania"*, ed. Ekaterina Velmezova, 40: 311–335. Toulouse.

Burini, Silvia. 2015. Jurij Lotman e le arti: l'originalità coma una forma di corragio. In *Le Muse fanno il girotondo: Jurij Lotman e le arti*, ed. Matteo Bertelé, Angela Bianco, and Alessia Cavallaro, 2–19. Venezia: Foscari.

Egorov, B.F. 1999. *Zhizn' i tvorchestvo Yu. M. Lotmana.* Moscow: Novoe literaturnoe obozrenie.

Eimermacher, Karl, and Serge Shishkoff. 1977. *Subject Bibliography of Soviet Semiotics: the Moscow-Tartu School.* Michigan Slavic Publications. Ann Arbor: University of Michigan Press.

Frank, Susi K., Cornelia Ruhe, and Alexander Schmitz, eds. 2012. *Explosion und Peripherie. Jurij Lotmans Semiotik der kulturellen Dynamik revisited.* Bielefeld: Transcript.

Grishakova, Marina, and Silvi Salupere, eds. 2015. *Theoretical Schools and Circles in the Twentieth-Century Humanities: Literary Theory, History, Philosophy.* New York, London: Routledge.

Ibrus, Indrek, and Peeter Torop. 2015. Remembering and Reinventing Juri Lotman for the Digital Age. *International Journal of Cultural Studies* 18 (1): 3–9.

Jakobson, Roman. 1985. O lingvisticheskikh aspektakh perevoda. In *Izbrannye raboty.* Trans. L.A. Cherniakhovskaia, 361–368. Moscow: Progress.

Koshelev, Aleksei D., ed. 1994. *Lotman i tartusko-moskovskaia semioticheskaia shkola.* Moscow: Gnozis.

Kristeva, Julia. 1994. On Yuri Lotman. *PMLA* 109: 375.

Kull, Kalevi. 2011. Lotman in English. Bibliography. *Sign Systems Studies* 39 (2/4): 343–356.

Kull, Kalevi, and Remo Gramigna. 2014. Juri Lotman in English: Updates to Bibliography. *Sign Systems Studies* 42 (4): 549–552.

Landolt, Emanuel. 2011. Odin nevozmozhnyi dialog vokrug semiotiki: Julia Kristeva-Yuri Lotman. *Novoe literaturnoe obozrenie* 109: 135–150.

Levchenko, Jan S., and Silvi Salupere, eds. 1999. *Materialy k slovariu terminov Tartusko-Moskovskoi semioticheskoi shkoly.* Tartu: Tartuskii universitet.

Lotman, Yuri M. 1964. Lektsii po struktural'noi poetike. (Vvedenie, teoriia stikha). In *Trudy po znakovym sistemam* 1: 1–160. Tartu: Uchenye Zapiski Taruskogo Universiteta.

———. 1967. Literaturovedenie dolzhno byt' naukoi. *Voprosy literatury* 1: 90–100.

———. 1992. *Izbrannye stat'ii v 3-kh tomakh.* Tallinn: Alexandra.

752   N. S. AVTONOMOVA

————. 1994. Tezisy k semiotike russkoi kul'tury. In *Lotman i tartusko-moskovskaia semioticheskaia shkola*, ed. Aleksei D. Koshelev, 407–416. Moscow: Gnozis.

————. 1995. *Pushkin. Biografia pisatelia. Stat'i i zametki 1960–1990. 'Evgenii Onegin'. Kommentarii.* St. Petersburg: Iskusstvo.

————. 1998. Semiotika. In *Kul'turologiia. XX vek. Entsiklopediia*, 194–196. St. Petersburg: Universitetskaia kniga.

————. 2001. *O poetakh i poezii. Analiz poeticheskogo teksta. Stat'i. Issledovaniia. Zametki.* St. Petersburg: Iskusstvo.

————. 2003a. O sud'bakh 'Tartuskoi shkoly.' Interview with Peeter Torop. In *Vospitanie dushi*, ed. L.N. Kiseleva et al., 146–157. St. Petersburg: Iskusstvo-SPb.

————. 2003b. Nam vse neobkhodimo, lishnego v mire net. In *Vospitanie dushi*, ed. L.N. Kiseleva et al., 287–295. St. Petersburg: Iskusstvo-SPb.

————. 2003c. Na poroge nepredskazuemogo. (Poslednee interview Lotmana s L.F. Glushkovskoi 6 iulia 1993 goda). In *Vospitanie dushi*, ed. L.N. Kiseleva et al., 298–306. St. Petersburg: Iskusstvo-SPb.

————. 2003d. *Vospitanie dushi.* St. Petersburg: Iskusstvo-SPb.

————. 2010a. *Semiosfera. Kul'tura i vzryv. Vnutri mysliashchikh mirov. Stat'i. Issledovaniia. Zametki.* St. Petersburg: Iskusstvo-SPb.

————. 2010b. *Nepredskazuemye mekhanizmy kul'tury.* Tallinn: Tallinn University Press.

Lotman, Yuri M., and Boris A. Uspensky. 1993. O Semioticheskom mekhanizme kul'tury. In *Izbrannye Trudy*, 3: 326–344. Tallinn: Aleksandra.

Makarychev, Andrey, and Alexandra Yatsyk. 2017. *Lotman's Cultural Semiotics and the Political.* London: Rowman & Littlefield International.

Monticelli, Daniele. 2012. Self-Description, Dialogue, and Periphery in Lotman's Later Thought. In *Explosion und Peripherie. Jurij Lotmans Semiotik der kulturellen Dynamik revisited*, ed. Susi K. Frank, Cornelia Ruhe, and Alexander Schmitz, 57–78. Bielefeld: Transcript.

————. 2016. Critique of Ideology or/and Analysis of Culture? Barthes and Lotman on Secondary Semiotic Systems. *Sign Systems Studies* 44 (3): 432–451.

Nekliudov, Sergei Yu., ed. 1998. *Moskovsko-tartuskaia semioticheskaia shkola: Istoriia, vospominaniia, razmyshleniia.* Moscow: Iazyki russkoi kul'tury.

Nikolaeva, Tat'iana M., ed. 1997. *Iz rabot moskovskogo semioticheskogo kruga.* Moscow: Iazyki russkoi kul'tury.

Paert, Irina. 2017. Ot sostavitelia rubriki. Antropologiia i fenomenologiia vizual'nosti: semiotika Iu.M. Lotmana i analiz kino: novoe prochtenie. *Novoe literaturnoe obozrenie* 5 (147): 56–58.

Pilshchikov, Igor A. 2012. Nevyshedshaia stat'ia Yu.M. Lotmana 'Strukturalizm v literaturovedenii. *Russkaia literatura* 4: 46–69.

Podoroga, Valerii A. 1996. Vystuplenie v diskussii 'Filosofiia filologii.' Kruglyi stol. *Novoe literaturnoe obozrenie* 17: 45–93.

Poselyagin, Nikolai. 2011. Rannii rossiiskii strukturalizm: 'dolotmanovskii' period. *Novoe literaturnoe obozrenie* 109: 118–134.

Schönle, Andreas, ed. 2006. *Lotman and Cultural Studies: Encounters and Extensions.* Madison, WI: University of Wisconsin Press.

Schönle, Andreas, and Jeremy Shines (eds). 2006. Introduction. In *Lotman and Cultural Studies: Encounters and Extensions*, ed. Andreas Schönle, 3–35. Madison, WI: University of Wisconsin Press.

Selg, Peter, and Andreas Ventsel. 2012. On a Semiotic Theory of Hegemony: Conceptual Foundations and a Brief Sketch for Future Research. In *Explosion und Peripherie. Jurij Lotmans Semiotik der kulturellen Dynamik revisited*, ed. Susi K. Frank, Cornelia Ruhe, and Alexander Schmitz, 41–55. Bielefeld: Transcript.

Sériot, Patrick. 2016. Barthes and Lotman: Ideology vs. Culture. *Sign Systems Studies* 44 (3): 402–414.

Tynyanov, Yuri, and Roman Jakobson. 1928. Problemy izucheniia literatury i iazyka. *Novyi LEF* 12: 35–37.

Velmezova, Ekaterina, ed. 2015. Douze questions à Tatiana Nikolaieva sur l'Ecole sémiotique de Moscou-Tartu (ou de Tartu-Moscou). Entretien avec Tatiana Nikolaieva. In *L'Ecole sémiotique de Moscou-Tartu, Tartu-Moscou: histoire, épistémologie, actualité*. Special issue edited by Ekaterina Velmezova. *Slavica Occitania* 40: 35–38. Toulouse: Université de Toulouse-Le Mirail.

Yanshin, Aleksandr L., Andrei V. Lapo, et al., eds. 2000. *Vernadsky: pro et contra. Antologia literatury o V.I. Vernadskom*. Petersburg: Izdatel'stvo russkogo khristianskogo gumanitarnogo universiteta.

Zhivov, Viktor M. 2009. Moskovsko-tartuskaia semiotika: ee dostizheniia i ee ogranicheniia. *Novoe literaturnoe obozrenie* 98: 11–26.

Żyłko, Bogusław. 2015. Notes on Yuri Lotman's Structuralism. *International Journal of Cultural Studies* 18 (1): 27–42.

CHAPTER 35

Art as an Instrument of Philosophy

Helen Petrovsky

In the eyes of Western readers, Russian philosophy—if indeed such an entity can be conceived of—has always been primarily associated with two basic cultural phenomena: literature and religion. I am tempted to write *Literature* with a capital letter, because since the nineteenth century and throughout a large part of the twentieth, it was an important social force and, in many ways, the actual "place" of philosophy, although no one would deny that philosophy as a discipline in its various guises existed independently as well. It has become commonplace to think of Russian culture as centered on literature [*literaturo-tsentrichnaia*], which has very much to do with the role of the intelligentsia—writers and critically minded scholars—in Russian and Soviet society. But this also has to do with literature's powers in creating a national mythology, at first linked to an imperial state and then to its Soviet successor. At the same time, despite its importance in the construction of a national identity, Russian literature had its various conflicting trends, including those that were marginal and also subversive. Even today, when it has lost its defining character for post-Soviet culture, literature remains a battlefield of sorts and a way of expressing the "emotional ground tone" of the current moment. It is therefore hard to overestimate its role for Russian culture, past and present.

Religious philosophy, on the other hand, is largely a historical phenomenon that dates back to nineteenth- and early twentieth-century Orthodox Christianity and especially its reappraisal by the thinkers of the Russian Silver

---

The original version of the chapter was updated. Correction to this chapter can be found at: https://doi.org/10.1007/978-3-030-62982-3_37

H. Petrovsky (✉)
Department of Aesthetics at the Institute of Philosophy, Russian Academy of Sciences, Moscow, Russia
e-mail: epetrovs@iph.ras.ru

© The Author(s), under exclusive license to Springer Nature
Switzerland AG 2021, corrected publication 2021
M. F. Bykova et al. (eds.), *The Palgrave Handbook of Russian Thought*,
https://doi.org/10.1007/978-3-030-62982-3_35

755

Age. Of course, even in Soviet times, there were religious authors, and some of them managed to openly express their ideas after the demise of the Soviet Union. However, now that Orthodox Christianity has come to replace an essentially atheistic outlook, one can hardly speak of a renaissance of religious thinking. It is not my concern here to shed light on this rather complicated topic. All I want to say is that the two faces of Russian philosophy—one that is turned toward literature and the other toward religion—are perhaps largely intact in the mind of the Western onlooker. In my exposé, I will examine contemporary Russian thought in its relation to art. Art will not be treated as some hiding place for philosophy, as was the case with classic Russian literature. Quite the contrary, it will be seen as an instrument of philosophy and also as that which replaces philosophy itself, offering a new way of thinking. In singling out this palpable tendency in contemporary Russian thought, I am inevitably—and deliberately—omitting other approaches. These could be organized into three main groups: first, there is a study of art within the general framework of culture. This tendency is most notably represented by the works of Alexander Dobrokhotov, for whom culture is endowed with a teleology of its own and, to a certain extent, replaces the concept of Being (Dobrokhotov 2016). Second, art has been analyzed in connection with design and, more generally, a project-oriented approach, which dates back to the Soviet time when it went against the grain of official Soviet ideology. This theoretical position is primarily associated with the name of Oleg Genisaretsky (1994). Third and finally, some Russian scholars display a firm interest in art as part of traditional aesthetics, insisting on a continuity of aesthetic ideas and experience, however transformed they may all be at the moment. This tendency is most clearly seen in the writings of Viktor Bychkov and Nadezhda Mankovskaya, who often engage in joint authorial projects (Bychkov 2015, 8–26; Mankovskaya 2015, 54–71).[1]

In this chapter, I will limit myself to the works of several contemporary scholars whose contribution to the field is significant and/or exemplary. Some still prefer to call this field "aesthetics." However, I hope to show, if only in passing, that even if we keep this designation, referring to a branch of knowledge or a specific type of experience, it will at the very least have to be extended.

Valery Podoroga's Analytical Anthropology

Valery Podoroga, a renowned and original Russian thinker, has developed a method of his own which he calls analytical anthropology.[2] It should be noted, though, that for him this is not so much a formalized methodology as it is an ongoing research project that takes on different shapes and forms. His own definition of the project runs as follows: "Mimesis. The analytical anthropology of literature and art" (Podoroga 2013, 12). This calls for some clarification. Why anthropology? And what exactly does it mean in the context of a profound exploration of one's own culture? I would suggest that this definition emerges at the intersection of philosophical anthropology, particularly the phenomenological ideas of Max Scheler whom Podoroga appreciates very much, and anthropology in the more conventional sense of the study of human societies for which the exemplary model (for Podoroga) would perhaps be Victor Turner or Claude Lévi-Strauss. Podoroga's interest is focused on classic and modern Russian literature of the nineteenth and early twentieth centuries. In describing his specific anthropology, he singles out and comments on the position of the observer who is engaged in the massive operation of reconstructing the inner logic of outstanding literary works. He insists on the position of non-participant—that is, exclusive—observation, by which he means distancing oneself from the literary work in question and at the same time (or rather, thanks to this procedure not unlike phenomenological reduction, i.e., the famous *epoché*) acquiring access to those layers of the literary work that are governed by the writer's instincts and not any one of the existing cultural conventions. The task of the analytical anthropologist, therefore, is to dismantle the object of his or her research and then to put it back together again—in the new (contemporary) time of reading. This is how Podoroga explains the work to be done: "The object of analysis is gradually but radically stripped of its mimetic properties, presenting itself as *it is* prior to any discourse about the world, i.e., freed from the national and imperial myth, from habits of morality and taste" (Podoroga 2017a, 25).[3]

This brings us back to mimesis, the key concept of the whole intellectual undertaking. Indeed, whatever the critical observer is called, in dealing with literature he or she is clearly dealing with what, since ancient times, is generally known as mimesis (imitation, (re)presentation, etc.). Without going into the history of philosophy, let us name at least two writers whose thoughts on mimesis are especially relevant for Podoroga: Erich Auerbach and Paul Ricœur, even though Podoroga is polemical toward their concepts. If one might say that the problem of representing reality is still very much to the point ("Reality remains the necessary condition and goal of observation" [Podoroga 2017a, 13]), an extended understanding of literature as organized human speech split into different linguistic codes calls for an elaboration of the very notion of mimesis. Conscious of Ricœur's three-fold mimesis, Podoroga offers his own tripartite scheme.[4] In doing so, he criticizes the French philosopher for a preunderstanding of mimesis that is based on human action. For Podoroga, human action already carries meaning and is defined accordingly. However, a literary work is not a series of actions that the reader tends to imitate (recalling Aristotle), but a host of meaningless movements (impulses, urges, restraints, etc.). They are understood as a "play of mimetic forces" and are linked to the reader's corporeal, that is, unconscious, activity. "It is not so much we who understand as it is our body that understands (instead of us and before us)," concludes Podoroga (2017a, 17).

In mentioning this body-image that precedes human understanding and that is turned or advances toward Being itself, Podoroga is implicitly referring to Maurice Merleau-Ponty whose phenomenology of the body is an important source for his thinking. Perhaps, it would not be an exaggeration to say that this is the most intriguing and original part of his conception of mimesis. However, before drawing any conclusions, we need to take a closer look at the scheme itself. As I have already said, mimesis is divided into three basic components or levels. Mimesis-I is the zone of contact between a literary work and reality that may well evolve into a conflict. This is where the style of nineteenth-century realism seems to take root. Mimesis-II is defined as inherent to the literary work itself. It is that which accounts for the unique character of the work of art, for its distinct features, indeed for its autonomy and freedom. This is the specific (and closed) reality of the work in question that resists anything outside itself, including its very creator. Finally, mimesis-III regulates the relations between different literary works; it accounts for the influence exerted by the already existing works on a singular work that is still in the making. In an earlier version of this scheme, mimesis-II was defined in terms of "communicative strategies" that the literary work develops in reaction to the outside world by way of appropriating, transforming, and finally, overturning its impact. Here the technique of anthropological analysis is linked to pure observation, devoid of any understanding whatsoever, and is explained in the following way: "The anthropology of seeing, being no artificial device, is the only condition for a *direct* apprehension (prior to interpretation) of the constructive forces of a literary work" (Podoroga 2006, 16).

What then can we make out of this unusual interpretation of mimesis? In Podoroga's reflections, we find a constant polemic against the imperial myth that for him largely accounts for the origins of nineteenth-century classic Russian literature. It is in opposition to this myth that he defines the kind of literature that he himself will be closely analyzing—he terms it "an other literature" or "minor literature," which reminds one of Deleuze and Guattari and their specific approaches to the subject.[5] The imperial myth is inseparable from the literature of the Russian nobility, that is, literature as both institution and norm. No wonder it exemplifies the kind of mimesis that Podoroga plainly wants to contest. Generally speaking, this line of classic literature is marked by a total transparency of language and the creation of various kinds of spatial images (unlike the temporal images that are the hallmark of a minor literature). In one way or another, the imperial tradition is associated with the names of Pushkin, Lermontov, Tolstoy, Turgenev, and Chekhov, to name a few. It is counterpoised by writers such as Dostoevsky and Gogol or, from a more recent period, Bely and Platonov. Indeed, minor literature seems to be charged with the exclusive task of attacking "the dominant realistic illusion, the form of Aristotelian mimesis that allegedly guarantees an adequate rendering of the image of the real and without which narration ('storytelling') is simply impossible" (Podoroga 2017a, 35). But minor literature for Podoroga *is* mimesis par excellence, for it is only by removing ("sublating") our dependence on myth that we are able to reach that level of a literary work where it presents itself as preconceptual Image (*Gestalt*). Preceding the appearance of the work itself, this Image turns out to be the "ultimate condition of mimesis" (Podoroga 2017a, 24).

So, let us repeat: the object of analysis, stripped of its mimetic qualities, is essentially anti-mimetic. If we are still speaking of a literary work (and we most certainly are), then the work itself is redefined in a radical manner. We already know that it is a field of forces that have everything to do with the body and that are therefore beyond the writer's control. Yet they follow a logic of their own, and none other than the analytical anthropologist can discover these subtle connections. This move might appear unexpected or even exotic if we fail to take into account the incredibly rich intellectual heritage of the Russian formalist school. Valery Podoroga follows and develops this tradition. Already in Boris Eikhenbaum and Yuri Tynyanov, we find brilliant analyses of classic Russian literature, addressing the question of how this or that piece of writing "is made."[6] The makeup of a literary work has nothing in common with the author's intentions and/or the reader's expectations; indeed, it is precisely the inner—pre-semantic—logic of the text, the interaction of its signifying elements that explain its "moral," ideology, and the overall impression it produces. Thus, it is impossible to overestimate the role of the so-called *skaz*, the unmediated or improvisational speech in Gogol, creating strong but false psychological effects (Eikhenbaum), as well as of a set of changing masks in his fantastic tale "The Nose," replacing the canonical development of characters (Tynyanov). As we remember, Podoroga is attentive to the construction of a literary work, that is, to the composition of its basic elements or its constitution. And this is where the writer's and reader's Ego, along with understanding and reflection, inevitably come to a halt. What is at stake, instead, is a literary work transformed into a complex "living" form, in other words, that which receives the rather brief denomination of Work proper [*Proizvedenie*]—this time, however, enhanced with a capital letter (Podoroga 2006, 13).

The two volumes of Podoroga's fundamental *Mimesis. Materialy k analiticheskoi antropologii literatury* [Mimesis. Studies in the Analytical Anthropology of Literature] are devoted to the reconstruction of concrete Works or, to put it another way, worlds (Podoroga 2006, 2011). Even if those worlds bear the names of well-known writers (Dostoevsky, Gogol, Bely, Platonov, etc.), they are in no way exhausted by the figure of the writer who succeeds in giving expression to his sentiments and thoughts. Indeed, it is the living form itself that calls for expression that expresses itself *via* this or that writer without the writer being able to encompass—to comprehend—all its transformations and mutations. I would suggest that the living form is that which remains essentially affected by the outside and maintains a constant relation with it, although Podoroga insists on the Work resembling a monad—a metaphor implying its closed and self-sufficient character. And yet, the Work is full of internal energy (the word belongs to Podoroga), and it is the observer—the analytical anthropologist—who manages to appropriate and "tie down" this energy by uncovering (creating) an anthropological matrix or anthropogram. An anthropogram accounts for the "speed of sensual reactions," the movement—unfolding—of writing itself (Podoroga 2017a, 48). It is that which traditional philosophic contemplation or reflection would simply overlook: the realm of the empirical. In Gogol, it is the corporeal image of the "heap" as a specific indication of the energies of dissolution and accumulation; in Dostoevsky, an accelerated time, affecting his characters' physique and provoking the appearance of doubles. In Bely, one is confronted with "explosions" as both a recurring motif in his works and the inner speed of his writing, while in Platonov one discovers a collision, indeed an ongoing war, between machines (standing for depth) and Nature (presented as surface).[7] Finally, the literature of the OBERIU avant-garde collective displays a deceleration of time, leading to the visible disintegration of all organic connections, and this is where occurrence (contingency) boldly steps in. All of those are corporeal images that the reader identifies with upon entering the imaginary space of the Work.

Another important take on the Work (and another influential exploration) is Valery Podoroga's book on the pioneering filmmaker Sergei Eisenstein, *The Second Screen: Sergei Eisenstein and the Cinema of Violence* [*Vtoroi ekran. Sergei Eizenshtein i kinematograf nasiliia*], the first volume of which finally appeared in 2017. This is another continuing project that began with Podoroga's presentation at the inter-university course in Dubrovnik, which he co-directed in October 1990 with the acclaimed American scholar Susan Buck-Morss under the title "Modern Problems of Power and Culture."[8] The 1990s saw a series of exciting lecture courses that marked the progress of this study.[9] The project is indeed ambitious. Podoroga's intention is to offer his reader nothing less than Eisenstein's "psychobiography." The amount of literature on Eisenstein and his oeuvre is colossal. And yet, once again, Podoroga's approach proves to be fresh and innovative. He is interested neither in the genre and its constraints nor in delving exclusively into psychoanalytic theory, the more so in that Eisenstein himself indulged in auto-psychoanalysis during his entire life and produced an astonishing amount of writing (diaries, essays, notes, dossiers, memoirs, etc.) which directly and indirectly corroborates this fact along with his own expertise in the subject. Eisenstein's written archive is close to being boundless and no film scholar can boast of having been able to embrace it. Still, Podoroga demonstrates an admirable knowledge of the various archival sources. However, his task is not an archival or psychoanalytic reconstruction in the traditional sense, but the (re)creation of another Work, namely, "Work-Eisenstein," or (as I would put it) the Work that goes under the name of Eisenstein and yet is not confined to the filmmaker's body of works (Podoroga 2017b, 10, 14 et seq.).

Since we have moved away from literature into the realm of cinema, let us take a moment to follow Podoroga's own elucidation:

> As for the general outline of research, the book project on E. is defined by one specific task, namely, to attempt, to the extent to which my analytic dexterity, will, and knowledge permit me, to recreate a dynamic image of the Work—"Work-Eisenstein." [...] [T]he Work is not a work in the usual sense of the word (collected writings, a book, a textual fragment), that which is produced [*proizvedeno*], created by someone, and which later acquires the author's name and the quality

of some kind of end-product [*proizvedennosti*]. The Work, rather, is an *Opus* or *Deal* (like, for example, the "deal of a lifetime"). The Work is made, produced [*pro-izvoditsia*], but it can never become complete [*proizvedennym*] or actual in the "here and now;" it is neither final product nor Book, but the condition of producing [*pro-izvedeniia*], making, i.e., it is always outside the time in which it seeks possibilities for expression. [...] The Work is not a result, a production [*proizvedennoe*], but the *possibility* of the Work. (Podoroga 2017b, 46–47)

In Eisenstein's case, the Work will be a combination of open series defined by the filmmaker's childhood experience: his father dissolving, indeed exploding, into a set of incompatible and changing fetishes such as small gods, an impotent knight, patent-leather shoes, and bones; his mother oscillating between at least two poles—that of the "phallic mother" and of the mother-womb, a powerful image of plasticity in Eisenstein's own writings. The series in question are nothing other than the living energies of what Podoroga calls "Work-Eisenstein." They are the "eidetic" images of Eisenstein's own memory, the "lifetime archive" that holds together and preserves the artist's existential ("psychological") experience defined precisely by the "here and now" (Podoroga 2017b, 14–16). Again, we are dealing with prefigural images, something that points toward representation and even informs it (Eisenstein's films and drawings) and yet remains unrepresentable or "archetypal."

I will not go into the important psychoanalytic sources for this study or even into Eisenstein's cinematic method (Podoroga makes a compelling connection between the two; it would suffice to mention that it covers how desire to return to the womb is transformed into Eisenstein's theory of ecstasy). Instead, I will conclude this section by pointing to a tension inherent in this type of analysis. Although Podoroga seeks to uncover and give expression to the dynamic forces that underlie a work of art, his method results in a kind of stasis, indeed in the "tying down" of those very energies or forces. Perhaps one of the reasons for this can be found in his essentially metaphysical outlook.[10] Despite his truly novel and original techniques, he speaks and thinks in terms of Being, drawing a sharp dividing line between the inside and the outside. To a certain extent this tension is present in the very notion of a work (with a small or capital letter), because at some point the work becomes impervious to the outside world with its endlessly changing relationships, ties, and connections. And in this capacity, the work lends itself to observation, with the observer engaged in an essentially anthropological task. But this is not what literature teaches us, even and especially according to Valery Podoroga. Indeed, it demonstrates the limits of thinking itself by subverting language and resisting any possible closure. In the end, it denies us the very privilege of observation since it continually shifts distances as well. It is perhaps contemporary culture (and not classic literature) that goes against the grain of a reflexive doubling of reality, in other words, metaphysics itself. To explore this insight, as well as the transformation of philosophy in these new conditions, we will have to turn to some alternative strategies of conceptualizing cinema, literature, and art.

Philosophy in Mass Societies: Thinking with Art

Although thinking is a relatively independent and autonomous activity, one has to admit that the very structure and functioning of contemporary post-industrial societies (or what is termed globalization) pose new palpable challenges to theory, especially if it wants to maintain its critical and explorative status. The beginnings of the world we live in go back to industrial modernity, that is, roughly to the second half of the nineteenth century, marked by the advent and rapid development of technological devices. This condition, famously known as the "age of mechanical reproduction"[11] (Walter Benjamin) and accompanied by the emergence of a new collective subject—the masses—calls for a dramatic reconsideration of some of the basic concepts concerning art, and in turn aesthetics. One might say that this work was largely begun by the historical avant-garde, as well as by some outstanding cultural theorists of the early twentieth century. The past century witnessed two world wars with their unprecedented techniques of mass extermination, which left an indelible imprint on humanity itself. Indeed, this was a turning point, affecting the problematics, language, and very tone of the humanities. And although we seem to be living in a different world, the impact of those events continues to determine the methods and ethics of contemporary thinking, even when it does not engage in the subject directly. This holds true for new reflections that are associated in one way or another with art. In this section, I will concentrate on the works of two contemporary Russian scholars, one of them formally affiliated with the Russian Academy of Sciences and the other an independent researcher, in fact, a celebrated composer. They are Oleg Aronson[12] and Vladimir Martynov.

Having begun his research with an inquiry into the cinematic space, Oleg Aronson has never given up his involvement with and theoretical interest in cinema.[13] However, cinema for him is not so much an art form with its own history and distinctive means of expression as it is a way of reflecting on present-day mass media societies, characterized by the essentially shared practices of perception and communication. This idea is best expressed in his concept of communicative image, developed in his book of the same name analyzing a number of cinematic and literary texts. First of all, why images, and what exactly do they denote? For Aronson, image is not identical with representation. If it fits into any rational theories of communication at all, it points to that which disrupts communication, opening up an additional dimension within its proper space. The image thus appears to be a "*temporary material combination of disparate signs*" (Aronson 2007, 8). Such signs, however, have nothing to do with traditional semiotics. They can be reduced neither to representations nor to artistic tropes. Remaining resolutely meaningless and contradictory in respect to each other, the signs in question are invariably excluded by the macro theories of both cinema and communication. Yet it is precisely through these kinds of signs that we become aware of that specific non-institutional community that is nothing other than the combination of subjectless forces operating in the new global media environment.

Before going any further, we should examine the theoretical sources at the heart of this unorthodox approach. Aronson clearly mentions two such sources, namely, the philosophy of community and the philosophy of the image. Community is an influential conception developed by contemporary French philosophers such as Maurice Blanchot, Georges Bataille, and Jean-Luc Nancy. To summarize, what is at stake is a critique of existing societies, a nostalgia for a lost community (even if only a mythological one), as well as an experience of the "we" that does not translate into philosophical substance, remaining essentially open, relational, and heterogeneous. For Aronson, it is an "affective community of singular existences" (and this is reminiscent of Nancy)—a "community of non-citizens," that is, that which stands in opposition to the individual in politics or to the subject in philosophy (Aronson 2007, 11). The other source for his concept of communicative image is Henri Bergson and, most importantly, Gilles Deleuze with his groundbreaking and intricate *Cinema*.[14] If Bergson's presence accounts for the materiality of images and their embeddedness in matter (they *are* matter, according to Bergson), it is Deleuze who allows us to conceive of images (and signs) in an entirely new way: they are immanent to the very fabric of cinema, while their impact on the viewer remains weak, indeed almost imperceptible. Such images, being traces of shared memories, expectations, and desires, are "forms of collective sensibility"; they surface only as some kind of "'misunderstanding,' the impossibility of capturing meaning directly" (Aronson 2007, 13).

Deleuze's ideas are not only crucial for a new understanding of cinema, but they are also conducive to the emergence of alternative semiotics, allowing for a different interpretation of films. What is perhaps of the utmost importance is that cinema, stripped of its generic and/or aesthetic qualities, becomes a new ground for philosophy itself, and this development—this expansion—very much in line with the changes taking place in contemporary technological societies, should by no means be overlooked. So, to repeat: images, in the Deleuzian sense, are prior to language and rational understanding in general. Still, they carry a message of their own, being implicated in a state of becoming that challenges metaphysics and politics by putting into question each and every predetermined essence. Everything is in a state of flux and thinking has to cope with a world that is permeated with the "powers of the false" (Aronson 2007, 14). This Deleuzian expression paradoxically stands for the new, for that which has no name because it cannot be represented or imagined. For Aronson, it implies those alternative values that resist appropriation and at the same time are indicative of collective affects. Affects, to remember Spinoza, are passages from one bodily state or constitution to another or, one might say, the dynamics of becoming itself. We grasp what has happened only after the fact, that is, we are always too late (or too slow) in seizing becoming. And yet we are always part of the process. It is this subtle and captivating topic with specific implications for contemporary culture that Aronson examines in his book. Thus, the communicative image is not only an analytic tool enabling a fresh reading of Stanley Kubrick or Virginia Woolf, but an effective means of "redefining philosophy and its problematic" (Aronson 2007, 16).[15]

What is at stake is the breaking down of the dichotomy between the sensual and the rational, between feeling and thinking. Images, the way Aronson sees them, are the very texture of a life whose forces and multiple connections are infinitely greater than our cognizing capacities. It is the side of those forces that Aronson unconditionally takes. In his recent book *Sily lozhnogo* [Powers of the False], he elaborates on the already familiar concept. Again, these powers are equated with non-representational images that are another way of conceptualizing what Jean-Luc Nancy would call "being-together." According to Aronson, such "powers," however weak, manage to make their action felt; still, they are "false," since the relationships that they reveal have nothing to do with the opposition between truth and falsity. Among other things, falsity is a characteristic of contemporary mediatized societies, indeed a way of life—we are surrounded by countless clichés, deceitful images, and simulations. Yet, they are at the core of our daily existence. When speaking of the "false," Aronson is vindicating not only mass culture that is *a priori* collective, defying individual perception, but what he generally terms the "non-valuable," referring first and foremost to the democratic—or rather democratizing—tendencies of contemporary mass societies. They may be traced in different areas, ranging from art that has completely lost its specificity (the "post-medium condition," according to Rosalind Krauss) to politics where institutional democracy is giving way to the steady worldwide tumult of the multitude.[16] In this new picture, art and politics are inseparable from each other. However, both are treated beyond respective institutions as the "energy of affective ties, engendering its own logic and its own sensibility" (Aronson 2017, 14).

Besides the non-valuable and community, which are the main motifs of his book, Aronson also singles out contamination. One may think of contamination as a metaphor, as one is perhaps inclined to interpret his expression "the virus of communality." However, Aronson warns us against such a simplistic reading by suggesting that the three motifs (and the three sections his book is divided into) are at the same time the "characteristic functions of contemporaneity" (Aronson 2017, 17). He goes on to explain that those are ways of defining the special logic of the multitude. This calls for an explanation. In *A Grammar of the Multitude*, a well-known book by the Italian Marxist theorist Paolo Vino, he sketches out what he calls the "emotional tonalities of the multitude" which for him is a designation of the new subject—new agent—of collective action: "With the expression 'emotional situation' I do not refer [...] to a cluster of psychological tendencies, but to ways of being and feeling so pervasive that they end up being common to the most diverse contexts of experience (work, leisure, feelings, politics, etc.)" (Vino 2004, 84). Surprisingly, the multitude today manifests itself with "bad sentiments," such as opportunism, cynicism, "idle talk," and "curiosity" (Heidegger). However, one must change the valences of those definitions (to remember Fredric Jameson) to understand the specific situation of the masses in the post-Ford era of production, communication, and consumption. All these terms (and this brings us back to Oleg Aronson) are ways of describing the largely unobservable but vital relations that define contemporary post-industrial societies. Since such relations are constantly changing (suffice it to mention precariousness as a new economic and social condition), it is important to find ways of grasping this very dynamic. Contamination is one such means.

It should be noted that none other than Leo Tolstoy seemed to be aware of the connection between contamination and art.[17] Amazingly, for Tolstoy art is *not* so many things, namely, the manifestation of transcendent ideas, a psychological outlet, the expression of emotions through external signs, the production of pleasing objects, and, consequently, pleasure itself; but instead, it is a means of communication among human beings, "joining them together in the same feelings" (Tolstoy 1904, 50). This is possible through "infection," which turns out to be both the test and the real subject of art. Anything can be art (jokes, home decoration, church services, etc.), so long as it is infectious, while the "quality of the feelings" thus transmitted may be safely put aside (Tolstoy 1904, 153). Aronson picks up on this insight. Besides being the discovery of a purely sensual level of communication, "infection" (contamination) points to an archaic "economy of poverty" that knows nothing of property, accumulation, and exchange (Aronson 2017, 301). It is, in fact, the action of pure communication, undermining the distinctions between aesthetics, ethics, and economy.[18] Also, this material act is the conductor of life itself, allowing for the emergence of an affective egalitarian "union [communion]" (to cite Tolstoy's favorite word). We may come to the conclusion that contamination now functions in the double capacity of analytic instrument *and* empirical phenomenon: on the one hand, it is a way of uncovering the "anti-mimetic logic of the image," while on the other hand, it is the "materialization of the relations of communication" (Aronson 2017, 18). Clearly, no place here is left for transcendence.

The difficulty in introducing Vladimir Martynov is that he is, first and foremost, a musician. This gives a special turn to his reflections on culture, the more so in that some of his colleagues insist on his compositions being at odds with his writings. (One has to admit that his music is equally rich and enjoyable.) Nevertheless, I will try to touch on some of his ideas, which display an affinity with an international trend in philosophy and critical thinking. It would not be an exaggeration to say that Martynov's name immediately brings up an association with the waning of composers' music. Indeed, such is the title of his perhaps most provocative book, namely *The End of the Composers' Era* [*Konets Vremeni Kompozitorov*] (Martynov 2002). The postulation of this end has produced an ongoing polemic, especially on the part of the composers themselves. However, if one comes to think of other "ends," such as the end of art in Hegel's lectures on aesthetics, the death of the author in post-structuralist theory, and, finally, the end of history itself (from Spengler's "Eurocentric" version to the postmodern all-embracing diagnosis), then one will realize that

Martynov's narrative fits into a larger picture. But before treating the subject itself, we need to take a brief look at Martynov's musical biography in order to better understand what exactly he is trying to communicate with those rather unsettling words. In doing so, I will be relying on the comments of the advanced music scholar Tatiana Cherednichenko,[19] who offers the readers of Martynov's book her professional experience of "long-term listening" [*naslushannost'*] to his music rather than a list of discrepancies concerning his treatment of musical and historical facts (Cherednichenko 2002, 275).

Majoring in composition and piano performance, Vladimir Martynov began composing avant-garde music in the early 1970s, which means that he was still using the twelve-tone music technique at the time. However, through rock music (an active cooperation with the Boomerang rock group), ethnomusicology (expeditions to the Caucasus, Tajikistan, central part of the Pamirs), and a serious study of Western Medieval and Renaissance music, Martynov rapidly evolves into a "minimalist" composer. Even without being experts in the field, we may remember such renowned figures as Terry Riley or Philip Glass, who, incidentally, prefers to think of his musical compositions in terms of repetitive structures. Indeed, minimal music may be described as the technique of microscopic changes, accumulating gradually within protracted repetitions. Although this might hold true for Martynov in the most general sense, his path and style appear to be exceptional. As early as his first avant-garde compositions, Martynov was interested in what he called "still" (or immobilized) time (Cherednichenko 2012, 282). Technically, this results in a lack of notable contrasts, although dodecaphony (twelve-tone serialism) has always been known for its rigid compositional time structure. Another influence on Martynov was the New Simplicity movement [*die neue Einfachheit*] that was skeptical of the recent avant-garde and, more generally, of objectivity in twentieth-century music. Both minimalism and New Simplicity called for a return to the past. However, it is precisely the understanding and implementation of this move that separate Martynov from his counterparts.

From 1980 to 1983, Martynov took a long break from composing. He spent his entire time on one musical score only—the reconstruction of a piece of old Russian church music based on a religious chant. After three years of hard work on anonymous canonical sources, Martynov creates his first *Opus posth* (1984), *posth* standing here for *post-authorial, post-compositional*.[20] In the process of reconstructing liturgy, the composer seems to have arrived at the following conclusion: "real music exists outside the author. Therefore, new techniques are of no concern; what is important is the arrangement of available models" (Cherednichenko 2012, 278). If one comes to think of it, non-authorial music takes on different guises. It encompasses not only folklore or hymnography, but also recreational music, as well as authorial music that has lost every trace of its origin and for this reason has become clichéd. Such is the vast domain of so-called "non-composition." In using this specific material of the past in his works (which is not unlike Duchamp's ready-mades), Martynov performs a recombination of existing models. This, in Cherednichenko's view, largely accounts for Martynov's Christian vocabulary and manner of self-explanation. Indeed, the recombination (or subordination) in question is reminiscent of the Christian doctrine, namely, a twofold movement—of the highest descending downward [*kenosis*] and of the lowest ascending upward [*theosis*]. But, most importantly, what is affected is musical time itself, since "only 'non-horizontal' time constitutes the substance of post-composition" (Cherednichenko 2012, 279).

So here we are, on the ruins of composition—nothing to be sad about. The implications of Martynov's musical experiments are many. What is put into question, in purely musical terms, is equal temperament—a whole tuning system in which the octave is divided into twelve semitones of equal size. Its practical embodiment is found in J. S. Bach's *The Well-Tempered Clavier* (1722), while theoretically it was elaborated by music scholars, both European and Chinese, beginning in the sixteenth century. This system, predominant in European classical music, accounts for an acoustic space delineated by the octave, which remains essentially indifferent to its content. Moreover, any improvisation of the kind one finds in folk choir singing, where the idea of the whole can be and is conveyed by different means (depending on the number of performers, for example), is not only alien to the system, but is interpreted as being out-of-tune. However, equal temperament is not just a way of tuning instruments and introducing universal calculus in music. It also correlates with a Newtonian worldview, according to which space and time are homogeneous and relationships are basically linear. Martynov's interest in pre-classical (or non-classical) music and its incorporation in his works is nothing less than a challenge to this paradigm.

And this is where his own ideas finally come into the picture: the basic distinction that Martynov draws in his book is between composition and bricolage (all the others are derivative and only serve to elucidate this opposition). Now, if the notion of composition needs no special explanation whatsoever, being identical with that of the author and/or individual expression, bricolage is a concept borrowed from the French anthropologist Claude Lévi-Strauss, who uses it to describe the patterns of mythological ("untamed") human thought. For the bricoleur, everything depends on the materials at hand: preexisting things are organized together in new ways, and although their repertoire is fairly large and whimsical, it does have its limits. This operation of the "savage mind" with its ability to transpose—reuse—whole structures is very close to Martynov. He reacts to it with his own understanding of a similar practice in music: "bricolage is the technique of manipulating intonational or melodic and rhythmic formulas-blocks." The formulas in question may have various melodic patterns, yet they should be "stable structures, not allowing for internal dynamism." Likewise, however vast, their number should be limited. This results in "a closed system, providing only for a permutation [combinatorial rearrangement] of the formulas" (Martynov 2002, 17). This quotation could serve as a helpful definition of minimal music. For Martynov, however, composition and bricolage, two separate types of music, have significant ramifications for the

768 H. PETROVSKY

history of culture. They explain not only the two distinct modes of dealing with an "archetypal model" (a departure from it regarded as novelty versus its faithful reproduction), but also the vagaries of history itself. For Martynov the end of history, coinciding with the end of the composers' era, is a symptom of a major transformation: it indicates that the historical vision of the world has itself come to an end.

These motifs have much in common with the reflections of postmodern philosophers, such as Michel Foucault and Fredric Jameson (which Martynov willingly admits). Moreover, the end of the composers' era is welcomed as new possibilities opening up for music after the yoke of composition has been finally removed. Having said all this, let us now take a more sweeping view of the concept. Martynov's hopes are inspired by an archaic vision of the world in which man was at one with the Universe. Music was then an element of ritual expressing this very connection. Today we seem to be able to regain this experience, however altered it may be. According to Martynov, ritual is repetition, while composition is a form of accretion. The music we play and listen to today is highly repetitive, if only for technological reasons. In fact, repetition is the mode of our sensual experience in the contemporary world: experience is structured as repetitive. As I have implied, Martynov resorts to Christianity (and church music) to explain the kind of transformation that is much anticipated. I would suggest that it somehow stands in a line with Tolstoy's idea of a "universal brotherhood" of men, which for him becomes the definition of religious consciousness, thereby turning it into a form of ethics (Tolstoy 1904, 159). It is also turned into aesthetics (especially if we remember the context—art is infectious). In Martynov, we witness a return to archaic practices that guarantee a new type of musical experience. However, it is based on samples. Sampling in music (the reusing of existing fragments) tells us a lot about ourselves. Such units ("formulas-blocks")[21] are nothing other than units of collective sensibility. They are not about the past but about our own experience as listeners *and* members of a global technological community. Thus, we might conclude that art, having given up transcendence, provides us with new and unexpected means for reflecting on our cultural condition.

CONCLUSION

In conclusion, I would like to sketch out some of the themes and topics that are characteristic of the way younger scholars engage in thinking through art. Before mentioning their respective works, we need to take a look at the broader picture. There is an increasing understanding that art has lost its privileged position. This does not mean, however, that art is becoming marginalized. It means that art—experimental art—is freeing itself from institutional constraints and at the same time opening onto a wide range of non-artistic practices. But, most importantly, it means that art today is the expression of the common, be it the experience of living in a global world or the means for conceptualizing this experience. I would say that art today is a synonym for action.[22] Indeed, having lost its specificity, it is the very trajectory of a new social dynamic, the trace of changing forces and relations. If such is the case, then there is no need for it to invent a special language, that is, to double what is happening with a separate "aesthetics." It *is* aesthetic in the sense that it manifests a shared sensual (empirical) experience and does so by avoiding any mediation whatsoever. It is for this reason that the old aesthetic categories are inoperative in the world we live in now: we are no longer dealing with isolated works of art, but with dynamic processes that the philosophy of representation fails to grasp or even to acknowledge.[23]

It comes as no surprise that the younger scholars are interested in "minor" art, to remember Deleuze and Guattari's signal definition. I would say that the philosophy of Gilles Deleuze is, for them, a constant source of inspiration. Thus, Alexandra Volodina is directly engaged in a study of Deleuzian "aesthetics."[24] It should be noted, though, that for Deleuze this is essentially the question of sensation that does not translate into any single or isolated discipline. Volodina has been applying his methods in her readings of marginal artistic phenomena, emerging at the crossroads of genres, ideologies, and trends. The difficulty lies in reconstructing a specific type of subjectivity that is itself part of sensation, as well as its constantly shifting dynamics. This, of course, affects the very concept of art. Instead of reproducing or representing what is already known, art opens up the space for the new in every subsequent act of perception. It is therefore redefined as an encounter with the world, shaping (and entering) sensation itself. Art produces signs or images of a specific kind that are dynamic and heterogeneous, combining different elements together. In other words, art becomes the manifestation of the operation of physical forces, removing the longstanding chasm between subject and object. Among other case studies, I would single out Volodina's increasing interest in the phenomenon of outsider art. Until recently synonymous with "art brut," outsider art denotes any work of art produced by a typically untrained artist who has no connections with the conventional art world. Volodina suggests that such practices should be treated as open processes rather than stable objects, that is, works of art. This calls for an extended understanding of aesthetics. If it stands for the space of sensation where an experiment with meanings is always underway, then any relevant material involved in this process (the author's life circumstances, his or her self-image, etc.) may also be seen as functioning in the newly defined aesthetic regime (Volodina 2016, 131–136).

For Denis Larionov,[25] "minor" art is an apt designation of the uncensored—underground—practices in Soviet literature dating back to the distinct period of the 1950s to the 1980s. "Minor" art is not a simple opposition to the literary mainstream; again, we are dealing with centrifugal forces, operating within Soviet literature itself. "Minor" here accounts for a will to transgress, and an ability to drift away from the grand narratives and conventions that define official Soviet literature. Although eventually many of the underground practices become part of the cultural mainstream, it is important not to lose sight of their anti-institutional, indeed subversive, drive. Likewise, their semiotic "poverty" should not be seen in terms of deficiency, but rather as the necessary condition that allows for this type of literature to come into existence. Larionov focuses on two writers of the period in question, namely, Evgenii Kharitonov and Pavel Ulitin. Both had little hopes of ever being published—or read—during their lifetime. Partly for this reason they switched their attention to practices that seem to be a far cry from literature, but eventually contributed to expanding its field. In Kharitonov's case, it is a serious engagement with theatrical pantomime, while Ulitin conspicuously uses the film techniques of montage in his unconventional writings. Following Foucault and Deleuze in their institutional critiques of art, Larionov highlights the elements of a literary work that are apparently non-literary (pantomimic gestures and montage) and that open onto a field of unrestricted social interactions. He interprets those elements as the non-verbal components of a literary work that end up being the conductors or bearers of its social meanings (Larionov 2017, 185–198).[26] Here again we see that literature, like every other kind of aesthetic activity, does not enjoy any privileged position, but is treated as one of the many manifestations of a "life."[27]

We might, predictably enough, ask ourselves the following question: why is immanent thinking, in one way or another, gaining ground among Russian scholars belonging to different generations? I would suggest both an ethical and a political answer. What we lack in present-day Russia is a real public sphere, and although the Constitution defines the country's political regime as democratic, citizens do not actually participate in the work of democratic institutions or influence the process of policymaking in other noticeable ways. Russian citizens are essentially alienated from politics, and it is not their voluntary choice. The only way to make oneself heard is to join public rallies and demonstrations that paradoxically have to be approved by the authorities. Change is conceivable only as the effect of the many, that is, of a grouping of forces that come together and that may not be politically or institutionally organized. Such was the case of the years 2011–2013, when the Russian protest movement made itself known almost all around the world. Ethics, then, is a way of being together, of changing the existing state of affairs through collective and unmediated action. It is the re-appropriation of publicity itself. And aesthetics (to go on with the list) is nothing other than the corporeal experience of this togetherness, preceding any institution or representation, whether political (representative democracy) or philosophical (the order of representation per se). Many Russian scholars are sensitive to their peculiar social and political situation, and yet are hopeful that change can be brought about regardless. There are no institutional or other guarantees that this will happen—only the dynamic of collective affectivity that increases (or decreases) our ability to act.

NOTES

1. For a clash of various approaches, see the seminal roundtable discussion *"Chto takoe iskusstvo?"* ["What Is Art?"] held at the Institute of Philosophy of the Russian Academy of Sciences (Bakshtein et al. 2016, 18–47).
2. Presently, he is acting head of the department of the same name at the Institute of Philosophy, Russian Academy of Sciences.
3. For an English translation of a shortened version of *Antropogrammy. Opyt samokritiki* [Anthropograms: An Essay in Self-Criticism], see the special issue of *Russian Studies in Philosophy* (Peter Golub offers a different translation for the second part of the title) (Podoroga 2016).
4. See Paul Ricœur's fundamental *Time and Narrative* in three volumes, originally published in French as *Temps et récit* (Ricœur 1983–1985).
5. Among other writings, see, for example, their influential and widely cited book *Kafka: Toward a Minor Literature* (Deleuze and Guattari 1986).
6. See the exemplary essay "How Gogol's *Overcoat* Is Made" by Boris Eikhenbaum (Eikhenbaum 1974) and Yuri Tynyanov's famous study "Dostoevsky and Gogol: Towards a Theory of Parody" (Tynyanov 1975, 1979).
7. An available and highly competent English translation of an earlier version of Podoroga's text on Platonov is "The Eunuch of the Soul: Positions of Reading and the World of Platonov" made by Gene Kuperman (Podoroga 1991).
8. For a description of the course itself and other forms of joint collaboration, see Buck-Morss's *Dreamworld and Catastrophe. The Passing of Mass Utopia in East and West* (Buck-Morss 2000, 230 ff.).
9. One important landmark is the book *Avto-bio-grafiia. K voprosu o metode. Tetradi po analiticheskoi antropologii. № 1* [Auto-bio-graphy. On the Question of Method. Papers on Analytical Anthropology. № 1]. In addition to Podoroga, who was also editor of the volume, it was coauthored by his pupils and/or members of his department at the time, including, among others, Mikhail Ryklin, Oleg Aronson, Elena Oznobkina, Andrei Paramonov, Oleg Nikiforov, and myself (Podoroga et al. 2001).
10. On the connection between Podoroga's conception of mimesis and the problematic of death and, more generally, for an introduction to his thinking, see Oleg Aronson's article "Forms of Thought within the Limits of the Body (On the Analytical Metaphysics of Valery Podoroga)" (Aronson 2016b).
11. One of the latest translations of *"technische Reproduzierbarkeit"* is "technological reproducibility," which is probably closer to the point.
12. He is senior research associate of the Department of Aesthetics of the Institute of Philosophy, Russian Academy of Sciences.
13. See, for example, *Metakino* [Metacinema] (Aronson 2003).
14. Although a great deal has been published on this book worldwide, one of the few competent Russian commentaries to date is Aronson's foreword *"Iazyk vremeni"* ["The Language of Time"] to its Russian edition (Aronson 2004).
15. The thesis reappears and is further developed in his most recent book *Kino i filosofiia: ot teksta k obrazu* [Cinema and Philosophy: From Text to Image] (Aronson 2018). This is close to my own understanding of photography, which is instrumental in uncovering spaces of collective affectivity (Petrovsky 2015).

16. See Aronson's compelling contribution "Maidan: Redefining Democracy" (tr. Peter Golub) to the special issue of *Russian Studies in Philosophy* on the pivotal events in Ukraine that commenced in the Fall of 2013 (Aronson 2016a).
17. His famous book *What Is Art?* (1897) was first published in English due to difficulties with the Russian censors.
18. For an explicit critique of the economic, or financial, dimension of art in the contemporary world, see Aronson's chapter "Iskusstvo i abstraktnyi kapitalism" ["Art and Abstract Capitalism"] in our joint book *Chto ostaetsia ot iskusstva* [What Remains of Art] (Aronson and Petrovsky 2015, 172–189).
19. See, among her other books, the posthumously published *Izbrannoe* [Selected Writings] (Cherednichenko 2012).
20. All the while he is supported by a group of talented and versatile musicians, including his future wife, the violinist Tatiana Grindenko, who will later set up her own ensemble of the same name (*Opus Posth* 1999). In 2002, Martynov and Grindenko were awarded the State Prize of the Russian Federation for their outstanding musical achievements.
21. It is interesting that Martynov's latest experimental book *Kniga peremen* [Book of Changes] (2016a), named after the famous Chinese divination text, is more like a music score. Consisting of various "samples" or "blocks," among them excerpts from Proust, Joyce, and family diaries, as well as the Composers' Union directives and newspaper dating ads, this masterfully structured oeuvre is meant for meditation rather than linear reading. In Martynov's own words, he "would like to be a DJ in literature" (Martynov 2016). For an account of Martynov's ideas on visuality and its social implications, see my book *Bezymiannye soobshchestva* [Anonymous Communities] (Petrovsky 2012, 178–186).
22. See, for example, my analysis of Pussy Riot and their actionism in terms of Bakhtin's philosophy of the act (Pyotrovsky [Petrovsky] 2017, 70–81). Actionism of this kind is not just political art engaged in the moment. It serves as a catalyst for the emergence of the new (new social interactions), for which we necessarily lack designations or names.
23. For a discussion of these and other closely related issues, see the special issue of my theoretical and philosophical journal *Sinii divan* [Blue Couch] on contemporary art (Petrovsky 2016).
24. She is preparing her dissertation in the Department of Aesthetics of the RAS Institute of Philosophy. See, for example, one of her most recent articles: "Estetika Zhilia Deleza: k immanentistskoi filosofii iskusstva" (Volodina 2018, 49–63).
25. Besides being a post-graduate student in the Department of Aesthetics of the RAS Institute of Philosophy, Larionov is a poet and literary critic.
26. Both Alexandra Volodina and Denis Larionov took part in an extensive round-table discussion on the social function of contemporary art organized and conducted by a group of young scholars from various establishments (Petrovsky 2016, 83–113).
27. A reference to the Deleuzian philosophy of immanence. For an elucidation of the term, see *Pure Immanence: Essays on A Life* (Deleuze 2001).

BIBLIOGRAPHY

Aronson, Oleg. 2003. *Metakino*. Moscow: Ad Marginem.

———. 2004. Iazyk vremeni. In Deleuze, Gilles. *Kino*. Translated by Boris Skuratov, 11–36. Moscow: Ad Marginem.

———. 2007. *Kommunikativnyi obraz (Kino. Literatura. Filosofiia)*. Moscow: Novoe literaturnoe obozrenie.

Aronson, Oleg V. 2016a. Maidan: Redefining Democracy. *Russian Studies in Philosophy. Special Issue: Maidan*, guest edited by Helen V. Petrovsky, 54 (3): 223–232.

———. 2016b. Forms of Thought within the Limits of the Body (On the Analytical Metaphysics of Valery Podoroga). *Russian Studies in Philosophy* 54 (4): 257–266.

Aronson, Oleg. 2017. *Sily lozhnogo. Opyty nepoliticheskoi demokratii*. Moscow: Falanster.

———. 2018. *Kino i filosofiia: ot teksta k obrazu*. Moscow: Institut filosofii Rossiiskoi akademii nauk.

Aronson, Oleg, and Helen Petrovsky. 2015. *Chto ostaetsia ot iskusstva*. Moscow: Institut problem sovremennogo iskusstva (Trudy IPSI, Tom II).

Bakshtein, Iosif, Evgenii Barabanov, Viktor Bychkov, Yakov Krotov, Nadezhda Man'kovskaya, Helen Petrovsky, and Valery Podoroga. 2016. Chto takoe iskusstvo? Kruglyi stol. *Filosofskii zhurnal / Philosophy Journal*. 9 (4): 18–47.

Buck-Morss, Susan. 2000. *Dreamworld and Catastrophe: The Passing of Mass Utopia in East and West*. Cambridge, MA and London: The MIT Press.

Bychkov, Viktor V. 2015. The Post-Nonclassical Sense of Contemporary Aesthetics. *Russian Studies in Philosophy. Special Issue: Contemporary Aesthetics in Russia*. Guest edited by Nadezhda B. Mankovskaya, 53 (1): 8–26.

Cherednichenko, Tatiana. 2002. Ob avtore (Posleslovie). In *Konets vremeni kompozitorov*, ed. Vladimir Martynov, 275–294. Moscow: Russkii put'.

———. 2012. *Izbrannoe*. Edited by Tatiana S. Kiuregian. Moscow: Nauchno-izdatel'skii tsentr 'Moskovskaia konservatoriia'.

Deleuze, Gilles. 2001. *Pure Immanence: Essays on a Life*. Translated by Anne Boyman, with an introduction by John Rajchman. New York: Zone Books.

Deleuze, Gilles, and Félix Guattari. 1986. *Kafka: Toward a Minor Literature*. Translated by Dana Polan, foreword by Réda Bensmaïa. Minneapolis, London: University of Minnesota Press.

Dobrokhotov, Alexander L. 2016. *Teleologiia kul'tury*. Moscow: Progress-Traditsiia.

Eikhenbaum, Boris. 1974. How Gogol's *Overcoat* Is Made. In *Gogol from the Twentieth Century: Eleven Essays*, ed. and trans. Robert A. Maguire, 269–291. Princeton: Princeton University Press.

Genisaretsky, Oleg. 1994. *Dizain i kul'tura*. Moscow: VNIITE.

Larionov, Denis. 2017. Neprochitannaia pantomima: dissertatsiia Evgeniia Kharitonova v svete ego khudozhestvennogo tvorchestva i sovetskikh teorii tantsa. *Shagi* 3 (1): 185–198.

Mankovskaya, Nadezhda B. 2015. French Symbolism: Aesthetic Dominants. *Russian Studies in Philosophy. Special Issue: Contemporary Aesthetics in Russia*. Guest edited by Nadezhda B. Mankovskaia, 53 (1): 54–71.

Martynov, Vladimir. 2002. *Konets vremeni kompozitorov*. Moscow: Russkii put'.

———. 2016a. *Kniga peremen*. Moscow: Klassika-XXI, Art-tranzit.

———. 2016b. Mne khotelos' by stat' didzheem v literature. *Gor'kii* [Gorky], September 26. https://gorky.media/intervyu/mne-hotelos-by-stat-didzheem-v-literature/.

Petrovsky, Helen. 2012. *Bezymiannye soobshchestva*. Moscow: Falanster.

———. 2015. *Antifotografiia 2. 2-e izd., dop*, 7. Moscow: Tri kvadrata (seriia 'Artes et media,' Vyp.

———, ed. 2016. *Sinii divan. Filosofsko-teoreticheskii zhurnal. Tema nomera: iskusstvo segodnia*. Moscow: Tri kvadrata.

Podoroga, Valery. 1991. The Eunuch of the Soul: Positions of Reading and the World of Platonov. *The South Atlantic Quarterly* 90 (2): 357–408.

———. 2006. *Mimesis. Materialy k analiticheskoi antropologii literatury*, 1. Moscow: Kul'turnaia revoliutsiia, Logos, Logos-altera.

———. 2011. *Mimesis. Materialy k analiticheskoi antropologii literatury*, 2/1. Moscow: Kul'turnaia revoliutsiia.

———. 2013. *Kairos, kriticheskii moment. Aktual'noe proizvedenie iskusstva na marshe*. Moscow: Grundrisse.

Podoroga, Valery A. 2016. Anthropograms: A Self-Critical Approach. *Russian Studies in Philosophy* 54 (4): 267–358.

Podoroga, Valery. 2017a. *Antropogrammy. Opyt samokritiki. S prilozheniem diskussii*. St. Petersburg: Izdatel'stvo Evropeiskogo universiteta v Sankt-Peterburge.

———. 2017b. *Vtoroi ekran. Sergei Eizenshtein i kinematograf nasiliia*. Moscow: Breus.

Podoroga, Valery, Helen Petrovsky, Elena Oznobkina, Oleg Aronson, Oleg Nikiforov, Andrei Paramonov, Mikhail Ryklin, Igor Chubarov, and Vladimir Maikov. 2001. *Avto-bio-grafiia. K voprosu o metode. Tetradi po analiticheskoi antropologii. № 1*. Edited by Valery A. Podoroga. Moscow: Logos.

Pyotrovsky [Petrovsky], Helen. 2017. Pussy Riot: From Intervention to Action. In *Art Riot. Post-Soviet Actionism, Saatchi Gallery, 16 November–31 December 2017 [Catalogue]*, curated by Marat Guelman, edited by Andrei Kovalev, 70–81. London: ABC Design Studio.

Ricœur, Paul. 1983–1985. *Temps et récit*. 3 vols. Paris: Éditions du Seuil.

Tolstoy, Leo. 1904. *What Is Art?* Translated, with an introduction by Aylmer Maude. New York: Funk & Wagnalls Co. https://archive.org/stream/whatisart00tolsuoft/whatisart00tolsuoft_djvu.txt.

Tynyanov, Yuri [Yuri N.]. 1975. Dostoevsky and Gogol: Towards a Theory of Parody [Part 2]. *Twentieth-Century Russian Literary Criticism*, edited [and translated] by Victor Erlich. 102–116. New Haven and London: Yale University Press.

———. 1979. Dostoevsky and Gogol: Towards a Theory of Parody [Part 1]. In *Dostoevsky & Gogol: Texts and Criticism*, edited and translated by Priscilla Meyer and Stephen Rudy, 101–118. Ann Arbor: Ardis.

Vino, Paolo. 2004. *A Grammar of the Multitude. For an Analysis of Contemporary Forms of Life*. Translated by Isabella Bertoletti, James Cascaito, Andrea Casson, foreword by Sylvère Lotringer. New York, Los Angeles: Semiotext(e).

Volodina, Alexandra. 2016. Narrativ vs. misteriia: neskol'ko zamechanii o dvoistvennoi strukture naivnogo iskusstva. In *Amplituda kolebanii. Naiv i ar brut: ot klassiki k sovremennosti. Materialy nauchnoi konferentsii*, 131–136. Moscow: Muzei russkogo lubka i naivnogo iskusstva.

———. 2018. Estetika Zhilia Deleza: k immanentistskoi filosofii iskusstva. *Filosofiia i kul'tura* 3: 49–63.

PART III

Afterword

CHAPTER 36

Russian Thought and *Russian Thinkers*

Michael N. Forster

Like many non-specialists on Russian thought, I first became broadly acquainted with it by reading Isaiah Berlin's *Russian Thinkers* (first published in 1978). Written by a thinker of importance in his own right who was partly raised and educated in Russia, this book became, and remains, the gold standard for the treatment of its subject. The present volume is (among other things) an attempt to extend, and where necessary correct, Berlin's account.

Berlin was a moral and political philosopher who had very definite views of his own. In particular, he was a champion of a pluralism about values, liberalism, democracy, and cosmopolitanism—all admirable principles, in my view. Perhaps inevitably, this led him to foreground thinkers from the Russian tradition who shared similar principles—especially, Herzen and Turgenev (neither of whom had previously enjoyed the sort of high profile in European representations of Russian thought that he lent them), as well as Belinsky and Tolstoy. By contrast, he wrote dismissively of the more politically radical side of Russian thought (Bakunin) or even passed over it in silence (Lenin and other Marxists). This all arguably led to certain distortions in his representation of Russian thought.

As a liberal and cosmopolitan like Berlin himself, Herzen is the main intellectual hero of Berlin's book (see its chapters "Herzen and Bakunin on Individual Liberty" and "Alexander Herzen"; Berlin 1978, 93–129, 212–239). According to Berlin, Herzen "is a political (and consequently a moral) thinker

M. N. Forster (✉)
University of Bonn, Bonn, Germany
e-mail: mnforste@uchicago.edu

© The Author(s), under exclusive license to Springer Nature   777
Switzerland AG 2021
M. F. Bykova et al. (eds.), *The Palgrave Handbook of Russian Thought*,
https://doi.org/10.1007/978-3-030-62982-3_36

of the first importance" (Berlin 1978, 94), "his political and social views were arrestingly original" (ibid., 238).

There are good grounds for this strong praise of Herzen. For example, as Berlin emphasizes, Herzen admirably defended the freedom of individual action, thought, and expression; included the disadvantaged and oppressed under the aegis of this defense; identified and resisted the threats to such freedom posed both by abstract political ideals, including those of the Left, and by fanciful teleological philosophies of history (such as Hegel's, to which Herzen had himself at one time been attracted, or that of Marx and Engels); and recognized that the masses who were supposed to be the main beneficiaries of his liberal ideals often did not want them (a theme that he develops poignantly in his autobiography *My Past and Thoughts* [1870] in connection with the political disappointment of the British socialist Robert Owen). Moreover, some of these positions were quite original, in particular those directed against the threats to liberty posed by abstract political ideals on the Left and by teleological philosophies of history (which had to wait for the flourishing of an organized Left and philosophies of history of the sort in question in the nineteenth century in order to acquire their targets).

Nonetheless, Berlin's praise of Herzen is perhaps slightly exaggerated. In particular, it seems doubtful that Herzen developed his positions with quite as much philosophical depth or quite as much ingenuity in devising mechanisms of implementation as several other great liberals had already achieved before him—for instance, Diderot, Wilhelm von Humboldt, and John Stuart Mill. Thus, concerning philosophical depth, not only does one miss in Herzen the sophistication of philosophical argument that one finds in such classic liberal works as Wilhelm von Humboldt's *Ideas for an Attempt to Determine the Limits of the Operation of the State* [*Ideen zu einem Versuch die Grenzen der Wirksamkeit des Staates zu bestimmen*] (written in 1791/1792, first published in 1854) or Mill's *On Liberty* (1859), but one also encounters a number of disturbing inconsistencies. For example, Herzen in certain passages preaches the unpredictability of the historical future but in others confidently prophesies a dire one (cf. Berlin 1978, 102–112), and he also contradicts himself on the subject of free will and determinism, sometimes holding that determinism is a fact and free will therefore an illusion, but at other times holding that free will is real (cf. Copleston 1986, 94–96). Similarly, concerning mechanisms of implementation, while Herzen's activities as a political publicist (especially in his journal *The Bell*), autobiographer, and novelist are certainly impressive, it is not clear that they can compete in quality and effectiveness with Diderot's astonishingly influential *Encyclopedia*, almost equally influential *History of the Two Indias* (nominally authored by his friend Raynal, but largely written by Diderot himself), brilliant socially critical novels (*Jacques le fataliste*, *Le neveu de Rameau*, and *La religieuse*), and various other ingenious mechanisms of influence, or with Humboldt's very different but equally impressive mechanisms of reforming the whole Prussian system of education in a liberal direction in his capacity as Prussia's de facto Minister of Education and leaving behind theoretical writings that continue to constitute a central part of the liberal canon to this day. Moreover, where Berlin sees in Herzen's writings only intellectual depth, literary brilliance, and deep humanity, some readers will be no less struck by his self-centredness, superficial rhetoric, and—perhaps worst of all—indulgence in a sort of ignorant and prejudiced stereotyping of other nations (especially the Germans, the British, and the French) that was all too common in the nineteenth century and that jars with his official cosmopolitanism. Finally (this time a more ad hominem point against Berlin), the impression that Berlin leaves of Herzen as a fellow liberal, democrat, and cosmopolitan is also misleading in a further respect (besides the national prejudices just mentioned), for the mature Herzen, rather than being a liberal democrat in Berlin's mold, was actually a radical who advocated a sort of communism modeled on the Russian *mir* or village commune.

If Berlin's praise of Herzen seems slightly exaggerated, his neglect or dismissal of the radicals seems a good deal more so. Berlin does not even deign to discuss Lenin, despite the fact that Lenin was not only in many ways an admirable political figure but also a philosopher of some ability (as Marina F. Bykova's contribution to the present volume well illustrates [see Chap. 12]). By contrast, Berlin does at least discuss Bakunin (see his chapter "Herzen and Bakunin on Individual Liberty"; Berlin 1978, 93–129). But he does so only in order to dismiss him.

Berlin indeed depicts Bakunin as little more than a sort of destructive poser lacking in any coherent political or philosophical position. However, Bakunin *did* have a coherent position, and moreover one that deserves serious consideration. As Berlin's own discussion shows despite itself, Bakunin's negative emphasis on destroying the state and the Church that supports it was not mere willful destructiveness. It was rather founded on a conviction that these institutions were artificial constructs that had corrupted a human nature that was fundamentally social and good, so that the main political task was just to eliminate these distorting institutions in order to liberate human beings' good social impulses (Berlin 1978, 122–125). Moreover, Bakunin complemented this destructive project with a positive picture of the better institutions that were to emerge from the destruction which was at least somewhat attractive, namely, a set of loosely affiliated communes modeled (as with Herzen) on the Russian *mir*. And if he refrained from characterizing these better institutions in much detail that was not from any lack of seriousness but because his assumption that human nature was fundamentally social and good, combined with a belief (broadly shared with Herder, Hegel, Marx, and Herzen—and moreover arguably correct) that the historical future could not be predicted in any detail, made him consider more elaborate projections for the future to be both unnecessary and futile.

Whether or not this position is defensible in the end, it is hardly an incoherent, or even a foolish, one. It seems especially plausible on its negative side. For example, it could be argued that Bakunin's skepticism about the state and its supporting institutions on grounds of the internal oppression, war, and imperialism/colonialism that they generate not only already had strong empirical support in the history of states that was known to him, but has since been emphatically confirmed by the even more appalling behavior of states in the twentieth century. And his more specific repudiation of the statist tendencies of the international labor movement of his day (tendencies with which his contemporaries Marx and Engels, by contrast, tended to sympathize) as merely a recipe for continuing the pernicious state of the past in a new guise now looks little less than prophetic given the way in which the Soviet Union would subsequently develop after its birth from the October Revolution of 1917.

Indeed, it could be argued that Bakunin saw a good deal further here than liberal democratic thinkers like Berlin who are content to retain the state and merely seek to (re)cast it in an optimal form, recognizing—as they do not—that the real problem of modern societies lies not just in specific types of state as contrasted with others—say, undemocratic, illiberal, inegalitarian ones as opposed to democratic, liberal, egalitarian ones—but in the state itself. This is certainly a line of thought that has seemed more plausible to German and Russian thinkers (e.g., Herder, Humboldt, Marx, and Engels on the German side; Bakunin himself, Tolstoy, and some Marxists on the Russian) than to Anglophone ones. And no doubt this asymmetry is in part due to the fact that the state has tended to be even more autocratic, internally repressive, and militaristic in Germany and Russia than in Britain or the USA. However, it would be hasty to infer from this situation that the line of thought in question is therefore merely an overreaction to a local trauma specific to Germany and Russia. For one thing, perhaps it is rather that these two countries have revealed the deep structure of the state more clearly than Britain or the USA. For another thing, the state oppression that troubled Bakunin (and some of the other German and Russian critics of the state as such just mentioned) prominently included *outward* forms of oppression such as imperialism and colonialism, which have been even more prevalent in Britain and the USA than in Germany or Russia, but which have tended to be (all too conveniently) ignored by Anglophone liberal democrats such as John Stuart Mill and Berlin.

If there is a real weakness in Bakunin's position, it arguably rather lies on its positive side: his optimistic assumption that, unlike the state, which is merely artificial and harmful, human nature is fundamentally social and good, and his consequent expectation that the elimination of the state and its supporting institutions will inevitably lead to an amelioration of the human condition. These positions were probably errors (albeit not merely foolish ones). The choice between the state and its abolition may therefore ultimately be a choice between different evils, the question being which is the lesser one.

But being half right on such difficult and important questions as these would still be a major theoretical achievement, and being half mistaken is not the same as being merely incoherent or superficial. So in the end one is inclined to say that Berlin's dismissal of Bakunin is something of an intellectual injustice. (For another, somewhat differently argued, defense of Bakunin against Berlin's dismissive treatment of him, see Jeff Love's contribution to the present volume [Chap. 7].)

Nonetheless, Berlin performed a very important service in drawing attention to the attractive but previously neglected liberal and cosmopolitan strand in Russian thought represented by thinkers such as Herzen and Turgenev. Indeed, he could well have strengthened his case on their behalf even more than he did in certain ways. For example, he could have added that in sharp contrast to the patriarchal and sexist tendencies of many nineteenth-century Russian thinkers (even relatively enlightened ones such as Tolstoy), Herzen and Turgenev were both champions of a form of feminism—Herzen especially in passages of *My Past and Thoughts*, Turgenev in several of his novels and novellas, including *On the Eve* (1860).

Another valuable service that Berlin performed was to point out that the Russian contributions to political and social thought are to be found less in pure philosophy or theory than in *literature* (Berlin 1978, 167–168). Accordingly, his presentation of Russian political and social thought treats primarily literary authors such as Herzen, Turgenev, and Tolstoy alongside, and with considerably greater respect than, more purely philosophical or theoretical authors such as Bakunin and less well-known figures. This judgment of Berlin's seems to be broadly correct and important.

Russian literature *typically* involves political and social thought in deep (if often implicit) ways. For, like much of the best literature of the French Enlightenment (e.g., the novels of Voltaire and Diderot) or of Germany in the age of Goethe (e.g., the literary works of Goethe himself in certain moods, Schiller, and, again in certain moods, the German Romantics), it is in general both politically-socially committed and theoretically informed. A good example of this is Turgenev's collection of interconnected short stories *Sketches from a Hunter's Album* (1852). Turgenev was a committed liberal who had studied philosophy in Berlin (especially Hegel's philosophy). Thanks to its superb artistry and its theoretically informed critical depiction of serfdom, his book came to play an important—indeed, perhaps even decisive—role in the movement to abolish serfdom in nineteenth-century Russia. *Much* of the best Russian literature of the nineteenth century shares this character of infusion with political-social commitment and thought. An interesting exception that in a way proves the rule is Gogol's novel *Dead Souls* (1842). When this work first appeared, many readers (not unreasonably) interpreted it as a critical satire on the institution of serfdom, the institution of owning serfs (the "souls" of the book's title and of its wonderfully weird plot, which involves its main character going round buying deceased serfs from their owners)—a sort of Russian counterpart to Swift's *A Modest Proposal*, written in a spirit critical of serfdom similar to that of Turgenev's work from a decade later. However, Gogol subsequently went on to deny that this had been his intention and indeed to make it clear that on the contrary, he held very conservative political and social views. Yet when he did so he provoked outrage, especially in the form of a famous response by the influential liberal literary critic Belinsky. Both the public's initial interpretation and the outrage that people like Belinsky later expressed say much about the predominantly social and political character of the Russian literature of the age. (For fuller discussion of Belinsky and this episode, see Vadim Shkolnikov's contribution to the present volume [Chap. 23].)

In connection with this central role of political-social commitment and thought in Russian literature, Berlin focuses not only on Turgenev, but also on an even more important example: Tolstoy. More specifically, he devotes considerable attention to Tolstoy's philosophies of history and education (see his chapters "The Hedgehog and the Fox" and "Tolstoy and Enlightenment"; Berlin 1978, 24–92, 273–298).

Tolstoy does indeed constitute a powerful example in support of Berlin's general thesis. However, as Lina Steiner implies in her contributions to the present volume (see Chaps. 21 and 26) and in previous work, such as her important book *For Humanity's Sake: The Bildungsroman in Russian Culture* (Steiner 2011), the details of Berlin's interpretation of this case require some correction.

To make the required points in my own terms rather than hers: As a Jew working in England in the decades immediately following the Nazi period and World War II, Berlin, like many other Jewish and non-Jewish Europeans of his generation, was understandably ambivalent about Germany. Perhaps in part because of this, his account of Tolstoy's philosophies of history and education does not emphasize German influences (with the exception of Schopenhauer), but rather French ones. Specifically, in connection with the philosophy of history, Berlin emphasizes de Maistre, and in connection with the philosophy of education Rousseau. No doubt, these French influences *did* play an important role, but it seems clear that German influences were at least as strong, if not stronger, and moreover that they are essential for understanding the character, and for assessing the strengths and weaknesses, of Tolstoy's positions.

For example, Tolstoy's famous reflections on the philosophy of history in the main text and the epilogue of *War and Peace* (1865)—especially, his recognition there of a sort of historical determinism; his insistence, though, on the great multiplicity and complexity of the determining causes involved; and his consequent denials that "great" individuals such as Napoleon are ever really in control of the course of historical events or that such events can ever really be predicted—were all strongly anticipated by Herder's philosophy of history (cf. Forster 2018, 242–245) and seem to be largely borrowed from it. It should therefore in principle be possible to arrive at a deeper understanding of Tolstoy's reflections by taking Herder's original versions of them into account.

Likewise, in the philosophy of education, whereas Berlin identifies Rousseau as the main influence on Tolstoy, the more important sources of Tolstoy's position were probably in fact again German. Moreover, whereas Berlin's emphasis on Rousseau leads him to suppose that there are deep problems in Tolstoy's position—in particular, a contradiction, revealed in his efforts at educating peasant children, between a Rousseauian aspiration to let pupils develop autonomously and a practical need to influence them as their teacher—the German background in question shows that this is not so. A strong clue to this whole situation lies in the fact that, as Berlin himself mentions in passing, Tolstoy in his reflections on education uses the German term *Bildung* [formation] and expresses pride at having found a Russian equivalent for it (Berlin 1978, 296). For this points to a strong connection with the German tradition of Herder and Wilhelm von Humboldt in the philosophy of education, for which *Bildung* was the central ideal. This ideal was rather complex. Its classic definition can be found in the work of Humboldt's that has already been mentioned, *Ideas for an Attempt to Determine the Limits of the Operation of the State*. Roughly speaking, what it meant was the free, individualistic, language-based, and unending self-development of the human individual in harmoniously unified theoretical, practical, and aesthetic respects, conceived as something at bottom natural but only realized through culture and education, and as the highest purpose of education, or even of the body politic as a whole (cf. Forster 2012, 2013). Moreover, while for these German thinkers the ideal of *Bildung* did include a certain sort of autonomy, as contrasted with mere steering from the outside, they rejected the naïve Rousseauian conception that the autonomy in question excluded influence by culture or teachers, but on the contrary considered such influence to be inevitable and essential for it. The sort of contradiction that Berlin thinks he detects in Tolstoy's position is therefore not really there at all.

Furthermore, a commitment to the German ideal of *Bildung*, or *Selbstbildung* [self-formation], accounts for Tolstoy's stance on education more adequately than a Rousseauian model could do in several additional respects as well. For example, whereas Tolstoy's own unending lifelong striving for new knowledge and insight would be difficult to square with Rousseauian ideals, it reflects the German ideal of *(Selbst)bildung* perfectly. So too does his biographically manifest effort to achieve a sort of unified and harmonious many-siddedness that included, for example, philosophical theory, literary art, crafts (such as shoe-making), and physical exercise.

Moreover, the nature of Tolstoy's greatest literary works—especially *War and Peace*—reflects the closely related German genre of the *Bildungsroman* [novel of formation], as it was developed above all by Herder's follower Goethe. Indeed, it reflects that genre in all of its complexity: as a type of writing that not only depicts the *(Selbst)bildung* of a central character (in Goethe's paradigmatic *Bildungsroman, Wilhelm Meisters Lehrjahre*, the character Wilhelm Meister; in *War and Peace*, Pierre), but that also, thereby, contributes to the *(Selbst)bildung* of readers, and (an aspect of the *Bildungsroman* that is often overlooked) in addition advances the *(Selbst)bildung* of the author himself, as he writes his work over a number of years in an exploratory and creative spirit (concerning this last aspect, compare Goethe's manner of writing *Wilhelm Meisters Lehrjahre* with Tolstoy's manner of writing *War and Peace*).

Similar points apply to several further areas of Tolstoy's thought as well. One of these is his philosophy of art. His main theoretical work on this subject is *What is art?* (1897–1898) (which is discussed in helpful detail by Henry Pickford in his contribution to the present volume [see Chap. 27]). Tolstoy sees the primary function of art as lying, not in the creation of beauty, but in *moral pedagogy*, the inculcation of moral attitudes, and he equates the moral attitudes involved with *feelings*. But (once again) these positions had already been central to Herder's philosophy of art (cf. Forster 2018, 12–14, 205–208, 210–211). Similarly, Tolstoy's liberal interpretation of Christianity—including his naturalistic re-conception of the soul's immortality—is very reminiscent of Herder's (cf. Forster 2018, Chap. 10). Finally, Tolstoy's fundamental practice of fusing literature with philosophy or theory in the novel (as in the case of *War and Peace*) is the realization of a conception of the novel that was originally developed by Herder in his *Letters for the Advancement of Humanity* (1793–1797) and then in continuity with him the German Romantics, especially Friedrich Schlegel (albeit that Tolstoy no doubt largely became acquainted with it as it had since been filtered through intermediaries, such as Victor Hugo's *Les Misérables* [1862]).

This whole revision of Berlin's picture of Tolstoy also makes possible a deeper explanation of the Russian tradition's emphasis on literature rather than pure philosophy or theory as the locus for political and social thought. Berlin explains this emphasis as merely a sort of *pis aller* due to the heavy hand of authoritarian censorship in Russia, which precluded more purely philosophical or theoretical presentations of political and social ideas (Berlin 1978, 304). That is no doubt *part* of the explanation. But another important part of it is connected with the German *Bildung* tradition and is both more principled and deeper in nature. For German theorists of *Bildung* such as Herder, literature was a powerful instrument of moral character formation, indeed the most powerful instrument of all. Moreover, they were probably right about this! Modern ideas of *l'art pour l'art* and literature written in their spirit have tended to obscure this important fact. But it can be seen, for example, from the fundamental role that the Homeric epics and tragedy played in the moral character formation of the ancient Greeks, and from the way in which ancient Greek philosophers like Protagoras and Plato took this role for granted (albeit in Plato's case as a severe critic of it). Russian authors such as Tolstoy and Turgenev simply absorbed this lesson from the German *Bildung* tradition and acted on it (Tolstoy's enthusiastic invocation of the word *Bildung* already shows this clearly enough in his case; concerning Turgenev's absorption of the same lesson, see, for example, his character Potugin in *Smoke* [1867]).

Finally, this revised version of Berlin's account also supports two further points that go beyond, and in the second case even against, things that he himself says. The first of these further points is that the greatest glory of the Russian intellectual tradition lies not in its pure philosophy or theory but instead in its philosophically-theoretically informed literature. With few if any exceptions, the purely philosophical side of the tradition turns out to be rather disappointing (a fact that has often been remarked on and which the contributions to the present volume tend to confirm rather than disconfirm). More precisely,

Russian philosophy usually falls into one or other of three equally problematic categories: a set of relatively unoriginal and sometimes even crude appropriations of ideas from German philosophers such as Kant, Schelling, Hegel, Marx, and Husserl; a rather dogmatic and heavy-handed official Marxism (as with Plekhanov, Lenin, Stalin, and many others); and a religious philosophy strongly influenced by the Russian Orthodox Church (as with Solovyov, Berdyaev, and others). As Sergei Horujy suggests in his very interesting contribution to the present volume (see Chap. 3), only the last of these three categories constitutes a significant exception to the general rule of Russian philosophy's lack of originality. However, if Russian philosophy's claims to originality are going to depend on its acceptance of the general worldview of the Russian Orthodox Church, then its cause seems *well and truly* lost. A related point applies to *explicit* treatments of philosophical ideas in Russian *literature* as well—for example, Turgenev's depiction of the materialist nihilist Bazarov in *Fathers and Sons* (1862), and Dostoevsky's depiction of philosophical positions in novels such as *The Possessed* (1873). Here again the philosophical ideas involved are rather unoriginal and crude—though in this case that is less the fault of the literary authors in question than of the Russian philosophical milieu that they were depicting or reflecting.

In sharp contrast with Russian philosophy, however, Russian *literature* itself is world class. Indeed, it would be no exaggeration to say that the Russian literary tradition that emerged in the nineteenth century is one of the greatest flowerings of literature in all of world history: comparable in quality to the flowering of tragedy and comedy in fifth-century Athens; the flowering of the poetry of Dante, Petrarch, and Boccaccio in late medieval Italy; the flowering of drama in Elizabethan and Jacobean England; the flowering of the English novel in the eighteenth through twentieth centuries; or the flowering of the French novel during the same period.

This great flowering of Russian literature began in the first half of the nineteenth century with Pushkin, Lermontov, and Gogol, then continued with the authors on whom this Afterword has mainly focused, Turgenev and Tolstoy, as well as several others. In its mature form it saliently included Dostoevsky, for example, whose greatness—aside from the extraordinary gift for storytelling that he shares with all of the other authors just mentioned—arguably lies less in his philosophy or in his agonizing over Christianity (an atavistic *faible* that he shares with Tolstoy) than in his psychology, especially his insight into the more pathological and criminal side of human nature (as perhaps most stunningly exemplified by his *Notes from the Underground* [1864]). The greatness of Russian literature then continued virtually unabated in the twentieth century with such authors as Gorky, Pasternak, Nabokov, and Solzhenitsyn.

This great burgeoning of Russian literature that began early in the nineteenth century was in part made possible by a long tradition of story-telling in Russia, the historical roots of which have been traced in fascinating and admirable detail by Prince Mirsky in his book *A History of Russian Literature* (Mirsky 1934). Importantly, this tradition included the sort of living practice of peasant story-telling that Turgenev depicts in certain passages of *Sketches from a Hunter's Album* and that Tolstoy admired in his own peasant pupils. But the great burgeoning in question was also in part made possible by several other advantages, including a massive infusion of enriching literary and philosophical influences from Europe and the sort of nineteenth-century fusion of narration with political-social commitment and thought that I discussed above.

Moreover, some of the most outstanding achievements of the Russian intellectual tradition that lie *beyond* literature were still largely *about* literature. These mainly belong to the twentieth century. They include the achievements of the literary theorist Mikhail Bakhtin (especially, his theory of genre in general and of the novel in particular); the literary theorist and linguist Roman Jakobson (e.g., his theory of translation and his theory of the reflexive nature of language); the novelist, literary theorist, translator, and translation theorist Vladimir Nabokov (whose views on translation continue to play a significant role in contemporary translation theory, for example); and the literary and cultural theorist Yuri Lotman (whose quasi-structuralist theory of literary texts and semiotic theory of culture have been influential). (For helpful presentations of the ideas of Bakhtin and Lotman, see Chaps. 30 and 34 in the present volume by Galin Tihanov and Natalia Avtonomova respectively).)

It is natural to wonder *why* this striking asymmetry between relatively modest achievements in pure philosophy and spectacularly high achievements in literature came about. There is no doubt some temptation to offer a sociopolitical explanation: whereas literature, as an activity that is largely solitary and that can communicate its controversial contents in indirect rather than direct ways, can thrive even in a politically repressive society like Russia, philosophy, as a more essentially social activity that is committed to explicit communication, cannot. However, as the example of the flourishing of Kant, German Idealism, and German Romanticism in the hardly less politically repressive German states of the late eighteenth and early nineteenth centuries shows, this explanation is inadequate; philosophy can very well flourish in the interstices of even politically repressive states.

I suspect that a better explanation lies in the more mysterious domain of individual genius and good fortune. However favorable the soil in an area of open ground may be, a cluster of, say, primroses will only come to grow there if one or two strong seeds fall on it and have sufficient good fortune to survive. In the "area" of literature in nineteenth-century Russia, not only was the "soil" favorable, but in addition the "seed" of Pushkin, followed by those of Lermontov, Gogol, and others, fell on it and then had enough good fortune to be able to grow. Similarly, in the "area" of philosophy in eighteenth-century Germany not only was the "soil" favorable, but in addition the "seed" of Kant, followed by those of his Idealist and Romantic successors, fell on it and then had sufficient good fortune to be able to thrive. By contrast, in the "area" of philosophy in nineteenth-century Russia, although the "soil" was hardly less favorable than it was in those other two cases, no Pushkin- or Kant-like "seed" fell on it. Perhaps that is about as close as one can come to an explanation in this case.

36 RUSSIAN THOUGHT AND *RUSSIAN THINKERS*   787

A second additional point that is supported by the revised version of Berlin's account that I advocated above is that the achievements of the Russian intellectual tradition as a whole were much more strongly enabled by *German* thought than he himself realized. Certainly, the influence of French philosophy and literature on that tradition was enormous: the aristocrats who dominated the tradition in the nineteenth century—for example, Pushkin, Herzen, Turgenev, and Tolstoy—were all strongly francophone, intimately familiar with French culture, and steeped in French philosophy and literature in particular. But the influence of German philosophy and literature was no less important and in some ways even more so. For the same aristocrats were almost as much at home in German language, culture, philosophy, and literature as they were in French. Accordingly, even the earliest generation of great Russian literary authors—especially Pushkin, Lermontov, and Gogol—was heavily indebted to German Romanticism (e.g., Pushkin's *Eugene Onegin* [1833] adopts techniques of deliberate fragmentariness and playful self-reflexivity from German Romanticism, Lermontov's *A Hero of Our Time* (1840) does so as well, and Gogol's work is heavily indebted to the German Romantic E.T.A. Hoffmann in particular). As has been mentioned, the main influences on Russian philosophy since the early nineteenth century have likewise been German, especially Kant, Schelling, Hegel, Marx, and Husserl. And finally, as we have now seen, there was also a deep, if often implicit, dependence of some of the best Russian literature of the later nineteenth century, especially that of Turgenev and Tolstoy, on the German *Bildung* tradition.

In sum, Isaiah Berlin's *Russian Thinkers* was a pathbreaking achievement and still constitutes the gold standard for work on the Russian intellectual tradition. But in many ways it was only a beginning rather than an end. The publication of the present volume will have been amply worthwhile if it has managed to take a few more steps down the path that he opened up.

BIBLIOGRAPHY

Berlin, Isaiah. 1978. *Russian Thinkers*. Edited by Henry Hardy and Aileen Kelly. London: Penguin.

Copleston, Frederick C. 1986. *Philosophy in Russia: From Herzen to Lenin and Berdyaev*. Notre Dame, IN: University of Notre Dame Press.

Forster, Michael N. 2012. Bildung bei Herder und seinen Nachfolgern: drei Begriffe. In *Bildung und Freiheit. Ein vergessener Zusammenhang*, ed. K. Vieweg and M. Winkler, 75–89. Paderborn: Schöningh.

———. 2013. Humboldts Bildungsideal und sein Modell der Universität. In *Die Bildung der Moderne*, ed. M. Dreyer, M.N. Forster, K.-U. Hoffmann, and K. Vieweg, 11–37. Marburg: Francke Verlag.

———. 2018. *Herder's Philosophy*. Oxford: Oxford University Press.

Mirsky, Dmitrii S. Prince. 1934. *A History of Russian Literature: From the Earliest Times to the Death of Dostoyevsky (1881)*. New York: Knopf.

Steiner, Lina. 2011. *For Humanity's Sake: The Bildungsroman in Russian Culture*. Toronto and London: University of Toronto Press.

Correction to: Art as an Instrument of Philosophy

Helen Petrovsky

CORRECTION TO:

Chapter 35 in: M. F. Bykova et al. (eds.), *The Palgrave Handbook of Russian Thought*, https://doi.org/10.1007/978-3-030-62982-3_35

An older version of the abstract has been published online erroneously which is corrected now and given below.

The chapter focuses on two distinct tendencies in contemporary Russian thought regarding its approach to art. The first is exemplified in the original method developed by the philosopher Valery Podoroga, namely, his analytical anthropology of literature and art. Offering a fresh reading of the Russian formalists as well as of phenomenology, Podoroga develops his own conception of mimesis and what he terms as "Work." The second trend has to do with the understanding of art as a phenomenon of mass societies. This approach emphasizes collective affectivity and is associated with the work of Oleg Aronson and the ideas of the composer Vladimir Martynov. Here art is no longer the object of reflection, but a new ground for thinking itself. The same perspective is shared by younger scholars, such as Alexandra Volodina and Denis Larionov, who explore the various manifestations of "minor" art.

The updated version of this chapter can be found at
https://doi.org/10.1007/978-3-030-62982-3_35

© The Author(s), under exclusive license to Springer Nature
Switzerland AG 2021
M. F. Bykova et al. (eds.), *The Palgrave Handbook of Russian Thought*,
https://doi.org/10.1007/978-3-030-62982-3_37

NAME INDEX

A

Adorno, Theodor W., 221, 708
Aksel'rod, Liubov' I., 83, 192
Aldanov, Mark (pseudonym of Mark
    Alexandrovich Landau), 131n3, 295
Alembert, Jean d, 25, 33, 46
Alexander I (The Emperor of Russia), 6,
    7, 26, 29, 96, 99, 102, 120, 128,
    299, 482n37
Alexander II (The Emperor of Russia), 3,
    10, 80, 89, 180, 300, 467, 563, 565
Alexander III (The Emperor of
    Russia), 80, 467
Alighieri, Dante, 206, 458, 743, 748,
    750n19, 785
Althusser, Louis, 86, 265n10,
    265–266n19
Arendt, Hannah, 73, 83, 87, 154,
    649, 653n7
Aristotle, 28, 69, 155n1, 225, 226,
    236n14, 481n21, 540, 542, 578,
    591n27, 652, 655n14, 674, 757
Asmus, Valentin F., 115, 130, 131,
    131n5, 132n17, 133–135, 138, 393
Astafiev, Viktor P., 541
Avenarius, Richard, 191, 194, 195,
    246–250, 275
Averintsev, Sergei S., 644, 655n14

B

Baader, Franz, 229
Bacon, Francis, 392
Badiou, Alain, 748
Bakhtin, Mikhail M., 2, 13–15, 17,
    19n16, 287, 420, 451, 456, 464,
    479n5, 481n21, 481n22, 482n41,
    482n42, 491, 570, 571, 643–652,
    659–669, 675, 676, 708, 709n8,
    719, 750n16, 772n22, 786
Bakunin, Mikhail A., 3, 75–79, 82, 89,
    139–145, 147, 149, 153, 154,
    155n2, 155n4, 155n7, 155–156n8,
    156n9, 156n10, 453, 481n24,
    482n33, 508, 510, 513–517,
    564–566, 568, 777, 779–781
Bataille, George, 763
Batishchev, Genrikh S., 287, 373, 396,
    403n2, 411–414, 416, 418, 419,
    421n2, 708
Bazarov, Vladimir A., 81, 180–182,
    196n4, 274, 275, 279, 521
Beccaria, Cesare, 34, 35
Belinsky, Vissarion G., 17, 76, 140, 213,
    449–455, 461, 464, 480n13,
    480n17, 481n19, 507–524,
    549–552, 554, 555, 567, 571n2,
    703, 709n9, 777, 781, 782

© The Author(s), under exclusive license to Springer Nature
Switzerland AG 2021
M. F. Bykova et al. (eds.), *The Palgrave Handbook of Russian Thought*,
https://doi.org/10.1007/978-3-030-62982-3

789

790 NAME INDEX

Bely, Andrei (pseudonym of Boris
  Nikolaevich Bugaev), 11, 58, 106,
  111, 470, 680, 758–760
Benjamin, Walter, 83, 661, 708, 762
Berdyaev, Nikolai A., 10–13, 17, 19n12,
  56–58, 60, 61, 83–85, 98, 99, 110,
  155n1, 190, 217–235, 274, 295,
  425, 426, 652, 673, 674, 686, 785
Bergson, Henri, 684, 763
Berkeley, George, 247, 248, 251,
  259, 260
Berlin, Sir Isaiah, v, vi, 17, 19n14, 145,
  147–149, 155n2, 509, 519, 589n6,
  777–784, 787
Berman, Jakov A., 288n13
Bervi, Wilhelm, 180
Bestuzhev, Nikolai A., 101
Bestuzhev-Marlinskii, Alexander A., 449
Bestuzhev-Riumin, Mikhail P., 99
Betskoi, Ivan I., 33, 34
Bibikhin, Vladimir V., 68, 69, 71n4,
  88, 89, 98
Bibler, Vladimir S., 287, 403n2
Bielfeld, Jacob von, 34
Blanchot, Maurice, 763
Bocharov, Sergei G., 647, 648,
  652, 653n5
Bogdanov, Alexander, 13, 28, 30, 81,
  188, 191, 192, 241, 249–252,
  254–257, 259, 261, 265n15,
  272–281, 285, 286, 288n10,
  288n15, 288n16, 289n19, 378n23,
  416, 695, 712n31
Bonch-Bruevich, Vladimir D., 194
Botkin, Vasilii P., 480n13, 517, 518
Brezhnev, Leonid I., 83, 392, 712n36
Briullov, Karl P., 634, 635
Broyde, Stephen, 630, 631
Bruno, Giordano, 168, 533, 536,
  538, 540
Buber, Martin, 646, 650,
  654n11, 654n12
Büchner, Ludwig, 180, 255, 577
Bukharin, Nikolai I., 83, 283–285,
  289n18, 289n19
Bulgakov, Mikhail A., 15, 131n3,
  266n23, 456, 549
Bulgakov, Sergei N. (Fr.), 11, 12, 56–61,
  63, 65, 68, 83, 85, 98, 190, 191,

218, 219, 228, 274, 295, 552,
  674, 720, a
Bulgarin, Faddei V., 493, 518
Bunin, Ivan A., 11, 104, 105,
  110, 295
Burke, Edmund, 661

C

Cabet, Étienne, 550
Carnap, Rudolf, 650
Cassirer, Ernst, 132n7, 281, 650
Catherine I (Empress of Russia), 31
Catherine II (Empress of Russia), 5,
  26–29, 31–42, 46, 128, 299, 302,
  303, 461, 479n3
Cervantes, Miguel de, 232, 453,
  483n54, 668
Chaadaev, Pyotr Ya, 3, 8, 69, 425, 449,
  479n3, 513, 557
Chekhov, Anton P., 207, 208, 213, 491,
  492, 608, 720, 758
Chelpanov, Georgii I., 341, 426
Chernyshevsky, Nikolai G., 3, 11, 17,
  180–182, 188, 234, 359, 449, 452,
  471, 509, 510, 549–571,
  571n2, 572n5
Chizhevsky Dmitry (Dmitro)
  (Tchizhevsky or Tchizhevskij),
  155n1, 665, 674
Chukhrai, Grigorii Ya., 385
Chukovsky, Korney I., 683
Clausewitz, Carl von, 241
Cohen, Hermann, 409
Comte, Auguste, 184, 275, 532, 538,
  540, 544n12
Copleston, Frederick C., 18n2, 19n11,
  19n17, 52, 244, 245, 253,
  265n16, 778

D

Dal', Vladimir I., 521
Danilevskii, Nikolai Ia., 3, 110
Dashkova, Ekaterina R. Princess.,
  6, 480n9
Davydov, Vasily V., 378n21, 410,
  411, 413
Deborin, Abram M., 129, 264n2, 699

NAME INDEX 791

Deleuze, Gilles, 70, 87, 546n41, 660, 758, 763, 769, 770
Derrida, Jacques, 149, 233, 628
Descartes, René, 369, 392, 411, 532, 540, 601
Diderot, Denis, 33–42, 46, 605, 778, 781
Dilthey, Wilhelm, 270, 650
Dobrokhotov, Alexander L., 756
Dobrolyubov (Dobroliubov), Nikolai (Nikolay) A., 11, 180, 234, 449, 509, 557, 559, 709n9
Dostoevsky, Fyodor M., 3, 10–12, 17, 96, 105, 155, 180, 182, 183, 185, 206–211, 213, 447, 450, 454, 455, 457, 458, 463–469, 472, 473, 475, 478, 479, 480n17, 481n22, 481n26, 482n36, 482n39, 482n40, 483n55, 484n64, 484n65, 484n75, 485n79, 491, 509, 520, 523, 549–571, 646, 647, 649, 651, 653n5, 662, 663, 665, 666, 675, 758–760, 785
Drobnitskii, Oleg, 708
Druzhinin, Alexander V., 555, 557

E

Ebner, Ferdinand, 650, 654n11
Egorov, Boris F., 739, 750n16
Ehrenburg, Ilya G., 391
Eikhenbaum, Boris M., 575, 589n4, 591n23, 662, 748n4, 759
Eisenstein, Sergei M., 760, 761
Elizabeth I (Empress of Russia), 31
Emerson, Caryl, 481n21, 601, 607, 616n3, 643, 647, 649, 655n14, 665, 669
Engels, Friedrich, 78, 119, 190, 243–245, 251, 256, 258–260, 265n11, 265n15, 270, 273, 282, 287n2, 362, 386, 394, 408, 564, 693–697, 709n6, 710n16, 711n27, 778, 780
Epicurus, 578
Epstein, Mikhail, 2, 15
Eriugena (John Duns Scotus), 55
Ern, Vladimir F., 56, 57, 68, 98, 129

F

Fedotov, Georgii P., 63, 209, 295
Fet, Afanasy A., 509, 566
Feuerbach, Ludwig, 181, 188, 369, 577, 695, 702
Fichte, Johann Gottlieb, 7, 130, 153, 155–156n8, 171, 368, 411, 511, 519, 540–542, 546n36, 684
Florensky, Pavel A., 11, 12, 56–58, 60, 61, 68, 125, 126, 218, 228, 237n18, 425, 427, 433, 440, 621–637, 674, 686, 748
Florovsky, Georgii V. (Georges), 9, 63, 64, 66, 67, 104, 105, 181, 295, 426
Fondaminsky, Ilya I., 293–314
Foucault, Michel, 87, 149, 748, 768, 770
Frank, Semyon L., 11, 52, 56–58, 60, 61, 63, 75, 83–85, 90, 185, 218, 295, 314n1, 626, 674, 720
Freidenberg Ol'ga M., 668
Freud, Sigmund, 476
Fyodorov (Fedorov), Nikolai F., 3, 52, 363, 470

G

Galich, Alexander I., 7
Gasparov, Mikhail L., 636, 638n11, 638n16, 665
Gershenzon, Mikhail O., 52, 53, 455
Gnedich, Pyotr P., 102
Goethe, Johann Wolfgang von, 7, 222, 371, 456, 517, 592n36, 653n2, 662, 697, 731, 781, 783
Gogol, Nikolai V., 17, 447, 450, 454, 458, 464, 465, 472, 481n18, 491–505, 509, 512, 519–523, 549, 551, 552, 554, 556, 566, 758–760, 781, 785–787
Golitsyn, Dmitri A. Prince, 33
Goncharov, Ivan A., 11, 450, 452, 509, 520, 522
Gorbachev, Mikhail S., 87, 89, 399, 402, 707
Gorky, Maxim (pseudonym of Alexei Maximovich Peshkov), 241, 242, 456, 482n42, 654n8, 785
Griboedov, Alexander S., 516, 517

792 NAME INDEX

Grigorovich, Dmitrii V., 554, 555, 557
Grot, Nikolai Ya., 17, 424, 525–543, 578, 580, 581
Gulyga, Arsenii (Arsenij) V., 222, 395, 733n1

H

Habermas, Jürgen, 154
Hegel, Georg Wilhelm Friedrich, 10, 53, 55, 76–78, 86, 96, 100, 103, 105, 118, 130, 131, 131n2, 132n9, 139–155, 160–162, 165, 168, 171, 174, 175, 185, 186, 190, 208, 211, 217, 220, 222, 227, 228, 230, 234, 236n10, 237n21, 241, 243, 253, 271–273, 317–332, 332n4, 333n8, 333n11, 333–334n14, 334n16, 362, 369, 377n10, 394, 396, 409, 411, 416, 450, 452, 508, 510–519, 557, 578, 593n41, 593n46, 673, 674, 683, 684, 695–697, 703, 705, 709n2, 709n9, 765, 778, 779, 781, 785, 787
Heidegger, Martin, 60, 69, 149, 5 29, 543, 546n34, 583, 592n37, 646, 649–652, 654n10, 654n12, 764
Heine, Heinrich, 206, 566, 697
Herder, Johann Gottfried, 116, 450, 480n16, 483n52, 512, 578, 580–582, 590n18, 591n23, 591n25, 592n32, 592n34, 593n41, 653n2, 779, 780, 782–784
Hertz, Heinrich, 188
Herzen, Alexander I., 3, 54, 75–77, 89, 90, 96, 98–100, 102–105, 110, 111n5, 140, 141, 145–149, 154, 155, 155n2, 450, 453, 455, 458, 462, 463, 480n9, 481n24, 482n33, 482n39, 485n79, 491, 495, 497, 502, 504, 509, 511, 514, 516, 520, 523, 553, 554, 557, 560, 568, 577, 590n10, 709n9, 777–779, 781, 787
Hessen, Sergei I., 96–98, 100, 103, 105, 111n2, 111n4
Hessen, Sergei Ya., 95, 100–103
Humboldt, Alexander von, 7

Humboldt, Wilhelm von, 347, 352, 353, 355n18, 450, 623, 624, 661, 778, 780, 783
Hume, David, 246–248, 251, 259
Husserl, Edmund, 60, 70, 236n12, 270, 319, 323, 339–341, 343, 344, 346, 348, 351, 353, 354, 354n1, 354n2, 354n3, 354n4, 355n14, 355n17, 355n18, 355n20, 356n24, 356n25, 529, 650–652, 654n10, 654n12, 662, 673, 785, 787

I

Ilyenkov, Evald V., 14, 245, 253, 259, 265n18, 273, 287, 359–376, 387–391, 394–397, 400, 403n2, 411–413, 416, 418, 420, 708, 709n2, 711n25
Ilyin (Il'in), Ivan A., 12, 17, 56, 58, 59, 66, 68, 74, 75, 84, 85, 87, 90, 242, 245, 273, 317–332
Ivan III (Grand Duke of Moscow), 5
Ivan IV (the Terrible) (Grand Duke of Moscow, the first Russian Tsar), 5, 717
Ivanov, Vyacheslav I., 52, 56–58, 60, 219, 225, 228, 237n20, 455, 570, 637n4, 674, 678, 738, 740

J

Jakobson, Roman O., 427, 433, 434, 746, 747, 786

K

Kagan, Matvei I., 662
Kakhovskii, Petr G., 99
Kant, Immanuel, 7, 19n9, 86, 88, 115–131, 153, 161, 171, 204, 211, 212, 222, 232, 234, 237n21, 243, 246, 248, 259, 274, 346, 350, 368, 392, 394, 408, 427, 428, 450, 480n15, 512, 527, 529, 530, 532–534, 536–541, 543, 544n9, 544n11, 546n35, 557, 567, 577, 578, 580, 581, 585, 591n23, 592n39, 684, 696, 697, 705, 710n19, 720, 721, 785–787

NAME INDEX

Karamzin, Nikolai M., 115, 118, 448, 457, 459, 460, 466, 473, 482n37, 483n52, 483n55, 581, 591n23, 591n29, 592n30, 593n41, 740, 741, 749n11
Karsavin, Lev P., 12, 56–58, 218, 652
Kavelin, Konstantin D., 529, 533, 544n10
Kedrov, Bonifaty (Bonifatii) M., 375, 403n2
Kerensky (Kerenskii), Alexander S., 295
Khomiakov, Alexei S., 10, 54
Khrapovitskii, Alexander V., 45, 128
Khrushchev, Nikita S., 14, 83, 86, 391, 694, 707, 709n1
Kireevskii, Ivan V., 54, 139, 140, 435
Kline, George L., 321, 481n25
Kliuchevsky (Klyuchevsky; Kliuchevskii), Vasilii O., 717
Kojève, Alexandre, 142, 147–149, 153, 155n6, 156n9
Kollontai, Alexandra M., 83
Kopnin, Pavel V., 272, 374, 375, 403n2
Korovikov, Valentin I., 360, 361, 372, 376, 377n6, 377n7, 388, 389
Koyré, Alexandre, 7, 10, 155n1, 155n2, 222, 223
Kraevskii, Andrei A., 516, 557
Kropotkin, Pyotr A. Prince., 79, 196n2
Krupskaya, Nadezhda K., 253
Küchelbecker, Wilhelm K., 100

L

Lassalle, Ferdinand, 241
Lavrov, Pyotr L., 183–185, 194
Lenin, Vladimir I. (pseudonym of Vladimir Il'ich Ulyanov), 74, 75, 79–82, 89, 90, 119, 192, 193, 239–264, 270–276, 278, 279, 287n4, 288n6, 288n9, 306–308, 314, 333n11, 362, 378n23, 386, 394, 564, 568, 693, 695, 696, 699, 701, 703, 709n3, 709n9, 710n18, 711n26, 722, 777, 779, 785
Leontiev, Alexei N., 360, 410, 413, 417, 421n1, 708
Lermontov, Mikhail Yu., 450, 451, 462, 483n59, 566, 758, 785–787
Leskov, Nikolai S., 492

Lifshits, Mikhail A., 403n2, 694, 697–701, 704–706, 708, 709n2, 710n14, 710n16, 710n18, 712n35
Lomonosov, Mikhail V., 6, 31, 32
Lopatin, Lev M., 318, 424, 425, 526, 541
Lopukhin, Ivan V., 43
Losev, Alexei (Aleksei) F., 2, 13, 14, 52, 57, 58, 68, 98, 159, 230, 235, 236n11, 237n22, 287, 403n2, 440, 552, 673–687, 705, 708, 709n8, 710n16
Lossky (Losski), Nikolai O., 6, 12, 18n2, 19n17, 52, 56–60, 63, 64, 66, 67, 180, 185, 295, 426, 542, 543, 544n5
Lossky (Losski), Vladimir N., 64, 65, 67
Lotman, Yuri M., 14, 17, 18n6, 102, 403n2, 448, 459, 460, 592n30, 621, 624, 625, 630, 633, 675, 708, 737–748, 786
Lubkin, Alexander S., 118, 122
Lunacharsky, Anatoly V., 83, 192, 219, 241, 249, 251, 274, 695
Lunin, Mikhail S., 100

M

Mach, Ernst, 189, 191, 192, 194, 246–250, 252, 256, 259, 261, 274, 275, 288n6, 288n10
Mamardashvili, Merab K., 14, 287, 385, 389, 398, 399, 403n2
Mandelstam (Mandel'shtam), Nadezhda Ya, 637n1
Mandelstam (Mandel'shtam), Osip E., 11, 17, 621–637
Marr, Nikolai Ya., 668
Marx, Karl, 78, 86, 87, 105, 132n16, 139, 186, 187, 190, 194, 239, 242–244, 251, 259, 265n11, 265n15, 270, 273, 282, 285, 287n2, 288n7, 333n11, 364–368, 370, 378n22, 385, 389, 394, 407, 408, 411, 416, 418, 510, 564, 694–699, 702–708, 709n2, 710n13, 710n16, 710n18, 711n27, 778–780, 785, 787
Masaryk, Thomas, 1

794 NAME INDEX

Mechnikov, Ilya I., 533
Medvedev, Pavel N., 27, 644, 654n7, 662, 669n3
Mendeleev, Dmitrii (Dmitri) I., 189, 190
Merezhkovskii (Merezhkovskij), Dmitrii S., 52, 102, 218
Mikhailov, Felix T., 373, 374, 616n4, 708
Mikhailovsky (Mikhajlovskii), Nikolai K., 184
Miliukov, Pavel N., 297
Mirsky, D. S. (pseudonym of Prince Dmitry Petrovich Svyatopolk-Mirsky), 18n5, 484n71, 785
Muraviov-Apostol, Sergei I., 99

N
Nabokov, Vladimir V., 295, 447–459, 463, 483n51, 484n63, 484n71, 484n73, 484n75, 484n76, 484n77, 484n78, 551, 785, 786
Nadezhdin, Nikolai I., 511
Natorp, Paul, 341
Nechaev, Sergei G., 564, 566, 568
Neizvestny, Ernst I., 385
Nekrasov, Nikolai A., 102, 509, 520, 554, 555
Nestor (the chronicler of Kievan Rus'), 4
Nicholas I (Emperor of Russia), 10, 77, 139, 179, 299, 304, 453, 482n37, 584, 586
Nietzsche, Friedrich, 12, 70, 162, 171, 190, 206–209, 214, 224–226, 232–234, 455, 459, 482n39, 482n40, 483n49, 537–540, 598, 621, 626, 634, 637n2, 637n7, 639n29, 650, 678
Nikon (Patriarch of Moscow), 29
Novgorodtsev, Pavel I., 56, 58, 187, 319, 323
Novikov, Nikolai I., 6, 27, 29, 43, 733n1

O
Obolenskii, Evgenii P. Prince, 101, 102
Odoevskii, Vladimir F. Prince, 7, 449, 480n12
Ogurtsov, Alexander P., 395, 719

P
Paleologue (Paleologina), Zoe (Sophia) (Grand Duchess of Moscow), 5
Panaeva, Avdot'ia P., 554
Paul I (Emperor of Russia), 6, 26, 480n9
Pestel, Pavel I., 99, 100
Piatigorsky, Alexander M., 91, 738
Pirogov, Nikolai I., 577
Pisarev, Dmitrii I., 181, 234, 449, 509
Plato, 28, 116, 119, 127, 155n1, 168, 233, 234, 258, 424, 427, 532, 538, 540–542, 578, 622, 624, 638n13, 652, 673, 784
Platonov, Andrei P., 17, 549, 715–733, 758–760, 771n7
Plekhanov, Georgii V., 119, 129, 185–188, 190–194, 245, 249–251, 260, 265n13, 265n17, 266n26, 270–279, 282–284, 287n2, 287n3, 288n12, 304, 516, 521, 589n3, 695, 785
Podoroga, Valery A., 88, 749n7, 756–761, 771n3, 771n7, 771n9, 771n10
Portugeis, Semen O., 293–314
Potebnia, Alexander A., 623, 624, 628, 629
Prigogine, Ilya, 750n17
Prokopovich, Feofan, 28
Pugachev, Emel'ian I., 6, 37–39, 45, 303, 461, 494
Pushkin, Alexander S., 100, 102, 132n8, 180, 303, 319, 439, 450, 453–455, 457, 459–462, 465, 467, 471–473, 475, 478, 479n2, 479n4, 480n9, 482n36, 482n37, 482n45, 483n46, 483n47, 483n57, 504, 505n3, 512, 518–521, 549, 554, 556, 557, 564, 743, 758, 785–787

R
Radishchev, Alexander N., 27, 44–46, 302, 303, 740, 741
Rickert, Heinrich, 96–98, 109, 111n2, 319, 651
Rimsky-Korsakov, Nikolai A., 673, 678
Rousseau, Jean-Jacques, 33, 156n14, 459, 474, 566, 578, 581, 589, 593n43, 610–612, 709n9, 782

NAME INDEX   795

Rozanov, Vasily (Vasilii) V., 3, 11, 12, 52, 56, 68, 69, 236n16

Rozhdestvenskii, Nikolai P., 127

Rubinstein, Sergei L., 407–410, 417–419, 426, 708

Russel, Bertrand, 257, 526, 529

Ryleev, Kondratii F., 99–102, 111n5, 449

S

Samarin, Yurii F., 28, 76

Scanlan, James, 86, 289n20, 590n15, 704, 705, 710n16, 711n21, 711n31

Schelling, Friedrich Wilhelm Joseph, 7, 10, 53, 55, 118, 131n2, 149, 150, 153, 168, 225, 227, 236n13, 368, 511, 512, 528, 541, 673, 705, 785, 787

Schiller, Friedrich, 549, 593n43, 697, 698, 709n9, 781

Schnittke, Alfred, 385

Schopenhauer, Arthur, 171, 190, 226, 482n33, 527, 534, 537, 539, 541, 545n24, 576, 578–580, 593n42, 607, 621, 624, 630, 637n2, 684, 782

Scriabin, Alexander N., 11, 639n28, 678–682, 684, 687, 688n13

Sechenov, Ivan M., 533

Shalamov, Varlam T., 17, 715–733

Shchedrovitsky, Georgy K., 287, 389, 395, 397, 398, 403n2, 412, 415, 416, 418, 421n3, 421n4

Shcherbatov, Mikhail M. Prince, 32, 42, 43

Shostakovich, Dmitri S., 233

Shpet, Gustav G., 17, 19n17, 54, 156n11, 339–356, 424–425, 427, 429, 433–435, 438, 440, 441n1, 441n4, 508, 519, 712n32

Shuvalov, Ivan I. Count, 33

Sinyavsky, Andrei D., 504, 505

Sof'ia Alexeevna, Tsarevna (the Regent of Russia), 29

Solovyov (Solov'ev), Vladimir S., 3, 12, 17, 55–58, 66, 68, 69, 75, 79–82, 84, 85, 88, 90, 98, 107, 119, 123,

141, 142, 149–155, 156n13, 159–177, 214, 218, 227, 231, 236n17, 424, 425, 429, 435, 441n1, 455, 525, 526, 532, 538, 541, 544n12, 546n38, 552, 582, 623, 652, 673, 676, 785

Solzhenitsyn, Alexander I., 86, 447, 456, 707, 785

Spinoza, Baruch, 160, 186, 187, 190, 208, 362, 369, 394, 396, 763

St. Gregory Palamas, 61, 65, 66, 68, 676

St. Vladimir Monomakh (Grand Prince of Kiev), 4

Stalin, Joseph V. (pseudonym of Iosif Vissarionovich Dzhugashvili), 13, 14, 81, 130, 233, 240, 264n2, 308, 314, 318, 384, 387, 391, 694, 695, 697, 707, 709n1, 709n4, 709n5, 717, 719, 722, 725, 726, 730, 732, 785

Stankevich, Nikolai V., 53, 140, 141, 145, 155n4, 450, 480n13, 481n24, 508, 510, 511, 513, 514, 518, 522

Stepin, Vyacheslav S., 392, 412, 415

Stepun, Fyodor (Fedor) A., 56, 96–98, 106–110, 111n6, 295, 314n2, 568

Strakhov, Nikolai N., 11, 567, 568, 579, 580, 591n20, 591n21

Struve, Peter (Pyotr) B., 58, 59, 274, 319, 674

Suvorin, Alexei S., 566

T

Tarkovsky, Andrei A., 385, 470

Tatishchev, Vasily N., 31, 32

Tchaikovsky, Pyotr I., 233

Timiriazev, Kliment A., 189

Tiutchev, Fyodor I., 566, 638n11

Tolstoy, Lev (Leo) N., 3, 102, 123, 206, 447, 526, 554, 575, 598, 729, 745, 758, 777

Toporov, Vladimir N., 460, 738, 740

Torop, Peeter, 739, 745

Trifonov, Yuri V., 385

796 NAME INDEX

Trubetskoi, Evgenii N. Prince, 56–59, 98, 123, 172, 177n2, 218, 319, 323
Trubetskoi, Sergei N. (Philosopher), 55, 58, 424
Trubetskoi, Sergei P. Prince (Decembrist), 58, 59, 99, 218, 425
Turgenev, Ivan S., 11, 180, 182, 447, 452–455, 458, 463, 466, 469, 481n24, 481n29, 482n33, 482n39, 491, 508, 509, 520, 521, 550, 554, 555, 557, 576, 729, 758, 777, 781, 782, 784–787
Tynyanov (Tynianov), Yuri N., 747, 748n4, 759, 771n6

U
Uspensky, Boris A., 18n6, 624, 625, 738, 740, 744, 745, 747
Uvarov, Sergei S. Count, 7, 179, 450, 480n14, 717

V
Vernadsky, Vladimir I., 362, 741, 742, 749n15
Voloshinov, Valentin N., 664, 665
Voltaire (pseudonym of François-Marie Arouet), 33, 39, 46, 79, 299, 461, 588, 589, 668, 781
Vvedensky, Alexander I., 525, 543
Vyazemsky (Viazemskii), Pyotr A. Prince, 557, 558

Vygotsky, Lev S., 2, 13, 360, 365, 410, 413, 420, 426, 433, 434, 708, 711n25
Vysheslavtsev, Boris P., 12, 58, 63

W
Wagner, Richard, 464, 604, 678, 680, 681, 684, 685, 688n10, 688n12
Walicki, Andrzej, 10, 19n17, 26, 77, 89, 142, 183, 184, 463, 542, 543, 544n5
Wittgenstein, Ludwig, 60, 69, 342, 411, 529, 613, 615
Woolf, Virgnia, 455, 764

Y
Yaroslav the Wise (Grand Prince of Kiev), 32
Yeltsin, Boris N.(Eltsin), 121
Yudin, Eric G., 403n2, 412, 417
Yurkevich (Iurkevich), Pamphil D., 557
Yushkevitch (Iushkevich), Pavel S., 275–279, 281

Z
Zamoshkin, Yuri A., 88
Zamyatin (Zamiatin), Evgenii I., 455, 456, 649
Zenkovsky, Vasilii V., 59, 63
Zinchenko, Vladimir P., 434
Zinoviev, Alexander A., 14, 87, 366, 385, 388–391, 394–397, 399–402, 403n2, 707
Žižek, Slavoj, 82, 87

Subject Index

A

Absolute, the
  in German idealism, 147, 148,
    150–153, 324–326, 329, 334n14,
    452, 539, 622, 623, 627, 628
  in Vl. Solovyov, 161–162, 167, 171,
    173, 175–176
  See also Unity, unity of all
Academy of Sciences, Russian/Soviet, 5,
  18n7, 28, 30–32, 34, 120, 130,
  394, 403n1, 403n2, 403n5, 738,
  762, 771n1, 771n2, 771n12
Action
  human, 172, 184, 186, 187, 757
  mediated, 770
  moral, 204
  political, 193, 195, 242, 251
  revolutionary, 271
  social, 54
Activity
  approach, 407–421, 428
  collective, 279, 410, 411, 413, 415
  communication and, 414, 419, 746
  conception (of), 408, 415, 708
  contemplation and, 418
  idea of, 413
  object-oriented, 410, 413, 414,
    418, 419
  ontology of, 702
  theory, 360, 407, 409–416,
    418–420, 711n25
  thinking and, 280
Ada (Nabokov), 470–479
Aesthetic(s)
  discussion, 694, 698, 705–707,
    709, 709n2
  Marxist-Leninist, 693, 700,
    708
  neo-Marxist, 708
  nature of, 168–169
  properties/qualities, 700, 701,
    704, 711n25
  relation to reality, 697, 698, 700
  soviet, 693, 705, 708, 709n8,
    711n21
Agency
  historical, 282, 519
  practical, 369
A Hero of Our Time (Lermontov),
  451–452, 787
Alienation
  criticism of, 411, 697
  of human, 203, 396, 411, 515, 625,
    706, 707
  of labor, 706
  self-alienation, 215

© The Author(s), under exclusive license to Springer Nature
Switzerland AG 2021
M. F. Bykova et al. (eds.), *The Palgrave Handbook of Russian Thought*,
https://doi.org/10.1007/978-3-030-62982-3

798   SUBJECT INDEX

All-unity (Vl. Solovyov), 12, 55–58, 61,
    85, 161, 163n3, 164–173, 177n3,
    538, 622, 623, 626
  expression of, 168, 636
Anarchism, Russian, 78, 84, 141, 153
And Quiet Flows the Don (Sholokhov),
    718, 720, 722, 725–726
Anna Karenina (Tolstoy), 467, 468,
    473, 477, 616n4, 616n7
Anthropocentrism, 123, 223, 681, 684,
    685, 693, 709
Anthropogram, 759, 771n3
Anthropology
  philosophical, 163n2, 164, 170, 756
    See also Ontology
Antiquity, 9, 170, 224, 236n7, 417,
    502, 675
Antisemitism, 85
Aristocracy
  Russian, 7, 85, 466, 483n62, 509, 740
  Western, 478
Aristos, 96, 103, 110
Army
  Red, 297, 360, 722, 723, 725
  White, 724
Art
  movement; avant-garde, 228, 229,
    233, 235, 468, 760, 762, 766;
    Futurism, 12; modernism, 452,
    454, 483n60; realism, 222, 451,
    507, 509, 510, 512, 700,
    726, 758
  Russian; contemporary, 17; theory of,
    17, 467, 597–598, 600, 604–605,
    613–614, 617n8, 703
  visual; architecture, 30, 47, 298, 498,
    538, 626; filmmaking, 360, 384,
    475, 666, 760, 761, 763, 770 (*see
    also* Cinema); painting, 33, 228,
    451, 467, 474, 502, 600,
    605–607, 616n3, 629, 739;
    photography, 771n15; sculpture,
    600, 677
  works of, 470, 600, 601, 614
Artistry, 95–111, 504, 781
  artistic many-souledness, 108
Atheism
  and God, 7, 125, 127
  militant, 242

Author and Hero in Aesthetic Activity
    (Bakhtin), 665–666
Autocracy
  Russian, 32, 35, 73–91, 95, 99, 102,
    121, 299, 302, 312, 331, 459,
    494, 516, 551, 552, 568, 716,
    717, 725, 732
  Soviet, 551, 717, 725
Autonomy
  human, 12, 392, 399, 458, 667, 783
  moral, 534, 577
  national, 783
  political, 392
    See also Freedom; Liberty

B
Base, 56, 60, 171, 185–186, 282–286,
    305, 329, 484n66, 544n5, 592n39,
    728, 746
  and superstructure, 282, 284, 286
Beauty/beautiful
  in Berdyaev, 219, 227–228
  ideal of, 168, 170, 171, 687
  in Losev, 679, 687
  in Russian literature, 453, 459, 465,
    471, 527, 535, 552–553, 558,
    623, 629–630
  in Vl. Solovyov, 165, 167–171
  soul, 93n43, 453, 458, 481n31,
    513–515, 518–519, 585
  in Tolstoy, 598–599, 603, 606, 612,
    613, 616n2, 784
Being/being
  event of, 649
  social, 96, 283, 339, 341, 683, 702
Bible, 28, 209, 210, 212, 229, 626
  character of Abraham, 213
  story of Job, 213
Bildung, 585, 590n11, 591n28, 783,
    784, 787
    See also Culture; Education
Bildungsroman, 452–454, 457, 463,
    468, 469, 480n10, 481n27,
    782, 783
Bohemian, 96, 99, 100, 103–110
Bolshevik(s), 13, 62, 76, 109, 130, 194,
    241, 249–251, 264n1, 265n14,
    265n17, 293, 296, 304–310, 312,

313, 314n4, 318, 324, 331,
333n11, 526, 551, 575, 654n8,
695, 718, 721, 722, 724,
725, 733n7
See also Menshevik(s)
Bolshevism, 108, 109, 250, 251,
265n17, 297, 306–313,
568, 733n14
Lenin's understanding of,
250–251, 265n17
programs of, 568
and Russian modernism, 313
theoretical credo of, the, 251
Bourgeoisie/bourgeois, 78, 79, 86, 129,
130, 153, 190, 192, 194, 223, 257,
305–306, 309–310, 312, 369, 389,
396, 451–452, 463, 473, 685,
686, 727
Brothers Karamazov, The (Dostoevsky),
181–182, 467, 556

C

Capital (city), 18, 37, 61, 153,
493, 495, 498–501, 503, 504,
560, 728
Capital (Das Kapital) (Marx), 78–79,
86, 129–130, 153, 190, 192, 194,
223, 257, 305–306, 309–310, 312,
389, 396, 451–452, 463, 476,
684–686, 727, 733n13
Captain's Daughter, The (Pushkin),
460–462
Carnival/carnivalization (Bakhtin), 464,
644, 651
Censorship, 76, 80, 111n3, 185, 376n2,
513, 524, 572n7, 575, 784
Chevengur (Platonov), 718, 729, 733n7,
733n11, 733n13
Children, 28, 29, 34, 35, 37, 90, 213,
223, 294, 341, 360, 370, 371, 384,
413, 419, 451, 458, 463, 477, 478,
482n33, 494, 521, 557, 563, 570,
588, 600, 604, 606, 608, 612, 626,
631, 632, 728, 782
Church
c. Fathers, 5, 28, 54, 64,
127
Ecumenical Orthodox, 68

Roman Catholic, 90, 124, 128,
132n15, 205, 552, 654n11 (*see
also* Religion, Catholicism)
Russian Orthodox, 10, 28, 85, 124,
128, 585, 622, 674, 785 (*see also*
Religion, Orthodox)
See also Religion
Cinema(tography)/cinematic
and communication, 762
fabric of, 763
method, 761
realm of, 760
studies, 17, 737, 747
Civilization
Asian, 5
bourgeois, 452
cultural, 53, 728
European, 454–455, 552
Greco-Roman, 9
human, 173
Russian, 297, 454, 523, 742
Western, 141, 150, 300, 454, 473
Class
antagonistic, 252
bourgeois, 78
consciousness, 285, 286
ideology (of), 242, 286
interest, 191
lower vs. upper, 300–301, 303
middle, 8
ruling, 78, 82, 312, 613
social, 42
of society, 36
working, 78, 239, 274, 286
in zoology, 179
Class struggle, 81, 86, 129, 270, 273,
284, 311, 613, 677, 699, 730
ideological criteria of, the, 391
populist perception of, the, 244
Cognition
cultural and historical character,
343, 437–439
embodied, 418
materialist form(s) of, 274, 279
semiotic nature of, 433
theory of, 176, 189, 259, 274, 279,
281, 288n9, 426
Commodity, 364–366, 479, 706
fetishism, 706

800 SUBJECT INDEX

"Common Human Roots of Idealism"
(Vl. Solovyov), 621–623, 626, 631
Commune, 179
See also Kommuna/village *mir*
Communication
and activity, 410, 413, 414, 419, 742
(*see also* Activity,
communication and)
deep, 414
dialogical, 69
theory of, 747
Concept(s)
being, of, 174, 756
deep communication, of, 414
dialectic(s), of, 273
freedom, of, 201
human action, of, 172, 186–187, 757
human spirit, of, 202, 219, 221, 226
individual development, of, 522
man/human subject, of, 186, 310
moral behavior, of, 604
religion, of, 26, 124, 231, 612
scientific theory, of, 415
social nature, of, 279
the world, of, 146–147, 166, 173,
191, 203, 210, 212, 219, 221,
242, 246, 248, 542
Conceptualism, 708
non-c, 276
Consciousness
form of, 523
individual, 682
self-c., 54, 103, 142, 170, 361, 362,
377n9, 449, 457, 468, 504, 509,
518, 520, 527, 536, 540, 556,
577, 581, 583–586, 588, 590n18,
593n43, 715, 719, 741–743
social/social nature of, 283, 307, 386,
507, 509, 522, 716–717
See also Mind; Self-awareness
Conservative/conservatism, 6, 26, 37,
84, 85, 102, 139, 142, 145, 148,
153, 221, 232, 285, 448, 461, 467,
479n4, 514, 553, 566, 592n33,
661, 740, 741, 781
Constructivism
epistemological, 281, 417
philosophical, 418

social, 419
Contradiction
dialectical, 365
non-c., 366, 625
Cosmism/Cosmists, Russian, 12,
591n22, 678
worldview, 678
Cosmology, 28, 161, 163, 165, 222,
236n11, 362
Cossacks, 100, 718, 721–724, 727
Don, 24
Creativity, 213, 217–235, 235n1, 235n2,
236n5, 305, 306, 370, 395, 408,
411, 420, 450, 503, 532, 537, 538,
582, 660, 662, 663, 681, 743
Crisis
economic, 87, 576
revolutionary, 59
spiritual, 450, 464
value, 451, 455, 577, 591n20
Criticism
art, 449
cultural, 234
empirical, 248 (*see also*
Empiriocriticism)
German Romantic, 448
Hegel, of, 149
humanism, of, 411, 686
Kant, of, 118, 121–123
Kantian, 354n3
literary, 11, 17, 107, 433, 449, 472,
512, 519, 556, 559, 647, 650,
697, 739, 741
musical, 677–679
philosophical, 653n5, 653n6
"a reactionary philosophy," of (Lenin),
81, 191–195, 241, 245, 248–257,
259, 264, 275, 288n6
self-c., 373, 378n19, 513, 517, 771n3
social, 3, 44, 411, 517, 519
sophiology, of, 58
Soviet society, of, 396
Critique of Abstract Principles (Vl.
Solovyov), 123, 160, 163, 165, 176
Critique of Pure Reason (Kant), 11,
116–117, 123, 125–127, 392, 529
Cult
Stalin's personality, 384, 391

SUBJECT INDEX   801

Culture
  Russian, 11, 15–17, 26, 51, 53, 62, 66,
    100, 102, 131, 319, 330, 424, 426,
    448, 450, 454, 455, 457, 468,
    479n2, 482n36, 493, 503, 509,
    510, 550, 555, 743, 744, 755, 782
  Western/Western European, 11, 55,
    300, 463, 556, 686, 743
Cultural studies, 3, 645, 737
Cybernetics, 369–371, 737, 738

D
Dead Souls (Gogol), 450, 464, 492–493,
    495–496, 498–504, 522, 781
Debate(s), Russian
  about the nature of beauty, 693, 696,
    698, 699, 703, 704, 710n19
  academic, 81
  aesthetic, 17, 693–696, 708,
    709n8, 711n22
  between; dialecticians (Deborinists)
    and mechanists, 264n2, 709n1;
    Marxist and non-Marxist thinkers,
    86; Narodniki and Marxists, 185;
    Slavophiles and Westernizers, 8–9,
    425; societalists
    (obshchestvenniki) and the
    naturists (*prirodniki*), 700–704
  epistemological, 427–429, 437
  freedom, 139–140
  Hesychast, 61, 65–66
  imiaslavie (Florensky), 638n17
  intellectual, vi, 98, 106, 455,
    457, 575–576
  on; Ilyenkov-Korovikov theses, the,
    372–388; Kant, Russian,
    116–117, 119, 122, 124, 127,
    129, 131; literary nationalism
    (*narodnost'*), 450; materialism,
    278; the nature of Christ
    (Solovyov), 152, 156n13; Russian
    identity/spirit, 139–140, 425,
    534, 570
  public (*publitsistika*), 80
  with Russian Machists
    (Lenin), 251–261
  within; the Orthodox Church, 26;
    Russian émigré politics, 250;
    Russian Marxism, 188

Decembrist(s)
  uprising, 7, 76
Deification (*theosis*), 70
  art, of, 681
  matter, of, 677
  man, of (*chelovekobozhestvo*), 82
  self-d., 678, 681
  self-interest, of, 153
  Solovyov's idea of, 82
Demons, The (Dostoevsky), 180, 473, 554
Despotism, 36, 37, 40, 41, 151,
    300, 309
Determinism, 77–78, 82, 110, 183,
    185–186, 188, 190, 195, 282–284,
    286, 778, 782
Devilry, 132n15, 554
Dialectical Logic (Ilyenkov), 369, 396
Dialectics
  absolute, 676–677
  Hegelian, 151, 242, 253, 695
  idealist, 375
  materialist, 81, 190, 194, 240,
    244–246, 251, 253–254, 256,
    259, 269–272, 274, 360–362,
    375, 386, 695, 707
"Dialectics of the Ideal" (Ilyenkov),
    375, 396
Dialectics of Myth, The (Losev), 674, 677,
    680, 684
Dialogism
  and monologism, 654n12, 664
Dialogue, 13, 15, 18, 36, 70–71,
    116, 375, 448, 470, 514,
    537, 621
  Bakhtin's conception of,
    644, 646, 654n9,
    662–666, 750n16
  Lotman's idea of, 740, 742
  Plato's, 152, 231, 233, 546n38
  Tolstoy's, 578, 584, 591n2
Dissidents, 13, 76, 86, 101, 384,
    402, 749n7
Dogma
  church/religious, 28, 57, 60,
    177, 577
  ideological, 246 (*see also* Marxism)
Dogmatism, 14, 61, 65, 128, 176, 177,
    246, 387, 528
Duel(s), 457, 462, 463, 475, 483n62,
    484n63, 586

E

East, v, 18n6, 293–314, 645, 647, 649, 650
Ecclesiastization (*vostserkovlenie*), 63
Economic and Philosophical Manuscripts of 1844 (Marx), 86, 693–695, 697–698
Economy, 26, 74, 185, 249, 269, 285, 286, 301, 365, 370, 492, 565, 612, 695, 765
Education
  moral, 459
  theological, 6, 63
  See also Bildung
Egoism, 122, 125, 147, 172, 181, 182, 567, 583
Embodiment, 167–170, 172, 215, 509, 629, 742, 749n7, 767
Emigration, Russian philosophical, 52, 62, 64, 75, 83, 317–318, 329–330, 402, 426, 472, 554, 563, 739
Émigré, 19n14, 19n15, 63–65, 67, 83–86, 242, 250, 293–315, 332n4, 425, 426, 471, 484n63, 589n1, 665
Emotion, 127, 184, 210, 211, 476, 530, 536, 537, 544n9, 600, 605–607, 614, 684, 765
Empire, 5, 27, 30, 39, 44, 77, 87, 179, 299, 301–304, 314, 493, 565, 716–718, 721, 727, 732
Empirical, 174, 180, 189, 210
Empiriocriticism, 81, 191–195, 241, 248–252, 254–257, 275, 288n6
Empiriomonism, 1, 241, 245, 250, 275, 288n11
Empiriosymbolism, 241, 275, 281, 288n11
Enlightenment (*prosveshchenie*)
  European, 425, 453
  Russian, 8, 11, 26, 32, 448
Epic, 217, 458, 470, 522, 660, 668, 715, 725–727, 750n19, 784
Epistemology
  classical, 428, 430–431
  constructivism in, 417
  cultural-historical, 428, 432, 433
  Marxist, 274
  neo-classical, 431

Russian, 423–441
  social, 281, 428, 431–432, 676
Equality, 25, 41, 120, 145, 232, 401, 570
Eros, 12, 630
Esoteric/esotericism, 146, 393
Eternity, 84, 95, 125, 223, 627, 632, 651, 728
Ethical life (*Sittlichkeit*), 320, 593n42
Ethics
  Drobnitski's, 708, 711n25
  Soviet, 396
  See also Moral philosophy
Eugene Onegin (Pushkin), 102, 450, 453–455, 787
Eurasianism/Eurasianists, 52, 88
Eurocentrism, 668
Evil
  "the annulment of past evil" (Shestov), 201, 207, 212, 214
  existence, 144, 201, 210
  God and, 213
  good and, 83, 128, 165, 313, 473, 602–603, 609
  necessary, 81, 179, 210–211
  problem of, 210–213, 223, 483n55, 518
  radical, 538, 567, 569, 584
  as wrongs, 37, 81, 107, 205, 697, 780
Evolution
  economic, 283
  evolutionary theory, 130, 170, 181, 249, 252, 286, 530
Existentialism
  French, 203, 455
  Russian, 12, 60, 203
Explosion (Lotman), 233, 742–744, 750n17, 760
Expression (theory), 9, 34, 53, 146, 168–170, 201, 207, 219, 225, 235, 261, 281, 303, 305, 331, 340, 343, 344, 347, 348, 351, 354n9, 355n10, 355n14, 356n24, 356n25, 365, 391, 396, 435, 436, 460, 512, 520, 525, 527, 538, 553, 598, 600, 603–605, 611, 613, 614, 616n2, 617n8, 624, 635–637, 637n3, 655n13, 667, 675, 678, 679, 684

F

Faith
religious, 10
Fanaticism, 40, 78, 206, 384
Fathers and Children (Turgenev), 180, 182, 463, 521, 576
Festival, homecoming (Bakhtin), 15, 645, 646, 648, 651
See also Carnival (Bakhtin)
Fiction, 101, 116, 119, 131n2, 195, 272, 295, 416, 449, 451, 453, 457, 459, 460, 463, 470, 472, 473, 477, 479, 566, 577, 580, 584, 590n16, 591n19, 682
Finitude, 74, 147, 155, 202, 467, 471, 580
Form/forms
artistic, 401, 424, 609, 677
expression, of, 706
literary, 509, 738
logical, 347, 348, 351
thinking, of, 523 (*see also* Consciousness, form of)
Foundation Pit, The (Platonov), 456, 718, 727–730
Frankfurt School (*see* Theory, critical)
Freedom
intellectual, 15, 87
political, 76, 140, 141
See also Autonomy; Liberty
Freemasons, 43, 45
From the Other Shore (Herzen), 77, 103
Future-in-the-past (Bakhtin), 643–652

G

Geography
symbolic, 491–505
Gift, the (Dar) (Nabokov), 471–472
Glasnost' (openness), 87, 89, 402
Globalization, 399, 762
Gnoseology, 271, 544n5
See also Epistemology
Gnostic(s), 209–210, 221
God
Biblical, the, 213
G.-man/Godmanhood (*bogochelovechestvo*) (Vl. Solovyov),

55–56, 58, 82, 151, 156n13, 455, 677–678
Gulag, 239, 675, 719

H

Happiness, 36, 40, 127, 181, 452, 473, 474, 476, 478, 485n79, 534, 538, 540, 568, 579, 580, 582, 583, 588, 592n39, 608, 727, 728, 741
Hegelian(s)/Hegelianism, 17, 77, 116–117, 119, 141, 149, 162, 165, 174–176, 245, 253, 321, 325, 328–329, 331, 395, 396, 481n32, 667
circles (in Moscow), 77
left, 76–77, 132n7, 140, 143, 145, 149, 151, 155n6, 156n9, 265n15
"non-Hegelian," 317, 333n11
right, 77, 84, 140, 145, 155n4
Russian, 141–147, 149, 152–153, 163, 508, 510–511, 515, 517–519
spirit, 514, 702
Hell, 126, 182, 373, 474, 627, 632, 715–733, 742
Hermeneutics, 340, 343, 346, 348–349, 354n6, 355n18, 429, 438, 585, 649, 651, 673–687
Hesychasm, 61, 622
Historicism, 282, 434, 437–440, 644, 648, 678
Historicity, 436, 450, 481n22, 518, 643–647, 649, 651, 738, 746
History
art and culture, of, 450, 697
end of, 233, 252, 585, 646, 765, 768
philosophy, of, 56, 58, 69, 74, 88, 117, 126, 159, 165, 232, 245, 258, 264, 287, 339, 368, 374, 387, 388, 390, 526, 529, 531, 532, 541, 650, 651, 709n1, 757
science, of, 412, 427, 737, 741
Soviet philosophy, of, 88, 117, 709n1
Holiness, 587
Holistic, 70, 96, 98, 153, 217, 398, 424, 434, 440, 441n1

804 SUBJECT INDEX

Homo sovieticus, 87, 707
Human
  development, 143
  dignity, 9, 43, 46, 453, 522, 523,
    607, 722
  essence, 696, 699, 701–702, 704, 706
  See also Person; Self, the
Humanism
  anti-h., 749n7
  European, 27–28, 456
  Russian, 8–9, 11, 411
  Soviet, 384
Humility, 10, 142, 145, 154, 155, 205,
  539, 583, 586, 614, 615

I

Idea, Russian, vi, 1, 10, 84, 426, 576
Ideal(s)
  moral, 202, 372, 538, 539
  and norms, 97, 102
Idealism
  German, 2, 57, 123, 156n14, 221,
    335, 511, 528n8, 590n10, 786
  and materialism, 2, 119 (*see also*
    Materialism)
  menshevizing, 372
  Russian, 140, 354n9, 526
Identity
  national, 8–9, 458, 755
  Russian, vi, 10, 139, 293–315,
    492, 493
Ideology
  Marxist, 2, 18n6, 80, 81, 185,
    240, 244
  state, 18n6, 269, 302, 385–387, 391,
    393, 401, 647
Idiot, The (Dostoevsky), 458, 463, 466,
  472, 483
Immanentism, 219–222
Immortality, 31, 321, 533, 534,
  582–584, 784
Imperialism, 458, 718, 728, 780
Individualism, 96, 98, 104, 224, 280,
  367, 452, 457, 463, 577, 653n6,
  678, 681, 684, 685
Infinite, 125, 142, 147–154, 210, 217,
  220, 221, 278, 327, 328, 415, 470,
  471, 511, 512, 515, 516, 741
Infinitism, 220–223, 226

Influence
  German classical philosophy, of, 130,
    162, 386
  German idealism, of, 57, 76, 787
  Western, vi, 299
Inspector General, The (Gogol), 492,
  495, 498–500, 503
Integrity
  self-i., 429, 435
Intellect/*Verstand*, 220–221, 223,
  225–226, 230–231, 279, 350, 371,
  515, 532, 537, 609, 623, 682, 740
Intelligentsia, vi, 8, 14–15, 27, 63,
  79–81, 83, 140, 179–195, 249,
  301–304, 310, 372, 425, 457, 462,
  471, 480n15, 507–509, 515, 517,
  522–523, 558, 577, 727, 755
Intentionality, 194, 340, 345,
  353, 711n30
Interpretation
  literary problems of, 514
  music, of, 677
  philosophical, 18, 121, 419, 426, 427
    (*see also* Hermeneutics)
  text(s)/classic text(s), 206, 207, 209,
    210, 386
Intuition(s)
  as *Anschauung*, 147, 541
  intelligible, 339, 341, 344, 345, 350,
    355n11, 356n26
Irrationalism, 104, 201, 207

J

Jazz, 684–687
Jew(s)/Jewish, 5, 83, 205, 294, 295,
  297, 312, 314n1, 468, 471, 493,
  626, 782
Judaism, 979
Justification of the Good, The (Vl.
  Solovyov), 80, 123, 163

K

Kantianism
  neo-K., 13, 81, 96–98, 116, 119, 123,
    191, 275, 288n5, 408, 409, 427
  Russian/Russian Kant Studies, 17, 116
Kiev Rus' 4, 32, 42, 56, 75, 100, 119,
  126, 296

SUBJECT INDEX   **805**

Knowledge
  holistic, 424, 425, 433, 434
  Lenin's copy/reflection theory of,
      259–262, 266n25, 271, 274, 278,
      439, 693, 695, 699–703
  philosophical, 160, 163n1, 173, 174,
      387, 427
  scientific, 81, 188, 191, 193–194, 234,
      263, 343, 363, 386, 390, 417,
      425, 427–428, 433, 749n7
  self-integrity theory of, 429–430,
      435
  socio-philosophical, 271
Kommuna/village *mir*, 779

L
Labor (*trud*)
  and action, 704
  alienation of, 706 (*see also* Alienation,
      labor, of)
  free, 79
Landmarks/*Signposts*, 10, 59, 83,
      296, 455
Language
  development of, 480n16
  problems of, 349
Law(s)
  causal, 283, 364
  criminal, 532, 564
  historical, 185, 309
  moral, 122, 191, 409
  and morality, 122
  natural, 35, 120–122, 156n9, 156n10,
      185, 186, 282
Liberalism
  Russian, 479n4, 777
  Western, 6, 26
Liberty, 9, 25, 27, 34–36, 40, 41, 78,
      82, 147, 153, 156n10, 664, 778
  See also Autonomy; Freedom
Life
  horror(s) of, 213
  meaning of, 105, 203, 204, 215, 477,
      577, 602, 609–612, 615, 727, 728
  See also Existentialism, Russian
Linguistic(s)
  turn, 651, 655n13
"Literary Reveries" (Belinsky), 449,
      508, 520

Literature
  criticism, 11, 17, 107, 433,
      472, 512, 519, 559, 647,
      650, 697, 739, 741;
      formalism, 122, 128, 175,
      433, 665, 708, 738, 740, 747;
      formalism, Russian, 738, 740;
      historicism, 644, 648; literary
      theory, 19n13; poststructural/ism,
      221, 740, 744, 745, 747;
      secondary modeling systems, 737,
      739; semiotics, 17, 346, 427,
      433–435, 624, 676, 737–748,
      762, 763, 769, 786; semiotics,
      (Moscow-)Tartu school of, 17,
      675, 737–748; structuralism/
      structuralist, 427, 433, 665, 666,
      738, 740, 741, 744–747, 750n21
  genres of; autobiography, 463, 473, 475,
      485n79, 526, 653n3, 778;
      dialogue, 31, 480n12, 664,
      750n17; epic, 458, 522, 581, 660,
      665, 726, 727; memoires, 36–39,
      473; novel(s), 11, 15, 17, 42, 44,
      87, 102, 131n3, 181, 206, 240,
      269, 360, 391, 401, 402, 447–479,
      499, 501, 510, 520, 522, 523,
      550–552, 559, 564–571, 580, 600,
      608, 653n2, 662, 663, 665, 666,
      668, 675, 682–684, 686, 718, 721,
      723, 725–729, 733n14, 761, 778,
      781, 783–786; novella(s), 458,
      459, 465, 473, 569, 607, 781;
      poetry, 14, 17, 32, 80, 104, 117,
      119, 166, 169, 227, 229, 231, 384,
      385, 449, 450, 458, 464, 504, 508,
      509, 520, 530, 559, 621, 629–633,
      637, 638n11, 660, 731, 739, 785
  minor, 758, 771n5
  national, 449, 520, 521
  periods and movements; feminism,
      781; postmodernism, 428, 437,
      484n77, 644, 645; realism, 451,
      507, 512, 521–522; Renaissance,
      458, 653n2; Romanticism/
      Romantics, 453; Silver Age, 12,
      119, 459; socialist realism, 360,
      456, 468, 509, 589n3, 696, 703,
      707–708, 709n9, 710n15, 725;
      Westernizers, 522

806 SUBJECT INDEX

Literature (*cont.*)
Russian, vi, 4, 9, 18n1, 32, 100, 106,
126, 447, 450, 452, 453, 455,
459, 470, 472, 481n20, 491,
498, 503, 507–510, 512,
519–521, 523, 524, 551,
553–556, 558, 559, 568, 570,
644, 683, 715–733, 738, 748n1,
755–759, 781, 782, 785, 787
techniques/devices; defamiliarization,
604; dialogue/dialogic, 36, 116,
152, 231, 233, 410, 449, 472,
478, 480n12, 514, 584, 644,
646, 662–666, 669n8;
imagination, 448, 464, 477, 659;
metaphor, 582, 593n46, 639n21,
759; mimesis, 756–759, 771n10;
narration, 758, 786; narrative,
454, 458, 465, 469, 470, 474,
475, 477, 485n79, 498, 510,
520, 529, 589, 668, 719, 732,
743, 750n18, 766;
personification, 96, 98, 675;
polyphony/polyphonic, 471–472,
481n22, 570, 663
Western, 709n7
world, 454, 459, 470, 665–669
Logic
dialectical, 258, 259, 272, 362,
373, 378n20
Hegelian, 174–175
Logicism, 96, 104
Logos, 98, 106–107

M
Machism/Machists, 191–194, 246, 249,
251, 252, 254, 255, 260, 266n26,
274–275, 288n6
Marxism
forms of, 244
Ilyenkov's, 363–376
Lenin's version of, 246
M.-Leninism, 13, 86–88, 90, 130,
286, 287, 387, 390, 693–696
Orthodox, v, 2, 13, 14, 86, 288n7
Russian, 119, 188, 249, 250,
264, 269–287
Soviet, 269, 272, 286, 376

Marxist(s)
legal, 274, 287–288n5
orthodox/dogmatic, 190, 192–193,
274, 284
theory, 243–244
Master and Margarita (Bulgakov), 15,
131n3, 456
Materialism
dialectical (*diamat*), 81, 83, 190, 194,
240, 244–246, 251, 253, 254,
256, 259, 264, 269–271, 274,
287, 288n7, 362, 375, 386,
693, 695
historical (*istmat*), 75, 81, 83, 86,
96, 98, 192, 282–287,
288n7, 289n19, 375,
693–695, 700
non-dialectical, 81
socialist, 270
Materialism and Empiriocriticism
(Lenin), 81, 192, 239–264, 264n6,
265n15, 288n6, 709n3
Meaning of Creative Act, The (Berdyaev),
61, 218–219, 222, 224–225, 227,
231, 235–237
Mechanicists/mechanists, 287n2,
709n1
See also Debate, between dialecticians
(Deborinists) and mechanicists
Men of the sixties/Sixtiers, the
(*shestidesiatniki*), 86, 383–402,
403n5, 435, 712n36
Menshevik(s), 249–251, 265n14,
266n26, 293, 296, 297
See also Bolshevik(s)
Menshivism, 249–251, 265n14, 266n26,
293, 296, 297
Metaphysics/metaphysical
classical, 57, 59, 60, 66
postulate(s), 60
Methodology
dialectical, 243, 273, 322, 323, 369,
386, 389
genetic-constructive, 415
history of philosophy, 10, 244,
441n4, 515
philosophical, 10, 244, 319, 515
science, 270, 345, 366, 374, 391, 392,
397, 532, 542

SUBJECT INDEX   807

Middle Ages, 219, 224, 231, 236n7,
    417, 685, 687
Mimesis, 756–759, 771n10
Mind
    social theory of, 371
    See also Consciousness
Modernity/modern, 5, 13, 16, 18n6, 29,
    30, 56, 69, 76, 81, 88, 97, 110,
    117, 118, 139, 141, 152, 154,
    155n4, 211, 217–235, 246, 247,
    251, 252, 255, 262, 281, 286, 293,
    298, 301, 304, 305, 309, 392, 396,
    397, 423–428, 430–432, 435, 437,
    438, 440, 448, 450, 452, 453, 458,
    464, 466, 470, 472, 479, 479n5,
    509, 514, 522, 531, 533, 549,
    552, 570, 577, 585, 611, 622, 623,
    632, 645, 646, 648, 659–662, 667,
    668, 678, 684–687, 757, 762,
    780, 784
Monarchy
    Russian, 32, 40–42, 46, 99, 304,
        332, 552
    Western/European, 300
Moral duty, 521
Moralism, 128, 229, 232, 234
Moralists, 201, 235, 451, 617
Morality, 128, 229–232, 234
    See also Ethics; Moralists; Moral
        philosophy
Moral philosophy, 122–124, 584,
    614, 664
Moscow Methodological Circle
    (MMC), 398
Moscow State University (MGU), 361,
    387, 403n5
Music, 106, 384, 602, 606, 739
    as art/culture, 14, 37, 384,
        739, 765–768
    influence of, 616n3, 711n28, 728
    and language/the word, 628–630,
        638n11, 638n12, 638n16
    Losev's mythology of,
        673–687, 688n9
    Schopenhauer on, 607, 630
My Past and Thoughts (Herzen), 76, 110,
    455, 463, 481–482, 523, 778, 781
Mysticism, 108, 140, 159, 173, 175,
    221, 229, 480n13, 523

Myth, 58, 154, 195, 207, 209, 214, 218,
    227, 229–231, 240, 277, 428, 458,
    466, 582, 644, 668, 674–683, 687,
    695, 738, 757, 758
Mythology
    absolute, 676–677
    in Berdyaev, 227–229
    finitude, of, 155
    intelligentsia, of the, 523
    as the medium, 227
    musical (*see* Music, Losev's
        mythology of)
    national, 755

N

Nakaz (Catherine II), 34, 35, 39–42
Nationalism
    nationality, 538, 696, 717, 718
    See also Debate(s), on literary
        nationalism (*narodnost'*)
Naturalism, 176, 190, 220, 279,
    449, 695
Negation, 78, 88, 89, 142–145, 147,
    150, 153, 154, 156n9, 156n10,
    213, 272, 273, 327, 329, 455, 518,
    519, 616n1, 662, 749n14
Negativity, 88, 462
Neo-
    Neo-Kantianism (*see*
        Kantianism, neo-K.)
    neopalamism, 66, 68, 71
    neopatristics, 66
    neoplatonism, 55
Nihilism/nihilist, 153, 155n8, 162,
    180, 452, 463, 469, 473, 478,
    482n33, 482n39, 485n79, 521,
    539, 560, 568, 576, 577, 685,
    687, 785
Norm/normativity
    moral, 453

O

Oblomov (Goncharov), 452
Of Idols and Ideals (Ilyenkov),
    369–370, 374
On Life (Tolstoy), 526–527, 545, 578,
    580–583, 586, 590–591

808 SUBJECT INDEX

Ontology, 56, 159, 271, 340, 552
  Berdyev's, 224–225
  hermeneutical, 651
  Lenin's, 256, 262
  Marx's, 702
  Nietzsche's, 226
  Orthodox, 61
  positivist, 247
  religious, 626
  social, 650, 652, 654n12, 711n24
  as subject matter of traditional
    metaphysics, 161, 163, 165
Order
  political, 26, 91, 154, 289n18, 577
  social, 239, 280, 370, 386, 391,
    395, 514
Orthodoxy
  debate about, 26, 124
  Marxist, 192, 279, 281, 286
  religious, 43, 52, 61, 66, 71n4, 85,
    106, 121, 124, 128, 544n11,
    551, 552, 593n46, 622, 694, 696
  Russian, 10, 28, 622
Other, the/otherness, 329, 435, 635,
    646, 649, 678
  See also Self, the

P
Paris Manuscripts (Marx), see Economic
  and Philosophical Manuscripts of
  1844 (Marx))
Partiinost' (partisanship), 240, 373,
  378n18, 696, 709n9
Party
  All-Union Communist Party
    (AUCP), 311–312
  Bolshevik, 83, 240
  Communist Party, Russian/of
    the USSR, 82, 130, 311,
    361, 386, 411, 416,
    469, 730
  Constitutional Democratic Party
    (Kadets), 89
  as the main institution of
    Bolshevism, 311
  Menshevik, 250, 293, 297
  Russian Social Democratic Labor Party
    (RSDLP), 232, 293
  Socialist Revolutionary Party
    (SRP), 293–294

Penal servitude, 551, 554, 558–559,
    563, 565, 571
Perestroika, 87, 89, 384, 402
Person/personality/personhood
  and consciousness, 70, 97, 371, 649, 697
  and culture, 53, 236n7, 719
  and group, 13
  in Marxism, 408, 686
  as part of social system, 371,
    411, 730–731
  in relation to God, 321, 458
  in relation to others, 184, 409, 411, 719
  as rooted in social life, 420
  as a whole, 687
Personalism, Russian, 12, 85, 654n10
Pesant(s), 10, 37, 44, 45, 77, 107, 184,
    194, 302, 458, 460, 461, 469, 498,
    502, 521, 554, 587, 588, 593n44,
    604, 607, 613, 616n7, 718, 721,
    722, 724, 727, 729, 782, 786
Peter and Paul Fortress, 77, 101, 564, 565
Petrashevskii Circle, 550, 551, 562
Phenomenology
  Husserlian, 341, 345, 347, 349, 353
  Russian, 60, 104, 118, 339–354, 411,
    428, 584, 586, 614, 650, 666,
    673, 677, 679, 757
Philology, 19n13, 348, 437, 511, 531,
    546n39, 650, 663, 745
"Philosophical Letters" (Chaadaev),
    508, 513
Philosophical ship/philosopher's ship/
    philosophy steamer, 15, 62
Philosophes, 25, 27, 33, 35, 36, 38,
    39, 46, 668
Philosophy
  academic, 73, 89, 126, 418, 694
  action, of, 193
  analytic, 395
  anti-academic, 73
  art, of, 58, 219–220, 226, 232, 598,
    609, 684, 704, 710n12, 715,
    733, 783–784
  culture, of, 58, 97, 663
  economy, of, 58, 69
  energy, of, 69
  first/Philosophia prima, 4, 6, 7,
    55, 69, 264
  history, of, 58, 163n2, 165, 184, 185,
    190, 220, 226, 348, 517,
    591n25, 715, 716, 720, 782

language, of, 69, 339–342, 349, 351, 353, 581, 638n10, 655n13, 675
law, of, 88, 117, 121, 122, 163n2, 165, 319, 427
life, of, 69, 575–589, 609
property, of, 69
psychology, of, 426
right, of, 450, 514, 532
science, of, 81, 363, 390, 392, 397, 428, 431, 436
state, of the, 58, 165
symbols, of, 278, 281
time, of, 69
political, 16, 33, 34, 73–91, 317, 575
positive, 150, 254, 346, 354n3, 424–428, 431, 433, 434, 437, 440 (*see also* Positivism)
postmodernist, 428, 437
poststructuralist, 744–745, 747
pragmatist, 95, 145, 187, 288n13, 411
quasi-academic, 73
Russian idealistic, 140, 354n9, 526 (*see also* Idealism, Russian)
Russian religious, 3, 11, 16, 51–71, 84, 85, 124, 434, 549, 575, 652, 712n32
See also Aesthetics; Epistemology; Ethics; Existentialism; Hermeneutics; Ontology; Phenomenology
Platonism, 55, 61, 540, 543
Pluralism, 777
methodological, 98, 100–105, 110
Plurality, 74, 81, 289n20, 746
Polis, 394, 430
Politics/political
theory, 192
Poor Liza (Karamzin), 460
Positivism
Russian, 118, 218, 223, 261, 263, 396, 435, 532, 534, 540, 544n11, 577, 581
Western/European, 162, 176, 190, 191, 246, 247, 252, 261, 264, 265n12, 275, 288n6, 529, 530, 532
Postmodernism, 428, 437
Practice/praxis
communal/social, 264n2
concept of, 708

intellectual, 3, 427
political, 252
revolutionary, 242–244
as social production, 235, 698–699
and theory (*see* Theory, and practice/praxis)
See also Activity
Prague Spring, 374
Praxis (Yugoslav group), 374, 411–412
Priest(s), 8, 28, 40, 80, 124, 126, 235, 295, 549, 635, 723
Principium individuationis, 537, 579, 588, 598
Prison, 76, 77, 102, 182, 213, 219, 294, 314, 333n11, 554, 559, 563–565, 671, 683, 731, 732
Progressivism, 220, 233–234
Proletariat
dictatorship of, 8, 82, 310, 456, 684, 687, 730
Property
intellectual, 659
private, 706
Province(s), 448, 472, 491, 492, 494–504, 506
Psychologism, 350–352, 438, 662
Psychoanalysis, 70
Psychology
Sociocultural, 360, 420, 434
Soviet, 310, 407, 410, 420
Pugachev Rebellion, 37, 302, 494

R
Radicalism, 9–11, 14, 25–27, 31, 35, 44–46, 73, 76–78, 81, 82, 87–90, 100, 129, 142–149, 153–155, 155n8, 206, 232, 248, 252, 276, 281, 294, 301, 306, 428, 439, 448, 454, 458, 471, 482n33, 491, 509, 521, 532, 538, 539, 553, 559, 560, 562–564, 575, 577, 581, 583, 584, 600, 645, 652, 715, 740, 742, 744, 759, 777, 779
Rationality
in historical development, 517–518
of the law, 330
universal, 9, 141
value-, 610, 612
Western, 469

810 SUBJECT INDEX

Realisms
anti-r., 675, 700, 711n22
as art movement (*see* Art, movement;
realism)
as literary movement (*see* Literature,
movement; realism)
philosophical, 257, 258,
266n22, 408
socialist, 456, 468, 509, 589n3, 696,
708, 710n15, 725 (*see also*
Literature, movement; socialist
realism)
Reality
absolute, 324, 326
historical, 97, 108, 132n6, 676,
703, 718
objective, 414, 630
political, 75, 90, 141, 743
social, 96, 234, 247, 285,
411, 416, 420, 511,
516, 702
Soviet, 83, 707
subjective, 367
virtual, 70
Reason (*Vernunft*)
collective, 441, 511
dialogical, 220
and faith, 5, 10, 569
power of, 146, 392
sovereignty of, 393
speculative, 230
Reconciliation, 140, 148, 149,
153, 282, 335n22, 485n79,
514–519, 523
Reform(s)
great, 576
liberal/progressive, 6, 76
Petrine, 53, 298, 522
Relativism, 81, 257, 344, 353, 428,
598, 687
Religion
Catholicism, 124, 128, 205
Protestantism, 106, 124, 128
Byzantine, 10, 71n4, 300
Eastern Christianity, 55
Russian Orthodox, 57 (*see*
Orthodoxy)
secularization, 63, 82, 448, 479n5
See also Church

Renaissance, 4, 11–15, 17, 25, 28, 106,
159, 320, 389, 448, 455–458, 470,
653n2, 668, 685–687, 743,
756, 766
religious-philosophical, 51, 56, 58,
60–65, 67, 69
Revisionism, 129, 251, 265n17,
372–374, 707
Revolt, 35, 74, 79, 96, 99, 102, 103,
180, 205, 217–235, 301–303, 554,
560, 674
Decembrist, 95, 96, 99, 103, 140, 302
(*see also* Decembrists)
Revolution
Bolshevik, 58, 61, 62, 295, 317, 331,
349, 354n1
bureaucratic (Peter I), 30
cultural, 30–31, 454–455
February 1917, 6, 7, 12, 84, 95,
191, 455
French, 6, 88, 111n1, 120, 121,
459, 518
liberal, 76
October 1917, 13, 81, 96, 98, 99,
103, 104, 109, 129, 218, 241,
284, 653n3, 687, 716, 780
paradigm, 95–111, 111n1
socialist, 77–78, 80, 314, 314n2,
314n4, 385
Rhythm, 59, 660, 677, 679, 685, 738
Right(s)
civil, 305, 674
individual, 13, 82, 171
political, 79, 239
Romanticism
German, 7, 106, 448–450, 464, 660,
680, 683, 781, 784, 786–787
Russian, 100, 102, 104, 218, 222,
451, 454, 681, 685, 687, 697
Russian
Christian thought, 51, 57, 67, 68, 71,
147, 295
Empire, 5, 26, 33, 35, 37, 76, 79,
239, 298, 300, 301, 304, 314,
459, 492, 493, 531, 717
history, 2, 6, 18n6, 31–32, 54, 59–60,
68, 80, 241, 293, 301, 308, 387,
450, 715–719, 727, 732
idea (*see* Idea, Russian)

literature, vi, 4, 9, 18n1, 32, 100, 106, 126, 447, 450, 452, 453, 455, 459, 470, 472, 481n20, 491, 498, 503, 507–510, 512, 519–521, 523, 524, 551, 553–556, 558, 559, 568, 570, 644, 683, 715–733, 738, 748n1, 755–759, 781, 782, 785, 787

monks, 68

philosophy, vi, 2–4, 8, 11, 12, 15–17, 18n1, 18n2, 19n11, 51–56, 59, 61–63, 66, 68, 69, 73, 90, 116, 119, 132n9, 159, 221, 236n8, 287n1, 342, 359, 383, 385, 387–389, 392, 396, 399, 420, 423–428, 430, 431, 433–435, 440, 441, 441n3, 525–543, 577, 647, 652, 686, 688n7, 755, 756, 785, 787

politics, 16, 32

state, 18n6, 299, 459, 482n37, 505n2, 741

Russian Idea, The (Bedyaev), 2, 84, 425–426

Russian Thinkers (Berlin), 202, 777, 787

S

Samizdat, 75, 86

Scholastics, 25, 28, 155n1, 258, 512

Science(s)

cognitive, 407, 418, 420, 428, 747

crises of, 190

human/of man, vii, 15, 71, 182, 190, 195, 349, 397, 411, 417, 429, 430, 432–434, 437

life, 377n11, 530

modern, 221, 223, 247, 255, 281, 427, 428, 431–432, 437, 585, 674

natural, 169, 179–195, 246, 343, 346, 377n11, 415, 521, 532, 535, 613

social, 14, 25, 81, 183–185, 246, 286, 346, 354n8, 417, 709n1, 715

Secularization, 63, 82, 448, 479n5

Self

s.-assertion, 140–142, 144, 172, 228

s.-awareness, 8, 274, 390, 681

s.-determination, 9, 84, 523

s.-transcendent, 582

Self, the/selfhood

deification of, 153, 678

sense of, 8, 166, 507, 511, 513, 516, 519, 522, 523, 730

See also Other, the

Semiosphere (Lotman), 741–742, 748

Sensualism, 176

Serf(s), 35, 37, 41, 43–45, 186, 303, 448, 453, 460–461, 511, 556, 560, 564, 781

Serfdom, 26, 35, 37, 43–44, 79, 99, 139, 300–301, 303, 448, 492, 523, 576, 781

Short Course (*Istoriia Vsesoiuznoi Kommunisticheskoi Partii (Bol'shevikov): Kratkii Kurs*), 286, 387, 695, 709n1, 709n4

Silentium (Mandelshtam), 621, 628–629

Silver Age (*serebryannyi vek*)

eschatology in, 58, 653n2

literature, 12, 385, 459, 470, 683

philosophy (*see* Time, period(s) (evolution of Russian philosophy))

poetry, 470

See also Literature, Silver Age

Skepticism/skeptical, v, 81, 90, 104, 147, 152, 154, 190, 206, 209, 224, 248, 255, 260, 262, 352, 368, 369, 533, 540, 591n23, 592n32, 625–628, 630, 632–635, 637, 766, 779

Slavery/slaves, 6, 35, 41, 43, 222, 301

Slavophiles, 7–10, 19n11, 53, 54, 76, 107, 129, 153, 308, 425, 458, 463, 464, 522, 551

political philosophy, 8–10, 54, 425, 463

See also Idea, Russian; Westernizers

Sobornost', 10, 54, 84, 224, 463, 467

Sociality, 84, 433, 480n13, 507–524

Social order, 239, 280, 370, 386, 391, 395, 514

Social science, 14, 25, 81, 183–185, 246, 270, 286, 346, 354n8, 417, 709n1, 715

Society

autocratic, 75, 87, 90, 302, 499, 780

communist, 67, 78, 82, 86, 685, 705, 706

812   SUBJECT INDEX

Sociology, 17, 346, 397, 401, 433, 437,
    677, 682–687, 697, 726
Sola Fide (Shestov), 205, 207, 213, 216
Sophia (Divine Wisdom) (Vl. Solovyov),
    5, 55–58, 65, 80, 151, 152, 223
Sophiology (Vl. Solovyov), 57, 58, 61,
    65, 68, 71n1, 150
Soul, 31, 97, 100, 108, 125, 126, 146,
    166, 169, 175, 183, 195, 298, 299,
    302–304, 321, 331, 432, 453, 460,
    465, 467, 477, 478, 480n13, 493,
    513–515, 521, 525, 527, 529–533,
    535, 539, 542, 544n11, 545n25,
    555, 581, 586–588, 589n7,
    593n43, 603, 608, 616n7, 622,
    623, 628, 635, 638n11, 667, 686,
    728, 781, 784
Soviet Union, the/USSR, v–vi, 14, 76,
    80, 81, 83–88, 91, 119, 129–131,
    147, 269, 287, 295, 311, 359, 360,
    366, 369, 374, 378n21, 384, 387,
    394, 400, 411, 415, 509, 647, 666,
    674, 694, 695, 708, 709n1,
    710n14, 715, 717, 719, 737–739,
    743, 749n7, 756, 780
Spiritual
    culture, 203, 367, 370, 374, 673
    strength, 13, 519
    unity, 331, 424, 541
Stagnation, 86, 469, 694, 744
Stalinism, 13, 147, 318, 384, 709,
    719, 740
    de-Stalinisation, 390, 391 (*see also*
        Thaw/*ottepel'*)
Study/studies
    Byzantological, 66
    Hegel, 117, 321
    interdisciplinary, 432, 433, 537
    Kant, 117, 119–122, 124
    patrological, 65
Style, 16, 52, 69, 76, 102, 168–170,
    175, 264, 276, 313, 349, 355n15,
    362, 365, 389, 393, 395, 396,
    423–441, 454, 471, 474, 481n18,
    502, 512, 521, 529, 557, 559, 614,
    653n6, 666, 675, 680, 685, 726,
    732, 739, 758, 766
Subjectivism, 183, 194, 248, 276, 352,
    598, 700, 702

Subjectivity, 143, 147, 221, 222, 225,
    416, 477, 536, 662, 769
Suicide, 116, 126, 149, 155, 359, 391,
    475, 477, 485n79, 729
Symbol, 52, 58, 183, 218, 260, 262,
    278, 281, 386, 454, 492, 623–625,
    629, 637n3, 637n4, 637n5,
    638n15, 674, 675, 682, 684, 685,
    687, 729, 750n18
Syncretism, 503
Synthesis, 150, 163, 165, 166, 176,
    177, 211, 227–230, 271, 278, 363,
    399, 529, 541, 553, 623, 678,
    682, 683
System(s), economic
    capitalism; anti-c., 308; crisis of,
        695
    communism, 86, 269, 318, 370, 372,
        376, 384, 396, 400–401, 695,
        707, 710n16, 718, 722, 779
    open, 55
    political; democracy, 25, 85, 87, 89,
        129, 144, 243, 307, 308, 331,
        334n18, 462, 740, 764, 770,
        777; despotism, 36–37, 40–41,
        151, 300, 309
    sign, 416, 738–739, 748n1, 748n2,
        749n6; theory, 286
    social; Russian, 523
    socialism, 74, 76–77, 82–84, 86,
        87, 89, 98, 109, 130, 185,
        189, 190, 242, 264n2, 274,
        277, 286, 297, 304–306, 308,
        374, 384, 387, 399–401, 411,
        516, 518, 576, 652, 677, 685,
        686, 695

T
Tamizdat, 75, 86
Teleology, 194, 232, 756
Terror(ism), 13, 74, 88, 294, 308, 312,
    361, 456, 467
Testament
    New, 5, 205, 230, 469, 568, 569, 575
    Old, 57, 208
Text(s)
    classic, 386
    theological, 66

Thaw (*ottepel'*)/de-Stalinization, 14, 83, 86, 359, 366, 372, 375, 390–391, 694, 707, 709n1, 738
Theater, Russian, 107
Theology
    Byzantine, 66 (*see also* Eastern Orthodoxy)
    Orthodox, 5, 61, 63–66
Theory
    aesthetic, 2, 17, 471, 601–602, 608–609, 611, 613–614, 616n1, 617n10
    creativity, of, 17, 226
    cultural/culture, of, 2, 31, 95, 110, 286, 708, 711n25, 786
    ethical, 122, 463
    life, of, 447, 580, 682
    literary, 13, 19n13, 645, 648, 663, 667–668, 737
    and method, 270–271, 348, 398
    philosophical, 17, 246, 254, 259, 264n2, 270, 783–784
    and practice/praxis, 77, 81, 239–240, 244, 252, 259, 365
    progress, of, 104, 184
    revolutionary, 130, 249–250, 252, 284, 517
    scientific, 390, 401, 415, 420, 436
    social, 282, 305, 463, 715
    translation, of, 659, 786
    values, of, 95–97, 694, 708, 711n25
    See also Activity, theory; Cognition, theory of; Knowledge, Lenin's copy/reflection theory of; Marxist, theory; Myth, theory of
Theurgy, 105, 222, 226–229, 235
Thought
    Christian, 51, 67, 68, 71, 147
    German, 57, 124, 448, 787
    Greek, 162
    Russian, v–vii, 1–18, 53–55, 58, 61, 64, 66–68, 129, 139, 153, 189, 194, 235n1, 349, 529, 531, 544n12, 643, 652, 676, 756, 777–787
    science of, 359–376
Time
    period(s) (evolution of Russian philosophy); awakening, of

1830s, 8–11, 302, 448; dark ages, 7, 9, 15; early, 4–8, 56; new awakening, 13–15; Silver Age (*serebriannyi vek*), 4, 11–13, 51, 58, 64–65, 67, 73, 89, 99, 111n3, 119, 207, 217, 218, 227, 314n1, 385, 459, 470, 621, 623, 628, 683, 755
    period(s) (in Russian political history); enlightenment, 5–6, 8, 11, 25–46, 448, 743; post-Revolutionary, 63, 295, 470, 722; pre-Revolutionary, 104, 109, 180, 305, 676; post-Soviet, 68, 84, 86–89, 124, 261; Soviet, v, 2, 15, 76, 120, 240, 242, 246, 287, 469, 507, 509, 575
    and space, 152, 217, 220, 629
Totalitarianism, 4, 83, 686, 687
Transcendentism, 222
Tsar, 3, 6, 28–30, 42, 77, 78, 80, 99, 111n5, 180, 298, 300, 302, 304, 462, 560, 564
Tsardom/tsarism, 5, 568
Tyranny, 28, 32, 44, 90, 147, 730

U
Ukraine, 100, 492, 493, 498, 505n2, 726, 772n16
Unity
    unity of all, 12, 55–58, 61, 161, 163–173, 177n3, 538, 541, 622, 623, 626–630, 635–637, 682, 683 (*see also* All-unity)
University, 3, 5, 6, 27, 30, 32, 34, 43, 68, 115–117, 120, 121, 125, 131, 180, 188, 232n1, 319, 327, 330, 341, 354n1, 355n19, 371, 389, 394, 511–513, 525, 529, 531–534, 536, 541, 542, 550, 558, 560, 571n2, 646, 649, 673, 738, 739, 743, 748n1
Untranslatability, 746–747
USSR, *see* Soviet Union
Utopia, 65, 309, 385, 428, 472, 630

814 SUBJECT INDEX

V

Village(s), 10, 44, 301, 304, 307, 334n18, 493, 499, 500, 560, 721–724, 729, 730, 779
Virgin Soul Upturned (Sholokhov), 723, 725–726, 730, 761
Voluntarism, 82, 188, 201, 207, 226, 231–233
Voprosy filosofii, 374, 399, 403n5, 425, 429
Voprosy filosofii i psikhologii/ VFP, 342, 424, 525–526, 536–537, 543n2, 546n35

W

War
1812 Patriotic, the, 53, 99
Civil, the, 13, 74, 79, 83, 217–218, 312, 318, 324, 332n4, 384, 722
Communism, 242
Crimean, the, 181, 576–577
Napoleonic, the, 76, 102, 218, 448
World War I, the, 13, 119, 129, 130, 241, 654n9
World War II, the, 119, 129, 130, 332n4, 470, 739, 782
War and Peace, 577, 580, 581, 583, 584, 589n3, 590n12, 590n18, 591n26, 592n32, 604, 783, 784
Westernizers, 8–10, 53–54, 76, 107, 425, 510, 522, 576
See also Idea, Russian; Slavophiles
What is Art? (Tolstoy), 526, 597–599, 603–604, 609–611, 614, 616
What is to be Done? (Chernyshevsky), 180–181, 471, 564–565
Will, 225, 228, 578, 669
free will, 77, 142, 182, 187, 282, 284, 778
Woman Thinker (Losev), 675, 682–684, 686–687

Y

Yawning Heights, The (Zinoviev), 87, 401
Yellow House, The (Zinoviev), 87, 401
Youth, 185, 190, 295, 312, 317, 363, 394, 453, 454, 473, 531, 562, 566, 576, 580, 585, 590n12, 592n36, 653n3, 740

Printed in the United States
by Baker & Taylor Publisher Services